Easy Learning

Italian

Dictionary

BEGINNER'S

ITALIAN

DICTIONARY

 HarperResource

An Imprint of HarperCollins*Publishers*

Easy Learning
Italian
Dictionary

HarperCollins*Publishers*

first edition 2002

© HarperCollins Publishers 2002

HarperCollins Publishers
Westerhill Road, Bishopbriggs, Glasgow G64 2QT
Great Britain

www.collinsdictionaries.com

Collins® and Bank of English® are registered trademarks of
HarperCollins Publishers Limited

ISBN 0-00-471030-4

HarperCollins Publishers, Inc
10 East 53rd Street, New York, NY 10022

ISBN 0-06-050856-6

Library of Congress Cataloging-in-Publication Data has been applied for

www.harpercollins.com

general editor
Michela Clari

contributors
Daphne Day   Gabriella Bacchelli   Loredana Riu
Anne Convery   Angela Jack   Phyllis Gautier

editorial coordination
Joyce Littlejohn

editorial staff
Cindy Mitchell

computing staff
Paul Ritchie

illustrations
Richard Anderson

series editor
Lorna Sinclair Knight

Corpus Acknowledgements
We would like to acknowledge the assistance of the many hundreds of individuals and
companies who have kindly given permission for copyright material to be used in the
Bank of English. The written sources include many national and regional newspapers in
Britain and overseas; magazine and periodical publishers; and book publishers in Britain,
the United States and Australia. Extensive spoken data has been provided by radio and
television broadcasting companies; research workers at many universities and other
institutions; and numerous individual contributors. We are grateful to them all.

A catalogue record for this book is available from the British Library

Printed and bound in Italy by Amadeus S.p.A.

INDICE

La pronuncia dell'inglese 6
Come usare il dizionario 7
ITALIANO ~ INGLESE 27
Inglese attivo 303
I verbi inglesi 325
I verbi italiani 339
INGLESE ~ ITALIANO 356

CONTENTS

Italian pronunciation 17
Dictionary Skills 18
ITALIAN ~ ENGLISH 27
Italian in Action 303
English verbs 325
Italian verbs 339
ENGLISH ~ ITALIAN 356

INTRODUZIONE

Il dizionario *Collins Easy Learning* è un'opera di nuova concezione studiata per chi si appresta ad imparare l'inglese. Desideriamo ringraziare tutti coloro che hanno collaborato alla realizzazione della serie Easy Learning. Un grazie particolare va a tutti gli insegnanti di lingue e ai consulenti didattici che ci hanno fornito materiali e consigli preziosi per aiutarci a venire incontro alle reali esigenze di degli studenti.

INTRODUCTION

Collins Easy Learning Italian Dictionary is an innovative dictionary designed specifically for anyone starting to learn Italian. We are grateful to everyone who has contributed to the development of the Easy Learning series, and acknowledge the help of the examining boards in providing us with word lists and exam papers, which we carefully studied when compiling this dictionary.

I Marchi registrati

I termini che a nostro parere costituiscono un marcho registrato sono stati designati come tali. In ogni caso, né la presenza né l'assenza di tale designazione implicano alcuna valutazione del loro reale stato giuridico.

Note on trademarks

Words which we have reason to believe constitute trademarks have been designated as such. However, neither the presence nor the absence of such designation should be regarded as affecting the legal status of any trademark.

LA PRONUNCIA DELL' INGLESE

► VOCALI

calm, part	[ɑː]
hat	[æ]
fiancé	[ɑ̃ː]
egg, set	[ɛ]
above	[ə]
earn, girl	[əː]
hit, fairly	[ɪ]
green, peace	[iː]
rot	[ɔ]
born, jaw	[ɔː]
hut	[ʌ]
full	[u]
pool	[uː]

► DITTONGHI

buy, die, my	[aɪ]
house, now	[au]
pay, mate	[eɪ]
pair, mare	[ɛə]
no, boat	[əu]
here, near	[ɪə]
boy, coin	[ɔɪ]
tour, poor	[uə]

► CONSONANTI

ball	[b]
child	[tʃ]
field	[f]
good	[g]
hand	[h]
just	[dʒ]
kind, catch	[k]
left, little	[l]
mat	[m]
nest	[n]
long	[ŋ]
put	[p]
run	[r]
sit	[s]
shall	[ʃ]
tag	[t]
thing	[θ]
this	[ð]
very	[v]
loch	[x]
ours, zip	[z]
measure	[ʒ]

► SEMIVOCALI

yet, million	[j]
wet, why	[w]

► ALTRI SIMBOLI

Accento	[']
r finale pronunciata se seguita da una vocale	[ʳ]

Nella parte inglese-italiano in tutte le voci la trascrizione fonetica segue il termine cui si referisce.

COME USARE IL DIZIONARIO

Con un po' di pratica e seguendo alcune semplici regole si può imparare ad usare correttamente il dizionario e a ricavarne tutte le informazioni di cui si ha bisogno. Questa sezione riporta le informazioni necessarie per utilizzare al meglio questo strumento.

Le risposte alle domande contenute in questa sezione sono riportate a pag.16.

▶ COME ASSICURARSI CHE SI STA CERCANDO NELLA PARTE GIUSTA DEL DIZIONARIO

La parte italiano-inglese appare per prima, ed è seguita dalla parte inglese-italiano. Nella parte superiore interna di ogni pagina compare l'iscrizione **Italiano ~ Inglese** o **Inglese ~ Italiano** che aiuta a capire immediatamente quale parte del dizionario si sta consultando. Le pagine centrali bordate di blu segnalano dove finisce la sezione italiano-inglese e dove comincia quella inglese-italiano.

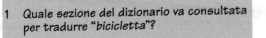

> 1 Quale sezione del dizionario va consultata per tradurre "*bicicletta*"?

▶ COME TROVARE LA PAROLA CHE SI CERCA

Per trovare una parola, come per esempio **temporale**, occorre innanzitutto vedere qual è la lettera con cui inizia, che in questo caso è T. Si dovrà quindi consultare la lettera T della parte italiano-inglese. Sulla parte superiore esterna di ogni pagina, compaiono la prima e l'ultima parola presenti in quella pagina. Per trovare "temporale" va consultata in ordine alfabetico la pagina contenente le parole che iniziano per **tem**.

> 2 A che pagina si trova la parola "*domani*" e quali sono la prima e l'ultima parola della pagina?
> 3 Nel dizionario compare prima la parola "*candela*" o la parola "*centro*"?

▶ PER CONTROLLARE CHE LA PAROLA TROVATA SIA QUELLA CHE SI
  VUOLE TRADURRE

Una voce del dizionario è composta dalla parola, dalle sue traduzioni e spesso
da alcuni esempi che servono da guida per l'uso delle traduzioni. Se c'è più di
una voce per la stessa parola, come nell'esempio riportato qui sotto, compare un
riquadro che rimanda anche all'altra voce.

piano AVVERBIO
    vedi anche **piano** NOME
    [1] slowly (adagio) ◇ Guida piano! Drive
    slowly!
    ♦ Fai piano, è fragile! Be careful, it's fragile!
    [2] quietly (a bassa voce) ◇ Parla più piano
    Speak more quietly.
    ♦ pian piano little by little

il **piano** NOME MASC
    vedi anche **piano** AVVERBIO
    [1] floor (di edificio) ◇ Abito al terzo piano. I
    live on the third floor. ◇ all'ultimo piano on
    the top floor ◇ al piano terra on the ground
    floor, US: on the first floor

4 Quale delle due voci "*piano*" bisogna consultare per tradurre la
   frase "Abito al terzo piano"?

▶ COME SCEGLIERE LA TRADUZIONE GIUSTA

La traduzione della parola è facilmente distinguibile in quanto compare a capo ed
è sottolineata. Se per una stessa parola esistono più traduzioni, ciascuna di esse
è preceduta da un numero. Se una voce continua alla pagina seguente, compare
il segno ☞.

Spesso all'interno della voce si trovano alcuni esempi in corsivo preceduti da una
losanga bianca ◇, che indicano come può essere usata la traduzione che li precede e quindi aiutano a scegliere la traduzione giusta.

5 Consulta gli esempi della voce "*interessare*" e traduci "Silvia si interessa di politica".

Spesso le parole hanno più di un significato e di una traduzione e quindi, quando
si traduce dall'italiano all'inglese, occorre essere sicuri di scegliere la parola che
ha il significato giusto. L'*Easy Learning* semplifica la ricerca delle varie traduzioni,
come si può vedere nell'esempio qui sotto.

il **nastro** NOME MASC
    [1] ribbon (di stoffa) ◇ un nastro di seta a
    silk ribbon
    [2] tape (magnetico) ◇ Ha fatto tornare
    indietro il nastro. He rewound the tape.
    ♦ nastro adesivo adhesive tape
    ♦ nastro trasportatore conveyor belt

È importante ricordare che tutte le traduzioni sono sottolineate, che la presenza
di numeri indica che vi è più di una traduzione e che le indicazioni in corsivo tra
parentesi dopo le parole guidano nella scelta della traduzione corretta.

Va ricordato che non si deve mai usare la prima traduzione che compare nella voce senza prima leggere anche le altre. Occorre sempre controllare se esiste più di una parola sottolineata nella stessa voce.

Le espressioni in **grassetto** che si trovano nella voce caccia, precedute da una losanga **nera** ◆ sono espressioni particolarmente comuni o importanti. A volte, all'interno di queste espressioni, la parola ha una traduzione completamente diversa rispetto a quella principale, a volte la traduzione è la stessa.

> la **caccia** NOME FEM
> <u>hunting</u> ◇ *Sono contro la caccia.* I'm
> against hunting.
> ◆ **andare a caccia** to go* hunting ◇ *La*
> *domenica vanno a caccia.* They go hunting
> on Sundays.
> ◆ **dare la caccia a qualcuno** to go* after
> somebody ◇ *La polizia gli dava la caccia.*
> The police went after him.
> ◆ **caccia al tesoro** treasure hunt

Quando si consulta una voce si deve sempre controllare le espressioni in grassetto che eventualmente vi compaiono.

▶ COME UTILIZZARE GLI ESEMPI E LE ESPRESSIONI DEL DIZIONARIO

A volte, consultando il dizionario non si troverà solamente la parola ma tutta la frase che si vuole tradurre. Ad esempio, se vogliamo dire *"Che tempo fa?"* occorrerà consultare la voce **tempo**, dove si trova proprio la frase che vogliamo tradurre.

In altri casi bisognerà adattare la traduzione dell'esempio. Supponiamo di voler tradurre la frase *"Gloria dice che li aiuterà"*. Alla voce **aiutare** troviamo:

> **aiutare** VERBO
> to help ◇ *Ha detto che ci avrebbe aiutati.* He
> said he would help us. ◇ *Mi puoi aiutare a*
> *compilare questo modulo?* Can you help me
> to fill in this form?

In questo caso occorrerà sostituire i pronomi e il tempo verbale, ricordando che alla terza persona singolare del presente va aggiunta una **-s**. Spesso occorrerà adattare gli esempi, e in particolare le forme verbali. In caso di necessità va consultata la sezione sui verbi che si trova nelle pagine centrali del dizionario e che fornisce una guida per la coniugazione.

Anche gli esempi che contengono aggettivi e nomi andranno adattati, e si dovrà fare particolare attenzione ai nomi inglesi che hanno un plurale irregolare.

> 9 Come si traduce "I bambini giocano nel parco"?

▶ COME UTILIZZARE AL MEGLIO IL DIZIONARIO

Cercare le parole richiede tempo, e quindi conviene evitare di usare il dizionario se non è necessario. Prima di consultare il dizionario si può cercare di esprimere quello che si vuole dire usando parole o espressioni comuni già conosciute. Per esempio:

◇ si può utilizzare una parola con un significato simile, cosa che è particolarmente facile con alcuni aggettivi e avverbi. Ci sono molti aggettivi, per esempio, che vogliono dire *buono*, *bello* o *grande*. Quindi, non sapendo come si dice "*squisito*" in inglese, si può sempre usare l'aggettivo "*good*", che sicuramente tutti conoscono.

◇ si può utilizzare la forma negativa. Per dire che un certo sapore è "*disgustoso*" si può sempre dire che "*non è buono*".

◇ si può utilizzare esempi concreti al posto di parole astratte o complesse. Invece di dire "*Nella mia città ci sono diversi impianti sportivi*" si può ad esempio dire "*Nella mia città ci sono due palestre e una piscina*".

> 10 Come si potrebbe dire con altre parole "Si è trattato di un banale incidente"?

Spesso è possibile indovinare il significato di una parola inglese in base alle parole o alle espressioni che la circondano. Supponiamo ad esempio di dover tradurre "*Bikes for hire – £5 per day*" e di non sapere cosa vuol dire "*for hire*". Dal fatto che queste biciclette costino 5 sterline al giorno possiamo facilmente dedurre che "*for hire*" vuol dire "*a noleggio*". Pensandoci un po' si può scoprire di essere ugualmente in grado di tradurla.

> 11 Senza usare il dizionario cerca di capire il significato della parola "essay" nella frase "We have to write a four-page essay about our favourite artist".

LE CATEGORIE GRAMMATICALI

Se si cerca la parola **piano** si vedrà che l'*Easy Learning* riporta due voci distinte, dato che "piano" può essere un avverbio oppure un nome. Ecco perché, se si vuole essere in grado di riconoscere la voce corretta, è importante imparare a distinguere tra un tipo di parola ed un altro.

Qui di seguito sono riportate alcune informazioni sulle varie categorie grammaticali e alcuni consigli su come tradurre correttamente in inglese nomi, preposizioni e così via, e su come individuare la funzione grammaticale di alcune parole inglesi di cui non si conosce il significato quando si trovano in un determinato contesto.

▶ NOMI

I nomi servono per descrivere le persone, gli animali o le cose. In inglese sono spesso preceduti da parole come *a, the, this, that, your* o *his*. Nella parte inglese-italiano accanto a tutti i nomi compare la dicitura NOUN.

his **dog**   her **cat**   a **street**

Se si vuole tradurre un sostantivo plurale occorre innanzitutto cercarlo al singolare. Per esempio, per tradurre "i quadri" occorrerà cercare la parola "quadro".

12 Come si traduce la frase "Si è messo il maglione"?

In inglese il plurale normalmente si forma aggiungendo una **-s** alla forma singolare.

many book**s**   two house**s**

Il plurale dei sostantivi che terminano in **-ch**, **-o**, **-ss**, **-sh** o **-x** si forma aggiungendo **-es.**:

many kiss**es**   three brush**es**   some box**es**

Per formare il plurale dei nomi che terminano in **-y**, se la "y" è preceduta da una vocale va aggiunta la desinenza **-s** (valley → valleys). Se invece prima della "y" vi è una consonante la "y" cade e va aggiunta la desinenza **-ies** (hobby → hobbies).

several bab**ies**   two pupp**ies**

Alcuni nomi hanno il plurale irregolare in inglese.

two **women**   many **mice**   six **loaves** of bread

one child   two children

I plurali irregolari dei sostantivi inglesi compaiono anche come voci a se stanti nella parte inglese-italiano con un rimando alla voce singolare.

children ['tʃɪldrən] NOUN PL *see* **child**

Normalmente i nomi compaiono al singolare nel dizionario. Tuttavia quando hanno solamente la forma plurale si trovano al plurale.

French fries ['frɛntʃfraɪz] NOUN
le <u>patate fritte</u> FEM PL

The children gave their teacher a box of chocolates.

13 Quanti nomi compaiono nella frase qui sopra?
14 Quanti di questi nomi sono plurali?
15 Qual è il singolare di "*children*"?
16 Consulta il dizionario per trovare il plurale della parola inglese "*calf*".

▶ AGGETTIVI

Gli aggettivi sono parole che descrivono la qualità del nome cui si riferiscono. Nella parte inglese-italiano sono contraddistinti dalla dicitura ADJECTIVE. Gli aggettivi, che in italiano possono cambiare di genere e di numero a seconda del nome che li accompagna, sono invariabili in inglese.

a **black** cat   **black** dogs   the cat is **black**

Bisogna consultare "*sweet*" NOUN oppure "*sweet*" ADJECTIVE per tradurre le seguenti frasi?

17   The cake is very sweet.
18   Sweets are bad for your teeth.
19   How sweet of you!

▶ PRONOMI

I pronomi sono parole come *io, tu, noi, me, te* eccetera che si possono usare al posto di un nome. Nella parte inglese-italiano sono seguiti dall'indicazione PRONOUN.

A differenza dell'italiano, in inglese il soggetto non può rimanere sottinteso e occorre sempre mettere il pronome personale (I, you, he ecc.) quando il soggetto della frase non è un nome.

▶ VERBI

I verbi si utilizzano per esprimere azioni o stati, e in inglese sono sempre preceduti da nomi o pronomi. In questo dizionario i verbi inglesi sono preceduti dalla particella **to** e seguiti dall'indicazione VERB.

Bisogna consultare "*fight*" NOUN oppure "*to fight*" VERB per tradurre le seguenti frasi?

20   He and his brother fight a lot.
21   He was injured in the fight.

I verbi possono avere tempi diversi. Per esempio possono essere al presente (**faccio**), al futuro (**farò**) al passato (**ho fatto**) e così via. Nel dizionario, ovviamente, compare solamente l'infinito dei verbi. Per tradurre la forma verbale della frase "*Hai fatto i compiti?*" occorrerà quindi cercare il verbo fare all'infinito.

Qual è la forma dell'infinito da consultare per tradurre le seguenti forme verbali coniugate?

22   Non so nuotare.
23   È difficile.

Come in italiano, anche in inglese ci sono parecchi verbi irregolari. Per agevolare la ricerca della forma all'infinito, nel dizionario le forme del passato e del participio passato dei verbi irregolari più importanti sono state inserite come voci indipendenti con un rimando alla forma infinita.

found [faund] VERB *see* **find**

Nella parte inglese-italiano tutti i verbi irregolari sono seguiti dalla forma del passato e del participio passato.

to **sew** [səu] VERB (**sewed, sewn**)
cucire ◇ *She was sewing.* Cuciva. ◇ *It was sewn by hand.* Era cucito a mano.

A pagina 325 del dizionario si trovano alcune informazioni sulla coniugazione dei più importanti verbi inglesi e le tavole di quelli irregolari.

> **Traduci le seguenti frasi in inglese.**
> 24   Dove vai?
> 25   Era al cinema.
> 26   Sono già partiti.

▶ AVVERBI

Gli avverbi si utilizzano in genere per specificare il significato di aggettivi e verbi. Nella sezione inglese-italiano del dizionario sono seguiti dalla dicitura inglese ADVERB.

Normalmente gli avverbi si formano in inglese aggiungendo **-ly** all'aggettivo, ma non sempre. Va ricordato che sia in inglese che in italiano esistono parole che possono fungere sia da avverbio che da aggettivo, ed è quindi importante saperne distinguere le funzioni grammaticali per poter essere in grado di scegliere la traduzione corretta.

spesso AGGETTIVO (FEM **spessa**)
| *vedi anche* **spesso** AVVERBIO |
thick (*carta, vetro, muro*) ◇ *È spesso cinque millimetri.* It's five millimetres thick.
spesso AVVERBIO
| *vedi anche* **spesso** AGGETTIVO |
often ◇ *Vai spesso al cinema?* Do you go to the cinema often?

> **Quale delle due voci va consultata per tradurre le frasi riportate qui sotto?**
> 27   Il vetro dev'essere più spesso.
> 28   Peccato che non ci vediamo più spesso.
> 29   Succede spesso.

▶ PREPOSIZIONI

Le preposizioni sono parole come *di*, *su* e *per* che normalmente si trovano prima di sostantivi e pronomi. Nella parte inglese-italiano le preposizioni sono seguite dalla dicitura PREPOSITION. È importante imparare a riconoscerne la funzione grammaticale in quanto alcune parole possono essere sia preposizioni che avverbi.

30   In quale delle due frasi seguenti *"over"* è usato come preposizione?

The party is over.
The ball went over the wall.

31   Traduci in inglese *"un film sull'Africa"*.

1 La parte **italiano-inglese**

2 A pagina 100; **dodicenne, dopo**

3 **candela**

4 piano NOME

5 **Silvia is interested in politics.**

6 **We're listening to a tape.**

7 **Abbiamo finito la benzina.**

8 **Paolo never plays football.**

9 **The children are playing in the park.**

10 **È stato un incidente non molto grave.**

11 **tema**

12 **He put on his jumper.**

13 **4**: children, teacher, box, chocolates

14 **2**: children, chocolates

15 **child**

16 **calves**

17 sweet **ADJECTIVE**

18 sweet **NOUN**

19 sweet **ADJECTIVE**

20 fight **VERB**

21 fight **NOUN**

22 **sapere**

23 **essere**

24 **Where are you going?**

25 **He was at the cinema.**

26 **They've already left.**

27 spesso **AGGETTIVO**

28 spesso **AVVERBIO**

29 spesso **AVVERBIO**

30 **The ball went over the wall.**

31 **a film about Africa.**

ITALIAN PRONUNCIATION

▶ ITALIAN VOWELS

Italian vowels are always clearly pronounced.

a — like the *a* in **apple**

e — like the *e* in **set**

i — like the *ee* in **sheep**

o — like the *o* in **orange**

u — like the *oo* in **soon**

Remember that if a word ends with an accented vowel, the stress is on this final syllable e.g. università, ragù.

▶ ITALIAN CONSONANTS

c — before **e** or **i** is pronounced *tch*.

ch — is pronounced like the **k** in **kit**.

g — before **e** or **i** is pronounced like the **j** in **jet**.

gh — is pronounced like the **g** in **get**.

gl — before **e** or **i** is normally pronounced like the **lli** in **million**, and only in a few cases like the **gl** in **glove**.

gn — is pronounced like the **ny** in **canyon**.

sc — before **e** or **i** is pronounced *sh*.

z — is pronounced like the **ts** in **stetson**, or like the **d's** in **bird's-eye**.

NB All double consonants in Italian are fully sounded: e.g. the **tt** in **tutto** is pronounced as in **hat trick**.

DICTIONARY SKILLS

Using a dictionary is a skill you can improve with practice and by following some basic guidelines. This section gives you a detailed explanation of how to use this dictionary to ensure you get the most out of it.

The answers to all the questions in this section are on page 26.

▶ MAKE SURE YOU LOOK ON THE RIGHT SIDE OF THE DICTIONARY

The Italian-English side comes first, followed by the English-Italian. At the top of the page, you will see either **Italian ~ English** or **English ~ Italian**, so you know immediately if you're looking up the side you want. The middle pages of the book have a blue border so that you can see where one side finishes and the other starts.

1   Which side of the dictionary would you look up to translate "*la bicicletta*"?

▶ FINDING THE WORD YOU WANT

When looking for a word, for example **felice**, look at the first letter - **f** - and find the F section in the Italian-English side. At the top of each page, you'll find the first and last words on that page. When you find the page with the words starting with **fe**, scan down the page until you find the word you want.

2   On which page will you find the word "*gelateria*"?
3   Which comes first – "*filo*" or "*fila*"?

▶ MAKE SURE YOU LOOK AT THE RIGHT ENTRY

An entry is made up of a **word**, its <u>translations</u>, and, often, example phrases to show you how to use the translations. If there is more than one entry for the same word, then there is a warning box to tell you so. Look at the following example entries:

flat [flæt] ADJECTIVE
| *see also* **flat** NOUN |
piatto ◇ *a flat surface* una superficie piatta
♦ **flat shoes** scarpe basse
♦ **I've got a flat tyre**. Ho una gomma a terra.

flat [flæt] NOUN
| *see also* **flat** ADJECTIVE |
l' appartamento

4   Which entry should you look at if you want to translate the
    phrase "My car has a flat tyre"?

Always pay attention to information boxes – they tell you if there is more than one entry for the same word, give you guidance on grammatical points, or tell you about Italian culture.

▶ CHOOSING THE RIGHT TRANSLATION

The main <u>translation</u> of a word is shown on a new line and is underlined to make it stand out from the rest of the entry. If there is more than one main translation for a word, each one is numbered. If an entry continues over the page there is a signpost to indicate this: ☞.

Often you will see phrases in *italics*, preceded by a white diamond ◊. These help you to choose the translation you want because they show how the translation they follow can be used.

5   Use the phrases given at the entry "*hard*" to help you
    translate: "*This bread is hard*".

Words often have more than one meaning and more than one translation. For example, a **pool** can be a puddle, a pond or a swimming pool; **pool** can also be a game. When you are translating from English into Italian, be careful to choose the Italian word that has the particular meaning you want. The dictionary offers you a lot of help with this. Look at the following entry:

pool [pu:l] NOUN
see also **pool** VERB
1   la <u>pozza</u> ◊ *a pool of blood* una pozza di sangue
2   lo <u>stagno</u> (*pond*)
3   la <u>piscina</u> (*swimming bath*)
4   il <u>biliardo</u> ◊ *Let's play pool.* Giochiamo a biliardo.

The underlining highlights all the main translations, the numbers tell you that there is more than one possible translation and the words in brackets in *italics* after the translations help you choose which translation you want.

> 6 How would you translate "*I like playing pool*"?

Never take the first translation you see without looking at the others. Always look to see if there is more than one underlined translation.

Phrases in **bold type** preceded by a black diamond ♦ are phrases which are particularly common or important. Sometimes these phrases have a completely different translation from the main translation; sometimes the translation is the same. For example:

cancer ['kænsəʳ] NOUN
  il cancro ◇ *He's got cancer.* Ha il cancro.
  ♦ **Cancer** Cancro ◇ *I'm Cancer.* Sono del Cancro.

to **fulfil** [ful'fil] VERB
  realizzare ◇ *He fulfilled his dream to visit China.* Ha realizzato il suo sogno di fare un viaggio in Cina.
  ♦ **to fulfil a promise** mantenere una promessa

When you look up a word, make sure you look beyond the main translations to see if the entry includes any **bold phrases**.

> 7 Look up "*andare*" to help you translate the sentence "*Vai in bicicletta?*"

▶ MAKING USE OF THE PHRASES IN THE DICTIONARY

Sometimes when you look up a word you will find not only the word, but the exact phrase you want. For example, you might want to say *"What's the date today"*? Look up **date** and you will find that exact phrase and its translation.

Sometimes you have to adapt what you find in the dictionary. If you want to say *"I ate a sandwich"* and look up **eat** you will find:

to **eat** [iːt] VERB (**ate, eaten**)
  mangiare ◇ *Would you like something to eat?* Vuoi mangiare qualcosa? ◇ *We slowly ate our sandwiches.* Abbiamo mangiato lentamente i nostri panini.

You have to substitute *ho mangiato* for the infinitive form *mangiare*. You will often have to adapt the infinitive in this way, adding the correct ending and choosing the present, future or past form. For help with this look at the verb tables on page 339, **mangiare** is a regular verb like parlare.

> 8 How would you say "*I don't eat meat*"?

Phrases containing nouns and adjectives also need to be adapted. You may need to make the noun plural, or the adjective feminine or plural.

> 9   How would you say "*The boys are French*"?

▶ DON'T OVERUSE THE DICTIONARY

It takes time to look up words so try to avoid using the dictionary unnecessarily, especially in exams. Think carefully about what you want to say and see if you can put it another way, using words you already know. To rephrase things you can:

◇ Use a word with a similar meaning. This is particularly easy with adjectives, as there are a lot of words which mean *good*, *bad*, *big* etc and you're sure to know at least one.

◇ Use negatives: if the cake you made was a total disaster, you could just say it wasn't very good.

◇ Use particular examples instead of general terms. If you are asked to describe the sports facilities in your area, and time is short, you could say something like "*In our town there is a swimming pool and a football ground*," without using the words "*sports facilities*".

> 10 How could you say "*Canada is huge*" without looking up the word "*huge*"?

You can also often guess the meaning of an Italian word by using others to give you a clue. If you see the sentence "*Maria legge un buon libro*", you may not know the meaning of the word *legge*, but you know it's a verb because it's preceded by *Maria*. Therefore it must be something you can do to a book: *read*. The translation is: *Maria is reading a good book*.

> 11 Try NOT to use your dictionary to work out the meaning of the sentence "*La ragazza sta mandando una cartolina alla sua amica*."

PARTS OF SPEECH

If you look up the word **flat**, you will see that there are two entries for this word as it can be a noun or an adjective. It helps to choose correctly between entries if you know how to recognize these different types of words.

▶ NOUNS AND PRONOUNS

Nouns often appear with words like *a, the, this, that, my, your* and *his*. They can be singular (abbreviated to SING in the dictionary):

      his **dog**   *her* **cat**   *a* **street**

or plural (abbreviated to PL in the dictionary):

   the **facts**   *those* **people**   *his* **shoes**   *our* **holidays**

They can be the subject of a verb:

                 Vegetables are good for you

or the object of a verb:

                     I play ***tennis***

Words like *I, me, you, he, she, him, her* and *they* are pronouns. They can be used instead of nouns. You can refer to a person as *he* or *she* or to a thing as *it*.

> *I bought my mother a box of chocolates.*
>
> 12   Which three words in this sentence are nouns?
> 13   Which of the nouns is plural?
> 14   Which word is a pronoun in this sentence?

Italian nouns are either masculine or feminine (abbreviated to MASC or FEM in the dictionary). Masculine nouns are shown by **il**, **l'** or **lo**:

     il *giorno*   **l'***uomo*   **lo** *zio*

feminine nouns are shown by **la** or **l'**:

| la donna | l'economia | l'amica |

The article for plural masculine nouns is **i** or **gli** and for plural feminine nouns it is le.

| i bambini | **gli** amici | **le** donne |

▶ ADJECTIVES

Adjectives describe nouns: your tyre can be **flat**, you can have a pair of **flat** shoes.

> I'm afraid of the dark.
> The girl has dark hair.
>
> 15   In which sentence is "dark" an adjective?

Italian adjectives may change their endings depending on the gender and number of the noun they are describing:

un ragazzo *alto* (MASCULINE SINGULAR)
une ragazza *alta* (FEMININE SINGULAR: replace -o of masculine with -a)
due ragazzi *alti* (MASCULINE PLURAL : replace -o with -i)
due ragazze *alte* (FEMININE PLURAL : replace -a with -e)

The masculine singular form of adjectives ending in "-o" is shown first in the dictionary. So if you want to find out what kind of houses "**case vecchie**" are, look under **vecchio**.

> 16 What is the feminine singular form of "*nero*"?
> 17 What is the masculine singular form of the adjective in the sentence "*I fiori sono belli*"?

▶ VERBS

> She's going to record the programme for me.
> His time in the race was a new world record.

Record is a verb in the first sentence, and a noun in the second.

One way to recognize a verb is that it frequently comes with a pronoun such as **I**,

you or **she**, or with somebody's name. Verbs can relate to the present, the past or the future. They have a number of different forms to show this: **I'm going** (present), **he will go** (future), and **Nicola went by herself** (past). Often verbs appear with **to: they promised to go**. This basic form of the verb is called the infinitive.

In this dictionary, verbs are preceded by "to", so you can identify them at a glance. No matter which of the four previous examples you want to translate, you should look up to **go**, not **going** or **went**. If you want to translate **I thought**, look up to **think**.

---

18 What would you look up to translate the verbs in these phrases?

I *came*   she's *crying*   they've *done* it   he's out

Verbs have different endings in Italian, depending on whether you are talking about **io, tu, noi** etc: **io parlo, tu parli, noi parliamo** etc. They also have different forms for the present, future, past etc. **Parliamo** (we *speak* = present), **abbiamo parlato** (we *spoke* = past), **parleremo** (we *will speak* = future). **Parlare** is the infinitive and is the form that appears in the dictionary.

Sometimes the verb changes completely between the infinitive form and the **io, tu, lui** etc form. For example, *to go out* is **uscire**, but *I go out* is **esco**, and **dico** comes from **dire** (*to say*).

On pages 342–357 of the dictionary you will find tables of Italian verbs. Each type of regular verb is shown, together with important irregular verbs. On pages 358–363 there are 95 numbered verbs, with irregular tenses set out. Finally, on page 364 there is a further list of irregular verbs, marked with the number of the verb they are like. Irregular Italian verbs are marked in the dictionary with an asterisk.

> **accadere*** VERBO
> to happen ◊ *È accaduto l'anno scorso.* It
> happened last year.

---

19 Look up the dictionary to find the imperfect and future tenses of "fare".

▶ ADVERBS

An adverb is a word that describes a verb or an adjective:

Write **soon.**   Check your work **carefully.**
The film was **very** good.

In the sentence *"The swimming pool is open daily"*, **daily** is an adverb describing the adjective **open**. In the phrase *"my daily routine"*, **daily** is an adjective describing the noun **routine**. We use the same word in English for both adjective and adverb forms, but to get the right Italian translation, it is important to know if it's being used as an adjective or an adverb. When you look up **daily** you find:

daily ['deɪlɪ] ADJECTIVE
see also **daily** ADVERB
quotidiano ◇ *It's part of my daily routine.* Fa parte del mio tran tran quotidiano.
♦ **a daily paper** un quotidiano

daily ['deɪlɪ] ADVERB
see also **daily** ADJECTIVE
ogni giorno ◇ *The pool is open daily from nine until six.* La piscina è aperta ogni giorno dalle nove alle diciotto.

The examples show you **daily** being used as an adjective and as an adverb and will help you choose the right Italian translation.

Take the sentence "The menu changes daily".

20   Is "*daily*" an adverb or an adjective here?

▶ PREPOSITIONS

Prepositions are words like **for**, **with** and **across**, which are followed by nouns or pronouns:

I've got a present **for** David.   Come **with** me.   He ran **across** the road.

The party's over.
The shop's just over the road.

21   Which sentence shows a preposition followed by a noun?

► ANSWERS

1 the **Italian-English** side
2 on page 123
3 **fila** comes first
4 the first (ADJECTIVE) entry
5 **Questo pane è duro.**
6 **Mi piace giocare a biliardo.**
7 **Are you cycling?**
8 **Non mangio carne.**
9 **I ragazzi sono francesi.**
10 **Il Canada è molto grande.**
11 **The girl is sending her friend a postcard.**

12 **mother**, **box** and **chocolates** are nouns
13 **chocolates** is plural
14 **I** is a pronoun
15 in the second sentence
16 **nera**
17 **bello**
18 to **come**, to **cry**, to **do**, to **be**
19 the imperfect tense is **facevo**, the future tense is **farò**
20 daily is an **adverb**
21 the second sentence

A

a PREPOSIZIONE

La preposizione a si può tradurre in molti modi in inglese. Leggi gli esempi e cerca di trovare quello che più si avvicina alla frase che vuoi tradurre.

1 at ◊ *Devo essere all'aeroporto alle quattro.* I've got to be at the airport at four o'clock. ◊ *Scendo alla prossima fermata.* I'm getting off at the next stop. ◊ *Arriverò a mezzogiorno.* I'll arrive at midday.

In genere **at** *non va messo all'inizio di una frase interrogativa.*

◊ *A che ora parti?* What time are you leaving?

2 in ◊ *Abita a Bologna.* She lives in Bologna. ◊ *Sono nato a maggio.* I was born in May. ◊ *Era ancora a letto.* He was still in bed.

3 to ◊ *Sei mai stato a New York?* Have you ever been to New York? ◊ *Andiamo al cinema?* Shall we go to the cinema? ◊ *Veramente l'ha dato a me.* Actually she gave it to me. ◊ *La cartolina era indirizzata a Paola.* The card was addressed to Paola.

4 on ◊ *Abito al terzo piano.* I live on the third floor. ◊ *L'ho sentito alla radio.* I heard it on the radio.

5 by ◊ *La lettera è stata recapitata a mano.* The letter was delivered by hand. ◊ *Sono entrati uno a uno.* They came in one by one. ◊ *È pagato a giornata.* He's paid by the day.

♦ **gelato alla fragola** strawberry ice-cream
♦ **pentola a pressione** pressure cooker
♦ **TV a colori** colour TV
♦ **A domani!** See you tomorrow!

gli abbaglianti NOME MASC PL
headlights ◊ *Aveva gli abbaglianti accesi.* He had his headlights on full beam.

abbaiare VERBO
to bark

abbandonare VERBO
1 to abandon ◊ *I suoi genitori lo hanno abbandonato quando era piccolo.* His parents abandoned him when he was small.
♦ **Non mi abbandonare!** Don't leave me!
2 to give* up ◊ *Hanno abbandonato tutte le speranze.* They gave up all hope.

abbassare VERBO
1 to lower ◊ *Il governo ha abbassato i tassi di interesse.* The government has lowered interest rates.
2 to turn down ◊ *Ti dispiace abbassare il volume?* Would you mind turning down the volume?
♦ **Abbassa la voce!** Don't speak so loud!
♦ **abbassarsi (1)** (*temperatura, prezzi, livello*) to fall*
♦ **abbassarsi (2)** (*persona*) to bend* down

abbastanza AVVERBIO
1 quite ◊ *È abbastanza alto.* He's quite

tall. ◊ *L'esame era abbastanza difficile.* The exam was quite difficult.
2 enough (*a sufficienza*) ◊ *Non avevo studiato abbastanza.* I hadn't studied enough. ◊ *Non ho abbastanza soldi per comprarlo.* I haven't got enough money to buy it.

A volte si traduce usando la parola **okay**.

◊ *Ti è piaciuto il film? – Sì, abbastanza.* Did you like the film? – Yes, it was okay. ◊ *Vanno abbastanza d'accordo.* They get on okay.

abbattere VERBO
1 to knock down ◊ *Hanno dovuto abbattere molti edifici pericolanti.* They had to knock down many unsafe buildings.
2 to put* down (*cane, cavallo*)

abbattuto AGGETTIVO (FEM **abbattuta**)
depressed ◊ *Mi è sembrato un po' abbattuto.* He seemed a bit depressed.

l' abbazia NOME FEM
abbey ◊ *l'abbazia di Westminster* Westminster abbey

l' abbigliamento NOME MASC
clothes PL ◊ *Spende molto per l'abbigliamento.* He spends a lot on clothes.

abboccare VERBO
to take* the bait

l' abbonamento NOME MASC
♦ **abbonamento mensile** (*per treno, per autobus*) monthly season ticket
♦ **un abbonamento alla televisione** a television licence
♦ **un abbonamento ad una rivista** a magazine subscription

abbonarsi VERBO
♦ **abbonarsi a** (*teatro, cinema*) to buy* a season ticket for ◊ *Vorrei abbonarmi a teatro quest'anno.* I'd like to buy a season ticket for the theatre this year.
♦ **Mi sono abbonato ad una rivista di moto.** I've got a subscription to a motorbike magazine.

abbondante AGGETTIVO
big ◊ *un'abbondante colazione* a big breakfast ◊ *In quel ristorante le porzioni sono più abbondanti.* The portions are bigger in that restaurant.
♦ **Ne ho comprato un chilo abbondante.** I bought over a kilo.

l' abbondanza NOME FEM
♦ **in abbondanza** plenty ◊ *Ne ho in abbondanza.* I've got plenty. ◊ *Dovresti mangiare frutta e verdura in abbondanza.* You should eat plenty of fruit and vegetables.

abbottonare VERBO
to button up ◊ *Abbottonati il cappotto.* Button your coat up.

abbracciarsi VERBO
to hug

l' **abbraccio** NOME MASC
- **Ci siamo salutati con un abbraccio.** We hugged and said goodbye.
- **Un abbraccio, Francesca** (*su cartolina ecc.*) Lots of love, Francesca

l' **abbreviazione** NOME FEM
abbreviation

l' **abbronzante** NOME MASC
suntan lotion

abbronzarsi VERBO
to get* tanned

abbronzato AGGETTIVO (FEM **abbronzata**)
tanned ◇ *È abbronzatissima.* She's very tanned.

abbuffarsi VERBO
- **abbuffarsi di qualcosa** to stuff oneself with something

l' **abete** NOME MASC
fir

abile AGGETTIVO
skilful
skillful US
◇ *un abile politico* a skilful politician
- **essere abile in qualcosa** to be* good at something ◇ *È molto abile nel suo lavoro.* He's very good at his job.

l' **abilità** NOME FEM (PL le **abilità**)
skill ◇ *Questo lavoro richiede una grande abilità.* This work requires great skill.

l' **abitante** NOME MASC/FEM
inhabitant

abitare VERBO
to live ◇ *Dove abiti?* Where do you live? ◇ *Abito a Firenze.* I live in Florence. ◇ *Abito qui da sei anni.* I've been living here for six years. ◇ *Loredana abita al numero quarantanove.* Loredana lives at number forty nine.

l' **abitazione** NOME FEM
house

l' **abito** NOME MASC
1 suit (*da uomo*)
2 dress (*da donna*)

abituarsi VERBO
- **abituarsi a qualcosa** to get* used to something
- **abituarsi a fare qualcosa** to get* used to doing something
to get used to regge il gerundio.
◇ *Dovrò abituarmi ad alzarmi presto.* I'll have to get used to getting up early.

abituato AGGETTIVO (FEM **abituata**)
- **essere abituato a qualcosa** to be* used to something ◇ *Sono abituato al caldo.* I'm used to the heat.
- **essere abituato a fare qualcosa** to be* used to doing something
to be used to regge il gerundio.
◇ *Non sono abituato a cenare così presto.* I'm not used to having dinner so early.

l' **abitudine** NOME FEM
habit ◇ *una brutta abitudine* a bad habit
- **Ha l'abitudine di dormire dopo pranzo.** He usually has a sleep after lunch.
- **Ci ho fatto l'abitudine.** I've got used to it.

abolire VERBO
to abolish

l' **aborto** NOME MASC
1 abortion (*provocato*)
2 miscarriage (*spontaneo*)

abusare VERBO
to take* advantage ◇ *Non vorrei abusare della tua gentilezza.* I don't want to take advantage of your kindness.

abusivo AGGETTIVO (PL **abusiva**)
illegal ◇ *un altro esempio di edilizia abusiva* another example of illegal building
- **un taxi abusivo** an unlicensed taxi
*In inglese esiste la parola **abusive** che però vuol dire **ingiurioso** oppure "violento".*

l' **accademia** NOME FEM
- **accademia militare** military academy
- **accademia di Belle Arti** art school
- **accademia d'arte drammatica** drama school

accadere* VERBO
to happen ◇ *È accaduto l'anno scorso.* It happened last year.

accalcarsi VERBO
to crowd

accaldato AGGETTIVO (FEM **accaldata**)
hot ◇ *Ero troppo stanco ed accaldato per fermarmi a chiacchierare.* I was too tired and hot to stop to talk.

l' **accampamento** NOME MASC
camp (*militare, di zingari*)

accamparsi VERBO
to camp ◇ *Ci siamo accampati vicino al lago.* We camped near the lake.

accanto AVVERBIO
near ◇ *Abita qui accanto.* She lives near here.
- **Abita nella casa accanto.** He lives next door.
- **accanto a** next to ◇ *La tua camera è accanto alla mia.* Your room's next to mine. ◇ *Siediti accanto a me.* Sit next to me.

accantonare VERBO
1 to shelve ◇ *Abbiamo deciso di accantonare il progetto per il momento.* We decided to shelve the project for the moment.
2 to set* aside ◇ *Sono riusciti ad accantonare una bella somma.* They managed to set aside a considerable sum of money.

l' **accappatoio** NOME MASC
bathrobe

accarezzare VERBO
to stroke ◇ *Stava accarezzando il gatto.* He was stroking the cat.

---

* *I verbi seguiti da questo simbolo sono irregolari. Si veda anche alle pp.328–338.*

accavallare VERBO
- **accavallare le gambe** to cross one's legs

accelerare VERBO
to accelerate

l' **acceleratore** NOME MASC
accelerator

accendere* VERBO
[1] to light* (*fiammifero, sigaretta, fuoco*) ◇ *Abbiamo acceso le candeline.* We lit the candles.
- **Mi fai accendere?** Have you got a light?
[2] to turn on (*luce, TV, gas*) ◇ *Accendi la TV.* Turn on the TV.

l' **accendino** NOME MASC
lighter ◇ *Ho perso l'accendino.* I've lost my lighter.

accennare VERBO
- **accennare a** to mention ◇ *Ti ha accennato al suo progetto?* Did he mention his plan to you?
- **Mi ha accennato qualcosa.** She mentioned something to me.

l' **accento** NOME MASC
[1] accent ◇ *Si scrive con l'accento sulla "u".* It's spelled with an accent on the "u". ◇ *Ha un forte accento scozzese.* She's got a strong Scottish accent.
[2] stress ◇ *L'accento cade sulla penultima sillaba.* The stress is on the penultimate syllable.

accertarsi VERBO
to make* sure ◇ *Accertati che Luca abbia chiuso bene la porta.* Make sure that Luca shut the door properly.

acceso AGGETTIVO (FEM **accesa**)
[1] on (*luce, radio, TV, motore*) ◇ *C'era la luce accesa.* The light was on.
[2] burning (*candela*)
[3] lit (*sigaretta*)
- **Quel fiammifero è ancora acceso.** That match is still alight.

l' **accesso** NOME MASC
access ◇ *Nessuno aveva accesso all'edificio.* Nobody had access to the building.
- **Vietato l'accesso.** No entry.

gli **accessori** NOME MASC PL
accessories (*d'abbigliamento, per auto*)

accettare VERBO
to accept ◇ *Ha accettato l'invito.* She accepted the invitaton.

l' **accettazione** NOME FEM
reception (*di albergo, di ospedale*)
- **"accettazione bagagli"** "check-in"

acchiappare VERBO
to catch* ◇ *L'ho rincorso ma non sono riuscito ad acchiapparlo.* I ran after him but couldn't catch him.

l' **acciaio** NOME MASC
steel

accidenti ESCLAMAZIONE

[1] damn! (*per rabbia*) ◇ *Accidenti a lui!* Damn him!
[2] wow! (*per meraviglia*) ◇ *Accidenti, che bella moto!* Wow, what a great bike!

accingersi* VERBO
- **accingersi a fare qualcosa** to be* about to do something ◇ *Mi accingevo ad andare a letto.* I was about to go to bed.

l' **acciuga** NOME FEM (PL le **acciughe**)
anchovy (PL anchovies)

accludere* VERBO
to enclose ◇ *Accludo una copia di...* I enclose a copy of...

accogliente AGGETTIVO
[1] pleasant (*casa, stanza*)
[2] welcoming (*atmosfera*)

accogliere* VERBO
to welcome ◇ *Mi ha accolto a braccia aperte.* She welcomed me with open arms.
- **Ci hanno accolto benissimo.** They gave us a warm welcome.

accoltellare VERBO
to stab ◇ *L'hanno accoltellato in una rissa.* He was stabbed in a fight.

accomodarsi VERBO
to sit* down ◇ *Si è accomodato sul divano.* He sat down on the sofa.
- **Prego, si accomodi! (1)** (*si sieda*) Please take a seat!
- **Prego, si accomodi! (2)** (*venga avanti*) Please come in!

accompagnare VERBO
to take* ◇ *Ti accompagno io all'aeroporto.* I'll take you to the airport. ◇ *Mi ha accompagnato a casa in macchina.* She took me home in her car.

accontentare VERBO
to please ◇ *È molto difficile da accontentare.* She's very difficult to please.
- **Voleva lo scooter e i suoi l'hanno accontentato.** He wanted a moped and his parents got him one.
- **accontentarsi di** to make* do with ◇ *Mi dovrò accontentare di vederlo in TV.* I'll have to make do with seeing it on TV.

l' **acconto** NOME MASC
deposit ◇ *Ho versato un acconto per il viaggio.* I've paid a deposit for the trip.

accorciare VERBO
to shorten ◇ *Devo accorciare questi jeans.* I need to shorten these jeans.
- **accorciarsi** to get shorter ◇ *Le giornate si stanno accorciando.* The days are getting shorter.

accordare VERBO
to tune (*chitarra, piano*)

l' **accordo** NOME MASC
[1] agreement ◇ *un accordo commerciale* a trade agreement
- **stringere un accordo** to sign an agreement
- **essere d'accordo** to agree ◇ *Su questo* ☞

siamo tutti d'accordo. We all agree on this.
* **D'accordo.** Okay.
* **andare d'accordo con qualcuno** to get* on well with somebody ◊ *Non vado d'accordo con i miei.* I don't get on well with my parents. ◊ *Vanno abbastanza d'accordo.* They get on quite well.
* **mettersi d'accordo per fare qualcosa** to arrange to do something ◊ *Ci siamo messi d'accordo per andare al cinema.* We arranged to go to the cinema.
* **rimanere d'accordo** to agree ◊ *Siamo rimasti d'accordo che sarebbe venuto a prendermi.* We agreed that he'd come and pick me up.
  2 chord (*di chitarra*)

accorgersi* VERBO
  1 to notice ◊ *Non si sono accorti di niente.* They didn't notice anything. ◊ *Si è accorto del furto solo il giorno dopo.* He only noticed it had been stolen the next day.
* **L'ho urtato senza accorgermene.** I accidentally bumped into him.
  2 to realize ◊ *Mi sono accorto subito che qualcosa non andava.* I immediately realized something was wrong.

accudire VERBO
  to look after

accurato AGGETTIVO (FEM **accurata**)
  detailed ◊ *una descrizione accurata* a detailed description
* **un lavoro accurato** a careful piece of work

l' **accusa** NOME FEM
  accusation

accusare VERBO
  to accuse ◊ *Mi ha accusato di avergli rotto lo stereo.* He accused me of breaking his stereo.

acerbo AGGETTIVO (FEM **acerba**)
  unripe

l' **aceto** NOME MASC
  vinegar

l' **acetone** NOME MASC
  nail varnish remover

l' **acido** NOME MASC
  vedi anche **acido** AGGETTIVO
  acid

acido AGGETTIVO (FEM **acida**)
  vedi anche **acido** NOME
  1 acid ◊ *Il vino è un po' acido.* The wine is rather acid.
  2 sour ◊ *latte acido* sour milk

l' **acino** NOME MASC
* **acino d'uva** grape

l' **acne** NOME FEM
  acne

l' **acqua** NOME FEM
  water ◊ *Mi dai un bicchiere d'acqua, per favore?* Could I have a glass of water please?
* **acqua dolce** fresh water

* **acqua gassata** fizzy water
* **acqua minerale** mineral water
* **acqua potabile** drinking water
* **acqua del rubinetto** tap water
* **acqua tonica** tonic water

l' **acquaio** NOME MASC
  sink

Acquario NOME MASC
  Aquarius (*dello zodiaco*) ◊ *Sono dell'Acquario.* I'm Aquarius.

l' **acquario** NOME MASC
  aquarium (*per i pesci*)

l' **acquazzone** NOME MASC
  downpour

l' **acquerello** NOME MASC
  watercolour
  watercolor US

acquistare VERBO
  to buy* ◊ *Abbiamo acquistato una casa nuova.* We've bought a new house.

gli **acquisti** NOME MASC PL
* **andare a fare acquisti** to go* shopping

l' **acquolina** NOME FEM
* **far venire l'acquolina in bocca a qualcuno** to make* somebody's mouth water ◊ *Solo a vederlo ti fa venire l'acquolina in bocca!* It makes your mouth water just to look at it!
* **Mmm, ho già l'acquolina in bocca!** Mmm, my mouth's watering!

l' **acustica** NOME FEM
  vedi anche **acustica** AGGETTIVO
  acoustics PL ◊ *La sala ha un'ottima acustica.* The hall has excellent acoustics.

acustico AGGETTIVO (FEM **acustica**, MASC PL **acustici**, FEM PL **acustiche**)
  vedi anche **acustica** NOME
  acoustic ◊ *una chitarra acustica* an acoustic guitar
* **un apparecchio acustico** a hearing aid

acutizzarsi VERBO
  to become* worse

acuto AGGETTIVO (FEM **acuta**)
  1 high ◊ *Ha una voce acuta.* She's got a high voice.
  2 sharp ◊ *Ho sentito un dolore acuto al braccio.* I felt a sharp pain in my arm.
  3 acute (*accento, angolo*)

adatto AGGETTIVO (FEM **adatta**)
  right ◊ *È la persona adatta per quel lavoro.* He's the right person for that job. ◊ *Non è il momento adatto.* It's not the right moment.

l' **addestramento** NOME MASC
  training ◊ *Il corso di addestramento dura un mese.* The training course lasts a month.

addestrare VERBO
  to train

l' **addio** NOME MASC, ESCLAMAZIONE
  goodbye
* **addio al celibato** stag night

addirittura AVVERBIO

* I verbi seguiti da questo simbolo sono irregolari. Si veda anche alle pp.328–338.

even ◇ *Gli hanno addirittura proibito di uscire di casa.* They've even forbidden him to leave the house.
◆ **Addirittura?!** Really?! ◇ *Gli hanno proibito di uscire di casa. – Addirittura?!* They've forbidden him to leave the house. – Really?!

addizione NOME FEM
sum

addobbo NOME MASC
decoration ◇ *gli addobbi natalizi* the Christmas decorations

addormentarsi VERBO
[1] to go* to sleep ◇ *Non voleva addormentarsi.* He didn't want to go to sleep. ◇ *Mi si è addormentato un piede.* My foot has gone to sleep.
◆ **Non riesco ad addormentarmi.** I can't get to sleep.
[2] to fall* asleep (*involontariamente*) ◇ *Mi sono addormentato davanti alla TV.* I fell asleep in front of the TV.

addormentato AGGETTIVO (FEM **addormentata**)
[1] sleeping ◇ *un bambino addormentato* a sleeping baby
[2] asleep (*dopo il verbo*) ◇ *Ero ancora mezzo addormentato.* I was still half asleep.

addosso AVVERBIO
◆ **avere addosso** to wear* ◇ *Aveva addosso un vecchio impermeabile.* She was wearing an old raincoat.
◆ **cadere addosso a qualcuno** to fall* on top of somebody
◆ **mettere le mani addosso a qualcuno** (*picchiare*) to hit* somebody

aderente AGGETTIVO
tight (*gonna, abito*)

adesivo AGGETTIVO (FEM **adesiva**)
vedi anche **adesivo** NOME
◆ **nastro adesivo** sticky tape

l' **adesivo** NOME MASC
vedi anche **adesivo** AGGETTIVO
sticker ◇ *Faccio collezione di adesivi.* I collect stickers.

adesso AVVERBIO
now ◇ *Adesso non posso, sto studiando.* I can't do it now, I'm studying. ◇ *E me lo dici adesso?* Now you tell me!
◆ **È arrivato proprio adesso.** He's just arrived.
◆ **Ho finito adesso.** I've just finished.

adirarsi VERBO
to get* angry ◇ *Si è adirato moltissimo.* He got very angry.

l' **adolescente** NOME MASC/FEM
vedi anche **adolescente** AGGETTIVO
teenager

adolescente AGGETTIVO
vedi anche **adolescente** NOME
teenage

adoperare VERBO
to use

adorare VERBO
to love ◇ *Adoro le ciliegie!* I love cherries!

adottare VERBO
[1] to adopt (*figlio*) ◇ *È stato adottato.* He was adopted.
[2] to find* (*soluzione*) ◇ *Dovremo adottare una soluzione diversa.* We'll have to find another solution.
[3] to pass (*provvedimento*)

adottivo AGGETTIVO (FEM **adottiva**)
[1] adopted (*figlio*)
[2] adoptive (*genitori*)

adulto, adulta NOME, AGGETTIVO
adult

aereo AGGETTIVO (FEM **aerea**)
vedi anche **aereo** NOME
◆ **per via aerea** by airmail

l' **aereo** NOME MASC
vedi anche **aereo** AGGETTIVO
plane ◇ *L'aereo era in ritardo.* The plane was late.
◆ **viaggiare in aereo** to fly* ◇ *Mi piace viaggiare in aereo.* I like flying.

l' **aerobica** NOME FEM
aerobics ◇ *Faccio aerobica due volte alla settimana.* I do aerobics twice a week.
aerobics è in genere seguito dal verbo al singolare.

l' **aeronautica** NOME FEM
◆ **aeronautica militare** air force

l' **aeroplano** NOME MASC
aeroplane
airplane US

l' **aeroporto** NOME MASC
airport ◇ *Ci vediamo in aeroporto.* I'll meet you at the airport. ◇ *l'aeroporto di Heathrow* Heathrow airport

l' **afa** NOME FEM
◆ **C'è un'afa terribile.** It's terribly close.

affacciarsi VERBO
◆ **affacciarsi alla finestra** to appear at the window

affamato AGGETTIVO (FEM **affamata**)
◆ **essere affamato** to be* starving

l' **affare** NOME MASC
[1] deal ◇ *Mi ha proposto un affare interessante.* He offered me a good deal.
◆ **Affare fatto!** It's a deal!
◆ **affari** business ◇ *Come vanno gli affari?* How's business? ◇ *un viaggio d'affari* a business trip ◇ *È via per affari.* He's away on business. ◇ *Sono affari miei.* That's my business. ◇ *Fatti gli affari tuoi!* Mind your own business!
[2] bargain (*occasione*) ◇ *A quel prezzo è proprio un affare.* It's a real bargain at that price.
[3] thing (*aggeggio*) ◇ *Come funziona quest'affare?* How does this thing work?

affascinante AGGETTIVO
[1] very attractive (*persona*)

☞

2 fascinating (*esperienza*)

affaticato AGGETTIVO (FEM **affaticata**)

tired

affatto AVVERBIO

at all ◊ *Non mi sono affatto divertita.* I didn't enjoy myself at all.

• **Niente affatto.** Not at all.

l' **affermazione** NOME FEM

statement

afferrare VERBO

1 to grab ◊ *L'hanno afferrato per un braccio.* They grabbed him by the arm.

2 to catch* (*parola, nome*) ◊ *Scusa, non ho afferrato il tuo nome.* Sorry, I didn't catch your name.

• **afferrare un concetto** to get* an idea ◊ *Afferri il concetto?* Do you get the idea?

affettare VERBO

to slice

l' **affetto** NOME MASC

affection ◊ *Trova difficile dimostrare il suo affetto.* He finds it difficult to show affection.

• **Con affetto, Simona** (*su lettera*) Love, Simona

affettuoso AGGETTIVO (FEM **affettuosa**)

affectionate ◊ *Il mio gatto è molto affettuoso.* My cat's very affectionate.

• **Un saluto affettuoso, Roberta** (*su lettera, su cartolina*) Love, Roberta

affezionato AGGETTIVO (FEM **affezionata**)

• **essere affezionato a** to be* fond of ◊ *Sono molto affezionato a mia zia.* I'm very fond of my aunt.

affiatato AGGETTIVO (FEM **affiatata**)

• **una squadra affiatata** a united team

• **una coppia molto affiatata** a very close couple

affibbiare VERBO

• **affibbiare un compito a qualcuno** to saddle somebody with a task

• **affibbiare un soprannome a qualcuno** to give* somebody a nickname

affidabile AGGETTIVO

reliable ◊ *una macchina affidabile* a reliable car

l' **affidamento** NOME MASC

• **fare affidamento su** to rely on ◊ *Sai che puoi fare affidamento su di me.* You know you can rely on me. ◊ *Non si può fare affidamento sui mezzi pubblici!* You can't rely on public transport!

affidare VERBO

• **affidare un incarico** to give* a task ◊ *Gli hanno affidato un incarico importante da svolgere.* He's been given an important task to do.

affilato AGGETTIVO (FEM **affilata**)

sharp ◊ *Attento, quel coltello è molto affilato.* Be careful, that knife's very sharp!

affinché CONGIUNZIONE

so that

affittare VERBO

to rent ◊ *Hanno affittato la casa a degli studenti.* They've rented the house to students. ◊ *Ho affittato una casa al mare.* I rented a house at the seaside.

• **"affittasi"** "to let"

l' **affitto** NOME MASC

rent ◊ *Quant'è l'affitto?* How much is the rent?

affogare VERBO

to drown ◊ *Per poco non affogavo.* I nearly drowned.

affollato AGGETTIVO (FEM **affollata**)

crowded ◊ *La spiaggia era molto affollata.* The beach was very crowded.

affondare VERBO

to sink* ◊ *La nave è affondata rapidamente.* The ship sank quickly. ◊ *Sono affondato nella neve fino al ginocchio.* I sank up to my knees in the snow.

affrettarsi VERBO

to hurry up ◊ *Affrettati o perderai il treno.* Hurry up, or you'll miss the train.

affrontare VERBO

1 to face up to (*situazione, problema*) ◊ *Prima o poi dovrai affrontare il problema.* Sooner or later you'll have to face up to the problem.

2 to face (*prova, avversario*) ◊ *Affrontano domani la prova decisiva per il campionato.* Tomorrow they face the decider for the championship.

3 to talk about (*argomento*) ◊ *È un argomento difficile da affrontare.* It's a difficult thing to talk about.

affumicato AGGETTIVO (FEM **affumicata**)

smoked (*salmone, prosciutto*)

afoso AGGETTIVO (FEM **afosa**)

muggy ◊ *Oggi è una giornata afosa.* It's muggy today.

l' **Africa** NOME FEM

Africa

africano, africana NOME, AGGETTIVO

African

l' **agenda** NOME FEM

diary (PL diaries) ◊ *L'ho segnato sull'agenda.* I noted it in my diary.

In inglese esiste la parola agenda che però vuol dire ordine del giorno.

l' **agendina** NOME FEM

• **agendina tascabile** pocket diary

l' **agente** NOME MASC/FEM

officer (*di polizia*)

• **agente segreto** secret agent

• **agente immobiliare** estate agent, US: realtor ®

• **agente di cambio** stockbroker

l' **agenzia** NOME FEM

1 agency (PL agencies) ◊ *un'agenzia*

pubblicitaria an advertising agency
- **agenzia di viaggi** travel agent's
- **agenzia immobiliare** estate agent's, US: real estate office
  2 branch office (*di banca*)

l' **agevolazioni** NOME FEM PL
- **agevolazioni di pagamento** payment on easy terms
- **agevolazioni fiscali** tax concessions

agganciare VERBO
to hook (*con gancio*)
- **agganciare il ricevitore** to hang* up

l' **aggeggio** NOME MASC
thing ◊ *A cosa serve quest'aggeggio?* What's this thing for?

l' **aggettivo** NOME MASC
adjective

aggiornato AGGETTIVO (FEM **aggiornata**)
up-to-date ◊ *un orario aggiornato* an up-to-date timetable
Si scrive con i trattini quando precede un nome.
- **tenersi aggiornato su qualcosa** to keep* up to date with something ◊ *Mi tengo aggiornato sulle novità discografiche.* I keep up to date with the new releases.

aggiungere* VERBO
to add ◊ *Aggiungi ancora un po' di latte.* Add a bit more milk.

aggiustare VERBO
1 to mend ◊ *Mi ha aggiustato la bicicletta.* He mended my bike for me.
2 to straighten ◊ *Si è aggiustato la cravatta.* He straightened his tie.

aggrapparsi VERBO
- **aggrapparsi a** to hold* onto ◊ *Si è aggrappato alla ringhiera.* He held onto the banister. ◊ *Aggrappati a me!* Hold onto me!

aggravare VERBO
to make*...worse ◊ *La pioggia ha aggravato ulteriormente la situazione.* The rain has made the situation even worse.
- **aggravarsi** to get* worse ◊ *La situazione si è aggravata.* The situation got worse.

aggredire VERBO
to attack ◊ *È stato aggredito mentre tornava in albergo.* He was attacked as he was going back to his hotel.

aggressivo AGGETTIVO (FEM **aggressiva**)
aggressive

l' **agguato** NOME MASC
ambush ◊ *È stato ucciso in un agguato.* He was killed in an ambush.
- **tendere un agguato a qualcuno** to set* a trap for somebody ◊ *Ci hanno teso un agguato.* They set a trap for us.

agile AGGETTIVO
agile

l' **agio** NOME MASC
ease

- **sentirsi a proprio agio** to feel* at ease ◊ *Mi sono sentito subito a mio agio.* I immediately felt at ease.
- **mettere qualcuno a proprio agio** to put* somebody at their ease ◊ *Ha fatto del suo meglio per mettermi a mio agio.* He did his best to put me at my ease.

agire VERBO
to act ◊ *Agisce senza riflettere.* He acts without thinking.

agitare VERBO
to shake* ◊ *Agitalo bene prima di aprirlo.* Shake it well before you open it.
- **agitarsi** to worry ◊ *Non è il caso di agitarsi tanto.* There's no need to worry so much.

agitato AGGETTIVO (FEM **agitata**)
nervous ◊ *Era molto agitato.* He was very nervous.

l' **aglio** NOME MASC
garlic ◊ *uno spicchio d'aglio* a clove of garlic

l' **agnello** NOME MASC
lamb ◊ *agnello arrosto* roast lamb

l' **ago** NOME MASC (PL gli **aghi**)
needle

l' **agopuntura** NOME FEM
acupuncture

agosto NOME MASC
August
Si noti l'uso della maiuscola in inglese.
◊ *in agosto* in August

l' **agricoltore** NOME MASC
farmer ◊ *Fa l'agricoltore.* He is a farmer.

l' **agricoltura** NOME FEM
agriculture

l' **agriturismo** NOME MASC
holiday accommodation on farms

l' **agrodolce** NOME MASC
- **in agrodolce** sweet and sour ◊ *maiale in agrodolce* sweet and sour pork

gli **agrumi** NOME MASC PL
citrus fruit SING

l' **AIDS** NOME MASC
Aids ◊ *Ha l'AIDS.* He's got Aids.

l' **airone** NOME MASC
heron

l' **aiuola** NOME FEM
flower bed

aiutare VERBO
to help ◊ *Ha detto che ci avrebbe aiutati.* He said he would help us. ◊ *Mi puoi aiutare a compilare questo modulo?* Can you help me to fill in this form?

l' **aiuto** NOME MASC
help ◊ *Mi serve il tuo aiuto.* I need your help. ◊ *Aiuto!* Help!
- **essere d'aiuto (1)** (*persona*) to be* of help ◊ *Se posso esserti d'aiuto...* If I can be of help to you...
- **essere d'aiuto (2)** (*cosa*) to be* useful ◊ *Grazie per la guida, mi è stata di grande*

☞

aiuto. Thanks for the guidebook, it was very useful.

• **gridare aiuto** to shout for help ◊ *C'è qualcuno che grida aiuto.* There's somebody shouting for help.

l' **ala** NOME FEM
wing ◊ *Il piccione aveva un'ala spezzata.* The pigeon had a broken wing. ◊ *Gioco nel ruolo di ala destra.* I play on the right wing.

l' **alba** NOME FEM
dawn ◊ *Ci siamo alzati all'alba.* We got up at dawn.

alberghiero AGGETTIVO (FEM **alberghiera**)
• **scuola alberghiera** catering college ◊ *Faccio la scuola alberghiera.* I'm at catering college.

l' **albergo** NOME MASC (PL gli **alberghi**)
hotel ◊ *Ho dormito in albergo.* I spent the night in a hotel.

l' **albero** NOME MASC
1 tree ◊ *un albero di mele* an apple tree
• **albero di Natale** Christmas tree
• **albero genealogico** family tree
2 mast (*di barca*)

l' **albicocca** NOME FEM (PL le **albicocche**)
apricot ◊ *marmellata di albicocche* apricot jam

l' **album** NOME MASC (PL gli **album**)
album ◊ *Hai sentito il suo ultimo album?* Have you heard her latest album? ◊ *un album di fotografie* a photograph album
• **album da disegno** sketch book

l' **albume** NOME MASC
egg white

l' **alcol** NOME MASC
1 surgical spirit (*disinfettante*)
2 alcohol (*liquori*)

alcolico AGGETTIVO (FEM **alcolica**, MASC PL **alcolici**, FEM PL **alcoliche**)
vedi anche **alcolico** NOME
alcoholic ◊ *È alcolico?* Is it alcoholic?

l' **alcolico** NOME MASC (PL gli **alcolici**)
vedi anche **alcolico** AGGETTIVO
alcoholic drink
• **Non vendono alcolici.** They don't sell alcoholic drinks.

alcolizzato NOME, AGGETTIVO (FEM **alcolizzata**)
alcoholic

alcuno AGGETTIVO, PRONOME (FEM **alcuna**)
• **non...alcuno** no... ◊ *Non c'è alcuna fretta.* There's no hurry.
• **alcuni** some ◊ *Sono uscito con alcuni amici.* I went out with some friends. ◊ *Ne ho prese alcune.* I took some.

alfabetico AGGETTIVO (FEM **alfabetica**, MASC PL **alfabetici**, FEM PL **alfabetiche**)
alphabetical ◊ *in ordine alfabetico* in alphabetical order

l' **alfabeto** NOME MASC
alphabet

l' **alfiere** NOME MASC
bishop (*negli scacchi*)

le **alghe** NOME FEM PL
seaweed SING

l' **aliante** NOME MASC
glider

l' **alibi** NOME MASC (PL gli **alibi**)
alibi ◊ *Aveva un alibi di ferro.* He had a cast-iron alibi.

gli **alimentari** NOME MASC PL
• **negozio di alimentari** grocer's, US: grocery store ◊ *C'è un negozio di alimentari qui vicino?* Is there a grocer's near here?

l' **alimentazione** NOME FEM
diet ◊ *un'alimentazione equilibrata* a balanced diet

l' **aliscafo** NOME MASC
hydrofoil

l' **alito** NOME MASC
breath ◊ *Ha l'alito cattivo.* He's got bad breath.

allacciare VERBO
1 to fasten (*vestito, cintura*) ◊ *Non avevo allacciato la cintura di sicurezza.* I hadn't fastened my seat belt.
2 to lace up (*scarpe*) ◊ *Allacciati le scarpe.* Lace up your shoes.
3 to connect (*telefono, luce*) ◊ *Il telefono non è ancora allacciato.* The phone hasn't been connected yet.

allagare VERBO
to flood ◊ *La pioggia aveva allagato le strade.* The rain had flooded the roads. ◊ *Si è allagato lo scantinato.* The basement is flooded.

allargare VERBO
to widen ◊ *Stanno allargando la strada.* They're widening the road.

allarmare VERBO
to alarm ◊ *Non volevo allarmarti.* I didn't want to alarm you.

l' **allarme** NOME MASC
alarm ◊ *I ladri hanno fatto scattare l'allarme.* The burglars set off the alarm. ◊ *Era solo un falso allarme.* It was just a false alarm.

allearsi VERBO
to join forces ◊ *Si sono alleate contro di me.* They joined forces against me.

l' **alleato,** l' **alleata** NOME MASC, FEM
ally (PL allies)

allegare VERBO
to enclose ◊ *Allego una copia di...* I enclose a copy of...

l' **allegato** NOME MASC
attachment ◊ *L'allegato può contenere un virus.* The attachment may contain a virus.
• **Le invio in allegato...** Please find enclosed...

allegro AGGETTIVO (FEM **allegra**)

---

* I verbi seguiti da questo simbolo sono irregolari. Si veda anche alle pp.328–338.

cheerful ◇ *È un tipo sempre allegro.* He's always cheerful.

• **un colore allegro** a bright colour

l' **allenamento** NOME MASC
   training ◇ *Si è fatto male al braccio durante l'allenamento.* He hurt his arm while training.

• **essere fuori allenamento** to be* out of practice ◇ *Sono un po' fuori allenamento.* I'm a bit out of practice.

allenare VERBO
   to train ◇ *Ha allenato la squadra per due anni.* He trained the team for two years. ◇ *Ci alleniamo ogni giovedì.* We train every Thursday.

• **Si sta allenando per la maratona.** She's in training for the marathon.

l' **allenatore**, l' **allenatrice** NOME MASC, FEM
   coach ◇ *l'allenatore della nazionale italiana* the Italian coach

allergico AGGETTIVO (FEM **allergica**, MASC PL **allergici**, FEM PL **allergiche**)

• **essere allergico a qualcosa** to be* allergic to something ◇ *Sono allergico alle fragole.* I'm allergic to strawberries.

l' **allievo**, l' **allieva** NOME MASC, FEM
   pupil ◇ *È uno dei miei migliori allievi.* He's one of my best pupils.

allineare VERBO
   to line up ◇ *Ci ha allineati in fondo alla palestra.* He lined us up at the back of the gym.

alloggiare VERBO
   to stay ◇ *Ho alloggiato presso una famiglia scozzese.* I stayed with a Scottish family.

l' **alloggio** NOME MASC
   accommodation

*Nell'inglese britannico **accommodation** si usa solo al singolare, mentre l'equivalente americano è **accommodations**.*
   ◇ *L'alloggio è compreso nel prezzo.* Accommodation is included in the price.

• **vitto e alloggio** board and lodging

• **la crisi degli alloggi** the housing problem

allontanare VERBO
   to move away ◇ *La polizia ha fatto allontanare tutti.* The police moved everybody away.

• **allontanarsi da** to move away from ◇ *Allontanati dall'orlo, è pericoloso.* Move away from the edge, it's dangerous.

• **Ci eravamo allontanati troppo dalla riva.** We had got too far away from the shore.

allora AVVERBIO, CONGIUNZIONE

1 then ◇ *Allora non lo sapevo.* I didn't know about it then. ◇ *È stato allora che ho capito che tipo era.* It was then that I realized what kind of person he was.

• **da allora** since then ◇ *Da allora non l'ho più visto.* I haven't seen him since then.

2 at that moment (*in quel momento*) ◇ *Proprio allora ha squillato il telefono.* Just at that moment the phone rang.

3 at that time (*in quel periodo*) ◇ *Allora aveva ancora i capelli lunghi.* At that time she still had long hair.

4 so ◇ *Allora, che facciamo stasera?* So, what are we going to do this evening? ◇ *Allora? Com'è andata?* So, how did it go?

• **E allora?** So what?

l' **alloro** NOME MASC
   bay ◇ *una foglia d'alloro* a bay leaf

l' **alluce** NOME MASC
   big toe

allucinante AGGETTIVO
   awful (*terribile*) ◇ *uno spettacolo allucinante* an awful sight

• **C'era un freddo allucinante.** It was awfully cold.

l' **alluminio** NOME MASC
   aluminium
   aluminum *US*

allungare VERBO
   to lengthen ◇ *Basterebbe allungare un po' la gonna.* The skirt just needs lengthening a bit.

• **allungare le gambe** to stretch one's legs ◇ *Non c'era posto per allungare le gambe.* There was no room to stretch one's legs.

• **Su, allunga il passo.** Come on, hurry up.

• **allungarsi** to get* longer ◇ *Le giornate si stanno allungando.* The days are getting longer.

l' **allusione** NOME FEM
   hint ◇ *un'allusione velata* a veiled hint

l' **alluvione** NOME FEM
   flood ◇ *L'alluvione ha causato molti danni.* The flood caused a lot of damage.

almeno AVVERBIO
   at least ◇ *Potevi almeno telefonare, no?* You could at least have phoned, couldn't you? ◇ *Dammene almeno uno!* At least give me one! ◇ *Ci saranno state almeno tremila persone.* There must have been at least three thousand people.

• **se almeno...** if only... ◇ *Se almeno sapessi dov'è!* If only I knew where it was!

l' **altalena** NOME FEM
   1 swing (*a funi*)
   2 seesaw (*a bilico*)

l' **altare** NOME MASC
   altar

l' **alternativa** NOME FEM
   alternative ◇ *Non abbiamo alternative.* We have no alternative.

alternativo AGGETTIVO (FEM **alternativa**)
   alternative ◇ *medicina alternativa* alternative medicine

alterno AGGETTIVO (FEM **alterna**)
   alternate ◇ *Ci vado a giorni alterni.* I go on alternate days.

l' **altezza** NOME FEM
   height ◇ *È di altezza media.* She's of

☞

medium height.
- **avere un'altezza di...** to be*...high ◇ *Ha un'altezza di cinque centimetri* It's five centimetres high.
- **all'altezza di** (*vicino a*) near ◇ *L'albergo è all'altezza di piazza Verdi.* The hotel is near Piazza Verdi.
- **Non è all'altezza della situazione.** He's not equal to the situation.

alto AGGETTIVO (FEM **alta**)

vedi anche **alto** NOME

[1] high (*monte, livello, prezzo*) ◇ *un muro alto cinque metri* a wall five metres high ◇ *Aveva la febbre alta.* She had a high temperature.

[2] tall (*persona, palazzo*) ◇ *un edificio alto a* tall building ◇ *Quanto sei alto?* How tall are you? ◇ *Marisa è più alta di me.* Marisa's taller than me. ◇ *Matteo è il più alto della famiglia.* Matteo is the tallest in the family.
- **Sono alto un metro e settanta.** I'm one metre seventy.

[3] deep ◇ *In quel punto l'acqua è molto alta.* The water's very deep there.

[4] loud ◇ *L'ha detto a voce alta perché sentissero tutti.* She said it in a loud voice so that everybody would hear. ◇ *Abbassa un po', è troppo alto.* Turn it down a bit, it's too loud.
- **Leggilo a voce alta.** Read it out.

l' **alto** NOME MASC

vedi anche **alto** AGGETTIVO

top ◇ *Dall'alto della torre si vede tutta la città.* From the top of the tower you can see the whole city.
- **È là in alto.** It's up there.
- **alti e bassi** ups and downs ◇ *La sua carriera ha avuto degli alti e bassi.* His career has had its ups and downs.
- **salto in alto** high jump

l' **altoparlante** NOME MASC
loudspeaker

altrettanto PRONOME

vedi anche **altrettanto** AVVERBIO

the same ◇ *Anna ne ha preso uno e io ho fatto altrettanto.* Anna took one and I did the same. ◇ *Buon Natale! – Grazie, altrettanto.* Merry Christmas! – Thank you, the same to you.

altrettanto AVVERBIO

vedi anche **altrettanto** PRONOME

equally ◇ *Paolo è altrettanto bravo.* Paolo is equally good.

altrimenti AVVERBIO

[1] or ◇ *Sbrigati, altrimenti arriveremo in ritardo.* Hurry up or we'll be late.

[2] another way ◇ *È fatto altrimenti.* It's done another way.

altro AGGETTIVO, PRONOME (FEM **altra**)

other ◇ *Non trovo l'altra scarpa.* I can't find the other shoe. ◇ *L'ho visto l'altro giorno.* I

saw him the other day.
- **un altro (1)** (*ancora uno*) another one ◇ *Ne hanno inciso un altro.* They've recorded another one.
- **un altro (2)** (*uno diverso*) a different one ◇ *Quello era esaurito, ne ho preso un altro.* That one was sold out, so I bought a different one.
- **Tu o un altro è lo stesso.** You or somebody else, it doesn't matter.
- **gli altri** (*la gente*) other people ◇ *Non m'interessa quello che dicono gli altri.* I don't care what other people say.
- **né l'uno né l'altro** neither of them
- **l'altro ieri** the day before yesterday
- **domani l'altro** the day after tomorrow
- **Desidera altro?** Would you like anything else?
- **Non fa altro che lamentarsi.** All he does is complain.

l' **alunno,** l' **alunna** NOME MASC, FEM
pupil

alzare VERBO

to lift ◇ *È troppo pesante, non riesco nemmeno ad alzarla.* It's too heavy, I can't even lift it. ◇ *Non ha alzato un dito per aiutarmi.* He didn't lift a finger to help me.
- **alzare la voce** to speak* up ◇ *Alza la voce, non ti sento.* Speak up, I can't hear you.
- **Non alzare la voce con me!** Don't shout at me!
- **alzarsi** to get* up ◇ *A che ora ti alzi la mattina?* What time do you get up in the morning? ◇ *Si è alzato e se n'è andato.* He got up and went away.

l' **amante** NOME MASC/FEM

vedi anche **amante** AGGETTIVO

lover ◇ *Sono amanti da anni.* They've been lovers for years.

amante AGGETTIVO

vedi anche **amante** NOME

- **essere amante di** (*appassionato*) to be* very keen on ◇ *È amante del jazz.* He's very keen on jazz.

amare VERBO

to love ◇ *Ti amo.* I love you. ◇ *Mi ami?* Do you love me? ◇ *Si amano.* They love each other.
- **Non amo i sapori forti.** I'm not fond of strong flavours.

amaro AGGETTIVO (PL **amara**)

bitter ◇ *un sapore amaro* a bitter taste
- **Il caffè lo prendo amaro.** I take my coffee without sugar.

l' **ambasciata** NOME FEM

embassy (PL embassies) ◇ *l'ambasciata britannica* the British Embassy

l' **ambasciatore,** l' **ambasciatrice** NOME
MASC, FEM
ambassador

---

* I verbi seguiti da questo simbolo sono irregolari. Si veda anche alle pp.328–338.

ambedue AGGETTIVO, PRONOME
both ◇ *ambedue i ragazzi* both boys

ambientare VERBO
to set* ◇ *Il film è ambientato nella Chicago degli anni venti.* The film is set in Chicago in the twenties.
* **ambientarsi** to settle ◇ *Ti stai ambientando nella nuova scuola?* Are you settling into your new school?

l' **ambiente** NOME MASC
environment ◇ *la difesa dell'ambiente* the protection of the environment
* **temperatura ambiente** room temperature

ambiguo AGGETTIVO (FEM **ambigua**)
ambiguous ◇ *una risposta ambigua* an ambiguous answer

l' **ambizione** NOME FEM
ambition ◇ *La mia ambizione è fare il giornalista.* My ambition is to be a journalist.

l' **ambulanza** NOME FEM
ambulance ◇ *Devo chiamare l'ambulanza?* Shall I call an ambulance?

l' **ambulatorio** NOME MASC
surgery (PL surgeries)
doctor's office US
◇ *A che ora apre l'ambulatorio?* What time does the surgery open?

l' **America** NOME FEM
America

americano, americana NOME, AGGETTIVO
American

amichevole AGGETTIVO
friendly (*relazione, partita*) ◇ *Potresti avere un atteggiamento un po' più amichevole.* You could be a bit friendlier.

l' **amicizia** NOME FEM
friendship ◇ *Ci tengo molto alla sua amicizia.* Her friendship is very important to me.
* **fare amicizia** to become* friends ◇ *Abbiamo fatto subito amicizia.* We immediately became friends.

l' **amico,** l' **amica** NOME MASC, FEM (MASC PL gli **amici,** FEM PL le **amiche**)
friend ◇ *la mia migliore amica* my best friend ◇ *Ha molti amici.* She's got a lot of friends. ◇ *È un mio amico.* He's a friend of mine.

l' **ammaccatura** NOME FEM
dent ◇ *C'è un'ammaccatura sullo sportello.* There's a dent in the door.

ammaestrato AGGETTIVO (FEM **ammaestrata**)
1 trained ◇ *È un cane ben ammaestrato.* It's a well-trained dog.
2 performing (*per spettacoli*) ◇ *foche ammaestrate* performing seals

ammalarsi VERBO
to get* ill ◇ *Mi sono ammalato e non sono potuto partire.* I got ill and couldn't go.

ammalato AGGETTIVO (FEM **ammalata**)
ill ◇ *Metà della classe era ammalata.* Half the class was ill.

ammazzare VERBO
to kill

ammettere* VERBO
1 to admit ◇ *Ha ammesso di avere torto.* She admitted she was wrong.
* **ammettere qualcuno ad un club** to admit somebody to a club
* **Sono ammessi solo i soci.** It's only open to members.
* **Non mi hanno ammesso agli esami.** They didn't let me take the exams.
2 to suppose

amministrare VERBO
to run* (*ditta, stato*)

l' **ammiraglio** NOME MASC
admiral

ammirare VERBO
to admire ◇ *Ci siamo fermati ad ammirare il paesaggio.* We stopped to admire the view. ◇ *Lo ammiro.* I admire him.

l' **ammirazione** NOME FEM
admiration

ammobiliato AGGETTIVO (FEM **ammobiliata**)
furnished ◇ *un appartamento ammobiliato* a furnished flat, US: a furnished apartment

l' **ammoniaca** NOME FEM
ammonia

ammonire VERBO
1 to reprimand (*scolaro*) ◇ *È stato ammonito dall'insegnante.* He was reprimanded by the teacher.
2 to book (*nello sport*) ◇ *È stato ammonito dall'arbitro.* He was booked by the referee.

l' **ammorbidente** NOME MASC
fabric softener

l' **ammortizzatore** NOME MASC
shock absorber (*di auto*)

ammucchiare VERBO
to pile up ◇ *Ha ammucchiato le sue cose in un angolo.* She piled up her things in a corner.

ammuffire VERBO
to go* mouldy
to go* moldy US
◇ *Il pane è ammuffito.* The bread's gone mouldy.

l' **amo** NOME MASC
fish hook

l' **amore** NOME MASC
love ◇ *una canzone d'amore* a love song
* **Che amore questo gattino!** Isn't this kitten sweet!

ampio AGGETTIVO (FEM **ampia**)
1 spacious (*sala, stanza*)
2 loose (*vestito, maniche*)
* **una gonna ampia** a full skirt

l' **amplificatore** NOME MASC

amplifier

gli **anabbaglianti** NOME MASC PL
dipped headlights
* **mettere gli anabbaglianti** to dip one's headlights

analcolico AGGETTIVO (FEM **analcolica**, MASC PL **analcolici**, FEM PL **analcoliche**)
* **bibita analcolica** soft drink
* **birra analcolica** alcohol-free beer

l' **analfabeta** NOME MASC/FEM (MASC PL gli **analfabeti**, FEM PL le **analfabete**)
illiterate

l' **analgesico** NOME MASC (PL gli **analgesici**)
painkiller

l' **analisi** NOME FEM (PL le **analisi**)
analysis (PL analyses)
* **analisi del sangue** blood test

l' **ananas** NOME MASC (PL gli **ananas**)
pineapple

l' **anatra** NOME FEM
duck ◇ *anatra all'arancia* duck with orange sauce

l' **anatroccolo** NOME MASC
duckling

anche CONGIUNZIONE
[1] too ◇ *Parla italiano e anche francese.* She speaks Italian and French too. ◇ *Sono stanchissimo! – Anch'io!* I'm really tired! – Me too! ◇ *Vengo anch'io.* I'll come too.
[2] even (*persino*) ◇ *Lo saprebbe fare anche un bambino.* Even a child could do it.
Qualche volta **anche** *non si traduce.*
◇ *Vieni anche tu?* Are you coming?
◇ *Avresti anche potuto avvertirmi.* You could have let me know.

ancora AVVERBIO, CONGIUNZIONE
[1] still ◇ *Stava ancora dormendo.* He was still asleep.
* **non ancora** not yet ◇ *Non è ancora arrivato.* He hasn't arrived yet. ◇ *È pronto? – No, non ancora.* Is it ready? – No, not yet.
[2] more (*in più*) ◇ *Mi dai ancora un po' di gelato?* Could I have a bit more ice cream? ◇ *Vorrei ancora latte.* I'd like more milk.
[3] again (*di nuovo*) ◇ *Ancora tu!* You again!
[4] even
even *si usa per rafforzare un comparativo.*
◇ *Oggi fa ancora più freddo.* It's even colder today.

andare* VERBO
to go* ◇ *Andremo in Grecia quest'estate.* We're going to Greece this summer. ◇ *Dove vai in vacanza?* Where are you going on holiday? ◇ *Andiamo in macchina o a piedi?* Shall we go by car or walk? ◇ *Su, andiamo!* Come on, let's go! ◇ *Dove vanno questi bicchieri?* Where do these glasses go? ◇ *Com'è andata?* How did it go? ◇ *Come va con Jason?* How are things going with Jason?
* **Come va? – Bene, grazie!** How are you? – Fine thanks!
* **Come va la scuola?** How's school?
* **andare a sciare** to go* skiing
* **andare a cavallo** to ride*
* **andare in bicicletta** to cycle
* **andarsene** to leave* ◇ *Si è alzato e se n'è andato.* He got up and left.

l' **andata** NOME FEM
* **un biglietto di sola andata** a single ticket
* **un biglietto di andata e ritorno** a return ticket
* **All'andata ci ho messo due ore.** It took me two hours to get there.

l' **anello** NOME MASC
ring ◇ *un anello d'oro* a gold ring

l' **anestesia** NOME FEM
anaesthesia
anesthesia $\boxed{US}$

l' **angelo** NOME MASC
angel

l' **angolo** NOME MASC
[1] corner ◇ *Il cinema è proprio dietro l'angolo.* The cinema's just round the corner. ◇ *È la casa all'angolo con via Verdi.* It's the house on the corner of Via Verdi.
[2] angle ◇ *Formano un angolo retto.* They form a right angle.

l' **anguilla** NOME FEM
eel

l' **anguria** NOME FEM
watermelon

l' **anima** NOME FEM
soul ◇ *Non c'era anima viva.* There wasn't a soul there.

l' **animale** NOME MASC
vedi anche **animale** AGGETTIVO
animal

animale AGGETTIVO
vedi anche **animale** NOME
animal ◇ *grasso animale* animal fat

annaffiare VERBO
to water

annegare VERBO
to drown ◇ *Non sapeva nuotare ed è annegato.* He couldn't swim and drowned.

l' **anniversario** NOME MASC
anniversary (PL anniversaries) ◇ *È il loro anniversario di matrimonio.* It's their wedding anniversary.

l' **anno** NOME MASC
year ◇ *l'anno scorso* last year ◇ *l'anno prossimo* next year
* **Buon Anno!** Happy New Year!
* **Quanti anni hai? – Ho sedici anni.** How old are you? – I'm sixteen.
* **una ragazza di vent'anni** a girl of twenty
* **gli anni novanta** the nineties

annoiare VERBO

Italian ~ English

annotare → anziano 39

A

to bore ◇ *Scusa, ti sto annoiando?* Sorry, am I boring you?
* **annoiarsi** to get* bored ◇ *A stare a casa mi annoio.* I get bored staying at home.
*Attenzione! In inglese esiste il verbo **to annoy** che però vuol dire **dare fastidio**.*

annotare VERBO
to note

annuale AGGETTIVO
annual

annullare VERBO
to cancel ◇ *Hanno annullato il viaggio.* They cancelled the trip.

annunciare VERBO
to announce

l' **annuncio** NOME MASC
announcement ◇ *Hanno dato l'annuncio ieri.* They made the announcement yesterday.
* **annunci economici** small ads

annusare VERBO
to sniff ◇ *Il cane mi ha annusato le mani.* The dog sniffed my hands.

annuvolarsi VERBO
to cloud over ◇ *Si sta annuvolando.* It's clouding over.

anonimo AGGETTIVO (FEM **anonima**)
anonymous ◇ *una telefonata anonima* an anonymous phone call

anoressico AGGETTIVO (FEM **anoressica**, MASC PL **anoressici**, FEM PL **anoressiche**)
anorexic

Antartico NOME MASC
* **l'Antartico** the Antarctic

l' **antenna** NOME FEM
aerial
antenna US
◇ *Bisogna regolare l'antenna.* The aerial needs adjusting.
* **antenna parabolica** satellite dish

l' **anteprima** NOME FEM
preview

anteriore AGGETTIVO
front ◇ *lo sportello anteriore* the front door

l' **antibiotico** NOME MASC (PL gli **antibiotici**)
antibiotic

l' **anticipo** NOME MASC
advance ◇ *Gli hanno dato un anticipo.* They gave him an advance.
* **pagare in anticipo** to pay* in advance
* **in anticipo** early ◇ *Sei in anticipo.* You're early.
* **con mezz'ora di anticipo** half an hour early

l' **antico** NOME MASC (PL gli **antichi**)
vedi anche **antico** AGGETTIVO
* **gli antichi** the ancients

antico AGGETTIVO (FEM **antica**, MASC PL **antichi**, FEM PL **antiche**)
vedi anche **antico** NOME
1 old (*palazzo, monumento*) ◇ *Abitano in un'antica villa di campagna.* They live in an

old house in the country.
* **un mobile antico** an antique
2 ancient ◇ *gli antichi Romani* the ancient Romans ◇ *nei tempi antichi* in ancient times
* **un uomo all'antica** an old-fashioned man

l' **anticoncezionale** NOME MASC
contraceptive

l' **antidoping** NOME MASC (PL gli **antidoping**)
drugs test
* **risultare positivo all'antidoping** to fail a drugs test

l' **antifona** NOME FEM
* **capire l'antifona** to take* the hint ◇ *Ha capito l'antifona e se n'è andato.* He took the hint and left.

antiforfora AGGETTIVO
* **shampoo antiforfora** anti-dandruff shampoo

l' **antifurto** NOME MASC (PL gli **antifurto**)
1 burglar alarm (*in casa, in negozio*)
2 car alarm (*in auto*)

antincendio AGGETTIVO (FEM **antincendia**)
* **scala antincendio** fire escape

gli **antinebbia** NOME MASC PL
fog lights

antiorario AGGETTIVO (FEM **antioraria**)
* **in senso antiorario** anticlockwise

l' **antipasto** NOME MASC
starter

l' **antipatia** NOME FEM
* **prendere in antipatia** to take* a dislike to ◇ *L'ha preso subito in antipatia.* She took an instant dislike to him.
* **avere antipatia per** not to like ◇ *Ho una certa antipatia per i viaggi in pullman.* I don't really like travelling by coach.

antipatico AGGETTIVO (FEM **antipatica**, MASC PL **antipatici**, FEM PL **antipatiche**)
unpleasant ◇ *un tipo antipatico* an unpleasant person
* **Mi è proprio antipatica!** I really hate her!

antiproiettile AGGETTIVO
* **giubbotto antiproiettile** bulletproof vest

l' **antiquariato** NOME MASC
* **negozio d'antiquariato** antique shop

l' **antiquario**, l' **antiquaria** NOME MASC, FEM
antique dealer ◇ *Fa l'antiquario.* He is an antique dealer.

antiquato AGGETTIVO (FEM **antiquata**)
old-fashioned (*idea, stile, metodo*)

l' **anulare** NOME MASC
ring finger

anzi CONGIUNZIONE
in fact ◇ *Non mi dispiace, anzi sono contento.* I don't mind, in fact I'm glad.
* **Prendo un'aranciata, anzi una limonata.** I'll have an orangeade, no...a lemonade

anziano AGGETTIVO (FEM **anziana**)
vedi anche **anziano** NOME
old ◇ *È tuo nonno, quel signore anziano?* Is that old gentleman your grandfather?

l' **anziano,** l' **anziana** NOME MASC, FEM
* **gli anziani** the elderly

anziché CONGIUNZIONE

[1] rather than ◇ *Preferisco telefonare anziché scrivere.* I prefer to phone rather than write. ◇ *Ho comprato quello giallo anziché quello rosso.* I bought the yellow one rather than the red one.

[2] instead of ◇ *Quest'anno andiamo al mare anziché in montagna.* This year we're going to the seaside instead of to the mountains.

l' **ape** NOME FEM
bee

l' **aperitivo** NOME MASC
aperitif ◇ *Prendiamo un aperitivo?* Shall we have an aperitif?

apertamente AVVERBIO
frankly ◇ *Ne abbiamo parlato apertamente.* We talked about it frankly.

aperto AGGETTIVO (FEM **aperta**)
vedi anche **aperto** NOME

[1] open ◇ *Hai lasciato la porta aperta.* You've left the door open.

[2] open-minded (*persona*) ◇ *I miei sono molto aperti.* My parents are very open-minded.

l' **aperto** NOME MASC
* **all'aperto** outdoors ◇ *Abbiamo dormito all'aperto.* We slept outdoors.

l' **apertura** NOME FEM
opening ◇ *orario di apertura* opening times

l' **apnea** NOME FEM
* **immergersi in apnea** to dive without breathing apparatus

l' **apostrofo** NOME MASC
apostrophe

appannarsi VERBO

[1] to mist up ◇ *Il parabrezza si era appannato.* The windscreen had misted up.

[2] to steam up ◇ *Mi si sono appannati gli occhiali.* My glasses steamed up.

apparecchiare VERBO
to set* the table ◇ *Ti aiuto ad apparecchiare?* Shall I help you to set the table?

l' **apparecchio** NOME MASC

[1] device ◇ *un complicato apparecchio elettronico* a complex electronic device

[2] brace (*per i denti*) ◇ *Porta l'apparecchio.* He wears a brace.

* **apparecchio acustico** hearing aid

apparire* VERBO
to appear

l' **appartamento** NOME MASC
flat
apartment US
◇ *un appartamento ammobiliato* a furnished flat

appartenere* VERBO

to belong ◇ *Questa collana apparteneva a mia nonna.* This necklace belonged to my grandma. ◇ *A chi appartiene questo libro?* Who does this book belong to?

appassionato AGGETTIVO (FEM **appassionata**)
* **essere appassionato di qualcosa** to love something ◇ *È appassionato di musica jazz.* He loves jazz.

appassito AGGETTIVO (FEM **appassita**)
dead ◇ *fiori appassiti* dead flowers

l' **appello** NOME MASC
* **fare l'appello** to take* the register

appena AVVERBIO, CONGIUNZIONE

[1] just ◇ *Se n'è appena andato.* He's just left. ◇ *Un po' di latte? – Grazie, appena un goccio.* Milk? – Yes please, just a drop.

[2] only just (*a malapena*) ◇ *L'indirizzo era appena leggibile.* The address was only just legible. ◇ *Sono appena le nove, resta ancora un po'.* It's only just nine o'clock, stay a bit longer. ◇ *Era appena tornato ed è dovuto uscire di nuovo.* He'd only just got back when he had to go out again.

* **Lo conosco appena.** I hardly know him.

[3] as soon as ◇ *Ha detto che sarebbe venuto appena possibile.* He said he'd come as soon as possible. ◇ *L'ho riconosciuto appena l'ho visto.* I recognized him as soon as I saw him.

appendere* VERBO
to hang* ◇ *Dove posso appendere il cappotto?* Where can I hang my coat?

l' **appendicite** NOME FEM
appendicitis ◇ *Ha un'appendicite acuta.* He's got acute appendicitis.

l' **appetito** NOME MASC
appetite ◇ *La camminata mi ha messo appetito.* The walk has given me an appetite.

* **Buon appetito!** (*detto da cameriere*) Enjoy your meal!

> ❶ *In inglese non si usa augurare* **buon appetito** *quando ci si mette a tavola.*

appiccicare VERBO
to stick*

appisolarsi VERBO
to doze off ◇ *Mi ero appisolato un attimo.* I dozed off for a moment.

applaudire VERBO
to clap ◇ *Applaudivano tutti.* Everybody was clapping.

l' **applauso** NOME MASC
applause

applause non ha plurale e non è mai preceduto dall'articolo "an".

◇ *un applauso* a round of applause
◇ *Hanno ricevuto molti applausi.* They got a lot of applause.

appoggiare VERBO

[1] to put* (*sopra qualcosa*) ◇ *Puoi appoggiare il pacco sul tavolo.* You can put the parcel on the table.

[2] to lean* (*contro qualcosa*) ◇ *Appoggia la scala al muro.* Lean the ladder against the wall.

♦ **appoggiarsi a** to lean* against ◇ *Si è dovuto appoggiare al muro per sostenersi.* He had to lean against the wall for support.

l' **appoggio** NOME MASC
support ◇ *Ho bisogno di tutto il vostro appoggio.* I need all your support.

apposta AVVERBIO

[1] on purpose ◇ *Scusa, non l'ho fatto apposta.* I'm sorry, I didn't do it on purpose.

[2] specially ◇ *Siamo venuti apposta per parlare con te.* We came specially to speak to you.

l' **apprendimento** NOME MASC
learning

approfittare VERBO

♦ **approfittare di qualcosa** to make* the most of something ◇ *Approfittiamo della bella giornata e andiamo al parco!* Let's make the most of the weather and go to the park! ◇ *Approfittane!* Make the most of it!

approfondire VERBO
to study in depth ◇ *Vorrei approfondire l'argomento.* I'd like to study the subject in depth.

approfondito AGGETTIVO (FEM **approfondita**)
thorough ◇ *un'analisi approfondita* a thorough analysis

approssimativo AGGETTIVO (FEM **approssimativa**)
rough ◇ *È solo un calcolo approssimativo.* It's only a rough estimate.

approvare VERBO

[1] to approve of (*ritenere giusto*) ◇ *Non approvo ciò che hai fatto.* I don't approve of what you've done.

[2] to approve (*votare favorevolmente*) ◇ *Hanno approvato il progetto.* They approved the project.

l' **appuntamento** NOME MASC

[1] appointment ◇ *Venerdì ho un appuntamento dal dentista.* I've got a dental appointment on Friday.

[2] date (*amoroso*) ◇ *Stasera ho appuntamento con il mio ragazzo.* I've got a date with my boyfriend tonight.

♦ **darsi appuntamento** to arrange to meet ◇ *Ci siamo dati appuntamento alle otto davanti al cinema.* We arranged to meet at eight in front of the cinema.

appuntito AGGETTIVO (FEM **appuntita**)
sharp ◇ *una matita appuntita* a sharp pencil

l' **appunto** NOME MASC
vedi anche **appunto** AVVERBIO
note ◇ *Non avevo preso appunti.* I hadn't

taken notes.

appunto AVVERBIO
vedi anche **appunto** NOME
just ◇ *Parlavamo appunto di questo.* We were just talking about that. ◇ *Stavo appunto per chiederti di venire.* I was just going to ask you to come.

♦ **Appunto!** Exactly!

l' **apribottiglie** NOME MASC (PL gli **apribottiglie**)
bottle-opener

aprile NOME MASC
April
Si noti l'uso della maiuscola in inglese.
◇ *in aprile* in April

♦ **Pesce d'aprile!** April Fool!

aprire* VERBO

[1] to open ◇ *Posso aprire la finestra?* Can I open the window? ◇ *Dai, non apri i regali?* Come on, aren't you going to open your presents? ◇ *A che ora apre la banca?* What time does the bank open?

♦ **Non ha aperto bocca.** She didn't say a word.

[2] to turn on ◇ *Non riesco ad aprire il rubinetto.* I can't turn the tap on.

l' **apriscatole** NOME MASC (PL gli **apriscatole**)
tin opener
can opener [US]

l' **aquila** NOME FEM
eagle

l' **aquilone** NOME MASC
kite ◇ *Facciamo volare l'aquilone!* Let's fly the kite!

l' **Arabia Saudita** NOME FEM
Saudi Arabia

arabo, araba NOME, AGGETTIVO
vedi anche **arabo** NOME
Arab

l' **arabo** NOME MASC
vedi anche **arabo** NOME, AGGETTIVO
Arabic (*lingua*) ◇ *Parlano l'arabo.* They speak Arabic.

l' **arachide** NOME FEM
peanut

l' **aragosta** NOME FEM
lobster

l' **arancia** NOME FEM (PL le **arance**)
orange ◇ *succo d'arancia* orange juice

l' **aranciata** NOME FEM
orangeade

arancione AGGETTIVO, NOME
orange ◇ *una maglietta arancione* an orange T-shirt

l' **arbitro** NOME MASC

[1] referee (*in genere*)

[2] umpire (*nel tennis*)

l' **arbusto** NOME MASC
shrub

l' **archeologia** NOME FEM
archaeology
archeology [US]

◊ *È laureata in archeologia.* She's got a degree in archaeology.

l' **archeologo,** l' **archeologa** NOME MASC, FEM (MASC PL gli **archeologi,** FEM PL le **archeologhe**)
archaeologist
archeologist US

l' **architetto** NOME MASC
architect ◊ *Sua madre fa l'architetto.* His mother is an architect.

l' **architettura** NOME FEM
architecture ◊ *Studia architettura.* He's studying architecture.

archiviare VERBO
to file *(pratica)*
♦ **archiviare un caso** to dismiss a case

l' **arco** NOME MASC (PL gli **archi**)
1 arch *(di edificio, di ponte)*
2 bow ◊ *arco e frecce* bow and arrows
♦ **nell'arco di tre settimane** within the space of three weeks

l' **arcobaleno** NOME MASC
rainbow

l' **area** NOME FEM
area ◊ *un'area di venticinque chilometri quadrati* an area of twenty-five square kilometres
♦ **area di rigore** penalty area

l' **argento** NOME MASC
silver ◊ *un anello d'argento* a silver ring

l' **argilla** NOME FEM
clay ◊ *un vaso d'argilla* a clay pot

l' **argomento** NOME MASC
subject ◊ *Cambiamo argomento.* Let's change the subject. ◊ *Visto che siamo in argomento...* Since we're on the subject...

l' **aria** NOME FEM
air ◊ *un po' d'aria fresca* a bit of fresh air
♦ **aria condizionata** air conditioning
♦ **all'aria aperta** in the open air
♦ **avere l'aria allegra** to look happy
♦ **avere l'aria stanca** to look tired
♦ **Si dà un sacco di arie.** He thinks he's so important!

l' **Ariete** NOME MASC
Aries ◊ *Sono dell'Ariete.* I'm Aries.

l' **aringa** NOME FEM (PL le **aringhe**)
herring ◊ *Le aringhe vivono in acque fredde.* Herrings are cold water fish.
♦ **un'aringa affumicata** a kipper

l' **arma** NOME FEM (PL le **armi**)
weapon ◊ *un'arma pericolosa* a dangerous weapon
♦ **essere alle prime armi** to have* just started ◊ *Come batterista sono ancora alle prime armi.* I've just started playing the drums.

l' **armadietto** NOME MASC
1 cabinet ◊ *l'armadietto dei medicinali* the medicine cabinet
2 locker *(con serratura)*

l' **armadio** NOME MASC
wardrobe

armato AGGETTIVO (FEM **armata**)
armed ◊ *Era armato di coltello.* He was armed with a knife.
♦ **rapina a mano armata** armed robbery

l' **armatura** NOME FEM
armour
armor US

l' **armonica** NOME FEM (PL le **armoniche**)
harmonica ◊ *Suono l'armonica.* I play the harmonica.

arrabbiare VERBO
♦ **far arrabbiare qualcuno** to make* somebody angry ◊ *Mi ha fatto veramente arrabbiare.* He really made me angry.
♦ **arrabbiarsi** to get* angry ◊ *Non ti arrabbiare!* Don't get angry!

arrabbiato AGGETTIVO (FEM **arrabbiata**)
angry ◊ *Era molto arrabbiato.* He was very angry. ◊ *È più arrabbiato di lei.* He's angrier than she is. ◊ *Gianni era il più arrabbiato di tutti.* Gianni was angriest of all.

arrampicarsi VERBO
to climb ◊ *Ci siamo arrampicati sull'albero.* We climbed the tree.

arrangiarsi VERBO
to manage ◊ *In un modo o nell'altro ci arrangeremo.* We'll manage somehow or other.

l' **arredamento** NOME MASC
furniture

arredato AGGETTIVO (FEM **arredata**)
furnished ◊ *un appartamento arredato* a furnished flat

arrendersi* VERBO
to surrender ◊ *Si sono arresi alla polizia.* They surrendered to the police.

arrestare VERBO
to arrest ◊ *I rapinatori sono stati arrestati ieri.* The robbers were arrested yesterday.

l' **arresto** NOME MASC
arrest ◊ *in stato d'arresto* under arrest

gli **arretrati** NOME MASC PL
back pay SING *(di stipendio)*

arretrato AGGETTIVO (FEM **arretrata**)
backward *(paese, zona)* ◊ *un paese arretrato* a backward country
♦ **numero arretrato** *(di giornale)* back number
♦ **Ho un sacco di lavoro arretrato.** I've got a huge backlog of work.

arrivare VERBO
to arrive ◊ *A che ora arrivi a scuola?* What time do you arrive at school?
Con i nomi di città e di paesi la preposizione da usare è **in**.
◊ *Sono arrivato a Londra alle sette.* I arrived in London at seven.
♦ **arrivare in orario** to arrive on time
♦ **arrivare in ritardo** to arrive late

---

* *I verbi seguiti da questo simbolo sono irregolari. Si veda anche alle pp.328–338.*

◆ **Come si arriva al castello?** How do you get to the castle?

◆ **Aspettami, arrivo!** Wait for me, I'm coming!

◆ **È troppo in alto, non ci arrivo.** It's too high, I can't reach it.

arrivederci ESCLAMAZIONE
goodbye! ◇ *Arrivederci, signora Cooper!* Goodbye, Mrs Cooper!

l' **arrivo** NOME MASC
arrival ◇ *al mio arrivo* on my arrival

◆ **essere in arrivo** to be* arriving ◇ *Il treno per Roma è in arrivo al binario uno.* The train to Rome is arriving at platform one.

◆ **"arrivi"** (*in aeroporto*) "arrivals"

arrogante AGGETTIVO
arrogant

arrossire VERBO
to go* red ◇ *È arrossito per l'imbarazzo.* He went red with embarrassment.

l' **arrosto** NOME MASC
vedi anche **arrosto** AGGETTIVO
roast meat

◆ **arrosto di manzo** roast beef

arrosto AGGETTIVO (FEM **arrosta**)
vedi anche **arrosto** NOME
roast ◇ *pollo arrosto* roast chicken

arrotondare VERBO
to supplement (*stipendio*) ◇ *Fa dei lavoretti extra per arrotondare lo stipendio.* He does part-time jobs to supplement his salary.

◆ **arrotondare una cifra (1)** (*per eccesso*) to round up a figure

◆ **arrotondare una cifra (2)** (*per difetto*) to round down a figure

arrugginito AGGETTIVO (FEM **arrugginita**)
rusty ◇ *un lucchetto arrugginito* a rusty padlock

arruolarsi VERBO
to join ◇ *Si è arruolato in marina.* He's joined the navy.

l' **arte** NOME FEM
art ◇ *una galleria d'arte* an art gallery ◇ *un'opera d'arte* a work of art

l' **articolo** NOME MASC
article (*in grammatica, su giornale*) ◇ *Abbiamo letto un articolo sull'effetto serra.* We read an article about the greenhouse effect.

◆ **negozio di articoli sportivi** sports shop

artificiale AGGETTIVO
artificial

l' **artigianato** NOME MASC
crafts PL ◇ *un negozio di artigianato locale* a shop selling local crafts

◆ **fiera dell'artigianato** craft fair

l' **artista** NOME MASC/FEM (MASC PL gli **artisti**, FEM PL le **artiste**)
artist ◇ *È un artista.* He's an artist.

artistico AGGETTIVO (FEM **artistica**, MASC PL **artistici**, FEM PL **artistiche**)
artistic ◇ *Non ho nessuna inclinazione artistica.* I'm not at all artistic.

◆ **liceo artistico** secondary school specializing in art

l' **ascella** NOME FEM
armpit

l' **ascensore** NOME MASC
lift
elevator │US│
◇ *L'ascensore è guasto.* The lift's out of order.

l' **asciugacapelli** NOME MASC (PL gli **asciugacapelli**)
hairdryer

l' **asciugamano** NOME MASC
towel

asciugare VERBO
to dry ◇ *Asciugati i capelli.* Dry your hair.

◆ **asciugarsi** to get* dry ◇ *La maglietta si è asciugata in fretta.* The T-shirt soon got dry.

asciutto AGGETTIVO (FEM **asciutta**)
dry ◇ *È asciutta la maglietta?* Is the T-shirt dry?

ascoltare VERBO
to listen to ◇ *Mi stai ascoltando?* Are you listening to me?

l' **Asia** NOME FEM
Asia

asiatico, asiatica NOME, AGGETTIVO (MASC PL **asiatici**, FEM PL **asiatiche**)
Asian

l' **asilo** NOME MASC
nursery school ◇ *Paolo va all'asilo.* Paolo goes to nursery school.

◆ **asilo politico** political asylum ◇ *Hanno chiesto asilo politico.* They've asked for political asylum.

l' **asino** NOME MASC
donkey

l' **asma** NOME FEM
asthma

l' **asparago** NOME MASC (PL gli **asparagi**)
asparagus ◇ *un mazzo di asparagi* a bunch of asparagus ◇ *Gli asparagi sono buoni.* Asparagus is nice.

aspettare VERBO
1 to wait ◇ *Aspetta un attimo!* Wait a minute! ◇ *È un'ora che aspetto.* I've been waiting for an hour.
Si noti la costruzione verbale in inglese.

◆ **aspettare qualcuno** to wait for somebody ◇ *Sto aspettando un'amica.* I'm waiting for a friend. ◇ *Aspettami, vengo anch'io!* Wait for me, I'm coming too!

◆ **fare aspettare qualcuno** to keep* somebody waiting ◇ *Mi ha fatto aspettare un'ora.* He kept me waiting for an hour.

2 to expect (*telefonata, lettera, ospiti*) ◇ *Sto aspettando una telefonata importante.* I'm expecting an important phone call. ◇ *Era meglio di quanto mi aspettassi.* It was better than I expected.

☞

♦ **aspettare un bambino** to be* expecting a
baby ◊ *Mia sorella aspetta un bambino.* My
sister's expecting a baby.

l' **aspetto** NOME MASC
appearance ◊ *Cura molto il suo aspetto.* He
takes great care of his appearance.

♦ **di bell'aspetto** good-looking

l' **aspirapolvere** NOME MASC (PL gli
aspirapolvere)
vacuum cleaner

♦ **passare l'aspirapolvere** to vacuum

l' **aspirina** ® NOME FEM
aspirin ◊ *Prendi due aspirine.* Take two
aspirins.

aspro AGGETTIVO (FEM **aspra**)
sour ◊ *Questo pompelmo è molto aspro.*
This grapefruit is very sour.

assaggiare VERBO
to taste ◊ *Vuoi assaggiare?* Would you like
to taste it?

assai AVVERBIO
1 very ◊ *Sono assai contento.* I'm very
pleased.
2 much (*con comparativo*) ◊ *È assai più
giovane di me.* He's much younger than me.

l' **assassino**, l' **assassina** NOME MASC, FEM
1 murderer (*in generale*)
2 assassin (*di uomo politico, di capo di
stato*)

l' **asse** NOME FEM
board (*di legno*)

♦ **asse da stiro** ironing board

l' **assegno** NOME MASC
cheque
check US
◊ *Ha pagato con un assegno.* He paid by
cheque.

l' **assemblea** NOME FEM
meeting

assente AGGETTIVO
absent ◊ *Oggi sono assenti due scolari.*
Two pupils are absent today.

♦ **La mia segretaria oggi è assente.** My
secretary is not at work today.

♦ **Sono stato assente da scuola per due
settimane.** I was off school for two weeks.

l' **assenza** NOME FEM
absence ◊ *in mia assenza* in my absence

♦ **Ho fatto molte assenze da scuola.** I've
missed a lot of school.

assetato AGGETTIVO (FEM **assetata**)
thirsty

assicurare VERBO
1 to insure ◊ *La macchina non era
assicurata contro il furto.* The car wasn't
insured against theft.
2 to assure (*garantire*) ◊ *Mi ha assicurato
che sarebbe venuto.* He assured me that
he'd come.

♦ **assicurarsi** to make* sure ◊ *Assicurati che*

la porta sia ben chiusa. Make sure the door's
closed properly.

l' **assicurazione** NOME FEM
insurance ◊ *Ho fatto un'assicurazione sulla
vita.* I took out life insurance.

assieme AVVERBIO
together

l' **assistente** NOME MASC/FEM
assistant ◊ *Il direttore ha chiamato una sua
assistente.* The manager called one of his
assistants.

♦ **assistente di volo** flight attendant

♦ **assistente sociale** social worker

assistere* VERBO
to look after (*malato*) ◊ *Assiste la madre
ammalata.* She's looking after her sick
mother.

♦ **assistere a (1)** (*spettacolo*) to watch

♦ **assistere a (2)** (*incidente*) to witness

l' **asso** NOME MASC
ace ◊ *l'asso di picche* the ace of spades ◊ *È
un asso del volante.* He's an ace driver.

l' **associazione** NOME FEM
association

assolutamente AVVERBIO
absolutely ◊ *È assolutamente incredibile.*
It's absolutely incredible.

♦ **Devi assolutamente vedere quel film, è
fantastico.** You really must see that film, it's
fantastic.

assolvere* VERBO
to acquit ◊ *È stato assolto.* He was
acquitted.

assomigliare VERBO

♦ **assomigliare a** to look like ◊ *Assomiglia
alla madre.* She looks like her mother.

♦ **assomigliarsi** to look alike ◊ *Si
assomigliano molto.* They look very alike.

assonnato AGGETTIVO (FEM **assonnata**)
sleepy ◊ *Hai l'aria assonnata.* You look
sleepy.

assopirsi VERBO
to doze off ◊ *Mi sono assopito un attimo.* I
dozed off for a moment.

l' **assorbente** NOME MASC

♦ **assorbente igienico** sanitary towel

♦ **assorbente interno** tampon

assordare VERBO
to deafen ◊ *Abbassa il volume, mi stai
assordando!* Turn down the volume, you're
deafening me!

assortito AGGETTIVO (FEM **assortita**)
assorted ◊ *una scatola di cioccolatini
assortiti* a box of assorted chocolates

assumere* VERBO
to take* on ◊ *L'azienda assumerà due
operai.* The company is going to take on two
workers.

♦ **essere assunto** to get* a job ◊ *È stata
assunta come programmatrice.* She's got a

job as a programmer.

assurdo AGGETTIVO (FEM **assurda**)
ridiculous ◇ *Che idea assurda!* What a
ridiculous idea! ◇ *È assurdo!* It's
ridiculous!

l' **asta** NOME FEM
pole ◇ *salto con l'asta* pole vault
♦ **vendita all'asta** auction

astemio AGGETTIVO (FEM **astemia**)
teetotal
Attenzione! In inglese esiste la parola
***abstemious** che però vuol dire **moderato**.*

l' **astenuto**, l' **astenuta** NOME MASC, FEM
abstention ◇ *Dieci a favore, tre contrari e
due astenuti.* Ten in favour, three against
and two abstentions.

l' **asterisco** NOME MASC (PL l' **asterischi**)
asterisk

astratto AGGETTIVO (FEM **astratta**)
abstract

l' **astrologia** NOME FEM
astrology

l' **astronauta** NOME MASC/FEM (MASC PL gli
astronauti, FEM PL le **astronaute**)
astronaut

l' **astronave** NOME FEM
spacecraft

l' **astronomia** NOME FEM
astronomy

astronomico AGGETTIVO (FEM **astronomica**,
MASC PL **astronomici**, FEM PL **astronomiche**)
astronomical ◇ *prezzi astronomici*
astronomical prices

l' **astuccio** NOME MASC
case ◇ *un astuccio portapenne* a pencil
case

astuto AGGETTIVO (FEM **astuta**)
cunning ◇ *È astuto come una volpe.* He's
cunning as a fox.

Atene NOME FEM
Athens ◇ *Quest'estate andremo ad Atene.*
We're going to Athens this summer. ◇ *Abita
ad Atene.* She lives in Athens.

l' **atleta** NOME MASC/FEM (MASC PL gli **atleti**, FEM PL
le **atlete**)
athlete

l' **atletica** NOME FEM
athletics SING ◇ *Guardo sempre l'atletica in
TV.* I always watch the athletics on TV.

l' **atmosfera** NOME FEM
atmosphere ◇ *C'era una bella atmosfera.*
There was a nice atmosphere.

atomico AGGETTIVO (FEM **atomica**, MASC PL
atomici, FEM PL **atomiche**)
atomic ◇ *la bomba atomica* the atomic
bomb

l' **atrio** NOME MASC
1 entrance (*di albergo*)
2 concourse (*di stazione*)

atroce AGGETTIVO
terrible ◇ *un mal di testa atroce* a terrible
headache

l' **attaccante** NOME MASC/FEM
forward ◇ *Gioca da attaccante.* He's a
forward.

l' **attaccapanni** NOME MASC (PL gli
attaccapanni)
hook ◇ *Appendi la giacca all'attaccapanni.*
Hang your jacket on the hook.

attaccare VERBO
1 to stick* ◇ *Non so dove attaccare questo
poster.* I don't know where to stick this
poster. ◇ *Il sugo si sta attaccando.* The
sauce is sticking. ◇ *Le pagine si sono
attaccate.* The pages are stuck together.
2 to sew* on (*cucire*) ◇ *Devo attaccare due
bottoni.* I've got to sew two buttons on.
3 to start (*cominciare*) ◇ *Quando attacca a
lamentarsi non la smette più.* Once she
starts moaning she never stops.
4 to give* (*malattia*) ◇ *Non vorrei
attaccarti il raffreddore.* I wouldn't want to
give you my cold.

l' **attacco** NOME MASC (PL gli **attacchi**)
1 attack ◇ *un attacco d'asma* an asthma
attack
♦ **giocare in attacco** (*squadra*) to play an
attacking game
2 binding (*di sci*)

l' **atteggiamento** NOME MASC
attitude ◇ *Non mi piace il suo
atteggiamento.* I don't like his attitude.

l' **attentato** NOME MASC
attack ◇ *un attentato terroristico* a terrorist
attack

attento AGGETTIVO (FEM **attenta**)
careful ◇ *Stai attento quando attraversi la
strada.* Be careful when you cross the road.
♦ **Non sono stato attento alla lezione.** I didn't
pay attention in class.
♦ **Attento!** Watch out!
♦ **Attento alle dita!** Mind your fingers!
♦ **"attenti al cane"** "beware of the dog"

l' **attenzione** NOME FEM
attention ◇ *Gli piace essere al centro
dell'attenzione.* He likes to be the centre of
attention. ◇ *Cerca di richiamare
l'attenzione del cameriere.* Try and attract
the waiter's attention.
♦ **Attenzione al gradino!** Mind the step!

l' **atterraggio** NOME MASC
landing ◇ *un atterraggio di fortuna* an
emergency landing

atterrare VERBO
to land ◇ *L'aereo ha appena atterrato.* The
plane has just landed.

l' **attesa** NOME FEM
wait ◇ *dopo una lunga attesa* after a long
wait
♦ **lista d'attesa** waiting list
♦ **sala d'attesa** waiting room

attillato AGGETTIVO (FEM **attillata**)
tight

l' **attimo** NOME MASC
minute ◊ *Aspetta un attimo.* Wait a minute.
◊ *Torno tra un attimo.* I'll be back in a
minute.

attirare VERBO
[1] to attract ◊ *L'ha fatto per attirare la sua
attenzione.* He did it to attract her attention.
[2] to appeal to ◊ *L'idea non mi attira per
niente.* The idea doesn't appeal to me at all.

l' **attività** NOME FEM (PL le **attività**)
activity (PL activities) ◊ *Mi piacciono le
attività all'aria aperta* I like outdoor
activities.

attivo AGGETTIVO (FEM **attiva**)
active

l' **atto** NOME MASC
act ◊ *atti di sabotaggio* acts of sabotage
◊ *durante il secondo atto* during the second
act

l' **attore** NOME MASC
actor ◊ *un attore famoso* a famous actor

attorno AVVERBIO
round ◊ *È entrato e si è guardato attorno.*
He came in and looked round. ◊ *Seduti
attorno al fuoco abbiamo cantato fino
all'alba.* We sat round the fire and sang until
dawn.

attraversare VERBO
[1] to cross ◊ *Stai attento quando attraversi
la strada.* Be careful when you cross the
road.
[2] to go* through ◊ *Sta attraversando un
periodo difficile.* She's going through a
difficult time.

attraverso PREPOSIZIONE
through ◊ *Sono entrati attraverso la
finestra.* They got in through the window.

attrezzato AGGETTIVO (FEM **attrezzata**)
♦ **ben attrezzato** well-equipped ◊ *una
palestra ben attrezzata* a well-equipped gym

l' **attrezzo** NOME MASC
tool ◊ *attrezzi da giardinaggio* gardening
tools
♦ **carro attrezzi** breakdown truck

l' **attrice** NOME FEM
actress ◊ *un'attrice famosa* a famous
actress

attuale AGGETTIVO
[1] present ◊ *al momento attuale* at the
present moment ◊ *l'attuale proprietario*
the present owner
[2] current ◊ *l'attuale situazione politica*
the current political situation
*Attenzione! In inglese esiste la parola **actual**
che però vuol dire **effettivo**.*

l' **attualità** NOME FEM
current affairs PL ◊ *un programma di
attualità* a current affairs programme
♦ **un problema di attualità** a topical issue

attualmente AVVERBIO

at the moment ◊ *Attualmente sono in
tournée in America.* They're on tour in
America at the moment.
*Attenzione! In inglese esiste la parola
actually che però vuol dire **effettivamente**
oppure "veramente".*

l' **audio** NOME MASC
sound ◊ *Il video funziona ma l'audio no.*
There's a picture but no sound.

l' **audizione** NOME FEM
audition

gli **auguri** NOME MASC PL
♦ **Auguri! (1)** (*di compleanno*) Happy birthday!
♦ **Auguri! (2)** (*buona fortuna*) Good luck!
♦ **fare gli auguri di Natale a qualcuno** to wish
somebody happy Christmas

l' **aula** NOME FEM
classroom

aumentare VERBO
to go* up ◊ *Il prezzo della benzina è
aumentato.* The price of petrol has gone up.
◊ *La disoccupazione è aumentata del dieci
per cento.* Unemployment's gone up by ten
per cent. ◊ *Gli hanno aumentato l'affitto.*
His rent's gone up.
♦ **Gli hanno aumentato lo stipendio.** They've
given him a pay rise.

l' **aumento** NOME MASC
increase ◊ *C'è stato un aumento del tre per
cento sul prezzo.* There's been a three per
cent increase in the price.
♦ **essere in aumento** to rise* ◊ *I prezzi sono in
aumento.* Prices are rising.
♦ **aumento di stipendio** pay rise

l' **Australia** NOME FEM
Australia ◊ *Ti è piaciuta l'Australia?* Did you
like Australia? ◊ *Quest'estate andremo in
Australia.* We're going to Australia this
summer.

australiano, australiana NOME,
AGGETTIVO
Australian

l' **Austria** NOME FEM
Austria ◊ *Ti è piaciuta l'Austria?* Did you
like Austria? ◊ *Quest'estate andremo in
Austria.* We're going to Austria this
summer.

austriaco, austriaca NOME, AGGETTIVO
(MASC PL **austriaci**, FEM PL **austriache**)
Austrian

autentico AGGETTIVO (FEM **autentica**, MASC PL
autentici, FEM PL **autentiche**)
genuine ◊ *La firma è autentica.* The
signature is genuine.

l' **autista** NOME MASC/FEM (MASC PL gli **autisti**, FEM
PL le **autiste**)
driver ◊ *Fa l'autista di autobus.* He is a bus
driver.

l' **auto** NOME FEM (PL le **auto**)
car ◊ *Verremo in auto.* We'll come by car.

* I verbi seguiti da questo simbolo sono irregolari. Si veda anche alle pp.328–338.

A

autobiografico AGGETTIVO (FEM
autobiografica, MASC PL **autobiografici**, FEM PL
autobiografiche)
autobiographical ◇ *un romanzo
autobiografico* an autobiographical novel

l' **autobus** NOME MASC (PL gli **autobus**)
bus ◇ *Vado a scuola in autobus.* I go to
school by bus. ◇ *un autobus a due piani* a
double-decker bus

l' **autocarro** NOME MASC
lorry (PL lorries)
truck US

l' **autogol** NOME MASC (PL gli **autogol**)
own goal ◇ *Ha fatto autogol.* He scored an
own goal.

l' **autografo** NOME MASC
autograph ◇ *Mi ha fatto l'autografo!* He
gave me his autograph!

automatico AGGETTIVO (FEM **automatica**,
MASC PL **automatici**, FEM PL **automatiche**)
automatic ◇ *porte a chiusura automatica*
automatic doors

l' **automobile** NOME FEM
car

l' **automobilista** NOME MASC/FEM (MASC PL gli
automobilisti, FEM PL le **automobiliste**)
motorist

l' **autonoleggio** NOME MASC
car hire place ◇ *C'è un autonoleggio da
queste parti?* Is there a car hire place near
here?

l' **autoradio** NOME FEM (PL le **autoradio**)
car radio ◇ *Gli hanno rubato l'autoradio.*
His car radio has been stolen.

l' **autore** NOME MASC
author

l' **autorità** NOME FEM (PL le **autorità**)
authority (PL authorities)

autorizzare VERBO
 ♦ **autorizzare qualcuno a fare qualcosa** to
give* somebody permission to do
something ◇ *Mi hanno autorizzato ad
aprire la corrispondenza.* I was given
permission to open correspondence.
 ♦ **La manifestazione non era stata
autorizzata.** Permission for the march had
not been granted.

l' **autrice** NOME FEM
author

gli **autoscontri** NOME MASC PL
Dodgems® ◇ *Facciamo un giro sugli
autoscontri.* Let's go on the dodgems.

l' **autoscuola** NOME FEM
driving school

l' **autostop** NOME MASC
 ♦ **fare l'autostop** to hitchhike ◇ *Abbiamo
fatto l'autostop fino a Reggio Calabria.* We
hitchhiked to Reggio Calabria.

l' **autostoppista** NOME MASC/FEM (MASC PL gli
autostoppisti, FEM PL le **autostoppiste**)
hitchhiker ◇ *Abbiamo dato un passaggio ad*

un autostoppista. We gave a hitchhiker a lift.

l' **autostrada** NOME FEM
motorway
freeway US

> ❶ *Sia in Gran Bretagna che negli Stati Uniti
l'accesso all'**autostrada** è gratuito.*

l' **autunno** NOME MASC
autumn
fall US
 ◇ *in autunno* in autumn

avanti AVVERBIO
forward ◇ *Ho fatto un passo avanti.* I took a
step forward. ◇ *Bisogna mettere l'orologio
avanti di un'ora.* You have to put the clock
forward an hour.
 ♦ **Il mio orologio è avanti.** My watch's fast.
 ♦ **in avanti** forward ◇ *Spostalo un po' in
avanti.* Move it forward a bit.
 ♦ **andare avanti (1)** (*continuare*) to go* on
 ◇ *Non si può andare avanti così.* We can't
go on like this.
 ♦ **andare avanti (2)** (*precedere*) to go* on
ahead ◇ *Vai pure avanti, ti raggiungo dopo.*
Go on ahead, I'll catch you up later.
 ♦ **Avanti!** (*entra*) Come in!
 ♦ **Avanti il prossimo!** Next please!
 ♦ **Avanti, assaggialo!** Go on, taste it!
 ♦ **avanti Cristo** BC ◇ *nel cinquantacinque
avanti Cristo* in fifty-five BC

avanzare VERBO
to be* left over ◇ *È avanzato del pollo da
ieri.* There's some chicken left over from
yesterday.
 ♦ **Basta e avanza.** That's more than enough.

gli **avanzi** NOME MASC PL
left-overs (*di cibo*)

avaro AGGETTIVO (FEM **avara**)
stingy ◇ *È più avara di lui.* She's stingier
than him. ◇ *È la persona più avara che abbia
mai incontrato.* He's the stingiest person
I've ever met.

avere* VERBO
[1] to have* ◇ *Non sapevo che avessi una
moto.* I didn't know you had a motorbike.
◇ *All'inizio ha avuto un sacco di problemi.*
He had a lot of problems at first.

*have è l'ausiliare usato per formare i tempi
composti in inglese.*

 ◇ *Ho già mangiato.* I've already eaten.
 ◇ *Hai visto quel film?* Have you seen that
film? ◇ *Se me l'avessi detto prima l'avrei
portato.* If you'd told me sooner I'd have
brought it.

*Spesso il passato prossimo italiano viene
tradotto con il "simple past" inglese.*

 ◇ *Gli ho parlato ieri.* I spoke to him
yesterday.

*Quando si usa **have** per esprimere possesso
al presente, spesso si aggiunge **got**.*

 ◇ *Ha la macchina nuova.* She's got a new

car. ◇ *Ho due fratelli.* I've got two brothers.
◇ *Ha gli occhi azzurri.* He's got blue eyes.
[2] to be* ◇ *Ho diciassette anni.* I'm
seventeen. ◇ *Aveva la mia età.* He was the
same age as me. ◇ *Ho fame.* I'm hungry.
* **Cos'hai?** What's the matter?
* **Quanti ne abbiamo oggi?** What's the date
today?

l' **avorio** NOME MASC
ivory

avvelenare VERBO
to poison

l' **avvenimento** NOME MASC
event ◇ *i principali avvenimenti sportivi* the
main sporting events

avvenire* VERBO
| vedi anche **avvenire** NOME |
to happen ◇ *È avvenuto nel 1999.* It
happened in 1999.

l' **avvenire** NOME MASC
| vedi anche **avvenire** VERBO |
future ◇ *Fa progetti per l'avvenire.* She's
making plans for the future.

avventato AGGETTIVO (FEM **avventata**)
rash ◇ *È stata una decisione avventata.* It
was a rash decision.

l' **avventura** NOME FEM
[1] adventure ◇ *È la vacanza ideale per chi
ama l'avventura.* It's an ideal holiday for
anyone who likes adventure.
[2] affair (*amorosa*) ◇ *Ha avuto
un'avventura con una donna sposata.* He
had an affair with a married woman.

avverarsi VERBO
to come* true ◇ *Il suo sogno si è avverato.*
Her dream came true.

l' **avverbio** NOME MASC
adverb

avversario AGGETTIVO (FEM **avversaria**)
| vedi anche **avversario** NOME |
opposing ◇ *la squadra avversaria* the
opposing team

l' **avversario**, l' **avversaria** NOME MASC, FEM
| vedi anche **avversario** AGGETTIVO |
opponent ◇ *Ha battuto l'avversario.* He
beat his opponent.

avvertire VERBO
to tell* ◇ *Se mi avessi avvertito sarei
arrivato prima.* If you'd told me I'd have
come sooner. ◇ *Avresti anche potuto
avvertirmi.* You could have told me.
* **Ti avverto, ogni tanto la doccia fa scherzi.**
Watch out, the shower doesn't always work
properly.

avvicinare VERBO
to move...closer ◇ *Avvicina la sedia al
tavolo.* Move your chair closer to the table.
◇ *Dovrò avvicinare il tavolo alla finestra.* I'll
have to move the table closer to the window.
* **avvicinarsi** to come* closer ◇ *Mi ha fatto*

cenno di avvicinarmi. He beckoned to me to
come closer. ◇ *Avvicinati!* Come closer!
* **Non ti avvicinare troppo al cane, morde.**
Don't go too near the dog, he bites.
* **Si avvicina il giorno della partenza.** We'll
soon be leaving.

l' **avviso** NOME MASC
[1] notice ◇ *Hai letto l'avviso in bacheca?*
Have you read the notice on the board?
◇ *fino a nuovo avviso* until further notice
[2] opinion ◇ *A mio avviso è una montatura
pubblicitaria.* In my opinion it's a publicity
stunt.
Attenzione! In inglese esiste la parola **advice**
che però vuol dire **consiglio**.

avvitare VERBO
* **avvitare una vite** to put* in a screw
* **avvitare una lampadina** to screw in a light
bulb

l' **avvocato** NOME MASC
lawyer
attorney [US]
◇ *Suo padre fa l'avvocato.* His father is a
lawyer.

avvolgere* VERBO
to wrap ◇ *Puoi avvolgere la scatola con
questa carta.* You can wrap the box in this
paper.
* **avvolgersi** to wrap oneself up ◇ *Si è avvolto
nella coperta.* He wrapped himself up in the
blanket.

l' **avvolgibile** NOME MASC
roller blind

l' **azienda** NOME FEM
business ◇ *È un'azienda familiare.* It's a
family business.

l' **azione** NOME FEM
[1] action ◇ *un film d'azione* an action
movie
[2] deed ◇ *una buona azione* a good deed
[3] share (*di società*)

azzardarsi VERBO
* **azzardarsi a fare qualcosa** to dare to do
something ◇ *Nessuno si azzardò a parlare.*
Nobody dared to speak.

l' **azzardo** NOME MASC
* **gioco d'azzardo** gambling ◇ *Gli piace il
gioco d'azzardo.* He likes gambling.

azzeccare VERBO
to get* right ◇ *Non ne azzecca mai una!* He
never gets anything right!

azzuffarsi VERBO
to fight* ◇ *S'azzuffa sempre col fratello.*
She's always fighting with her brother.

azzurro AGGETTIVO (FEM **azzurra**)
| vedi anche **azzurro** NOME |
blue ◇ *occhi azzurri* blue eyes

l' **azzurro** NOME MASC
| vedi anche **azzurro** AGGETTIVO |
* **gli azzurri** the Italian team

---

* *I verbi seguiti da questo simbolo sono irregolari. Si veda anche alle pp.328–338.*

B

il **babbo** NOME MASC

dad ◊ *È un regalo per il mio babbo.* It's a little present for my dad.
+ **Babbo Natale** Father Christmas

il/la **baby sitter** NOME MASC/FEM (PL i/le **baby sitter**)

babysitter ◊ *Non sono riusciti a trovare una baby sitter.* They couldn't find a babysitter.
+ **fare la baby sitter** (*di sera*) to babysit ◊ *Fa la babysitter il sabato sera.* She babysits on Saturday evenings.
+ **Durante le vacanze fa la baby sitter.** She looks after children during the holidays.

la **bacchetta** NOME FEM

+ **bacchetta magica** magic wand
+ **bacchette (1)** (*per mangiare alla cinese*) chopsticks
+ **bacchette (2)** (*per suonare*) drumsticks

la **bacheca** NOME FEM (PL le **bacheche**)

1 notice board ◊ *Appendilo in bacheca.* Put it on the notice board.
2 bulletin board (*elettronica*)

baciare VERBO

to kiss ◊ *L'ha baciato sulla guancia.* She kissed him on the cheek.
+ **baciarsi** to kiss ◊ *Ci siamo baciati.* We kissed.

la **bacinella** NOME FEM

bowl ◊ *una bacinella di plastica* a plastic bowl

il **bacio** NOME MASC

kiss ◊ *un bacio sulla guancia* a kiss on the cheek
+ **Tanti baci, Anna** (*su lettera*) Lots of love, Anna

il **baco** NOME MASC (PL i **bachi**)

1 worm ◊ *Questa mela ha il baco.* There's a worm in this apple.
2 bug (*di computer*)
+ **baco da seta** silkworm

badare VERBO

1 to pay* attention ◊ *Nessuno gli ha badato.* Nobody paid any attention to him.
2 to mind ◊ *Bada a non cadere.* Mind you don't fall. ◊ *È un tipo che non bada a spese.* He doesn't mind how much he spends.

i **baffi** NOME MASC PL

1 moustache SING
mustache SING [US]
◊ *Ha i baffi.* He's got a moustache.
2 whiskers (*di gatto*) ◊ *Non tirare i baffi al gatto.* Don't pull the cat's whiskers.
+ **leccarsi i baffi** to lick one's lips

il **bagagliaio** NOME MASC

boot
trunk [US]
(*di macchina*)
◊ *Puoi mettere la valigia nel bagagliaio.* You can put your case in the boot.

il **bagaglio** NOME MASC

luggage
luggage non ha plurale.
◊ *Hai molti bagagli?* Have you got a lot of luggage? ◊ *Ho lasciato i miei bagagli all'albergo.* I left my luggage at the hotel.
+ **Dove si ritirano i bagagli?** Where's the baggage reclaim?
+ **bagaglio a mano** hand luggage
+ **fare i bagagli** to pack ◊ *Hai già fatto i bagagli?* Have you packed?

bagnare VERBO

1 to get* wet ◊ *Non voglio bagnarmi le scarpe.* I don't want to get my shoes wet.
2 to water ◊ *Hai bagnato le piante?* Did you water the plants?
+ **bagnarsi** to get* soaked ◊ *Ci siamo bagnati anche se avevamo l'ombrello.* We got soaked even though we had an umbrella.

bagnato AGGETTIVO (FEM **bagnata**)

wet ◊ *Ho i capelli bagnati.* My hair's wet.
◊ *Sei bagnato fradicio!* You're soaking wet!

il **bagnino**, la **bagnina** NOME MASC, FEM

lifeguard ◊ *Fa il bagnino.* He is a lifeguard.

il **bagno** NOME MASC

1 bathroom ◊ *Qui c'è il bagno e lì la camera da letto.* The bathroom's here, and the bedroom's there.
2 toilet ◊ *Scusi, dov'è il bagno?* Where's the toilet, please?
3 bath ◊ *Preferisci il bagno o la doccia?* Which do you prefer, a bath or a shower?
+ **fare il bagno (1)** (*nella vasca*) to have* a bath
+ **fare il bagno (2)** (*nel mare*) to go* for a swim

il **bagnoschiuma** NOME MASC (PL i **bagnoschiuma**)

bubble bath

la **baia** NOME FEM

bay

balbettare VERBO

to stammer

il **balcone** NOME MASC

balcony (PL balconies) ◊ *Il balcone dà sul giardino.* The balcony looks onto the garden.

la **balena** NOME FEM

whale

ballare VERBO

to dance ◊ *Abbiamo ballato tutta la sera.* We danced all night.
+ **andare a ballare** to go* dancing ◊ *Andiamo a ballare?* Shall we go dancing?

il **ballerino**, la **ballerina** NOME MASC, FEM

dancer ◊ *un ottimo ballerino* a very good dancer ◊ *Voleva fare la ballerina.* She wanted to be a dancer.
+ **ballerino classico** ballet dancer
+ **ballerina classica** ballerina

il **ballo** NOME MASC

dance ◊ *un ballo sudamericano* a Latin American dance

☞

♦ **ballo mascherato** fancy-dress ball

il **balsamo** NOME MASC
hair conditioner (*per capelli*)

la **bambina** NOME FEM
little girl

il **bambino** NOME MASC
[1] child (PL children) ◇ *Lo saprebbe fare anche un bambino!* A child could do it!
◇ *C'erano dei bambini che giocavano nel parco.* There were some children playing in the park.
[2] baby (PL babies) ◇ *Aspetta un bambino.* She's expecting a baby.
[3] little boy (*maschietto*) ◇ *Chi è quel bambino?* Who's that little boy?

la **bambola** NOME FEM
doll

banale AGGETTIVO
[1] minor ◇ *Si è trattato di un banale incidente.* It was a minor accident.
[2] ordinary ◇ *È solo un banale raffreddore.* It's just an ordinary cold.
[3] banal ◇ *La trama del libro era un po' banale.* The plot of the book was rather banal.

la **banana** NOME FEM
banana

la **banca** NOME FEM (PL FEM le **banche**)
bank ◇ *Devo andare in banca.* I need to go to the bank.

la **bancarella** NOME FEM
stall ◇ *L'ho comprato in una bancarella al mercato.* I bought it from a stall in the market.

la **banchina** NOME FEM
quay (*di porto*)

il **banco** NOME MASC (PL i **banchi**)
[1] desk (*a scuola*)
[2] counter (*in negozio*)

la **banconota** NOME FEM
note
bill │US│
◇ *una banconota da cento euro* a hundred euro note

la **banda** NOME FEM
[1] gang ◇ *una banda di rapinatori* a gang of robbers
[2] band ◇ *Suona nella banda del paese.* She plays in the village band.

la **bandiera** NOME FEM
flag ◇ *la bandiera italiana* the Italian flag

il **bar** NOME MASC (PL i **bar**)
café

> ❶ *The main drink served in Italian* **bars** *is coffee, although alcoholic drinks are available. Many people go to a* **bar** *in the morning to have coffee and a cake for breakfast.*

la **bara** NOME FEM
coffin

la **baracca** NOME FEM (PL le **baracche**)
hut

barare VERBO
to cheat ◇ *Hai barato!* You cheated!

il **barattolo** NOME MASC
[1] jar (*di vetro*)
[2] tin (*di latta*)
[3] pot (*di plastica*)

la **barba** NOME FEM
beard ◇ *Ha la barba.* He's got a beard.
♦ **farsi la barba** to shave

la **barbabietola** NOME FEM
beetroot (*da insalata*)
♦ **barbabietola da zucchero** sugar beet

il **barbiere** NOME MASC
barber ◇ *Fa il barbiere.* He is a barber.
♦ **Devo andare dal barbiere.** I need a haircut.

il **barboncino** NOME MASC
poodle

il **barbone,** la **barbona** NOME MASC, FEM
tramp

la **barca** NOME FEM (PL le **barche**)
boat ◇ *Si è comprato una barca.* He's bought himself a boat.
♦ **barca a vela** sailing boat
♦ **una barca di** loads of ◇ *Ha una barca di soldi.* She's got loads of money.

barcollare VERBO
to stagger ◇ *Ha barcollato ed è caduto.* He staggered and fell.

la **barella** NOME FEM
stretcher ◇ *L'hanno portato via in barella.* He was carried away on a stretcher.

il/la **barista** NOME MASC/FEM (MASC PL i **baristi**, FEM PL le **bariste**)
♦ **Fa la barista.** She works in a bar.

barocco AGGETTIVO, NOME MASC (FEM **barocca**, MASC PL **barocchi**, FEM PL **barocche**)
baroque

la **barzelletta** NOME FEM
joke ◇ *Mi ha raccontato una barzelletta molto divertente.* He told me a very funny joke.

basare VERBO
to base ◇ *Il film è basato su un fatto realmente accaduto.* The film is based on a true story.
♦ **Mi baso sulle esperienze precedenti.** I'm going on past experience.

la **base** NOME FEM
[1] base ◇ *la base della lampada* the lamp base
[2] basis ◇ *La fiducia stava alla base della nostra amicizia.* Trust was the basis of our friendship.
♦ **di base** basic ◇ *Il suo stipendio di base è piuttosto basso.* Her basic salary is quite low.

B

◆ **in base a** according to ◇ *In base a questo depliant ci sono tre alberghi.* According to this brochure there are three hotels.

◆ **liquore a base di caffè** coffee liqueur

le **basette** NOME FEM PL
sideburns

il **basilico** NOME MASC
basil

il **basket** NOME MASC
basketball ◇ *Gioco a basket.* I play basketball.

il/la **bassista** NOME MASC/FEM (MASC PL **i bassisti**, FEM PL le **bassiste**)
bass player

basso AGGETTIVO (FEM **bassa**)
vedi anche **basso** NOME

[1] low ◇ *Il volume è troppo basso.* The sound's too low. ◇ *in bassa stagione* in the low season

[2] short (*persona*) ◇ *È basso e grasso.* He's short and fat. ◇ *Simona è più bassa di me.* Simona is shorter than me.

[3] shallow (*acqua*) ◇ *In quel punto l'acqua è bassa.* The water's shallow there.

il **basso** NOME MASC
vedi anche **basso** AGGETTIVO
bass guitar (*strumento*)

◆ **suonare il basso** to play bass guitar

◆ **in basso** at the bottom ◇ *Io sono quella in basso a destra nella foto.* I'm the one in the bottom right of the photo.

◆ **È là in basso.** It's down there.

◆ **più in basso** lower down ◇ *Mettilo un po' più in basso.* Put it a bit lower down.

bastare VERBO
to be* enough ◇ *Sei sicuro che venti sterline bastino?* Are you sure twenty pounds is enough? ◇ *Questa pasta non basta per cinque persone.* This pasta isn't enough for five people.

◆ **Basta e avanza!** That's more than enough!

◆ **Basta!** That's enough!

◆ **Basta così?** (*al bar, in negozio*) Will that be all?

◆ **Basta così, grazie.** That's all, thank you.

◆ **Dimmi basta.** (*servendo da bere o da mangiare*) Say when.

◆ **Basta chiedere a un poliziotto.** Just ask a policeman.

i **bastoncini** NOME MASC PL
[1] chopsticks (*per mangiare alla cinese*)
[2] ski poles (*per sciare*)

◆ **bastoncini di pesce** fish fingers, [US:] fish sticks

il **bastone** NOME MASC
[1] stick ◇ *L'ha picchiato con un bastone.* He hit him with a stick.
[2] walking stick (*da passeggio*)

la **battaglia** NOME FEM
battle

battere VERBO
[1] to beat* ◇ *Li abbiamo battuti due a zero.*

We beat them two nil. ◇ *Gli batteva forte il cuore.* His heart was beating fast. ◇ *Ha battuto il record mondiale.* She's beaten the world record.

[2] to hit* (*urtare*) ◇ *Ha battuto il mento sul gradino.* He hit his chin on the step.

◆ **battere a macchina** to type

◆ **battere un rigore** to take* a penalty

◆ **battersi** to fight*

la **batteria** NOME FEM
[1] drums PL ◇ *Suona la batteria.* He plays the drums.
[2] battery (PL batteries) ◇ *La batteria è scarica.* The battery's flat.

il/la **batterista** NOME MASC/FEM (MASC PL **i batteristi**, FEM PL le **batteriste**)
drummer

il **battesimo** NOME MASC
christening

◆ **nome di battesimo** Christian name

la **battuta** NOME FEM
joke ◇ *Ma dai, era solo una battuta.* Come on, it was only a joke.

◆ **Ha sempre la battuta pronta.** He's always ready with a witty remark.

◆ **fare una battuta su qualcosa** to make* a joke about something

il **batuffolo** NOME MASC
wad ◇ *un batuffolo di cotone* a wad of cotton wool

il **baule** NOME MASC
trunk

il **bavaglio** NOME MASC
gag ◇ *Si è liberato del bavaglio.* He got the gag off.

beato AGGETTIVO (FEM **beata**)
◆ **Beato te!** Lucky you!

il **beauty case** NOME MASC (PL **i beauty case**)
vanity case ◇ *Le ho regalato un beauty case.* I gave her a vanity case.

beccare VERBO
to catch* ◇ *Mi sono beccato un raffreddore.* I've caught a cold. ◇ *L'hanno beccato a rubare in un negozio.* They caught him shoplifting.

il **becco** NOME MASC (PL **i becchi**)
beak

la **Befana** NOME FEM

> ⓘ The **Befana** is an old woman who, according to legend, brings children presents at Epiphany (January 6).

belga NOME, AGGETTIVO (MASC PL **belgi**, FEM PL **belghe**)
Belgian

il **Belgio** NOME MASC
Belgium

la **bellezza** NOME FEM
beauty (PL beauties) ◇ *un istituto di bellezza* a beauty salon

☞

♦ **Mi è costato la bellezza di tre cento euro.** I paid three hundred euros for it.
♦ **Che bellezza!** Fantastic!

bello AGGETTIVO (FEM **bella**)
> *vedi anche* **bello** NOME

[1] lovely ◇ *Che bella giornata!* What a lovely day! ◇ *Ha dei bellissimi occhi.* He's got really lovely eyes.

[2] good-looking (*persona*) ◇ *Paolo è proprio un bel ragazzo.* Paolo is a very good-looking boy. ◇ *È più bello di me.* He's better-looking than me.

[3] good ◇ *un bel film* a good film ◇ *È troppo bello per essere vero.* It's too good to be true.

[4] nice ◇ *una bella tazza di tè* a nice cup of tea

♦ **un bel niente** absolutely nothing
♦ **bella copia** final copy

il **bello** NOME MASC
> *vedi anche* **bello** AGGETTIVO

♦ **Il bello è che...** The best bit about it is that...
♦ **Che fai di bello stasera?** What are you doing this evening?
♦ **proprio sul più bello** at that very moment

il **belvedere** NOME MASC (PL i **belvedere**)
viewing point

la **benda** NOME FEM
[1] bandage (*fascia*)
[2] blindfold (*sugli occhi*)

bendare VERBO
[1] to bandage ◇ *Mi ha bendato la mano.* He bandaged my hand.
[2] to blindfold ◇ *L'hanno bendato e imbavagliato.* He was blindfolded and gagged.

bene AVVERBIO
well ◇ *Parli molto bene l'italiano.* You speak Italian very well. ◇ *Non mi sento troppo bene.* I don't feel very well.
♦ **andare bene a** (*vestiti*) to fit ◇ *Questi jeans non mi vanno bene.* These jeans don't fit me.
♦ **Va bene.** OK. ◇ *Va bene, ho capito.* OK, I understand. ◇ *A che ora? – Va bene alle due?* What time? – Is two o'clock OK?
♦ **stare bene** (*persona*) to be* fine ◇ *Sto bene, grazie.* I'm fine, thanks.
♦ **Stai bene?** Are you OK?
♦ **stare bene a** (*vestiti*) to suit ◇ *Questi jeans ti stanno molto bene.* Those jeans really suit you.
♦ **voler bene a qualcuno** to love somebody ◇ *È la mia migliore amica e le voglio molto bene.* She's my best friend and I really love her.
♦ **Hai fatto bene.** You did the right thing.
♦ **La frutta fa bene.** Fruit is good for you.
♦ **Bevi un po' d'acqua, ti farà bene.** Drink some water, it'll make you feel better.
♦ **Ben gli sta!** It serves him right!
♦ **Lì si mangia molto bene.** The food is excellent there.
♦ **Sono pronta. – Bene, andiamo.** I'm ready. – OK, let's go.

la **beneficenza** NOME FEM
charity ◇ *un concerto di beneficenza* a charity concert

benestante AGGETTIVO
well-off ◇ *una famiglia benestante* a well-off family ◇ *Viene da una famiglia più benestante della mia.* His family is better off than mine.

benvenuto AGGETTIVO (FEM **benvenuta**)
welcome ◇ *Benvenuti a Roma!* Welcome to Rome!

la **benzina** NOME FEM
petrol
gas US
◇ *Siamo rimasti senza benzina.* We ran out of petrol.
♦ **benzina verde** unleaded petrol

bere* VERBO
to drink* ◇ *Vuoi bere qualcosa?* Would you like something to drink?
♦ **Chi porta da bere?** Who's going to bring the drinks?

la **berlina** NOME FEM
saloon car
sedan US

i **bermuda** NOME MASC PL
♦ **un paio di bermuda** a pair of Bermuda shorts

il **bernoccolo** NOME MASC
bump ◇ *Ho un bernoccolo in fronte.* I've got a bump on my forehead.

il **berretto** NOME MASC
cap ◇ *un berretto da baseball* a baseball cap

il **bersaglio** NOME MASC
target ◇ *Ha mancato il bersaglio.* He missed the target.

la **besciamella** NOME FEM
béchamel sauce

bestemmiare VERBO
to swear* ◇ *Non l'ho mai sentito bestemmiare.* I've never heard him swear.

la **bestia** NOME FEM
animal ◇ *Non voglio bestie in casa!* I don't want animals in the house!

bestiale AGGETTIVO
♦ **Fa un caldo bestiale.** It's absolutely boiling.
♦ **Ho una fame bestiale!** I'm starving!

la **bevanda** NOME FEM
drink ◇ *una bevanda alcolica* an alcoholic drink

la **biancheria** NOME FEM
sheets and towels PL (*per la casa*)
♦ **biancheria intima** underwear

bianco AGGETTIVO, NOME MASC (FEM **bianca**, MASC PL **bianchi**, FEM PL **bianche**)
white ◇ *Ha i capelli bianchi.* She's got white

* *I verbi seguiti da questo simbolo sono irregolari. Si veda anche alle pp.328–338.*

Italian ~ English

B

hair.
* **TV in bianco e nero** black and white TV

la **Bibbia** NOME FEM
  Bible

la **bibita** NOME FEM
  soft drink ◊ *Vendono gelati e bibite.* They
  sell ice cream and soft drinks.

la **biblioteca** NOME FEM (PL le **biblioteche**)
  library (PL libraries)

il **bicchiere** NOME MASC
  glass ◊ *un bicchiere di vino* a glass of wine
  ◊ *un bicchiere da vino* a wine glass
* **un bicchiere di carta** a paper cup

la **bici** NOME FEM (PL le **bici**)
  bike

la **bicicletta** NOME FEM
  bike ◊ *Ci sono andato in bicicletta.* I went
  there on my bike.

il **bidé** NOME MASC (PL i **bidé**)
  bidet

il **bidello**, la **bidella** NOME MASC, FEM
  school caretaker

il **bidone** NOME MASC
* **bidone dell'immondizia** dustbin

la **bigiotteria** NOME FEM
  costume jewellery
  costume jewelry [US]

la **biglietteria** NOME FEM
  booking office

il **biglietto** NOME MASC
  [1] ticket ◊ *Hai fatto il biglietto?* Have you
  bought a ticket?
* **biglietto di andata e ritorno** return ticket
  [2] card ◊ *Mi ha mandato un biglietto per il
  compleanno.* He sent me a card for my
  birthday.
  [3] note
  bill [US]
  ◊ *Ho solo un biglietto da venti sterline.* I've
  only got a twenty-pound note.

il **bigodino** NOME MASC
  roller

il **bikini** NOME MASC (PL i **bikini**)
  bikini

Bilancia NOME FEM
  Libra (*dello zodiaco*) ◊ *Sono della Bilancia.*
  I'm Libra.

la **bilancia** NOME FEM (PL le **bilance**)
  scales PL ◊ *Hai una bilancia?* Have you got
  scales?

il **biliardo** NOME MASC
  pool ◊ *Sai giocare a biliardo?* Can you play
  pool?
* **sala da biliardo** poolroom

bilingue AGGETTIVO
  bilingual

il **binario** NOME MASC
  [1] track ◊ *Camminava lungo il binario.* He
  was walking along the track.
  [2] platform (*in stazione*) ◊ *Da quale binario
  parte il treno per Cambridge?* Which

platform does the Cambridge train go from?

il **binocolo** NOME MASC
  [1] binoculars PL ◊ *Guardava gli uccelli con
  il binocolo.* She was looking at the birds
  through binoculars.
  [2] opera glasses PL (*da teatro*)

biondo AGGETTIVO (FEM **bionda**)
  [1] blond (*uomo*)
  [2] blonde (*donna*)

la **biro** ® NOME FEM (PL le **biro**)
  Biro ®

la **birra** NOME FEM
  beer ◊ *una birra alla spina* a draught beer
* **birra chiara** lager
* **birra scura** stout

la **birreria** NOME FEM
  pub

il **bis** NOME MASC (PL i **bis**)
* **fare il bis di** to have* some more
  ◊ *Facciamo il bis di gelato?* Shall we have
  some more ice cream?
* **Bis!** Encore!

bisbigliare VERBO
  to whisper ◊ *Mi ha bisbigliato qualcosa
  all'orecchio.* He whispered something in my
  ear.

il **biscotto** NOME MASC
  biscuit
  cookie [US]

bisestile AGGETTIVO
* **anno bisestile** leap year

il **bisnonno**, la **bisnonna** NOME MASC, FEM
  great-grandfather
  great-grandmother
* **i miei bisnonni** my great-grandparents

bisognare VERBO
* **Bisogna prenotare?** Is it necessary to book?
* **Bisogna arrivare un'ora prima per il
  check-in.** You have to get there an hour
  earlier to check in.
* **Bisognerebbe telefonargli.** We should
  phone him.

il **bisogno** NOME MASC
  need ◊ *Non c'è bisogno di prenotare.*
  There's no need to book.
* **aver bisogno di qualcosa** to need
  something ◊ *Hai bisogno di qualcosa?* Do
  you need anything?
* **aver bisogno di fare qualcosa** to need to do
  something ◊ *Ho bisogno di cambiare dei
  soldi.* I need to change some money.

la **bistecca** NOME FEM (PL le **bistecche**)
  steak ◊ *una bistecca ai ferri* a grilled steak

bisticciare VERBO
  to quarrel ◊ *Bisticciano sempre.* They're
  always quarrelling.

il **bivio** NOME MASC
  junction ◊ *Al bivio prendi la strada che va a
  destra.* Go right at the junction.

bloccare VERBO
  to block ◊ *La strada è bloccata da una frana.* ☞

The road is blocked by a landslide.
- **rimanere bloccato** to be* stuck ◊ *Siamo rimasti bloccati in un ingorgo.* We were stuck in a traffic jam.
- **bloccarsi** to get* stuck ◊ *L'ascensore si è bloccato.* The lift got stuck.

il **blocchetto** NOME MASC
notebook (*per appunti*)
- **un blocchetto di biglietti per l'autobus** a book of tickets for the bus

blu AGGETTIVO, NOME MASC
navy ◊ *una maglietta blu* a navy T-shirt

la **boa** NOME FEM
buoy

la **bocca** NOME FEM (PL le **bocche**)
mouth ◊ *Non ha aperto bocca.* He didn't open his mouth.
- **respirazione bocca a bocca** mouth-to-mouth resuscitation
- **In bocca al lupo!** Good luck!

bocciare VERBO
- **essere bocciato agli esami** to fail one's exams
- **Andava male in tutte le materie ed è stato bocciato.** He did badly in all subjects and was kept down.

> **ⓘ** *If Italian school students fail their end of year exams they have to retake them. They cannot move up into the next year until they have passed them.*

la **bolla** NOME FEM
bubble

bollente AGGETTIVO
1 boiling ◊ *Cuocere in acqua bollente.* Cook in boiling water.
2 boiling hot ◊ *La minestra è bollente!* The soup is boiling hot!

la **bolletta** NOME FEM
bill ◊ *la bolletta del telefono* the phone bill

bollire VERBO
to boil ◊ *L'acqua bolle.* The water's boiling.

il **bollitore** NOME MASC
kettle

la **bomba** NOME FEM
bomb ◊ *È scoppiata una bomba alla stazione.* A bomb went off at the station.
- **bomba ad orologeria** time bomb
- **bomba a mano** hand grenade

la **bombetta** NOME FEM
bowler hat ◊ *la classica bombetta inglese* the famous English bowler hat

la **bombola** NOME FEM
cylinder ◊ *una bombola di gas* a gas cylinder

il **bordo** NOME MASC
1 edge ◊ *Eravamo seduti sul bordo della piscina.* We were sitting on the edge of the pool.

2 border ◊ *È nero, con un bordo rosso.* It's black, with a red border.
- **a bordo di** (*nave, aereo, treno*) on board ◊ *C'erano cento passeggeri a bordo dell'aereo.* There were a hundred passengers on board the plane.
- **salire a bordo** to get* on ◊ *Siamo saliti a bordo del'aereo.* We got on the plane.

borghese AGGETTIVO
middle-class ◊ *una famiglia borghese* a middle-class family
- **un poliziotto in borghese** a plainclothes policeman

il **borotalco** NOME MASC
talcum powder

la **borraccia** NOME FEM (PL le **borracce**)
flask

la **borsa** NOME FEM
bag ◊ *Ho una valigia e una borsa.* I've got one case and one bag.
- **borsa dell'acqua calda** hot water bottle
- **borsa di studio** scholarship ◊ *Ha vinto una borsa di studio.* He won a scholarship.
- **la Borsa** the Stock Exchange

il **borsellino** NOME MASC
purse

la **borsetta** NOME FEM
handbag

il **bosco** NOME MASC (PL i **boschi**)
wood ◊ *un bosco di querce* an oak wood ◊ *una passeggiata nel bosco* a walk in the woods PL

la **Bosnia** NOME FEM
Bosnia

bosniaco, bosniaca NOME, AGGETTIVO
(MASC PL **bosniaci**, FEM PL **bosniache**)
Bosnian

la **botta** NOME FEM
- **prendere una botta** to be* hit ◊ *Ha preso una botta sulla testa.* He was hit on the head.
- **fare a botte** to fight*
- **dare un sacco di botte a qualcuno** (1) (*per punizione*) to give* somebody a hiding
- **dare un sacco di botte a qualcuno** (2) (*in un'aggressione*) to beat* somebody up

la **bottiglia** NOME FEM
bottle ◊ *una bottiglia di vino* a bottle of wine

il **botto** NOME MASC
bang ◊ *Abbiamo sentito un gran botto.* We heard a loud bang.
- **di botto** suddenly ◊ *Si è fermato di botto.* He stopped suddenly.

il **bottone** NOME MASC
button

bovino AGGETTIVO, NOME MASC (FEM **bovina**)
- **carne bovina** beef
- **bovini** cattle ◊ *allevamento di bovini* cattle farming

la **boxe** NOME FEM

B

boxing ◇ *un incontro di boxe* a boxing match

i **boxer** NOME MASC PL
+ **un paio di boxer** a pair of boxer shorts

il **braccetto** NOME MASC
+ **a braccetto** arm in arm ◇ *Si tenevano a braccetto.* They were arm in arm.

il **braccialetto** NOME MASC
bracelet ◇ *un braccialetto d'argento* a silver bracelet

il **braccio** NOME MASC (PL le **braccia**)
arm ◇ *Mi fa male il braccio.* My arm hurts.
+ **braccio di ferro** arm wrestling

il **bracciolo** NOME MASC
armrest

il **Brasile** NOME MASC
Brazil ◇ *Mi è piaciuto molto il Brasile.* I really liked Brazil. ◇ *Andremo in Brasile quest'estate.* We're going to Brazil this summer.

brasiliano, brasiliana AGGETTIVO, NOME
Brazilian

bravo AGGETTIVO (FEM **brava**)
good ◇ *un attore molto bravo* a very good actor
+ **il più bravo** the best ◇ *È il più bravo della classe.* He's the best in the class.
+ **essere bravo in qualcosa** to be* good at something ◇ *Sono abbastanza bravo in inglese.* I'm quite good at English.
+ **Bravo!** Well done!

le **bretelle** NOME FEM PL
1 braces
suspenders US
(*per pantaloni*)
2 straps (*di abito, di reggiseno*)

breve AGGETTIVO
short ◇ *una breve visita* a short visit

la **briciola** NOME FEM
crumb

il **briciolo** NOME MASC
bit ◇ *Non ha un briciolo di cervello.* She hasn't got a bit of sense.

brillante AGGETTIVO
vedi anche **brillante** NOME
bright ◇ *una camicia verde brillante* a bright green shirt

il **brillante** NOME MASC
vedi anche **brillante** AGGETTIVO
diamond ◇ *un anello con brillanti* a diamond ring

brillare VERBO
to shine* ◇ *Le stelle brillano in cielo.* The stars are shining in the sky.

brillo AGGETTIVO (FEM **brilla**)
drunk ◇ *Era un po' brillo.* He was a bit drunk.

la **brina** NOME FEM
frost ◇ *C'è ancora la brina sui campi.* There's still frost on the fields.

il **brindisi** NOME MASC (PL i **brindisi**)

toast ◇ *Facciamo un brindisi!* Let's drink a toast!

la **brioche** NOME FEM (PL le **brioche**)
brioche

britannico, britannica AGGETTIVO (MASC PL **britannici**, FEM PL **britanniche**)
British ◇ *le isole britanniche* the British Isles

il **brivido** NOME MASC
shiver ◇ *Ho i brividi.* I've got the shivers.
+ **racconto del brivido** thriller ◇ *Mi piacciono i racconti del brivido.* I like thrillers.

la **brocca** NOME FEM (PL le **brocche**)
jug

i **broccoli** NOME MASC PL
broccoli SING ◇ *I broccoli fanno bene.* Broccoli is good for you.

il **brodo** NOME MASC
1 soup ◇ *brodo di pollo* chicken soup
2 stock (*per cucinare*)
+ **dadi da brodo** stock cubes

brontolare VERBO
to moan ◇ *Non fa altro che brontolare.* He's always moaning.
+ **Mi brontola lo stomaco per la fame.** My stomach is rumbling.

il **bronzo** NOME MASC
bronze ◇ *Ha vinto la medaglia di bronzo.* She won the bronze medal.

bruciare VERBO
to burn* ◇ *Oh no, ho bruciato la torta!* Oh no, I've burnt the cake! ◇ *Mi sono bruciata un dito.* I've burnt my finger.
+ **Mi bruciano gli occhi.** My eyes are smarting.
+ **bruciarsi** to burn* oneself ◇ *Mi sono bruciata!* I've burnt myself!

il **bruciato** NOME MASC
+ **Sento odore di bruciato.** I can smell burning.

il **brufolo** NOME MASC
spot

bruno AGGETTIVO (FEM **bruna**)
+ **È bruno.** He's got dark hair.

brusco AGGETTIVO (FEM **brusca**, MASC PL **bruschi**, FEM PL **brusche**)
abrupt ◇ *È stato un po' brusco con me.* He was a bit abrupt with me.
+ **Ha fatto una brusca frenata.** He braked suddenly.

brutto AGGETTIVO (FEM **brutta**)
1 ugly (*di aspetto*) ◇ *È proprio brutto!* He's really ugly. ◇ *È il posto più brutto che abbia mai visto.* It's the ugliest place I've ever seen.
2 bad ◇ *Ho un brutto raffreddore.* I've got a bad cold. ◇ *Ho fatto un brutto sogno.* I had a bad dream. ◇ *Ho preso un brutto voto in matematica.* I got a bad mark in maths.
+ **Che brutta giornata!** What a horrible day!

la **Bruxelles** NOME FEM
Brussels ◇ *Vivo a Bruxelles.* I live in

☞

Brussels.

la **buca** NOME FEM (PL le **buche**)
<u>hole</u> ◊ *La strada è piena di buche.* The road is full of holes.
- **buca delle lettere** post box, US: mail box

bucare VERBO
<u>to have* a puncture</u> ◊ *Abbiamo bucato e siamo arrivati in ritardo.* We had a puncture and arrived late.
- **bucarsi** (*drogarsi*) to be* on heroin

il **bucato** NOME MASC
- **fare il bucato** to do* the washing

la **buccia** NOME FEM (PL le **bucce**)
1 <u>peel</u> (*di frutto, di patata*) ◊ *bucce di patata* potato peel SING
2 <u>rind</u> ◊ *Aggiungi un po' di una buccia di limone grattugiata.* Add some grated lemon rind.
- **una buccia di banana** a banana skin

il **buco** NOME MASC (PL i **buchi**)
<u>hole</u> ◊ *C'è un buco nella tasca.* There's a hole in the pocket.
- **buco della serratura** keyhole

il **budino** NOME MASC
<u>pudding</u> ◊ *budino al cioccolato* chocolate pudding

buffo AGGETTIVO (FEM **buffa**)
<u>funny</u> ◊ *Pensa a qualcosa di più buffo.* Think of something funnier. ◊ *È la cosa più buffa che abbia mai sentito.* It's the funniest thing I've ever heard.

la **bugia** NOME FEM (PL le **bugie**)
<u>lie</u> ◊ *Non dico mai le bugie.* I never tell lies.

il **bugiardo**, la **bugiarda** NOME MASC, FEM
vedi anche **bugiardo** AGGETTIVO
<u>liar</u> ◊ *Mi ha dato del bugiardo.* He called me a liar.

bugiardo AGGETTIVO (FEM **bugiarda**)
vedi anche **bugiardo** NOME
- **essere bugiardo** to be* a liar

buio AGGETTIVO (FEM **buia**)
vedi anche **buio** NOME
<u>dark</u> ◊ *un vicolo buio* a dark alley

il **buio** NOME MASC
<u>dark</u>
vedi anche **buio** AGGETTIVO ◊ *Ha paura del buio.* She's afraid of the dark.

il **bullone** NOME MASC
<u>bolt</u>

buonanotte ESCLAMAZIONE
<u>good night!</u>

buonasera ESCLAMAZIONE
1 <u>good evening!</u> (*dopo le sei; quando si arriva*)
2 <u>good afternoon!</u> (*prima delle sei; quando si arriva*)
3 <u>goodbye!</u> (*quando si va via*)

buongiorno ESCLAMAZIONE
1 <u>good morning!</u> (*prima dell'una; quando si arriva*)
2 <u>goodbye!</u> (*quando si va via*)

buono AGGETTIVO (FEM **buona**)
vedi anche **buono** NOME
<u>good</u> ◊ *un buon ristorante* a good restaurant ◊ *Ha un buon sapore.* It tastes good.
- **Buona fortuna!** Good luck!
- **Buon viaggio!** Have a good trip!
- **Buon compleanno!** Happy birthday!
- **Buon Natale!** Happy Christmas!
- **Buon divertimento!** Have a nice time!

il **buono** NOME MASC
vedi anche **buono** AGGETTIVO
- **i buoni e i cattivi** the goodies and the baddies
- **C'è di buono che...** The good thing about it is that...
- **buono sconto** coupon

il **buonsenso** NOME MASC
<u>common sense</u> ◊ *Non ha un briciolo di buonsenso.* She hasn't a bit of common sense.

il **buonumore** NOME MASC
- **essere di buonumore** to be* in a good mood ◊ *Oggi sono di buonumore.* I'm in a good mood today.

il **burattino** NOME MASC
<u>puppet</u>

il **burro** NOME MASC
<u>butter</u> ◊ *pane e burro* bread and butter

il **burrone** NOME MASC
<u>ravine</u>

bussare VERBO
<u>to knock</u> ◊ *Ho bussato alla porta.* I knocked at the door.
- **Hanno bussato.** There's somebody at the door.

la **bussola** NOME FEM
<u>compass</u>

la **busta** NOME FEM
<u>envelope</u>

la **bustarella** NOME FEM
<u>bribe</u> ◊ *lo scandalo delle bustarelle* the bribes scandal

la **bustina** NOME FEM
- **una bustina di tè** a tea bag
- **una bustina di zucchero** a sachet of sugar

buttare VERBO
<u>to throw*</u> ◊ *Ha buttato il cappotto sul letto.* He threw his coat onto the bed.
- **buttare via** to throw* away ◊ *Era rotto e l'ho buttato via.* It was broken and I threw it away.
- **buttare giù un muro** to knock down a wall
- **buttare la pasta** to put* the pasta on ◊ *Hai già buttato la pasta?* Have you put the pasta on?
- **buttarsi in acqua** to jump into the water

C

la **cabina** NOME FEM
cabin (*di nave*) ◇ *una cabina di seconda classe* a second-class cabin
◆ **cabina telefonica** phone box
◆ **cabina di pilotaggio** cockpit

il **cacao** NOME MASC
cocoa

la **caccia** NOME FEM
hunting ◇ *Sono contro la caccia.* I'm against hunting.
◆ **andare a caccia** to go* hunting ◇ *La domenica vanno a caccia.* They go hunting on Sundays.
◆ **dare la caccia a qualcuno** to go* after somebody ◇ *La polizia gli dava la caccia.* The police went after him.
◆ **caccia al tesoro** treasure hunt

cacciare VERBO
1 to hunt ◇ *Ha imparato a cacciare e a pescare da bambino.* He learned to hunt and fish as a child.
2 to throw* out (*mandare via*) ◇ *Se continua così lo cacceranno dalla squadra.* If he goes on like this they'll throw him out of the team.
3 to put* (*mettere*) ◇ *Dove hai cacciato quel libro?* Where did you put that book?
◆ **cacciarsi nei guai** to get* into trouble ◇ *Si caccia sempre nei guai.* She's always getting into trouble.

il **cacciatore** NOME MASC
hunter

il **cacciavite** NOME MASC (PL i **cacciavite**)
screwdriver

il **cadavere** NOME MASC
dead body (PL dead bodies)

cadere* VERBO
to fall* ◇ *Ho inciampato e sono caduta.* I tripped and fell. ◇ *È caduto dalla bicicletta.* He fell off his bike. ◇ *Sono caduto dal letto.* I fell out of bed.
◆ **Il mio compleanno cade di lunedì.** My birthday is on a Monday.
◆ **Ti è caduta la sciarpa.** You've dropped your scarf.
◆ **far cadere** (*urtando*) to knock over ◇ *Attento che fai cadere il bicchiere.* Mind you don't knock over your glass.
◆ **Ha fatto cadere il vassoio.** (*dall'alto*) She dropped the tray.
◆ **cadere dalle nuvole** to be* very surprised ◇ *Quando gliel'ho detto è caduto dalle nuvole.* When I told him about it he was very surprised.
◆ **È caduta la linea.** We were cut off.

la **caduta** NOME FEM
1 fall ◇ *Ha fatto una brutta caduta.* He had a nasty fall.
2 loss ◇ *contro la caduta dei capelli* against hair loss

il **caffè** NOME (PL i **caffè**)
1 coffee ◇ *un gelato al caffè* a coffee ice cream
◆ **caffè macchiato** coffee with a dash of milk
◆ **caffè espresso** expresso
2 café (*locale*) ◇ *Si sono incontrati in un caffè.* They met in a café.

il **caffellatte** NOME MASC (PL i **caffellatte**)
milky coffee

la **caffettiera** NOME FEM
coffee maker

il **calamaro** NOME MASC
squid (PL squid) ◇ *calamari alla griglia* grilled squid

la **calamita** NOME FEM
magnet

calare VERBO
1 to decrease (*di numero, di quantità*) ◇ *La popolazione è calata del dieci per cento.* The population has decreased by ten percent.
◆ **calare di peso** to lose* weight
2 to fall* (*prezzi, valore*) ◇ *Il prezzo della benzina è calato.* The price of petrol has fallen.
3 to drop (*temperatura, vento*) ◇ *La temperatura è calata improvvisamente.* The temperature suddenly dropped.
4 to lower (*far scendere*)
◆ **calare il sipario** to lower the curtain

il **calcagno** NOME MASC
heel

il **calcetto** NOME MASC
table football (*calcio-balilla*)

il **calciatore** NOME MASC
football player

calcio NOME (PL i **calci**)
1 football (*sport*) ◇ *una partita di calcio* a football match ◇ *Giochi a calcio?* Do you play football?
2 kick (*pedata*) ◇ *Mi ha dato un calcio.* He gave me a kick.
◆ **calcio d'angolo** corner kick
◆ **calcio di punizione** free kick
◆ **calcio di rigore** penalty kick

calcolare VERBO
to work out ◇ *Hai calcolato quanto viene a testa?* Have you worked out how much it comes to each?

la **calcolatrice** NOME FEM
calculator

il **calcolo** NOME MASC
calculation ◇ *Ho fatto un rapido calcolo.* I did a quick calculation.
◆ **fare il calcolo di** to work out ◇ *Ho fatto il calcolo di quanto gli dovevo.* I worked out how much I owed him.

la **caldaia** NOME FEM
boiler

caldo AGGETTIVO (FEM **calda**)

☞

vedi anche **caldo** NOME

1 hot ◇ *l'acqua calda* hot water ◇ *La minestra è troppo calda.* The soup's too hot. ◇ *È il mese più caldo.* It's the hottest month.

2 warm *(tiepido)* ◇ *una bella coperta calda* a nice warm blanket ◇ *Il tuo cappotto è più caldo del mio.* Your coat is warmer than mine.

hot *descrive una temperatura superiore a* **warm; warm** *ha spesso una connotazione positiva.*

il **caldo** NOME MASC

vedi anche **caldo** AGGETTIVO

heat ◇ *Non sopporto il caldo.* I can't stand the heat.

- **avere caldo** to be* hot ◇ *Io ho caldo, e tu?* I'm hot, what about you?
- **fare caldo** to be* hot ◇ *Fa caldo qui, non trovi?* It's hot here, isn't it?

il **calendario** NOME MASC
calendar

la **calligrafia** NOME FEM
handwriting ◇ *Non capisco la sua calligrafia.* I can't read her writing.

la **calma** NOME FEM
peace ◇ *Finalmente un po' di calma.* A bit of peace at last.

- **Fai pure con calma.** Take your time.
- **Calma!** Steady on! ◇ *Calma, non spingete!* Steady on! Don't push.

calmare VERBO ◇ *Ho cercato di calmarlo.* I tried to calm him down.
to relieve *(dolore)* ◇ *Non riusciva a calmare i dolori.* He couldn't relieve the pain.

- **calmarsi** to calm down ◇ *Calmati e dimmi tutto.* Calm down and tell me everything.

calmo AGGETTIVO (FEM **calma**)
calm ◇ *Il mare è calmo, oggi.* The sea's calm today.

- **stare calmo** to keep* calm ◇ *State calmi, non c'è pericolo.* Keep calm, there's no danger.

il **calo** NOME MASC
drop ◇ *un forte calo delle vendite* a big drop in sales

il **calore** NOME MASC
heat

il **calorifero** NOME MASC
heater

caloroso AGGETTIVO (FEM **calorosa**)
warm ◇ *un'accoglienza calorosa* a warm welcome

- **È un tipo caloroso.** He doesn't feel the cold.

calpestare VERBO

- **"vietato calpestare l'erba"** "keep off the grass"

calvo AGGETTIVO (FEM **calva**)
bald

la **calza** NOME FEM
sock *(calzino)* ◇ *una calza bucata* a sock

with a hole in it

- **calze (1)** *(calzini, calzettoni)* socks
- **calze (2)** *(collant)* tights
- **calze (3)** *(con reggicalze)* stockings

la **calzamaglia** NOME FEM

- **una calzamaglia** a pair of tights ◇ *una calzamaglia di lana* a pair of woollen tights

il **calzettone** NOME MASC
knee sock ◇ *un paio di calzettoni* a pair of knee socks

il **calzino** NOME MASC
sock ◇ *un paio di calzini* a pair of socks

il **calzolaio** NOME MASC
cobbler ◇ *Mio padre fa il calzolaio.* My father is a cobbler.

i **calzoncini** NOME MASC PL
shorts ◇ *Vorrei un paio di calzoncini rossi.* I'd like a pair of red shorts.

- **calzoncini da bagno** swimming trunks

i **calzoni** NOME MASC PL
trousers ◇ *un paio di calzoni rossi* a pair of red trousers

il **cambiamento** NOME MASC
change ◇ *un cambiamento di orario* a change in the timetable

cambiare VERBO
to change ◇ *Ultimamente è molto cambiato.* He's changed a lot recently. ◇ *Cambiamo argomento.* Let's change the subject. ◇ *Vorrei cambiare questi euro in sterline.* I'd like to change these euros into pounds. ◇ *Se non va bene me lo cambia?* If it's not right will you change it?

- **cambiare idea** to change one's mind ◇ *Scusi, ho cambiato idea. Prendo quell'altro.* Sorry, I've changed my mind. I'll have that one.
- **cambiare casa** to move house ◇ *Ha cambiato casa il mese scorso.* She moved house last month.
- **cambiarsi** to get* changed ◇ *Devo andare a casa a cambiarmi.* I've got to go home and get changed.

Il verbo **to change** *non va confuso con* **to exchange,** *che significa* **scambiare.**

il **cambiavalute** NOME MASC (PL i **cambiavalute**)
bureau de change (PL bureaux de change)

il **cambio** NOME MASC
change ◇ *Ho portato solo un cambio d'abito.* I've only brought one change of clothes.

- **agenzia di cambio** bureau de change
- **in cambio di** in exchange for ◇ *Mi ha dato una cassetta in cambio del pallone.* He gave me a cassette in exchange for the football.
- **dare il cambio a qualcuno** to take* over from somebody ◇ *Se sei stanco ti do il cambio.* If you're tired I'll take over from you.
- **il cambio della guardia** the changing of the

---

* *I verbi seguiti da questo simbolo sono irregolari. Si veda anche alle pp.328–338.*

guard

la **camera** NOME FEM

1 room (*stanza*) ◇ *una camera grande* a big room

2 bedroom (*da letto*) ◇ *È rimasto in camera sua tutto il pomeriggio.* He stayed in his bedroom the whole afternoon.

• **camera da letto** bedroom
• **camera matrimoniale** double room
• **camera singola** single room

Attenzione! In inglese esiste la parola **camera**, *che però significa* **macchina fotografica**.

la **cameriera** NOME FEM

1 waitress (*che serve a tavola*)

2 chambermaid (*che fa le camere*)

il **cameriere** NOME MASC

waiter ◇ *Fa il cameriere.* He is a waiter. ◇ *Scusi, cameriere!* Waiter!

la **camicetta** NOME FEM

blouse

camicia NOME (PL le **camicie**)

shirt ◇ *una camicia rossa* a red shirt

• **camicia da notte** nightdress

il **caminetto** NOME MASC

fireplace

il **camino** NOME MASC

chimney (*sul tetto*)

il **camion** NOME (PL i **camion**)

lorry (PL lorries)

truck US

la **camionista** NOME MASC/FEM (MASC PL i **camionisti**, FEM PL le **camioniste**)

lorry driver

trucker US

◇ *Mio padre fa il camionista.* My father is a lorry driver.

il **cammello** NOME MASC

camel

camminare VERBO

to walk ◇ *Non sono abituato a camminare tanto.* I'm not used to walking so much.

la **camomilla** NOME FEM

camomile tea

la **campagna** NOME FEM

1 country ◇ *Abita in campagna.* She lives in the country. ◇ *Siamo andati in campagna a passeggiare.* We went for a walk in the country.

2 countryside (*paesaggio*) ◇ *La campagna inglese è proprio bella.* The English countryside is really beautiful.

3 campaign ◇ *una campagna pubblicitaria* a publicity campaign

la **campana** NOME FEM

bell

il **campanello** NOME MASC

bell ◇ *Hai suonato il campanello?* Have you rung the bell?

il **campanile** NOME MASC

bell tower

il **campeggio** NOME MASC

camp site (*luogo*) ◇ *C'è un campeggio qui vicino?* Is there a camp site near here?

• **andare in campeggio** to go* camping ◇ *Quest'estate andremo in campeggio.* We're going camping this summer.

il **camper** NOME (PL i **camper**)

camper van

il **campionato** NOME MASC

championship ◇ *il campionato di calcio* the league championship

• **il campionato di serie A** the premier league

il **campione** NOME MASC

1 champion ◇ *il campione del mondo di sci* the world skiing champion

2 sample ◇ *un campione gratuito* a free sample

la **campionessa** NOME FEM

champion

il **campo** NOME MASC

field ◇ *un campo di grano* a field of wheat ◇ *Nel suo campo è uno dei migliori.* He's one of the best in his field.

• **campo di calcio** football ground
• **campo giochi** playground
• **campo sportivo** sports ground
• **campo da tennis** tennis court

il **Canada** NOME MASC

Canada ◇ *Mi è piaciuto molto il Canada.* I really liked Canada. ◇ *Andremo in Canada quest'estate.* We're going to Canada this summer.

canadese NOME, AGGETTIVO

Canadian

Si noti l'uso della maiuscola in inglese.

il **canale** NOME MASC

1 channel ◇ *Su che canale è il film?* Which channel is the film on?

• **il canale della Manica** the Channel

2 canal (*artificiale*) ◇ *i canali di Venezia* the canals of Venice

il **canarino** NOME MASC

canary (PL canaries)

cancellare VERBO

1 to rub out (*con la gomma*)

2 to cross out (*con la penna*)

3 to delete (*con il computer*)

il **cancello** NOME MASC

gate

Cancro NOME MASC

Cancer (*dello zodiaco*) ◇ *Sono del Cancro.* I'm Cancer.

il **cancro** NOME MASC

cancer ◇ *cancro ai polmoni* lung cancer

la **candeggina** NOME FEM

bleach

la **candela** NOME FEM

1 candle (*di cera*)

2 spark plug (*dell'auto*)

il **candidato**, la **candidata** NOME MASC, FEM

candidate

il **cane** NOME MASC
dog
* **cane da caccia** hunting dog
* **cane da guardia** guard dog

il **canestro** NOME MASC
basket
* **fare canestro** to shoot* a basket

il **canguro** NOME MASC
kangaroo

il **canile** NOME MASC
kennel

la **canna** NOME FEM
reed (*pianta*)
* **canna da zucchero** sugar cane
* **canna da pesca** fishing rod

la **cannuccia** NOME (PL le **cannucce**)
straw

la **canoa** NOME FEM
canoe
* **andare in canoa** to go* canoeing

la **canottiera** NOME FEM
vest
undershirt [US]

il **canotto** NOME MASC
dinghy (PL dinghies)

il/la **cantante** NOME MASC/FEM
singer

cantare VERBO
to sing* ◇ *Ha cantato per tutta la sera.* He
sang all evening.

il **cantiere** NOME MASC
shipyard (*navale*)

la **cantina** NOME FEM
cellar ◇ *È in cantina.* It's in the cellar.
Attenzione! In inglese esiste la parola
canteen, *che però significa* **mensa**.

la **canzone** NOME FEM
song

capace AGGETTIVO
[1] able ◇ *un insegnante molto capace* a
very able teacher
* **essere capace di** to be* able to ◇ *Sarai
capace di farlo?* Will you be able to do it?
* **Sei capace di nuotare?** Can you swim?
* **Non è stata capace di farlo.** She couldn't do
it.
[2] large (*spazioso*) ◇ *una stanza capace* a
large room
* **La mia borsa è molto capace.** My bag holds
a lot.

la **capanna** NOME FEM
hut

il **capello** NOME MASC
hair ◇ *C'è un capello nella minestra.*
There's a hair in the soup.
* **i capelli** hair
i capelli si traduce con **hair** *singolare, quasi
sempre senza articolo.*
◇ *Ha i capelli ricci.* She's got curly hair. ◇ *Mi
lavo i capelli ogni giorno.* I wash my hair

every day. ◇ *Ho i capelli ancora bagnati.* My
hair is still wet.

capire VERBO
to understand* ◇ *Va bene, capisco.* OK, I
understand. ◇ *Non ho capito una parola.* I
didn't understand a word. ◇ *Non ho capito,
puoi ripetere?* I don't understand, could you
say it again?
* **Fammi capire…** Let me get this straight…
* **capire male** to misunderstand*

la **capitale** NOME FEM
capital

il **capitano** NOME MASC
captain

capitare VERBO
to happen ◇ *Sono cose che capitano.* These
things happen. ◇ *Non mi è mai capitato.* It's
never happened to me.

il **capitello** NOME MASC
capital

il **capitolo** NOME MASC
chapter

il **capo** NOME MASC
[1] head (*testa*)
* **da capo a piedi** from head to foot ◇ *Era
coperto di fango da capo a piedi.* He was
covered in mud from head to foot.
* **fare un discorso senza né capo né coda** to
talk nonsense
[2] boss (*principale*) ◇ *Il mio capo è molto
esigente.* My boss is very demanding.
* **il capo di stato** the head of state
[3] end (*estremità*) ◇ *Era seduto all'altro
capo del tavolo.* He was sitting at the other
end of the table.
* **a capo** (*dettando*) new paragraph
* **da capo** all over again ◇ *Ha sbagliato e ha
dovuto ricominciare da capo.* He made a
mistake and had to start all over again.

Capodanno NOME MASC
New Year's Day (*il 1° gennaio*)
* **il veglione di Capodanno** New Year's Eve

il **capogiro** NOME MASC
* **avere un capogiro** to feel* dizzy ◇ *Ho avuto
un capogiro.* I felt dizzy.

il **capolavoro** NOME MASC
masterpiece

il **capolinea** NOME MASC (PL i **capolinea**)
terminus (PL termini)

il **capostazione** NOME MASC (PL i
capistazione)
station master

il/la **capotavola** NOME MASC/FEM
* **sedere a capotavola** to sit* at the head of the
table

capovolgere* VERBO
to turn upside down (*bicchiere, piatto*)
* **capovolgersi (1)** (*auto*) to overturn
* **capovolgersi (2)** (*barca*) to capsize
* **capovolgersi (3)** (*situazione*) to be* reversed

* *I verbi seguiti da questo simbolo sono irregolari. Si veda anche alle pp.328–338.*

Italian ~ English

C

la **cappella** NOME FEM
chapel

il **cappello** NOME MASC
hat ◇ *un cappello di paglia* a straw hat

i **capperi** NOME MASC PL
capers

cappottare VERBO
to overturn ◇ *La macchina ha cappottato in curva.* The car overturned on the bend.

il **cappotto** NOME MASC
coat ◇ *M'infilo il cappotto e sono pronta.* I'll put my coat on and I'll be ready.

il **cappuccino** NOME MASC
cappuccino

il **cappuccio** NOME MASC
hood ◇ *una felpa col cappuccio* a sweatshirt with a hood

la **capra** NOME FEM
goat ◇ *formaggio di capra* goat's cheese

il **capriccio** NOME MASC
whim ◇ *È solo un capriccio.* It's just a whim.
♦ **fare i capricci** to be* naughty

capriccioso AGGETTIVO (FEM **capricciosa**)
naughty ◇ *un bambino capriccioso* a naughty boy

il **Capricorno** NOME MASC
Capricorn ◇ *Sono del Capricorno.* I'm Capricorn.

la **capriola** NOME FEM
somersault ◇ *Sai fare le capriole?* Can you do somersaults?

la **caraffa** NOME FEM
carafe

la **caramella** NOME FEM
sweet
candy (PL candies) US
◇ *Vuoi una caramella?* Would you like a sweet?
♦ **una caramella alla menta** a mint

il **carattere** NOME MASC
1 personality (PL personalities) ◇ *C'è una certa incompatibilità di carattere tra noi.* There's a bit of a personality clash between us.
♦ **avere un brutto carattere** to be* bad-tempered
♦ **avere un bel carattere** to be* good-natured
2 letter (dell'alfabeto)

caratteristica NOME (PL le **caratteristiche**)
feature

caratteristico AGGETTIVO (FEM **caratteristica**, MASC PL **caratteristici**, FEM PL **caratteristiche**)
1 special ◇ *il sapore caratteristico del caviale* the special taste of caviar
2 distinctive ◇ *un elemento caratteristico dell'architettura locale* a distinctive feature of the local architecture
3 traditional ◇ *un ristorante caratteristico* a traditional restaurant

il **carburante** NOME MASC
fuel ◇ *Siamo rimasti senza carburante.* We ran out of fuel.

il **carburatore** NOME MASC
carburettor

il **carcere** NOME MASC
prison ◇ *Sono evasi dal carcere.* They escaped from prison. ◇ *Gli hanno dato dieci anni di carcere.* He was sent to prison for ten years.

il **carciofo** NOME MASC
artichoke

la **carestia** NOME FEM
famine ◇ *Migliaia di persone rischiano di morire a causa della carestia.* Thousands of people may die as a result of the famine.

cariarsi VERBO
♦ **Mi si è cariato un dente.** I've got a hole in one of my teeth.

la **carica** NOME FEM (PL le **cariche**)
♦ **in carica** in office ◇ *il presidente in carica* the president in office
♦ **rimanere in carica per...** to hold* office for... ◇ *Il Presidente è rimasto in carica per cinque anni.* The President held office for five years.

caricare VERBO
1 to load ◇ *Ho caricato le valigie in macchina.* I've loaded the cases into the car. ◇ *Hai caricato il programma?* Have you loaded the program?
♦ **Come si carica questa macchina fotografica?** How do you put the film in this camera?
2 to wind* (orologio) ◇ *Avevo dimenticato di caricare la sveglia.* I'd forgotten to wind the alarm clock.
3 to charge ◇ *La polizia ha caricato i dimostranti.* The police charged the demonstrators.

carico AGGETTIVO (FEM **carica**, MASC PL **carichi**, FEM PL **cariche**)
vedi anche **carico** NOME
loaded ◇ *Il fucile era carico.* The gun was loaded.
♦ **carico di** loaded with ◇ *È tornato carico di pacchi e pacchetti.* He came back loaded with parcels.
♦ **un camion carico di mattoni** a lorry with a load of bricks

il **carico** NOME MASC (PL i **carichi**)
vedi anche **carico** AGGETTIVO
load ◇ *Trasportava un carico di arance.* It was carrying a load of oranges.

la **carie** NOME FEM (PL le **carie**)
♦ **Ho una carie.** I've got a hole in one of my teeth.

carino AGGETTIVO (FEM **carina**)
1 nice ◇ *Carina questa maglietta!* That's a nice T-shirt! ◇ *Ha una casa molto carina.* She's got a very nice house. ◇ *È stato molto carino da parte tua.* It was really nice of you.
♦ **essere carino con qualcuno** to be* nice to somebody ◇ *Sono stati molto carini con*

me. They were very nice to me.

[2] nice-looking ◇ *È carino tuo fratello.* Your brother's nice-looking.

la **carità** NOME FEM

♦ **chiedere la carità** to beg* ◇ *C'era uno che chiedeva la carità fuori dalla chiesa.* There was a man begging outside the church.

♦ **Per carità!** You're joking! ◇ *Uscire con lui? Per carità!* Go out with him? You're joking!

la **carnagione** NOME FEM

complexion ◇ *Ha la carnagione chiara.* She's got a fair complexion.

la **carne** NOME FEM

meat ◇ *Preferisci la carne o il pesce?* Which do you prefer, meat or fish?

♦ **carne di maiale** pork

♦ **carne di manzo** beef

♦ **carne tritata** mince, US: ground beef

♦ **in carne e ossa** in the flesh ◇ *Era proprio lui, in carne e ossa!* It was really him, in the flesh!

il **carnevale** NOME MASC

carnival ◇ *il carnevale di Venezia* the Venice Carnival

> **❶ Carnevale** in Italy is a period when there are parties, often in costume, bonfires and processions. It begins at the end of January and ends on Shrove Tuesday, before the start of Lent.

caro AGGETTIVO (FEM **cara**)

[1] dear ◇ *Caro Paul* Dear Paul ◇ *Carissima Cinzia* Dearest Cinzia

♦ **cari saluti** best wishes

[2] expensive (*costoso*) ◇ *È troppo caro, non lo compro.* It's too expensive, I won't buy it.

la **carota** NOME FEM

carrot

il **carrello** NOME MASC

trolley
cart US

la **carriera** NOME FEM

career ◇ *una carriera brillante* a brilliant career

♦ **fare carriera** to have* a career ◇ *Non è facile far carriera per una donna con figli.* It's not easy for a woman with children to have a career.

♦ **Farà sicuramente carriera.** He'll get on.

il **carro** NOME MASC

cart (*in campagna*)

♦ **carro attrezzi (1)** (*per macchine in avaria*) breakdown truck

♦ **carro attrezzi (2)** (*per macchine in divieto*) tow truck

♦ **carro armato** tank

la **carrozza** NOME FEM

carriage

la **carrozzina** NOME FEM

[1] pram
baby carriage US
(*per bambini*)

[2] wheelchair (*per invalidi*)

la **carta** NOME FEM

paper ◇ *un foglio di carta* a sheet of paper

♦ **carta di credito** credit card

♦ **carta geografica** map

♦ **carta d'identità** identity card

♦ **carta igienica** toilet paper

♦ **carta d'imbarco** boarding card

♦ **carta da lettere** writing paper

♦ **carta da regalo** wrapping paper

♦ **carte da gioco** playing cards

la **cartella** NOME FEM

[1] folder (*raccoglitore*)

[2] briefcase (*valigetta*)

il **cartellino** NOME MASC

price label (*del prezzo*)

♦ **timbrare il cartellino (1)** (*all'entrata*) to clock in

♦ **timbrare il cartellino (2)** (*all'uscita*) to clock out

il **cartello** NOME MASC

sign ◇ *Cosa indica quel cartello?* What does that sign say? ◇ *Sul cartello c'era scritto "Tutto esaurito".* The sign said "Sold out".

il **cartellone** NOME MASC

hoarding
billboard US
(*pubblicitario*)

la **cartina** NOME FEM

map (*piantina*)

la **cartoleria** NOME FEM

stationer's ◇ *Lo trovi in cartoleria.* You'll get it at a stationer's.

la **cartolina** NOME FEM

postcard ◇ *Mandami una cartolina.* Send me a postcard.

il **cartone** NOME MASC

[1] cardboard (*materiale*) ◇ *una scatola di cartone* a cardboard box

[2] carton (*scatola*) ◇ *un cartone di latte* a carton of milk

♦ **cartone animato** cartoon ◇ *i cartoni animati di Tom e Jerry* Tom and Jerry cartoons

cartuccia NOME (PL le **cartucce**)

cartridge (*di arma, di penna*)

la **casa** NOME FEM

[1] house ◇ *una bella casa grande* a nice big house ◇ *una casa in campagna* a house in the country ◇ *Eravamo a casa mia.* We were at my house. ◇ *Andiamo a casa tua.* Let's go to your house.

♦ **casa editrice** publishing house

♦ **casa popolare** council house

[2] home (*in senso più astratto*) ◇ *Sono stato in casa tutta la sera.* I was at home all

evening. ◇ *Non è a casa.* She isn't at home. ◇ *Sarò a casa tra un'ora.* I'll be home in an hour.

senza preposizione.

◇ *Fai come se fossi a casa tua!* Make yourself at home!

♦ **andare a casa** to go* home ◇ *Io vado a casa.* I'm going home.

♦ **tornare a casa** to get* home ◇ *È tornato a casa tardi.* He got home late.

♦ **fatto in casa** home-made ◇ *pane fatto in casa* home-made bread

3 **flat** (*appartamento*) ◇ *Hanno una bella casa.* They have a nice flat.

♦ **"Tanti saluti a casa."** "Best wishes to all the family."

♦ **casa discografica** record company

♦ **casa dello studente** hall of residence

a **casalinga** NOME FEM (PL le **casalinghe**)
    housewife (PL housewives) ◇ *Fa la casalinga.* She is a housewife.

cascare VERBO
    to fall* ◇ *È cascato dal letto.* He fell out of bed.

♦ **cascarci** to fall* for it ◇ *Gli ho detto che era mia e lui c'è cascato.* I told him it was mine and he fell for it.

a **cascata** NOME FEM
    waterfall ◇ *Sono le cascate più alte del mondo.* They're the biggest waterfalls in the world.

♦ **le cascate del Niagara** the Niagara Falls

il **casco** NOME MASC (PL i **caschi**)
    crash helmet (*per moto*)

♦ **i Caschi blu** the Blue Helmets

a **caserma** NOME FEM
    barracks PL

il **casino** NOME MASC
    1 **bloody racket** (*rumore*) ◇ *Cos'è questo casino?* What's this bloody racket?
    2 **mess** (*disordine*) ◇ *In camera mia c'è un gran casino.* My bedroom is in a hell of a mess.
    3 **problem** (*problema*) ◇ *In questo periodo ho tanti casini.* I've got loads of problems at the moment.

♦ **un casino di** loads of ◇ *C'era un casino di gente.* There were loads of people.

il **casinò** NOME MASC (PL i **casinò**)
    casino

il **caso** NOME MASC
    case

♦ **in ogni caso** in any case ◇ *In ogni caso non ci perdi niente.* In any case you won't lose anything.

♦ **in tal caso** in that case ◇ *Be', in tal caso dovremo rimandare la partenza.* Well, in that case we'll have to put off our departure.

♦ **nel caso che** in case ◇ *Ti do il mio numero di telefono, nel caso che tu venga a Roma.* I'll give you my phone number, in case you come to Rome.

♦ **per caso** by chance ◇ *L'ho incontrato per caso.* I met him by chance.

♦ **a caso** at random ◇ *Ho aperto il libro a caso.* I opened the book at random.

♦ **caso mai** if ◇ *Caso mai non possiate venire, telefonate.* If you can't come, phone. ◇ *Dovrei essere lì alle cinque, caso mai aspetta.* I should be there at five, if I'm not, wait for me.

♦ **far caso a** (*vedere*) to notice ◇ *Hai fatto caso a come ti guardava?* Did you notice how he was looking at you? ◇ *Non ci ho fatto caso.* I didn't notice.

♦ **Non farci caso, è così con tutti.** Don't pay any attention, he's like that with everybody.

♦ **I casi sono due...** There are two possibilities...

♦ **mettiamo il caso che** supposing ◇ *Mettiamo il caso che ti inviti: accetteresti?* Supposing he invited you, would you go?

♦ **non è il caso di** there's no point ◇ *Non è il caso di prendersela!* There's no point getting upset!

♦ **Forse sarebbe il caso di andarcene.** Perhaps we'd better go.

caspita ESCLAMAZIONE
    1 **wow!** (*sorpresa*)
    2 **for goodness' sake!** (*impazienza*)

la **cassa** NOME FEM
    1 **case** ◇ *Ho comprato una cassa di birra.* I bought a case of beer.

♦ **cassa da imballaggio** packing case
    2 **cash desk** (*al bar, in negozio*)
    3 **checkout** (*al supermercato*)

la **cassaforte** NOME FEM (PL le **casseforti**)
    safe ◇ *Hanno forzato la cassaforte.* They forced open the safe.

la **cassetta** NOME FEM
    1 **box** ◇ *una cassetta di mele* a box of apples
    2 **cassette** ◇ *Ce l'ho sia su CD che su cassetta.* I've got it on CD and on cassette.
    3 **post box**
    mailbox US
    (*per imbucare*)

♦ **cassetta delle lettere** letterbox

la **cassettiera** NOME FEM
    chest of drawers

il **cassetto** NOME MASC
    drawer ◇ *È nel primo cassetto.* It's in the top drawer.

il **cassiere**, la **cassiera** NOME MASC, FEM
    1 **cashier** (*al bar, in negozio, di banca*)
    2 **checkout operator** (*al supermercato*)

il **cassonetto** NOME MASC
    wheelie bin

la **castagna** NOME FEM
    chestnut

castano AGGETTIVO (FEM **castana**)
    brown ◇ *Ha gli occhi e i capelli castani.* She's got brown eyes and brown hair.

il **castello** NOME MASC

☞

castle ◇ *un castello di sabbia* a sand castle

il **castigo** NOME MASC (PL i **castighi**)
punishment ◇ *per castigo* as a punishment
- **Sono in castigo e non posso uscire.** I'm being punished and I'm not allowed to go out.
- **mettere in castigo** to punish

il **catalogo** NOME MASC (PL i **cataloghi**)
catalogue

la **categoria** NOME FEM
class (*di albergo, nello sport*)

la **catena** NOME FEM
chain (*di bici, di negozi*)

la **catenina** NOME FEM
chain

il **catino** NOME MASC
basin

il **catrame** NOME MASC
tar

la **cattedra** NOME FEM
teacher's desk

la **cattedrale** NOME FEM
cathedral

la **cattiveria** NOME FEM
- **fare una cattiveria** to do* something bad
- **dire una cattiveria** to say* something spiteful

cattolico, cattolica NOME, AGGETTIVO (MASC PL **cattolici**, FEM PL **cattoliche**)
Catholic
Si noti l'uso della maiuscola in inglese.

la **causa** NOME FEM
cause ◇ *Quella è stata la causa principale.* That was the main cause.
- **a causa di** because of ◇ *L'aeroporto è chiuso a causa della nebbia.* The airport is closed because of the fog.
- **fare causa a qualcuno** to take* legal action against somebody ◇ *Mi ha fatto causa.* He took legal action against me.

causare VERBO
to cause ◇ *Potrebbe causare dei problemi.* It might cause problems.

cavalcare VERBO
to ride* ◇ *Sai cavalcare?* Can you ride?
- **andare a cavalcare** to go* riding

la **cavalcata** NOME FEM
ride ◇ *Abbiamo fatto una cavalcata nel bosco.* We went for a ride in the woods.

il **cavalcavia** NOME MASC (PL i **cavalcavia**)
flyover

cavalcioni AVVERBIO
- **a cavalcioni di** astride ◇ *Era seduto a cavalcioni del muretto.* He was sitting astride the wall.

la **cavalletta** NOME FEM
grasshopper

il **cavalletto** NOME MASC
1 tripod (*per foto*)
2 easel (*da pittore*)

il **cavallo** NOME MASC
1 horse ◇ *Ti piacciono i cavalli?* Do you like horses?
- **andare a cavallo** to ride* ◇ *Sai andare a cavallo?* Can you ride?
- **cavallo a dondolo** rocking horse
- **cavallo da corsa** racehorse
2 knight (*negli scacchi*)
3 crotch (*dei pantaloni*)

cavarsi VERBO
- **cavarsela** to do* all right ◇ *Se l'è cavata all'esame.* He did all right in the exam.
- **Se l'è cavata con qualche graffio.** He came out of it with only a few scratches.

il **cavatappi** NOME MASC (PL i **cavatappi**)
corkscrew

la **cavia** NOME FEM
guinea pig
- **fare da cavia** to be* a guinea pig

la **caviglia** NOME FEM
ankle ◇ *Mi sono slogato la caviglia.* I've sprained my ankle.

il **cavo** NOME MASC
cable ◇ *televisione via cavo* cable television
- **cavo di traino** towrope

la **cavolata** NOME FEM
- **fare una cavolata** to do* something stupid
- **dire una cavolata** to talk rubbish

il **cavolfiore** NOME MASC
cauliflower

il **cavolo** NOME MASC
cabbage ◇ *una minestra di cavolo* a cabbage soup
- **Che cavolo vuoi?** What the hell do you want?
- **Non fa un cavolo tutto il giorno.** He doesn't do a damn thing all day.

il **cazzo** NOME MASC
prick (*volgare*)
- **Fatti i cazzi tuoi!** Mind your own bloody business!

ce *vedi* **ci**

i **ceci** NOME MASC PL
chickpeas

ceco, ceca NOME, AGGETTIVO (MASC PL **cechi**, FEM PL **ceche**)
Czech
Si noti l'uso della maiuscola in inglese.

cedere VERBO
1 to give* (*dare*)
- **cedere qualcosa a qualcuno** to give* somebody something ◇ *Le ho ceduto il posto.* I gave her my seat.
2 to collapse (*rompersi*) ◇ *La sedia a sdraio ha ceduto sotto il suo peso.* The deckchair collapsed under his weight.
3 to give* in (*arrendersi*) ◇ *Ha insistito tanto che alla fine ho ceduto.* She was so insistent that in the end I gave in.

celebre AGGETTIVO
famous

* I verbi seguiti da questo simbolo sono irregolari. Si veda anche alle pp.328–338.

celeste AGGETTIVO, NOME MASC
pale blue ◇ *una gonna celeste* a pale blue skirt
+ **Ha gli occhi celesti.** She's got blue eyes.

la cella NOME FEM
cell (*in prigione*)

il cellulare NOME MASC
cell phone

la cellulite NOME FEM
cellulite ◇ *una crema contro la cellulite* an anti-cellulite cream

il cemento NOME MASC
cement (*per mattoni*)
+ **cemento armato** reinforced concrete

la cena NOME FEM
dinner ◇ *Vieni a cena da noi?* Would you like to come to dinner with us? ◇ *Mi hanno invitato a cena.* They've invited me to dinner. ◇ *Ti telefono all'ora di cena.* I'll phone you at dinner time.

cenare VERBO
to have* dinner ◇ *Hai cenato?* Have you had dinner?

la cenere NOME FEM
ash

la Cenerentola NOME FEM
Cinderella

il cenno NOME MASC
1 nod (*col capo*)
+ **far cenno di sì** to nod
+ **far cenno di no** to shake* one's head
2 wave (*con la mano*)
+ **far cenno di no** (*col dito*) to wag one's finger
+ **far cenno a qualcuno** to gesture to somebody ◇ *Mi ha fatto cenno di avvicinarmi.* He gestured to me to come closer.

il centenario NOME MASC
centenary (PL centenaries)

il centesimo NOME MASC
vedi anche **centesimo** AGGETTIVO
1 cent ◇ *Costa ottanta centesimi.* It costs eighty cents.
2 hundredth ◇ *pochi centesimi di secondo* a few hundredths of a second

centesimo AGGETTIVO (FEM **centesima**)
vedi anche **centesimo** NOME
hundredth

centigrado AGGETTIVO
centigrade ◇ *venti gradi centigradi* twenty degrees centigrade

il centimetro NOME MASC
centimetre
centimeter *US*
◇ *lungo venti centimetri* twenty centimetres long

il centinaio NOME MASC (PL FEM le **centinaia**)
+ **un centinaio di** about a hundred ◇ *un centinaio di persone* about a hundred people
+ **centinaia** hundreds ◇ *Ci sono stato centinaia di volte.* I've been there hundreds of times.
+ **diverse centinaia di sterline** several thousand pounds

cento NUMERO
a hundred ◇ *cento sterline* a hundred pounds
+ **per cento** per cent ◇ *cinque per cento* five per cent
+ **al cento per cento** a hundred per cent ◇ *Ne sono sicuro al cento per cento.* I'm a hundred per cent sure.
+ **Cento di questi giorni!** Many happy returns!

centodieci NUMERO
one hundred and ten
+ **laurearsi con centodieci e lode** to get* a first class degree

centomila NUMERO
a hundred thousand

centrale AGGETTIVO
vedi anche **centrale** NOME
central ◇ *Dov'è la stazione centrale?* Where's the central station? ◇ *L'albergo è molto centrale.* The hotel is very central.
+ **sede centrale** head office ◇ *La sede centrale è a Roma.* The head office is in Rome.

la centrale NOME FEM
vedi anche **centrale** AGGETTIVO
+ **centrale di polizia** police headquarters SING

il/la centralinista NOME MASC/FEM (MASC PL i **centralinisti**, FEM PL le **centraliniste**)
switchboard operator

il centralino NOME MASC
switchboard

centralizzato AGGETTIVO (FEM **centralizzata**)
central
+ **riscaldamento centralizzato** central heating
+ **chiusura centralizzata** (*di portiere*) central locking

il centravanti NOME MASC (PL i **centravanti**)
centre forward

il centro NOME MASC
1 centre
center *US*
◇ *Al centro della piazza c'è una fontana.* There's a fountain in the centre of the square.
+ **centro commerciale** shopping centre
2 town centre (*di città*) ◇ *Siamo andati in centro a fare spese.* We went into the town centre to do some shopping. ◇ *Abiti in centro o in periferia?* Do you live in the town centre or in the suburbs?

il centrocampo NOME MASC (PL i **centrocampo**)
midfield

la cera NOME FEM
wax
+ **il museo delle cere** the waxworks
waxworks è sia la forma singolare che quella plurale.

cercare VERBO

⸤1⸥ to look for ◇ *Le ho cercate dappertutto.* I've looked for them everywhere. ◇ *Stai cercando lavoro?* Are you looking for a job?

⸤2⸥ to look up (*parola, numero di telefono*) ◇ *Devo cercare la parola sul dizionario.* I'll have to look the word up in the dictionary.

⸤3⸥ to try (*tentare*) ◇ *Ho cercato di spiegargli il motivo.* I tried to explain the reason to him. ◇ *Cerca di non fare tardi.* Try not to be late.

il **cerchietto** NOME MASC
hairband (*per capelli*)

il **cerchio** NOME MASC
circle ◇ *Eravamo seduti in cerchio.* We were sitting in a circle.

i **cereali** NOME MASC PL

⸤1⸥ cereals ◇ *la produzione annuale di cereali* the annual production of cereals

⸤2⸥ cereal (*per colazione*) ◇ *A colazione mangio sempre cereali.* I always have cereal for breakfast.

la **cerimonia** NOME FEM
ceremony (PL ceremonies)

il **cerino** NOME MASC
wax match ◇ *una scatola di cerini* a box of wax matches

cerniera NOME

♦ **cerniera lampo** zip, ⸤US:⸥ zipper

il **cerotto** NOME MASC
sticking plaster
Band-Aid ® ⸤US⸥

il **certificato** NOME MASC
certificate ◇ *un certificato medico* a medical certificate

certo AGGETTIVO (FEM **certa**)

⸤vedi anche **certo** AVVERBIO⸥

⸤1⸥ sure (*sicuro*) ◇ *Sono certo che verrà.* I'm sure she'll come. ◇ *Ne sono più che certo.* I'm absolutely sure of it. ◇ *Non sono certo di poter venire.* I'm not sure I can come.

Quasi sempre è possibile usare **certain** *al posto di* **sure**, *ma* **certain** *è un po' più formale.*

⸤2⸥ certain (*tale*) ◇ *un certo signor Smith* a certain Mr Smith

♦ **C'è un certo Sam che ti cerca.** Someone called Sam is looking for you.

⸤3⸥ some (*qualche; con valore intensivo*) ◇ *Certi giorni l'ufficio apre più tardi.* Some days the office opens later. ◇ *Certa gente non è mai contenta.* Some people are never satisfied. ◇ *Non vado a vedere certi film.* There are some films I don't go to see.

♦ **certe volte** sometimes ◇ *Certe volte non ti capisco proprio!* Sometimes I just don't understand you!

♦ **in un certo senso** in a way

certo AVVERBIO

⸤vedi anche **certo** AGGETTIVO⸥

of course (*certamente*) ◇ *Posso portare un*

amico? – Ma certo! May I bring a friend? – Yes, of course! ◇ *Certo che no!* Of course not!

il **cervello** NOME MASC
brain

il **cervo** NOME MASC

⸤1⸥ deer (PL deer) (*animale*)

⸤2⸥ venison (*carne*)

il **cespuglio** NOME MASC
bush

cessare VERBO
to stop

Quando **to stop** *ha questo significato regge sempre il gerundio.*

◇ *Non ha ancora cessato di piovere.* It hasn't stopped raining yet.

il **cestino** NOME MASC

⸤1⸥ basket ◇ *un cestino di vimini* a wicker basket

♦ **cestino dei rifiuti** litter bin

⸤2⸥ punnet ◇ *un cestino di fragole* a punnet of strawberries

il **cetriolo** NOME MASC
cucumber

che PRONOME, AGGETTIVO, CONGIUNZIONE

⸤1⸥ what ◇ *Che giorno è oggi?* What day is it today? ◇ *Che ore sono?* What time is it? ◇ *Che tipo di musica ti piace?* What sort of music do you like? ◇ *A che ora parti?* What time are you leaving?

♦ **che cosa** what ◇ *Che cosa fai?* What are you doing? ◇ *Che cosa vuoi?* What do you want? ◇ *A che cosa pensi?* What are you thinking about?

La preposizione va alla fine.

⸤2⸥ which (*quando la scelta è ristretta*) ◇ *Che gusto preferisci? Limone o cioccolato?* Which flavour would you like? Lemon or chocolate? ◇ *Che film hai visto?* Which film did you see?

⸤3⸥ that (*in subordinazione*) ◇ *Ha detto che farà tardi.* He said that he'll be late. ◇ *la squadra che ha vinto il campionato* the team that won the championship

⸤4⸥ who (*riferito a persona*) ◇ *il ragazzo che è seduto laggiù* the boy who's sitting over there ◇ *Ha un fratello che abita a Roma.* She's got a brother who lives in Rome.

Quando **che** *è complemento spesso non si traduce.*

◇ *la ragazza che hai visto* the girl you saw ◇ *il libro che mi hai prestato* the book you lent me ◇ *la sera che ti ho visto* the evening I saw you

Nelle esclamazioni, quando **che** *è seguito da un nome al singolare, si traduce con* **what a**, *quando è seguito da un nome al plurale si traduce con* **what**.

◇ *Che bella ragazza!* What a pretty girl! ◇ *Che brutte scarpe!* What horrible shoes!

Quando **che** *è seguito da un aggettivo*

---

* *I verbi seguiti da questo simbolo sono irregolari. Si veda anche alle pp.328–338.*

spesso si traduce con **it's.**
◇ *Che buono!* It's delicious! ◇ *Che carino!*
It's lovely! ◇ *Che freddo!* It's freezing!

chef NOME MASC (PL **gli chef**)
chef

chi PRONOME

[1] who ◇ *Chi è?* Who is it? ◇ *Ma chi crede
di essere?* Who does he think he is?

Se il pronome interrogativo **chi** *è preceduto
da preposizione, la preposizione va messa
alla fine della frase in inglese.*

◇ *Con chi desidera parlare?* Who do you
wish to speak to? ◇ *Con chi parli?* Who are
you talking to? ◇ *Di chi è?* Who does it
belong to?

◆ **Di chi è l'idea?** Whose idea is it?

[2] whoever (*pronome relativo*) ◇ *Chi arriva
prima vince.* Whoever gets there first is the
winner. ◇ *Esco con chi mi pare.* I go out with
whoever I like. ◇ *Puoi invitare chi vuoi.* You
can invite whoever you like.

◆ **Chi non vuole andarci non ci vada.** Anyone
who doesn't want to go doesn't have to.

chiacchierare VERBO

to chat ◇ *Ci siamo fermati a chiacchierare
sotto casa sua.* We stopped to chat outside
her house.

chiacchiere NOME FEM PL

◆ **fare due chiacchiere** to have* a chat

chiamare VERBO

[1] to call ◇ *Hanno chiamato la polizia.*
They called the police.

[2] to call to (*ad alta voce*) ◇ *L'ho chiamato
ma non mi ha sentito.* I called to him but he
didn't hear me.

◆ **chiamarsi** to be* called ◇ *Come si chiama il
tuo amico?* What is your friend called?

◆ **Come ti chiami? – Mi chiamo Paolo.** What's
your name? – My name's Paolo.

◆ **Questa si chiama fortuna!** That's what I call
luck!

[3] to phone (*al telefono*) ◇ *Ha chiamato
Loredana.* Loredana phoned.

chiamata NOME FEM

call (*telefonica*) ◇ *una chiamata urbana* a
local call

chiarire VERBO

[1] to get* clear ◇ *Vorrei chiarire alcuni
punti.* I'd like to get some points clear.

[2] to solve (*svelare*) ◇ *Alla fine il mistero è
stato chiarito.* In the end the mystery was
solved.

chiaro AGGETTIVO (FEM **chiara**)

[1] clear ◇ *Non voglio averci niente a che
fare, è chiaro?* I want nothing to do with it, is
that clear?

◆ **Era chiaro che non se l'aspettava.** He clearly
wasn't expecting it.

[2] light (*colore*) ◇ *verde chiaro* light green

[3] fair (*capelli, carnagione*) ◇ *Ha i capelli
chiari.* She's got fair hair.

chiasso NOME MASC

noise ◇ *Cos'è tutto questo chiasso?* What's
all this noise?

◆ **Smettetela di fare chiasso!** Be quiet!

la **chiave** NOME FEM

key ◇ *Ho perso le chiavi di casa.* I've lost my
house keys.

◆ **chiudere a chiave** to lock ◇ *Mi raccomando,
chiudi a chiave la porta.* Make sure you lock
the door.

la **chiavetta** NOME FEM

[1] key ◇ *la chiavetta d'accensione* the
ignition key

[2] winder (*di sveglia, di giocattolo*)

chiedere* VERBO

[1] to ask ◇ *Chiedi dov'è l'albergo.* Ask
where the hotel is.

◆ **chiedere qualcosa a qualcuno** to ask
somebody something ◇ *Chiedi a Lidia
come si chiama il suo cane.* Ask Lidia what
her dog's called. ◇ *Mi ha chiesto l'ora.* He
asked me the time. ◇ *Chiedi a Giulia di
spostarsi un po'.* Ask Giulia to move over a
bit.

[2] to ask for (*per avere*)

◆ **chiedere qualcosa a qualcuno** to ask
somebody for something ◇ *Ho chiesto il
conto al cameriere.* I asked the waiter for the
bill. ◇ *Mi ha chiesto degli spiccioli.* He
asked me for some change.

◆ **chiedere di qualcuno** to ask after somebody
◇ *Tutti i miei amici chiedono di te.* All my
friends are asking after you.

◆ **C'è un certo Andrea che chiede di te.**
Someone called Andrea is looking for you.

◆ **chiedere scusa a qualcuno** to apologize to
somebody ◇ *Ho chiesto scusa a Marco.* I
apologized to Marco.

◆ **chiedersi** to wonder ◇ *Mi chiedo cosa stia
facendo.* I wonder what she's doing.

la **chiesa** NOME FEM

church ◇ *Va in chiesa ogni domenica.* He
goes to church every Sunday.

il **chilo** NOME MASC

kilo ◇ *quarantacinque chili* forty five kilos
◇ *mezzo chilo di ciliegie* half a kilo of
cherries

> **ⓘ** *Un* **chilo** *corrisponde a 2.2 libbre,
> "pounds" in inglese, un'unità di misura che a
> volte viene ancora usata nei negozi. In Gran
> Bretagna il peso delle persone si misura
> normalmente in "stones" – uno "stone"
> corrisponde a 6,35 chili – mentre negli Stati
> Uniti si misura in "pounds".*

il **chilometro** NOME MASC

kilometre
kilometer US

> **ⓘ** *Un* **chilometro** *equivale a 0.62 miglia,
> unità di misura del sistema imperiale.*

◇ *cinquanta chilometri all'ora* thirty miles per hour

• **Abbiamo fatto chilometri a piedi.** We walked miles.

la **chimica** NOME FEM
chemistry ◇ *la professoressa di chimica* the chemistry teacher

chimico NOME (PL i **chimici**)
chemist

chinarsi VERBO
to bend* down ◇ *Si è chinata a raccogliere la borsa.* She bent down to pick up the bag.

la **chiocciola** NOME FEM
[1] snail *(animale)*
[2] @ sign *(nei messaggi di posta elettronica)*
• **scala a chiocciola** spiral staircase

il **chiodo** NOME MASC
nail

chiosco NOME (PL i **chioschi**)
kiosk

chirurgo NOME (PL i **chirurghi**)
surgeon ◇ *Fa il chirurgo.* He is a surgeon.

chissà AVVERBIO
I wonder ◇ *Chissà se verrà alla festa.* I wonder if he'll come to the party. ◇ *Chissà chi gliel'ha detto.* I wonder who told him.

la **chitarra** NOME FEM
guitar ◇ *una chitarra elettrica* an electric guitar ◇ *Suona la chitarra.* He plays the guitar.

il/la **chitarrista** NOME MASC/FEM (MASC PL i **chitarristi**, FEM PL le **chitarriste**)
guitarist

chiudere* VERBO
[1] to close ◇ *Chiudi la finestra, per favore.* Close the window please. ◇ *A che ora chiude il negozio?* What time does the shop close? ◇ *La fabbrica ha chiuso due anni fa.* The factory closed two years ago. ◇ *Il centro è stato chiuso al traffico.* The town centre is closed to traffic.
• **Con lui ho chiuso.** I've finished with him.
• **chiudersi** to close ◇ *La porta si è chiusa.* The door closed.
• **chiudere a chiave** to lock ◇ *Sei sicuro di aver chiuso a chiave?* Are you sure you locked it?
[2] to turn off *(gas, acqua)* ◇ *Ricordati di chiudere il gas.* Remember to turn off the gas. ◇ *Chiudi bene il rubinetto.* Turn the tap off properly.

chiunque PRONOME
[1] whoever *(pronome relativo)* ◇ *Chiunque l'abbia fatto ha sbagliato.* Whoever did it made a mistake.
• **chiunque sia** whoever it is ◇ *Chiunque sia, digli che non ci sono.* Whoever it is, tell them I'm not here.
[2] anyone *(pronome indefinito)* ◇ *Attacca*

discorso con chiunque. She'll talk to anyone.

chiuso AGGETTIVO (FEM **chiusa**)
[1] closed ◇ *una finestra chiusa* a closed window
Spesso si può usare anche shut, ma shut non va mai messo prima del nome cui si riferisce.
◇ *La porta era chiusa.* The door was shut.
◇ *La banca è chiusa per sciopero.* The bank is closed because of a strike.
• **a occhi chiusi** with one's eyes closed ◇ *Lo saprei fare ad occhi chiusi.* I could do it with my eyes closed.
[2] locked *(a chiave)* ◇ *La porta era chiusa.* The door was locked. ◇ *Sono rimasto chiuso fuori.* I was locked out.
• **chiuso a chiave** locked
[3] quiet *(poco espansivo)* ◇ *un ragazzo molto chiuso* a very quiet boy
[4] blocked-up *(naso)* ◇ *Ho il naso chiuso.* I've got a blocked-up nose.

la **chiusura** NOME FEM
• **chiusura lampo** zip, [US:] zipper
• **a chiusura ermetica** airtight ◇ *un recipiente a chiusura ermetica* an airtight container
• **orario di chiusura** closing time

ci PRONOME
vedi anche **ci** AVVERBIO
[1] us ◇ *Ci hanno visto.* They saw us.
Spesso us è preceduto da una preposizione, a seconda del verbo usato.
◇ *Ci chiamava.* He was calling to us. ◇ *Ci sembrava una buona idea.* It seemed a good idea to us. ◇ *Ci ha sorriso.* He smiled at us.
[2] ourselves *(in riflessivi)* ◇ *Ci siamo preparati.* We prepared ourselves.
Spesso ci non viene tradotto.
◇ *Ci siamo stancati.* We got tired. ◇ *Ci siamo lavati i denti.* We brushed our teeth.
[3] each other *(riflessivo reciproco)* ◇ *Ci vogliamo bene.* We love each other.
• **Ci vediamo domani!** See you tomorrow!
[4] it ◇ *Non ci credo.* I don't believe it.
Spesso it è preceduto da una preposizione, a seconda del verbo usato.
◇ *Ci penserò.* I'll think about it. ◇ *Ci puoi scommettere.* You can bet on it. ◇ *Cosa c'entra?* What's that got to do with it?

ci AVVERBIO
vedi anche **ci** PRONOME
[1] there *(là)* ◇ *Ci sei mai stato?* Have you ever been there?
Spesso ci non viene tradotto.
◇ *Ci andrò domani.* I'll go tomorrow.
[2] here *(qua)* ◇ *Qui non ci torno più!* I'm not coming back here again!

la **ciabatta** NOME FEM
[1] slipper *(pantofola)*
[2] ciabatta *(pane)*

ciao ESCLAMAZIONE
[1] hello! *(all'arrivo)*

* *I verbi seguiti da questo simbolo sono irregolari. Si veda anche alle pp.328–338.*

Italian ~ English

[2] goodbye! (*alla partenza*)

ciascuno AGGETTIVO, PRONOME (FEM **ciascuna**)
each ◇ *Ciascun candidato deve presentare un tema.* Each candidate has to submit an essay. ◇ *Ne avevamo uno per ciascuno.* We had one each. ◇ *Costano cinquanta euro ciascuno.* They cost fifty euros each.

cibo NOME MASC
food

cicatrice NOME FEM
scar

ciccione, la cicciona NOME MASC, FEM
fatty (PL fatties)

ciclamino NOME MASC
cyclamen

ciclismo NOME MASC
cycling ◇ *un campione di ciclismo* a cycling champion

ciclista NOME MASC/FEM (MASC PL **i ciclisti**, FEM PL **le cicliste**)
cyclist ◇ *un ciclista professionista* a professional cyclist

ciclo NOME MASC
[1] series ◇ *un ciclo di film di fantascienza* a series of sci-fi films
[2] cycle (*mestruale*)

cicogna NOME FEM
stork

cieca NOME FEM (PL **le cieche**)
blind woman (PL blind women)

cieco AGGETTIVO (FEM **cieca**, MASC PL **ciechi**, FEM PL **cieche**)
vedi anche **cieco** NOME
blind ◇ *Il mio cane è cieco da un occhio.* My dog's blind in one eye.

cieco NOME MASC (PL **i ciechi**)
vedi anche **cieco** AGGETTIVO
blind man (PL blind men)
• **i ciechi** (*uomini e donne*) the blind

cielo NOME MASC
sky (PL skies) ◇ *un cielo azzurro* a blue sky
• **Santo cielo!** Good heavens!

cifra NOME FEM
figure ◇ *un numero di cinque cifre* a five-figure number
• **scrivere un numero in cifre** to write* a number in figures
• **L'ha pagato una bella cifra.** He paid a lot for it.

ciglio NOME MASC
[1] eyelash (*di occhio*)
When **ciglio** *means* **eyelash** *the plural is* **le ciglia.**
◇ *ciglia finte* false eyelashes
[2] edge (*bordo*) ◇ *sul ciglio della strada* at the edge of the road

cigno NOME MASC
swan

ciliegia NOME (PL **le ciliegie** *o* **le ciliege**)
cherry (PL cherries) ◇ *marmellata di ciliegie* cherry jam

---

il cilindro NOME MASC
[1] cylinder (*di auto*)
[2] top hat (*cappello*)

la cima NOME FEM
[1] top ◇ *sulla cima del monte* on the top of the mountain ◇ *Si è posato sulla cima dell'albero.* It landed in the top of the tree. ◇ *Sono in cima alla classifica.* They're at the top of the league.
• **da cima a fondo** (*dappertutto*) from top to bottom ◇ *Hanno perquisito la casa da cima a fondo.* They searched the house from top to bottom.
• **L'ho letto da cima a fondo.** I read it from beginning to end.
• **essere una cima** to be* a genius ◇ *Non è una cima, ma se la cava.* He's not a genius, but he does OK.
[2] peak (*montagna*)

il cimitero NOME MASC
graveyard

la Cina NOME FEM
China

cincin ESCLAMAZIONE
cheers!

il cinema NOME (PL **i cinema**)
cinema ◇ *Andiamo al cinema?* Shall we go to the cinema? ◇ *Cosa danno al cinema stasera?* What's on at the cinema tonight?

cinese AGGETTIVO
vedi anche **cinese** NOME MASC, NOME FEM
Chinese

il cinese NOME MASC
vedi anche **cinese** NOME FEM, AGGETTIVO
[1] Chinese man (PL Chinese men) (*persona*)
• **i cinesi** (*uomini e donne*) the Chinese
[2] Chinese (*lingua*) ◇ *Parla cinese.* She speaks Chinese.
Si noti l'uso della maiuscola in inglese.

la cinese NOME FEM
vedi anche **cinese** NOME MASC, AGGETTIVO
Chinese woman (PL Chinese women)

la cinghia NOME FEM
[1] strap (*di valigia, di zaino*)
[2] belt (*per calzoni*)

il cinghiale NOME MASC
wild boar

cinquanta NUMERO
fifty ◇ *Ha cinquant'anni.* He is fifty.

cinquantesimo AGGETTIVO, NOME MASC (FEM **cinquantesima**)
fiftieth

la cinquantina NOME FEM
about fifty ◇ *È sulla cinquantina.* He's about fifty.

cinque NUMERO
five ◇ *Ha cinque anni.* She is five. ◇ *le cinque di sera* five o'clock in the evening ◇ *Eravamo in cinque.* There were five of us.
• **il cinque dicembre** the fifth of December

cinquecento NUMERO

C

☞

five hundred ◇ *cinquecento sterline* five
hundred pounds

♦ **il Cinquecento** the sixteenth century

la **cintura** NOME FEM
belt ◇ *una cintura di pelle* a leather belt

♦ **cintura di sicurezza** seat belt ◇ *Allacciati la
cintura di sicurezza.* Fasten your seat belt.

il **cinturino** NOME MASC
strap (*di orologio, di scarpa*)

ciò PRONOME
this ◇ *Ciò significa che...* This means that...
◇ *Da ciò deduco che...* From this I deduce
that... ◇ *Di ciò parleremo più tardi.* We'll talk
about this later.

♦ **ciò che** what ◇ *L'hanno sgridato per ciò che
ha fatto.* He got told off for what he did.

♦ **ciò nonostante** anyway ◇ *Aveva la febbre e
ciò nonostante è uscito.* He had a
temperature, but went out anyway.

♦ **E con ciò?** So what?

la **cioccolata** NOME FEM
chocolate ◇ *una tavoletta di cioccolata* a
bar of chocolate ◇ *Io vorrei una cioccolata
calda.* I'd like a hot chocolate.

il **cioccolatino** NOME MASC
chocolate ◇ *una scatola di cioccolatini* a
box of chocolates

il **cioccolato** NOME MASC
chocolate

♦ **cioccolato al latte** milk chocolate

♦ **cioccolato fondente** plain chocolate

cioè AVVERBIO
that is ◇ *Partirò il tredici, cioè domenica
prossima.* I'm leaving on the thirteenth,
that's next Sunday.

♦ **Vengo tra poco. – Cioè?** I'll come in a bit. –
Meaning...?

la **ciotola** NOME FEM
bowl

la **cipolla** NOME FEM
onion

il **cipresso** NOME MASC
cypress

circa AVVERBIO, PREPOSIZIONE
about ◇ *Costerà circa venti sterline.* It'll cost
about twenty pounds. ◇ *Sarà mezzogiorno
circa.* It must be about twelve o'clock.
◇ *Non mi ha detto niente circa i suoi
progetti.* He didn't tell me anything about
his plans.

il **circo** NOME MASC (PL i **circhi**)
circus

circolare VERBO

> vedi anche **circolare** AGGETTIVO, NOME

[1] to pass round ◇ *Luca ne ha fatto
circolare una copia in classe.* Luca passed a
copy round the class.

[2] to drive* (*in macchina*) ◇ *Circolare in
città diventa sempre più difficile.* Driving in
town is getting more and more difficult.

♦ **Circola voce che...** There's a rumour going
round that...

circolare AGGETTIVO

> vedi anche **circolare** VERBO, NOME

circular ◇ *un movimento circolare* a
circular movement

la **circolare** NOME FEM

> vedi anche **circolare** VERBO, AGGETTIVO

circular ◇ *Ha inviato una circolare.* He's
sent out a circular.

il **circolo** NOME MASC
[1] circle (*cerchio*)

♦ **un circolo vizioso** a vicious circle

[2] club ◇ *un circolo giovanile* a youth club

circondare VERBO
to surround ◇ *La polizia aveva circondato il
palazzo.* The police had surrounded the
building.

la **circonvallazione** NOME FEM
ring road
beltway US

la **circostanza** NOME FEM
circumstance ◇ *Date le circostanze, è stato
un buon risultato.* In the circumstances, it
was a good result.

il **circuito** NOME MASC
circuit ◇ *televisione a circuito chiuso*
closed-circuit television

♦ **fare corto circuito** to short-circuit

il **citofono** NOME MASC
[1] entry phone (*di appartamento*)
[2] intercom (*in ufficio*)

la **città** NOME (PL le **città**)
[1] town ◇ *Abiti in città o in campagna?* Do
you live in town or in the country? ◇ *Ti
faccio visitare la città.* I'll show you round
the town.

♦ **la mia città** my home town

[2] city (PL cities) (*più grande*) ◇ *Firenze è
una bella città.* Florence is a beautiful city.

la **cittadinanza** NOME FEM
citizenship ◇ *Ha la cittadinanza britannica.*
He has British citizenship.

il **cittadino,** la **cittadina** NOME MASC, FEM
citizen

il **ciuccio** NOME MASC
dummy (PL dummies)
pacifier US

il **ciuffo** NOME MASC
strand

la **civetta** NOME FEM
owl

civile AGGETTIVO
civil (*guerra, diritti*)

♦ **un paese civile** a civilized country

la **civiltà** NOME FEM (PL le **civiltà**)
civilization ◇ *un'antica civiltà* an ancient
civilization

il **clacson** NOME (PL i **clacson**)
horn

---

* I verbi seguiti da questo simbolo sono irregolari. Si veda anche alle pp.328–338.

C

* **suonare il clacson** to sound the horn

classe NOME FEM
[1] class ◇ *Che classe fai?* What class are you in? ◇ *Viaggiano in prima classe?* Do they travel first class? ◇ *un mio compagno di classe* a boy in my class
[2] classroom (*aula*) ◇ *Siamo rimasti in classe durante l'intervallo.* We stayed in the classroom during the break.

classico AGGETTIVO (FEM **classica**, MASC PL **classici**, FEM PL **classiche**)
vedi anche **classico** NOME
classical ◇ *Non mi piace la musica classica.* I don't like classical music.
* **liceo classico** school specializing in arts subjects

classico NOME MASC (PL i **classici**)
vedi anche **classico** AGGETTIVO
classic ◇ *un classico del cinema francese* a classic of the French cinema

classifica NOME FEM (PL le **classifiche**)
[1] results PL (*di gara*) ◇ *la classifica finale* the final results
[2] charts PL (*di dischi*)
[3] league table (*di campionato*)
* **essere primo in classifica (1)** (*concorrente*) to come* first
* **essere primo in classifica (2)** (*disco*) to be* number one in the charts
* **essere primo in classifica (3)** (*squadra*) to be* top of the league

clavicola NOME FEM
collarbone ◇ *Si è fratturato la clavicola.* He broke his collarbone.

cliccare VERBO
* **cliccare su** to click on

cliente NOME MASC/FEM
[1] customer ◇ *Il negozio era pieno di clienti.* The shop was full of customers.
[2] client (*di avvocato*)
cliente si usa per indicare il cliente di un libero professionista e non quello di un negozio.

clima NOME MASC (PL i **climi**)
climate

clinica NOME FEM (PL le **cliniche**)
[1] private hospital (*ospedale*)
[2] department (*reparto*)

coca NOME FEM
coke (*droga, bevanda*)

cocaina NOME FEM
cocaine

cocainomane NOME MASC/FEM
cocaine addict ◇ *È un cocainomane.* He's a cocaine addict.

coccinella NOME FEM
[1] ladybird
[2] ladybug [US]

cocco NOME MASC
coconut ◇ *gelato al cocco* coconut ice cream
* **noce di cocco** coconut

coccodrillo NOME MASC
crocodile

le coccole NOME FEM PL
* **fare le coccole a qualcuno** to give* somebody a cuddle

cocomero NOME MASC
watermelon

coda NOME FEM
[1] tail (*di animale*)
[2] queue (*fila*)
* **mettersi in coda** to join the queue ◇ *Prendi il vassoio e mettiti in coda.* Take a tray and join the queue.
* **fare la coda** to queue ◇ *La coda si fa da questa parte.* Queue this side.
* **guardare con la coda dell'occhio** to look out of the corner of one's eye ◇ *Mi guardava con la coda dell'occhio.* She was looking at me out of the corner of her eye.
* **coda di cavallo** ponytail ◇ *Ha la coda di cavallo.* She's got a ponytail.

codice NOME MASC
code ◇ *un messaggio in codice* a message in code
* **codice postale** postcode, [US] zip code ◇ *Sai qual è il codice postale?* Do you know what the postcode is?
* **codice della strada** highway code

codino NOME MASC
ponytail ◇ *Ha il codino.* He's got a ponytail.

coetaneo AGGETTIVO (FEM **coetanea**)
* **essere coetaneo di...** to be* the same age as... ◇ *Ma allora siamo coetanei!* So we're the same age!

cofano NOME MASC
bonnet
hood [US]

cogliere* VERBO
to pick (*fiori*) ◇ *Ho colto una mela dall'albero.* I picked an apple off the tree.
* **cogliere qualcuno sul fatto** to catch* somebody red-handed ◇ *L'ho colto sul fatto.* I caught him red-handed.

cognata NOME FEM
sister-in-law (PL sisters-in-law)

cognato NOME MASC
brother-in-law (PL brothers-in-law)

cognome NOME MASC
surname ◇ *Come ti chiami di cognome?* What's your surname?

coincidenza NOME FEM
[1] coincidence ◇ *Che coincidenza, vado anch'io a Bologna.* What a coincidence, I'm going to Bologna too.
[2] connection (*di treni*) ◇ *Ho perso la coincidenza.* I missed my connection.

coinvolgere* VERBO
to involve ◇ *Non mi coinvolgere in questa storia.* Don't involve me in this business.

colapasta NOME (PL i **colapasta**)
colander

colare VERBO

1 to drain ◊ *Hai colato la pasta?* Have you drained the pasta?

2 to strain (*brodo, tè*)

la **colazione** NOME FEM

breakfast ◊ *Cosa mangi a colazione?* What do you have for breakfast?

♦ **fare colazione** to have* breakfast

♦ **colazione all'inglese** English breakfast

il **colino** NOME MASC

strainer

la **colla** NOME FEM

glue ◊ *un tubetto di colla* a tube of glue

collaborare VERBO

1 to work together (*lavorare insieme*) ◊ *Tu e Luca dovete cercare di collaborare.* You and Luca must try to work together.

2 to work (*a progetto*) ◊ *Ho collaborato ad un progetto molto interessante.* I worked on a very interesting project.

il **collaboratore,** la **collaboratrice** NOME MASC, FEM

1 member of a team ◊ *tutti i nostri collaboratori* all the members of our team

♦ **È uno dei nostri collaboratori più validi.** He's one of our best people.

♦ **Stiamo cercando due collaboratori per questo progetto.** We're looking for two people to work on this project.

♦ **collaboratrice domestica** home help

♦ **collaboratore esterno** freelancer

2 contributor (*a giornale*)

la **collana** NOME FEM

necklace

il **collant** NOME MASC (PL i **collant**)

tights PL

pantyhose US

◊ *un paio di collant* a pair of tights

il **collare** NOME MASC

collar

il **collasso** NOME MASC

collapse

♦ **avere un collasso** to collapse ◊ *Ha avuto un collasso mentre giocava a pallone.* He collapsed while playing football.

il/la **collega** NOME MASC/FEM (MASC PL i **colleghi,** FEM PL le **colleghe**)

colleague ◊ *un suo collega* a colleague of hers

il **collegamento** NOME MASC

link (*ferroviario, ipertestuale*)

collegare VERBO

1 to connect ◊ *Devi collegare la stampante al computer.* You have to connect the printer to the computer.

♦ **collegarsi a** (*Internet*) to connect to

2 to link ◊ *L'autostrada collega Bologna a Firenze.* The motorway links Bologna and Florence.

il **collegio** NOME MASC (PL i **collegi**)

boarding school

*Con il termine **college** in Gran Bretagna e negli Stati Uniti generalmente si intende un'università.*

la **collera** NOME FEM

♦ **essere in collera con qualcuno** to be* angry with somebody

la **colletta** NOME FEM

collection ◊ *Abbiamo fatto una colletta per comprarle un regalo.* We had a collection to buy her a present.

il **colletto** NOME MASC

collar

collezionare VERBO

to collect ◊ *Colleziono cartoline da tutto il mondo.* I collect postcards from all over the world.

la **collezione** NOME FEM

collection ◊ *una collezione di francobolli* a collection of stamps

♦ **fare collezione di qualcosa** to collect something

la **collina** NOME FEM

hill

il **collirio** NOME MASC

eyedrops PL ◊ *Vorrei un collirio.* I'd like some eyedrops.

il **collo** NOME MASC

neck ◊ *Portava un foulard al collo.* She had a scarf round her neck.

♦ **essere nei guai fino al collo** to be* in deep trouble

♦ **maglione a collo alto** polo neck jumper

il **colloquio** NOME MASC

interview ◊ *Domani ha un colloquio di lavoro.* She's got a job interview tomorrow.

il **colombo** NOME MASC

pigeon

la **colonia** NOME FEM

colony (PL colonies) ◊ *Era una colonia britannica.* It was a British colony.

♦ **colonia marina** seaside summer camp

la **colonna** NOME FEM

column ◊ *le colonne di un tempio* the columns of a temple

♦ **colonna sonora** soundtrack

♦ **colonna vertebrale** spine

il **colonnello** NOME MASC

colonel

colorato AGGETTIVO (FEM **colorata**)

coloured

colored US

◊ *una camicia colorata* a coloured shirt

◊ *una maglietta molto colorata* a brightly coloured T-shirt

il **colore** NOME MASC

colour

color US

◊ *Di che colore è?* What colour is it?

senza preposizione.

◊ *un cappotto color ruggine* a rust-coloured coat

- **TV a colori** colour TV
- **di colore** black ◊ *una ragazza di colore* a black girl
- **diventare di tutti i colori** to go* red ◊ *È diventato di tutti i colori per l'imbarazzo.* He went red with embarrassment.
- **farne di tutti i colori** to get* up to all sorts of things ◊ *In gita ne abbiamo fatte di tutti i colori.* On the trip we got up to all sorts of things.

colpa NOME FEM

[1] fault ◊ *Di chi è la colpa?* Whose fault is it? ◊ *È colpa mia.* It's my fault.
◊ *L'incidente è successo per colpa sua.* The accident was his fault. ◊ *Per colpa sua non possiamo uscire.* It's his fault we can't go out.

- **sentirsi in colpa** to feel* guilty ◊ *Se non ci vado mi sento in colpa.* If I don't go I feel guilty.

[2] blame (*biasimo*)
- **addossarsi la colpa** to take* the blame ◊ *Si è addossato lui la colpa.* He took the blame.
- **dare la colpa a qualcuno** to blame somebody ◊ *Non dare la colpa a me!* Don't blame me!

colpevole AGGETTIVO

vedi anche **colpevole** NOME

guilty ◊ *colpevole di omicidio* guilty of murder

colpevole NOME MASC/FEM

vedi anche **colpevole** AGGETTIVO

culprit ◊ *Non hanno trovato il colpevole.* They haven't found the culprit.

colpire VERBO

[1] to hit* ◊ *È stata colpita alla testa.* She was hit on the head.
- **colpire qualcuno con un pugno** to punch somebody

[2] to strike* (*stupire*) ◊ *Qual è la cosa che ti ha colpito di più?* What's the thing that struck you most?
- **rimanere colpito da qualcosa** to be* shocked by something ◊ *Sono rimasto colpito dalla sua reazione.* I was shocked by his reaction.

colpo NOME MASC

[1] blow ◊ *un colpo in testa* a blow on the head ◊ *Il divorzio dei suoi è stato un brutto colpo per lei.* Her parents' divorce was a terrible blow for her.
- **Mi hai fatto venire un colpo!** You gave me a fright!
- **Ti venisse un colpo!** Drop dead!
- **dare un colpo a qualcuno** to hit* somebody ◊ *Gli ha dato un colpo in testa.* He hit him on the head.
- **di colpo** suddenly ◊ *Si è fermato di colpo.* He stopped suddenly.
- **sul colpo** instantly ◊ *È morto sul colpo.* He

died instantly.
- **fare colpo** to be* a hit ◊ *Hai fatto colpo sulla mia amica!* You were a hit with my friend!
- **colpo d'aria** chill ◊ *Ho preso un colpo d'aria.* I've caught a chill.
- **colpo di fulmine** love at first sight ◊ *È stato un colpo di fulmine.* It was love at first sight.
- **colpo di telefono** ring ◊ *Ti do un colpo di telefono domani sera.* I'll give you a ring tomorrow evening.

[2] shot (*sparo*) ◊ *Abbiamo sentito dei colpi.* We heard shots.
- **sparare un colpo** to fire ◊ *Ha sparato dei colpi in aria.* He fired into the air.

[3] raid (*rapina*) ◊ *un colpo in banca* a bank raid

il coltello NOME MASC

knife (PL knives)

coltivare VERBO

to grow* ◊ *Coltivavano pomodori.* They grew tomatoes.

colto AGGETTIVO (FEM **colta**)

well-educated ◊ *una persona molto colta* a very well-educated person

il coma NOME MASC (PL i **coma**)

coma ◊ *È entrato in coma.* He's gone into a coma.
- **Oggi sono in coma!** I'm half dead today!

il comandante NOME MASC

captain (*di nave, di aereo*)

comandare VERBO

[1] to be* the boss ◊ *È lei che comanda in casa.* She's the boss in the house.

[2] to command (*esercito*)

combattere VERBO

to fight* ◊ *Hanno sempre combattuto contro l'ingiustizia.* They've always fought against injustice.

combinare VERBO

to do* ◊ *Che cosa stai combinando?* What are you doing?
- **Che cosa hai combinato?** What have you gone and done?
- **Oggi non ho combinato nulla.** I haven't got anything done today.

la combinazione NOME FEM

[1] combination (*di serratura, di cassaforte*)

[2] coincidence ◊ *Che combinazione!* What a coincidence!
- **per combinazione** by chance ◊ *Per combinazione era lì anche lui.* By chance he was there too.

come AVVERBIO, CONGIUNZIONE

[1] how ◊ *Come stai?* How are you?
◊ *Com'è andato il viaggio?* How was the journey? ◊ *Com'è successo?* How did it happen? ◊ *Mi ha spiegato come l'ha conosciuto.* She told me how she met him.
- **Com'è carino!** Isn't it pretty!
- **Come mai? (1)** (*con sorpresa*) How come?
- **Come mai? (2)** (*perché*) Why?

[2] what ◊ *Scusa, come hai detto?* Sorry,

what did you say? ◇ *Ma come! Aveva detto che sarebbe venuto!* What! He said he'd come! ◇ *Come ti chiami?* What's your name? ◇ *Com'è la tua città?* What's your town like? ◇ *Com'è la cucina scozzese?* What's Scottish food like? ◇ *Come sarebbe a dire?* What do you mean?

♦ **Come?** Sorry?

③ like *(per paragoni)* ◇ *Ne ho uno come il tuo.* I've got one like yours. ◇ *Piangeva come un bambino.* He was crying like a child.

④ as ◇ *Ho fatto come hai detto tu.* I did as you said. ◇ *bianco come la neve* white as snow ◇ *Mi piace così com'è.* I like it as it is. ◇ *come puoi ben vedere* as you can see ◇ *come sai* as you know

♦ **come se** as if ◇ *Sì, come se non lo sapessi!* Yes, as if you didn't know!

♦ **come se niente fosse** as if nothing had happened ◇ *Si comportava come se niente fosse.* He behaved as if nothing had happened.

♦ **come non detto** let's forget it ◇ *Va bene, come non detto.* OK, let's forget it.

♦ **A come Andrea** A for Andrew

comico AGGETTIVO (FEM **comica**, MASC PL **comici**, FEM PL **comiche**)

vedi anche **comico** NOME

funny ◇ *una scena comica* a funny scene

il **comico** NOME MASC (PL i **comici**)

vedi anche **comico** AGGETTIVO

comedian ◇ *È un comico famoso.* He's a well-known comedian.

cominciare VERBO

to start ◇ *Il film comincia con un'esplosione.* The film starts with an explosion. ◇ *Hai cominciato il libro che ti ho prestato?* Have you started the book I lent you? ◇ *La prima parola comincia per F.* The first word starts with F.

Quando start è seguito da un verbo in genere si possono usare sia l'infinito che il gerundio. ◇ *Ha cominciato a ridere.* She started to laugh. ◇ *Ha cominciato a piangere.* She started crying.

♦ **tanto per cominciare** in the first place ◇ *Tanto per cominciare non sappiamo se funzionerà.* In the first place we don't know if it'll work.

♦ **Cominciamo bene!** *(ironico)* This is a fine start!

la **comitiva** NOME FEM

group ◇ *una comitiva di turisti* a group of tourists

♦ **sconto per comitive** group discount

la **commedia** NOME FEM

① play *(opera teatrale)*

② comedy *(che fa ridere)* (PL comedies)

commerciale AGGETTIVO

commercial ◇ *le attività industriali e*

commerciali industrial and commercial activities

♦ **un'attività commerciale** *(ditta)* a business

♦ **avere rapporti commerciali con** to trade with

il/la **commerciante** NOME MASC/FEM

shopkeeper *(negoziante)* ◇ *i commercianti del centro* the shopkeepers in the town centre

♦ **commerciante all'ingrosso** wholesaler

il **commercio** NOME MASC

trade ◇ *commercio all'ingrosso* wholesale trade

♦ **economia e commercio** *(all'università)* economics and business

il **commesso**, la **commessa** NOME MASC, FEM

shop assistant

sales clerk US

◇ *Fa la commessa.* She is a shop assistant.

il **commissario** NOME MASC (PL i **commissari**)

♦ **commissario di polizia** police superintendent

♦ **commissario tecnico** *(calcio)* national team manager

la **commissione** NOME FEM

commission ◇ *Ha una commissione sulle vendite.* He gets commission on sales.

♦ **la Commissione europea** the European Commission

♦ **commissione esaminatrice** panel of examiners

commovente AGGETTIVO

moving ◇ *una storia commovente* a moving story

la **commozione** NOME FEM

emotion ◇ *Non riusciva a nascondere la commozione.* He couldn't hide his emotion.

♦ **Si è messa a piangere per la commozione.** She got emotional and started to cry.

commuoversi* VERBO

to get* emotional ◇ *Si è commossa.* She got emotional.

il **comodino** NOME MASC

bedside table

la **comodità** NOME FEM (PL le **comodità**)

convenience ◇ *la comodità di abitare in centro* the convenience of living in the town centre

♦ **Ho la comodità di avere la fermata sotto casa.** Conveniently for me, the stop is outside my house.

comodo AGGETTIVO (FEM **comoda**)

① comfortable ◇ *una poltrona comoda* a comfortable chair ◇ *Stai comodo lì?* Are you comfortable there?

♦ **State comodi!** Please don't get up!

② easy *(facile)* ◇ *È comodo dare la colpa agli altri.* It's easy to blame other people.

③ convenient *(pratico)* ◇ *Sarebbe più*

comodo incontrarci in centro. It would be more convenient to meet in the town centre.

♦ **far comodo** to be* a help ◇ *Quei soldi mi hanno fatto proprio comodo.* That money was a great help.

la **compagnia** NOME FEM
company (PL companies) ◇ *Lavora in una compagnia di assicurazioni.* He works in an insurance company.

♦ **fare compagnia a qualcuno** to keep* somebody company ◇ *Quand'era malato andavo a fargli compagnia.* When he was ill I used to go and keep him company.

♦ **essere di compagnia** to be* sociable ◇ *È un tipo di compagnia.* He's a sociable kind of person.

il **compagno,** la **compagna** NOME MASC, FEM
[1] schoolfriend (*di scuola*) ◇ *È una mia compagna di scuola.* She's one of my schoolfriends.

♦ **un mio compagno di classe** a boy in my class
♦ **un compagno di squadra** a team-mate
[2] partner (*in coppia*)

il **compenso** NOME MASC
payment (*per lavoro*)

♦ **È brutto ma in compenso è molto simpatico.** He's not handsome, but he's very nice.
♦ **Ha un lavoro noiosissimo. In compenso è pagato molto bene.** His job is very boring – the plus side is that it's very well paid.

le **compere** NOME FEM PL
♦ **andare a fare le compere** to go* shopping

la **competizione** NOME FEM
competition

compiere VERBO
♦ **Quando compi gli anni?** When is your birthday?
♦ **Quanti anni compi?** How old will you be?
♦ **Ho compiuto sedici anni il mese scorso.** I was sixteen last month.

compilare VERBO
to fill in ◇ *Compilare il modulo in stampatello.* Fill in the form in block letters.

il **compito** NOME MASC
[1] test (*in classe*) ◇ *Domani c'è il compito in classe di matematica.* We've got a maths test tomorrow.
[2] homework (*a casa*)
homework non ha plurale e non è mai preceduto dall'articolo a.

♦ **fare i compiti** to do* one's homework ◇ *Non posso, devo fare i compiti.* I can't, I've got to do my homework.
[3] job (*incarico*) ◇ *A me è toccato il compito di portare le bibite.* It was my job to bring the drinks.

il **compleanno** NOME MASC
birthday ◇ *Buon compleanno!* Happy birthday!

complesso AGGETTIVO (FEM **complessa**)
vedi anche **complesso** NOME
complex ◇ *un problema complesso* a complex problem

il **complesso** NOME MASC
vedi anche **complesso** AGGETTIVO
[1] complex ◇ *un complesso d'inferiorità* an inferiority complex ◇ *Ha il complesso del naso grosso.* She's got a complex about the size of her nose.
[2] band ◇ *Suona in un complesso.* He plays in a band.

♦ **nel complesso** on the whole ◇ *Nel complesso mi è piaciuto abbastanza.* On the whole I quite liked it.

completamente AVVERBIO
completely

completo AGGETTIVO (FEM **completa**)
vedi anche **completo** NOME
complete ◇ *È stato un disastro completo!* It was a complete disaster! ◇ *un frullatore completo di accessori* a blender complete with accessories

♦ **al completo** full ◇ *L'albergo era al completo.* The hotel was full.

il **completo** NOME MASC
vedi anche **completo** AGGETTIVO
suit ◇ *Portava un completo grigio.* He was wearing a grey suit.

♦ **completo da sci** ski suit

complicato AGGETTIVO (FEM **complicata**)
complicated ◇ *una faccenda complicata* a complicated affair ◇ *È un po' complicato da spiegare.* It's a bit complicated to explain.

il/la **complice** NOME MASC/FEM
accomplice

la **complicità** NOME FEM (PL le **complicità**)
collusion

il **complimento** NOME MASC
compliment

♦ **fare un complimento a qualcuno** to pay* somebody a compliment
♦ **Complimenti!** Congratulations! ◇ *Complimenti per la promozione!* Congratulations on your promotion!
A volte complimenti non si traduce.
◇ *Complimenti, parli molto bene l'italiano!* You speak very good Italian!
◇ *Complimenti, che bella casa!* Your house is lovely!

il **complotto** NOME MASC
plot

comporre* VERBO
[1] to dial (*numero*) ◇ *Alzare il ricevitore e comporre il numero.* Lift the receiver and dial the number.
[2] to compose (*musica*) ◇ *Ha composto la colonna sonora.* He composed the soundtrack.

♦ **essere composto da** to consist of ◇ *La casa è composta da tre stanze.* The house consists of three rooms.

il **comportamento** NOME MASC
behaviour
behavior [US]

◊ *Non capisco il suo comportamento.* I don't understand her behaviour.

comportarsi VERBO
to behave ◊ *Si è comportato da vigliacco.* He behaved like a coward. ◊ *Non si è comportato molto bene con me.* He didn't behave very well towards me.

comprare VERBO
to buy* ◊ *Cosa hai comprato?* What did you buy? ◊ *Ho comprato un regalino per mia sorella.* I bought a little present for my sister.

comprensivo AGGETTIVO (FEM **comprensiva**)
understanding ◊ *È molto comprensivo.* He's very understanding.
Attenzione! In inglese esiste la parola **comprehensive**, *che però non significa* **comprensivo**.

compreso AGGETTIVO (FEM **compresa**)
inclusive ◊ *dall'otto al ventidue compreso* from the eighth to the twenty-second inclusive

♦ **È aperto tutta la settimana, domenica compresa.** It's open all week, including Sunday.

♦ **tutto compreso** all-inclusive ◊ *La vacanza, tutto compreso, costa mille euro.* The holiday costs one thousand euros, all-inclusive.

comunale AGGETTIVO

♦ **palazzo comunale** town hall

♦ **Fa l'impiegato comunale.** He works for the council.

comune AGGETTIVO
vedi anche **comune** NOME
common ◊ *È un problema molto comune.* It's a very common problem.

♦ **avere in comune** to have* in common ◊ *Non abbiamo niente in comune.* We haven't got anything in common.

♦ **Abbiamo un amico in comune.** We've got a mutual friend.

il **comune** NOME MASC
vedi anche **comune** AGGETTIVO
[1] council ◊ *Lavora per il comune.* She works for the council.
[2] town hall (*edificio*) ◊ *Devi andare al comune per richiedere il certificato.* You have to go to the town hall to get the certificate.

la **comunione** NOME FEM

♦ **prima comunione** first communion

la **comunità** NOME (PL le **comunità**)
community (PL communities) ◊ *C'è una grossa comunità britannica in Toscana.* There's a big British community in Tuscany.

♦ **Comunità Europea** European Community

comunque AVVERBIO, CONGIUNZIONE
anyway ◊ *I miei non vogliono, ma ci vado comunque.* My parents don't want me to, but I'm going anyway. ◊ *Comunque,*

avresti potuto telefonare. Anyway, you could have phoned.

♦ **Comunque vada...** However it turns out... ◊ *Comunque vada, sono contento che sia finita.* However it turns out, I'm glad it's over.

con PREPOSIZIONE
[1] with ◊ *Ci andrò con lei.* I'll go with her.
◊ *Con chi sei stato?* Who were you with?
◊ *un ragazzo con gli occhi azzurri* a boy with blue eyes

♦ **con la forza** by force

♦ **Con questo freddo non potremo partire.** We can't set off in this cold weather.

♦ **E con questo?** So what?
[2] to ◊ *È sposata con uno scozzese.* She's married to a Scot. ◊ *Hai parlato con lui?* Have you spoken to him? ◊ *È gentile con tutti.* She's nice to everybody.

concentrarsi VERBO
to concentrate ◊ *Non riuscivo a concentrarmi.* I couldn't concentrate.

il **concerto** NOME MASC
concert

il **concetto** NOME MASC
idea ◊ *Non ho afferrato bene il concetto.* I haven't quite got the idea.

la **conchiglia** NOME FEM
shell

conciare VERBO
to make* a mess of ◊ *Come hai conciato quei jeans!* What a mess you've made of those jeans!

♦ **Ma come ti sei conciato? (1)** (*vestito in modo strano*) What on earth have you got on?

♦ **Ma come ti sei conciato? (2)** (*sporco*) How did you get into that state?

il/la **concorrente** NOME MASC/FEM
[1] competitor (*in gara sportiva*)
[2] contestant (*a un quiz*)

la **concorrenza** NOME FEM
competition

il **concorso** NOME MASC
exam (*per un impiego*)

♦ **concorso a premi** competition ◊ *Ha partecipato ad un concorso a premi ed ha vinto.* She went in for a competition and won.

♦ **concorso di bellezza** beauty contest

concreto AGGETTIVO (FEM **concreta**)
concrete ◊ *una prova concreta* concrete evidence

♦ **in concreto** actually ◊ *Ma cosa fa in concreto?* What's he actually doing?

condannare VERBO
[1] to sentence ◊ *L'hanno condannato a cinque anni di prigione.* He's been sentenced to five years in prison.

♦ **condannare qualcuno per** to convict somebody of ◊ *Li hanno condannati per* rapina a mano armata. They were convicted of armed robbery.

[2] to condemn ◇ Non me la sento di condannarlo. I don't condemn him.

condire VERBO
[1] to dress (insalata)
[2] to season (con spezie)
◆ una salsa per condire la pasta a sauce for pasta

condividere* VERBO
to share ◇ Condivide l'appartamento con il fratello. He shares the flat with his brother.
◆ condividere l'opinione di qualcuno to agree with somebody ◇ Non condivido le tue opinioni. I don't agree with you.

la condizione NOME FEM
condition ◇ Lo farò ad una sola condizione. I'll do it on one condition.
◆ Non sei in condizione di guidare. You're not in a fit state to drive.
◆ in buone condizioni in good condition al singolare.
◇ La macchina è ancora in buone condizioni. The car is still in good condition.

la conducente NOME MASC/FEM
driver ◇ il conducente dell'autobus the bus driver

la conferenza NOME FEM
[1] conference ◇ una conferenza sull'inquinamento atmosferico a conference on air pollution
◆ conferenza stampa press conference
[2] lecture (discorso) ◇ Terrà una conferenza nell'aula magna. He's going to give a lecture in the main hall.

confermare VERBO
to confirm ◇ Devo confermare la prenotazione. I've got to confirm the booking. ◇ Ha confermato che verrà. He's confirmed that he's coming.

confessare VERBO
to confess ◇ L'assassino ha confessato. The murderer has confessed. ◇ Ti confesso che... I must confess that...
◆ andare a confessarsi to go* to confession

il confetto NOME MASC
sugared almond
Attenzione! In inglese esiste la parola confetti, che però significa coriandoli.

la confettura NOME FEM
jam

la confezione NOME FEM
packet ◇ una confezione di caramelle a packet of sweets
◆ confezione risparmio economy size
◆ fare una confezione regalo to giftwrap ◇ Mi può fare una confezione regalo? Can you giftwrap it for me?

conficcare VERBO
◆ conficcare in to stick* into ◇ Mi si è conficcata una spina nel dito. A thorn stuck into my finger.

confidare VERBO
◆ confidare qualcosa a qualcuno to tell* somebody something ◇ Ti voglio confidare un segreto. I want to tell you a secret.
◆ confidarsi con to confide in ◇ Aveva bisogno di confidarsi con qualcuno. She needed to confide in somebody.

il confine NOME MASC
border ◇ Abbiamo passato il confine. We crossed the border.

il conflitto NOME MASC
conflict

confondere* VERBO
to mix up ◇ Ho confuso le date. I mixed up the dates. ◇ Non starai confondendo i nomi? You're not mixing up the names, are you?
◆ confondersi to get* mixed up ◇ No, scusa, mi sono confuso: era ieri. No, sorry, I've got mixed up: it was yesterday.
◆ confondere le idee a qualcuno to get* somebody confused ◇ Tutti questi discorsi mi confondono le idee. All this talk is getting me confused.

confrontare VERBO
to compare ◇ Abbiamo confrontato le nostre scuole. We compared our schools.

il confronto NOME MASC
comparison ◇ Non c'è confronto! There's no comparison!
◆ fare un confronto fra due cose to compare two things
◆ in confronto a compared to ◇ In confronto ai tuoi, i miei sono più piccoli. Mine are small, compared to yours.
◆ nei confronti di qualcuno towards somebody ◇ Non ho risentimento nei suoi confronti. I don't feel any resentment towards him.

la confusione NOME FEM
[1] noise (chiasso) ◇ Smettetela di fare confusione! Stop making this noise!
[2] confusion (caos) ◇ Ha approfittato della confusione per scappare. He took advantage of the confusion to escape.
[3] mess (disordine) ◇ Che confusione! What a mess!
◆ far confusione (confondersi) to get* mixed up

confuso AGGETTIVO (FEM **confusa**)
confused ◇ Sono un po' confuso. I'm a bit confused. ◇ La situazione è ancora confusa. The situation is still confused.

il congegno NOME MASC
device

congelato AGGETTIVO (FEM **congelata**)
frozen ◇ Sono congelato! I'm frozen!

il congelatore NOME MASC
freezer

congiungere* VERBO
to link ◇ Il ponte congiunge l'isoletta alla terraferma. The bridge links the island to the ☞

mainland.

il **congiuntivo** NOME MASC
subjunctive

le **congratulazioni** NOME FEM PL
congratulations ◇ *Congratulazioni per la promozione!* Congratulations on your promotion!

il **congresso** NOME MASC
[1] conference ◇ *il congresso del partito socialista* the Socialist Party conference
[2] meeting (*scientifico, letterario*)

il **coniglietto** NOME MASC
bunny (PL bunnies)

il **coniglio** NOME MASC
rabbit

la **connessione** NOME FEM
connection

connettere* VERBO
[1] to connect (*collegare*) ◇ *Non avevo connessi i due fatti.* I hadn't connected the two facts.
[2] to think* straight (*pensare*) ◇ *La mattina non riesco a connettere.* I can't think straight in the morning.

il **cono** NOME MASC
cone ◇ *un cono al cioccolato* a chocolate cone

il/la **conoscente** NOME MASC/FEM
acquaintance ◇ *una mia conoscente* an acquaintance of mine

conoscere* VERBO
to know* ◇ *Non conosco bene la città.* I don't know the town well.
♦ **conoscere qualcuno di vista** to know* somebody by sight ◇ *Lo conosco solo di vista.* I only know him by sight. ◇ *Da quanto vi conoscete?* How long have you known each other? ◇ *Ci conosciamo da poco tempo.* We haven't known each other long.
♦ **conoscersi** (*per la prima volta*) to meet* ◇ *Ci siamo conosciuti in vacanza.* We met on holiday. ◇ *Ci siamo conosciuti a Firenze.* We first met in Florence.

conosciuto AGGETTIVO (FEM **conosciuta**)
well-known ◇ *un attore conosciuto* a well-known actor

la **consegna** NOME FEM
delivery (PL deliveries) ◇ *La consegna è garantita in giornata.* Same-day delivery is guaranteed.
♦ **alla consegna** on delivery ◇ *Si può pagare alla consegna.* You can pay on delivery.
♦ **consegna a domicilio** home delivery

consegnare VERBO
to deliver ◇ *Mi hanno consegnato il pacco stamattina.* The parcel was delivered this morning.

la **conseguenza** NOME FEM
consequence ◇ *Non aveva pensato alle conseguenze.* He hadn't thought of the consequences.

conservare VERBO
to keep* ◇ *Lo conservo in una scatola.* I keep it in a box. ◇ *Si conserva bene per alcune settimane.* It keeps well for several weeks.

il **conservatorio** NOME MASC
music school ◇ *Studio al conservatorio.* I'm at music school.

considerare VERBO
[1] to consider ◇ *Bisogna considerare i pro e i contro.* You have to consider the pros and cons.
[2] to regard as ◇ *La considero un'amica.* I regard her as a friend.
♦ **considerarsi** to think* oneself ◇ *Puoi considerarti fortunato!* You can think yourself lucky!
♦ **Si considera il migliore.** He thinks he's the best.

considerato AGGETTIVO
♦ **tutto considerato** all things considered ◇ *Tutto considerato non è male.* It's not bad, all things considered.
♦ **considerato che** considering that ◇ *Giochi bene, considerato che hai cominciato da poco.* You play well, considering that you only started recently.

consigliare VERBO
[1] to recommend ◇ *Che cosa mi consigli?* What do you recommend? ◇ *Ti consiglio la pizza.* I'd recommend the pizza.
senza pronome personale in inglese.
[2] to advise ◇ *Gli ha consigliato di andarsene prima possibile.* She advised him to leave as soon as possible. ◇ *Ti consiglierei di sbrigarti.* I'd advise you to get a move on.
♦ **Ti consiglio di non accettare l'invito.** I don't advise you to accept the invitation.

il **consiglio** NOME MASC
advice ◇ *Mi ha chiesto un consiglio.* She asked me for advice.
advice non ha plurale e non è mai preceduto dall'articolo "an".
◇ *Ho seguito i tuoi consigli.* I followed your advice. ◇ *Ti do due consigli...* I'll give you two bits of advice...

consolare VERBO
to cheer up ◇ *Ho cercato di consolarla un po'.* I tried to cheer her up a bit.

il **consolato** NOME MASC
consulate ◇ *il consolato italiano* the Italian consulate

la **consolazione** NOME FEM
consolation ◇ *L'unica consolazione è che...* The only consolation is that...
♦ **premio di consolazione** consolation prize

la **consonante** NOME FEM
consonant

consumare VERBO

[1] to wear* out (*scarpe, vestiti*) ◇ *Ho consumato la suola delle scarpe.* I've worn the soles of my shoes out.

[2] to use ◇ *Quanto consuma la tua macchina?* How much petrol does your car use?

il **contachilometri** NOME MASC (PL i **contachilometri**)

mileometer

il **contadino,** la **contadina** NOME MASC, FEM

peasant ◇ *A quel tempo i contadini erano molto poveri.* At that time peasants were very poor.

◆ **Mio zio è contadino.** My uncle works on the land.

contagioso AGGETTIVO (FEM **contagiosa**)

[1] infectious (*in medicina*) ◇ *una malattia contagiosa* an infectious disease

[2] catching (*nell'uso comune*) ◇ *Non preoccuparti, non è contagioso.* Don't worry, it's not catching.

i **contanti** NOME MASC PL

cash SING ◇ *mille euro in contanti* a thousand euros in cash

◆ **pagare in contanti** to pay* cash

contare VERBO

to count ◇ *Li ho contati, sono quindici.* I've counted them, there are fifteen. ◇ *Conta fino a cinquanta e poi vieni a cercarci.* Count to fifty and then come and look for us.

◆ **senza contare** not counting ◇ *Eravamo in dieci, senza contare i professori.* There were ten of us, not counting the teachers.

◆ **contare su qualcuno** to count on somebody ◇ *Sai che puoi contare su di me.* You know you can count on me.

◆ **contare di** (*ripromettersi*) to think* of ◇ *Contavamo di partire nel pomeriggio.* We were thinking of leaving in the afternoon.

◆ **Conto di essere lì per mezzogiorno.** I think I'll be there by midday.

il **contatto** NOME MASC

contact ◇ *Il loro contatto negli Stati Uniti era Chris.* Their contact in the United States was Chris.

◆ **mettersi in contatto con** to contact ◇ *Devo mettermi in contatto con John.* I must contact John.

◆ **mantenersi in contatto** to keep* in touch ◇ *Ci siamo mantenuti in contatto.* We've kept in touch.

contemporaneamente AVVERBIO

at the same time ◇ *Sono arrivati contemporaneamente.* They arrived at the same time.

contenere* VERBO

to contain ◇ *Questo succo non contiene zucchero.* This juice does not contain sugar.

◆ **Lo stadio può contenere centomila spettatori.** The stadium can hold a hundred thousand spectators.

il **contenitore** NOME MASC

container ◇ *un contenitore di plastica* a plastic container

contento AGGETTIVO (FEM **contenta**)

[1] happy ◇ *Sei contento adesso?* Are you happy now? ◇ *Oggi sono più contento.* I'm happier today.

◆ **far contento qualcuno** to make* somebody happy ◇ *Sono andato per far contenta la mamma.* I went to make my mum happy.

[2] glad ◇ *Sono contento di vederti.* I'm glad to see you. ◇ *Sono contenta che ti piaccia.* I'm glad you like it.

il **contenuto** NOME MASC

contents PL ◇ *Ha rovesciato sul tavolo il contenuto della borsa.* He tipped the contents of the bag out onto the table.

il **continente** NOME MASC

[1] continent (*Europa, Asia*)

[2] mainland (*terraferma: rispetto ad un'isola*)

continuamente AVVERBIO

nonstop (*senza interruzione*) ◇ *È piovuto continuamente.* It rained nonstop.

◆ **Cambia idea continuamente.** She keeps changing her mind.

continuare VERBO

to carry on ◇ *Per oggi basta, continueremo domani.* That's enough for today, we'll carry on tomorrow. ◇ *Se continua così...* If he carries on like this...

◆ **continuare a fare qualcosa** to go* on doing something ◇ *Ha continuato a dormire nonostante il chiasso.* She went on sleeping despite the noise.

◆ **Continua a piovere.** It's still raining.

◆ **Continui pure.** Do go on.

*In inglese esiste anche il verbo **to continue**, che è leggermente più formale.*

◇ *Continuano le trattative.* Negotiations are continuing. ◇ *Continuava a credere in lei.* He continued to believe in her.

__to continue__ può anche reggere il gerundio.

continuo AGGETTIVO (FEM **continua**)

constant ◇ *Sono stufa delle sue lamentele continue.* I'm fed up with her constant complaints.

◆ **C'è un continuo viavai di gente.** There are people constantly coming and going.

◆ **di continuo** nonstop ◇ *Piove di continuo da tre giorni.* It's been raining nonstop for three days.

il **conto** NOME MASC

[1] bill ◇ *Il conto, per favore.* Could I have the bill, please?

[2] account (*in banca*) ◇ *un conto corrente* a current account, US: a checking account

[3] calculation (*calcolo*) ◇ *Ho fatto un rapido conto.* I did a quick calculation.

◆ **rendersi conto** to realize ◇ *Non si era reso conto che c'ero anch'io.* He hadn't realized I was there too. ◇ *Non ti rendi conto delle*

☞

conseguenze! You don't realize what will happen!

♦ **tener conto di** to allow for ◇ *Non avevo tenuto conto del fuso orario.* I hadn't allowed for the time difference.

♦ **per conto di** on behalf of ◇ *Telefono per conto di Sara.* I'm phoning on behalf of Sara.

♦ **per conto mio (1)** (*a mio parere*) in my opinion ◇ *Per conto mio la faccenda è un po' strana.* In my opinion it's all rather strange.

♦ **per conto mio (2)** (*da solo*) on my own ◇ *Ci vado per conto mio.* I'm going on my own.

♦ **in fin dei conti** after all ◇ *Be', in fin dei conti non ha tutti i torti.* Well, after all, he's quite right.

♦ **sul conto di** about ◇ *Girano strane voci sul conto di Luca.* I've heard some strange things about Luca.

♦ **Con te faccio i conti più tardi!** I'll sort you out later!

♦ **conto alla rovescia** countdown

il **contorno** NOME MASC
vegetables PL

> ❶ *In restaurants in Italy meat and fish dishes don't usually come with vegetables. These are ordered separately from the section of the menu headed* **Contorni**.

◇ *Non prendo il contorno.* I don't want any vegetables.

♦ **Cosa prendi come contorno?** What would you like to go with it?

♦ **arrosto con contorno di patate** roast meat and potatoes

il **contrabbandiere** NOME MASC
smuggler

il **contrabbando** NOME MASC
smuggling ◇ *contrabbando di droga* drug smuggling

♦ **sigarette di contrabbando** contraband cigarettes

il **contrabbasso** NOME MASC
double bass

contraddire* VERBO
to contradict ◇ *Mi contraddice sempre.* He's always contradicting me.

contrario AGGETTIVO (FEM **contraria**)
vedi anche **contrario** NOME
opposite ◇ *in direzione contraria* in the opposite direction

♦ **essere contrario a qualcosa** to be* against something ◇ *Sono contrario alla vivisezione.* I'm against vivisection.

il **contrario** NOME MASC
vedi anche **contrario** AGGETTIVO
opposite ◇ *Fa tutto il contrario di quello che dice.* He does the complete opposite of what he says.

♦ **al contrario di** contrary to ◇ *Al contrario di*

quanto si crede, è piuttosto grande. Contrary to what people think, it's quite big.

♦ **avere qualcosa in contrario** to have* an objection ◇ *Io avrei qualcosa in contrario.* I have an objection. ◇ *Se qualcuno ha qualcosa in contrario lo dica subito.* If anyone has an objection they should say so at once. ◇ *Non ho niente in contrario.* I have no objection.

il **contrattempo** NOME MASC
problem ◇ *Sono arrivato in ritardo per un contrattempo.* There was a problem, and I arrived late.

il **contratto** NOME MASC
contract ◇ *Il contratto sarà firmato domani.* The contract will be signed tomorrow.

contribuire VERBO
to contribute ◇ *Abbiamo contribuito tutti alla spesa.* We all contributed to the cost.

contro PREPOSIZIONE, AVVERBIO
against ◇ *la lotta contro la droga* the fight against drugs ◇ *Non ho niente contro di lui.* I've nothing against him. ◇ *Hanno votato contro.* They voted against it. ◇ *Stava appoggiato contro la porta.* He was leaning against the door.

♦ **Si è schiantato contro un albero.** It crashed into a tree.

♦ **Ho battuto la testa contro lo spigolo.** I banged my head on the corner.

♦ **pastiglie contro la tosse** cough sweets

la **controfigura** NOME FEM
stuntman (PL stuntmen)

controllare VERBO
to check ◇ *Controlla che la porta sia ben chiusa.* Check that the door is shut properly. ◇ *Mi hanno controllato il passaporto.* My passport was checked.

♦ **controllarsi** to control oneself ◇ *Non riuscivo a controllarmi.* I couldn't control myself.

> *to control si usa in genere nel significato di "avere il controllo di" e nel senso di "ispezionare".*

il **controllo** NOME MASC
[1] control ◇ *Ha perso il controllo della macchina.* He lost control of the car.

♦ **sotto controllo** under control ◇ *La situazione è sotto controllo.* The situation is under control.

♦ **Avevano il telefono sotto controllo.** Their phone was bugged.

[2] check ◇ *un controllo di sicurezza* a security check

♦ **controllo bagagli** baggage check

♦ **controllo passaporti** passport control

il **controllore** NOME MASC
ticket inspector (*su treno, su autobus*) ◇ *Chiedi al controllore.* Ask the ticket inspector.

♦ **controllore di volo** air traffic controller

---

* *I verbi seguiti da questo simbolo sono irregolari. Si veda anche alle pp.328–338.*

controluce AVVERBIO
against the light ◇ *Guardala controluce.*
Look at it against the light.

contromano AVVERBIO
* **guidare contromano (1)** (*su due corsie*) to drive* on the wrong side of the road
* **guidare contromano (2)** (*in un senso unico*) to drive* the wrong way along a one-way street

controvoglia AVVERBIO
* **L'ho mangiato controvoglia.** I ate it, though I didn't want to.
* **È andato alla festa controvoglia.** He went to the party, though he didn't want to.

convalidare VERBO
to stamp (*biglietto*)

conveniente AGGETTIVO
cheap (*economico*)
*Attenzione! In inglese esiste la parola **convenient**, che però non significa **conveniente**.*

convenire* VERBO
to be* cheaper (*essere meno caro*)
◇ *Comprare al supermercato conviene sempre.* It's always cheaper to shop at the supermarket.
*Per tradurre **convenire** nel senso di "essere opportuno" si può usare in genere **had better**, seguito dall'infinito senza "to".*
◇ *Converrebbe rimandare la gita.* We'd better put off the trip. ◇ *Se vuoi evitare il traffico ti conviene partire presto.* If you want to avoid the traffic you'd better leave early.

il convento NOME MASC
convent

la conversazione NOME FEM
conversation

convertire VERBO
to convert (*file, programma, moneta*)
* **Si è convertito al buddismo.** He has become a Buddhist.

convincente AGGETTIVO
convincing ◇ *una spiegazione convincente* a convincing explanation

convincere* VERBO
to convince ◇ *Va bene, mi hai convinto.* OK, you've convinced me.
* **convincere qualcuno a fare qualcosa** to persuade somebody to do something ◇ *Mi ha convinto a comprarlo.* She persuaded me to buy it.

la cooperativa NOME FEM
cooperative

il coperchio NOME MASC
lid (*di pentola, di barattolo*)

la coperta NOME FEM
blanket ◇ *una bella coperta calda* a nice warm blanket
* **stare sotto le coperte** to be* in bed

la copertina NOME FEM

1. cover ◇ *La sua faccia è sulla copertina di questa settimana.* Her picture is on this week's cover.
2. jacket (*di libro*)

coperto AGGETTIVO (FEM **coperta**)
vedi anche **coperto** NOME
1. indoor ◇ *una piscina coperta* an indoor pool
2. overcast (*nuvoloso*) ◇ *Il cielo è coperto.* The sky is overcast.
* **coperto di** covered with ◇ *libri coperti di polvere* books covered with dust ◇ *una parete coperta di poster* a wall covered with posters
* **essere ben coperto** (*vestito*) to be* wearing warm clothes ◇ *Sei ben coperto?* Are you wearing warm clothes?

il coperto NOME MASC
vedi anche **coperto** AGGETTIVO
cover charge (*al ristorante*) ◇ *Il coperto è compreso nel conto.* The cover charge is included in the bill.
* **al coperto** indoors ◇ *In caso di pioggia la festa si svolgerà al coperto.* If it rains, the party will be held indoors.

la copia NOME FEM
1. copy (PL copies) ◇ *Non è l'originale, è una copia.* It's not the original, it's a copy.
◇ *Hanno venduto un milione di copie dell'album.* A million copies of the album have been sold.
* **brutta copia** first draft
* **bella copia** final draft
2. print (*di foto*) ◇ *Vorrei due copie di ciascuna foto.* I'd like two prints of each photo.

copiare VERBO
to copy ◇ *Non dovete copiare.* You mustn't copy.

la coppa NOME FEM
1. cup ◇ *La nostra squadra ha vinto la coppa.* Our team won the cup.
2. tub (*di gelato*) ◇ *Prendi un cono o una coppa?* Are you going to have a cone or a tub?
* **una coppa di champagne** a glass of champagne

la coppia NOME FEM
1. couple ◇ *Sono una bella coppia.* They're a nice-looking couple.
2. pair (*due*) ◇ *una coppia di canarini* a pair of canaries

il copriletto NOME MASC
bedspread

coprire* VERBO
to cover ◇ *Ho coperto la bici con un telo di plastica.* I covered the bike with a plastic sheet.
* **coprirsi** (*cielo*) to cloud over

la coque NOME FEM
* **uovo alla coque** soft-boiled egg

il coraggio NOME MASC

☞

[1] courage ◇ *Ha dimostrato molto coraggio.* She showed great courage.
- **avere il coraggio di fare qualcosa** to be* brave enough to do something ◇ *Ha avuto il coraggio di dire la verità.* He was brave enough to tell the truth.
- **farsi coraggio** to pluck up courage ◇ *Si è fatto coraggio e le ha chiesto di uscire con lui.* He plucked up courage and asked her to go out with him.
- **Coraggio!** Come on! ◇ *Coraggio, siamo quasi arrivati!* Come on, we're nearly there!
  [2] nerve (*sfacciataggine*) ◇ *Hai un bel coraggio!* You've got a nerve!

il **corallo** NOME MASC
coral

la **corda** NOME FEM
[1] rope ◇ *una corda per saltare* a skipping rope
- **saltare con la corda** to skip
[2] string (*di chitarra, di racchetta*)
- **essere giù di corda** to feel* down ◇ *Oggi sono un po' giù di corda.* I'm feeling a bit down today.

cordiale AGGETTIVO
friendly ◇ *una persona molto cordiale* a very friendly person ◇ *È la ragazza più cordiale che abbia mai conosciuto.* She the friendliest girl I've ever met.

i **coriandoli** NOME MASC PL
confetti SING

coricarsi VERBO
to go* to bed ◇ *Ieri mi sono coricato presto.* I went to bed early yesterday.

la **cornacchia** NOME FEM
crow

la **cornamusa** NOME FEM
bagpipes PL

la **cornetta** NOME FEM
receiver ◇ *Sollevare la cornetta e comporre il numero.* Lift the receiver and dial the number.

il **cornetto** NOME MASC
[1] croissant (*brioche*)
[2] cornet (*gelato*)

la **cornice** NOME FEM
frame ◇ *una cornice d'argento* a silver frame

il **corno** NOME MASC
horn (*strumento musicale, di toro*)

la **Cornovaglia** NOME FEM
Cornwall ◇ *Andremo in Cornovaglia a Pasqua.* We're going to Cornwall at Easter. ◇ *Mi è piaciuta molto la Cornovaglia.* I really liked Cornwall.

il **coro** NOME MASC
choir ◇ *Canta in un coro.* He sings in a choir.
- **un coro di proteste** a chorus of protests
- **tutti in coro** all together

la **corona** NOME FEM
crown

il **corpo** NOME MASC
body (PL bodies)

la **corporatura** NOME FEM
build ◇ *di corporatura media* of medium build

correggere* VERBO
[1] to correct ◇ *Correggimi se faccio un errore.* Correct me if I make a mistake.
[2] to mark (*a penna*) ◇ *Deve ancora correggere i compiti di ieri.* She hasn't marked yesterday's homework yet.

la **corrente** NOME FEM
vedi anche **corrente** NOME MASC, AGGETTIVO
[1] power (*elettricità*) ◇ *È andata via la corrente.* The electricity's gone off.
- **presa di corrente** socket, US: outlet
[2] current (*d'acqua*) ◇ *La corrente l'ha trascinato al largo.* The current carried him out to sea.
[3] draught (*spiffero*) draft US ◇ *Chiudi la porta, c'è corrente.* Shut the door, there's a draught.

il **corrente** NOME MASC
vedi anche **corrente** NOME FEM, AGGETTIVO
- **mettere qualcuno al corrente di qualcosa** to tell* somebody about something ◇ *Mi ha messo al corrente degli ultimi sviluppi.* She told me about the latest developments.

corrente AGGETTIVO
vedi anche **corrente** NOME FEM, NOME MASC
- **acqua corrente** running water

correntemente AVVERBIO
- **parlare correntemente una lingua** to speak* a language fluently ◇ *Parla correntemente il francese.* She speaks French fluently.

correre* VERBO
[1] to run* ◇ *Abbiamo corso come pazzi per non perdere il treno.* We ran like mad to catch the train. ◇ *Paolo vuole correre i cento metri.* Paolo wants to run in the hundred metres.
- **Sono corso subito fuori.** I immediately rushed outside.
- **correre il rischio** to risk ◇ *Non voglio correre il rischio di non trovare posto.* I don't want to risk not getting a seat.
  to risk regge il gerundio.
[2] to go* running (*per ginnastica*) ◇ *Oggi ho corso un'ora.* I went running for an hour today.
- **Corre troppo in macchina.** He drives too fast.

la **correzione** NOME FEM
correction

la **corrida** NOME FEM
bullfight

il **corridoio** NOME MASC
[1] corridor
hall US

(*in casa*)

[2] aisle (*in aereo, al cinema*)

il **corridore** NOME MASC (PL i **corridori**)

[1] runner (*a piedi*)

[2] racer (*su veicolo*)

la **corriera** NOME FEM

coach

il **corrimano** NOME MASC

handrail

a **corrispondenza** NOME FEM

correspondence ◇ *un corso per corrispondenza* a correspondence course

corrispondere* VERBO

to correspond ◇ *A ciascun numero corrisponde una lettera.* Each number corresponds to a letter.

la **corsa** NOME FEM

race ◇ *una corsa automobilistica* a motor race

◆ **da corsa** racing ◇ *un'auto da corsa* a racing car

◆ **fare una corsa** to run* ◇ *Ho fatto una corsa per non perdere il treno.* I ran to catch the train.

◆ **fare qualcosa di corsa** to do* something quickly ◇ *Ho fatto i compiti di corsa e sono uscito.* I did my homework quickly and went out.

◆ **Ho mangiato di corsa un panino e sono uscito.** I had a quick sandwich and went out.

◆ **arrivare di corsa** to rush in

◆ **andarsene di corsa** to rush off

◆ **A che ora c'è l'ultima corsa?** When's the last bus?

la **corsia** NOME FEM

[1] lane ◇ *la corsia di sorpasso* the overtaking lane

◆ **corsia di emergenza** hard shoulder

[2] ward (*di ospedale*)

il **corso** NOME MASC

[1] course ◇ *un corso d'inglese* an English course

◆ **nel corso di** during

[2] main street (*via*) ◇ *Ha un negozio sul corso.* She's got a shop in the main street.

la **corte** NOME FEM

court (*giudiziaria, regale*)

la **cortesia** NOME FEM

favour ◇ *Mi faresti una cortesia?* Would you do me a favour? ◇ *Fammi la cortesia di star zitto!* Do me a favour and shut up!

◆ **Per cortesia...** Excuse me... ◇ *Per cortesia, dov'è il bagno?* Excuse me, where's the toilet?

il **cortile** NOME MASC

courtyard

corto AGGETTIVO (FEM **corta**)

short ◇ *maniche corte* short sleeves ◇ *Questi pantaloni sono troppo corti.* These trousers are too short.

◆ **essere a corto di qualcosa** to be* short of something ◇ *Sono a corto di soldi.* I'm short of money.

il **corvo** NOME MASC

raven

la **cosa** NOME FEM

[1] thing ◇ *La cosa migliore sarebbe partire di mattina.* The best thing would be to leave in the morning. ◇ *E no, non è la stessa cosa!* But that's not the same thing! ◇ *Sono cose che capitano!* These things happen! ◇ *Le cose stanno così.* That's how things are.

◆ **Devo dirti una cosa.** I've got to tell you something.

◆ **ogni cosa** everything ◇ *Il terremoto ha distrutto ogni cosa.* The earthquake destroyed everything.

◆ **qualche cosa** something ◇ *C'è qualche altra cosa da discutere.* There's something else to discuss. ◇ *Vuole qualche cosa da mangiare?* Would you like something to eat?

[2] what (*nelle domande*) ◇ *Cosa stai facendo?* What are you doing? ◇ *Che cos'è?* What is it? ◇ *Che cosa ha detto?* What did he say? ◇ *Cosa?!* What?!

la **coscia** NOME FEM (PL le **cosce**)

[1] thigh (*di persona*)

[2] leg (*di animale*) ◇ *una coscia di pollo* a chicken leg ◇ *una coscia d'agnello* a leg of lamb

così AVVERBIO, CONGIUNZIONE, AGGETTIVO

[1] so ◇ *Pioveva, così siamo rimasti a casa.* It was raining so we stayed at home. ◇ *Com'era il concerto? – Così così.* What was the concert like? – So-so. ◇ *È così o no?* Isn't that so? ◇ *È così simpatica!* She's so nice!

◆ **È un ragazzo così simpatico.** He's such a nice boy.

◆ **così...che...** so...that... ◇ *Era così stanco che è andato subito a letto.* He was so tired that he went to bed immediately.

[2] like this (*in questo modo*) ◇ *Devi ripiegarlo così.* You have to fold it like this.

[3] like that (*in quel modo*) ◇ *Se lo tiri così lo rompi.* If you pull it like that you'll break it. ◇ *I tipi così mi danno ai nervi.* People like that get on my nerves.

◆ **Non ho detto così.** That's not what I said.

◆ **Basta così!** That's enough!

◆ **così...come...** as...as... ◇ *Non è così lontano come credi.* It isn't as far as you think.

i **cosmetici** NOME MASC PL

cosmetics

la **costa** NOME FEM

coast ◇ *una città sulla costa* a town on the coast

◆ **la Costa Azzurra** the French Riviera

costante AGGETTIVO

constant

costare VERBO

to cost* ◇ *Quanto costa quell'anello?* How much does that ring cost? ◇ *È costato trenta* 🖙

euro. It cost thirty euros. ◇ *Quanto t'è costato?* How much did it cost you?

♦ **costare caro** to be* expensive ◇ *Mangiare fuori tutte le sere costa caro.* Eating out every evening is expensive.

♦ **costare poco** to be* cheap

il **costo** NOME MASC
cost ◇ *il costo della vacanza* the cost of the holiday

♦ **a tutti i costi** at all costs ◇ *Dev'essere evitato a tutti i costi.* It must be avoided at all costs.

♦ **L'ha voluto portare a tutti i costi.** He was determined to bring it, no matter what.

la **costola** NOME FEM
rib ◇ *Mi sono rotto una costola.* I broke a rib.

costoso AGGETTIVO (FEM **costosa**)
expensive ◇ *un albergo costoso* an expensive hotel

costringere* VERBO

♦ **costringere qualcuno a fare qualcosa** to make* somebody do something ◇ *Mi ha costretto a dire la verità.* She made me tell the truth.

♦ **È stato costretto a ritirarsi dalla gara.** He had to withdraw from the competition.

costruire VERBO
to build* ◇ *Qui costruiranno il nuovo stadio.* They're going to build the new stadium here.

la **costruzione** NOME FEM
building ◇ *una costruzione in vetro e acciaio* a building made of glass and steel

♦ **La costruzione del ponte è durata sette anni.** It took seven years to build the bridge.

♦ **essere in costruzione** to be* under construction ◇ *L'autostrada è in costruzione.* The motorway is under construction.

il **costume** NOME MASC
custom ◇ *gli usi e i costumi di un paese* the traditions and customs of a country

♦ **costume da bagno (1)** (*da donna*) swimsuit

♦ **costume da bagno (2)** (*da uomo*) swimming trunks PL

la **cotoletta** NOME FEM
chop (*di maiale, di agnello*) ◇ *una cotoletta di maiale* a pork chop

♦ **una cotoletta di vitello** a veal cutlet

il **cotone** NOME MASC
cotton ◇ *una maglietta di cotone* a cotton T-shirt

♦ **cotone idrofilo** cotton wool, US: absorbent cotton

la **cotta** NOME FEM

♦ **prendersi una cotta per qualcuno** to get* a crush on somebody

cotto AGGETTIVO (FEM **cotta**)
[1] cooked ◇ *Cotta o cruda?* Cooked or raw?
[2] done (*pronto*) ◇ *Sono cotti gli spaghetti?*

Is the spaghetti done?

♦ **ben cotto** (*carne*) well done

♦ **poco cotto** (*carne*) rare

♦ **troppo cotto** overcooked

♦ **mele cotte** stewed apples

♦ **essere cotto di qualcuno** to have* a crush on somebody

il **cotton fioc®** NOME MASC (PL i **cotton fioc**)
cotton bud

la **cottura** NOME FEM
cooking ◇ *Tempo di cottura: due ore.* Cooking time: two hours.

la **cozza** NOME FEM
mussel ◇ *spaghetti con le cozze* spaghetti with mussels

il **crampo** NOME MASC
cramp ◇ *Ho un crampo alla gamba.* I've got cramp in my leg.

il **cranio** NOME MASC
skull

la **cravatta** NOME FEM
tie

creare VERBO
[1] to create (*inventare*) ◇ *Ha creato un personaggio molto divertente.* He created a very funny character.
[2] to cause (*suscitare*) ◇ *La notizia ha creato il panico.* The news caused panic. ◇ *Mi ha creato un sacco di problemi.* It's caused me a lot of problems.

credere VERBO
[1] to believe ◇ *Non posso crederci!* I can't believe it! ◇ *Non dirmi che credi ai fantasmi!* Don't tell me you believe in ghosts! ◇ *Come puoi credere a una cosa simile?* How can you believe such a thing? ◇ *Non credeva ai suoi occhi.* She couldn't believe her eyes.

♦ **credere a qualcuno** to believe somebody ◇ *Non ti credo.* I don't believe you.

♦ **Ti credo sulla parola.** I'll take your word for it.

[2] to think* (*ritenere*) ◇ *Credo che arrivi domani.* I think he's arriving tomorrow. ◇ *Credeva di aver perso le chiavi.* She thought she had lost her keys. ◇ *Ma chi si crede di essere?* Who does she think she is? ◇ *Ti credevo meno ingenuo.* I didn't think you were so naive. ◇ *Credo di sì.* I think so. ◇ *Credo di no.* I don't think so. ◇ *Lo credo bene!* I should think so too!

il **credito** NOME MASC
credit ◇ *Non si fa credito.* We do not give credit.

la **crema** NOME FEM
[1] cream (*per la pelle*)

♦ **crema idratante** moisturizing cream

♦ **crema solare** sun cream

[2] custard (*pasticciera*) ◇ *una pasta con la crema* a cake with a custard filling

* I verbi seguiti da questo simbolo sono irregolari. Si veda anche alle pp.328–338.

+ **un gelato alla crema** a vanilla ice cream

la **crepa** NOME FEM
crack ◇ *una crepa sul muro* a crack in the wall

la **crêpe** NOME FEM (PL le **crêpe**)
pancake ◇ *una crêpe al cioccolato* a chocolate pancake

crescere* VERBO
to grow* ◇ *Com'è cresciuto tuo fratello!* Hasn't your brother grown!
+ **È cresciuto in campagna.** He grew up in the country.
+ **farsi crescere i capelli** to grow* one's hair ◇ *Si sta facendo crescere i capelli.* She's growing her hair.

la **cresima** NOME FEM
+ **fare la cresima** to be* confirmed

crespo AGGETTIVO (FEM **crespa**)
+ **capelli crespi** frizzy hair

la **creta** NOME FEM
clay

la **cretinata** NOME FEM
stupid thing

il **cretino**, la **cretina** NOME MASC, FEM
vedi anche **cretino** AGGETTIVO
idiot ◇ *Quel cretino mi ha quasi investito.* That idiot nearly ran me over.

cretino AGGETTIVO (FEM **cretina**)
vedi anche **cretino** NOME
stupid ◇ *Ma come sei cretina!* You're so stupid!

il **cric** NOME MASC (PL i **cric**)
jack (*per cambiare la ruota*)

il **criceto** NOME MASC
hamster

criminale AGGETTIVO, NOME MASC/FEM
criminal

il **crimine** NOME MASC
crime

il **crisantemo** NOME MASC
chrysanthemum

la **crisi** NOME FEM (PL le **crisi**)
[1] crisis (PL crises) ◇ *la crisi economica* the economic crisis
+ **In questo periodo sono in crisi.** I've got a lot of problems at the moment.
[2] fit (*di epilessia, di nervi*)

il **cristallo** NOME MASC
crystal ◇ *un bicchiere di cristallo* a crystal glass

cristiano, cristiana NOME, AGGETTIVO
Christian
Si noti l'uso della maiuscola in inglese.

Cristo NOME MASC
Christ

criticare VERBO
to criticize ◇ *Ha sempre qualcosa da criticare.* She always finds something to criticize.

critico AGGETTIVO (FEM **critica**, MASC PL **critici**, FEM PL **critiche**)
vedi anche **critico** NOME
critical ◇ *un momento critico* a critical moment

il **critico** NOME MASC (PL i **critici**)
vedi anche **critico** AGGETTIVO
critic ◇ *un critico cinematografico* a film critic

croccante AGGETTIVO
[1] crisp ◇ *un biscotto croccante* a crisp biscuit
[2] crusty ◇ *un panino croccante* a crusty roll

la **croce** NOME FEM
cross

la **crociera** NOME FEM
cruise ◇ *Sono andati in crociera nel Mediterraneo.* They went on a Mediterranean cruise.

il **crocifisso** NOME MASC
crucifix

crollare VERBO
to collapse ◇ *Il ponte è crollato.* The bridge collapsed. ◇ *È crollato sul letto, stanco morto.* He collapsed onto the bed, absolutely exhausted.

il **crollo** NOME MASC
collapse (*di palazzo, di azienda*)

la **cronaca** NOME FEM (PL le **cronache**)
news SING ◇ *un fatto di cronaca* a news item
+ **la cronaca rosa** the gossip column

il **cronometro** NOME MASC
stopwatch

la **crosta** NOME FEM
[1] crust (*di pane*)
[2] scab (*di ferita*)

la **crostata** NOME FEM
tart ◇ *una crostata di albicocche* an apricot tart

il **crostino** NOME MASC
[1] crostino (*da antipasto*)
[2] croûton (*da brodo*)

il **cruciverba** NOME MASC (PL i **cruciverba**)
crossword puzzle

crudele AGGETTIVO
cruel ◇ *Non essere così crudele!* Don't be so cruel!

crudo AGGETTIVO (FEM **cruda**)
raw ◇ *Mangia carne cruda.* He eats raw meat.
+ **La bistecca è un po' cruda.** The steak is rather underdone.

il **cruscotto** NOME MASC
dashboard (*in auto*)

il **cubetto** NOME MASC
cube ◇ *un cubetto di ghiaccio* an ice cube

il **cubo** NOME MASC
cube

la **cuccetta** NOME FEM
[1] couchette (*in treno*)
[2] berth (*su nave*)

il **cucchiaino** NOME MASC ☞

teaspoon (*posata*) ◊ *due cucchiaini di zucchero* two teaspoons of sugar

il **cucchiaio** NOME MASC
1 spoon (*posata*) ◊ *forchetta, coltello e cucchiaio* fork, knife and spoon
2 spoonful (*quantità*) ◊ *Aggiungere un cucchiaio di farina.* Add a spoonful of flour. ◊ *Ha mangiato qualche cucchiaio di minestra.* She ate a few spoonfuls of soup.

la **cuccia** NOME FEM (PL le **cucce**)
1 kennel (*casetta*)
2 dog basket (*cestino*)
• **A cuccia!** Down!

la **cucciolata** NOME FEM
litter ◊ *Era il più piccolo della cucciolata.* It was the smallest of the litter.

il **cucciolo** NOME MASC
1 puppy (PL puppies) (*di cane*)
2 cub (*di leone, di lupo*)

la **cucina** NOME FEM
1 kitchen (*stanza*) ◊ *una cucina spaziosa* a big kitchen
2 cooker (*elettrodomestico*) ◊ *una cucina a gas* a gas cooker
3 food (*le pietanze*) ◊ *Mi piace la cucina cinese.* I like Chinese food.

cucinare VERBO
to cook ◊ *Oggi cucino io!* I'll cook today!

il **cucinino** NOME MASC
kitchenette

cucire VERBO
to sew* ◊ *Non so cucire.* I can't sew.

la **cucitrice** NOME FEM
stapler (*per fogli*)

il **cucù** NOME MASC (PL i **cucù**)
cuckoo ◊ *un orologio a cucù* a cuckoo clock

la **cuffia** NOME FEM
1 headphones PL (*per ascoltare*)
2 bathing cap (*per nuotare*)
3 shower cap (*per la doccia*)

il **cugino,** la **cugina** NOME MASC, FEM
cousin

cui PRONOME

Quando cui è accompagnato da una preposizione di solito non si traduce e la preposizione va messa alla fine della frase.
◊ *la persona a cui si riferiva* the person he was referring to ◊ *le ragazze di cui ti ho parlato* the girls I told you about ◊ *il ponte su cui camminavamo* the bridge we were walking on ◊ *la casa in cui abito* the house I live in

Quando cui ha valore di complemento di specificazione si traduce con whose.
whose ◊ *un'attrice il cui nome mi sfugge* an actress whose name I can't remember ◊ *la persona di cui ti ho dato il numero di telefono ieri* the person whose phone number I gave you yesterday

• **per cui** (*perciò*) so ◊ *Io non c'ero, per cui*

non chiedere a me. I wasn't there, so don't ask me.
• **il motivo per cui non sono venuto** the reason why I didn't come

la **culla** NOME FEM
cradle

il **culo** NOME MASC
bum
butt $\boxed{US}$ (*volgare:deretano*)
• **aver culo** (*fortuna*) to be* lucky

la **cultura** NOME FEM
culture ◊ *la cultura occidentale* Western culture
• **avere una certa cultura** to be* educated
• **una donna di grande cultura** a well-educated woman
• **una persona di scarsa cultura** a person without much education
• **cultura generale** general knowledge ◊ *una domanda di cultura generale* a general knowledge question

culturale AGGETTIVO
cultural ◊ *una serie di manifestazioni culturali* a series of cultural events ◊ *scambi culturali* cultural exchanges

il **culturismo** NOME MASC
body-building

la **cunetta** NOME FEM
dip (*avvallamento*)

la **cuoca** NOME FEM (PL le **cuoche**)
cook ◊ *Tua madre è una cuoca eccezionale!* Your mother is a wonderful cook!

cuocere* VERBO
to cook ◊ *Lascialo cuocere per mezz'ora.* Cook it for half an hour.
• **cuocere in umido** to stew
• **cuocere a vapore** to steam
• **cuocere al forno (1)** (*pane, torta, pesce*) to bake
• **cuocere al forno (2)** (*carne*) to roast

il **cuoco** NOME MASC (PL i **cuochi**)
cook

il **cuoio** NOME MASC
leather ◊ *scarpe di cuoio* leather shoes
• **cuoio capelluto** scalp

il **cuore** NOME MASC
heart ◊ *La ginnastica fa bene al cuore.* Exercise is good for your heart.
◊ *un'operazione al cuore* a heart operation
◊ *nel cuore della città* in the heart of the city
◊ *una scatola a forma di cuore* a heart-shaped box
• **nel cuore della notte** in the middle of the night

la **cupola** NOME FEM
dome

la **cura** NOME FEM
cure ◊ *Non hanno ancora trovato una cura.* They haven't found a cure yet.
• **fare una cura** to have* treatment ◊ *Sto*

---

* I verbi seguiti da questo simbolo sono irregolari. Si veda anche alle pp.328–338.

facendo una cura contro l'acne. I'm having treatment for my acne.

curare VERBO
to treat (*malato, malattia*)

a **curiosità** NOME FEM
curiosity ◇ *Siamo andati per curiosità.* We went out of curiosity.

* **Per curiosità, quanto l'hai pagato?** As a matter of interest, how much did you pay for it?

curioso AGGETTIVO (FEM **curiosa**)
[1] curious ◇ *Sono curioso di vedere cosa succederà.* I'm curious to see what will happen.
[2] nosy (*ficcanaso*) ◇ *È un po' troppo curioso.* He's a bit too nosy.

a **curva** NOME FEM
bend ◇ *Ha sorpassato in curva.* He overtook on a bend.

curvo AGGETTIVO (FEM **curva**)
curved ◇ *una linea curva* a curved line

* **stare curvo** to slouch ◇ *Non stare curvo!* Don't slouch!

il **cuscino** NOME MASC
[1] cushion (*su divano, su sedia*)
[2] pillow (*guanciale*)

il/la **custode** NOME MASC/FEM
[1] attendant (*di museo*)
[2] keeper (*di parco*)

la **custodia** NOME FEM
case (*di occhiali, di chitarra*)

* **agente di custodia** prison warder

custodire VERBO
to keep* ◇ *I gioielli sono custoditi in cassaforte.* The jewels are kept in a safe.

il **cybercaffè** NOME (PL i **cybercaffè**)
cybercafé

D

da PREPOSIZIONE

[1] from (*provenienza, distanza*) ◇ *a tre chilometri da qui* three kilometres from here ◇ *Viene da Roma.* He comes from Rome.
* **scendere dalla macchina** to get* out of the car
* **uscire dalla finestra** to get* out through the window
* **cadere dal terrazzo** to fall* off the balcony

[2] to (*moto a luogo*) ◇ *Vado dal giornalaio.* I'm going to the paper shop.

[3] at (*stato in luogo*) ◇ *Sono da Pietro.* I'm at Pietro's.

[4] for (*periodo di tempo*) ◇ *Vivo qui da un anno.* I've been living here for a year.
Si noti la costruzione verbale inglese.

[5] since (*a partire da*) ◇ *È a Londra da martedì.* He's been in London since Tuesday. ◇ *Ti aspetto dalle tre.* I've been waiting for you since three o'clock.
Si noti la costruzione verbale inglese.
* **da allora** since then
* **d'ora in poi** from now on
* **da...a** from...to ◇ *dalle otto alle dieci* from eight to ten

[6] by (*agente*) ◇ *dipinto da un grande artista* painted by a great artist

[7] with (*causa*) ◇ *Tremava dal freddo.* He was shivering with cold.
* **qualcosa da bere** something to drink
* **una ragazza dagli occhi azzurri** a girl with blue eyes
* **un vestito da cento euro** a dress costing one hundred euros
* **Da giovane andavo a ballare spesso.** When I was young I often went dancing.

daccapo AVVERBIO
* **ricominciare daccapo** to start all over again

il **dado** NOME MASC

[1] dice (PL dice) (*da gioco*)
* **giocare a dadi** to play dice

[2] nut (*di vite*)
* **dado da brodo** stock cube

il **daino** NOME MASC
fallow deer (PL fallow deer)
* **pelle di daino** chamois leather

la **dama** NOME FEM

[1] draughts SING
checkers SING *US*
(*gioco*)
* **giocare a dama** to play draughts

[2] partner (*nel ballo*)

danese AGGETTIVO
vedi anche **danese** NOME MASC, NOME FEM
Danish

il **danese** NOME MASC
vedi anche **danese** NOME FEM, AGGETTIVO

[1] Dane (*persona*) ◇ *i danesi* the Danes

[2] Danish (*lingua*) ◇ *Parli danese?* Do you

speak Danish?

la **danese** NOME FEM
vedi anche **danese** NOME MASC, AGGETTIVO
Dane

la **Danimarca** NOME FEM
Denmark ◇ *Ti è piaciuta la Danimarca?* Did you like Denmark? ◇ *Andrò in Danimarca quest'estate.* I'm going to Denmark this summer.

dannazione ESCLAMAZIONE
damn!

danneggiare VERBO
to damage

il **danno** NOME MASC
damage ◇ *Il danno ormai è fatto.* The damage has been done. ◇ *due milioni di risarcimento danni* two million in damages
* **Ho provocato un piccolo danno alla macchina.** I damaged the car slightly.
* **fare danni** to do* damage ◇ *La grandine ha fatto molti danni.* The hail did a lot of damage. ◇ *senza fare danni* without doing any damage

dannoso AGGETTIVO (FEM **dannosa**)
harmful ◇ *una sostanza dannosa* a harmful substance
* **Il fumo è dannoso alla salute.** Smoking is bad for your health.

il **Danubio** NOME MASC
Danube

la **danza** NOME FEM
dance ◇ *una danza tribale* a tribal dance
* **danza classica** ballet

dappertutto AVVERBIO
everywhere

dare* VERBO
to give*
* **dare qualcosa a qualcuno** to give* somebody something
Notate le diverse costruzioni in inglese a seconda della posizione del complemento oggetto.
◇ *Gli ho dato un libro.* I gave him a book.
◇ *Gli ho dato la cartina.* I gave the map to him. ◇ *Dammelo.* Give it to me.
* **dare su** to look onto ◇ *La mia finestra dà sul giardino.* My window looks onto the garden.
* **può darsi** maybe
* **Quanti anni mi dai?** How old do you think I am?
* **Danno ancora quel film?** Is that film still showing?
* **Devi darti da fare.** You'll have to get busy.

la **data** NOME FEM
date ◇ *Che data è oggi?* What's the date today? ◇ *la mia data di nascita* my date of birth

i **dati** NOME MASC PL

---

* I verbi seguiti da questo simbolo sono irregolari. Si veda anche alle pp.328–338.

Italian ~ English

data

data è in genere seguito dal verbo al singolare.

◊ *I dati sono sbagliati.* The data is wrong.

+ **elaborazione dati** data processing
+ **dati personali** personal details

dato AGGETTIVO (FEM **data**)

given ◊ *in un dato periodo* at a given time
◊ *dato che...* given that...

+ **entro quel dato giorno** by that particular day

il **datore** NOME MASC

+ **datore di lavoro** employer

il **dattero** NOME MASC

date (*frutto*)

la **dattilografia** NOME FEM

typing

il **dattilografo**, la **dattilografa** NOME MASC, FEM

typist ◊ *Fa la dattilografa.* She is a typist.

davanti AVVERBIO, PREPOSIZIONE

vedi anche **davanti** AGGETTIVO

at the front (*in pullman, al cinema*) ◊ *Posso sedermi davanti?* Can I sit at the front?

+ **davanti a (1)** in front of ◊ *Era seduto davanti a me al cinema.* He was sitting in front of me at the cinema.
+ **davanti a (2)** (*dirimpetto a*) ◊ *la casa davanti alla mia* the house opposite mine

davanti AGGETTIVO

vedi anche **davanti** AVVERBIO, PREPOSIZIONE

front ◊ *le file davanti* the front rows

il **davanzale** NOME MASC

windowsill

davvero AVVERBIO

really ◊ *È successo davvero.* It really happened.

d.C. ABBREVIAZIONE (= *dopo Cristo*)

AD

il **debito** NOME MASC

debt ◊ *Ha molti debiti.* He's got a lot of debts.

+ **debito formativo** failure to achieve the required standard

debole AGGETTIVO

vedi anche **debole** NOME

1. weak ◊ *Mi sento debole.* I feel weak.
2. faint ◊ *un debole suono* a faint sound
3. dim ◊ *una luce debole* a dim light

il **debole** NOME MASC

vedi anche **debole** AGGETTIVO

weakness ◊ *Ha un debole per la cioccolata.* He's got a weakness for chocolate.

+ **Ha un debole per me.** She's got a soft spot for me.

la **debolezza** NOME FEM

weakness

decaffeinato AGGETTIVO, NOME

+ **caffè decaffeinato** decaffeinated coffee
+ **un decaffeinato** a cup of decaffeinated coffee

decappottabile AGGETTIVO

+ **una macchina decappottabile** a convertible

il **decennio** NOME MASC

decade

decente AGGETTIVO

decent

decidere* VERBO

to decide ◊ *Hai deciso?* Have you decided?

+ **decidere di fare qualcosa** to decide to do something ◊ *Ho deciso di non andarci.* I decided not to go.
+ **decidersi** to decide ◊ *Non so decidermi.* I can't decide.

decifrare VERBO

1. to decode (*messaggio in codice*)
2. to decipher (*calligrafia*)

decimo AGGETTIVO, NOME MASC (FEM **decima**)

tenth

la **decina** NOME FEM

+ **una decina** about a dozen ◊ *una decina di macchine* about a dozen cars

*Letteralmente **dozen** vuol dire "dozzina", ma corrisponde nell'uso a **decina**.*

la **decisione** NOME FEM

decision

+ **prendere una decisione** to make* a decision ◊ *Ho preso una decisione.* I've made a decision.
+ **agire con decisione** to act decisively

decisivo AGGETTIVO (FEM **decisiva**)

decisive ◊ *Il suo voto è stato decisivo.* His vote was decisive.

deciso AGGETTIVO (FEM **decisa**)

1. determined (*persona, carattere*)
2. firm (*tono*)

declinare VERBO

1. to turn down ◊ *Ho declinato l'offerta.* I turned down the offer.
2. to decline (*in grammatica*)

il **declino** NOME MASC

decline ◊ *in declino* in decline

decollare VERBO

to take* off ◊ *L'aereo è decollato alle otto.* The plane took off at eight o'clock.

il **decollo** NOME MASC

take-off

decorare VERBO

to decorate

la **decorazione** NOME FEM

decoration

la **dedica** NOME FEM (PL le **dediche**)

dedication

dedicare VERBO

to dedicate ◊ *Le ha dedicano una canzone.* He dedicated a song to her.

dedurre* VERBO

1. to deduce (*concludere*) ◊ *Ne deduco che...* I deduce from this that...
2. to deduct (*detrarre*) ◊ *L'IVA va dedotta alla fine.* VAT is deducted at the end.

il/la **deficiente** NOME MASC/FEM

idiot

il **deficit** NOME MASC (PL i **deficit**)
deficit

definire VERBO
[1] to settle (*questione*) ◇ *Dobbiamo definire la questione al più presto.* We must settle this matter as soon as possible.
[2] to define (*parola*)

la **definitiva** NOME FEM
◆ **in definitiva** (1) (*alla fine*) in the end
◆ **in definitiva** (2) (*tutto sommato*) all in all

definitivo AGGETTIVO (FEM **definitiva**)
[1] definitive (*risposta, soluzione*)
[2] final (*decisione*)

la **definizione** NOME FEM
definition (*di parola*)

deformare VERBO
[1] to put* out of shape (*oggetto*)
[2] to deform (*corpo*)
◆ **deformarsi** to go* out of shape

defunto AGGETTIVO (FEM **defunta**)
│ *vedi anche* **defunto** NOME │
late ◇ *il defunto presidente* the late president

il **defunto**, la **defunta** NOME MASC, FEM
│ *vedi anche* **defunto** AGGETTIVO │
◆ **il defunto** the deceased
◆ **i defunti** the dead

il/la **degente** NOME MASC/FEM
patient

deglutire VERBO
to swallow

degnare VERBO
◆ **Non mi ha degnato di uno sguardo.** He didn't even look at me.
◆ **Non si è degnato di rispondermi.** He didn't bother to answer me.

degno AGGETTIVO (FEM **degna**)
◆ **degno di fiducia** trustworthy

il **degrado** NOME MASC
◆ **degrado urbano** urban decay

il **delfino** NOME MASC
dolphin

delicato AGGETTIVO (FEM **delicata**)
delicate

il/la **delinquente** NOME MASC/FEM
[1] criminal ◇ *La polizia ha arrestato il delinquente.* The police arrested the criminal.
[2] scoundrel (*mascalzone*)

la **delinquenza** NOME FEM
crime ◇ *un aumento della delinquenza* an increase in crime
◆ **la delinquenza minorile** juvenile delinquency

il **delitto** NOME MASC
crime ◇ *Ha commesso un terribile delitto.* He committed a terrible crime.

delizioso AGGETTIVO (FEM **deliziosa**)
[1] delicious (*odore, cibo*)
[2] charming (*persona*)

il **deltaplano** NOME MASC
hang-glider
◆ **andare in deltaplano** to hang-glide

deludente AGGETTIVO
disappointing ◇ *un film un po' deludente* a rather disappointing film

deludere* VERBO
to disappoint ◇ *Mi hai molto deluso.* You've really disappointed me.
◆ **Il suo ultimo film mi ha deluso.** His last film was disappointing.

la **delusione** NOME FEM
disappointment ◇ *È stata una delusione.* It was a disappointment. ◇ *Che delusione!* What a disappointment!

deluso AGGETTIVO (FEM **delusa**)
disappointed ◇ *Sono deluso del voto che ho preso.* I'm disappointed with the mark I got.

democratico AGGETTIVO (FEM **democratica**, MASC PL **democratici**, FEM PL **democratiche**)
democratic

la **democrazia** NOME FEM
democracy (PL democracies)

demolire VERBO
to demolish

il **demonio** NOME MASC
devil

il **denaro** NOME MASC
money ◇ *Non ho molto denaro con me.* I haven't got much money with me.

denso AGGETTIVO (FEM **densa**)
thick ◇ *una minestra densa* a thick soup

il **dente** NOME MASC
tooth (PL teeth) ◇ *Mi lavo i denti dopo ogni pasto.* I clean my teeth after every meal.
◆ **denti del giudizio** wisdom teeth
◆ **avere mal di denti** to have* toothache
◆ **mettere qualcosa sotto i denti** to have* a bite to eat
◆ **al dente** (*pasta*) al dente

la **dentiera** NOME FEM
false teeth PL ◇ *Porta la dentiera.* She's got false teeth.

il **dentifricio** NOME MASC
toothpaste ◇ *dentifricio al fluoro* fluoride toothpaste

il/la **dentista** NOME MASC/FEM (MASC PL i **dentisti**, FEM PL le **dentiste**)
dentist ◇ *Fa la dentista.* She is a dentist.

dentro AVVERBIO
│ *vedi anche* **dentro** PREPOSIZIONE │
inside ◇ *Vai dentro.* Go inside.
◆ **qui dentro** in here
◆ **tenere tutto dentro** to keep* everything bottled up

dentro PREPOSIZIONE
│ *vedi anche* **dentro** AVVERBIO │
in ◇ *È dentro l'armadio.* It's in the wardrobe.

* I verbi seguiti da questo simbolo sono irregolari. Si veda anche alle pp.328–338.

la **denuncia** NOME FEM (PL le **denunce**)
- **sporgere denuncia contro qualcuno** to report somebody to the police
- **denuncia dei redditi** tax return

denunciare VERBO
[1] to report ◊ *Lo ha denunciato alla polizia.* He reported him to the police.
[2] to expose ◊ *Ha denunciato la corruzione all'interno del partito.* He exposed the corruption within the party.

denutrito AGGETTIVO (FEM **denutrita**)
undernourished

il **deodorante** NOME MASC
deodorant

depilarsi VERBO
- **depilarsi le gambe** to shave one's legs

depilatorio AGGETTIVO (FEM **depilatoria**)
- **crema depilatoria** hair-removing cream

il **dépliant** NOME MASC (PL i **dépliant**)
[1] leaflet (*pubblicitario*)
[2] brochure (*turistico*)

depositare VERBO
to deposit (*in banca*)

il **deposito** NOME MASC
[1] warehouse (*magazzino*)
- **deposito bagagli** left-luggage office
[2] deposit (*di denaro*)

la **depressione** NOME FEM
depression

depresso AGGETTIVO (FEM **depressa**)
depressed

deprimente AGGETTIVO
depressing ◊ *una storia deprimente* a depressing story

deprimere* VERBO
to depress

il **deputato**, la **deputata** NOME MASC, FEM
[1] MP (*in Gran Bretagna*)
MP vuol dire "Member of Parliament".
[2] congressman (PL congressmen)
congresswoman (PL congresswomen)
(*negli Stati Uniti*)

deragliare VERBO
to be* derailed

deridere* VERBO
to mock

la **deriva** NOME FEM
- **andare alla deriva** to drift

derivare VERBO
to derive ◊ *"Gas" deriva dalla parola greca "chaos".* "Gas" derives from the Greek word "chaos".
- **Questa parola deriva dal francese.** This word is of French derivation.

il **dermatologo**, la **dermatologa** NOME MASC, FEM (MASC PL i **dermatologi**, FEM PL le **dermatologhe**)
dermatologist

derubare VERBO
to rob ◊ *Lo hanno picchiato e derubato.* He was attacked and robbed.
- **Mi hanno derubato del portafoglio.** I had my wallet stolen.

descrivere* VERBO
to describe
- **descrivere qualcosa a qualcuno** to describe something to somebody ◊ *Mi ha descritto ciò che aveva trovato.* He described to me what he had found.

la **descrizione** NOME FEM
description
- **fare una descrizione** to give* a description

deserto AGGETTIVO (FEM **deserta**)
vedi anche **deserto** NOME
deserted ◊ *Le strade erano deserte.* The streets were deserted.
- **isola deserta** desert island

il **deserto** NOME MASC
vedi anche **deserto** AGGETTIVO
desert

desiderare VERBO
to want ◊ *Desiderava migliorare il suo inglese.* He wanted to improve his English. ◊ *Sei desiderato al telefono.* You're wanted on the phone.
- **Desidero parlarvi subito.** I'd like to speak to you immediately.
- **Cosa desidera? (1)** (*al bar*) What would you like?
- **Cosa desidera? (2)** (*in negozio*) Can I help you?

il **desiderio** NOME MASC
[1] wish ◊ *Esprimi un desiderio.* Make a wish.
[2] desire (*sessuale*)

la **desinenza** NOME FEM
ending

desolato AGGETTIVO (FEM **desolata**)
- **Sono desolato!** I'm terribly sorry!

il **dessert** NOME MASC (PL i **dessert**)
dessert

il **destinatario**, la **destinataria** NOME MASC, FEM
addressee (*di lettera*)

la **destinazione** NOME FEM
destination ◊ *Sono giunti a destinazione.* They reached their destination.

il **destino** NOME MASC
destiny ◊ *il mio destino* my destiny ◊ *Era destino che ci incontrassimo.* It was our destiny to meet.

la **destra** NOME FEM
[1] right (*parte*) ◊ *Sulla destra, nella foto...* On the right of the photograph...
- **voltare a destra** to turn right
- **spostarsi verso destra** to move to the right
[2] right hand (*mano*) ◊ *Scrivo con la destra.* I write with my right hand.
- **la destra** (*in politica*) the right
- **un partito di destra** a right-wing party

destro AGGETTIVO (FEM **destra**)
right (*mano, braccio*)

D

il **detenuto,** la **detenuta** NOME MASC, FEM
prisoner

detergente AGGETTIVO
cleansing ◊ *latte detergente* cleansing milk
Attenzione! In inglese esiste la parola
detergent *che però significa* **detersivo.**

determinativo AGGETTIVO (FEM
determinativa)
♦ **articolo determinativo** definite article

determinato AGGETTIVO (FEM **determinata**)
[1] certain ◊ *in determinate circostanze* in
certain circumstances
[2] determined ◊ *È molto determinato.*
He's very determined.

il **detersivo** NOME MASC
detergent ◊ *un detersivo neutro* a mild
detergent
♦ **detersivo per bucato** washing powder
♦ **detersivo per pavimenti** floor cleaner
♦ **detersivo per i piatti** washing-up liquid

detestare VERBO
to detest *(persona, cibo)* ◊ *Lo detesto!* I
detest him!
♦ **Detesto mentire.** I hate lying.

detrarre* VERBO
to deduct

il **dettaglio** NOME MASC
detail ◊ *in dettaglio* in detail
♦ **prezzo al dettaglio** retail price

dettare VERBO
to dictate

il **dettato** NOME MASC
dictation

detto AGGETTIVO (FEM **detta**)
vedi anche **detto** NOME
called *(soprannominato)*

il **detto** NOME MASC
vedi anche **detto** AGGETTIVO
saying ◊ *un detto cinese* a Chinese saying

deviare VERBO
to divert ◊ *Il traffico è stato deviato.* The
traffic has been diverted.

la **deviazione** NOME FEM
diversion *(del traffico)*

di PREPOSIZIONE, ARTICOLO PARTITIVO
[1] of ◊ *un gruppo di studenti* a group of
students ◊ *un bicchiere di vino* a glass of
wine ◊ *È fatto di legno.* It's made of wood.
◊ *Era pieno di gente.* It was full of people.
◊ *Ho paura di volare.* I'm afraid of flying.
Spesso di non viene tradotto e il secondo
nome viene anteposto al primo, come negli
esempi.
◊ *le chiavi della macchina* the car keys ◊ *un*
orologio d'oro a gold watch ◊ *un bambino*
di tre anni a three-year-old child ◊ *il*
professore di inglese the English teacher
♦ **due milioni di lire** two thousand lire
Per indicare possesso, in genere si usa il
genitivo sassone, cioè si aggiunge 's dopo il

sostantivo. Ricorda che nei nomi plurali va
messo solo l'apostrofo senza "s".
◊ *la moto di Gianni* Gianni's bike ◊ *i libri di*
mio padre my father's books ◊ *la sorella di*
mia madre my mother's sister ◊ *la*
reputazione di un'attrice an actress's
reputation ◊ *la casa dei miei genitori* my
parents' house
[2] than *(in comparativi)* ◊ *È più alto di me.*
He's taller than me. ◊ *È più brava di lui.*
She's better than him.
♦ **il migliore della classe** the best in the class
[3] in *(in espressioni di tempo)* ◊ *d'estate* in
the summer ◊ *di mattina* in the morning
◊ *di sera* in the evening
♦ **di domenica** on Sundays
♦ **di notte** at night
[4] by *(autore)* ◊ *un poesia di Montale* a
poem by Montale
L'articolo partitivo "del" ("della", "dei",
"delle") si traduce in inglese con some.
◊ *C'erano delle persone che aspettavano.*
There were some people waiting. ◊ *Vuoi dei*
biscotti? Do you want some biscuits?
[5] to *(seguito dall'infinito)* ◊ *Sto tentando*
di concentrarmi. I'm trying to concentrate.
◊ *Ho dimenticato di fare l'esercizio.* I forgot
to do the exercise.
♦ **Credo di capire.** I think* I understand.

il **diabete** NOME MASC
diabetes SING

diabetico AGGETTIVO (FEM **diabetica**, MASC PL
diabetici, FEM PL **diabetiche**)
diabetic

il **diaframma** NOME MASC (PL i **diaframmi**)
diaphragm

la **diagnosi** NOME FEM (PL le **diagnosi**)
diagnosis *(PL* diagnoses*)*

il **dialetto** NOME MASC
dialect

il **dialogo** NOME MASC (PL i **dialoghi**)
dialogue *(in libro, a teatro)*
♦ **Non c'è più dialogo tra noi.** We don't talk to
each other any more.

il **diamante** NOME MASC
diamond ◊ *un anello con diamante* a
diamond ring

il **diametro** NOME MASC
diameter

la **diapositiva** NOME FEM
slide

il **diario** NOME MASC
diary *(PL* diaries*)*
♦ **tenere un diario** to keep* a diary

la **diarrea** NOME FEM
diarrhoea
diarrhea US

il **diavolo** NOME MASC
devil ◊ *Povero diavolo!* Poor devil!
♦ **mandare qualcuno al diavolo** to tell*

somebody to go to hell ◇ *L'ho mandato al diavolo.* I told him to go to hell.
+ **Va al diavolo!** Go to hell!
+ **Cosa diavolo vuoi?** What the hell do you want?

il **dibattito** NOME MASC
debate

dicembre NOME
December
Si noti l'uso della maiuscola in inglese.
◇ *in dicembre* in December

la **diceria** NOME FEM
rumour
rumor [US]
◇ *Sono solo dicerie.* They're only rumours.

dichiarare VERBO
[1] to declare ◇ *Niente da dichiarare?* Anything to declare?
[2] to say* ◇ *Il ministro ha dichiarato che...* The minister said that...

la **dichiarazione** NOME FEM
[1] declaration ◇ *una dichiarazione d'indipendenza* a declaration of independence
+ **Le ha fatto una dichiarazione d'amore.** He told her he loved her.
+ **dichiarazione dei redditi** tax return
[2] statement ◇ *Ha rilasciato una dichiarazione alla polizia.* He made a statement to the police.

diciannove NUMERO
nineteen ◇ *Ho diciannove anni.* I'm nineteen.
+ **alle diciannove** at seven p.m.
+ **il diciannove maggio** the nineteenth of May

diciannovenne AGGETTIVO, NOME
nineteen-year-old

diciannovesimo AGGETTIVO (FEM **diciannovesima**)
nineteenth

diciassette NUMERO
seventeen ◇ *Ho diciassette anni.* I'm seventeen.
+ **alle diciassette** at five p.m.
+ **il diciassette maggio** the seventeenth of May

diciassettenne AGGETTIVO, NOME
seventeen-year-old

diciassettesimo AGGETTIVO (FEM **diciassettesima**)
seventeenth

diciottenne AGGETTIVO, NOME
eighteen-year-old

diciottesimo AGGETTIVO (FEM **diciottesima**)
eighteenth

diciotto NUMERO
eighteen ◇ *Ho diciotto anni.* I'm eighteen.
+ **alle diciotto** at six p.m.
+ **il diciotto maggio** the eighteenth of May

la **didascalia** NOME FEM
[1] caption (*di illustrazione*)

[2] subtitle (*al cinema*)

dieci NUMERO
ten ◇ *Ho dieci anni.* I'm ten. ◇ *alle dieci* at ten a.m.
+ **il dieci maggio** the tenth of May

diesel AGGETTIVO (MASC, FEM, PL **diesel**)
+ **motore diesel** diesel engine
+ **macchina diesel** diesel car

la **dieta** NOME FEM
diet
+ **essere in dieta** to be* on a diet

dietro AVVERBIO, PREPOSIZIONE
vedi anche **dietro** AGGETTIVO
behind ◇ *dietro la porta* behind the door ◇ *Dev'essere qua dietro.* It must be behind here.
+ **Abita qua dietro.** He lives round the corner.
+ **essere seduto dietro (1)** (*in macchina*) to be* sitting in the back
+ **essere seduto dietro (2)** (*in autobus*) to be* sitting at the back
+ **dietro l'angolo** round the corner
+ **dietro a** behind ◇ *Era dietro alla scrivania.* He was behind his desk.
+ **dietro di** behind ◇ *Sono seduti dietro di me.* They're sitting behind me.
+ **stare dietro a qualcuno (1)** (*sorvegliare*) to keep* an eye on somebody
+ **stare dietro a qualcuno (2)** (*corteggiare*) to be* after somebody
+ **uno dietro l'altro (1)** (*dopo*) one after the other
+ **uno dietro l'altro (2)** (*in fila*) one behind the other

dietro AGGETTIVO (MASC, FEM, PL **dietro**)
vedi anche **dietro** AVVERBIO, PREPOSIZIONE
back ◇ *le file dietro* the back rows

difendere* VERBO
to defend
+ **difendersi** to defend oneself

il **difensore** NOME MASC
[1] lawyer for the defence (*in tribunale*)
[2] defender (*nello sport*)

la **difesa** NOME FEM
defence
defense [US]
◇ *giocare in difesa* to play in defence
+ **per legittima difesa** in self-defence
+ **la difesa** (*in tribunale*) the defence

il **difetto** NOME MASC
fault ◇ *Ha molti difetti.* He has many faults.

difettoso AGGETTIVO (FEM **difettosa**)
faulty

differente AGGETTIVO
different

la **differenza** NOME FEM
difference ◇ *Non c'è alcuna differenza.* There's no difference.
+ **a differenza di** unlike ◇ *A differenza del calcio qui il rugby non è molto diffuso.* Unlike football, rugby isn't very popular here.

difficile AGGETTIVO

[1] difficult ◇ *un esercizio difficile* a difficult exercise

[2] unlikely ◇ *È difficile che venga.* It's unlikely he'll come.

la **difficoltà** NOME FEM (PL le **difficoltà**)

difficulty (PL difficulties) ◇ *Non arrenderti alla prima difficoltà.* Don't give up at the first difficulty.

◆ **trovarsi in difficoltà** to have* problems

diffidente AGGETTIVO

suspicious ◇ *È diffidente nei miei confronti.* He's suspicious of me.

la **diffidenza** NOME FEM

◆ **con diffidenza** suspiciously

diffondere* VERBO

[1] to spread* (*notizie, malattia*)

[2] to give* out (*luce, calore*)

◆ **diffondersi*** to spread*

diffuso AGGETTIVO (FEM **diffusa**)

common ◇ *un'usanza diffusa* a common custom

la **diga** NOME FEM (PL le **dighe**)

[1] dam (*di fiume*)

[2] breakwater (*di porto*)

digerire VERBO

to digest ◇ *Ci vogliono otto ore per digerire.* It takes eight hours to digest.

◆ **Non ho digerito bene.** I've got indigestion.

la **digestione** NOME FEM

digestion

il **digestivo** NOME MASC

after-dinner liqueur

> ❶ *Nei paesi anglosassoni l'usanza di bere un* **digestivo** *dopo il pasto non è molto diffusa.*

digitale AGGETTIVO

digital ◇ *un orologio digitale* a digital watch ◇ *TV digitale* digital TV

il **digiuno** NOME

fasting ◇ *Alcune diete prevedono il digiuno.* Some diets involve fasting.

◆ **Sono a digiuno da ieri.** I haven't eaten since yesterday.

◆ **stare a digiuno** to fast

la **dignità** NOME FEM

dignity

dilettante NOME MASC/FEM, AGGETTIVO

amateur ◇ *un fotografo dilettante* an amateur photographer

diligente AGGETTIVO

hard-working ◇ *un alunno diligente* a hard-working student

diluviare VERBO

to pour ◇ *Sta diluviando.* It's pouring

dimagrante AGGETTIVO

◆ **fare una cura dimagrante** to go* on a diet

dimagrire VERBO

to lose* weight ◇ *È dimagrita.* She's lost weight.

◆ **È dimagrito di dieci chili.** He's lost ten kilos.

la **dimensione** NOME FEM

dimension ◇ *la dimensione politica* the political dimension

◆ **dimensioni** (*grandezza*) size SING ◇ *le dimensioni della stanza* the size of the room

◆ **di piccole dimensioni** small

◆ **di grandi dimensioni** big

la **dimenticanza** NOME FEM

oversight ◇ *È stata una dimenticanza.* It was an oversight.

dimenticare VERBO

to forget* ◇ *Ho dimenticato il tuo numero di telefono.* I've forgotten your phone number.

◆ **Ho dimenticato a casa l'ombrello.** I left my umbrella at home.

◆ **dimenticarsi di qualcosa** to forget* something

dimettere* VERBO

◆ **dimettere qualcuno dall'ospedale** to discharge somebody from hospital

◆ **dimettersi** to resign ◇ *Si è dimesso ieri.* He resigned yesterday.

diminuire VERBO

[1] to decrease (*di numero, di quantità*) ◇ *La popolazione è diminuita del dieci per cento.* The population has decreased by ten percent.

◆ **diminuire di peso** to lose* weight

[2] to fall* (*prezzi, valore*) ◇ *Il prezzo della carne è diminuito.* The price of meat has fallen.

[3] to drop (*temperatura, vento*)

[4] to die down (*rumore*)

[5] to cut* (*ridurre*) ◇ *La ditta ha deciso di diminuire i prezzi.* The company has decided to cut its prices. ◇ *Dobbiamo diminuire le spese del venti per cento.* We must cut spending by twenty percent.

diminutivo AGGETTIVO, NOME MASC

diminutive

la **diminuzione** NOME FEM

drop ◇ *una forte diminuzione della temperatura* a big drop in temperature

◆ **essere in diminuzione** to be* dropping ◇ *La temperatura è in diminuzione.* The temperature is dropping.

le **dimissioni** NOME FEM PL

◆ **dare le dimissioni** to hand in one's resignation

al singolare.

◇ *Ha dato le dimissioni.* He handed in his resignation.

dimostrare VERBO

[1] to prove ◇ *Questo dimostra che hai ragione.* This proves you're right.

[2] to show* (*affetto, simpatia*)

◆ **Non dimostra la sua età.** He doesn't look his age.

---

* I verbi seguiti da questo simbolo sono irregolari. Si veda anche alle pp.328–338.

la dimostrazione NOME FEM
demonstration ◇ *una dimostrazione studentesca* a student demonstration
+ **una dimostrazione d'affetto** a show of affection

la dinamite NOME FEM
dynamite

il dinosauro NOME MASC
dinosaur

i dintorni NOME MASC PL
+ **nei dintorni** nearby ◇ *Abita nei dintorni.* She lives nearby.
+ **nei dintorni di** (*città*) outside ◇ *un paese nei dintorni di Milano* a village outside Milan

il dio NOME MASC (PL gli **dei**)
god ◇ *gli dei* the gods ◇ *Credi in Dio?* Do you believe in God? ◇ *Grazie a Dio!* Thank God!

senza preposizione.

+ **Dio mio!** My goodness!

la dipendente NOME MASC/FEM
vedi anche **dipendente** AGGETTIVO
employee ◇ *un dipendente della ditta* an employee of the firm

dipendente AGGETTIVO
vedi anche **dipendente** NOME
+ **essere dipendente da** (*alcol, droga*) to be* addicted to

dipendere* VERBO
[1] to depend ◇ *Dipende!* It depends!
◇ *Andiamo? – Non lo so. Dipende da Mario.* Are we going? – I don't know. It depends on Mario.
+ **Puoi farlo o meno, dipende solo da te.** You can do it or not, it's up to you.
[2] to be* dependent (*economicamente*)
◇ *Non voglio più dipendere dai miei genitori.* I don't want to be dependent on my parents any longer.

dipingere* VERBO
to paint

il dipinto NOME MASC
painting

il diploma NOME MASC (PL i **diplomi**)
+ **diploma di laurea** degree
+ **diploma di maturità** school-leaving certificate

> ❶ *The education system in Italy is different, and students generally finish secondary school a year later than in Britain or America.*

diplomatico AGGETTIVO (FEM **diplomatica**, MASC PL **diplomatici**, FEM PL **diplomatiche**)
vedi anche **diplomatico** NOME
diplomatic ◇ *Cerca di essere diplomatico.* Try to be diplomatic.

il diplomatico NOME MASC (PL i **diplomatici**)
vedi anche **diplomatico** AGGETTIVO
diplomat (*agente*)

diradare VERBO

+ **diradare le visite** to call less frequently
+ **diradarsi (1)** (*nebbia*) to clear
+ **diradarsi (2)** (*folla*) to disperse
+ **diradarsi (3)** (*vegetazione*) to thin out

dire* VERBO
[1] to say* ◇ *"Grazie," disse.* "Thank you," she said. ◇ *Ha detto che verrà.* He said he'll come. ◇ *Non disse una parola.* She didn't say a word. ◇ *Si dice che...* They say that...
◇ *Come si dice "quadro" in inglese?* How do you say "quadro" in English?
+ **dire di sì** to say* yes
+ **dire di no** to say* no
+ **Come sarebbe a dire?** What do you mean?
+ **Che ne diresti di andarcene?** Shall we leave?
[2] to tell* ◇ *Hai detto troppe bugie.* You've told too many lies.
+ **dire qualcosa a qualcuno** to tell* somebody something ◇ *Mi ha detto la verità.* He told me the truth. ◇ *Ti dirò un segreto.* I'll tell you a secret. ◇ *Dimmi dov'è.* Tell me where it is.
+ **dire a qualcuno di fare qualcosa** to tell* somebody to do something ◇ *Gli ho detto di andarsene.* I told him to go away.

la diretta NOME FEM
+ **in diretta** live ◇ *un incontro di calcio in diretta* a live football match

diretto AGGETTIVO (FEM **diretta**)
direct ◇ *la strada più diretta* the most direct route
+ **il mio diretto superiore** my immediate superior
+ **treno diretto** through train

il direttore, **la direttrice** NOME MASC, FEM
[1] manager (*di banca, di fabbrica*)
[2] head (*di scuola*)
+ **direttore d'orchestra** conductor
+ **direttore tecnico** team manager

la direzione NOME FEM
[1] direction ◇ *È nella direzione opposta.* It's in the opposite direction.
+ **In che direzione vai?** Which way are you going?
[2] management (*di società*)
[3] leadership (*di partito*)

il/la dirigente NOME MASC/FEM
vedi anche **dirigente** AGGETTIVO
[1] executive (*di ditta*)
[2] leading figure (*di partito*)

dirigente AGGETTIVO
vedi anche **dirigente** NOME
+ **la classe dirigente** the ruling class

dirigere* VERBO
+ **dirigere il traffico** to direct the traffic
+ **dirigere una ditta** to run* a company
+ **dirigere un'orchestra** to conduct an orchestra
+ **dirigere i lavori** to be* in charge of the work
+ **dirigersi verso** to make* for ◇ *Si è diretto verso la porta.* He made for the door.
+ **essere diretti a nord** to be* heading north

diritto AGGETTIVO (FEM **diritta**)

> vedi anche **diritto** NOME, AVVERBIO

straight ◇ *una strada diritta* a straight road

diritto AVVERBIO

> vedi anche **diritto** AGGETTIVO, AVVERBIO

straight ◇ *Vai sempre diritto fino al semaforo.* Keep straight on until you get to the traffic lights.

il **diritto** NOME MASC

> vedi anche **diritto** AGGETTIVO, AVVERBIO

1 right ◇ *Ho il diritto di sapere.* I've got a right to know. ◇ *il diritto di voto* the right to vote

2 law (*legge*) ◇ *Studia diritto.* He's studying law.

3 forehand (*nel tennis*)

il **dirottamento** NOME MASC

♦ **dirottamento aereo** hijack

dirottare VERBO

1 to hijack (*aereo*)

2 to divert (*traffico*)

il **dirottatore,** la **dirottatrice** NOME MASC, FEM

hijacker

dirotto AGGETTIVO (FEM **dirotta**)

♦ **Piove a dirotto.** It's pouring.

♦ **scoppiare in un pianto dirotto** to burst* into tears

disabitato AGGETTIVO (FEM **disabitata**)

uninhabited

il **disagio** NOME MASC

♦ **sentirsi a disagio** to feel* ill at ease

disapprovare VERBO

♦ **disapprovare qualcosa** to disapprove of something ◇ *Disapprovano il mio comportamento.* They disapprove of my behaviour.

la **disapprovazione** NOME FEM

disapproval

disarmato AGGETTIVO (FEM **disarmata**)

disarmed

il **disarmo** NOME MASC

disarmament

il **disastro** NOME MASC

disaster ◇ *È il più grande disastro aereo mai avvenuto.* It's the worst air disaster there has ever been.

♦ **Quel cameriere è un disastro!** That waiter is awful!

disastroso AGGETTIVO (FEM **disastrosa**)

disastrous ◇ *effetti disastrosi* disastrous effects

♦ **in condizioni disastrose** in a terrible state

disattento AGGETTIVO (FEM **disattenta**)

inattentive

la **disattenzione** NOME FEM

♦ **un errore di disattenzione** a careless mistake

la **disavventura** NOME FEM

misadventure

la **discarica** NOME FEM (PL le **discariche**)

tip

dump *US*

la **discesa** NOME FEM

slope ◇ *una discesa ripida* a steep slope

♦ **in discesa** downhill ◇ *Da casa nostra al paese la strada è in discesa.* It's downhill from our house to the village.

♦ **discesa libera** downhill race

la **disciplina** NOME FEM

discipline

il **disco** NOME MASC (PL i **dischi**)

1 record ◇ *uno dei miei dischi preferiti* one of my favourite records

2 disk (*di computer*) ◇ *il disco rigido* the hard disk

3 discus (*nello sport*)

♦ **il lancio del disco** the discus ◇ *Chi ha vinto il lancio del disco?* Who won the discus?

♦ **disco orario** parking disc

♦ **disco volante** flying saucer

discografico AGGETTIVO (FEM **discografica**, MASC PL **discografici**, FEM PL **discografiche**)

♦ **casa discografica** record company

il **discorso** NOME MASC

speech

♦ **fare un discorso** to make* a speech

♦ **discorso diretto** direct speech

♦ **discorso indiretto** indirect speech

la **discoteca** NOME FEM (PL le **discoteche**)

club ◇ *una discoteca alla moda* a popular club

♦ **Vado in discoteca di sabato.** I go clubbing on Saturdays.

discreto AGGETTIVO (FEM **discreta**)

1 reasonable ◇ *un voto discreto* a reasonable mark

2 discreet ◇ *È una persona molto discreta.* He's very discreet.

la **discriminazione** NOME FEM

discrimination ◇ *la discriminazione razziale* racial discrimination

la **discussione** NOME FEM

1 discussion (*dibattito*)

♦ **fare una discussione** to have* a discussion

♦ **mettere in discussione** to bring* into question

♦ **È fuori discussione.** It's out of the question.

2 argument (*litigio*) ◇ *Abbiamo avuto una discussione.* We had an argument.

discutere* VERBO

1 to discuss

♦ **discutere di qualcosa** to discuss something ◇ *Discutono spesso di politica.* They often discuss politics.

♦ **Ho discusso a lungo con lui.** I had a long discussion with him.

> *to discuss* è sempre seguito dal complemento oggetto. Di conseguenza non si può dire "I discussed with him".

---

* *I verbi seguiti da questo simbolo sono irregolari. Si veda anche alle pp.328–338.*

[2] to argue (*litigare*) ◇ *Non voglio mettermi a discutere con te.* I don't want to argue with you.

♦ **Mi ha ubbidito senza discutere.** He obeyed me without question.

disdire* VERBO
to cancel (*prenotazione, appuntamento*)

disegnare VERBO
[1] to draw* ◇ *Mio fratello sta disegnando.* My brother is drawing.
[2] to design ◇ *Disegna mobili.* He designs furniture.

disegnatore, la **disegnatrice** NOME MASC, FEM
designer

disegno NOME MASC
[1] drawing ◇ *un bel disegno* a beautiful drawing
[2] design ◇ *un disegno a fiori* a floral design

disfare* VERBO
to undo* (*pacco, nodo, maglia*) ◇ *Ha disfatto il pacco.* He undid the parcel.

♦ **disfare la valigia** to unpack ◇ *Ha disfatto la valigia.* He's unpacked.

♦ **disfare il letto** to strip the bed

disfatto AGGETTIVO (FEM **disfatta**)
♦ **un letto disfatto** an unmade bed

disgrazia NOME FEM
♦ **È successa una disgrazia.** Something terrible has happened.

disgustoso AGGETTIVO (FEM **disgustosa**)
disgusting

disinfettante NOME MASC
disinfectant

disinfettare VERBO
to disinfect

disinibito AGGETTIVO (FEM **disinibita**)
uninhibited

disintegrare VERBO
to disintegrate

disinteresse NOME MASC
indifference

disintossicante AGGETTIVO
♦ **una cura disintossicante** a detox

disintossicarsi VERBO
♦ **disintossicarsi dall'alcol** to be* treated for alcoholism
♦ **disintossicarsi dalla droga** to be* treated for drug addiction

disinvolto AGGETTIVO (FEM **disinvolta**)
relaxed (*spigliato*) ◇ *Ha un modo di fare molto disinvolto.* She's got a very relaxed manner.

disobbediente AGGETTIVO
disobedient

disobbidire VERBO
♦ **disobbidire a qualcuno** to disobey somebody ◇ *Mi ha disobbidito.* He disobeyed me.

disoccupato, disoccupata NOME,

AGGETTIVO
unemployed ◇ *È ancora disoccupato.* He's still unemployed.
♦ **i disoccupati** the unemployed

la **disoccupazione** NOME FEM
unemployment ◇ *La disoccupazione è in aumento.* Unemployment is rising.

disonesto AGGETTIVO (FEM **disonesta**)
dishonest

disordinato AGGETTIVO (FEM **disordinata**)
untidy ◇ *un ragazzo disordinato* an untidy boy

il **disordine** NOME MASC
mess ◇ *Non sopporto il disordine.* I can't stand mess. ◇ *Che disordine!* What a mess!
♦ **essere in disordine** (*stanza, casa*) to be* in a mess
♦ **disordini** (*tumulti*) disturbances ◇ *i disturbi della settimana scorsa* the disturbances of last week

disorientato AGGETTIVO (FEM **disorientata**)
disorientated

dispari AGGETTIVO
♦ **numeri dispari** odd numbers

disparte NOME
♦ **starsene in disparte** to stand* by oneself ◇ *Se ne stava in disparte.* He was standing by himself.

la **dispensa** NOME FEM
sideboard (*mobile*)

disperato AGGETTIVO (FEM **disperata**)
desperate ◇ *un gesto disperato* a desperate gesture
♦ **Ho un disperato bisogno di soldi.** I desperately need money.

la **disperazione** NOME FEM
despair

il **disperso,** la **dispersa** NOME MASC, FEM
missing person

il **dispetto** NOME MASC
♦ **fare dispetti a qualcuno** to tease somebody ◇ *Smettila di fargli dispetti.* Stop teasing him.
♦ **per dispetto** out of spite

dispettoso AGGETTIVO (FEM **dispettosa**)
spiteful

il **dispiacere** NOME MASC
  vedi anche **dispiacere** VERBO
♦ **dare un dispiacere a qualcuno** to upset someone ◇ *Non voglio dare un dispiacere ai miei genitori.* I don't want to upset my parents.
♦ **Le ha dato molti dispiaceri.** He's made her very unhappy.
♦ **È un gran dispiacere dovervelo dire.** I'm really sorry to have to tell you this.

dispiacere* VERBO
  vedi anche **dispiacere** NOME
♦ **Mi dispiace.** I'm sorry.
♦ **Le dispiace se fumo?** Do you mind if I smoke?

☞

• **Se non le dispiace** If you don't mind

disponibile AGGETTIVO

[1] available ◊ *È disponibile in molti colori.* It's available in many colours.

[2] ready to help ◊ *Luca è sempre molto disponibile.* Luca's always very ready to help.

il **dispositivo** NOME MASC

device ◊ *un dispositivo di sicurezza* a safety device

la **disposizione** NOME FEM

[1] order ◊ *Ho dato disposizioni precise.* I gave precise orders.

• **a tua disposizione** at your disposal

• **avere a disposizione** to have at one's disposal ◊ *Abbiamo a disposizione cinque computer nuovi.* We've got five new computers at our disposal.

[2] arrangement ◊ *la disposizione dei mobili* the arrangement of the furniture

• **Ha cambiato la disposizione dei mobili.** He rearranged the furniture.

disposto AGGETTIVO (FEM **disposta**)

• **essere disposto a** to be* prepared to ◊ *Non sono disposto ad aiutarti se non mi paghi.* I'm not prepared to help you if you don't pay me.

• **essere ben disposto nei confronti di** to be well disposed towards

disprezzare VERBO

to despise

il **disprezzo** NOME MASC

contempt ◊ *Mi ha guardato con disprezzo.* He looked at me with contempt.

dissetante AGGETTIVO

refreshing ◊ *una bevanda dissetante* a refreshing drink

distaccare VERBO

• **distaccare qualcuno** to leave* somebody behind ◊ *Li ha distaccati di parecchi metri.* He left them several metres behind.

il **distacco** NOME MASC (PL i **distacchi**)

• **con distacco** coldly ◊ *Mi guardava con distacco.* He looked at me coldly.

• **Il distacco dalla famiglia è spesso difficile.** Leaving home is often difficult.

• **vincere con un distacco di cento metri** to win* by a hundred metres

distante AVVERBIO, AGGETTIVO

far away ◊ *Non abitano distante.* They don't live far away.

• **essere distante da** to be* a long way from ◊ *La casa è distante dal centro.* The house is a long way from the centre. ◊ *È distante da qui?* Is it a long way from here?

la **distanza** NOME FEM

distance ◊ *la distanza tra Roma e Milano* the distance between Rome and Milan

• **Era a due metri di distanza.** She was two metres away.

• **a poca distanza da qui** not far from here

• **a distanza di due giorni** two days later

• **distanza di sicurezza** braking distance

distare* VERBO

to be* far ◊ *Dista molto da qui?* Is it far from here?

• **Dista pochi chilometri da Roma.** It's a few kilometres from Rome.

distendere* VERBO

to stretch *(gambe, braccia)* ◊ *Non c'era posto per distendere le gambe.* There was no room to stretch your legs.

• **distendere i nervi** to relax

• **distendersi (1)** *(sdraiarsi)* to lie* down

• **distendersi (2)** *(rilassarsi)* to relax

disteso AGGETTIVO (FEM **distesa**)

• **essere disteso** to be* lying ◊ *Era distesa sul letto.* She was lying on the bed.

distinguere* VERBO

to see* ◊ *Non riesco a distinguere il numero dell'autobus.* I can't see the number of the bus.

• **distinguere tra** to tell* the difference between ◊ *Non li distinguo tra loro.* I can't tell the difference between them.

• **Si distingue per efficienza.** He's outstandingly efficient.

il **distintivo** NOME MASC

badge

distinto AGGETTIVO (FEM **distinta**)

[1] distinguished *(raffinato)* ◊ *un signore dall'aspetto distinto* a distinguished-looking man

• **modi distinti** excellent manners

[2] distinct *(separato)* ◊ *due materie distinte* two distinct subjects

• **Distinti saluti** Yours sincerely *Se la lettera non è indirizzata ad una persona in particolare si usa invece "Yours faithfully".*

la **distorsione** NOME FEM

sprain *(di caviglia)*

distrarre* VERBO

to distract ◊ *Non distrarlo dal lavoro.* Don't distract him from his work.

• **distrarsi** to take* one's mind off things ◊ *Ho bisogno di distrarmi un po'.* I need to take my mind off things.

• **Si distrae spesso durante le lezioni.** His mind often wanders during lessons.

• **Non distrarti!** Pay attention!

distratto AGGETTIVO (FEM **distratta**)

absent-minded ◊ *È molto distratto.* He's very absent-minded.

• **Scusa, ero distratta.** I'm sorry, I wasn't paying attention.

la **distrazione** NOME FEM

• **un errore di distrazione** a careless mistake

• **Mi scusi, è stato un attimo di distrazione.** I'm sorry, I wasn't thinking.

distribuire VERBO

---

to hand out ◇ *Distribuisci i quaderni.* Hand out the exercise books.
- **distribuire le carte** to deal* the cards

il **distributore** NOME MASC
pump (*di benzina*)
- **distributore automatico** (*di sigarette, di bibite*) vending machine

distruggere* VERBO
to destroy

la **distruzione** NOME FEM
destruction

disturbare VERBO
to disturb ◇ *Ti disturbo?* Am I disturbing you? ◇ *"non disturbare"* "do not disturb"
- **La disturba se fumo?** Do you mind if I smoke?
- **Grazie del regalo, ma non dovevi disturbarti!** Thank you for the present, but you shouldn't have!

il **disturbo** NOME MASC
trouble ◇ *Non è affatto un disturbo.* It's no trouble at all.
- **disturbi di stomaco** stomach trouble SING

disubbidiente AGGETTIVO
disobedient

disubbidire VERBO
- **disubbidire a qualcuno** to disobey somebody ◇ *Mi ha disubbidito.* He disobeyed me.

il **dito** NOME MASC (PL FEM le **dita**)
1 finger (*di mano*) ◇ *Non ha mosso un dito per aiutarmi.* He didn't lift a finger to help me.
2 toe (*di piede*)

la **ditta** NOME FEM
firm
- **Spett. Ditta,...** (*in lettera*) Dear Sirs,...

il **dittatore** NOME MASC
dictator

la **dittatura** NOME FEM
dictatorship

il **divano** NOME MASC
sofa ◇ *sul divano* on the sofa
- **divano letto** sofa-bed

diventare VERBO
1 to become* ◇ *È diventato famoso.* He became famous. ◇ *La situazione è diventata pericolosa.* The situation has become dangerous.
2 to go* (*con gusto, colore*) ◇ *Il latte è diventato acido.* The milk has gone sour. ◇ *La maglietta è diventata rosa dopo il lavaggio.* The T-shirt went pink in the wash.
- **diventare vecchio** to grow* old

diverso AGGETTIVO (FEM **diversa**)
different ◇ *È diverso da me.* He's different from me.
- **diversi** (*parecchi*) several ◇ *diversi amici* several friends ◇ *Gliel'ho detto diverse volte.* I told him several times.

divertente AGGETTIVO

funny ◇ *una barzelletta divertente* a funny joke ◇ *Mario è molto divertente.* Mario is very funny.
- **È un gioco molto divertente.** This game is really fun.

il **divertimento** NOME MASC
- **Buon divertimento!** Have fun!

divertire VERBO
to amuse ◇ *Mi ha divertito molto la sua storia.* I was very amused by her story.
- **divertirsi** to have* a good time ◇ *Ti sei divertito alla festa?* Did you have a good time at the party? ◇ *Divertiti!* Have a good time!

dividere* VERBO
to divide ◇ *L'ho diviso in tre parti.* I've divided it into three parts. ◇ *otto diviso quattro fa due* eight divided by four is two
- **dividersi** to be* divided ◇ *Il libro si divide in tre parti.* The book is divided into three parts.

il **divieto** NOME MASC
- **"divieto di accesso"** "no entry"
- **"divieto di sosta"** "no parking"

la **divisa** NOME FEM
uniform
- **un ufficiale in divisa** a uniformed officer

la **divisione** NOME FEM
division

il **divo**, la **diva** NOME MASC, FEM
star ◇ *un divo del cinema* a film star

divorare VERBO
to devour

divorziare VERBO
to get* divorced ◇ *Hanno divorziato.* They got divorced.

il **divorzio** NOME MASC
divorce

il **dizionario** NOME MASC
dictionary (PL dictionaries) ◇ *un dizionario di inglese* an English dictionary

il **do** NOME MASC (PL i **do**)
C (*nota*)

doc AGGETTIVO (MASC, FEM, PL **doc**)
- **vino doc** quality wine

la **doccia** NOME FEM (PL le **docce**)
shower
- **fare la doccia** to have* a shower

docile AGGETTIVO
docile (*persona, animale*)

il **documentario** NOME MASC
documentary (PL documentaries)

il **documento** NOME MASC
- **documento di identità** proof of identity
- **documenti** papers ◇ *È andato a ritirare i documenti.* He went to pick up the papers. ◇ *Il poliziotto mi ha chiesto i documenti.* The policeman asked for my papers.

🛈 *In Italy everyone has an identity card.*

D

dodicenne AGGETTIVO, NOME
twelve-year-old

dodicesimo AGGETTIVO, NOME MASC (FEM
dodicesima)
twelfth

dodici NUMERO
twelve ◇ *Ha dodici anni.* He's twelve. ◇ *alle dodici* at twelve o'clock
* **il dodici dicembre** the twelfth of December

la **dogana** NOME FEM
customs PL
* **passare la dogana** to go* through customs

il **doganiere** NOME MASC
customs officer

dolce AGGETTIVO
vedi anche **dolce** NOME
sweet ◇ *Il caffè è troppo dolce.* The coffee's too sweet. ◇ *È molto dolce con me.* He's very sweet to me.
* **un formaggio dolce** a mild cheese

il **dolce** NOME MASC
vedi anche **dolce** AGGETTIVO
dessert ◇ *Hai ordinato il dolce?* Have you ordered a dessert?

il **dolcificante** NOME MASC
sweetener

il **dollaro** NOME MASC
dollar

il **dolore** NOME MASC
[1] pain ◇ *un dolore acuto* a sharp pain ◇ *Ho un dolore al braccio.* I've got a pain in my arm.
[2] sorrow ◇ *È con grande dolore che annunciamo la scomparsa di...* With great sorrow we announce the death of...
[3] grief
* **morire di dolore** to die of grief

doloroso AGGETTIVO (FEM **dolorosa**)
[1] painful ◇ *È un'operazione dolorosa.* It's a painful operation.
[2] sad ◇ *una notizia dolorosa* a sad piece of news

la **domanda** NOME FEM
[1] question
* **fare una domanda a qualcuno** to ask somebody a question ◇ *Ti ha fatto molte domande?* Did he ask you a lot of questions?
[2] application (*richiesta scritta*) ◇ *Hai spedito la domanda?* Have you sent off your application?
* **fare domanda per un lavoro** to apply for a job

domandare VERBO
to ask
* **domandare qualcosa a qualcuno** to ask somebody something ◇ *Mi ha domandato l'ora.* He asked me the time. ◇ *Mi ha domandato se volevo andare alla festa.* He asked me if I wanted to go to the party.
* **domandarsi** to wonder ◇ *Mi domando*

dove possa essere. I wonder where it can be.
* **domandare di qualcuno** to ask after somebody ◇ *Mi ha domandato di te.* She asked after you.

domani AVVERBIO
tomorrow ◇ *Domani è sabato.* Tomorrow's Saturday.
* **domani stesso** tomorrow
* **domani l'altro** the day after tomorrow
* **domani a otto** a week tomorrow
* **A domani!** See you tomorrow!

la **domenica** NOME FEM (PL le **domeniche**)
Sunday
Si noti l'uso della maiuscola in inglese.
◇ *L'ho visto domenica.* I saw him on Sunday.
* **di domenica** on Sundays ◇ *Di domenica vado al cinema.* I go to the cinema on Sundays.
* **domenica scorsa** last Sunday
* **domenica prossima** next Sunday

la **domestica** NOME FEM (PL le **domestiche**)
cleaning lady (PL cleaning ladies)

il **domestico** NOME MASC (PL i **domestici**)
vedi anche **domestico** AGGETTIVO
servant

domestico AGGETTIVO (FEM **domestica**, MASC
PL **domestici**, FEM PL **domestiche**)
vedi anche **domestico** NOME
* **lavori domestici** housework SING
* **animale domestico** pet

il **donatore**, la **donatrice** NOME MASC, FEM
* **donatore di sangue** blood donor
* **donatore di organi** organ donor

dondolarsi VERBO
[1] to rock (*su sedia*)
[2] to swing* (*su altalena*)

il **dondolo** NOME MASC
* **cavallo a dondolo** rocking horse
* **sedia a dondolo** rocking chair

la **donna** NOME FEM
[1] woman (PL women) ◇ *Ho visto due donne giovani.* I saw two young women.
* **donna delle pulizie** cleaning lady (PL cleaning ladies)
[2] queen (*nei giochi di carte*)

dopo AVVERBIO, PREPOSIZIONE, CONGIUNZIONE
[1] later (*più tardi*) ◇ *Ci vediamo dopo.* See you later. ◇ *È successo un anno dopo.* It happened a year later.
[2] then (*poi*) ◇ *Ora studia, e dopo potrai uscire.* First do your homework, then you can go out.
[3] after ◇ *il giorno dopo* the day after ◇ *Ci vediamo dopo le vacanze.* See you after the holidays. ◇ *È arrivato dopo di me.* He arrived after me. ◇ *Dopo aver telefonato è uscito.* After making a phone call he went out. ◇ *uno dopo l'altro* one after the other
* **dopo che** after ◇ *dopo che è partito* after he

left

dopobarba NOME MASC (PL i **dopobarba**)
aftershave

dopodomani AVVERBIO
the day after tomorrow ◇ *Ci vediamo dopodomani.* See you the day after tomorrow.

doposcì NOME MASC (PL i **doposcì**)
après-ski boot

doppiare VERBO
1. to dub (*film*)
2. to lap (*concorrente*)

doppio AGGETTIVO (FEM **doppia**)
vedi anche **doppio** NOME, AVVERBIO
double ◇ *un doppio whisky* a double whisky
* **frase a doppio senso** double entendre
* **doppi vetri** double-glazing
* **chiudere a doppia mandata** to double-lock
* **strada a doppio senso** two-way street

doppio AVVERBIO
vedi anche **doppio** AGGETTIVO, NOME
double
* **vedere doppio** to see* double

doppio NOME MASC
vedi anche **doppio** AGGETTIVO, AVVERBIO
* **il doppio** twice as much ◇ *Ho pagato il doppio.* I paid twice as much.
* **fare un doppio** (*a tennis*) to play a game of doubles

dormiglione, la **dormigliona** NOME MASC, FEM
sleepyhead ◇ *Sveglia, dormiglione!* Wake up, sleepyhead!

dormire* VERBO
to sleep* ◇ *Sta dormendo.* She's sleeping.
* **andare a dormire** to go* to bed ◇ *Vado a dormire.* I'm going to bed.
* **dormire come un ghiro** to sleep* like a log
* **dormire in piedi** to be* asleep on one's feet

dormita NOME FEM
* **farsi una bella dormita** to have* a good sleep

dorso NOME MASC
back ◇ *Sdraiati sul dorso.* Lie on your back.
* **nuotare a dorso** to do* the backstroke

dose NOME FEM
dose (*di droga, di medicina*)

dotato AGGETTIVO (FEM **dotata**)
* **un bambino dotato** a gifted child

dottorato NOME MASC
doctorate

dottore, la **dottoressa** NOME MASC, FEM
doctor

> **❶** In Italy **dottore** is a title used by anyone who has a degree.

dove AVVERBIO
where ◇ *Dove abiti?* Where do you live?
◇ *Di dove sei?* Where are you from? ◇ *La città dove abito è sul mare.* The town where I

live is by the sea.

il **dovere** NOME MASC
vedi anche **dovere** VERBO
duty (PL duties) ◇ *Credeva che fosse suo dovere.* He thought it was his duty.
* **Avevi il dovere di dirmelo.** You should have told me.
* **Mi sono sentito in dovere di dirtelo.** I felt I should tell you.

dovere* VERBO
vedi anche **dovere** NOME
1. to have* to (*obbligo*) ◇ *È dovuto partire.* He had to leave. ◇ *Devi tornare a casa presto stasera?* Do you have to go home early this evening? ◇ *Non devi andarci se non vuoi.* You don't have to go if you don't want to.

> Al presente si può usare anche **to have got to**.

◇ *Ora devo proprio andare.* I've really got to go now.

2. must

> **must** si usa quando chi parla sta dando un ordine e nelle deduzioni.

◇ *Devi farlo subito.* You must do it at once.
◇ *Devi finire i compiti prima di uscire.* You must finish your homework before you go out. ◇ *Non devi dirglielo per nessun motivo.* You mustn't on any account tell him. ◇ *Dev'essere tardi.* It must be late.
◇ *Devi essere stanco dopo un viaggio così lungo.* You must be tired after such a long journey.

> Per tradurre **dovere** al condizionale si usa **should**.

◇ *Dovresti studiare di più.* You should study more. ◇ *Pensi che avrebbe dovuto dirmelo?* Do you think he should have told me?
◇ *Dovrebbe arrivare alle dieci.* He should arrive at ten.

3. to owe (*essere debitore*)
* **dovere qualcosa a qualcuno** to owe somebody something ◇ *Gli devo quindici euro.* I owe him fifteen euros.

dovunque AVVERBIO
1. wherever ◇ *Ti troverò dovunque tu vada.* I'll find you wherever you go.
2. everywhere ◇ *L'ho cercato dovunque.* I've looked for it everywhere.

dovuto AGGETTIVO (FEM **dovuta**)
* **essere dovuto a** to be* due to ◇ *Il ritardo è dovuto al maltempo.* The delay is due to the bad weather.

la **dozzina** NOME FEM
dozen ◇ *una dozzina di uova* a dozen eggs

il **dramma** NOME MASC (PL i **drammi**)
drama
* **fare un dramma di qualcosa** to make* a drama out of something

drammatico AGGETTIVO (FEM **drammatica**, MASC PL **drammatici**, FEM PL **drammatiche**)
terrible (*situazione, momento*)
* **arte drammatica** drama

drastico AGGETTIVO (FEM **drastica**, MASC PL
drastici, FEM PL **drastiche**)
drastic

dritto = **diritto**

la **droga** NOME FEM (PL le **droghe**)
drug (*stupefacente*)
♦ **fare uso di droga** to be* on drugs
al plurale.
♦ **droghe leggere** soft drugs
♦ **droghe pesanti** hard drugs

drogarsi VERBO
to take* drugs

il **drogato**, la **drogata** NOME MASC, FEM
drug addict

il **dromedario** NOME MASC
dromedary (PL dromedaries)

il **dubbio** NOME MASC
doubt ◊ *Ho i miei dubbi in proposito.* I have
my doubts about it.
♦ **mettere in dubbio qualcosa** to question
something ◊ *Ha messo in dubbio la mia
onestà.* He questioned my honesty.
♦ **avere il dubbio che...** to suspect that... ◊ *Ho
il dubbio che sia stato lui.* I suspect that it
was him.
♦ **senza dubbio** undoubtedly ◊ *È senza
dubbio uno dei suoi quadri più belli.* It's
undoubtedly one of his finest paintings.

dubitare VERBO
to doubt ◊ *Pensi che telefonerà? – Dubito.*
Do you think he'll phone? – I doubt it.
◊ *Dubito che verrà.* I doubt he'll come.
♦ **dubitare di** (*onestà, capacità*) to doubt
◊ *Nessuno dubita della tua onestà.* Nobody
doubts your honesty.

Dublino NOME FEM
Dublin ◊ *Vive a Dublino.* He lives in Dublin.

il **duca** NOME MASC (PL i **duchi**)
duke

la **duchessa** NOME FEM
duchess

due NUMERO
two ◊ *due bambini* two children ◊ *Ha due
anni.* She's two. ◊ *alle due* at two o'clock
♦ **il due dicembre** the second of December

♦ **Vorrei dire due parole.** I'd like to say a few
words.
♦ **Ci metto due minuti.** It'll only take me a
couple of minutes.
♦ **due volte** twice ◊ *L'ho fatto due volte.* I did
it twice.

duecento NUMERO
two hundred
♦ **il Duecento** the thirteenth century

il **duepezzi** NOME MASC (PL i **duepezzi**)
two-piece swimsuit

dunque CONGIUNZIONE
[1] so ◊ *Ho sbagliato, dunque è giusto che
paghi.* It was my mistake, so it's fair I should
pay.
[2] well ◊ *Dunque, come dicevo...* Well, as I
was saying...

il **duomo** NOME MASC
cathedral
Attenzione! In inglese esiste la parola **dome**,
che però significa **cupola.**

il **duplicato** NOME MASC
duplicate

durante PREPOSIZIONE
during

durare VERBO
to last ◊ *Le batterie non sono durate a
lungo.* The batteries didn't last long. ◊ *Il
film dura circa due ore.* The film lasts about
two hours.
♦ **Così non può durare!** This can't go on any
longer!

duro AGGETTIVO (FEM **dura**)
vedi anche **duro** NOME
hard ◊ *Il materasso è troppo duro per me.*
The mattress is too hard for me. ◊ *Non
essere troppo duro con lui.* Don't be too
hard on him. ◊ *L'insegnamento è un lavoro
duro.* Teaching is hard work.
♦ **duro d'orecchi** hard of hearing
♦ **fare il duro** to act tough

il **duro** NOME
vedi anche **duro** AGGETTIVO
♦ **fare il duro** to act tough

E

e CONGIUNZIONE

[1] and ◇ *Io e Davide ci andremo.* David and I will go.

[2] but (*invece*) ◇ *Lo credevo onesto e non lo è.* I thought he was honest but he isn't. ◇ *Sapeva di sbagliare e l'ha fatto lo stesso.* She knew she was making a mistake, but she did it all the same.

[3] how about ◇ *Io non ci vado, e tu?* I'm not going, how about you?

A volte e non si traduce.

◇ *Ho pagato quattro sterline e cinquanta.* I paid four pounds fifty. ◇ *A me piace molto, e a te?* I like it a lot, do you? ◇ *E smettila!* Stop it!

ebreo, l' ebrea NOME MASC, FEM

vedi anche **ebreo** AGGETTIVO

Jew

• **gli ebrei** the Jews

ebreo AGGETTIVO (FEM **ebrea**)

vedi anche **ebreo** NOME

Jewish ◇ *È ebreo.* He's Jewish.

ecc. ABBREVIAZIONE

etc ◇ *Vendono libri, dischi, magliette, poster ecc.* They sell books, records, T-shirts, posters etc.

eccellente AGGETTIVO

excellent

eccentrico AGGETTIVO (FEM **eccentrica**, MASC PL **eccentrici**, FEM PL **eccentriche**)

eccentric ◇ *Suo zio è un po' eccentrico.* His uncle's a bit eccentric.

• **Si veste in modo eccentrico.** She wears unusual clothes.

eccessivo AGGETTIVO (FEM **eccessiva**)

excessive ◇ *Proibirgli di uscire mi sembra un po' eccessivo.* I think it's a bit excessive to forbid him to go out.

eccesso NOME MASC

excess ◇ *Devo smaltire il peso in eccesso.* I must lose some excess weight.

• **eccesso di velocità** speeding ◇ *Ha preso una multa per eccesso di velocità.* She was fined for speeding.

eccetto PREPOSIZIONE

except ◇ *Tutti lo sapevano, eccetto io.* Everybody except me knew about it.

eccezionale AGGETTIVO

[1] really good ◇ *È un film eccezionale.* It's a really good film.

[2] exceptional (*inusuale*) ◇ *in circostanze eccezionali* in exceptional circumstances

eccezione NOME FEM

exception ◇ *Va bene, ma lui è un'eccezione.* Okay, but he's an exception. ◇ *Mi dispiace, non posso fare eccezioni.* I'm sorry, I can't make exceptions.

eccitato AGGETTIVO (FEM **eccitata**)

[1] excited (*agitato*)

[2] aroused (*sessualmente*)

ecco AVVERBIO

• **Ecco il treno!** Here's the train!

• **Eccomi!** Here I am!

• **Ecco, tieni.** Here you are.

• **Ah, ecco perché non è venuto!** So that's why he didn't come!

eccome AVVERBIO

• **Ti piace? – Eccome!** Do you like it? – Yes I do!

• **Era difficile? – Eccome!** Was it difficult? – Yes it was!

• **Ti sei divertito? – Eccome!** Did you enjoy yourself? – Yes I did!

l' eclisse NOME FEM

eclipse

l' eco NOME MASC (PL gli **echi**)

echo

ecologico AGGETTIVO (FEM **ecologica**, MASC PL **ecologici**, FEM PL **ecologiche**)

[1] ecological ◇ *una catastrofe ecologica* an ecological disaster

[2] environmentally friendly ◇ *un detersivo ecologico* an environmentally friendly detergent

l' economia NOME FEM

[1] economy (PL economies) ◇ *L'economia è in crisi.* The economy is in crisis.

[2] economics SING (*disciplina*) ◇ *Studia economia.* He's studying economics.

economico AGGETTIVO (FEM **economica**, MASC PL **economici**, FEM PL **economiche**)

inexpensive ◇ *un albergo economico* an inexpensive hotel

• **più economico** cheaper ◇ *È più economico viaggiare in pullman.* It's cheaper to travel by coach.

• **crisi economica** economic crisis

• **viaggiare in classe economica** to travel economy class

l' edera NOME FEM

ivy

l' edicola NOME FEM

newspaper kiosk

l' edificio NOME MASC

building

edile AGGETTIVO

• **un cantiere edile** a building site

• **un operaio edile** a construction worker

la Edimburgo NOME FEM

Edinburgh ◇ *Domani andremo a Edimburgo.* We're going to Edinburgh tomorrow. ◇ *Abita ad Edimburgo.* She lives in Edinburgh.

l' editore NOME MASC

publisher

Attenzione! In inglese esiste la parola **editor***, che però significa* **redattore***, oppure* **direttore** *di giornale.*

l' edizione NOME FEM

edition ◇ *la seconda edizione del libro* the ☞

second edition of the book
* **edizione economica** paperback ◊ *Si trova anche in edizione economica.* It's also available in paperback.

educato AGGETTIVO (FEM **educata**)
polite ◊ *È un ragazzo molto educato.* He's a very polite boy.
* **Non è educato fissare la gente.** It's rude to stare at people.
Attenzione! In inglese esiste la parola educated, che però significa istruito.

l' **educazione** NOME FEM
underline upbringing ◊ *Ha avuto un'educazione molto severa.* He had a very strict upbringing.
* **Ma che razza di educazione!** How rude!
* **educazione fisica** physical education

effervescente AGGETTIVO
underline fizzy (*bibita*)

l' **effetto** NOME MASC
underline effect ◊ *un film ricco di effetti speciali* a film with lots of special effects ◊ *La pastiglia farà effetto tra una mezz'ora.* You'll feel the effect of the pill in about half an hour.
* **Che effetto fa?** What's it like?
* **in effetti** in fact ◊ *In effetti non ha tutti i torti.* In fact she's quite right.
* **effetto serra** greenhouse effect

efficace AGGETTIVO
underline effective ◊ *un rimedio efficace contro il raffreddore* an effective remedy for colds

efficiente AGGETTIVO
underline efficient ◊ *un impiegato efficiente* an efficient worker

l' **Egitto** NOME MASC
underline Egypt ◊ *Mi è piaciuto molto l'Egitto.* I really liked Egypt. ◊ *Andremo in Egitto questa primavera.* We're going to Egypt this spring.

egli PRONOME
underline he

egoista AGGETTIVO (MASC PL **egoisti**, FEM PL **egoiste**)
vedi anche **egoista** NOME
underline selfish ◊ *Penso di essere stato molto egoista.* I think I've been very selfish. ◊ *Sei egoista!* You're selfish!

l' **egoista** NOME MASC/FEM (MASC PL gli **egoisti**, FEM PL le **egoiste**)
vedi anche **egoista** AGGETTIVO
underline selfish person ◊ *È un grande egoista.* He's a very selfish person.

elasticizzato AGGETTIVO (FEM **elasticizzata**)
underline stretch ◊ *tessuto elasticizzato* stretch material

l' **elastico** NOME MASC (PL gli **elastici**)
vedi anche **elastico** AGGETTIVO
underline elastic band

elastico AGGETTIVO (FEM **elastica**, MASC PL **elastici**, FEM PL **elastiche**)
vedi anche **elastico** NOME
underline elastic

l' **elefante** NOME MASC
underline elephant

elegante AGGETTIVO
underline smart ◊ *una giacca elegante* a smart jacket ◊ *È sempre elegante.* She's always smart.

eleggere VERBO
underline elect ◊ *Hanno eletto il nuovo presidente.* They've elected the new president.

elementare AGGETTIVO
underline basic ◊ *alcune nozioni elementari di informatica* some basic knowledge of computing
* **scuola elementare** primary school, US: elementary school
* **la seconda elementare** the second year at primary school

l' **elemento** NOME MASC
underline element ◊ *un elemento chimico* a chemical element
* **Enrico è il miglior elemento della squadra.** Enrico's the best player in the team.

l' **elemosina** NOME FEM
* **chiedere l'elemosina** to beg ◊ *Per strada tanti chiedevano l'elemosina.* There were a lot of people begging in the street.

l' **elenco** NOME MASC (PL gli **elenchi**)
underline list ◊ *C'è un elenco di ostelli della gioventù.* There's a list of youth hostels.
* **fare un elenco di** to list
* **elenco telefonico** phone book ◊ *L'ho cercato sull'elenco telefonico.* I looked him up in the phone book.

elettorale AGGETTIVO
* **campagna elettorale** election campaign
* **sistema elettorale** electoral system

l' **elettore,** l' **elettrice** NOME MASC, FEM
underline voter

l' **elettricista** NOME MASC (PL gli **elettricisti**)
underline electrician ◊ *Fa l'elettricista.* He is an electrician.

l' **elettricità** NOME FEM
underline electricity

elettrico AGGETTIVO (FEM **elettrica**, MASC PL **elettrici**, FEM PL **elettriche**)
underline electric ◊ *un filo elettrico* an electric wire

elettrizzante AGGETTIVO
underline thrilling

l' **elettrodomestico** NOME MASC (PL gli **elettrodomestici**)
underline domestic appliance

elettronico AGGETTIVO (FEM **elettronica**, MASC PL **elettronici**, FEM PL **elettroniche**)
underline electronic ◊ *musica elettronica* electronic music
* **posta elettronica** e-mail

l' **elica** NOME FEM (PL le **eliche**)
underline propeller

l' **elicottero** NOME MASC
underline helicopter

eliminare VERBO

to eliminate ◇ *La nostra squadra è stata eliminata alle semifinali.* Our team was eliminated in the semi-final.

emarginati NOME MASC PL

• **gli emarginati** the socially excluded

emergenza NOME FEM

emergency (PL emergencies) ◇ *È un'emergenza.* It's an emergency.

• **in caso di emergenza** in case of emergency ◇ *In caso di emergenza chiama questo numero.* In case of emergency call this number.

emicrania NOME FEM

migraine ◇ *Aveva l'emicrania.* He had a migraine.

emigrare VERBO

to emigrate ◇ *Erano emigrati in Germania.* They emigrated to Germany.

emittente NOME FEM

station ◇ *un'emittente radiofonica locale* a local radio station ◇ *un'emittente televisiva privata* an independent television station

emorragia NOME FEM (PL le **emorragie**)

bleeding ◇ *un'emorragia interna* internal bleeding

bleeding non ha plurale.

emorroidi NOME FEM PL

piles

emotivo AGGETTIVO (FEM **emotiva**)

emotional ◇ *È molto emotiva.* She's very emotional.

emozionante AGGETTIVO

exciting ◇ *È stata un'avventura emozionante.* It was an exciting adventure.

emozionare VERBO

1 to move (*commuovere*)

2 to excite (*appassionare*)

• **emozionarsi (1)** (*commuoversi*) to be* moved

• **emozionarsi (2)** (*appassionarsi*) to be* excited

emozionato AGGETTIVO (FEM **emozionata**)

1 moved ◇ *Era stupita ed emozionata per l'accoglienza ricevuta.* She was amazed and moved by the welcome she got.

2 emotional ◇ *Ero troppo emozionato per fare un discorso.* I was too emotional to make a speech.

emozione NOME FEM

emotion ◇ *Le tremava la voce per l'emozione.* Her voice trembled with emotion.

• **a caccia di emozioni** in search of excitement

enciclopedia NOME FEM

encyclopaedia

encyclopedia US

energia NOME FEM

energy ◇ *Come fai ad essere così pieno di energia?* How do you manage to be so full of energy?

• **energia nucleare** nuclear energy

energico AGGETTIVO (FEM **energica**, MASC PL **energici**, FEM PL **energiche**)

energetic

enorme AGGETTIVO

huge ◇ *È un negozio enorme.* It's a huge shop. ◇ *Ha avuto un enorme successo.* It was a huge success.

entrambi AGGETTIVO, PRONOME

both ◇ *Si può parcheggiare su entrambi i lati della strada.* You can park on both sides of the street. ◇ *Sono partiti entrambi.* They've both left.

entrare VERBO

1 to go* in ◇ *Ho bussato e sono entrato.* I knocked and went in. ◇ *Siamo entrati in aula.* We went into the classroom.

2 to come* in ◇ *Permesso? Posso entrare?* Excuse me, can I come in?

3 to get* in ◇ *I ladri sono entrati dalla finestra.* The thieves got in through the window.

• **Questo non c'entra.** That's got nothing to do with it.

• **Io non c'entro.** It's got nothing to do with me.

• **La matematica non mi entra in testa.** I can't understand maths.

l' **entrata** NOME FEM

entrance ◇ *L'entrata principale è sulla via laterale.* The main entrance is in the side street.

• **"entrata libera"** "admission free"

entro PREPOSIZIONE

1 by ◇ *Devo pagare entro il dodici febbraio.* I've got to pay by the twelfth of February. ◇ *entro domani* by tomorrow ◇ *entro aprile* by the end of April

2 within (*con le parole "settimana", "giorno" ecc.*) ◇ *Avremo i risultati entro un mese.* We'll have the results within a month. ◇ *entro quattro anni* within four years

l' **entusiasmo** NOME MASC

enthusiasm ◇ *All'inizio era pieno di entusiasmo.* At the start he was full of enthusiasm.

entusiasta AGGETTIVO (MASC PL **entusiasti**, FEM PL **entusiaste**)

delighted ◇ *Non era troppo entusiasta, ma ha accettato.* He wasn't exactly delighted, but he agreed.

• **essere entusiasta di** to be* extremely pleased with ◇ *Sono entusiasta dei risultati.* I'm extremely pleased with the results.

l' **epidemia** NOME FEM

epidemic ◇ *un'epidemia di influenza* a flu epidemic

epilettico AGGETTIVO (FEM **epilettica**, MASC PL **epilettici**, FEM PL **epilettiche**)

epileptic ◇ *una crisi epilettica* an epileptic fit

l' **episodio** NOME MASC

episode ◇ *un episodio imbarazzante della*

E

sua vita an embarrassing episode in her life
♦ **un grave episodio di intolleranza razziale** a serious instance of racism

l' **epoca** NOME FEM (PL le **epoche**)
era ◊ *in epoca bizantina* in the Byzantine era
♦ **a quell'epoca** at that time ◊ *A quell'epoca mi trovavo a Londra.* At that time I was in London.
♦ **mobili d'epoca** period furniture SING

eppure CONGIUNZIONE
and yet ◊ *Sembra impossibile, eppure è vero!* It seems impossible, and yet it's true!
♦ **Non è venuto all'appuntamento. Eppure aveva promesso.** He didn't come to the meeting, though he'd promised he would.

l' **equatore** NOME MASC
equator

equatoriale AGGETTIVO
equatorial ◊ *clima equatoriale* equatorial climate

l' **equilibrio** NOME MASC
balance ◊ *Ha perso l'equilibrio ed è caduto.* He lost his balance and fell.

l' **equipaggiamento** NOME MASC
equipment

equipaggiato AGGETTIVO (FEM **equipaggiata**)
equipped ◊ *Erano ben equipaggiati per la montagna.* They were well-equipped for climbing.

l' **equipaggio** NOME MASC
crew ◊ *l'equipaggio dell'aereo* the cabin crew

l' **equitazione** NOME FEM
riding ◊ *C'è una scuola di equitazione qua vicino.* There's a riding school near here.

l' **equivoco** NOME MASC (PL gli **equivoci**)
vedi anche **equivoco** AGGETTIVO
misunderstanding ◊ *È stato tutto un equivoco.* It was all a misunderstanding.

equivoco AGGETTIVO (FEM **equivoca**, MASC PL **equivoci**, FEM PL **equivoche**)
vedi anche **equivoco** NOME
ambiguous

equo AGGETTIVO (FEM **equa**)
fair ◊ *un compenso equo* fair payment

l' **erba** NOME FEM
grass ◊ *Eravamo sdraiati sull'erba.* We were lying on the grass.
♦ **erbe aromatiche** herbs

l' **erbaccia** NOME FEM (PL le **erbacce**)
weed

l' **erboristeria** NOME FEM
herbalist's shop

l' **erede** NOME MASC/FEM
heir ◊ *Lei è l'unica erede.* She's the only heir.

l' **eredità** NOME FEM
inheritance ◊ *Aveva paura di perdere l'eredità.* He was afraid of losing his

inheritance.
♦ **lasciare in eredità** to leave* ◊ *Suo padre gli ha lasciato in eredità una bella casa.* His father left him a beautiful house.

ereditare VERBO
to inherit ◊ *Ha ereditato la casa del nonno.* She inherited her grandfather's house.

ereditario AGGETTIVO (FEM **ereditaria**)
hereditary ◊ *una malattia ereditaria* a hereditary disease

l' **ergastolo** NOME MASC
life sentence ◊ *Gli hanno dato l'ergastolo.* He was given a life sentence.

l' **erica** NOME FEM
heather

l' **eroe** NOME MASC
hero (PL heroes)

l' **eroina** NOME FEM
1 heroine ◊ *l'eroina del romanzo* the heroine of the novel
2 heroin ◊ *L'eroina è una droga pesante.* Heroin is a hard drug.

errato AGGETTIVO (FEM **errata**)
wrong

l' **errore** NOME MASC
mistake ◊ *Non ho fatto neanche un errore.* I didn't make a single mistake. ◊ *un errore di ortografia* a spelling mistake

esagerare VERBO
to exaggerate ◊ *Non esagerare!* Don't exaggerate!
♦ **Ha esagerato un po' nel bere.** He had a bit too much to drink.

l' **esame** NOME MASC
1 exam ◊ *Non ho passato l'esame.* I didn't pass the exam. ◊ *Quando saprai il risultato degli esami?* When will you get your exam results?
2 test
♦ **esame di guida** driving test
♦ **esame del sangue** blood test

esaminare VERBO
to examine

esattamente AVVERBIO
exactly ◊ *È esattamente quello che intendevo.* It's exactly what I meant.

esatto AGGETTIVO (FEM **esatta**)
exact ◊ *Non mi ricordo le parole esatte.* I can't remember the exact words.

l' **esaurimento** NOME MASC
♦ **esaurimento nervoso** nervous breakdown

esaurire VERBO
1 to sell* out ◊ *Vorrei una borsa di paglia. – Mi spiace, le abbiamo esaurite.* I'd like a straw bag. – I'm sorry, we've sold out of them.
2 to run* out of ◊ *L'aereo aveva esaurito il carburante.* The plane had run out of fuel.

esaurito AGGETTIVO (FEM **esaurita**)
1 sold out ◊ *I biglietti erano tutti esauriti.*

All the tickets were sold out.

[2] run-down ◇ *Sono un po' esaurito.* I'm a bit run-down.

esausto AGGETTIVO (FEM **esausta**)
exhausted ◇ *Sono esausta!* I'm exhausted!

esca NOME FEM (PL le **esche**)
bait

eschimese NOME MASC/FEM, AGGETTIVO
Eskimo

esclamativo AGGETTIVO (FEM **esclamativa**)
• **punto esclamativo** exclamation mark

esclamazione NOME FEM
exclamation

escludere* VERBO
to exclude ◇ *È stato escluso dalla gara.* He was excluded from the competition.

esclusivamente AVVERBIO
[1] entirely ◇ *La colpa è esclusivamente tua.* The fault is entirely yours.
[2] exclusively ◇ *Non è una professione esclusivamente femminile.* It's not an exclusively female profession.

esclusivo AGGETTIVO (FEM **esclusiva**)
exclusive ◇ *un ristorante esclusivo* an exclusive restaurant

escluso AGGETTIVO (FEM **esclusa**)
except ◇ *Tutti lo sapevano, escluso me.* Everybody knew about it, except me.
• **Le bevande sono gratuite, escluse quelle alcoliche.** Drinks, apart from alcoholic ones, are free.
• **Costa cinquecento sterline, escluso l'albergo.** It costs five hundred pounds, not including the hotel.

esecuzione NOME FEM
[1] execution (*di un compito*)
• **È responsabile dell'esecuzione dei lavori.** He's responsible for carrying out the work.
• **esecuzione capitale** execution
[2] performance (*musicale*)

eseguire VERBO
[1] to carry out ◇ *Stava solo eseguendo gli ordini.* He was only carrying out orders.
[2] to perform (*musica*) ◇ *Ha eseguito un valzer di Chopin.* She performed a waltz by Chopin.

esempio NOME MASC
example ◇ *Fammi un esempio.* Give me an example.
• **per esempio** for example

esemplare NOME MASC
specimen ◇ *un esemplare rarissimo* a very rare specimen

esercitare VERBO
[1] to practise
to practice US
(*professione*)
[2] to train (*corpo, mente*)
• **esercitare il proprio controllo su qualcuno** to exert control over somebody
• **esercitarsi** to practise ◇ *esercitarsi nella guida* to practise one's driving

l' **esercito** NOME MASC
army (PL armies)

l' **esercizio** NOME MASC
exercise ◇ *un esercizio di matematica* a maths exercise ◇ *Questi esercizi sviluppano gli addominali.* These exercises develop the abdominal muscles.

esigente AGGETTIVO
demanding ◇ *Il suo capo è molto esigente.* His boss is very demanding.

esigere* VERBO
to demand ◇ *Il proprietario esige il pagamento immediato.* The owner is demanding immediate payment. ◇ *È un lavoro che esige molta concentrazione.* It's a job which demands a lot of concentration.

l' **esilio** NOME MASC
exile ◇ *Vive in esilio da alcuni anni.* He's been living in exile for several years.
• **mandare in esilio** to exile

esistere VERBO
to exist ◇ *Babbo Natale non esiste.* Santa Claus doesn't exist.
• **Non esiste!** (*neanche per sogno*) No way!

esitare VERBO
to hesitate ◇ *Ha esitato prima di rispondere.* He hesitated before answering.

l' **esito** NOME MASC
result ◇ *l'esito degli esami* the exam results al plurale.

l' **esodo** NOME MASC
exodus ◇ *È cominciato l'esodo per le vacanze estive.* The summer holiday exodus has begun.

l' **esordio** NOME MASC
debut ◇ *Questo è il suo esordio in nazionale.* This is his debut in the national team.
• **La sua carriera è ancora agli esordi.** His career is just beginning.

esotico AGGETTIVO (FEM **esotica**, MASC PL **esotici**, FEM PL **esotiche**)
exotic ◇ *frutta esotica* exotic fruit

espellere* VERBO
[1] to expel ◇ *L'hanno espulso dalla scuola.* He was expelled from the school.
[2] to send* off (*nel calcio*) ◇ *Tutt'e due i calciatori sono stati espulsi.* Both players were sent off.

l' **esperienza** NOME FEM
experience ◇ *È stata un'esperienza molto utile.* It was a very useful experience.
• **parlare per esperienza** to speak* from experience

l' **esperimento** NOME MASC
experiment ◇ *esperimenti sugli animali* experiments on animals

l' **esperto,** l' **esperta** NOME MASC, FEM
expert ◇ *un esperto di computer* a computer expert

E

esplicito AGGETTIVO (FEM **esplicita**)
explicit

esplodere* VERBO
to explode ◊ *L'ordigno è esploso uccidendo tre persone.* The bomb exploded, killing three people.

esplorare VERBO
to explore ◊ *Appena arrivati siamo usciti ad esplorare la città.* As soon as we arrived we went out to explore the town.

l' **esplosione** NOME FEM
explosion ◊ *L'esplosione ha distrutto il palazzo.* The explosion destroyed the building.

esporre* VERBO
1 to display ◊ *Ha esposto la merce in vetrina.* He displayed the goods in the window.
2 to explain ◊ *Ha esposto i fatti con grande chiarezza.* She explained the facts very clearly.
3 to show ◊ *Espone i suoi quadri in una galleria d'arte.* He's showing his paintings in an art gallery.
◆ **esporsi al sole** to expose oneself to the sun

esportare VERBO
to export

esposto AGGETTIVO (FEM **esposta**)
◆ **essere esposto a** (*edificio*) to face ◊ *La casa è esposta a nord.* The house faces north.

l' **espressione** NOME FEM
expression ◊ *libertà di espressione* freedom of expression ◊ *Ha usato un'espressione volgare.* He used a coarse expression.

l' **espresso** NOME MASC
1 espresso ◊ *Un espresso e un cappuccino, per favore.* An espresso and a cappuccino, please.
2 express train ◊ *Abbiamo preso l'espresso per Roma.* We took the express train to Rome.
◆ **per espresso** express ◊ *Vorrei spedirlo per espresso.* I'd like to send it express.

esprimere* VERBO
to express ◊ *Ognuno è libero di esprimere il proprio parere.* Everybody's free to express their own opinion.
◆ **esprimere un desiderio** to make* a wish ◊ *Dai, esprimi un desiderio!* Go on, make a wish!
◆ **esprimersi** to express oneself ◊ *Trovo difficile esprimermi in inglese.* I find it difficult to express myself in English.
◆ **esprimersi a gesti** to communicate by gestures

l' **essenziale** NOME MASC
◆ **l'essenziale è...** the main thing is...
◊ *L'essenziale è che tu sia arrivato sano e salvo.* The main thing is that you got here

safe and sound.

essenzialmente AVVERBIO
essentially

essere* VERBO
vedi anche **essere** NOME
1 to be* ◊ *Sono italiana.* I'm Italian. ◊ *Sei sicuro?* Are you sure? ◊ *Chi è?* Who is it? ◊ *È l'una.* It's one o'clock. ◊ *Sono le otto.* It's eight o'clock. ◊ *Siamo in dieci.* There are ten of us. ◊ *È di Manchester.* She's from Manchester. ◊ *È di mio fratello.* It's my brother's. ◊ *Ce ne sono due.* There are two of them. ◊ *Cosa c'è che non va?* What's wrong?
2 to have*
have è l'ausiliare usato per formare i tempi composti in inglese.
◊ *Sono appena arrivato.* I've just arrived. ◊ *Mario è appena partito.* Mario has just left.

l' **essere** NOME MASC
vedi anche **essere** VERBO
◆ **essere umano** human being

essi, esse PRONOME
they

esso, essa PRONOME
it

est NOME MASC, AGGETTIVO
east ◊ *Il vento viene da est.* The wind comes from the east.
◆ **ad est** east ◊ *ad est di Palermo* east of Palermo ◊ *Il sole sorge ad est.* The sun rises in the east.
◆ **ad est di** east of ◊ *Si trova ad est della città.* It's east of the city.
◆ **i paesi dell'Est** Eastern Europe

l' **estate** NOME FEM
summer ◊ *d'estate* in the summer

esteriore AGGETTIVO
◆ **La sua sicurezza è solo esteriore.** He seems confident, but he isn't really.

esterno AGGETTIVO, NOME MASC (FEM **esterna**)
outside ◊ *il muro esterno* the outside wall ◊ *l'esterno del palazzo* the outside of the building

estero AGGETTIVO (FEM **estera**)
vedi anche **estero** NOME
foreign ◊ *Vendono giornali esteri?* Do they sell foreign newspapers?

l' **estero** NOME MASC
vedi anche **estero** AGGETTIVO
◆ **all'estero** abroad ◊ *Non è mai stato all'estero.* He's never been abroad.

l' **estetista** NOME FEM
beautician ◊ *Fa l'estetista.* She is a beautician.

l' **estintore** NOME MASC
fire extinguisher

l' **estinzione** NOME FEM
extinction ◊ *una specie in via di estinzione*

Italian ~ English

a species on the verge of extinction

estivo AGGETTIVO (FEM **estiva**)
summer ◇ *le vacanze estive* the summer holidays
+ *una giornata estiva* a summer's day

estraneo, l' estranea NOME MASC, FEM
stranger ◇ *È difficile parlare di sé con un estraneo.* It's difficult to talk about yourself to a stranger.

estrarre* VERBO
to extract

estremamente AVVERBIO
extremely ◇ *È stato estremamente gentile.* He was extremely kind. ◇ *Mi sarà estremamente difficile poter venire lunedì.* It'll be extremely difficult for me to come on Monday.

estremità NOME FEM (PL le **estremità**)
end ◇ *C'è una scala alle due estremità del corridoio.* There are stairs at both ends of the corridor.

estremo AGGETTIVO, NOME MASC (FEM **estrema**)
extreme ◇ *l'estrema destra* the extreme right ◇ *Passa da un estremo all'altro.* She goes from one extreme to the other.
+ **l'Estremo Oriente** the Far East

estroverso AGGETTIVO (FEM **estroversa**)
outgoing ◇ *Claudia è molto estroversa.* Claudia's very outgoing.

età NOME FEM (PL le **età**)
age ◇ *Sandra ha la mia età.* Sandra's the same age as me.
+ **di mezza età** middle-aged

eternità NOME FEM
eternity ◇ *È durato pochi minuti ma mi è sembrato un'eternità.* It only lasted a few minutes but it seemed like an eternity.

etichetta NOME FEM
label ◇ *Si è staccata l'etichetta.* The label's come off.

etto NOME MASC
one hundred grams ◇ *Ci vogliono tre etti di farina.* You need three hundred grams of flour.

euro NOME MASC (PL gli **euro**)
euro ◇ *dieci euro* ten euros

euroconvertitore NOME MASC
euro-converter

Europa NOME FEM
Europe

europeo, europea NOME, AGGETTIVO
European ◇ *l'Unione Europea* the European Union

evadere* VERBO
to escape ◇ *Sono evasi dal carcere.* They escaped from prison.

eventuale AGGETTIVO
any ◇ *Siamo assicurati contro eventuali danni.* We're insured against any damage. ◇ *Per eventuali domande rivolgersi a...* If you have any queries contact...
Attenzione! In inglese esiste la parola eventual, che però significa finale.

eventualmente AVVERBIO
by any chance ◇ *Se eventualmente cambiassi idea, sai dove trovarci.* If by any chance you change your mind, you know where to find us.
Qualche volta eventualmente non si traduce.
+ **Eventualmente potremmo sempre andare in treno.** We could always go by train.
Attenzione! In inglese esiste la parola eventually, che però significa alla fine.

evidente AGGETTIVO
obvious ◇ *Era evidente che non voleva venire.* It was obvious he didn't want to come.

evidentemente AVVERBIO
obviously ◇ *Era evidentemente seccato.* He was obviously annoyed. ◇ *Evidentemente avevo capito male.* I obviously misunderstood.

evitare VERBO
to avoid ◇ *Passiamo di qui per evitare il traffico.* We're going this way to avoid the traffic.
+ **evitare di fare qualcosa** to avoid doing something
to avoid regge sempre il gerundio.
◇ *Evita di uscire da sola la notte.* Avoid going out alone at night.

evviva ESCLAMAZIONE
hurrah!

ex AGGETTIVO, NOME MASC/FEM (MASC, FEM, PL **ex**)
former ◇ *l'ex Primo ministro* the former Prime Minister
+ **il mio ex** my ex

extra AGGETTIVO (MASC, FEM, PL **extra**)
vedi anche **extra** NOME MASC
extra ◇ *una spesa extra* an extra expense

l' extra NOME MASC (PL gli **extra**)
vedi anche **extra** AGGETTIVO ◇ *Nel conto c'erano molti extra.* There were a lot of extras on the bill.

extracomunitario AGGETTIVO (FEM **extracomunitaria**)
vedi anche **extracomunitario** NOME
+ **i paesi extracomunitari** countries outside the European Union

l' extracomunitario, l' extracomunitaria NOME MASC, FEM
vedi anche **extracomunitario** AGGETTIVO
+ **gli extracomunitari** people from outside the European Union

extraterrestre NOME MASC/FEM, AGGETTIVO
extraterrestrial

E

F

il **fa** NOME MASC (PL i **fa**)
> *vedi anche* **fa** AVVERBIO

F (*nota*)

fa AVVERBIO
> *vedi anche* **fa** NOME

ago ◇ *L'ho incontrata due ore fa.* I met her two hours ago.

ago non si usa mai con il "present perfect".

la **fabbrica** NOME FEM (PL le **fabbriche**)
factory (PL factories)
Attenzione! In inglese esiste la parola **fabric**, *che però significa* **tessuto**.

fabbricare VERBO
to make* (*produrre*) ◇ *È fabbricato in Cina.* It's made in China.

la **faccenda** NOME FEM
matter ◇ *È una faccenda complicata.* It's a complicated matter.
- **Devo sbrigare alcune faccende.** I've got a few things to do.
- **faccende domestiche** housework SING

il **facchino** NOME MASC
porter

la **faccia** NOME FEM (PL le **facce**)
face ◇ *Cosa ti sei messa in faccia?* What have you got on your face?
- **faccia a faccia** face to face
- **avere faccia tosta** to have* a cheek ◇ *Hai una bella faccia tosta!* You've got a real cheek!

la **facciata** NOME FEM
[1] façade (*di palazzo*)
[2] side (*di foglio*) ◇ *Scrivi su entrambe le facciate.* Write on both sides.

facile AGGETTIVO
[1] easy ◇ *Non era facile come pensavo.* It wasn't as easy as I thought. ◇ *Il francese è più facile del tedesco.* French is easier than German. ◇ *È la lezione più facile del libro.* It's the easiest exercise in the book.
[2] likely ◇ *È facile che piova.* It's likely to rain. ◇ *È facile che venga.* He's likely to come.

la **facoltà** NOME FEM (PL le **facoltà**)
department ◇ *È iscritta alla facoltà di legge.* She's a student in the law department.

facoltativo AGGETTIVO (FEM **facoltativa**)
optional ◇ *un corso facoltativo* an optional course
- **una fermata facoltativa** a request stop

il **faggio** NOME MASC
beech

i **fagiolini** NOME MASC PL
French beans

il **fagiolo** NOME MASC
bean

il **fai-da-te** NOME MASC
DIY (*do-it-yourself*)

il **falco** NOME MASC (PL i **falchi**)
hawk

il **falegname** NOME MASC
carpenter ◇ *Mio padre fa il falegname.* My father is a carpenter.

il **fallimento** NOME MASC
[1] bankruptcy (PL bankruptcies) ◇ *Molte aziende rischiavano il fallimento.* Many firms were facing bankruptcy.
- **andare in fallimento** to go* bankrupt
[2] failure ◇ *È stato un fallimento totale.* It was a total failure.

fallire VERBO
[1] to go* bankrupt ◇ *La ditta è fallita.* The firm has gone bankrupt.
[2] to fail (*non riuscire*) ◇ *Il nostro piano è destinato a fallire.* Our plan is bound to fail.
[3] to miss (*mancare*) ◇ *Sampras ha fallito il colpo.* Sampras missed the ball.

il **fallo** NOME MASC
foul (*nello sport*) ◇ *È stato espulso per un fallo sul portiere.* He was sent off for a foul on the goalkeeper.
- **mettere il piede in fallo** to lose* one's footing ◇ *Ha messo il piede in fallo ed è caduto.* He lost his footing and fell.
- **cogliere qualcuno in fallo** to catch* somebody out ◇ *Mi ha colto in fallo.* He caught me out.

il **falò** NOME MASC (PL i **falò**)
bonfire

falsificare VERBO
to forge (*firma*)

falso AGGETTIVO (FEM **falsa**)
> *vedi anche* **falso** NOME

[1] false ◇ *un nome falso* a false name
[2] forged (*denaro, documenti*) ◇ *Aveva un passaporto falso.* He had a forged passport.
[3] fake (*pietra, gioiello*) ◇ *un diamante falso* a fake diamond

il **falso** NOME MASC
> *vedi anche* **falso** AGGETTIVO

fake (*quadro, opera d'arte*) ◇ *Il quadro era un falso.* The painting was a fake.

la **fama** NOME FEM
[1] fame ◇ *Voglio fama e successo.* I want fame and success.
- **un attore di fama mondiale** a world-famous actor
[2] reputation ◇ *Ha una cattiva fama.* He's got a bad reputation.

la **fame** NOME FEM
hunger ◇ *il problema della fame nel terzo mondo* the problem of hunger in the Third World
- **avere fame** to be* hungry ◇ *Hai fame?* Are you hungry?
- **morire di fame** to be* starving

---

* *I verbi seguiti da questo simbolo sono irregolari. Si veda anche alle pp.328–338.*

F

famiglia NOME FEM
family (PL families) ◇ *Viene da una famiglia numerosa.* He comes from a large family.

familiare AGGETTIVO
vedi anche **familiare** NOME
familiar ◇ *un viso familiare* a familiar face

familiare NOME MASC/FEM
vedi anche **familiare** AGGETTIVO
relative (*parente*) ◇ *Va in vacanza con dei familiari.* He's going on holiday with relatives.

famoso AGGETTIVO (FEM **famosa**)
famous

fanatico AGGETTIVO (FEM **fanatica**, MASC PL **fanatici**, FEM PL **fanatiche**)
vedi anche **fanatico** NOME
◆ **essere fanatico di** to be* mad about ◇ *È fanatico di calcio.* He's mad about football.

fanatico, la fanatica NOME MASC, FEM (MASC PL i **fanatici**, FEM PL le **fanatiche**)
vedi anche **fanatico** AGGETTIVO
fanatic ◇ *È un fanatico della pallacanestro.* He's a basketball fanatic.

fango NOME MASC (PL i **fanghi**)
mud ◇ *Ero coperto di fango.* I was covered with mud.
◆ **farsi* i fanghi** to have a mud treatment

fannullone, la fannullona NOME MASC, FEM
layabout

fantascienza NOME FEM
science fiction ◇ *un film di fantascienza* a science fiction film

fantasia NOME FEM
[1] imagination ◇ *Non hai fantasia.* You've got no imagination.
[2] pattern (*su stoffa*) ◇ *Non mi piace questa fantasia.* I don't like this pattern.
◆ **camicia fantasia** patterned shirt

fantasma NOME MASC (PL i **fantasmi**)
ghost

fantastico AGGETTIVO (FEM **fantastica**, MASC PL **fantastici**, FEM PL **fantastiche**)
great ◇ *È una festa fantastica.* It's a great party. ◇ *Fantastico!* Great!

fantino NOME MASC
jockey

fare* VERBO
Quando si usa to do e quando to make? Leggi gli esempi per orientarti.
[1] to make* ◇ *Ho fatto un errore.* I made a mistake. ◇ *Posso fare una telefonata?* Can I make a phone call? ◇ *Due più due fa quattro.* Two and two makes four.
[2] to do* ◇ *Ho già fatto i compiti.* I've already done my homework. ◇ *Cosa fai stasera?* What are you doing this evening? ◇ *Cosa stai facendo?* What are you doing? ◇ *Cosa fa tuo padre?* What does your father do? ◇ *Abbiamo fatto cinque chilometri.* We did five kilometres. ◇ *Non farlo.* Don't do it.
◆ **andare a fare qualcosa** to go* and do

something ◇ *Andiamo a fare la spesa.* Let's go and do some shopping.
[3] to be* ◇ *Fa il medico.* He is a doctor.
◇ *Fa caldo.* It's hot. ◇ *Fa freddo.* It's cold.
◇ *Le ha fatto da madre* She was like a mother to her.
[4] to have* (*vacanza, sogno, pausa*)
◇ *Vorrei fare una vacanza.* I'd like to have a holiday.
◆ **far fare qualcosa** to have* something done ◇ *Ho fatto riparare la macchina.* I had the car repaired.
◆ **far fare qualcosa a qualcuno** to make* somebody do something ◇ *Mi ha fatto riordinare la camera.* She made me tidy up my room. ◇ *Mi ha fatto ridere.* He made me laugh.
◆ **Lascia stare, lo farò fare a lui.** Don't bother, I'll get him to do it.
◆ **farsi* fare qualcosa** to have* something done ◇ *Mi sono fatta tagliare i capelli.* I had my hair cut.
◆ **fare un passeggiata** to go* for a walk
◆ **fare un viaggio** to go* on a trip
◆ **Fammi vedere.** Let me see.
◆ **Non fa niente.** It doesn't matter.
◆ **farcela** to do* it ◇ *Ce l'abbiamo fatta!* We did it!
◆ **Ce la fai?** Can you manage?
◆ **Non ce la faremo ad arrivare in tempo.** We won't make it in time.
◆ **Non ce la faccio più. (1)** (*a camminare*) I can't go on any further.
◆ **Non ce la faccio più. (2)** (*a sopportare*) I can't take it any more.
◆ **farsi** (*drogarsi*) to do* drugs

la farfalla NOME FEM
butterfly (PL butterflies) ◇ *i cento metri farfalla* the hundred metres butterfly

la farina NOME FEM
flour

la farmacia NOME FEM (PL le **farmacie**)
chemist's
druggist's US
◇ *Sto andando in farmacia.* I'm going to the chemist's.
◆ **farmacia di turno** duty chemist

il/la farmacista NOME MASC/FEM (MASC PL i **farmacisti**, FEM PL le **farmaciste**)
chemist

il faro NOME MASC
lighthouse (*edificio*)
◆ **fari** (*di macchina*) headlights ◇ *Accendi i fari.* Switch on your headlights.

la fascia NOME FEM (PL le **fasce**)
bandage (*per medicare*) ◇ *una fascia elastica* a crepe bandage

fasciare VERBO
to bandage ◇ *Gli hanno fasciato il ginocchio.* They bandaged his knee.

il fascicolo NOME MASC
file (*in ufficio*)

il **fascino** NOME MASC
charm ◇ *una donna di gran fascino* a
woman of great charm

la **fase** NOME FEM
phase

il **fastidio** NOME MASC
* **dare fastidio a qualcuno (1)** (*irritare*) to get*
on somebody's nerves ◇ *Smettila! Mi dai
fastidio!* Stop it! You're getting on my
nerves!
* **Il suo modo di fare mi dà fastidio.** I find his
manner irritating.
* **dare fastidio a qualcuno (2)** (*seccare*) to
bother somebody ◇ *Ti dà fastidio il rumore?*
Is the noise bothering you? ◇ *La caviglia mi
dà ancora fastidio.* My ankle is still
bothering me.
* **Le dà fastidio se fumo?** Do you mind if I
smoke?

fastidioso AGGETTIVO (FEM **fastidiosa**)
annoying ◇ *È un bambino fastidioso.* He's
an annoying child.
* **un dolore fastidioso** a nagging pain
Attenzione! In inglese esiste la parola
fastidious*, che però significa* **pignolo**.

la **fata** NOME FEM
fairy (PL fairies)

fatale AGGETTIVO
fatal ◇ *un errore fatale* a fatal mistake

la **fatica** NOME FEM (PL le **fatiche**)
effort ◇ *Ci vuole tempo e fatica.* It takes time
and effort.
* **Che fatica!** It's hard work!
* **L'ho convinto a fatica.** It was hard work
convincing him.
* **fare fatica a fare qualcosa** to find* it difficult
to do something ◇ *Faccio fatica a capire la
matematica.* I find it difficult to understand
maths.

faticoso AGGETTIVO (FEM **faticosa**)
tiring

fatto AGGETTIVO (FEM **fatta**)
vedi anche **fatto** NOME
[1] made
* **fatto a mano** handmade
* **fatto in casa** home-made
[2] stoned (*drogato, ubriaco*) ◇ *È
completamente fatto.* He's completely
stoned.

il **fatto** NOME MASC
vedi anche **fatto** AGGETTIVO
fact ◇ *I fatti parlano chiaro.* The facts speak
for themselves. ◇ *Il fatto è che ha ragione
lui.* The fact is that he's right.
* **È successo un fatto strano.** Something
strange happened.
* **un fatto di cronaca** a news item
* **cogliere qualcuno sul fatto** to catch*
somebody red-handed ◇ *Li hanno colti sul
fatto.* They caught them red-handed.

* **Pensa ai fatti tuoi!** Mind your own business!

la **fattoria** NOME FEM
farm
Attenzione! In inglese esiste la parola
factory*, che però significa* **fabbrica**.

il **fattorino** NOME MASC
errand boy

la **fattura** NOME FEM
invoice (*commerciale*)

la **fava** NOME FEM
broad bean

la **favola** NOME FEM
fairy tale

favoloso AGGETTIVO (FEM **favolosa**)
fabulous ◇ *una casa favolosa* a fabulous
house

il **favore** NOME MASC
favour
favor US
* **fare un favore a qualcuno** to do* somebody
a favour ◇ *Mi faresti un favore?* Would you
do me a favour?
* **chiedere un favore a qualcuno** to ask
somebody a favour ◇ *Posso chiederti un
favore?* Can I ask you a favour?
* **per favore** please

il **fax** NOME MASC (PL i **fax**)
fax ◇ *Gli ho mandato un fax.* I sent him a
fax.

il **fazzoletto** NOME MASC
handkerchief (*di stoffa*)
* **fazzoletto di carta** tissue

il **febbraio** NOME MASC
February
Si noti l'uso della maiuscola in inglese.
◇ *in febbraio* in February

la **febbre** NOME FEM
temperature
* **avere la febbre** to have* a temperature
◇ *Hai la febbre?* Have you got a
temperature?

la **fede** NOME FEM
[1] faith
* **in buona fede** in good faith ◇ *Ho agito in
buona fede.* I acted in good faith.
[2] wedding ring (*anello*)

fedele AGGETTIVO
faithful ◇ *un marito fedele* a faithful
husband
* **essere fedele a** to be* faithful to ◇ *Gli è
sempre stata fedele.* She's always been
faithful to him.

la **federa** NOME FEM
pillowcase

il **fegato** NOME MASC
liver ◇ *Non mi piace il fegato.* I don't like
liver.
* **Ha fegato!** He's got guts!

la **felce** NOME FEM
fern

* I verbi seguiti da questo simbolo sono irregolari. Si veda anche alle pp.328–338.

felice AGGETTIVO
  happy ◇ *Adesso sono più felice.* I'm
  happier now. ◇ *È stato il giorno più felice
  della mia vita.* It was the happiest day of my
  life.

felicità NOME FEM
  happiness

felpa NOME FEM
  sweatshirt

femmina NOME FEM
  | vedi anche **femmina** AGGETTIVO |
  girl (*figlia*) ◇ *Ha un maschio e una femmina.*
  She has a boy and a girl.

femmina AGGETTIVO
  | vedi anche **femmina** NOME |
  female ◇ *una giraffa femmina* a female
  giraffe

femminile AGGETTIVO
  feminine ◇ *È molto femminile.* She's very
  feminine.
  ◆ *una rivista femminile* a women's magazine

il femore NOME MASC
  femur

il fenomeno NOME MASC
  phenomenon (PL phenomena) ◇ *un
  fenomeno inspiegabile* an inexplicable
  phenomenon

feriale AGGETTIVO
  ◆ *giorno feriale* week day

ferie NOME FEM PL
  holiday SING ◇ *Ho due settimane di ferie.* I
  have two weeks' holiday.
  ◆ *un giorno di ferie* a day off
  ◆ *andare in ferie* to go* on holiday ◇ *Dove vai
  in ferie?* Where are you going on holiday?
  ◆ *prendere un giorno di ferie* to take* a day off
  ◇ *Ho preso un giorno di ferie.* I took a day
  off.

ferire VERBO
  1 to injure (*in generale*) ◇ *La bomba ha
  ferito tre persone.* The bomb injured three
  people.
  ◆ *Mi sono ferito ad una mano.* I've hurt my
  hand.
  2 to wound (*con arma*) ◇ *Il soldato è stato
  ferito ad una gamba.* The soldier was
  wounded in the leg.

la ferita NOME FEM
  1 injury (PL injuries) ◇ *La sue ferite non
  erano gravi.* His injuries were not serious.
  2 wound (*con arma*)

il ferito NOME MASC
  casualty (PL casualties) ◇ *Hanno portato i
  feriti all'ospedale.* The casualties were taken
  to hospital.
  ◆ *Nell'incidente ci sono stati due feriti.* Two
  people were injured in the accident.

il fermaglio NOME MASC
  1 clasp (*di collana, di braccialetto*)
  2 clip (*per documenti, per capelli*)

fermare VERBO

to stop* ◇ *Non cercare di fermarmi.* Don't
try and stop me.
  ◆ **fermarsi** to stop* ◇ *Fermati!* Stop!
  ◇ *L'orologio si è fermato alle tre e cinque.*
  The clock stopped at five past three. ◇ *Mi
  sono fermato a salutarla.* I stopped to say
  hello to her.

la fermata NOME FEM
  stop ◇ *la fermata dell'autobus* the bus stop
  ◆ *una fermata a richiesta* a request stop

fermo AGGETTIVO (FEM **ferma**)
  still
  ◆ *stare fermo* to keep* still ◇ *Non sta fermo
  un attimo.* He can't keep still for a minute.
  ◆ *Fermo!* Don't move!
  ◆ *Ero fermo al semaforo.* I was waiting at the
  traffic lights.
  ◆ *La macchina era ferma in mezzo alla strada.*
  The car had stopped in the middle of the
  road.
  ◆ *Il treno era fermo in stazione.* The train was
  standing in the station.
  ◆ *Quell'orologio è fermo.* That clock has
  stopped.

il ferragosto NOME MASC
  August fifteenth

  > **ⓘ** In Italy **August 15** is a public holiday. Many
  > shops, restaurants and businesses are
  > closed on this day for a week or so.

il ferro NOME MASC
  iron
  ◆ *di ferro* iron ◇ *una sbarra di ferro* an iron
  bar
  ◆ *ferro battuto* wrought iron
  ◆ *ferro da stiro* iron
  ◆ *ai ferri* (*cibo*) grilled ◇ *una bistecca ai ferri* a
  grilled steak
  ◆ *ferro di cavallo* horseshoe
  ◆ *Tocca ferro!* Touch wood!

  > **ⓘ** Italians touch iron, rather than wood,
  > when they are hoping for good luck.

la ferrovia NOME FEM
  railway
  railroad US

ferroviario AGGETTIVO (FEM **ferroviaria**)
  railway
  railroad US
  ◇ *la stazione ferroviaria* the railway station

il ferroviere NOME MASC
  railwayman (PL railwaymen)

la fessura NOME FEM
  1 crack (*crepa*)
  2 slot (*per moneta*)

la festa NOME FEM
  1 holiday ◇ *Oggi è festa.* Today's a
  holiday.
  2 party (PL parties) (*ricevimento*) ◇ *Ha dato
  una festa per il suo compleanno.* He gave a ☞

F

party for his birthday.

[3] birthday (*compleanno*) ◇ *Quando è la tua festa?* When is your birthday?

• **festa della mamma** Mother's Day
• **festa del papà** Father's Day

festeggiare VERBO

to celebrate (*compleanno, promozione*)

festivo AGGETTIVO (FEM **festiva**)

• **giorno festivo** holiday
• **"sabato e festivi"** "Saturdays, Sundays and public holidays"

la **fetta** NOME FEM

slice ◇ *una fetta di pane* a slice of bread

• **tagliare a fette** to slice ◇ *Può tagliarmelo a fette?* Can you slice it for me?

la **fiaba** NOME FEM

fairy tale

la **fiala** NOME FEM

phial

la **fiamma** NOME FEM

flame ◇ *La casa è andata in fiamme.* The house went up in flames. ◇ *È una sua vecchia fiamma.* She's an old flame of his.

• **Morì tra le fiamme.** He died in the blaze.

il **fiammifero** NOME MASC

match ◇ *una scatola di fiammiferi* a box of matches

il **fianco** NOME MASC (PL i **fianchi**)

[1] hip ◇ *Ha i fianchi larghi.* She's got wide hips.

[2] side (*lato*) ◇ *Dormo sempre su un fianco.* I always sleep on my side.

• **Starò sempre al tuo fianco.** I'll always stand by you.
• **fianco a fianco** side by side
• **a fianco di** next to ◇ *Si trova a fianco della chiesa.* It's next to the church.

il **fiasco** NOME MASC (PL i **fiaschi**)

bottle ◇ *un fiasco di vino* a bottle of wine

• **essere un fiasco** to be* a fiasco ◇ *La festa è stata un fiasco completo.* The party was a complete fiasco.

fiatare VERBO

• **Non fiatate!** Don't say a word!

il **fiato** NOME MASC

[1] breath ◇ *Sono senza fiato.* I'm out of breath.

• **riprendere fiato** to get* one's breath back ◇ *Mi sono fermato a riprendere fiato.* I stopped to get my breath back.
• **rimanere senza fiato** to be* speechless ◇ *Quando l'ho saputo sono rimasto senza fiato.* I was speechless when I heard about it.
• **tutto d'un fiato** all in one go ◇ *Bevilo tutto d'un fiato.* Drink it all in one go.
• **strumenti a fiato** wind instruments

[2] stamina (*resistenza*) ◇ *Non ho più molto fiato.* I haven't got much stamina these days.

la **fibbia** NOME FEM

buckle

la **fibra** NOME FEM

fibre
fiber US

ficcare VERBO

[1] to put* ◇ *Dove lo hai ficcato?* Where did you put it?

• **Ha ficcato tutti i libri in borsa.** She crammed all the books into her bag.

[2] to stick* (*infilare*) ◇ *Mi ha ficcato un dito nell'occhio.* He stuck his finger in my eye. ◇ *Non ficcare il naso nei miei affari.* Don't stick your nose into my business.

• **ficcarsi** (*andare a finire*) to get* to ◇ *Dove si sarà ficcato?* Where's he got to?

il **fico** NOME MASC (PL i **fichi**)

[1] fig tree (*albero*)

[2] fig (*frutto*)

• **fico d'India** prickly pear
• **fico secco** dried fig

il **fidanzamento** NOME MASC

engagement

fidanzarsi VERBO

to get* engaged ◇ *Si sono appena fidanzati.* They've just got engaged.

la **fidanzata** NOME FEM

fiancée

il **fidanzato** NOME MASC

fiancé

fidarsi VERBO

• **fidarsi di qualcuno** to trust somebody ◇ *Mi fido di lui.* I trust him.
• **Non mi fido.** I'm not sure.

fidato AGGETTIVO (FEM **fidata**)

trustworthy

la **fiducia** NOME FEM

trust ◇ *Ha tradito la nostra fiducia.* He has betrayed our trust.

• **avere fiducia in** to trust ◇ *Ho fiducia in lui.* I trust him.
• **fiducia in se stesso** self-confidence ◇ *Devi avere più fiducia in te stesso.* You should have more self-confidence.
• **una persona di fiducia** a trustworthy person

la **fiera** NOME FEM

fair (*esposizione*)

fiero AGGETTIVO (FEM **fiera**)

proud

• **andare fiero di** to be* proud of ◇ *I suoi vanno molto fieri di lui.* His parents are very proud of him.

la **fifa** NOME FEM

• **avere fifa** to have* the jitters ◇ *Ho fifa.* I've got the jitters.

la **figlia** NOME FEM

daughter

il **figlio** NOME MASC

[1] child (PL children) (*senza specificare il sesso*) ◇ *Aspetta il secondo figlio.* She's expecting her second child. ◇ *Ho due figli.*

---

* *I verbi seguiti da questo simbolo sono irregolari. Si veda anche alle pp.328–338.*

I've got two children. ◇ *Non vuole avere figli.* She doesn't want to have children.
+ **figlio unico** only child
2 **son** (*maschietto*) ◇ *Mio figlio ha sette anni.* My son is seven.

la **figura** NOME FEM
1 **picture** (*illustrazione*) ◇ *Questo libro ha molte figure.* This book has lots of pictures.
2 **impression**
+ **fare una brutta figura** to make* a bad impression ◇ *Ho fatto una brutta figura al colloquio.* I made a bad impression at the interview.
+ **fare una bella figura** to make* a good impression
+ **Che figura!** How embarrassing!

figurarsi VERBO
+ **Ti disturbo? – Ma figurati!** Am I disturbing you? – Not at all!

la **figurina** NOME FEM
picture card

la **fila** NOME FEM
1 **line** ◇ *una fila di alberi* a line of trees
+ **Ci hanno messo in fila per due.** They lined us up in twos.
+ **in fila indiana** in single file
2 **row** (*al cinema, a teatro*) ◇ *Ero seduto in seconda fila.* I was sitting in the second row.
3 **queue** (*coda*) ◇ *C'era una lunga fila alla fermata dell'autobus.* There was a long queue at the bus stop.
+ **fare la fila** to queue

la **filastrocca** NOME FEM (PL le **filastrocche**)
nursery rhyme

il **filetto** NOME MASC
fillet

la **filiale** NOME FEM
branch (*di banca, di negozio*)

il **film** NOME MASC (PL i **film**)
film
movie US

il **filo** NOME MASC
1 **thread** (*di cotone*)
2 **yarn** (*di lana*)
3 **wire** (*elettrico, del telefono*)
+ **filo interdentale** dental floss
+ **filo spinato** barbed wire

il **filone** NOME MASC
baguette (*di pane*)

la **filosofia** NOME FEM
philosophy (PL philosophies)

il **filosofo**, la **filosofa** NOME MASC, FEM
philosopher

il **filtro** NOME MASC
filter

finale AGGETTIVO
vedi anche **finale** NOME MASC, NOME FEM
final

il **finale** NOME MASC
vedi anche **finale** AGGETTIVO, NOME FEM
ending ◇ *Non mi è piaciuto il finale.* I didn't

like the ending.

la **finale** NOME FEM
vedi anche **finale** AGGETTIVO, NOME MASC
final ◇ *Sono entrati in finale.* They reached the final.
+ **la finale di Coppa** the Cup Final

finalmente AVVERBIO
at last ◇ *Finalmente sei arrivato!* You're here at last!

la **finanza** NOME FEM
finance

finché CONGIUNZIONE
1 **until** (*fino a quando*) ◇ *Aspetta finché non sarò tornato.* Wait until I come back.
I verbi che seguono until non vanno al futuro.
2 **as long as** (*per tutto il tempo che*)
◇ *Rimani finché vuoi.* Stay as long as you like.

fine AGGETTIVO
vedi anche **fine** NOME MASC, NOME FEM
1 **thin** (*lamina, carta*)
2 **fine** (*capelli, polvere*)
3 **good** (*vista, udito*)
4 **refined** (*persona*)

il **fine** NOME MASC
vedi anche **fine** AGGETTIVO, NOME FEM
end ◇ *Il fine giustifica i mezzi.* The end justifies the means.
+ **a fin di bene** with good intentions ◇ *L'ho fatto a fin di bene.* I did it with good intentions.
+ **a lieto fine** (*romanzo, film*) with a happy ending ◇ *Mi piacciono le storie a lieto fine.* I like stories with a happy ending.
+ **in fin dei conti** (*tutto sommato*) after all
+ **un secondo fine** an ulterior motive
+ **fine settimana** weekend

la **fine** NOME FEM
vedi anche **fine** AGGETTIVO, **fine** NOME MASC
end ◇ *verso la fine dell'anno* towards the end of the year ◇ *dall'inizio alla fine* from beginning to end
+ **Che fine ha fatto?** What became of him?
+ **alla fine** in the end ◇ *Alla fine lo ha perdonato.* In the end she forgave him.

la **finestra** NOME FEM
window

il **finestrino** NOME MASC
window (*di macchina, di treno*)

fingere* VERBO
to pretend ◇ *Fingiamo di dormire.* Let's pretend we're asleep. ◇ *Ha finto di non conoscermi.* He pretended he didn't recognize me. ◇ *Si è finto ubriaco.* He pretended he was drunk.

finire* VERBO
1 **to finish** ◇ *Non ho ancora finito i compiti.* I haven't finished my homework yet. ◇ *Il film finisce alle dieci.* The film finishes at ten.
+ **finire di fare qualcosa** to finish doing something

to finish *regge sempre il gerundio.*
◊ *Ho finito di leggere il libro.* I've finished reading the book.

[2] **to end** ◊ *L'anno scolastico finisce a giugno.* The school year ends in June.
◊ *Com'è finita la partita?* How did the match end?

[3] **to be* over** ◊ *La festa è finita.* The party's over. ◊ *Tra noi è tutto finito.* It's all over between us.

[4] **to run* out of** (*esaurire*) ◊ *Abbiamo finito il pane.* We've run out of bread.

• **andare a finire** to get* to ◊ *Dov'è andato a finire quel libro?* Where's that book got to?
• **Com'è andata a finire?** What happened in the end?
• **Finiscila!** Stop it!

finlandese AGGETTIVO

vedi anche **finlandese** NOME MASC, NOME FEM
Finnish

il **finlandese** NOME MASC

vedi anche **finlandese** AGGETTIVO, NOME FEM
[1] Finn (*persona*) ◊ *i finlandesi* the Finns
[2] Finnish (*lingua*) ◊ *Parli finlandese?* Do you speak Finnish?

la **finlandese** NOME FEM

vedi anche **finlandese** AGGETTIVO, NOME MASC
Finn (*persona*)

la **Finlandia** NOME FEM
Finland ◊ *Ti è piaciuta la Finlandia?* Did you like Finland? ◊ *Andrò in Finlandia quest'estate.* I'm going to Finland this summer.

fino PREPOSIZIONE
• **fino a (1)** (*tempo*) until ◊ *Resto fino a venerdì.* I'm staying until Friday.
• **Fino a quando puoi rimanere?** How long can you stay?
• **fino a (2)** (*luogo*) as far as ◊ *Vengo con te fino alla chiesa.* I'll come with you as far as the church.

il **finocchio** NOME MASC
fennel

finora AVVERBIO
[1] yet (*nelle frasi negative*) ◊ *Finora non è arrivato.* He hasn't arrived yet.
Si noti la posizione di **yet**.
[2] so far (*nelle frasi positive*) ◊ *Finora abbiamo fatto solo il presente.* So far we've only studied the present tense.

la **finta** NOME FEM
• **far finta** to pretend ◊ *Facciamo finta di dormire.* Let's pretend we're asleep.
• **L'ho detto per finta.** (*per scherzo*) I was only joking.
• **fare una finta** (*nello sport*) to feint

finto AGGETTIVO (FEM **finta**)
[1] false (*denti, barba*)
[2] artificial (*fiori*)
[3] imitation (*cuoio*) ◊ *una giacca in finta*

pelle an imitation leather jacket

il **fiocco** NOME MASC (PL **i fiocchi**)
bow (*di nastro*)
• **un fiocco di neve** a snowflake
• **fiocchi di granturco** cornflakes

il **fioraio**, la **fioraia** NOME MASC, FEM
florist ◊ *Sto andando dal fioraio.* I'm going to the florist's.

il **fiore** NOME MASC
flower ◊ *fiori di campo* wild flowers
• **a fiori** with a flower pattern ◊ *una gonna a fiori* a skirt with a flower pattern
• **fiori** (*nei giochi di carte*) clubs
• **fior di latte** cream

la **fiorentina** NOME FEM
[1] Florentine (*persona*)
[2] T-bone steak (*bistecca*)
Si noti l'uso della maiuscola in inglese.

fiorentino AGGETTIVO, NOME MASC (FEM **fiorentina**)
Florentine (*persona*)
• **i fiorentini** the people of Florence

la **Firenze** NOME FEM
Florence ◊ *Sto andando a Firenze.* I'm going to Florence. ◊ *Vive a Firenze.* He lives in Florence.

la **firma** NOME FEM
signature
Attenzione! In inglese esiste la parola **firm**, *che però significa* **ditta**.

firmare VERBO
to sign ◊ *Dove devo firmare?* Where shall I sign?

firmato AGGETTIVO (FEM **firmata**)
• **un abito firmato** a designer dress

la **fisarmonica** NOME FEM (PL **le fisarmoniche**)
accordion

fiscale AGGETTIVO
• **evasione fiscale** tax evasion

fischiare VERBO
[1] to whistle ◊ *Sai fischiare?* Can you whistle?
• **fischiare un rigore** to give* a penalty
[2] to boo ◊ *Il pubblico lo ha fischiato.* The audience booed him.

il **fischietto** NOME MASC
whistle

il **fischio** NOME MASC
whistle ◊ *il fischio dell'arbitro* the referee's whistle
• **fare un fischio** to whistle

il **fisco** NOME MASC
tax authorities PL

la **fisica** NOME FEM
physics SING

fisico AGGETTIVO (FEM **fisica**, MASC PL **fisici**, FEM PL **fisiche**)
vedi anche **fisico** NOME
physical ◊ *il contatto fisico* physical contact
• **educazione fisica** physical education

---

* *I verbi seguiti da questo simbolo sono irregolari. Si veda anche alle pp.328–338.*

◆ aspetto fisico appearance

il **fisico** NOME MASC (PL i **fisici**)
vedi anche **fisico** AGGETTIVO
[1] physique (*corporatura: uomo*) ◇ *Ha un bel fisico.* He has a good physique.
[2] figure (*donna*) ◇ *Ha un bel fisico.* She has a good figure.
[3] physicist (*studioso*) ◇ *un fisico nucleare* a nuclear physicist

la **fisioterapia** NOME FEM
physiotherapy

la **fisioterapista** NOME MASC/FEM (MASC PL i **fisioterapisti**, FEM PL le **fisioterapiste**)
physiotherapist

fissare VERBO
[1] to fix ◇ *È fissato al muro.* It's fixed to the wall. ◇ *Hai fissato la data?* Have you fixed the date?
[2] to book (*prenotare*) ◇ *Ho fissato una stanza per lunedì.* I've booked a room for Monday.
[3] to stare at (*guardare*) ◇ *Non fissarlo tutto il tempo.* Don't keep staring at him.

fisso AGGETTIVO (FEM **fissa**)
fixed ◇ *prezzo fisso* fixed price
◆ un lavoro fisso a permanent job
◆ uno stipendio fisso a regular income
◆ un ragazzo fisso a steady boyfriend

la **fitta** NOME FEM
sharp pain ◇ *A volte ho delle fitte al petto.* I sometimes get sharp pains in my chest.

fitto AGGETTIVO (FEM **fitta**)
thick (*bosco, nebbia*)
◆ È buio fitto. It's pitch dark.

il **fiume** NOME MASC
river

il **flagrante** NOME MASC
◆ cogliere qualcuno in flagrante to catch* somebody red-handed ◇ *Hanno colto il ladro in flagrante.* They caught the burglar red-handed.

il **flauto** NOME MASC
◆ flauto traverso flute
◆ flauto dolce recorder

flessibile AGGETTIVO
flexible (*persona, materiale*)
◆ orario flessibile flexitime

la **flessione** NOME FEM
[1] knee-bend (*sulle gambe*)
[2] forward bend (*in piedi*)
[3] sit-up (*da seduto*)
[4] press-up (*sulle braccia*)

il **flipper** NOME MASC (PL i **flipper**)
pinball machine

la **flotta** NOME FEM
fleet

il **fluoro** NOME MASC
◆ un dentifricio al fluoro a fluoride toothpaste

la **foca** NOME FEM (PL le **foche**)
seal

la **foce** NOME FEM

mouth ◇ *la foce del Po* the mouth of the Po

la **fodera** NOME FEM
[1] lining (*di vestito*)
[2] cover (*di divano, di poltrona*)

la **foglia** NOME FEM
leaf (PL leaves)

il **foglio** NOME MASC
sheet (*di carta*)
◆ un foglio a righe a sheet of lined paper
◆ foglio elettronico (*in informatica*) spreadsheet
◆ foglio rosa (*per guidare*) provisional licence

la **fogna** NOME FEM
sewer

il **föhn** NOME MASC (PL i **föhn**)
hair dryer

la **folla** NOME FEM
crowd

folle AGGETTIVO
mad (*persona, idea*)
◆ in folle in neutral ◇ *Assicurati che sia in folle.* Make sure it's in neutral.

la **follia** NOME FEM
madness ◇ *in un momento di follia* in a moment of madness
◆ È una follia! It's crazy!
◆ amare qualcuno alla follia to be* madly in love with somebody ◇ *Lo amo alla follia.* I'm madly in love with him.
◆ costare una follia to cost* the earth ◇ *La sua macchina nuova dev'essere costata una follia.* His new car must have cost the earth.

folto AGGETTIVO (FEM **folta**)
thick (*capelli, bosco*)

il **fon** NOME MASC (PL i **fon**)
hair dryer

le **fondamenta** NOME FEM PL
foundations

fondamentale AGGETTIVO
fundamental

fondente AGGETTIVO
◆ cioccolato fondente plain chocolate

fondo AGGETTIVO (FEM **fonda**)
vedi anche **fondo** NOME
deep ◇ *Qui l'acqua è fonda.* The water is deep here. ◇ *una buca fonda tre metri* a hole three metres deep
◆ un piatto fondo a soup dish

il **fondo** NOME MASC
vedi anche **fondo** AGGETTIVO
[1] bottom ◇ *il fondo del bicchiere* the bottom of the glass
◆ in fondo a at the bottom of ◇ *in fondo al mare* at the bottom of the sea
◆ andare a fondo to sink* ◇ *La nave è andata a fondo.* The ship sank.
◆ in fondo alla strada at the end of the street
◆ in fondo alla sala at the back of the room
◆ laggiù in fondo (1) (*lontano*) over there
◆ laggiù in fondo (2) (*in profondità*) down there

[2] background (*sfondo*) ◊ *bianco su fondo nero* white on a black background
[3] fund (*somma di denaro*)
- **in fondo** (*tutto sommato*) after all
- **in fondo in fondo** deep down
- **conoscere a fondo** to know* inside out
  ◊ *Conosco a fondo la materia.* I know this subject inside out.
- **dar fondo a** (*provviste, risparmi*) to use up
  ◊ *Abbiamo dato fondo alle provviste.* We've used up all the food.
- **sci di fondo** cross-country skiing

il **fondotinta** NOME MASC (PL i **fondotinta**)
foundation

la **fonetica** NOME FEM
phonetics SING

la **fontana** NOME FEM
fountain

la **fonte** NOME FEM
source ◊ *una fonte di informazioni* a source of information

forare VERBO
to punch (*biglietto*)
- **Abbiamo forato.** We've got a puncture.

le **forbici** NOME FEM PL
scissors ◊ *un paio di forbici* a pair of scissors

la **forchetta** NOME FEM
fork

la **forcina** NOME FEM
hairpin

la **foresta** NOME FEM
forest ◊ *foresta pluviale* rain forest

la **forfora** NOME FEM
dandruff

la **forma** NOME FEM
[1] shape ◊ *Di che forma è?* What shape is it?
senza preposizione.
  ◊ *a forma di cuore* heart-shaped
[2] form ◊ *una forma rara di cancro* a rare form of cancer
- **essere in forma** to be* in good form ◊ *Era in ottima forma e ha segnato tre gol.* He was in great form and scored three goals.
- **non essere in forma** to be* off form ◊ *La squadra non era in forma.* The team was off form.
- **tenersi in forma** to keep* fit ◊ *Mi tengo in forma nuotando tutti i giorni.* I keep fit by swimming every day.

il **formaggio** NOME MASC
cheese ◊ *un panino al formaggio* a cheese sandwich

formale AGGETTIVO
formal

formare VERBO
[1] to form ◊ *Abbiamo formato un gruppo.* We formed a group.
- **formare una famiglia** to start a family

- **formarsi** to form ◊ *Si è formata la fila allo sportello.* A queue formed at the counter.
[2] to dial* (*numero di telefono*) ◊ *Sollevate il ricevitore prima di formare il numero.* Lift the receiver before dialling the number.

il **formato** NOME MASC
size ◊ *formato A4* A4 size ◊ *una confezione formato gigante* a giant-size pack

la **formazione** NOME FEM
[1] training ◊ *un corso di formazione professionale* a vocational training course
[2] line-up (*di squadra sportiva*)

la **formica** NOME FEM (PL le **formiche**)
ant

la **formula** NOME FEM
formula

il **fornaio**, la **fornaia** NOME MASC, FEM
baker

il **fornello** NOME MASC
- **fornello a gas (1)** (*di cucina*) gas ring
- **fornello a gas (2)** (*da campeggio*) camping stove
- **fornello elettrico** hotplate

fornire VERBO
- **fornire qualcosa a qualcuno** to supply somebody with something ◊ *Ci forniscono le materie prime.* They supply us with raw materials.
- **Ci ha fornito tutte le informazioni necessarie.** He gave us all the necessary information.

il **forno** NOME MASC
[1] oven (*di cucina*) ◊ *Metti la torta nel forno.* Put the cake in the oven.
- **pollo al forno** roast chicken
- **forno a microonde** microwave oven
[2] bakery (PL bakeries) (*panetteria*)

il **foro** NOME MASC
hole

forse AVVERBIO
maybe ◊ *Forse hai ragione.* Maybe you're right. ◊ *Forse dovremmo andarcene.* Maybe we should leave. ◊ *Verrà? – Non so. Forse.* Will he come? – I don't know. Maybe.

forte AGGETTIVO
vedi anche **forte** AVVERBIO
[1] strong ◊ *un vento forte* a strong wind
  ◊ *È più forte di me.* He's stronger than me.
- **un forte fumatore** a heavy smoker
- **il piatto forte** the main dish
[2] hard (*violento*) ◊ *un forte colpo in testa* a hard knock on the head
[3] bad (*mal di testa, raffreddore*) ◊ *Ho un forte mal di testa.* I've got a bad headache.
[4] loud ◊ *un rumore forte* a loud noise
[5] good (*bravo*) ◊ *È proprio forte!* He's really good!
- **essere forte in qualcosa** to be* good at something ◊ *È forte in matematica.* She's good at maths.

forte AVVERBIO

vedi anche **forte** AGGETTIVO

1 fast ◇ *Correva forte.* He was running fast.

2 hard ◇ *Ha picchiato forte la testa.* She hit her head hard.

3 loud ◇ *Non parlare così forte.* Don't speak so loud. ◇ *Potresti parlare più forte?* Could you speak louder?

4 tight ◇ *Tieniti forte!* Hold tight!

la **fortezza** NOME FEM
fortress

la **fortuna** NOME FEM

1 luck ◇ *Buona fortuna!* Good luck!

+ **portare fortuna** to bring* good luck ◇ *Mi ha sempre portato fortuna.* It's always brought me good luck.

+ **avere fortuna** to be* lucky

+ **per fortuna** luckily ◇ *Per fortuna sei arrivato in tempo.* Luckily, you arrived in time.

+ **atterraggio di fortuna** emergency landing

2 fortune (*ricchezza*) ◇ *Costa una fortuna.* It costs a fortune.

fortunato AGGETTIVO (FEM **fortunata**)
lucky ◇ *Sei più fortunato di me.* You're luckier than me. ◇ *È la persona più fortunata che conosca.* She's the luckiest person I know.

il **foruncolo** NOME MASC
boil

la **forza** NOME FEM

1 force ◇ *la forza dell'esplosione* the force of the explosion

2 strength SING ◇ *È per misurare la forza dei muscoli.* It's to test the strength of the muscles. ◇ *la forza del vento* the strength of the wind ◇ *Ha riacquistato presto le forze.* He quickly regained his strength.

+ **Ha molta forza.** He's very strong.

+ **Forza!** Come on!

+ **Per forza!** (*naturalmente*) Obviously!

+ **Mi ha costretto con la forza.** He forced me to do it.

+ **Lo ha fatto per forza.** He was forced to do it.

+ **Perderai la voce a forza di gridare.** You'll lose your voice if you shout so much.

+ **forza di volontà** willpower

+ **le forze armate** the armed forces

forzare VERBO
to force ◇ *La serratura è stata forzata.* The lock has been forced.

la **foschia** NOME FEM

+ **Oggi c'è molta foschia.** It's very hazy today.

la **fossa** NOME FEM
pit

la **fossetta** NOME FEM
dimple

il **fosso** NOME MASC
ditch

la **foto** NOME FEM (PL le **foto**)
photo ◇ *una foto in bianco e nero* a black and white photo

+ **fare una foto** to take* a photo ◇ *Ha fatto molte foto.* He took a lot of photos.

la **fotocopia** NOME FEM
photocopy (PL photocopies)

fotocopiare VERBO
to photocopy

la **fotocopiatrice** NOME FEM
photocopier

fotografare VERBO
to photograph

la **fotografia** NOME FEM
photograph ◇ *una fotografia a colori* a colour photograph

+ **un corso di fotografia** a photography course

fotografico AGGETTIVO (FEM **fotografica**, MASC PL **fotografici**, FEM PL **fotografiche**)

+ **macchina fotografica** camera

+ **servizio fotografico** (*per giornale*) photo feature

il **fotografo**, la **fotografa** NOME MASC, FEM
photographer

il **fotoromanzo** NOME MASC
photo love story (PL photo love stories)

la **fototessera** NOME FEM
passport-size photo

il **foulard** NOME MASC (PL i **foulard**)
scarf (PL scarves)

fra PREPOSIZIONE

1 between (*tra due*) ◇ *Era seduto fra il padre e lo zio.* He was sitting between his father and his uncle. ◇ *Detto fra noi, non piace neanche a me.* Between you and me, I don't like it either.

2 among (*tra più di due*) ◇ *Fra i feriti c'era anche il pilota dell'aereo.* The pilot of the plane was among the injured.

3 in (*in espressioni di tempo*) ◇ *Torno fra un'ora.* I'll be back in an hour. ◇ *fra cinque giorni* in five days

+ **fra poco** soon

+ **Fra venti chilometri c'è un'area di servizio.** It's twenty kilometres to the next services.

fradicio AGGETTIVO (FEM **fradicia**, MASC PL **fradici**, FEM PL **fradice**)
soaked ◇ *Ho la camicia fradicia.* My shirt is soaked.

+ **bagnato fradicio** soaking wet

+ **Era ubriaco fradicio.** He was blind drunk.

fragile AGGETTIVO
fragile

la **fragola** NOME FEM
strawberry (PL strawberries)

fraintendere* VERBO
to misunderstand ◇ *Mi hai frainteso.* You misunderstood me.

la **frana** NOME FEM
landslide

francese AGGETTIVO

vedi anche **francese** NOME MASC, NOME FEM

French

il **francese** NOME MASC

☞

vedi anche **francese** AGGETTIVO, NOME FEM
  [1] Frenchman (PL Frenchmen) (persona)
  ◆ **i Francesi** (uomini e donne) the French
  [2] French (lingua) ◇ Parli francese? Do you speak French?
la **francese** NOME FEM
vedi anche **francese** NOME MASC, AGGETTIVO
  Frenchwoman (PL Frenchwomen)
la **Francia** NOME FEM
  France ◇ Ti piace la Francia? Do you like France? ◇ Andrò in Francia quest'estate. I'm going to France this summer.
franco AGGETTIVO (FEM **franca**, MASC PL **franchi**, FEM PL **franche**)
vedi anche **franco** NOME
  frank
il **franco** NOME MASC (PL i **franchi**)
vedi anche **franco** AGGETTIVO
  franc (moneta)
il **francobollo** NOME MASC
  stamp
la **frangia** NOME FEM (PL le **frange**)
  fringe
  bangs PL US
il **frappé** NOME MASC (PL i **frappé**)
  milk shake
la **frase** NOME FEM
  sentence ◇ Traduci questa frase. Translate this sentence.
  ◆ **una frase fatta** a set phrase
il **frate** NOME MASC
  friar
il **fratello** NOME MASC
  brother ◇ Questo è mio fratello. This is my brother.
  ◆ **Hai fratelli?** (maschi e femmine) Have you any brothers or sisters?
  ◆ **Marina e Piero sono fratelli.** Marina and Piero are brother and sister.
frattempo NOME MASC
  ◆ **nel frattempo** in the meantime
la **frattura** NOME FEM
  fracture ◇ una grave frattura a serious fracture
  ◆ **Ha una frattura alla gamba.** He's broken his leg.
le **freccette** NOME FEM PL
  darts ◇ Giochiamo a freccette. Let's play darts.
la **freccia** NOME FEM (PL le **frecce**)
  [1] arrow (di arco)
  [2] indicator (di auto)
  ◆ **mettere la freccia** to indicate ◇ Ha messo la freccia per voltare a destra. He indicated he was turning right.
freddo AGGETTIVO, NOME MASC (FEM **fredda**)
  cold ◇ La minestra è fredda. The soup is cold.
  ◆ **Fa freddo.** It's cold.
  ◆ **avere freddo** to be* cold ◇ Hai freddo? Are you cold?

freddoloso AGGETTIVO (FEM **freddolosa**)
  ◆ **essere freddoloso** to feel* the cold
fregare VERBO
  [1] to pinch (rubare) ◇ Mi ha fregato il portafoglio. He pinched my wallet.
  [2] to cheat (truffare) ◇ Ha cercato di fregarmi. He tried to cheat me.
  [3] to rub* (strofinare) ◇ Si fregava le mani. He was rubbing his hands.
  ◆ **Chi se ne frega?** Who cares?
frenare VERBO
  to brake ◇ Ha frenato per evitare un cane. He braked to avoid a dog.
  ◆ **Non riusciva a frenare le lacrime.** She couldn't hold back her tears.
il **freno** NOME MASC
  brake
  ◆ **freno a mano** handbrake ◇ Tira il freno a mano. Put the handbrake on.
frequentare VERBO
  [1] to go* to (scuola, corso) ◇ Frequento un corso di inglese. I go to English classes.
  [2] to see* (persona) ◇ Non li frequento più. I don't see them any more. ◇ La frequento poco. I don't see much of her.
  ◆ **Non mi piace la gente che frequenta.** I don't like the people she mixes with.
frequentato AGGETTIVO (FEM **frequentata**)
  popular ◇ È la pizzeria più frequentata della città. It's the most popular pizzeria in town.
frequente AGGETTIVO
  frequent
  ◆ **di frequente** frequently
fresco AGGETTIVO (FEM **fresca**, MASC PL **freschi**, FEM PL **fresche**)
  [1] fresh ◇ frutta fresca fresh fruit
  [2] cool ◇ Fa fresco stasera. It's cool this evening.
  ◆ **mettere in fresco** to put* in the fridge ◇ Metti il vino in fresco. Put the wine in the fridge.
  ◆ **"vernice fresca"** "wet paint"
la **fretta** NOME FEM
  hurry ◇ Che fretta c'è? What's the hurry?
  ◆ **avere fretta** to be* in a hurry ◇ Scusa ma ho un po' di fretta. I'm sorry but I'm in a bit of a hurry. ◇ Aveva fretta di andarsene. He was in a hurry to leave.
  ◆ **in fretta** (velocemente) quickly ◇ Fallo in fretta. Do it quickly.
  ◆ **Fa' in fretta!** Hurry up!
  ◆ **far fretta a qualcuno** to hurry somebody ◇ Non farmi fretta. Don't hurry me.
friggere* VERBO
  to fry*
il **frigo** NOME MASC (PL i **frigo**)
  fridge ◇ Mettilo in frigo. Put it in the fridge.
la **frittata** NOME FEM
  omelette

fritto AGGETTIVO (FEM **fritta**)
> *vedi anche* **fritto** NOME

fried ◊ *pollo fritto* fried chicken
+ **patate fritte** chips, US: french fries

il **fritto** NOME
> *vedi anche* **fritto** AGGETTIVO

+ **fritto misto** mixed fried fish

la **frizione** NOME FEM
clutch (*di auto*)

frizzante AGGETTIVO
sparkling ◊ *acqua minerale frizzante* sparkling mineral water

frontale AGGETTIVO
+ **uno scontro frontale** a head-on collision

la **fronte** NOME FEM
> *vedi anche* **fronte** NOME MASC

forehead ◊ *Gli ha dato un bacio in fronte.* She gave him a kiss on the forehead.
+ **di fronte** opposite ◊ *l'edificio di fronte* the building opposite ◊ *Abita qui di fronte.* He lives in the house opposite.
+ **di fronte a** opposite ◊ *Si è seduto di fronte a me.* He sat down opposite me. ◊ *la casa di fronte alla mia* the house opposite mine

il **fronte** NOME MASC
> *vedi anche* **fronte** NOME FEM

front ◊ *Parti per il fronte a diciotto anni.* He left for the front when he was eighteen.

la **frontiera** NOME FEM
border

il **frullato** NOME MASC
milk shake

il **frullatore** NOME MASC
electric mixer

la **frusta** NOME FEM
whip

la **frutta** NOME FEM
fruit ◊ *frutta fresca* fresh fruit ◊ *Vuoi della frutta?* Would you like some fruit? ◊ *Mi piace molto la frutta.* I love fruit.
+ **frutta candita** candied fruit
+ **frutta secca (1)** (*noci, mandorle ecc.*) nuts PL
+ **frutta secca (2)** (*fichi, prugne ecc.*) dried fruit

il **fruttivendolo**, la **fruttivendola** NOME MASC, FEM
greengrocer

il **frutto** NOME MASC
fruit ◊ *un frutto tropicale* a tropical fruit
+ **frutti di mare** seafood SING

il **fucile** NOME MASC
① rifle (*di soldato*)
② shotgun (*da caccia*)

la **fuga** NOME FEM (PL le **fughe**)
escape
+ **tentare la fuga** to try to escape
+ **fuga di gas** gas leak

fuggire VERBO
① to escape (*prigioniero*) ◊ *È fuggito di prigione.* He escaped from jail.
② to run* away ◊ *È fuggita di casa.* She ran away from home.

il **fulmine** NOME MASC
lightning ◊ *È stato colpito da un fulmine.* He was struck by lightning.
+ **fulmini** lightning SING ◊ *tuoni e fulmini* thunder and lightning

fumare VERBO
to smoke ◊ *Ha smesso di fumare.* She's given up smoking.
+ **"è vietato fumare"** "no smoking"

il **fumatore**, la **fumatrice** NOME MASC, FEM
smoker ◊ *È un forte fumatore.* He's a heavy smoker.
+ **uno scompartimento fumatori** a smoking compartment

il **fumetto** NOME MASC
① comic strip (*vignetta*)
② comic (*giornalino*) ◊ *Le piacciono i fumetti.* She likes comics.

il **fumo** NOME MASC
① smoke (*di incendio ecc.*) ◊ *Sento odore di fumo.* I can smell smoke.
② smoking (*il fumare*) ◊ *Il fumo fa male.* Smoking is bad for you.
+ **fumo passivo** passive smoking

la **fune** NOME FEM
① rope ◊ *Hanno tirato con forza e la fune si è spezzata.* They pulled hard and the rope broke.
② cable (*più grossa*)

il **funerale** NOME MASC
funeral

il **fungo** NOME MASC (PL i **funghi**)
① mushroom
+ **fungo velenoso** toadstool
② fungus (*in medicina*)

la **funivia** NOME FEM
cablecar

funzionare VERBO
to work ◊ *Come funziona?* How does it work? ◊ *L'ascensore non funziona.* The lift isn't working.

la **funzione** NOME FEM
function ◊ *La funzione principale di...* The main function of...
+ **essere in funzione** (*macchina*) to be* on ◊ *Non si apre quand'è in funzione.* It won't open when it's on.

il **fuoco** NOME MASC (PL i **fuochi**)
fire
+ **prendere fuoco** to catch* fire ◊ *La tenda ha preso fuoco subito.* The curtain caught fire immediately.
+ **dare fuoco a qualcosa** to set* fire to something ◊ *Ha dato fuoco alla casa.* He set fire to the house.
+ **far fuoco** (*sparare*) to fire
+ **fuochi d'artificio** fireworks

fuori AVVERBIO, PREPOSIZIONE
① outside ◊ *Ti aspetto fuori.* I'll wait for you outside. ◊ *Fuori è ancora buio.* It's still dark outside. ◊ *Abito fuori Roma.* I live outside Rome.

F

- **fuori città** out of town
- **fuori da** outside ◊ *C'era molta gente fuori dal teatro.* There were lots of people outside the theatre.

  2 out ◊ *Cosa fai là fuori?* What are you doing out there? ◊ *Andiamo a mangiare fuori?* Shall we eat out?
- **Fuori!** Get out!
- **Fuori dai piedi!** Get out of the way!
- **Ha i denti in fuori.** Her teeth stick out.
- **far fuori qualcuno** to kill somebody
- **essere fuori di sé** to be* furious
- **fuori mano** out of the way
- **fuori pasto** between meals
- **fuori pericolo** out of danger
- **fuori servizio** out of order
- **fuori stagione** out of season
- **fuori uso** out of use

il **fuorigioco** NOME MASC
- **in fuorigioco** offside ◊ *Quando ha segnato era in fuorigioco.* He was offside when he scored.

il **fuoristrada** NOME MASC (PL i **fuoristrada**)
  all-terrain vehicle

furbo AGGETTIVO (FEM **furba**)
  vedi anche **furbo** NOME
  clever ◊ *un ragazzo furbo* a clever boy

il **furbo,** la **furba** NOME MASC, FEM

  vedi anche **furbo** AGGETTIVO
- **fare il furbo** to be* clever ◊ *Vuoi fare il furbo?* Are you trying to be clever?

il **furgone** NOME MASC
  van

la **furia** NOME FEM
- **andare su tutte le furie** to fly* into a rage
- **Perderai la voce a furia di gridare.** You'll lose your voice if you shout so much.

furibondo AGGETTIVO (FEM **furibonda**)
  furious

il **furto** NOME MASC
  theft ◊ *Vorrei denunciare un furto.* I'd like to report a theft.
- **furto con scasso** burglary (PL burglaries)

le **fusa** NOME FEM PL
- **fare le fusa** to purr

i **fuseaux** NOME MASC PL
  leggings

il **fuso** NOME MASC
- **fuso orario** time difference ◊ *Non ho tenuto conto del fuso orario.* I forgot about the time difference.

il **fustino** NOME MASC
  tub (*di detersivo*)

futuro AGGETTIVO, NOME MASC (FEM **futura**)
  future

---

* I verbi seguiti da questo simbolo sono irregolari. Si veda anche alle pp.328–338.

G

la **gabbia** NOME FEM
cage
  ◆ **gabbia toracica** rib cage

il **gabbiano** NOME MASC
seagull

il **gabinetto** NOME MASC
toilet ◇ *Dov'è il gabinetto?* Where's the toilet? ◇ *Posso andare al gabinetto?* Can I go to the toilet, please?

la **gaffe** NOME FEM (PL le **gaffe**)
  ◆ **fare una gaffe** to put* one's foot in it ◇ *Ho fatto una gaffe.* I've put my foot in it.

la **galera** NOME FEM
prison ◇ *Ha fatto due anni di galera.* He spent two years in prison.
  ◆ **mandare qualcuno in galera** to send* someone to prison ◇ *Li hanno mandati in galera.* They sent them to prison.

galla NOME FEM
  ◆ **venire a galla** to come* to the surface
  ◆ **stare a galla** to float ◇ *Non so nuotare, ma sto a galla.* I can't swim, but I can float.

galleggiare VERBO
to float

la **galleria** NOME FEM
  [1] tunnel ◇ *la galleria del Monte Bianco* the Mont Blanc tunnel
  [2] circle (*in teatro*) ◇ *due poltrone in galleria* two seats in the circle
  ◆ **galleria d'arte** art gallery

il **Galles** NOME MASC
Wales ◇ *Mi è piaciuto molto il Galles.* I really liked Wales. ◇ *Andremo in Galles quest'estate.* We're going to Wales this summer.

gallese AGGETTIVO
  vedi anche **gallese** NOME MASC, NOME FEM
Welsh ◇ *la squadra gallese* the Welsh team

il **gallese** NOME MASC
  vedi anche **gallese** AGGETTIVO, NOME FEM
  [1] Welshman (PL Welshmen) (*persona*)
  ◆ **i gallesi** (*uomini e donne*) the Welsh
  [2] Welsh (*lingua*)

la **gallese** NOME FEM
  vedi anche **gallese** AGGETTIVO, NOME MASC
Welshwoman (PL Welshwomen)

la **gallina** NOME FEM
hen

il **gallo** NOME MASC
cock

il **galoppo** NOME MASC
  ◆ **andare al galoppo** to gallop

la **gamba** NOME FEM
leg (*di persona, di tavolo*) ◇ *Mi fa male la gamba.* My leg hurts.
  ◆ **in gamba (1)** clever ◇ *Gloria è una ragazza in gamba.* Gloria's a clever girl.
  ◆ **in gamba (2)** (*al lavoro*) good ◇ *Il nostro professore è molto in gamba.* Our teacher's

very good.

il **gamberetto** NOME MASC
prawn

il **gambero** NOME MASC
  [1] king prawn (*di mare*)
  [2] crayfish (*di fiume*)

il **gambo** NOME MASC
stem (*di fiore*)

la **gamma** NOME FEM
range ◇ *una vasta gamma di articoli sportivi* a wide range of sports goods

il **gancio** NOME MASC
hook ◇ *Le chiavi erano appese ad un gancio.* The keys were hanging on a hook.

la **gara** NOME FEM
competition
  ◆ **partecipare a una gara** to take* part in a competition
  ◆ **gara di nuoto** swimming gala
  ◆ **gara ciclistica** cycle race
  ◆ **Facciamo a gara a chi arriva primo!** I'll race you!

il **garage** NOME MASC (PL i **garage**)
garage ◇ *Hai messo la macchina in garage?* Have you put the car in the garage?

garantire VERBO
  [1] to guarantee ◇ *Questo televisore è garantito tre anni.* This television is guaranteed for three years.
  [2] to assure ◇ *Ti garantisco che...* I assure you that...

la **garanzia** NOME FEM
guarantee ◇ *L'orologio è ancora in garanzia.* The watch is still under guarantee.
  ◆ **essere in garanzia** (*automobile*) to be* under warranty

il **garofano** NOME MASC
carnation

il **gas** NOME MASC (PL i **gas**)
gas ◇ *una stufa a gas* a gas heater ◇ *Hai spento il gas?* Have you turned off the gas?
  ◆ **gas lacrimogeno** tear gas

il **gasolio** NOME MASC
diesel

gassato AGGETTIVO (FEM **gassata**)
fizzy

il **gattino** NOME MASC
kitten

il **gatto**, la **gatta** NOME MASC, FEM
cat
  ◆ **gatto delle nevi** snow cat

gelare VERBO
to freeze* ◇ *Il lago gela durante l'inverno.* The lake freezes in winter. ◇ *Si gela qui dentro!* It's freezing in here!

la **gelateria** NOME FEM
ice-cream shop

il **gelato** NOME MASC
  vedi anche **gelato** AGGETTIVO

ice cream ◇ *un gelato alla fragola* a strawberry ice cream

gelato AGGETTIVO (FEM **gelata**)
vedi anche **gelato** NOME
frozen ◇ *Ho le mani gelate.* My hands are frozen.

gelido AGGETTIVO (FEM **gelida**)
icy ◇ *un vento gelido* an icy wind

la **gelosia** NOME FEM
jealousy

geloso AGGETTIVO (FEM **gelosa**)
jealous ◇ *È geloso del fratellino.* He's jealous of his baby brother.

Gemelli NOME MASC PL
Gemini (*dello zodiaco*) ◇ *Sono dei Gemelli.* I'm Gemini.

il **gemello,** la **gemella** NOME MASC, FEM
twin ◇ *Sono gemelli.* They're twins.

il **gemello** NOME MASC
cufflink (*su polsino*) ◇ *un paio di gemelli* a pair of cufflinks

generale AGGETTIVO
vedi anche **generale** NOME MASC
general ◇ *uno sciopero generale* a general strike
◆ **in generale** on the whole ◇ *In generale le cose vanno bene.* On the whole things are going well.
◆ **In generale le ragazze sono più brave.** Girls are generally better.

il **generale** NOME MASC
vedi anche **generale** AGGETTIVO
general

la **generazione** NOME FEM
generation

il **genere** NOME MASC
1 kind ◇ *È il genere di musica che mi piace.* It's the kind of music I like.
◆ **qualcosa del genere** something like that
◆ **Non ho mai visto una cosa del genere!** I've never seen anything like it!
◆ **in genere** usually ◇ *In genere mi alzo alle sette.* I usually get up at seven.
◆ **generi di prima necessità** basic essentials
2 gender (*in grammatica*)

il **genero** NOME MASC
son-in-law (PL sons-in-law)

generoso AGGETTIVO (FEM **generosa**)
generous ◇ *un'offerta generosa* a generous offer

la **gengiva** NOME FEM
gum

geniale AGGETTIVO
brilliant ◇ *un'idea geniale* a brilliant idea

il **genio** NOME MASC
genius ◇ *Sei un genio!* You're a genius!
◆ **un colpo di genio** a brainwave ◇ *Ho avuto un colpo di genio.* I've had a brainwave.

il **genitore** NOME MASC
parent ◇ *i miei genitori* my parents

gennaio NOME MASC
January
Si noti l'uso della maiuscola in inglese.
◇ *in gennaio* in January

Genova NOME FEM
Genoa ◇ *Domani vado a Genova.* I'm going to Genoa tomorrow. ◇ *Abitiamo a Genova.* We live in Genoa.

la **gente** NOME FEM
people PL ◇ *C'era tanta gente.* There were lots of people. ◇ *C'era poca gente in spiaggia.* There weren't many people on the beach. ◇ *È gente molto simpatica.* They're very nice people.

gentile AGGETTIVO
nice ◇ *È molto gentile da parte vostra.* It's very nice of you.
◆ **Gent. Sig. Rossi (1)** (*su busta*) Mr Rossi
◆ **Gent. Sig. Rossi (2)** (*in lettera*) Dear Mr Rossi

la **geografia** NOME FEM
geography

la **geometria** NOME FEM
geometry

la **Germania** NOME FEM
Germany ◇ *Mi è piaciuta molto la Germania.* I really liked Germany. ◇ *Andremo in Germania quest'estate.* We're going to Germany this summer.

il **gerundio** NOME MASC
gerund

il **gesso** NOME MASC
1 chalk (*per lavagna*)
2 plaster ◇ *Ha una gamba in gesso.* He's got his leg in plaster.

la **gestione** NOME FEM
management

gestire VERBO
to manage

il **gesto** NOME MASC
gesture ◇ *un gesto di rabbia* an angry gesture

Gesù NOME MASC
Jesus ◇ *Gesù Bambino* baby Jesus

gettare VERBO
to throw* ◇ *Ha gettato il libro dalla finestra.* He threw the book out of the window. ◇ *Non gettare il giornale per terra.* Don't throw the paper on the floor.
◆ **gettarsi in acqua** to jump into water

il **gettone** NOME MASC
token

ghiacciato AGGETTIVO (FEM **ghiacciata**)
1 frozen ◇ *Ho i piedi ghiacciati.* My feet are frozen.
2 ice-cold ◇ *una birra ghiacciata* an ice-cold beer

il **ghiaccio** NOME MASC
ice ◇ *un cubetto di ghiaccio* an ice cube

il **ghiacciolo** NOME MASC
ice lolly (PL ice lollies)

---

* *I verbi seguiti da questo simbolo sono irregolari. Si veda anche alle pp.328–338.*

Popsicle® US
◇ **un ghiacciolo al limone** a lemon ice lolly

la **ghiaia** NOME FEM
gravel

la **ghiandola** NOME FEM
gland

già AVVERBIO
already ◇ *Te l'ho già detto.* I've already told you. ◇ *Sei già di ritorno?* Are you back already?
♦ **Ma non ci conosciamo già?** Haven't we met before?

la **giacca** NOME FEM (PL le **giacche**)
jacket ◇ *una giacca sportiva* a sports jacket
♦ **giacca a vento** anorak

il **giaccone** NOME MASC
winter jacket

giallo AGGETTIVO, NOME MASC (FEM **gialla**)
1 yellow ◇ *una sciarpa gialla* a yellow scarf ◇ *le Pagine gialle* the Yellow Pages
2 amber (*di semaforo*) ◇ *Non attraversare con il giallo.* You mustn't cross on an amber light.
♦ **romanzo giallo** detective story
♦ **film giallo** thriller

il **Giappone** NOME MASC
Japan ◇ *Mi è piaciuto molto il Giappone.* I really liked Japan. ◇ *Andremo in Giappone quest'estate.* We're going to Japan this summer.

giapponese AGGETTIVO
vedi anche **giapponese** NOME MASC, NOME FEM
Japanese

il **giapponese** NOME MASC
vedi anche **giapponese** NOME FEM, AGGETTIVO
1 Japanese man (PL Japanese men) (*persona*)
♦ **i giapponesi** (*uomini e donne*) the Japanese
2 Japanese (*lingua*) ◇ *Parla giapponese.* She speaks Japanese.

la **giapponese** NOME FEM
vedi anche **giapponese** NOME MASC, AGGETTIVO
Japanese woman (PL Japanese women)

il **giardiniere** NOME MASC
gardener

il **giardino** NOME MASC
garden
yard US
◇ *Sono in giardino.* They're in the garden.
♦ **giardino pubblico** park

il **gigante** NOME MASC
vedi anche **gigante** AGGETTIVO
giant

gigante AGGETTIVO
vedi anche **gigante** NOME
giant ◇ *un cavolfiore gigante* a giant cauliflower
♦ **confezione gigante** economy-size packet

il **giglio** NOME MASC
lily (PL lilies)

il **gilè** NOME MASC (PL i **gilè**)

waistcoat
vest US

il **ginecologo**, la **ginecologa** NOME MASC, FEM (MASC PL i **ginecologi**, FEM PL le **ginecologhe**)
gynaecologist
gynecologist US

Ginevra NOME FEM
Geneva ◇ *Domani vado a Ginevra.* I'm going to Geneva tomorrow. ◇ *Abitano a Ginevra.* They live in Geneva.

la **ginnastica** NOME FEM
exercise ◇ *Dovresti fare un po' di ginnastica.* You should do some exercise.
♦ **Vado a fare ginnastica due volte alla settimana.** I go to the gym twice a week.

il **ginocchio** NOME MASC (PL FEM le **ginocchia**)
knee
♦ **mettersi in ginocchio** to kneel* down

giocare VERBO
to play ◇ *Sai giocare a scacchi?* Can you play chess? ◇ *Gioca nel Milan.* He plays for Milan.
♦ **giocare d'azzardo** to gamble

il **giocatore**, la **giocatrice** NOME MASC, FEM
player ◇ *un giocatore di scacchi* a chess player
♦ **un giocatore d'azzardo** a gambler

il **giocattolo** NOME MASC
toy

il **gioco** NOME MASC (PL i **giochi**)
game ◇ *un gioco da tavolo* a board game ◇ *Facciamo un gioco.* Let's play a game.
♦ **i giochi olimpici** the Olympic Games
♦ **È stato un gioco da ragazzi.** It was dead easy.

il **giocoliere** NOME MASC
juggler

la **gioia** NOME FEM
joy

la **gioielleria** NOME FEM
jeweller's
jeweler's US

il **gioiello** NOME MASC
♦ **un gioiello** a piece of jewellery
♦ **i gioielli di mia madre** my mother's jewellery

la **Giordania** NOME FEM
Jordan

il **giornalaio** NOME MASC
newsagent's
news dealer US
(*negozio*)

il **giornale** NOME MASC
newspaper ◇ *L'ho letto sul giornale.* I read it in the newspaper.
♦ **il giornale radio** the radio news SING

giornaliero AGGETTIVO (FEM **giornaliera**)
daily

il **giornalismo** NOME MASC
journalism

G

il/la **giornalista** NOME MASC/FEM (MASC PL i
giornalisti, FEM PL le **giornaliste**)
journalist ◇ *Fa la giornalista.* She is a
journalist.

la **giornata** NOME FEM
day ◇ *Bella giornata, vero?* Lovely day, isn't
it?
+ **giornata lavorativa** working day

il **giorno** NOME MASC
day ◇ *due giorni fa* two days ago ◇ *uno di
questi giorni* one of these days
+ **di giorno** during the day ◇ *Preferisco
guidare di giorno.* I prefer driving during the
day.
+ **tre volte al giorno** three times a day
+ **Che giorno è oggi? (1)** (*giorno della
settimana*) What day is it today?
+ **Che giorno è oggi? (2)** (*data*) What date is it
today?
+ **al giorno d'oggi** nowadays
+ **un giorno feriale** a weekday
+ **un giorno festivo** a holiday

la **giostra** NOME FEM
roundabout
carousel US
+ **le giostre** (*luna park*) funfair

giovane AGGETTIVO
vedi anche **giovane** NOME MASC, NOME FEM
young ◇ *Sei troppo giovane.* You're too
young. ◇ *È più giovane di me.* He's younger
than me. ◇ *È il più giovane della squadra.*
He's the youngest in the team.

il **giovane** NOME MASC
vedi anche **giovane** AGGETTIVO, NOME FEM
young man (PL young men) ◇ *da giovane*
when he was a young man
+ **i giovani** (*uomini e donne*) young people

la **giovane** NOME FEM
vedi anche **giovane** AGGETTIVO, NOME MASC
young woman (PL young women)

il **giovedì** NOME MASC (PL i **giovedì**)
Thursday
Si noti l'uso della maiuscola in inglese.
◇ *L'ho vista giovedì.* I saw her on Thursday.
+ **di giovedì** on Thursdays ◇ *Vado in piscina
di giovedì.* I go swimming on Thursdays.
+ **giovedì scorso** last Thursday
+ **giovedì prossimo** next Thursday

il **giradischi** NOME MASC (PL i **giradischi**)
record player

la **giraffa** NOME FEM
giraffe

girare VERBO
to turn ◇ *Gira a destra.* Turn right.
+ **Mi gira la testa.** I feel dizzy.
+ **girarsi** to turn round ◇ *Si è girata e mi ha
guardato.* She turned round and looked at
me.
+ **girare un film** to make* a film
+ **Ho girato tutta la città** I've been all over

il **girasole** NOME MASC
sunflower

girevole AGGETTIVO
+ **porta girevole** revolving door
+ **sedia girevole** swivel chair

il **giro** NOME MASC
+ **fare un giro (1)** (*passeggiata*) to go* for a
walk
+ **fare un giro (2)** (*in bici*) to go* for a ride
+ **fare un giro (3)** (*in macchina*) to go* for a
drive
+ **fare un giro in centro** to have* a look round
the city centre
+ **guardarsi in giro** to look around
+ **lasciare tutto in giro** to leave* everything
lying about
+ **prendere in giro qualcuno** to make* fun of
somebody ◇ *Mi prendono in giro perché
sono grasso.* They make fun of me because
I'm fat.
+ **Ma va', mi stai prendendo in giro!** Come on,
you're pulling my leg!
+ **giro turistico** sightseeing tour

il **girocollo** NOME MASC
+ **maglia a girocollo** crewneck sweater

il **girone** NOME MASC
+ **girone d'andata** first leg
+ **girone di ritorno** second leg

la **gita** NOME FEM
trip ◇ *una gita scolastica* a school trip
+ **fare una gita** to go* on a trip

giù AVVERBIO
down ◇ *Vieni giù!* Come down! ◇ *Oggi
sono un po' giù.* I'm a bit down today.
+ **più in giù** further down ◇ *Spostalo più in
giù.* Move it further down.
+ **bambini dai sette anni in giù** children of
seven and under
+ **Giù le mani!** Hands off!

il **giubbotto** NOME MASC
bomber jacket
+ **giubbotto salvagente** life jacket
+ **giubbotto antiproiettile** bulletproof vest

giudicare VERBO
to judge ◇ *a giudicare da quello che dice*
judging by what he says

il **giudice** NOME MASC
judge

il **giudizio** NOME MASC
opinion ◇ *a mio giudizio* in my opinion
+ **denti del giudizio** wisdom teeth

il **giugno** NOME MASC
June
Si noti l'uso della maiuscola in inglese.
◇ *in giugno* in June

la **giungla** NOME FEM
jungle

giurare VERBO
to swear* ◇ *È vero, te lo giuro!* It's true, I

---

* *I verbi seguiti da questo simbolo sono irregolari. Si veda anche alle pp.328–338.*

swear! ◇ *Ti giuro che non sono stato io.* I swear it wasn't me. ◇ *Mi pare che fosse lui, ma non potrei giurarci.* I think it was him, but I couldn't swear to it.

la **giuria** NOME FEM
jury (PL juries)

giustificare VERBO
to excuse ◇ *Non lo giustifico, però capisco perché l'ha fatto.* I don't excuse him but I understand why he did it.
♦ **Si è giustificato dicendo che era stanco.** His excuse was that he was tired.

la **giustificazione** NOME FEM
excuse ◇ *Non c'è alcuna giustificazione per quello che hai fatto.* There's no excuse for what you did.

la **giustizia** NOME FEM
justice ◇ *In questo mondo non c'è giustizia!* There's no justice in this world!
♦ **farsi giustizia da sé** to take* the law into one's own hands

giustiziare VERBO
to execute

giusto AGGETTIVO (FEM **giusta**)
vedi anche **giusto** AVVERBIO
[1] right ◇ *Dobbiamo aspettare il momento giusto.* We'll have to wait for the right moment. ◇ *Non trovo la parola giusta.* I can't find the right word.
[2] fair ◇ *Non è giusto! Vince sempre lui.* It's not fair! He always wins.

giusto AVVERBIO
vedi anche **giusto** AGGETTIVO
just ◇ *Sono arrivato giusto in tempo.* I arrived just in time. ◇ *Volevo vedere giusto te.* You're just the person I wanted to see.
♦ **Giusto!** Of course! ◇ *Ah sì, giusto! Quasi mi dimenticavo.* Yes, of course! I was nearly forgetting.
♦ **stare giusto** to fit perfectly ◇ *I tuoi stivali mi stanno giusti.* Your boots fit me perfectly.

gli ARTICOLO PL
vedi anche **gli** PRONOME
the ◇ *Gli spari provenivano dal parco.* The shots came from the park.
*Spesso **gli** non viene tradotto.*
◇ *Gli inglesi amano gli animali.* English people love animals. ◇ *Ti piacciono gli spaghetti?* Do you like spaghetti? ◇ *gli amici di Mario* Mario's friends
*A volte **gli** viene tradotto con il pronome possessivo.*
◇ *Si è tolto gli stivali.* He took off his boots.
◇ *Chiudi gli occhi.* Close your eyes.

gli PRONOME
vedi anche **gli** ARTICOLO
[1] him ◇ *Gli ho detto tutto.* I told him everything. ◇ *Dagli qualcosa da mangiare.* Give him something to eat.
*Spesso **him** è preceduto da una preposizione, a seconda del verbo usato.*
◇ *Scrivigli!* Write to him! ◇ *Gli sembrava una buona idea.* It seemed a good idea to him. ◇ *Gli ha sorriso.* He smiled at him.
[2] it (*oggetto*) ◇ *Dagli una lucidata.* Give it a polish.
*Spesso **it** è preceduto da una preposizione, a seconda del verbo usato.*
◇ *Aggiungili un po' di sale.* Add a bit of salt to it. ◇ *Dagli un'occhiata.* Have a look at it.
Quando si traduce "glielo", ("gliela", "glieli", "gliele" e "gliene") bisogna scegliere il pronome inglese corretto.
◇ *Gabriele lo sa? – Sì, gliel'ho detto.* Does Gabriele know? – Yes, I've told him. ◇ *Lidia lo sa? – Sì, gliel'ho detto.* Does Lidia know? – Yes, I've told her. ◇ *I tuoi lo sanno? – Sì, gliel'ho detto.* Do your parents know? – Yes, I've told them. ◇ *Dagliela domani.* Give it to him tomorrow. ◇ *Glieli hai promessi.* You promised them to her. ◇ *Gliel'ha spedite.* He sent them to them. ◇ *Gliene ho parlato.* I spoke to her about it.

la **gloria** NOME FEM
glory ◇ *gloria e fama* glory and fame

gli **gnocchi** NOME MASC PL
gnocchi

la **goccia** NOME FEM (PL le **gocce**)
drop
♦ **una goccia d'olio** a drop of oil
♦ **gocce per gli occhi** eye drops
♦ **Questa è la goccia che fa traboccare il vaso!** That's the last straw!

il **goccio** NOME MASC
drop ◇ *Vuoi un goccio di vino?* Would you like a drop of wine?

gocciolare VERBO
to drip ◇ *Il rubinetto gocciola.* The tap's dripping.
♦ **Mi gocciola il naso.** My nose is running.

goffo AGGETTIVO (FEM **goffa**)
clumsy ◇ *È un po' goffo.* He's a bit clumsy. ◇ *È la persona la più goffa che abbia mai conosciuto.* He's the clumsiest person I've ever met.

la **gola** NOME FEM
throat
♦ **avere mal di gola** to have* a sore throat ◇ *Ho mal di gola.* I've got a sore throat.

il **golf** NOME MASC (PL i **golf**)
[1] golf (*sport*)
♦ **giocare a golf** to play golf
[2] cardigan (*con bottoni*)
[3] jumper (*senza bottoni*)

il **golfo** NOME MASC
gulf
♦ **il golfo del Messico** the Gulf of Mexico
♦ **il golfo di Napoli** the Bay of Naples
♦ **il golfo Persico** the Gulf

goloso AGGETTIVO (FEM **golosa**)
♦ **essere goloso di dolci** to love sweets ◇ *Sono golosa di dolci.* I love sweets.

la **gomitata** NOME FEM
♦ **dare una gomitata a qualcuno** to elbow

G

somebody ◇ *Mi ha dato una gomitata nello stomaco.* He elbowed me in the stomach.

il **gomito** NOME MASC
elbow

il **gomitolo** NOME MASC
• **un gomitolo di lana** a ball of wool

la **gomma** NOME FEM
[1] rubber ◇ *Mi presti la gomma?* Can I borrow your rubber?
• **gomma da masticare** chewing gum
• **guanti di gomma** rubber gloves
[2] tyre
tire [US]
(*di macchina, di bici*)
◇ *Ho una gomma a terra.* I've got a flat tyre.

il **gommone** NOME MASC
rubber dinghy (PL rubber dinghies)

gonfiare VERBO
to blow* up ◇ *Devo gonfiare le gomme della bici.* I need to blow up the tyres on my bike.
• **gonfiarsi** to swell* ◇ *Mi si è gonfiata la caviglia.* My ankle is swollen.

gonfio AGGETTIVO (FEM **gonfia**)
[1] swollen ◇ *Ho il piede gonfio.* My foot's swollen.
[2] puffy (*viso, occhi*) ◇ *Aveva gli occhi gonfi per il pianto.* Her eyes were puffy with crying.

il **gonfiore** NOME MASC
swelling

la **gonna** NOME FEM
skirt ◇ *una gonna lunga* a long skirt
• **una gonna pantalone** a pair of culottes

il **gorilla** NOME MASC (PL i **gorilla**)
[1] gorilla (*animale*)
[2] bodyguard (*guardia del corpo*)

gotico AGGETTIVO (FEM **gotica**, MASC PL **gotici**, FEM PL **gotiche**)
Gothic
Si noti l'uso della maiuscola in inglese.

il **governo** NOME MASC
government ◇ *il governo britannico* the British government
• **il partito al governo** the party in power

la **gradinata** NOME FEM
[1] flight of steps (*scalinata*)
[2] terraces PL (*allo stadio*) ◇ *Abbiamo seguito la partita dalla gradinata.* We watched the match from the terraces.

il **gradino** NOME MASC
step ◇ *Attento al gradino.* Mind the step.

il **grado** NOME MASC
degree ◇ *cinque gradi sotto zero* five degrees below zero
• **essere in grado di fare qualcosa** to be* able to do something ◇ *Presto sarà in grado di camminare di nuovo.* He'll soon be able to walk again.
• **Non sono in grado di farlo da solo.** I can't do

it by myself.

graffiare VERBO
to scratch ◇ *Il gatto mi ha graffiato la mano.* The cat scratched my hand.

il **graffio** NOME MASC
scratch

il **grafico** NOME MASC (PL i **grafici**)
[1] graph ◇ *Il grafico illustra il calo nelle vendite.* The graph shows the drop in sales.
[2] graphic designer ◇ *Fa il grafico.* He is a graphic designer.

la **grammatica** NOME FEM (PL le **grammatiche**)
grammar ◇ *un libro di grammatica* a grammar book
• **C'erano molti errori di grammatica.** There were lots of grammatical errors.

il **grammo** NOME MASC
gram

la **Gran Bretagna** NOME FEM
Great Britain ◇ *Mi piace la Gran Bretagna.* I like Great Britain. ◇ *Andremo in Gran Bretagna quest'estate.* We're going to Great Britain this summer.

il **granchio** NOME MASC
crab

grande AGGETTIVO
vedi anche **grande** NOME
*Quando si usa **big** e quando **large**? Leggi gli esempi per orientarti, e ricorda che per descrivere un oggetto si possono usare entrambi, ma **large** è un po' più formale.*
[1] big ◇ *La stanza non è molto grande.* The room isn't very big. ◇ *Quant'è grande questa stanza?* How big is this room? ◇ *Come ti sei fatto grande!* How big you've got! ◇ *Milano è più grande di Genova.* Milan is bigger than Genoa. ◇ *lo stadio più grande d'Italia* the biggest stadium in Italy
[2] large ◇ *un gran numero di macchine* a large number of cars ◇ *Importano una grande quantità di materie prime.* They import large quantities of raw materials. ◇ *Si è radunata una gran folla.* A large crowd gathered.
[3] old ◇ *Sei abbastanza grande per capire.* You're old enough to understand. ◇ *È più grande di me.* He's older than me. ◇ *Sono la più grande.* I'm the oldest.
• **Hanno due figli grandi.** They have two grown-up children.
[4] great ◇ *un grande poeta* a great poet ◇ *Sei stato di grande aiuto.* You've been a great help.
• **Ho una gran fame.** I'm starving.
• **Fa un gran caldo oggi.** It's terribly hot today.
• **Con mia grande sorpresa l'ho trovato lì.** To my great surprise I found it there.
• **un gran bel film** an excellent film
• **Sei un gran bugiardo!** You're such a liar!
• **grandi magazzini** department store SING

---

* I verbi seguiti da questo simbolo sono irregolari. Si veda anche alle pp.328–338.

a grande NOME MASC/FEM
vedi anche **grande** AGGETTIVO
grown-up ◇ *I bambini pensano che i grandi sappiano tutto.* Children think grown-ups know everything.
✦ **Cosa farai da grande?** What are you going to be when you grow up?

grandinare VERBO
to hail ◇ *Ieri è grandinato.* It hailed yesterday.

a grandine NOME FEM
hail
✦ **chicco di grandine** hailstone

il granello NOME MASC
1 grain ◇ *un granello di sabbia* a grain of sand
2 speck ◇ *un granello di polvere* a speck of dust

il grano NOME MASC
wheat

il granturco NOME MASC
maize

il grappolo NOME MASC
✦ **grappolo d'uva** bunch of grapes

grasso AGGETTIVO (FEM **grassa**)
vedi anche **grasso** NOME
1 fat ◇ *un signore grasso* a fat man ◇ *È più grasso di te.* He's fatter than you.
2 greasy ◇ *Ho i capelli grassi.* My hair is greasy. ◇ *Ho i capelli più grassi dei tuoi.* My hair is greasier than yours.
3 fatty ◇ *Dovresti evitare i cibi grassi.* You should avoid fatty food.

il grasso NOME MASC
vedi anche **grasso** AGGETTIVO
1 fat ◇ *grassi animali e vegetali* animal and vegetable fats
2 grease ◇ *una macchia di grasso* a grease stain

gratis AVVERBIO
free ◇ *I bambini viaggiano gratis.* Children travel free.
✦ **Me l'ha riparato gratis.** He repaired it for me for nothing.

il grattacielo NOME MASC
skyscraper

grattarsi VERBO
to scratch ◇ *Smettila di grattarti!* Stop scratching! ◇ *Si grattava la schiena.* He was scratching his back.

la grattugia NOME (PL le **grattugie**)
grater

grattugiare VERBO
to grate

gratuito AGGETTIVO (FEM **gratuita**)
free ◇ *L'ingresso è gratuito.* Admission is free.

grave AGGETTIVO
serious ◇ *Non è niente di grave.* It's nothing serious. ◇ *una malattia grave* a serious illness

✦ **un malato grave** a seriously-ill patient

gravemente AVVERBIO
seriously ◇ *È rimasto gravemente ferito.* He was seriously injured.

la gravidanza NOME FEM
pregnancy (PL pregnancies) ◇ *una gravidanza difficile* a difficult pregnancy

la gravità NOME FEM
seriousness ◇ *la gravità della situazione* the seriousness of the situation
✦ **la legge di gravità** the law of gravity
✦ **la forza di gravità** gravity

la grazia NOME FEM
grace ◇ *la grazia di una ballerina* the grace of a ballerina
✦ **concedere la grazia a qualcuno** (*a condannato*) to pardon somebody
✦ **ottenere la grazia** (*condannato*) to be* pardoned

grazie ESCLAMAZIONE
1 thank you ◇ *Vuoi un caffè? – No grazie.* Would you like a coffee? – No, thank you.
✦ **Vuoi un tè? – Sì grazie.** Would you like some tea? – Yes, please.
2 thanks (*meno formale*) ◇ *Hai trovato i libri? – Sì grazie.* Did you find the books? – Yes, thanks.
✦ **mille grazie** many thanks
✦ **grazie a lui** thanks to him
✦ **Grazie a Dio!** Thank God!
thank, e non "thanks".

grazioso AGGETTIVO (FEM **graziosa**)
charming

la Grecia NOME FEM
Greece ◇ *Mi piace la Grecia.* I like Greece. ◇ *Andremo in Grecia quest'estate.* We're going to Greece this summer.

greco, greca NOME, AGGETTIVO (MASC PL **greci**, FEM PL **greche**)
vedi anche **greco** NOME
Greek

il greco NOME MASC
vedi anche **greco** NOME, AGGETTIVO
Greek (*lingua*) ◇ *Parla il greco?* Do you speak Greek?

il gregge NOME MASC (PL FEM le **greggi**)
flock ◇ *un gregge di pecore* a flock of sheep

il grembiule NOME MASC
1 apron (*da cucina*)
2 overall (*da lavoro*)

il grembo NOME MASC
lap

gridare VERBO
to shout ◇ *Smettila di gridare!* Stop shouting!
✦ **gridare aiuto** to shout for help ◇ *Abbiamo sentito qualcuno che gridava aiuto.* We heard someone shouting for help.

il grido NOME MASC (PL FEM le **grida**)
1 shout ◇ *le grida dei bambini* the children's shouts

G

2 **cry** (PL cries) ◇ *I soccorritori hanno sentito le sue grida di aiuto.* The rescuers heard his cries for help.

grigio AGGETTIVO, NOME MASC (FEM **grigia,** MASC PL **grigi,** FEM PL **grigie**)
grey
gray US
◇ *Ha i capelli grigi* She's got grey hair.

la **griglia** NOME FEM
◆ **alla griglia** grilled ◇ *una bistecca alla griglia* a grilled steak

il **grilletto** NOME MASC
trigger ◇ *Ha premuto il grilletto.* He pulled the trigger.

il **grillo** NOME MASC
cricket

il **grissino** NOME MASC
breadstick

la **grondaia** NOME FEM
gutter

grosso AGGETTIVO (FEM **grossa**)
1 big ◇ *un grosso macigno* a big rock ◇ *È più grossa della mia.* It's bigger than mine. ◇ *È il più grosso del mondo.* It's the biggest in the world.
◆ **Stavolta l'hai fatta grossa.** This time you're in big trouble.
◆ **Ti sbagli di grosso.** You're very much mistaken.
2 thick ◇ *una grossa fune* a thick rope
3 large ◇ *una grossa somma* a large sum
4 serious ◇ *Sarebbe un grosso errore.* It would be a serious mistake.

la **grotta** NOME FEM
cave

la **gru** NOME FEM (PL le **gru**)
crane (*uccello, macchina*)

la **gruccia** NOME FEM (PL le **grucce**)
1 crutch (*per camminare*)
2 coat hanger (*per abiti*)

il **grumo** NOME MASC
lump ◇ *C'erano dei grumi nella besciamella.* There were lumps in the béchamel sauce.

il **gruppo** NOME MASC
group ◇ *Dividiamoli in gruppi di tre.* Let's divide them into groups of three.
◆ **Sono arrivati a gruppi di tre.** They came in threes.
◆ **gruppo sanguigno** blood group

guadagnare VERBO
1 to earn ◇ *Guadagna bene.* He earns a lot. ◇ *Quanto guadagni al mese?* How much do you earn per month?
◆ **E io che cosa ci guadagno?** What's in it for me?
2 to gain ◇ *Non ci guadagni niente a fare così.* There's nothing to be gained by doing that.
◆ **guadagnare tempo** to gain time ◇ *L'ha*

detto per guadagnare tempo. He said it to gain time.

il **guadagno** NOME MASC
earnings PL

guai ESCLAMAZIONE
◆ **Guai a te!** Don't you dare!
◆ **Guai a te se lo fai un'altra volta!** Don't you dare do that again!

il **guaio** NOME MASC
trouble ◇ *Il guaio è che sono già partiti.* The trouble is that they've already left.
◆ **Sono in un bel guaio.** I'm in a real mess.

la **guancia** NOME FEM (PL le **guance**)
cheek

il **guanto** NOME MASC
glove ◇ *un paio di guanti di lana* a pair of woollen gloves

il **guardalinee** NOME MASC (PL i **guardalinee**)
linesman (PL linesmen)

guardare VERBO
1 to look ◇ *Guarda qui!* Look here! ◇ *Guarda cos'hai combinato!* Look what you've done! ◇ *Guarda chi si vede!* Look who's here! ◇ *Si guardavano negli occhi.* They were looking into each other's eyes.
2 to look at ◇ *Si girò a guardarlo.* She turned to look at him. ◇ *Cos'hai da guardare?* What are you looking at? ◇ *Si guardò allo specchio.* He looked at himself in the mirror.
3 to watch ◇ *Hai guardato la partita ieri sera?* Did you watch the match last night? ◇ *Stasera guardo la tivù.* I'm going to watch TV tonight.

Si ricordi che in genere quando si guarda qualcosa di fermo va usato **to look at**, *mentre quando si guarda qualcosa in movimento va usato* **to watch**.
◇ *L'ho guardata mentre correve giù per le scale.* I watched her run down the stairs.

il **guardaroba** NOME MASC (PL i **guardaroba**)
1 wardrobe ◇ *Metti in ordine il tuo guardaroba!* Tidy up your wardrobe!
2 cloakroom (*a teatro, al ristorante*) ◇ *Ho lasciato l'impermeabile al guardaroba.* I left my raincoat in the cloakroom.

la **guardia** NOME FEM
◆ **guardia carceraria** prison warder
◆ **guardia del corpo** bodyguard
◆ **Guardia di Finanza** financial police
◆ **guardia giurata** security guard
◆ **guardia medica** emergency doctor service
◆ **il cambio della guardia** the changing of the guard
◆ **fare la guardia** to keep* watch ◇ *Stavo facendo la guardia.* I was keeping watch.
◆ **essere di guardia** to be* on duty ◇ *Al cancello c'era un poliziotto di guardia.* There was a policeman on duty at the gate.
◆ **cane da guardia** guard dog

guardiano NOME MASC
caretaker
janitor US
◇ *il guardiano della scuola* the school
caretaker
+ **guardiano notturno** night watchman

guarigione NOME FEM
recovery (PL recoveries) ◇ *Auguri di pronta
guarigione!* Best wishes for a speedy
recovery!

guarire VERBO
[1] to be* better ◇ *Spero che tu guarisca
presto.* I hope you'll be better soon. ◇ *Non
sono ancora completamente guarito.* I'm
not completely better yet.
[2] to cure ◇ *I medici non sono riusciti a
guarirlo.* The doctors couldn't cure him.
[3] to heal up ◇ *La ferita guarirà in dieci
giorni.* The wound will heal up in ten days.

guastafeste NOME MASC/FEM
killjoy ◇ *Non fare il guastafeste!* Don't be
such a killjoy!

guastarsi VERBO
to break* down ◇ *Mi si è guastata la
macchina in autostrada.* My car broke down
on the motorway.
+ **Speriamo che il tempo non si guasti.** Let's
hope the weather doesn't change for the
worse.

guasto AGGETTIVO (FEM **guasta**)
vedi anche **guasto** NOME
[1] not working ◇ *Il mio televisore è guasto.*
My television isn't working.
+ **"guasto"** "out of order"
[2] bad ◇ *Quella mela è guasta.* That apple
is bad.

guasto NOME MASC
vedi anche **guasto** AGGETTIVO
failure ◇ *L'aereo è precipitato per un guasto
al motore.* The plane crashed because of
engine failure
+ **Il meccanico ha riparato un guasto al
motore.** The mechanic repaired a fault in the
engine.

guerra NOME FEM
war ◇ *Ha combattuto nella guerra del
Vietnam.* He fought in the Vietnam war.
+ **guerra civile** civil war
+ **guerra mondiale** world war ◇ *la seconda
guerra mondiale* the Second World War
+ **guerra chimica** chemical warfare

gufo NOME MASC
owl

la **guida** NOME FEM
[1] guide ◇ *Ho comprato una guida di
Londra.* I bought a guide to London. ◇ *Fa la
guida turistica.* He is a tourist guide.
+ **la guida telefonica** the phone book
[2] driving (*di veicolo*) ◇ *Ha preso la multa
per guida in stato di ebbrezza.* He was fined
for drink-driving. ◇ *lezioni di guida* driving
lessons
+ **una macchina con la guida a destra** a
right-hand drive car

guidare VERBO
[1] to drive* ◇ *Sai guidare?* Can you drive?
◇ *Ha guidato per tutta la notte.* She drove all
night. ◇ *Ha mai guidato in Gran Bretagna?*
Have you ever driven in Britain?
[2] to lead* ◇ *Ha guidato una spedizione in
Antartide.* He led an expedition to
Antarctica.
+ **Lasciati guidare dall'istinto.** Let your
instinct be your guide.

il **guidatore,** la **guidatrice** NOME MASC, FEM
driver

il **guinzaglio** NOME MASC
lead ◇ *un cane al guinzaglio* a dog on a lead

il **guscio** NOME MASC (PL i **gusci**)
shell (*di uovo, di noce*)

il **gusto** NOME MASC
[1] flavour
flavor US
◇ *disponibile in tre nuovi gusti* available in
three new flavours
+ **al gusto di fragola** strawberry-flavoured
[2] taste ◇ *un gusto amaro* a bitter taste
◇ *Veste con gusto.* She's got good taste in
clothes. ◇ *uno scherzo di cattivo gusto* a
joke in bad taste ◇ *Abbiamo gusti diversi in
fatto di musica.* We have different tastes in
music.
+ **Abbiamo gli stessi gusti.** We like the same
things.
+ **Ci ha preso gusto.** He got to like it.
+ **Per i miei gusti tu corri un po' troppo.** You
drive too fast for my liking.
+ **Lo fa per il gusto di farlo.** He does it for the
fun of it.

gustoso AGGETTIVO (FEM **gustosa**)
tasty ◇ *un piatto gustoso* a tasty dish ◇ *La
carne è più gustosa cucinata così.* Meat is
tastier when it's cooked like this.

G

H

l' **handicappato,** l' **handicappata** NOME
MASC, FEM
vedi anche **handicappato** AGGETTIVO
handicapped person (PL handicapped
people)
handicappato AGGETTIVO (FEM
handicappata)
vedi anche **handicappato** NOME MASC/FEM
handicapped
l' **hascisc** NOME MASC
hashish
l' **hi-fi** NOME MASC (PL gli **hi-fi**)

hi-fi

l' **hobby** NOME MASC (PL gli **hobby**)
hobby (PL hobbies)

l' **hockey** NOME MASC
hockey
  • **hockey su ghiaccio** ice hockey

l' **hostess** NOME FEM (PL le **hostess**)
air hostess

l' **hotel** NOME MASC (PL gli **hotel**)
hotel

I

i ARTICOLO PL

the ◇ *I bambini erano già a letto.* The children were already in bed. ◇ *Chi ha preso i libri?* Who's taken the books?

*Spesso **i** non viene tradotto.*

◇ *I bambini viaggiano gratis.* Children travel free. ◇ *Non mi piacciono i funghi.* I don't like mushrooms. ◇ *i genitori di Mario* Mario's parents

*A volte **i** viene tradotto con l'aggettivo possessivo.*

◇ *Si è tolto i guanti.* He took off his gloves. ◇ *Va' a lavarti i denti.* Go and brush your teeth. ◇ *Ho i piedi gonfi.* My feet are swollen.

l' **iceberg** NOME MASC (PL gli **iceberg**)

iceberg ◇ *la punta dell'iceberg* the tip of the iceberg

l' **idea** NOME FEM

idea ◇ *È un'idea geniale!* It's a brilliant idea! ◇ *Non hai idea del traffico che c'era.* You've no idea how much traffic there was. ◇ *Non ne ho la più pallida idea.* I haven't the faintest idea.

+ **Neanche per idea!** No way! ◇ *Pensi di andarci? – Neanche per idea!* Are you thinking of going? – No way!

+ **cambiare idea** to change one's mind ◇ *Ho cambiato idea.* I've changed my mind.

ideale AGGETTIVO

vedi anche **ideale** NOME

ideal ◇ *Secondo me è la soluzione ideale.* In my opinion it's the ideal solution.

l' **ideale** NOME MASC

vedi anche **ideale** AGGETTIVO

ideal ◇ *Hanno fatto sacrifici per i loro ideali.* They have made sacrifices for their ideals.

+ **L'ideale sarebbe andarsene adesso.** The best thing would be to leave now.

identico AGGETTIVO (FEM **identica**, MASC PL **identici**, FEM PL **identiche**)

identical ◇ *Sono indentici.* They're identical.

+ **essere identico a** to be* exactly the same as ◇ *È identico al mio.* It's exactly the same as mine.

l' **identità** NOME FEM (PL le **identità**)

identity (PL identities) ◇ *la carta d'identità* the identity card

idiomatico AGGETTIVO (FEM **idiomatica**, MASC PL **idiomatici**, FEM PL **idiomatiche**)

+ **una frase idiomatica** an idiom

idiota AGGETTIVO (MASC PL **idioti**, FEM PL **idiote**)

vedi anche **idiota** NOME

stupid

l' **idiota** NOME MASC/FEM (MASC PL gli **idioti**, FEM PL le **idiote**)

vedi anche **idiota** AGGETTIVO

idiot

l' **idolo** NOME MASC

idol

idratante AGGETTIVO

+ **crema idratante** moisturizing cream

l' **idraulico** NOME MASC (PL gli **idraulici**)

plumber ◇ *Fa l'idraulico.* He is a plumber.

l' **iena** NOME FEM

hyena

ieri AVVERBIO

yesterday ◇ *Sono tornato ieri.* I got back yesterday. ◇ *il giornale di ieri* yesterday's paper

con il genitivo sassone.

◇ *ieri mattina* yesterday morning ◇ *ieri sera* yesterday evening

+ **ieri notte** last night

+ **ieri l'altro** the day before yesterday

igienico AGGETTIVO (FEM **igienica**, MASC PL **igienici**, FEM PL **igieniche**)

1. hygiene *(norme)*
2. hygienic *(condizioni)*

+ **carta igienica** toilet paper

ignorante AGGETTIVO

ignorant ◇ *Non ho fatto domande per paura di sembrare ignorante.* I didn't ask any questions for fear of appearing ignorant.

+ **Come sei ignorante!** Don't you know anything!

ignorare VERBO

1. to ignore ◇ *Mi ha ignorato completamente.* She completely ignored me.
2. to be* unaware ◇ *Ignoravo che tu tu fossi qui.* I was unaware that you were here.

il ARTICOLO

the ◇ *Il bambino ha fame.* The baby is hungry. ◇ *il Tamigi* the Thames

*Spesso **il** non viene tradotto.*

◇ *Il nuoto è il mio sport preferito.* Swimming is my favourite sport. ◇ *Non mi piace il riso.* I don't like rice. ◇ *Il Milan gioca in casa.* A.C. Milan is playing at home. ◇ *il padre di Mario* Mario's father

*A volte **il** viene tradotto con l'aggettivo possessivo.*

◇ *Si è tolto il cappotto.* He took off his coat. ◇ *Soffiati il naso.* Blow your nose. ◇ *Mi fa male il piede.* My foot hurts.

illegale AGGETTIVO

illegal

illeggibile AGGETTIVO

illegible

illeso AGGETTIVO (FEM **illesa**)

unhurt ◇ *È uscito illeso dall'incidente.* He escaped unhurt from the accident.

illudersi VERBO

to deceive oneself ◇ *Ti illudi se pensi di riavere i soldi.* You're deceiving yourself if you think you'll get the money back.

+ **Si illudeva di trovare qualcuno pronto ad aiutarlo.** He mistakenly thought he might

☞

find somebody ready to help him.

illuminare VERBO
to light* ◇ *La stanza era illuminata da un'unica lampada.* The room was lit by a single lamp.
• **illuminare a giorno** to floodlight ◇ *Lo stadio era illuminato a giorno.* The stadium was floodlit.

l' **illuminazione** NOME FEM
lighting

l' **illusione** NOME FEM
illusion ◇ *un'illusione ottica* an optical illusion
• **Non farti illusioni, non è sicuro che vengano.** Don't get your hopes up, it's not certain they're coming.

l' **illuso,** l' **illusa** NOME MASC, FEM
• **Sei un illuso!** You're fooling yourself!

illustrare VERBO
to illustrate

l' **illustrazione** NOME FEM
illustration

l' **imballaggio** NOME MASC
packing ◇ *una cassa da imballaggio* a packing case
• **carta da imballaggio** brown paper

imbarazzante AGGETTIVO
[1] awkward ◇ *una domanda imbarazzante* an awkward question
[2] embarrassing ◇ *una situazione imbarazzante* an embarrassing situation

imbarazzato AGGETTIVO (FEM **imbarazzata**)
embarrassed ◇ *Ero così imbarazzato che non sapevo cosa dire.* I was so embarrassed I didn't know what to say.

l' **imbarazzo** NOME MASC
embarrassment ◇ *Non è riuscito a mascherare il suo imbarazzo.* He couldn't hide his embarrassment.
• **mettere in imbarazzo** to embarrass ◇ *La sua domanda mi ha messo in imbarazzo.* Her question embarrassed me.
• **avere solo l'imbarazzo della scelta** to be* spoilt for choice ◇ *Hai solo l'imbarazzo della scelta.* You're spoilt for choice.

l' **imbarcazione** NOME FEM
boat

l' **imbarco** NOME MASC (PL gli **imbarchi**)
boarding ◇ *È già cominciato l'imbarco del mio volo?* Has boarding started for my flight yet?
• **carta d'imbarco** boarding card

imbattibile AGGETTIVO
unbeatable

imbavagliare VERBO
to gag ◇ *L'hanno legato e imbavagliato.* They bound and gagged him.

imbecille AGGETTIVO
vedi anche **imbecille** NOME
stupid

l' **imbecille** NOME MASC/FEM
vedi anche **imbecille** AGGETTIVO
idiot

imbiancare VERBO
[1] to whitewash (*con bianco di calce*)
[2] to paint (*con altra pittura*)

l' **imbianchino** NOME MASC
painter and decorator ◇ *Fa l'imbianchino.* He is a painter and decorator.

l' **imboscata** NOME FEM
ambush ◇ *L'hanno ucciso in un'imboscata.* He was killed in an ambush.

imbottire VERBO
[1] to fill (*panino*)
[2] to pad (*giacca*)
[3] to stuff (*sedia, cuscino*)
• **imbottirsi di** (*rimpinzarsi*) to stuff oneself with

imbottito AGGETTIVO (FEM **imbottita**)
[1] filled ◇ *un panino imbottito* a filled roll
[2] padded ◇ *un reggiseno imbottito* a padded bra

imbranato AGGETTIVO (FEM **imbranata**)
hopeless ◇ *Con le ragazze è proprio imbranato.* He's hopeless with girls.
◇ *Quell'imbranata non ne combina una giusta!* She's hopeless, she never does anything right!

imbrogliare VERBO
to cheat ◇ *Non imbrogliare!* Don't cheat!

l' **imbroglione,** l' **imbrogliona** NOME MASC, FEM
cheat (*in gioco*) ◇ *Sei un imbroglione!* You're a cheat!
• **un affarista imbroglione** a dishonest businessman

imbronciato AGGETTIVO (FEM **imbronciata**)
sulky

imbucare VERBO
to post
to mail US

imburrare VERBO
[1] to grease (*teglia*)
[2] to butter (*pane*)

l' **imbuto** NOME MASC
funnel

imitare VERBO
to imitate

immaginare VERBO
[1] to imagine ◇ *Non riesco ad immaginarlo.* I can't imagine it.
◇ *Immagina di essere su un'isola deserta...* Imagine you're on a desert island...
[2] to think* ◇ *Me lo immaginavo più giovane.* I thought he was younger. ◇ *Me lo immaginavo!* I thought so!
• **Grazie mille! – S'immagini!** Thank you very much! – Don't mention it!

l' **immaginazione** NOME FEM
imagination

* I verbi seguiti da questo simbolo sono irregolari. Si veda anche alle pp.328–338.

Italian ~ English

immagine NOME FEM
picture

immangiabile AGGETTIVO
inedible ◇ *Il cibo era immangiabile.* The food was inedible.

immaturo AGGETTIVO (FEM **immatura**)
immature ◇ *un ragazzo immaturo* an immature boy

immediatamente AVVERBIO
immediately ◇ *Vai immediatamente dal medico!* Go and see the doctor immediately!

immenso AGGETTIVO (FEM **immensa**)
huge ◇ *C'era un giardino immenso.* There was a huge garden.

immergere* VERBO
to plunge ◇ *Ha immerso il metallo incandescente nell'acqua.* He plunged the red-hot metal into the water.
♦ **immergersi (1)** (*bagnante*) to plunge
♦ **immergersi (2)** (*sommozzatore*) to dive
♦ **immergersi in** (*studio ecc.*) to immerse oneself in

immigrato, immigrata AGGETTIVO, NOME MASC, FEM
immigrant

immischiarsi VERBO
to interfere ◇ *Non t'immischiare, non sono fatti tuoi.* Don't interfere, it's nothing to do with you.

immobile AGGETTIVO
motionless ◇ *È rimasto lì, immobile.* He stood there, motionless.

immobiliare AGGETTIVO
♦ **agenzia immobiliare** estate agent's, US: real estate office

immondizie NOME FEM PL
rubbish SING
garbage SING US
◇ *L'ha gettato nelle immondizie.* He threw it in the rubbish.

impacchettare VERBO
to wrap up ◇ *Devo impacchettare il regalo.* I've got to wrap up the present.

impacciato AGGETTIVO (FEM **impacciata**)
awkward ◇ *Mi sentivo un po' impacciato.* I felt a bit awkward.

impacco NOME MASC (PL gli **impacchi**)
compress ◇ *Dovrai fare degli impacchi freddi.* You'll have to apply cold compresses.

impalato AGGETTIVO (FEM **impalata**)
♦ **Non stare lì impalato, fa' qualcosa!** Don't just stand there, do something!

impalcatura NOME FEM
scaffolding
scaffolding non ha plurale.

impallidire VERBO
to go* pale ◇ *È impallidito per la paura.* He went pale with fear.

impanato AGGETTIVO (FEM **impanata**)
fried in breadcrumbs ◇ *una cotoletta di vitello impanata* a veal cutlet fried in breadcrumbs

impantanarsi VERBO
to get* stuck in the mud ◇ *La nostra macchina si è impantanata.* Our car got stuck in the mud.

impappinarsi VERBO
to stammer ◇ *Si è impappinata per l'emozione.* She stammered with emotion.

imparare VERBO
to learn* ◇ *Sto imparando a suonare la chitarra.* I'm learning to play the guitar. ◇ *L'ha imparata a memoria.* He's learnt it by heart.

imparziale AGGETTIVO
impartial

impasticcarsi VERBO
to pop pills

impatto NOME MASC
impact

impaurire VERBO
to frighten ◇ *Mi hai impaurito.* You frightened me.

impaziente AGGETTIVO
impatient

impazzire VERBO
to go* mad ◇ *Ma sei impazzito?* Have you gone mad?
♦ **far impazzire qualcuno** to drive* somebody mad ◇ *Questo compito mi sta facendo impazzire.* This homework is driving me mad.
♦ **Ho un prurito da impazzire.** I've got an itch that's driving me mad.

impeccabile AGGETTIVO
impeccable ◇ *Ha un gusto impeccabile.* She's got impeccable taste.
♦ **in modo impeccabile** impeccably ◇ *Si veste sempre in modo impeccabile.* He's always impeccably dressed.

impedire VERBO
♦ **impedire a qualcuno di fare qualcosa** to stop somebody doing something
stop è seguito dal gerundio.
◇ *Il rumore mi ha impedito di dormire.* The noise stopped me sleeping. ◇ *L'hanno messo per impedire alle macchine di parcheggiare.* They put it there to stop cars parking.
♦ **Chi ti impedisce di farlo?** Who's stopping you?

impegnarsi VERBO
♦ **impegnarsi a fare qualcosa** to promise to do something ◇ *Si è impegnato a darmi una mano.* He promised to give me a hand.
♦ **impegnarsi nello studio** to study hard ◇ *Non s'impegna abbastanza nello studio.* She doesn't study hard enough.

impegnativo AGGETTIVO (FEM **impegnativa**)
demanding ◇ *un lavoro impegnativo* a ☞

demanding job

impegnato AGGETTIVO (FEM **impegnata**)
busy ◊ *Oggi sono molto impegnato.* I'm
very busy today. ◊ *Mi sembra che sia più
impegnato di te.* I think he's busier than you.
◆ **Mi dispiace, stasera sono già impegnata.**
I'm sorry, I'm already doing something
tonight.

l' **impegno** NOME MASC
[1] engagement ◊ *un impegno precedente*
a previous engagement
◆ **Domani non posso, ho un impegno.** I can't
tomorrow, I've got something on.
[2] commitment (*responsabilità*) ◊ *Ha molti
impegni di lavoro.* She has a lot of work
commitments.
◆ **studiare con impegno** to study hard

impellente AGGETTIVO
urgent ◊ *un bisogno impellente* an urgent
need

l' **imperativo** NOME MASC
imperative

l' **imperatore** NOME MASC
emperor

l' **imperatrice** NOME FEM
empress

imperfetto NOME MASC, AGGETTIVO
imperfect

impermeabile AGGETTIVO
vedi anche **impermeabile** NOME
waterproof ◊ *tessuto impermeabile*
waterproof material

l' **impermeabile** NOME MASC
vedi anche **impermeabile** AGGETTIVO
raincoat

l' **impero** NOME MASC
empire ◊ *l'impero romano* the Roman
Empire

impertinente AGGETTIVO
impertinent

impiantarsi VERBO
to hang* (*computer, programma*)

l' **impianto** NOME MASC
system ◊ *l'impianto di riscaldamento* the
heating system ◊ *un impianto stereo* a
stereo system
◆ **impianti di risalita** ski lifts

impiccare VERBO
to hang* ◊ *L'hanno impiccato.* He was
hanged.
◆ **impiccarsi** to hang* oneself ◊ *Si è
impiccato.* He hanged himself.

impicciarsi VERBO
◆ **Non t'impicciare!** Keep out of this!
◆ **Impicciati degli affari tuoi!** Mind your own
business!

impiegare VERBO
◆ **Ho impiegato più di due ore a fare i compiti.**
It took me more than two hours to do my
homework.

◆ **Quanto ci impieghi per arrivare a scuola?**
How long does it take you to get to school?

l' **impiegato**, l' **impiegata** NOME MASC, FEM
clerk ◊ *un'impiegata di banca* a bank clerk
◆ **un impiegato statale** a clerical worker in the
public sector

l' **impiego** NOME MASC (PL gli **impieghi**)
job ◊ *un impiego fisso* a permanent job

impigliarsi VERBO
to get* caught ◊ *Mi si è impigliato il vestito
in un chiodo.* My dress got caught on a nail.

impolverato AGGETTIVO (FEM **impolverata**)
dusty ◊ *È sempre più impolverato.* It's
getting dustier and dustier.

imponente AGGETTIVO
impressive ◊ *un edificio imponente* an
impressive building

impopolare AGGETTIVO
unpopular ◊ *un provvedimento
impopolare* an unpopular measure

importante AGGETTIVO
vedi anche **importante** NOME MASC
important ◊ *Questo è molto importante.*
This is very important.
◆ **una partita importante** a big match

l' **importante** NOME MASC
vedi anche **importante** AGGETTIVO
important thing ◊ *L'importante è arrivare
entro domani.* The important thing is to get
there by tomorrow.

l' **importanza** NOME FEM
importance ◊ *un fatto della massima
importanza* a matter of the greatest
importance
◆ **dare importanza a qualcosa** to think*
something is important ◊ *Danno molta
importanza all'abbigliamento.* They think
clothes are very important.
◆ **avere importanza** to matter ◊ *Che
importanza ha sapere chi è stato?* What
does it matter who it was?

importare VERBO
[1] to matter ◊ *Oggi o domani non importa.*
Today or tomorrow, it doesn't matter.
◊ *Non preoccuparti, non importa.* Don't
worry, it doesn't matter. ◊ *Non m'importa
niente di quello che pensano.* It doesn't
matter to me what they think.
◆ **Sembra che non gli importi degli esami.** He
doesn't seem to care about the exams.
[2] to import (*merci*) ◊ *La vodka viene
importata dalla Russia.* Vodka is imported
from Russia.

l' **importo** NOME MASC
amount

impossibile AGGETTIVO
impossible ◊ *Ma va', è impossibile!* Come
off it, it's impossible!
◆ **È impossibile che lo sappia.** She can't know
about it.

---

* I verbi seguiti da questo simbolo sono irregolari. Si veda anche alle pp.328–338.

imposta NOME FEM
1. shutter (*di finestra*)
2. tax (*tassa*)

impostazioni NOME FEM PL
settings (*di computer*)

impraticabile AGGETTIVO
1. impassable (*strada*)
2. unplayable (*campo di gioco*)

imprecazione NOME FEM
+ **lanciare un'imprecazione** to curse

imprenditore NOME MASC
entrepreneur

imprenditrice NOME FEM
entrepreneur

impresa NOME FEM
business ◇ *Lavora nell'impresa del padre.*
He works in his father's business. ◇ *le piccole e medie imprese* small and medium-sized businesses
+ **un'impresa edile** a building firm
+ **Sarà un'impresa riuscire a convincerlo!** It'll be hard work persuading him!

impressionante AGGETTIVO
1. terrible ◇ *una scena impressionante* a terrible scene
2. amazing ◇ *una velocità impressionante* an amazing speed

impressione NOME FEM
1. feeling (*sensazione*) ◇ *Ho avuto l'impressione che non si fidasse di me.* I had the feeling that she didn't trust me.
2. impression ◇ *Che impressione ti ha fatto?* What was your impression of him?
+ **Il sangue mi fa impressione.** I can't stand the sight of blood.

imprevedibile AGGETTIVO
unpredictable

imprevisto AGGETTIVO (FEM **imprevista**)
vedi anche **imprevisto** NOME
unexpected ◇ *una spesa imprevista* an unexpected expense

imprevisto NOME MASC
vedi anche **imprevisto** AGGETTIVO
something unexpected ◇ *salvo imprevisti* unless something unexpected happens

improbabile AGGETTIVO
unlikely ◇ *È improbabile che venga.* He's unlikely to come.

impronta NOME FEM
print (*di piede, di mano*)
+ **impronte digitali** fingerprints

improvvisamente AVVERBIO
1. suddenly ◇ *Improvvisamente si è messo a piovere.* It suddenly started to rain.
2. unexpectedly (*senza preavviso*) ◇ *È arrivato improvvisamente.* He arrived unexpectedly.

improvvisare VERBO
1. to improvise (*in musica, a teatro*)
2. to put* together ◇ *Abbiamo improvvisato una cenetta alla buona.* We put together a simple meal.

improvviso AGGETTIVO (FEM **improvvisa**)
sudden ◇ *un improvviso cambiamento di programma* a sudden change of plan
+ **all'improvviso** suddenly ◇ *All'improvviso si è spalancata la porta.* The door suddenly opened. ◇ *È partita all'improvviso.* She left suddenly.

imprudente AGGETTIVO
careless ◇ *un guidatore imprudente* a careless driver

impugnare VERBO
to hold* (*arma, racchetta*)

impulsivo AGGETTIVO (FEM **impulsiva**)
impulsive ◇ *Ha un carattere impulsivo.*
He's got an impulsive nature.

l' **impulso** NOME MASC
impulse ◇ *Ho agito d'impulso.* I acted on impulse.

l' **imputato,** l' **imputata** NOME MASC, FEM
defendant

in PREPOSIZIONE
1. in ◇ *Vive in Canada.* He lives in Canada.
◇ *È nel cassetto.* It's in the drawer.
◇ *millenovecentonovantanove* nineteen-ninety nine ◇ *in estate* in summer
◇ *L'ha fatto in sei mesi.* He did it in six months. ◇ *Camminavano in silenzio.* They walked in silence. ◇ *Parlavano in tedesco.* They were speaking in German. ◇ *L'ha tagliato in due.* She cut it in two.
2. to (*moto a luogo*) ◇ *Andrò in Germania quest'estate.* I'm going to Germany this summer. ◇ *È andato in ufficio.* He's gone to the office.
3. into (*dentro*) ◇ *Su, sali in macchina.* Come on, get into the car. ◇ *Come sono penetrati nella banca?* How did they get into the bank? ◇ *L'ha gettato in acqua.* He threw it into the water.
4. by (*mezzo*) ◇ *Siamo andati in treno.* We went by train.
+ **essere in vacanza** to be* on holiday
+ **andare in vacanza** to go* on holiday

inabitabile AGGETTIVO
uninhabitable

inaccettabile AGGETTIVO
unacceptable

inacidirsi VERBO
to go* sour

inaffidabile AGGETTIVO
unreliable ◇ *È una persona totalmente inaffidabile.* He's totally unreliable.

inamidato AGGETTIVO (FEM **inamidata**)
starched (*colletto*)

inaspettato AGGETTIVO (FEM **inaspettata**)
unexpected ◇ *una visita inaspettata* an unexpected visit

inaudito AGGETTIVO (FEM **inaudita**)
+ **È inaudito!** It's outrageous!

inaugurare VERBO ☞

to open ◊ *Il nuovo stadio sarà inaugurato domani.* The new stadium is being opened tomorrow.
♦ **Oggi ho inaugurato le scarpe nuove.** I wore my new shoes for the first time today.

l' **inaugurazione** NOME FEM
opening ◊ *l'inaugurazione di una mostra* the opening of an exhibition

incamminarsi VERBO
to set* off ◊ *Ci siamo incamminati verso la spiaggia.* We set off towards the beach.

incantevole AGGETTIVO
lovely ◊ *C'era un paesaggio incantevole.* The scenery was lovely. ◊ *È ancora più incantevole del solito.* It's even lovelier than usual.

l' **incanto** NOME MASC
♦ **Questo paesino è un incanto!** This village is lovely!
♦ **come per incanto** as if by magic ◊ *L'eczema è scomparso come per incanto.* The eczema disappeared as if by magic.

incapace AGGETTIVO
♦ **essere incapace di** to be* incapable of ◊ *È incapace di mentire.* She's incapable of lying.

incaricare VERBO
♦ **incaricare qualcuno di fare qualcosa** to ask somebody to do something ◊ *Mi hanno incaricato di rispondere al telefono.* They asked me to answer the phone.
♦ **Me ne incarico io.** I'll see to it.

l' **incarico** NOME MASC (PL gli **incarichi**)
job ◊ *un incarico importante* an important job
♦ **Chi aveva l'incarico di comprare i biglietti?** Who was supposed to get the tickets?

incarnita AGGETTIVO
♦ **unghia incarnita** ingrown toenail

incartare VERBO
to wrap ◊ *Devo ancora incartare i regali.* I still have to wrap the presents. ◊ *Me lo incarta, per favore?* Could you wrap it for me please?

incasinare VERBO
to mess up ◊ *Mio fratello ha incasinato i miei CD.* My brother has messed up my CDs.

incasinato AGGETTIVO (FEM **incasinata**)
in a mess ◊ *In questo periodo sono proprio incasinata.* I'm in a real mess at the moment.

incassare VERBO
to cash ◊ *Puoi incassare l'assegno in qualunque banca.* You can cash the cheque at any bank.

l' **incasso** NOME MASC
takings PL ◊ *I ladri sono fuggiti con l'incasso della giornata.* The thieves escaped with the day's takings.
♦ **Il film ha battuto ogni record d'incasso.** The film has been a great box office success.

incastrare VERBO
to frame ◊ *Era ovvio che l'ave o incastrato.* It was obvious that he'd been framed.
♦ **incastrarsi (1)** (*bloccarsi*) to get* stuck ◊ *La chiave si è incastrata nella serratura.* The key got stuck in the lock.
♦ **incastrarsi (2)** (*andare*) to fit ◊ *Quel pezzo si incastra qui.* That piece fits here.

incatenare VERBO
to chain ◊ *I prigionieri venivano incatenati al muro.* The prisoners were chained to the wall.

incavato AGGETTIVO (FEM **incavata**)
1. hollow (*guance*)
2. sunken (*occhi*)

incavolarsi VERBO
to get* angry ◊ *S'incavola per ogni sciocchezza.* She gets angry about the slightest thing. ◊ *Non t'incavolare con me!* Don't get angry with me!

incazzarsi VERBO
to get* pissed off (*volgare*) ◊ *Mi sono incazzato da morire!* I was really pissed off!

incendiare VERBO
to set* fire to ◊ *Dei vandali hanno incendiato la scuola.* Vandals set fire to the school.

l' **incendio** NOME MASC
fire ◊ *I vigili del fuoco hanno domato l'incendio.* The firemen have got the fire under control.

l' **inceneritore** NOME MASC
incinerator

l' **incenso** NOME MASC
incense ◊ *odore d'incenso* smell of incense
♦ **bastoncini d'incenso** joss sticks

incepparsi VERBO
to jam ◊ *La serratura si è inceppata.* The lock jammed.

l' **incertezza** NOME FEM
uncertainty (PL uncertainties) ◊ *un periodo di incertezza politica* a period of political uncertainty
♦ **Ha avuto un momento d'incertezza nel rispondere.** He hesitated for a moment before answering.

incerto AGGETTIVO (FEM **incerta**)
uncertain ◊ *La situazione è ancora incerta.* The situation is still uncertain. ◊ *Ero incerto se dirglielo o no.* I was uncertain whether to tell him or not.

l' **inchiesta** NOME FEM
1. inquiry (PL inquiries) (*della polizia*) ◊ *È stata aperta un'inchiesta.* An inquiry has been opened.
2. special report (*di giornale*) ◊ *un'inchiesta sui giovani e la droga* a special report on young people and drugs

l' **inchiostro** NOME MASC
ink ◊ *una macchia d'inchiostro* an ink stain

---

* I verbi seguiti da questo simbolo sono irregolari. Si veda anche alle pp.328–338.

inciampare VERBO
to trip ◇ *Sono inciampato nel tappeto.* I tripped over the carpet.

incidente NOME MASC
accident ◇ *Sono rimasti feriti in un incidente d'auto.* They were injured in a car accident.
• **incidente aereo** plane crash ◇ *È il terzo incidente aereo in un mese.* It's the third plane crash in a month.
• **un incidente ferroviario** a train crash

incinta AGGETTIVO
pregnant ◇ *È incinta di cinque mesi.* She's five months pregnant.
• **rimanere incinta** to get* pregnant ◇ *È rimasta incinta.* She got pregnant.

incirca AVVERBIO
• **all'incirca** about ◇ *È grande all'incirca così.* It's about this big. ◇ *Saranno all'incirca le tre.* It must be about three.

incivile AGGETTIVO
rude ◇ *una persona incivile* a rude person
• **Che modi incivili!** What bad manners!

inclinare VERBO
to tilt ◇ *Inclina un po' il tavolo.* Tilt the table a bit.

includere* VERBO
to include

incluso AGGETTIVO (FEM **inclusa**)
[1] included ◇ *È inclusa la colazione?* Is breakfast included?
[2] including ◇ *Tutti lo sapevano, incluso John.* Everyone, including John, knew about it.
• **Leggere da pagina cinque a pagina sette inclusa.** Read from the beginning of page five to the end of page seven.

incollare VERBO
to stick* ◇ *Ha incollato le sue foto sul diario.* She stuck the photos of him into her diary.

incollato AGGETTIVO (FEM **incollata**)
glued ◇ *Passa il pomeriggio incollata al computer.* She spends the afternoon glued to the computer.

incolpare VERBO
to blame ◇ *Hanno incolpato me.* They blamed me.
• **Mi ha incolpato di avergli rotto il motorino.** He accused me of damaging his bike.

incolume AGGETTIVO
unhurt ◇ *È uscito incolume dall'incidente.* He escaped from the accident unhurt.

incominciare VERBO
to start ◇ *La partita incomincia alle sette.* The match starts at seven. ◇ *La prima parola incomincia per F.* The first word starts with F.
*Quando **start** è seguito da un verbo in genere si possono usare sia l'infinito che il gerundio.*
◇ *Ha incominciato a ridere.* She started to laugh. ◇ *Ha incominciato a piangere.* She started crying.

incompetente AGGETTIVO
vedi anche **incompetente** NOME MASC/FEM
incompetent

l' **incompetente** NOME MASC/FEM
vedi anche **incompetente** AGGETTIVO
incompetent person

incompiuto AGGETTIVO (FEM **incompiuta**)
unfinished ◇ *una sinfonia incompiuta* an unfinished symphony

incomprensibile AGGETTIVO
incomprehensible

inconcepibile AGGETTIVO
incredible ◇ *È inconcepibile!* It's incredible!

inconfondibile AGGETTIVO
unmistakable ◇ *Il suo stile è inconfondibile.* His style is unmistakable.

inconsueto AGGETTIVO (FEM **inconsueta**)
unusual

incontrare VERBO
[1] to meet* ◇ *Incontriamoci davanti al cinema.* Let's meet in front of the cinema. ◇ *Ci siamo incontrati ad una festa.* We met at a party.
[2] to bump into (*imbattersi*) ◇ *Ho incontrato Maurizio per strada.* I bumped into Maurizio in the street.
[3] to play ◇ *L'Inter incontrerà la Juve domenica prossima.* Inter Milan are playing Juventus next Sunday.

l' **incontro** NOME MASC
vedi anche **incontro** PREPOSIZIONE
[1] meeting ◇ *un incontro casuale* a chance meeting
[2] match (*sportivo*) ◇ *un incontro di pugilato* a boxing match

incontro PREPOSIZIONE
vedi anche **incontro** NOME
• **incontro a** towards ◇ *Mi è venuto incontro sorridente.* He came towards me smiling.

l' **inconveniente** NOME MASC
[1] drawback (*svantaggio*) ◇ *Ha un unico inconveniente: è troppo piccolo.* It's only got one drawback: it's too small.
[2] problem (*noia*) ◇ *Ho avuto qualche inconveniente con la moto.* I had some problems with my motorbike.

incoraggiare VERBO
to encourage ◇ *I suoi l'hanno incoraggiato a studiare musica.* His parents encouraged him to study music.

incorniciare VERBO
to frame ◇ *Ho incorniciato la foto.* I've framed the photo.

incosciente AGGETTIVO
vedi anche **incosciente** NOME MASC/FEM
[1] unconscious (*privo di sensi*) ◇ *È rimasto incosciente per alcuni minuti.* He was unconscious for several minutes.
[2] reckless ◇ *un automobilista incosciente* a reckless driver

l' **incosciente** NOME MASC/FEM
>vedi anche **incosciente** AGGETTIVO

reckless person

incredibile AGGETTIVO
incredible ◊ *È incredibile!* That's incredible!

incrinare VERBO
to crack ◊ *Non l'ho rotto, l'ho solo incrinato.* I didn't break it, I just cracked it.

incrociare VERBO
1 to cross ◊ *Ha incrociato le braccia.* He crossed his arms.
2 to meet* ◊ *Ci siamo incrociati nel corridoio.* We met in the corridor.

l' **incrocio** NOME MASC (PL gli **incroci**)
1 junction (*tra strade*) ◊ *All'incrocio gira a destra.* Turn right at the junction.
2 cross (*tra razze*) ◊ *un incrocio tra un collie e un labrador* a cross between a collie and a labrador

l' **incubo** NOME MASC
nightmare ◊ *Stanotte ho avuto un incubo.* I had a nightmare last night.

incurabile AGGETTIVO
incurable ◊ *un male incurabile* an incurable disease

l' **incursione** NOME FEM
raid ◊ *un'incursione aerea* an air raid

incustodito AGGETTIVO (FEM **incustodita**)
unattended ◊ *Il parcheggio è incustodito.* The car park is unattended. ◊ *Non lasciare il bagaglio incustodito.* Don't leave your luggage unattended.

indaffarato AGGETTIVO (FEM **indaffarata**)
busy ◊ *Era indaffarato a riparare la bici.* He was busy mending his bike. ◊ *È sempre più indaffarato.* He's busier and busier.

indagare VERBO
♦ **indagare su** to investigate ◊ *La polizia sta indagando sul delitto.* The police are investigating the crime.
>senza preposizione.

l' **indagine** NOME FEM
investigation ◊ *le indagini della polizia* police investigations

indebitarsi VERBO
♦ **indebitarsi con** to borrow money from ◊ *Si è indebitato con la banca.* He borrowed money from the bank.

indebolirsi VERBO
1 to get* weak (*persona*) ◊ *Si è molto indebolito.* He's got very weak.
2 to deteriorate (*vista*)

indecente AGGETTIVO
indecent ◊ *Quella minigonna è indecente!* That mini skirt is indecent!

indeciso AGGETTIVO (FEM **indecisa**)
♦ **Sono indeciso tra questi due.** I can't decide between these two.
♦ **Era indeciso su cosa regalarle.** He couldn't

decide what to give her.

indeterminativo AGGETTIVO (FEM **indeterminativa**)
♦ **articolo indeterminativo** indefinite article

l' **India** NOME FEM
India ◊ *Mi è piaciuta molto l'India.* I really liked India. ◊ *Andremo in India quest'estate.* We're going to India this summer.

indiano, indiana NOME, AGGETTIVO
Indian ◊ *un ristorante indiano* an Indian restaurant ◊ *gli indiani* the Indians
>Si noti l'uso della maiuscola in inglese.

indicare VERBO
to show* ◊ *Gli indicherò la strada.* I'll show him the way.
♦ **indicare qualcosa** (*col dito*) to point to something

l' **indicativo** NOME MASC
indicative

le **indicazioni** NOME FEM PL
1 directions (*istruzioni*) ◊ *Mi ha dato le indicazioni per arrivarci.* She gave me directions to get here.
2 signs (*cartelli*) ◊ *Segui le indicazioni.* Follow the signs.

l' **indice** NOME MASC
1 index finger (*dito*)
2 index (*di libro*)

indietro AVVERBIO
back ◊ *Ho fatto un passo indietro.* I took a step back. ◊ *Ha voluto indietro i soldi.* She wanted her money back. ◊ *Bisogna mettere l'orologio indietro di un'ora.* The clock has to be put back an hour.
♦ **tornare indietro** to turn back ◊ *Torniamo indietro?* Shall we turn back?
♦ **all'indietro** backwards ◊ *È caduta all'indietro.* She fell backwards.
♦ **essere indietro (1)** (*orologio*) to be* slow ◊ *Il mio orologio è indietro.* My watch is slow.
♦ **essere indietro (2)** (*in matematica ecc.*) to be* behind

indifeso AGGETTIVO (FEM **indifesa**)
defenceless ◊ *un povero bambino indifeso* a poor defenceless child

indifferente AGGETTIVO
>vedi anche **indifferente** NOME MASC/FEM
♦ **A piedi o in auto, per me è indifferente.** We can walk or drive, I don't mind which.
♦ **lasciare indifferente** to leave* cold ◊ *La notizia mi ha lasciato del tutto indifferente.* The news left me completely cold.

l' **indifferente** NOME MASC/FEM
>vedi anche **indifferente** AGGETTIVO
♦ **fare l'indifferente** to act casual ◊ *Cerca di fare l'indifferente, sta venendo da questa parte.* Try to act casual, she's coming this way.

---

* *I verbi seguiti da questo simbolo sono irregolari. Si veda anche alle pp.328–338.*

- **Non fare l'indifferente, sto parlando di te.** Don't pretend you don't understand, I'm talking about you.

indigestione NOME FEM
- **Ho fatto un'indigestione di dolci.** I've eaten too many cakes.

indimenticabile AGGETTIVO
unforgettable ◊ *una vacanza indimenticabile* an unforgettable holiday

indipendente AGGETTIVO
independent ◊ *Ha un carattere molto indipendente.* She's got a very independent nature.
- **essere economicamente indipendente** to be* financially independent ◊ *Non sono ancora economicamente indipendente.* I'm not yet financially independent.

indiretto AGGETTIVO (FEM **indiretta**)
indirect ◊ *discorso indiretto* indirect speech
- **per vie indirette** indirectly

indirizzare VERBO
① to address ◊ *La lettera era indirizzata a me.* The letter was addressed to me.
② to send* ◊ *Mi hanno indirizzato qui.* They sent me here.

indirizzo NOME MASC
address ◊ *Mi dai il tuo indirizzo?* Can I have your address?

indispensabile AGGETTIVO
vedi anche **indispensabile** NOME MASC
essential ◊ *È uno strumento indispensabile.* It's an essential tool. ◊ *Non è indispensabile che ci sia anche tu.* It's not essential for you to be here.

indispensabile NOME MASC
vedi anche **indispensabile** AGGETTIVO
what's necessary ◊ *Ho portato solo l'indispensabile per una notte.* I've just brought what's necessary for one night.

individuale AGGETTIVO
personal ◊ *libertà individuale* personal freedom
- **lezioni individuali** one-to-one tuition SING

indizio NOME MASC
clue ◊ *La polizia non ha trovato alcun indizio.* The police haven't found any clues.

indolenzito AGGETTIVO (FEM **indolenzita**)
aching ◊ *Sono tutto indolenzito.* I'm aching all over.

indomani NOME MASC
- **l'indomani** the next day ◊ *Ha detto che sarebbe tornata l'indomani.* She said she'd come back the next day.

indossare VERBO
to wear*

indossatore, l' **indossatrice** NOME MASC, FEM
model ◊ *Fa l'indossatrice.* She is a model.

indovinare VERBO
to guess ◊ *Indovina chi ho incontrato ieri!* Guess who I met yesterday!

- **Bravo, hai indovinato!** Well done, you've got it right!
- **tirare a indovinare** to have* a guess ◊ *Non lo sapevo, quindi ho tirato a indovinare.* I didn't know, so I had a guess.

l' **indovinello** NOME MASC
riddle ◊ *Sai risolvere questo indovinello?* Do you know the answer to this riddle?

indubbiamente AVVERBIO
definitely ◊ *È indubbiamente uno dei migliori.* It's definitely one of the best.

indurire VERBO
to harden ◊ *Viene usato per indurire l'acciaio.* It's used to harden steel.
- **indurirsi** to go* hard ◊ *Il terreno si è indurito.* The ground has gone hard.

l' **industria** NOME FEM
industry (PL industries) ◊ *Lavora nell'industria automobilistica.* He works in the car industry.

industriale AGGETTIVO
vedi anche **industriale** NOME
industrial ◊ *una città industriale* an industrial town

l' **industriale** NOME MASC/FEM
vedi anche **industriale** AGGETTIVO
industrialist ◊ *È un industriale.* He is an industrialist.

inedito AGGETTIVO (FEM **inedita**)
unpublished

l' **inesperienza** NOME FEM
inexperience ◊ *un errore dovuto all'inesperienza* a mistake caused by inexperience

inesperto AGGETTIVO (FEM **inesperta**)
inexperienced ◊ *un giovane medico inesperto* an inexperienced young doctor

inevitabile AGGETTIVO
inevitable

infallibile AGGETTIVO
① excellent ◊ *un rimedio infallibile contro il raffreddore* an excellent remedy for colds
② infallible ◊ *Nessuno è infallibile.* Nobody is infallible.

infangato AGGETTIVO (FEM **infangata**)
covered with mud ◊ *Ho le scarpe infangate.* My shoes are covered with mud.

infantile AGGETTIVO
childish ◊ *comportamento infantile* childish behaviour
- **asilo infantile** nursery school

l' **infarinatura** NOME FEM
- **Ho solo un'infarinatura di informatica.** I only know a bit about computing.

l' **infarto** NOME MASC
heart attack ◊ *Ha avuto un infarto.* He had a heart attack.

infatti CONGIUNZIONE
- **Mi aveva promesso un regalo e infatti me l'ha portato.** She'd promised me a present and she brought me one.

♦ **Penso che sia uscito. – Infatti non risponde nessuno.** I think he's out. – Yes, no one's answering.

♦ **Ha detto che avrebbe telefonato. -Sì, infatti...** She said she'd phone. – Yes, well... *Attenzione! In inglese esiste l'espressione in* **fact** *che però vuol dire* **in effetti.**

infedele AGGETTIVO
unfaithful

infelice AGGETTIVO
unhappy ◊ *il giorno più infelice della mia vita* the unhappiest day of my life

inferiore AGGETTIVO
1 lower ◊ *il labbro inferiore* the lower lip
2 inferior ◊ *un prodotto di qualità inferiore* a product of inferior quality

♦ **i bambini di età inferiore ai cinque anni** children under five

l' **inferiorità** NOME FEM
inferiority ◊ *un complesso d'inferiorità* an inferiority complex

l' **infermiere,** l' **infermiera** NOME MASC, FEM
nurse ◊ *Fa l'infermiere.* He is a nurse.

infernale AGGETTIVO
terrible ◊ *C'era un chiasso infernale.* There was a terrible noise.

♦ **Qui dentro fa un caldo infernale!** It's terribly hot in here!

l' **inferno** NOME MASC
hell

l' **inferriata** NOME FEM
railings PL

l' **infezione** NOME FEM
infection

infiammabile AGGETTIVO
inflammable

l' **infiammazione** NOME FEM
inflammation

infilare VERBO
to put* ◊ *Ho infilato la chiave nella serratura.* I put the key into the lock.

♦ **infilarsi (1)** to put* on ◊ *Si è infilato la giacca ed è uscito.* He put on his jacket and went out.

♦ **infilarsi (2)** to get* ◊ *Il gatto si è infilato sotto il letto.* The cat got under the bed.

infine AVVERBIO
finally ◊ *Vorrei dire, infine...* Finally I would like to say...

infinito AGGETTIVO (FEM **infinita**)
vedi anche **infinito** NOME
endless ◊ *Ha una pazienza infinita.* She has endless patience.

♦ **Grazie infinite!** Many thanks!

l' **infinito** NOME MASC
vedi anche **infinito** AGGETTIVO
infinitive (*in grammatica*)

l' **influenza** NOME FEM
flu ◊ *Ho l'influenza.* I've got flu.

influenzare VERBO

to influence ◊ *Si lascia influenzare troppo dagli amici.* She's too easily influenced by her friends.

influire VERBO

♦ **influire su** to influence ◊ *Non ha influito sulla sua decisione.* It didn't influence his decision.

infondato AGGETTIVO (FEM **infondata**)
unfounded ◊ *un sospetto infondato* an unfounded suspicion

informare VERBO
to inform ◊ *Avete informato la polizia?* Have you informed the police?

♦ **informarsi su qualcosa** to ask about something ◊ *Mi sono informato sugli orari dei treni.* I asked about train times.

l' **informatica** NOME FEM
computing ◊ *un corso d'informatica* a computing course

informato AGGETTIVO (FEM **informata**)
informed ◊ *Tienimi informato.* Keep me informed.

♦ **È sempre informato sulle novità discografiche.** He always knows about the latest releases.

l' **informatore,** l' **informatrice** NOME MASC, FEM
informer

l' **informazione** NOME FEM
information
information non ha il plurale e non è mai preceduto dall'articolo indeterminativo.
◊ *Scusi, può darmi un'informazione?* Excuse me, can you give me some information? ◊ *Mi ha dato un'informazione utile.* He gave me some useful information. ◊ *Ho chiesto un'informazione ad un poliziotto.* I asked a policeman for information. ◊ *Per ulteriori informazioni telefonare al numero...* For further information call... ◊ *Dov'è l'ufficio informazioni?* Where's the information office?

infortunato AGGETTIVO (FEM **infortunata**)
injured

l' **infortunio** NOME MASC
accident ◊ *Ha avuto un infortunio sul lavoro.* He had an accident at work.

infreddolito AGGETTIVO (FEM **infreddolita**)
cold ◊ *Sono un po' infreddolito.* I'm a bit cold.

infuori AVVERBIO
out ◊ *Sporge un po' infuori.* It sticks out a bit.

♦ **all'infuori di** except ◊ *Lo sapevano tutti all'infuori di lui.* They all knew except him.

ingaggiare VERBO

♦ **essere ingaggiato** (*giocatore*) to sign ◊ *È stato ingaggiato per la prossima stagione.* He's signed for next season.

Italian ~ English

ingannare VERBO
1. to deceive ◊ *Mi hai ingannato!* You deceived me!
+ **Le apparenze spesso ingannano.** Appearances are often deceptive.
2. to take* in ◊ *Non lasciarti ingannare dalla sua aria innocente.* Don't be taken in by his air of innocence.
+ **ingannarsi** (*sbagliarsi*) to be* mistaken
+ **ingannare il tempo** to while away the time

ingarbugliarsi VERBO
1. to get* tangled (*corda*)
2. to get* complicated ◊ *A questo punto la faccenda s'ingarbuglia.* At this point things get complicated.

ingegnere NOME MASC
engineer ◊ *Fa l'ingegnere.* He is an engineer.

ingegneria NOME FEM
engineering ◊ *È laureata in ingegneria.* She's got a degree in engineering.

ingelosire VERBO
to make* jealous ◊ *L'ha fatto solo per farlo ingelosire.* She just did it to make him jealous.

ingenuo AGGETTIVO (FEM **ingenua**)
vedi anche **ingenuo** NOME MASC/FEM
naïve ◊ *È molto ingenua.* She's very naïve. ◊ *Ma come fai ad essere così ingenuo?* How can you be so naïve?
Attenzione! In inglese esiste la parola **ingenious**, *che però significa* **ingegnoso**.

ingenuo, l' **ingenua** NOME MASC, FEM
vedi anche **ingenuo** AGGETTIVO
+ **fare l'ingenuo** to act the innocent ◊ *Non fare l'ingenuo, sai benissimo di cosa parlo.* Don't act the innocent, you know perfectly well what I'm talking about.

ingessare VERBO
to put* in plaster ◊ *Gli hanno ingessato il braccio.* They put his arm in plaster.

ingessatura NOME FEM
plaster ◊ *Mi hanno tolto l'ingessatura.* They took off the plaster.

Inghilterra NOME FEM
England ◊ *Mi è piaciuta molto l'Inghilterra.* I really liked England. ◊ *Andrò in Inghilterra quest'estate.* I'm going to England this summer.

> ❶ *Italians often refer to Britain as a whole as* **l'Inghilterra**.

inghiottire VERBO
to swallow

inginocchiarsi VERBO
to kneel* down ◊ *Si è inginocchiato accanto al cane.* He knelt down beside the dog.

ingiusto AGGETTIVO (FEM **ingiusta**)
unfair ◊ *Questo è profondamente ingiusto.* This is utterly unfair.

inglese AGGETTIVO
vedi anche **inglese** NOME MASC, NOME FEM
English

> ❶ *Gli scozzesi, i gallesi e gli irlandesi si possono offendere se vengono chiamati* **English**. *Quando si vuole parlare degli abitanti del Regno Unito si deve usare "the British".*

◊ *la squadra inglese* the English team

l' **inglese** NOME MASC
vedi anche **inglese** NOME FEM, AGGETTIVO
1. Englishman (PL Englishmen) (*persona*)
+ **gli inglesi** (*uomini e donne*) English people
2. English (*lingua*) ◊ *Parli inglese?* Do you speak English?

l' **inglese** NOME FEM
vedi anche **inglese** NOME MASC, AGGETTIVO
Englishwoman (PL Englishwomen)

ingoiare VERBO
to swallow

ingolfarsi VERBO
to flood ◊ *Il motore si è ingolfato.* The engine has flooded.

ingombrante AGGETTIVO
cumbersome ◊ *una valigia ingombrante* a cumbersome case

ingombrare VERBO
to block ◊ *Si prega di non ingombrare il corridoio.* Please don't block the corridor.
+ **I bagagli ingombravano la stanza.** The room was full of luggage.

ingordo AGGETTIVO (FEM **ingorda**)
greedy ◊ *Non essere ingordo!* Don't be greedy! ◊ *È più ingordo di me.* He's greedier than me.

l' **ingorgo** NOME MASC (PL gli **ingorghi**)
hold-up ◊ *C'era un ingorgo all'incrocio.* There was a hold-up at the junction.

ingranare VERBO
+ **ingranare la marcia** to get* into gear ◊ *Non riesco a ingranare la marcia.* I can't get into gear.

l' **ingrandimento** NOME MASC
enlargement ◊ *Vorrei un ingrandimento di questa foto.* I'd like an enlargement of this photo.
+ **far fare un ingrandimento** to get* an enlargement
+ **una lente d'ingrandimento** a magnifying glass

ingrandire VERBO
1. to enlarge (*foto*)
2. to extend ◊ *Ho deciso di ingrandire la casa.* I've decided to extend my house.
+ **ingrandirsi** to get* bigger ◊ *La città si sta ingrandendo.* The town is getting bigger.

ingrassare VERBO
to put* on weight ◊ *Sei un po' ingrassata.* You've put on a bit of weight.
+ **ingrassare di** to put* on ◊ *Sono ingrassato* ☞

di due chili. I've put on two kilos.
- **far ingrassare** (*cibo*) to be* fattening ◇ *I dolci fanno ingrassare.* Puddings are fattening.

l' **ingrediente** NOME MASC
ingredient

l' **ingresso** NOME MASC
[1] entrance ◇ *L'ingresso principale è sulla via laterale.* The main entrance is in the side street.
[2] doorway ◇ *Non stare qui nell'ingresso, accomodati.* Don't stand there in the doorway, come in.
- **"ingresso libero"** "admission free"
- **"vietato l'ingresso"** "no admittance"

ingrosso AVVERBIO
- **all'ingrosso**
wholesale

l' **inguine** NOME MASC
groin ◇ *Ho uno strappo all'inguine.* I've strained my groin.

inibito AGGETTIVO (FEM **inibita**)
inhibited ◇ *Non pensavo che fossi così inibito!* I didn't think you were so inhibited!

l' **iniezione** NOME FEM
injection
- **fare un'iniezione** to give* an injection ◇ *Mi hanno fatto un'iniezione di penicillina.* They gave me an injection of penicillin.
- **motore a iniezione** fuel injection engine

ininterrottamente AVVERBIO
non-stop ◇ *Ha parlato ininterrottamente per tre ore.* He talked non-stop for three hours.

iniziale AGGETTIVO
vedi anche **iniziale** NOME FEM
initial ◇ *la fase iniziale* the initial phase
- **lo stipendio iniziale** the starting salary

l' **iniziale** NOME FEM
vedi anche **iniziale** AGGETTIVO
initial ◇ *un accendino con le sue iniziali* a lighter with his initials

iniziare VERBO
to start ◇ *Il film sta per iniziare.* The film is about to start.
- **iniziare a fare qualcosa** to start doing something ◇ *Hai iniziato a cucinare?* Have you started cooking?

l' **iniziativa** NOME FEM
initiative ◇ *È venuta di propria iniziativa.* She came on her own initiative.
- **prendere l'iniziativa** to take* the initiative ◇ *Se vuoi rivederla, devi prendere tu l'iniziativa.* If you want to see her again, you'll have to take the initiative.
- **una serie di iniziative culturali** a series of arts events

l' **inizio** NOME MASC
beginning ◇ *Ho riletto l'inizio della lettera dieci volte.* I read the beginning of the letter

ten times. ◇ *Il pareggio è arrivato all'inizio del secondo tempo.* The equalizer came at the beginning of the second half.
- **L'inizio dei lavori è previsto per la fine del mese.** Work will begin at the end of the month.
- **avere inizio** to begin* ◇ *Il film ha inizio con una scena d'azione.* The film begins with an action scene.
- **all'inizio** at first ◇ *All'inizio pensavo che scherzasse.* At first I thought he was joking.
- **all'inizio di** at the beginning of ◇ *Abito proprio all'inizio della strada.* I live at the beginning of the street.

innaffiare VERBO
to water

innamorarsi VERBO
to fall* in love ◇ *Si è subito innamorato di lei.* He instantly fell in love with her.

innamorato AGGETTIVO (FEM **innamorata**)
in love ◇ *È innamorata persa.* She's madly in love.
- **essere innamorato di qualcuno** to be* in love with someone ◇ *Sei innamorato di lei?* Are you in love with her?

innanzitutto AVVERBIO
first of all ◇ *Innanzitutto bisogna informarsi degli orari.* First of all you need to ask about the times.

innervosire VERBO
- **innervosire qualcuno** to get* on somebody's nerves ◇ *Il traffico mi innervosisce.* The traffic gets on my nerves.
- **Si è innervosito per il rumore.** The noise got on his nerves.

l' **inno** NOME MASC
- **inno nazionale** national anthem

innocente AGGETTIVO
innocent ◇ *Secondo me è innocente.* In my opinion he's innocent.
- **dichiararsi innocente** to maintain one's innocence ◇ *Si è sempre dichiarato innocente.* He has always maintained his innocence.
- **uno scherzo innocente** a harmless joke

inodore AGGETTIVO
odourless
odorless US
◇ *un gas inodore* an odourless gas

inoltre AVVERBIO
besides

inosservato AGGETTIVO (FEM **inosservata**)
unnoticed ◇ *L'errore non è passato inosservato.* The mistake didn't go unnoticed.

inossidabile AGGETTIVO
- **acciaio inossidabile** stainless steel

l' **inquilino,** l' **inquilina** NOME MASC, FEM
tenant

l' **inquinamento** NOME MASC

---

pollution ◊ *la lotta contro l'inquinamento* the fight against pollution

inquinare VERBO

to pollute ◊ *Le fabbriche hanno inquinato il mare.* The factories have polluted the sea.

insalata NOME FEM

1 salad ◊ *un'insalata verde* a green salad ◊ *un'insalata di pomodori* a tomato salad ◊ *un'insalata di mare* a seafood salad

2 lettuce ◊ *Hai lavato l'insalata?* Have you washed the lettuce?

insalatiera NOME FEM

salad bowl

insaputa NOME FEM

◆ **all'insaputa di qualcuno** without somebody's knowledge ◊ *L'ha comprato all'insaputa dei suoi.* She bought it without her parents' knowledge.

insegna NOME FEM

sign ◊ *un'insegna al neon* a neon sign

insegnamento NOME MASC

teaching ◊ *il suo metodo d'insegnamento* her way of teaching

insegnante NOME MASC/FEM

teacher ◊ *Fa l'insegnante.* She is a teacher. ◊ *l'insegnante d'inglese* the English teacher

insegnare VERBO

to teach*

◆ **insegnare qualcosa a qualcuno** to teach* somebody something ◊ *Ha insegnato ai bambini i nomi delle piante.* She taught the children the names of plants.

◆ **insegnare a qualcuno a fare qualcosa** to teach* somebody to do something ◊ *Mi ha insegnato a suonare la chitarra.* He taught me to play the guitar.

inseguire VERBO

to chase ◊ *La polizia ha inseguito i rapinatori.* The police chased the robbers.

insenatura NOME FEM

inlet

inserire VERBO

to put* ◊ *Bisogna inserire la vite nel foro.* You need to put the screw in the hole.

◆ **inserire la spina della TV** to plug in the TV

◆ **inserirsi in** to settle into ◊ *Non si è ancora inserito bene nella nuova scuola.* He hasn't settled into his new school yet.

inserzione NOME FEM

advert

ad US

◊ *Ho messo un'inserzione sul giornale.* I put an advert in the paper.

insetticida NOME MASC (PL gli **insetticidi**)

◆ **una bomboletta d'insetticida** a can of fly spray

insetto NOME MASC

insect

insicuro AGGETTIVO (FEM **insicura**)

insecure

insieme AVVERBIO

vedi anche **insieme** NOME

together ◊ *Da quanto tempo state insieme?* How long have you been together? ◊ *colori che stanno bene insieme* colours that go well together ◊ *Forza, spingete tutti insieme!* Come on, everyone push together!

◆ **Non parlate tutti insieme, per favore.** Don't all speak at the same time, please.

◆ **mettersi insieme** to start going out together ◊ *Si sono messi insieme due anni fa.* They started going out together two years ago.

◆ **insieme a** with ◊ *Ha cenato insieme a noi.* He had dinner with us.

l' insieme NOME MASC

vedi anche **insieme** AVVERBIO

◆ **nell'insieme** on the whole ◊ *Nell'insieme mi sembra buono.* It seems okay on the whole.

◆ **nel suo insieme** as a whole ◊ *Bisogna considerarlo nel suo insieme.* It needs to be considered as a whole.

insignificante AGGETTIVO

insignificant ◊ *un particolare insignificante* an insignificant detail

insinuare VERBO

to insinuate ◊ *Cosa vorresti insinuare?* What are you insinuating?

insipido AGGETTIVO (FEM **insipida**)

insipid

insistere* VERBO

1 to insist ◊ *Se proprio insisti, vengo.* If you really insist, I'll come.

2 to keep* on ◊ *Non insistere, tanto non te lo presto.* Don't keep on, I'm not going to lend it to you. ◊ *È inutile insistere su quell'argomento.* There's no point keeping on about this.

l' insolazione NOME FEM

sunstroke ◊ *Ho preso un'insolazione.* I got sunstroke.

insolito AGGETTIVO (FEM **insolita**)

unusual

insomma AVVERBIO, ESCLAMAZIONE

1 well ◊ *Insomma, sei pronta o no?* Well, are you ready or not? ◊ *Insomma, cosa ti hanno detto?* Well, what did they say to you?

2 all in all ◊ *Era sporco, scomodo e caro, insomma un disastro!* It was dirty, uncomfortable and expensive. All in all – a disaster!

◆ **Come stai? – Insomma.** How are you? – Not too bad.

◆ **Insomma, basta!** That's enough!

l' insonnia NOME FEM

◆ **soffrire d'insonnia** not to be* able to sleep ◊ *Da un po' di tempo soffro d'insonnia.* I haven't been able to sleep lately.

insonnolito AGGETTIVO (FEM **insonnolita**)

sleepy ◊ *È sempre più insonnolito.* He's getting sleepier and sleepier.

insopportabile AGGETTIVO
horrible ◇ C'è una puzza insopportabile qui dentro. There's a horrible smell in here.
* È una ragazza proprio insopportabile. That girl is a real pain.

insospettire VERBO
to make* suspicious ◇ Il suo atteggiamento mi ha insospettito. Her behaviour made me suspicious.
* insospettirsi to become* suspicious ◇ Si è insospettito e ha chiamato la polizia. He became suspicious and called the police.

instabile AGGETTIVO
1 unstable ◇ Il situazione politica è un po' instabile. The political situation is rather unstable.
2 unsettled ◇ Il tempo è ancora instabile. The weather is still unsettled.
3 unsteady ◇ La sedia è un po' instabile. The chair is a bit unsteady.

insufficiente AGGETTIVO
1 unsatisfactory (voto)
2 below standard (compito)
* Il cibo è insufficiente. There's not enough food.

l' **insufficienza** NOME FEM
* prendere un'insufficienza in to fail ◇ Ho preso un'insufficienza in chimica. I failed chemistry.
* insufficienza di prove lack of evidence ◇ L'hanno assolto per insufficienza di prove. He was acquitted because of lack of evidence.

l' **insulto** NOME MASC
insult

intanto AVVERBIO
1 for now ◇ Intanto prendi questo, poi ti darò il resto. Take this for now, I'll give you the rest later.
2 but ◇ Sì, sì, intanto tocca sempre a me farlo! Yes, yes, but it's always me who has to do it!
* Mettiti il cappotto, io intanto chiamo un taxi. Put on your coat while I get a taxi.

intasarsi VERBO
to be* blocked ◇ Si è intasato il lavandino. The sink's blocked.

intascare VERBO
to pocket

integrale AGGETTIVO
* pane integrale wholemeal bread
* abbronzatura integrale all-over tan
* edizione integrale unabridged edition
* auto a trazione integrale four-wheel drive vehicle

intellettuale AGGETTIVO, NOME MASC/FEM
intellectual

intelligente AGGETTIVO
intelligent

intendere* VERBO

to mean* ◇ Cosa intendevi? What did you mean? ◇ Dipende da cosa intendi per "giustizia". It depends what you mean by "justice".
* intendersi to understand* each other ◇ Cominciamo a intenderci. We're beginning to understand each other.
* Ci siamo intesi? Is that clear?
* intendersi di qualcosa to know* about something ◇ Si intende di fotografia. She knows about photography.

l' **intenditore**, l' **intenditrice** NOME MASC, FEM
expert

intenso AGGETTIVO (FEM **intensa**)
1 intense ◇ un calore intenso intense heat
2 bright ◇ una luce intensa a bright light
3 heavy ◇ Il traffico è più intenso attorno alle otto. The traffic is heaviest around eight.

l' **intenzione** NOME FEM
intention ◇ Non so quali sono le sue intenzioni. I don't know what her intentions are.
* avere intenzione di fare qualcosa to mean* to do something ◇ Avevo intenzione di andare ma poi ho cambiato idea. I meant to go but then I changed my mind. ◇ Non avevo intenzione di offenderti. I didn't mean to offend you.

interessante AGGETTIVO
interesting

interessare VERBO
* Se ti interessa ti posso dare il suo indirizzo. If you're interested I can give you his address.
* Non mi interessa dove sei stato. I'm not interested where you've been.
* interessarsi di qualcosa to be* interested in something ◇ Non mi interesso di politica. I'm not interested in politics.

l' **interesse** NOME MASC
interest ◇ Ha ascoltato con grande interesse. She listened with great interest. ◇ un interesse del cinque % five per cent interest
* Lo dico nel tuo interesse. I'm saying this for your own good.

l' **interferenza** NOME FEM
interference
interference non ha plurale.
◇ Ci sono delle interferenze sulla linea. There's interference on the line.

interferire VERBO
to interfere ◇ Non interferire in questa faccenda! Don't interfere in this!

l' **intermezzo** NOME MASC
interval

internazionale AGGETTIVO
international

Internet NOME MASC

the Internet ◇ *L'ho trovato su Internet.* I've found it on the Internet.
+ **navigare in Internet** to surf the net

interno AGGETTIVO (FEM **interna**)
vedi anche **interno** NOME MASC
inside ◇ *la tasca interna della giacca* the inside pocket of the jacket

interno NOME MASC
vedi anche **interno** AGGETTIVO
1 inside ◇ *L'interno della scatola è rosso.* The inside of the box is red.
+ **dall'interno di** from inside ◇ *Le urla provenivano dall'interno della casa.* The screams were coming from inside the house.
+ **all'interno di** inside ◇ *C'erano ancora venti persone all'interno della discoteca.* There were still twenty people inside the club.
2 extension ◇ *Vorrei l'interno trentadue.* Can I have extension thirty two, please?

intero AGGETTIVO (FEM **intera**)
whole ◇ *Ho trascorso l'intera settimana a studiare.* I spent the whole week studying.
+ **latte intero** full-cream milk

interpretare VERBO
1 to interpret ◇ *Non so come interpretare il suo comportamento.* I don't know how to interpret his behaviour.
+ **interpretare male** to misunderstand*
◇ *Forse hai interpretato male quello che ha detto.* Perhaps you misunderstood what he said.
2 to play (*a teatro, al cinema*) ◇ *Ha interpretato il ruolo di Robin Hood.* He played the part of Robin Hood.

interprete NOME MASC/FEM
1 interpreter ◇ *Fa l'interprete.* She is an interpreter.
2 actor (*di cinema*)
3 performer (*di teatro*)

interrogare VERBO
1 to test (*insegnante*) ◇ *L'insegnante di inglese mi ha interrogato sul futuro.* The English teacher tested me on the future tense.
+ **essere interrogato** to have* an oral test
◇ *Sono stato interrogato in matematica oggi.* I had an oral test in maths today.
2 to question (*polizia, giudice*) ◇ *La polizia vuole interrogarlo.* The police want to question him.

interrogazione NOME FEM
oral test

interrompere* VERBO
to interrupt ◇ *Scusa se t'interrompo.* Excuse me for interrupting.

interruttore NOME MASC
switch ◇ *l'interruttore della luce* the light switch

interurbana NOME FEM
long-distance call ◇ *Posso fare un'interurbana?* Can I make a long-distance call?

intervallo NOME MASC
1 interval (*al cinema*) ◇ *nell'intervallo* in the interval
2 half-time (*di partita*) ◇ *nell'intervallo* at half-time
3 break (*a scuola*) ◇ *nell'intervallo* during break

intervenire* VERBO
to intervene ◇ *È intervenuto nella discussione.* He intervened in the discussion.
+ **intervenire a** (*manifestazione, riunione*) to take* part in ◇ *Tutti possono intervenire alla riunione.* Everybody can take part in the meeting.

intervento NOME MASC
1 operation ◇ *Ha subito un intervento delicato.* He's had a complicated operation.
2 speech (*a dibattito*) ◇ *un intervento interessante* an interesting speech

intervista NOME FEM
interview ◇ *Non concede interviste.* She doesn't give interviews.

intervistare VERBO
to interview ◇ *È stato intervistato alla TV.* He was interviewed on TV.

intestato AGGETTIVO (FEM **intestata**)
+ **essere intestato** to be* registered ◇ *La macchina è intestata a lui.* The car is registered in his name.

intestino NOME MASC
intestine

intimità NOME FEM
privacy ◇ *nell'intimità della propria casa* in the privacy of one's own home

intimo AGGETTIVO (FEM **intima**)
intimate ◇ *una cenetta intima* an intimate dinner
+ **amico intimo** close friend
+ **biancheria intima** underwear

intitolare VERBO
to call ◇ *Questo quadro l'ho intitolato "Mattina e Sera".* I've called this picture "Morning and Evening".
+ **intitolarsi** to be* called ◇ *Come s'intitola il film?* What's the film called?

intonaco NOME MASC (PL gli **intonaci**)
plaster

intonato AGGETTIVO (FEM **intonata**)
matching ◇ *Portava una cravatta intonata alla camicia.* He was wearing a shirt and matching tie.
+ **essere intonato** (*nel cantare*) to be* in tune

intorno AVVERBIO
round ◇ *Qui intorno non c'è neanche un giornalaio.* There's isn't even a paper shop round here. ◇ *un giardino con una siepe intorno* a garden with a hedge round it
+ **intorno a** round ◇ *Erano seduti intorno al tavolo.* They were sitting round the table.

intorpidito AGGETTIVO (FEM **intorpidita**)

♦ **Ho la gamba intorpidita.** My leg's gone to sleep.

l' **intossicazione** NOME FEM
♦ **intossicazione alimentare** food poisoning

intransitivo AGGETTIVO (FEM **intransitiva**)
intransitive

intraprendente AGGETTIVO
enterprising ◇ *un giovane intraprendente* an enterprising young man

intrattabile AGGETTIVO
awkward ◇ *Oggi sei proprio intrattabile.* You're being really awkward today.

intravedere* VERBO
to catch* sight of ◇ *L'ho intravisto tra la folla.* I caught sight of him in the crowd.

introdurre* VERBO
to put* ◇ *Introdurre la moneta nella fessura.* Put the coin in the slot.

l' **introduzione** NOME FEM
introduction ◇ *Dobbiamo leggere solo l'introduzione.* We only have to read the introduction.

intromettersi* VERBO
to interfere ◇ *S'intromette sempre nei fatti degli altri.* She's always interfering in other people's business.

intuire VERBO
to realize ◇ *Ha intuito la verità.* She realized the truth. ◇ *Ho intuito subito che c'era qualcosa che non andava.* I realized at once that something was wrong.

l' **intuito** NOME MASC
intuition

inumano AGGETTIVO (FEM **inumana**)
inhuman

inutile AGGETTIVO
[1] useless ◇ *un aggeggio inutile* a useless gadget ◇ *Mi sento inutile qui.* I feel useless here.
[2] pointless ◇ *È inutile, tanto non lo convinci.* It's pointless, you won't persuade him.
♦ **È inutile arrabbiarsi!** There's no point getting angry!

inutilmente AVVERBIO
unnecessarily ◇ *Non volevo preoccuparti inutilmente.* I didn't want to worry you unnecessarily.

invadente AGGETTIVO
interfering ◇ *un vicino di casa invadente* an interfering neighbour

invadere* VERBO
to invade ◇ *I tifosi hanno invaso il campo.* The fans invaded the pitch.

invalido AGGETTIVO (FEM **invalida**)
vedi anche **invalido** NOME MASC/FEM
disabled

l' **invalido**, l' **invalida** NOME MASC, FEM
vedi anche **invalido** AGGETTIVO
disabled person (PL disabled people)

invecchiare VERBO
to get* old ◇ *Molti hanno paura di invecchiare.* A lot of people are afraid of getting old.

invece AVVERBIO
but ◇ *Pensavo di potercela fare e invece ho visto che era troppo difficile.* I thought I could do it, but I saw that it was too difficult.
*Spesso **invece** non viene tradotto.*
◇ *A me piace il rock, a Luca invece il rap.* I like rock, Luca likes rap.
♦ **invece di** instead of ◇ *Potresti aiutarmi invece di stare lì a guardare la TV.* You could help me instead of sitting there watching TV. ◇ *Prendo un tè invece del caffè.* I'll have tea instead of coffee.

inventare VERBO
[1] to make* up ◇ *Ho inventato una scusa per uscire prima.* I made up an excuse to leave early.
[2] to invent (*invenzione*) ◇ *Ha inventato un nuovo gioco.* He invented a new game.

invernale AGGETTIVO
winter ◇ *una giornata invernale* a winter's day

l' **inverno** NOME MASC
winter
♦ **d'inverno** in winter

l' **inversione** NOME FEM
♦ **inversione di marcia** U-turn

inverso AGGETTIVO (FEM **inversa**)
opposite ◇ *un'auto che veniva in senso inverso* a car coming in the opposite direction

l' **investigatore**, l' **investigatrice** NOME MASC, FEM
detective ◇ *un investigatore privato* a private detective

l' **investimento** NOME MASC
investment ◇ *un buon investimento* a good investment

investire VERBO
[1] to run* over ◇ *È stato investito da un camion.* He was run over by a lorry.
[2] to invest ◇ *Ha investito i suoi risparmi in titoli di stato.* He has invested his savings in government bonds.

inviare VERBO
to send* (*lettera, e-mail*)

l' **inviato**, l' **inviata** NOME MASC, FEM
correspondent ◇ *un inviato speciale* a special correspondent

l' **invidia** NOME FEM
envy ◇ *Sta morendo d'invidia.* He's green with envy.
♦ **È tutta invidia, la tua.** You're just jealous.

invidiare VERBO
to envy ◇ *L'ha sempre invidiato.* He's always envied him.

invidioso AGGETTIVO (FEM **invidiosa**)

jealous ◇ *È invidioso perché io ce l'ho e lui no.* He's jealous because I've got one and he hasn't.

l' **invio** NOME MASC
return (*tasto*)

invitare VERBO
to invite ◇ *Mi hanno invitato ad una festa.* They've invited me to a party.
* **invitare qualcuno a ballare** to ask someone to dance

l' **invitato**, l' **invitata** NOME MASC, FEM
guest

l' **invito** NOME MASC
invitation ◇ *Hai ricevuto l'invito?* Did you get the invitation?

l' **involtini** NOME MASC PL
* **involtini di manzo** beef olives

inzuppare VERBO
to dip ◇ *Inzuppo sempre il pane nel latte.* I always dip my bread in my milk.

io PRONOME
I

Si noti l'uso della maiuscola in inglese.

◇ *Io ci vado, tu fai come vuoi.* I'm going, you do what you like. ◇ *Fallo tu, io non ci riesco.* You do it, I can't. ◇ *Ho fame. – Anch'io.* I'm hungry. – So am I. ◇ *Vengo anch'io.* I'll come too.
* **Non lo sapevo nemmeno io.** I didn't even know it myself.
* **Chi è? – Sono io, apri.** Who's that? – It's me, open the door.
* **Pronto, c'è Paola? – Sì, sono io.** Hello, is Paola there? – Yes, speaking.

lo **iodio** NOME MASC
iodine

lo **Ionio** NOME MASC
* **il mar Ionio** the Ionian Sea

l' **ipertesto** NOME MASC
hypertext

ipnotizzare VERBO
to hypnotize ◇ *L'hanno ipnotizzato.* He was hypnotized.

l' **ipocrita** NOME MASC/FEM (MASC PL gli **ipocriti**, FEM PL le **ipocrite**)
hypocrite

l' **ipotesi** NOME FEM (PL le **ipotesi**)
possibility (PL possibilities) ◇ *Le ipotesi sono due.* There are two possibilities.
* **Facciamo l'ipotesi che non venga.** Supposing he doesn't come.
* **nella migliore delle ipotesi** at best ◇ *Nella migliore delle ipotesi lo finirò sabato.* At best I'll finish it on Saturday.
* **nella peggiore delle ipotesi** if the worst comes to the worst

l' **ippica** NOME FEM
horseracing

l' **ippodromo** NOME MASC
racecourse

l' **ippopotamo** NOME MASC

hippo

la **ipsilon** NOME FEM (PL le **ipsilon**)
y ◇ *Si scrive con la "i" o con la "ipsilon"?* Do you spell it with an "i" or with a "y"?

iracheno, irachena NOME, AGGETTIVO
Iraqi

l' **Irak** NOME MASC
Iraq

l' **Iran** NOME MASC
Iran

iraniano, iraniana NOME, AGGETTIVO
Iranian

l' **Irlanda** NOME FEM
Ireland ◇ *Mi è piaciuta molto l'Irlanda.* I really liked Ireland. ◇ *Andremo in Irlanda quest'estate.* We're going to Ireland this summer.
* **l'Irlanda del Nord** Northern Ireland
* **il mar d'Irlanda** the Irish Sea

irlandese AGGETTIVO
vedi anche **irlandese** NOME
Irish ◇ *la squadra irlandese* the Irish team

l' **irlandese** NOME MASC
vedi anche **irlandese** AGGETTIVO, NOME
[1] Irishman (PL Irishmen) (*persona*)
* **gli irlandesi** (*uomini e donne*) the Irish
[2] Irish (*lingua*)

l' **irlandese** NOME FEM
vedi anche **irlandese** AGGETTIVO, NOME
Irishwoman (PL Irishwomen)

ironico AGGETTIVO (FEM **ironica**, MASC PL **ironici**, FEM PL **ironiche**)
ironic ◇ *un sorrisetto ironico* an ironic smile

irregolare AGGETTIVO
[1] irregular ◇ *un verbo irregolare* an irregular verb ◇ *lineamenti irregolari* irregular features
[2] uneven (*terreno*)

irritare VERBO
to irritate (*gola, occhi*)
* **irritare qualcuno** (*persona*) to get* on somebody's nerves ◇ *Il suo modo di ridere mi irrita.* His laugh gets on my nerves.
* **irritarsi** to get* annoyed ◇ *Si irrita moltissimo se qualcuno lo interrompe.* He gets very annoyed if anyone interrupts him.

l' **iscritto**, l' **iscritta** NOME MASC, FEM
[1] student (*a scuola*) ◇ *gli iscritti al primo anno di università* first year university students
[2] competitor (*a gara*)
[3] member (*a club*)
* **mettere per iscritto** to put* something in writing

iscriversi* VERBO
[1] to register ◇ *Si è iscritto all'università.* He's registered at the university.
[2] to enrol ◇ *Mi iscriverò ad un corso di lingue.* I'm going to enrol on a language course.
[3] to join ◇ *Non si è mai iscritto a un partito.* ☞

He never joined a political party.

l' **iscrizione** NOME FEM
- **tassa di iscrizione (1)** (*a università*) registration fee
- **tassa di iscrizione (2)** (*a club*) membership fee

l' **Islam** NOME MASC
Islam

l' **Islanda** NOME FEM
Iceland

l' **isola** NOME FEM
island ◇ *un'isola deserta* a desert island
- **le isole britanniche** the British Isles
- **isola pedonale** pedestrian precinct

l' **isolamento** NOME MASC
isolation ◇ *È ricoverata nel reparto d'isolamento.* She's been admitted to the isolation ward.

isolare VERBO
to cut* off ◇ *La bufera di neve ha isolato il paese.* The village was cut off by the snowstorm.
- **isolarsi** to cut* oneself off ◇ *Non isolarti, frequenta un po' di gente.* Don't cut yourself off, go out and meet people.

isolato AGGETTIVO (FEM **isolata**)
vedi anche **isolato** NOME
isolated ◇ *C'è stato un caso isolato di epatite.* There was an isolated case of hepatitis.
- **Vivono isolati, in campagna.** They live in a remote place in the country.
- **rimanere isolato** to be* cut off ◇ *Il paese è rimasto isolato a causa della neve.* The village was cut off by the snow.

l' **isolato** NOME MASC
vedi anche **isolato** AGGETTIVO
block ◇ *Ho fatto il giro dell'isolato.* I went round the block. ◇ *Il cinema è a due isolati da qui.* The cinema is two blocks from here.

l' **ispettore,** l' **ispettrice** NOME MASC, FEM
inspector

ispirare VERBO
to inspire ◇ *Non mi ha ispirato fiducia.* He didn't inspire confidence.
- **L'idea non mi ispira.** The idea doesn't attract me.
- **ispirarsi a** to get* one's idea from ◇ *Per il romanzo si è ispirato a un fatto di cronaca.* He got the idea for the novel from a news story.

l' **Israele** NOME MASC
Israel ◇ *Andremo in Israele quest'estate.* We're going to Israel this summer.

israeliano, israeliana NOME, AGGETTIVO
Israeli

l' **istante** NOME MASC
moment ◇ *Sarò pronta tra un istante.* I'll be ready in a moment. ◇ *In quell'istante è entrata Paola.* At that moment Paola came in.

l' **istinto** NOME MASC
instinct ◇ *Ho seguito il mio istinto.* I followed my instinct.

l' **istituto** NOME MASC
college ◇ *un istituto tecnico* a technical college
- **istituto magistrale** teacher training school
- **istituto d'arte** art school
- **istituto di bellezza** beauty salon

istruito AGGETTIVO (FEM **istruita**)
well-educated ◇ *una persona molto istruita* a very well-educated person

l' **istruttore,** l' **istruttrice** NOME MASC, FEM
instructor ◇ *un istruttore di nuoto* a swimming instructor ◇ *un istruttore di scuola guida* a driving instructor

l' **istruzione** NOME FEM
education ◇ *Ha avuto una buona istruzione.* He had a good education.
- **Ministero della pubblica istruzione** Ministry of Education
- **istruzioni** instructions ◇ *Siamo in attesa di istruzioni.* We're waiting for instructions. ◇ *istruzioni per l'uso* instructions for use

l' **Italia** NOME FEM
Italy ◇ *Ti è piaciuta l'Italia?* Did you like Italy? ◇ *Verranno in Italia quest'estate.* They're coming to Italy this summer.

l' **italiana** NOME FEM
Italian

italiano AGGETTIVO (FEM **italiana**)
vedi anche **italiano** NOME
Italian

l' **italiano** NOME MASC
vedi anche **italiano** AGGETTIVO
Italian (*persona, lingua*) ◇ *gli italiani* the Italians ◇ *Parli italiano?* Do you speak Italian? ◇ *l'insegnante di italiano* the Italian teacher

l' **itinerario** NOME MASC
itinerary (PL itineraries)

l' **Iugoslavia** NOME FEM
- **la ex Iugoslavia** the former Yugoslavia

IVA ABBREVIAZIONE
VAT (= Value Added Tax) ◇ *cento euro + IVA* one hundred euros plus VAT

J

il **jazz** NOME MASC
  jazz

i **jeans** NOME MASC PL
  jeans

a **jeep** NOME FEM (PL le **jeep**)
  Jeep®

il **jogging** NOME MASC
  jogging
  ♦ **fare jogging** to go* jogging

il **jolly** NOME MASC (PL i **jolly**)
  joker

il **judo** NOME MASC
  judo

la **Jugoslavia** NOME FEM
  ♦ **la ex Jugoslavia** the former Yugoslavia

il **jukebox** NOME MASC (PL i **jukebox**)
  jukebox

K

il **karatè** NOME MASC
  karate

il **kayak** NOME MASC (PL i **kayak**)
  kayak

il **koala** NOME MASC (PL i **koala**)
  koala

il **krapfen** NOME MASC (PL i **krapfen**)
  doughnut

L

la ARTICOLO FEM
vedi anche **la** PRONOME, NOME
the ◇ *La bambina ha fame.* The baby is hungry. ◇ *Chi ha rotto la finestra?* Who broke the window? ◇ *la Senna* the Seine
Spesso la non viene tradotto.
◇ *La pallacanestro è il mio sport preferito.* Basketball is my favourite sport. ◇ *Non mi piace la pastasciutta.* I don't like pasta. ◇ *La Juventus gioca in casa.* Juventus is playing at home. ◇ *la madre di Mario* Mario's mother
A volte la viene tradotto con l'aggettivo possessivo.
◇ *Si è tolto la giacca.* He took off his jacket. ◇ *Dammi la mano.* Give me your hand. ◇ *Mi fa male la gamba.* My leg hurts.

la PRONOME
vedi anche **la** ARTICOLO, NOME
[1] her ◇ *La chiamerò domani mattina.* I'll call her tomorrow morning. ◇ *Chiamala!* Call her!
[2] it ◇ *La compro io.* I'll buy it. ◇ *Riesci ad alzarla?* Can you lift it?
[3] you (*forma di cortesia*) ◇ *La ringrazio molto, signore.* Thank you very much, sir. ◇ *Lieto di conoscerla.* Pleased to meet you.

la **la** NOME FEM (PL le **la**)
vedi anche **la** ARTICOLO, PRONOME
A (*nota musicale*)

là AVVERBIO
there ◇ *Mettilo là.* Put it there. ◇ *Vieni via di là.* Come away from there.
♦ **Mia madre è di là.** My mother's in the other room.
♦ **per di là** that way ◇ *Non passo mai per di là.* I never go that way.
♦ **più in là (1)** (*luogo*) further on ◇ *La mia casa è un po' più in là.* My house is a bit further on.
♦ **Potresti sederti un po' più in là?** Could you move along a bit?
♦ **più in là (2)** (*tempo*) later on ◇ *Deciderò più in là.* I'll decide later on.
♦ **là dentro** in there
♦ **là fuori** out there
♦ **là sopra** up there
♦ **là sotto** under there

il labbro NOME MASC (PL FEM le **labbra**)
lip

il labirinto NOME MASC
maze

il laboratorio NOME MASC
laboratory (PL laboratories)
♦ **laboratorio linguistico** language laboratory

la lacca NOME FEM (PL le **lacche**)
[1] hair spray (*per capelli*)
[2] nail varnish (*per unghie*)

i lacci NOME MASC PL
♦ **lacci per scarpe** shoelaces

la lacrima NOME FEM
tear ◇ *Mi ha guardato con le lacrime agli occhi.* He looked at me with tears in his eyes.
♦ **scoppiare in lacrime** to burst* into tears ◇ *Quando ha visto la foto è scoppiata in lacrime.* When she saw the photo she burst into tears.

lacrimogeno AGGETTIVO (FEM **lacrimogena**)
♦ **gas lacrimogeno** tear gas

la lacuna NOME FEM
♦ **Ho molte lacune in matematica.** My knowledge of maths is rather sketchy.

il ladro, la ladra NOME MASC, FEM
[1] thief (PL thieves) (*di macchina, di portafoglio*)
♦ **Al ladro!** Stop thief!
[2] burglar (*in casa*)

laggiù AVVERBIO
[1] down there (*in basso*)
[2] over there (*lontano*)

il lago NOME MASC (PL i **laghi**)
lake ◇ *il lago di Garda* Lake Garda

la laguna NOME FEM
lagoon

la lama NOME FEM
blade (*di coltello*)

lamentarsi VERBO
to complain ◇ *Si sono lamentati del cibo.* They complained about the food. ◇ *Non mi lamento!* I can't complain!

la lamentela NOME FEM
complaint ◇ *Ci sono state molte lamentele sul servizio.* There have been a lot of complaints about the service.

la lametta NOME FEM
razor blade

la lampada NOME FEM
lamp ◇ *Accendi quella lampada.* Switch that lamp on.

il lampadario NOME MASC
chandelier

la lampadina NOME FEM
light bulb ◇ *una lampadina da cento watt* a hundred watt light bulb
♦ **lampadina tascabile** torch

il lampeggiatore NOME MASC
indicator (*di auto*)

il lampione NOME MASC
street lamp

il lampo NOME MASC
vedi anche **lampo** AGGETTIVO
flash of lightning (*fulmine*)
♦ **tuoni e lampi** thunder and lightning
al singolare.
♦ **un lampo di luce** a flash of light

lampo AGGETTIVO (FEM **lampa**)
vedi anche **lampo** NOME
♦ **cerniera lampo** zip, US: zipper

---

* *I verbi seguiti da questo simbolo sono irregolari. Si veda anche alle pp.328–338.*

lampone NOME MASC
raspberry (PL raspberries)

lana NOME FEM
wool ◇ *un maglione di lana* a wool sweater
• **pura lana vergine** pure new wool

lancetta NOME FEM
1 hand (*di orologio*)
2 needle (*di strumento*)

lanciare VERBO
1 to throw* ◇ *Ho lanciato la palla a Piero.* I
threw the ball to Piero. ◇ *Mi ha lanciato un
sasso.* He threw a stone at me.
2 to launch ◇ *La NASA ha lanciato un
razzo la settimana scorsa.* NASA launched a
rocket last week.
3 to start ◇ *Hanno lanciato una nuova
moda.* They've started a new fashion.
• **lanciare un grido** to let* out a cry ◇ *Ha
lanciato un grido di dolore.* He let out a cry of
pain.

lancinante AGGETTIVO
• **un dolore lancinante** a shooting pain

lancio NOME MASC
• **lancio del disco** discus
• **lancio del giavellotto** javelin
• **lancio del peso** shot put

lapide NOME FEM
tombstone

lapsus NOME MASC (PL i **lapsus**)
slip ◇ *un lapsus freudiano* a Freudian slip

larga NOME FEM
• **stare alla larga** to keep* away ◇ *Stai alla
larga da casa mia!* Keep away from my
house!

larghezza NOME FEM
width ◇ *Larghezza: 20 cm.* Width: 20 cm.
• **La stanza ha tre metri di larghezza.** The
room is three metres wide.

largo AGGETTIVO (FEM **larga**, MASC PL **larghi**, FEM
PL **larghe**)
vedi anche **largo** NOME
1 wide ◇ *Il corridoio è largo due metri.*
The corridor is two metres wide. ◇ *Ha i
fianchi larghi.* She's got wide hips.
• **Ha le spalle larghe.** He's got broad
shoulders.
2 loose (*abito*) ◇ *Questa gonna è troppo
larga.* This skirt is too loose.

largo NOME MASC
vedi anche **largo** AGGETTIVO
• **Fate largo!** Make way!
• **farsi largo tra la folla** to push one's way
through the crowd ◇ *Si è fatta largo tra la
folla ed è salita sul palco.* She pushed her
way through the crowd and went up on the
stage.
• **al largo di Genova** off the coast of Genoa

lasagne NOME FEM PL
lasagne SING

lasciare VERBO
to leave* ◇ *Il marito l'ha lasciata per
un'altra.* Her husband left her for another
woman. ◇ *Hai lasciato a casa il maglione?*
Did you leave your jumper at home? ◇ *Non
lasciare la finestra aperta.* Don't leave the
window open.
• **lasciare fare qualcosa a qualcuno** to let*
somebody do something ◇ *Mio padre non
mi lascia uscire fino a tardi.* My father
doesn't let me stay out late. ◇ *Lascia fare a
me.* Let me do it.
• **lasciar stare qualcuno** to leave* somebody
alone ◇ *Lascia stare mia sorella!* Leave my
sister alone!
• **Lascialo stare, non vale la pena arrabbiarsi.**
Just ignore him, it's not worth getting
annoyed.
• **Lasciami in pace!** Leave me alone!
• **lasciarsi** to split up ◇ *I miei si sono lasciati
un anno fa.* My parents split up a year ago.

laser AGGETTIVO (MASC, FEM, PL **laser**)
laser ◇ *una stampante laser* a laser printer

il **lassativo** NOME MASC
laxative

lassù AVVERBIO
up there ◇ *Guarda lassù!* Look up there!

la **lastra** NOME FEM
1 slab (*di pietra*)
2 sheet (*di ghiaccio, di vetro*)
3 X-ray (*radiografia*)
• **Ho fatto una lastra alla gamba.** I had my leg
X-rayed.

laterale AGGETTIVO
side ◇ *una strada laterale* a side street

latino AGGETTIVO, NOME MASC (FEM **latina**)
Latin
Si noti l'uso della maiuscola in inglese.

il **lato** NOME MASC
1 side ◇ *l'altro lato della strada* the other
side of the street
2 aspect ◇ *Questo è un lato del problema
che non avevo considerato.* This is an
aspect of the problem I hadn't considered.
• **da un lato...dall'altro...** on the one hand...on
the other hand...

la **latta** NOME FEM
tin ◇ *un barattolo di latta* a tin can

il **latte** NOME MASC
milk
• **latte intero** full-cream milk
• **latte scremato** skimmed milk
• **latte parzialmente scremato**
semi-skimmed milk
• **latte detergente** cleansing milk

i **latticini** NOME MASC PL
dairy products ◇ *Sono allergico ai latticini.*
I'm allergic to dairy products.

la **lattina** NOME FEM
can ◇ *una lattina di birra* a can of beer

la **lattuga** NOME FEM (PL le **lattughe**)
lettuce

la **laurea** NOME FEM

degree

laurearsi VERBO
to graduate

il **laureato**, la **laureata** NOME MASC, FEM
graduate

il **lavabo** NOME MASC
washbasin

il **lavaggio** NOME MASC
washing ◊ *istruzioni per il lavaggio*
washing instructions
* **fare il lavaggio del cervello a qualcuno** to
brainwash somebody ◊ *Gli hanno fatto il
lavaggio del cervello.* He's been
brainwashed.

la **lavagna** NOME FEM
blackboard ◊ *Scrivilo sulla lavagna.* Write it
on the blackboard.
* **lavagna luminosa** overhead projector

la **lavanda** NOME FEM
lavender (*erba*)
* **Gli hanno fatto una lavanda gastrica.** He
had his stomach pumped.

la **lavanderia** NOME FEM
* **lavanderia automatica** Launderette® US:
Laundromat®
* **lavanderia a secco** dry-cleaner's

il **lavandino** NOME MASC
[1] sink (*di cucina*)
[2] washbasin (*del bagno*)

lavare VERBO
to wash ◊ *Lava la macchina tutte le
domeniche.* He washes his car every
Sunday.
* **lavare a secco** to dry-clean
* **lavare i piatti** to wash up
* **lavarsi le mani** to wash one's hands ◊ *Si è
lavata le mani.* She washed her hands.
* **lavarsi i capelli** to wash one's hair ◊ *Mi lavo
i capelli ogni mattina.* I wash my hair every
morning.
* **lavarsi i denti** to brush one's teeth ◊ *Lavati i
denti prima di andare a letto.* Brush your
teeth before you go to bed.

la **lavastoviglie** NOME FEM (PL le **lavastoviglie**)
dishwasher

la **lavatrice** NOME FEM
washing machine

lavorare VERBO
to work ◊ *Lavoro dalle otto alle cinque.* I
work from eight to five.
* **andare a lavorare** to go* to work ◊ *Vado a
lavorare alle sette.* I go to work at seven.

lavorativo AGGETTIVO (FEM **lavorativa**)
* **giorno lavorativo** working day

il **lavoratore**, la **lavoratrice** NOME MASC, FEM
worker

il **lavoro** NOME MASC
[1] work ◊ *Ho molto lavoro da fare.* I've got
a lot of work to do. ◊ *Il papà è al lavoro.* Dad
is at work.

[2] job (*occupazione*) ◊ *Ho un buon lavoro.*
I've got a good job. ◊ *È rimasto senza
lavoro.* He's lost his job.
* **lavori di casa** housework SING
* **lavori stradali** roadworks

le ARTICOLO FEM PL
vedi anche **le** PRONOME
the ◊ *Le ragazze erano già a letto.* The girls
were already in bed. ◊ *Chi ha preso le
forbici?* Who's taken the scissors?
*Spesso **le** non viene tradotto.*
◊ *Le macchine nuove costano troppo.* New
cars cost too much. ◊ *Non mi piacciono le
melanzane.* I don't like aubergines. ◊ *le
sorelle di Mario* Mario's sisters
*A volte **le** viene tradotto con l'aggettivo
possessivo.*
◊ *Si è tolto le scarpe.* He took off his shoes.
◊ *Va' a lavarti le mani.* Go and wash your
hands. ◊ *Ho le mani gonfie.* My hands are
swollen.

le PRONOME
vedi anche **le** ARTICOLO
[1] her ◊ *Le ho detto tutto.* I told her
everything. ◊ *Dalle qualcosa da mangiare.*
Give her something to eat.
*Spesso **her** è preceduto da una preposizione,
a seconda del verbo usato.*
◊ *Le ho già scritto.* I've already written to
her. ◊ *Le ho spiegato il motivo.* I explained
the reason to her. ◊ *Le ha sorriso.* He
smiled at her.
[2] you (*forma di cortesia*) ◊ *Le posso offrire
qualcosa da bere?* Can I get you something
to drink? ◊ *Le ho prenotato una stanza nello
stesso albergo.* I've booked you a room at
the same hotel.
[3] them ◊ *Mettile nel frigo.* Put them in the
fridge. ◊ *Guardale!* Look at them!

leale AGGETTIVO
loyal

il **lecca lecca** NOME MASC (PL i **lecca lecca**)
lollipop

leccare VERBO
to lick
* **leccarsi i baffi** to lick one's lips

legale AGGETTIVO
legal

legalizzare VERBO
to legalize

il **legame** NOME MASC
link ◊ *Dev'esserci un legame tra i due
episodi.* There must be a link between the
two events.
* **C'è un legame molto forte tra di loro.**
They're very close.
* **legame di parentela** family tie

legare VERBO
to tie ◊ *Hai legato bene il pacco?* Have you
tied the parcel securely? ◊ *Legagli le mani.*

*** I verbi seguiti da questo simbolo sono irregolari. Si veda anche alle pp.328–338.**

Tie his hands. ◊ *I rapinatori lo hanno legato ad una sedia.* The robbers tied him to a chair.
* **Non ho mai legato con lui.** I've never been very friendly with him.
* **essere legato a qualcuno** to be* close to somebody ◊ *Sono molto legato a mia madre.* I'm very close to my mother.
* **essere legato a qualcosa** to be* attached to something ◊ *È molto legato alla sua vecchia bici.* He's very attached to his old bike.
* **legarsi le scarpe** to do* up one's shoes ◊ *Non sa ancora legarsi le scarpe.* He doesn't know how to do up his shoes yet.

a **legge** NOME FEM
law ◊ *una nuova legge* a new law ◊ *Studia legge.* He's studying law.

a **leggenda** NOME FEM
legend

leggere* VERBO
to read* ◊ *Non ho ancora letto quel libro.* I haven't read that book yet.

leggero AGGETTIVO (FEM **leggera**)
1 light ◊ *un pacco leggero* a light parcel ◊ *un pasto leggero* a light meal
* **Questo caffè è un po' troppo leggero.** This coffee is a bit weak.
2 slight ◊ *Ho un leggero mal di testa.* I've got a slight headache. ◊ *Ha un leggero accento francese.* She's got a slight French accent.

a **legna** NOME FEM
wood ◊ *una stufa a legna* a wood stove

l **legno** NOME MASC
wood ◊ *un pezzo di legno* a piece of wood
* **di legno** wooden ◊ *un tavolo di legno* a wooden table

lei PRONOME
1 she (*soggetto*) ◊ *Lei è molto bella.* She's very beautiful. ◊ *Viene anche lei?* Is she coming too?
* **Non lo sapeva nemmeno lei.** She didn't even know it herself.
2 her (*complemento*) ◊ *Vado alla festa con lei.* I'm going to the party with her. ◊ *Dimmi qualcosa di lei.* Tell me something about her. ◊ *È lei, apri la porta.* It's her, open the door. ◊ *senza di lei* without her
3 you (*forma di cortesia*) ◊ *Posso venire con lei?* May I come with you?

lentamente AVVERBIO
slowly

a **lente** NOME FEM
lens
* **lenti a contatto** contact lenses ◊ *Porto le lenti a contatto.* I wear contact lenses.
* **lenti morbide** soft lenses
* **lenti rigide** hard lenses
* **lente d'ingrandimento** magnifying glass

e **lenticchie** NOME FEM PL
lentils

e **lentiggini** NOME FEM PL
freckles

lento AGGETTIVO (FEM **lenta**)
slow ◊ *Il mio computer è troppo lento.* My computer is too slow. ◊ *È molto più lenta di me.* She's much slower than me. ◊ *È il ragazzo più lento della squadra.* He's the slowest boy in the team.

la **lenza** NOME FEM
fishing line

il **lenzuolo** NOME MASC (PL FEM le **lenzuola**)
sheet (*per letto*)

Leone NOME MASC
Leo (*dello zodiaco*)
* **essere del Leone** to be* Leo

il **leone** NOME MASC
lion (*animale*)

la **lepre** NOME FEM
hare

lercio AGGETTIVO (FEM **lercia**)
filthy

la **lesbica** NOME FEM (PL le **lesbiche**)
lesbian

lesso AGGETTIVO (FEM **lessa**)
boiled ◊ *carne lessa* boiled meat

il **letame** NOME MASC
manure

il **letargo** NOME MASC
hibernation ◊ *Gli orsi vanno in letargo d'inverno.* Bears go into hibernation in the winter.

la **lettera** NOME FEM
letter ◊ *Hai ricevuto la mia lettera?* Did you get my letter? ◊ *una lettera d'amore* a love letter ◊ *Era scritto a lettere minuscole.* It was written in tiny letters.
* **lettere** (*all'università*) arts ◊ *Fa lettere all'università.* She's doing arts at university.

letteralmente AVVERBIO
literally

la **letteratura** NOME FEM
literature

il **letto** NOME MASC
bed
* **andare a letto** to go* to bed ◊ *Ieri sera sono andato a letto molto tardi.* I went to bed very late last night.
* **letto a castello** bunk bed
* **letto a una piazza** single bed
* **letto matrimoniale** double bed

il **lettore,** la **lettrice** NOME MASC, FEM
reader ◊ *Sono un avido lettore di fantascienza.* I'm an avid reader of science fiction.
* **lettore universitario** language assistant
* **lettore CD** CD player

la **lettura** NOME FEM
reading
*Attenzione! In inglese esiste la parola **lecture**, che però significa **lezione** oppure **conferenza**.*

la **leva** NOME FEM

L

lever ◇ *Ha premuto una leva.* He pressed a lever.
* **la leva del cambio** the gear lever, US: the gearshift

levare VERBO
to take* off ◇ *Leva i tuoi libri dal tavolo.* Take your books off the table. ◇ *Leva il coperchio dalla pentola.* Take the lid off the saucepan.
* **levare un dente** to take* a tooth out ◇ *Il dentista mi ha levato un dente.* The dentist took one of my teeth out.
* **levarsi** (*indumenti, scarpe*) to take* off ◇ *Levati il maglione.* Take your jumper off.
* **Levati di mezzo!** Get out of the way!

il **levriero** NOME MASC
greyhound

la **lezione** NOME FEM
1 lesson ◇ *una lezione di inglese* an English lesson ◇ *Do lezioni private.* I give private lessons.
2 lecture (*all'università*)

li PRONOME PL
them ◇ *Li ho visti ieri.* I saw them yesterday. ◇ *Guardali!* Look at them!

lì AVVERBIO
there ◇ *Mettilo lì.* Put it there. ◇ *Vieni via di lì.* Come away from there.
* **lì dentro** in there
* **lì fuori** out there
* **lì sopra** up there
* **lì sotto** under there

il **Libano** NOME MASC
Lebanon ◇ *Andremo in Libano.* We're going to Lebanon.

il **libellula** NOME MASC
dragonfly (PL dragonflies)

liberale AGGETTIVO
liberal

liberalizzare VERBO
to liberalize

liberare VERBO
to set* free ◇ *Hanno curato il cigno e poi l'hanno liberato.* They treated the swan and then set it free.
* **liberare un prigioniero** to release a prisoner
* **liberare una stanza** to vacate a room ◇ *Dobbiamo liberare la stanza entro le undici.* We have to vacate the room by eleven.
* **liberarsi** to get* away ◇ *Finalmente mi sono liberata di lui.* I finally got away from him. ◇ *Spero di liberarmi per le cinque.* I hope to get away by five o'clock.
* **È riuscito a liberarsi ed è scappato.** He managed to get free and escaped.

libero AGGETTIVO (FEM **libera**)
free ◇ *Sei libera domani sera?* Are you free tomorrow evening? ◇ *Siete liberi di andarvene.* You're free to go. ◇ *L'ingresso è*

libero. Admission is free. ◇ *Finalmente è libero!* (*telefono*) The line is free at last! ◇ *È libero questo posto?* Is this seat free?
* **Avete una camera libera per questa sera?** Have you got a room available for tonight?
* **La strada è libera.** The road is clear.
* **tempo libero** spare time ◇ *Cosa fai nel tempo libero?* What do you do in your spare time?

la **libertà** NOME FEM (PL le **libertà**)
1 freedom ◇ *libertà di scelta* freedom of choice
2 liberty ◇ *le libertà civili* civil liberties
* **libertà provvisoria** bail

la **Libia** NOME FEM
Libya

il **libraio** NOME MASC
bookseller

la **libreria** NOME FEM
1 bookshop (*negozio*)
2 bookcase (*mobile*)
Attenzione! **library** *vuol dire* **biblioteca**.

il **libretto** NOME MASC
little book ◇ *un libretto di proverbi* a little book of proverbs
* **libretto d'istruzioni** instruction booklet
* **libretto degli assegni** chequebook, US: checkbook

il **libro** NOME MASC
book
* **libro di testo** textbook

la **licenza** NOME FEM
licence
license US
(*di pesca, di caccia*)
* **andare in licenza** (*militare*) to go* on leave

licenziare VERBO
1 to sack (*in generale*) ◇ *Ha minacciato di licenziarla.* He threatened to sack her.
2 to make* redundant (*per eccesso di personale*) ◇ *Mio padre è stato licenziato dopo trent'anni di lavoro.* My father was made redundant after working there for thirty years.
* **licenziarsi** to give* up one's job ◇ *Si è licenziata per occuparsi del bambino.* She gave up her job to look after her little boy.

il **liceo** NOME MASC
secondary school

ⓘ *The two main types of* **liceo** *are the "liceo classico", which specializes in arts subjects, and the "liceo scientifico", which specializes in science subjects.*

lieto AGGETTIVO (FEM **lieta**)
happy ◇ *una storia a lieto fine* a story with a happy ending
* **Molto lieto!** (*nelle presentazioni*) Pleased to meet you!

lievito NOME MASC
yeast

lilla AGGETTIVO, NOME MASC (MASC, FEM, PL **lilla**)
lilac (*colore*)

lillà NOME MASC (PL i **lillà**)
lilac (*fiore*)

lima NOME FEM
* **lima da unghie** nailfile

limite NOME MASC
vedi anche **limite** AGGETTIVO
limit
* **limite di velocità** speed limit
* **nei limiti del possibile** as far as possible ◇ *Ti aiuterò nei limiti del possibile.* I'll help you as far as possible.
* **al limite** if necessary ◇ *Non portare l'ombrello; al limite te ne presto uno.* Don't bring your umbrella; if necessary I'll lend you one.
* **Hai passato ogni limite!** You've gone too far!

limite AGGETTIVO (MASC, FEM, PL **limite**)
vedi anche **limite** NOME
* **un caso limite** an extreme case

limonata NOME FEM
1. lemonade (*frizzante*)
2. lemon squash (*spremuta*)

limone NOME MASC
lemon (*frutto*)

limpido AGGETTIVO (FEM **limpida**)
clear (*acqua, cielo*)

linea NOME FEM
line ◇ *linea di partenza* starting line
* **È caduta la linea.** I've been cut off.
* **in linea d'aria** as the crow flies ◇ *Il paese dista dieci chilometri da qui in linea d'aria.* The village is ten kilometres from here as the crow flies.
* **in linea di massima** on the whole ◇ *In linea di massima penso che tu abbia ragione.* On the whole I think you're right.
* **linea aerea** airline
* **volo di linea** scheduled flight

lineamenti NOME MASC PL
features

lineetta NOME FEM
1. hyphen (*nelle parole composte*)
2. dash (*all'interno di una frase*)

lingua NOME FEM
1. tongue ◇ *Ce l'ho sulla punta della lingua.* It's on the tip of my tongue.
2. language ◇ *Parla tre lingue.* He speaks three languages. ◇ *Studio lingue all'università.* I'm studying languages at university.
* **paesi di lingua inglese** English-speaking countries

lino NOME MASC
linen ◇ *una giacca di lino* a linen jacket

liofilizzato AGGETTIVO (FEM **liofilizzata**)
freeze-dried ◇ *caffè liofilizzato* freeze-dried

coffee granules

liquefatto AGGETTIVO (FEM **liquefatta**)
melted ◇ *Aggiungere il burro liquefatto all'impasto.* Add the melted butter to the mixture.

liquidazione NOME FEM
clearance sale (*svendita*)
* **in liquidazione** in a sale ◇ *Ho comprato questa gonna in liquidazione.* I bought this skirt in a sale.

liquido AGGETTIVO (FEM **liquida**)
vedi anche **liquido** NOME
liquid ◇ *un gas liquido* a liquid gas
* **denaro liquido** cash

liquido NOME MASC
vedi anche **liquido** AGGETTIVO
1. liquid ◇ *un liquido verde* a green liquid
2. cash (*soldi*)

liquirizia NOME FEM
liquorice
licorice US
◇ *un bastoncino di liquirizia* a stick of liquorice

liquore NOME MASC
liqueur

lira NOME FEM
lira ◇ *una banconota da diecimila lire* a ten thousand lire note
* **lira sterlina** pound sterling

lirico AGGETTIVO (FEM **lirica**, MASC PL **lirici**, FEM PL **liriche**)
* **musica lirica** opera ◇ *una cantante lirica* an opera singer

Lisbona NOME FEM
Lisbon ◇ *Andrò a Lisbona quest'estate.* I'm going to Lisbon this summer. ◇ *Abita a Lisbona.* He lives in Lisbon.

lisca NOME FEM (PL le **lische**)
fishbone (*di pesce*)

liscio AGGETTIVO (FEM **liscia**, MASC PL **lisci**, FEM PL **lisce**)
vedi anche **liscio** AVVERBIO
smooth ◇ *Ha la pelle liscia.* She's got smooth skin.
* **passarla liscia** to get* away with it ◇ *Questa volta non la passerà liscia.* He won't get away with it this time.
* **Un whisky, per favore. – Liscio o con ghiaccio?** A whisky, please. – Neat or with ice?
* **avere i capelli lisci** to have* straight hair

liscio AVVERBIO
vedi anche **liscio** AGGETTIVO
smoothly ◇ *È andato tutto liscio.* It went smoothly.

lista NOME FEM
list ◇ *la lista della spesa* the shopping list ◇ *la lista degli invitati* the guest list
* **lista elettorale** electoral register
* **lista delle vivande** menu

lite NOME FEM

L

☞

quarrel
litigare VERBO
to quarrel ◇ *Litigo spesso con il mio
ragazzo.* I often quarrel with my boyfriend.
* **Ho litigato con il mio capo.** I had an
argument with my boss.

il **litigio** NOME MASC
quarrel

il **litro** NOME MASC
litre
liter [US]
◇ *un litro d'acqua* a litre of water

il **livello** NOME MASC
level ◇ *allo stesso livello* at the same level

il **livido** NOME MASC
bruise

lo **ARTICOLO MASC**
vedi anche **la** PRONOME
the ◇ *Chiudi lo sportello.* Close the door.
◇ *Mi passeresti lo zucchero?* Could you
pass me the sugar, please?
Spesso lo non viene tradotto.
◇ *Lo sci è il mio sport preferito.* Skiing is my
favourite sport. ◇ *Non metto mai lo
zucchero nel caffè.* I never take sugar in my
coffee. ◇ *lo zio di Mario* Mario's uncle
*A volte lo viene tradotto con l'aggetivo
possessivo.*
◇ *Si è tolto lo stivale.* He took off his boot.

lo **PRONOME**
vedi anche **la** ARTICOLO
[1] him ◇ *Lo chiamerò domani mattina.* I'll
call him tomorrow morning. ◇ *Vuoi
conoscerlo?* Would you like to meet him?
◇ *Guardalo!* Look at him!
[2] it ◇ *Lo compro io.* I'll buy it. ◇ *Riesci ad
alzarlo?* Can you lift it?

locale AGGETTIVO
vedi anche **locale** NOME
local ◇ *il giornale locale* the local paper
* **treno locale** stopping train

il **locale** NOME MASC
vedi anche **locale** AGGETTIVO
place (*luogo pubblico*) ◇ *È un locale molto
costoso.* It's a very expensive place.
* **locale notturno** nightclub

la **località** NOME FEM (PL le **località**)
* **località turistica** holiday resort
* **località balneare** seaside resort

lodare VERBO
to praise

la **lode** NOME FEM
* **laurearsi con centodieci e lode** to graduate
with first-class honours

il **loggione** NOME MASC
* **il loggione** the gods (*a teatro*)

logicamente AVVERBIO
obviously

logico AGGETTIVO (FEM **logica**, MASC PL **logici**,
FEM PL **logiche**)

logical ◇ *Quello che dici non è molto logico.*
What you're saying isn't very logical.

logoro AGGETTIVO (FEM **logora**)
threadbare ◇ *un tappeto logoro* a
threadbare rug
* **Indossava un cappotto logoro.** He was
wearing a shabby overcoat.

il/la **londinese** NOME MASC/FEM
vedi anche **londinese** AGGETTIVO
Londoner

londinese AGGETTIVO
vedi anche **londinese** NOME
London ◇ *il traffico londinese* London
traffic
* **la vita londinese** life in London

Londra NOME FEM
London ◇ *Domani vado a Londra.* I'm going
to London tomorrow. ◇ *Abita a Londra.* He
lives in London.

la **lontananza** NOME FEM
* **in lontananza** in the distance ◇ *Vedo una
casa in lontananza.* I can see a house in the
distance.
* **La lontananza da casa lo faceva soffrire.**
Being away from home made him unhappy.

lontano AGGETTIVO (FEM **lontana**)
vedi anche **lontano** AVVERBIO
[1] a long way ◇ *È lontano.* It's a long way.
*far viene usato nelle frasi interrogative e
negative.*
◇ *Il mare non è lontano da qui.* The sea isn't
far from here. ◇ *È lontana la casa?* Is the
house far from here? ◇ *la città più lontana
dal mare* the city farthest from the sea
* **La città è ancora molto lontana.** The city is
still a long way off.
[2] distant ◇ *paesi lontani* distant countries
◇ *Sento delle voci lontane.* I can hear
distant voices.

lontano AVVERBIO
vedi anche **lontano** AGGETTIVO
far ◇ *Abiti lontano dalla scuola?* Do you live
far from school? ◇ *È più lontano di quanto
pensassi.* It's farther than I thought.
* **Abita lontano.** He lives a long way from
here.
* **da lontano** from a distance ◇ *Da lontano mi
sembravi tuo fratello.* From a distance you
looked like your brother.

lordo AGGETTIVO (FEM **lorda**)
gross (*peso, stipendio*)

loro PRONOME
vedi anche **loro** AGGETTIVO
[1] they (*soggetto*) ◇ *Loro abitano qui.* They
live here. ◇ *Vengono anche loro?* Are they
coming too?
* **Non lo sapevano nemmeno loro.** They
didn't even know it themselves.
* **Sono loro, apri la porta.** It's them, open the
door.

[2] them (*complemento*) ◇ *Vado alla festa con loro.* I'm going to the party with them. ◇ *Dimmi qualcosa di loro.* Tell me something about them. ◇ *Ho spedito loro una cartolina.* I sent them a postcard. ◇ *senza di loro* without them

[3] theirs (*pronome possessivo*) ◇ *La nostra casa è più grande della loro.* Our house is bigger than theirs. ◇ *Di chi è questo? – È loro.* Whose is this? – It's theirs.

loro AGGETTIVO (FEM **lora**)
vedi anche **loro** PRONOME
their ◇ *i loro libri* their books ◇ *Verranno con la loro macchina.* They'll come in their car. ◇ *È colpa loro.* It's their fault.
• **un loro amico** a friend of theirs

losco AGGETTIVO (FEM **losca**, MASC PL **loschi**, FEM PL **losche**)
• **un tipo losco** a shady character

a **lotta** NOME FEM
struggle ◇ *la lotta per la sopravvivenza* the struggle for survival ◇ *la lotta politica* the political struggle
• **la lotta contro la droga** the fight against drugs
• **lotta libera** all-in wrestling

lottare VERBO
to fight* ◇ *Dobbiamo lottare per i nostri diritti.* We must fight for our rights. ◇ *Ha sempre lottato contro il razzismo.* She's always fought against racism.

a **lotteria** NOME FEM
lottery (PL lotteries)
• **vincere alla lotteria** to win* the lottery ◇ *Hanno vinto alla lotteria l'anno scorso.* They won the lottery last year.

a **lozione** NOME FEM
lotion

il **lucchetto** NOME MASC
padlock

luccicare VERBO
[1] to sparkle (*cristallo, diamanti, occhi*)
[2] to glitter (*oro*)
[3] to twinkle (*stella*)

a **lucciola** NOME FEM
glow-worm (*insetto*)

a **luce** NOME FEM
light ◇ *Accendi la luce.* Switch the light on.
• **luce del sole** sunlight
• **luci di posizione** (*in auto*) sidelights

a **lucertola** NOME FEM
lizard

il **lucidalabbra** NOME MASC (PL i **lucidalabbra**)
lip gloss

lucidare VERBO
to polish

lucido AGGETTIVO (FEM **lucida**)
vedi anche **lucido** NOME
[1] shiny ◇ *una camicia di raso nero lucido* a shiny black satin blouse ◇ *Ha le scarpe più lucide delle tue.* His shoes are shinier than

yours.
[2] lucid (*di mente*) ◇ *È ancora lucido.* He's still lucid.

il **lucido** NOME MASC
vedi anche **lucido** AGGETTIVO
• **lucido per scarpe** shoe polish

il **lucro** NOME MASC
• **a scopo di lucro** for money ◇ *Non lo fa a scopo di lucro.* He doesn't do it for money.
• **organizzazione senza scopo di lucro** non-profit organization

luglio NOME MASC
July
Si noti l'uso della maiuscola in inglese.
◇ *in luglio* in July

lugubre AGGETTIVO
gloomy ◇ *un'atmosfera lugubre* a gloomy atmosphere ◇ *sempre più lugubre* gloomier and gloomier

lui PRONOME
[1] he (*soggetto*) ◇ *Ha ragione lui.* He's right. ◇ *Viene anche lui?* Is he coming too?
• **Non lo sapeva nemmeno lui.** He didn't even know it himself.
[2] him (*complemento*) ◇ *Vado alla festa con lui.* I'm going to the party with him. ◇ *Dimmi qualcosa di lui.* Tell me something about him. ◇ *È lui, apri la porta.* It's him, open the door. ◇ *senza di lui* without him

la **lumaca** NOME FEM (PL le **lumache**)
[1] slug (*senza guscio*)
[2] snail (*con guscio*)

luminoso AGGETTIVO (FEM **luminosa**)
[1] bright ◇ *Il soggiorno è molto luminoso.* The living room is very bright.
[2] luminous (*lancetta, quadrante*)
• **un'insegna luminosa** a neon sign

la **luna** NOME FEM
moon ◇ *il sole e la luna* the sun and the moon
• **avere la luna** to be* in a bad mood ◇ *Oggi ha la luna.* He's in a bad mood today.
• **luna di miele** honeymoon

il **luna park** NOME MASC (PL i **luna park**)
funfair

il **lunario** NOME MASC
• **sbarcare il lunario** to make* ends meet ◇ *Riesco a malapena a sbarcare il lunario.* I can only just make ends meet.

lunatico AGGETTIVO (FEM **lunatica**, MASC PL **lunatici**, FEM PL **lunatiche**)
temperamental

il **lunedì** NOME MASC (PL i **lunedì**)
Monday
Si noti l'uso della maiuscola in inglese.
◇ *L'ho vista lunedì.* I saw her on Monday.
• **di lunedì** on Mondays ◇ *Vado in piscina di lunedì.* I go swimming on Mondays.
• **lunedì scorso** last Monday
• **lunedì prossimo** next Monday

la **lunga** NOME FEM

L

☞

- **di gran lunga** far and away ◇ *È di gran lunga il migliore.* It's far and away the best.
- **alla lunga** in the end ◇ *Alla lunga si stuferà.* He'll get fed up with it in the end.

la **lunghezza** NOME FEM
length ◇ *Lunghezza: 20 cm.* Length: 20 cm.
- **La stanza ha tre metri di lunghezza.** The room is three metres long.

lungo AGGETTIVO, NOME MASC (FEM **lunga**, MASC PL **lunghi**, FEM PL **lunghe**)
vedi anche **lungo** PREPOSIZIONE
long ◇ *È lungo quattro metri.* It's four metres long. ◇ *Questa gonna è troppo lunga.* This skirt is too long. ◇ *Hanno fatto una lunga passeggiata.* They went for a long walk.
- **a lungo** for a long time ◇ *Abbiamo parlato a lungo.* We talked for a long time.
- **un caffè lungo** a weak coffee
- **a lungo andare** in the end ◇ *A lungo andare si stuferà.* He'll get fed up with it in the end.
- **in lungo e in largo** everywhere ◇ *L'ho cercato in lungo e in largo.* I looked for it everywhere.

lungo PREPOSIZIONE
vedi anche **lungo** AGGETTIVO, NOME
along ◇ *Camminava lungo la riva del fiume.* He was walking along the river bank.

il **luogo** NOME MASC (PL **i luoghi**)
place ◇ *È un luogo sicuro.* It's a safe place.
- **in primo luogo** in the first place
- **aver luogo** to take* place ◇ *L'incontro ha avuto luogo in maggio.* The meeting took place in May.
- **luogo del delitto** scene of the crime
- **luogo di villeggiatura** holiday resort
- **luogo comune** cliché

il **lupo** NOME MASC
wolf (PL wolves) ◇ *Ho visto un lupo.* I saw a wolf.
- **cane lupo** Alsatian, US: German shepherd
- **lupo mannaro** werewolf
- **Ho una fame da lupi.** I'm starving.
- **In bocca al lupo!** Good luck!

lurido AGGETTIVO (FEM **lurida**)
filthy ◇ *sempre più lurido* filthier and filthier

il **lusso** NOME MASC
luxury ◇ *Non posso permettermi il lusso di una vacanza.* I can't afford the luxury of a holiday.
- **di lusso** luxury ◇ *un'auto di lusso* a luxury car

lussuoso AGGETTIVO (FEM **lussuosa**)
luxury ◇ *un albergo lussuoso* a luxury hotel

il **lutto** NOME MASC
loss ◇ *È stato un grave lutto per il paese.* It was a great loss to the country.
- **essere in lutto** to be* in mourning ◇ *È ancora in lutto per suo marito.* She's still in mourning for her husband.

M

ma CONGIUNZIONE
  but ◇ *Strano, ma vero.* Strange, but true.
+ **Ti dispiace? – Ma no!** Do you mind? – Of
  course I don't!
+ **Ma insomma! Vuoi smetterla?** Stop it, for
  heaven's sake!

macché ESCLAMAZIONE
+ **Sei innamorata di lui? – Macché! È solo un
  amico.** Are you in love with him? – Of course
  not! He's just a friend.
+ **Hai finito il compito? – Macché! Sono
  ancora a metà.** Have you finished your
  homework? – You're joking! I've only done
  half of it.

i maccheroni NOME MASC PL
  macaroni SING ◇ *Sono buoni i maccheroni?*
  Is the macaroni nice?

a macchia NOME FEM
  stain ◇ *una macchia di caffè* a coffee stain

macchiare VERBO
+ **Hai macchiato la tovaglia di caffè.** You've
  got coffee on the tablecloth.
+ **Mi sono macchiata il vestito.** I've got a mark
  on my dress.

macchiato AGGETTIVO (FEM **macchiata**)
+ **macchiato di** stained with ◇ *I suoi vestiti
  erano macchiati di fango.* His clothes were
  stained with mud.
+ **caffè macchiato** espresso coffee with a dash
  of milk

a macchina NOME FEM
  [1] car ◇ *Sali in macchina!* Get into the car!
+ **andare in macchina** to go by car ◇ *Ci andate
  in macchina o in treno?* Are you going there
  by car or by train?
  [2] machine (*apparecchio*) ◇ *La macchina
  funziona premendo il pulsante.* The
  machine works when you press the button.
+ **macchina da cucire** sewing machine
+ **macchina fotografica** camera
+ **macchina da scrivere** typewriter

il macchinario NOME MASC
  machinery
+ **macchinari** machinery SING

il macchinista NOME MASC (PL i **macchinisti**)
  engine driver (*di treno*)

a macedonia NOME FEM
  fruit salad

il macellaio NOME MASC
  butcher

a macelleria NOME FEM
  butcher's ◇ *Sono andato in macelleria.* I
  went to the butcher's.

le macerie NOME FEM PL
  rubble SING

il macigno NOME MASC
  rock

macinare VERBO
  [1] to grind* (*grano, pepe*) ◇ *caffè macinato*

ground coffee
  [2] to mince (*carne*)
+ **carne macinata** mince

macrobiotico AGGETTIVO (FEM
  macrobiotica, MASC PL **macrobiotici**, FEM PL
  macrobiotiche)
  macrobiotic

madornale AGGETTIVO
+ **un errore madornale** a huge mistake

la madre NOME FEM
  mother ◇ *mia madre* my mother ◇ *la
  madre dei due bambini* the mother of the
  two children ◇ *la madre di Matteo* Matteo's
  mother

la madrelingua NOME FEM
  mother tongue ◇ *Non è di madrelingua
  inglese.* English isn't his mother tongue.

la maestà NOME FEM
+ **Sua Maestà la regina** Her Majesty the
  Queen

la maestra NOME FEM
  teacher ◇ *maestra di scuola* primary school
  teacher ◇ *maestra d'asilo* nursery school
  teacher
+ **Scusi, signora maestra...** Excuse me, Miss...

il maestro NOME MASC
  teacher ◇ *maestro di scuola* primary school
  teacher
+ **Scusi, signor maestro...** Excuse me, sir...
+ **maestro di sci** ski instructor
+ **maestro d'orchestra** conductor

la maga NOME FEM (PL le **maghe**)
  sorceress

magari ESCLAMAZIONE, AVVERBIO
  [1] if only ◇ *Magari fosse vero!* If only it
  were true!
+ **Ti piacerebbe andare a Londra? – Magari!**
  Would you like to go to London? – I certainly
  would!
  [2] maybe ◇ *Saremo in cinque, magari in
  sei.* There will be five of us, or maybe six.

il magazzino NOME MASC
  warehouse ◇ *Lo tengono in un magazzino.*
  They keep it in a warehouse.
+ **grandi magazzini** department store SING
  Attenzione! In inglese esiste la parola
  magazine *che però significa* ***rivista***.

maggio NOME MASC
  May
  Si noti l'uso della maiuscola in inglese.
  ◇ *in maggio* in May

la maggioranza NOME FEM
  majority (PL majorities)

maggiore AGGETTIVO
  vedi anche **maggiore** NOME
  [1] more ◇ *con maggiore entusiasmo* with
  more enthusiasm
+ **Le spese sono state maggiori del previsto.**
  Costs were higher than expected.

+ **la maggior parte di** most of ◊ *la maggior parte dei miei amici* most of my friends
+ **la maggior parte della gente** most people
+ **la maggiore industria automobilistica d'Italia** the biggest car maker in Italy
+ **il maggiore poeta francese del secolo** the most important French poet of the century
  [2] older ◊ *il mio fratello maggiore* my older brother
  [3] major ◊ *in re maggiore* in D major

il/la **maggiore** NOME MASC/FEM
  vedi anche **maggiore** AGGETTIVO
  [1] older (*tra due*) ◊ *la maggiore delle due sorelle* the older of the two sisters
  [2] oldest (*tra più di due*) ◊ *il maggiore dei tre fratelli* the oldest of the three brothers

maggiorenne AGGETTIVO
  of age ◊ *Adesso sono maggiorenne.* Now I'm of age.
+ **diventare maggiorenne** to come* of age
+ **Quando sarai maggiorenne...** When you're eighteen...

la **magia** NOME FEM
  magic ◊ *Scomparve come per magia.* It disappeared as if by magic.

magico AGGETTIVO (FEM **magica**, MASC PL **magici**, FEM PL **magiche**)
  magic

il **magistrato** NOME MASC
  magistrate

la **maglia** NOME FEM
  [1] sweater (*maglione*)
  [2] T-shirt (*maglietta*)
+ **maglia di lana** (*indumento intimo*) vest, [US:] undershirt
+ **lavorare a maglia** to knit ◊ *Mi piace lavorare a maglia.* I like knitting.

la **maglietta** NOME FEM
  T-shirt

il **maglione** NOME MASC
  sweater

magnetico AGGETTIVO (FEM **magnetica**, MASC PL **magnetici**, FEM PL **magnetiche**)
  magnetic

magnifico AGGETTIVO (FEM **magnifica**, MASC PL **magnifici**, FEM PL **magnifiche**)
  wonderful ◊ *uno scenario magnifico* wonderful scenery

il **mago** NOME MASC (PL i **maghi**)
  magician

magro AGGETTIVO (FEM **magra**)
  thin ◊ *È alta e magra.* She's tall and thin.
  ◊ *È più magra di me.* She's thinner than me.
+ **formaggio magro** low-fat cheese

mai AVVERBIO
  never

  ***never** va posto dopo l'ausiliare e prima di tutti gli altri verbi.*
  ◊ *Non esco mai.* I never go out. ◊ *Non l'ho mai visto.* I've never seen it.

+ **il più bello che abbia mai visto** the best I've ever seen

  *Nelle frasi interrogative e in frasi che in inglese contengono una negazione **mai** si traduce con **ever**.*
  ◊ *Sei mai stato in Russia?* Have you ever been to Russia? ◊ *Non lo aveva mai visto nessuno.* Nobody had ever seen it.

+ **quasi mai** hardly ever ◊ *Non esco quasi mai.* I hardly ever go out. ◊ *Mai, o quasi mai.* Never, or hardly ever.
+ **mai più** never again ◊ *Non lo farò mai più.* I'll never do it again.
+ **Come mai?** Why? ◊ *Come mai sei arrivato in ritardo?* Why were you late? ◊ *Hai fatto molti errori nel tema, come mai?* You made a lot of mistakes in your essay, why was that?

il **maiale** NOME MASC
  [1] pig (*animale, persona*) ◊ *Sei proprio un maiale!* You're a real pig!
  [2] pork (*carne*) ◊ *una cotoletta di maiale* a pork chop

la **maionese** NOME FEM
  mayonnaise

il **mais** NOME MASC
  [1] corn (*coltura*)
  [2] sweetcorn (*in scatola*)

maiuscolo AGGETTIVO (FEM **maiuscola**)
  vedi anche **maiuscolo** NOME
  capital (*lettera*) ◊ *a lettere maiuscole* in capital letters

il **maiuscolo** NOME MASC
  vedi anche **maiuscolo** AGGETTIVO
+ **in maiuscolo** in capital letters

la **malafede** NOME FEM
+ **È sicuramente in malafede.** He's certainly not sincere.
+ **Questo dimostra la tua malafede.** This shows you aren't sincere.

il **malanno** NOME MASC
+ **prendersi un malanno** to catch* something ◊ *Mi devo essere preso un malanno.* I must have caught something.

malapena AVVERBIO
+ **a malapena**
  hardly ◊ *Ti vedo a malapena.* I can hardly see you.

la **malaria** NOME FEM
  malaria

malato AGGETTIVO (FEM **malata**)
  vedi anche **malato** NOME
  [1] ill (*dopo il verbo*) ◊ *Mio nonno è molto malato.* My grandfather is very ill.
+ **È malata di cuore.** She has heart trouble.
+ **È malato di cancro.** He's got cancer.
  [2] sick (*prima del nome*) ◊ *un bambino malato* a sick child

il **malato**, la **malata** NOME MASC, FEM
  vedi anche **malato** AGGETTIVO

patient (*in ospedale*) ◇ *un malato di cancro* a cancer patient

• **i malati di mente** mentally ill people

la **malattia** NOME FEM

1 illness ◇ *È morto dopo una lunga malattia.* He died after a long illness.

2 disease (*come malaria, AIDS, TBC*) ◇ *una malattia infettiva* an infectious disease ◇ *L'AIDS è una terribile malattia.* Aids is a terrible disease.

• **mettersi in malattia** to go* on sick leave

la **malavita** NOME FEM

• **la malavita** the underworld

malavoglia AVVERBIO

• **di malavoglia** reluctantly ◇ *Lo fece di malavoglia.* She did it reluctantly.

maldestro AGGETTIVO (FEM **maldestra**)

clumsy ◇ *È la persona più maldestra che conosca.* He's the clumsiest person I know.

male AVVERBIO

vedi anche **male** NOME

badly ◇ *Oggi ho giocato male.* I played badly today.

• **Male! Non avresti dovuto farlo.** That was wrong of you. You shouldn't have done it.

• **sentirsi male** to feel* ill ◇ *Mi sono sentita male.* I felt ill.

• **capire male** to misunderstand* ◇ *Hai capito male.* You've misunderstood.

• **Mi ha parlato male di te.** He said bad things about you.

il **male** NOME MASC

vedi anche **male** AVVERBIO

evil ◇ *Questo è il male minore.* This is the lesser evil. ◇ *il bene e il male* good and evil

• **far male** to hurt* ◇ *Mi fa male una gamba.* My leg hurts. ◇ *Ahi! Mi hai fatto male!* Ouch! You've hurt me!

• **Fumare fa male.** Smoking is bad for you.

• **Ho mal di testa.** I've got a headache.

• **Ho mal di stomaco.** I've got a stomach ache.

• **Ho mal di gola.** I've got a sore throat.

• **soffrire di mal di mare** to get* sea sick

• **soffrire di mal d'auto** to get* car sick

maledetto AGGETTIVO (FEM **maledetta**)

damn ◇ *Spegni quella maledetta radio!* Turn off that damn radio!

maledire* VERBO

to curse

la **maledizione** NOME FEM

curse ◇ *la maledizione del faraone* the curse of the Pharaoh

• **Maledizione!** Damn!

maleducato AGGETTIVO (FEM **maleducata**)

rude

la **maleducazione** NOME FEM

bad manners ◇ *È maleducazione parlare con la bocca piena.* It's bad manners to speak with your mouth full.

il **malessere** NOME MASC

• **Ho avuto un leggero malessere.** I didn't feel very well.

malfamato AGGETTIVO (FEM **malfamata**)

• **un quartiere malfamato** a rough area

malgrado PREPOSIZIONE

in spite of ◇ *Malgrado tutto sono ancora amici.* They're still friends, in spite of everything.

maligno AGGETTIVO (FEM **maligna**)

malicious (*persona, parole*) ◇ *delle insinuazioni maligne* malicious gossip

• **un tumore maligno** a malignant tumour

la **malinconia** NOME FEM

melancholy

malinconico AGGETTIVO (FEM **malinconica**, MASC PL **malinconici**, FEM PL **malinconiche**)

sad ◇ *Cantava una canzone malinconica.* She was singing a sad song. ◇ *sempre più maliconico* sadder and sadder

malincuore:

• **a malincuore** AVVERBIO reluctantly ◇ *Gliel'ho dato a malincuore.* I gave it to him reluctantly.

il **malinteso** NOME MASC

misunderstanding

malizioso AGGETTIVO (FEM **maliziosa**)

mischievous (*sguardo, sorriso*)

il **malore** NOME MASC

• **È stato colto da malore.** He was suddenly taken ill.

la **malta** NOME FEM

mortar

il **maltempo** NOME MASC

bad weather

maltrattare VERBO

to ill-treat ◇ *Gli ostaggi non sono stati maltrattati.* The hostages weren't ill-treated.

il **malumore** NOME MASC

• **di malumore** in a bad mood ◇ *Oggi il capo è di malumore.* The boss is in a bad mood today.

la **malva** NOME FEM

mallow

malvagio AGGETTIVO (FEM **malvagia**, MASC PL **malvagi**, FEM PL **malvagie**)

wicked

malvolentieri AVVERBIO

unwillingly

la **mamma** NOME FEM

mum ◇ *Me l'ha detto la mamma.* Mum told me that. ◇ *la mia mamma* my mum

• **Mamma mia!** Good heavens!

il **mammifero** NOME MASC

mammal

la **mancanza** NOME FEM

lack ◇ *per mancanza di soldi* because of lack of money

• **sentire la mancanza di qualcuno** to miss somebody ◇ *Sento la tua mancanza.* I miss you.

mancare VERBO

to be* missing (*non esserci*) ◇ *Quanti pezzi mancano?* How many pieces are missing? ☞

M

◆ **Mancano ancora dieci sterline.** We're still ten pounds short.

◆ **Fammi sapere se ti manca qualcosa.** Let me know if you need anything.

◆ **Mi manchi.** I miss you.

◆ **Manca un quarto alle due.** It's a quarter to two.

la **mancia** NOME FEM (PL le **mance**)
tip

◆ **dare la mancia a qualcuno** to tip somebody ◇ *Ha dato la mancia al cameriere.* He tipped the waiter.

la **manciata** NOME FEM
handful

mancino AGGETTIVO (FEM **mancina**)
left-handed

mandare VERBO
to send*

◆ **mandare qualcosa a qualcuno** to send* somebody something ◇ *Manderò una cartolina a Loredana.* I'll send Loredana a postcard. ◇ *Mi puoi mandare un po' di denaro?* Can you send me some money?

◆ **Glielo manderò.** I'll send it to him.

◆ **Mando sempre una cartolina a tutti i miei amici.** I always send postcards to all my friends.

◆ **mandare in onda** to broadcast

il **mandarino** NOME MASC
mandarin

il **mandato** NOME MASC

◆ **mandato di arresto** arrest warrant

◆ **mandato di perquisizione** search warrant

la **mandibola** NOME FEM
jaw

la **mandorla** NOME FEM
almond

la **mandria** NOME FEM
herd

il **maneggio** NOME MASC (PL i **maneggi**)
riding school

le **manette** NOME FEM PL
handcuffs

◆ **mettere le manette a qualcuno** to handcuff somebody

il **mangianastri** NOME MASC (PL i **mangianastri**)
cassette recorder

mangiare VERBO
to eat* ◇ *Non mangio carne.* I don't eat meat. ◇ *Vuoi mangiare qualcosa?* Would you like something to eat?

◆ **Si mangia bene in quel ristorante.** The food is good in that restaurant.

◆ **fare da mangiare** to cook ◇ *La mamma sta facendo da mangiare.* Mum is cooking.

il **mangime** NOME MASC
1 birdseed (*per uccelli*)
2 fish food (*per pesci*)

la **mania** NOME FEM

◆ **Ha la mania dell'ordine.** He's obsessively tidy.

◆ **una delle sue manie** one of his strange habits

il **maniaco**, la **maniaca** NOME MASC, FEM (MASC PL i **maniaci**, FEM PL le **maniache**)
maniac

la **Manica** NOME FEM
the Channel

◆ **il Canale della Manica** the Channel

la **manica** NOME FEM (PL le **maniche**)
sleeve ◇ *Le maniche sono troppo corte.* The sleeves are too short.

◆ **una maglia con le maniche lunghe** a long-sleeved sweater

il **manichino** NOME MASC
dummy (PL dummies)

il **manico** NOME MASC (PL i **manici**)
1 handle (*di tazza, di coltello*)
2 neck (*di chitarra*)

il **manicomio** NOME MASC
mental hospital

la **maniera** NOME FEM
way ◇ *in maniera strana* in an odd way

◆ **maniere** manners ◇ *Non conosce le buone maniere.* Her manners are awful.

la **manifestazione** NOME FEM
1 demonstration (*politica*) ◇ *una manifestazione contro il governo* a demonstration against the government
2 event ◇ *una manifestazione sportiva* a sporting event

il **manifesto** NOME MASC
poster

la **maniglia** NOME FEM
handle

la **mano** NOME FEM (PL le **mani**)
hand ◇ *Mi sono scottato la mano.* I've burnt my hand.

◆ **Mani in alto!** Hands up!

◆ **stringersi la mano** (*per salutarsi*) to shake* hands ◇ *I due ministri si strinsero la mano.* The two ministers shook hands.

◆ **tenersi per mano** to hold* hands ◇ *Si tenevano per mano.* They were holding hands.

◆ **dare una mano a qualcuno** to give* somebody a hand ◇ *Dammi una mano, per favore.* Give me a hand, please.

◆ **a portata di mano** within reach ◇ *Tienilo sempre a portata di mano.* Always keep it within reach.

◆ **fatto a mano** handmade

◆ **di seconda mano** second-hand ◇ *Ha comprato una macchina di seconda mano.* She bought a second-hand car.

◆ **una mano di vernice** a coat of paint

la **manodopera** NOME FEM
labour
labor US

manomettere* VERBO
to tamper with

la **manopola** NOME FEM
[1] knob ◇ *Girò la manopola per cercare il canale.* He turned the knob to find the station.
[2] mitten (*guanto*)

il **manovale** NOME MASC
labourer
laborer US

la **manovella** NOME FEM
handle

la **manovra** NOME FEM
manoeuvre
maneuver US

la **mansarda** NOME FEM
attic

il **mantello** NOME MASC
cloak (*indumento*)

mantenere* VERBO
[1] to keep* ◇ *Pensi che manterrà la promessa?* Do you think she'll keep her promise? ◇ *Cerca di mantenere la calma.* Try to keep calm.
[2] to support (*finanziaramente*) ◇ *Ha una famiglia da mantenere.* He's got a family to support.
◆ **Lavora per mantenersi.** She works for a living.

Mantova NOME FEM
Mantua ◇ *Abito a Mantova.* I live in Mantua.

manuale AGGETTIVO, NOME MASC
manual ◇ *il lavoro manuale* manual work ◇ *il manuale di istruzioni* the instructions manual

il **manubrio** NOME MASC
handlebars PL (*di bicicletta, di motorino*)

la **manutenzione** NOME FEM
maintenance

il **manzo** NOME MASC
[1] beef (*carne*) ◇ *uno spezzatino di manzo* a beef stew
[2] steer (*animale*)

il **mappamondo** NOME MASC
globe

la **maratona** NOME FEM
marathon

la **marca** NOME FEM (PL le **marche**)
[1] make (*di vestito, di orologio*) ◇ *Di che marca è il tuo stereo?* What make is your stereo?
◆ **capi di marca** designer clothes
[2] brand (*di sigarette, di caffè*)

marcare VERBO
[1] to mark (*avversario*) ◇ *Devi marcare il numero otto.* Mark number eight.
[2] to score (*segnare*) ◇ *La squadra ha marcato all'ultimo minuto.* The team scored in the final minute.

la **marchesa** NOME FEM
marchioness

la **marcia** NOME FEM (PL le **marce**)
[1] march (*militare*)
[2] walking (*sportiva*)
[3] gear (*di automobile*) ◇ *Cambiò marcia.* She changed gear.
◆ **fare marcia indietro** to reverse
◆ **Mettiamoci in marcia.** Let's get going.

il **marciapiede** NOME MASC
pavement
sidewalk US

marciare VERBO
to march

marcio AGGETTIVO (FEM **marcia**, MASC PL **marci**, FEM PL **marce**)
rotten (*uovo, legno, frutta*)

marcire VERBO
to go* rotten (*cibi, frutta*)

il **marco** NOME MASC (PL i **marchi**)
mark (*moneta*)

il **mare** NOME MASC
[1] sea ◇ *Il mare era mosso.* The sea was rough. ◇ *È morto in mare.* He died at sea.
◆ **il Mar Adriatico** the Adriatic
[2] seaside (*località*) ◇ *una casa al mare* a house at the seaside
◆ **andare al mare** to go* to the seaside ◇ *Sono andati al mare.* They went to the seaside.

la **marea** NOME FEM
◆ **alta marea** high tide
◆ **bassa marea** low tide ◇ *C'era bassa marea.* It was low tide.

la **margarina** NOME FEM
margarine

la **margherita** NOME FEM
daisy (PL daisies)

il **margine** NOME MASC
margin

la **marina** NOME FEM
marina (*per barche da diporto*)
◆ **la marina militare** the navy (*militare*)
◆ **la marina mercantile** the merchant navy

il **marinaio** NOME MASC
sailor

marinare VERBO
◆ **marinare la scuola** to play truant

la **marionetta** NOME FEM
puppet

il **marito** NOME MASC
husband ◇ *suo marito* her husband ◇ *il marito di mia sorella* my sister's husband

la **marmellata** NOME FEM
jam
jelly US
◇ *marmellata di fragole* strawberry jam
◆ **marmellata di arance** marmalade

la **marmitta** NOME FEM
silencer
◆ **marmitta catalitica** catalytic converter

il **marmo** NOME MASC
marble ◇ *una statua di marmo* a marble

M

statue

marocchino, marocchina NOME, AGGETTIVO
Moroccan

il **Marocco** NOME MASC
Morocco ◊ *Mi è piaciuto molto il Marocco. I really liked Morocco.* ◊ *Andremo in Marocco quest'estate. We're going to Morocco this summer.*

marrone AGGETTIVO
brown
*Attenzione! In inglese esiste la parola **maroon**, che però indica un altro colore, il rosso bordeaux.*

il **marsupio** NOME MASC
[1] pouch *(di canguro)*
[2] bumbag *(borsellino)*

il **martedì** NOME MASC (PL i **martedì**)
Tuesday
Si noti l'uso della maiuscola in inglese.
◊ *L'ho vista martedì. I saw her on Tuesday.*
• **di martedì** on Tuesdays ◊ *Vado in piscina di martedì. I go swimming on Tuesdays.*
• **martedì scorso** last Tuesday
• **martedì prossimo** next Tuesday
• **martedì grasso** Shrove Tuesday

> **ⓘ martedì grasso** *is the last day of the Italian "Carnevale", which begins at the end of January.*

il **martello** NOME MASC
hammer

il **marzapane** NOME MASC
marzipan

marzo NOME MASC
March
Si noti l'uso della maiuscola in inglese.
◊ *in marzo in March*

il **mascara** NOME MASC (PL i **mascara**)
mascara

la **mascella** NOME FEM
jaw

la **maschera** NOME FEM
mask ◊ *una maschera di carnevale a carnival mask* ◊ *Ho comprato la maschera e le pinne. I bought a mask and flippers.*
• **vestirsi in maschera** to wear* fancy dress
• **un ballo in maschera** a fancy dress ball

mascherare VERBO
to hide* *(sentimenti, paura)*

maschile AGGETTIVO
[1] male ◊ *una voce maschile a male voice* ◊ *Sesso: maschile. Sex: male.*
[2] masculine *(in grammatica)* ◊ *un nome maschile a masculine noun*

maschilista NOME MASC (PL i **maschilisti**)
male chauvinist

il **maschio** NOME MASC
vedi anche **maschio** AGGETTIVO

[1] boy *(bambino)* ◊ *Hanno un maschio e una femmina. They've got a boy and a girl.*
[2] male ◊ *un maschio bianco a white male*
• **i maschi** *(adulti)* the men

maschio AGGETTIVO (FEM **maschia**)
vedi anche **maschio** NOME
male ◊ *i miei colleghi maschi my male colleagues*

la **massa** NOME FEM
• **una massa di** masses of ◊ *una massa di persone masses of people*
• **di massa** mass ◊ *turismo di massa mass tourism*

il **massacro** NOME MASC
massacre

il **massaggio** NOME MASC
massage

massiccio AGGETTIVO (FEM **massiccia**, MASC PL **massicci**, FEM PL **massicce**)
• **oro massiccio** solid gold
• **legno massiccio** solid wood

massimo AGGETTIVO (FEM **massima**)
vedi anche **massimo** NOME
maximum ◊ *la temperatura massima the maximum temperature*
• **È una questione della massima importanza.** It's a question of the greatest importance.

il **massimo** NOME MASC
vedi anche **massimo** AGGETTIVO
• **al massimo** at the most ◊ *Può portare al massimo cinque persone. It can take five people at the most.*
• **Cerca di impegnarti al massimo.** Try to do your best.

il **masso** NOME MASC
rock ◊ *"Attenzione! Caduta massi." "Beware! Falling rocks."*

masticare VERBO
to chew
• **gomma da masticare** chewing gum

la **matematica** NOME FEM
maths SING
math *US*
◊ *È brava in matematica. She's good at maths.*

il **materassino** NOME MASC
mat *(per la ginnastica)*
• **materassino gonfiabile** airbed

il **materasso** NOME MASC
mattress

la **materia** NOME FEM
[1] subject *(a scuola)* ◊ *È una materia difficile. It's a difficult subject.*
[2] material *(sostanza)*
• **materie prime** raw materials

il **materiale** NOME MASC
material ◊ *Sto raccogliendo materiale per il mio progetto. I'm collecting material for my project.*
• **materiale da costruzione** building materials

PL
la **maternità** NOME FEM
maternity ◊ *reparto maternità* maternity ward
- **Essere in maternità.** To be* on maternity leave.

materno AGGETTIVO (FEM **materna**)
maternal ◊ *l'istinto materno* the maternal instinct
- **i miei nonni materni** my mother's parents
- **la mia lingua materna** my mother tongue
- **scuola materna** nursery school

la **matita** NOME FEM
pencil
- **a matita** in pencil ◊ *Scrivi le note a matita.* Write your notes in pencil. ◊ *un disegno a matita* a pencil drawing

la **matrigna** NOME FEM
stepmother

matrimoniale AGGETTIVO
- **una camera matrimoniale** a double room
- **un letto matrimoniale** a double bed

il **matrimonio** NOME MASC
[1] marriage ◊ *dopo dieci anni di matrimonio* after ten years of marriage
[2] wedding (*cerimonia*) ◊ *Non mi hanno invitato al matrimonio.* They didn't invite me to the wedding.

la **mattina** NOME FEM
morning
- **di mattina** in the morning ◊ *alle sette di mattina* at seven in the morning
- **domani mattina** tomorrow morning
- **ogni mattina** every morning

matto AGGETTIVO (FEM **matta**)
mad ◊ *Sei matto!* You're mad! ◊ *sempre più matto* madder and madder
- **diventare matto** to go* mad ◊ *Sto diventando matta!* I'm going mad!
- **far diventare matto qualcuno** to drive* somebody mad ◊ *Mi ha fatto diventar matto.* He drove me mad.
- **andar matto per** to be* mad about ◊ *Va matto per il calcio.* He's mad about football.

il **mattone** NOME MASC
brick ◊ *un muro di mattoni* a brick wall
- **Questo libro è un mattone.** This book is really hard going.

la **mattonella** NOME FEM
tile

la **maturità** NOME FEM
- **esame di maturità** school-leaving examination

maturo AGGETTIVO (FEM **matura**)
[1] ripe (*frutto*) ◊ *una pesca matura* a ripe peach
[2] mature (*persona*) ◊ *È molto matura per la sua età.* She's very mature for her age.

la **mazza** NOME FEM
[1] bat (*da baseball*)
[2] club (*da golf*)

la **mazzetta** NOME FEM
[1] bundle (*pacchetto di banconote*)
[2] bribe (*tangente*)

il **mazzo** NOME MASC
bunch ◊ *un mazzo di fiori* a bunch of flowers ◊ *un mazzo di chiavi* a bunch of keys
- **un mazzo di carte** a pack of cards

me PRONOME
me ◊ *Vieni con me!* Come with me! ◊ *senza di me* without me ◊ *Dopo di me tocca a te.* It's your turn after me. ◊ *È alta come me.* She's as tall as me. ◊ *Me la dai?* Will you give it to me?

il **meccanico** NOME MASC (PL **i meccanici**)
mechanic ◊ *Fa il meccanico.* He is a mechanic.
- **Devo portare la macchina dal meccanico.** I've got to take my car to the garage.

il **meccanismo** NOME MASC
mechanism

la **medaglia** NOME FEM
medal ◊ *Ha vinto una medaglia d'oro.* He won a gold medal.

medesimo AGGETTIVO (FEM **medesima**)
same ◊ *Mi ha detto le medesime cose.* He said the same things to me.

la **media** NOME FEM
average ◊ *al di sopra della media* above average ◊ *al di sotto della media* below average ◊ *con la media dell'otto* with an average of eight out of ten
- **in media** on average ◊ *Guadagna in media cinquecento euro al mese.* On average she earns five hundred euros a month.
- **Abbiamo fatto in media settanta chilometri all'ora.** We did an average of seventy kilometres an hour.

mediante PREPOSIZIONE
by means of

medicare VERBO
[1] to treat (*paziente*) ◊ *La medicò e la rimandò a casa.* He treated her and sent her home.
[2] to dress (*ferita*) ◊ *Gli medicò la ferita.* She dressed his wound.

la **medicina** NOME FEM
medicine ◊ *una medicina contro la tosse* a cough medicine ◊ *Voglio studiare medicina.* I want to study medicine.

il **medico** NOME MASC (PL **i medici**)
vedi anche **medico** AGGETTIVO
doctor ◊ *il medico di famiglia* the family doctor ◊ *Chi è il tuo medico curante?* Who's your doctor?

medico AGGETTIVO (FEM **medica**, MASC PL **medici**, FEM PL **mediche**)
vedi anche **medico** NOME
medical SING ◊ *cure mediche* medical treatment
- **fare una visita medica** (*malato*) to have* a medical examination ◊ *Ha fatto una visita* ☞

M

medica. He had a medical examination.

medio AGGETTIVO (FEM **media**)
average ◊ *una persona di statura media* a person of average height
* **il dito medio** the middle finger
* **il Medio Oriente** the Middle East

mediocre AGGETTIVO
mediocre ◊ *Il suo ultimo disco è mediocre.* His latest record is mediocre.
* **un prodotto di qualità mediocre** a poor quality product

il **medioevo** NOME MASC
Middle Ages PL ◊ *nel medioevo* in the Middle Ages

mediterraneo AGGETTIVO (FEM **mediterranea**)
Mediterranean (*clima, dieta*)
Si noti l'uso della maiuscola in inglese.
* **il mare Mediterraneo** the Mediterranean

la **medusa** NOME FEM
jellyfish (PL jellyfish)

meglio AVVERBIO, AGGETTIVO
better ◊ *Sto meglio.* I feel better. ◊ *È molto meglio così.* It's much better like this. ◊ *Franca gioca meglio di lui.* Franca plays better than him. ◊ *È meglio che tu te ne vada.* You'd better leave. ◊ *meglio tardi che mai* better late than never

la **mela** NOME FEM
apple ◊ *una torta di mele* an apple tart
* **mela cotogna** quince

la **melagrana** NOME FEM
pomegranate

la **melanzana** NOME FEM
aubergine
eggplant US

il **melo** NOME MASC
apple tree

la **melodia** NOME FEM
tune

il **melone** NOME MASC
melon

il **membro** NOME MASC
member ◊ *Diventò membro del partito socialista.* He became a member of the Socialist Party.

la **memoria** NOME FEM
memory (PL memories) ◊ *Ho una buona memoria.* I've got a good memory. ◊ *Non ho molta memoria.* I haven't got a good memory. ◊ *Il mio computer non ha abbastanza memoria.* My computer hasn't got enough memory.
* **imparare qualcosa a memoria** to learn* something by heart ◊ *Ha imparato a memoria la poesia.* She learnt the poem by heart.

il/la **mendicante** NOME MASC/FEM
beggar

meno AVVERBIO, AGGETTIVO

vedi anche **meno** PREPOSIZIONE

[1] less ◊ *Dovresti mangiare meno.* You should eat less. ◊ *La birra costa meno in Italia.* Beer costs less in Italy. ◊ *C'è meno lavoro.* There's less work.
* **di meno** less ◊ *Ho speso di meno.* I spent less.
* **quello che mi è piaciuto di meno** the one I liked least
* **più o meno** more or less
* **meno...di** less...than ◊ *Sono meno stanca di lei.* I'm less tired than her.
* **Ha due anni meno di me.** He's two years younger than me.
* **Sono meno brava di te in matematica.** I'm not as good at maths as you.
* **il meno intelligente** the least intelligent
[2] fewer ◊ *Quest'anno ci sono meno turisti.* There are fewer tourists this year.
[3] minus ◊ *Quattro meno uno fa tre.* Four minus one makes three. ◊ *meno tre gradi* minus three degrees
* **Sono le tre meno un quarto.** It's a quarter to three.
* **Meno male!** Thank goodness!

meno PREPOSIZIONE

vedi anche **meno** AVVERBIO, AGGETTIVO

except ◊ *Ci siamo tutti meno lui.* Everybody's here except him.
* **a meno che** unless ◊ *Ci andrò, a meno che non piova.* I'll go, unless it rains.

la **menopausa** NOME FEM
menopause
* **essere in menopausa** to be* going through the menopause

la **mensa** NOME FEM
canteen

mensile AGGETTIVO
monthly ◊ *un abbonamento mensile* a monthly ticket

la **mensola** NOME FEM
shelf (PL shelves)

la **menta** NOME FEM
mint (*erba, caramella*)
* **una caramella alla menta** a mint

mentale AGGETTIVO
mental

la **mentalità** NOME FEM (PL le **mentalità**)
* **Ha una mentalità aperta.** He's open-minded.
* **Ha una mentalità ristretta.** He's narrow-minded.

la **mente** NOME FEM
mind ◊ *Ha una mente logica.* He's got a logical mind. ◊ *Ha qualcosa in mente.* He's got something in mind.
* **Ma cosa ti salta in mente?** You must be crazy!

mentire VERBO
to lie* ◊ *Mente.* He's lying.

---

* *I verbi seguiti da questo simbolo sono irregolari. Si veda anche alle pp.328–338.*

il mento NOME MASC
chin

mentre CONGIUNZIONE
while ◇ *È successo mentre eri fuori.* It happened while you were out.

il menù NOME MASC (PL i **menù**)
menu ◇ *menù turistico* tourist menu ◇ *Potrei avere il menù, per favore?* Could I have the menu please?

la menzogna NOME FEM
lie ◇ *dire menzogne* to tell* lies

la meraviglia NOME FEM
surprise ◇ *con mia grande meraviglia* to my great surprise
• **Tutto va a meraviglia.** Everything is going perfectly.
• **È una meraviglia!** It's wonderful!

meravigliarsi VERBO
to be* surprised ◇ *Mi meraviglio di te!* I'm surprised at you!

meraviglioso AGGETTIVO (FEM **meravigliosa**)
wonderful

il mercatino NOME MASC
local street market

il mercato NOME MASC
market ◇ *Vado al mercato.* I'm going to the market.

la merce NOME FEM
goods PL

il mercoledì NOME MASC (PL i **mercoledì**)
Wednesday
Si noti l'uso della maiuscola in inglese.
◇ *L'ho vista mercoledì.* I saw her on Wednesday.
• **di mercoledì** on Wednesdays ◇ *Vado in piscina di mercoledì.* I go swimming on Wednesdays.
• **mercoledì scorso** last Wednesday
• **mercoledì prossimo** next Wednesday

la merda NOME FEM
shit (*volgare*)

la merenda NOME FEM
snack ◇ *Ragazzi, venite a fare merenda.* Children, come and have a snack.

meridionale AGGETTIVO
vedi anche **meridionale** NOME
southern (*regione*)

la meridionale NOME MASC/FEM
vedi anche **meridionale** AGGETTIVO
• **i meridionali** people from Southern Italy

il meridione NOME MASC
• **il meridione** Southern Italy

la meringa NOME FEM (PL le **meringhe**)
meringue

meritare VERBO
1 to deserve ◇ *Meriti un premio.* You deserve a prize.
2 to be* worth ◇ *Non merita neanche parlarne.* It's not worth talking about.

il merito NOME MASC
• **È merito suo se hanno vinto.** It's thanks to him that they won.
• **in merito a** with regard to

il merletto NOME MASC
lace

il merlo NOME MASC
blackbird

il merluzzo NOME MASC
cod

meschino AGGETTIVO (FEM **meschina**)
mean (*persona*)
• **fare una figura meschina** to look silly

mescolare VERBO
to mix ◇ *Mescolate la farina e lo zucchero.* Mix the flour and sugar.

il mese NOME MASC
month ◇ *fra due mesi* in two months ◇ *alla fine del mese* at the end of the month

la messa NOME FEM
Mass
Si noti l'uso della maiuscola in inglese.
◇ *Andiamo a messa di domenica.* We go to Mass on Sundays.

il messaggio NOME MASC
message ◇ *Vuole lasciare un messaggio?* Would you like to leave a message?
• **messaggio di posta elettronica** e-mail

il Messico NOME MASC
Mexico ◇ *Mi è piaciuto molto il Messico.* I really liked Mexico. ◇ *Quest'estate andremo in Messico.* We're going to Mexico this summer.

il mestiere NOME MASC
job ◇ *un mestiere difficile* a difficult job
• **Cosa fa tuo padre di mestiere?** What does your father do?

il mestolo NOME MASC
ladle

le mestruazioni NOME FEM PL
period SING ◇ *Ho le mestruazioni.* I've got my period.

la meta NOME FEM
destination ◇ *Finalmente giunsero alla meta.* They finally reached their destination.
• **senza meta** aimlessly ◇ *Vagava senza meta.* He was wandering aimlessly.

la metà NOME FEM (PL le **metà**)
half (PL halves) ◇ *Dammene metà.* Give me half. ◇ *Dividilo a metà.* Divide it in half. ◇ *Lo vendono a metà prezzo.* They're selling it at half price. ◇ *le due metà* the two halves ◇ *Facciamo a metà.* Let's go halves.
• **a metà strada** halfway ◇ *Incontriamoci a metà strada.* Let's meet halfway.

il metallo NOME MASC
metal ◇ *un portacenere di metallo* a metal ashtray

il metano NOME MASC
methane (*gas*)
• **riscaldamento a metano** gas heating

il metodo NOME MASC
method

il **metro** NOME MASC

[1] metre

meter US

◇ *un metro quadrato* a square metre ◇ *un metro cubo* a cubic metre

[2] tape measure (*per misurare*)

la **metropolitana** NOME FEM

underground

subway US

◇ *Ha preso la metropolitana.* He took the underground.

> ❶ *A Londra* **la metropolitana** *viene chiamata anche "the tube".*

mettere* VERBO

[1] to put* ◇ *Dove hai messo la mia penna?* Where did you put my pen? ◇ *Hai messo i bambini a letto?* Have you put the children to bed? ◇ *Metterò un annuncio sul giornale.* I'll put an advert in the paper.

♦ **Mettiti là e aspetta.** Wait there.

♦ **Quanto tempo ci hai messo?** How long did it take you?

♦ **mettersi a sedere** to sit* down

[2] to put* on ◇ *Mettiti il maglione.* Put your jumper on. ◇ *Si mise le scarpe.* He put his shoes on.

♦ **Non metto più quelle scarpe.** I don't wear those shoes any more.

[3] to set* ◇ *Hai messo la sveglia?* Have you set the alarm?

♦ **mettersi a fare qualcosa** to start to do something ◇ *Si mise a piangere.* She started to cry.

la **mezzanotte** NOME FEM

midnight ◇ *a mezzanotte* at midnight

mezzo AGGETTIVO (FEM **mezza**)

> *vedi anche* **mezzo** NOME

half ◇ *mezza bottiglia di vino* half a bottle of wine ◇ *un chilo e mezzo* one and a half kilos ◇ *Sono le due e mezza.* It's half past two. ◇ *mezz'ora* half an hour

♦ **un uomo di mezza età** a middle-aged man

il **mezzo** NOME

> *vedi anche* **mezzo** AGGETTIVO

[1] middle ◇ *Era in mezzo alla strada.* He was in the middle of the road. ◇ *il sedile di mezzo* the middle seat

[2] means SING ◇ *un mezzo di trasporto* a means of transport

♦ **i mezzi pubblici** public transport

♦ **per mezzo di** by means of ◇ *per mezzo della nuova tecnologia* by means of new technology

il **mezzogiorno** NOME MASC

midday ◇ *a mezzogiorno* at midday

♦ **È mezzogiorno e mezzo.** It's half past twelve.

♦ **Il Mezzogiorno** the South of Italy

mi PRONOME

> *vedi anche* **mi** NOME

[1] me ◇ *Mi aiuti?* Could you help me?
◇ *Dammi quel libro.* Give me that book.
◇ *Mi scusi!* Excuse me! ◇ *Puoi prestarmi la penna?* Can you lend me your pen?

> *Spesso* **me** *è preceduto da una preposizione, a seconda del verbo usato.*

◇ *Mi chiamava.* He was calling to me. ◇ *Mi sembrava una buona idea.* It seemed a good idea to me. ◇ *Mi ha sorriso.* He smiled at me. ◇ *Aspettami!* Wait for me!

[2] myself (*riflessivo*) ◇ *Mi sono divertita.* I enjoyed myself. ◇ *Mi sono fatto male.* I've hurt myself. ◇ *Mi guardai allo specchio.* I looked at myself in the mirror.

♦ **Mi sono lavato i denti.** I brushed my teeth.

il **mi** NOME MASC (PL i **mi**)

> *vedi anche* **mi** PRONOME

E (*nota musicale*)

miagolare VERBO

to miaow

mica AVVERBIO

♦ **Non ci crederai mica!** You won't believe it!

♦ **Non sono mica stanco.** I'm not a bit tired.

♦ **Non sarà mica partito?** He wouldn't have left, would he?

la **miccia** NOME FEM (PL le **micce**)

fuse

♦ **accendere la miccia** to light* the fuse

il **microfono** NOME MASC

microphone

il **microscopio** NOME MASC

microscope

il **midollo** NOME MASC

♦ **midollo osseo** bone marrow

♦ **midollo spinale** spinal cord

il **miele** NOME MASC

honey

il **migliaio** NOME MASC (PL FEM le **migliaia**)

about a thousand ◇ *un migliaio di persone* about a thousand people

> *Quando* **thousand** *si riferisce ad un numero, va al singolare.*

◇ *due migliaia di persone* about two thousand people ◇ *parecchie migliaia di copie* several thousand copies

> *Il plurale* **thousands** *si usa solo quando* **migliaia** *significa "una grande quantità".*

◇ *L'ho fatto migliaia di volte.* I've done it thousands of times.

il **miglio** NOME MASC (PL F le **miglia**)

mile ◇ *Camminò per miglia e miglia.* She walked for miles and miles.

♦ **miglio marino** nautical mile

il **miglioramento** NOME MASC

improvement ◇ *Non c'è ancora nessun miglioramento.* There hasn't been any improvement yet.

migliorare VERBO

to improve ◇ *Partiremo domani, se il tempo*

migliora. We'll set off tomorrow, if the weather improves. ◇ *Fa un corso per migliorare il suo inglese.* He's doing a course to improve his English.

migliore AGGETTIVO, NOME MASC/FEM
1 better (*usato nel comparativo*) ◇ *molto migliore* much better ◇ *Il libro è migliore del film.* The book is better than the film.
2 best (*usato nel superlativo*) ◇ *la migliore della classe* the best in the class ◇ *Questo è il miglior ristorante della città.* This is the best restaurant in town.

il **mignolo** NOME MASC
1 little finger (*di mano*)
2 little toe (*di piede*)

-**mila** SUFFISSO
thousand
al singolare.
♦ **tremila sterline** three thousand pounds
♦ **seicentomila** six hundred thousand

Milano NOME FEM
Milan ◇ *Domani vado a Milano.* I'm going to Milan tomorrow. ◇ *Abitiamo a Milano.* We live in Milan.

miliardario AGGETTIVO (FEM **miliardaria**)
billionaire ◇ *È miliardario.* He's a billionaire.

il **miliardo** NOME MASC
thousand million ◇ *un miliardo di euro* one thousand million euros
♦ **miliardi di persone** millions of people
Quando million si riferisce ad un numero si usa sempre al singolare.
◇ *tre miliardi di lire* three thousand million lire

il **milione** NOME MASC
million ◇ *un milione di dollari* one million dollars
Quando million si riferisce ad un numero si usa sempre al singolare.
◇ *due milioni di sterline* two million pounds
◇ *parecchi milioni di lire* several million lire
Il plurale millions si usa solo quando milioni significa "una gran quantità".
◇ *milioni di persone* millions of people

militare AGGETTIVO
vedi anche **militare** NOME
military ◇ *il servizio militare* military service

> ❶ Until recently young men in Italy had to do military service.

♦ **un ufficiale militare** an army officer

il **militare** NOME MASC
vedi anche **militare** AGGETTIVO
serviceman (PL servicemen) ◇ *due militari* two servicemen
♦ **fare il militare** to do* one's military service
◇ *Non ho fatto il militare.* I didn't do military service.

mille AGGETTIVO

a thousand ◇ *mille persone* a thousand people
♦ **Grazie mille.** Thank you very much.

il **millimetro** NOME MASC
millimetre
millimeter [US]

la **milza** NOME FEM
spleen

mimetizzarsi VERBO
to camouflage oneself

il **mimo** NOME MASC
mime

la **mimosa** NOME FEM
mimosa

la **mina** NOME FEM
mine

la **minaccia** NOME FEM (PL le **minacce**)
threat ◇ *una minaccia per l'ambiente* a threat to the environment
♦ **fare delle minacce a qualcuno** to threaten somebody

minacciare VERBO
to threaten ◇ *Mi minacciò con la pistola.* He threatened me with a gun. ◇ *Lo hanno minacciato di morte.* They threatened to kill him.
♦ **Minaccia di piovere.** It looks like rain.

il **minatore** NOME MASC
miner

minerale AGGETTIVO, NOME MASC
mineral ◇ *acqua minerale* mineral water
◇ *un minerale* a mineral

la **minestra** NOME FEM
soup ◇ *minestra di verdura* vegetable soup

la **miniera** NOME FEM
mine ◇ *una miniera d'oro* a gold mine
◇ *una miniera di carbone* a coal mine

la **minigonna** NOME FEM
miniskirt

minimo AGGETTIVO (FEM **minima**)
vedi anche **minimo** NOME
1 minimum ◇ *la temperatura minima* the minimum temperature
2 minimal (*molto piccolo*) ◇ *ad un costo minimo* at a minimal cost
♦ **La differenza è minima.** There's hardly any difference.
3 slightest ◇ *Non ne ho la minima idea.* I haven't the slightest idea. ◇ *Non c'è stato il minimo cambiamento.* There hasn't been the slightest change.

il **minimo** NOME MASC
vedi anche **minimo** AGGETTIVO
minimum ◇ *il minimo indispensabile* the bare minimum
♦ **È il minimo che tu possa fare.** It's the least you can do.

il **ministero** NOME MASC
ministry (PL ministries)

il **ministro** NOME MASC
minister

• **il ministro della Pubblica Istruzione** the Minister of Education

la **minoranza** NOME FEM
minority (PL minorities)

minore AGGETTIVO
vedi anche **minore** NOME
1 lower ◊ con minore entusiasmo with less enthusiasm
2 lower ◊ Le spese sono state minori del previsto. Costs were lower than expected.
• **un numero minore di studenti** a smaller number of students
3 younger ◊ il mio fratello minore my younger brother
4 minor ◊ le opere minori di Shakespeare Shakespeare's minor works ◊ in do minore in C minor

il/la **minore** NOME MASC/FEM
vedi anche **minore** AGGETTIVO
1 younger (tra due) ◊ la minore delle due sorelle the younger of the two sisters
2 youngest (tra più di due) ◊ il minore dei tre fratelli the youngest of the three brothers
3 minor (minorenne)
• **vietato ai minori di 18 anni** 18 certificate

minorenne AGGETTIVO
under age ◊ Mia sorella è minorenne. My sister is under age.

minuscolo AGGETTIVO (FEM **minuscola**)
vedi anche **minuscolo** NOME
1 small ◊ a lettere minuscole in small letters
2 tiny ◊ un appartamento minuscolo a tiny flat

il **minuscolo** NOME MASC
vedi anche **minuscolo** AGGETTIVO
• **in minuscolo** in small letters

il **minuto** NOME MASC
minute ◊ tra pochi minuti in a few minutes

mio AGGETTIVO (FEM **mia**, MASC PL **miei**, FEM PL **mie**)
vedi anche **mio** PRONOME
my (aggettivo possessivo) ◊ i miei libri my books ◊ È colpa mia. It's my fault.
• **un mio amico** a friend of mine

mio PRONOME (FEM **mia**, MASC PL **miei**, FEM PL **mie**)
vedi anche **mio** AGGETTIVO
mine (pronome possessivo) ◊ È questo il tuo cappotto? – No, il mio è nero. Is this your coat? – No, mine's black. ◊ La tua casa è più grande della mia. Your house is bigger than mine. ◊ Di chi è questo? – È mio. Whose is this? – It's mine.
• **i miei** (genitori) my parents ◊ Vivo con i miei. I live with my parents.

miope AGGETTIVO
short-sighted

la **mira** NOME FEM
• **prendere la mira** to take* aim

• **prendere di mira qualcuno** to target somebody

il **miracolo** NOME MASC
miracle

mirare VERBO
• **mirare a qualcosa** to aim at something ◊ Mirai al bersaglio e sparai. I aimed at the target and fired.

il **mirino** NOME MASC
1 viewfinder (di macchina fotografica)
2 sight (di arma)

il **mirtillo** NOME MASC
bilberry (PL bilberries)

la **miseria** NOME FEM
poverty ◊ Vivono nella miseria. They live in poverty.
• **Porca miseria!** Bloody hell!

il **missile** NOME MASC
missile

il **missionario,** la **missionaria** NOME MASC, FEM
missionary (PL missionaries)

misterioso AGGETTIVO (FEM **misteriosa**)
mysterious

il **mistero** NOME MASC
mystery (PL mysteries)

misto AGGETTIVO (FEM **mista**)
mixed ◊ un'insalata mista a mixed salad ◊ una grigliata mista a mixed grill ◊ una scuola mista a mixed school

la **misura** NOME FEM
1 size (taglia) ◊ Ha una misura più piccola? Have you got a smaller size?
2 measurement (dimensioni) ◊ Può prendermi le misure? Can you take my measurements?
• **fatto su misura** made-to-measure ◊ un completo fatto su misura a made-to-measure suit
• **unità di misura** unit of measurement
3 measure (provvedimento) ◊ misure di sicurezza safety measures

misurare VERBO
to measure ◊ Misura la distanza fra questi due punti. Measure the distance between these two points.
• **Quanto misura questa stanza?** How big is this room?

il **mito** NOME MASC
myth

la **mitologia** NOME FEM
mythology

il **mitra** NOME MASC (PL i **mitra**)
machine gun

il/la **mittente** NOME MASC/FEM
sender ◊ Rispedire al mittente. Return to sender.

il **mobile** NOME MASC
• **un mobile** a piece of furniture
furniture non ha plurale e non è mai

---

* I verbi seguiti da questo simbolo sono irregolari. Si veda anche alle pp.328–338.

preceduto dall'articolo "a"

* **i mobili** the furniture SING ◇ *un negozio di mobili* a furniture shop

a **moda** NOME FEM
fashion ◇ *una sfilata di moda* a fashion show
* **essere di moda** to be* in fashion ◇ *È di moda il nero.* Black is in fashion.
* **essere fuori moda** to be* out of fashion

il **modello**, la **modella** NOME MASC, FEM
model

moderno AGGETTIVO (FEM **moderna**)
modern

modesto AGGETTIVO (FEM **modesta**)
modest

a **modifica** NOME FEM (PL le **modifiche**)
1 modification ◇ *Sono necessarie alcune modifiche.* Some modifications need to be made.
2 alteration (*su abito*)

modificare VERBO
to modify

il **modo** NOME MASC
1 way ◇ *Lo farò a modo mio.* I'll do it my own way. ◇ *in modo strano* in an odd way
* **in modo eccessivo** excessively
* **in questo modo** this way ◇ *Fallo in questo modo.* Do it this way.
* **ad ogni modo** anyway ◇ *Ad ogni modo, non ha importanza.* Anyway, it doesn't matter.
* **in qualche modo** somehow ◇ *In qualche modo riuscirò a farlo.* I'll manage it somehow.
* **in modo da** so as to ◇ *Entrai in punta di piedi in modo da non disturbarlo.* I went in on tiptoe so as not to disturb him.
* **fare in modo di** to try to ◇ *Fate in modo di tornare per le cinque.* Try to be back by five o'clock.
* **Che modi!** What bad manners!
* **un modo di dire** an expression
2 mood (*in grammatica*)

il **modulo** NOME MASC
form ◇ *Riempite il modulo in stampatello.* Fill in the form in block letters.

a **moglie** NOME FEM
wife (PL wives) ◇ *Questa è mia moglie Anna.* This is my wife Anna.

il **molare** NOME MASC
molar

molestare VERBO
1 to torment (*dar fastidio a*) ◇ *Non molestare quel povero cane.* Don't torment that poor dog.
2 to sexually harass (*con molestie sessuali*)

le **molestie** NOME FEM PL
* **molestie sessuali** sexual harassment SING

la **molla** NOME FEM
spring

mollare VERBO

1 to chuck ◇ *Ha mollato il lavoro.* She's chucked her job.
2 to dump ◇ *Ha mollato il suo ragazzo.* She's dumped her boyfriend.
3 to give* up (*rinunciare*) ◇ *Non mollare proprio adesso!* Don't give up now!
* **mollare un ceffone a qualcuno** to give* somebody a slap ◇ *Gli mollò un ceffone.* She gave him a slap.

molle AGGETTIVO
soft

la **molletta** NOME FEM
1 clothes peg
clothespin US
(*per i panni*)
2 hairgrip (*per capelli*)

la **mollica** NOME FEM
soft part (*di pane*)

il **molo** NOME MASC
jetty (PL jetties)

moltiplicare VERBO
to multiply ◇ *Moltiplicate otto per cinque.* Multiply eight by five.

la **moltiplicazione** NOME FEM
multiplication

molto AGGETTIVO (FEM **molta**)
vedi anche **molto** AVVERBIO
Nelle frasi affermative si usa in genere **a lot of.**
◇ *Hai molti libri.* You've got a lot of books.
◇ *Bevo molta acqua.* I drink a lot of water.
◇ *C'era molta gente.* There were a lot of people.
Nelle frasi negative ed interrogative si usa **much** *per indicare una gran quantità.*
◇ *Non ho molto denaro.* I haven't got much money. ◇ *Hai ancora molto lavoro da fare?* Have you got much work left to do?
Nelle frasi negative ed interrogative si usa **many** *per indicare un gran numero.*
◇ *Non ha molti amici.* He hasn't got many friends. ◇ *Hai visto molti film ultimamente? – Non molti.* Have you seen many films lately? – No, not many.

molto AVVERBIO
vedi anche **molto** AGGETTIVO
1 a lot ◇ *Leggo molto.* I read a lot.
◇ *Viaggi molto?* Do you travel a lot?
* **Ci vorrà molto?** Will it take long?
2 much
Nelle frasi negative e nei comparativi si usa **much.**
◇ *Non esco molto.* I don't go out much.
◇ *Chiara è molto più alta di me.* Chiara is much taller than me.
* **molto meglio** much better ◇ *Ora mi sento molto meglio.* I feel much better now.
3 very
seguito da aggettivo o avverbio.
◇ *L'ha fatto molto bene.* He did it very well.
◇ *Sono molto stanco.* I'm very tired.
* **moltissimo** very much ◇ *Mi sono divertita* ☞

M

moltissimo. I enjoyed myself very much.
+ **Mi dispiace moltissimo.** I'm terribly sorry.
momentaneamente AVVERBIO
  at the moment ◊ *È momentaneamente
  assente.* She's not here at the moment.
il **momento** NOME MASC
  moment ◊ *Un momento, per favore!* Just a
  moment please!
+ **in questo momento** at the moment ◊ *In
  questo momento è al telefono.* He's on the
  phone at the moment.
+ **da un momento all'altro** any moment now
  ◊ *Può arrivare da un momento all'altro.*
  He'll be here any moment now.
+ **È un momento difficile.** It's a difficult time.
la **monaca** NOME FEM (PL le **monache**)
  nun
Monaco NOME FEM
+ **Monaco di Baviera** Munich
+ **il Principato di Monaco** Monaco
il **monaco** NOME MASC (PL i **monaci**)
  monk
la **monarchia** NOME FEM
  monarchy (PL monarchies)
il **monastero** NOME MASC
  1 monastery (PL monasteries) (*di monaci*)
  2 convent (*di monache*)
mondiale AGGETTIVO
  world ◊ *la seconda guerra mondiale* the
  Second World War
+ **i mondiali di calcio** the World Cup
il **mondo** NOME MASC
  world ◊ *il migliore del mondo* the best in
  the world ◊ *in tutto il mondo* all over the
  world
la **moneta** NOME FEM
  1 coin ◊ *una moneta da due euro* a two
  euro coin
  2 change (*spiccioli*) ◊ *Non ho moneta.* I
  haven't got any change.
  3 currency (PL currencies) (*di paese*) ◊ *La
  sterlina è una moneta forte.* The pound is a
  strong currency.
la **mongolfiera** NOME FEM
  hot-air balloon
il **monitor** NOME MASC (PL i **monitor**)
  monitor
il **monolocale** NOME MASC
  studio flat
il **monopolio** NOME MASC
  monopoly (PL monopolies)
monotono AGGETTIVO (FEM **monotona**)
  monotonous
il **montaggio** NOME MASC (PL i **montaggi**)
  1 assembly (*di pezzi*)
  2 editing (*di film*)
la **montagna** NOME FEM
  1 mountain ◊ *Il Ben Nevis è la montagna
  più alta della Scozia.* Ben Nevis is the
  highest mountain in Scotland. ◊ *un paesino*

di montagna a mountain village
  2 mountains PL ◊ *Mi piace la montagna.* I
  like the mountains. ◊ *Andremo in vacanza
  in montagna.* We're going to the mountains
  for our holiday. ◊ *Ha una casa in montagna.*
  He's got a house in the mountains.
+ **montagne russe** roller coaster SING
montare VERBO
  1 to assemble ◊ *Ha montato l'armadio da
  solo.* He assembled the wardrobe himself.
+ **Montarono la tenda vicino al lago.** They
  pitched their tent near the lake.
  2 to whip (*panna*)
+ **montare a neve** to whisk until stiff
  ◊ *Montate a neve gli albumi.* Whisk the egg
  whites until stiff.
+ **montare in (1)** (*macchina*) to get* into
+ **montare in (2)** (*treno, bicicletta*) to get* on
+ **montare su una scala** to climb a ladder
+ **montarsi la testa** to get* big-headed ◊ *Si è
  montato la testa.* He's got big-headed.
la **montatura** NOME FEM
  frames PL (*di occhiali*)
il **monte** NOME MASC
  mountain ◊ *Qual è il monte più alto
  d'Europa?* Which is the highest mountain in
  Europe?
+ **il monte Everest** Mount Everest
il **montone** NOME MASC
  1 ram (*animale*)
  2 mutton (*carne*)
+ **una giacca di montone** a sheepskin jacket
montuoso AGGETTIVO (FEM **montuosa**)
  mountainous
il **monumento** NOME MASC
+ **visitare i monumenti** to go* sightseeing
+ **un monumento ai caduti** a war memorial
la **moquette** NOME FEM (PL le **moquette**)
  carpet
la **mora** NOME FEM
  1 blackberry (PL blackberries) (*di rovo*)
  2 mulberry (PL mulberries) (*di gelso*)
il **morale** NOME MASC
  vedi anche **morale** AGGETTIVO, NOME
  morale ◊ *Bisogna tenere alto il morale della
  squadra.* We must keep the team's morale
  high.
+ **Sono giù di morale.** I'm feeling down.
+ **Su col morale!** Cheer up!
la **morale** NOME FEM
  vedi anche **morale** AGGETTIVO, NOME
  1 moral ◊ *la morale della favola* the moral
  of the story
  2 morals PL ◊ *Non hanno morale.* They
  haven't got any morals.
morale AGGETTIVO
  vedi anche **morale** NOME
  moral
morbido AGGETTIVO (FEM **morbida**)
  soft ◊ *Ha la pelle morbida.* She's got soft

skin.

*Attenzione! In inglese esiste la parola **morbid**, che però significa **morboso**.*

morbillo NOME MASC
measles SING ◇ *Giorgio ha il morbillo.* Giorgio has got measles.

morbo NOME MASC
disease

mordere* VERBO
to bite* ◇ *Il cane mi ha morso la gamba.* The dog bit my leg.

morire* VERBO
to die* ◇ *Morì nel 1857.* He died in 1857.
◇ *Muoio di sete.* I'm dying of thirst.
◆ **Muoio di fame.** I'm starving.
◆ **Fa un caldo da morire.** It's terribly hot.
◆ **morire dalla voglia di fare qualcosa** to be* dying to do something ◇ *Moriva dalla voglia di raccontarle tutto.* He was dying to tell her everything.

mormorare VERBO
to mutter

morsicare VERBO
to bite*

morso NOME MASC
bite ◇ *Mi dai un morso del tuo panino?* Can I have a bite of your roll?
◆ **dare un morso a qualcosa** to bite* into something ◇ *Diede un morso al panino.* He bit into his roll.

mortale AGGETTIVO
1 fatal (*incidente*)
2 deadly (*veleno*)

morte NOME FEM
death

morto NOME MASC
vedi anche **morto** AGGETTIVO
◆ **i morti** the dead ◇ *Il due novembre commemoriamo i morti.* We remember the dead on November the second.
◆ **Ci sono stati tre morti nella sparatoria.** Three people were killed in the shooting.
◆ **fare il morto** (*nuotando*) to float

morto AGGETTIVO (FEM **morta**)
vedi anche **morto** NOME
dead ◇ *il loro fratello morto* their dead brother
◆ **essere morto di paura** to be* scared to death
◆ **essere stanco morto** to be* knackered
◆ **essere morto di freddo** to be* frozen stiff

mosaico NOME MASC (PL i **mosaici**)
mosaic

Mosca NOME FEM
Moscow ◇ *Vado a Mosca.* I'm going to Moscow. ◇ *Abitano a Mosca.* They live in Moscow.

mosca NOME FEM (PL le **mosche**)
fly (PL flies)

moscerino NOME MASC
midge

moschea NOME FEM
mosque

la mossa NOME FEM
move ◇ *Ha fatto una mossa sbagliata.* He made a bad move.

mosso AGGETTIVO (FEM **mossa**)
1 rough ◇ *Oggi c'è mare mosso.* The sea's rough today.
2 wavy ◇ *Ha i capelli mossi.* He's got wavy hair.
3 blurred ◇ *La fotografia è un po' mossa.* The photo is a bit blurred.

la mostarda NOME FEM
mustard

la mostra NOME FEM
exhibition ◇ *una mostra d'arte* an art exhibition
◆ **mostra canina** dog show
◆ **Le piace mettersi in mostra.** She likes to be the centre of attention.

mostrare VERBO
to show*
◆ **mostrare qualcosa a qualcuno** to show* somebody something ◇ *Ho mostrato le foto a Paolo.* I showed Paolo the photos.
◇ *Le ho mostrato il mio vestito nuovo.* I showed her my new dress. ◇ *Mi mostri come si fa?* Will you show me how to do it?
◆ **mostrare la lingua a** to stick* out one's tongue at

il mostro NOME MASC
monster

mostruoso AGGETTIVO (FEM **mostruosa**)
terrible ◇ *un delitto mostruoso* a terrible crime
◆ **Ha una cultura mostruosa.** She knows an awful lot.

il motel NOME MASC (PL i **motel**)
motel

il motivo NOME MASC
reason ◇ *Ho un motivo valido per farlo.* I've got a good reason for doing it. ◇ *Si è dimesso per motivi personali.* He resigned for personal reasons.
◆ **Per quale motivo?** Why?
◆ **senza motivo** for no reason

la moto NOME FEM (PL le **moto**)
vedi anche **moto** NOME
motorbike ◇ *Vado a scuola in moto.* I go to school on my motorbike.

il moto NOME MASC
vedi anche **moto** NOME
exercise ◇ *Devi fare un po' di moto.* You should take some exercise.
◆ **mettere in moto la macchina** to start the car

il/la motociclista NOME MASC/FEM (MASC PL i **motociclisti**, FEM PL le **motocicliste**)
motorcyclist

il motore NOME MASC
engine ◇ *Spegni il motore.* Switch off the engine. ◇ *un motore diesel* a diesel engine
◆ **motore di ricerca** search engine

M

♦ **a motore** motor ◊ *una barca a motore* a motor boat

il **motorino** NOME MASC
moped ◊ *Vado a scuola in motorino.* I go to school on my moped.

il **motoscafo** NOME MASC
motorboat

il **movente** NOME MASC
motive ◊ *Avevano un movente per ucciderlo.* They had a motive for killing him.

il **movimento** NOME MASC
movement ◊ *un movimento politico* a political movement ◊ *un movimento brusco* a sudden movement
♦ **È sempre in movimento.** She's always on the go.

il **mozzicone** NOME MASC
butt (*di sigaretta*)

la **mucca** NOME FEM (PL le **mucche**)
cow

il **mucchio** NOME MASC
heap ◊ *un mucchio di sassi* a heap of stones
♦ **un mucchio di** (*molti*) loads of ◊ *Ho un mucchio di cose da fare.* I've got loads of things to do. ◊ *Ha detto un mucchio di sciocchezze.* He talked a load of rubbish.

la **muffa** NOME FEM
mould
mold US
♦ **fare la muffa** to go* mouldy

il **mulino** NOME MASC
mill
♦ **un mulino a vento** a windmill

il **mulo** NOME MASC
mule

la **multa** NOME FEM
fine ◊ *una multa di cinquanta euro* a fine of fifty euros
♦ **Ho preso una multa per divieto di sosta.** I got a parking ticket.
♦ **dare la multa a qualcuno** to fine somebody ◊ *Il controllore le ha dato la multa.* The inspector fined her.

il **municipio** NOME MASC
town hall

le **munizioni** NOME FEM PL
ammunition SING

muovere* VERBO
to move ◊ *Non riesco a muovere la gamba.* I can't move my leg.
♦ **muoversi** to move ◊ *Non si muove.* It won't move.
♦ **Muoviti!** Hurry up! ◊ *Muoviti, o perdiamo il treno!* Hurry up, or we'll miss the train!

le **mura** NOME FEM PL
walls ◊ *le mura della città* the city walls

il **muratore** NOME MASC

bricklayer ◊ *Fa il muratore.* He is a bricklayer.

il **muro** NOME MASC
wall ◊ *un muro alto* a high wall
♦ **un armadio a muro** a built-in cupboard

il **muschio** NOME MASC
moss

il **muscolo** NOME MASC
muscle ◊ *muscoli forti* strong muscles
♦ **scaldare i muscoli** to warm up

il **museo** NOME MASC
museum

la **museruola** NOME FEM
muzzle
♦ **mettere la museruola a un cane** to muzzle a dog
♦ **I cani devono avere la museruola.** Dogs have to be muzzled.

la **musica** NOME FEM
music ◊ *Mi piace la musica classica.* I like classical music.

musicale AGGETTIVO
musical

il/la **musicista** NOME MASC/FEM (MASC PL i **musicisti**, FEM PL le **musiciste**)
1 musician ◊ *Fa il musicista.* He is a musician.
2 player ◊ *uno dei musicisti dell'orchestra* one of the players in the orchestra

il **muso** NOME MASC
1 muzzle (*di cane*)
2 face ◊ *Gli diede un pugno sul muso.* He punched him in the face.
♦ **fare il muso** to sulk ◊ *Fa il muso.* She's sulking.

mussulmano, mussulmana NOME, AGGETTIVO
Muslim

la **muta** NOME FEM
♦ **una muta subacquea** a wet suit

le **mutande** NOME FEM PL
1 underpants (*da uomo*) ◊ *Venne ad aprire la porta in mutande.* He came to open the door in his underpants.
2 pants (*da donna*)

muto AGGETTIVO (FEM **muta**)
1 dumb ◊ *un ragazzo muto* a dumb boy
♦ **Giuro che sarò muto come un pesce.** I swear I won't say a word.
2 silent ◊ *il cinema muto* the silent cinema ◊ *La h è muta.* The h is silent.

il **mutuo** NOME MASC
mortgage
♦ **fare un mutuo** to take* out a mortgage ◊ *Ho dovuto fare un mutuo per comprare la casa.* I had to take out a mortgage to buy the house.

N

nafta NOME FEM
diesel

nanna NOME FEM
+ **andare a nanna** to go* to beddy-byes ◇ *Andiamo a nanna.* Let's go to beddy-byes.
+ **Fai la nanna, ora.** Go to sleep now.

nano, la nana NOME MASC, FEM
dwarf (PL dwarves)

Napoli NOME FEM
Naples ◇ *Domani vado a Napoli.* I'm going to Naples tomorrow. ◇ *Abitiamo a Napoli.* We live in Naples.

narice NOME FEM
nostril

narrativa NOME FEM
fiction ◇ *È uno dei capolavori della narrativa europea.* It's one of the greatest works of European fiction.

nasale AGGETTIVO
nasal

nascere* VERBO
to be* born ◇ *È nato nel 1977.* He was born in 1977. ◇ *Sono nata il 28 aprile.* I was born on the 28th of April.

nascita NOME FEM
birth ◇ *dopo la nascita della bambina* after the baby's birth ◇ *È cieco dalla nascita.* He has been blind from birth.

nascondere* VERBO
to hide* ◇ *Dove hai nascosto la lettera?* Where have you hidden the letter?
+ **nascondersi** to hide* ◇ *Si è nascosto dietro al divano.* He hid behind the sofa.

nascondiglio NOME MASC
hiding place

nascondino NOME MASC
+ **giocare a nascondino** to play hide-and-seek

nascosto AGGETTIVO (FEM **nascosta**)
hidden ◇ *un pericolo nascosto* a hidden danger
+ **di nascosto** secretly ◇ *L'abbiamo fatto di nascosto.* We did it secretly.

naso NOME MASC
nose ◇ *Si è soffiato il naso.* He blew his nose.
+ **Ha naso per gli affari.** He has a flair for business.

nastro NOME MASC
[1] ribbon (*di stoffa*) ◇ *un nastro di seta* a silk ribbon
[2] tape (*magnetico*) ◇ *Ha fatto tornare indietro il nastro.* He rewound the tape.
+ **nastro adesivo** adhesive tape
+ **nastro trasportatore** conveyor belt

Natale NOME MASC
Christmas ◇ *Cosa fai a Natale?* What are you doing at Christmas? ◇ *albero di Natale* Christmas tree ◇ *Buon Natale!* Merry Christmas!

natalizio AGGETTIVO (FEM **natalizia**)
Christmas ◇ *gli addobbi natalizi* Christmas decorations

la natica NOME FEM (PL le **natiche**)
buttock

nato AGGETTIVO (FEM **nata**)
+ **un attore nato** a born actor

la natura NOME FEM
nature ◇ *gli amanti della natura* nature lovers ◇ *la natura umana* human nature
+ **È allegra di natura.** She's got a cheerful personality.
+ **una natura morta** a still life

naturale AGGETTIVO
[1] natural ◇ *risorse naturali* natural resources
+ **acqua minerale naturale** still mineral water
[2] of course ◇ *Posso venire anch'io? – Naturale!* Can I come with you? – Of course!

naturalmente AVVERBIO
of course ◇ *Mi telefonerai? – Sì, naturalmente.* Will you phone me? – Yes, of course.

naturista NOME MASC/FEM, AGGETTIVO (MASC PL **naturisti**, FEM PL **naturiste**)
nudist

naufragare VERBO
[1] to be* wrecked (*nave*) ◇ *La nave è naufragata a causa della tempesta.* The ship was wrecked in the storm.
[2] to be* shipwrecked (*persona*) ◇ *Naufragarono poco lontano dall'isola.* They were shipwrecked not far from the island.

il naufrago, la naufraga NOME MASC, FEM (MASC PL i **naufraghi**, FEM PL le **naufraghe**)
[1] shipwrecked person (*in mare*)
[2] castaway (*su un'isola*)

la nausea NOME FEM
+ **avere la nausea** to feel* sick ◇ *Avevo un po' di nausea.* I felt a bit sick.

nauseante AGGETTIVO
disgusting ◇ *un odore nauseante* a disgusting smell

la navata NOME FEM
+ **navata centrale** nave
+ **navata laterale** aisle

la nave NOME FEM
ship
+ **nave da guerra** warship
+ **nave da crociera** cruise liner

la navicella NOME FEM
+ **una navicella spaziale** a spaceship

navigare VERBO
to sail ◇ *Navigarono per tre mesi prima di raggiungere la costa.* They sailed for three months before they reached land.
+ **navigare in Internet** to surf the Net

la navigazione NOME FEM

☞

◆ **dopo una settimana di navigazione** after a week at sea

nazionale AGGETTIVO
> vedi anche **nazionale** NOME

national ◇ *l'inno nazionale* the national anthem ◇ *un parco nazionale* a national park

la **nazionale** NOME FEM
> vedi anche **nazionale** AGGETTIVO

◆ **la nazionale azzurra** the Italian team

la **nazionalità** NOME FEM (PL le **nazionalità**)
nationality (PL nationalities) ◇ *Nazionalità: Italiana.* Nationality: Italian.

◆ **È di nazionalità britannica.** She's British.

la **nazione** NOME FEM
nation

ne AVVERBIO, PRONOME
Spesso ne non viene tradotto.
◇ *È meglio che tu te ne vada.* You'd better leave. ◇ *Dammene uno, per favore.* Give me one, please. ◇ *Ne voglio ancora un po'.* I want a bit more. ◇ *Hai del pane? – No, non ne ho.* Have you got any bread? – No, I haven't. ◇ *Quanti anni hai? – Ne ho diciasette.* How old are you? – I'm seventeen.
Quando ne significa "riguardo a", va tradotto con about it.
◇ *Non parliamone più!* Let's not talk about it any more! ◇ *Non me ne importa niente.* I couldn't care less about it.

né CONGIUNZIONE
◆ **né...né...** neither...nor... ◇ *Non verranno né Chiara né Donatella.* Neither Chiara nor Donatella are coming.
Se si traduce il verbo con una forma negativa va usato either...or.
◇ *Non parla né l'italiano né il tedesco.* He doesn't speak either Italian or German.
◆ **Non l'ho più vista né sentita.** I didn't see or hear from her again.
◆ **né l'uno né l'altro** neither of them ◇ *Né l'uno né l'altro gioca a tennis.* Neither of them plays tennis.
◆ **Non conosco né l'uno né l'altro.** I don't know either of them.

neanche AVVERBIO, CONGIUNZIONE
[1] not even ◇ *Neanche un bambino ci crederebbe.* Not even a child would believe it.
◆ **non...neanche** not even... ◇ *Non mi ha neanche pagato.* She didn't even pay me.
◆ **neanche se** even if ◇ *Non potrebbe venire neanche se volesse.* He couldn't come even if he wanted to.
[2] neither ◇ *Non l'ho visto. – Neanch'io.* I didn't see him. – Neither did I. ◇ *Non ne ero sicuro. – Neanche lei.* I wasn't sure. – Neither was she.
Si noti la costruzione verbale in inglese.
◆ **Neanche per idea!** Certainly not!

◆ **Non ci penso neanche!** I wouldn't dream of it!

la **nebbia** NOME FEM
fog ◇ *Odio la nebbia.* I hate fog.
◆ **Oggi c'è nebbia.** It's foggy today.

necessario AGGETTIVO (FEM **necessaria**)
> vedi anche **necessario** NOME

necessary ◇ *Porta i documenti necessari.* Bring the necessary documents.
◆ **È necessario far presto.** We've got to hurry.

il **necessario** NOME MASC
> vedi anche **necessario** AGGETTIVO

◆ **lo stretto necessario** the bare essentials PL ◇ *Ha messo in valigia lo stretto necessario.* She packed the bare essentials.

la **necessità** NOME FEM (PL le **necessità**)
necessity (PL necessities) ◇ *Non è un lusso, è una necessità.* It isn't a luxury, it's a necessity.
◆ **L'ho fatto per necessità.** I did it because I had to.
◆ **in caso di necessità** if necessary

negare VERBO
to deny ◇ *Non puoi negarlo.* You can't deny it.
◆ **negare di aver fatto qualcosa** to deny doing something
deny regge il gerundio.
◇ *Ha negato di aver preso i soldi.* He denied taking the money.
È possibile anche la costruzione: "He denied he had taken the money".
◆ **negare qualcosa a qualcuno** to refuse to give somebody something ◇ *Mi ha negato il suo appoggio.* He refused to give me his support.

la **negativa** NOME FEM
negative (di fotografia)

negativo AGGETTIVO (FEM **negativa**)
negative ◇ *Il risultato del test è stato negativo.* The result of the test was negative.

negato AGGETTIVO (FEM **negata**)
◆ **essere negato per** to be* no good at ◇ *Sono negato per lo sport.* I'm no good at sport.

il/la **negoziante** NOME MASC/FEM
shopkeeper

il **negoziato** NOME MASC
◆ **negoziati per la pace** peace talks

il **negozio** NOME MASC
shop
store US
◇ *un negozio di scarpe* a shoe shop

negro AGGETTIVO (FEM **negra**)
black ◇ *un ragazzo negro* a black boy

nemico NOME MASC/FEM, AGGETTIVO (FEM **nemica**, MASC PL **nemici**, FEM PL **nemiche**)
enemy (PL enemies) ◇ *Ha molti nemici.* He's got a lot of enemies. ◇ *territorio nemico* enemy territory

---

* *I verbi seguiti da questo simbolo sono irregolari. Si veda anche alle pp.328–338.*

Italian ~ English

nemmeno AVVERBIO, CONGIUNZIONE
[1] not even ◇ *Nemmeno un bambino ci crederebbe.* Not even a child would believe it.
* **non...nemmeno** not even... ◇ *Non mi ha nemmeno pagato.* She didn't even pay me.
* **nemmeno se** even if ◇ *Non potrebbe venire nemmeno se volesse.* He couldn't come even if he wanted to.
[2] neither ◇ *Non l'ho visto. – Nemmeno io.* I didn't see him. – Neither did I. ◇ *Non ne ero sicuro. – Nemmeno lei.* I wasn't sure. – Neither was she.
Si noti la costruzione verbale in inglese.
* **Nemmeno per idea!** Certainly not!
* **Non ci penso nemmeno!** I wouldn't dream of it!

neo NOME MASC
mole *(sulla pelle)*

neon NOME MASC
neon ◇ *una luce al neon* a neon light

neonato, la neonata NOME MASC, FEM
newborn baby *(PL newborn babies)*

neozelandese AGGETTIVO
vedi anche **neozelandese** NOME
New Zealand ◇ *la squadra neozelandese* the New Zealand team

neozelandese NOME MASC/FEM
vedi anche **neozelandese** AGGETTIVO
New Zealander

neppure = **nemmeno**

nero AGGETTIVO, NOME MASC (FEM **nera**)
black ◇ *Ha i capelli neri.* She's got black hair. ◇ *È vestita di nero.* She's dressed in black.
* **essere di umore nero** to be* in a very bad mood ◇ *Oggi sono di umore nero.* I'm in a very bad mood today.
* **mercato nero** black market
* **lavoro nero** work in the black economy

nervo NOME MASC
nerve
* **dare sui nervi a qualcuno** to get* on somebody's nerves ◇ *Quando fa così mi dà proprio sui nervi.* It really gets on my nerves when he does that.
* **avere i nervi saldi** to be* calm
* **avere i nervi a fior di pelle** to be* edgy

nervoso AGGETTIVO (FEM **nervosa**)
[1] irritable ◇ *È sempre nervoso e si arrabbia spesso.* He's always irritable and often loses his temper.
[2] stressed
* **essere nervoso** to feel* stressed ◇ *Ero nervoso e gli ho risposto male.* I was feeling stressed and didn't give him a proper answer.
[3] nervous *(spaventato)* ◇ *Sono sempre un po' nervoso prima di un compito in classe.* I'm always a bit nervous before a test at school.

nessuno, nessuna PRONOME

vedi anche **nessuno** AGGETTIVO
Quando **nessuno** *è soggetto e il verbo inglese non contiene negazione, va tradotto con* **nobody** *o* **no one**.
◇ *Non è venuto nessuno.* Nobody came.
◇ *Nessuno mi crede.* No one believes me.
◇ *Non c'era nessuno.* There was no one there.
Quando invece il verbo inglese contiene negazione, **nessuno** *va tradotto con* **anybody** *o* **anyone**.
◇ *Non c'era nessuno.* There wasn't anyone there. ◇ *Non dirlo a nessuno.* Don't tell that to anybody.
Nelle frasi interrogative si usa **anybody** *o* **anyone**.
◇ *Ha telefonato nessuno?* Did anybody phone? ◇ *Hai visto nessuno?* Did you see anyone?
* **nessuno di loro** none of them ◇ *Non è venuto nessuno di loro.* None of them came.

nessuno AGGETTIVO (FEM **nessuna**)
vedi anche **nessuno** PRONOME
[1] no ◇ *Non c'è nessun bisogno di andare.* There's no need to go.
Quando il verbo inglese è usato nella forma negativa **nessuno** *si traduce con* **any**.
◇ *Non ha fatto nessun commento.* He didn't make any comment.
[2] any *(qualche)* ◇ *Nessuna obiezione?* Any objections?
* **nessun altro** no one else ◇ *Nessun altro voleva andarci.* No one else wanted to go.
* **Non ho incontrato nessun altro.** I didn't meet anyone else.
* **da nessuna parte** not...anywhere ◇ *Non riesco a trovarlo da nessuna parte.* I can't find it anywhere.

netto AGGETTIVO (FEM **netta**)
[1] clear ◇ *La squadra ha riportato una netta vittoria.* The team won a clear victory.
[2] net ◇ *peso netto* net weight

il netturbino NOME MASC
dustman *(PL dustmen)*
garbage collector [US]

neutrale AGGETTIVO
neutral

neutro AGGETTIVO (FEM **neutra**)
[1] neutral *(colore)*
[2] neuter *(genere grammaticale)*

la neve NOME FEM
snow ◇ *Mi piace camminare sulla neve.* I like walking in the snow.
* **È caduta tanta neve ieri.** It snowed a lot yesterday.

nevicare VERBO
to snow ◇ *Nevica.* It's snowing.

la nevicata NOME FEM
snowfall

il nevischio NOME MASC
sleet

la nicotina NOME FEM

☞

nicotine

il **nido** NOME MASC
  [1] nest (di uccello)
  [2] crèche (asilo)

niente PRONOME, AVVERBIO
  nothing ◇ Cos'hai comprato? – Niente.
  What did you buy? – Nothing. ◇ Cosa c'è? –
  Niente. What's the matter? – Nothing.
  ◇ Non è successo niente. Nothing
  happened.

  Quando la traduzione contiene una
  *negazione, e nelle frasi interrogative, **niente***
  *si traduce in genere con **anything**.*

  ◇ Non ho visto niente. I didn't see anything.
  ◇ Hai bisogno di niente? Do you need
  anything?
  ◆ **Non mi sono fatto niente.** I didn't hurt
  myself.
  ◆ **poco o niente** next to nothing
  ◆ **Nient'altro?** (in negozio) Will that be all?
  ◆ **Grazie. – Di niente.** Thanks. – You're
  welcome.
  ◆ **niente affatto** not at all ◇ Le dispiace se
  fumo? – Niente affatto. Do you mind if I
  smoke? – Not at all.
  ◆ **non...per niente** not...at all ◇ Non mi sono
  divertito per niente. I didn't enjoy it at all.
  ◆ **Niente male!** Not bad at all!
  ◆ **Niente paura!** Don't worry!
  ◆ **Non fa niente.** It doesn't matter.

la **ninnananna** NOME FEM
  lullaby (PL lullabies)

il/la **nipote** NOME MASC/FEM
  ◆ **il nipote (1)** (di nonni) grandson
  ◆ **il nipote (2)** (di zii) nephew
  ◆ **la nipote (1)** (di nonni) granddaughter
  ◆ **la nipote (2)** (di zii) niece
  ◆ **nipoti (1)** (di nonni: maschi e femmine)
  grandchildren
  ◆ **nipoti (2)** (di zii: maschi e femmine) nieces
  and nephews

nitido AGGETTIVO (FEM **nitida**)
  sharp ◇ un'immagine nitida a sharp image

no AVVERBIO
  [1] no (nelle risposte) ◇ Vieni? – No. Are you
  coming? – No, I'm not. ◇ Ti piace? – No. Do
  you like it? – No, I don't. ◇ Ne vuoi ancora? –
  No, grazie. Would you like some more? – No
  thank you.
  [2] not ◇ Perché no? Why not? ◇ Vieni o
  no? Are you coming or not? ◇ Spero di no. I
  hope not.

  *Per tradurre ...**no?** alla fine di una frase leggi*
  gli esempi qui sotto.

  ◇ Mi scriverai, no? You'll write to me, won't
  you? ◇ Può venire, no? He can come, can't
  he? ◇ Vieni anche tu, no? You're coming
  too, aren't you? ◇ Hai finito, no? You've
  finished, haven't you?

nobile AGGETTIVO
  *vedi anche **nobile** NOME*

  [1] aristocratic ◇ una famiglia nobile an
  aristocratic family
  [2] noble ◇ nobili sentimenti noble
  sentiments

il/la **nobile** NOME MASC/FEM
  *vedi anche **nobile** AGGETTIVO*
  [1] aristocrat (oggi)
  [2] nobleman (PL noblemen)
  noblewoman (PL noblewomen) (in passato)
  ◆ **i nobili** (uomini e donne) the aristocracy

la **nocca** NOME FEM (PL le **nocche**)
  knuckle

la **nocciola** NOME FEM
  *vedi anche **nocciola** AGGETTIVO*
  hazelnut ◇ gelato alla nocciola hazelnut ice
  cream

nocciola AGGETTIVO (MASC, FEM, PL **nocciola**)
  *vedi anche **nocciola** NOME*
  hazel (colore)

la **nocciolina** NOME FEM
  ◆ **nocciolina americana** peanut

il **nòcciolo** NOME MASC
  stone (di frutto) ◇ un nocciolo di pesca a
  peach stone
  ◆ **Il nocciolo della questione è...** The main
  point is...

il **nocciòlo** NOME MASC
  hazel (albero)

la **noce** NOME FEM
  *vedi anche **noce** NOME*
  walnut
  ◆ **noce di cocco** coconut
  ◆ **noce moscata** nutmeg

il **noce** NOME MASC
  *vedi anche **noce** NOME*
  walnut tree

nocivo AGGETTIVO (FEM **nociva**)
  harmful ◇ Non contiene sostanze nocive. It
  doesn't contain any harmful substances.

il **nodo** NOME MASC
  [1] knot (di cravatta, di fune)
  ◆ **fare un nodo** to tie a knot
  ◆ **sciogliere un nodo** to untie a knot
  [2] tangle (nei capelli)

noi PRONOME
  [1] we (soggetto) ◇ Noi andiamo al cinema.
  We're going to the cinema.
  ◆ **Non lo sapevamo nemmeno noi.** We didn't
  even know it ourselves.
  [2] us (complemento) ◇ Chi viene con noi?
  Who's coming with us? ◇ Sono più giovani
  di noi. They are younger than us. ◇ Chi è? –
  Siamo noi. Who is it? – It's us.

la **noia** NOME FEM
  boredom ◇ Stavano morendo di noia. They
  were dying of boredom.
  ◆ **Che noia, quel film!** The film was so boring!
  ◆ **noie** (problemi) trouble SING ◇ Ha avuto
  delle noie con i vicini. She had trouble with
  the neighbours. ◇ Ha avuto delle noie con la

polizia. He was in trouble with the police.
* **dare noia a qualcuno** to bother somebody
  ◇ *Finiscila di dar noia a tua sorella.* Stop
  bothering your sister.
* **Le dà noia se fumo?** Do you mind if I smoke?
* **Mi è venuto a noia.** I'm tired of it.

noioso AGGETTIVO (FEM **noiosa**)
  boring
  Attenzione! In inglese esiste la parola **noisy**,
  che però significa **rumoroso**.

noleggiare VERBO
  [1] to hire ◇ *Dove possiamo noleggiare una
  macchina?* Where can we hire a car?
  [2] to hire out (*dare a noleggio*)
  ◇ *Noleggiano biciclette ai turisti.* They hire
  out bikes to tourists.

il **noleggio** NOME MASC
  hire (*di auto, di bicicletta, di sci*)
* **prendere a noleggio** to hire ◇ *Prenderemo
  gli sci a noleggio.* We're going to hire skis.

il **nomade** NOME MASC/FEM
  nomad

il **nome** NOME MASC
  [1] name ◇ *Che bel nome!* What a nice
  name! ◇ *Lo conosco di nome.* I know the
  name. ◇ *Li conosce tutti per nome.* She
  knows them all by name. ◇ *Posso chiamarti
  per nome?* Can I call you by your first name?
* **Gli hanno dato il nome del nonno.** He is
  named after his grandfather.
* **a nome di** in the name of ◇ *La macchina è a
  nome di mio marito.* The car is in my
  husband's name.
* **Tanti saluti anche a nome di mia moglie.** My
  wife asked me to give you her regards.
* **nome di battesimo** Christian name
  [2] noun (*in grammatica*)

la **nomina** NOME FEM
  appointment

nominare VERBO
  [1] to mention (*citare*) ◇ *L'ha nominata nel
  suo discorso.* He mentioned her in his
  speech.
* **Non l'ho mai sentito nominare.** I've never
  heard of it.
  [2] to appoint ◇ *È stato nominato segretario
  generale.* He has been appointed
  secretary-general.

non AVVERBIO
  not ◇ *La legge non è stata ancora
  approvata.* The law has not yet been passed.
  In genere **not** *viene abbreviato nella lingua
  parlata o meno formale.*
  ◇ *Mario non c'è.* Mario isn't here. ◇ *Non
  sono inglesi.* They aren't English. ◇ *Non ci
  sono andato.* I didn't go. ◇ *Non lo so.* I don't
  know. ◇ *Non andarci!* Don't go! ◇ *Non
  avresti dovuto farlo.* You shouldn't have
  done that.

la **nonna** NOME FEM
  grandmother
  Il termine più familiare è "granny" o
  "grandma".

il **nonno** NOME MASC
  grandfather
  Il termine più familiare è "grandad" o
  "grandpa".
* **i miei nonni** (*nonno e nonna*) my
  grandparents

nono AGGETTIVO, NOME MASC (FEM **nona**)
  ninth ◇ *Abita al nono piano.* He lives on the
  ninth floor.

nonostante PREPOSIZIONE
  vedi anche **nonostante** CONGIUNZIONE
  in spite of ◇ *Ci è riuscita nonostante tutto.*
  She succeeded in spite of everything.

nonostante CONGIUNZIONE
  vedi anche **nonostante** PREPOSIZIONE
  even though ◇ *Ha voluto alzarsi nonostante
  fosse ancora malato.* He wanted to get up
  even though he was still ill.

il **nord** NOME MASC
  north ◇ *La sua famiglia è del nord.* His
  family comes from the north.
* **a nord** north ◇ *Si è diretto a nord.* He
  headed north. ◇ *Piove di più a nord.* It rains
  more in the north.
* **a nord di** north of ◇ *Si trova a nord della
  città.* It's north of the city.
* **l'America del Nord** North America
* **l'Italia del nord** Northern Italy

il **nordest** NOME MASC
  north-east
* **a nordest di** north-east of

il **nordovest** NOME MASC
  north-west
* **a nordovest di** north-west of

la **norma** NOME FEM
  norm ◇ *le norme sociali* social norms
* **di norma** as a rule ◇ *Di norma chiudo a
  chiave la porta.* I lock the door as a rule.
* **norme di sicurezza** safety regulations
* **norme per l'uso** instructions for use

normale AGGETTIVO
  normal

norvegese AGGETTIVO
  vedi anche **norvegese** NOME MASC, FEM
  Norwegian

il **norvegese** NOME MASC
  vedi anche **norvegese** AGGETTIVO, NOME FEM
  Norwegian (*persona, lingua*) ◇ *Parla
  norvegese.* He speaks Norwegian. ◇ *i
  norvegesi* the Norwegians

la **norvegese** NOME FEM
  vedi anche **norvegese** AGGETTIVO, NOME MASC
  Norwegian (*persona*)

la **Norvegia** NOME FEM
  Norway ◇ *Ti è piaciuta la Norvegia?* Did you
  like Norway? ◇ *Andremo in Norvegia
  quest'estate.* We're going to Norway this
  summer.

la **nostalgia** NOME FEM
* **Ho nostalgia di casa.** I'm homesick. ☞

N

♦ **Ho nostalgia dei vecchi tempi.** I'm nostalgic for the good old days.

nostro AGGETTIVO (FEM **nostra**)
vedi anche **nostro** PRONOME
our (aggettivo possessivo) ◊ il nostro giardino our garden ◊ la nostra macchina our car ◊ i nostri libri our books ◊ nostro padre our father ◊ È colpa nostra. It's our fault.
♦ **un nostro amico** a friend of ours
♦ **Alla nostra!** To us!

nostro PRONOME (FEM **nostra**)
vedi anche **nostro** AGGETTIVO
ours (pronome possessivo) ◊ È questa la vostra macchina? – No, la nostra è nera. Is this your car? – No, ours is black. ◊ Le sue foto sono più belle delle nostre. His pictures are better than ours. ◊ Di chi è questo? – È nostro. Whose is this? – It's ours.

la **nota** NOME FEM
note ◊ Leggi la nota a pagina cinquantasei. Read the note on page fifty six.
♦ **prendere nota di qualcosa** to make* a note of something ◊ Ho preso nota di tutto quello che ha detto. I made a note of everything she said.
♦ **degno di nota** noteworthy
♦ **una nota musicale** a note
♦ **note a piè di pagina** footnotes

il **notaio** NOME MASC
notary (PL notaries)

notare VERBO
to notice ◊ Hai notato com'era strano? Did you notice how strange he was?
♦ **Gli ho fatto notare che l'errore era suo.** I pointed out that it was his mistake.
♦ **farsi notare** to draw* attention to oneself ◊ Le piace farsi notare. She likes to draw attention to herself.

notevole AGGETTIVO
♦ **Quell'anello ha un valore notevole.** That ring is very valuable.
♦ **una donna di notevole bellezza** a very beautiful woman

la **notizia** NOME FEM
news SING
news non è mai preceduto dall'articolo indeterminativo.
◊ Questa è una notizia interessante. That's interesting news. ◊ Ho sentito la notizia della sua morte per radio. I heard the news of his death on the radio. ◊ La notizia è stata uno shock per lui. The news was a shock to him.
♦ **notizie** news ◊ Ho delle buone notizie per te. I've got some good news for you.
◊ Brutte notizie, purtroppo! Bad news, unfortunately! ◊ Non abbiamo sue notizie da un anno. It's a year since we had any news of her.
♦ **Fammi avere tue notizie!** Keep in touch!

il **notiziario** NOME MASC
news SING ◊ L'hanno detto al notiziario delle otto. It was on the eight o'clock news.

noto AGGETTIVO (FEM **nota**)
well-known ◊ un noto politico a well-known politician ◊ Suo fratello è più noto. His brother is better known.

la **notte** NOME FEM
night
♦ **di notte** at night ◊ Ha paura di uscire di notte. She's afraid to go out at night.
♦ **È successo di notte.** It happened during the night.
♦ **questa notte (1)** (quella passata) last night
♦ **questa notte (2)** (quella che viene) tonight

notturno AGGETTIVO (FEM **notturna**)
night ◊ Non c'è un servizio notturno. There is no night service.

novanta NUMERO
ninety

novantesimo AGGETTIVO, NOME MASC (FEM **novantesima**)
ninetieth

nove NUMERO
nine ◊ Ho nove anni. I'm nine. ◊ le nove di sera nine o'clock in the evening
♦ **il nove dicembre** the ninth of December

novecento NUMERO
nine hundred
♦ **il Novecento** the twentieth century

novembre NOME MASC
November
Si noti l'uso della maiuscola in inglese.
◊ in novembre in November

la **novità** NOME FEM (PL le **novità**)
news SING
news non è mai preceduto dall'articolo indeterminativo.
◊ Ci sono novità? Is there any news?
♦ **Questa è una novità!** That's something new!
♦ **l'ultima novità in fatto di lettori CD** the latest thing in CD players

le **nozze** NOME FEM PL
wedding SING ◊ un regalo di nozze a wedding present
♦ **nozze d'argento** silver wedding
♦ **nozze d'oro** golden wedding
♦ **viaggio di nozze** honeymoon ◊ Dove andrete in viaggio di nozze? Where are you going on your honeymoon?

nubile AGGETTIVO
unmarried ◊ una donna nubile an unmarried woman

la **nuca** NOME FEM (PL le **nuche**)
nape of the neck

nucleare AGGETTIVO
nuclear ◊ l'energia nucleare nuclear energy

il **nucleo** NOME MASC
♦ **il nucleo familiare** the family unit

N

* **il nucleo antidroga** the anti-drugs squad

nudista NOME MASC/FEM, AGGETTIVO (MASC PL **nudisti,** FEM PL **nudiste)**
nudist

nudo AGGETTIVO (FEM **nuda)**
naked ◊ *un uomo nudo* a naked man ◊ *Era completamente nuda.* She was completely naked.

* **a piedi nudi** barefoot ◊ *Camminava a piedi nudi in giardino.* He was walking barefoot in the garden.
* **a occhio nudo** to the naked eye ◊ *È invisibile a occhio nudo.* It's not visible to the naked eye.

nulla PRONOME, AVVERBIO
nothing ◊ *Cos'hai comprato? – Nulla.* What did you buy? – Nothing. ◊ *Cosa c'è? – Nulla.* What's the matter? – Nothing. ◊ *Non è successo nulla.* Nothing happened.
*Quando la traduzione contiene una negazione, e nelle frasi interrogative, **nulla** si traduce in genere con **anything**.*
◊ *Non ho visto nulla.* I didn't see anything.
◊ *Hai bisogno di nulla?* Do you need anything?

* **non mi sono fatto nulla.** I didn't hurt myself.
* **Grazie. – Di nulla.** Thanks. – You're welcome.
* **non...per nulla** not...at all ◊ *Non mi sono divertito per nulla.* I didn't enjoy it at all.

il numero NOME MASC
① number ◊ *Abito al numero sei.* I live at number six. ◊ *Qual è il tuo numero di telefono?* What's your phone number?
② size ◊ *Che numero di scarpe porti?* What size shoe do you take?

> ⓘ *Italian shoe sizes are different: for example, 38 is the equivalent of a British size 5, and 40 is the equivalent of size 6 1/2.*

③ act (*di spettacolo*) ◊ *Il suo numero è stato molto divertente.* His act was very entertaining.

numeroso AGGETTIVO (FEM **numerosa)**
① numerous ◊ *Ci sono stati numerosi casi di morbillo quest'anno.* There have been numerous cases of measles this year.
② large ◊ *Ha una famiglia numerosa.* He's got a large family.

nuocere* VERBO
* **nuocere a** to be* bad for ◊ *Il fumo nuoce alla salute.* Smoking is bad for your health.

la **nuora** NOME FEM
daughter-in-law (PL daughters-in-law)

nuotare VERBO
to swim* ◊ *Sai nuotare?* Can you swim?
* **nuotare a rana** to do* the breast stroke

* **nuotare sul dorso** to do* the backstroke

il **nuotatore,** la **nuotatrice** NOME MASC, FEM
swimmer ◊ *È un bravo nuotatore.* He's a good swimmer.

il **nuoto** NOME MASC
swimming ◊ *una gara di nuoto* a swimming gala
* **Ho attraversato il lago a nuoto.** I swam across the lake.

nuovamente AVVERBIO
again ◊ *Si è nuovamente ammalato.* He's ill again.

la **Nuova Zelanda** NOME FEM
New Zealand ◊ *Ti è piaciuta la Nuova Zelanda?* Did you like New Zealand?
◊ *Andremo in Nuova Zelanda.* We're going to New Zealand.

nuovo AGGETTIVO (FEM **nuova)**
new ◊ *un vestito nuovo* a new dress
◊ *Sono nuovo di qui.* I'm new here.
* **Il suo volto non mi è nuovo.** I know his face.
* **nuovo di zecca** brand-new ◊ *Ha una macchina nuova di zecca.* He's got a brand-new car.
* **di nuovo** again ◊ *È successo di nuovo.* It happened again. ◊ *Sei di nuovo tu?* Is it you again?
* **Che c'è di nuovo?** What's new?
* **Non c'è niente di nuovo.** There's nothing new.

nutriente AGGETTIVO
nourishing ◊ *una crema nutriente* a nourishing cream

nutrire VERBO
to feed* ◊ *La madre nutriva i piccoli.* The mother was feeding her young.
* **nutrirsi di** to eat* ◊ *I leoni si nutrono esclusivamente di carne.* Lions only eat meat.

la **nuvola** NOME FEM
cloud
* **avere la testa fra le nuvole** to have* one's head in the clouds ◊ *Ha sempre la testa tra le nuvole.* He always has his head in the clouds.
* **cadere dalle nuvole** to be* astonished ◊ *Quando gliel'ho detto è caduto dalle nuvole.* When I told him he was astonished.

nuvoloso AGGETTIVO (FEM **nuvolosa)**
cloudy ◊ *Oggi è più nuvoloso di ieri.* It's cloudier today than it was yesterday.

nuziale AGGETTIVO
wedding ◊ *la cerimonia nuziale* the wedding ceremony

il **nylon** NOME MASC
nylon

O

o CONGIUNZIONE
or ◊ *due o tre volte* two or three times
- **o...o...** either...or... ◊ *o oggi o domani*
either today or tomorrow

obbediente AGGETTIVO
obedient

obbedire* VERBO
to obey ◊ *Ha obbedito alla madre senza fare
storie.* He obeyed his mother without
making a fuss.

obbligare VERBO
- **obbligare qualcuno a fare qualcosa** to
make* somebody do something
*dopo **make** si usa l'infinito senza "to".*
◊ *Mi ha obbligato a fare i compiti.* She made
me do my homework.
- **essere obbligato a fare qualcosa** to have* to
do something ◊ *Non sei obbligato a farlo.*
You don't have to do it.

obbligatorio AGGETTIVO (FEM **obbligatoria**)
compulsory

l' **obbligo** NOME MASC (PL gli **obblighi**)
obligation ◊ *Ho degli obblighi nei confronti
dei miei genitori.* I've got obligations to my
parents.
- **Non ho l'obbligo di timbrare il cartellino al
lavoro.** I don't have to clock in at work.
- **la scuola dell'obbligo** compulsory
education

obiettare VERBO
- **Non ho nulla da obiettare.** I haven't got any
objections.

l' **obiettivo** NOME MASC
vedi anche **obiettivo** AGGETTIVO
1 lens SING (*di macchina fotografica*)
2 aim (*scopo*) ◊ *Il suo obiettivo è quello di
vincere la gara.* His aim is to win the
competition.

obiettivo AGGETTIVO (FEM **obiettiva**)
vedi anche **obiettivo** NOME
objective

l' **obiettore** NOME MASC
- **obiettore di coscienza** conscientious
objector

l' **obiezione** NOME FEM
objection ◊ *Ci sono obiezioni?* Any
objections?

obliquo AGGETTIVO (FEM **obliqua**)
oblique ◊ *una linea obliqua* an oblique line

obliterare VERBO
to stamp ◊ *Il biglietto va obliterato prima di
partire.* The ticket must be stamped before
you start your journey.

l' **obliteratrice** NOME FEM
stamping machine

l' **oblò** NOME MASC (PL gli **oblò**)
porthole

l' **oca** NOME FEM (PL le **oche**)

goose (PL geese)

l' **occasione** NOME FEM
1 opportunity (PL opportunities) ◊ *Lo farò
alla prima occasione.* I'll do it at the first
opportunity.
2 occasion ◊ *in occasione del suo
compleanno* on the occasion of his birthday
3 bargain ◊ *Compralo! È un'occasione.*
Buy it! It's a bargain.
- **comprare qualcosa d'occasione** to get*
something cheap

le **occhiaie** NOME FEM PL
bags under one's eyes ◊ *Ho le occhiaie.* I've
got bags under my eyes.

gli **occhiali** NOME MASC PL
glasses ◊ *Porto gli occhiali.* I wear glasses.
- **occhiali da sole** sunglasses

l' **occhiata** NOME FEM
- **dare un'occhiata a qualcosa** to have* a look
at something ◊ *Vorrei dare un'occhiata a
quel libro.* I'd like to have a look at that book.
- **Potresti dare un'occhiata alle mie valigie?**
Could you keep an eye on my cases?

l' **occhio** NOME MASC
eye ◊ *Ha gli occhi azzurri.* He's got blue
eyes.
- **tenere d'occhio** to keep* an eye on ◊ *Per
favore, tieni d'occhio le mie valigie.* Please
could you keep an eye on my cases?
- **chiudere un occhio** to turn a blind eye ◊ *Per
questa volta chiuderò un occhio.* I'll turn a
blind eye this once.
- **dare nell'occhio** to attract attention
◊ *Vestiti in modo da non dare troppo
nell'occhio.* Dress so as not to attract too
much attention.
- **a occhio e croce** round about ◊ *A occhio e
croce costerà cento euro.* It'll cost round
about one hundred euros.
- **Costa un occhio della testa.** It costs an arm
and a leg.
- **Occhio!** Watch out!

l' **occhiolino** NOME MASC
- **fare l'occhiolino a qualcuno** to wink at
somebody ◊ *Le fece l'occhiolino.* He
winked at her.

occidentale AGGETTIVO
western ◊ *i paesi occidentali* western
countries
- **la costa occidentale della Francia** the west
coast of France

l' **occidente** NOME MASC
west
- **a occidente** in the west ◊ *Il sole tramonta
ad occidente.* The sun sets in the west.

occorrere* VERBO
- **Ti occorre qualcosa?** Do you need anything?
- **Mi occorre del denaro.** I need some money.

---

* I verbi seguiti da questo simbolo sono irregolari. Si veda anche alle pp.328–338.

◆ **Non occorre che mi telefoni.** You don't need to phone me.

◆ **Occorre farlo subito.** It should be done at once.

Attenzione! In inglese esiste il verbo **to occur**, *che però significa* **succedere**.

occupare VERBO

[1] to take* up ◇ *L'armadio occupa tutta la parete.* The cupboard takes up the whole wall. ◇ *Lo sport mi occupa tutto il tempo libero.* Sport takes up all my spare time.

[2] to occupy ◇ *Gli studenti hanno occupato la scuola.* The students have occupied the school. ◇ *La città è stata occupata durante la guerra.* The city was occupied during the war.

◆ **occuparsi di** (*prendersi cura di*) to look after ◇ *Potresti occuparti dei bambini?* Could you look after the children?

◆ **Si occupa di computer.** He's in computers.

◆ **Occupati dei fatti tuoi!** Mind your own business!

occupato AGGETTIVO (FEM **occupata**)

[1] occupied ◇ *La scuola è ancora occupata.* The school is still occupied. ◇ *una città occupata* an occupied city

[2] busy (*indaffarato*) ◇ *In questo momento il signor Rossi è molto occupato.* Mr Rossi is very busy at the moment. ◇ *Domani sarò ancora più occupato.* I'll be even busier tomorrow.

[3] taken (*posto, sedia*) ◇ *È occupato quel posto?* Is that seat taken?

[4] engaged (*toilette, telefono*) ◇ *La toilette è occupata.* The toilet is engaged. ◇ *Non riesco a telefonargli. È sempre occupato.* I can't get through to him. The line's always engaged.

l' **occupazione** NOME FEM

[1] job ◇ *Sto cercando un'occupazione.* I'm looking for a job.

[2] occupation ◇ *Occupazione: Infermiere* Occupation: Nurse

l' **oceano** NOME MASC

ocean

l' **oculista** NOME MASC/FEM (MASC PL gli **oculisti**, FEM PL le **oculiste**)

eye specialist ◇ *Devo andare dall'oculista.* I need to go to the eye specialist.

odiare VERBO

to hate ◇ *Ti odio!* I hate you! ◇ *Odio le persone egoiste.* I hate selfish people.

◆ **odiare fare qualcosa** to hate doing something

to hate è seguito dal gerundio.

◇ *Odio alzarmi presto al mattino.* I hate getting up early in the morning.

◆ **odiarsi** to hate each other ◇ *Marco e Matteo si odiano.* Marco and Matteo hate each other.

l' **odio** NOME MASC

hatred

odioso AGGETTIVO (FEM **odiosa**)

horrible ◇ *Sei odioso.* You're horrible.

l' **odore** NOME MASC

smell ◇ *un buon odore* a nice smell ◇ *un cattivo odore* a bad smell

◆ **Ha un buon odore.** It smells nice.

◆ **Ha un cattivo odore.** It smells awful.

◆ **sentire odore di qualcosa** to smell* something ◇ *Sento odore di pesce.* I can smell fish.

◆ **gli odori** (*in cucina*) herbs

offendere* VERBO

to insult ◇ *Non avevo intenzione di offenderti.* I didn't mean to insult you.

◆ **offendersi** to take* offence ◇ *Se non vieni mi offendo.* I'll be offended if you don't come. ◇ *Si è offeso per non essere stato invitato.* He took offence because they didn't invite him.

l' **offerta** NOME FEM

offer ◇ *Mi ha fatto un'offerta generosa.* He made me a generous offer. ◇ *È in offerta speciale.* It's on special offer. ◇ *Ho accettato la sua offerta di lavoro.* I've accepted his offer of a job.

◆ **"offerte d'impiego"** "situations vacant"

l' **offesa** NOME FEM

insult

offeso AGGETTIVO (FEM **offesa**)

offended ◇ *È terribilmente offesa per quello che hai detto.* She's terribly offended about what you said.

l' **officina** NOME FEM

garage ◇ *Devo portare la macchina in officina.* I have to take the car to the garage.

offrire* VERBO

to offer

◆ **offrire qualcosa a qualcuno** to offer somebody something ◇ *Mi ha offerto un passaggio.* He offered me a lift. ◇ *Le hanno offerto un lavoro.* They've offered her a job. ◇ *Mi ha offerto un caffè.* She offered me a coffee. ◇ *L'ha offerto prima a me.* He offered it to me first.

◆ **Mi offri una sigaretta?** Could I have a cigarette?

◆ **Vieni, ti offro da bere.** Come on, I'll buy you a drink.

◆ **Offro io, questa volta!** I'll pay this time!

◆ **offrirsi volontario** to volunteer ◇ *Nessuno si è offerto volontario.* Nobody volunteered.

◆ **offrirsi di fare qualcosa** to offer to do something ◇ *Si è offerto di aiutarci.* He offered to help us.

l' **oggetto** NOME MASC

object ◇ *un oggetto rotondo* a round object

◆ **oggetti smarriti** lost property SING ◇ *Dov'è l'ufficio oggetti smarriti?* Where's the lost property office?, US: Where's the lost-and-found?

oggi AVVERBIO

today ◇ *Oggi è venerdì.* It's Friday today. ☞

◇ *il giornale di oggi* today's paper *con il genitivo sassone.*

* **oggi stesso** today ◇ *Lo farò oggi stesso.* I'll do it today.
* **dall'oggi al domani** from one day to the next ◇ *Potrebbe cambiare tutto dall'oggi al domani.* Everything could change from one day to the next.
* **oggi a otto** a week today

oggigiorno AVVERBIO
nowadays

ogni AGGETTIVO
every ◇ *Lo vedo ogni giorno.* I see him every day. ◇ *Viene ogni due giorni.* He comes every two days.

* **C'era gente di ogni tipo.** There were all sorts of people.
* **in ogni caso** anyway ◇ *Penso che dovresti telefonargli in ogni caso.* I think you should phone him anyway.
* **ogni tanto** every so often ◇ *Ogni tanto le scrivo.* I write to her every so often.

ognuno, ognuna PRONOME
① each (*ciascuno*) ◇ *Ad ognuno di voi verrà dato un questionario.* Each of you will be given a questionnaire.
② everybody (*tutti*)
*È possibile anche usare **everyone**.*
◇ *Ognuno ha il diritto di dire quello che pensa.* Everybody has the right to say what they think.

l' **Olanda** NOME FEM
Holland ◇ *Mi è piaciuta molto l'Olanda.* I liked Holland very much. ◇ *Andrò in Olanda in giugno.* I'm going to Holland in June.

olandese AGGETTIVO
*vedi anche **olandese** NOME MASC, NOME FEM*
Dutch

l' **olandese** NOME MASC
*vedi anche **olandese** AGGETTIVO, NOME FEM*
① Dutchman (PL Dutchmen) (*persona*)
* **gli olandesi** (*uomini e donne*) the Dutch
② Dutch (*lingua*) ◇ *Parla olandese.* He speaks Dutch.

l' **olandese** NOME FEM
*vedi anche **olandese** AGGETTIVO, NOME MASC*
Dutchwoman (PL Dutchwomen)

l' **oleandro** NOME MASC
oleander

l' **oliera** NOME FEM
oil and vinegar set

le **Olimpiadi** NOME FEM PL
the Olympic Games

olimpico AGGETTIVO (FEM **olimpica**, MASC PL **olimpici**, FEM PL **olimpiche**)
Olympic

l' **olio** NOME MASC
oil ◇ *un quadro a olio* an oil painting ◇ *una lampada ad olio* an oil lamp
* **olio d'oliva** olive oil

* **olio di semi** vegetable oil
* **olio solare** suntan oil
* **olio dei freni** brake fluid
* **sott'olio** in oil ◇ *funghi sott'olio* mushrooms in oil

l' **oliva** NOME FEM
olive

l' **olivo** NOME MASC
olive tree

oltre PREPOSIZIONE, AVVERBIO
over ◇ *L'ho gettato oltre il muro.* I threw it over the wall. ◇ *gli uomini oltre i cinquant'anni* men over fifty ◇ *Non la vedo da oltre tre mesi.* I haven't seen her for over three months.

* **Non posso aspettare oltre.** I can't wait any longer.
* **oltre a** apart from ◇ *Oltre a te non voglio vedere nessuno.* Apart from you, I don't want to see anyone.
* **È anche piccola, oltre ad essere cara.** It's small as well as being expensive.

oltrepassare VERBO
to cross ◇ *Oltrepassarono il confine.* They crossed the border.

* **Questa volta hai oltrepassato ogni limite!** This time you've gone too far!

l' **omaggio** NOME
*vedi anche **omaggio** AGGETTIVO*
gift ◇ *Ecco un piccolo omaggio per le signore.* Here's a little gift for the ladies.

omaggio AGGETTIVO (MASC, FEM, PL **omaggio**)
*vedi anche **omaggio** NOME*
free ◇ *un biglietto omaggio* a free ticket

l' **ombelico** NOME MASC (PL gli **ombelichi**)
navel
Il termine più familiare è "belly button".

l' **ombra** NOME FEM
① shade ◇ *Mi sedetti all'ombra.* I sat down in the shade.
② shadow (*sagoma*) ◇ *l'ombra di un grattacielo* the shadow of a skyscraper
* **senza ombra di dubbio** without a shadow of a doubt

l' **ombrello** NOME MASC
umbrella

l' **ombrellone** NOME MASC
beach umbrella

l' **ombretto** NOME MASC
eyeshadow

l' **omelette** NOME FEM (PL le **omelette**)
omelette ◇ *un'omelette al prosciutto* a ham omelette

l' **omeopata** NOME MASC/FEM (MASC PL gli **omeopati**, FEM PL le **omeopate**)
homeopath

l' **omeopatia** NOME FEM
homeopathy

l' **omicida** NOME MASC/FEM (MASC PL gli **omicidi**, FEM PL le **omicide**)

murderer

omicidio NOME MASC
murder
+ **commettere un omicidio** to commit a murder

omogeneizzati NOME MASC PL
baby food SING

omonimo, omonima NOME MASC/FEM, AGGETTIVO
+ **È un mio omonimo.** He's got the same name as me.
+ **il film tratto dall'omonimo romanzo** the film based on the novel of the same name

omosessuale NOME MASC/FEM, AGGETTIVO
homosexual

onda NOME FEM
wave ◇ *Si è tuffato tra le onde.* He dived into the waves.
+ **andare in onda** to be* on ◇ *Il programma va in onda alle sei.* The programme is on at six o'clock.
+ **mandare in onda** to broadcast

onestà NOME FEM
honesty

onesto AGGETTIVO (FEM **onesta**)
[1] honest ◇ *È una persona onesta.* He's an honest person.
[2] fair *(equo)* ◇ *Mi sembra un prezzo onesto.* It seems a fair price.

onomastico NOME MASC (PL gli **onomastici**)
name day ◇ *Oggi è il mio onomastico.* Today's my name day.

ⓘ *In Italy people celebrate their **name day** – that is, the day of the saint with the same name. For someone called Giorgio, for example, this would be April 23, which is St George's Day.*

onore NOME MASC
honour
honor *US*
◇ *È un onore per me.* It's an honour for me.
+ **fare gli onori di casa** to act as host ◇ *Paolo ha fatto gli onori di casa.* Paolo acted as host.
+ **farsi onore** to do* well ◇ *Si è fatto onore agli esami.* He did well in the exams.

O.N.U. NOME FEM
the UN (= the United Nations)

opaco AGGETTIVO (FEM **opaca**, MASC PL **opachi**, FEM PL **opache**)
[1] opaque *(vetro)*
[2] matt *(carta)*

opera NOME FEM
work ◇ *le opere più importanti di Dante* Dante's most important works
+ **mettersi all'opera** to get* down to work
+ **opera d'arte** work of art
+ **opera lirica** opera

operaio, l' operaia NOME MASC, FEM
vedi anche **operaio** AGGETTIVO

worker

operaio AGGETTIVO (FEM **operaia**)
vedi anche **operaio** NOME
+ **il movimento operaio** the labour movement
+ **un quartiere operaio** a working-class district
+ **la classe operaia** the working class

operare VERBO
to do* an operation ◇ *Hanno dovuto operare d'urgenza.* They had to do an emergency operation.
+ **Matteo è stato operato allo stomaco.** Matteo had an operation on his stomach.
+ **operarsi** to have* an operation ◇ *Dovrò operarmi la prossima settimana.* I'm going to have an operation next week.
+ **Si è operato d'appendicite.** He had his appendix removed.

l' **operazione** NOME FEM
operation

l' **opinione** NOME FEM
opinion ◇ *Vorrei sapere qual è la tua opinione su di lui.* I'd like to know your opinion of him.
+ **l'opinione pubblica** public opinion

opporre* VERBO
+ **opporre resistenza** to put* up a struggle ◇ *Si sono arresi senza opporre resistenza.* They surrendered without putting up a struggle.
+ **opporsi** to object ◇ *Ci siamo opposti alla proposta.* We objected to the proposal.

l' **opportunista** NOME MASC/FEM (MASC PL gli **opportunisti**, FEM PL le **opportuniste**)
opportunist ◇ *È un opportunista.* He's an opportunist.

l' **opportunità** NOME FEM
opportunity (PL opportunities) ◇ *Non ho avuto l'opportunità di parlargli.* I didn't have the opportunity to speak to him.

opportuno AGGETTIVO (FEM **opportuna**)
right ◇ *Non era il momento opportuno per parlarne.* It wasn't the right moment to talk about it.

l' **opposizione** NOME FEM
opposition ◇ *i partiti dell'opposizione* the opposition parties

opposto AGGETTIVO, NOME MASC (FEM **opposta**)
opposite ◇ *Veniva dalla direzione opposta.* She was coming from the opposite direction. ◇ *l'opposto* the opposite
+ **Hanno opinioni opposte.** They have very different ideas.

oppure CONGIUNZIONE
or ◇ *Possiamo guardare la TV oppure noleggiare un video.* We can watch TV or rent a video.

l' **opuscolo** NOME MASC
booklet *(in generale)*
+ **opuscolo pubblicitario** brochure

l' **ora** NOME FEM

O

vedi anche **ora** AVVERBIO

1 hour ◊ *Aspetto da un'ora.* I've been waiting for an hour. ◊ *tre ore e mezza* three and a half hours

♦ **mezz'ora** half an hour

♦ **all'ora** an hour ◊ *Lo pagano trenta euro all'ora.* They pay him thirty euros an hour. ◊ *70 km all'ora* 70 km an hour

♦ **ora di punta** rush hour ◊ *il traffico dell'ora di punta* the rush hour traffic

♦ **di buon'ora** early

♦ **Non vedo l'ora di dirglielo.** I can't wait to tell him.

2 time ◊ *Che ora è?* What time is it? ◊ *A che ora parti?* What time are you leaving? ◊ *È ora di partire.* It's time we went. ◊ *domani a quest'ora* this time tomorrow

♦ **ora di pranzo** lunchtime

♦ **ora legale** summer time

♦ **ora locale** local time

ora AVVERBIO

vedi anche **ora** NOME

now ◊ *Ora sto meglio.* I'm better now.

♦ **Ora sono molto occupata.** I'm very busy at the moment.

*A volte **ora** si traduce usando **just.***

◊ *È uscito proprio ora.* He's just gone out.

◊ *Ora arrivo.* I'm just coming.

♦ **d'ora in avanti** from now on

♦ **per ora** for now

orale AGGETTIVO

oral ◊ *un esame orale* an oral exam

orario AGGETTIVO (FEM **oraria**)

vedi anche **orario** NOME

time ◊ *il segnale orario* the time signal

♦ **in senso orario** clockwise

♦ **la tariffa oraria** the hourly rate

l' **orario** NOME MASC

vedi anche **orario** AGGETTIVO

1 timetable ◊ *l'orario ferroviario* the railway timetable

2 hours PL ◊ *l'orario di lavoro* working hours ◊ *orario di ufficio* business hours

3 time ◊ *Qual è l'orario delle visite?* When's visiting time?

♦ **l'orario di apertura** opening time

♦ **l'orario di chiusura** closing time

l' **orbita** NOME FEM

orbit ◊ *Il razzo fu lanciato in orbita.* The rocket was launched into orbit.

le **Orcadi** NOME FEM PL

the Orkneys

l' **orchestra** NOME FEM

orchestra

l' **orchidea** NOME FEM

orchid

l' **ordigno** NOME MASC

♦ **un ordigno esplosivo** an explosive device

ordinale AGGETTIVO

ordinal

ordinare VERBO

to order ◊ *Hai già ordinato?* Have you already ordered?

♦ **ordinare a qualcuno di fare qualcosa** to order somebody to do something ◊ *Gli hanno ordinato di andarsene subito.* They ordered him to leave immediately.

♦ **Il medico mi ha ordinato di riposare.** The doctor told me to rest.

ordinato AGGETTIVO (FEM **ordinata**)

tidy (*camera, persona*) ◊ *È la persona la più ordinata cha abbia mai conosciuto.* He's the tidiest person I've ever met.

l' **ordine** NOME MASC

order ◊ *in ordine alfabetico* in alphabetical order ◊ *in ordine d'importanza* in order of importance ◊ *per ordine del preside* by order of the headmaster

♦ **Ho l'ordine di non farvi entrare.** I've been told not to let you in.

♦ **mettere in ordine** to tidy up ◊ *Stavano mettendo in ordine la loro camera.* They were tidying up their room.

♦ **in ordine** (*a posto*) tidy ◊ *La casa è in ordine.* The house is tidy.

♦ **le forze dell'ordine** the police

l' **orecchino** NOME MASC

earring ◊ *un paio di orecchini d'oro* a pair of gold earrings

l' **orecchio** NOME MASC (PLUR FEM le **orecchie**)

ear

♦ **farsi fare i buchi nelle orecchie** to have* one's ears pierced ◊ *Mi sono fatta fare i buchi nelle orecchie.* I've had my ears pierced.

♦ **Ha orecchio.** He's got a good ear.

♦ **Mi fa male un orecchio.** I've got earache.

gli **orecchioni** NOME MASC PL

mumps SING

l' **orefice** NOME MASC/FEM

jeweller

jeweler US

l' **oreficeria** NOME FEM

jeweller's

jeweler's US

l' **orfano**, l' **orfana** NOME MASC, FEM

vedi anche **orfano** AGGETTIVO

orphan

orfano AGGETTIVO (FEM **orfana**)

vedi anche **orfano** NOME

♦ **rimanere orfano** to be* orphaned ◊ *È rimasto orfano a dieci anni.* He was orphaned at the age of ten.

♦ **È orfano di madre.** His mother is dead.

organizzare VERBO

to organize ◊ *Hanno organizzato un concerto.* They organized a concert.

♦ **Abbiamo organizzato una gita in campagna.** We've arranged a trip to the country.

* I verbi seguiti da questo simbolo sono irregolari. Si veda anche alle pp.328–338.

organizzazione NOME FEM
organization ◇ *un'organizzazione studentesca* a student organization
◆ **Ci occuperemo dell'organizzazione della festa.** We'll organize the party.

organo NOME MASC
organ ◇ *trapianto d'organi* organ transplants ◇ *Suona l'organo.* She plays the organ.

orgoglio NOME MASC
pride

orgoglioso AGGETTIVO (FEM **orgogliosa**)
proud

orientale AGGETTIVO
① eastern ◇ *l'Europa orientale* eastern Europe
◆ **la costa orientale della Gran Bretagna** the east coast of Britain
② oriental ◇ *un tappeto orientale* an oriental carpet

orientamento NOME MASC
◆ **perdere l'orientamento** to lose* one's bearings ◇ *Ho perso l'orientamento.* I've lost my bearings.
◆ **senso di orientamento** sense of direction

orientarsi VERBO
to know* one's way ◇ *Si orientava bene in città.* He knew his way around the city.

oriente NOME MASC
east ◇ *a oriente* in the east
◆ **il Medio Oriente** the Middle East
◆ **l'Estremo Oriente** the Far East

origano NOME MASC
oregano

originale AGGETTIVO, NOME MASC
original ◇ *un'idea originale* an original idea ◇ *Vuoi una copia o l'originale?* Do you want a copy, or the original?
◆ **È un tipo originale.** He's a bit eccentric.

origine NOME FEM
origin

origliare VERBO
to eavesdrop

orizzontale AGGETTIVO
horizontal

orizzonte NOME MASC
horizon
◆ **all'orizzonte** on the horizon
◇ *Improvvisamente compare un'isola all'orizzonte.* Suddenly an island appeared on the horizon.

orlo NOME MASC
① edge ◇ *La macchina era sull'orlo del precipizio.* The car was on the edge of the precipice.
② brink ◇ *È sull'orlo della rovina.* He's on the brink of ruin.
③ brim ◇ *Ha riempito il bicchiere fino all'orlo.* She filled the glass to the brim.
④ hem ◇ *L'orlo della tovaglia si è scucito.* The hem of the tablecloth has come

unstitched.

orma NOME FEM
① track (*di animale*) ◇ *Segui le orme della volpe.* Follow the fox's tracks.
② footprint (*di persona*) ◇ *La polizia ha trovato delle orme in giardino.* The police found footprints in the garden.
◆ **seguire le orme di qualcuno** to follow in somebody's footsteps ◇ *Ha seguito le orme del padre.* He followed in his father's footsteps.

ormai AVVERBIO
by now ◇ *Ormai dovrebbe essere partito.* He must have left by now.
Qualche volta ormai non viene tradotto.
◇ *Non fermarti! Ormai siamo quasi arrivati.* Don't stop! We're nearly there.

l' **ormone** NOME MASC
hormone

l' **oro** NOME MASC
gold
◆ **d'oro** gold ◇ *un orologio d'oro* a gold watch ◇ *Ha vinto la medaglia d'oro.* He won the gold medal.
◆ **un'occasione d'oro** a golden opportunity
◆ **Ha un cuore d'oro.** He has a heart of gold.
◆ **È un affare d'oro.** It's a real bargain.

l' **orologio** NOME MASC
① clock (*da muro*)
② watch (*da polso*)
◆ **un orologio da polso** a wristwatch

l' **oroscopo** NOME MASC
horoscope

orrendo AGGETTIVO (FEM **orrenda**)
awful

orribile AGGETTIVO
horrible

l' **orrore** NOME MASC
horror ◇ *un film dell'orrore* a horror film
◆ **I ragni mi fanno orrore.** I hate spiders.

l' **orsacchiotto** NOME MASC
teddy bear

l' **orso** NOME MASC
bear
◆ **un orso bianco** a polar bear
◆ **un orso bruno** a brown bear

l' **ortica** NOME FEM (PL le **ortiche**)
nettle ◇ *Mi sono punto con le ortiche.* I stung myself on the nettles.

l' **orticaria** NOME FEM
nettle rash

l' **orto** NOME MASC
vegetable garden

l' **ortografia** NOME FEM
spelling ◇ *un errore di ortografia* a spelling mistake

l' **ortopedico** NOME MASC (PL gli **ortopedici**)
orthopaedic specialist
orthopedist US

l' **orzaiolo** NOME MASC
stye

O

l' **orzo** NOME MASC
barley

osare VERBO
to dare

♦ **osare fare qualcosa** to dare to do something
◇ *Ha osato sfidarlo.* She dared to defy him.
◇ *Non osavo dirlo.* I didn't dare to say it.

to dare a volte si comporta come un verbo modale ed è seguito dall'infinito del verbo senza "to".
◇ *Oserei dire che...* I dare say...

♦ **Come osi?** How dare you?

osceno AGGETTIVO (FEM **oscena**)
obscene

oscillare VERBO
1 to swing* to and fro (*lampadario, pendolo*)
2 to fluctuate (*temperatura*)

l' **oscurità** NOME FEM
darkness ◇ *La stanza piombò nell'oscurità.* The room was plunged into darkness.

oscuro AGGETTIVO (FEM **oscura**)
vedi anche **oscuro** NOME
unclear ◇ *Ci sono alcuni punti oscuri nel suo racconto.* There are some unclear points in his account.

♦ **È morto in circostanze oscure.** He died in mysterious circumstances.

l' **oscuro** NOME MASC
vedi anche **oscuro** AGGETTIVO

♦ **all'oscuro** in the dark ◇ *Mi hanno sempre tenuto all'oscuro della faccenda.* They've always kept me in the dark about this.

l' **ospedale** NOME MASC
hospital

♦ **essere ricoverato in ospedale** to be* admitted to hospital

♦ **essere all'ospedale** (*paziente*) to be* in hospital ◇ *Luigi è all'ospedale da una settimana.* Luigi's been in hospital for a week.

ospitale AGGETTIVO
hospitable

ospitare VERBO
to put* up ◇ *Mi hanno ospitato per una settimana.* They put me up for a week.

l' **ospite** NOME MASC/FEM
1 guest (*chi viene ospitato*) ◇ *Ero l'unico ospite dell'albergo* I was the only guest at the hotel.

♦ **la stanza degli ospiti** the guest room
al singolare.
2 host
hostess
(*chi ospita*)

l' **ospizio** NOME MASC
old people's home

osservare VERBO
1 to watch ◇ *Osservava attentamente quello che stavo facendo.* He was carefully watching what I was doing.
2 to notice ◇ *Hai osservato che zoppica un po'?* Have you noticed that she limps a bit?

♦ **far osservare qualcosa a qualcuno** to point something out to somebody ◇ *Vorrei farvi osservare alcune cose.* I'd like to point out a few things to you.

l' **osservazione** NOME FEM
1 observation ◇ *L'hanno tenuto sotto osservazione per due giorni.* He was kept under observation for two days.
2 remark ◇ *Questa è un'osservazione molto acuta.* That's a very intelligent remark.

♦ **Nessuno ha delle osservazioni da fare?** Has anyone got any comments?

♦ **Il professore mi ha fatto un'osservazione ingiusta.** The teacher criticized me unfairly.

l' **ossigeno** NOME MASC
oxygen

l' **osso** NOME MASC (PL FEM le **ossa**)
bone (*umano*) ◇ *le ossa della gamba* the bones of the leg

♦ **essere bagnato fino all'osso** to be* soaked to the skin

♦ **rompersi l'osso del collo** to break* one's neck

♦ **essere un osso duro** to be* a tough nut

ostacolare VERBO
to hinder ◇ *Le gonne strette ostacolano i movimenti.* Tight skirts hinder one's movements.

♦ **Maurizio ha cercato di ostacolare il mio piano.** Maurizio tried to spoil my plan.

♦ **Hanno cercato di ostacolarmi.** They tried to make things difficult for me.

♦ **ostacolare la giustizia** to obstruct justice

l' **ostacolo** NOME MASC
1 difficulty (PL difficulties) ◇ *Ha superato molti ostacoli.* She has overcome many difficulties.
2 hurdle (*in atletica*) ◇ *i quattrocento metri a ostacoli* the four hundred meter hurdles
3 jump (*in equitazione*)

l' **ostaggio** NOME MASC
hostage

♦ **prendere qualcuno in ostaggio** to take* somebody hostage ◇ *I dirottatori hanno preso in ostaggio due donne.* The hijackers have taken two women hostage.

l' **ostello** NOME MASC
♦ **ostello della gioventù** youth hostel

l' **osteria** NOME FEM
inn

l' **ostetrica** NOME FEM (PL le **ostetriche**)
midwife (PL midwives) ◇ *Mia madre fa l'ostetrica.* My mother is a midwife.

ostile AGGETTIVO
hostile

ostinarsi VERBO
♦ **ostinarsi a fare qualcosa** to keep* on doing

something ◇ *È inutile che ti ostini a negarlo.* It's no use keeping on denying it.

ostinato AGGETTIVO (FEM **ostinata**)
stubborn

ostrica NOME FEM (PL le **ostriche**)
oyster
Attenzione! In inglese esiste la parola ostrich, che però significa struzzo.

ostruire VERBO
to block ◇ *C'è qualcosa che ostruisce il tubo.* There's something blocking the pipe.

otite NOME FEM
ear infection ◇ *Ho l'otite.* I've got an ear infection.

otorino NOME MASC
ear, nose and throat specialist

ottanta NUMERO
eighty

ottantesimo AGGETTIVO (FEM **ottantesima**)
eightieth

ottavo AGGETTIVO (FEM **ottava**)
vedi anche **ottavo** NOME
eighth ◇ *Abita all'ottavo piano.* He lives on the eighth floor.

ottavo NOME
vedi anche **ottavo**
eighth (*frazione*)
♦ **superare gli ottavi di finale** to reach the quarter-finals

ottenere* VERBO
to get* ◇ *Ha ottenuto il permesso di uscire.* She got permisssion to go out. ◇ *Abbiamo ottenuto un buon risultato.* We got a good result.

ottico AGGETTIVO (FEM **ottica**, MASC PL **ottici**, FEM PL **ottiche**)
vedi anche **ottico** NOME
♦ **un'illusione ottica** an optical illusion

ottico NOME MASC (PL gli **ottici**)
vedi anche **ottico** AGGETTIVO
optician

ottimismo NOME MASC
optimism

ottimista NOME MASC/FEM (MASC PL gli **ottimisti**, FEM PL le **ottimiste**)
vedi anche **ottimista** AGGETTIVO
optimist

ottimista AGGETTIVO (MASC PL **ottimisti**, FEM PL **ottimiste**)
vedi anche **ottimista** NOME
optimistic

ottimo AGGETTIVO (FEM **ottima**)
excellent ◇ *risultati ottimi* excellent results
♦ **La cena è stata ottima.** The dinner was delicious.

otto NUMERO

eight ◇ *Ha otto anni.* He is eight. ◇ *le otto di sera* eight o'clock in the evening
♦ **l'otto dicembre** the eighth of December

ottobre NOME MASC
October
Si noti l'uso della maiuscola in inglese.
◇ *in ottobre* in October

ottocento NUMERO
eight hundred
♦ **l'Ottocento** the nineteenth century

l' **ottone** NOME MASC
brass ◇ *un campanello di ottone* a brass bell

otturare VERBO
1 to seal ◇ *Bisogna otturare la falla.* We need to seal the leak.
2 to block ◇ *Ci dev'essere qualcosa che ottura il lavandino.* There must be something blocking the sink.
3 to fill (*dente*) ◇ *Il dentista mi ha otturato due denti.* The dentist has filled two of my teeth.

l' **otturatore** NOME MASC
shutter (*di macchina fotografica*)

l' **otturazione** NOME FEM
filling (*di dente*)

ovale AGGETTIVO
oval

l' **ovatta** NOME FEM
cotton wool
cotton US

l' **ovest** NOME MASC
west ◇ *Il vento viene da ovest.* The wind comes from the west.
♦ **ad ovest** west ◇ *Si è diretto ad ovest.* He headed west.
♦ **Il sole tramonta ad ovest.** The sun sets in the west.
♦ **L'Italia confina ad ovest con la Francia.** Italy has a border to the west with France.
♦ **ad ovest di** west of ◇ *Si trova ad ovest della città.* It's west of the city.

ovunque AVVERBIO
1 wherever ◇ *Ti troverò ovunque tu vada.* I'll find you wherever you go.
2 everywhere ◇ *L'ho cercato ovunque.* I've looked for it everywhere.

ovvio AGGETTIVO (FEM **ovvia**)
obvious

l' **ozio** NOME MASC
♦ **Se ne sta tutto il giorno in ozio.** He sits around doing nothing all day.

l' **ozono** NOME MASC
ozone ◇ *il buco nello strato ozono* the hole in the ozone layer

O

P

il **pacchetto** NOME MASC

    1 packet ◇ *un pacchetto di sigarette* a packet of cigarettes

    2 parcel ◇ *Le ho spedito un pacchetto.* I sent her a parcel.

    ♦ **un pacchetto software** a software package

    ♦ **un pacchetto turistico** a package holiday

il **pacco** NOME MASC (PL i **pacchi**)

    parcel ◇ *un grosso pacco marrone* a large brown parcel ◇ *C'era un grosso pacco per lui sotto l'albero.* There was a big parcel for him under the tree.

    ♦ **un pacco di zucchero** a packet of sugar

la **pace** NOME FEM

    peace ◇ *un trattato di pace* a peace treaty

    ♦ **fare la pace con qualcuno** to make* it up with somebody ◇ *Ho fatto la pace con Luciana.* I've made it up with Luciana.

    ♦ **Lasciami in pace!** Leave me alone!

pacifico AGGETTIVO (FEM **pacifica**, MASC PL **pacifici**, FEM PL **pacifiche**)

    peaceful (*manifestazione, protesta*)

    ♦ **l'Oceano Pacifico** the Pacific Ocean

pacifista AGGETTIVO, NOME MASC/FEM (MASC PL **pacifisti**, FEM PL **pacifiste**)

    pacifist ◇ *È pacifista.* He's a pacifist.

la **padella** NOME FEM

    frying pan

il **padre** NOME MASC

    father ◇ *mio padre* my father ◇ *il padre di Roberto* Roberto's father

il **padrone**, la **padrona** NOME MASC, FEM

    owner (*proprietario*) ◇ *Chi è il padrone di questo cane?* Who's the owner of this dog?

    ♦ **padrone di casa** landlord

    ♦ **padrona di casa** landlady (PL landladies)

il **paesaggio** NOME MASC

    landscape

il **paese** NOME MASC

    1 country (PL countries) ◇ *i paesi in via di sviluppo* developing countries

    2 village ◇ *Vivo in un paese.* I live in a village.

    ♦ **i Paesi Bassi** the Netherlands

la **paga** NOME FEM (PL le **paghe**)

    pay ◇ *La paga non è molto alta.* The pay's not very good.

    Per i lavori manuali si usa la parola plurale **wages**. *Le* **wages** *vengono corrisposte alla fine di ogni settimana in contanti.*

    ◇ *Dava tutta la paga alla moglie.* He gave all his wages to his wife.

il **pagamento** NOME MASC

    payment

    ♦ **fare un pagamento** to make* a payment

pagare VERBO

    to pay* ◇ *Hai pagato il conto?* Have you paid the bill? ◇ *Posso pagare con la carta di credito?* Can I pay by credit card? ◇ *Te la farò pagare!* You'll pay for this!

    Quando si acquista qualcosa **pagare** *si traduce con* **pay for**.

    ◇ *Quanto l'hai pagato?* How much did you pay for it? ◇ *L'ho pagato venti euro.* I paid twenty euros for it.

    ♦ **Pago io.** (*al bar*) I'll get it.

la **pagella** NOME FEM

    school report

la **pagina** NOME FEM

    page ◇ *Fate l'esercizio due a pagina dieci.* Do exercise two on page ten. ◇ *Andate a pagina cinque.* Turn to page five. ◇ *Ha scritto un tema di tre pagine.* He wrote a three-page essay.

la **paglia** NOME FEM

    straw ◇ *un cappello di paglia* a straw hat

il **pagliaccio** NOME MASC

    clown

il **paio** NOME MASC (PL FEM le **paia**)

    pair ◇ *un paio di occhiali* a pair of glasses ◇ *un paio di guanti* a pair of gloves

    ♦ **un paio di** (*alcuni*) a couple of ◇ *un paio di giorni* a couple of days

il **palato** NOME MASC

    palate

il **palazzo** NOME MASC

    1 building (*edificio*)

    2 palace (*reggia*)

    ♦ **palazzo dello sport** sports centre

il **palco** NOME MASC (PL i **palchi**)

    box (*a teatro*)

il **palcoscenico** NOME MASC (PL i **palcoscenici**)

    stage

la **palestra** NOME FEM

    gym ◇ *Vado in palestra due volte alla settimana.* I go to the gym twice a week.

    ♦ **fare palestra** to work out ◇ *Fa palestra un'ora al giorno.* He works out for an hour every day.

la **paletta** NOME FEM

    1 spade (*giocattolo*)

    2 dustpan (*per spazzatura*)

il **palio** NOME MASC

    ♦ **mettere qualcosa in palio** to offer something as a prize

la **palla** NOME FEM

    ball ◇ *una palla da tennis* a tennis ball

    ♦ **giocare a palla** to play ball

    ♦ **una palla di neve** a snowball

la **pallacanestro** NOME FEM

    basketball

la **pallamano** NOME FEM

    handball

la **pallanuoto** NOME FEM

    water polo

la **pallavolo** NOME FEM

volleyball

pallido AGGETTIVO (FEM **pallida**)
pale ◊ *Sei pallida.* You're pale.
* **Non ne ho la più pallida idea.** I haven't the faintest idea.

i **pallini** NOME MASC PL
spots ◊ *rosso a pallini bianchi* red with white spots

il **palloncino** NOME MASC
balloon

il **pallone** NOME MASC
ball
* **giocare a pallone** to play football

la **pallottola** NOME FEM
bullet

la **palma** NOME FEM
palm (*albero*)

il **palmo** NOME MASC
palm (*della mano*)
* **restare con un palmo di naso** to be* very disappointed

il **palo** NOME MASC
1 pole ◊ *un palo della luce* a telegraph pole
2 goalpost (*nel calcio*)
* **fare il palo** (*in rapina*) to act as look-out

la **palpebra** NOME FEM
eyelid

la **palude** NOME FEM
marsh

la **pancetta** NOME FEM
bacon

la **panchina** NOME FEM
bench

la **pancia** NOME FEM (PL le **pance**)
belly (PL bellies) ◊ *Mio padre ha un po' di pancia.* My dad's got a bit of a belly.
* **avere mal di pancia** to have* stomach ache

il **panciotto** NOME MASC
waistcoat
vest US

il **pane** NOME MASC
bread ◊ *una fetta di pane* a slice of bread
* **pane a cassetta** sliced bread
* **pane di segale** rye bread
* **pane integrale** wholemeal bread
* **pane tostato** toast ◊ *una fetta di pane tostato* a slice of toast

la **panetteria** NOME FEM
bakery (PL bakeries) ◊ *la panetteria all'angolo* the bakery on the corner
* **Vado in panetteria.** I'm going to the baker's.

il **panettiere** NOME MASC
baker ◊ *Fa il panettiere.* He is a baker.

il **pangrattato** NOME MASC
breadcrumbs PL

il **panico** NOME MASC
panic
* **essere in preda al panico** to panic
* **farsi prendere dal panico** to panic ◊ *Si è fatta prendere dal panico.* She panicked.

il **panificio** NOME MASC = **panetteria**

il **panino** NOME MASC
roll ◊ *un panino al prosciutto* a ham roll

la **panna** NOME FEM
cream
* **panna da cucina** single cream
* **panna montata** whipped cream

la **panne** NOME FEM
* **rimanere in panne** to break* down ◊ *Siamo rimasti in panne sull'autostrada.* We broke down on the motorway.

il **pannello** NOME MASC
panel
* **pannello di controllo** control panel
* **pannello solare** solar panel

il **panno** NOME MASC
cloth ◊ *un panno umido* a damp cloth
* **Mettiti nei miei panni.** Put yourself in my shoes.

il **pannolino** NOME MASC
nappy (PL nappies)
diaper US
(*per bambini*)

il **panorama** NOME MASC (PL i **panorami**)
view ◊ *Che bel panorama!* What a lovely view!

i **pantaloni** NOME MASC PL
trousers
pants US
◊ *un paio di pantaloni nuovi* a pair of new trousers

le **pantofole** NOME FEM PL
slippers ◊ *Era in pantofole.* He was in his slippers.

il **Papa** NOME MASC
Pope ◊ *Papa Wojtyla* Pope John Paul II
II si legge "the second".

il **papà** NOME MASC (PL i **papà**)
dad ◊ *il mio papà* my dad ◊ *il papà di Claudio* Claudio's father

il **papavero** NOME MASC
poppy (PL poppies)

la **pappa** NOME FEM
baby food

il **pappagallo** NOME MASC
parrot

parabolico AGGETTIVO (FEM **parabolica**)
* **antenna parabolica** satellite dish

il **parabrezza** NOME MASC (PL i **parabrezza**)
windscreen
windshield US

il **paracadute** NOME MASC (PL i **paracadute**)
parachute

il **paradiso** NOME MASC
heaven

i **paraggi** NOME MASC PL
* **nei paraggi di** near ◊ *nei paraggi della stazione* near the station
* **Dev'essere qui nei paraggi.** It's around here somewhere.

paragonare VERBO

P

☞

to compare ◊ *Paragonate le due frasi.*
Compare the two sentences.
* **paragonare a** to compare with ◊ *Lo*
paragona sempre al fratello. She's always
comparing him with his brother.
il **paragone** NOME MASC
* **fare un paragone tra** to compare ◊ *Se*
facciamo un paragone tra le due macchine...
If we compare the two cars...
il **paragrafo** NOME MASC
paragraph
paralizzato AGGETTIVO (FEM **paralizzata**)
paralyzed
le **parallele** NOME FEM PL
parallel bars (*attrezzo*)
parallelo AGGETTIVO, NOME MASC (FEM
parallela)
parallel
paranoico AGGETTIVO (FEM **paranoica**, MASC PL
paranoici, FEM PL **paranoiche**)
paranoid
il **parapetto** NOME MASC
parapet
parare VERBO
to save (*nel calcio*) ◊ *Ha parato il rigore.* He
saved the penalty.
la **parata** NOME FEM
save (*nel calcio*)
* **una parata militare** a military parade
il **paraurti** NOME MASC (PL i **paraurti**)
bumper
parcheggiare VERBO
to park
il **parcheggio** NOME MASC
1 car park
parking lot US
◊ *Hanno costruito un nuovo parcheggio.* A
new car park has been built.
2 parking space ◊ *Non riesco a trovare*
parcheggio. I can't find a parking space.
* **Qui c'è divieto di parcheggio.** You can't park
here.
il **parchimetro** NOME MASC
parking meter
il **parco** NOME MASC (PL i **parchi**)
park
* **parco dei divertimenti** amusement park
* **parco giochi** playground
parecchio PRONOME (FEM **parecchia**)
vedi anche **parecchio** AGGETTIVO
quite a lot ◊ *Mi è costato parecchio.* It cost
me quite a lot. ◊ *Ce n'è parecchio.* There's
quite a lot.
* **parecchi di noi** quite a few of us
parecchio AGGETTIVO (FEM **parecchia**)
vedi anche **parecchio** PRO NOME, AVVERBIO
quite a lot of ◊ *C'era parecchia gente alla*
festa. There were quite a lot of people at the
party. ◊ *C'erano parecchie ragazze.* There
were quite a lot of girls.

* **Non lo vedo da parecchio tempo.** I haven't
seen him for ages.
* **parecchio tempo fa** a long time ago
pareggiare VERBO
to draw* (*nello sport*) ◊ *Hanno pareggiato*
due a due. They drew two all.
il **pareggio** NOME MASC
draw (*nello sport*)
il/la **parente** NOME MASC/FEM
relative ◊ *È un mio parente.* He's a relative
of mine.
Attenzione! In inglese esiste la parola **parent,**
che però significa **genitore.**
la **parentesi** NOME FEM (PL le **parentesi**)
bracket ◊ *parentesi tonde* round brackets
* **tra parentesi** in brackets
il **parere** NOME MASC
vedi anche **parere** VERBO
opinion ◊ *Vuoi il mio parere?* Do you want
my opinion?
* **a mio parere** in my opinion
parere* VERBO
vedi anche **parere** NOME
* **Mi pare che...** I think that... ◊ *Mi pare che sia*
già arrivato. I think he's already here.
* **Fa' come ti pare!** Do as you like!
* **Mi pare di sì.** I think so.
* **Mi pare di no.** I don't think so.
* **Che te ne pare?** What do you think?
* **pare che** apparently ◊ *Pare che voglia*
cambiare squadra. Apparently he wants to
change teams. ◊ *Pare che sia stato lui.*
Apparently it was him.
* **Ma ti pare!** Not at all. ◊ *Disturbo? – Ma ti*
pare! Am I disturbing you? – Not at all.
la **parete** NOME FEM
wall
pari AGGETTIVO (MASC, FEM, PL **pari**)
1 even ◊ *numeri pari* even numbers
2 equal ◊ *Hanno pari diritti e doveri.* They
have equal rights and duties.
* **La partita è finita pari.** The match was a
draw.
* **Siamo pari.** (*in gioco*) It's a draw.
* **Hanno vinto a pari merito.** They were joint
winners.
* **rimettersi in pari** to catch* up ◊ *Cercherò di*
rimettermi in pari. I'll try to catch up.
* **una ragazza alla pari** an au pair girl
Parigi NOME FEM
Paris ◊ *Vado a Parigi quest'estate.* I'm
going to Paris this summer. ◊ *Vive a Parigi.*
He lives in Paris.
parlamentare AGGETTIVO
vedi anche **parlamentare** NOME
parliamentary
il/la **parlamentare** NOME MASC/FEM
vedi anche **parlamentare** AGGETTIVO
Member of Parliament
il **parlamento** NOME MASC

* I verbi seguiti da questo simbolo sono irregolari. Si veda anche alle pp.328–338.

parliament ◇ *il parlamento europeo* the European Parliament

la **parlantina** NOME FEM
+ **avere la parlantina** to have* the gift of the gab

parlare VERBO
*Si usa **to speak** o **to talk**? Leggi gli esempi e scegli la traduzione giusta a seconda del contesto. Ricorda che **to talk** si riferisce in genere ad una conversazione, ad una discussione o all'attività del parlare.*
[1] to speak* ◇ *Sai parlare l'inglese?* Can you speak English? ◇ *Parla più forte.* Speak louder. ◇ *Pronto, chi parla?* Hello, who's speaking? ◇ *Posso parlare con Marina?* Can I speak to Marina? ◇ *Voglio parlare con il direttore!* I want to speak to the manager!
+ **Ne ho sentito parlare.** I've heard about it.
+ **Non parliamone più.** Let's just forget about it.
[2] to talk ◇ *Abbiamo parlato per ore.* We talked for hours. ◇ *Non parlate tutti insieme.* Don't all talk at once. ◇ *Non sa ancora parlare.* He can't talk yet.
+ **parlare di qualcosa** to talk about something ◇ *Di che cosa avete parlato?* What did you talk about? ◇ *Parliamone.* Let's talk about it.
+ **parlare a qualcuno** to talk to somebody ◇ *Lascia che gli parli io.* Let me talk to him. ◇ *Gli parlerò di te.* I'll talk to him about you.
+ **parlare del più e del meno** to talk about this and that
+ **parlare male di qualcuno** to say* nasty things about somebody
+ **parlare bene di qualcuno** to say* nice things about somebody
[3] to be* about (*libro, film*) ◇ *Di cosa parla quel libro?* What is that book about?
+ **Ne parlano tutti i giornali.** It's in all the newspapers.

il **parmigiano** NOME MASC
Parmesan cheese
Si noti l'uso della maiuscola in inglese.

la **parola** NOME FEM
word ◇ *una parola difficile* a difficult word
+ **rivolgere la parola a qualcuno** to speak* to somebody
+ **dare la propria parola a qualcuno** to give* somebody one's word ◇ *Gli ho dato la mia parola.* I gave him my word.
+ **mantenere la parola** to keep* one's word ◇ *Ho mantenuto la parola.* I've kept my word.
+ **rimangiarsi la parola** to break* one's promise ◇ *Si è rimangiato la parola.* He broke his promise.
+ **parola d'ordine** password
+ **parole incrociate** crossword SING ◇ *Sta facendo le parole incrociate.* She's doing the crossword.

la **parolaccia** NOME FEM (PL le **parolacce**)
swearword
+ **dire le parolacce** to swear*

la **parrucca** NOME FEM (PL le **parruche**)
wig

il **parrucchiere**, la **parrucchiera** NOME MASC, FEM
hairdresser ◇ *Fa la parrucchiera.* She is a hairdresser.

la **parte** NOME FEM
[1] part ◇ *la prima parte del libro* the first part of the book
[2] side (*lato*) ◇ *È dall'altra parte della strada.* It's on the other side of the road.
[3] share (*quota*) ◇ *Ognuno ebbe la sua parte.* Everyone had their share.
+ **la maggior parte di** most of ◇ *la maggior parte dei ragazzi* most of the boys
+ **fare parte di** to belong to ◇ *Fa parte di un club sportivo.* He belongs to a sports club.
+ **prendere parte a** to take* part in ◇ *Non ha preso parte alla discussione.* He didn't take part in the discussion.
+ **mettere da parte** (*denaro*) to save up ◇ *Ha messo da parte un bel po' di denaro.* He's saved up quite a lot of money.
+ **a parte questo** apart from that
+ **d'altra parte** on the other hand
+ **da parte di** (*per conto di*) from ◇ *Questo è da parte di Giorgio.* This is from Giorgio.
+ **da qualche parte** somewhere
+ **da nessuna parte** not...anywhere ◇ *Non riesco a trovarlo da nessuna parte.* I can't find it anywhere.
+ **da questa parte** this way
+ **prendere le parti di qualcuno** to side with somebody ◇ *Hanno preso le sue parti.* They sided with him.
+ **scherzi a parte** but, seriously

partecipare VERBO
+ **partecipare a** (*gara, manifestazione*) to take* part in ◇ *Parteciperai alla gara?* Are you going to take part in the competition?
+ **Posso partecipare alle spese?** Can I help pay?

la **partenza** NOME FEM
[1] departure ◇ *il tabellone delle partenze* the departure board
+ **Dobbiamo decidere prima della mia partenza.** We must decide before I leave.
+ **essere in partenza** to be* about to leave ◇ *Fa' presto, il treno è in partenza.* Hurry up, the train is about to leave.
+ **I passeggeri in partenza per...** Passengers travelling to...
[2] start (*in gara sportiva*) ◇ *una falsa partenza* a false start

il **participio** NOME MASC
+ **participio passato** past participle

particolare AGGETTIVO
vedi anche **particolare** NOME
[1] particular (*specifico*) ◇ *in questo caso particolare* in this particular case
[2] distinctive (*caratteristico*) ◇ *Ha un*

P

sapore particolare. It has a distinctive flavour.

il **particolare** NOME MASC
vedi anche **particolare** AGGETTIVO
detail ◇ *Vorrei sapere i particolari*. I'd like to know the details.
- **in particolare** in particular

partire VERBO
to leave* ◇ *A che ora parte il treno?* What time does the train leave? ◇ *Il volo parte da Ciampino*. The flight leaves from Ciampino. ◇ *Sono partita da Roma alle sei*. I left Rome at six.
- **La macchina non parte.** The car won't start.
- **partendo da** from ◇ *È la seconda partendo da destra*. It's the second from the right.

la **partita** NOME FEM
[1] match (*competizione*) ◇ *Sono andata alla partita di calcio ieri*. I went to the football match yesterday.
[2] game (*per gioco*) ◇ *una partita a carte* a game of cards ◇ *Facciamo una partita a tennis*. Let's have a game of tennis.

il **partito** NOME MASC
party (PL parties) (*politico*)

il **parto** NOME MASC
birth ◇ *È stato un parto difficile*. It was a difficult birth.
- **parto cesareo** Caesarean
Si noti l'uso della maiuscola in inglese.
- **parto naturale** natural childbirth

parziale AGGETTIVO
partial ◇ *un successo parziale* a partial success

il **pascolo** NOME MASC
pasture

la **Pasqua** NOME FEM
Easter ◇ *Cosa fai per Pasqua?* What are you doing at Easter? ◇ *le vacanze di Pasqua* the Easter holidays ◇ *il lunedì di Pasqua* Easter Monday ◇ *un uovo di Pasqua* an Easter egg

il **passaggio** NOME MASC
[1] lift (*in macchina*) ◇ *Può darmi un passaggio?* Can you give me a lift?
[2] pass (*nello sport*) ◇ *un passaggio indietro* a back pass
[3] passage (*apertura, brano*) ◇ *uno stretto passaggio tra le rocce* a narrow passage between the rocks ◇ *un passaggio da I Promessi Sposi* a passage from I Promessi Sposi
- **passaggio a livello** level crossing, US: grade crossing
- **passaggio pedonale** pedestrian crossing

il/la **passante** NOME MASC/FEM
vedi anche **passante** NOME MASC
passer-by (PL passers-by)

il **passante** NOME MASC
vedi anche **passante** NOME MASC/FEM
loop (*di cintura*)

il **passaporto** NOME MASC
passport

passare VERBO
[1] to pass ◇ *Hai passato l'esame?* Did you pass the exam? ◇ *Ha passato la palla a Enrico*. He passed the ball to Enrico.
◇ *Potresti passarmi il sale?* Could you pass me the salt, please? ◇ *Sono passati molti anni dalla fine della guerra*. Many years have passed since the end of the war.
- **Non è passata neanche una macchina.** Not one car went by.
- **Mi hai passato l'influenza.** You gave me the flu.
- **Può passarmi Daniela?** (*al telefono*) Can I speak to Daniela?
- **Ti passo Michele.** Here's Michele.
- **lasciar passare qualcuno** to let* somebody through ◇ *Non mi hanno lasciato passare*. They didn't let me through.
- **passare davanti a** to go* past ◇ *Siamo passati davanti a casa tua*. We went past your house.
[2] to call in (*fare una breve sosta*) ◇ *Passa quando vuoi*. Call in whenever you like.
◇ *Passo da te dopo cena*. I'll call in after dinner.
- **Devo passare in banca.** I've got to go to the bank.
- **passare a prendere qualcuno** to come* and pick somebody up ◇ *Ti passo a prendere alle otto*. I'll come and pick you up at eight o'clock.
[3] to spend* (*trascorrere*) ◇ *Ho passato due giorni in montagna*. I spent two days in the mountains.
[4] to be* over (*finire*) ◇ *Il peggio è passato*. The worst is over.
- **Ti è passato il mal di testa?** Has your headache gone?

il **passatempo** NOME MASC
pastime

passato AGGETTIVO (FEM **passata**)
vedi anche **passato** NOME
last (*scorso*) ◇ *l'anno passato* last year
- **Sono le otto passate.** It's past eight o'clock.
- **participio passato** past participle

il **passato** NOME MASC
vedi anche **passato** AGGETTIVO
past
- **in passato** in the past
- **passato prossimo** present perfect
- **passato remoto** simple past

il **passeggero**, la **passeggera** NOME MASC, FEM
passenger

passeggiare VERBO
to stroll

la **passeggiata** NOME FEM
- **fare una passeggiata** to go* for a walk

il **passeggino** NOME MASC

* I verbi seguiti da questo simbolo sono irregolari. Si veda anche alle pp.328–338.

pushchair
stroller *US*

la **passerella** NOME FEM
1 catwalk (*per sfilate*)
2 gangway (*di nave*)

il **passero** NOME MASC
sparrow

la **passione** NOME FEM
passion ◇ *amore e passione* love and
passion
• **Il giardinaggio è la mia più grande passione.**
Gardening is my greatest pleasure.

passivo AGGETTIVO (FEM **passiva**)
passive

il **passo** NOME MASC
1 step ◇ *un passo di danza* a dance step
◇ *Fai un passo avanti.* Take a step forward.
• **Camminava con passo veloce.** He was
walking fast.
• **fare due passi** to go* for a walk
• **di questo passo** at this rate ◇ *Di questo
passo non finiremo mai.* We'll never finish
at this rate.
2 pass (*valico*)

la **pasta** NOME FEM
1 pasta (*pastasciutta*)
2 cake (*pasticcino*)
3 dough (*impasto*)
• **pasta frolla** shortcrust pastry
• **pasta sfoglia** puff pastry

il **pastello** NOME MASC
pastel

la **pasticceria** NOME FEM
cake shop

il **pasticciere**, la **pasticciera** NOME MASC,
FEM
baker ◇ *Fa il pasticciere.* He is a baker.

il **pasticcino** NOME MASC
cake

il **pasticcio** NOME MASC
1 pie ◇ *un pasticcio di carne* a meat pie
2 mess ◇ *È proprio un bel pasticcio.* It's a
real mess.
• **mettersi nei pasticci** to get* into trouble

la **pastiglia** NOME FEM
tablet (*in generale*)
• **pastiglie per il mal di gola** throat sweets

il **pasto** NOME MASC
meal

il **pastore** NOME MASC
shepherd
• **cane da pastore** sheepdog
• **pastore tedesco** Alsatian, *US:* German
shepherd

la **patata** NOME FEM
potato ◇ *patate arrosto* roast potatoes
• **patate fritte** chips, *US:* French fries

le **patatine** NOME FEM PL
1 crisps
potato chips *US*
(*confezionate*)
2 chips
French fries *US*
(*fritte*)

la **patente** NOME FEM
driving licence
driver's license *US*
◇ *Ho perso la patente.* I've lost my driving
licence.
• **Mio fratello non ha la patente.** My brother
doesn't drive.
*Attenzione! In inglese esiste la parola **patent**,
che però significa **brevetto**.*

patetico AGGETTIVO (FEM **patetica**, MASC PL
patetici, FEM PL **patetiche**)
pathetic ◇ *Non essere patetico!* Don't be
pathetic!

il **patito**, la **patita** NOME MASC, FEM
fan ◇ *È un patito del calcio.* He's a football
fan.
• **un patito di musica classica** a classical
music lover

la **patria** NOME FEM
country (PL countries)

il **patrigno** NOME MASC
stepfather

il **patrimonio** NOME MASC
1 fortune ◇ *Mi è costato un patrimonio.* It
cost me a fortune.
2 heritage ◇ *il nostro patrimonio artistico*
our artistic heritage

il **pattinaggio** NOME MASC
skating
• **fare pattinaggio** to go* skating
• **pattinaggio a rotelle** roller skating
• **pattinaggio su ghiaccio** ice skating

pattinare VERBO
to skate

il **pattinatore**, la **pattinatrice** NOME MASC,
FEM
skater

il **pattino** NOME MASC
skate
• **pattini a rotelle** roller skates
• **pattini da ghiaccio** ice skates
• **pattini in linea** Rollerblades®

il **patto** NOME MASC
pact
• **fare un patto** to make* a pact
• **a patto che** on condition that

la **pattuglia** NOME FEM
patrol

la **pattumiera** NOME FEM
bin

la **paura** NOME FEM
fear ◇ *Stava tremando dalla paura.* She
was trembling with fear.
• **Era morto di paura.** He was scared to death.
• **avere paura** to be* scared ◇ *Avevo molta
paura.* I was really scared.
• **aver paura di qualcosa** to be* scared of
something ◇ *Ho paura dei ragni.* I'm scared ☞

P

of spiders.

È possibile anche dire "to be afraid of".
◇ *Hai paura del buio?* Are you afraid of the dark?

* **aver paura di fare qualcosa** to be* scared of doing something ◇ *Ha paura di volare.* He's scared of flying.
* **Ho paura di uscire da sola la sera.** I'm afraid to go out alone at night.
* **far paura a qualcuno** to frighten somebody ◇ *Mi hai fatto paura.* You frightened me.
* **Ho paura di sì.** I'm afraid so.
* **Ho paura di no.** I'm afraid not.

pauroso AGGETTIVO (FEM **paurosa**)
  awful ◇ *un pauroso incidente stradale* an awful road accident
* **essere pauroso** to get* scared easily ◇ *È pauroso.* He gets scared easily.

la **pausa** NOME FEM
  [1] break ◇ *una pausa di un'ora* an hour's break ◇ *Facciamo una pausa.* Let's have a break.
  [2] pause (*nel parlare*) ◇ *dopo una pausa* after a pause

il **pavimento** NOME MASC
  floor
  *Attenzione! In inglese esiste la parola **pavement**, che però significa **marciapiede**.*

il **pavone** NOME MASC
  peacock

paziente AGGETTIVO, NOME MASC/FEM
  patient

la **pazienza** NOME FEM
  patience ◇ *Alla fine ha perso la pazienza e se n'è andato.* Finally he lost patience and left.
* **avere pazienza** to be* patient
* **Pazienza!** Never mind!

pazzesco AGGETTIVO (FEM **pazzesca**, MASC PL **pazzeschi**, FEM PL **pazzesche**)
  [1] crazy ◇ *un'idea pazzesca* a crazy idea ◇ *Quest'idea è ancora più pazzesca.* This idea is even crazier.
  [2] incredible ◇ *una somma pazzesca* an incredible amount of money

la **pazzia** NOME FEM
  madness ◇ *È stata una pazzia!* It was madness!
* **Ho paura che possa fare una pazzia.** I'm afraid he'll do something crazy.

pazzo AGGETTIVO (FEM **pazza**)
  vedi anche **pazzo** NOME
  crazy ◇ *È pazzo!* He's crazy! ◇ *È pazzo di lei.* He's crazy about her. ◇ *È il ragazzo più pazzo che abbia mai conosciuto.* He's the craziest boy I've ever known.
* **essere innamorato pazzo** to be* madly in love
* **essere pazzo da legare** to be* raving mad

il **pazzo**, la **pazza** NOME MASC, FEM

  vedi anche **pazzo** AGGETTIVO
  madman (PL madmen)
  madwoman (PL madwomen)
  ◇ *Guidava come un pazzo.* He was driving like a madman.
* **Dovremo lavorare come pazzi per finire in tempo.** We'll have to work like mad to finish in time.

il **peccato** NOME MASC
  [1] shame ◇ *È un peccato che non sia potuto venire.* It's a shame that he couldn't come. ◇ *Che peccato!* What a shame!
  [2] sin (*in senso religioso*) ◇ *un peccato mortale* a mortal sin

la **pecora** NOME FEM
  sheep (PL sheep) ◇ *C'erano solo due pecore nel campo.* There were only two sheep in the field.
* **la pecora nera della famiglia** the black sheep of the family

il **pedaggio** NOME MASC
  toll

pedalare VERBO
  to pedal

il **pedale** NOME MASC
  pedal

la **pedata** NOME FEM
* **dare una pedata a** to kick ◇ *Mi ha dato una pedata.* He kicked me.

il/la **pediatra** NOME MASC/FEM (MASC PL i **pediatri**, FEM PL le **pediatre**)
  paediatrician
  pediatrician US
  ◇ *Fa il pediatra.* He is a paediatrician.

pedonale AGGETTIVO
  pedestrian ◇ *una zona pedonale* a pedestrian precinct

il **pedone** NOME MASC
  pedestrian

peggio AVVERBIO
  vedi anche **peggio** NOME
  worse ◇ *Luca è andato peggio di me all'esame.* Luca did worse than me in the exam. ◇ *Sta sempre peggio.* He's getting worse and worse.
* **Peggio per te.** That's your loss. ◇ *Non vuoi venire? Peggio per te.* You don't want to come? That's your loss.

la **peggio** NOME FEM
  vedi anche **peggio** AVVERBIO
* **alla peggio** if the worst comes to the worst
* **avere la peggio** to come* off worst ◇ *Hanno litigato e Gigi ha avuto la peggio.* They had an argument and Gigi came off worst.

peggiorare VERBO
  to get* worse (*tempo, ammalato*)

peggiore AGGETTIVO
  vedi anche **peggiore** NOME
  worse ◇ *È peggiore di lui.* She's worse than him.

---

* *I verbi seguiti da questo simbolo sono irregolari. Si veda anche alle pp.328–338.*

peggiore NOME MASC/FEM
vedi anche **peggiore** AGGETTIVO
worst ◊ *È il peggiore della classe.* He's the worst in the class.
• **nel peggiore dei casi** if the worst comes to the worst

pegno NOME MASC
• **dare in pegno** to leave* as security ◊ *Posso darle in pegno l'orologio.* I can leave you my watch as security.
• **un pegno d'amore** a token of love

pelare VERBO
to peel (*frutta, patate*)

pelato AGGETTIVO (FEM **pelata**)
bald (*calvo*) ◊ *È pelato.* He's bald.
• **pomodori pelati** peeled tomatoes

pelle NOME FEM
1 skin ◊ *Ho la pelle secca.* I've got dry skin.
• **avere la pelle d'oca** to have* goosepimples
2 leather (*cuoio*) ◊ *una giacca di pelle* a leather jacket

pellerossa NOME MASC/FEM (PL i/le **pellirosse**)
Indian

pelliccia NOME FEM (PL le **pellicce**)
fur coat

pellicola NOME FEM
film

pelo NOME MASC
1 fur ◊ *Il gatto ha il pelo morbido.* The cat has soft fur.
2 hair (*sul corpo*)
• **per un pelo** nearly ◊ *Per un pelo non ho perso il treno.* I nearly missed the train.
• **L'ha mancato per un pelo.** He just missed him.

peloso AGGETTIVO (FEM **pelosa**)
hairy

peluche NOME MASC
• **un pupazzo di peluche** a cuddly toy

pena NOME FEM
• **essere in pena per qualcuno** to worry about somebody ◊ *Ero in pena per te.* I was worried about you.
• **Mi fa pena.** I feel sorry for him.
• **valere la pena** to be* worth it ◊ *Non ne vale la pena.* It's not worth it.
to be worth regge il gerundio.
◊ *Vale la pena farlo.* It's worth doing.
• **la pena di morte** the death penalty ◊ *Sono contrario alla pena di morte.* I'm against the death penalty.
• **È stato condannato alla pena di morte.** He was sentenced to death.

penale AGGETTIVO
• **codice penale** penal code
• **precedenti penali** criminal record SING

pendere* VERBO
to hang* ◊ *la lampada che pende dal soffitto* the lamp that hangs from the ceiling

pendio NOME MASC (PL i **pendii**)
slope

il/la pendolare NOME MASC/FEM
commuter
• **fare il pendolare** to commute

penetrare VERBO
• **penetrare in** to go* into ◊ *Il proiettile gli è penetrato nel cuore.* The bullet went into his heart.
• **I ladri sono penetrati in casa di notte.** The thieves entered the house at night.

la penisola NOME FEM
peninsula

la penna NOME FEM
1 pen
• **penna a sfera** ballpoint pen
• **penna stilografica** fountain pen
2 feather (*di uccello*)

il pennarello NOME MASC
felt-tip pen

il pennello NOME MASC
paintbrush (*per dipingere*)
• **pennello da barba** shaving brush
• **stare a pennello** to fit perfectly ◊ *Quel vestito ti sta a pennello.* That dress fits you perfectly.

la penombra NOME FEM
• **in penombra** in the half-light ◊ *Mi è sembrato di vedere qualcuno nella penombra.* I thought I saw someone in the half-light.

pensare VERBO
to think* ◊ *Penso che* I think that ◊ *Cosa ne pensi?* What do you think of it?
• **Penso di sì.** I think so.
• **Penso di no.** I don't think so.
• **a pensarci bene** on second thoughts
• **pensare a** to think* about ◊ *A chi stai pensando?* Who are you thinking about? ◊ *Non voglio nemmeno pensarci.* I don't even want to think about it.
• **Vorrei pensarci su.** I'd like to think it over.
• **Ci penso io.** I'll see to it.
• **pensare di fare qualcosa** to think* of doing something ◊ *Pensavo di invitare anche lui.* I was thinking of inviting him too.

il pensiero NOME MASC
1 thought ◊ *libertà di pensiero* freedom of thought ◊ *È un pensiero gentile.* It's a kind thought. ◊ *Era immerso nei suoi pensieri.* He was deep in thought.
al singolare.
2 worry (PL worries) (*preoccupazione*) ◊ *Ha tanti pensieri.* He has so many worries.
• **stare in pensiero per qualcuno** to be* worried about somebody

pensieroso AGGETTIVO (FEM **pensierosa**)
thoughtful

il pensionato, la **pensionata** NOME MASC, FEM
pensioner

la pensione NOME FEM
1 pension (*somma di denaro*)
• **andare in pensione** to retire

P

☞

+ **essere in pensione** to be* retired
+ [2] boarding house (*albergo*)
+ **mezza pensione** half board
+ **pensione completa** full board

pentirsi VERBO

+ **pentirsi di qualcosa** to regret something
  ◇ *Vieni con noi e non te ne pentirai.* If you come with us you won't regret it.
+ **pentirsi di aver fatto qualcosa** to regret doing something
  regret regge il gerundio.
  ◇ *Mi pento di averglielo detto.* I regret telling him.
  È possibile anche dire "I regret that I told him".

la **pentola** NOME FEM
  pot ◇ *Metti la pentola sul fuoco.* Put the pot on the gas.

+ **pentola a pressione** pressure cooker

penultimo AGGETTIVO (FEM **penultima**)
  second from last ◇ *È arrivato penultimo.* He arrived second from last.

il **pepe** NOME MASC
  pepper

il **peperoncino** NOME MASC
  chilli pepper

il **peperone** NOME MASC
  pepper ◇ *un peperone rosso* a red pepper
  ◇ *peperoni ripieni* stuffed peppers

+ **rosso come un peperone** as red as a beetroot

per PREPOSIZIONE

+ [1] for ◇ *Questo è per te.* This is for you.
  ◇ *Ho comprato un poster per la mia stanza.* I bought a poster for my room. ◇ *È troppo difficile per lui.* It's too difficult for him. ◇ *È partito per l'Inghilterra.* He left for England. ◇ *L'ho comprato per trenta centesimi.* I bought it for thirty cents. ◇ *Ho guidato per dieci chilometri.* I drove for ten kilometres.
  ◇ *per molto tempo* for a long time
+ **per tutto il giorno** all day long
  [2] through (*moto attraverso luogo*) ◇ *I ladri sono passati per la finestra.* The thieves got in through the window. ◇ *Sono passata per Londra.* I came through London.
+ **L'ho incontrato per le scale.** I met him on the stairs.
  [3] by (*modo o maniera*) ◇ *per posta* by post
  ◇ *per ferrovia* by rail ◇ *L'ho preso per mano.* I took him by the hand.
+ **Abbiamo parlato per telefono.** We spoke on the phone.
  [4] out of (*causa*) ◇ *per abitudine* out of habit ◇ *per curiosità* out of curiosity ◇ *Non l'ho fatto per pigrizia.* I didn't do it out of laziness.
+ **per errore** by mistake
+ **Tremava per il freddo.** She was shivering with cold.
  [5] to ◇ *L'ho fatto per aiutarti.* I did it to help

you.
+ **uno per uno** one by one
+ **giorno per giorno** day by day
+ **moltiplicare due per tre** to multiply two by three
+ **Due per tre fa sei.** Two times three equals six.
+ **uno per volta** one at a time
+ **per cento** per cent ◇ *il dieci per cento* ten per cent
+ **sedersi per terra** to sit* on the ground
+ **L'ha fatto per gioco.** He did it as a joke.

la **pera** NOME FEM
  pear

perbene AGGETTIVO
  respectable ◇ *gente perbene* respectable people

la **percentuale** NOME FEM
  percentage

perché AVVERBIO
  [1] why ◇ *Perché?* Why? ◇ *Perché l'hai fatto?* Why did you do it? ◇ *Spiegami perché sei arrabbiato.* Tell me why you're angry. ◇ *Non so perché.* I don't know why.
  [2] because ◇ *Perché vai via? – Perché è tardi.* Why are you going? – Because it's late. ◇ *Non posso uscire perché ho molto da fare.* I can't go out because I've got a lot to do.
  [3] so that (*affinché*) ◇ *Ho telefonato perché non si preoccupassero.* I phoned so that they wouldn't worry.

perciò CONGIUNZIONE
  so

percorrere* VERBO
  to cover ◇ *Abbiamo percorso venti chilometri al giorno.* We covered twenty kilometres a day.

il **percorso** NOME MASC
  route ◇ *Ho seguito il percorso più breve.* I took the shortest route.

+ **lungo il percorso** along the way

perdere* VERBO
  [1] to lose* ◇ *Ho perso il portafoglio.* I've lost my wallet. ◇ *Non perdere la speranza.* Don't lose hope. ◇ *Non ho niente da perdere.* I've got nothing to lose. ◇ *Il libro è andato perso.* The book got lost.
+ **perdere di vista qualcuno** to lose* sight of somebody ◇ *L'ho perso di vista dopo mezzora.* I lost sight of him after half an hour.
+ **Dopo la scuola si sono persi di vista.** They lost touch after leaving school.
+ **Lascia perdere!** (*non insistere*) Forget it!
+ **Lascialo perdere!** (*non ascoltarlo*) Don't listen to him.
  [2] to miss (*treno, autobus, aereo*) ◇ *Ho perso il treno.* I've missed the train.
+ **È un'occasione da non perdere.** It's an opportunity not to be missed.
  [3] to waste (*sprecare*) ◇ *Hai perso tempo e denaro.* You've wasted time and money.

* I verbi seguiti da questo simbolo sono irregolari. Si veda anche alle pp.328–338.

Italian ~ English

perdita → persona 201

[4] to leak (*serbatoio, tubo*) ◇ *Il tubo perde.* The pipe is leaking.
- **perdersi** to get* lost ◇ *Ci siamo persi.* We got lost.

perdita NOME FEM
[1] loss ◇ *È una grave perdita.* It's a great loss.
[2] waste (*spreco*) ◇ *È una perdita di tempo.* It's a waste of time.

perdonare VERBO
to forgive* ◇ *Mi perdoni?* Do you forgive me? ◇ *Non glielo perdonerò mai.* I'll never forgive him for that.
- **Le ha comprato dei fiori per farsi perdonare.** He bought her flowers as a peace offering.

perfettamente AVVERBIO
perfectly ◇ *Funziona perfettamente.* It works perfectly. ◇ *Sai perfettamente che...* You know perfectly well that...

perfetto AGGETTIVO (FEM **perfetta**)
perfect

perfezionamento NOME MASC
- **un corso di perfezionamento di inglese** a course to improve one's English

perfezionare VERBO
to improve

perfino AVVERBIO
even

pericolante AGGETTIVO
unsafe (*muro, edificio*)

pericolo NOME MASC
danger
- **essere in pericolo** to be* in danger
- **essere fuori pericolo** to be* out of danger

pericoloso AGGETTIVO (FEM **pericolosa**)
dangerous

periferia NOME FEM
outskirts PL ◇ *la periferia di Milano* the outskirts of Milan
- **Vivo in periferia.** I live on the edge of town.

periodico NOME MASC (PL i **periodici**)
periodical (*pubblicazione*)

periodo NOME MASC
period ◇ *un periodo di tre anni* a period of three years ◇ *un periodo di prova* a trial period

perito NOME MASC
- **È perito chimico.** He has a qualification in chemistry.

perla NOME FEM
pearl ◇ *una collana di perle* a pearl necklace

perlina NOME FEM
bead

permaloso AGGETTIVO (FEM **permalosa**)
touchy

permanente NOME FEM
vedi anche **permanente** AGGETTIVO
perm ◇ *Ha la permanente.* She's got a perm.
- **farsi fare la permanente** to have* one's hair permed ◇ *Mi sono fatta fare la permanente.*

I had my hair permed.

permanente AGGETTIVO
vedi anche **permanente** NOME
permanent

la **permanenza** NOME FEM
stay ◇ *Buona permanenza!* Enjoy your stay!

il **permesso** NOME MASC
[1] permission ◇ *Ho chiesto il permesso di uscire.* I asked permission to leave the room.
[2] permit (*documento*)
- **permesso di lavoro** work permit
- **permesso di soggiorno** residence permit

permettere* VERBO
to allow
- **permettere a qualcuno di fare qualcosa** to allow somebody to do something ◇ *Non mi ha permesso di vederla.* He didn't allow me to see her.
- **Permettete che mi presenti.** Let me introduce myself.
  Il verbo to permit esiste, ma è piuttosto formale.
- **Permesso? (1)** (*posso entrare?*) May I come in?
- **Permesso? (2)** (*posso passare?*) Excuse me.
- **permettersi (1)** (*poter comprare*) to afford ◇ *Non può permettersi una macchina nuova.* He can't afford a new car.
- **permettersi (2)** (*osare*) to dare ◇ *Come ti permetti?* How dare you?

la **pernacchia** NOME FEM
raspberry (PL raspberries)
- **fare una pernacchia** to blow* a raspberry

pernottare VERBO
to spend* the night

però CONGIUNZIONE
but ◇ *Mi piace, però è troppo caro.* I like it, but it's too expensive.

perplesso AGGETTIVO (FEM **perplessa**)
puzzled

perquisire VERBO
to search ◇ *All'aeroporto siamo stati perquisiti.* We were searched at the airport.

la **perquisizione** NOME FEM
search ◇ *un mandato di perquisizione* a search warrant

la **persiana** NOME FEM
shutter (*di finestra*)

persino AVVERBIO
even

perso AGGETTIVO (FEM **persa**)
- **a tempo perso** in one's spare time ◇ *Dipinge a tempo perso.* She paints in her spare time.
- **È tempo perso.** It's a waste of time.

la **persona** NOME FEM
person ◇ *una persona intelligente* an intelligent person
- **persone** people PL ◇ *C'erano molte*

P

☞

persone. There were a lot of people.

il **personaggio** NOME MASC
character ◇ *i personaggi del romanzo* the characters in the novel

* **un importante personaggio politico** an important political figure

personale AGGETTIVO
| *vedi anche* **personale** NOME |
personal

il **personale** NOME MASC
| *vedi anche* **personale** AGGETTIVO |
staff ◇ *il personale dell'azienda* the staff of the company

* **ufficio personale** personnel office

la **personalità** NOME FEM (PL le **personalità**)
personality (PL personalities) ◇ *Ha una forte personalità.* He's got a strong personality.

perspicace AGGETTIVO
shrewd

pertanto CONGIUNZIONE
therefore

la **pertica** NOME FEM (PL le **pertiche**)
pole (*in palestra*)

la **pertosse** NOME FEM
whooping cough

perverso AGGETTIVO (FEM **perversa**)
perverse

il **pervertito**, la **pervertita** NOME MASC, FEM
pervert

p.es. ABBREVIAZIONE (= *per esempio*)
e.g.

pesante AGGETTIVO
1 heavy (*borsa, pranzo*) ◇ *Quella valigia è troppo pesante.* That suitcase is too heavy. ◇ *La mia è la più pesante.* Mine is the heaviest.
2 heavy going (*libro, film*) ◇ *Il film era un po' pesante.* The film was rather heavy going.

* **droghe pesanti** hard drugs

pesare VERBO
to weigh ◇ *Quanto pesa?* How much does it weigh? ◇ *L'ho già pesato.* I've already weighed it.

* **Come pesa!** It weighs a ton!
* **pesarsi** to weigh oneself

la **pesca** NOME FEM (PL le **pesche**)
1 peach (*frutto*)
2 fishing (*il pescare*)

* **andare a pesca** to go* fishing
* **pesca subacquea** underwater fishing
* **pesca con la lenza** angling
* **pesca di beneficenza** lucky dip

pescare VERBO
1 to fish ◇ *Ti insegnerò a pescare.* I'll teach you how to fish.

* **Ho pescato un pesce enorme.** I caught an enormous fish.
2 to get* (*trovare*) ◇ *Dove diavolo hai pescato quella giacca?* Where on earth did

you get that jacket?

il **pescatore** NOME MASC
fisherman (PL fishermen)

il **pesce** NOME MASC
fish (PL fish) ◇ *Ho pescato due pesci.* I caught two fish. ◇ *Ti piace il pesce?* Do you like fish?

* **pesce rosso** goldfish
* **pesce spada** swordfish
* **pesce d'aprile** April Fool

Pesci NOME MASC PL
Pisces (*dello zodiaco*) ◇ *Sono dei Pesci.* I'm Pisces.

il **pescecane** NOME MASC
shark

il **peschereccio** NOME MASC (PL i **pescherecci**)
fishing boat

la **pescheria** NOME FEM
fishmonger's

il **peso** NOME MASC
weight

* **peso lordo** gross weight
* **peso netto** net weight
* **dar peso a qualcosa** to attach importance to something ◇ *Non ho dato molto peso alle sue parole.* I didn't attach much importance to his words.
* **essere di peso a qualcuno** to be* a burden to somebody ◇ *Non voglio essere di peso a nessuno.* I don't want to be a burden to anybody.
* **portare qualcuno via di peso** to carry somebody away bodily
* **avere due pesi e due misure** to have* double standards
* **fare pesi** to do* weight training
* **sollevamento pesi** weightlifting
* **lancio del peso** shot put

pessimista AGGETTIVO (MASC PL **pessimisti**, FEM PL **pessimiste**)
| *vedi anche* **pessimista** NOME |
pessimistic

il/la **pessimista** NOME MASC/FEM (MASC PL i **pessimisti**, FEM PL le **pessimiste**)
| *vedi anche* **pessimista** AGGETTIVO |
pessimist

pessimo AGGETTIVO (FEM **pessima**)
1 very bad ◇ *un pessimo insegnante* a very bad teacher
2 terrible ◇ *un odore pessimo* a terrible smell

* **essere di pessimo umore** to be* in a very bad mood

pestare VERBO
1 to beat* (*picchiare*) ◇ *Suo marito la pesta.* Her husband beats her.
2 to crush (*aglio, ecc.*)

la **peste** NOME FEM
1 plague (*malattia*)
2 pest (*persona fastidiosa*) ◇ *Sei una*

* I verbi seguiti da questo simbolo sono irregolari. Si veda anche alle pp.328–338.

peste! You're a pest!

petalo NOME MASC
petal

petardo NOME MASC
firecracker

petroliera NOME FEM
oil tanker

petrolio NOME MASC
oil

*Attenzione! In inglese esiste la parola **petrol** che però significa **benzina**.*

pettegolezzo NOME MASC
gossip ◇ *Sono solo pettegolezzi.* It's just gossip.

al singolare.

◇ *Vuoi sentire un pettegolezzo?* Do you want to hear a bit of gossip?

+ **fare pettegolezzi** to gossip

pettegolo, pettegola NOME MASC/FEM, AGGETTIVO
gossip ◇ *Lucia è un po' pettegola.* Lucia is a bit of a gossip.

pettinare VERBO
to comb ◇ *Le ho pettinato con cura i capelli.* I combed her hair carefully.

+ **pettinarsi** to comb one's hair ◇ *Ti sei pettinata?* Have you combed your hair?

pettinatura NOME FEM
hairstyle

pettine NOME MASC
comb

pettirosso NOME MASC
robin

petto NOME MASC
chest ◇ *Ho un dolore al petto.* I've got a pain in my chest.

+ **petto di pollo** chicken breast

+ **giacca a doppio petto** double-breasted jacket

pezza NOME FEM
patch *(toppa)* ◇ *Ha una pezza sui pantaloni.* He has a patch on his trousers.

+ **una bambola di pezza** a rag doll

pezzo NOME MASC
[1] piece ◇ *un pezzo di pane* a piece of bread
[2] part *(di macchina, di motore)* ◇ *Ha cambiato un pezzo.* He's replaced a part.

+ **un pezzo di ricambio** a spare part

+ **andare in pezzi** to break* ◇ *Il bicchiere è andato in pezzi.* The glass broke.

+ **essere a pezzi** *(persona)* to be* shattered ◇ *Ho lavorato tutto il giorno e sono a pezzi.* I've been working all day and I'm shattered.

+ **un due pezzi** *(costume)* a bikini

+ **da un pezzo** for a while ◇ *È qui da un pezzo.* He has been here for a while.

piacere* VERBO
vedi anche **piacere** NOME

+ **Mi piace.** I like it.

+ **Questa musica non mi piace.** I don't like this music.

+ **Cosa ti piacerebbe fare?** What would you like to do?

il **piacere** NOME MASC
vedi anche **piacere** VERBO
[1] pleasure ◇ *È un viaggio d'affari o di piacere?* Is this trip for business or for pleasure? ◇ *Con piacere!* With pleasure!

+ **Mi farebbe piacere rivederlo.** It would be nice to see him again.

+ **Mi fa piacere per lui.** I'm pleased for him.

+ **"Piacere!"** *(nelle presentazioni)* "Pleased to meet you!"

+ **Che piacere vederti!** How nice to see you!
[2] favour
favor US
(cortesia)
◇ *Mi faresti un piacere?* Would you do me a favour?

+ **per piacere** please

piacevole AGGETTIVO
pleasant

la **piaga** NOME FEM (PL le **piaghe**)
sore

+ **piaghe da decubito** bedsores

piagnucolare VERBO
to whimper

il **pianerottolo** NOME MASC
landing

il **pianeta** NOME MASC (PL i **pianeti**)
planet

piangere* VERBO
to cry

il/la **pianista** NOME MASC/FEM (MASC PL i **pianisti**, FEM PL le **pianiste**)
pianist

piano AVVERBIO
vedi anche **piano** NOME
[1] slowly *(adagio)* ◇ *Guida piano!* Drive slowly!

+ **Fai piano, è fragile!** Be careful, it's fragile!
[2] quietly *(a bassa voce)* ◇ *Parla più piano.* Speak more quietly.

+ **pian piano** little by little

il **piano** NOME MASC
vedi anche **piano** AVVERBIO
[1] floor *(di edificio)* ◇ *Abito al terzo piano.* I live on the third floor. ◇ *all'ultimo piano* on the top floor ◇ *al piano terra* on the ground floor, US: on the first floor

🛈 *Negli Stati Uniti la numerazione dei piani comincia dal piano terra, il "first floor". Di conseguenza il primo piano è il "second floor" e così via.*

◇ *al piano di sopra* on the floor above ◇ *al piano di sotto* on the floor below

+ **una casa di tre piani** a three-storey house

+ **autobus a due piani** double-decker bus
[2] plan *(programma)* ◇ *un piano di pace* a peace plan ◇ *Tutto va secondo i piani.*

P

☞

Everything's going according to plan. *al singolare.*

3 piano (*pianoforte*)

• **in primo piano** in the foreground ◊ *una figura in primo piano* a figure in the foreground

• **primo piano** (*fotografia*) close-up

il **pianoforte** NOME MASC
piano

la **pianta** NOME FEM
1 plant ◊ *una pianta d'appartamento* a house plant

• **pianta grassa** succulent
2 map (*cartina*) ◊ *una pianta della città* a map of the city

• **pianta del piede** sole of the foot
piantare VERBO
1 to plant ◊ *Ho piantato un albero in giardino.* I've planted a tree in the garden.

• **piantare una tenda** to put* up a tent
2 to dump (*lasciare*) ◊ *Ha piantato il ragazzo.* She's dumped her boyfriend.

• **piantare qualcuno in asso** to leave* somebody in the lurch ◊ *Mi ha piantata in asso.* He left me in the lurch.

• **Piantala!** Stop it!

la **pianura** NOME FEM
plain

la **piastra** NOME FEM
slab (*di pietra*)

• **una piastra di registrazione** a tape deck

la **piastrella** NOME FEM
tile

la **piattaforma** NOME FEM
platform

il **piattino** NOME MASC
saucer

piatto AGGETTIVO (FEM **piatta**)
vedi anche **piatto** NOME
flat ◊ *Questa zona è più piatta.* This area is flatter.

il **piatto** NOME MASC
vedi anche **piatto** AGGETTIVO
1 dish ◊ *Lavo io i piatti.* I'll wash the dishes. ◊ *un piatto tipico spagnolo* a traditional Spanish dish

• **piatto del giorno** dish of the day
2 plate (*di portata*) ◊ *un piatto di carne* a plate of meat ◊ *Metti più piselli nel mio piatto.* Put more peas on my plate.

• **un piatto di minestra** a bowl of soup

• **piatto fondo** soup plate

• **piatto piano** dinner plate

• **i piatti** (*strumento*) the cymbals

la **piazza** NOME FEM
square ◊ *Piazza San Marco* St Mark's Square

• **scendere in piazza** (*dimostrare*) to take* to the streets ◊ *Gli operai sono scesi in piazza.* The workers took to the streets.

• **a una piazza** single ◊ *un lenzuolo ad una piazza* a single sheet

• **a due piazze** double

il **piazzale** NOME MASC
square

piccante AGGETTIVO
1 hot (*cibo*) ◊ *È molto piccante?* Is it very hot? ◊ *A me piace più piccante.* I like it hotter.
2 risqué ◊ *una barzelletta piccante* a risqué joke

le **picche** NOME FEM PL
spades (*nei giochi di carte*)

il **picchetto** NOME MASC
peg (*di tenda*)

picchiare VERBO
1 to hit* ◊ *È lui che mi ha picchiato!* It was him who hit me!
2 to beat* (*ripetutamente*) ◊ *Picchia la moglie.* He beats his wife.
3 to bang (*sbattere*) ◊ *Ho picchiato la testa.* I banged my head.
4 to knock (*bussare*) ◊ *Qualcuno picchiava alla porta.* Somebody was knocking at the door.

picchiata NOME FEM
• **scendere in picchiata** (*aeroplano*) to nosedive

piccino AGGETTIVO (FEM **piccina**)
tiny ◊ *Ha preso in braccio il più piccino.* He took the tiniest one in his arms.

il **piccione** NOME MASC
pigeon

il **picco** NOME MASC (PL i **picchi**)
peak (*in grafico*)

• **una roccia a picco sul mare** a sheer cliff

• **colare a picco** (*nave*) to sink*

piccolo AGGETTIVO (FEM **piccola**)
vedi anche **piccolo** NOME
Si usa **small** *o* **little**? *Leggi gli esempi e scegli la traduzione giusta a seconda del contesto ricordando che in genere* **little** *è un po' meno formale di* **small** *e non si usa dopo il verbo.*
1 small ◊ *Ho una macchina molto piccola.* I have a very small car. ◊ *Me ne dia uno più piccolo.* Give me a smaller one. ◊ *Qual è la stanza più piccola della casa?* Which is the smallest room in the house?
2 little ◊ *una piccola casetta in campagna* a little house in the country ◊ *un bambino piccolo* a little boy
3 young (*giovane*) ◊ *È ancora troppo piccolo.* He's still too young. ◊ *i bambini piccoli* young children ◊ *mio fratello più piccolo* my younger brother ◊ *Paolo è il più piccolo dei fratelli.* Paolo is the youngest of the brothers.

il **piccolo**, la **piccola** NOME MASC, FEM
vedi anche **piccolo** AGGETTIVO
small child (PL small children)

* I verbi seguiti da questo simbolo sono irregolari. Si veda anche alle pp.328–338.

‹ **da piccolo** as a child ◇ *Da piccola ero molto timida.* I was very shy as a child.

il picnic NOME MASC (PL i **picnic**)
picnic
‹ **fare un picnic** to have* a picnic

il pidocchio NOME MASC (PL i **pidocchi**)
louse (PL lice)

il piede NOME MASC
foot (PL feet) ◇ *Mi fanno male i piedi.* My feet are sore.
‹ **andare a piedi** to walk ◇ *Ci andrò a piedi.* I'll walk.
‹ **a piedi nudi** barefoot
‹ **stare in piedi** to be* standing ◇ *Stava in piedi in un angolo.* He was standing in a corner.
‹ **tra i piedi** in the way ◇ *È sempre tra i piedi.* He's always in the way.
‹ **Fuori dai piedi!** Get out of the way!

la piega NOME FEM (PL le **pieghe**)
[1] fold (*nella carta*)
[2] pleat (*di gonna*)
[3] crease (*di pantaloni*)

piegare VERBO
[1] to fold (*vestito, foglio*) ◇ *Piega la cartina e mettila via.* Fold the map and put it away.
[2] to bend* (*braccia, gambe*) ◇ *Piegate le braccia.* Bend your arms.
[3] to bow (*testa*)
‹ **piegarsi** (*persona*) to bend*

pieghevole AGGETTIVO
folding ◇ *una sedia pieghevole* a folding chair

il Piemonte NOME MASC
Piedmont

la piena NOME FEM
‹ **essere in piena** to be* in flood ◇ *Il fiume è in piena.* The river is in flood.

pieno AGGETTIVO (FEM **piena**)
vedi anche **pieno** NOME
full ◇ *La mia valigia è piena.* My suitcase is full.
‹ **pieno di** full of ◇ *una borsa piena di libri* a bag full of books
‹ **Sono pieno di lavoro.** I have a lot of work to do.
‹ **pieno zeppo** packed ◇ *Il cinema era pieno zeppo.* The cinema was packed.
‹ **a tempo pieno** full-time ◇ *Cerco un lavoro a tempo pieno.* I'm looking for a full-time job.
‹ **in pieno giorno** in broad daylight
‹ **in pieno inverno** in the depths of winter
‹ **in piena notte** in the middle of the night

il pieno NOME MASC
vedi anche **pieno** AGGETTIVO
‹ **Mi fa il pieno per favore?** Can you fill it up, please?

la pietà NOME FEM
pity ◇ *Non voglio la vostra pietà.* I don't want your pity.

pietoso AGGETTIVO (FEM **pietosa**)
pitiful ◇ *uno spettacolo pietoso* a pitiful sight ◇ *È in uno stato pietoso.* It's in a pitiful state.

la pietra NOME FEM
stone
‹ **una pietra preziosa** a precious stone
‹ **Mettiamoci una pietra sopra.** Let bygones be bygones.
‹ **di pietra** stone ◇ *una casa di pietra* a stone house

il pigiama NOME MASC (PL i **pigiami**)
pyjamas PL
pajamas PL [US]
◇ *Questo pigiama mi è un po' stretto.* These pyjamas are a bit tight on me.
‹ **essere in pigiama** to be* in one's pyjamas ◇ *Siamo ancora in pigiama.* We're still in our pyjamas.

la pigna NOME FEM
pine cone

pignolo AGGETTIVO (FEM **pignola**)
fussy ◇ *È più pignolo di me.* He's fussier than me.

la pigrizia NOME FEM
laziness ◇ *Non l'ho fatto per pigrizia.* I didn't do it out of laziness.

pigro AGGETTIVO (FEM **pigra**)
lazy ◇ *È il ragazzo più pigro che abbia mai conosciuto.* He's the laziest boy I've ever known.

la pila NOME FEM
[1] pile ◇ *una pila di libri* a pile of books
[2] battery (PL batteries) (*batteria*) ◇ *Funziona a pile.* It works on batteries.
[3] torch (*torcia*)

il pilastro NOME MASC
pillar

la pillola NOME FEM
pill
‹ **prendere la pillola** (*contraccettivo*) to be* on the pill

il pilone NOME MASC
[1] pylon (*di linea elettrica*)
[2] pier (*di ponte*)

il/la pilota NOME MASC/FEM (MASC PL i **piloti**, FEM PL le **pilote**)
[1] pilot (*di aereo, di nave*)
[2] driver (*di macchina*)
‹ **pilota automatico** automatic pilot

la pinacoteca NOME FEM (PL le **pinacoteche**)
art gallery (PL art galleries)

la pineta NOME FEM
pinewood

il ping-pong NOME MASC
table tennis

il pinguino NOME MASC
penguin

la pinna NOME FEM
[1] fin (*di pesce*)
[2] flipper (*di delfino, per nuotare*)

il pino NOME MASC
pine tree

P

il **pinolo** NOME MASC
pine kernel

la **pinza** NOME FEM
pliers PL

le **pinzette** NOME FEM PL
tweezers

la **pioggia** NOME FEM (PL le **piogge**)
rain ◇ *sotto la pioggia* in the rain
♦ **pioggia acida** acid rain

il **piolo** NOME MASC
rung ◇ *un piolo rotto* a broken rung
♦ **scala a pioli** ladder

il **piombo** NOME MASC
lead
♦ **benzina senza piombo** unleaded petrol

il **pioniere,** la **pioniera** NOME MASC, FEM
pioneer

il **pioppo** NOME MASC
poplar

piovere* VERBO
to rain ◇ *Piove.* It's raining.

piovigginare VERBO
to drizzle

piovoso AGGETTIVO (FEM **piovosa**)
rainy

la **pipa** NOME FEM
pipe ◇ *Fuma la pipa.* He smokes a pipe.

la **pipì** NOME FEM
♦ **fare pipì** to have* a pee

il **pipistrello** NOME MASC
bat

il **pirata** NOME MASC (PL i **pirati**)
pirate
♦ **un pirata della strada** a hit-and-run driver

pisciare VERBO
to piss (*volgare*)

la **piscina** NOME FEM
swimming pool

i **piselli** NOME MASC PL
peas

il **pisolino** NOME MASC
nap
♦ **fare un pisolino** to have* a nap

la **pista** NOME FEM
1 track ◇ *I corridori erano in pista.* The runners were on the track.
♦ **Pista!** Out of the way!
♦ **pista ciclabile** cycle track
♦ **pista da sci** ski run
♦ **pista da pattinaggio** skating rink
♦ **pista da ballo** dance floor
2 lead (*traccia*) ◇ *La polizia sta seguendo una pista.* The police are following a lead.
3 runway (*di aeroporto*)

il **pistacchio** NOME MASC (PL i **pistacchi**)
pistachio

la **pistola** NOME FEM
gun

il **pittore,** la **pittrice** NOME MASC, FEM
painter

pittoresco AGGETTIVO (FEM **pittoresca**, MASC PL **pittoreschi**, FEM PL **pittoresche**)
picturesque (*paesino, veduta*)

la **pittura** NOME FEM
painting ◇ *la pittura astratta* abstract painting
♦ **pittura fresca** wet paint

pitturare VERBO
to paint

più AVVERBIO
more ◇ *Quella gonna è più costosa.* That skirt is more expensive. ◇ *Può parlare più lentamente?* Could you speak more slowly?

Il comparativo spesso si forma con l'aggiunta del suffisso **-er** *all'aggettivo.*
◇ *Lucia è più carina.* Lucia is prettier.
◇ *Quella stanza è più luminosa.* That room is brighter.

♦ **più di** more than ◇ *Paolo le piace più di Marco.* She likes Paolo more than Marco. ◇ *Ho speso più di 10 sterline.* I spent more than 10 pounds. ◇ *Studia più di me.* She studies more than I do.

♦ **più...di** more...than ◇ *È più intelligente di me.* He's more intelligent than me. ◇ *Ho più compiti di te.* I've got more homework than you.

♦ **È più veloce di me.** He's quicker than me.

♦ **il più** the most ◇ *il ristorante più caro della città* the most expensive restaurant in the town ◇ *Sono le ragazze più belle della classe.* They're the most attractive girls in the class.

Il superlativo spesso si forma con l'aggiunta del suffisso **-est** *all'aggettivo.*
◇ *Questa è la cabina telefonica più vicina.* This is the nearest phone box.

♦ **non...più** not...any more ◇ *Non lavora più.* He doesn't work any more. ◇ *Non ce n'è più.* There isn't any more.

Se si usa il verbo inglese senza la negazione, **non...più** *va tradotto con* **no more.**
◇ *Non c'è più birra.* There's no more beer.

♦ **Non c'è più nessuno.** There's no one left.

♦ **Non c'è più niente da fare.** There's nothing else to do.

♦ **di più** more ◇ *Costa molto di più.* It costs a lot more.

♦ **È la persona che odio di più.** He's the person I hate most.

♦ **in più** more ◇ *Ci sono tre persone in più.* There are three more people.

♦ **più o meno** more or less

♦ **più che mai** more than ever

♦ **mai più** never again

♦ **per lo più** mostly

♦ **al più presto** as soon as possible

♦ **al più tardi** at the latest

♦ **il più delle volte** more often than not

♦ **sempre più veloce** faster and faster

♦ **due più due fa quattro** two plus two equals

I verbi seguiti da questo simbolo sono irregolari. Si veda anche alle pp.328–338.

four

a **piuma** NOME FEM
feather

il **piumino** NOME MASC
1 duvet (*coperta*)
2 quilted jacket (*giacca*)

piuttosto AVVERBIO
rather ◇ *Prenderei piuttosto un'acqua minerale.* I'd rather have some mineral water. ◇ *Fa piuttosto caldo.* It's rather hot.

a **pizza** NOME FEM
pizza

a **pizzeria** NOME FEM
pizzeria

pizzicare VERBO
1 to pinch ◇ *Gli ho pizzicato un braccio.* I pinched his arm.
◆ **Mi sono pizzicato un dito nella porta.** I caught my finger in the door.
2 to itch (*prudere*) ◇ *Mi pizzica il naso.* My nose is itching.

il **pizzico** NOME MASC (PL i **pizzichi**)
pinch ◇ *un pizzico di sale* a pinch of salt

il **pizzicotto** NOME MASC
pinch

il **pizzo** NOME MASC
lace (*merletto*)

il **plaid** NOME MASC (PL i **plaid**)
travelling rug

la **plastica** NOME FEM
plastic
◆ **di plastica** plastic ◇ *un piatto di plastica* a plastic plate
◆ **farsi fare la plastica** to have* plastic surgery

il **platano** NOME MASC
plane tree

la **platea** NOME FEM
1 the stalls PL (*a teatro*) ◇ *un posto in platea* a seat in the stalls
2 audience (*pubblico*) ◇ *La platea ha applaudito.* The audience applauded.

plausibile AGGETTIVO
plausible

il **plico** NOME MASC (PL i **plichi**)
parcel

il **plotone** NOME MASC
platoon
◆ **plotone d'esecuzione** firing squad

plurale AGGETTIVO, NOME MASC
plural

lo **pneumatico** NOME MASC (PL gli **pneumatici**)
tyre
tire US

po' AVVERBIO, NOME MASC
◆ **un po'** a bit ◇ *Sono un po' stanco.* I'm a bit tired. ◇ *Zoppica un po'.* He limps a bit.
◆ **un po' di** some ◇ *Potrei avere ancora un po' di tè?* Could I have some more tea?
◇ *Mettici un po' di zucchero.* Put some sugar in it. ◇ *un po' di soldi* some money
◆ **un bel po'** quite a lot ◇ *un bel po' di soldi* quite a lot of money
◆ **tra un po'** shortly

poco AGGETTIVO, AVVERBIO, NOME MASC (FEM **poca**, MASC PL **pochi**, FEM PL **poche**)
1 not much (*per indicare quantità*) ◇ *Bevo poco vino.* I don't drink much wine. ◇ *C'è poco spazio.* There's not much room.
2 not many (*per indicare numero*)
◇ *C'erano poche ragazze alla festa.* There weren't many girls at the party. ◇ *Questa macchina ha fatto pochi chilometri.* This car hasn't done many kilometres. ◇ *Pochi ci crederebbero.* Not many people would believe that.
◆ **È poco più alta di lui.** She's a bit taller than him.
◆ **Studia troppo poco.** He doesn't study enough.
◆ **a poco a poco** little by little
◆ **poco fa** a short time ago
◆ **per poco** nearly ◇ *Per poco non cadevo.* I nearly fell.
◆ **poco dopo** shortly afterwards
◆ **poco prima** shortly before
◆ **fra poco** soon
◆ **poco spesso** not very often
◆ **Sono arrivato da poco.** I have just arrived.
◆ **Sta poco bene.** He's not very well.

il **podio** NOME MASC
podium

la **poesia** NOME FEM
1 poem ◇ *una poesia di Foscolo* a poem by Foscolo
2 poetry (*arte*) ◇ *la poesia e la prosa* poetry and prose

il **poeta**, la **poetessa** NOME MASC, FEM
poet

poggiare VERBO
1 to put* (*sopra qualcosa*) ◇ *Puoi poggiare il pacco sul tavolo.* You can put the parcel on the table.
2 to lean* (*contro qualcosa*) ◇ *Poggia la scala al muro.* Lean the ladder against the wall.
◆ **poggiarsi a** to lean* against ◇ *Si è dovuto poggiare al muro per sostenersi.* He had to lean against the wall for support.

il **poggiatesta** NOME MASC (PL i **poggiatesta**)
headrest

poi AVVERBIO
1 then (*in seguito*) ◇ *E poi cos'è successo?* And then what happened?
2 later (*più tardi*) ◇ *Poi te lo dico.* I'll tell you later.
◆ **prima o poi** sooner or later
◆ **d'ora in poi** from now on
◆ **da domani in poi** from tomorrow onwards

poiché CONGIUNZIONE
since

la **polacca** NOME
(*vedi anche* **polacco** AGGETTIVO PL le **polacche**)
Pole

P

polacco AGGETTIVO (FEM **polacca**, MASC PL **polacchi**, FEM PL **polacche**)
vedi anche **polacco** NOME
Polish

il **polacco** NOME (PL **i polacchi**)
  ☐1 Pole (*persona*) ◊ *i polacchi* the Poles
  ☐2 Polish (*lingua*) ◊ *Parli polacco?* Do you speak Polish?

la **polemica** NOME FEM (PL le **polemiche**)
controversy (PL controversies)

polemico AGGETTIVO (FEM **polemica**, MASC PL **polemici**, FEM PL **polemiche**)
argumentative

il **polipo** NOME MASC
polyp

il **polistirolo** NOME MASC
polystyrene

la **politica** NOME FEM (PL le **politiche**)
  ☐1 politics SING ◊ *Si interessa di politica.* He's interested in politics.
  ☐2 policy (PL policies) ◊ *la politica economica del governo* the government's economic policy

politico AGGETTIVO (FEM **politica**, MASC PL **politici**, FEM PL **politiche**)
political ◊ *la situazione politica* the political situation
  • **elezioni politiche** general election
  • **un uomo politico** a politician

la **polizia** NOME FEM
police PL ◊ *È arrivata la polizia?* Have the police arrived? ◊ *Chiama la polizia!* Call the police!

poliziesco AGGETTIVO (FEM **poliziesca**, MASC PL **polizieschi**, FEM PL **poliziesche**)
  • **un film poliziesco** a detective film

la **poliziotta** NOME FEM
policewoman (PL policewomen)

il **poliziotto** NOME MASC
policeman (PL policemen)
  • **cane poliziotto** police dog

il **pollaio** NOME MASC
henhouse

il **pollice** NOME MASC
  ☐1 thumb
  • **girarsi i pollici** to twiddle one's thumbs
  ☐2 inch (= 2,45 cm) ◊ *un televisore a 24 pollici* a 24-inch TV

il **polline** NOME MASC
pollen
  • **Sono allergico al polline.** I suffer from hay fever.

il **pollo** NOME MASC
chicken

il **polmone** NOME MASC
lung

la **polmonite** NOME FEM
pneumonia

il **polo** NOME MASC
  • **il Polo nord** the North Pole
  • **il Polo sud** the South Pole

la **Polonia** NOME FEM
Poland ◊ *Ti è piaciuta la Polonia?* Did you like Poland? ◊ *Sei mai stato in Polonia?* Have you ever been to Poland?

il **polpaccio** NOME MASC
calf (PL calves)

il **polpastrello** NOME MASC
fingertip

la **polpetta** NOME FEM
meatball

il **polpo** NOME MASC
octopus

il **polsino** NOME MASC
cuff

il **polso** NOME MASC
wrist ◊ *Ha un braccialetto al polso.* She's got a bracelet on her wrist.
  • **avere polso** to be* firm

poltrire VERBO
to laze about

la **poltrona** NOME FEM
armchair

la **polvere** NOME FEM
dust ◊ *C'è uno strato di polvere sul pavimento.* There's a layer of dust on the floor.
  • **polvere da sparo** gunpowder

la **pomata** NOME FEM
ointment

il **pomeriggio** NOME MASC
afternoon
  • **nel pomeriggio** in the afternoon
  • **alle due del pomeriggio** at two o'clock in the afternoon
  • **domani pomeriggio** tomorrow afternoon
  • **ogni pomeriggio** every afternoon

il **pomodoro** NOME MASC
tomato
  • **spaghetti al pomodoro** spaghetti with tomato sauce

la **pompa** NOME FEM
pump ◊ *una pompa da bicicletta* a bicycle pump
  • **pompa antincendio** fire hose
  • **pompa di benzina** petrol pump

pompare VERBO
to pump up ◊ *Devo pompare il materassino.* I need to pump up my airbed.

il **pompelmo** NOME MASC
grapefruit

il **pompiere** NOME MASC
fireman (PL firemen) ◊ *Fa il pompiere.* He is a fireman.
  • **i pompieri** the fire brigade SING ◊ *Chiamate i pompieri!* Call the fire brigade!

il **ponte** NOME MASC
  ☐1 bridge ◊ *È dell'altra parte del ponte.* It's across the bridge.
  • **ponte levatoio** drawbridge

[2] deck (di nave)
+ **fare ponte** to have* a long weekend
popolare AGGETTIVO

popular ◇ *un cantante molto popolare* a very popular singer ◇ *la stampa popolare* the popular press
+ **un quartiere popolare** a poor area
+ **una casa popolare** a council house
la **popolazione** NOME FEM
population
il **popolo** NOME MASC
people PL
la **porcellana** NOME FEM
porcelain
il **porcellino** NOME MASC
piglet
+ **porcellino d'India** guinea pig
la **porcheria** NOME FEM
rubbish
junk US
*Sia **rubbish** che **junk** non hanno il plurale.*
◇ *Mangia un sacco di porcherie.* He eats a lot of rubbish.
il **porcino** NOME MASC
cep (fungo)
il **porco** NOME MASC (PL i **porci**)
pig
il **porcospino** NOME MASC
porcupine
porno AGGETTIVO (MASC, FEM, PL **porno**)
+ **un film porno** a porn film
la **pornografia** NOME FEM
pornography
porre* VERBO
[1] to put* (mettere)
[2] to place (collocare)
[3] to lay* down (appoggiare)
+ **Poniamo che...** Let's suppose that...
+ **porre una domanda a qualcuno** to ask somebody a question
+ **porre fine a** to put* an end to
+ **porsi in salvo** to save oneself
il **porro** NOME MASC
leek ◇ *una minestra di porri* leek soup
la **porta** NOME FEM
[1] door ◇ *Chiudi la porta, per favore.* Close the door, please.
+ **mettere qualcuno alla porta** to throw* somebody out ◇ *Lo hanno messo alla porta.* They threw him out.
+ **vendita porta a porta** door-to-door selling
[2] goal (nel calcio)
il **portabagagli** NOME MASC (PL i **portabagagli**)
boot
trunk US
il **portacenere** NOME MASC (PL i **portacenere**)
ashtray
il **portachiavi** NOME MASC (PL i **portachiavi**)
[1] key ring (anello)
[2] key case (astuccio)
la **portaerei** NOME FEM (PL le **portaerei**)

aircraft carrier
la **portafinestra** NOME FEM (PL le **portefinestre**)
French window
il **portafoglio** NOME MASC
wallet
il **portafortuna** NOME MASC (PL i **portafortuna**)
lucky charm
il **portamatite** NOME MASC (PL i **portamatite**)
pencil case
il **portamonete** NOME MASC (PL i **portamonete**)
purse
change purse US
il **portaombrelli** NOME MASC (PL i **portaombrelli**)
umbrella stand
il **portapacchi** NOME MASC (PL i **portapacchi**)
luggage rack
portare VERBO
[1] to take* (lontano da chi parla) ◇ *Sta portando i bambini a scuola.* She's taking the children to school. ◇ *Puoi portarlo laggiù?* Can you take it down? ◇ *Porta questa lettera a Lucia.* Take this letter to Lucia.
[2] to bring* (vicino a chi parla) ◇ *Portalo qui.* Bring it here. ◇ *Puoi portarmi quel libro?* Can you bring me that book?
[3] to carry (tenere) ◇ *Portava un pacco sottobraccio.* He was carrying a parcel under his arm.
[4] to wear* (indossare) ◇ *Portava un bel vestito.* She was wearing a beautiful dress.
[5] to lead* (condurre) ◇ *Dove porta questa strada?* Where does this street lead?
+ **portare fortuna** to bring* good luck
il **portariviste** NOME MASC (PL i **portariviste**)
magazine rack
il **portasigarette** NOME MASC (PL i **portasigarette**)
cigarette case
la **portata** NOME FEM
course (di pranzo) ◇ *la portata principale* the main course
+ **a portata di mano** within reach
portatile AGGETTIVO
portable ◇ *una TV portatile* a portable TV
portato AGGETTIVO (FEM **portata**)
+ **essere portato per qualcosa** to have* a gift for something ◇ *È portato per le lingue.* He has a gift for languages.
il **portauovo** NOME MASC (PL i **portauova**)
egg cup
il/la **portavoce** NOME MASC/FEM (MASC/FEM PL i/le **portavoce**)
spokesperson
la **portiera** NOME FEM
door (di auto, ecc.)
il **portiere** NOME MASC
[1] goalkeeper (nel calcio)
[2] porter (di albergo)

P

☞

3 concierge (*di casa*)

il **porto** NOME MASC

1 harbour

harbor *US*

◇ *un porto riparato* a sheltered harbour

2 port (*struttura commerciale*) ◇ *un importante porto fluviale* an important river port

• **porto d'armi** gun licence, *US*: gun license

il **Portogallo** NOME MASC

Portugal ◇ *Ti è piaciuto il Portogallo?* Did you like Portugal? ◇ *Sei mai stato in Portogallo?* Have you ever been to Portugal?

portoghese AGGETTIVO, NOME MASC/FEM

Portuguese

• **i portoghesi** the Portuguese

il **portone** NOME MASC

main entrance

la **porzione** NOME FEM

portion ◇ *una porzione abbondante* a big portion

la **posa** NOME FEM

1 exposure ◇ *un rullino a 24 pose* a 24 exposure film

2 pose (*atteggiamento, di modello*)

• **mettersi in posa** to pose

• **lavorare senza posa** to work without a break

posare VERBO

to put* ◇ *Ha posato la penna sul tavolo.* He put the pen on the table.

le **posate** NOME FEM PL

cutlery SING

positivo AGGETTIVO (FEM **positiva**)

positive

la **posizione** NOME FEM

position ◇ *una posizione scomoda* an uncomfortable position

• **Si è fatto una posizione.** He's done well.

• **luci di posizione** sidelights

posporre* VERBO

to postpone

possedere* VERBO

1 to have* ◇ *Quasi tutti possiedono una macchina.* Most people have a car.

2 to own (*casa, terreni*) ◇ *Possiede una casa in campagna.* She owns a house in the country.

possessivo AGGETTIVO (FEM **possessiva**)

possessive

possibile AGGETTIVO, NOME MASC

possible ◇ *Pensi che sia possibile?* Do you think it's possible?

• **fare tutto il possibile** to do* everything possible

• **il più presto possibile** as soon as possible

la **possibilità** NOME FEM (PL le **possibilità**)

1 possibility (PL possibilities) ◇ *Ci sono varie possibilità.* There are various possibilities.

2 opportunity (PL opportunities) (*occasione*) ◇ *Non ha avuto la possibilità di andare all'università.* He didn't have the opportunity to go to university.

la **posta** NOME FEM

1 post

mail *US*

◇ *C'è posta per me?* Is there any post for me?

• **per posta** by post ◇ *Mandalo per posta.* Send it by post.

• **posta aerea** airmail

• **posta elettronica** e-mail

2 post office (*ufficio*) ◇ *Sto andando alla posta.* I'm going to the post office.

postale AGGETTIVO

postal ◇ *servizio postale* postal service

• **impiegato postale** post office employee

• **timbro postale** postmark

posteggiare VERBO

to park

il **posteggio** NOME MASC

1 car park

parking lot *US*

(*piazzale*)

◇ *un posteggio gratuito* a free car park

2 parking space (*posto*) ◇ *Non riesco a trovare posteggio.* I can't find a parking space.

• **posteggio taxi** taxi rank

il **poster** NOME MASC (PL i **poster**)

poster

posteriore AGGETTIVO

back ◇ *il sedile posteriore* the back seat

posticipare VERBO

to postpone

la **postina** NOME FEM

postwoman (PL postwomen)

il **postino** NOME MASC

postman (PL postmen)

mailman (PL mailmen) *US*

il **posto** NOME MASC

1 place ◇ *È un posto magnifico.* It's a beautiful place. ◇ *Rimetti il libro al suo posto.* Put the book back in its place.

2 room (*spazio libero*) ◇ *Non c'è più posto in macchina.* There's no more room in the car.

3 seat (*a teatro, in treno*) ◇ *Vorrei prenotare due posti.* I'd like to book two seats.

• **un posto a sedere** a seat

• **posti in piedi** standing room

• **a posto** (*in ordine*) tidy ◇ *La casa era a posto.* The house was tidy.

• **Tutto a posto?** Is everything OK?

• **mettere a posto** (*riordinare*) to tidy ◇ *Metti a posto la tua camera.* Tidy your room.

• **al posto di** instead of ◇ *C'è un film al posto della partita.* There's a film instead of the

match. ◇ *Andrò io al suo posto.* I'll go instead of him.
* **Se fossi al tuo posto ci andrei.** If I were you I would go.
* **posto di blocco** roadblock
* **posto di lavoro** job

potabile AGGETTIVO
* **acqua potabile** drinking water

potente AGGETTIVO
powerful ◇ *un motore potente* a powerful engine

potenza NOME FEM
power

potere VERBO
vedi anche **potere** NOME

can*

can è usato per tradurre il presente di potere.
◇ *Non posso venire.* I can't come. ◇ *Posso entrare?* Can I come in? ◇ *Si può visitare il castello tutti i giorni dell'anno.* You can visit the castle any day of the year.

Per tradurre il passato o il condizionale di potere si usa could.
◇ *Non è potuto venire.* He couldn't come.
◇ *Potresti aprire la finestra?* Could you open the window?

Dato che can non ha né l'infinito né il participio, per tradurre alcuni tempi verbali si deve usare to be able to.
◇ *Non potrò venire domani.* I won't be able to come tomorrow. ◇ *Dovresti potercela fare da solo.* You should be able to do it by yourself.

Per formulare un'ipotesi si possono usare may o could.
◇ *Può aver avuto un incidente.* He may have had an accident. ◇ *Potrebbe essere vero.* It could be true.
* **può darsi** perhaps ◇ *Pensi di andarci? – Può darsi.* Do you think you'll go? – Perhaps.
* **Può darsi che non venga.** He may not come.
* **Non ne posso più!** I can't take any more!

potere NOME MASC
vedi anche **potere** VERBO
power ◇ *una lotta per il potere* a power struggle
* **essere al potere** to be* in power

povero AGGETTIVO, NOME MASC/FEM (FEM **povera**)
poor ◇ *Sono molto poveri.* They're very poor.
* **i poveri** the poor

povertà NOME FEM
poverty

pozzanghera NOME FEM
puddle

pozzo NOME MASC
well
* **pozzo petrolifero** oil well

pranzare VERBO
to have* lunch ◇ *Abbiamo appena pranzato.* We've just had lunch.

* **pranzare fuori** to go* out for lunch
il **pranzo** NOME MASC
lunch ◇ *un pranzo di lavoro* a business lunch ◇ *Vieni a pranzo da me?* Will you come and have lunch with me?

la **pratica** NOME FEM (PL le **pratiche**)
[1] practice ◇ *Devi solo fare un po' di pratica.* You only need a bit of practice. ◇ *la pratica e la teoria* practice and theory
* **in pratica** in practice
* **mettere in pratica** to put* into practice
◇ *Cercate di mettere in pratica questa idea.* Try to put this idea into practice.
[2] experience (*esperienza*) ◇ *Non ho molta pratica di queste cose.* I haven't got much experience in these things.
[3] file (*incartamento*) ◇ *Può cercarmi quella pratica?* Can you get that file for me?
* **fare le pratiche per** to do* the paperwork for

praticamente AVVERBIO
practically

praticare VERBO
[1] to do* (*scherma, judo*) ◇ *Pratica molti sport.* He does a lot of different sports.
[2] to play (*calcio, pallacanestro*)

pratico AGGETTIVO (FEM **pratica**, MASC PL **pratici**, FEM PL **pratiche**)
[1] practical ◇ *un metodo pratico* a practical method
[2] handy (*utile*) ◇ *un aggeggio molto pratico* a very handy tool ◇ *l'aggeggio più pratico* the handiest tool
[3] convenient (*facile*) ◇ *Mi è più pratico venire di pomeriggio.* It's more convenient for me to come in the afternoon.
* **essere pratico di qualcosa** to know* something ◇ *È pratico del mestiere.* He knows the job. ◇ *Non sono pratica di queste parti.* I don't know this area very well.

il **prato** NOME MASC
[1] meadow ◇ *Giocavano sul prato.* They were playing in the meadow.
[2] lawn (*di giardino*) ◇ *Giocavano sul prato.* They were playing on the lawn.
* **prato all'inglese** lawn

la **precauzione** NOME FEM
precaution
* **prendere delle precauzioni** to take* precautions

precedente AGGETTIVO
previous ◇ *il giorno precedente* the previous day

la **precedenza** NOME FEM
* **avere la precedenza** (*in macchina*) to have* the right of way
* **dare la precedenza (1)** (*in macchina*) to give* way
* **dare la precedenza (2)** (*priorità*) to give* priority

precedere* VERBO
to precede

precipitare VERBO

P

☞

to fall* ◇ *Sono precipitati in un burrone.* They fell into a ravine.
- **La situazione sta precipitando.** The situation is getting out of control.

precipitoso AGGETTIVO (FEM **precipitosa**)
rash ◇ *È un po' troppo precipitoso.* He's a bit too rash.
- **una fuga precipitosa** a hasty escape

il **precipizio** NOME MASC
precipice ◇ *È caduto da un precipizio.* He fell over a precipice.

precisamente AVVERBIO
precisely ◇ *È precisamente quello che intendevo.* That's precisely what I meant.

precisare VERBO
to point out ◇ *Vorrei precisare che...* I'd like to point out that...

preciso AGGETTIVO (FEM **precisa**)
① precise ◇ *le sue precise parole* his precise words ◇ *in quel preciso istante* at that precise moment
- **Non ho un'idea precisa di come funzioni.** I don't know precisely how it works.
- **Sono le 9 precise.** It's exactly 9 o'clock.
② careful (*accurato*) ◇ *È molto preciso nel suo lavoro.* He's very careful in his work.

il **preconcetto** NOME MASC
prejudice

la **preda** NOME FEM
prey (*di animale*)
- **essere in preda al panico** to panic ◇ *Era in preda al panico.* He was panicking.

predire* VERBO
to predict ◇ *Aveva predetto che sarebbe successo.* He had predicted it would happen.
- **predire il futuro** to tell* the future

la **predisposizione** NOME FEM
- **avere predisposizione a** to have* a gift for ◇ *Ha predisposizione alla musica.* He has a gift for music.

la **prefazione** NOME FEM
preface

la **preferenza** NOME FEM
preference ◇ *Non ho preferenze.* I have no preference.
- **Qui non si fanno preferenze.** There is no favouritism here.

preferire VERBO
to prefer ◇ *Preferisco il caffè al tè.* I prefer coffee to tea. ◇ *Preferisce spendere i suoi soldi in vestiti.* He prefers to spend his money on clothes.
- **Cosa preferisci, caffè o tè?** Which would you like, coffee or tea?
- **Preferirei un'insalata.** I'd rather have a salad.

Se preferire è seguito da un verbo si traduce anche con would rather.
◇ *Preferisco non parlarne.* I would rather not talk about it. ◇ *Preferirei lavorare a casa.*

I'd rather work at home.

preferito AGGETTIVO (FEM **preferita**)
favourite
favorite [US]

prefiggersi* VERBO
- **prefiggersi uno scopo** to set* oneself a goal ◇ *Questo era lo scopo che mi ero prefissa.* This was the goal that I had set myself.

il **prefisso** NOME MASC
① code (*del telefono*) ◇ *Qual è il prefisso di Londra?* What's the code for London?
② prefix (*in grammatica*)

pregare VERBO
to pray ◇ *Stava pregando.* She was praying.
- **pregare qualcuno di fare qualcosa** to ask somebody to do something ◇ *L'ho pregata di venire.* I asked her to come.
- **I passeggeri sono pregati di...** Passengers are kindly requested to...
- **Ti prego!** Please! ◇ *Ti prego, lasciami in pace.* Please leave me alone.

la **preghiera** NOME FEM
prayer

pregiato AGGETTIVO (FEM **pregiata**)
valuable ◇ *un tappeto pregiato* a valuable carpet

il **pregio** NOME MASC
good quality (PL good qualities) (*di persona*) ◇ *Ha molti pregi.* He has a lot of good qualities.
- **i pregi e i difetti** the good points and the bad points

il **pregiudizio** NOME MASC
prejudice ◇ *pregiudizio razziale* racial prejudice
- **avere dei pregiudizi nei confronti di qualcuno** to be* prejudiced against somebody

prego ESCLAMAZIONE
you're welcome (*di niente*) ◇ *Grazie dell'aiuto. – Prego!* Thank you for your help. – You're welcome!
- **Prego, si accomodi. (1)** (*entri*) Please come in.
- **Prego, si accomodi. (2)** (*si sieda*) Please take a seat.
- **Prego?** (*come?*) Pardon?

prelevare VERBO
to withdraw* ◇ *Vorrei prelevare cinquanta sterline.* I'd like to withdraw fifty pounds, please.

il **prelievo** NOME MASC
withdrawal (*di denaro*)
- **fare un prelievo di sangue** to take* a blood sample

premere* VERBO
to press ◇ *Premi forte!* Press hard!
- **premere il grilletto** to pull the trigger

premiare VERBO
to give* a prize to (*persona*) ◇ *Il preside ha*

premiato due studenti. The headmaster gave prizes to two students.

• **essere premiato** to win* a prize ◇ *Il film è stato premiato.* The film won a prize.

premiazione NOME FEM

[1] prize-giving (*a scuola*)

[2] award ceremony (PL award ceremonies) (*di film, di libro*)

premio NOME MASC

prize ◇ *Ho ricevuto un premio.* I was given a prize.

• **premio di consolazione** consolation prize

• **premio Nobel** Nobel prize

premura NOME FEM

• **aver premura** to be* in a hurry ◇ *Svelto, che ho premura!* Quick, I'm in a hurry!

• **fare premura a qualcuno** to hurry somebody ◇ *Mi dispiace farti premura, ma devo andare.* I'm sorry to hurry you, but I have to go.

• **circondare qualcuno di premure** to make* a fuss of somebody

premuroso AGGETTIVO (FEM **premurosa**)

thoughtful

prendere* VERBO

[1] to take* ◇ *Prendi quella borsa.* Take that bag. ◇ *Hai preso l'ombrello?* Have you taken your umbrella? ◇ *Ho preso il treno delle dieci.* I took the ten o'clock train.

[2] to get* (*ottenere*) ◇ *Ho preso un bel voto.* I got a good mark.

• **andare a prendere qualcosa** to go* and get something ◇ *Vai a prendermi gli occhiali.* Go and get my glasses.

• **venire a prendere qualcuno** to come* and get somebody ◇ *Potresti venire a prendermi alla stazione?* Could you come and get me at the station?

• **prendere paura** to get* a fright

[3] to have* (*al bar, al ristorante*) ◇ *Prendo un caffè.* I'll have a coffee.

• **Prende qualcosa da bere?** Would you like something to drink?

[4] to earn (*guadagnare*) ◇ *Quanto prende al mese?* How much does he earn a month?

[5] to charge (*far pagare*) ◇ *Quanto prende per un taglio di capelli?* How much do you charge for a haircut?

[6] to catch* (*catturare*) ◇ *Ho preso un grosso pesce.* I caught a huge fish.

[7] to handle (*trattare*) ◇ *So come prenderlo.* I know how to handle him.

• **prendere l'influenza** to catch* the flu

• **prendere fuoco** to catch* fire

• **prendere qualcuno per** to mistake* somebody for ◇ *Mi ha preso per mio fratello.* He mistook me for my brother.

• **Per chi mi prendi?** Who do you think I am?

• **prendersi a calci** to kick each other

• **prendersi a pugni** to punch each other

• **prendersela (1)** (*arrabbiarsi*) to get* annoyed

• **prendersela (2)** (*preoccuparsi*) to get* upset

• **Perché te la prendi sempre con me?** Why do you always pick on me?

• **Cosa ti prende?** What's got into you?

prenotare VERBO

to book

la **prenotazione** NOME FEM

booking

• **fare una prenotazione** to make* a booking

preoccupare VERBO

to worry

• **preoccuparsi** to worry ◇ *Non preoccuparti.* Don't worry.

• **preoccuparsi per qualcosa** to worry about something

preoccupato AGGETTIVO (FEM **preoccupata**)

worried

la **preoccupazione** NOME FEM

worry (PL worries) ◇ *Ha molte preoccupazioni.* He has a lot of worries.

preparare VERBO

to prepare

• **preparare da mangiare** to prepare a meal

• **prepararsi** (*vestirsi*) to get* ready

• **prepararsi ad un esame** to prepare for an exam

i **preparativi** NOME MASC PL

preparations ◇ *Stanno facendo i preparativi per la festa.* They're making preparations for the party.

la **preposizione** NOME FEM

preposition

prepotente AGGETTIVO, NOME MASC/FEM

bully (PL bullies) ◇ *È un prepotente.* He's a bully.

• **un ragazzo prepotente** a bully

la **presa** NOME FEM

grip ◇ *Ha allentato la presa.* He loosened his grip.

• **presa di corrente** socket, US: outlet

• **macchina da presa** cine camera

presbite AGGETTIVO

long-sighted

prescrivere* VERBO

to prescribe

presentare VERBO

[1] to introduce (*persona*) ◇ *L'ha presentata ai suoi amici.* He introduced her to his friends.

[2] to present (*trasmissione, ecc.*) ◇ *Chi ha presentato lo spettacolo?* Who presented the show?

[3] to put* in (*domanda*) ◇ *Ha presentato una domanda di assunzione.* He put in a job application.

• **presentarsi (1)** (*farsi conoscere*) to introduce oneself

• **presentarsi (2)** (*occasione*) to arise*

presente AGGETTIVO, NOME MASC

present ◇ *Erano tutti presenti alla lezione.* Everybody was present at the class.

P

♦ **Presente!** (*ad appello*) Here!

♦ **il presente** (*in grammatica*) the present tense

♦ **i presenti** those present

♦ **aver presente qualcosa** to know* something ◇ *Hai presente la casa rossa vicino alla mia?* You know the red house near mine?

♦ **tener presente qualcosa** to remember something ◇ *Tieni presente che non ho molto tempo libero.* Remember I don't have much spare time.

il **presentimento** NOME MASC

♦ **Ho il presentimento che...** I've a feeling that...

la **presenza** NOME FEM
presence

il **presepio** NOME MASC
crib

il **preservativo** NOME MASC
condom

il/la **preside** NOME MASC/FEM
[1] head (*di scuola*)
[2] dean (*di facoltà universitaria*)

il/la **presidente** NOME MASC/FEM
[1] president (*di nazione*)
[2] chairman (PL chairmen)
chairwoman (PL chairwomen) (*di assemblea, di società commerciale*)

pressappoco AVVERBIO
about ◇ *Ha pressappoco quarant'anni.* He's about forty.

pressi NOME MASC PL

♦ **nei pressi di** near ◇ *L'albergo si trova nei pressi della stazione.* The hotel is near the station.

la **pressione** NOME FEM
[1] pressure

♦ **pentola a pressione** pressure cooker
[2] blood pressure (*del sangue*) ◇ *Ha la pressione alta.* He's got high blood pressure.

♦ **far pressione su qualcuno** to put* pressure on somebody

♦ **essere sotto pressione** to be* under pressure

presso PREPOSIZIONE
c/o (*nelle lettere*) ◇ *Lucia Micoli, presso fam. Bianchi* Lucia Micoli, c/o Mr and Mrs Bianchi *c/o si legge "care of".*

♦ **Abita presso una zia.** He lives with an aunt.

♦ **Lavora presso di noi.** He works for us.

prestare VERBO

♦ **prestare qualcosa a qualcuno** to lend* somebody something ◇ *Mi ha prestato venticinque euro.* He lent me twenty five euros. ◇ *Gliel'ho prestato.* I lent it to him.

♦ **farsi prestare qualcosa da qualcuno** to borrow something from somebody ◇ *Mi sono fatto prestare una penna da Luca.* I borrowed a pen from Luca.

♦ **prestare attenzione** to pay* attention

la **prestazione** NOME FEM
performance (*di auto, di atleta*)

il **prestigiatore** NOME MASC
conjurer

il **prestigio** NOME MASC
prestige ◇ *È una questione di prestigio.* It's a matter of prestige.

♦ **gioco di prestigio** conjuring trick

il **prestito** NOME MASC
loan ◇ *un prestito bancario* a bank loan

♦ **dare in prestito qualcosa a qualcuno** to lend* somebody something ◇ *Gli ho dato in prestito la mia bici.* I lent him my bike.

♦ **prendere in prestito qualcosa da qualcuno** to borrow something from somebody ◇ *Ha preso in prestito cento euro da sua madre.* She borrowed a hundred euros from her mother.

♦ **fare un prestito** to give* a loan ◇ *Mi faresti un prestito?* Could you give me a loan?

presto AVVERBIO
[1] soon (*tra poco*) ◇ *Arriverà presto.* He'll be here soon. ◇ *il più presto possibile* as soon as possible

♦ **presto o tardi** sooner or later

♦ **Presto!** Hurry up!

♦ **A presto!** See you soon!
[2] early (*di buon'ora*) ◇ *Mi alzo sempre presto.* I always get up early. ◇ *Mi alzo più presto di te.* I get up earlier than you.
◇ *Sono arrivato troppo presto.* I arrived too early.

presumere* VERBO
to presume

presuntuoso AGGETTIVO (FEM **presuntuosa**)
conceited

il **prete** NOME MASC
priest

pretendere* VERBO
to expect (*aspettarsi*) ◇ *Pretende di essere pagato in anticipo.* He expects to be paid in advance.

♦ **Pretende di aver sempre ragione.** He thinks he's always right.

Attenzione! In inglese esiste il verbo ***to pretend***, *che però significa* ***fingere***.

la **pretesa** NOME FEM

♦ **Non ho molte pretese.** I'm easily pleased.

♦ **senza pretese** (*persona, casa, locale*)
unpretentious

il **pretesto** NOME MASC
pretext

♦ **con il pretesto di** on the pretext of

prevedere* VERBO
[1] to foresee* ◇ *Non possiamo prevedere cosa succederà.* We can't foresee what will happen.

♦ **come previsto** as expected
[2] to plan ◇ *È previsto per martedì.* It's planned for Tuesday.

---

* *I verbi seguiti da questo simbolo sono irregolari. Si veda anche alle pp.328–338.*

[3] to forecast* (*tempo*) ◇ *È previsto maltempo per il fine settimana.* Bad weather is forecast for the weekend.

preventivo NOME MASC
estimate

◆ **fare un preventivo** to give* an estimate

prevenzione NOME FEM
prevention ◇ *prevenzione degli infortuni* prevention of accidents

previdenza NOME FEM

◆ **la previdenza sociale** social security

previsioni NOME FEM PL

◆ **previsioni del tempo** weather forecast SING ◇ *Cosa dicono le previsioni del tempo per domani?* What is the weather forecast for tomorrow?

previsto NOME MASC

◆ **più del previsto** more than expected

◆ **prima del previsto** earlier than expected

prezioso AGGETTIVO (FEM **preziosa**)

[1] precious (*oggetto*) ◇ *una pietra preziosa* a precious stone

[2] invaluable (*aiuto, consiglio*) ◇ *Il loro consiglio mi è stato prezioso.* Their advice was invaluable to me.

prezzemolo NOME MASC
parsley

prezzo NOME MASC
price ◇ *il prezzo della benzina* the price of petrol ◇ *a metà prezzo* half price ◇ *a prezzo scontato* at a reduced price

prigione NOME FEM
prison

prigioniero, la **prigioniera** NOME MASC, FEM
prisoner

prima AVVERBIO, CONGIUNZIONE

vedi anche **prima** NOME

[1] before ◇ *due giorni prima* two days before ◇ *Prima non lo sapevo.* I didn't know that before.

◆ **prima di** before ◇ *Sono andati via prima di noi.* They left before us. ◇ *Mi sono alzato prima delle sette.* I got up before seven. ◇ *Dobbiamo decidere prima della mia partenza.* We must decide before I leave. ◇ *prima d'ora* before now

[2] earlier (*più presto*) ◇ *È arrivato prima del previsto.* He arrived earlier than expected. ◇ *Domani devo alzarmi un po' prima.* Tomorrow I have to get up a bit earlier.

◆ **prima o poi** sooner or later

◆ **prima possibile** as soon as possible

[3] in advance (*in anticipo*) ◇ *La prossima volta dimmelo prima.* Next time let me know in advance.

prima NOME FEM

vedi anche **prima** AVVERBIO, CONGIUNZIONE

[1] opening night (*a teatro*)

[2] première (*di film*)

◆ **prima elementare** first year at primary school

◆ **prima media** first year at secondary school

◆ **prima superiore** fourth year at secondary school

il **primario** NOME MASC
consultant (*medico*)

il/la **primatista** NOME MASC/FEM (MASC PL i **primatisti**, FEM PL le **primatiste**)
record holder ◇ *il primatista mondiale del salto in lungo* the world record holder for the long jump

il **primato** NOME MASC
record

la **primavera** NOME FEM
spring ◇ *in primavera* in spring

primitivo AGGETTIVO (FEM **primitiva**)
primitive (*popolazione, usanza*)

primo AGGETTIVO, NOME MASC/FEM (FEM **prima**)
first ◇ *le prime due pagine* the first two pages ◇ *il primo luglio* the first of July ◇ *Prendi la prima strada a destra.* Take the first street on the right.

◆ **le prime ore del mattino** the early hours of the morning

◆ **prima classe** first class ◇ *un biglietto di prima classe* a first class ticket ◇ *viaggiare in prima classe* to travel first-class

◆ **essere primo in classifica (1)** (*squadra*) to be* top of the league

◆ **essere primo in classifica (2)** (*disco*) to be* number one in the charts

◆ **in prima pagina** on the front page

◆ **ai primi di maggio** at the beginning of May

◆ **per prima cosa** firstly

◆ **in primo luogo** first of all

◆ **di prima qualità** first-class

◆ **in un primo momento** at first

la **primula** NOME FEM
primrose

principale AGGETTIVO

vedi anche **principale** NOME

main ◇ *È questa la strada principale?* Is this the main road? ◇ *proposizione principale* main clause

il/la **principale** NOME MASC/FEM

vedi anche **principale** AGGETTIVO

boss (*colloquiale*) ◇ *Il principale ti vuole parlare.* The boss wants to speak to you.

principalmente AVVERBIO
mainly

il **principe** NOME MASC
prince

la **principessa** NOME FEM
princess

il/la **principiante** NOME MASC/FEM
beginner

il **principio** NOME MASC

[1] beginning (*inizio*) ◇ *dal principio alla fine* from beginning to end

◆ **al principio** at first

◆ **fin dal principio** right from the start

[2] principle (*concetto, norma*) ◇ *una*

☞

P

questione di principio a matter of principle
◊ *per principio* on principle

privato AGGETTIVO, NOME MASC (FEM **privata**)
private ◊ *la proprietà privata* private
property
◆ **in privato** in private

privilegiato AGGETTIVO (FEM **privilegiata**)
privileged (*individuo, classe*)

il **privilegio** NOME MASC
privilege

privo AGGETTIVO (FEM **priva**)
◆ **privo di** without ◊ *un'albero privo di foglie*
a tree without leaves
◆ **parole prive di significato** meaningless
words
◆ **essere privo di** to have* no ◊ *È privo di
scrupoli.* He's got no scruples.
◆ **privo di sensi** unconscious

i **pro** NOME MASC PL ◊ *i pro e i contro* the pros
and cons

probabile AGGETTIVO
probable

la **probabilità** NOME FEM (PL le **probabilità**)
chance ◊ *Che probabilità hanno di vincere?*
What are their chances of winning? ◊ *Ha
buone probabilità di ottenere il lavoro.* He's
got a good chance of getting the job.
al singolare.
◊ *una probabilità su mille* a chance in a
thousand
◆ **una probabilità su due** a fifty-fifty chance
◆ **con molta probabilità** very probably

probabilmente AVVERBIO
probably

il **problema** NOME MASC (PL i **problemi**)
problem

la **proboscide** NOME FEM
trunk

procedere VERBO
to get* on ◊ *Come procede il lavoro?* How's
the work getting on?
◆ **Gli affari procedono bene.** Business is going
well.
◆ **Il traffico procede lentamente.** The traffic is
moving slowly.

processare VERBO
to try

il **processo** NOME MASC
trial ◊ *un processo per omicidio* a murder
trial
◆ **essere sotto processo** to be* on trial

procurare VERBO
to get* (*trovare*) ◊ *Hai procurato i biglietti?*
Did you get the tickets?

il **prodotto** NOME MASC
product ◊ *È un buon prodotto.* It's a good
product.
◆ **prodotti agricoli** farm produce SING
◆ **prodotti alimentari** foodstuffs
◆ **prodotti di bellezza** cosmetics

◆ **prodotti chimici** chemicals

produrre* VERBO
to produce

la **produzione** NOME FEM
production

professionale AGGETTIVO
professional

la **professione** NOME FEM
occupation ◊ *Professione: infermiera.*
Occupation: nurse.
◆ **la professione medica** the medical
profession

professionista NOME MASC/FEM, AGGETTIVO
(MASC PL **professionisti**, FEM PL **professioniste**)
professional ◊ *un fotografo professionista*
a professional photographer
◆ **i liberi professionisti** the self-employed

il **professore**, la **professoressa** NOME
MASC, FEM
1 teacher (*di scuola*)
2 lecturer (*di università*)
3 professor (*titolare di cattedra
universitaria*)

il **profilo** NOME MASC
profile
◆ **di profilo** in profile

il **profitto** NOME MASC
profit ◊ *un profitto di ottomila euro* an eight
thousand euro profit

la **profondità** NOME FEM (PL le **profondità**)
depth ◊ *la profondità del mare* the depth of
the sea
◆ **avere una profondità di...** to be*...deep ◊ *Il
fiume qui ha una profondità di cinque metri.*
The river here is five metres deep.

profondo AGGETTIVO (FEM **profonda**)
deep ◊ *È profondo otto metri.* It's eight
metres deep.

il **profugo**, la **profuga** NOME MASC, FEM (MASC
PL i **profughi**, FEM PL le **profughe**)
refugee

profumato AGGETTIVO (FEM **profumata**)
1 fragrant (*fiore*)
2 scented (*fazzoletto, saponetta*)

la **profumeria** NOME FEM
perfume shop

> **ⓘ** As well as perfume a **profumeria** sells
> cosmetics, jewellery and gift items.

il **profumo** NOME MASC
perfume (*prodotto*)
◆ **mettersi il profumo** to put* perfume on
◆ **Questi fiori hanno un buon profumo.** These
flowers smell lovely.
◆ **Questa saponetta ha un profumo di limone.**
This soap smells of lemon.

progettare VERBO
to plan

il **progetto** NOME MASC

plan ◊ *i miei progetti per il futuro* my plans
for the future ◊ *il progetto della casa* the
plan of the house
+ **progetto di legge** bill

programma NOME MASC (PL i **programmi**)
1 programme (*televisivo, politico*)
+ **Hai programmi per stasera?** Have you
anything planned for this evening?
2 program (*informatico*)
3 syllabus (*scolastico*)

programmare VERBO
1 to plan (*gita, lavoro*)
2 to program (*al computer*)

programmatore, la **programmatrice**
NOME MASC, FEM
computer programmer

progresso NOME MASC
progress ◊ *i progressi della scienza*
scientific progress
al singolare.
+ **fare progressi** to make* progress ◊ *Sta
facendo progressi in matematica.* She's
making progress in maths.

proibire VERBO
to forbid* ◊ *Mi ha proibito di uscire.* She
has forbidden me to go out.

proiettile NOME MASC
bullet (*pallottola*)

proiettore NOME MASC
projector

prolunga NOME FEM (PL le **prolunghe**)
extension (*di cavo*)

promemoria NOME MASC (PL i **promemoria**)
note

promessa NOME FEM
promise
+ **fare una promessa** to make* a promise
+ **mantenere una promessa** to keep* a
promise

promettere* VERBO
to promise ◊ *Promettimi che scriverai.*
Promise me that you'll write.
+ **Promette bene.** It looks promising.

promuovere* VERBO
+ **essere promosso agli esami** to pass one's
exams
+ **essere promosso** (*squadra, impiegato*) to
be* promoted

pronome NOME MASC
pronoun

pronto AGGETTIVO (FEM **pronta**)
ready ◊ *È pronto il pranzo?* Is lunch ready?
◊ *Sono pronto a tutto.* I'm ready for
anything.
+ **Pronto?** (*al telefono*) Hello!
+ **pronto soccorso** first aid
+ **Pronti? Attenti! Via!** (*nelle gare*) Ready,
steady, go!

pronuncia NOME FEM
pronunciation

pronunciare VERBO

to pronounce (*parola*)

proporre* VERBO
to suggest
+ **proporre di fare qualcosa** to suggest doing
something
suggest regge il gerundio.
◊ *Ho proposto di andare al cinema.* I
suggested going to the cinema.
*È possibile anche dire "I suggested we went
to the cinema".*
+ **proporre un brindisi** to propose a toast

proporzionale AGGETTIVO
proportional

proposito NOME MASC
intention ◊ *È pieno di buoni propositi.* He's
full of good intentions.
+ **di proposito** on purpose ◊ *L'ha fatto di
proposito.* He did it on purpose.
+ **a proposito** by the way ◊ *A proposito, come
sta tua madre?* By the way, how's your
mother?
+ **A proposito di Roberto...** Speaking of
Roberto...

proposizione NOME FEM
clause (*in grammatica*)
+ **proposizione principale** main clause
+ **proposizione secondaria** subordinate
clause

proposta NOME FEM
suggestion ◊ *Ha fatto una proposta.* He
made a suggestion.

proprietà NOME FEM (PL le **proprietà**)
property (PL properties) ◊ *la proprietà
privata* private property

proprietario, la **proprietaria** NOME MASC,
FEM
owner (*di casa, di macchina*)

proprio, propria AGGETTIVO, NOME
vedi anche **proprio** AVVERBIO
own ◊ *L'ha visto con i propri occhi.* He saw
it with his own eyes. ◊ *Ognuno è arrivato
con la propria macchina.* Everybody arrived
in their own car.
+ **Ognuno è tornato a casa propria.**
Everybody went back home.
+ **un nome proprio** a proper noun
+ **mettersi in proprio** to set* up one's own
business ◊ *Si è messo in proprio.* He set up
his own business.

proprio AVVERBIO
vedi anche **proprio** AGGETTIVO, NOME
1 just (*precisamente*) ◊ *Le cose sono
andate proprio così.* That's just how things
went.
2 really (*davvero*) ◊ *Sono proprio stanco.*
I'm really tired.
+ **non...proprio** not...at all ◊ *Non mi piace
proprio.* I don't like it at all.

prosa NOME FEM
prose ◊ *la prosa e la poesia* prose and
poetry
+ **un attore di prosa** a theatre actor

P

il **prosciutto** NOME MASC
ham

♦ **prosciutto cotto** cooked ham
♦ **prosciutto crudo** Parma ham

proseguire VERBO
to continue ◇ *Decise di proseguire il viaggio.* He decided to continue his journey.

la **prospettiva** NOME FEM
[1] prospect *(possibilità)* ◇ *Non ci sono molte prospettive di lavoro.* There aren't many job prospects.
[2] perspective *(di quadro)* ◇ *in prospettiva* in perspective

prossimo AGGETTIVO, NOME MASC/FEM (FEM **prossima**)
next ◇ *Ci vediamo venerdì prossimo.* See you next Friday. ◇ *Scende alla prossima fermata?* Are you getting off at the next stop? ◇ *Avanti il prossimo.* Next please.
♦ **un parente prossimo** a close relative
♦ **passato prossimo** perfect tense

la **prostituta** NOME FEM
prostitute

il/la **protagonista** NOME MASC/FEM (MASC PL i **protagonisti**, FEM PL le **protagoniste**)
protagonist

proteggere* VERBO
to protect

la **protesta** NOME FEM
protest

protestante AGGETTIVO, NOME MASC/FEM
Protestant
Si noti l'uso della maiuscola in inglese.

protestare VERBO
to protest

protetto AGGETTIVO (FEM **protetta**)
sheltered ◇ *un porto protetto* a sheltered harbour
♦ **una specie protetta** a protected species

la **protezione** NOME FEM
protection

la **prova** NOME FEM
[1] test ◇ *un giro di prova* a test run
♦ **Facciamo una prova.** Let's try it.
♦ **prova scritta** written test
♦ **prova orale** oral exam
♦ **in prova** *(assumere)* on a trial basis
[2] proof *(dimostrazione)* ◇ *Ho la prova che è stato lui.* I've got proof that it was him.
[3] evidence *(in tribunale)* ◇ *Non ci sono abbastanza prove per incriminarlo.* There isn't enough evidence to charge him.
al singolare.
[4] rehearsal *(a teatro)*
♦ **prova generale** dress rehearsal

provare VERBO
[1] to try ◇ *Ho provato una nuova crema.* I've tried a new cream. ◇ *Prova questo gelato, ti piacerà.* Try this ice cream. You'll like it. ◇ *Ho provato il suo motorino.* I tried

out his moped. ◇ *Perché non provi a parlargli?* Why don't you try talking to him?
[2] to try on *(abito, scarpe)* ◇ *Provati questo maglione.* Try this jumper on.
[3] to feel* *(sentire)* ◇ *Ho provato rabbia quando l'ho saputo.* I felt angry when I found out.
[4] to prove *(dimostrare)* ◇ *Posso provare che ero a casa.* I can prove I was at home.

provenire* VERBO
to come* ◇ *Proviene dagli Stati Uniti.* It comes from the United States.

il **proverbio** NOME MASC
proverb

la **provetta** NOME FEM
test tube
♦ **bambino in provetta** test-tube baby

il **provider** NOME MASC (PL i **provider**)
provider

la **provincia** NOME FEM (PL le **province**)
province

il **provino** NOME MASC
[1] screen test *(per il cinema)* ◇ *Ha fatto un provino.* She did a screen test.
[2] trailer *(anteprima di film)*

provocare VERBO
[1] to cause ◇ *La nebbia ha provocato molti incidenti.* The fog caused a lot of accidents.
[2] to provoke *(persona)* ◇ *Non provocarmi!* Don't provoke me!

la **provocazione** NOME FEM
provocation

il **provvedimento** NOME MASC
measure ◇ *un provvedimento disciplinare* a disciplinary measure

provvisorio AGGETTIVO (FEM **provvisoria**)
♦ **orario provvisorio** provisional timetable
♦ **un lavoro provvisorio** a temporary job
♦ **un governo provvisorio** an interim government

le **provviste** NOME FEM PL
provisions ◇ *Abbiamo abbastanza provviste per due settimane.* We've got enough provisions for two weeks.
♦ **fare provviste** to stock up

la **prua** NOME FEM
bow

prudente AGGETTIVO
careful ◇ *un guidatore prudente* a careful driver ◇ *Sii prudente!* Be careful!
♦ **Non è prudente guidare quando si è stanchi.** It's not a good idea to drive when you're tired.
♦ **È più prudente aspettare qui.** It would be better to wait here.

la **prudenza** NOME FEM
♦ **Guida con prudenza!** Drive carefully!
♦ **per prudenza** as a precaution

prudere VERBO
to itch ◇ *Mi prude il naso.* My nose is

itching.

la **prugna** NOME FEM
plum
+ **prugna secca** prune

l **prurito** NOME MASC
+ **Ho prurito alla mano.** My hand is itching.

a **psicanalista** NOME MASC/FEM (MASC PL gli **psicanalisti**, FEM PL le **psicanaliste**)
psychoanalyst

a **psichiatra** NOME MASC/FEM (MASC PL gli **psichiatri**, FEM PL le **psichiatre**)
psychiatrist

psichiatrico AGGETTIVO (FEM **psichiatrica**, MASC PL **psichiatrici**, FEM PL **psichiatriche**)
psychiatric

a **psicologia** NOME FEM
psychology

psicologico AGGETTIVO (FEM **psicologica**, MASC PL **psicologi**, FEM PL **psicologhe**)
psychological

o **psicologo**, la **psicologa** NOME MASC, FEM (MASC PL gli **psicologi**, FEM PL le **psicologhe**)
psychologist

pubblicare VERBO
to publish

a **pubblicazione** NOME FEM
publication
+ **le pubblicazioni** (di matrimonio) the banns

a **pubblicità** NOME FEM (PL le **pubblicità**)
[1] advert
ad `US`
(singolo annuncio)
◇ Ho visto la pubblicità sul giornale. I saw the advert in the paper.
[2] adverts PL
ads PL `US`
(insieme degli annunci)
◇ C'è troppa pubblicità in TV. There are too many adverts on TV.
+ **fare pubblicità a qualcosa** to advertise something ◇ Fa pubblicità ad uno shampoo. She advertises a shampoo.
[3] advertising (attività) ◇ Si occupa di pubblicità. He's in advertising.

pubblico AGGETTIVO (FEM **pubblica**, MASC PL **pubblici**, FEM PL **pubbliche**)
`vedi anche **pubblico** NOME`
public ◇ la pubblica amministrazione public administration ◇ pubbliche relazioni public relations
+ **una scuola pubblica** a state school

il **pubblico** NOME MASC
`vedi anche **pubblico** AGGETTIVO`
[1] public ◇ È aperto al pubblico di domenica. It's open to the public on Sundays.
+ **in pubblico** in public
[2] audience (spettatori)

pudico AGGETTIVO (FEM **pudica**, MASC PL **pudici**, FEM PL **pudiche**)
modest

il **pugilato** NOME MASC
boxing ◇ un incontro di pugilato a boxing match

il **pugile** NOME MASC
boxer

pugnalare VERBO
to stab

il **pugnale** NOME MASC
dagger

il **pugno** NOME MASC
fist ◇ con i pugni stretti with clenched fists
+ **dare un pugno a qualcuno** to punch somebody ◇ Gli ho dato un pugno sul naso. I punched him on the nose.

la **pulce** NOME FEM
flea

il **pulcino** NOME MASC
chick

pulire VERBO
to clean ◇ Stava pulendo l'interno della macchina. She was cleaning the inside of the car.
+ **pulirsi i piedi** to wipe one's feet
+ **far pulire qualcosa** to have* something cleaned ◇ Ho fatto pulire la macchina. I had my car cleaned.
+ **pulire a secco** to dry-clean

pulito AGGETTIVO (FEM **pulita**)
clean ◇ un pavimento pulito a clean floor
+ **avere la coscienza pulita** to have* a clear conscience

la **pulitura** NOME FEM
+ **pulitura a secco** (negozio) dry cleaner's

le **pulizie** NOME FEM PL
+ **fare le pulizie** to do* the cleaning

il **pullman** NOME MASC (PL i **pullman**)
coach

il **pulmino** NOME MASC
minibus

il **pulsante** NOME MASC
button ◇ Premi il pulsante. Press the button.

pungere* VERBO
to sting* (insetto, ortica) ◇ L'ha punto una vespa. A wasp stung him.
+ **pungersi un dito** to prick one's finger

punire VERBO
to punish

la **punizione** NOME FEM
punishment ◇ una punizione severa a harsh punishment
+ **calcio di punizione** free kick

la **punta** NOME FEM
[1] point (di matita, di ago, di coltello)
+ **fare la punta alla matita** to sharpen a pencil
[2] top (di campanile, di albero, di monte)
[3] touch (minima parte) ◇ una punta di invidia a touch of envy
+ **a punta** pointed ◇ un paio di scarpe a punta a pair of pointed shoes
+ **in punta di piedi** on tiptoe

P

☞

◆ **ore di punta** peak hours
◆ **doppie punte** (*capelli*) split ends
puntare VERBO
  to point (*arma, dito*) ◇ *Le ha puntato un fucile contro.* He pointed a gun at her.
  ◆ **puntare su** (*scommettere*) to bet* on ◇ *Ha puntato su quel cavallo.* He bet on that horse.
la **puntata** NOME FEM
  ☐ episode (*di sceneggiato*) ◇ *Hai visto la prima puntata?* Did you see the first episode?
  ☐ flying visit (*breve sosta*) ◇ *Farò una puntata a Parigi.* I'm going to pay a flying visit to Paris.
la **punteggiatura** NOME FEM
  punctuation
il **punteggio** NOME MASC
  score (*in gara*) ◇ *Qual è il punteggio?* What's the score?
la **puntina** NOME FEM
  ◆ **puntina da disegno** drawing pin, US: thumbtack
il **puntino** NOME MASC
  dot
  ◆ **cotto a puntino** cooked to perfection
il **punto** NOME MASC
  ☐ point ◇ *Ha segnato tre punti.* He scored three points. ◇ *Su questo punto siamo d'accordo.* We agree on this point.
  ◆ **A che punto sei?** How are you getting on?
  ◆ **alle sei in punto** at six o'clock sharp
  ◆ **di punto in bianco** suddenly
  ◆ **punto debole** weak point
  ◆ **punto di partenza** starting point
  ◆ **punto d'incontro** meeting place
  ◆ **punto di vista** point of view
  ◆ **punti neri** (*sul viso*) blackheads
  ☐ stitch (*con ago*)
  ☐ full stop
  period US
  (*segno di punteggiatura*)
  ◆ **due punti** colon
  ◆ **punto e virgola** semicolon
  ◆ **punto esclamativo** exclamation mark
  ◆ **punto interrogativo** question mark
puntuale AGGETTIVO
  punctual ◇ *È sempre puntuale.* He's always punctual.
  ◆ **arrivare puntuale** to arrive on time
la **puntura** NOME FEM

☐ injection ◇ *Gli ha fatto una puntura sul braccio.* She gave him an injection in his arm.
☐ sting (*di insetto*)
☐ bite (*di zanzara*)
Attenzione! In inglese esiste la parola **puncture**, *che si usa per indicare la foratura di una gomma.*
il **pupazzo** NOME MASC
  puppet
  ◆ **pupazzo di neve** snowman
la **pupilla** NOME FEM
  pupil
purché CONGIUNZIONE
  as long as ◇ *Verrò con te purché non piova.* I'll come with you as long as it doesn't rain.
pure CONGIUNZIONE, AVVERBIO
  ☐ too (*anche*) ◇ *È venuto pure lui.* He came too.
  ☐ even though (*anche se*) ◇ *Pur non volendolo ho dovuto farlo.* I had to do it even though I didn't want to.
  ◆ **Faccia pure!** Please do!
il **purè** NOME MASC
  ◆ **purè di patate** mashed potatoes
il **purgante** NOME MASC
  laxative
puro AGGETTIVO (FEM **pura**)
  pure ◇ *pura lana vergine* pure new wool
  ◆ **È la pura verità.** It's the honest truth.
  ◆ **per puro caso** by sheer chance
  ◆ **per pura curiosità** out of sheer curiosity
il/la **purosangue** NOME MASC/FEM (PL i/le **purosangue**)
  thoroughbred (*cavallo*)
purtroppo AVVERBIO
  unfortunately
il **pus** NOME MASC
  pus
la **puttana** NOME FEM
  whore (*volgare*)
  ◆ **figlio di puttana** son of a bitch (*volgare*)
la **puzza** NOME FEM
  stink
puzzare VERBO
  to stink* ◇ *Puzza di fumo.* It stinks of smoke.
  ◆ **La faccenda puzza d'imbroglio.** There's something fishy about the whole thing.
puzzolente AGGETTIVO
  stinking

---

* I verbi seguiti da questo simbolo sono irregolari. Si veda anche alle pp.328–338.

Q

qua AVVERBIO

here ◇ *Vieni qua.* Come here. ◇ *Eccomi qua.* Here I am.

- **qua dentro** in here ◇ *Le penne e le matite sono qua dentro.* The pens and pencils are in here.
- **qua sotto** under here ◇ *Qua sotto c'è la tua camicia.* Your shirt is under here.
- **Abita qua sotto.** She lives on the floor below.
- **Vieni più in qua.** Come closer.
- **di qua** this way ◇ *Passavo di qua.* I was passing this way.
- **al di qua del fiume** on this side of the river
- **Da quando in qua?** Since when? ◇ *Da quando in qua ti interessi di musica classica?* Since when have you been interested in classical music?

il quaderno NOME MASC
exercise book

il quadrante NOME MASC
face (*di orologio*)

quadrare VERBO

- **Qui c'è qualcosa che non quadra.** There's something wrong here.

quadrato AGGETTIVO (FEM quadrata)
vedi anche **quadrato** NOME
square ◇ *una tovaglia quadrata* a square tablecloth ◇ *due metri quadrati* two square metres

il quadrato NOME MASC
vedi anche **quadrato** AGGETTIVO
1 square ◇ *un quadrato rosso* a red square
2 ring (*nel pugilato*)

il quadrifoglio NOME MASC
four-leaf clover

il quadrimestre NOME MASC
term (*a scuola*)

il quadro NOME MASC
painting ◇ *un quadro di Van Gogh* a painting by Van Gogh ◇ *un quadro a olio* an oil painting

- **dipingere un quadro** to paint a picture
- **quadri** (*nei giochi di carte*) diamonds
- **a quadri** checked ◇ *una giacca a quadri* a checked jacket

quaggiù AVVERBIO
down here

la quaglia NOME FEM
quail

qualche AGGETTIVO

Nelle frasi affermative in genere si usa **some** *seguito dal nome al plurale.*

◇ *Ho comprato qualche disco.* I've bought some records. ◇ *Ha qualche amico a Londra.* He has some friends in London.

Nelle domande dirette e indirette in genere si usa **any** *seguito dal nome al plurale.*

◇ *Hai qualche sigaretta?* Have you got any cigarettes? ◇ *Mi ha chiesto se c'era qualche problema.* He asked me if there were any problems.

Quando si offre o si richiede qualcosa in genere si usa **some** *anche nelle domande.*

◇ *Vuole qualche rivista mentre aspetta?* Would you like some magazines while you're waiting? ◇ *Posso prendere in prestito qualche CD?* Can I borrow some CDs?

- **qualche volta** sometimes ◇ *Qualche volta si sente un po' giù.* She sometimes feels a bit down.
- **Vieni a trovarmi qualche volta.** Come and see me some time.
- **L'ho incontrato qualche volta.** I've met him a couple of times.
- **fra qualche mese** in a few months
- **per qualche giorno** for a few days
- **in qualche modo** somehow ◇ *In qualche modo riuscirò a trovarlo.* I'll manage to find him somehow.

qualcosa PRONOME

Nelle frasi affermative in genere si usa **something**.

◇ *Ci dev'essere qualcosa che non va.* There must be something wrong. ◇ *Voglio fare qualcos'altro.* I'd like to do something else.

Nelle domande dirette e indirette si usa in genere **anything**.

◇ *Qualcosa da dichiarare?* Anything to declare? ◇ *Vedi qualcosa?* Can you see anything? ◇ *Fammi sapere se hai bisogno di qualcosa.* Let me know if you need anything. ◇ *Gli ho chiesto se c'era qualcosa che non andava.* I asked him if anything was wrong.

Quando si offre o si richiede qualcosa in genere si usa **something** *anche nelle domande.*

◇ *Vuole qualcosa da mangiare?* Would you like something to eat? ◇ *Mi dai qualcosa da bere, per favore?* Can I have something to drink, please?

Quando si vuole tradurre **qualcosa di** *si noti che* **something** *e* **anything** *non vogliono la preposizione "of".*

◇ *Vorrei qualcosa di nuovo.* I'd like something new. ◇ *Hai visto qualcosa di bello?* Did you see anything nice?

qualcuno PRONOME

1 somebody (*persona*) ◇ *Ha telefonato qualcuno per te.* Somebody phoned for you. ◇ *Chiedilo a qualcun altro.* Ask somebody else. ◇ *Cosa fai qui? Aspetti qualcuno?* What are you doing here? Are you waiting for somebody? ◇ *Qualcuno ha perso la sua borsa.* Somebody has lost their bag.

Si può usare anche **someone**.

◇ *C'è qualcuno alla porta.* There's someone ☞

at the door.

Nelle domande si usa anybody o anyone quando non si intende una persona in particolare.

◇ *C'è qualcuno in casa?* Is there anybody at home? ◇ *Qualcuno ha visto il mio ombrello?* Has anyone seen my umbrella? ◇ *Hai incontrato qualcun altro alla festa?* Did you meet anybody else at the party?

2 some *(oggetto)* ◇ *Prendine ancora qualcuno.* Take some more. ◇ *Hai visto i suoi film? – Ne ho visto qualcuno.* Have you seen his films? – I've seen some of them.

quale AGGETTIVO, PRONOME

Nelle frasi interrogative, se la domanda è generale si usa what per gli oggetti, e who per le persone; quando quale significa "quale di questi" si usa which sia per gli oggetti che per le persone.

1 what *(oggetto)* ◇ *Qual è il tuo colore preferito?* What's your favourite colour? ◇ *Quali programmi hai?* What are your plans?

◆ **Per quale ragione?** Why?

2 who *(persona)* ◇ *Qual è il tuo cantante preferito?* Who's your favourite singer?

3 which *(oggetto, persona)* ◇ *Quale dei due vuoi?* Which one do you want? ◇ *Quali giocatori hanno scelto per la squadra?* Which players have they chosen for the team?

Il pronome relativo il quale viene spesso omesso in inglese.

◇ *La ragione per la quale sono venuto è semplice.* The reason why I came is simple. ◇ *Il ragazzo con il quale esco è molto alto.* The boy I go out with is very tall. ◇ *Questi sono gli amici con i quali siamo andati in vacanza.* These are the friends we went on holiday with. ◇ *La signora alla quale ho telefonato è un'amica di mia madre.* The lady I phoned is a friend of my mother's.

la **qualifica** NOME FEM (PL le **qualifiche**)
qualification

qualificarsi VERBO

to qualify ◇ *La squadra si è qualificata per i mondiali.* The team has qualified for the World Cup.

qualificato AGGETTIVO (FEM **qualificata**)

1 qualified ◇ *Non penso che sia qualificato per quel lavoro.* I don't think he's qualified for that job.

2 skilled ◇ *un operaio qualificato* a skilled worker

la **qualificazione** NOME FEM

◆ **una partita di qualificazione** a qualifying match

◆ **un corso di qualificazione professionale** a vocational training course

la **qualità** NOME FEM (PL le **qualità**)
quality (PL qualities) ◇ *Preferisco la qualità*

alla quantità. I prefer quality to quantity.

◆ **di qualità** quality ◇ *un prodotto di qualità* a quality product

◆ **di ottima qualità** top-quality ◇ *È una stoffa di ottima qualità.* It's top-quality fabric.

qualsiasi AGGETTIVO

any ◇ *in qualsiasi momento* at any time

◆ **qualsiasi cosa** anything ◇ *Farei qualsiasi cosa per lei.* I'd do anything for her.

◆ **Qualsiasi cosa accada, telefonami.** Whatever happens, phone me.

◆ **Mettiti un vestito qualsiasi.** Wear anything you like.

◆ **a qualsiasi costo** no matter what ◇ *Ci riuscirò a qualsiasi costo.* I'll manage it no matter what.

qualunque = **qualsiasi**

quando CONGIUNZIONE, AVVERBIO

when ◇ *Quando vai in vacanza?* When are you going on holiday? ◇ *Quando arriverà?* When's he arriving? ◇ *Non so quando abbia telefonato.* I don't know when he phoned. ◇ *Passerò a trovarti, ma non so quando.* I'll come and see you, but I don't know when. ◇ *Quando finirò verrò da te.* When I finish I'll come to your place. ◇ *Lo comprerò quando avrò abbastanza denaro.* I'll buy it when I have enough money. ◇ *Quando avrò finito verrò da te.* When I've finished I'll come to your place.

◆ **da quando** since ◇ *Abita qui da quando era piccola.* She has lived here since she was a child.

◆ **Da quando sei qui?** How long have you been here?

◆ **di quando in quando** from time to time ◇ *Ci penso di quando in quando.* I think about it from time to time.

la **quantità** NOME FEM (PL le **quantità**)
quantity (PL quantities) ◇ *Preferisco la qualità alla quantità.* I prefer quality to quantity.

◆ **in grande quantità** in large quantities

al plurale

◆ **una quantità di** lots of ◇ *Hanno invitato una quantità di gente.* They invited lots of people. ◇ *Ho una quantità di cose da fare.* I've got lots of things to do.

quanto AGGETTIVO, PRONOME, AVVERBIO (FEM **quanta**)

1 how much ◇ *Quanto pane hai comprato?* How much bread did you buy? ◇ *Quanto costa?* How much does it cost? ◇ *Quanto pesi?* How much do you weigh? ◇ *Quant'è?* How much is it?

◆ **Quanti?** How many? ◇ *Quanti ne vuoi?* How many do you want?

◆ **Quanti anni hai?** How old are you?

◆ **Quante?** How many? ◇ *Quante ragazze ci sono in classe?* How many girls are there in the class?

2 <u>how long</u> (*tempo*) ◊ *Quanto starai via?* How long will you be away? ◊ *Da quanto sei qui?* How long have you been here? ◊ *Quanto tempo ci vorrà?* How long will it take?

3 <u>what a</u> (*nelle esclamazioni*) ◊ *Quanto tempo sprecato!* What a waste of time! ◊ *Quante storie!* What a fuss!
* **Quanta gente!** What a lot of people!
* **Quanti ne abbiamo oggi?** What's the date today?
* **per quanto ne sappia** as far as I know

quaranta NUMERO
forty

quarantesimo AGGETTIVO, NOME MASC (FEM **quarantesima**)
fortieth

quarantina NUMERO
* **È sulla quarantina.** He's about forty.

la **quaresima** NOME FEM
Lent
Si noti l'uso della maiuscola in inglese.

la **quarta** NOME FEM
vedi anche **quarta** NOME, AGGETTIVO
fourth gear (*marcia*)
* **quarta elementare** fourth year at primary school
* **quarta superiore** seventh year at secondary school

il **quartiere** NOME MASC
area ◊ *un quartiere malfamato* a rough area ◊ *un quartiere residenziale* a residential area
* **quartier generale** headquarters PL

quarto AGGETTIVO (FEM **quarta**)
vedi anche **quarto** NOME
fourth ◊ *Abito al quarto piano.* I live on the fourth floor. ◊ *È arrivato quarto nella gara.* He came fourth in the competition. ◊ *La squadra è quarta in classifica.* The team is fourth in the league.

il **quarto** NOME MASC
vedi anche **quarto** AGGETTIVO
quarter ◊ *un quarto della miscela* a quarter of the mixture ◊ *un quarto di vino* a quarter-litre bottle of wine ◊ *un quarto di pollo* a quarter chicken ◊ *un quarto d'ora* a quarter of an hour ◊ *tre quarti d'ora* three quarters of an hour ◊ *Sono le tre e un quarto.* It's a quarter past three. ◊ *Sono le due meno un quarto.* It's a quarter to two. ◊ *Sono le otto e tre quarti.* It's a quarter to nine.
* **quarti di finale** quarterfinals

il **quarzo** NOME MASC
quartz

quasi AVVERBIO
1 <u>nearly</u> ◊ *Ha quasi vent'anni.* He's nearly twenty.
2 <u>hardly</u> ◊ *Non è venuto quasi nessuno.* Hardly anybody came. ◊ *Non sento quasi niente.* I can hardly hear anything.

La negazione "non" non va tradotta.
* **quasi mai** hardly ever ◊ *Non lo vedo quasi mai.* I hardly ever see him.

quassù AVVERBIO
up here

quattordicenne AGGETTIVO
fourteen-year-old

quattordicesimo AGGETTIVO (FEM **quattordicesima**)
fourteenth

quattordici NUMERO
fourteen ◊ *Ho quattordici anni.* I'm fourteen.
* **le quattordici** two p.m.
* **il quattordici dicembre** the fourteenth of December

quattro NUMERO
four ◊ *Ha quattro anni.* He's four. ◊ *le quattro del pomeriggio* four o'clock in the afternoon
* **il quattro dicembre** the fourth of December
* **fare quattro chiacchiere** to have* a chat ◊ *Abbiamo fatto quattro chiacchiere.* We had a chat.
* **fare quattro passi** to go* for a little walk ◊ *Facciamo quattro passi.* Let's go for a little walk.
* **a quattr'occhi** face to face ◊ *Vorrei parlarti a quattr'occhi.* I'd like to speak to you face to face.

quattrocento NUMERO
four hundred ◊ *quattrocento sterline* four hundred pounds
* **il Quattrocento** the fifteenth century

quello AGGETTIVO, PRONOME (FEM **quella**)
1 <u>that</u> ◊ *Dammi quel libro.* Give me that book. ◊ *Chi è quella donna?* Who's that woman? ◊ *Cos'è quello?* What's that?
2 <u>that one</u> ◊ *Preferisci questo o quello?* Do you prefer this one or that one?
* **il mio cappotto e quello di Sara** my coat and Sara's
* **quello là** that ◊ *Quello là è il mio professore.* That's my teacher.
* **Prendo quello là.** I'll take that one.
* **quelli** those ◊ *Dove hai comprato quei pantaloni?* Where did you buy those trousers? ◊ *Quelle ragazze abitano qui vicino.* Those girls live near here. ◊ *Penso che quelle siano le mie scarpe.* I think those are my shoes. ◊ *Prendo quelli.* I'll have those.
* **quello che** what ◊ *Ho fatto quello che potevo.* I did what I could. ◊ *Da quello che ho sentito sei molto bravo a tennis.* From what I've heard you're very good at tennis.

la **quercia** NOME FEM (PL le **querce**)
oak

il **questionario** NOME MASC
questionnaire

la **questione** NOME FEM
matter ◊ *Si tratta di una questione*

personale. It's a personal matter. ◊ *È solo questione di tempo*. It's only a matter of time. ◊ *È una questione di vita o di morte*. It's a matter of life and death.

questo AGGETTIVO, PRONOME (FEM **questa**)
this ◊ *Questa gonna è troppo stretta*. This skirt is too tight. ◊ *Cos'è questo?* What's this? ◊ *Questo è il tuo posto*. This is your seat.
+ **Dove hai comprato questo quadro?** Where did you buy that picture?
+ **questi** these ◊ *Queste scarpe sono comode*. These shoes are comfortable.
+ **questo qua** this ◊ *Questo qua è il mio migliore amico*. This is my best friend.
+ **Prendo questo qua.** I'll have this one.
+ **E con questo?** So what?
+ **Questo è quanto.** That's all.

la **questura** NOME FEM
police headquarters SING

qui AVVERBIO
here ◊ *Vieni qui*. Come here. ◊ *Eccomi qui*. Here I am.
+ **qui dentro** in here ◊ *Non c'è molto spazio qui dentro*. There's not much room in here.
+ **qui sotto** under here ◊ *Qui sotto c'è la tua camicia*. Your shirt's under here.
+ **Abita qui sotto.** She lives on the floor below.

quindi AVVERBIO, CONGIUNZIONE
[1] then (*poi*) ◊ *Ho cenato e quindi sono andato al cinema*. I had dinner and then went to the cinema.
[2] so (*di conseguenza*) ◊ *Avevo freddo e quindi mi sono messo il maglione*. I was cold, so I put on a sweater.

quindicenne AGGETTIVO
fifteen-year-old

quindicesimo AGGETTIVO (FEM **quindicesima**)
fifteenth

quindici NUMERO
fifteen ◊ *Ho quindici anni*. I'm fifteen.
+ **le quindici** three p.m.
+ **il quindici dicembre** the fifteenth of December

+ **quindici giorni** a fortnight, US: two weeks

la **quindicina** NOME FEM
+ **una quindicina** about fifteen ◊ *C'erano una quindicina di persone a tavola*. There were about fifteen people round the table.
+ **una quindicina di giorni** a fortnight, US: two weeks

la **quinta** NOME FEM
vedi anche **quinto** NOME, AGGETTIVO
fifth gear (*marcia*)
+ **quinta elementare** fifth year at primary school
+ **quinta superiore** final year at secondary school

il **quintale** NOME MASC
one hundred kilos ◊ *Questa cassa pesa più di un quintale*. This box weighs more than a hundred kilos.
+ **Pesa un quintale!** (*moltissimo*) It weighs a ton!

quinto AGGETTIVO, NOME MASC (FEM **quinta**)
fifth ◊ *Abito al quinto piano*. I live on the fifth floor. ◊ *È arrivato quinto nella gara*. He came fifth in the competition. ◊ *La squadra è quinta in classifica*. The team is fifth in the league. ◊ *un quinto* a fifth ◊ *un quinto della popolazione* a fifth of the population

il **quiz** NOME MASC (PL **i quiz**)
question ◊ *i quiz della patente* the questions for the driving test
+ **gioco a quiz** quiz show

la **quota** NOME FEM
+ **L'aereo volava a bassa quota.** The plane was flying low.
+ **prendere quota** to gain height
+ **quota d'iscrizione** (*ad un club*) membership fee

quotidiano AGGETTIVO (FEM **quotidiana**)
vedi anche **quotidiano** NOME
daily ◊ *la vita quotidiana* daily life

il **quotidiano** NOME MASC
vedi anche **quotidiano** AGGETTIVO
daily paper

R

rabbia NOME FEM
  [1] rage ◊ *Urlava dalla rabbia.* He howled with rage.
  • **Mi fanno una rabbia!** They make me so angry!
  • **Che rabbia!** That's so annoying!
  [2] rabies SING (*malattia*)

rabbrividire VERBO
  to shiver

raccapricciante AGGETTIVO
  horrifying ◊ *una scena raccapricciante* a horrifying scene

il **raccattapalle** NOME MASC (PL i **raccattapalle**)
  ballboy

la **racchetta** NOME FEM
  [1] racket (*da tennis*)
  [2] bat (*da ping-pong*)

raccogliere* VERBO
  [1] to pick up ◊ *Mi ero chinato a raccogliere la penna.* I had bent down to pick up the pen.
  [2] to pick (*fiori, frutta*) ◊ *Abbiamo raccolto un mazzo di fiori.* We picked a bunch of flowers.
  [3] to collect ◊ *Stiamo raccogliendo libri usati per la biblioteca.* We're collecting second-hand books for the library.

la **raccolta** NOME FEM
  collection ◊ *la mia raccolta di CD* my CD collection
  • **fare raccolta di** to collect ◊ *Faccio raccolta di cartoline.* I collect postcards.

il **raccolto** NOME MASC
  harvest

raccomandabile AGGETTIVO
  • **poco raccomandabile** not to be trusted ◊ *È un tipo poco raccomandabile.* He's not to be trusted.

raccomandare VERBO
  to recommend ◊ *L'albergo è raccomandato dalla guida.* The hotel is recommended by the guide.
  • **mi raccomando** please ◊ *Mi raccomando, scrivimi!* Please write to me!
  • **Non perderlo, mi raccomando!** Please don't lose it!

la **raccomandata** NOME FEM
  recorded delivery (PL recorded deliveries) ◊ *Spediscilo per raccomandata.* Send it by recorded delivery.

raccontare VERBO
  to tell* ◊ *Mi ha raccontato una barzelletta molto divertente.* He told me a very funny joke. ◊ *Dai, raccontami tutto.* Come on, tell me all about it.

il **racconto** NOME MASC
  short story (PL short stories) ◊ *un racconto di Calvino* a short story by Calvino
  • **racconti per bambini** children's stories

il **radar** NOME MASC (PL i **radar**)
  radar

raddoppiare VERBO
  to double ◊ *Il prezzo del biglietto è raddoppiato.* The price of the ticket has doubled.

raddrizzare VERBO
  to straighten

radere* VERBO
  to shave ◊ *S'è fatto radere i capelli a zero.* He's had his head shaved.
  • **radersi** to shave ◊ *Si rade ogni mattina.* He shaves every morning.

il **radiatore** NOME MASC
  radiator

la **radiazione** NOME FEM
  radiation

radicale AGGETTIVO
  radical ◊ *un cambiamento radicale* a radical change

la **radice** NOME FEM
  root

la **radio** NOME FEM (PL le **radio**)
  radio ◊ *L'ho sentito alla radio.* I heard it on the radio.

radioattivo AGGETTIVO (FEM **radioattiva**)
  radioactive ◊ *scorie radioattive* radioactive waste

la **radiocronaca** NOME FEM (PL le **radiocronache**)
  commentary (PL commentaries) ◊ *la radiocronaca della partita* the commentary on the match

la **radiografia** NOME FEM
  X-ray

il **radioregistratore** NOME MASC
  radio cassette player

la **radiosveglia** NOME FEM
  radio alarm

rado AGGETTIVO (FEM **rada**)
  thin (*capelli*) ◊ *sempre più radi* thinner and thinner
  • **di rado** rarely ◊ *Vanno di rado al ristorante.* They rarely go to a restaurant.

la **raffica** NOME FEM (PL le **raffiche**)
  • **una raffica di vento** a gust of wind
  • **una raffica di mitra** a burst of machine-gun fire

raffigurare VERBO
  to show* ◊ *Il quadro raffigura la presa della Bastiglia.* The picture shows the storming of the Bastille.

raffinato AGGETTIVO (FEM **raffinata**)
  sophisticated ◊ *una donna raffinata* a sophisticated woman

il **raffreddamento** NOME MASC
  cooling ◊ *raffreddamento ad aria* air cooling

raffreddare VERBO
  to cool ◊ *Lascia raffreddare la torta.* Leave ☞

the cake to cool.
* **raffreddarsi** to get* cold ◊ *Non lasciare che la minestra si raffreddi.* Don't let the soup get cold.

raffreddato AGGETTIVO (FEM **raffreddata**)
* **essere raffreddato** to have* a cold ◊ *Sono raffreddata.* I've got a cold.

il **raffreddore** NOME MASC
cold ◊ *Prenderai un raffreddore!* You'll get a cold! *Ha il raffreddore.* He's got a cold.
* **raffreddore da fieno** hay fever

la **ragazza** NOME FEM
[1] girl ◊ *una ragazza alta e bionda* a tall blonde girl
[2] girlfriend ◊ *È la mia ragazza.* She's my girlfriend.
* **ragazza alla pari** au-pair ◊ *È una ragazza alla pari.* She's an au-pair.

il **ragazzo** NOME MASC
[1] boy ◊ *un ragazzo irlandese* an Irish boy
[2] boyfriend ◊ *Ha litigato con il suo ragazzo.* She's quarrelled with her boyfriend.
Quando ragazzi indica maschi e femmine non si traduce boys ma children.
◊ *È in vacanza con sua moglie e i ragazzi.* He's on holiday with his wife and children.
A volte ragazzi non viene tradotto.
◊ *Dai ragazzi, andiamo via.* Come on, let's go!

il **raggio** NOME MASC
ray ◊ *un raggio di sole* a ray of sunlight
* **raggi X** X-rays

raggiungere* VERBO
to reach ◊ *La temperatura può raggiungere i quaranta gradi.* The temperature can reach forty degrees.
* **Vi raggiungo più tardi.** I'll join you later.

ragionare VERBO
to think* ◊ *Ragionaci su!* Think about it!
◊ *Quando ho fame non ragiono più.* I can't think when I'm hungry.

la **ragione** NOME FEM
reason ◊ *Avrà le sue buone ragioni per dire di no.* He must have his reasons for refusing.
* **aver ragione** to be* right ◊ *Sì, hai perfettamente ragione.* Yes, you're quite right.

la **ragioneria** NOME FEM
accounting ◊ *Studia ragioneria.* She's studying accounting

ragionevole AGGETTIVO
[1] sensible (*persona, proposta*) ◊ *Sii ragionevole!* Be sensible!
[2] reasonable (*prezzo, offerta*) ◊ *Il prezzo mi sembra ragionevole.* The price seems reasonable.

il **ragioniere**, la **ragioniera** NOME MASC, FEM
accountant ◊ *È ragioniere.* He is an accountant.

la **ragnatela** NOME FEM
cobweb ◊ *C'erano un sacco di ragnatele.* There were lots of cobwebs.

il **ragno** NOME MASC
spider ◊ *Ho paura dei ragni.* I'm scared of spiders.

il **ragù** NOME MASC (PL i **ragù**)
meat sauce ◊ *spaghetti al ragù* spaghetti with meat sauce

rallegrare VERBO
[1] to cheer up ◊ *La notizia ha rallegrato tutti.* The news cheered everyone up.
[2] to brighten up ◊ *Quel bel tappeto giallo rallegra la stanza.* That lovely yellow carpet brightens up the room.

rallentare VERBO
to slow down ◊ *Rallenta, c'è un passaggio pedonale.* Slow down, there's a pedestrian crossing.

il **rallentatore** NOME MASC
* **al rallentatore** in slow motion

il **rally** NOME MASC (PL i **rally**)
rally (PL rallies) ◊ *il rally di Montecarlo* the Monte Carlo rally

il **rame** NOME MASC
copper

rammendare VERBO
[1] to darn (*calzini*)
[2] to mend (*giacca, pantaloni*)

il **ramo** NOME MASC
[1] branch (*di albero*)
[2] field (*campo*) ◊ *Non è il suo ramo.* It's not his field.

il **ramoscello** NOME MASC
twig

la **rampa** NOME FEM
* **rampa di scale** flight of stairs
* **rampa d'accesso** ramp

il **rampicante** NOME MASC
climber

la **rana** NOME FEM
frog (*animale*)
* **nuotare a rana** to do* the breaststroke
◊ *Sai nuotare a rana?* Can you do the breaststroke?

rancido AGGETTIVO (FEM **rancida**)
rancid

randagio AGGETTIVO (FEM **randagia**, MASC PL **randagi**, FEM PL **randage**)
stray ◊ *un cane randagio* a stray dog

rannicchiarsi VERBO
to crouch ◊ *Era rannicchiato dietro la macchina.* He was crouching behind the car.

la **rapa** NOME FEM
turnip

rapace AGGETTIVO
* **uccello rapace** bird of prey

rapidamente AVVERBIO
quickly ◊ *L'incendio si è esteso rapidamente.* The fire spread quickly.

rapido AGGETTIVO (FEM **rapida**)
quick ◊ *Gli ho dato solo una rapida occhiata.* I just had a quick look at it.

il **rapimento** NOME MASC
kidnapping ◊ *Il rapimento è avvenuto in pieno giorno.* The kidnapping happened in broad daylight.

la **rapina** NOME FEM
robbery (PL robberies) ◊ *C'è stata una rapina in banca ieri.* There was a bank robbery yesterday.

rapinare VERBO
to rob ◊ *Quella banca è stata rapinata tre volte in un mese.* That bank has been robbed three times in a month.

il **rapinatore**, la **rapinatrice** NOME MASC, FEM
robber ◊ *I rapinatori sono fuggiti a piedi.* The robbers ran away.

rapire VERBO
to kidnap* ◊ *L'hanno rapito due mesi fa.* He was kidnapped two months ago.

il **rapitore**, la **rapitrice** NOME MASC, FEM
kidnapper ◊ *I rapitori hanno minacciato di uccidere l'ostaggio.* The kidnappers threatened to kill the hostage.

il **rapporto** NOME MASC
① relationship ◊ *Abbiamo un ottimo rapporto.* We have a very good relationship.
♦ **avere rapporti sessuali** to have* intercourse
② report ◊ *Scrivi un rapporto sulla situazione.* Write a report on the situation.

il **rappresentante** NOME MASC/FEM
① representative ◊ *il rappresentante di classe* the class representative
② rep (*di commercio*) ◊ *Fa il rappresentante.* He is a rep.

rappresentare VERBO
to represent ◊ *Questo rappresenta un passo avanti nella scienza.* This represents a step forward for science.

la **rappresentazione** NOME FEM
① representation (*raffigurazione*)
② play (*a teatro*)

raramente AVVERBIO
rarely ◊ *Ci vediamo raramente.* We rarely see each other.

raro AGGETTIVO (FEM **rara**)
rare ◊ *una pianta rara* a rare plant

rasare VERBO
to shave off ◊ *Si è rasato la barba.* He's shaved his beard off.

raschiare VERBO
to scrape (*grattare*)
♦ **raschiarsi la gola** to clear one's thoat

raso AGGETTIVO, AVVERBIO (FEM **rasa**)
vedi anche **raso** NOME
♦ **un cucchiaio raso di farina** a level spoonful of flour
♦ **raso terra** close to the ground ◊ *Volava raso terra.* It flew close to the ground.

il **raso** NOME MASC

vedi anche **raso** AGGETTIVO, AVVERBIO
satin ◊ *una camicetta di raso* a satin blouse

il **rasoio** NOME MASC
razor ◊ *un rasoio radi e getta* a disposable razor
♦ **rasoio elettrico** electric shaver

la **rassegna** NOME FEM
♦ **una rassegna del cinema latino-americano** a season of Latin American films

rassegnarsi VERBO
♦ **rassegnarsi a qualcosa** to accept something ◊ *Si è rassegnato alla decisione del padre.* He accepted his father's decision. ◊ *È stato difficile ma alla fine si è rassegnata.* It was difficult, but she eventually accepted it.

rassicurare VERBO
to reassure ◊ *Il medico ci ha rassicurato sulla sua salute.* The doctor reassured us about his health. ◊ *Ho cercato di rassicurarla, ma non è servito.* I tried to reassure her, but with no success.

rassodare VERBO
to tone ◊ *Il nuoto aiuta a rassodare i muscoli.* Swimming helps to tone the muscles.

rassomigliare VERBO
to look like ◊ *Rassomigli molto a tua madre.* You look very like your mother.
♦ **rassomigliarsi** to look alike ◊ *Vi rassomigliate moltissimo.* You look very alike.

il **rastrello** NOME MASC
rake

la **rata** NOME FEM
instalment
installment [US]
◊ *Si può pagare a rate.* You can pay by instalments.

il **ratto** NOME MASC
rat

rattoppare VERBO
to patch ◊ *Devo rattoppare i jeans.* I need to patch my jeans.

rattrappito AGGETTIVO (FEM **rattrappita**)
stiff ◊ *Ho le gambe rattrappite.* My legs are stiff.

rauco AGGETTIVO (FEM **rauca**, MASC PL **rauchi**, FEM PL **rauche**)
hoarse

il **ravanello** NOME MASC
radish

i **ravioli** NOME MASC PL
ravioli SING

ravvicinato AGGETTIVO (FEM **ravvicinata**)
♦ **a distanza ravvicinata** at close range ◊ *Gli hanno sparato a distanza ravvicinata.* He was shot at close range.

razionale AGGETTIVO
rational ◊ *Ci dev'essere una spiegazione razionale.* There must be a rational explanation.

R

il **razionamento** NOME MASC
rationing ◊ *il razionamento della benzina*
petrol rationing

razionare VERBO
to ration ◊ *Stanno razionando l'acqua.*
Water is being rationed.

la **razza** NOME FEM
1 race ◊ *studenti di tutte le razze* students
of all races
2 breed ◊ *Di che razza è il tuo cane?* What
breed is your dog?
3 sort ◊ *Ma che razza di discorso è?* What
sort of argument is that?
◆ **Che razza di cretino!** What an idiot!

il **razzismo** NOME MASC
racism

razzista AGGETTIVO, NOME MASC/FEM
racist

il **razzo** NOME MASC
rocket

il **re** NOME MASC (PL i **re**)
1 king ◊ *Re Artù* King Arthur
2 D (*nota musicale*) ◊ *in re maggiore* in D
major

reagire VERBO
to react ◊ *Come ha reagito Kate alla notizia?*
How did Kate react to the news?

reale AGGETTIVO
1 true ◊ *È basato su un fatto reale.* It's
based on a true story.
2 royal ◊ *la famiglia reale* the royal family

realizzare VERBO
1 achieve ◊ *Ho realizzato il mio sogno di
viaggiare.* I've achieved my ambition to
travel.
◆ **realizzarsi** (*sogno*) to come* true
2 to realize (*capire*) ◊ *Quando Luca ha
realizzato quello che era successo...* When
Luca realized what had happened...

realmente AVVERBIO
really ◊ *È un fatto realmente accaduto?* Did
it really happen?

la **realtà** NOME FEM (PL le **realtà**)
reality (PL realities) ◊ *La realtà era molto
diversa.* The reality was very different.
◆ **realtà virtuale** virtual reality
◆ **in realtà** in fact ◊ *Sembra un ragazzino, in
realtà ha quasi quarant'anni.* He looks very
young, but in fact he's nearly forty.

il **reato** NOME MASC
crime

la **reazione** NOME FEM
reaction ◊ *La sua prima reazione è stata
scappare.* Her immediate reaction was to
run away.

il **rebus** NOME MASC (PL i **rebus**)
picture puzzle (*gioco*)

recapitare VERBO
to deliver

il **recapito** NOME MASC
address ◊ *Puoi lasciarmi il tuo recapito?*
Can you give me your address?
◆ **recapito telefonico** telephone number

la **recensione** NOME FEM
review ◊ *Il film ha avuto delle ottime
recensioni.* The film has had excellent
reviews.

recente AGGETTIVO
recent ◊ *una scoperta recente* a recent
discovery
◆ **di recente** recently ◊ *Questo ristorante è
stato aperto di recente.* This restaurant
opened recently.

recentemente AVVERBIO
recently ◊ *Ha cominciato a lavorare lì solo
recentemente.* She started working there
only recently.

recintare VERBO
◆ **recintare qualcosa** to put* a fence round
something ◊ *Hanno recintato il giardino.*
They've put a fence round the garden.

il **recinto** NOME MASC
fence

il **recipiente** NOME MASC
container ◊ *I recipienti di plastica sono più
pratici.* Plastic containers are more
practical.

reciproco AGGETTIVO (FEM **reciproca**, MASC PL
reciproci, FEM PL **reciproche**)
mutual ◊ *È chiaro che la adora, e l'affetto è
reciproco.* He obviously adores her, and the
affection is mutual.

recitare VERBO
to act ◊ *Non sa recitare.* He can't act. ◊ *Mi
piace recitare.* I like acting.
◆ **Recita molto bene.** He's a very good actor.
◆ **recitare una parte** to play a part ◊ *Ha
recitato la parte di Giulietta.* She played the
part of Juliet.

il **reclamo** NOME MASC
◆ **fare reclamo** to complain ◊ *Hanno fatto
reclamo alla direzione per il chiasso.* They
complained to the manager about the noise.

reclinabile AGGETTIVO
◆ **sedile reclinabile** reclining seat

la **reclusione** NOME FEM
imprisonment ◊ *dieci anni di reclusione* ten
years' imprisonment
◆ **L'hanno condannato a un anno di
reclusione.** He was sentenced to a year in
prison.

il **record** NOME MASC (PL i **record**)
record ◊ *Ha battuto il record mondiale del
salto in alto.* He beat the world record for the
high jump.
◆ **a tempo di record** in record time

recuperare VERBO
1 to recover ◊ *Parte della refurtiva è stata
recuperata.* Some of the stolen goods have
been recovered.

---

* *I verbi seguiti da questo simbolo sono irregolari. Si veda anche alle pp.328–338.*

[2] to get* back ◇ *Ho recuperato la borsa che avevo smarrito.* I've got back the bag I lost.
+ **recuperare il tempo perduto** to make* up for lost time

redditizio AGGETTIVO (FEM **redditizia**)
profitable ◇ *un'attività redditizia* a profitable business

il **reddito** NOME MASC
income

le **redini** NOME FEM PL
reins ◇ *Tiene le redini dell'azienda* He holds the reins of the company

le **referenze** NOME FEM PL
references ◇ *Martin aveva delle buone referenze.* Martin had good references.

regalare VERBO
to give* ◇ *Mia sorella mi ha regalato un suo CD.* My sister gave me one of her CDs.
+ **Non so cosa regalare a mia madre per Natale.** I don't know what to get my mother for Christmas.

il **regalo** NOME MASC
present ◇ *regali di Natale* Christmas presents ◇ *Ho ricevuto un sacco di regali.* I got lots of presents.
+ **fare un regalo a qualcuno** to give* somebody a present
+ **Mi può fare una confezione regalo?** Could you gift-wrap it for me?

reggere* VERBO
to hold* ◇ *Reggi questa borsa, per favore.* Hold this bag, please.
+ **reggersi** to hold* on ◇ *Reggiti a me.* Hold on to me. ◇ *Reggiti forte.* Hold on tight.
+ **Non mi reggo in piedi dalla stanchezza.** I'm so tired I can hardly stand.

il **reggimento** NOME MASC
regiment

il **reggiseno** NOME MASC
bra

il **regime** NOME MASC
regime ◇ *un regime totalitario* a totalitarian regime

la **regina** NOME FEM
queen ◇ *la regina Elisabetta* Queen Elizabeth ◇ *la regina madre* the Queen Mother

regionale AGGETTIVO
regional

la **regione** NOME FEM
region ◇ *L'Italia è suddivisa in venti regioni.* Italy is divided into twenty regions.

la **regista** NOME MASC/FEM (MASC PL **i registi**, FEM PL **le registe**)
director

registrare VERBO
to record ◇ *Voglio registrare questo programma.* I want to record this programme.

il **registratore** NOME MASC
tape recorder
+ **registratore di cassa** till

il **registro** NOME MASC
register ◇ *il registro di classe* the class register

regnare VERBO
to reign

il **regno** NOME MASC
kingdom
+ **il Regno Unito** the United Kingdom

la **regola** NOME FEM
rule ◇ *Le regole del gioco sono molto semplici.* The rules of the game are very simple.
+ **essere in regola** to be* in order ◇ *Tutti i documenti erano in regola.* All the papers were in order.

il **regolamento** NOME MASC
rules PL
+ **essere proibito dal regolamento** to be* against the rules ◇ *Fumare è proibito dal regolamento scolastico.* Smoking is against the school rules.

regolare AGGETTIVO
vedi anche **regolare** VERBO
regular ◇ *a intervalli regolari* at regular intervals

regolare VERBO
vedi anche **regolare** AGGETTIVO
to adjust ◇ *Non riesco a regolare il volume.* I can't adjust the sound.
+ **Ricordati di regolare l'orologio.** Remember to set the clock.
+ **Non so come regolarmi.** I don't know what to do.

relativo AGGETTIVO (FEM **relativa**)
relative ◇ *un pronome relativo* a relative pronoun
+ **relativo a** relating to

la **relazione** NOME FEM
[1] relationship ◇ *La loro relazione è un po' in crisi.* Their relationship isn't going well.
[2] affair (*amorosa*) ◇ *Ha scoperto che il marito ha una relazione.* She's discovered that her husband is having an affair.
[3] report ◇ *Devo scrivere una relazione sulla visita al museo.* I've got to write a report on our visit to the museum.

la **religione** NOME FEM
religion

remare VERBO
to row ◇ *Ora tocca a te remare.* It's your turn to row now.

il **remo** NOME MASC
oar
+ **barca a remi** rowing boat

rendere* VERBO
[1] to give* back (*restituire*) ◇ *Potresti rendermi la penna?* Could you give me back my pen?
[2] to make* (*far diventare*) ◇ *Un po' di*

R

☞

diplomazia renderebbe tutto più facile. A bit of diplomacy would make everything easier.

◆ **rendersi utile** to make* oneself useful
◇ *Posso rendermi utile?* Can I make myself useful?

◆ **rendersi conto di qualcosa** to realize something ◇ *Forse non ti rendi conto di quanto sia pericoloso.* Maybe you don't realize how dangerous it is.

il **rene** NOME MASC
kidney

la **renna** NOME FEM
1 reindeer (*animale*)
2 suede (*pellame*) ◇ *una giacca di renna* a suede coat

il **reparto** NOME MASC
1 department (*nei grandi magazzini*) ◇ *Scusi, dov'è il reparto casalinghi?* Excuse me, where's the household department?
2 ward (*in ospedale*) ◇ *il reparto maternità* the maternity ward

la **replica** NOME FEM (PL le **repliche**)
repeat ◇ *Domani trasmettono la replica dell'ultima puntata.* The repeat of the final episode is on tomorrow.

la **repressione** NOME FEM
repression

la **repubblica** NOME FEM (PL le **repubbliche**)
republic

la **reputazione** NOME FEM
reputation ◇ *Si è rovinato la reputazione.* He has ruined his reputation.

il **requisito** NOME MASC
requirement ◇ *Uno dei requisiti era la conoscenza del tedesco.* One of the requirements was a knowledge of German.

il/la **residente** NOME MASC/FEM
vedi anche **residente** AGGETTIVO
resident ◇ *per i residenti dell'unione europea* for the residents of the European Union

residente AGGETTIVO
vedi anche **residente** NOME
◆ **È residente a Londra.** He lives in London.
◆ **Sono residenti all'estero.** They live abroad.

residenziale AGGETTIVO
residential ◇ *un quartiere residenziale* a residential area

la **resina** NOME FEM
resin

resistente AGGETTIVO
strong ◇ *un tessuto molto resistente* a very strong material

resistere VERBO
to resist ◇ *Non ho saputo resistere alla tentazione!* I couldn't resist the temptation!
senza preposizione.

respingere* VERBO
to reject ◇ *La sua domanda è stata respinta.* His application was rejected.

respirare VERBO
to breathe ◇ *Non riuscivo a respirare.* I couldn't breathe.

la **respirazione** NOME FEM
breathing ◇ *esercizi di respirazione* breathing exercises
◆ **respirazione bocca a bocca** mouth-to-mouth resuscitation ◇ *Gli hanno fatto la respirazione bocca a bocca.* He was given mouth-to-mouth resuscitation.

il **respiro** NOME MASC
breath ◇ *Prova a trattenere il respiro.* Try to hold your breath.

responsabile AGGETTIVO
vedi anche **responsabile** NOME
responsible ◇ *È un tipo molto responsabile.* He's a very responsible person. ◇ *Si sente responsabile dell'accaduto.* She feels responsible for what happened.

il/la **responsabile** NOME MASC/FEM
vedi anche **responsabile** AGGETTIVO
person in charge ◇ *Vorrei parlare con il responsabile.* I'd like to speak to the person in charge.

la **responsabilità** NOME FEM (PL le **responsabilità**)
responsibility (PL responsibilities) ◇ *Non voglio responsabilità.* I don't want responsibilities.

restare VERBO
1 to stay ◇ *Dai, resta ancora un po'.* Go on, stay a bit longer. ◇ *Sono restato a casa tutto il giorno.* I stayed at home all day.
2 to be* left ◇ *Ne restano solo due.* There are only two left.
◆ **Mi restano solo cinquanta sterline.** I've only got fifty pounds left.

restaurare VERBO
to restore ◇ *Stanno restaurando il quadro.* The painting is being restored.

restituire VERBO
to give*...back ◇ *Me lo presti? Te lo restituisco domani.* Will you lend it to me? I'll give it back to you tomorrow.

il **resto** NOME MASC
1 rest ◇ *Dove mettiamo il resto della roba?* Where shall we put the rest of the stuff?
2 change (*soldi*) ◇ *Tenga pure il resto.* Keep the change. ◇ *Signora, ha dimenticato il resto!* You've forgotten your change!

restringere* VERBO
to take* in (*vestito*)
◆ **restringersi (1)** (*stoffa, vestito*) to shrink*
◆ **restringersi (2)** (*strada*) to narrow

la **rete** NOME FEM
net ◇ *La pallina ha toccato la rete.* The ball touched the net.
◆ **collegarsi in rete** to get* connected to the Net

◆ segnare una rete to score a goal

il **retro** NOME MASC
<u>back</u> ◇ *Sul retro c'è un giardino.* There's a garden at the back.

retrocedere* VERBO
to relegate ◇ *La squadra è stata retrocessa in serie B.* The team has been relegated to the second division.

la **retromarcia** NOME FEM
reverse
◆ mettere la retromarcia to go* into reverse ◇ *Ha messo la retromarcia.* He went into reverse.
◆ fare retromarcia to reverse ◇ *Ho sbattuto facendo retromarcia.* I bumped the car when I was reversing.

retrovisore AGGETTIVO
◆ specchietto retrovisore rear-view mirror

la **retta** NOME FEM
1 straight line (*linea*)
◆ dar retta a to listen to ◇ *Non dargli retta, quello s'inventa le cose!* Don't listen to him, he makes things up! ◇ *Dammi retta, non vale la pena.* Listen to me, it's not worth it.
2 fee (*pagamento*)

rettangolare AGGETTIVO
rectangular

il **rettile** NOME
reptile

retto AGGETTIVO (FEM **retta**)
◆ linea retta straight line
◆ angolo retto right angle

il **reumatismo** NOME MASC
rheumatism ◇ *Soffre di reumatismi.* She suffers from rheumatism.
al singolare.

la **revisione** NOME FEM
1 revision (*di documento, di libro*)
2 servicing (*di macchina*)

il **revival** NOME MASC (PL i **revival**)
revival ◇ *un revival degli anni settanta* a Seventies revival

riabbracciare VERBO
◆ Spero di riabbracciarvi presto. Hope to see you again soon.

la **riabilitazione** NOME FEM
rehabilitation

riaddormentarsi VERBO
to go* back to sleep ◇ *Ho spento la sveglia e mi sono riaddormentata.* I switched off the alarm and went back to sleep.

riagganciare VERBO
to hang* up ◇ *Non riagganciare, premi il pulsante e rifai il numero.* Don't hang up, press the button and redial.

rialzarsi VERBO
to get* up ◇ *È caduto ma si è rialzato subito.* He fell, but got up immediately.

la **rianimazione** NOME FEM
◆ in rianimazione in intensive care

riaprire* VERBO

to reopen ◇ *Quando riaprono le scuole?* When do the schools reopen? ◇ *Il cinema ha riaperto dopo l'incendio.* The cinema has reopened after the fire.

riassumere* VERBO
to summarize

il **riassunto** NOME MASC
summary (PL summaries)

riattaccare VERBO
to hang* up ◇ *Ha riattaccato senza lasciarmi finire.* He hung up without letting me finish.

ribaltare VERBO
to turn over
◆ ribaltarsi to turn over

ribassare VERBO
to cut* ◇ *Hanno ribassato il prezzo dei CD.* They've cut the price of CDs.

ribellarsi VERBO
to rebel ◇ *Si è ribellato alla decisione del padre.* He rebelled against his father's decision.

ribelle AGGETTIVO, NOME MASC/FEM
rebel

il **ribes** NOME MASC (PL i **ribes**)
◆ ribes nero blackcurrants
◆ ribes rosso redcurrants

la **ricaduta** NOME FEM
◆ avere una ricaduta to relapse

ricamare VERBO
to embroider

ricamato AGGETTIVO (FEM **ricamata**)
embroidered

ricambiare VERBO
to return ◇ *Bisogna ricambiare l'invito.* We must return the invitation.

il **ricambio** NOME MASC
◆ pezzi di ricambio spare parts

ricapitolare VERBO
to sum up ◇ *Dunque, ricapitolando...* So, to sum up...

ricaricabile AGGETTIVO
rechargeable

ricaricare VERBO
1 to reload (*fucile, macchina fotografica*)
2 to wind* up (*giocattolo, orologio*)
3 to refill (*penna*)
4 to recharge (*batteria, pila*)

ricattare VERBO
to blackmail ◇ *Lo stavano ricattando.* They were blackmailing him.

il **ricatto** NOME MASC
blackmail ◇ *Ma questo è un ricatto!* This is blackmail!

la **ricca** NOME (PL le **ricche**)
rich woman (PL rich women)

riccio AGGETTIVO (FEM **riccia**, MASC PL **ricci**, FEM PL **ricce**)
vedi anche **riccio** NOME
curly ◇ *Ho i capelli ricci.* I've got curly hair.
◇ *I suoi capelli sono più ricci dei miei.* His

R

☞

hair is curlier than mine.

il **riccio** NOME MASC

> vedi anche **riccio** AGGETTIVO

  [1] hedgehog (*di terra*)

  [2] sea urchin (*di mare*)

il **ricciolo** NOME MASC

  curl

ricco AGGETTIVO (FEM **ricca**, MASC PL **ricchi**, FEM PL **ricche**)

> vedi anche **ricco** NOME

  rich ◊ *Viene da una famiglia ricca.* He comes from a rich family. ◊ *Le arance sono ricche di vitamina C.* Oranges are rich in vitamin C.

il **ricco** NOME (PL i **ricchi**)

> vedi anche **ricco** AGGETTIVO

  rich man (PL rich men) ◊ *Ha sposato un ricco.* She married a rich man.

  ◆ **i ricchi e i poveri** (*uomini e donne*) the rich and the poor

la **ricerca** NOME FEM (PL le **ricerche**)

  [1] search ◊ *Hanno abbandonato le ricerche.* The search has been abandoned. *al singolare.*

  ◆ **essere alla ricerca di qualcosa** to be* looking for something ◊ *Mia sorella è alla ricerca di un lavoro.* My sister is looking for a job.

  [2] research ◊ *la ricerca scientifica* scientific research

  [3] project (*studio*) ◊ *Devo fare una ricerca sulla Pop Art.* I've got to do a project on Pop Art.

ricercato AGGETTIVO (FEM **ricercata**)

  ◆ **È ricercato dalla polizia.** He's wanted by the police.

il **ricercatore**, la **ricercatrice** NOME MASC, FEM

  researcher

la **ricetta** NOME FEM

  [1] recipe (*di cucina*) ◊ *Mi dai la ricetta della torta di mele?* Could I have the recipe for apple pie?

  [2] prescription (*medica*) ◊ *Puoi comprare l'aspirina senza ricetta.* You can buy aspirin without a prescription.

ricevere VERBO

  to get* ◊ *Cara Denise, ho ricevuto ieri la tua lettera...* Dear Denise, I got your letter yesterday... ◊ *Non ha ancora ricevuto lo stipendio.* He hasn't got his pay yet.

il **ricevimento** NOME MASC

  reception ◊ *un ricevimento di nozze* a wedding reception

il **ricevitore** NOME MASC

  receiver

la **ricevuta** NOME FEM

  receipt ◊ *Mi dà la ricevuta, per favore?* Could you give me a receipt please?

richiamare VERBO

to call back ◊ *Richiamerò tra un quarto d'ora.* I'll call back in a quarter of an hour.

richiedere* VERBO

  [1] to ask for (*chiedere*) ◊ *Ha richiesto il parere di un avvocato.* He has asked for a lawyer's opinion.

  [2] to apply for (*far domanda*) ◊ *Ha richiesto il passaporto più d'un mese fa.* He applied for a passport more than a month ago.

  [3] to require (*necessitare*) ◊ *un lavoro che richiede molta concentrazione* a job that requires a lot of concentration

la **richiesta** NOME FEM

  request ◊ *una fermata a richiesta* a request stop

riciclare VERBO

  to recycle ◊ *carta riciclata* recycled paper

ricominciare VERBO

  to start again ◊ *Ho dovuto ricominciare tutto da capo.* I had to start all over again.

  ◆ **ricominciare a fare qualcosa** to start doing something again ◊ *Ha ricominciato a fumare.* He's started smoking again.

la **ricompensa** NOME FEM

  reward

riconoscente AGGETTIVO

  grateful

riconoscere* VERBO

  [1] to recognize ◊ *L'ho riconosciuto appena l'ho visto.* I recognized him as soon as I saw him.

  [2] to admit ◊ *Devo riconoscere che hai ragione.* I must admit you're right.

ricoperto AGGETTIVO (FEM **ricoperta**)

  covered ◊ *una torta ricoperta di panna* a cake covered with cream

ricordare VERBO

  [1] to remember ◊ *Il mio numero è facile da ricordare.* My number is easy to remember. ◊ *Ti ricordi di Laura?* Do you remember Laura?

  senza preposizione.

  ◊ *Non mi ricordo.* I can't remember.

  [2] to remind

  ◆ **ricordare a qualcuno qualcosa** to remind somebody of something ◊ *Mi ricorda un po' la Scozia.* It reminds me a bit of Scotland.

  ◆ **ricordare a qualcuno di fare qualcosa** to remind somebody to do something ◊ *Ricordami di spedire la lettera.* Remind me to post the letter.

il **ricordo** NOME MASC

  [1] memory (PL memories) ◊ *Ho dei bellissimi ricordi dell'Irlanda.* I have very happy memories of Ireland.

  [2] souvenir ◊ *Questo è un ricordo del viaggio in Marocco.* This is a souvenir of my trip to Morocco.

ricostruire VERBO

  [1] to rebuild* (*edifici*)

[2] to reconstruct (*fatti, delitto*)

la **ricotta** NOME FEM
ricotta

ricoverare VERBO
- **È stato ricoverato in ospedale.** He's been admitted to hospital.

la **ricreazione** NOME FEM
break ◇ *Facciamo quindici minuti di ricreazione.* We have a fifteen minute break.

ricredersi VERBO
to change one's mind ◇ *Mi sono ricreduto sul suo conto.* I've changed my mind about him.

ridare* VERBO
to give*...back ◇ *Me lo presti? Te lo ridò domani.* Will you lend it to me? I'll give it back to you tomorrow.

ridere* VERBO
to laugh ◇ *Perché ridi?* Why are you laughing? ◇ *Tutti sono scoppiati a ridere.* They all burst out laughing.
- **Che c'è da ridere?** What's so funny?
- **Non c'è niente da ridere.** It's not funny.

ridicolo AGGETTIVO (FEM **ridicola**)
[1] funny (*buffo*) ◇ *Era così ridicolo con quel cappello!* He was so funny in that hat! ◇ *ancora più ridicolo* even funnier
[2] ridiculous (*assurdo*) ◇ *Non essere ridicolo! Io non c'entro niente!* Don't be ridiculous! It's nothing to do with me!

ridire VERBO
- **trovare da ridire su** to criticize ◇ *Trova sempre da ridire sui miei amici.* She's always criticizing my friends.

ridotto AGGETTIVO (FEM **ridotta**)
reduced ◇ *L'ho comprata a prezzo ridotto.* I bought it at a reduced price.

ridurre* VERBO
to cut* ◇ *Hanno ridotto il prezzo da cinquanta a trentacinque sterline.* The price was cut from fifty pounds to thirty-five. ◇ *Ho dovuto ridurre il tema a sessanta righe.* I had to cut the essay to sixty lines.
- **Guarda come hai ridotto quei jeans!** Look at the state of your jeans!
- **Ma come ti sei ridotto?** What a state you're in!
- **essere ridotto proprio male** to be* in a terrible state

riempire* VERBO
[1] to fill ◇ *Tieni, ho riempito il termos di caffè, va bene?* Here, I've filled the flask with coffee, okay?
[2] to fill in (*modulo*) ◇ *Riempi il modulo, per favore.* Fill in the form, please.

rientrare VERBO
to get* back ◇ *Sono rientrato molto tardi.* I got back very late.
- **No, Daniela non è ancora rientrata.** No, Daniela isn't back yet.

riepilogare VERBO

to sum up ◇ *Dunque, riepilogando... So, to sum up...*

rifare* VERBO
to do* again ◇ *Lo devo rifare da capo.* I've got to do it all over again. ◇ *Stai tranquillo, non lo rifarà.* Don't worry, she won't do it again.
- **rifarsi il trucco** to redo* one's makeup
- **rifare il letto** to make* the bed

il **riferimento** NOME MASC
reference ◇ *Nell'articolo si fa riferimento al recente scandalo.* There's a reference in the article to the recent scandal.
- **punto di riferimento** reference point ◇ *Ho preso la stazione come punto di riferimento.* I took the station as my reference point.
- **in riferimento alla Vostra del...** with reference to your letter of the...

riferire VERBO
to tell* ◇ *È andato a riferire tutto al professore.* He went and told the teacher everything.
- **riferirsi a** to refer to ◇ *Non ho capito a cosa si riferisse.* I didn't understand what he was referring to.

rifinito AGGETTIVO (FEM **rifinita**)
- **ben rifinito** well finished

rifiutare VERBO
to refuse ◇ *Ha rifiutato di pagare la sua parte.* He refused to pay his share.

il **rifiuto** NOME MASC
refusal ◇ *un secco rifiuto* a flat refusal
- **rifiuti** rubbish SING, trash SING US:
◇ *L'ha buttato nei rifiuti.* She threw it in the rubbish.

la **riflessione** NOME
[1] remark ◇ *Ha fatto alcune riflessioni interessanti.* He made some interesting remarks.
[2] thought (*meditazione*) ◇ *Ha risposto dopo un attimo di riflessione.* She replied after a moment's thought.

riflessivo AGGETTIVO (FEM **riflessiva**)
reflexive

il **riflesso** NOME MASC
[1] reflection ◇ *il riflesso della luce sui vetri* the relection of the light on the windows ◇ *il riflesso della luna sul mare* the reflection of the moon in the sea
[2] reflex ◇ *Quando si beve non si ha i riflessi pronti.* Your reflexes are slower when you've been drinking.

riflettere* VERBO
to think* ◇ *Agisce senza riflettere.* He does things without thinking. ◇ *Ci ho riflettuto su e ho deciso di accettare.* I've thought about it and have decided to accept.

il **riflettore** NOME MASC
floodlight

la **riforma** NOME FEM
reform ◇ *la riforma del sistema sanitario*

R

☞

the reform of the health service
- **la riforma della scuola** educational reforms
  al plurale.

il **riformatorio** NOME MASC
community home

il **rifornimento** NOME MASC
- **fare rifornimento (1)** (*di benzina*) to get*
  petrol ◊ *Dove possiamo fare rifornimento?*
  Where can we get petrol?
- **fare rifornimento (2)** (*di provviste*) to stock
  up

il **rifugiato**, la **rifugiata** NOME MASC, FEM
refugee

il **rifugio** NOME MASC
shelter

la **riga** NOME FEM (PL le **righe**)
  [1] line ◊ *Ne ho letto solo poche righe.* I just
  read a few lines.
- **un foglio a righe** a piece of lined paper
- **mettersi in riga** to line up
  [2] stripe ◊ *giallo a righe rosse* yellow with
  red stripes
- **una camicia a righe** a striped shirt
  [3] parting
  part US
  (*di capelli*)

rigare VERBO
- **rigare dritto** to behave ◊ *Ti conviene rigare
  dritto!* You'd better behave!

rigido AGGETTIVO (FEM **rigida**)
  [1] stiff (*colletto, cartoncino*)
  [2] harsh (*clima*)
  [3] hard (*inverno*)
  [4] strict (*disciplina, educazione*)

il **rigore** NOME MASC
  [1] penalty (PL penalties) (*nel calcio*)
  [2] rigour
  rigor US
  (*severità*)

riguardare VERBO
  to concern ◊ *È un problema che ci riguarda
  tutti.* It's a problem which concerns us all.
- **Sono cose che non mi riguardano.** It's none
  of my business.
- **per quel che mi riguarda** as far as I'm
  concerned ◊ *Per quel che mi riguarda la
  faccenda è chiusa.* As far as I'm concerned
  the matter is closed.

il **riguardo** NOME MASC
  consideration ◊ *Non ha alcun riguardo per
  gli altri.* He has no consideration for other
  people.
- **riguardo a** about ◊ *Cos'hai deciso di fare
  riguardo all'offerta di lavoro?* What have
  you decided to do about the job offer?

rilasciare VERBO
  to release (*ostaggi, prigionieri*) ◊ *Gli ostaggi
  sono stati rilasciati ieri.* The hostages were
  released yesterday.
- **rilasciare un'intervista** to give* an interview

- **rilasciare una dichiarazione** to make* a
  statement

rilassarsi VERBO
  to relax ◊ *Rilassati! Andrà tutto bene.*
  Relax! Everything will be all right.

rileggere* VERBO
  to read* through ◊ *Ho consegnato il
  compito senza rileggerlo.* I gave in my
  homework without reading it through.

la **rima** NOME FEM
- **fare rima** to rhyme ◊ *"Head" fa rima con
  "red".* "Head" rhymes with "red".

rimandare VERBO
  to put* off ◊ *Abbiamo dovuto rimandare la
  gita di qualche giorno.* We had to put off the
  trip for a few days.

rimanere* VERBO
  [1] to stay ◊ *Sono rimasto a casa tutto il
  giorno.* I stayed at home all day. ◊ *Mi
  piacerebbe rimanere qualche altro giorno.*
  I'd like to stay a few more days.
  [2] to be* left ◊ *Ne è rimasto solo uno.*
  There's only one left. ◊ *È rimasto indietro.*
  He was left behind.
- **rimanere senza qualcosa** to run* out of
  something ◊ *Siamo rimasti senza benzina.*
  We ran out of petrol.
- **Sono rimasto senza parole.** I was
  speechless.
- **rimanere male** to be* hurt ◊ *C'è rimasta
  molto male.* She was really hurt.
- **rimanere ferito** to be* injured ◊ *È rimasto
  ferito in un incidente stradale.* He was
  injured in a car accident.

rimangiarsi VERBO
- **rimangiarsi la parola** to go* back on one's
  word ◊ *Aveva promesso e poi s'è
  rimangiato la parola.* He promised, and then
  went back on his word.

rimbalzare VERBO
  to bounce ◊ *La palla ha rimbalzato un paio
  di volte.* The ball bounced a couple of times.

rimborsare VERBO
  to refund ◊ *Mi hanno rimborsato il prezzo
  del biglietto.* They refunded the price of the
  ticket.

rimediare VERBO
- **rimediare a qualcosa** to try and find a
  solution to something

il **rimedio** NOME MASC
  cure ◊ *un ottimo rimedio contro il
  raffreddore* an excellent cure for a cold
- **Non c'è rimedio.** There's no way out.
- **porre rimedio a** to remedy ◊ *Occorre porre
  rimedio alla situazione.* We must remedy
  the situation.

rimettere* VERBO
  [1] to put* back ◊ *L'ho rimesso subito sul
  tavolo.* I put it back on the table
  immediately.

* I verbi seguiti da questo simbolo sono irregolari. Si veda anche alle pp.328–338.

2 to bring* up (*vomitare*)

* **rimettersi** to recover ◇ *Non si è ancora rimesso dall'operazione.* He hasn't yet recovered from the operation.
* **rimettersi in cammino** to set* off again ◇ *Dopo un breve sosta ci siamo rimessi in cammino.* After a short stop we set off again.
* **rimetterci** to lose* ◇ *Quando l'ho venduto ci ho rimesso un sacco di soldi.* When I sold it I lost a lot of money.

rimodernare VERBO
to modernize

rimorchiare VERBO
to tow ◇ *Ci può rimorchiare sino all'officina?* Could you tow us to the garage?

il **rimorchio** NOME MASC
trailer

il **rimorso** NOME MASC
remorse ◇ *Non ha dimostrato alcun rimorso.* He showed no remorse.

rimpiangere* VERBO
to be* sorry ◇ *Ora rimpiange di non essere andato all'università.* He's sorry now that he didn't go to university.

il **rimpianto** NOME MASC
regret ◇ *Non ho rimpianti.* I have no regrets.

rimpinzarsi VERBO
* **rimpinzarsi di** to stuff oneself with ◇ *Mi sono rimpinzato di biscotti.* I stuffed myself with biscuits.

rimproverare VERBO
to tell* off ◇ *L'hanno rimproverato per essere tornato tardi.* He was told off for coming home late.

il **Rinascimento** NOME MASC
Renaissance

rincarare VERBO
to go* up ◇ *La benzina è rincarata.* Petrol has gone up.

rincasare VERBO
to get* home ◇ *È rincasato molto tardi.* He got home very late.
* **No, Maria non è ancora rincasata.** No, Maria isn't back yet.

rinchiudere* VERBO
to lock up ◇ *Dovrebbero rinchiuderlo in galera.* He should be locked up.
* **Si è rinchiuso in camera.** He shut himself up in his bedroom.

rincorrere* VERBO
to run* after ◇ *L'ho rincorso ma non sono riuscito ad acchiapparlo.* I ran after him but I couldn't catch him.
* **giocare a rincorrersi** to play tag ◇ *Dei bambini giocavano a rincorrersi.* Some children were playing tag.

la **rincorsa** NOME FEM
run-up ◇ *Ha preso la rincorsa prima di saltare.* She took a run-up before she jumped.

rincrescere* VERBO
* **Mi rincresce che tu non stia bene.** I'm sorry you're not well.
* **Mi rincresce di non poter venire.** I'm sorry I can't come.
* **Se non ti rincresce vorrei pensarci su.** If you don't mind I'd like to think it over.

rinforzare VERBO
to reinforce (*muro, ponte*)

rinfrescare VERBO
to freshen ◇ *Il temporale ha rinfrescato l'aria.* The storm freshened the air.
* **rinfrescarsi** to freshen up ◇ *Vorrei rinfrescarmi un po'.* I'd like to freshen up a bit.

il **rinfresco** NOME MASC (PL i **rinfreschi**)
reception ◇ *un rinfresco di nozze* a wedding reception
* **rinfreschi** (*cibi e bevande*) refreshments

la **ringhiera** NOME FEM
1 railing (*di balcone*)
2 banisters PL (*di scale*)

ringiovanire VERBO
to make* look younger ◇ *Quella pettinatura la ringiovanisce molto.* That hair style makes her look much younger.

ringraziare VERBO
to thank ◇ *Non so proprio come ringraziarvi!* I don't know how to thank you!
* **ringraziare qualcuno per aver fatto qualcosa** to thank somebody for doing something ◇ *Vi ringrazio per avermi ospitato a Edimburgo.* Thank you for putting me up in Edinburgh.
* **Ti ringrazio.** Thank you.

rinnovare VERBO
to renew ◇ *Devo rinnovare l'abbonamento ferroviario.* I need to renew my season ticket. ◇ *Quest'anno non gli hanno rinnovato il contratto.* His contract hasn't been renewed this year.

il **rinoceronte** NOME MASC
rhino

rintracciare VERBO
to find* ◇ *La polizia sta cercando di rintracciare i testimoni.* The police are trying to find the witnesses.

rinunciare VERBO
* **rinunciare a** to give* up ◇ *Ho dovuto rinunciare al viaggio in Giappone.* I had to give up my trip to Japan. ◇ *È troppo difficile, ci rinuncio!* It's too difficult, I give up!

rinviare VERBO
to postpone ◇ *La riunione è stata rinviata a fine mese.* The meeting has been postponed till the end of the month.

il **rinvio** NOME
postponement

riordinare VERBO
to tidy ◇ *Devo riordinare la mia camera.* I

R

must tidy my room.

riparare VERBO
to repair ◇ *Me l'ha riparato in un attimo.* He repaired it for me in no time.

◆ **far riparare qualcosa** to get* something repaired ◇ *Ho fatto riparare il videoregistratore.* I got the video repaired.

◆ **ripararsi da** to shelter from ◇ *Siamo entrati in un bar per ripararci dalla pioggia.* We went into a bar to shelter from the rain.

la **riparazione** NOME FEM
repair

riparlare VERBO
◆ **Ne riparleremo domani.** We'll talk about it tomorrow.

il **riparo** NOME MASC
shelter ◇ *Dobbiamo trovare un riparo.* We need to find shelter.

◆ **Siamo al riparo!** We're safe!

ripartire VERBO
to leave* ◇ *È arrivato ieri e riparte domani.* He arrived yesterday and is leaving tomorrow.

ripassare VERBO
1️⃣ to come* back ◇ *In questo momento non c'è, può ripassare più tardi?* She's not here at the moment, could you come back later?
2️⃣ to revise ◇ *Devo ripassare, domani ho l'esame.* I've got to revise, I've got the exam tomorrow.

ripensare VERBO
1️⃣ to think* ◇ *Quando ci ripenso mi vergogno un po'.* When I think about it I feel rather ashamed.
2️⃣ to change one's mind ◇ *Ci ho ripensato, non vengo.* I've changed my mind, I'm not coming.

ripetere VERBO
to repeat ◇ *Scusi, può ripetere?* Excuse me, could you repeat that?

◆ **Non se l'è fatto ripetere due volte!** He didn't need to be asked twice!

la **ripetizione** NOME FEM
private lesson ◇ *Malcom dà ripetizioni di inglese.* Malcom gives private English lessons.

◆ **andare a ripetizione** to have* private lessons ◇ *Vado a ripetizione di matematica.* I have private maths lessons.

il **ripiano** NOME MASC
shelf (PL shelves) ◇ *L'ho messo sull'ultimo ripiano.* I put it on the top shelf.

la **ripicca** NOME FEM (PL le **ripicche**)
◆ **per ripicca** out of spite ◇ *L'ha fatto solo per ripicca.* She did it just out of spite.

ripido AGGETTIVO (FEM **ripida**)
steep ◇ *C'è una salita ripida per andare al castello.* It's a steep climb up to the castle.

ripiegare VERBO

to fold up ◇ *Ho ripiegato per bene il giornale.* I folded the newspaper up neatly.

◆ **ripiegare su qualcosa** to make* do with something ◇ *Era troppo caro, ho ripiegato su uno più economico.* It was too expensive, I made do with a cheaper one.

ripieno AGGETTIVO (FEM **ripiena**)
stuffed ◇ *peperoni ripieni* stuffed peppers

riportare VERBO
1️⃣ to take* back ◇ *Riportalo in cucina.* Take it back to the kitchen. ◇ *Mi ha riportato all'albergo a mezzanotte.* He took me back to the hotel at midnight.
2️⃣ to bring* back (*vicino a chi parla*) ◇ *Tieni, ti ho riportato il CD.* Here, I've brought you back your CD.

riposare VERBO
1️⃣ to rest ◇ *Sta riposando in camera sua.* She's resting in her room.
2️⃣ to sleep* ◇ *Avete riposato bene?* Did you sleep well?

il **riposo** NOME MASC
rest ◇ *cinque minuti di riposo* five minutes' rest

◆ **giorno di riposo** (*dal lavoro*) day off ◇ *Oggi ha preso un giorno di riposo.* He's taken a day off today.

il **ripostiglio** NOME MASC
junk room

riprendere VERBO
to take* back ◇ *Si è ripreso tutte le sue foto.* He's taken back all his photos.

◆ **Puoi riprenderlo, non mi serve più** You can have it back, I don't need it any more.

◆ **riprendere sonno** to get* back to sleep ◇ *Non sono riuscito a riprendere sonno.* I couldn't get back to sleep.

◆ **riprendersi** to recover ◇ *Si è appena ripreso dalla polmonite.* He's just recovered from pneumonia.

la **ripresa** NOME FEM
1️⃣ second half (*nel calcio*) ◇ *Ha segnato al 15° della ripresa.* He scored in the fifteenth minute of the second half.
2️⃣ round (*nella boxe*) ◇ *un incontro in 10 riprese* a ten-round fight
3️⃣ acceleration (*di auto*) ◇ *Questa macchina non ha ripresa.* This car hasn't got any acceleration.
4️⃣ shot (*con videocamera, ecc.*) ◇ *Ho fatto delle belle riprese nel Galles.* I got some nice shots in Wales.

◆ **ripresa economica** economic recovery

riprovare VERBO
to try again ◇ *Riproverò più tardi.* I'll try again later.

risalire VERBO
to date from ◇ *Il palazzo risale al Cinquecento.* The palace dates from the sixteenth century.

---

* I verbi seguiti da questo simbolo sono irregolari. Si veda anche alle pp.328–338.

risaputo AGGETTIVO (FEM **risaputa**)
- È risaputo che... Everyone knows that...

risarcimento NOME MASC
compensation ◊ *Ha ricevuto un risarcimento di diecimila euro.* He got ten thousand euros compensation.

risata NOME FEM
laugh ◊ *Ci siamo fatti una bella risata.* We had a good laugh.

riscaldamento NOME MASC
1 heating ◊ *Il riscaldamento non funziona.* The heating isn't working.
2 warm-up ◊ *Prima della partita facciamo riscaldamento.* Before a match we do a warm-up.

riscaldare VERBO
1 to warm up ◊ *Il pollo dev'essere solo riscaldato.* The chicken just needs warming up.
2 to heat ◊ *Un caminetto riscaldava la stanza.* The room was heated by an open fire.

riscatto NOME MASC
ransom

rischiare VERBO
to risk ◊ *Ha rischiato la vita.* He risked his life.
- rischiare di fare qualcosa to risk doing something ◊ *Non voglio rischiare di arrivare in ritardo.* I don't want to risk arriving late.

rischio NOME MASC
risk
- correre il rischio di fare qualcosa to risk doing something ◊ *Ha corso il rischio di essere licenziato.* He risked being sacked.

rischioso AGGETTIVO (FEM **rischiosa**)
risky ◊ *un'impresa rischiosa* a risky enterprise ◊ *l'operazione più rischiosa del secolo* the century's riskiest operation

risciacquare VERBO
to rinse

riserva NOME FEM
reserve ◊ *Domenica scorsa ho giocato come riserva.* Last Sunday I played as reserve.
- di riserva spare ◊ *Ne tengo sempre uno di riserva.* I've always got a spare one.
- riserva naturale nature reserve

riservare VERBO
to book ◊ *Vorrei riservare un tavolo per stasera.* I'd like to book a table for this evening.

riservato AGGETTIVO (FEM **riservata**)
reserved

riso NOME MASC (PL le **risa**)
1 rice ◊ *riso integrale* brown rice
2 laughter ◊ *il riso e il pianto* laughter and tears ◊ *risa allegre* cheerful laughter

risolto AGGETTIVO (FEM **risolta**)
solved

risolvere* VERBO
to solve ◊ *Ho risolto l'indovinello!* I've solved the riddle!

le **risorse** NOME FEM PL
- risorse naturali natural resources
- È una donna di grandi risorse. She's a very resourceful woman.

il **risotto** NOME MASC
risotto

risparmiare VERBO
to save ◊ *Sto risparmiando per comprare un videogame.* I'm saving to buy a video game.
- far risparmiare tempo to save time

il **risparmio** NOME MASC
saving ◊ *un grosso risparmio di tempo* a big saving in time ◊ *Ha speso tutti i suoi risparmi.* He spent all his savings.

rispettare VERBO
to respect ◊ *Bisogna rispettare le opinioni altrui.* You have to respect other people's opinions.

il **rispetto** NOME MASC
respect ◊ *Non ha alcun rispetto per le cose altrui.* She has no respect for other people's things.
- rispetto a compared to ◊ *Rispetto all'anno scorso è molto più caro.* Compared to last year it's much more expensive.

rispondere* VERBO
to answer ◊ *Ho telefonato ma non ha risposto nessuno.* I phoned, but nobody answered.
- rispondere a to answer ◊ *Sai rispondere alla mia domanda?* Can you answer my question? ◊ *Ha risposto alla tua lettera?* Has he answered your letter?
- rispondere di sì to say* yes
- rispondere di no to say* no
- rispondere di qualcosa to be* accountable for something

la **risposta** NOME FEM
answer ◊ *la risposta esatta* the right answer

la **rissa** NOME FEM
brawl ◊ *Ieri c'è stata una rissa nel bar.* There was a brawl in the bar yesterday.

il **ristorante** NOME MASC
restaurant ◊ *Abbiamo mangiato al ristorante.* We ate in a restaurant.

ristretto AGGETTIVO (FEM **ristretta**)
- caffè ristretto extra strong coffee
- una persona di idee ristrette a narrow-minded person

risultare VERBO
to emerge ◊ *Dalle indagini è risultato che...* It emerged from the inquiry that...
- La tue previsioni sono risultate errate. Your predictions proved to be wrong.
- Non mi risulta che... I don't think... ◊ *Non mi risulta che sia partito.* I don't think he's left.

R

il **risultato** NOME MASC
result ◇ *Domani sapremo il risultato degli esami.* We'll get the exam results tomorrow. *al plurale.*

ritagliare VERBO
to cut* out ◇ *Ho ritagliato l'articolo dal giornale.* I cut the article out of the paper.

il **ritardo** NOME MASC
delay ◇ *un ritardo di due ore* a two hour delay
♦ **Il volo ha avuto un ritardo di due ore.** The flight was two hours late.
♦ **in ritardo** late ◇ *Il treno è in ritardo.* The train is late. ◇ *Miriam arriva sempre in ritardo.* Miriam always arrives late.
♦ **Scusa il ritardo!** Sorry I'm late!

ritirare VERBO
[1] to take* out ◇ *Ha ritirato dei soldi.* He took out some money.
♦ **ritirare lo stipendio** to get* paid ◇ *Quando ritira lo stipendio?* When does he get paid?
[2] to collect ◇ *È andata alla posta a ritirare un pacco.* She's gone to the post office to collect a parcel.
♦ **Dove si ritirano i bagagli?** Where is the baggage reclaim?
[3] to take* away (*permesso, passaporto*)
♦ **Gli hanno ritirato la patente.** He lost his licence.

il **ritmo** NOME MASC
rhythm

ritornare VERBO
[1] to get* back ◇ *È appena ritornata da New York.* She's just got back from New York. ◇ *Parto il cinque e ritorno il dieci.* I leave on the fifth and get back on the tenth.
[2] to go* back ◇ *Mi piacerebbe ritornare in Irlanda.* I'd like to go back to Ireland.

il **ritornello** NOME MASC
chorus (*di canzone*)

il **ritorno** NOME MASC
♦ **essere di ritorno** to be* back ◇ *Sarò di ritorno venerdì prossimo.* I'll be back next Friday.
♦ **al ritorno** on the way back ◇ *Al ritorno siamo passati per Bristol.* We went through Bristol on the way back.
♦ **il viaggio di ritorno** the return journey ◇ *Il viaggio di ritorno è stato più breve.* The return journey was shorter.
♦ **due ore andata e ritorno** two hours there and back
♦ **un biglietto di andata e ritorno** a return ticket

il **ritratto** NOME MASC
portrait

ritrovare VERBO
to find* ◇ *Ho ritrovato la mia agendina.* I've found my diary.
♦ **ritrovarsi (1)** (*in una situazione*) to find* oneself

♦ **ritrovarsi (2)** (*reincontrarsi*) to meet* again

ritto AGGETTIVO (FEM **ritta**)
upright ◇ *Non riusciva a star ritto.* He couldn't stand upright.

la **riunione** NOME FEM
meeting ◇ *essere in riunione* to be* in a meeting

riunirsi VERBO
to meet* ◇ *Il consiglio si riunisce di giovedì.* The council meets on Thursdays. ◇ *Ci siamo riuniti a casa di Roberto.* We met at Roberto's house.

riuscire* VERBO
♦ **riuscire a fare qualcosa** to manage to do something ◇ *Siamo riusciti a convincerla.* We managed to persuade her.
♦ **Non riesco ad aprirlo.** I can't open it.
♦ **Spostalo un po'. – Non ci riesco.** Move it a bit. – I can't.
♦ **riuscire bene** to go* well ◇ *La festa è riuscita bene.* The party went well.

la **riva** NOME FEM
[1] shore (*di lago, di mare*)
♦ **in riva al mare** on the seashore
[2] bank (*di fiume*)

rivale NOME MASC/FEM, AGGETTIVO
rival ◇ *Come stilista non ha rivali.* As a designer he has no rivals. ◇ *Appartengono a bande rivali.* They belong to rival gangs.

la **rivalità** NOME FEM (PL le **rivalità**)
rivalry (PL rivalries)

rivedere* VERBO
to see* again ◇ *Non mi dispiacerebbe rivedere quel film.* I wouldn't mind seeing that film again.
♦ **Dalla scorsa estate non li ho più rivisti.** I haven't seen them since last summer.

rivelare VERBO
to reveal ◇ *Non ha voluto rivelare il nome dell'informatore.* She wouldn't reveal the name of her informant.
♦ **rivelarsi** to prove to be ◇ *Si è rivelato un ottimo portiere.* He proved to be an excellent goalkeeper.

la **rivelazione** NOME FEM
revelation ◇ *Come ballerina è stata una rivelazione!* Her dancing was a revelation!

riversarsi VERBO
to pour out ◇ *La folla si è riversata nelle strade.* The crowd poured out into the streets.

il **rivestimento** NOME MASC
covering ◇ *un rivestimento di plastica* a plastic covering

la **rivincita** NOME FEM
rematch ◇ *Mi ha chiesto la rivincita.* He challenged me to a rematch.

la **rivista** NOME FEM
magazine ◇ *una rivista di moda* a fashion

---

* *I verbi seguiti da questo simbolo sono irregolari. Si veda anche alle pp.328–338.*

magazine

rivolgere* VERBO
- **rivolgere la parola a qualcuno** to speak* to somebody ◇ *Sono due giorni che non mi rivolge la parola.* She hasn't spoken to me for two days.
- **rivolgersi a** to go* and ask ◇ *Dovrebbe rivolgersi all'impiegato laggiù.* You should go and ask the man over there.

la **rivolta** NOME FEM
revolt

la **rivoltella** NOME FEM
revolver

rivoluzionare VERBO
to revolutionize

rivoluzionario, rivoluzionaria
AGGETTIVO, NOME MASC/FEM
revolutionary (PL revolutionaries)

la **rivoluzione** NOME FEM
revolution

la **roba** NOME FEM
1 things PL ◇ *Ho ancora un sacco di roba da fare.* I've still got lots of things to do.
2 stuff (oggetti) ◇ *Cos'è quella roba sul tavolo?* What's that stuff on the table?
- **roba da mangiare** food ◇ *C'era un sacco di roba da mangiare.* There was lots of food.
- **roba da lavare** washing ◇ *Posso mettere la mia roba da lavare in lavatrice?* Can I put my washing in the machine?
- **Roba da matti!** It's just incredible!

robusto AGGETTIVO (FEM **robusta**)
strong ◇ *un ramo robusto* a strong branch ◇ *un uomo robusto* a strong man
- **È un po' robusta.** She's quite a big woman.

la **roccia** NOME FEM (PL le **rocce**)
rock

roco AGGETTIVO (FEM **roca**, MASC PL **rochi**, FEM PL **roche**)
hoarse

il **rodaggio** NOME MASC
- **essere in rodaggio** to be* being run in ◇ *La macchina è ancora in rodaggio.* The car is still being run in.

il **rognone** NOME MASC
kidney

Roma NOME FEM
Rome ◇ *Domani andremo a Roma.* We're going to Rome tomorrow. ◇ *Abita a Roma.* She lives in Rome.

la **Romania** NOME FEM
Romania

romano AGGETTIVO (FEM **romana**)
Roman
Si noti l'uso della maiuscola in inglese.

romantico AGGETTIVO (FEM **romantica**, MASC PL **romantici**, FEM PL **romantiche**)
romantic

il **romanzo** NOME MASC
novel ◇ *Leggo soprattutto romanzi.* I mainly read novels.
- **romanzo giallo** detective story (PL detective stories)

rompere* VERBO
to break* ◇ *Ho rotto un bicchiere!* I've broken a glass!
- **Uffa quanto rompi!** What a pain you are!
- **rompersi (1)** to break* ◇ *Il piatto si è rotto.* The plate broke. ◇ *Si è rotto una gamba.* He broke a leg.
- **rompersi (2)** (macchina, apparecchio) to break* down ◇ *La macchina si è rotta sull'autostrada.* The car broke down on the motorway.

il/la **rompiscatole** NOME MASC/FEM (PL i/le **rompiscatole**)
- **È un vero rompiscatole!** He's a real pain!

la **rondine** NOME FEM
swallow

la **rosa** NOME
vedi anche **rosa** AGGETTIVO
rose ◇ *un mazzo di rose* a bunch of roses

rosa AGGETTIVO (MASC, FEM, PL **rosa**)
vedi anche **rosa** NOME
pink ◇ *calzini rosa* pink socks
- **un romanzo rosa** a romantic novel

rosato AGGETTIVO (FEM **rosata**)
rosé ◇ *vino rosato* rosé wine

il **rosmarino** NOME MASC
rosemary

il **rospo** NOME MASC
toad

il **rossetto** NOME MASC
lipstick

rosso AGGETTIVO (FEM **rossa**)
vedi anche **rosso** NOME
red ◇ *Ha i capelli rossi.* She's got red hair.

il **rosso** NOME
vedi anche **rosso** AGGETTIVO
yolk ◇ *rosso d'uovo* egg yolk

la **rosticceria** NOME FEM
delicatessen

la **rotaia** NOME FEM
rail

la **rotella** NOME FEM
wheel ◇ *una valigia con le rotelle* a case with wheels
- **pattini a rotelle** roller skates
- **Gli manca una rotella!** He's got a screw loose!

rotolare VERBO
to roll ◇ *Il pallone è rotolato giù per le scale.* The ball rolled down the steps.

il **rotolo** NOME MASC
roll ◇ *un rotolo di carta igienica* a roll of toilet paper

rotondo AGGETTIVO (FEM **rotonda**)
round

il **rottame** NOME MASC
wreck ◇ *Questa macchina è un rottame!* This car is a wreck!

rotto AGGETTIVO (FEM **rotta**)

R

☞

broken ◊ *Il videoregistratore è rotto.* The video is broken. ◊ *Betty ha un braccio rotto.* Betty has a broken arm.

la **roulotte** NOME FEM (PL le **roulotte**)
caravan

il **rovere** NOME MASC
oak ◊ *una botte di rovere* an oak barrel

la **rovescia** NOME FEM
♦ **alla rovescia (1)** (*sottosopra*) upside down
♦ **alla rovescia (2)** (*con l'esterno all'interno*) inside out
♦ **alla rovescia (3)** (*con il davanti dietro*) back to front

rovesciare VERBO
  1 to knock over ◊ *Mi sono alzato di scatto e ho rovesciato la sedia.* I got up in a hurry and knocked over the chair.
  2 to spill (*liquido*) ◊ *Ha rovesciato il latte per terra.* She spilled the milk on the floor.
♦ **rovesciarsi** (*macchina*) to overturn

il **rovescio** NOME MASC (PL i **rovesci**)
  1 wrong side (*di abito, di stoffa*) ◊ *Stirala dal rovescio.* Iron it on the wrong side.
  2 backhand (*in tennis*) ◊ *Ha un rovescio potentissimo.* She has a very powerful backhand.

rovinare VERBO
to ruin ◊ *Si è rovinata il vestito.* She's ruined her dress.

rubare VERBO
to steal* ◊ *A Londra mi hanno rubato la macchina fotografica.* My camera was stolen in London.

il **rubinetto** NOME MASC
tap
faucet US

il **rubino** NOME MASC
ruby (PL rubies)

la **rubrica** NOME FEM (PL le **rubriche**)
♦ **rubrica telefonica** address book

la **ruga** NOME FEM (PL le **rughe**)
wrinkle

la **ruggine** NOME FEM
rust

la **rugiada** NOME FEM
dew

il **rullino** NOME MASC
film ◊ *un rullino da ventiquattro foto* a twenty-four exposure film

il **rum** NOME MASC
rum

rumeno AGGETTIVO (FEM **rumena**)
Romanian

il **rumore** NOME MASC
noise ◊ *Cos'è questo rumore?* What's that noise?
♦ **fare rumore** to make* a noise ◊ *Cerca di non far rumore, dormono tutti.* Try not to make a noise, everybody's asleep.
♦ **un rumore di passi** a sound of footsteps
Attenzione! In inglese esiste la parola **rumour**, *che però significa* **voce** *oppure* **diceria**.

rumoroso AGGETTIVO (FEM **rumorosa**)
noisy ◊ *una strada rumorosa* a noisy street ◊ *Mi ha dato una stanza ancora più rumorosa.* He gave me an even noisier room.

il **ruolo** NOME MASC
part ◊ *Recita nel ruolo di Capitan Uncino.* He's playing the part of Captain Hook.
senza preposizione.

la **ruota** NOME FEM
wheel ◊ *la ruota di scorta* the spare wheel

il **ruscello** NOME MASC
stream

russare VERBO
to snore

la **Russia** NOME FEM
Russia

russo, russa NOME, AGGETTIVO
Russian

il **rutto** NOME MASC
♦ **fare un rutto** to burp

ruvido AGGETTIVO (FEM **ruvida**)
rough

S

sabato NOME MASC
Saturday
Si noti l'uso della maiuscola in inglese.
◇ *L'ho visto sabato.* I saw him on Saturday.
- **di sabato** on Saturdays ◇ *Vado in piscina di sabato.* I go swimming on Saturdays.
- **sabato scorso** last Saturday
- **sabato prossimo** next Saturday

sabbia NOME FEM
sand ◇ *sulla sabbia* on the sand
- **sabbie mobili** quicksand SING

sabbioso AGGETTIVO (FEM **sabbiosa**)
sandy

sacca NOME FEM (PL le **sacche**)
bag ◇ *una sacca da viaggio* a travel bag

sacchetto NOME MASC
bag ◇ *un sacchetto di carta* a paper bag ◇ *un sacchetto di plastica* a plastic bag

sacco NOME MASC (PL i **sacchi**)
sack ◇ *un sacco di patate* a sack of potatoes
- **sacco a pelo** sleeping bag
- **un sacco di** (*molto*) lots of ◇ *C'era un sacco di gente.* There were lots of people.

sacerdote NOME MASC
priest

sacrificio NOME MASC
sacrifice
- **fare dei sacrifici** to make* sacrifices

sacro AGGETTIVO (FEM **sacra**)
sacred (*musica, luogo*)

sadico AGGETTIVO (FEM **sadica**, MASC PL **sadici**, FEM PL **sadiche**)
sadistic

saggio AGGETTIVO (FEM **saggia**, MASC PL **saggi**, FEM PL **sagge**)
vedi anche **saggio** NOME
wise

saggio NOME MASC (PL i **saggi**)
vedi anche **saggio** AGGETTIVO
essay ◇ *un saggio su Dante* an essay on Dante
- **un saggio di ginnastica** a gymnastics display
- **un saggio di musica** a recital

Sagittario NOME MASC
Sagittarius ◇ *Sono del Sagittario.* I'm Sagittarius.

sagoma NOME FEM
[1] outline (*profilo*) ◇ *Da lontano si vedeva la sagoma di una nave.* In the distance we saw the outline of a ship.
[2] shape (*forma*) ◇ *Ha una sagoma irregolare.* It has an irregular shape.

sala NOME FEM
[1] room (*stanza*) ◇ *C'era un tavolo rotondo in mezzo alla sala.* There was a round table in the middle of the room.
- **sala da pranzo** dining room
- **sala d'attesa** waiting room
- **sala di lettura** reading room
[2] hall (*molto grande*) ◇ *L'enorme sala era piena zeppa.* The enormous hall was packed.
- **sala giochi** amusement arcade
- **sala operatoria** operating theatre, US: operating room

salame NOME MASC
salami

salamoia NOME FEM
brine ◇ *olive in salamoia* olives in brine

salato AGGETTIVO (FEM **salata**)
salty (*sapore, cibo*) ◇ *È troppo salato.* It's too salty. ◇ *Questo è più salato.* This one is saltier.
- **acqua salata** salt water

saldare VERBO
[1] to settle ◇ *Devo saldare il conto.* I must settle the bill.
[2] to solder (*metallo*)

saldi NOME MASC PL
sales ◇ *I saldi cominciano a gennaio.* The sales start in January.

saldo AGGETTIVO (FEM **salda**)
- **Tieniti saldo!** Hold tight!
- **Non è più molto saldo sulle gambe.** He's not very steady on his feet any more.

sale NOME MASC
salt ◇ *C'è troppo sale.* There's too much salt in it.
- **sotto sale** salted ◇ *acciughe sotto sale* salted anchovies
- **sale fino** table salt
- **sale grosso** cooking salt
- **sali da bagno** bath salts

salice NOME MASC
willow
- **salice piangente** weeping willow

salire* VERBO
to go* up ◇ *I prezzi sono saliti.* Prices have gone up. ◇ *È appena salito in camera sua.* He's just gone up to his room.
Quando **salire** *descrive un movimento verso chi parla, va usato* **to come up***.*
◇ *Salì tu o scendo io?* Are you coming up or shall I come down?
- **salire su** (*monte, albero, scala*) to climb ◇ *È salito sull'albero per raccogliere ciliegie.* He climbed the tree to pick some cherries.
- **salire in** (*treno, autobus, aereo*) to get* on ◇ *È già salito in aereo?* Has he already got on the plane?
- **salire in macchina** to get* into the car

salita NOME FEM
[1] climb ◇ *La salita è stata molto faticosa.* The climb was very tiring.
[2] hill ◇ *Abbiamo dovuto fermarci a metà della salita.* We had to stop halfway up the hill.
- **una strada in salita** a road going uphill

la **saliva** NOME FEM
saliva

il **salmone** NOME MASC
salmon (PL salmon)

il **salone** NOME MASC
1 lounge (in albergo, in casa)
2 show (mostra)
* **salone dell'automobile** motor show
* **salone di bellezza** beauty salon

il **salotto** NOME MASC
sitting room

la **salsa** NOME FEM
sauce ◇ spaghetti con salsa di pomodoro spaghetti with tomato sauce

la **salsiccia** NOME FEM (PL le **salsicce**)
sausage

saltare VERBO
1 to jump ◇ Il gatto è saltato sul tavolo. The cat jumped on the table. ◇ È saltato giù dal treno. He jumped off the train.
* **Ma che ti salta in mente?** What on earth are you thinking of?
* **saltare fuori** (riapparire) to turn up ◇ Il libro è saltato fuori dopo una settimana. The book turned up a week later.
* **Da dove salta fuori questa camicia?** Where has this shirt appeared from?
* **saltare in aria** to blow* up ◇ I terroristi hanno fatto saltare in aria l'edificio. Terrorists blew up the building.
2 to skip ◇ Hai saltato il pranzo oggi? Did you skip lunch today? ◇ Ho saltato una riga. I've skipped a line.
* **saltare con la corda** to skip

il **salto** NOME MASC
jump ◇ un salto in avanti a jump forward
* **fare un salto** to jump
* **fare un salto da qualcuno** to drop in on somebody ◇ Faccio un salto da te questo pomeriggio. I'll drop in on you this afternoon.
* **salto con l'asta** pole vault
* **salto in alto** high jump
* **salto in lungo** long jump
* **salto mortale** somersault

saltuario AGGETTIVO (FEM **saltuaria**)
* **lavoro saltuario** occasional work

la **salumeria** NOME FEM
delicatessen

i **salumi** NOME MASC PL
cold meats

salutare VERBO
1 to say* hello to ◇ Non mi saluta mai. He never says hello to me. ◇ Salutami Giulia. Say hello to Giulia for me.
* **Mi saluti sua moglie.** Give my regards to your wife.
2 to say* goodbye to (congedandosi) ◇ È uscito senza salutare nessuno. He left without saying goodbye to anybody.

la **salute** NOME FEM
health ◇ Fumare fa male alla salute. Smoking is bad for your health.
* **godere di buona salute** to be* in good health
* **Salute! (1)** (a chi starnutisce) Bless you!
* **Salute! (2)** (nei brindisi) Cheers!

il **saluto** NOME MASC
* **tanti saluti** (in cartolina, in lettera) best wishes
* **Cordiali saluti.** (in lettera) Yours sincerely,...
*Se si comincia la lettera con "Dear Sir" o "Dear Madam", senza mettere il nome del destinatario, **Cordiali saluti** va tradotto invece con "Yours faithfully". Nell'inglese americano sia in presenza che in assenza del nome del destinatario normalmente si usa "Sincerely".*

il **salvadanaio** NOME MASC
money box

il **salvagente** NOME MASC
1 rubber ring (per bambini) ◇ Sai nuotare senza il salvagente? Can you swim without a rubber ring?
2 lifebelt (ciambella di salvataggio)
3 lifejacket (giubbotto di salvataggio)

salvare VERBO
1 to save (proteggere) ◇ La cintura di sicurezza lo ha salvato. The seat belt saved him.
* **salvare la vita a qualcuno** to save somebody's life ◇ Una volta mi ha salvato la vita. He once saved my life.
2 to rescue (soccorrere) ◇ I pompieri hanno salvato due bambini. The firemen rescued two children.
* **Non si è salvato nessuno nell'incidente.** Nobody survived the accident.

il **salvataggio** NOME MASC
rescue ◇ C'è stato un ferito durante le operazioni di salvataggio. One person was injured during the rescue operation.
* **scialuppa di salvataggio** lifeboat
* **giubbotto di salvataggio** life jacket

salve! ESCLAMAZIONE
hello!

la **salvia** NOME FEM
sage

la **salvietta** NOME FEM
serviette (tovagliolo)
* **salviette umidificate per bambini** baby wipes

salvo AGGETTIVO, NOME MASC (FEM **salva**)
vedi anche **salvo** PREPOSIZIONE
safe ◇ Sono salvo! I'm safe!
* **essere in salvo** to be* safe ◇ Non preoccuparti, ora sei in salvo. Don't worry, you're safe now.
* **mettersi in salvo** to reach safety

salvo PREPOSIZIONE
vedi anche **salvo** AGGETTIVO, NOME

except ◇ *Sono libero tutti i giorni salvo il lunedì.* I'm free every day except Monday.
* **Ci vediamo domani, salvo imprevisti.** I'll see you tomorrow, all being well.

San AGGETTIVO
Saint ◇ *San Francesco* Saint Francis

sandalo NOME MASC
[1] sandal (*calzatura*)
[2] sandalwood (*profumo*)

sangue NOME MASC
blood ◇ *Devo fare le analisi del sangue.* I've got to have a blood test.
* **una bistecca al sangue** a rare steak

sanguinare VERBO
to bleed*

sanità NOME FEM
* **Ministero della Sanità** Department of Health

sano AGGETTIVO (FEM **sana**)
healthy ◇ *un bambino sano* a healthy child ◇ *È più sana di lui.* She's healthier than him. ◇ *la dieta più sana di tutte* the healthiest diet of all
* **sano e salvo** safe and sound ◇ *È tornata a casa sana e salva.* She got home safe and sound.
* **sano come un pesce** fit as a fiddle
* **sano di mente** sane

San Silvestro NOME MASC
New Year's Eve ◇ *Cosa fai per San Silvestro?* What are you doing on New Year's Eve?

santo AGGETTIVO (FEM **santa**)
vedi anche **santo** NOME
holy

santo, la **santa** NOME MASC, FEM
vedi anche **santo** AGGETTIVO
saint ◇ *Non è un santo.* He's no saint.

santuario NOME MASC
sanctuary (PL sanctuaries)

sapere* VERBO
[1] to know* ◇ *Sai dove abita?* Do you know where he lives? ◇ *Lo so, non è colpa tua.* I know, it's not your fault. ◇ *Non ne so nulla.* I don't know anything about it.
* **far sapere qualcosa a qualcuno** to let* somebody know something ◇ *Fagli sapere che lo sto cercando.* Let him know I'm looking for him.
[2] to be* able to ◇ *È utile saper guidare.* It's useful to be able to drive.
Per tradurre questo significato spesso vengono usati i verbi modali **can** *e* **could.**
◇ *Sai nuotare?* Can you swim? ◇ *Non so guidare.* I can't drive. ◇ *Non sapeva andare in bicicletta.* He couldn't ride a bike.
[3] to taste (*avere sapore*) ◇ *Sa di fragola.* It tastes of strawberries.
[4] to smell* (*avere odore*) ◇ *Sa di pesce.* It smells of fish.

sapone NOME MASC
soap

il **sapore** NOME MASC
taste ◇ *Non ha nessun sapore.* It doesn't have any taste.
* **avere un buon sapore** to taste good

saporito AGGETTIVO (FEM **saporita**)
tasty ◇ *un piatto saporito* a tasty dish ◇ *È più saporito cucinato così.* It's tastier when it's cooked like this.

la **saracinesca** NOME FEM
shutter

la **Sardegna** NOME FEM
Sardinia ◇ *Mi è piaciuta molto la Sardegna.* I really liked Sardinia. ◇ *Andrò in Sardegna quest'estate.* I'm going to Sardinia this summer.

le **sardine** NOME FEM PL
sardines ◇ *una scatoletta di sardine* a tin of sardines

la **sarta** NOME FEM
dressmaker

il **sarto** NOME MASC
tailor

il **sasso** NOME MASC
stone

il **sassofono** NOME MASC
saxophone

il **satellite** NOME MASC
satellite ◇ *la TV via satellite* satellite TV

la **sauna** NOME FEM
sauna ◇ *Abbiamo fatto la sauna.* We had a sauna.

sazio AGGETTIVO (FEM **sazia**)
* **essere sazio** to be* full ◇ *Sono sazio.* I'm full.

sbadato AGGETTIVO (FEM **sbadata**)
careless

sbadigliare VERBO
to yawn

lo **sbadiglio** NOME MASC
yawn
* **fare uno sbadiglio** to yawn

sbagliare VERBO
to make* a mistake ◇ *Mi dispiace, ho sbagliato.* I'm sorry, I've made a mistake.
* **sbagliare numero** to get* the wrong number ◇ *Scusi, ho sbagliato numero.* Sorry, I've got the wrong number.
* **sbagliare strada** to take* the wrong road
* **sbagliarsi** to be* wrong ◇ *Pensavo fosse lei, ma mi sono sbagliato.* I thought it was her, but I was wrong.
* **Sbagliando s'impara.** You learn by your mistakes.

sbagliato AGGETTIVO (FEM **sbagliata**)
wrong

lo **sbaglio** NOME MASC
mistake ◇ *È stato uno sbaglio.* It was a mistake.
* **fare uno sbaglio** to make* a mistake

sbalordire VERBO
to stun ◇ *La notizia mi ha sbalordito.* I was ☞

S

stunned by the news.

sbalzare VERBO

to throw* ◇ *È stato sbalzato fuori dall'auto.* He was thrown out of the car.

sbandare VERBO

to skid (*auto*)

sbarazzarsi VERBO

◆ **sbarazzarsi di** to get* rid of ◇ *Mi sono sbarazzata di quei vecchi dischi.* I got rid of those old records.

sbarcare VERBO

① to disembark ◇ *I passeggeri stavano sbarcando.* The passengers were disembarking.

② to unload (*merci*)

la **sbarra** NOME FEM

bar (*di metallo*)

sbarrare VERBO

to block ◇ *Una macchina della polizia gli ha sbarrato la strada.* A police car blocked his way.

sbattere* VERBO

① to slam ◇ *Se n'è andato sbattendo la porta.* He went out slamming the door.

② to bang ◇ *La finestra sbatte per il vento.* The window is banging in the wind. ◇ *Ho sbattuto il ginocchio.* I banged my knee.

◆ **sbattere contro** to bump into ◇ *Era buio e ho sbattuto contro l'armadio.* It was dark and I bumped into the wardrobe.

◆ **sbattere fuori qualcuno** to throw* somebody out

la **sberla** NOME FEM

◆ **dare una sberla a qualcuno** to slap somebody

sbiadito AGGETTIVO (FEM **sbiadita**)

faded (*stoffa, disegno*)

sbocciare VERBO

to bloom (*fiore*)

la **sbornia** NOME FEM

◆ **prendersi una sbornia** to get* drunk

◆ **smaltire la sbornia** to sober up

sborsare VERBO

to pay* out

sbottonare VERBO

to unbutton ◇ *Si è sbottonato la camicia.* He unbuttoned his shirt.

sbriciolare VERBO

to crumble (*biscotti*)

◆ **sbriciolarsi** to crumble ◇ *La pietra mi si è sbriciolata in mano.* The stone crumbled in my hand.

◆ **La torta s'è tutta sbriciolata.** The cake got all broken.

sbrigare VERBO

to do* ◇ *Ho ancora alcune faccende da sbrigare.* I've still got a few things to do.

◆ **sbrigarsi** to hurry ◇ *Devi sbrigarti se non vuoi perdere il treno.* You'll have to hurry if you don't want to miss the train.

◆ **Sbrigatevi!** Hurry up!

la **sbronza** NOME FEM

◆ **prendersi una sbronza** to get* drunk

◆ **smaltire la sbronza** to sober up

sbronzarsi VERBO

to get* drunk

sbronzo AGGETTIVO (FEM **sbronza**)

drunk

sbucciare VERBO

① to peel (*frutto, patata*)

② to shell (*piselli*)

◆ **sbucciarsi un ginocchio** to graze one's knee ◇ *Mi sono sbucciato un ginocchio.* I grazed my knee.

sbuffare VERBO

① to pant ◇ *Saliva le scale sbuffando per la fatica.* He was panting with the effort of climbing the stairs.

② to grumble ◇ *Sbuffa sempre quando deve lavare i piatti.* He always grumbles when he has to wash the dishes.

gli **scacchi** NOME MASC PL

chess SING ◇ *Sai giocare a scacchi?* Can you play chess?

◆ **a scacchi** checked ◇ *una camicia a scacchi* a checked shirt

scadente AGGETTIVO

poor-quality ◇ *un prodotto scadente* a poor-quality product

la **scadenza** NOME FEM

① expiry date (*di documento*)

② sell-by date (*di alimento*)

③ use-by date (*di farmaco*)

scadere* VERBO

to expire (*contratto, documento*) ◇ *Il mio passaporto è scaduto.* My passport has expired.

◆ **Il latte è scaduto.** The milk is past its sell-by date.

lo **scaffale** NOME MASC

bookcase

scagliare VERBO

to hurl (*lanciare*)

la **scala** NOME FEM

① ladder (*a pioli, di corda*)

② staircase (*a gradini*)

◆ **scale (1)** (*in edificio*) stairs

◆ **scale (2)** (*all'esterno*) steps

◆ **salire le scale** (*in edificio*) to go* upstairs

◆ **scendere le scale** (*in edificio*) to go* downstairs

◆ **scala a chiocciola** spiral staircase

◆ **scala mobile** escalator

◆ **scala antincendio** fire escape

③ scale ◇ *una riproduzione in scala* a reproduction to scale

scalare VERBO

to climb (*monte*)

lo **scaldabagno** NOME MASC (PL gli **scaldabagno**)

water heater

scaldare VERBO

to heat (*cibo, stanza*) ◊ *Scalda un po' di latte.* Heat some milk.

• **scaldare il motore** to warm up the engine

• **scaldarsi (1)** (*al fuoco, al sole*) to warm oneself

• **scaldarsi (2)** (*aria, atleta, macchina*) to warm up

scalinata NOME FEM

1 staircase (*in edificio*)

2 flight of steps (*all'esterno*)

scalino NOME MASC

step

scalo NOME MASC

• **fare scalo a (1)** (*aereo*) to make* a stopover at

• **fare scalo a (2)** (*nave*) to call at

scaloppina NOME FEM

escalope ◊ *una scaloppina di vitello* a veal escalope

scalzo AGGETTIVO (FEM **scalza**)

barefoot ◊ *Era scalzo.* He was barefoot.

scambiare VERBO

to exchange (*barattare*) ◊ *Ho scambiato un CD con due cassette.* I exchanged a CD for two cassettes.

• **scambiare qualcuno per** (*confondere*) to mistake* somebody for ◊ *L'ho scambiato per suo fratello.* I mistook him for his brother.

scambio NOME MASC

exchange ◊ *uno scambio di prigionieri* an exchange of prisoners ◊ *scambi culturali* cultural exchanges ◊ *uno scambio di opinioni* an exchange of views

• **fare uno scambio** to do* a swap ◊ *Facciamo uno scambio?* Shall we do a swap?

scampagnata NOME FEM

• **fare una scampagnata** to go* for a day out in the country

scampare VERBO

• **scamparla bella** to have* a narrow escape

scampi NOME MASC PL

scampi SING

scampo NOME MASC

• **Non c'è scampo.** There's no way out.

scandalizzarsi VERBO

to be* shocked ◊ *Si scandalizza per un nonnulla.* She's easily shocked.

scandalo NOME MASC

scandal

scansafatiche NOME MASC/FEM (PL gli/le **scansafatiche**)

layabout

scansarsi VERBO

to dodge ◊ *Si è scansato per evitare il colpo.* He dodged to avoid the blow.

• **Potresti scansarti un po'?** Could you move over a bit?

lo scantinato NOME MASC

basement

la scapola NOME FEM

shoulder blade

lo scapolo NOME MASC

bachelor

lo scappamento NOME MASC

• **tubo di scappamento** exhaust pipe

scappare VERBO

to get* away ◊ *I ladri sono scappati.* The thieves got away.

• **scappare di prigione** to escape from prison

• **scappare di casa** to run* away from home

• **Scusa, ma devo scappare.** I'm sorry, but I must dash.

• **Non lasciarti scappare l'occasione.** Don't miss this opportunity.

• **Mi è scappato da ridere.** I burst out laughing.

• **Mi è scappato di mente.** It slipped my mind.

• **Mi scappa la pipì.** I'm bursting.

la scappatoia NOME FEM

way out (PL ways out)

lo scarabeo NOME MASC

1 beetle (*insetto*)

2 Scrabble® (*gioco*)

scarabocchiare VERBO

to scribble

lo scarabocchio NOME MASC

scribble

lo scarafaggio NOME MASC

cockroach

la scaramanzia NOME FEM

• **Incrocia le dita per scaramanzia.** Cross your fingers for luck.

• **Non gliel'ho ancora detto per scaramanzia.** I haven't told him yet, just in case.

scaricare VERBO

1 to unload ◊ *Stanno scaricando il camion.* They're unloading the lorry.

2 to download ◊ *Ci vuole un'ora per scaricare il file.* It takes an hour to download the file.

• **scaricarsi (1)** (*batteria di auto*) to go* flat

• **scaricarsi (2)** (*batteria, pila*) to run* out

• **scaricarsi (3)** (*sfogarsi*) to unwind

scarico AGGETTIVO (FEM **scarica**, MASC PL **scarichi**, FEM PL **scariche**)

1 not loaded (*arma*)

2 dead (*batteria, pila*)

3 flat (*batteria di auto*)

la scarlattina NOME FEM

scarlet fever

la scarpa NOME FEM

shoe ◊ *Mettiti le scarpe.* Put on your shoes. ◊ *scarpe coi tacchi alti* high-heeled shoes ◊ *scarpe coi tacchi bassi* flat shoes

• **scarpe da ginnastica** trainers, US: sneakers

la scarpiera NOME FEM

shoe rack

lo scarpone NOME MASC

S

boot

+ **scarponi da sci** ski boots
+ **scarponi da montagna** climbing boots

scarseggiare VERBO
to be* in short supply ◇ *I viveri scarseggiavano.* Food was in short supply.

+ **Cominciano a scarseggiare i medicinali.** Supplies of medicine are starting to run low.

scarso AGGETTIVO (FEM **scarsa**)
[1] rather small ◇ *Le porzioni erano scarse.* The portions were rather small.

+ **un chilo scarso** just under a kilo
+ **di scarso interesse** of little interest

[2] few ◇ *Hanno scarse risorse a disposizione.* They have few resources at their disposal.

[3] poor ◇ *scarsa visibilità* poor visibility

scartare VERBO
[1] to unwrap (*pacco, caramella*) ◇ *Hai scartato i regali?* Have you unwrapped your presents?

[2] to reject (*idee, suggerimenti*) ◇ *Hanno scartato tutte le mie proposte.* They rejected all my suggestions.

scassinare VERBO
to force (*porta, serratura, cassaforte*)

la **scatola** NOME FEM
[1] box ◇ *una scatola di cioccolatini* a box of chocolates

[2] can (*di latta*) ◇ *una scatola di fagioli* a can of beans

+ **cibi in scatola** canned foods

scattare VERBO
to go* off (*allarme*) ◇ *È scattato l'allarme.* The alarm went off.

+ **far scattare l'allarme** to set* off the alarm
+ **scattare una fotografia** to take* a picture
+ **scattare in piedi** to spring* to one's feet ◇ *Sono scattati in piedi.* They sprang to their feet.

lo **scatto** NOME MASC
[1] click (*rumore*) ◇ *Ho sentito lo scatto della serratura.* I heard the click of the lock.

[2] spurt (*di atleta*) ◇ *Ha sorpassato gli altri corridori con uno scatto.* He put on a spurt and overtook the other runners.

+ **alzarsi di scatto** to jump up ◇ *Si è alzato di scatto ed è uscito.* He jumped up and went out.

scavalcare VERBO
to climb over ◇ *Abbiamo scavalcato il muro.* We climbed over the wall.

scavare VERBO
to dig* (*terreno, buco*)

scegliere* VERBO
to choose* ◇ *Hai scelto il suo regalo?* Have you chosen her present?

la **scelta** NOME FEM
choice ◇ *Non ho scelta, devo accettare.* I've got no choice, I have to agree.

+ **fare una scelta** to make* a choice ◇ *Hai fatto la scelta giusta.* You made the right choice.

+ **di prima scelta** top-quality ◇ *verdura di prima scelta* top-quality vegetables

scemo AGGETTIVO (FEM **scema**)
stupid

la **scena** NOME FEM
scene ◇ *Compare nella prima scena.* He appears in the first scene.

+ **Ha fatto scena muta.** He didn't open his mouth.

+ **mettere in scena una commedia** to stage a play

lo **scenario** NOME MASC
scenery ◇ *La costa ligure offre un magnifico scenario.* The Italian Riviera has wonderful scenery.

la **scenata** NOME FEM
+ **fare una scenata** to make* a scene ◇ *Sandra ha fatto una scenata al ristorante.* Sandra made a scene at the restaurant.

scendere* VERBO
[1] to go* down (*andare giù*) ◇ *Sono arrivati. Scendi ad aprire la porta.* They're here. Go down and open the door.

[2] to come* down (*venire giù*) ◇ *Sali tu o scendo io?* Are you coming up or shall I come down?

+ **Scendo subito!** (*arrivo!*) I'm coming!
+ **scendere da (1)** (*macchina*) to get* out of
+ **scendere da (2)** (*treno, aereo, autobus*) to get* off

[3] to fall* (*prezzi, temperatura*) ◇ *La temperatura è scesa di due gradi.* The temperature fell by two degrees.

lo **sceneggiato** NOME MASC
TV drama

scettico AGGETTIVO (FEM **scettica**, MASC PL **scettici**, FEM PL **scettiche**)
sceptical
skeptical US

la **scheda** NOME FEM
card (*di schedario*)

+ **scheda telefonica** phonecard
+ **scheda elettorale** ballot paper

lo **schedario** NOME MASC
[1] card index (*raccolta di schede*)
[2] filing cabinet (*mobile*)

la **schedina** NOME FEM
+ **giocare la schedina** to do* the football pools

la **scheggia** NOME FEM (PL le **schegge**)
splinter

lo **scheletro** NOME MASC
skeleton

lo **schema** NOME MASC (PL gli **schemi**)
diagram ◇ *Ha disegnato lo schema alla lavagna.* He drew the diagram on the board.

+ **uno schema riassuntivo** an outline of the main points

* I verbi seguiti da questo simbolo sono irregolari. Si veda anche alle pp.328–338.

scherma NOME FEM
fencing ◊ *Faccio scherma.* I do fencing.
schermo NOME MASC
screen ◊ *il grande schermo* the big screen
◊ *il piccolo schermo* the small screen
scherzare VERBO
to joke ◊ *Stavo solo scherzando.* I was only
joking.
scherzo NOME MASC
joke
✦ **per scherzo** as a joke ◊ *L'ho detto per
scherzo.* I said it as a joke.
✦ **fare uno scherzo a qualcuno** to play a trick
on somebody ◊ *Facciamo uno scherzo a
Daniele!* Let's play a trick on Daniele!
✦ **scherzi a parte** seriously ◊ *Scherzi a parte,
penso che sia una ragazza intelligente.*
Seriously, I think she's a clever girl.
schiacciare VERBO
1 to squash ◊ *Si è seduta sul mio cappello
e l'ha schiacciato.* She sat on my hat and
squashed it.
2 to crush (*rompere*) ◊ *La macchina gli ha
schiacciato un piede.* The car crushed his
foot.
3 to crack (*noce*)
4 to press (*pulsante*)
✦ **schiacciare la palla** (*a pallavolo, a tennis*) to
smash the ball
✦ **schiacciare un pisolino** to have* a nap
schiaffo NOME MASC
✦ **dare uno schiaffo a qualcuno** to slap
somebody's face
✦ **prendere a schiaffi qualcuno** to slap
somebody's face
schiantarsi VERBO
to crash ◊ *La macchina si è schiantata
contro un albero.* The car crashed into a
tree.
schiarirsi VERBO
✦ **schiarirsi i capelli** to dye one's hair blonde
◊ *Si è schiarita i capelli.* She's dyed her hair
blonde.
✦ **schiarirsi la voce** to clear one's throat
schiavo, la **schiava** NOME MASC, FEM
slave
schiena NOME FEM
back ◊ *Mi voltava la schiena.* She had her
back to me. ◊ *Mi ha voltato la schiena
proprio quando avevo bisogno di lui.* He
turned his back on me just when I needed
him.
✦ **mal di schiena** backache ◊ *Ho mal di
schiena.* I've got backache.
schienale NOME MASC
back (*di sedia*)
schifo NOME MASC
✦ **fare schifo (1)** (*insetto, cibo*) to be*
disgusting
✦ **fare schifo (2)** (*film, libro*) to be* awful
✦ **Mi fai proprio schifo!** You really make me
sick!

✦ **Che schifo!** It's disgusting!
schifoso AGGETTIVO (FEM **schifosa**)
disgusting (*insetto, cibo*)
la **schiuma** NOME FEM
1 foam ◊ *schiuma da barba* shaving foam
2 lather (*di sapone, di shampoo*)
schizzare VERBO
to splash ◊ *Finiscila di schizzarmi.* Stop
splashing me.
✦ **Ti sei schizzato la giacca di vino.** You've got
wine on your jacket.
✦ **schizzare via** (*macchina, moto*) to speed* off
schizzinoso AGGETTIVO (FEM **schizzinosa**)
fussy ◊ *È più schizzinosa di me.* She's
fussier than me.
lo **schizzo** NOME MASC
1 splash ◊ *uno schizzo d'acqua* a splash
of water
2 sketch (*disegno*)
lo **sci** NOME MASC (PL gli **sci**)
1 ski ◊ *un nuovo paio di sci* a new pair of
skis ◊ *una gara di sci* a ski race
2 skiing (*attività*) ◊ *Lo sci mi piace molto.* I
love skiing.
✦ **sci da fondo** cross-country skiing
✦ **sci nautico** water-skiing
sciacquare VERBO
to rinse
la **sciagura** NOME FEM
disaster ◊ *una sciagura aerea* an air
disaster
lo **scialle** NOME MASC
shawl
la **scialuppa** NOME FEM
✦ **scialuppa di salvataggio** lifeboat
lo **sciame** NOME MASC
swarm
sciare VERBO
to ski ◊ *Sai sciare?* Can you ski?
✦ **andare a sciare** to go* skiing
la **sciarpa** NOME FEM
scarf (PL scarves)
lo **sciatore,** la **sciatrice** NOME MASC, FEM
skier
scientifico AGGETTIVO (FEM **scientifica**, MASC
PL **scientifici**, FEM PL **scientifiche**)
scientific (*metodo, approccio*) ◊ *la ricerca
scientifica* scientific research
✦ **una materia scientifica** a science subject
✦ **Ha scelto il ramo scientifico.** He chose
science.
la **scienza** NOME FEM
science ◊ *la scienza e la tecnologia* science
and technology
✦ **scienze** (*a scuola*) science SING
lo **scienziato,** la **scienziata** NOME MASC, FEM
scientist
la **scimmia** NOME FEM
monkey
lo **scimpanzé** NOME MASC (PL gli **scimpanzé**)
chimpanzee

S

scintillare VERBO
to sparkle

la **sciocchezza** NOME FEM

♦ **fare una sciocchezza** to do* something silly ◊ *Mi raccomando, non fare sciocchezze!* Make sure you don't do anything silly!

♦ **dire sciocchezze** to talk* nonsense

♦ **Sciocchezze!** Nonsense!

sciocco AGGETTIVO (FEM **sciocca**, MASC PL **sciocchi**, FEM PL **sciocche**)
silly ◊ *È l'idea più sciocca che abbia mai sentito.* It's the silliest idea I've ever heard.

sciogliere* VERBO

1 to melt (*neve, ghiaccio*) ◊ *Il sole ha sciolto il neve.* The sun has melted the snow.

♦ **sciogliersi** (*neve, ghiaccio*) to melt

2 to dissolve (*zucchero, sale*)

♦ **sciogliersi** (*zucchero, sale*) to dissolve

3 to untie (*nodo*)

♦ **sciogliersi** (*nodo*) to come* undone

4 to undo* (*capelli*)

♦ **esercizi per sciogliere i muscoli** warm-up exercises

lo **scioglilingua** NOME MASC (PL gli **scioglilingua**)
tongue-twister

lo **sciopero** NOME MASC
strike

♦ **essere in sciopero** to be* on strike

♦ **fare sciopero** to strike*

♦ **sciopero della fame** hunger strike ◊ *Sta facendo lo sciopero della fame.* He is on hunger strike.

la **sciovia** NOME FEM
ski tow

scippare VERBO

♦ **scippare qualcuno** to snatch somebody's bag ◊ *Mi hanno scippato.* My bag was snatched.

lo **sciroppo** NOME MASC
syrup ◊ *sciroppo per la tosse* cough syrup

sciupare VERBO
to ruin ◊ *Le scarpe nuove si sono sciupate.* My new shoes were ruined.

scivolare VERBO
to slip ◊ *È scivolato ed è caduto giù dalle scale.* He slipped and fell down the stairs.

♦ **Attento, si scivola!** Be careful, it's slippery!

♦ **scivolare sul ghiaccio (1)** (*persona*) to slip on the ice

♦ **scivolare sul ghiaccio (2)** (*macchina*) to skid on the ice

lo **scivolo** NOME MASC
slide (*gioco*)

scivoloso AGGETTIVO (FEM **scivolosa**)
slippery

la **scodella** NOME FEM
bowl

la **scogliera** NOME FEM

1 cliff (*rupe*) ◊ *le bianche scogliere di*

Dover the white cliffs of Dover

2 rocks PL (*scogli*) ◊ *La nave è finita sulla scogliera.* The ship went onto the rocks.

lo **scoglio** NOME MASC
rock (*al mare*)

lo **scoiattolo** NOME MASC
squirrel

lo **scolapasta** NOME MASC (PL gli **scolapasta**)
colander

lo **scolapiatti** NOME MASC (PL gli **scolapiatti**)
plate rack

scolare VERBO
to drain ◊ *Puoi scolare la pasta, per favore?* Can you drain the pasta, please?

lo **scolaro,** la **scolara** NOME MASC, FEM
pupil
Attenzione! In inglese esiste la parola **scholar,** *che però significa* **studioso.**

scolastico AGGETTIVO (FEM **scolastica**, MASC PL **scolastici**, FEM PL **scolastiche**)
school ◊ *l'anno scolastico* the school year

scollato AGGETTIVO (FEM **scollata**)
low-cut ◊ *un abito scollato* a low-cut dress

la **scollatura** NOME FEM
neckline

scollegarsi VERBO

1 to disconnect (*da Internet*)

2 to log off (*da chat-line*)

scolorirsi VERBO
to fade ◊ *La camicia si è scolorita.* The shirt has faded.

scolorito AGGETTIVO (FEM **scolorita**)
faded

scolpire VERBO
to carve (*legno, marmo*)

la **scommessa** NOME FEM
bet ◊ *Sergio ha mangiato cinquanta uova per scommessa.* Sergio ate fifty eggs for a bet.

♦ **fare una scommessa** to make* a bet ◊ *Ho fatto una scommessa con Martina.* I made a bet with Martina.

scommettere* VERBO
to bet* ◊ *Ha scommesso ottanta euro su un cavallo.* He bet eighty euros on a horse.

♦ **Scommettiamo che...?** I bet you... ◊ *Scommettiamo che Paola arriva in ritardo?* I bet you Paola will be late.

scomodo AGGETTIVO (FEM **scomoda**)

1 uncomfortable ◊ *una sedia scomoda* an uncomfortable chair

♦ **stare scomodo** to be* uncomfortable

2 difficult ◊ *Mi è un po' scomodo venire di pomeriggio.* It's a bit difficult for me to come in the afternoon.

♦ **L'orario della banca mi è scomodo.** The opening hours of the bank are inconvenient for me.

scomparire* VERBO
to disappear ◊ *La nave è scomparsa*

* I verbi seguiti da questo simbolo sono irregolari. Si veda anche alle pp.328–338.

all'orizzonte. The ship disappeared over the horizon.

♦ **Dov'eri scomparso?** Where did you get to?

scompartimento NOME MASC
<u>compartment</u> (*del treno*)

sconcio AGGETTIVO (FEM **sconcia**, MASC PL **sconci**, FEM PL **sconce**)

♦ **una barzelletta sconcia** a dirty joke

sconfiggere* VERBO
<u>to defeat</u>

sconfitta NOME FEM
<u>defeat</u>

scongelare VERBO
<u>to defrost</u>

scongiurare VERBO
<u>to beg*</u> ◊ *Ti scongiuro, aiutami.* I beg you, help me.

♦ **Il pericolo è scongiurato.** We're out of danger.

scongiuro NOME MASC

♦ **Facciamo gli scongiuri!** Touch wood!

sconosciuto* AGGETTIVO (FEM **sconosciuta**) ·
vedi anche **sconosciuto** NOME
<u>unknown</u> ◊ *un attore sconosciuto* an unknown actor

♦ **È una zona sconosciuta.** It's a little-known area.

sconosciuto, la sconosciuta NOME MASC, FEM
vedi anche **sconosciuto** AGGETTIVO
<u>stranger</u> ◊ *Non parlare agli sconosciuti.* Don't talk to strangers.

sconsigliare VERBO

♦ **sconsigliare a qualcuno di fare qualcosa** to advise somebody not to do something ◊ *Ti ho sconsigliato di telefonarle.* I advised you not to phone her.

♦ **Ti sconsiglio di telefonarle.** I wouldn't advise you to phone her.

♦ **Voleva dirtelo, ma l'ho sconsigliato.** He wanted to tell you, but I advised him not to.

scontare VERBO

♦ **scontare due anni di prigione** to serve two years in prison

scontato AGGETTIVO (FEM **scontata**)
1. <u>reduced</u> (*prezzo*) ◊ *tutto a prezzi scontati* everything at reduced prices
2. <u>predictable</u> (*prevedibile*) ◊ *Il finale del film era scontato.* The ending of the film was predictable.

♦ **essere scontato che** to be* bound to ◊ *Era scontato che finisse così.* It was bound to end that way.

♦ **dare qualcosa per scontato** to assume something ◊ *Davo per scontato che venissi.* I assumed that you would come.

scontento AGGETTIVO (FEM **scontenta**)
<u>unhappy</u> ◊ *È sempre scontento.* He's always unhappy. ◊ *Ora è più scontento.* He's unhappier now.

♦ **essere scontento di** to be* unhappy with

◊ *Sono molto scontento della squadra.* I'm very unhappy with the team.

lo sconto NOME MASC
<u>discount</u> ◊ *uno sconto del dieci per cento* a ten per cent discount ◊ *Mi ha fatto uno sconto.* He gave me a discount.

scontrarsi VERBO
<u>to crash</u> (*veicoli*) ◊ *La macchina si è scontrata con un autobus.* The car crashed into a bus.

lo scontrino NOME MASC
<u>receipt</u>

lo scontro NOME MASC
1. <u>crash</u> (*di veicoli*) ◊ *È rimasto ferito nello scontro.* He was injured in the crash.

♦ **uno scontro frontale** a head-on collision
2. <u>clash</u> ◊ *Ci sono stati scontri tra la polizia e i manifestanti.* There have been clashes between the police and the demonstrators.

♦ **uno scontro a fuoco** a shoot-out

sconvolgere* VERBO
<u>to upset</u> ◊ *La notizia mi ha sconvolto.* The news upset me.

sconvolto AGGETTIVO (FEM **sconvolta**)
<u>upset</u> ◊ *Era sconvolto.* He was upset.
◊ *Grazia aveva una faccia sconvolta.* Grazia looked upset.

la scopa NOME FEM
<u>broom</u>

scopare VERBO
1. <u>to sweep*</u> ◊ *Ho scopato la cucina.* I've swept the kitchen.
2. <u>to shag</u> (*fare sesso*)

la scoperta NOME FEM
<u>discovery</u> (PL discoveries)

scoperto AGGETTIVO (FEM **scoperta**)
1. <u>bare</u> (*braccia, spalle*)
♦ **a capo scoperto** bare-headed
2. <u>uncovered</u> (*pentola*)
♦ **una macchina scoperta** an open car
♦ **un assegno scoperto** a dud cheque

lo scopo NOME MASC
<u>aim</u> ◊ *lo scopo di questo studio* the aim of this research

♦ **A che scopo?** What for? ◊ *A che scopo lavori tanto?* What are you working so hard for?

♦ **a scopo di lucro** for money

scoppiare VERBO
1. <u>to go*</u> off (*bomba*) ◊ *La bomba è scoppiata alle 11 precise.* The bomb went off at exactly 11 o'clock.
2. <u>to burst*</u> (*gomma, pallone*) ◊ *Mi è scoppiata una gomma sull'autostrada.* My tyre burst on the motorway.

♦ **scoppiare a piangere** to burst* into tears
♦ **scoppiare dal caldo** to be* boiling
3. <u>to break*</u> out (*guerra, rivolta*) ◊ *La guerra è scoppiata nel 1939.* War broke out in 1939.

lo scoppio NOME MASC

1 explosion (*di bomba*)

2 bang (*di arma*)

scoprire* VERBO

1 to find* out ◇ *Ha scoperto la verità.* He's found out the truth.

2 to discover (*continente, cura*) ◇ *Chi ha scoperto l'America?* Who discovered America?

scoraggiarsi VERBO
to get* discouraged

la **scorciatoia** NOME FEM
short cut ◇ *Ho preso una scorciatoia.* I took a short cut.

scordare VERBO
to forget* ◇ *Ho scordato il tuo numero di telefono.* I've forgotten your phone number.

♦ **Ho scordato a casa l'ombrello.** I left my umbrella at home.

♦ **scordarsi di fare qualcosa** to forget* to do something ◇ *Mi sono scordato di telefonargli.* I forgot to phone him.

♦ **scordarsi di qualcuno** to forget* about somebody

le **scorie** NOME FEM PL

♦ **scorie radioattive** radioactive waste SING

Scorpione NOME MASC
Scorpio (*segno zodiacale*) ◇ *Sono dello Scorpione.* I'm Scorpio.

lo **scorpione** NOME MASC
scorpion (*animale*)

scorrere* VERBO
to run* (*liquido, fiume*) ◇ *Lascia scorrere l'acqua.* Let the water run.

scorretto AGGETTIVO (FEM **scorretta**)

1 incorrect ◇ *un uso scorretto* an incorrect use

2 unfair (*sleale*) ◇ *È stato scorretto da parte tua.* It was unfair of you.

scorrevole AGGETTIVO

♦ **porta scorrevole** sliding door

scorso AGGETTIVO (FEM **scorsa**)
last ◇ *lo scorso mese* last month

la **scorta** NOME FEM
police escort ◇ *Il ministro è arrivato con la scorta.* The minister arrived with a police escort.

♦ **di scorta** spare ◇ *la ruota di scorta* the spare wheel

♦ **fare scorta di** (*viveri, medicine*) to stock up with

scortese AGGETTIVO
rude (*risposta, persona*)

♦ **in modo scortese** rudely

la **scorza** NOME FEM
peel (*di agrumi*)

la **scossa** NOME FEM
electric shock ◇ *Ho preso la scossa accendendo la lampada.* I got an electric shock when I swiched on the lamp.

♦ **una scossa di terremoto** an earth tremor

scosso AGGETTIVO (FEM **scossa**)
shaken ◇ *Sono ancora scosso.* I'm still shaken.

♦ **Ho i nervi scossi.** I'm still in a nervous state.

lo **scotch** ® NOME MASC
Sellotape ®
Scotch tape ® *US*

scottare VERBO
to be* hot ◇ *Attento che scotta.* Be careful, it's hot. ◇ *Il sole scotta in agosto.* The sun is hot in August.

♦ **scottarsi (1)** to burn* oneself

♦ **scottarsi (2)** (*al sole*) to get* burnt

la **scottatura** NOME FEM

1 burn ◇ *Ho una scottatura sulla mano.* I've got a burn on my hand.

2 sunburn (*da esposizione al sole*)

scotto AGGETTIVO (FEM **scotta**)
overcooked (*cibo*)

la **Scozia** NOME FEM
Scotland ◇ *Mi è piaciuta molto la Scozia.* I really liked Scotland. ◇ *Andremo in Scozia quest'estate.* We're going to Scotland this summer.

lo/la **scozzese** NOME MASC/FEM
vedi anche **scozzese** AGGETTIVO
Scot ◇ *gli scozzesi* the Scots

scozzese AGGETTIVO
vedi anche **scozzese** NOME
Scottish ◇ *le isole scozzesi* the Scottish islands

scremato AGGETTIVO (FEM **scremata**)
skimmed ◇ *latte scremato* skimmed milk ◇ *latte parzialmente scremato* semi-skimmed milk

screpolato AGGETTIVO (FEM **screpolata**)
chapped (*labbra, mani*) ◇ *Ho le labbra screpolate.* My lips are chapped.

scricchiolare VERBO
to creak

lo **scrittore**, la **scrittrice** NOME MASC, FEM
writer

la **scrittura** NOME FEM
writing ◇ *Non riesco a leggere la sua scrittura.* I can't read his writing.

la **scrivania** NOME FEM
desk

scrivere* VERBO

1 to write* ◇ *Scrivimi presto.* Write to me soon.

♦ **scrivere qualcosa a qualcuno** to write* somebody something ◇ *Ho scritto una lettera a Luca.* I wrote Luca a letter. ◇ *Gli hai scritto una cartolina?* Have you written him a postcard?

♦ **Scrivo sempre cartoline a tutti i miei amici.** I always write postcards to all my friends.

♦ **scrivere a macchina** to type

♦ **scrivere a penna** to write* in pen

2 to spell* ◇ *Come si scrive?* How do you

* I verbi seguiti da questo simbolo sono irregolari. Si veda anche alle pp.328–338.

spell it? ◇ *Si scrive con la K.* It's spelt with a K.

scroccone, la **scroccona** NOME MASC, FEM
scrounger

scrollare VERBO
- **scrollare la testa** to shake* one's head ◇ *Ha scrollato la testa.* He shook his head.
- **scrollare le spalle** to shrug one's shoulders

scrupolo NOME MASC
scruple ◇ *Non mi farei degli scrupoli a chiederglielo.* I wouldn't have any scruples about asking him.
- **essere senza scrupoli** to be* unscrupulous

scrupoloso AGGETTIVO (FEM **scrupolosa**)
conscientious

scucirsi VERBO
to come* unstitched ◇ *Mi si è scucita una tasca.* One of my pockets has come unstitched.

scuderia NOME FEM
stable (*di cavalli*)

scudetto NOME MASC
- **vincere lo scudetto** to win* the championship ◇ *Il Milan ha vinto lo scudetto.* AC Milan has won the championship.

scudo NOME MASC
shield

sculacciare VERBO
to spank

scultore, la **scultrice** NOME MASC, FEM
sculptor

scultura NOME FEM
sculpture

scuola NOME FEM
school
- **andare a scuola** to go* to school ◇ *Vado a scuola ogni giorno.* I go to school every day. ◇ *I miei devono andare a scuola a parlare con i professori.* My parents have to go to the school to talk to the teachers.
  l'articolo va messo quando ci reca a scuola per motivi diversi dall'insegnare o dall'imparare.
- **scuola materna** nursery school
- **scuola elementare** primary school, $\boxed{US:}$ elementary school
- **scuola media inferiore** secondary school, $\boxed{US:}$ junior high school
- **scuola media superiore** secondary school, $\boxed{US:}$ high school

ⓘ *Secondary schooling in Italy comprises three years at the "scuola media inferiore" and four or five years at the "scuola media superiore".*

- **scuola privata** private school
- **scuola pubblica** state school, $\boxed{US:}$ public school
- **la scuola dell'obbligo** compulsory

education
- **scuola serale** night school
- **scuola guida** driving school

scuotere* VERBO
to shake* ◇ *Ha scosso la testa.* He shook his head.

scuro AGGETTIVO (FEM **scura**)
dark ◇ *un colore scuro* a dark colour ◇ *una gonna verde scuro* a dark green skirt

la **scusa** NOME FEM
excuse ◇ *Era solo una scusa per andarsene.* It was just an excuse to leave.
- **chiedere scusa a qualcuno** to apologize to somebody ◇ *Devi chiedere scusa all'insegnante.* You must apologize to the teacher.
- **Vi prego di accettare le mie scuse.** Please accept my apologies.
- **una lettera di scuse** a letter of apology

scusare VERBO
to excuse ◇ *Scusate un attimo, torno subito.* Excuse me, I'll be back in a minute.
- **scusarsi** to apologize ◇ *Si è scusato del ritardo.* He apologized for being late. ◇ *Ti sei scusato con lui?* Did you apologize to him?
- **Scusi! (1)** (*mi dispiace*) I'm sorry!
- **Scusi! (2)** (*per richiamare l'attenzione*) Excuse me!

sdraiarsi VERBO
to lie* down ◇ *Si è sdraiato sul letto.* He lay down on the bed.

la **sdraio** NOME FEM (PL le **sdraio**)
deck chair

se CONGIUNZIONE
$\boxed{1}$ if ◇ *Fammi sapere se c'è qualche problema.* Let me know if there are any problems. ◇ *Guarda se è lì.* See if it's there. ◇ *Se fosse più furbo verrebbe.* If he had more sense he would come. ◇ *Se fossi in te...* If I were you...
$\boxed{2}$ whether (*per indicare un'alternativa*)
◇ *Sono indecisa se scrivere o telefonare.* I'm not sure whether to write or to phone. ◇ *Non so se dirglielo o no.* I don't know whether to tell him or not.
- **se no** or else ◇ *Rispondigli, se no si arrabbia.* Answer him, or else he'll get angry.

sé PRONOME

*sé si traduce in genere con **himself, herself, itself** o **themselves** a seconda della persona a cui si riferisce.*

◇ *L'ha fatto da sé.* He did it himself.
◇ *Hanno tenuto la notizia per sé.* They kept the news to themselves. ◇ *È piena di sé.* She's full of herself.
- **L'ha portato con sé.** He took it with him.
- **se stesso** himself
- **se stessa** herself ◇ *Pensa solo a se stessa.* She only thinks of herself.

seccare VERBO

☞

⨂1 to dry ◇ *Il vento secca la pelle.* Wind dries the skin.
- **seccarsi** (*terra*) to dry up
⨂2 to annoy (*infastidire*) ◇ *Mi secca dover aspettare.* It annoys me to have to wait.
- **Smettila di seccarmi!** Stop bothering me!
- **seccarsi** (*persona*) to get* annoyed
⨂3 to mind (*dispiacere*) ◇ *Ti secca se ti faccio una domanda?* Do you mind if I ask you a question? ◇ *Ti secca abbassare il volume?* Would you mind turning down the volume?
mind è seguito dal gerundio.

seccato AGGETTIVO (FEM **seccata**)
annoyed

la **seccatura** NOME FEM
⨂1 nuisance (*fastidio*) ◇ *Che seccatura!* What a nuisance!
⨂2 bother (*problema*)
bother non ha plurale.
◇ *Non voglio seccature!* I don't want any bother!

il **secchiello** NOME MASC
bucket

il **secchio** NOME MASC
bucket ◇ *un secchio d'acqua* a bucket of water
- **secchio della spazzatura** dustbin, US: garbage can

secco AGGETTIVO (FEM **secca**, MASC PL **secchi**, FEM PL **secche**)
⨂1 dry (*pelle, clima, fiume*) ◇ *Ho la pelle molto secca.* I've got very dry skin. ◇ *La mia pelle è più secca della tua.* My skin is drier than yours.
- **frutta secca (1)** (*noci, mandorle ecc.*) nuts PL
- **frutta secca (2)** (*fichi, datteri ecc.*) dried fruit
- **avere la gola secca** to be* parched ◇ *Potrei avere qualcosa da bere? Ho la gola secca.* Could I have something to drink please, I'm parched.
- **far lavare a secco qualcosa** to get* something dry-cleaned ◇ *Devo far lavare a secco la giacca.* I need to get my jacket dry-cleaned.
⨂2 hard (*colpo*) ◇ *Devi dare un colpo secco.* You need to give it a hard bang.

il **secolo** NOME MASC
century (PL centuries) ◇ *nel XX secolo* in the 20th century
Si legge "in the twentieth century".

la **seconda** NOME FEM
⨂1 second year (*a scuola*)
- **seconda elementare** second year at primary school
- **seconda media** second year at secondary school
- **seconda superiore** fifth year at secondary school
⨂2 second gear (*marcia*) ◇ *mettere in seconda* to go* into second gear

- **a seconda di** according to ◇ *Le tariffe cambiano a seconda dell'ora del giorno.* Charges vary according to the time of day.

secondo AGGETTIVO (FEM **seconda**)
vedi anche **secondo** NOME MASC, PREPOSIZIONE
second (*in lista, di serie*) ◇ *in seconda fila* in the second row ◇ *Prendi la seconda strada a destra.* Take the second street on the right. ◇ *È arrivato secondo.* He came second.
- **Il suo disco è secondo in classifica.** His record is number two in the charts.
- **di seconda mano** second-hand ◇ *una moto di seconda mano* a second-hand motorbike
- **seconda classe** (*in treno*) second class ◇ *un biglietto di seconda classe* a second class ticket
- **viaggiare in seconda classe** to travel second-class

il **secondo** NOME MASC
vedi anche **secondo** AGGETTIVO, PREPOSIZIONE
⨂1 second (*di tempo*) ◇ *un minuto e dieci secondi* one minute and ten seconds
- **Un secondo, arrivo subito!** I won't be a minute!
⨂2 main course (*secondo piatto*) ◇ *Come secondo vorrei del salmone alla griglia.* I'd like grilled salmon for my main course.

secondo PREPOSIZIONE
vedi anche **secondo** AGGETTIVO, NOME
according to ◇ *Tutto sta andando secondo i piani.* Everything's going according to plan. ◇ *Secondo il giornale quel film è da non perdere.* According to the paper that film shouldn't be missed.
- **secondo me** in my opinion ◇ *Secondo me dovresti scrivergli.* In my opinion you should write to him.

il **sedano** NOME MASC
celery

la **sede** NOME FEM
office (*di ditta, di banca*)
- **sede centrale** head office

sedere* VERBO
vedi anche **sedere** NOME
to be* sitting ◇ *Era seduta accanto a me.* She was sitting beside me.
- **sedersi** to sit* ◇ *Si è seduto per terra.* He sat on the floor. ◇ *Siediti qui!* Sit here! ◇ *Sono così stanca che non vedo l'ora di sedermi!* I'm so tired I can't wait to sit down!
- **un posto a sedere** a seat

il **sedere** NOME MASC
vedi anche **sedere** VERBO
bottom

la **sedia** NOME FEM
chair
- **sedia a rotelle** wheelchair
- **sedia elettrica** electric chair

sedicenne AGGETTIVO
sixteen-year-old

---

* *I verbi seguiti da questo simbolo sono irregolari. Si veda anche alle pp.328–338.*

sedicesimo AGGETTIVO (FEM **sedicesima**)
sixteenth

sedici NUMERO
sixteen ◊ *Ha sedici anni.* She's sixteen.
• **alle sedici** at four p.m.
• **il sedici dicembre** the sixteenth of December

sedile NOME MASC
seat

sedurre* VERBO
to seduce

seduta NOME FEM
sitting ◊ *una seduta del parlamento* a parliamentary sitting
• **seduta spiritica** seance

sega NOME FEM (PL le **seghe**)
saw

segare VERBO
to saw*

seggio NOME MASC
• **seggio elettorale** polling station

seggiola NOME FEM
chair

seggiolone NOME MASC
highchair (*per bambini*)

seggiovia NOME FEM
chair lift

segnalare VERBO
1 to report ◊ *Ho segnalato il fatto alla polizia.* I reported the incident to the police. ◊ *Niente da segnalare.* Nothing to report.
2 to recommend (*consigliare*) ◊ *Potresti segnalarci un buon albergo?* Could you recommend a good hotel?
• *L'insegnante ha segnalato alcuni nomi per la borsa di studio.* The teacher suggested a few names for the scholarship.

segnale NOME MASC
signal ◊ *Al mio segnale spegnete la luce.* When I give the signal switch the light off.
• **segnale stradale** road sign
• **segnale orario** time signal
• *Lasciate un messaggio dopo il segnale acustico.* Leave a message after the tone.

segnalibro NOME MASC
bookmark

segnare VERBO
1 to mark ◊ *Gli errori sono segnati in rosso.* The mistakes are marked in red.
2 to show* (*indicare*) ◊ *Non segna la velocità giusta.* It's not showing the right speed.
3 to score (*nel calcio*) ◊ *Ha segnato nella ripresa.* He scored in the second half.
4 to make* a note of (*annotare*) ◊ *Segna quanto ti devo.* Make a note of what I owe you.

segno NOME MASC
1 sign ◊ *È un brutto segno.* It's a bad sign. ◊ *Di che segno sei?* What sign are you?
2 mark ◊ *Aveva dei segni rossi sul viso.*

She had red marks on her face.

il **segretario,** la **segretaria** NOME MASC, FEM
secretary (PL secretaries)

la **segreteria** NOME FEM
secretary's office (*di scuola, di ditta*)
• **segreteria telefonica** answering machine

segreto AGGETTIVO, NOME MASC (FEM **segreta**)
secret ◊ *un passaggio segreto* a secret passage
• **mantenere un segreto** to keep* a secret ◊ *Sai mantenere un segreto?* Can you keep a secret?
• **in segreto** in secret

seguente AGGETTIVO
following ◊ *il giorno seguente* the following day

seguire VERBO
to follow ◊ *Mi ha seguita fino a casa.* He followed me home. ◊ *Mi segui o vado troppo veloce?* Are you following me or am I going too fast?
• **Perché non segui i miei consigli?** Why don't you take my advice?
• **seguire un corso** to attend a course

il **seguito** NOME MASC
• **in seguito** then ◊ *Ora leggete; in seguito vi farò delle domande.* Now read it, then I'll ask you some questions.
• **di seguito** non-stop ◊ *È piovuto per tre giorni di seguito.* It rained non-stop for three days.

sei NUMERO
six ◊ *Ha sei anni.* She's six. ◊ *alle sei* at six o'clock
• **il sei dicembre** the sixth of December

seicento NUMERO
six hundred
• **il Seicento** the seventeenth century

selezionare VERBO
to select

la **sella** NOME FEM
saddle (*di cavallo, di moto*)

il **sellino** NOME MASC
saddle (*di bici*)

la **selvaggina** NOME FEM
game

selvaggio AGGETTIVO (FEM **selvaggia,** MASC PL **selvaggi,** FEM PL **selvagge**)
wild

selvatico AGGETTIVO (FEM **selvatica,** MASC PL **selvatici,** FEM PL **selvatiche**)
wild

il **semaforo** NOME MASC
traffic lights PL ◊ *Attento! Il semaforo è rosso.* Watch out! The traffic lights are red.

sembrare VERBO
1 to look ◊ *Ha quarant'anni, ma sembra più giovane.* She's forty, but she looks younger.
2 to seem ◊ *Non è facile come sembra.* It's not as easy as it seems. ◊ *Non mi* ☞

S

sembra possibile. It doesn't seem possible.

♦ **Mi sembra che...** (*penso che*) I think... ◊ *Mi sembra che tu abbia ragione.* I think you're right.

♦ **Non mi sembra vero!** I can't believe it!

il **seme** NOME MASC
[1] seed (*da piantare*)
[2] pip (*di agrumi, di mela, di pera*)
♦ **olio di semi** vegetable oil

la **semifinale** NOME FEM
semifinal

il **semifreddo** NOME MASC
frozen dessert

il **seminario** NOME MASC
seminar ◊ *Ho seguito un seminario di storia.* I attended a history seminar.

il **seminterrato** NOME MASC
basement

semplice AGGETTIVO
simple ◊ *L'esercizio è molto semplice.* The exercise is very simple. ◊ *Conduce una vita semplice.* He lives a simple life.
♦ **una semplice formalità** a mere formality

sempre AVVERBIO
[1] always ◊ *È sempre in ritardo.* He's always late. ◊ *Crede di avere sempre ragione.* He thinks he's always right.
♦ **per sempre** for ever ◊ *La situazione non durerà per sempre.* The situation won't last for ever.
♦ **una volta per sempre** once and for all
♦ **sempre più** more and more ◊ *Diventa sempre più difficile.* It's getting more and more difficult.
♦ **Diventa sempre più raro.** It's getting rarer and rarer.
♦ **sempre meno** less and less ◊ *L'attività è sempre meno redditizia.* The business is getting less and less profitable.
[2] still (*ancora, comunque*) ◊ *Esci sempre con lui?* Are you still going out with him? ◊ *È pur sempre tuo fratello.* He's still your brother.

la **senape** NOME FEM
mustard

il **Senato** NOME MASC
the Italian Senate

il **senatore,** la **senatrice** NOME MASC, FEM
senator

il **seno** NOME MASC
breast

sensazionale AGGETTIVO
sensational (*spettacolo, gara*)

la **sensazione** NOME FEM
feeling ◊ *Ho la sensazione di averlo già incontrato.* I've a feeling I've met him before.

sensibile AGGETTIVO
[1] sensitive ◊ *È un ragazzo sensibile.* He's a sensitive boy.

♦ **essere sensibile al freddo** to feel* the cold
[2] considerable (*notevole*) ◊ *C'è stato un sensibile aumento della temperatura.* There's been a considerable rise in the temperature.
Attenzione! In inglese esiste la parola **sensible,** *che però significa* **ragionevole.**

il **senso** NOME MASC
[1] sense ◊ *i cinque sensi* the five senses
♦ **avere senso** to make* sense ◊ *Questo non ha senso.* This doesn't make sense.
♦ **Che senso ha?** What's the sense in it?
♦ **Non capisco il senso della frase.** I can't understand the sentence.
♦ **un discorso senza senso** a meaningless speech
♦ **avere senso pratico** to be* practical ◊ *Ha molto senso pratico.* She's very practical.
♦ **senso dell'umorismo** sense of humour
♦ **senso di colpa** sense of guilt
♦ **riprendere i sensi** to regain consciousness
♦ **Mi fa senso.** It disgusts me.
[2] direction (*direzione*) ◊ *Veniva in senso contrario.* He was coming in the opposite direction.
♦ **in senso orario** clockwise
♦ **in senso antiorario** anticlockwise
♦ **una via a senso unico** a one-way street

sensuale AGGETTIVO
[1] sensual (*donna*)
[2] sensuous (*voce*)

il **sentiero** NOME MASC
path

sentimentale AGGETTIVO
sentimental

il **sentimento** NOME MASC
feeling ◊ *Aveva sempre nascosto i suoi sentimenti per lei.* He had always hidden his feelings for her.

sentire VERBO
[1] to hear* (*udire*) ◊ *Mi sentite?* Can you hear me? ◊ *Sento dei passi.* I can hear footsteps. ◊ *Ho sentito dire che...* I've heard that...
♦ **Ci sentiamo spesso.** We often talk on the phone.
♦ **Fatti sentire.** Keep in touch.
♦ **Stammi a sentire!** Listen to me!
[2] to feel* (*percepire*) ◊ *Sento freddo.* I feel cold. ◊ *Non sento niente per lui.* I don't feel anything for him.
♦ **Sento che succederà qualcosa.** I've got a feeling that something is going to happen.
♦ **sentirsi bene** to feel* well
♦ **sentirsi male** to feel* ill
♦ **Come ti senti?** How do you feel?
♦ **sentirsela di fare qualcosa** to feel* like doing something
to feel like regge il gerundio.
◊ *Non me la sento di continuare.* I don't feel like going on.

* I verbi seguiti da questo simbolo sono irregolari. Si veda anche alle pp.328–338.

senza PREPOSIZIONE

without ◇ *È uscito senza ombrello.* He went out without an umbrella. ◇ *È andato via senza dire niente.* He left without saying anything. ◇ *senza di te* without you

- **senz'altro** of course ◇ *Mi scriverai? – Senz'altro!* Will you write to me? – Of course!
- **Lo farò senz'altro domani.** I'll do it tomorrow without fail.

separare VERBO

1. to separate *(in generale)*
2. to distinguish *(aspetti, problemi)*

- **separarsi** to split up ◇ *I miei genitori si sono separati quando ero piccolo.* My parents split up when I was little.
- **Si è separata dal marito un anno fa.** She and her husband split up a year ago.

separato AGGETTIVO (FEM **separata**)

1. separate *(distinto)* ◇ *Abbiamo chiesto conti separati.* We asked for separate bills.
2. separated *(coppia)* ◇ *I miei genitori sono separati.* My parents are separated.

seppellire* VERBO

to bury

seppia NOME FEM

cuttlefish (PL cuttlefish)

sequestrare VERBO

to confiscate ◇ *I miei mi hanno sequestrato il motorino.* My parents have confiscated my moped.

sequestro NOME MASC

- **sequestro di persona** kidnapping

sera NOME FEM

evening

- **di sera** in the evening
- **domani sera** tomorrow evening
- **questa sera** this evening

serale AGGETTIVO

evening ◇ *un corso serale* an evening class

- **scuola serale** night school

serata NOME FEM

evening ◇ *Grazie per la bella serata.* Thanks for the lovely evening.

serbatoio NOME MASC

tank

serbo, serba NOME, AGGETTIVO

Serb

sereno AGGETTIVO (FEM **serena**)

1. calm *(persona, espressione)*
2. clear *(cielo)*

serie NOME FEM (PL le **serie**)

series ◇ *una serie di furti* a series of robberies

- **serie A** first division ◇ *Gioca in serie A.* He plays in the first division.
- **serie B** second division
- **produzione in serie** mass production

serio AGGETTIVO (FEM **seria**)

1. serious ◇ *È una faccenda seria.* It's a serious matter. ◇ *Aveva un'espressione molto seria.* He looked very serious.
2. reliable *(affidabile)* ◇ *È una ditta seria.* It's a reliable firm.

- **sul serio** *(davvero)* really ◇ *Sul serio vuoi andarci?* Do you really want to go?
- **Dico sul serio.** I'm serious.
- **Faccio sul serio.** I mean it.
- **prendere qualcosa sul serio** to take* something seriously ◇ *Prende lo studio molto sul serio.* He takes his schoolwork very seriously.

il serpente NOME MASC

snake

la serra NOME FEM

greenhouse ◇ *l'effetto serra* the greenhouse effect

la serratura NOME FEM

lock

il server NOME MASC (PL i **server**)

server

servire VERBO

to serve *(pranzo, cena, caffè)* ◇ *Dopo la cena ha servito il caffè.* After dinner she served coffee.

- **Serviti pure!** Help yourself!
- **servire a qualcosa** to be* for something ◇ *A che cosa serve?* What's it for?
- **servire per qualcosa** to be* for something ◇ *Serve per tagliare il formaggio.* It's for cutting cheese.
- **Non mi serve più.** I don't need it any more.

il servizio NOME MASC

1. service ◇ *Il servizio è compreso?* Is service included?

- **servizio militare** military service
- **i servizi segreti** the secret service SING
- **fuori servizio** *(telefono, ascensore)* out of order
- **una casa con doppi servizi** a house with two bathrooms

2. report *(articolo)* ◇ *un servizio sul terremoto in Afghanistan* a report on the earthquake in Afghanistan

3. serve *(nel tennis)* ◇ *Ha un servizio potentissimo.* She has a very powerful serve.

4. set *(da cucina)* ◇ *un servizio di posate* a set of cutlery ◇ *un servizio da tè* a tea set

sessanta NUMERO

sixty

sessantesimo AGGETTIVO, NOME MASC (FEM **sessantesima**)

sixtieth

il sesso NOME MASC

sex

- **fare sesso** to have* sex

sessuale AGGETTIVO

sexual

sesto AGGETTIVO, NOME MASC (FEM **sesta**)

sixth ◇ *Abito al sesto piano.* I live on the sixth floor. ◇ *È arrivato sesto nella gara.* He came sixth in the competition. ◇ *un sesto a* ☞

S

sixth ◇ *un sesto della popolazione* a sixth of the population

la **seta** NOME FEM
silk ◇ *una camicia di seta* a silk shirt

la **sete** NOME FEM
thirst ◇ *Muoio di sete.* I'm dying of thirst.
◆ **avere sete** to be* thirsty

settanta NUMERO
seventy

settantesimo AGGETTIVO, NOME MASC (FEM **settantesima**)
seventieth

sette NUMERO
seven ◇ *Ha sette anni.* She's seven. ◇ *alle sette di sera* at seven p.m.
◆ **il sette dicembre** the seventh of December

settecento NUMERO
seven hundred
◆ **il Settecento** the eighteenth century

il **settembre** NOME MASC
September
Si noti l'uso della maiuscola in inglese.
◇ *in settembre* in September

settentrionale AGGETTIVO
northern ◇ *l'Italia settentrionale* northern Italy

la **settimana** NOME FEM
week ◇ *la settimana scorsa* last week ◇ *la settimana prossima* next week ◇ *tra due settimane* in two weeks ◇ *Ho preso tre settimane di ferie.* I took three weeks' holiday.
con il genitivo sassone.

settimanale AGGETTIVO, NOME MASC
weekly

settimo AGGETTIVO, NOME MASC (FEM **settima**)
seventh ◇ *Abito al settimo piano.* I live on the seventh floor. ◇ *un settimo della popolazione* a seventh of the population

il **settore** NOME MASC
sector

severo AGGETTIVO (FEM **severa**)
[1] strict (*genitore, insegnante*)
[2] severe (*punizione*)

la **sezione** NOME FEM
section

la **sfacchinata** NOME FEM
◆ **È stata una bella sfacchinata!** It was really exhausting!

sfacciato AGGETTIVO (FEM **sfacciata**)
cheeky (*persona*) ◇ *È la ragazza più sfacciata della classe.* She's the cheekiest girl in the class.

sfasciare VERBO
to smash up (*macchina, moto*)

la **sfera** NOME FEM
◆ **sfera di cristallo** crystal ball
◆ **penna a sfera** ballpoint pen

la **sfida** NOME FEM
challenge

sfidare VERBO
to challenge ◇ *L'ho sfidato a scacchi.* I challenged him to a game of chess.
◆ **Sfido io!** No wonder! ◇ *Non si sente bene. – Sfido io, è tutto il giorno che mangia patatine!* He's not feeling well. – No wonder, he's been eating crisps all day!

sfilare VERBO
[1] to march (*manifestanti*)
[2] to slip off (*vestito, scarpe*)
◆ **sfilarsi** to take* off (*vestito, scarpe*) ◇ *Si è sfilata il vestito.* She took her dress off.

la **sfilata** NOME FEM
◆ **sfilata di moda** fashion show

sfinito AGGETTIVO (FEM **sfinita**)
exhausted

sfiorare VERBO
[1] to brush against ◇ *Qualcosa mi ha sfiorato la gamba.* Something brushed against my leg.
◆ **Il proiettile l'ha solo sfiorato.** The bullet only grazed him.
[2] to touch on ◇ *Non ha neppure sfiorato l'argomento.* He didn't even touch on the subject.

sfocato AGGETTIVO (FEM **sfocata**)
out of focus (*foto*)

sfogarsi VERBO
◆ **sfogarsi con qualcuno** to confide in someone ◇ *Avevo proprio bisogno di sfogarmi con qualcuno.* I really needed to confide in someone.
◆ **Non sfogarti su di me!** Don't take it out on me!

sfogliare VERBO
to leaf through ◇ *Stava sfogliando una rivista.* She was leafing through a magazine.

sfondare VERBO
[1] to break* down ◇ *Ha sfondato la porta.* He broke down the door.
[2] to be* successful ◇ *È difficile sfondare nel cinema.* It's difficult to be successful in the film world.

lo **sfondo** NOME MASC
background ◇ *bianco su sfondo rosso* white on a red background

la **sfortuna** NOME FEM
bad luck ◇ *Che sfortuna!* What bad luck!
◆ **portare sfortuna** to be* unlucky ◇ *Passare sotto una scala porta sfortuna.* It's unlucky to walk under a ladder.
◆ **avere sfortuna** to be* unlucky ◇ *Ho avuto sfortuna ieri sera, non ho vinto niente.* I was unlucky last night, I didn't win anything.

sfortunato AGGETTIVO (FEM **sfortunata**)
unlucky (*persona, numero*)

sforzarsi VERBO
◆ **sforzarsi di fare qualcosa** to try to do something ◇ *Sforzati di ricordare!* Try to remember!

sforzo NOME MASC
effort
+ **fare uno sforzo** to make* an effort
sfrattare VERBO
to evict
sfratto NOME MASC
+ **dare lo sfratto a qualcuno** to give*
somebody notice to quit ◇ *Ci hanno dato lo sfratto.* We've been given notice to quit.
sfregare VERBO
to rub ◇ *Si fregava gli occhi.* He was rubbing his eyes.
sfruttamento NOME MASC
exploitation
sfruttare VERBO
[1] to make* the most of (*tempo, spazio*)
◇ *Dobbiamo sfruttare lo spazio che abbiamo.* We have to make the most of the space we have.
[2] to exploit (*operai, risorse*)
[3] to take* advantage of (*opportunità*)
sfuggire VERBO
to escape ◇ *Mi sfugge il nome.* His name escapes me.
+ **È sfuggita alla polizia.** She got away from the police.
+ **sfuggire di mano a qualcuno** to slip out of somebody's hands ◇ *Il vaso mi è sfuggito di mano.* The vase slipped out of my hands.
+ **Mi è sfuggito di mente.** It slipped my mind.
+ **lasciarsi sfuggire** (*occasione, opportunità*) to miss ◇ *Non lasciarti sfuggire l'occasione.* Don't miss this opportunity.
sfumatura NOME FEM
shade (*di colore, di significato*)
sgabello NOME MASC
stool
sgabuzzino NOME MASC
junk room
sgambetto NOME MASC
+ **fare lo sgambetto a qualcuno** to trip somebody up
sganciare VERBO
to undo (*chiusura*)
sgarbato AGGETTIVO (FEM **sgarbata**)
rude (*persona*)
sgargiante AGGETTIVO
gaudy (*colore, vestito*)
sgobbare VERBO
[1] to swot (*scolaro*)
[2] to slog (*operaio*)
sgomberare VERBO
[1] to clear (*svuotare*) ◇ *Stanno sgomberando la stanza.* They're clearing the room.
[2] to move out (*andare via*) ◇ *Dobbiamo sgomberare entro lunedì.* We have to move out by Monday.
sgombro NOME MASC
mackerel (PL mackerel)
sgonfiare VERBO

to let* down ◇ *Sgonfia il materassino.* Let down the airbed.
+ **sgonfiarsi (1)** (*materassino*) to deflate
+ **sgonfiarsi (2)** (*gomma*) to go* flat
+ **La sua caviglia si è sgonfiata.** Her ankle is no longer swollen.
sgonfio AGGETTIVO (FEM **sgonfia**)
flat (*gomma, pallone*) ◇ *Hai una gomma sgonfia.* You've got a flat tyre.
sgradevole AGGETTIVO
unpleasant
sgranchirsi VERBO
+ **sgranchirsi le gambe** to stretch one's legs ◇ *Ho bisogno di sgranchirmi le gambe.* I need to stretch my legs.
sgranocchiare VERBO
to munch
sgraziato AGGETTIVO (FEM **sgraziata**)
clumsy (*persona, movimenti*) ◇ *Luigi è ancora più sgraziato.* Luigi is even clumsier.
sgridare VERBO
+ **sgridare qualcuno** to tell* somebody off ◇ *Perché mi sgridi?* Why are you telling me off?
sgualcire VERBO
to crease ◇ *Attenta a non sgualcire il vestito.* Mind you don't crease your dress.
+ **sgualcirsi** to get* creased
lo **sguardo** NOME MASC
look ◇ *Mi ha lanciato uno sguardo d'intesa.* He gave me a knowing look.
+ **Aveva lo sguardo triste.** He looked sad.
+ **sollevare lo sguardo** to look up
sguazzare VERBO
to splash about (*nell'acqua*)
lo **shampoo** NOME MASC
shampoo
si PRONOME
vedi anche **si** NOME

*Nel caso di alcuni verbi riflessivi **si** si traduce con **oneself, herself, himself, itself** o **themselves** a seconda della persona cui si riferisce.*

◇ *Si è scottata.* She's burned herself. ◇ *Si è tagliato.* He's cut himself. ◇ *Si sono già presentati.* They've already introduced themselves.

*Molto spesso però, **si** non si traduce, come negli esempi qui sotto.*

◇ *Si sta lavando le mani.* She's washing her hands. ◇ *Si è pettinato prima di uscire.* He combed his hair before going out. ◇ *Si è dimenticato l'ombrello a casa.* He left his umbrella at home. ◇ *L'orologio si è fermato.* The clock has stopped. ◇ *Si sono incontrati alle cinque.* They met at five o'clock.

*Nel caso dei verbi riflessivi reciproci, **si** si traduce spesso con **each other**.*

◇ *Si odiano.* They hate each other.
+ **Si stanno baciando?** Are they kissing?
il **si** NOME MASC (PL i **si**)

S

vedi anche **sì** PRONOME
B (*nota musicale*)

sì AVVERBIO
yes ◇ *Vuoi un caffè? – Sì, grazie.* Would you
like a coffee? – Yes, please. ◇ *Gli hai
telefonato? – Sì.* Have you phoned him? –
Yes, I have. ◇ *Siete andati al cinema ieri? –
Sì.* Did you go to the cinema yesterday? –
Yes, we did.
♦ **dire di sì** to say* yes
♦ **Penso di sì.** I think so.
♦ **Spero di sì.** I hope so.
♦ **un giorno sì e uno no** every other day

sia CONGIUNZIONE
♦ **sia...che...** both...and... ◇ *Verranno sia Luigi
che suo fratello.* Both Luigi and his brother
will be coming.

la **siccità** NOME FEM
drought

siccome CONGIUNZIONE
since ◇ *Siccome era tardi ho deciso di
tornare a casa.* Since it was late I decided to
go home.

la **Sicilia** NOME FEM
Sicily ◇ *Mi è piaciuta molto la Sicilia.* I really
liked Sicily. ◇ *Vado in Sicilia quest'estate.*
I'm going to Sicily this summer.

la **sicura** NOME FEM
safety catch (*di arma*)

la **sicurezza** NOME FEM
safety ◇ *una campagna per la sicurezza
sulle strade* a road safety campaign
♦ **di sicurezza** (*ago, valvola*) safety
♦ **cintura di sicurezza** seat belt ◇ *Mettiti la
cintura di sicurezza.* Fasten your seat belt.
♦ **per sicurezza** just in case ◇ *Per sicurezza
portati l'ombrello.* Take your umbrella, just
in case.
♦ **con sicurezza** confidently ◇ *Ha risposto con
molta sicurezza.* He answered very
confidently.
♦ **Lo so con sicurezza.** I'm quite certain.

sicuro AGGETTIVO (FEM **sicura**)
vedi anche **sicuro** NOME, AVVERBIO
1 safe ◇ *Questo non è un luogo sicuro.*
This isn't a safe place. ◇ *Non mi sento
sicuro qui.* I don't feel safe here.
2 sure (*certo*) ◇ *Sono sicuro che ce la farai.*
I'm sure you'll manage it. ◇ *Sei sicuro?* Are
you sure?
♦ **Ne ero sicuro!** I knew it!
♦ **L'ho saputo da fonte sicura.** I heard about it
from a reliable source.
♦ **di sicuro** for sure ◇ *Non sappiamo di sicuro
cosa sia successo.* We don't know for sure
what happened.
♦ **sicuro di sé** self-confident ◇ *È molto sicuro
di sé.* He's very self-confident.

il **sicuro** NOME MASC
vedi anche **sicuro** AGGETTIVO, AVVERBIO

♦ **essere al sicuro** to be* safe ◇ *Non
preoccuparti, qui siamo al sicuro.* Don't
worry, we're safe here.
♦ **mettere qualcosa al sicuro** to put*
something in a safe place ◇ *Ho messo il tuo
anello al sicuro.* I've put your ring in a safe
place.

sicuro AVVERBIO
vedi anche **sicuro** AGGETTIVO, NOME
of course ◇ *Verrai? – Sicuro!* Will you
come? – Of course I will!

la **siepe** NOME FEM
hedge

sieronegativo AGGETTIVO (FEM
sieronegativa)
HIV-negative

sieropositivo AGGETTIVO (FEM **sieropositiva**)
HIV-positive

la **sigaretta** NOME FEM
cigarette

il **sigaro** NOME MASC
cigar

la **sigla** NOME FEM
acronym (*abbreviazione*)

significare VERBO
to mean* ◇ *Cosa significa questa parola?*
What does this word mean?

il **significato** NOME MASC
meaning

la **signora** NOME FEM
lady (PL ladies) ◇ *È una signora molto
simpatica.* She's a very nice lady. ◇ *Signore
e signori!* Ladies and Gentlemen!
♦ **la signora Rossi** Mrs Rossi
Mrs si pronuncia "missis".
♦ **Gentile Signora,...** (*in una lettera*) Dear
Madam,...
♦ **Gentile Signora Rossi,...** Dear Mrs Rossi,...

il **signore** NOME MASC
gentleman (PL gentlemen) ◇ *C'è un signore
che ti cerca.* There's a gentleman looking for
you. ◇ *Signore e signori!* Ladies and
Gentlemen!
♦ **il signor Rossi** Mr Rossi
Mr si pronuncia "mister".
♦ **Gentile Signore,...** (*in una lettera*) Dear Sir,...
♦ **Gentile Signor Rossi,...** Dear Mr Rossi,...
♦ **i signori Bianchi** (*coniugi*) Mr and Mrs
Bianchi
♦ **il Signore** the Lord

la **signorina** NOME FEM
young woman (PL young women) ◇ *È la
signorina che abita al piano di sotto.* She's
the young woman who lives downstairs.
♦ **la signorina Rossi** Miss Rossi
♦ **Gentile Signorina,...** (*in una lettera*) Dear
Madam,...
♦ **Gentile Signorina Rossi,...** Dear Miss
Rossi,...

il **silenzio** NOME MASC

---

* *I verbi seguiti da questo simbolo sono irregolari. Si veda anche alle pp.328–338.*

silence

• **Fate silenzio!** Be quiet!

• **in silenzio** in silence ◊ *Ascoltavano in silenzio.* They listened in silence.

silenzioso AGGETTIVO (FEM **silenziosa**)
quiet ◊ *È un ragazzo silenzioso.* He's a quiet boy.

la **sillaba** NOME FEM
syllable

il **simbolo** NOME MASC
symbol

simile AGGETTIVO
similar ◊ *Abbiamo gusti simili.* We've got similar tastes. ◊ *Ha una gonna simile alla mia.* She's got a skirt similar to mine.

• **Non ho mai visto niente di simile.** I've never seen anything like it.

la **simpatia** NOME FEM

• **provare simpatia per qualcuno** to like somebody

simpatico AGGETTIVO (FEM **simpatica**, MASC PL **simpatici**, FEM PL **simpatiche**)
nice ◊ *È una ragazza simpatica.* She's a nice girl.

• **Mi è molto simpatico.** I really like him.
Attenzione! In inglese esiste la parola **sympathetic**, *che però significa* **comprensivo**.

sincero AGGETTIVO (FEM **sincera**)
[1] honest ◊ *Sii sincero con me.* Be honest with me.

• **un ragazzo sincero** a truthful boy
[2] sincere (*ammirazione, scuse*)

il **sindacato** NOME MASC
trade union

il **sindaco** NOME MASC (PL i **sindaci**)
mayor

la **sinfonia** NOME FEM
symphony (PL symphonies)

singhiozzare VERBO
to sob (*piangere*)

il **singhiozzo** NOME MASC

• **avere il singhiozzo** to have* hiccups

singolare AGGETTIVO, NOME MASC
singular (*in grammatica*) ◊ *la prima persona singolare* the first person singular ◊ *al singolare* in the singular

singolo AGGETTIVO (FEM **singola**)
vedi anche **singolo** NOME MASC
single ◊ *una camera singola* a single room

il **singolo** NOME
vedi anche **singolo** AGGETTIVO
singles ◊ *il singolo maschile* (*nel tennis*) the men's singles PL

la **sinistra** NOME FEM
[1] left (*parte*) ◊ *sulla sinistra, nella foto* on the left of the photo

• **voltare a sinistra** to turn left

• **spostarsi verso sinistra** to move to the left
[2] left hand (*mano*) ◊ *Scrive con la sinistra.* He writes with his left hand.

• **la sinistra** (*in politica*) the left ◊ *Ha vinto la sinistra.* The left won the election.

• **un partito di sinistra** a left-wing party

sinistro AGGETTIVO (FEM **sinistra**)
left (*mano, braccio*)

il **sinonimo** NOME MASC
synonym

sintetico AGGETTIVO (FEM **sintetica**, MASC PL **sintetici**, FEM PL **sintetiche**)
synthetic ◊ *materiali sintetici* synthetic materials

il **sintomo** NOME MASC
symptom

sintonizzarsi VERBO

• **sintonizzarsi su una stazione radio** to tune in to a radio station

la **sirena** NOME FEM
siren (*di polizia, di pompieri*)

la **siringa** NOME FEM (PL le **siringhe**)
syringe

il **sistema** NOME MASC (PL i **sistemi**)
[1] system ◊ *un sistema operativo* an operating system ◊ *il sistema nervoso* the nervous system ◊ *il sistema solare* the solar system
[2] way ◊ *È un nuovo sistema per imparare le lingue.* It's a new way to learn languages.

sistemare VERBO
[1] to arrange (*libri, mobili*) ◊ *Ha sistemato tutti i libri sullo scaffale.* He arranged all the books on the shelf.
[2] to settle ◊ *Abbiamo ancora una questione da sistemare.* We've still got one question to settle.

• **sistemarsi (1)** (*sposarsi*) to settle down

• **sistemarsi (2)** (*trovare un lavoro*) to find* a job

• **Vedrai, tutto si sistemerà.** You'll see, everything will work out.

la **sistemazione** NOME FEM
accommodation (*alloggio*) ◊ *È solo una sistemazione provvisoria.* It's only temporary accommodation.

il **sito** NOME MASC
site ◊ *un sito web* a web site

situato AGGETTIVO (FEM **situata**)
situated ◊ *La casa è situata nel centro del paese.* The house is situated in the middle of the village.

la **situazione** NOME FEM
situation

slacciare VERBO
to undo* (*vestito, nodo, scarpe*)

slavo AGGETTIVO (FEM **slava**)
Slav (*cultura, popolazioni*)

• **lingue slave** Slavonic languages

sleale AGGETTIVO
[1] disloyal (*persona*)
[2] unfair ◊ *concorrenza sleale* unfair competition

slegare VERBO

S

to untie (*corda, pacco*)

gli **slip** NOME MASC PL
briefs ◊ *un paio di slip nuovi* a new pair of briefs

la **slitta** NOME FEM
1 sledge (*giocattolo*)
2 sleigh (*trainata*)

slittare VERBO
1 to slip (*persona*)
2 to skid (*automobile*)

slogarsi VERBO
to sprain ◊ *Mi sono slogato la caviglia.* I've sprained my ankle.

la **Slovenia** NOME FEM
Slovenia

sloveno, slovena AGGETTIVO, NOME MASC/FEM
Slovene

lo **smacchiatore** NOME MASC
stain remover

smagliante AGGETTIVO
♦ *un sorriso smagliante* a dazzling smile

la **smagliatura** NOME FEM
1 ladder (*su calza*)
2 stretch mark (*sulla pelle*)

lo **smaltimento** NOME MASC
♦ *lo smaltimento dei rifiuti* waste disposal

smaltire VERBO
♦ *smaltire la sbornia* to sober up

lo **smalto** NOME MASC
♦ *smalto per unghie* nail varnish ◊ *Mi sto mettendo lo smalto.* I'm putting my nail varnish on.

smarrire VERBO
to lose* ◊ *Ho smarrito il portafoglio.* I've lost my wallet.
♦ *smarrirsi* (*perdersi*) to get* lost ◊ *Si sono smarriti nel bosco.* They got lost in the woods.

smentire VERBO
to deny ◊ *Il ministro ha smentito le voci.* The minister denied the rumours.

lo **smeraldo** NOME MASC
emerald ◊ *un anello con smeraldo* an emerald ring

smettere* VERBO
to stop ◊ *Smettila subito!* Stop it at once!
♦ *smettere di fare qualcosa* to stop doing something
con il gerundio.
◊ *Quando sono entrato hanno smesso di parlare.* When I came in they stopped talking. ◊ *Sta cercando di smettere di fumare.* He's trying to stop smoking.

smistare VERBO
to sort (*pacchi, lettere*)

smontare VERBO
1 to take* apart (*moto, macchina, mobile*)
2 to get* off (*da treno, da bicicletta, da autobus*) ◊ *Stava smontando dall'autobus.*

He was getting off the bus.
♦ *smontare dalla macchina* to get* out of the car

la **smorfia** NOME FEM
grimace ◊ *una smorfia di dolore* a grimace of pain
♦ *fare smorfie* to make* faces

snello AGGETTIVO (FEM **snella**)
slim ◊ *È la più snella.* She's the slimmest.

snervante AGGETTIVO
♦ *un lavoro snervante* a stressful job
♦ *L'attesa è stata snervante.* It was a strain having to wait.

lo/la **snob** NOME MASC/FEM (PL gli/le **snob**)
vedi anche **snob** AGGETTIVO
snob

snob AGGETTIVO (MASC, FEM, PL **snob**)
vedi anche **snob** NOME
snobbish (*persona*)

snobbare VERBO
to snub

snodare VERBO
to untie (*corda, lacci*)

sobrio AGGETTIVO (FEM **sobria**)
sober

socchiudere* VERBO
1 to leave* ajar (*porta, finestra*) ◊ *Ha socchiuso la porta.* He left the door ajar.
2 to half-close ◊ *Ha socchiuso gli occhi.* He half-closed his eyes.

socchiuso AGGETTIVO (FEM **socchiusa**)
1 ajar (*porta, finestra*) ◊ *Lascia la porta socchiusa.* Leave the door ajar.
2 half-closed ◊ *Aveva gli occhi socchiusi.* His eyes were half-closed.

soccorrere* VERBO
to help

il **soccorritore,** la **soccorritrice** NOME MASC, FEM
rescuer

il **soccorso** NOME MASC
♦ *prestare soccorso* to help ◊ *Nessuno si è fermato a prestare soccorso.* Nobody stopped to help.
♦ *pronto soccorso* first aid
♦ *soccorso stradale* breakdown service
♦ *soccorsi* aid SING ◊ *Stanno organizzando i soccorsi per i terremotati.* They are organizing aid for the earthquake victims.

sociale AGGETTIVO
social

la **società** NOME FEM (PL le **società**)
1 society (PL societies) ◊ *la società dei consumi* the consumer society
2 company (PL companies) ◊ *una società di assicurazioni* an insurance company
♦ *mettersi in società con qualcuno* to go* into business with somebody ◊ *Si è messo in società con suo fratello.* He went into business with his brother.

◆ società sportiva sports club

socievole AGGETTIVO
sociable

il socio, la socia NOME MASC, FEM
☐1 partner (*di ditta*)
☐2 member (*di associazione, di club*)

soddisfacente AGGETTIVO
satisfactory

soddisfare* VERBO
to satisfy ◇ *Il mio lavoro non mi soddisfa.*
My job doesn't satisfy me.

soddisfatto AGGETTIVO (FEM **soddisfatta**)
pleased ◇ *Sono soddisfatto del risultato.*
I'm pleased with the result.

la soddisfazione NOME FEM
satisfaction

sodo AGGETTIVO (FEM **soda**)
vedi anche **sodo** AVVERBIO, NOME
◆ un uovo sodo a hard-boiled egg

sodo AVVERBIO
vedi anche **sodo** AGGETTIVO, NOME
◆ lavorare sodo to work hard
◆ dormire sodo to sleep* soundly

sodo NOME MASC
vedi anche **sodo** AGGETTIVO, AVVERBIO
◆ venire al sodo to come* to the point ◇ *Vieni al sodo!* Come to the point!

sofferto AGGETTIVO (FEM **sofferta**)
◆ una vittoria sofferta a hard-won victory
◆ una decisione sofferta a painful decision

soffiare VERBO
to blow* ◇ *Soffiava un forte vento.* A strong wind was blowing.
◆ soffiarsi il naso to blow* one's nose ◇ *Si è soffiata il naso rumorosamente.* She blew her nose loudly.

la soffiata NOME FEM
◆ fare una soffiata alla polizia to tip off the police

soffice AGGETTIVO
soft

il soffio NOME MASC
breath (*di vento*) ◇ *Non c'era neanche un soffio di vento.* There wasn't a breath of wind.

la soffitta NOME FEM
attic

il soffitto NOME MASC
ceiling

soffocante AGGETTIVO
stifling (*caldo, atmosfera*)

soffocare VERBO
to suffocate ◇ *Ho rischiato di soffocare.* I nearly suffocated.
◆ Qua dentro si soffoca. It's stifling in here.

soffrire* VERBO
☐1 to suffer ◇ *Sta soffrendo molto.* He's suffering a lot.
◆ soffrire la fame to suffer from hunger
◆ soffrire la sete to suffer from thirst
◆ soffrire di to suffer from ◇ *Soffre di frequenti mal di testa.* He suffers from frequent headaches.
☐2 to stand* (*sopportare*) ◇ *Non lo posso soffrire.* I can't stand him.

sofisticato AGGETTIVO (FEM **sofisticata**)
sophisticated

il soggetto NOME MASC
subject (*di frase*)

la soggezione NOME FEM
◆ avere soggezione di qualcuno to be* in awe of somebody ◇ *Aveva soggezione del fratello maggiore.* He was in awe of his older brother.

il soggiorno NOME MASC
☐1 living room (*stanza*)
☐2 stay (*permanenza*) ◇ *un soggiorno di due settimane a Londra* a two-week stay in London

la sogliola NOME FEM
sole

sognare VERBO
to dream* ◇ *Ho sognato di essere sulla luna.* I dreamt I was on the moon. ◇ *Ho sempre sognato una casa così.* I've always dreamt of a house like this. ◇ *Stanotte ti ho sognato.* I dreamt about you last night.
◆ Te lo puoi sognare! In your dreams!
◆ sognare a occhi aperti to daydream*

il sogno NOME MASC
dream ◇ *un brutto sogno* a bad dream
◆ fare un sogno to have* a dream ◇ *Ho fatto uno strano sogno.* I had a strange dream.
◆ Neanche per sogno! No way!

la soia NOME FEM
soya

il sol NOME MASC (PL **i sol**)
G (*nota musicale*)

solamente AVVERBIO
only

solare AGGETTIVO
solar (*energia, sistema, pannelli*) ◇ *l'energia solare* solar power
◆ crema solare sun cream

il soldato NOME MASC
soldier
◆ soldato di leva conscript
◆ fare il soldato to serve in the army

i soldi NOME MASC PL
money SING ◇ *Mi presteresti dei soldi?* Could you lend me some money? ◇ *È pieno di soldi.* He's got lots of money.
◆ È roba da quattro soldi. It's cheap stuff.

il sole NOME MASC
sun ◇ *Preferirei stare al sole.* I'd rather stay in the sun. ◇ *Oggi c'è il sole.* The sun is shining today.
◆ una giornata di sole a sunny day
◆ prendere il sole to sunbathe

solenne AGGETTIVO
solemn

la solidarietà NOME FEM

S

☞

solidarity

solido AGGETTIVO (FEM **solida**)
[1] solid (*sostanza, rifiuti*)
[2] substantial (*edificio, muro*)

solitario AGGETTIVO (FEM **solitaria**)
vedi anche **solitario** NOME
lonely ◊ *una strada buia e solitaria* a dark, lonely road ◊ *una strada ancora più solitaria* an even lonelier road
♦ **È un tipo solitario.** He's a loner.

il **solitario** NOME MASC
vedi anche **solitario** AGGETTIVO
patience (*con le carte*) ◊ *Sto facendo un solitario.* I'm playing patience.

solito AGGETTIVO (FEM **solita**)
usual ◊ *più tardi del solito* later than usual ◊ *come al solito* as usual
♦ **di solito** usually ◊ *Di solito mi alzo alle sette.* I usually get up at seven o'clock.
Si noti la posizione di **usually**.

la **solitudine** NOME FEM
loneliness ◊ *La solitudine è un problema per gli anziani.* Loneliness is a problem for old people.
♦ **Soffre di solitudine.** He feels lonely.

il **solletico** NOME MASC
♦ **fare il solletico a qualcuno** to tickle somebody ◊ *Mi ha fatto il solletico.* He tickled me.
♦ **soffrire il solletico** to be* ticklish ◊ *Soffro molto il solletico.* I'm very ticklish.

il **sollevamento** NOME MASC
♦ **sollevamento pesi** weightlifting

sollevare VERBO
to lift ◊ *Non riesco a sollevare la valigia.* I can't lift the suitcase.
♦ **Ha sollevato gli occhi dal libro.** She raised her eyes from the book.
♦ **sollevarsi (1)** (*fumo, polvere*) to rise*
♦ **sollevarsi (2)** (*nebbia*) to lift
♦ **sentirsi sollevato** to feel* relieved

il **sollievo** NOME MASC
relief ◊ *Ho tirato un sospiro di sollievo.* I heaved a sigh of relief.

solo AGGETTIVO (FEM **sola**)
vedi anche **solo** AVVERBIO
[1] just one ◊ *Hanno un solo figlio.* They've just got one child.
[2] lonely (*abbandonato*) ◊ *Mi sento solo.* I feel lonely. ◊ *sempre più solo* lonelier and lonelier
[3] alone (*per conto suo*) ◊ *Vuole stare sola.* She wants to be alone.
♦ **da solo** on one's own
♦ **Vive da solo.** He lives on his own.
♦ **L'hai fatto da solo?** Did you do it on your own?
♦ **Ci vado da sola.** I'll go on my own.

solo AVVERBIO
vedi anche **solo** AGGETTIVO

only ◊ *L'ho incontrato solo due volte.* I've only met him twice.
♦ **Mancavi solo tu.** You were the only one who wasn't there.

soltanto AVVERBIO
only

solubile AGGETTIVO
instant (*caffè*)

la **soluzione** NOME FEM
solution ◊ *Non riesco a trovare una soluzione.* I can't find a solution.

il **somaro** NOME MASC
donkey (*animale*)
♦ **Sei un somaro!** You're an idiot!

somigliare VERBO
♦ **somigliare a** to look like ◊ *Somiglio moltissimo a mia madre.* I look very like my mother.

la **somma** NOME FEM
sum ◊ *una grossa somma di denaro* a large sum of money
♦ **fare le somme** to add up ◊ *Sai fare le somme?* Can you add up?

sommare VERBO
to add together ◊ *Somma i due numeri.* Add the two numbers together.
♦ **tutto sommato** all in all ◊ *Tutto sommato sono contento di essere venuto.* All in all I'm glad I came.

il **sommario** NOME MASC
summary (PL summaries)

il **sommergibile** NOME MASC
submarine

la **sommossa** NOME FEM
uprising

il **sondaggio** NOME MASC
♦ **sondaggio d'opinioni** opinion poll

il **sonnambulo,** la **sonnambula** NOME MASC, FEM
sleepwalker

il **sonnellino** NOME MASC
♦ **fare un sonnellino** to have* a nap

il **sonnifero** NOME MASC
sleeping pill

il **sonno** NOME MASC
sleep ◊ *Parli durante il sonno.* You talk in your sleep.
♦ **aver sonno** to be* sleepy
♦ **prendere sonno** to fall* asleep

sonoro AGGETTIVO (FEM **sonora**)
loud ◊ *una risata sonora* a loud laugh
♦ **colonna sonora** (*di film*) soundtrack

sopportare VERBO
[1] to stand* ◊ *Non lo sopporto.* I can't stand him. ◊ *Non sopporto il dolore fisico.* I can't stand physical pain.
[2] to put* up with ◊ *Hanno dovuto sopportare molte umiliazioni.* They had to put up with a lot of humiliation.
Attenzione! In inglese esiste il verbo **to**

support, *che però non significa* **sopportare**.

sopprimere* VERBO
to withdraw* ◇ *Il servizio di autobus è stato soppresso*. The bus service has been withdrawn.

sopra PREPOSIZIONE, AVVERBIO
[1] over ◇ *Indossava un maglione rosso sopra la camicia*. He was wearing a red jumper over his shirt. ◇ *le donne sopra i sessant'anni* women over sixty
[2] above (*più in alto di*) ◇ *L'aereo volava sopra le nuvole*. The plane was flying above the clouds. ◇ *cento metri sopra il livello del mare* a hundred metres above sea level ◇ *cinque gradi sopra lo zero* five degrees above zero
[3] on top of (*appoggiato*) ◇ *Il dizionario è sopra quella pila di libri*. The dictionary is on top of that pile of books.
◆ **là sopra** up there
◆ **qua sopra** up here
◆ **di sopra** upstairs ◇ *Abito di sopra*. I live upstairs.

l **soprabito** NOME MASC
coat

l **sopracciglio** NOME MASC (PL FEM le **sopracciglia**)
eyebrow

l **soprammobile** NOME MASC
ornament

soprannaturale AGGETTIVO
supernatural

l **soprannome** NOME MASC
nickname

a **soprano** NOME MASC/FEM
soprano

soprappensiero AVVERBIO
◆ **essere soprappensiero** to be* miles away

soprassalto NOME MASC
◆ **di soprassalto** with a start ◇ *Mi sono svegliata di soprassalto*. I woke up with a start.

soprattutto AVVERBIO
[1] mainly (*principalmente*) ◇ *Dipende soprattutto da lui*. It depends mainly on him.
[2] especially (*in particolare*) ◇ *Firenze è piena di turisti, soprattutto d'estate*. Florence is full of tourists, especially in the summer.

il **sopravvissuto**, la **sopravvissuta** NOME MASC, FEM
survivor

sopravvivere* VERBO
to survive ◇ *Riuscirà a sopravvivere?* Will he survive? ◇ *È sopravvissuto all'incidente*. He survived the accident.
senza preposizione.

il **sorbetto** NOME MASC
sorbet

sordo AGGETTIVO (FEM **sorda**)
deaf ◇ *È sordo da un orecchio*. He's deaf in one ear.
◆ **un rumore sordo** a dull sound

sordomuto AGGETTIVO (FEM **sordomuta**)
deaf-and-dumb

la **sorella** NOME FEM
sister ◇ *mia sorella* my sister ◇ *la sorella di Nadia* Nadia's sister

sorgere* VERBO
to rise* (*sole*)

sorpassare VERBO
to overtake* (*macchina*)

sorprendente AGGETTIVO
surprising

sorprendere* VERBO
[1] to catch* (*cogliere*) ◇ *Mia madre mi ha sorpreso a fumare*. My mother caught me smoking. ◇ *Sono stati sorpresi dal temporale*. They were caught in the storm.
[2] to surprise (*stupire*) ◇ *Mi ha sorpreso molto la sua risposta*. His answer really surprised me.

la **sorpresa** NOME FEM
surprise ◇ *Voglio fargli una sorpresa per il suo compleanno*. I want to give him a surprise for his birthday.

sorpreso AGGETTIVO (FEM **sorpresa**)
surprised ◇ *Sono sorpreso di vederti qui*. I'm surprised to see you here.

sorridente AGGETTIVO
smiling ◇ *un viso sorridente* a smiling face ◇ *È sempre sorridente*. He's always smiling.

sorridere* VERBO
to smile ◇ *Mi sorrideva*. She was smiling at me.

il **sorriso** NOME MASC
smile

il **sorso** NOME MASC
sip ◇ *Vuoi un sorso?* Do you want a sip?
◆ **tutto d'un sorso** all in one gulp ◇ *L'ho bevuto tutto d'un sorso*. I drank it all in one gulp.

la **sorte** NOME FEM
fate ◇ *Non sappiamo quale sarà la sua sorte*. We don't know what his fate will be.
◆ **tirare a sorte** to draw* lots ◇ *Hanno tirato a sorte per decidere chi doveva andare per primo*. They drew lots to decide who should go first.

sorvegliare VERBO
to watch ◇ *La polizia sorveglia la casa notte e giorno*. The police are watching the house night and day.

il/la **sosia** NOME MASC/FEM (PL i/le **sosia**)
double ◇ *È un tuo sosia!* He's your double!

sospendere* VERBO
to suspend ◇ *La partita è stata sospesa*. The match was suspended.

sospettare VERBO
to suspect ◇ *Nessuno sospettava niente*. Nobody suspected anything.

S

☞

* **sospettare di qualcuno** to suspect somebody ◊ *La polizia sospettava di loro.* The police suspected them.

il **sospetto** NOME MASC
  suspicion ◊ *Avevo dei sospetti su di lui.* I had my suspicions about him.

sospettoso AGGETTIVO (FEM **sospettosa**)
  suspicious

sospirare VERBO
  to sigh

il **sospiro** NOME MASC
  sigh ◊ *Ho tirato un sospiro di sollievo.* I heaved a sigh of relief.

la **sosta** NOME FEM
* **fare una sosta** to stop ◊ *Abbiamo fatto una sosta a Torino.* We stopped in Turin.
* **senza sosta** non-stop ◊ *Abbiamo lavorato senza sosta tutto il pomeriggio.* We worked non-stop all afternoon.
* **Qui è divieto di sosta.** You can't stop here.

il **sostantivo** NOME MASC
  noun

la **sostanza** NOME FEM
  substance

sostare VERBO
  to stop

sostenere* VERBO
  [1] to support ◊ *L'albero è sostenuto da una sbarra di ferro.* The tree is supported by a iron bar. ◊ *Il partito è sostenuto dall'industria.* The party is supported by industry.
  [2] to claim (*affermare*) ◊ *Sostiene di essere un tuo amico.* He claims to be a friend of yours.
* **Ha sempre sostenuto la propria innocenza.** He's always maintained his innocence.
* **sostenere che** to insist that ◊ *Sostiene che Paolo ha ragione.* He insists that Paolo is right.
* **sostenere gli esami** to sit* one's exams ◊ *Ho sostenuto gli esami in giugno.* I sat my exams in June.

sostituire VERBO
  [1] to change ◊ *Devo sostituire la cartuccia.* I need to change the cartridge.
  [2] to take* somebody's place ◊ *Era stanco e il suo collega l'ha sostituito.* He was tired and his colleague took his place.

la **sostituzione** NOME FEM
  substitution ◊ *Ha fatto una sostituzione all'ultimo minuto della partita.* He made a substitution in the last minute of the game.

i **sottaceti** NOME MASC PL
  pickles

sotterraneo AGGETTIVO (FEM **sotterranea**)
  underground ◊ *un fiume sotterraneo* an underground river

sotterrare VERBO
  to bury

sottile AGGETTIVO
  thin (*oggetto, strato, fetta*) ◊ *Le voglio più sottili.* I want them thinner.
* **capelli sottili** fine hair

sottinteso AGGETTIVO (FEM **sottintesa**)
  understood ◊ *Il verbo è sottinteso.* The verb is understood.
* **È sottinteso che...** It goes without saying that...

sotto PREPOSIZIONE
  [1] under ◊ *La cartina è sotto quel libro.* The map is under that book. ◊ *Si è nascosto sotto il letto.* He hid under the bed. ◊ *Ha un maglione verde sotto il cappotto.* She's wearing a green sweater under her coat. ◊ *Questo giocattolo non è adatto ai bambini sotto i tre anni.* This toy is not suitable for children under three.
  [2] below (*più in basso di*) ◊ *È sotto il livello del mare.* It's below sea level. ◊ *Abita sotto di noi.* He lives below us. ◊ *cinque gradi sotto zero* five degrees below zero
* **al piano di sotto** downstairs
* **là sotto** down there
* **qua sotto** down here
* **sotto la pioggia** in the rain
* **sotto il sole** in the sun

il **sottofondo** NOME MASC
* **sottofondo musicale** background music

sottolineare VERBO
  [1] to underline ◊ *Hai sottolineato le parole che non conosci?* Have you underlined the words you don't know?
  [2] to stress ◊ *Vorrei sottolineare l'importanza di quello che ha detto.* I'd like to stress the importance of what he said.

il **sottomarino** NOME MASC
  submarine

il **sottopassaggio** NOME MASC
  underpass

sottoporre* VERBO
  to submit* (*presentare*) ◊ *Gli ho sottoposto la mia richiesta.* I submitted my request to him.

sottosopra AVVERBIO
  upside down ◊ *Hanno messo la casa sottosopra.* They turned the house upside down.

sottoterra AVVERBIO
  underground

i **sottotitoli** NOME MASC PL
  subtitles ◊ *un film coi sottotitoli* a film with subtitles

sottovalutare VERBO
  to underestimate (*persona, prova*)

la **sottoveste** NOME FEM
  slip

sottovoce AVVERBIO
  in a low voice

sottovuoto AGGETTIVO (FEM **sottovuota**)

---

* I verbi seguiti da questo simbolo sono irregolari. Si veda anche alle pp.328–338.

+ **confezione sottovuoto** vacuum pack

sottrarre* VERBO
to subtract (*in matematica*)

+ **sottrarsi alle proprie responsabilità** to avoid one's responsibilities ◇ *Cerca di sottrarsi alle sue responsabilità.* He's trying to avoid his responsibilities.

sottrazione NOME FEM
subtraction

souvenir NOME MASC (PL i **souvenir**)
souvenir

sovietico AGGETTIVO (FEM **sovietica**, MASC PL **sovietici**, FEM PL **sovietiche**)
Soviet

sovraccarico AGGETTIVO (FEM **sovraccarica**, MASC PL **sovraccarichi**, FEM PL **sovraccariche**)
overloaded

sovraffollato AGGETTIVO (FEM **sovraffollata**)
overcrowded

sovvenzione NOME FEM
subsidy (PL subsidies)

spaccare VERBO
to break* ◇ *Ho spaccato il vaso.* I broke the vase.

+ **spaccarsi** to break* ◇ *Per poco non mi spaccavo un dente.* I nearly broke a tooth.

+ **spaccarsi la testa** to cut* one's head open ◇ *È caduto e si è spaccato la testa.* He fell and cut his head open.

spaccatura NOME FEM
split

spacciare VERBO

+ **spacciare droga** to sell* drugs

+ **spacciarsi per qualcuno** (*farsi credere*) to pretend to be somebody ◇ *Si è spacciata per tua cugina.* She pretended to be your cousin.

spacciatore, la **spacciatrice** NOME MASC, FEM
drug dealer

spaccio NOME MASC

+ **spaccio di droga** drug dealing

spacco NOME MASC (PL gli **spacchi**)
slit (*di gonna, di vestito*)

spada NOME FEM
sword

spaesato AGGETTIVO (FEM **spaesata**)
lost ◇ *Si sentiva spaesato nella grande città.* He felt lost in the big city.

+ **Mi sentivo spaesato tra quella gente.** I didn't feel comfortable with those people.

spaghetti NOME MASC PL
spaghetti SING ◇ *Sono buoni gli spaghetti?* Is the spaghetti nice?

Spagna NOME FEM
Spain ◇ *Mi è piaciuta molto la Spagna.* I really liked Spain. ◇ *Andrò in Spagna quest'estate.* I'm going to Spain this summer.

spagnola NOME FEM
Spanish woman (PL Spanish women)

(*persona*)

spagnolo AGGETTIVO (FEM **spagnola**)
| *vedi anche* **spagnolo** NOME |
Spanish

lo **spagnolo** NOME MASC
| *vedi anche* **spagnolo** AGGETTIVO |
[1] Spaniard (*persona*)

+ **gli Spagnoli** (*uomini e donne*) the Spanish
[2] Spanish (*lingua*) ◇ *Parli spagnolo?* Do you speak Spanish? ◇ *un insegnante di spagnolo* a Spanish teacher

lo **spago** NOME MASC (PL gli **spaghi**)
string

la **spalla** NOME FEM
shoulder ◇ *Mi fa male una spalla.* One of my shoulders hurts. ◇ *Ha le spalle curve.* He's got round shoulders.

+ **alle mie spalle** behind me

+ **voltare le spalle a qualcuno** to turn one's back on somebody ◇ *Mi ha voltato le spalle proprio quando avevo bisogno di lui.* He turned his back on me just when I needed him.

la **spalliera** NOME FEM
[1] back (*di sedia*)
[2] headboard (*di letto*)
[3] wall bars PL (*in ginnastica*)

la **spallina** NOME FEM
strap (*di vestito*)

spalmare VERBO
[1] to spread* ◇ *Spalma il burro sul pane.* Spread the butter on the bread.
[2] to rub (*crema*) ◇ *Stava spalmandosi la crema sulle gambe.* She was rubbing cream on her legs.

sparare VERBO

+ **sparare a qualcuno** to shoot* somebody ◇ *Le ha sparato.* He shot her.

+ **sparare un colpo** to fire a shot

la **sparatoria** NOME FEM
shoot-out

sparecchiare VERBO
to clear the table ◇ *Ti aiuto a sparecchiare?* Shall I help you clear the table?

lo **spareggio** NOME MASC
play-off

spargere* VERBO
to scatter ◇ *I miei fogli erano sparsi sulla scrivania.* My papers were scattered over the desk.

+ **Si è sparsa una voce sul suo conto.** There's a rumour going round about him.

sparire* VERBO
to disappear ◇ *La nave è sparita all'orizzonte.* The ship disappeared over the horizon.

+ **Dov'è sparita la mia penna?** Where has my pen gone?

sparlare VERBO

+ **sparlare di qualcuno** to say* nasty things about somebody ◇ *Sparla sempre di lei con* ☞

S

i suoi amici. He's always saying nasty things about her to his friends.

lo **sparo** NOME MASC
shot

sparpagliato AGGETTIVO (FEM **sparpagliata**)
scattered ◇ *I giocattoli erano sparpagliati sul pavimento.* The toys were scattered over the floor.

spartire VERBO
to share out (*eredità, bottino*)

lo **spartito** NOME MASC
score (*di musica*)

lo **spasso** NOME MASC
* **andare a spasso** to go* for a walk
* **portare a spasso il cane** to take* the dog for a walk

spavaldo AGGETTIVO (FEM **spavalda**)
cocky ◇ *Ora è più spavaldo che mai.* Now he's cockier than ever.

spaventare VERBO
to scare ◇ *L'idea mi spaventa un po'.* The idea scares me a bit.
* **spaventarsi** to be* scared ◇ *Si è spaventato molto vedendo la pistola.* He was very scared when he saw the gun.

lo **spavento** NOME MASC
* **far spavento a qualcuno** to scare somebody

spaventoso AGGETTIVO (FEM **spaventosa**)
terrible

spazientirsi VERBO
to lose* patience ◇ *Si è spazientito e se n'è andato.* He lost patience and left.

lo **spazio** NOME MASC
[1] room ◇ *Occupa molto spazio.* It takes up a lot of room. ◇ *Non c'è più spazio nell'armadio.* There's no more room in the wardrobe.
[2] space ◇ *grandi spazi aperti* wide open spaces ◇ *Hanno lanciato un satellite nello spazio.* They've launched a satellite into space. ◇ *È riuscita a parcheggiare in uno spazio piccolissimo.* She managed to park in a tiny space.

spazioso AGGETTIVO (FEM **spaziosa**)
spacious

lo **spazzaneve** NOME MASC (PL gli **spazzaneve**)
snowplough
snowplow US

spazzare VERBO
to sweep*

la **spazzatura** NOME FEM
rubbish
garbage US
◇ *Puoi portare fuori la spazzatura?* Can you take the rubbish out?
* **il secchio della spazzatura** the dustbin,
US: the garbage can

lo **spazzino** NOME MASC
road sweeper

la **spazzola** NOME FEM
brush
* **spazzola per capelli** hairbrush
* **spazzola per abiti** clothes brush

spazzolare VERBO
to brush

lo **spazzolino** NOME MASC
* **spazzolino da denti** toothbrush

lo **specchietto** NOME MASC
pocket mirror (*da borsetta*)
* **specchietto retrovisore** rear-view mirror
* **specchietto laterale** wing mirror

lo **specchio** NOME MASC
mirror ◇ *Mi sono guardata allo specchio.* I looked at myself in the mirror.

speciale AGGETTIVO
special

lo/la **specialista** NOME MASC/FEM (MASC PL gli **specialisti**, FEM PL le **specialiste**)
specialist

la **specialità** NOME FEM (PL le **specialità**)
speciality (PL specialities)

specialmente AVVERBIO
especially

la **specie** NOME FEM (PL le **specie**)
[1] sort (*tipo*) ◇ *È una specie di piatto con grandi manici.* It's a sort of dish with big handles.
[2] species ◇ *una specie in via di estinzione* an endangered species ◇ *alcune specie rare di piante* some rare species of plants

specificare VERBO
to specify

la **speculazione** NOME FEM
speculation

spedire VERBO
to send* ◇ *Non ho ancora spedito la lettera.* I haven't sent the letter yet.
* **spedire qualcosa a qualcuno** to send* somebody something ◇ *Gli ho spedito una cartolina.* I sent him a postcard. ◇ *Spedisco sempre una cartolina a tutti quelli che conosco.* I always send postcards to all the people I know. ◇ *Gliel'ho già spedito.* I've already sent it to him.

spegnere* VERBO
[1] to put* out (*fuoco, sigaretta*)
[2] to turn off (*luce, apparecchio elettrico, gas, motore*)
* **spegnersi (1)** (*luce, apparecchio elettrico*) to go* off ◇ *La luce si è spenta all'improvviso.* The light went off suddenly.
* **spegnersi (2)** (*motore*) to stall ◇ *Il motore si è spento al semaforo.* The engine stalled at the traffic lights.
* **spegnersi (3)** (*fuoco, sigaretta*) to go* out

spellarsi VERBO
to peel ◇ *Mi si sta spellando la schiena.* My back's peeling.

spendere* VERBO
to spend* ◇ *Quanto hai speso?* How much

* I verbi seguiti da questo simbolo sono irregolari. Si veda anche alle pp.328–338.

did you spend?
* **Si mangia bene e si spende poco.** The food's good and it doesn't cost much.

spensierato AGGETTIVO (FEM **spensierata**)
carefree

spento AGGETTIVO (FEM **spenta**)
off (*luce, apparecchio elettrico, motore*)

la **speranza** NOME FEM
hope ◇ *Hai qualche speranza di rivederlo?* Do you have any hope of seeing him again?

sperare VERBO
to hope ◇ *Spero che Luca arrivi in tempo.* I hope Luca arrives in time.
* **sperare di fare qualcosa** to hope to do something ◇ *Spero di trovare un lavoro presto.* I hope to find a job soon.
* **Spero di sì.** I hope so.
* **Spero di no.** I hope not.
* **Speriamo bene!** Let's hope it'll be okay.

la **spesa** NOME FEM
expense ◇ *una grossa spesa* a big expense ◇ *Le spese ti verranno rimborsate.* Your expenses will be reimbursed. ◇ *Sono andata a Parigi a spese della ditta.* I went to Paris at the company's expense.
al singolare.
* **fare la spesa** to do* the shopping
* **Adoro fare spese.** I love shopping.
* **ridurre le spese** to spend* less ◇ *Stiamo cercando di ridurre le spese del riscaldamento.* We're trying to spend less on heating.
* **spesa pubblica** public expenditure

spesso AGGETTIVO (FEM **spessa**)
vedi anche **spesso** AVVERBIO
thick (*carta, vetro, muro*) ◇ *È spesso cinque millimetri.* It's five millimetres thick.

spesso AVVERBIO
vedi anche **spesso** AGGETTIVO
often ◇ *Vai spesso al cinema?* Do you go to the cinema often?

lo **spessore** NOME MASC
* **avere uno spessore di...** to be*...thick ◇ *Ha uno spessore di due centimetri.* It's two centimetres thick.

Spett. ABBREVIAZIONE
* **Spett. Ditta,...** (*in lettera*) Dear Sirs,...

> ⓘ *Letters to companies also have* **Spett.** *before the name of the company on the envelope.*

lo **spettacolo** NOME MASC
show ◇ *uno spettacolo televisivo* a TV show
* **il primo spettacolo** (*al cinema*) the first showing ◇ *Andremo al primo spettacolo.* We'll go to the first showing.

spettare VERBO
* **spettare a qualcuno (1)** (*decisione*) to be* up to ◇ *Spetta a te decidere.* It's up to you to decide.
* **spettare a qualcuno (2)** (*denaro*) to be* due

to ◇ *Voglio solo quello che mi spetta.* I only want what's due to me.

lo **spettatore**, la **spettatrice** NOME MASC, FEM
[1] viewer (*di TV*)
[2] spectator (*di sport*)
* **gli spettatori** (*al cinema, a teatro*) the audience SING

spettegolare VERBO
to gossip

spettinato AGGETTIVO (FEM **spettinata**)
* **Sono tutta spettinata.** My hair's in a mess.

le **spezie** NOME FEM PL
spices

spezzare VERBO
to break* ◇ *Basta, mi spezzi il braccio!* Stop it! You're breaking my arm!
* **spezzarsi** to break* ◇ *La fune si è spezzata.* The rope broke.

spezzato AGGETTIVO (FEM **spezzata**)
broken (*unghia, ramo, braccio*)

la **spia** NOME FEM
[1] spy (*persona*) (PL spies)
* **Non fare la spia.** Don't be a sneak.
[2] light (*luce*) ◇ *la spia dell'olio* the oil light

spiacente AGGETTIVO
sorry ◇ *Spiacente, ma...* Sorry, but...

spiacevole AGGETTIVO
unpleasant

la **spiaggia** NOME FEM (PL le **spiagge**)
beach ◇ *una spiaggia sabbiosa* a sandy beach

spiare VERBO
* **spiare qualcuno** to spy on somebody ◇ *Ci stava spiando da dietro la porta.* He was spying on us from behind the door.

lo **spiazzo** NOME MASC
[1] piece of ground ◇ *Giocano in uno spiazzo davanti alla casa.* They play on a piece of ground in front of the house.
[2] clearing ◇ *Si fermarono in uno spiazzo nel bosco.* They stopped in a clearing in the forest.

lo **spicchio** NOME MASC
[1] segment (*di agrumi*)
[2] clove (*di aglio*)

spicciarsi VERBO
to hurry up ◇ *Digli di spicciarsi.* Tell him to hurry up.

gli **spiccioli** NOME MASC PL
change SING ◇ *Hai degli spiccioli per telefonare?* Have you got change for the phone?
* **Mi dispiace, ma non ho spiccioli.** I'm sorry, but I haven't got anything smaller.

lo **spiedino** NOME MASC
[1] kebab (*cibo*)
[2] skewer (*utensile*)

lo **spiedo** NOME MASC
spit
* **allo spiedo** spit-roasted ◇ *un pollo allo spiedo* a spit-roasted chicken

S

spiegare VERBO

1 to explain (far capire) ◇ Potresti spiegarci il motivo? Could you explain the reason to us? ◇ Gli ho spiegato la situazione. I explained the situation to him.

♦ **spiegarsi** (farsi capire) to make* oneself understood ◇ Era così agitato che non riusciva a spiegarsi. He was so upset that he couldn't make himself understood.

♦ **Mi sono spiegato?** Do you understand?

♦ **Non mi spiego come sia potuto accadere.** I can't understand how it could have happened.

2 to unfold (tovaglia, carta)

la **spiegazione** NOME FEM
explanation

spiegazzato AGGETTIVO (FEM **spiegazzata**)
creased

spietato AGGETTIVO (FEM **spietata**)
ruthless

lo **spiffero** NOME MASC
draught
draft US
◇ Questa stanza è piena di spifferi. This room is full of draughts.

lo **spigolo** NOME MASC
edge

la **spilla** NOME FEM
brooch ◇ una spilla d'oro a gold brooch

lo **spillo** NOME MASC
pin
♦ **tacchi a spillo** stiletto heels

spilorcio AGGETTIVO (FEM **spilorcia**, MASC PL **spilorci**, FEM PL **spilorce**)
mean

la **spina** NOME FEM
1 plug (elettrica)
2 thorn (di rosa, di rovo)
3 bone (di pesce)
♦ **spina dorsale** backbone
♦ **birra alla spina** draught beer

gli **spinaci** NOME MASC PL
spinach SING ◇ Gli spinaci fanno bene. Spinach is good for you.

lo **spinello** NOME MASC
joint (droga)

spingere* VERBO
1 to push ◇ Non spingete! Don't push!
2 to drive* ◇ È stato spinto dalla gelosia. He was driven by jealousy.

la **spinta** NOME FEM
push ◇ Mi aiuta a dare una spinta alla macchina? Could you help me give the car a push?

lo **spioncino** NOME MASC
peephole

spiritico AGGETTIVO (FEM **spiritica**, MASC PL **spiritici**, FEM PL **spiritiche**)
♦ **seduta spiritica** séance

lo **spirito** NOME MASC

spirit ◇ Ha preso lo scherzo con lo spirito giusto. He took the joke in the right spirit.

♦ **È una persona di spirito.** He's got a sense of humour.

♦ **lo Spirito Santo** the Holy Spirit

spiritoso AGGETTIVO (FEM **spiritosa**)
witty ◇ È il più spiritoso del gruppo. He's the wittiest in the group.

splendere VERBO
to shine* ◇ Il sole splende. The sun's shining.

splendido AGGETTIVO (FEM **splendida**)
wonderful

spogliare VERBO
to undress ◇ Ha spogliato il bambino e l'ha messo a letto. She undressed the baby and put him to bed.

♦ **spogliarsi** to get* undressed

lo **spogliarello** NOME MASC
striptease

lo **spogliatoio** NOME MASC
changing room

spolverare VERBO
to dust

spontaneo AGGETTIVO (FEM **spontanea**)
spontaneous ◇ È stato un gesto spontaneo da parte sua. It was a spontaneous gesture on his part.

♦ **I bambini sono sempre spontanei.** Children always act naturally.

♦ **di sua spontanea volontà** of his own free will

sporcare VERBO
to dirty ◇ Attento a non sporcare il tappeto. Mind you don't dirty the carpet.

♦ **sporcarsi** to get* dirty ◇ Deve essersi sporcato in giardino. He must have got dirty in the garden. ◇ Mi sono sporcato la camicia riparando la moto. I got my shirt dirty when I was fixing the motorbike.

♦ **Si è sporcato la camicia di sugo.** He's got sauce on his shirt.

sporco AGGETTIVO (FEM **sporca**, MASC PL **sporchi**, FEM PL **sporche**)
dirty ◇ Il fazzoletto è sporco. The handkerchief is dirty. ◇ sempre più sporco dirtier and dirtier

♦ **Il fazzoletto è sporco di sangue.** There's blood on the handkerchief.

♦ **avere la coscienza sporca** to have* a guilty conscience

sporgere* VERBO
to stick* out ◇ Sporge un po' troppo. It sticks out a bit too much.

♦ **sporgersi** to lean* out ◇ Non sporgerti dal finestrino. Don't lean out of the window.

lo **sport** NOME MASC (PL gli **sport**)
sport ◇ Fa diversi sport. He does various sports.

lo **sportello** NOME MASC

1️⃣ door (*di treno, di auto*)
2️⃣ window (*di banca, di ufficio*)
♦ **sportello automatico** (*di banca*) cash dispenser

sportivo AGGETTIVO (FEM **sportiva**)
1️⃣ sports ◇ *una macchina sportiva* a sports car ◇ *la pagina sportiva* the sports page
2️⃣ sporty (*persona*) ◇ *È molto sportiva.* She's very sporty. ◇ *Sei molto più sportiva di me.* You're much sportier than I am.
♦ **abbigliamento sportivo** casual clothes

sposa NOME FEM
bride ◇ *una bella sposa* a beautiful bride
♦ **un abito da sposa** a wedding dress

sposare VERBO
to marry ◇ *Le ha chiesto di sposarlo.* He asked her to marry him.
♦ **sposarsi** to get* married ◇ *Si sono sposati in giugno.* They got married in June.
♦ **sposarsi con qualcuno** to marry somebody ◇ *Si è sposato con Paola.* He married Paola.

sposato AGGETTIVO (FEM **sposata**)
married

sposo NOME MASC
bridegroom ◇ *un giovane sposo* a young bridegroom
♦ **gli sposi** the newlyweds
♦ **Viva gli sposi!** To the bride and groom!

spostare VERBO
to move ◇ *Mi aiuti a spostare il tavolo?* Can you help me move the table?
♦ **Hanno spostato la data.** They've changed the date.
♦ **spostarsi** to move ◇ *Potresti spostarti più in là?* Could you move along a bit?

sprecare VERBO
to waste ◇ *Stai sprecando tempo.* You're wasting time.

spremere VERBO
to squeeze (*arancia, limone*)
♦ **spremersi le meningi** to rack one's brains

spremiagrumi NOME MASC (PL gli **spremiagrumi**)
lemon squeezer

spremuta NOME FEM
♦ **spremuta d'arancia** freshly-squeezed orange juice

sproporzionato AGGETTIVO (FEM **sproporzionata**)
out of proportion ◇ *Il suo peso è sproporzionato all'altezza.* His weight is out of proportion to his height.

sproposito NOME MASC
♦ **parlare a sproposito** to go* off the point

sprovvista NOME FEM
♦ **prendere qualcuno alla sprovvista** to catch* somebody unawares

sprovvisto AGGETTIVO (FEM **sprovvista**)
♦ **sprovvisto di** without ◇ *I passeggeri sprovvisti di biglietto saranno multati.* Passengers without tickets will be fined.

♦ **Ne siamo rimasti sprovvisti.** (*in negozio*) We're out of it at the moment.

spruzzare VERBO
to spray (*profumo, lacca, insetticida ecc.*)

spugna NOME FEM
sponge ◇ *una spugna saponata* a soapy sponge
♦ **di spugna** towelling ◇ *un accappatoio di spugna* a towelling bathrobe

spuntare VERBO
1️⃣ to sprout (*germoglio*)
2️⃣ to rise* (*sole*)
3️⃣ to appear (*persona*) ◇ *È spuntato da chissà dove.* Heaven knows where he appeared from.
♦ **spuntarla** to get* one's own way ◇ *La spunta sempre lui.* He always gets his own way.

spuntino NOME MASC
snack
♦ **fare uno spuntino** to have* a snack

spunto NOME MASC
♦ **prendere spunto da qualcosa** (*scrittore, regista*) to take* inspiration from something ◇ *Il regista ha preso spunto da un fatto realmente accaduto.* The director took his inspiration from a real life story.

sputare VERBO
to spit*

squadra NOME FEM
team (*sportiva*) ◇ *una squadra di calcio* a football team
♦ **squadra del buon costume** vice squad
♦ **squadra mobile** flying squad

squagliarsi VERBO
to melt

squalificare VERBO
to disqualify

squallido AGGETTIVO (FEM **squallida**)
1️⃣ dingy (*albergo, casa*) ◇ *una squallida stanza d'albergo* a dingy hotel room
2️⃣ miserable ◇ *una vita squallida* a miserable life

squalo NOME MASC
shark

squarciagola:
♦ **a squarciagola** AVVERBIO at the top of one's voice ◇ *Gridava a squarciagola.* He was shouting at the top of his voice.

squilibrato AGGETTIVO (FEM **squilibrata**)
deranged (*persona, mente*)
♦ **una dieta squilibrata** an unbalanced diet

squillare VERBO
to ring* (*campanello, telefono*)

squillo NOME MASC
ring

squisito AGGETTIVO (FEM **squisita**)
delicious (*cibo, pranzo*)

srotolare VERBO
to unroll

stabile AGGETTIVO

S

☞

vedi anche **stabile** NOME

stable (prezzi, temperatura, situazione)

 • **un'occupazione stabile** a steady job
 • **La scala non è stabile.** The ladder's shaky.

lo **stabile** NOME MASC

vedi anche **stabile** AGGETTIVO

building (edificio)

lo **stabilimento** NOME MASC

 • **uno stabilimento industriale** an industrial plant

stabilire VERBO

to fix (prezzi, data)

 • **stabilirsi** to settle ◊ Si sono stabiliti qui tre anni fa. They settled here three years ago.

staccare VERBO

[1] to remove (etichetta, cerotto) ◊ Hai staccato l'etichetta dal dischetto? Did you remove the label from the disk?

 • **staccarsi** (bottone, etichetta, cerotto) to come* off ◊ Mi si è staccato un bottone della camicia. A button has come off my shirt.

[2] to pull away (allontanare) ◊ Stacca la sedia dal muro. Pull the chair away from the wall.

[3] to tear* out (foglio, pagina) ◊ Ha staccato una pagina dal quaderno. He tore a page out of the exercise book.

[4] disconnect (telefono) ◊ Se non paghi ti staccheranno il telefono. If you don't pay they'll disconnect your phone.

 • **Ho staccato il telefono perché la bambina dormiva.** I took the phone off the hook because the baby was sleeping.

 • **staccare la presa** to take* the plug out of the socket

 • **staccare la presa di** (TV, elettrodomestico) to unplug

lo **stadio** NOME MASC

[1] stadium (sportivo)

[2] stage (fase) ◊ durante l'ultimo stadio della malattia during the final stage of the illness

la **staffetta** NOME FEM

relay race

stagionato AGGETTIVO (FEM **stagionata**)

 • **formaggio stagionato** mature cheese

la **stagione** NOME FEM

season ◊ l'alta stagione the high season ◊ la bassa stagione the low season

 • **la bella stagione** the summer months PL

lo **stagno** NOME MASC

[1] pond (acquitrino)

[2] tin (materiale)

la **stagnola** NOME FEM

tinfoil

la **stalla** NOME FEM

[1] cowshed (per mucche)

[2] stable (per cavalli)

stamattina AVVERBIO

this morning

la **stampa** NOME FEM

print (disegno, quadro)

 • **la stampa** (giornali) the press

 • **"stampe"** (su busta) "printed matter"

la **stampante** NOME FEM

printer ◊ una stampante a getto d'inchiostro an ink jet printer

stampare VERBO

to print

lo **stampatello** NOME MASC

block letters PL ◊ Devo scrivere il mio nome in stampatello? Shall I write my name in block letters?

la **stampella** NOME FEM

crutch

stancare VERBO

to tire ◊ Non stancare i bambini con troppi giochi. Don't tire the children with too many games. ◊ Il viaggio lo ha stancato molto. The journey tired him out.

 • **Mi hai stancato con le tue lamentele.** I'm fed up of your complaining.

 • **stancarsi** to get* tired ◊ Non stancarti troppo. Don't get too tired. ◊ Mi sono stancato di aspettare. I got tired of waiting.

stanco AGGETTIVO (FEM **stanca**, MASC PL **stanchi**, FEM PL **stanche**)

tired ◊ Sei stanco? Are you tired? ◊ Sono stanco di ripetere la stessa cosa. I'm tired of repeating the same thing. ◊ Sono stanco morto. I'm dead tired.

la **stanghetta** NOME FEM

leg (di occhiali)

stanotte AVVERBIO

[1] tonight ◊ Stanotte ci saranno i fuochi d'artificio. There are going to be fireworks tonight.

[2] last night ◊ Stanotte non ho dormito bene. I didn't sleep well last night.

la **stanza** NOME FEM

room

 • **stanza da letto** bedroom

stappare VERBO

to open

stare* VERBO

[1] to be* ◊ Sei mai stato in Francia? Have you ever been to France? ◊ La casa sta sulla collina. The house is on the hill. ◊ Come stai? How are you? ◊ Sto bene, grazie. I'm fine, thanks. ◊ Sta studiando. He's studying. ◊ Stavo andando a casa. I was going home.

[2] to stay (rimanere) ◊ Stai ancora un po'! Stay a bit longer!

[3] to live (abitare) ◊ Sto con i miei. I live with my parents. ◊ Dove stai? Where do you live?

 • **A Londra starò da amici.** I'll be staying with friends in London.

---

* I verbi seguiti da questo simbolo sono irregolari. Si veda anche alle pp.328–338.

* **stare in piedi** to stand*
* **stare seduto** to be* sitting
* **stare fermo** to keep* still
* **stare zitto** to be* quiet
* **stare per fare qualcosa** to be* about to do something ◇ *Stavo per uscire quando ha squillato il telefono.* I was about to go out when the phone rang.
* **stare bene a qualcuno** to suit somebody ◇ *Quel vestito ti sta bene.* That dress suits you.
* **Nel bagagliaio non ci sta più niente.** There's no room for anything more in the boot.
* **Staremo a vedere.** Let's wait and see.
* **Sta a te decidere.** It's up to you to decide.
* **Ci sto!** OK!

starnutire VERBO
  to sneeze

lo **starnuto** NOME MASC
  sneeze

stasera AVVERBIO
  this evening

statale AGGETTIVO
  state ◇ *un impiegato statale* a state employee
* **un'industria statale** a state-owned industry

lo **stato** NOME MASC
  state ◇ *uno stato totalitario* a totalitarian state ◇ *un capo di stato* a head of state ◇ *Guarda in che stato si è ridotto!* Look at the state he's in!
* **La macchina è in buono stato.** The car is in good condition.
* **gli Stati Uniti d'America** the United States of America
* **in stato interessante** (*incinta*) pregnant

la **statua** NOME FEM
  statue

la **statura** NOME FEM
* **essere alto di statura** to be* tall
* **essere basso di statura** to be* short

stavolta AVVERBIO
  this time

la **stazione** NOME FEM
  station ◇ *la stazione ferroviaria* the railway station ◇ *la stazione degli autobus* the bus station
* **una stazione di servizio** a petrol station, US: a gas station

la **stecca** NOME FEM (PL le **stecche**)
* **una stecca di sigarette** a two hundred pack of cigarettes

lo **steccato** NOME MASC
  fence

la **stella** NOME FEM
  star ◇ *Stanotte si vedono le stelle.* You can see the stars tonight. ◇ *una stella cadente* a shooting star ◇ *una stella del cinema* a film star
* **stella alpina** edelweiss
* **stella di mare** starfish (PL starfish)

lo **stemma** NOME MASC (PL gli **stemmi**)
  coat of arms

stempiato AGGETTIVO (FEM **stempiata**)
* **essere stempiato** to have* a receding hairline

stendere* VERBO
  1 to stretch (*braccia, gambe*)
* **stendersi** to lie* down ◇ *Si è steso sul letto.* He lay down on the bed.
  2 to spread* out (*tovaglia*)
  3 to hang* out (*bucato*)

la **stenografia** NOME FEM
  shorthand

stentare VERBO
* **stentare a fare qualcosa** to find* it hard to do something ◇ *Stentavo a crederlo.* I found it hard to believe.

lo **stento** NOME MASC
* **Riesco a stento a pagare l'affitto.** I only just manage to pay the rent.

lo **stereo** NOME MASC (PL gli **stereo**)
  stereo

sterile AGGETTIVO
  sterile (*persona*)

la **sterlina** NOME FEM
  pound

sterminare VERBO
  to exterminate

sterminato AGGETTIVO (FEM **sterminata**)
  immense

lo **sterzo** NOME MASC
  steering wheel (*volante*)

stesso AGGETTIVO, PRONOME (FEM **stessa**)
  same ◇ *Aveva addosso lo stesso vestito.* She was wearing the same dress. ◇ *Abbiamo gli stessi gusti.* We have the same tastes. ◇ *Sei la stessa di sempre.* You're the same as ever. ◇ *In quello stesso istante ha suonato il campanello.* That same moment the bell rang.
* **L'ho sentito con le mie stesse orecchie.** I heard it with my own ears.
* **lo stesso** all the same ◇ *Per me fa lo stesso.* It's all the same to me. ◇ *Parto lo stesso.* I'm leaving all the same.

  *Quando **stesso** segue il pronome personale si traduce con **myself, yourself, himself, herself, ourselves, yourselves, themselves** a seconda del pronome.*
  ◇ *L'ho visto io stesso.* I saw it myself. ◇ *Lei stessa è venuta a dirmelo.* She came and told me herself.

lo **stile** NOME MASC
  style ◇ *gli stili architettonici* architectural styles ◇ *Bisogna ammettere che ha stile!* You have to admit he's got style!
* **Non è nel suo stile.** It's not like him.
* **stile libero** crawl ◇ *Sai nuotare a stile libero?* Can you do the crawl?
* **i cento metri stile libero** the hundred metres freestyle

S

☞

• **mobili in stile** period furniture SING

lo/la **stilista** NOME MASC/FEM (MASC PL gli **stilisti**, FEM PL le **stiliste**)
fashion designer

la **stilografica** NOME FEM (PL le **stilografiche**)
fountain pen

la **stima** NOME FEM
respect ◊ *Ho molta stima di lui.* I have great respect for him.

stimare VERBO
to respect ◊ *La stimo molto.* I really respect her.

stimolare VERBO
to stimulate

stinto AGGETTIVO (FEM **stinta**)
faded

lo **stipendio** NOME MASC
salary (PL salaries)

stirare VERBO
to iron

la **stitichezza** NOME FEM
constipation

lo **stivale** NOME MASC
boot

la **stoffa** NOME FEM
material

lo **stomaco** NOME MASC (PL gli **stomaci**)
stomach ◊ *Ho mal di stomaco.* I've got stomach ache.
• **dare di stomaco** to vomit

stonato AGGETTIVO (FEM **stonata**)
[1] tone-deaf (*persona*)
[2] out of tune (*voce*)

lo **stop** NOME MASC (PL gli **stop**)
[1] stop sign (*cartello stradale*)
[2] brake-light (*fanalino*)
• **Stop!** Stop!

storcere* VERBO
• **storcere il naso** to turn up one's nose
• **storcersi la caviglia** to twist one's ankle

stordire VERBO
to stun (*intontire*)

stordito AGGETTIVO (FEM **stordita**)
stunned

la **storia** NOME FEM
[1] story (PL stories) ◊ *una storia d'amore* a love story ◊ *Mi racconti una storia?* Will you tell me a story? ◊ *È sempre la stessa storia.* It's the same old story.
• **Non voglio più saperne di questa storia!** I don't want to hear any more about this!
[2] history ◊ *l'insegnante di storia* the history teacher
• **storie (1)** (*capricci*) fuss SING ◊ *Non ha fatto storie.* He didn't make a fuss.
• **storie (2)** (*fandonie*) nonsense SING ◊ *Racconta un sacco di storie.* He talks a lot of nonsense.

storico AGGETTIVO (FEM **storica**, MASC PL **storici**, FEM PL **storiche**)
[1] historical ◊ *un personaggio storico* a historical figure
[2] historic (*memorabile*) ◊ *È stato un momento storico.* It was a historic moment.

lo **stormo** NOME MASC
flock

la **storta** NOME FEM
• **prendersi una storta alla caviglia** to sprain one's ankle

storto AGGETTIVO (FEM **storta**)
[1] crooked (*quadro, gambe*)
[2] bent (*chiodo, tubo, manubrio*)
• **avere gli occhi storti** to be* cross-eyed
• **Mi va tutto storto.** Everything's going wrong for me.

le **stoviglie** NOME FEM PL
dishes

strabico AGGETTIVO (FEM **strabica**, MASC PL **strabici**, FEM PL **strabiche**)
• **essere strabico** to have* a squint

stracciare VERBO
to tear* up ◊ *Ho stracciato la lettera.* I tore up the letter.

lo **straccio** NOME MASC
vedi anche **straccio** AGGETTIVO
cloth (*per pulire*)

straccio AGGETTIVO (FEM **straccia**, MASC PL **stracchi**, FEM PL **stracce**)
vedi anche **straccio** NOME
• **carta straccia** waste paper

la **strada** NOME FEM
[1] road ◊ *Il bambino ha attraversato la strada senza guardare.* The child crossed the road without looking.
[2] way (*percorso*) ◊ *C'è tanta strada da fare?* Is it a long way? ◊ *Ti faccio strada.* I'll show you the way.
• **Sono tre ore di strada in macchina.** It's three hours' drive.
• **Facciamo la strada insieme?** Shall we walk along together?
[3] track
• **essere sulla buona strada** (*con indagine ecc.*) to be* on the right track
• **essere fuori strada** to be* on the wrong track
• **portare qualcuno sulla cattiva strada** to lead* somebody astray

stradale AGGETTIVO
road ◊ *un cartello stradale* a road sign

la **strage** NOME FEM
massacre

strambo AGGETTIVO (FEM **stramba**)
odd ◊ *un tipo strambo* an odd person

strangolare VERBO
to strangle

straniero AGGETTIVO (FEM **straniera**)
vedi anche **straniero** NOME
foreign ◊ *un paese straniero* a foreign country

lo **straniero**, la **straniera** NOME MASC, FEM

vedi anche **straniero** ADGETTIVO
foreigner

Attenzione! In inglese esiste la parola
stranger, *che però significa* **sconosciuto**
oppure **estraneo**.

strano AGGETTIVO (FEM **strana**)
strange

straordinario AGGETTIVO (FEM **straordinaria**)
vedi anche **straordinario** NOME
extraordinary (persona, fatto)

straordinario NOME MASC
vedi anche **straordinario** AGGETTIVO
overtime ◊ Ho fatto tre ore di straordinario.
I did three hours' overtime.

strappare VERBO
to tear* up ◊ Ha strappato la lettera. She
tore up the letter.
+ **Ho strappato una pagina dal quaderno.** I
tore a page out of the exercise book.
+ **strappare qualcosa a qualcuno** to snatch
something from somebody ◊ Mi ha
strappato la borsa. He snatched the bag
from me.
+ **strapparsi** to tear* ◊ La camicia si è
strappata sulla manica. The sleeve of the
shirt is torn.
+ **strapparsi un muscolo** to tear* a muscle

strappo NOME MASC
1 tear ◊ C'è uno strappo nella camicia.
There's a tear in the shirt.
+ **strappo muscolare** torn muscle
2 lift (passaggio) ◊ Mi dai uno strappo?
Could you give me a lift?

straripare VERBO
to overflow

stratagemma NOME MASC (PL gli
stratagemmi)
stratagem

strategico AGGETTIVO (FEM **strategica**, MASC PL
strategici, FEM PL **strategiche**)
strategic

strato NOME MASC
layer ◊ uno strato di polvere a layer of dust
+ **uno strato di pittura** a coat of paint

strattone NOME MASC
+ **Mi ha dato uno strattone.** He tugged at me.

stravagante AGGETTIVO
eccentric (persona, abbigliamento)

stravolto AGGETTIVO (FEM **stravolta**)
distraught ◊ Era stravolto. He was
distraught.
+ **Era stravolto dalla stanchezza.** He was
shattered.

strazio NOME MASC
+ **È uno strazio!** (libro, film, festa) It's dead
boring!

strega NOME FEM (PL le **streghe**)
witch

stremato AGGETTIVO (FEM **stremata**)
exhausted

strepitoso AGGETTIVO (FEM **strepitosa**)

+ **un successo strepitoso** a huge success

stressante AGGETTIVO
stressful ◊ Fa un lavoro stressante. He has
a stressful job.

stressato AGGETTIVO (FEM **stressata**)
stressed ◊ È un po' stressato ultimamente.
He's been rather stressed lately.

la stretta NOME FEM
+ **stretta di mano** handshake

stretto AGGETTIVO (FEM **stretta**)
1 narrow (strada, stanza) ◊ La strada
diventa stretta in quel punto. The road gets
narrow there.
2 tight (gonna, scarpe, nodo) ◊ Questa
gonna mi è stretta. This skirt's tight on me.
◊ Tienti stretto! Hold on tight!
+ **un parente stretto** a close relative
+ **lo stretto necessario** the bare minimum

la strettoia NOME FEM
bottleneck

stridulo AGGETTIVO (FEM **stridula**)
shrill (voce, suono)

strillare VERBO
to scream

lo strillo NOME MASC
scream

stringere* VERBO
to be* tight (vestito, scarpe) ◊ Queste
scarpe mi stringono. These shoes are tight
on me.
+ **stringere qualcosa (1)** (pugni, denti) to
clench something
+ **stringere qualcosa (2)** (vite, cintura, nodo) to
tighten something
+ **stringere qualcosa (3)** (vestito, gonna) to
take* something in
+ **stringersi la mano** to shake* hands ◊ Ci
siamo stretti la mano. We shook hands.
+ **stringersi** (persone) to squeeze up ◊ Se vi
stringete un po' posso sedermi anch'io. If
you squeeze up a bit I'll be able to sit down.

la striscia NOME FEM (PL le **strisce**)
strip (di carta, di stoffa)
+ **a strisce** striped ◊ una maglia a strisce blu e
bianche a blue and white striped jumper
+ **strisce pedonali** zebra crossing SING

strisciare VERBO
1 to crawl ◊ Stava strisciando sul
pavimento. He was crawling on the floor.
2 to scratch ◊ Scusami, ti ho strisciato la
macchina. I'm sorry, I've scratched your car.

lo striscione NOME MASC
banner

strizzare VERBO
to wring* out (vestiti)
+ **strizzare l'occhio** to wink ◊ Mi ha strizzato
l'occhio. She winked at me.

lo strofinaccio NOME MASC
1 duster (per la polvere)
2 dishcloth
dish towel US

S

☞

(*per piatti*)

strofinare VERBO
to rub

la **stronzata** NOME FEM
* **Non dire stronzate!** Don't talk crap!
* **Ho fatto una stronzata.** I've done something stupid.

stronzo AGGETTIVO (FEM **stronza**)
* **Stronzo!** You shit!

strozzare VERBO
to strangle

struccarsi VERBO
to take* off one's make-up ◇ *Mi sono struccata e sono andata a letto.* I took off my make-up and went to bed.

lo **strumento** NOME MASC
* **strumento musicale** musical instrument

la **struttura** NOME FEM
structure

lo **struzzo** NOME MASC
ostrich

lo **stucco** NOME MASC
⟦1⟧ plaster (*tipo di malta*)
⟦2⟧ stucco (*ornamentale*) ◇ *una stanza piena di stucchi* a room full of stucco work

lo **studente**, la **studentessa** NOME MASC, FEM
student

studiare VERBO
to study

lo **studio** NOME MASC
⟦1⟧ study (PL studies) ◇ *Ha interrotto gli studi per un anno.* He took a break from his studies for a year. ◇ *Il nonno legge nello studio.* Grandpa's reading in the study.
* **Ho letto uno studio recente sull'inquinamento.** I read a recent piece of research on pollution.
⟦2⟧ office (*di professionista*) ◇ *uno studio legale* a lawyer's office
* **studio fotografico** photographer's studio

studioso AGGETTIVO (FEM **studiosa**)
vedi anche **studioso** NOME
studious

lo **studioso**, la **studiosa** NOME MASC, FEM
vedi anche **studioso** AGGETTIVO
scholar

la **stufa** NOME FEM
* **stufa elettrica** electric heater
* **stufa a gas** gas heater

stufare VERBO
* **stufarsi di** to get* fed up with ◇ *Mi sono stufato di loro.* I got fed up with them.
* **stufarsi di fare qualcosa** to get* fed up of doing something ◇ *Mi sono stufato di aspettarlo.* I got fed up of waiting for him.
* **Mi hai proprio stufato!** I'm really fed up with you!

stufo AGGETTIVO (FEM **stufa**)
* **essere stufo** to be* fed up ◇ *Sei già stufa?* Are you fed up already?

* **essere stufo di fare qualcosa** to be* fed up of doing something ◇ *Sono stufo di studiare.* I'm fed up of studying.

stupefacente AGGETTIVO
* **sostanze stupefacenti** drugs

stupefatto AGGETTIVO (FEM **stupefatta**)
astonished

stupendo AGGETTIVO (FEM **stupenda**)
wonderful

la **stupidaggine** NOME FEM
* **Ho fatto una stupidaggine.** I did something stupid.
* **Non dire stupidaggini!** Don't talk nonsense!

stupido AGGETTIVO (FEM **stupida**)
stupid

stupire VERBO
to amaze ◇ *La sua risposta mi ha stupito molto.* His answer really amazed me.
* **stupirsi di qualcosa** to be* amazed at something ◇ *Mi sono stupito del suo coraggio.* I was amazed at his courage.
* **Non c'è da stupirsi.** It's not surprising.

lo **stupore** NOME MASC
amazement ◇ *Con mio grande stupore ho scoperto che...* Much to my amazement I discovered that...

stuprare VERBO
to rape

lo **stupro** NOME MASC
rape

lo **stuzzicadenti** NOME MASC (PL gli **stuzzicadenti**)
toothpick

stuzzicare VERBO
to tease (*persona*) ◇ *Smettila di stuzzicarlo.* Stop teasing him.
* **stuzzicare l'appetito** to whet the appetite

su PREPOSIZIONE
⟦1⟧ on ◇ *Il libro è sul tavolo.* The book's on the table. ◇ *Mettilo sulla sedia.* Put it on the chair. ◇ *È sulla destra.* It's on the right. ◇ *un libro sulla seconda guerra mondiale* a book on the Second World War
* **L'ho letto sul giornale.** I read it in the paper.
* **in tre casi su dieci** in three cases out of ten
* **Su, avanti!** Come on!
⟦2⟧ up (*in alto*) ◇ *Guarda su!* Look up!
* **Era su che aspettava.** She was waiting upstairs.
* **andare su e giù** to go* up and down
* **dai venti anni in su** from the age of twenty onwards
* **100 metri sul livello del mare** 100 metres above sea level
⟦3⟧ about (*circa*) ◇ *È costata sui cinquemila euro.* It cost about five thousand euros.

il **subacqueo**, la **subacquea** NOME MASC, FEM
vedi anche **subacqueo** AGGETTIVO
skin-diver

subacqueo AGGETTIVO (FEM **subacquea**)
vedi anche **subacqueo** NOME
underwater ◇ *esplorazione subacquea*
underwater exploration
+ **una muta subacquea** a wetsuit
subire* VERBO
1 to suffer ◇ *Dovrai subirne le consequenze.* You'll have to suffer the consequences. ◇ *Ha subito un torto.* He suffered an injustice.
2 to undergo* (*essere sottoposto a*) ◇ *Il progetto ha subito alcune modifiche.* The project has undergone some modifications.
subito AVVERBIO
immediately ◇ *È arrivato subito dopo di te.* He arrived immediately after you. ◇ *Fallo subito!* Do it immediately!
+ **Torno subito.** I'll be right back.
subordinato AGGETTIVO (FEM **subordinata**)
subordinate
+ **proposizione subordinata** subordinate clause
succedere* VERBO
to happen ◇ *Cos'è successo?* What happened? ◇ *Dev'essergli successo qualcosa.* Something must have happened to him. ◇ *Sono cose che succedono.* These things happen.
successivo AGGETTIVO (FEM **successiva**)
following ◇ *il giorno successivo* the following day
il **successo** NOME MASC
success ◇ *È stato un successo!* It was a success! ◇ *Ho provato ma senza successo.* I tried, but without success.
+ **di successo** successful ◇ *un film di successo* a successful film
+ **avere successo** (*persona, film, canzone*) to be* successful
succhiare VERBO
to suck
il **succhiotto** NOME MASC
dummy (PL dummies)
pacifier US
il **succo** NOME MASC (PL i **succhi**)
juice ◇ *succo di frutta* fruit juice ◇ *succo di pomodoro* tomato juice
il **sud** NOME MASC
south ◇ *La sua famiglia è del sud.* His family is from the south. ◇ *Il vento viene da sud.* The wind comes from the south.
+ **a sud** (*verso sud*) south ◇ *Si è diretto a sud.* He headed south.
+ **La Svizzera confina a sud con l'Italia.** To the south Switzerland has a border with Italy.
+ **a sud di** south of ◇ *Si trova a sud della città.* It's south of the city.
+ **l'Italia del Sud** Southern Italy
+ **l'America del Sud** South America
sudare VERBO
to sweat
sudato AGGETTIVO (FEM **sudata**)

sweaty (*persona, mani*) ◇ *sempre più sudato* sweatier and sweatier
+ **una vittoria sudata** a hard-won victory
sudicio AGGETTIVO (FEM **sudicia**, MASC PL **sudici**, FEM PL **sudice**)
dirty ◇ *sempre più sudicio* dirtier and dirtier
il **sudore** NOME MASC
sweat ◇ *Si è asciugato il sudore dalla fronte.* He wiped the sweat off his forehead.
sufficiente AGGETTIVO
enough ◇ *Pensi che il pane sia sufficiente?* Do you think there's enough bread? ◇ *È più che sufficiente.* It's more than enough.
la **sufficienza** NOME FEM
pass mark ◇ *Sono riuscito a prendere la sufficienza.* I managed to get a pass mark.
+ **a sufficienza** enough ◇ *Ne hai a sufficienza?* Have you got enough?
il **suggerimento** NOME MASC
suggestion ◇ *Qualcuno ha altri suggerimenti?* Has anyone got any other suggestions?
suggerire VERBO
to suggest ◇ *Cosa suggerisci?* What do you suggest? ◇ *Gli ho suggerito di dire tutto ai suoi genitori.* I suggested he told his parents everything.
Si noti la costruzione in inglese.
+ **Non suggerite!** (*in classe*) Don't help!
il **sughero** NOME MASC
cork
il **sugo** NOME MASC (PL i **sughi**)
sauce
+ **sugo di carne** gravy
suicidarsi VERBO
to commit suicide
il **suicidio** NOME MASC
suicide
suo AGGETTIVO (FEM **sua**)
vedi anche **suo** PRONOME
1 his (*di lui*) ◇ *Fabio ha preso i suoi libri.* Fabio took his books. ◇ *È colpa sua. Si è dimenticato i biglietti.* It's his fault. He forgot the tickets.
+ **un suo amico** a friend of his
2 her (*di lei*) ◇ *Luciana e le sue amiche* Luciana and her friends
3 its (*di animale, cosa*) ◇ *Il cane dorme nella sua cuccia.* The dog is sleeping in its kennel.
4 your (*forma di cortesia*) ◇ *Mi presta il suo ombrello?* Could you lend me your umbrella?
suo PRONOME (FEM **sua**)
vedi anche **suo** AGGETTIVO
1 his (*di lui*) ◇ *La mia casa è più grande della sua.* My house is bigger than his.
+ **i suoi genitori** his parents
2 hers (*di lei*) ◇ *È di Roberta questa macchina? – Sì, è sua.* Is this Roberta's car? – Yes, it's hers.
3 yours (*forma di cortesia*) ◇ *Scusi*

S

signore, È suo questo? Excuse me sir, is this yours?

la **suocera** NOME FEM
mother-in-law (PL mothers-in-law)

il **suocero** NOME MASC
father-in-law (PL fathers-in-law)
 • **i miei suoceri** my in-laws

la **suola** NOME FEM
sole (*di scarpa*)

suonare VERBO
1 to play (*strumento musicale*) ◊ *Sai suonare la chitarra?* Can you play the guitar?
 • **suonare il clacson** to hoot
2 to ring* (*telefono, campanello*) ◊ *Sta suonando il telefono.* The phone is ringing.
3 to sound ◊ *Mi suona strano.* It sounds strange to me.

il **suono** NOME MASC
sound

la **suora** NOME FEM
nun ◊ *Vuole farsi suora.* She wants to become a nun.
 • **Suor Maria** Sister Maria

la **super** NOME FEM
four-star petrol (*benzina*)

superare VERBO
1 to exceed (*livello, aspettative*) ◊ *Il risultato ha superato le aspettative.* The result exceeded expectations.
 • **Ha superato il limite di velocità.** He broke the speed limit.
2 to overcome* (*difficoltà, ostacolo, paura*) ◊ *Sono certo che riusciremo a superare queste difficoltà.* I'm sure we can overcome these difficulties.
3 to pass (*esame*) ◊ *Ha superato l'esame di guida.* He's passed his driving test.
 • **superare per primo il traguardo** to be* first to cross the finishing line
 • **aver superato la cinquantina** to be* over fifty

superbo AGGETTIVO (FEM **superba**)
haughty

superficiale AGGETTIVO
superficial ◊ *Fortunatamente è solo una ferita superficiale.* Fortunately, it's only a superficial wound. ◊ *È un po' superficiale.* She's a bit superficial.

la **superficie** NOME FEM (PL le **superfici**)
surface (*di acqua, di oggetto*)

superfluo AGGETTIVO (FEM **superflua**)
superfluous

superiore AGGETTIVO
vedi anche **superiore** NOME
1 upper ◊ *la parte superiore del corpo* the upper part of the body
2 above ◊ *La temperatura è superiore alla media.* The temperature is above average. ◊ *Sono superiore a queste cose.* I'm above such things.

 • **scuola superiore** secondary school, US: high school

il/la **superiore** NOME MASC/FEM
vedi anche **superiore** AGGETTIVO
superior ◊ *È il mio superiore.* He's my superior.

superlativo AGGETTIVO, NOME MASC (FEM **superlativa**)
superlative

il **supermercato** NOME MASC
supermarket

il/la **superstite** NOME MASC/FEM
survivor

la **superstizione** NOME FEM
superstition

superstizioso AGGETTIVO (FEM **superstiziosa**)
superstitious

supplementare AGGETTIVO
extra (*razione, servizi*)
 • **tempi supplementari** extra time SING ◊ *Hanno segnato nei tempi supplementari.* They scored in extra time.

il **supplemento** NOME MASC
supplement

il/la **supplente** NOME MASC/FEM
supply teacher

supplicare VERBO
to implore

supporre* VERBO
to suppose ◊ *Supponiamo che...* Let's suppose that... ◊ *Suppongo di sì.* I suppose so. ◊ *Suppongo di no.* I suppose not.

la **supposta** NOME FEM
suppository (PL suppositories)

surgelato AGGETTIVO (FEM **surgelata**)
frozen ◊ *cibo surgelato* frozen food

suscettibile AGGETTIVO
touchy ◊ *È molto suscettibile.* She's very touchy. ◊ *È più suscettibile di me.* She's touchier than me.

la **susina** NOME FEM
plum

il **sussidio** NOME MASC
 • **sussidi audiovisivi** audio-visual aids
 • **sussidio di disoccupazione** unemployment benefit

sussurrare VERBO
to whisper

il **sussurro** NOME MASC
whisper

svagarsi VERBO
to take* one's mind off things ◊ *Ho bisogno di svagarmi un po'.* I need to take my mind off things a bit.

svaligiare VERBO
 • **svaligiare una banca** to rob a bank
 • **svaligiare una casa** to burgle a house

la **svalutazione** NOME FEM
devaluation

---

* I verbi seguiti da questo simbolo sono irregolari. Si veda anche alle pp.328–338.

Italian ~ English

svanire VERBO
to disappear

svantaggiato AGGETTIVO (FEM **svantaggiata**)
disadvantaged ◊ *i bambini svantaggiati* disadvantaged children

svantaggio NOME MASC
disadvantage ◊ *i vantaggi e gli svantaggi della situazione* the advantages and disadvantages of the situation
• **essere in svantaggio di due punti** to be* two points down

svedese AGGETTIVO
vedi anche **svedese** NOME MASC, NOME FEM
Swedish ◊ *il governo svedese* the Swedish government

svedese NOME MASC
vedi anche **svedese** NOME FEM, AGGETTIVO
[1] Swede (*persona*) ◊ *gli svedesi* the Swedes
[2] Swedish (*lingua*) ◊ *Parla svedese.* He speaks Swedish.

svedese NOME FEM
vedi anche **svedese** NOME MASC, AGGETTIVO
Swede

sveglia NOME FEM
alarm clock ◊ *Hai puntato la sveglia?* Have you set the alarm clock? ◊ *Non ho sentito la sveglia stamattina.* I didn't hear the alarm clock this morning.

svegliare VERBO
• **svegliare qualcuno** to wake* somebody up ◊ *Svegliami alle sette.* Wake me up at seven.
• **svegliarsi** to wake* up ◊ *Mi sveglio sempre presto.* I always wake up early.

sveglio AGGETTIVO (FEM **sveglia**, MASC PL **svegli**, FEM PL **sveglie**)
[1] awake ◊ *Ero sveglio quando ha telefonato.* I was awake when he phoned.
[2] bright ◊ *un ragazzo sveglio* a bright boy

svelare VERBO
to reveal

svelto AGGETTIVO (FEM **svelta**)
quick ◊ *Svelto, vieni qua!* Quick, come here!

svendita NOME FEM
sale ◊ *una svendita di fine stagione* an end-of-season sale
• **in svendita** in a sale ◊ *Ho comprato questo cappotto in svendita.* I bought this coat in a sale.

svenire* VERBO
to faint

sventolare VERBO
to wave ◊ *Sulla torre del castello sventolavano delle bandiere.* Flags were waving on the castle tower.

svestirsi VERBO
to get* undressed

la **Svezia** NOME FEM
Sweden ◊ *Ti è piaciuta la Svezia?* Did you like Sweden? ◊ *Andrò in Svezia quest'estate.* I'm going to Sweden this summer.

sviluppare VERBO
to develop ◊ *Hai già fatto sviluppare le foto?* Have you had the photos developed yet?
• **svilupparsi** to develop

lo **sviluppo** NOME MASC
development (*di foto, di città*)
• **paesi in via di sviluppo** developing countries

la **svista** NOME FEM
oversight

svitare VERBO
to unscrew

la **Svizzera** NOME FEM
Switzerland ◊ *Ti è piaciuta la Svizzera?* Did you like Switzerland? ◊ *Andrò in Svizzera quest'inverno.* I'm going to Switzerland this winter.

la **svizzera** NOME FEM
Swiss woman (PL Swiss women)

svizzero AGGETTIVO (FEM **svizzera**)
vedi anche **svizzero** NOME
Swiss ◊ *il formaggio svizzero* Swiss cheese

lo **svizzero** NOME MASC
vedi anche **svizzero** AGGETTIVO
Swiss man (PL Swiss men)
• **gli svizzeri** (*uomini e donne*) the Swiss

svolgere* VERBO
• **svolgere un tema** to write* an essay
• **Che attività svolge?** What do you do?
• **svolgersi** (*aver luogo*) to happen ◊ *Tutto si è svolto rapidamente.* Everything happened quickly. ◊ *Come si sono svolti veramente i fatti?* How did it actually happen?

la **svolta** NOME FEM
turn (*curva*) ◊ *C'è un divieto di svolta a sinistra.* There's a no left turn sign.
• **Prendi la prima svolta a destra.** Take the first turning on the right.

svoltare VERBO
to turn ◊ *All'incrocio svolta a destra.* Turn right at the junction.

svuotare VERBO
to empty ◊ *Ho dovuto svuotare tutti i cassetti per trovarlo.* I had to empty all the drawers to find it.

S

T

la **tabaccheria** NOME FEM
tobacconist's shop

> **❶** *In Italy tobacco is a state monopoly.*

il **tabacco** NOME MASC (PL i **tabacchi**)
tobacco

la **tabella** NOME FEM
table

il **tabellone** NOME MASC
timetable (*in stazione, in aeroporto*)

il **tacchino** NOME MASC
turkey

il **tacco** NOME MASC (PL i **tacchi**)
heel ◊ *tacchi alti* high heels

tacere* VERBO
to be* quiet ◊ *Taci!* Be quiet!

la **taglia** NOME FEM
size ◊ *Che taglia porti?* What size do you
take? ◊ *taglia unica* one size

il **tagliando** NOME MASC
coupon

tagliare VERBO
to cut* ◊ *Taglialo in due.* Cut it in two.
♦ **tagliarsi** to cut* oneself ◊ *Mi sono tagliato.*
I've cut myself.
♦ **Mi sono tagliato un dito.** I've cut my finger.
♦ **tagliarsi i capelli** to have* one's hair cut
◊ *Devo tagliarmi i capelli.* I need to get my
hair cut. ◊ *Ti sei tagliato i capelli?* Have you
had your hair cut?

le **tagliatelle** NOME FEM PL
tagliatelle SING

tagliente AGGETTIVO
sharp

il **taglio** NOME MASC
cut ◊ *Ha un taglio sulla fronte.* He's got a cut
on his forehead.
♦ **taglio di capelli** hairstyle ◊ *Questo taglio di
capelli ti dona moltissimo.* That hairstyle
really suits you.

il **tailleur** NOME MASC (PL i **tailleur**)
suit

il **talco** NOME MASC
talcum powder

tale AGGETTIVO
such ◊ *Dice tali sciocchezze.* He says such
stupid things. ◊ *Mi son preso un tale
spavento!* I got such a fright!
Si noti la posizione dell'articolo "a".
♦ **essere tale quale** to be* exactly like ◊ *Il tuo
vestito è tale quale il mio.* Your dress is
exactly like mine.

il **talismano** NOME MASC
talisman

il **tallone** NOME MASC
heel

talmente AVVERBIO

1 so much ◊ *L'Irlanda mi è talmente
piaciuta che ci tornerei domani.* I liked
Ireland so much that I'd go back there
tomorrow.
2 so (+ *aggettivo*) ◊ *È talmente noioso!* It's
so boring!

la **talpa** NOME FEM
mole

il **tamburo** NOME MASC
drum

il **Tamigi** NOME MASC
Thames

tamponare VERBO
to crash into ◊ *Abbiamo tamponato un
furgone.* We crashed into a van.

il **tampone** NOME MASC
tampon (*assorbente*)

la **tangente** NOME FEM
kickback (*bustarella*)

la **tangenziale** NOME FEM
bypass (*strada*)

tanto AGGETTIVO, PRONOME (FEM **tanta**)
vedi anche **tanto** AVVERBIO
1 a lot of ◊ *Mangio sempre tanta pasta.* I
always eat a lot of pasta. ◊ *Alla festa c'erano
tante ragazze.* There were a lot of girls at the
party.
♦ **da tanto tempo** for a long time ◊ *Non lo
vedevo da tanto tempo.* I hadn't seen him
for a long time.
♦ **Tanti saluti ai tuoi!** Give my regards to your
family!
♦ **Ho ancora tanta strada da fare.** I've still got a
long way to go.
2 so much (*così tanto*) ◊ *Ho mangiato
tanta pasta che sono stato male.* I ate so
much pasta that I felt ill. ◊ *Non credevo che
costasse tanto.* I didn't think it cost so much.
♦ **tanti** (*così tanti*) so many ◊ *Non pensavo
che ce ne sarebbero stati tanti.* I didn't think
there would be so many.
♦ **ogni tanto** every so often
♦ **È da tanto che aspetti?** Have you been
waiting long?
♦ **tanto vale che tu** you may as well ◊ *Se lo
devi fare, tanto vale che lo faccia subito.* If
you're going to do it, you may as well do it at
once.

tanto AVVERBIO
vedi anche **tanto** AGGETTIVO, PRONOME
1 so (+ *aggettivo*) ◊ *È tanto simpatico!*
He's so nice!
2 so much (+ *verbo*) ◊ *Non capisco come
hai speso tanto.* I don't understand how you
spent so much.
♦ **tanto per cambiare** just for a change
◊ *Tanto per cambiare è in ritardo.* She's late,
just for a change.

---

* I verbi seguiti da questo simbolo sono irregolari. Si veda anche alle pp.328–338.

- **Parla tanto per parlare.** He just talks for the sake of talking.
- **L'abbiamo fatto così, tanto per ridere.** We just did it for a laugh.

tappa NOME FEM
stop ◇ *La prima tappa del nostro viaggio sarà Pisa.* The first stop on our journey will be Pisa.
- **fare tappa** to stop off ◇ *Abbiamo fatto tappa a Bath.* We stopped off at Bath.

tappare VERBO
to put* the cork in ◇ *Potresti tappare la bottiglia?* Could you put the cork in the bottle, please?
- **tapparsi il naso** to hold* one's nose
- **tapparsi le orecchie** to cover one's ears

tapparella NOME FEM
shutter

tappetino NOME MASC
mat (*sul pavimento*)
- **tappetino del mouse** mouse pad

tappeto NOME MASC
rug ◇ *un tappeto persiano* a Persian rug

tappezzeria NOME FEM
wallpaper ◇ *In camera da letto c'era la tappezzeria rosa.* There was pink wallpaper in the bedroom.

tappo NOME MASC
1. cork (*di sughero*)
2. plug (*di lavandino, di vasca*)

tardare VERBO
to be* late ◇ *Come mai hai tardato tanto?* How come you're so late?
- **Scusa se ho tardato a rispondere alla tua lettera, ma...** I'm sorry I've taken so long to reply to your letter, but...

tardi AVVERBIO
late ◇ *Oggi mi sono alzato tardi.* I got up late today. ◇ *Ormai è troppo tardi.* It's too late now. ◇ *Vi raggiungo più tardi.* I'll join you later.
- **A più tardi!** See you later!
- **Meglio tardi che mai!** Better late than never!
- **fare tardi** to be* late ◇ *Scusa se ho fatto tardi, ho perso l'autobus.* I'm sorry I'm late, I missed the bus.
- **Non devo fare tardi stasera, domani ho l'esame.** I mustn't stay up late tonight, I've got an exam tomorrow.
- **presto o tardi** sooner or later ◇ *Presto o tardi se ne pentirà.* Sooner or later he'll be sorry.

targa NOME FEM (PL le **targhe**)
number plate
license plate US
◇ *Non sono riuscito a leggere la targa.* I couldn't read the number plate.

targhetta NOME FEM
1. nameplate (*su porta*)
2. name tag (*su bagaglio*)

tariffa NOME FEM
1. fare (*di mezzi di trasporto*) ◇ *le tariffe ferroviarie* train fares ◇ *C'è una tariffa ridotta per i bambini.* There are reduced fares for children.
al plurale.
2. rate (*postale ecc.*)
3. charge (*di telefono*)

il tarlo NOME MASC
woodworm

la tarma NOME FEM
moth

i tarocchi NOME MASC PL
tarot cards

la tartaruga NOME FEM (PL le **tartarughe**)
1. tortoise (*terrestre*)
2. turtle (*di mare*)

la tartina NOME FEM
canapé

la tasca NOME FEM (PL le **tasche**)
pocket ◇ *L'ho messo nella tasca della giacca.* I put it in my jacket pocket.

tascabile AGGETTIVO
pocket ◇ *una calcolatrice tascabile* a pocket calculator ◇ *un'edizione tascabile* a pocket edition

la tassa NOME FEM
tax ◇ *Non aveva pagato le tasse.* He hadn't paid his taxes.
- **tasse scolastiche** school fees

il/la tassista NOME MASC/FEM (MASC PL i **tassisti**, FEM PL le **tassiste**)
taxi driver ◇ *Fa il tassista.* He is a taxi driver.

il tasso NOME MASC
- **tasso di cambio** rate of exchange
- **tasso di interesse** rate of interest

la tastiera NOME FEM
keyboard (*di computer, di piano*)

il/la tastierista NOME MASC/FEM (MASC PL i **tastieristi**, FEM PL le **tastieriste**)
1. keyboard player (*di strumento*)
2. keyboarder (*di computer*)

il tasto NOME MASC
key

il tatuaggio NOME MASC
tattoo ◇ *Ha un tatuaggio sul braccio.* He's got a tattoo on his arm.

la tavola NOME FEM
table ◇ *Apparecchio la tavola?* Shall I set the table?
- **A tavola!** Dinner's ready!

la tavoletta NOME FEM
- **una tavoletta di cioccolata** a bar of chocolate

il tavolino NOME MASC
table ◇ *un bar con i tavolini all'aperto* a café with tables outside

il tavolo NOME MASC
table ◇ *Vieni a sedere al nostro tavolo.* Come and sit at our table.

il taxi NOME MASC (PL i **taxi**)
taxi

la tazza NOME FEM

T

1 cup (*normale*)
2 mug (*più grande*)

te PRONOME
you ◇ *È alto come te.* He's as tall as you.
◇ *Parlavamo di te.* We were talking about you.

il **tè** NOME MASC (PL i **tè**)
tea

il **teatro** NOME MASC
theatre
theater US
◇ *Qualche volta vanno a teatro.* They sometimes go to the theatre.

la **tecnica** NOME FEM (PL le **tecniche**)
technique

tecnico AGGETTIVO (FEM **tecnica**, MASC PL **tecnici**, FEM PL **tecniche**)
vedi anche **tecnico** NOME
technical ◇ *Fa l'istituto tecnico.* He goes to the technical college.

il **tecnico** NOME MASC (PL i **tecnici**)
vedi anche **tecnico** AGGETTIVO
repair man (PL repair men) ◇ *È venuto il tecnico per riparare la TV.* The repair man's come to fix the TV.

la **tedesca** NOME FEM (PL le **tedesche**)
German

tedesco AGGETTIVO (FEM **tedesca**, MASC PL **tedeschi**, FEM PL **tedesche**)
vedi anche **tedesco** NOME
German ◇ *È tedesca.* She's German.

il **tedesco** NOME MASC (PL i **tedeschi**)
vedi anche **tedesco** AGGETTIVO
German (*persona, lingua*) ◇ *i tedeschi* the Germans ◇ *Parli tedesco?* Do you speak German?

il **tegame** NOME MASC
pan

la **teiera** NOME FEM
teapot

la **tela** NOME FEM
cloth ◇ *una pezza di tela* a piece of cloth
♦ **pantaloni di tela** cotton trousers
♦ **borsa di tela** canvas bag

la **telecamera** NOME FEM
TV camera

il **telecomando** NOME MASC
remote control

telefonare VERBO
to phone ◇ *Stamattina ha telefonato tua madre.* Your mother phoned this morning.
♦ **telefonare a qualcuno** to phone somebody ◇ *Ieri ho telefonato a Richard.* I phoned Richard yesterday.

la **telefonata** NOME FEM
phone call ◇ *Posso fare una telefonata?* Can I make a phone call?

telefonico AGGETTIVO (FEM **telefonica**, MASC PL **telefonici**, FEM PL **telefoniche**)
phone

♦ **cabina telefonica** phone box
♦ **elenco telefonico** phone book
♦ **scheda telefonica** phone card

il **telefonino** NOME MASC
mobile phone

il **telefono** NOME MASC
phone ◇ *È al telefono.* She's on the phone.
♦ **dare un colpo di telefono a qualcuno** to give* somebody a ring ◇ *Ti do un colpo di telefono più tardi.* I'll give you a ring later.
♦ **numero di telefono** phone number
♦ **telefono a monete** pay phone
♦ **telefono a scheda** cardphone
♦ **telefono pubblico** public phone

il **telegiornale** NOME MASC
news SING ◇ *L'hanno detto al telegiornale.* It was on the news. ◇ *Il telegiornale è alle otto.* The news is at eight.

il **telegramma** NOME MASC (PL i **telegrammi**)
telegram

il **telespettatore**, la **telespettatrice** NOME MASC, FEM
viewer

la **televisione** NOME FEM
television ◇ *L'ho visto alla televisione.* I saw it on television.

il **televisore** NOME MASC
television set ◇ *un televisore nuovo* a new television set

il **tema** NOME MASC (PL i **temi**)
essay ◇ *Ho consegnato il tema senza rileggerlo.* I handed in my essay without reading it through.

il **temperamatite** NOME MASC (PL i **temperamatite**)
pencil sharpener

la **temperatura** NOME FEM
temperature

il **temperino** NOME MASC
penknife (PL penknives)

la **tempesta** NOME FEM
tempest

le **tempie** NOME FEM PL
temples

il **tempio** NOME MASC
temple

il **tempo** NOME MASC
1 time ◇ *Scusa, adesso non ho tempo.* Sorry, I haven't got time at the moment.
◇ *Rilassati, abbiamo ancora tempo!* Relax, we've still got time!
♦ **al tempo stesso** at the same time
♦ **tempo libero** spare time ◇ *Cosa fai nel tempo libero?* What do you do in your spare time?
♦ **un po' di tempo** a while ◇ *Non lo vedo da un po' di tempo.* I haven't seen him for a while.
◇ *Era qui un po' di tempo fa.* She was here a while ago.
♦ **tempi supplementari** extra time SING

---

* *I verbi seguiti da questo simbolo sono irregolari. Si veda anche alle pp.328–338.*

2 weather (*metereologico*) ◇ *Che tempo fa?* What's the weather like? ◇ *brutto tempo* bad weather
• **le previsioni del tempo** the weather forecast SING
3 half (*di partita*) ◇ *Ha segnato nel secondo tempo.* He scored in the second half.
4 part (*di film, di commedia*) ◇ *Il primo tempo era un po' noioso.* The first part was a bit boring.

temporale NOME MASC
thunderstorm

temporaneo AGGETTIVO (FEM **temporanea**)
temporary ◇ *una sistemazione temporanea* temporary accommodation

tenaglie NOME FEM PL
pincers

tenda NOME FEM
1 tent (*da campeggio*)
2 awning (*per il sole*)
• **tende** (*di finestra*) curtains, US: drapes
• **tirare le tende** to draw* the curtains

tendere* VERBO
to stretch ◇ *Hanno teso una corda tra due alberi.* They stretched a rope between two trees.
• **tendere a** to tend to ◇ *Tende ad ingrassare.* She tends to put on weight.
• **blu che tende al verde** blue-green

tenente NOME MASC
lieutenant

tenere* VERBO
1 to hold* ◇ *Tiene la racchetta con la sinistra.* He holds the racket with his left hand.
• **tenere in braccio un bambino** to hold* a baby
• **tenersi a** to hold* onto ◇ *Tieniti al corrimano.* Hold onto the rail.
• **Tieniti forte!** Hold on tight!
• **tenersi per mano** to hold* hands ◇ *Si tenevano per mano.* They were holding hands.
• **Tieniti pronta per le cinque.** Be ready by five.
2 to keep* ◇ *Non mi serve, puoi tenerlo.* I don't need it, you can keep it. ◇ *Mi tieni il posto? Torno subito.* Will you keep my seat for me. I'll be right back.
• **tenere la destra** to keep* to the right
• **Tieni!** Here! ◇ *Tieni, usa il mio.* Here, use mine. ◇ *Tieni, questo è per te.* Here, this is for you.

tenero AGGETTIVO (FEM **tenera**)
1 soft ◇ *Il materasso è troppo tenero.* The mattress is too soft.
2 tender (*carne*)

tennis NOME MASC
tennis ◇ *Giochi a tennis?* Do you play tennis?
• **tennis da tavolo** table tennis

tennista NOME MASC/FEM (MASC PL i **tennisti**, FEM PL le **tenniste**)
tennis player

tentare VERBO
to try ◇ *Tenterà di battere il record mondiale.* She's going to try to beat the world record. ◇ *Le ho tentate tutte per convincerli.* I tried everything to persuade them.

il tentativo NOME MASC
attempt

la tentazione NOME FEM
temptation ◇ *Non ho saputo resistere alla tentazione!* I couldn't resist the temptation!

la teoria NOME FEM
theory (PL theories)
• **in teoria** in theory

il teppista NOME MASC (PL i **teppisti**)
hooligan

la terapia NOME FEM
therapy (PL therapies)

il tergicristallo NOME MASC
windscreen wiper
windshield wiper US

terminare VERBO
to finish ◇ *A che ora termina il film?* What time does the film finish?

il termine NOME MASC
end
• **avere termine** to end

il termometro NOME MASC
thermometer

il termos NOME MASC (PL i **termos**)
flask

il termosifone NOME MASC
radiator

il termostato NOME MASC
thermostat

la terra NOME FEM
ground ◇ *La terra è bagnata.* The ground's wet.
• **per terra (1)** (*terreno*) on the ground
• **per terra (2)** (*pavimento*) on the floor
• **cadere per terra** to fall* down
• **la Terra** the Earth

la terrazza NOME FEM
terrace ◇ *Erano seduti in terrazza.* They were sitting on the terrace.

il terrazzo NOME MASC
balcony (PL balconies)

il terremoto NOME MASC
earthquake

il terreno NOME MASC
1 land ◇ *una casa con 500 ettari di terreno* a house with 500 hectares of land ◇ *Hanno dei terreni in Toscana.* They've got land in Tuscany.
al singolare.
2 ground (*suolo*) ◇ *Il terreno è bagnato.* The ground's wet.

terribile AGGETTIVO
terrible

T

il **territorio** NOME MASC
territory (PL territories)

il **terrore** NOME MASC
* **avere il terrore di** to be* terrified of ◇ *Anna ha il terrore dei ragni.* Anna's terrified of spiders.
* **avere il terrore di fare qualcosa** to be* terrified of doing something ◇ *Sergio ha il terrore di volare.* Sergio's terrified of flying.

il **terrorismo** NOME MASC
terrorism

il/la **terrorista** NOME MASC/FEM (MASC PL i **terroristi**, FEM PL le **terroriste**)
terrorist

terrorizzato AGGETTIVO (FEM **terrorizzata**)
* **essere terrorizzato** to be* terrified

la **terza** NOME FEM
[vedi anche **terzo** NOME, AGGETTIVO]
third gear (*marcia*)
* **terza elementare** third year at primary school
* **terza media** third year at secondary school
* **terza superiore** sixth year at secondary school

il **terzino** NOME MASC
back ◇ *Gioca da terzino destro.* He plays right back.

terzo AGGETTIVO, NOME MASC (FEM **terza**)
third ◇ *Abito al terzo piano.* I live on the third floor. ◇ *È stato promosso solo un terzo della classe.* Only a third of the class have gone up to the next year.

il **teschio** NOME MASC
skull

la **tesi** NOME FEM (FEM le **tesi**)
dissertation ◇ *Presenterà una tesi su Jane Austen.* She's going to do a dissertation on Jane Austen.

teso AGGETTIVO (FEM **tesa**)
tense

il **tesoro** NOME MASC
treasure ◇ *caccia al tesoro* treasure hunt
* **Grazie tesoro!** Thank you darling!

la **tessera** NOME FEM
[1] card ◇ *una tessera magnetica* a swipe card
[2] membership card ◇ *Ho la tessera del Milan.* I've got a membership card for AC-Milan.
* **tessera dell'autobus** bus pass

il **tessuto** NOME MASC
fabric

la **testa** NOME FEM
head ◇ *Ho battuto la testa contro il pensile.* I banged my head on the cupboard.
* **dalla testa ai piedi** from head to foot
* **a testa** (*ciascuno*) a head ◇ *quindici euro a testa* fifteen euros a head
* **Testa o croce?** Heads or tails?
* **Facciamo a testa o croce?** Shall we toss for it?

* **essere in testa alla classifica (1)** (*pilota, disco*) to be* number one
* **essere in testa alla classifica (2)** (*squadra*) to be* top of the league

il **testamento** NOME MASC
will ◇ *Ha deciso di fare testamento.* He decided to make his will.

testardo AGGETTIVO (FEM **testarda**)
stubborn

il/la **testimone** NOME MASC/FEM
witness ◇ *Non c'erano testimoni.* There weren't any witnesses.

testimoniare VERBO
to give* evidence ◇ *Era disposta a testimoniare contro lui.* She was ready to give evidence against him.

la **testina** NOME FEM
head

il **testo** NOME MASC
text ◇ *un testo difficile* a difficult text
* **un libro di testo** a textbook

il **tetto** NOME MASC
roof

la **tettoia** NOME FEM
[1] canopy (PL canopies)
[2] roof (*di stazione*)

il **tettuccio** NOME MASC
* **tettuccio apribile** sunroof

il **Tevere** NOME MASC
Tiber

ti PRONOME
[1] you ◇ *Ti telefono più tardi.* I'll phone you later. ◇ *Ti piace?* Do you like it?
*Spesso **you** è preceduto da una preposizione, a seconda del verbo usato.* ◇ *Ti ha parlato?* Did she speak to you? ◇ *Ti ha sorriso.* He smiled at you.
[2] yourself (*riflessivo*) ◇ *Ti sei divertito?* Did you enjoy yourself?
* **Ti sei lavato i denti?** Have you brushed your teeth?
* **Ti ricordi?** Do you remember?

tiepido AGGETTIVO (FEM **tiepida**)
lukewarm ◇ *acqua tiepida* lukewarm water

il **tifo** NOME MASC
* **fare il tifo per** to support ◇ *Faccio il tifo per la Juventus.* I support Juventus.

il **tifoso**, la **tifosa** NOME MASC, FEM
supporter ◇ *i tifosi del Liverpool* the Liverpool supporters

la **tigre** NOME FEM
tiger

timbrare VERBO
to stamp ◇ *Hai timbrato il biglietto?* Have you stamped your ticket?

il **timbro** NOME MASC
stamp
* **mettere il timbro su qualcosa** to stamp something ◇ *Gli hanno messo il timbro sul*

---

* *I verbi seguiti da questo simbolo sono irregolari. Si veda anche alle pp.328–338.*

passaporto. They stamped his passport.
+ **timbro postale** postmark
timido AGGETTIVO (FEM **timida**)
shy
timone NOME MASC
rudder
tinta NOME FEM
[1] paint (*sostanza colorante*) ◇ *un barattolo di tinta* a tin of paint
[2] colour
color US
(*colore*)
◇ *una tinta vivace* a bright colour
+ **in tinta unita** plain ◇ *un vestito giallo in tinta unita* a plain yellow dress
tintoria NOME FEM
dry cleaner's ◇ *Devo portare il cappotto in tintoria.* I need to take my coat to the dry cleaner's.
tipico AGGETTIVO (FEM **tipica**, MASC PL **tipici**, FEM PL **tipiche**)
[1] typical ◇ *un esempio tipico* a typical example
[2] traditional ◇ *un tipico pub inglese* a traditional English pub ◇ *un tipico piatto scozzese* a traditional Scottish dish
tipo NOME MASC
[1] sort ◇ *Che tipo di bici hai?* What sort of bike have you got? ◇ *piante di tutti i tipi* all sorts of plants
[2] type ◇ *Non è il mio tipo.* He's not my type.
+ **Chi era quel tipo?** Who was that?
+ **Mi sembra un tipo simpatico.** He seems nice.
tirare VERBO
[1] to pull ◇ *Tira!* Pull! ◇ *Mi ha tirato i capelli.* She pulled my hair.
[2] to throw* (*lanciare*) ◇ *Tirami la palla!* Throw me the ball! ◇ *Ha tirato un sasso e poi si è nascosto.* He threw a stone and then hid.
+ **tirare un pugno a qualcuno** to punch somebody
+ **tirare uno schiaffo a qualcuno** to slap somebody
+ **tirare un calcio** to kick
+ **tirarsi indietro** to back out ◇ *Aveva promesso di aiutarmi ma poi si è tirato indietro.* He promised to help me and then backed out.
tirchio AGGETTIVO (FEM **tirchia**)
mean ◇ *Quant'è tirchio!* He's so mean!
titolo NOME MASC
title ◇ *Qual è il titolo di quella canzone?* What's the title of that song? ◇ *Ha conservato il titolo mondiale.* He retained the world title.
+ **i titoli** (*di giornale*) the headlines
tivù NOME FEM (PL le **tivù**)
TV ◇ *Cosa c'è in tivù stasera?* What's on TV tonight?

toast NOME MASC (PL i **toast**)
toastie
toccare VERBO
to touch ◇ *Non toccarlo!* Don't touch it! ◇ *Non vuole che si tocchi la sua roba.* He doesn't like people touching his things.
+ **A chi tocca?** Whose turn is it?
+ **Tocca a David.** It's David's turn.
+ **Perché tocca sempre a me farlo?** Why do I always have to do it?
+ **Mi è toccato pagare per tutti.** I had to pay for everybody.
togliere* VERBO
[1] to take* off ◇ *Togliti il cappotto.* Take off your coat. ◇ *Ho tolto il poster dalla parete.* I took the poster off the wall.
[2] to take* out (*estrarre*) ◇ *Mi hanno tolto due denti.* I had two teeth taken out.
la **toilette** NOME FEM (PL le **toilette**)
toilet ◇ *Dov'è la toilette?* Where's the toilet?
la **tomba** NOME FEM
grave
la **tombola** NOME FEM
bingo
+ **giocare a tombola** to play bingo
tondo AGGETTIVO (FEM **tonda**)
round ◇ *un cuscino tondo* a round cushion ◇ *parentesi tonde* round brackets
+ **chiaro e tondo** bluntly ◇ *Gli ho detto chiaro e tondo quello che pensavo.* I told him bluntly what I thought.
la **tonnellata** NOME FEM
ton ◇ *Questa valigia pesa una tonnellata!* This suitcase weighs a ton!
il **tonno** NOME MASC
tuna ◇ *un tramezzino al tonno* a tuna sandwich
il **tono** NOME MASC
tone ◇ *Dal tono di voce si capiva che era seccata.* You could tell she was annoyed by her tone of voice.
il **topo** NOME MASC
[1] mouse (PL mice)
[2] rat (*più grande*)
il **torace** NOME MASC
chest
la **torcia** NOME FEM (PL le **torce**)
+ **torcia elettrica** torch
il **torcicollo** NOME MASC
stiff neck ◇ *Ho il torcicollo.* I've got a stiff neck.
il **torero** NOME MASC
bullfighter
Torino NOME FEM
Turin ◇ *Domani andremo a Torino.* We're going to Turin tomorrow. ◇ *Abita a Torino.* She lives in Turin.
tormentare VERBO
to torment ◇ *Smettila di tormentare quel povero cane.* Stop tormenting that poor dog.

T

il **tornante** NOME MASC
hairpin bend
hairpin curve │US│

tornare VERBO
[1] to get* back ◊ *Quando sei tornato?*
When did you get back? ◊ *Sono tornato
domenica mattina.* I got back on Sunday
morning.
♦ **tornare a casa** to get* home
♦ **A che ora torni da scuola?** What time do you
get home from school?
[2] to be* back ◊ *Non sono ancora tornati
dalle vacanze.* They're not back from their
holidays yet. ◊ *Torno tra un attimo.* I'll be
back in a minute.

il **torneo** NOME MASC
tournament ◊ *un torneo di tennis* a tennis
tournament

Toro NOME MASC
Taurus (*dello zodiaco*) ◊ *Sono del Toro.* I'm
Taurus.

il **toro** NOME MASC
bull (*animale*)

la **torre** NOME FEM
[1] tower ◊ *la torre pendente di Pisa* the
Leaning Tower of Pisa
[2] rook (*negli scacchi*)

il **torrente** NOME MASC
torrent

il **torrone** NOME MASC
nougat

il **torsolo** NOME MASC
core ◊ *un torsolo di mela* an apple core

la **torta** NOME FEM
cake ◊ *una fetta di torta* a slice of cake

il **tortellini** NOME MASC
tortellini SING

il **torto** NOME MASC
♦ **avere torto** to be* wrong ◊ *Mi dispiace, ma
hai torto.* I'm sorry, but you're wrong.
♦ **In effetti non ha tutti i torti.** In fact she's
quite right.
♦ **Tutti hanno dato torto a Marina.** Everybody
said Marina was wrong.

la **tortura** NOME FEM
torture

torturare VERBO
[1] to torture (*prigioniero*)
[2] to torment ◊ *Smetti di torturare quel
povero gatto!* Stop tormenting that poor
cat!

Toscana NOME FEM
Tuscany ◊ *Andrò in Toscana quest'estate.*
I'm going to Tuscany this summer. ◊ *Ti è
piaciuta la Toscana?* Did you like Tuscany?

la **tosse** NOME FEM
cough ◊ *Ho la tosse.* I've got a cough.

il/la **tossicodipendente** NOME MASC/FEM
drug addict

tossire VERBO

to cough

il **tostapane** NOME MASC (PL i **tostapane**)
toaster

tostato AGGETTIVO (FEM **tostata**)
♦ **pane tostato** toast ◊ *una fetta di pane
tostato* a piece of toast

totale AGGETTIVO, NOME MASC
total ◊ *La festa è stata un fallimento totale.*
The party was a total failure. ◊ *Il totale è di
sessanta sterline.* The total is sixty pounds.

il **totocalcio** NOME MASC
the pools PL ◊ *Gioco al totocalcio ogni
settimana.* I do the pools every week.

la **tournée** NOME FEM (PL le **tournée**)
tour ◊ *Sono in tournée in Italia.* They're on
tour in Italy.

la **tovaglia** NOME FEM
tablecloth

il **tovagliolo** NOME MASC
napkin

tra PREPOSIZIONE
[1] between (*fra due*) ◊ *Era seduto tra il
padre e lo zio.* He was sitting between his
father and his uncle. ◊ *Detto tra noi, non
piace neanche a me.* Between you and me, I
don't like it either.
[2] among (*fra più di due*) ◊ *Tra i feriti c'era
anche il pilota dell'aereo.* The pilot of the
plane was among the injured.
[3] in (*in espressioni di tempo*) ◊ *Torno tra
un'ora.* I'll be back in an hour. ◊ *tra cinque
giorni* in five days
♦ **tra poco** soon
♦ **Tra venti chilometri c'è un'area di servizio.**
It's twenty kilometres to the next service
area.

la **traccia** NOME FEM (PL le **tracce**)
trace ◊ *Sul bicchiere c'erano tracce di
rossetto.* There were traces of lipstick on the
glass.
♦ **sparire senza lasciar traccia** to vanish
without trace

la **tracolla** NOME FEM
♦ **borsa a tracolla** shoulder bag

tradire VERBO
[1] to be* unfaithful to (*marito, moglie*) ◊ *Ha
tradito suo marito.* She was unfaithful to her
husband.
[2] to betray ◊ *Hai tradito la mia fiducia.*
You betrayed my trust.

tradizionale AGGETTIVO
traditional

la **tradizione** NOME FEM
tradition

tradurre* VERBO
to translate ◊ *Ho dovuto tradurlo
dall'inglese in italiano.* I had to translate it
from English into Italian.

la **traduzione** NOME FEM
translation

---

* *I verbi seguiti da questo simbolo sono irregolari. Si veda anche alle pp.328–338.*

trafficante NOME MASC/FEM
- **trafficante di droga** drug trafficker

traffico NOME MASC
traffic ◇ *C'è un traffico pazzesco.* The traffic's terrible.
- **traffico di droga** drug trafficking

tragedia NOME FEM
tragedy (PL tragedies) ◇ *una tragedia greca* a Greek tragedy
- **Non è il caso di farne una tragedia!** There's no need to make such a fuss about it!

traghetto NOME MASC
ferry (PL ferries) ◇ *Siamo andati in Irlanda col traghetto.* We went to Ireland by ferry.

tragico AGGETTIVO (FEM **tragica**, MASC PL **tragici**, FEM PL **tragiche**)
tragic

tragitto NOME MASC
journey ◇ *un breve tragitto* a short journey
- **lungo il tragitto** on the way ◇ *È scomparso lungo il tragitto da casa a scuola.* He disappeared on the way to school.

traguardo NOME MASC
finishing line ◇ *È stato il primo a tagliare il traguardo.* He was the first to cross the finishing line.

trainare VERBO
to tow (*macchina*) ◇ *Il carro attrezzi ha trainato la macchina fino alla città più vicina.* The breakdown van towed the car to the nearest town.

tram NOME MASC (PL i **tram**)
tram
streetcar US

trama NOME FEM
plot ◇ *La trama del film è un po' complicata.* The plot of the film is rather complicated.

tramezzino NOME MASC
sandwich ◇ *un tramezzino al prosciutto* a ham sandwich

tramonto NOME MASC
sunset

trampolino NOME MASC
diving board

tranne PREPOSIZIONE
except ◇ *Ha invitato tutti tranne me.* He invited everybody except me.

tranquillante NOME MASC
tranquillizer

tranquillizzare VERBO
to reassure ◇ *L'ho detto per tranquillizzarla.* I said it to reassure her.
*Attenzione! In inglese esiste il verbo **to tranquillize**, che però significa "calmare con un tranquillante".*

tranquillo AGGETTIVO (FEM **tranquilla**)
quiet ◇ *Cerchiamo un angolo tranquillo.* Let's find a quiet corner. ◇ *È un tipo molto tranquillo.* He's very quiet.
- **Sta' tranquillo!** Don't worry!

transitivo AGGETTIVO (FEM **transitiva**)
transitive

trapano NOME MASC
drill

trapianto NOME MASC
transplant

trappola NOME FEM
trap ◇ *Sono caduti nella trappola della polizia.* They fell into the police trap.

trapunta NOME FEM
quilt

trarre* VERBO
to draw* (*tirare*)
- **trarre le conclusioni** to draw* conclusions ◇ *Sta a te trarre le conclusioni.* You can draw your own conclusions.
- **trarre in inganno** to be* misleading ◇ *Il suo modo di fare trae in inganno.* His manner is misleading.
- **trarre in salvo** to rescue ◇ *Sono stati tratti in salvo dai vigili del fuoco.* They were rescued by the firemen.
- **un film tratto da un romanzo di A. Christie** a film based on a novel by A. Christie

trasandato AGGETTIVO (FEM **trasandata**)
- **È trasandato nel vestire.** He wears scruffy clothes.

trascinare VERBO
to drag

trascorrere* VERBO
1 to spend* ◇ *Trascorrono sempre le vacanze al mare.* They always spend their holidays at the seaside.
2 to pass ◇ *Sono già trascorsi sei giorni da allora.* Six days have passed since then.

trasferimento NOME MASC
transfer ◇ *Ha chiesto il trasferimento.* He's asked for a transfer.

trasferire* VERBO
to transfer ◇ *È stato trasferito a Milano.* He's been transferred to Milan.
- **trasferirsi** to move ◇ *Il mese prossimo ci trasferiamo a Firenze.* We're moving to Florence next month.

trasferta NOME FEM
- **giocare in trasferta** to play away from home ◇ *La prossima settimana giochiamo in trasferta.* We're playing away from home next week.

trasformare VERBO
1 to transform ◇ *Il soggiorno in America l'ha trasformato.* His stay in America has transformed him.
2 to convert ◇ *Hanno trasformato la stalla in un ristorante.* They converted the stable into a restaurant.
- **trasformarsi** to convert ◇ *un tavolo che si trasforma in asse da stiro* a table that converts into an ironing board

traslocare VERBO
to move

trasloco NOME MASC (PL i **traslochi**)

T

☞

removal ◇ *una ditta di traslochi* a removal firm
◆ **fare un trasloco** to move house ◇ *Li ho aiutati a fare il trasloco.* I helped them to move house.

trasmettere* VERBO
to broadcast
◆ **trasmettere in diretta** to broadcast live ◇ *Il concerto sarà trasmesso in diretta.* The concert will be broadcast live.

la **trasmissione** NOME FEM
programme
program US
◇ *una trasmissione radiofonica* a radio programme

trasparente AGGETTIVO
transparent

trasportare VERBO
to carry ◇ *Il camion trasportava un carico di arance.* The lorry was carrying a load of oranges.

il **trasporto** NOME MASC
transport
transport non ha plurale.
◇ *un sistema di trasporti efficiente* an efficient transport system
◆ **i trasporti pubblici** public transport SING
◇ *Qui i trasporti pubblici funzionano molto bene.* Public transport is very efficient here.

trattare VERBO
to treat ◇ *Lo tratta come un cane.* She treats him like a dog.
◆ **trattare con qualcuno** to deal* with somebody ◇ *Ho trattato direttamente con il proprietario.* I dealt directly with the owner.
◆ **trattare di** to be* about ◇ *Di cosa tratta il libro?* What's the book about? ◇ *Ti ha detto di cosa si tratta?* Did he tell you what it's about?
◆ **Si tratterebbe di poche ore.** It would just be a few hours.

trattenere* VERBO
1 to hold* ◇ *Prova a trattenere il respiro.* Try to hold your breath.
2 to hold* back ◇ *Se non l'avessimo trattenuto l'avrebbe picchiato.* If we hadn't held him back he would have hit him.
◆ **trattenersi (1)** (*rimanere*) to stay ◇ *Quanto ti trattieni?* How long are you staying?
◆ **trattenersi (2)** (*fermarsi*) to stop ◇ *Non sono più riuscito a trattenermi.* I just couldn't stop myself.

il **trattino** NOME MASC
hyphen ◇ *Si scrive con il trattino.* It's spelt with a hyphen.

il **tratto** NOME MASC
stetch (*di strada*) ◇ *È un tratto di strada molto pericoloso.* It's a very dangerous stretch of road.
◆ **C'è ancora un bel tratto da fare.** We've still

got a long way to go.
◆ **tutt'a un tratto** suddenly ◇ *Tutt'a un tratto ha cominciato a piovere.* It suddenly started to rain.

la **trattoria** NOME FEM
restaurant

il **trauma** NOME MASC (PL i **traumi**)
shock ◇ *La morte del padre è stata un trauma per lui.* His father's death was a shock to him.
◆ **trauma cranico** concussion

la **traversa** NOME FEM
1 sidestreet ◇ *Abita in una traversa di Via Roma.* She lives in a sidestreet off Via Roma.
◆ **Prendi la seconda traversa a destra.** Take the second right.
2 crossbar (*nel calcio*) ◇ *La palla ha colpito la traversa.* The ball hit the crossbar.

la **traversata** NOME FEM
crossing ◇ *la traversata dell'Atlantico* the crossing of the Atlantic

traverso AVVERBIO
◆ **di traverso** sideways ◇ *Mettilo di traverso.* Put it sideways.
◆ **andare di traverso** to go* down the wrong way ◇ *Il latte mi è andato di traverso.* The milk went down the wrong way.

travestirsi VERBO
to disguise oneself ◇ *Si erano travestiti da infermieri.* They were disguised as nurses.

tre NUMERO
three ◇ *Ha tre anni.* He is three. ◇ *alle tre* at three o'clock
◆ **il tre dicembre** the third of December

la **treccia** NOME FEM (PL le **trecce**)
plait ◇ *Anita ha le trecce.* Anita has plaits.

trecento NUMERO
three hundred
◆ **il Trecento** the fourteenth century

tredicenne AGGETTIVO
thirteen-year-old

tredicesimo AGGETTIVO (FEM **tredicesima**)
thirteenth

tredici NUMERO
thirteen ◇ *Ha tredici anni.* He is thirteen.
◆ **le tredici** one p.m.
◆ **il tredici dicembre** the thirteenth of December
◆ **fare tredici al totocalcio** to win* the pools

tremare VERBO
to shake* ◇ *Tremavo di paura.* I was shaking with fear. ◇ *Mi tremavano le mani.* My hands were shaking.
◆ **Tremava di freddo.** She was shivering with cold.

tremendo AGGETTIVO (FEM **tremenda**)
terrible ◇ *Aveva un mal di testa tremendo.* He had a terrible headache.
◆ **Ho una sete tremenda.** I'm terribly thirsty.
Attenzione! In inglese esiste la parola

tremendous, che però significa **fantastico** oppure **strepitoso**.

tremila NUMERO
three thousand

il **treno** NOME MASC
train ◇ *Ho perso il treno.* I missed the train.
◇ *Siamo andati in treno.* We went by train.

trenta NUMERO
thirty

trentesimo AGGETTIVO (FEM **trentesima**)
thirtieth

a **trentina** NOME FEM
about thirty ◇ *Eravamo una trentina.* There were about thirty of us. ◇ *Sarà sulla trentina.* He must be about thirty.

il **triangolo** NOME MASC
triangle

il **tribunale** NOME MASC
court

il **triciclo** NOME MASC
tricycle

il **trimestre** NOME MASC
term

a **trincea** NOME FEM
trench

il **trionfo** NOME MASC
triumph ◇ *il trionfo della nazionale italiana* the triumph of the Italian team

il **triplo** NOME MASC
three times as much ◇ *Guadagna il triplo di lei.* He earns three times as much as her.

triste AGGETTIVO
sad ◇ *Aveva un'aria molto triste.* He looked very sad. ◇ *una notizia ancora più triste* even sadder news

tritato AGGETTIVO (PL **tritata**)
chopped ◇ *cipolle tritate* chopped onions
◆ **carne tritata** minced meat, US: ground meat

a **tromba** NOME FEM
trumpet ◇ *Suono la tromba.* I play the trumpet.
◆ **tromba d'aria** whirlwind

il **tronco** NOME MASC (PL i **tronchi**)
trunk

il **trono** NOME MASC
throne

tropicale AGGETTIVO
tropical

troppo AGGETTIVO, PRONOME (FEM **troppa**)
vedi anche **troppo** AVVERBIO
[1] too much ◇ *Questa pasta è troppa per me.* This pasta is too much for me. ◇ *Ne vorrei ancora un po', ma non troppo.* I'd like a bit more, but not too much. ◇ *Ho mangiato troppo.* I've eaten too much.
[2] too many ◇ *C'erano troppi bambini.* There were too many children. ◇ *Siamo in troppi.* There are too many of us.

troppo AVVERBIO
vedi anche **troppo** AGGETTIVO, PRONOME

too (+ *aggettivo*) ◇ *Fa troppo caldo.* It's too hot.
◆ **È troppo poco.** It's not enough.

la **trota** NOME FEM
trout

la **trottola** NOME FEM
spinning top

trovare VERBO
[1] to find* ◇ *Ha trovato lavoro.* She's found a job. ◇ *Non riesco a trovare le chiavi.* I can't find my keys.
[2] to think* ◇ *L'ho trovato molto cambiato.* I thought he'd changed a lot. ◇ *Fa caldo, non trovi?* It's hot, don't you think?
◆ **trovarsi (1)** (*essere*) to be* ◇ *L'albergo si trova proprio al centro.* The hotel's right in the town centre. ◇ *In quel periodo mi trovavo a Napoli.* At that time I was in Naples.
◆ **trovarsi (2)** (*incontrarsi*) to meet*
◇ *Troviamoci alle cinque davanti al cinema.* Let's meet at five in front of the cinema.
◆ **trovarsi bene con qualcuno** to get* on well with somebody ◇ *Mi sono trovata benissimo con i suoi.* I got on very well with his parents.
◆ **andare a trovare qualcuno** to go* to see somebody ◇ *Ieri sono andato a trovare Chris.* I went to see Chris yesterday.

truccarsi VERBO
to do* one's make-up ◇ *Passa delle ore a truccarsi.* She spends hours doing her make-up.
◆ **Si trucca pochissimo.** She doesn't wear much make-up.

il **trucco** NOME MASC (PL i **trucchi**)
[1] make-up (*cosmetico*) ◇ *Aveva un trucco pesante.* She was wearing heavy make-up.
[2] trick (*giochetto*) ◇ *Ti mostro un trucco che riesce sempre.* I'll show you a trick that always works.

truffa VERBO
swindle

truffare VERBO
to swindle ◇ *Sono stato truffato.* I've been swindled.

il **truffatore**, la **truffatrice** NOME MASC, FEM
swindler

tu PRONOME
you

il **tubo** NOME MASC
pipe (*tubatura*)
◆ **i tubi dell'acqua** the pipes
◆ **un tubo di cartone** a cardboard tube

tuffarsi VERBO
to dive

il **tuffo** NOME
dive
◆ **fare un tuffo** to dive

il **tulipano** NOME MASC
tulip

T

il **tumore** NOME MASC
tumour
tumor US

tuo AGGETTIVO (FEM **tua**)
vedi anche **tuo** PRONOME
your ◇ *tuo fratello* your brother ◇ *la tua bici* your bike
* **una tua amica** a friend of yours

tuo PRONOME (FEM **tua**)
vedi anche **tuo** AGGETTIVO
yours ◇ *È questo il tuo?* Is this one yours?
◇ *La tua è più bella della mia.* Yours is nicer than mine.
* **i tuoi** (*genitori*) your parents ◇ *Cosa hanno detto i tuoi?* What did your parents say?

il **tuono** NOME MASC
thunder

il **tuorlo** NOME MASC
yolk

il **turbante** NOME MASC
turban

turbato AGGETTIVO (FEM **turbata**)
upset ◇ *Era molto turbato.* He was very upset.

la **turca** NOME FEM (PL le **turche**)
Turk

la **Turchia** NOME FEM
Turkey ◇ *Mi è piaciuta molto la Turchia.* I really liked Turkey. ◇ *Andremo in Turchia quest'estate.* We're going to Turkey this summer.

turco AGGETTIVO (FEM **turca**, MASC PL **turchi**, FEM PL **turche**)
vedi anche **turco** NOME
Turkish ◇ *È turca.* She's Turkish.

il **turco** NOME MASC (PL i **turchi**)
vedi anche **turco** AGGETTIVO
1 Turk (*persona*) ◇ *i turchi* the Turks
2 Turkish ◇ *Parla turco?* Does he speak Turkish?

il **turismo** NOME MASC
tourism

il/la **turista** NOME MASC/FEM (MASC PL i **turisti**, FEM PL le **turiste**)
tourist

turistico AGGETTIVO (FEM **turistica**, MASC PL **turistici**, FEM PL **turistiche**)
tourist ◇ *una località turistica* a tourist resort

il **turno** NOME MASC
1 turn ◇ *È il tuo turno.* It's your turn.
* **fare un turno a fare qualcosa** to take* turns to do something ◇ *Abbiamo fatto a turno a guidare.* We took turns to drive.
2 shift (*al lavoro*) ◇ *il turno di notte* the night shift ◇ *un turno di sei ore* a six-hour shift

la **tuta** NOME FEM
* **tuta da meccanico** overalls PL
* **tuta da ginnastica** tracksuit

tuttavia AVVERBIO
but ◇ *Il compito era difficile, tuttavia ce l'ho fatta.* The homework was difficult, but I managed to do it.

tutto AGGETTIVO (FEM **tutta**)
vedi anche **tutto** PRONOME
all ◇ *Ho bevuto tutto il latte.* I've drunk all the milk. ◇ *L'ho bevuto tutto.* I've drunk it all. ◇ *Sei tutto bagnato!* You're all wet!
◇ *tutto il giorno* all day
* **tutti** every ◇ *tutti i venerdì* every Friday
◇ *tutte le sere* every evening
In inglese il sostantivo va al singolare.

tutto PRONOME
vedi anche **tutto** AGGETTIVO
everything ◇ *Va tutto bene?* Is everything okay? ◇ *Mi hai detto tutto?* Have you told me everything?
* **In tutto sono venti sterline.** That's twenty pounds in all.
* **tutti** everybody ◇ *Vengono tutti.* Everybody's coming. ◇ *Lo sanno tutti tranne me.* Everybody knows except me.
everybody regge il verbo al singolare.
* **tutti e due** both ◇ *Ci siamo andati tutti e due.* We both went. ◇ *Sbagliate tutti e due.* You're both wrong.

la **TV** NOME FEM (PL le **TV**)
TV ◇ *L'hanno detto alla TV.* It was on TV.

U

ubriacarsi VERBO
to get* drunk ◇ *Gli basta una birra per ubriacarsi.* He gets drunk if he has just one beer.

ubriaco AGGETTIVO, NOME MASC/FEM (FEM **ubriaca**, MASC PL **ubriachi**, FEM PL **ubriache**)
drunk ◇ *Era un po' ubriaco.* He was a bit drunk. ◇ *Un ubriaco cantava a squarciagola.* A drunk was singing at the top of his voice.

uccello NOME MASC
bird

uccidere* VERBO
to kill ◇ *È rimasto ucciso in un incidente stradale.* He was killed in a road accident.

udito NOME MASC
hearing

ufficiale AGGETTIVO
vedi anche **ufficiale** NOME
official ◇ *È in visita ufficiale in Italia.* He's on an official visit to Italy.

ufficiale NOME MASC
vedi anche **ufficiale** AGGETTIVO
officer ◇ *un ufficiale di marina* a naval officer

ufficio NOME MASC
office ◇ *Oggi non è andata in ufficio.* She didn't go to the office today.
♦ **ufficio postale** post office
♦ **ufficio informazioni** information desk

uguagliare VERBO
to equal ◇ *Ha uguagliato il record mondiale.* He equalled the world record.

uguale AGGETTIVO
the same ◇ *Sono esattamente uguali.* They're exactly the same.
♦ **uguale a** the same as ◇ *Il tuo maglione è uguale al mio.* Your sweater's the same as mine.
♦ **per me è uguale** it doesn't matter to me ◇ *Che venga oppure no, per me è uguale.* It doesn't matter to me whether he comes or not.
♦ **Decidi tu, per me è uguale.** You decide, I don't mind.
♦ **due più due è uguale a quattro** two and two equals four

ultimamente AVVERBIO
lately ◇ *Non hanno giocato bene ultimamente.* They haven't been playing well lately.

ultimo AGGETTIVO (FEM **ultima**)
vedi anche **ultimo** NOME
[1] last ◇ *Quella è stata l'ultima volta che l'ho vista.* That was the last time I saw her.
♦ **all'ultimo momento** at the last moment ◇ *Ha cambiato idea all'ultimo momento.* He changed his mind at the last moment.
♦ **arrivare per ultimo** (*in un posto*) to arrive last ◇ *Marco è arrivato per ultimo.* Marco

arrived last.
♦ **arrivare ultimo** (*in una gara*) to come* last ◇ *Chiara è arrivata ultima.* Chiara came last.
♦ **l'ultimo anno** (*di scuola, di università*) the final year ◇ *Fa l'ultimo anno dell'università.* She is in her final year at university.
♦ **l'ultimo piano** the top floor ◇ *Abito all'ultimo piano.* I live on the top floor.
♦ **negli ultimi tempi** recently ◇ *Ci vediamo poco, negli ultimi tempi.* We haven't seen each other much recently.
[2] latest (*il più recente*) ◇ *Hai visto l'ultimo film di Spielberg?* Have you seen Spielberg's latest film? ◇ *Il loro ultimo album è in testa alla classifica.* Their latest album is at the top of the charts.

l' **ultimo**, l' **ultima** NOME MASC, FEM
vedi anche **ultimo** AGGETTIVO
last one ◇ *Lei è stata l'ultima ad arrivare.* She was the last one to arrive. ◇ *Questi sono gli ultimi.* These are the last ones.
♦ **Daniela è l'ultima della classe.** Daniela's bottom of the class.

umano AGGETTIVO (FEM **umana**)
human ◇ *il corpo umano* the human body

l' **umidità** NOME FEM
♦ **Nella casa c'era molta umidità.** The house was very damp.

umido AGGETTIVO (FEM **umida**)
[1] damp (*panni, clima*) ◇ *un clima caldo e umido* a hot, damp climate
[2] wet (*erba*) ◇ *L'erba è un po' umida.* The grass is a bit wet. ◇ *ancora più umido* even wetter

umile AGGETTIVO
humble ◇ *Era di umili origini.* He was of humble origins.
♦ **i lavori più umili** the most menial tasks

l' **umore** NOME MASC
mood ◇ *Di che umore è, oggi?* What mood is he in today?
♦ **essere di buon umore** to be* in a good mood
♦ **essere di cattivo umore** to be* in a bad mood

l' **umorismo** NOME MASC
♦ **avere il senso dell'umorismo** to have* a sense of humour

umoristico AGGETTIVO (FEM **umoristica**, MASC PL **umoristici**, FEM PL **umoristiche**)
funny ◇ *un racconto più umoristico* a funnier story

unanime AGGETTIVO
unanimous ◇ *È stata una decisione unanime.* It was a unanimous decision.

l' **uncino** NOME MASC
hook

undicenne AGGETTIVO, NOME
eleven-year-old

undicesimo AGGETTIVO, NOME MASC (FEM **undicesima**)

U

eleventh

undici NUMERO
eleven ◊ *Ha undici anni.* He's eleven. ◊ *alle undici* at eleven o'clock
• **l'undici dicembre** the eleventh of December

ungere* VERBO
[1] to oil *(lubrificare)* ◊ *Devo ungere la catena della bici.* I need to oil the chain of my bike.
[2] to grease ◊ *Ungi bene la teglia.* Grease the tin well.

ungherese NOME, AGGETTIVO
vedi anche **ungherese** NOME MASC
Hungarian

l' **ungherese** NOME MASC
vedi anche **ungherese** NOME, AGGETTIVO
Hungarian *(lingua)*

l' **Ungheria** NOME FEM
• **l'Ungheria** Hungary ◊ *Ti è piaciuta l'Ungheria?* Did you like Hungary? ◊ *Andrò in Ungheria quest'estate.* I'm going to Hungary this summer.

l' **unghia** NOME FEM
[1] nail ◊ *Marina si mangia le unghie.* Marina bites her nails.
• **unghie delle mani** fingernails
• **unghie dei piedi** toenails
[2] claw *(di gatto)*

unico AGGETTIVO (FEM **unica**, MASC PL **unici**, FEM PL **uniche**)
vedi anche **unico** NOME
only ◊ *È stata l'unica volta che l'ho visto.* It was the only time I saw him. ◊ *Robert è figlio unico.* Robert's an only child.

l' **unico**, l' **unica** NOME MASC, FEM (MASC PL gli **unici**, FEM PL le **uniche**)
vedi anche **unico** AGGETTIVO
the only one ◊ *Lei è stata l'unica a capire.* She was the only one who understood.

l' **unificazione** NOME FEM
unification ◊ *dopo l'unificazione della Germania* after the unification of Germany

l' **uniforme** NOME FEM
uniform ◊ *Indossava l'uniforme della marina.* He was wearing naval uniform.

l' **unione** NOME FEM
union ◊ *l'Unione Europea* the European Union

unire VERBO
[1] to put* together ◊ *Se uniamo i due tavoli ci stiamo tutti.* If we put the two tables together there'll be room for all of us.
[2] to join ◊ *Abbiamo deciso di unire i nostri sforzi.* We decided to join forces.
• **unirsi a** to join ◊ *Due ragazzi svizzeri si sono uniti a noi.* Two Swiss boys joined us.

l' **unità** NOME FEM (PL le **unità**)
unity ◊ *un passo avanti verso l'unità europea* a step towards European unity
• **unità di misura** unit of measurement

unito AGGETTIVO (FEM **unita**)
[1] close *(famiglia)* ◊ *La mia è una famiglia molto unita.* My family's very close.
[2] united *(squadra, partito)*
• **in tinta unita** plain ◊ *una cravatta in tinta unita* a plain tie

l' **università** NOME FEM (PL le **università**)
university (PL universities) ◊ *L'ho visto uscire dall'università.* I saw him coming out of the university.
*Quando si intende l'**università** come corso universitario non si usa l'articolo.*
◊ *Fa l'università.* She's at university.
◊ *Andrai all'università?* Are you going to go to university?

l' **universo** NOME MASC
universe

uno ARTICOLO (FEM **una**)
vedi anche **uno** PRONOME, NUMERO
[1] a ◊ *Era una giornata splendida.* It was a beautiful day. ◊ *un mio amico* a friend of mine
[2] an *(davanti a vocale)* ◊ *È un artista.* He's an artist. ◊ *un programma interessante* an interesting programme

uno NUMERO (FEM **una**)
vedi anche **uno** PRONOME, ARTICOLO
one ◊ *Ne ho comprato uno stamattina.* I bought one this morning. ◊ *Ce n'è uno a testa.* There's one each. ◊ *una camera solo per una notte* a room for one night only ◊ *a uno a uno* one by one ◊ *Che ore sono? – È l'una.* What time is it? – It's one o'clock.

uno PRONOME (FEM **una**)
vedi anche **uno** NUMERO, ARTICOLO
someone ◊ *Ho incontrato uno che ti conosce.* I met someone who knows you.
*Si può usare anche **somebody**.*
• **o l'uno o l'altro** either of them ◊ *O l'uno o l'altro per me va bene.* Either of them will be fine.
• **né l'uno né l'altro** neither of them ◊ *Quale prendi? – Né l'uno né l'altro.* Which one are you going to take? – Neither of them.
*Se nella frase ci sono due negazioni si usa **either**.*
◊ *Non prendo né l'uno né l'altro.* I'm not going to take either of them.

unto AGGETTIVO (FEM **unta**)
greasy ◊ *ancora più unti* even greasier

l' **uomo** NOME MASC (PL gli **uomini**)
man (PL men) ◊ *un uomo di mezz'età* a middle-aged man ◊ *C'erano due uomini nell'ufficio.* There were two men in the office.
• **scarpe da uomo** men's shoes

l' **uovo** NOME MASC (PL FEM le **uova**)
egg
• **uovo alla coque** soft-boiled egg
• **uovo fritto** fried egg
• **uovo sodo** hard-boiled egg

+ **uova strapazzate** scrambled eggs
+ **uovo di Pasqua** Easter egg

uragano NOME MASC
  hurricane

urgente AGGETTIVO
  urgent ◊ *Ha detto che era urgente.* He said it was urgent.

urgenza NOME FEM
  hurry (*fretta*) ◊ *Non c'è urgenza.* There's no hurry.
+ **Questo lavoro va fatto con molta urgenza.** This work is very urgent.
+ **essere ricoverato d'urgenza** to be* rushed into hospital ◊ *È stato ricoverato d'urgenza.* He's been rushed into hospital.

urlare VERBO
  to shout ◊ *Ho dovuto urlare per farmi sentire.* I had to shout to make myself heard.
+ **urlare di dolore** to scream with pain

urlo NOME MASC (PL FEM le **urla**)
  scream ◊ *urla di terrore* screams of terror
+ **lanciare un urlo** to scream ◊ *Quando l'ha visto ha lanciato un urlo.* She screamed when she saw him.

urtare VERBO
  to bump into ◊ *L'ha urtata e l'ha fatta cadere.* He bumped into her and knocked her down.

usanza NOME FEM
  custom ◊ *È un'usanza del posto.* It's a local custom.

usare VERBO
  to use ◊ *Non mi lascia usare il suo computer.* He doesn't let me use his computer. ◊ *Come si usa questo coso?* How do you use this thing?
+ **Quest'anno si usano le gonne lunghe.** This year long skirts are in fashion.

usato AGGETTIVO (FEM **usata**)
  second-hand ◊ *Ha comprato una macchina usata.* He bought a second-hand car.

uscire* VERBO
  ☐1 to go* out (*andare fuori*) ◊ *È uscito senza dire una parola.* He went out without saying a word. ◊ *È uscita a comprare il giornale.* She's gone out to buy a newspaper. ◊ *Ieri sono uscita con degli amici.* I went out with

friends yesterday.
  ☐2 to come* out (*venire fuori*) ◊ *Uscirà dall'ospedale domani.* He's coming out of hospital tomorrow. ◊ *L'ho incontrata che usciva dalla farmacia.* I met her coming out of the chemist's. ◊ *La rivista esce di lunedì.* The magazine comes out on Mondays. ◊ *È appena uscito il loro ultimo album.* Their latest album has just come out.
+ **uscire di strada** to leave* the road ◊ *La macchina è uscita di strada.* The car left the road.

l' **uscita** NOME FEM
  exit ◊ *Dov'è l'uscita?* Where's the exit?
+ **Ho incontrato Claudia all'uscita di scuola.** I met Claudia when we were coming out of school.
+ **uscita di sicurezza** emergency exit

l' **usignolo** NOME MASC
  nightingale

l' **uso** NOME MASC
  ☐1 use ◊ *per uso personale* for personal use
  ☐2 usage (*di parola*) ◊ *l'uso corretto di quella espressione* the correct usage of that expression
+ **gli usi e i costumi degli antichi romani** the customs of the ancient Romans

l' **ustione** NOME FEM
  burn ◊ *Aveva ustioni di terzo grado.* He had third-degree burns.

l' **utensile** NOME MASC
  tool

utile AGGETTIVO
  useful ◊ *Grazie per la guida, mi è stata molto utile.* Thanks for the guide book, it was very useful.
+ **rendersi utile** to make* oneself useful ◊ *Posso rendermi utile?* Can I make myself useful?

utilizzare VERBO
  to use ◊ *L'ho fatto utilizzando ritagli di stoffa.* I made it using scraps of material.

l' **uva** NOME FEM
  grapes PL ◊ *un grappolo d'uva* a bunch of grapes
+ **uva passa** raisins PL

U

V

la **vacanza** NOME FEM
  holiday
  vacation `US`
  ◇ *Ho fatto una lunga vacanza.* I had a long
  holiday. ◇ *le vacanze scolastiche* the school
  holidays ◇ *Trascorriamo sempre le vacanze
  al mare.* We always spend our holidays at
  the seaside.
  • **andare in vacanza** to go* on holiday ◇ *Dove
  andrai in vacanza quest'anno?* Where are
  you going on holiday this year?
  • **essere in vacanza** to be* on holiday
  Attenzione! In inglese esiste la parola
  vacancy che però indica un posto vacante o
  una camera disponibile.

vaccinare VERBO
  to vaccinate
  • **farsi vaccinare** to get* vaccinated ◇ *Si è
  fatto vaccinare contro l'influenza.* He got
  vaccinated against flu.

il **vagabondo**, la **vagabonda** NOME MASC,
  FEM
  tramp

vagare VERBO
  to wander ◇ *Vagava senza meta per la città.*
  He was wandering aimlessly around the
  town.

il **vaglia** NOME MASC (PL i **vaglia**)
  • **vaglia postale** postal order

vago AGGETTIVO (FEM **vaga**, MASC PL **vaghi**, FEM
  PL **vaghe**)
  vague

il **vagone** NOME MASC
  [1] carriage (*per passeggeri*)
  • **vagone letto** sleeping car
  • **vagone ristorante** restaurant car
  [2] truck (*per merci*)

la **valanga** NOME FEM (PL le **valanghe**)
  avalanche

valere* VERBO
  to be* worth ◇ *L'auto vale tremila euro.* The
  car is worth three thousand euros.
  • **non valere niente** to be* worthless
  • **valere la pena** to be* worth it ◇ *Non ne vale
  la pena.* It's not worth it. ◇ *Non vale la pena
  arrabbiarsi tanto.* It's not worth getting so
  angry.
  to be worth regge il gerundio.
  • **vale a dire** that is to say
  • **Tanto vale che te lo dica.** I might as well tell
  you.
  • **Questo vale anche per te.** This applies to
  you, too.
  • **Così non vale!** That's not fair!

il **valico** NOME MASC (PL i **valichi**)
  pass (*in montagna*)
  • **valico di frontiera** border crossing

valido AGGETTIVO (FEM **valida**)

valid ◇ *Il suo passaporto non è più valido.*
  Your passport is no longer valid.

la **valigia** NOME FEM (PL le **valigie** o le **valige**)
  suitcase
  • **fare le valigie** to pack
  • **disfare le valigie** to unpack

la **valle** NOME FEM
  valley

il **valore** NOME MASC
  value ◇ *il valore di un anello* the value of a
  ring ◇ *valori morali* moral values ◇ *Questo
  documento non ha valore legale.* This
  document has no legal value.
  • **È un anello di gran valore.** It's a very
  valuable ring.

la **valuta** NOME FEM
  • **valuta estera** foreign currency (PL foreign
  currencies)

valutare VERBO
  [1] to value (*casa, gioielli*) ◇ *La casa è stata
  valutata centomila euro.* The house has
  been valued at a hundred thousand euros.
  [2] to assess (*danni*) ◇ *I danni sono valutati
  attorno a cinquecentomila euro.* The
  damage has been assessed at about five
  hundred thousand euros.
  [3] to weigh up (*pro e contro, possibilità*)
  ◇ *Bisogna valutare i pro e i contro.* We need
  to weigh up the pros and cons.

la **valvola** NOME FEM
  valve ◇ *una valvola di sicurezza* a safety
  valve

il **valzer** NOME MASC (PL i **valzer**)
  waltz ◇ *Sai ballare il valzer?* Can you do the
  waltz?

il **vampiro** NOME MASC
  vampire

il **vandalismo** NOME MASC
  vandalism ◇ *un atto di vandalismo* an act of
  vandalism

il **vangelo** NOME MASC
  gospel

la **vaniglia** NOME FEM
  vanilla ◇ *un gelato alla vaniglia* a vanilla ice
  cream

vanitoso AGGETTIVO (FEM **vanitosa**)
  vain

vano AGGETTIVO (FEM **vana**)
  vain ◇ *vane speranze* vain hopes
  • **Tutti i nostri sforzi sono stati vani.** All our
  efforts were useless.

il **vantaggio** NOME MASC
  advantage ◇ *i vantaggi e gli svantaggi di
  vivere in città* the advantages and
  disadvantages of living in a city ◇ *Sei in una
  posizione di vantaggio.* You're at an
  advantage.
  • **essere in vantaggio** (*nello sport*) to be* in

the lead. ◇ *Siamo in vantaggio.* We're in the lead.

+ **Sono in vantaggio di due punti sugli avversari.** They have a two-point lead over their opponents.

vantaggioso AGGETTIVO (FEM **vantaggiosa**)
good ◇ *Mi ha fatto un'offerta molto vantaggiosa.* He made me a very good offer. ◇ *un prezzo vantaggioso* a good price

vantarsi VERBO
to boast ◇ *Si vanta sempre del proprio successo.* He's always boasting about his success.

vanvera NOME FEM

+ **parlare a vanvera** to talk nonsense

vapore NOME MASC
steam

+ **a vapore** steam ◇ *un ferro a vapore* a steam iron

+ **al vapore** steamed ◇ *verdure al vapore* steamed vegetables

varare VERBO

+ **varare una nave** to launch a ship

+ **varare una legge** to pass a law

varechina NOME FEM
bleach

variabile AGGETTIVO

1 variable ◇ *La qualità del prodotto è molto variabile.* The quality of the product is very variable.

2 unsettled ◇ *Il tempo si manterrà variabile.* The weather will continue unsettled.

varicella NOME FEM
chickenpox

varietà NOME FEM (PL le **varietà**)
variety (PL varieties) ◇ *Hanno una grande varietà di piatti.* They have a great variety of dishes.

vario AGGETTIVO (FEM **varia**)
varied ◇ *Il paesaggio è molto vario.* The landscape is very varied.

+ **vari** (*parecchi*) various ◇ *Devo vedere varie persone oggi.* I've got to see various people today.

vasca NOME FEM (PL le **vasche**)
tub

+ **vasca da bagno** bathtub

+ **vasca dei pesci** fish tank

vaschetta NOME FEM
tub ◇ *una vaschetta di gelato* a tub of ice cream

vaselina NOME FEM
Vaseline ®

vasetto NOME MASC
jar (*barattolo*) ◇ *un vasetto di marmellata* a jar of jam

vaso NOME MASC

1 vase (*per fiori, ornamentale*)

2 flowerpot (*per piante*)

vassoio NOME MASC

tray

vasto AGGETTIVO (FEM **vasta**)
vast ◇ *una vasta area* a vast area

+ **su vasta scala** on a huge scale

ve vedi **vi**

la **vecchia** NOME FEM
old woman (PL old women)

vecchio AGGETTIVO (FEM **vecchia**, MASC PL **vecchi**, FEM PL **vecchie**)
vedi anche **vecchio** NOME
old ◇ *Ho una macchina vecchia.* I've got an old car. ◇ *È un mio vecchio amico.* He's an old friend of mine. ◇ *È più vecchio di me.* He's older than me. ◇ *la casa più vecchia della via* the oldest house in the street

il **vecchio** NOME MASC (PL i **vecchi**)
vedi anche **vecchio** AGGETTIVO
old man (PL old men)

+ **i vecchi** (*uomini e donne*) the old

vedere* VERBO
to see* ◇ *Non ci vedo senza occhiali.* I can't see without my glasses. ◇ *Fammi vedere il tuo tema.* Let me see your essay. ◇ *Non lo vedo da molto tempo.* I haven't seen him for a long time.

+ **Ci vediamo domani!** See you tomorrow!

+ **farsi vedere** to be* seen ◇ *Da quella volta non si è fatto più vedere.* He hasn't been seen since.

+ **Si fa vedere ogni tanto.** He comes to see us from time to time.

+ **Non lo posso vedere.** I can't stand him.

+ **Non vedo l'ora di conoscerlo.** I can't wait to meet him.

la **vedova** NOME FEM
widow ◇ *Mia madre è vedova.* My mother is a widow.

+ **rimanere vedova** to be* widowed

il **vedovo** NOME MASC
widower ◇ *Mio padre è vedovo.* My father is a widower.

+ **rimanere vedovo** to be* widowed

la **veduta** NOME FEM
view ◇ *Da quassù si ha una stupenda veduta sul mare.* You get a wonderful view of the sea from up here.

+ **di larghe vedute** broad-minded ◇ *I miei sono di larghe vedute.* My parents are broad-minded.

+ **di vedute ristrette** narrow-minded

vegetale AGGETTIVO
vegetable

vegetariano, vegetariana AGGETTIVO, NOME MASC/FEM
vegetarian

la **vegetazione** NOME FEM
vegetation

il **veglione** NOME MASC
party (PL parties) ◇ *il veglione di Capodanno* New Year's Eve party

il **veicolo** NOME MASC

V

vehicle

la **vela** NOME FEM
> 1. sail (di barca)
> 2. sailing (sport)
- **barca a vela** sailing boat
- **Tutto va a gonfie vele.** Everything's going perfectly.

il **veleno** NOME MASC
> poison

velenoso AGGETTIVO (FEM **velenosa**)
> poisonous

la **velina** NOME FEM
- **carta velina** tissue paper

il **velluto** NOME MASC
> velvet ◇ un paio di pantaloni di velluto a pair of velvet trousers
- **velluto a coste** corduroy

il **velo** NOME MASC
> veil

veloce AGGETTIVO, AVVERBIO
> fast ◇ È una macchina veloce. It's a fast car. ◇ Guidi troppo veloce. You drive too fast. ◇ La mia moto è più veloce della tua. My motorbike is faster than yours. ◇ È uno dei corridori più veloci del mondo. He's one of the fastest drivers in the world.
- **Su, veloce, corri a casa!** Quick, go home!

la **velocità** NOME FEM (PL le **velocità**)
> speed ◇ Guidava a tutta velocità. He was driving at full speed.

la **vena** NOME FEM
> vein ◇ le vene e le arterie veins and arteries
- **Oggi non sono in vena.** I'm not in the mood today.

la **vendemmia** NOME FEM
> grape harvest

vendere* VERBO
> to sell* ◇ L'ho venduto per tremila euro. I sold it for three thousand euros.
- **"vendesi"** "for sale"

la **vendetta** NOME FEM
> revenge
- **farsi vendetta** to take* one's revenge ◇ Ha deciso di farsi vendetta da solo. He decided to take his revenge.

vendicarsi VERBO
> to take* revenge ◇ Vuole vendicarsi di loro. He wants to take revenge on them.
- **Voglio vendicarmi.** I want revenge.

la **vendita** NOME FEM
> sale ◇ reparto vendite sales department ◇ I biglietti saranno in vendita da venerdì. Tickets will be on sale from Friday. ◇ Hanno messo in vendita la casa. They have put their house up for sale.
- **vendita al minuto** retail
- **vendita all'ingrosso** wholesale

il **venerdì** NOME MASC
> Friday
> *Si noti l'uso della maiuscola in inglese.*

◇ L'ho vista venerdì. I saw her on Friday.
- **di venerdì** on Fridays ◇ Vado in piscina di venerdì. I go swimming on Fridays.
- **venerdì scorso** last Friday
- **venerdì prossimo** next Friday
- **venerdì santo** Good Friday

Venezia NOME FEM
> Venice ◇ Abito a Venezia. I live in Venice. ◇ Domani vado a Venezia. I'm going to Venice tomorrow.

venire* VERBO
> 1. to come* ◇ È venuto in macchina. He came by car. ◇ Da dove vieni? Where do you come from? ◇ Vieni a trovarci. Come and see us! ◇ È venuto il momento di dire la verità. The time has come to tell the truth.
- **Quanto viene?** How much is it?
- **Mi è venuta un'idea!** I've had an idea!
- **Gli è venuto il mal di testa.** He's got a headache.
- **Mi viene da piangere.** I feel like crying.
> 2. to turn out (riuscire) ◇ Il dolce è venuto bene. The cake turned out well.
> 3. to be* (ausiliare) ◇ Viene venduto al chilo. It's sold by the kilo. (came, come)

il **ventaglio** NOME MASC
> fan

ventenne AGGETTIVO, NOME
> twenty-year-old

ventesimo AGGETTIVO (FEM **ventesima**)
> twentieth ◇ il ventesimo secolo the twentieth century

venti NUMERO
> twenty ◇ Ha vent'anni. He is twenty.
- **alle venti** at eight p.m.
- **il venti dicembre** the twentieth of December

il **ventilatore** NOME MASC
> fan

il **vento** NOME MASC
> wind ◇ contro vento against the wind
- **C'è vento.** It's windy.

la **vera** NOME FEM
> wedding ring

veramente AVVERBIO
> 1. really ◇ È veramente bella. She's really beautiful.
> 2. actually ◇ Veramente non ne sapevo niente. Actually, I didn't know anything about it.

la **veranda** NOME FEM
> 1. veranda (aperta)
> 2. conservatory (PL conservatories) (chiusa, tutta di vetro)

il **verbo** NOME MASC
> verb ◇ un verbo transitivo a transitive verb

verde AGGETTIVO, NOME MASC
> green ◇ una camicia verde scuro a dark green shirt
- **essere al verde** to be* broke
- **i Verdi** (in politica) the Greens

verdura NOME FEM
vegetables PL ◇ *Non mi piace la verdura.* I don't like vegetables.
+ **negozio di frutta e verdura** greengrocer's

vergine AGGETTIVO
| *vedi anche* **vergine** NOME |
virgin
+ **essere vergine** (*persona*) to be* a virgin
+ **pura lana vergine** pure new wool

vergine NOME FEM
| *vedi anche* **vergine** AGGETTIVO |
virgin (*persona*)
+ **Vergine** (*dello zodiaco*) Virgo ◇ *Sono della Vergine.* I'm Virgo.

vergogna NOME FEM
embarrassment ◇ *È arrossito per la vergogna.* He went red with embarrassment.
+ **È una vergogna!** It's a disgrace!

vergognarsi VERBO
1 to be* ashamed ◇ *Non ti vergogni di aver copiato all'esame?* Aren't you ashamed that you copied in the exam?
+ **Vergognati!** You should be ashamed!
2 to be* embarrassed ◇ *Dai, suonaci qualcosa. – No, mi vergogno.* Come on, play something. – No, I'm embarrassed.

vergognoso AGGETTIVO (FEM **vergognosa**)
terrible ◇ *È vergognoso che debbano ancora succedere cose simili!* It's terrible that such things still happen!

verificare VERBO
to check (*controllare*)
+ **verificarsi** (*accadere*) to happen

verità NOME FEM (PL le **verità**)
truth ◇ *Hai detto la verità?* Did you tell the truth? ◇ *a dire la verità* to tell the truth

verme NOME MASC
worm

vernice NOME FEM
1 varnish (*trasparente*)
2 paint (*pittura*) ◇ *vernice fresca* wet paint
3 patent leather (*pelle*) ◇ *una borsetta di vernice* a patent leather bag

verniciare VERBO
1 to varnish (*con vernice trasparente*)
2 to paint (*pitturare*)

vero AGGETTIVO (FEM **vera**)
| *vedi anche* **vero** NOME |
1 true ◇ *Vero o falso?* True or false?
◇ *Questa è una storia vera.* This is a true story. ◇ *Magari fosse vero!* If only it were true!
2 real ◇ *Quei fiori sembrano veri.* Those flowers look real. ◇ *Il vero problema è...* The real problem is...
+ **vero e proprio** real ◇ *Questo è un vero e proprio affare.* This is a real bargain.
3 genuine (*autentico*) ◇ *perle vere* genuine pearls ◇ *È un vero Picasso.* It's a genuine Picasso.

Per tradurre **vero?** *alla fine della frase, si usano le forme negative inglesi "aren't you?", "isn't it?", "don't you?", "didn't he?" ecc., concordate col verbo principale della frase.*
◇ *Questa è la tua macchina, vero?* This is your car, isn't it? ◇ *Hai finito i compiti, vero?* You've finished your homework, haven't you? ◇ *Ti piace la cioccolata, vero?* You like chocolate, don't you?

il **vero** NOME MASC
| *vedi anche* **vero** AGGETTIVO |
truth ◇ *a dire il vero* to tell the truth

la **verruca** NOME FEM (PL le **verruche**)
1 wart (*sulla mano*)
2 verruca (*sul piede*)

la **versamento** NOME FEM
deposit (*in banca*)

versare VERBO
1 to pour ◇ *Mi versi un po' d'acqua?* Can you pour me some water?
2 to spill* (*involontariamente*) ◇ *Ho versato un po' di vino sulla tovaglia.* I spilt some wine on the tablecloth.
3 to pay* in ◇ *Vorrei versare duecentocinquanta euro nel mio conto corrente.* I'd like to pay two hundred and fifty euros into my current account.

la **versione** NOME FEM
version ◇ *Vorrei sentire la sua versione dell'accaduto.* I'd like to hear her version of what happened.
+ **una versione più aggiornata della guida** a more up-to-date edition of the guide
+ **in versione originale** (*film*) in the original language

il **verso** NOME MASC
| *vedi anche* **verso** PREPOSIZIONE |
1 line (*di poesia*)
2 noise (*di animale*) ◇ *Che verso fa il maiale?* What noise does a pig make?
+ **fare il verso a qualcuno** to mimic somebody ◇ *Faceva il verso al professore.* He mimicked the teacher.
+ **Non c'è verso di fargli cambiare idea.** There's no way of making him change his mind.

verso PREPOSIZIONE
| *vedi anche* **verso** NOME |
1 towards ◇ *Veniva verso di me.* He was coming towards me. ◇ *Stavo camminando verso la stazione quando l'ho visto.* I was walking towards the station when I saw him.
+ **È tardi. Faremmo bene ad avviarci verso casa.** It's late. We'd better head for home.
+ **verso l'alto** upwards ◇ *Tirare l'anello verso l'alto.* Pull the ring upwards.
+ **verso il basso** downwards
2 around ◇ *Ci rivediamo verso la fine di novembre.* I'll see you around the end of November. ◇ *Arriverò verso le sette.* I'll be there at around seven.

vertebrale AGGETTIVO

V

+ **colonna vertebrale** spine

verticale AGGETTIVO
vertical

le **vertigini** NOME FEM PL

+ **soffrire di vertigini** to be* afraid of heights ◇ *Non vengo lassù perché soffro di vertigini.* I'm not coming up because I'm afraid of heights.

la **vescica** NOME FEM (PL le **vesciche**)

[1] blister ◇ *Ho una vescica sul piede.* I've got a blister on my foot.

[2] bladder (*organo*)

il **vescovo** NOME MASC
bishop

la **vespa** NOME FEM
wasp (*insetto*)

la **vestaglia** NOME FEM
dressing gown

vestirsi VERBO

[1] to get* dressed ◇ *Si è vestito in fretta ed è uscito.* He got dressed quickly and went out. ◇ *Vestiti, che usciamo.* Get dressed, we're going out.

[2] to dress ◇ *Si veste bene.* She dresses well.

+ **vestirsi da** to dress up as ◇ *Si è vestito da donna.* He dressed up as a woman.

il **vestito** NOME MASC

[1] dress (*da donna*)

[2] suit (*da uomo*)

+ **vestiti** clothes ◇ *Ho messo alcuni vestiti in valigia.* I put some clothes in a suitcase.

il **veterinario**, la **veterinaria** NOME MASC, FEM
vet

il **vetraio** NOME MASC
glazier

la **vetrata** NOME FEM

[1] big window (*di salotto*)

[2] stained-glass window (*di chiesa*)

vetrato AGGETTIVO (FEM **vetrata**)
glazed (*porta*)

+ **carta vetrata** sandpaper

la **vetrina** NOME FEM
window (*di negozio*) ◇ *C'è una gonna che mi piace in vetrina.* There's a skirt I like in the window.

il/la **vetrinista** NOME MASC/FEM (MASC PL i **vetrinisti**, FEM PL le **vetriniste**)
window dresser ◇ *Fa la vetrinista.* She is a window dresser.

il **vetro** NOME MASC
glass ◇ *un vaso di vetro* a glass vase

+ **pulire i vetri** to clean the windows

la **vetta** NOME FEM
summit (*di montagna*) ◇ *Abbiamo raggiunto la vetta in quattro ore.* We reached the summit in four hours.

vi PRONOME
vedi anche **vi** AVVERBIO

[1] you ◇ *Vi darò un consiglio.* I'll give you some advice. ◇ *Vorrebbero aiutarvi.* They'd like to help you.

Spesso **you** *è preceduto da una preposizione, a seconda del verbo usato.*
◇ *Vi scriverò.* I'll write to you. ◇ *Vi ha salutato?* Did he say hello to you? ◇ *Ve lo do subito.* I'll give it to you in a moment. ◇ *Vi ha sorriso.* He smiled at you. ◇ *Vi stava cercando.* She was looking for you.

[2] yourselves (*riflessivo*) ◇ *Vi siete fatti male?* Did you hurt yourselves? ◇ *Vi siete divertiti?* Did you enjoy yourselves?

+ **Pettinatevi.** Comb your hair.

vi AVVERBIO
vedi anche **vi** PRONOME
there ◇ *Vi sono stato parecchie volte.* I've been there several times. ◇ *Vi sono molti modi per farlo.* There are many ways of doing it.

la **via** NOME FEM
vedi anche **via** AVVERBIO

[1] street ◇ *Abito in una via molto stretta.* I live in a very narrow street.

+ **Non c'è via d'uscita.** There's no way out.

+ **spedire per via aerea** to send* by airmail

[2] starting signal (*in gara*) ◇ *Quando darai il via?* When are you going to give the starting signal?

via AVVERBIO
vedi anche **via** NOME
away ◇ *Vai via!* Go away! ◇ *L'ho buttato via.* I threw it away.

+ **Pronti, attenti, via!** Ready, steady, go!

viaggiare VERBO
to travel ◇ *Viaggi spesso per lavoro?* Do you travel much for your job? ◇ *Mi piace viaggiare.* I like travelling.

il **viaggiatore**, la **viaggiatrice** NOME MASC, FEM
traveller
traveler US

il **viaggio** NOME MASC

[1] journey ◇ *È stato un viaggio molto faticoso.* It was a very tiring journey. ◇ *Avete fatto buon viaggio?* Did you have a good journey?

+ **Vorrei fare un viaggio in Cina.** I'd like to visit China.

[2] trip (*più breve*) ◇ *Buon viaggio!* Have a good trip! ◇ *Ha proposto di fare un viaggio in montagna domenica prossima.* He suggested taking a trip to the mountains next Sunday.

+ **viaggio d'affari** business trip ◇ *Papà è in viaggio d'affari.* Dad's on a business trip.

+ **spese di viaggio** travelling expenses

+ **agenzia di viaggi** travel agency

+ **viaggio di nozze** honeymoon ◇ *Dove andranno in viaggio di nozze?* Where are they going on their honeymoon?

* *I verbi seguiti da questo simbolo sono irregolari. Si veda anche alle pp.328–338.*

+ **viaggio organizzato** package tour ◇ *Sono andato a Praga con un viaggio organizzato.* I went to Prague on a package tour.

viale NOME MASC
avenue

vicenda NOME FEM

[1] event (*avvenimento*) ◇ *Il libro parla delle vicende che hanno portato alla guerra.* The book discusses the events that led to the war.

[2] story (PL stories) (*storia*) ◇ *È una vicenda estremamente complicata.* It's an extremely complicated story.

+ **a vicenda** each other ◇ *Ci siamo aiutati a vicenda.* We helped each other.

viceversa AVVERBIO
vice versa

vicino AGGETTIVO, AVVERBIO (FEM **vicina**)

vedi anche **vicino** NOME

near ◇ *Abitiamo qui vicino.* We live near here. ◇ *La stazione è abbastanza vicina.* The station is quite near. ◇ *La mia macchina è più vicina della tua.* My car is nearer than yours. ◇ *Dov'è il telefono più vicino?* Where's the nearest phone?

+ **un paese vicino** a nearby village
+ **Vieni più vicino.** Come closer.
+ **Mi sono stati molto vicini.** They were very supportive towards me.
+ **vicino a** near ◇ *L'interruttore della luce è vicino alla porta.* The light switch is near the door.
+ **Era seduta vicino a me.** She was sitting next to me.
+ **guardare qualcosa da vicino** to take* a close look at something ◇ *Guardalo da vicino!* Take a close look at it!

vicino, la **vicina** NOME MASC, FEM

vedi anche **vicino** AGGETTIVO, AVVERBIO

neighbour
neighbor US

◇ *i miei vicini di casa* my next-door neighbours

vicolo NOME MASC
alley

+ **vicolo cieco** blind alley

video NOME MASC (PL i **video**)
video

videocamera NOME FEM
camcorder

videocassetta NOME FEM
video ◇ *Abbiamo noleggiato una videocassetta.* We rented a video.

videogioco NOME MASC (PL i **videogiochi**)
video game

videoregistratore NOME MASC
video recorder

vietare VERBO
to forbid* ◇ *Il dottore gli ha vietato di fumare.* The doctor has forbidden him to smoke.

+ **Fallo, se vuoi. Chi te lo vieta?** Do it if you like.

Who's stopping you?

vietato AGGETTIVO (FEM **vietata**)

+ **Qui è vietato fumare.** Smoking is not allowed here.
+ **"Vietato fumare"** "No smoking"
+ **È un film vietato ai minori di 18 anni.** You have to be eighteen to see that film.

vigile NOME MASC
traffic warden ◇ *Il vigile mi ha dato la multa.* The traffic warden gave me a ticket.

+ **vigile del fuoco** firefighter
+ **i vigili del fuoco** (*istituzione*) the fire brigade SING,
the fire department SING US:
◇ *Qualcuno ha chiamato i vigili del fuoco.* Somebody called the fire brigade.

vigilia NOME FEM
eve ◇ *la vigilia di Natale* Christmas Eve ◇ *alla vigilia di* on the eve of

vigliacco, la **vigliacca** NOME MASC, FEM
(MASC PL i **vigliacchi**, FEM PL le **vigliacche**)
coward

vigneto NOME MASC
vineyard

vignetta NOME FEM
cartoon

vigore NOME MASC

+ **essere in vigore** (*legge*) to be* in force
+ **entrare in vigore** to come* into force

villa NOME FEM
house

villaggio NOME MASC
village ◇ *un villaggio africano* an African village

villetta NOME FEM
house with a garden

vimini NOME MASC PL

+ **una sedia di vimini** a wicker chair

vincere* VERBO
to win* ◇ *Ieri abbiamo vinto la partita.* We won the match yesterday.

vincitore, la **vincitrice** NOME MASC, FEM
winner

vino NOME MASC
wine ◇ *vino bianco* white wine ◇ *vino rosso* red wine

viola AGGETTIVO (MASC, FEM, PL **viola**)

vedi anche **viola** NOME FEM

purple (*colore*)

viola NOME FEM

vedi anche **viola** NOME MASC, AGGETTIVO

violet (*fiore*)

violentare VERBO
to rape

violento AGGETTIVO (FEM **violenta**)
violent

violenza NOME FEM
violence

+ **violenza carnale** rape

violetto AGGETTIVO, NOME MASC (FEM **violetta**)
violet (*colore*)

il/la **violinista** NOME MASC/FEM (MASC PL i **violinisti**, FEM PL le **violiniste**)
violinist

il **violino** NOME MASC
violin

il **violoncello** NOME MASC
cello

la **vipera** NOME FEM
viper

la **virgola** NOME FEM
☐1 comma (*segno di interpunzione*)
☐2 point (*in matematica*) ◊ *5,7%* 5.7%
Si legge **five point seven.**

le **virgolette** NOME FEM PL
inverted commas ◊ *una parola scritta tra virgolette* a word written in inverted commas

virtuale AGGETTIVO
♦ **realtà virtuale** virtual reality

il **virus** NOME MASC (PL i **virus**)
virus

viscido AGGETTIVO (FEM **viscida**)
slimy ◊ *ancora più viscido* even slimier

la **visione** NOME FEM
vision ◊ *Hanno avuto una visione della Madonna.* They had a vision of the Madonna.
♦ **film in prima visione** (*al cinema*) newly released film

la **visita** NOME FEM
visit
♦ **fare visita a qualcuno** to visit somebody ◊ *Andiamo a fargli visita.* Let's go and visit him.
♦ **orario delle visite** visiting hours
♦ **visita medica** medical, US: physical ◊ *Devi fare una visita medica prima di cominciare a lavorare.* You have to have a medical before you start the job.
♦ **visita di controllo** check-up ◊ *Ho fatto una visita di controllo.* I had a check-up.
♦ **visita guidata** guided tour ◊ *Quanto costa la visita guidata della città?* How much is a guided tour of the city?

visitare VERBO
☐1 to visit ◊ *Hai già visitato la National Gallery?* Have you visited the National Gallery? ◊ *Visitate il nostro sito Intenet.* Visit our web site.
☐2 to examine (*paziente*) ◊ *Siamo rimasti con lei finché il dottore l'ha visitata.* We stayed with her until the doctor examined her.

il **visitatore**, la **visitatrice** NOME MASC, FEM
visitor

il **viso** NOME MASC
face ◊ *Si è spalmata la crema sul viso.* She rubbed the cream into her face.

il **visone** NOME MASC
mink ◊ *una pelliccia di visone* a mink coat

la **vista** NOME FEM
☐1 sight (*facoltà*) ◊ *La vista mi si sta indebolendo.* My sight is deteriorating.
♦ **Ha la vista buona.** He has good eyesight.
♦ **a prima vista** at first sight ◊ *È stato amore a prima vista.* It was love at first sight.
♦ **conoscere qualcuno di vista** to know* somebody by sight ◊ *Lo conosco solo di vista.* I only know him by sight.
♦ **perdere qualcuno di vista** to lose* sight of somebody ◊ *Correva così veloce che l'ho perso di vista.* He was running so fast that I lost sight of him.
♦ **Dopo aver finito l'università si sono persi di vista.** They lost touch after they left university.
☐2 view (*veduta*) ◊ *una camera con vista sul lago* a room with a view of the lake

il **visto** NOME MASC
☐1 visa (*su passaporto*)
☐2 tick (*segno*)

la **vita** NOME FEM
☐1 life ◊ *Ha rischiato la vita per aiutarla.* He risked his life to help her. ◊ *È piena di vita.* She's full of life.
♦ **essere in vita** to be* alive ◊ *Quando sono arrivati era ancora in vita.* When they got there he was still alive.
☐2 waist ◊ *Mi è un po' largo in vita.* It's a bit loose round the waist.

la **vitamina** NOME FEM
vitamine

la **vite** NOME FEM
☐1 screw (*per avvitare*)
☐2 vine (*pianta*)

il **vitello** NOME MASC
☐1 calf (PL calves) (*animale*)
☐2 veal (*carne*) ◊ *una scaloppina di vitello* a veal escalope

la **vittima** NOME FEM
victim

il **vitto** NOME MASC
♦ **vitto e alloggio** board and lodging

la **vittoria** NOME FEM
victory (PL victories)

viva ESCLAMAZIONE
♦ **Viva gli sposi!** To the bride and groom!
♦ **Viva l'Italia!** Hooray for Italy!

vivace AGGETTIVO
lively ◊ *una ragazza vivace* a lively girl ◊ *È più vivace della sorella.* She's livelier than her sister.
♦ **un colore vivace** a bright colour

vivere VERBO
to live ◊ *Mi piacerebbe vivere in Scozia.* I'd like to live in Scotland.
♦ **modo di vivere** way of life

la **vivisezione** NOME FEM
vivisection

vivo AGGETTIVO (FEM **viva**)

* *I verbi seguiti da questo simbolo sono irregolari. Si veda anche alle pp.328–338.*

Italian ~ English

[1] alive ◇ *Il pesce era ancora vivo.* The fish was still alive.

[2] live (*prima di un nome*) ◇ *esperimenti su animali vivi* experiments on live animals

◆ **un colore vivo** a bright colour

◆ **farsi vivo** to keep* in touch ◇ *Fatti vivo!* Keep in touch!

◆ **È da tanto che non si fa viva.** She hasn't been in touch for a long time.

viziato AGGETTIVO (FEM **viziata**)

[1] spoilt ◇ *un bambino viziato* a spoilt child

[2] stale ◇ *aria viziata* stale air

vizio NOME MASC

[1] bad habit (*cattiva abitudine*) ◇ *Il mio unico vizio è quello di mangiarmi le unghie.* Biting my nails is my only bad habit.

◆ **Ha il vizio del gioco.** He's addicted to gambling.

[2] vice (*morale*) ◇ *i vizi e le virtù* vices and virtues

vocabolario NOME MASC

dictionary (PL dictionaries) ◇ *un vocabolario di italiano* an Italian dictionary

vocabolo NOME MASC

word

vocale NOME FEM

vowel

voce NOME FEM

voice ◇ *Ho perso la voce.* I've lost my voice.

◆ **parlare ad alta voce** to speak* loudly

◆ **parlare ad bassa voce** to speak* quietly

◆ **Leggi il brano ad alta voce.** Read the passage aloud.

◆ **voci di corridoio** rumours, US: rumors ◇ *Sono solo voci di corridoio.* They're only rumours.

voglia NOME FEM

◆ **aver voglia di fare qualcosa** to feel* like doing something

to feel like è seguito dal gerundio.

◇ *Adesso non ho voglia di mangiare.* I don't feel like eating just now.

◆ **morire dalla voglia di fare qualcosa** to be* dying to do something ◇ *Muoio dalla voglia di vederlo.* I'm dying to see him.

voi PRONOME

you ◇ *Io ci vado, voi fate come volete.* I'm going, you do what you like. ◇ *Venite anche voi?* Are you coming too? ◇ *Sono più giovani di voi.* They are younger than you.

◆ **Non lo sapevate nemmeno voi.** You didn't even know it yourselves.

volante NOME MASC

steering wheel

volantino NOME MASC

leaflet

volare VERBO

to fly*

volenteroso AGGETTIVO (FEM **volenterosa**)

willing ◇ *un alunno volenteroso* a willing pupil

volentieri AVVERBIO

willingly ◇ *L'ho fatto volentieri.* I did it willingly.

◆ **Volentieri! (1)** Certainly! ◇ *Mi aiuti? – Volentieri!* Will you help me? – Certainly!

◆ **Volentieri! (2)** (*in risposta ad invito*) I'd love to! ◇ *Verresti a cena da noi stasera? – Grazie, volentieri!* Would you like to come to dinner with us this evening? – Yes, I'd love to!

volere* VERBO

to want ◇ *Voglio comprare una macchina nuova.* I want to buy a new car. ◇ *Che cosa vuoi che faccia?* What do you want me to do? ◇ *Quanto vuole per quel quadro?* How much do you want for that picture?

◆ **Devo pagare subito o posso pagare domani? – Come vuole.** Do I have to pay now or can I pay tomorrow? – As you prefer.

*Quando si offre qualcosa e nelle frasi al condizionale presente **volere** si traduce con **would like**.*

◇ *Vuole un po' di caffè?* Would you like some coffee? ◇ *Adesso vorrei andarmene.* I'd like to go now. ◇ *Vorrebbe andare in America.* She'd like to go to America.

◆ **volerci (1)** (*tempo*) to take* ◇ *Quanto ci vuole per andare da Roma a Firenze?* How long does it take to get from Rome to Florence?

◆ **volerci (2)** (*soldi, pazienza, materiale*) to need ◇ *Per una giacca ci vogliono quattro metri di stoffa.* You need four metres of material to make a jacket. ◇ *Ci vuole il pane.* We need bread.

◆ **volere dire** to mean* ◇ *Cosa vuol dire questa parola?* What does this word mean?

◆ **senza volere** accidentally ◇ *L'ho spinto senza volere.* I accidentally pushed him.

volgare AGGETTIVO

vulgar

il **volo** NOME MASC

flight ◇ *Ci sono due ore di volo da Londra a Milano.* It's a two-hour flight from London to Milan.

◆ **volo charter** charter flight

◆ **volo di linea** scheduled flight

◆ **prendere al volo** (*autobus, treno*) to only just catch* ◇ *Ho preso il treno al volo.* I only just caught the train.

◆ **capire al volo** to understand* immediately ◇ *Ha capito al volo la situazione.* He understood the situation immediately.

la **volontà** NOME FEM

will ◇ *L'ha fatto di sua spontanea volontà.* He did it of his own free will.

il **volontario**, la **volontaria** NOME MASC, FEM

volunteer ◇ *C'è qualche volontario?* Are there any volunteers?

◆ **Lavoro come volontario.** I'm a voluntary worker.

la **volpe** NOME FEM

V

fox

la volta NOME FEM
time ◇ *La prima volta che l'ho visto...* The first time I saw him... ◇ *Ti ricordi quella volta che...* Do you remember the time when... ◇ *Questa volta ci vado io.* I'll go this time. ◇ *Gli telefonerò un'altra volta, adesso non ne ho voglia.* I'll phone him some other time, I don't feel like it now. ◇ *Tre volte quattro fa dodici.* Three times four makes twelve.

◆ **una volta** once ◇ *Le ho scritto una volta sola.* I wrote to her only once.
◆ **Una volta si camminava di più.** People used to walk more.
◆ **una volta alla settimana** once a week
◆ **due volte** twice ◇ *Gli ho telefonato due volte.* I phoned him twice.
◆ **tre volte** three times
◆ **certe volte** sometimes ◇ *Certe volte sono un po' triste.* I feel a bit down sometimes.
◆ **una volta tanto** just for once ◇ *Una volta tanto potresti pagare tu.* You could pay, just for once.
◆ **una volta o l'altra** one of these days ◇ *Una volta o l'altra glielo dirò.* I'll tell him one of these days.
◆ **una volta per tutte** once and for all ◇ *Deciditi una volta per tutte.* Make up your mind once and for all.
◆ **di volta in volta** as we go ◇ *Decideremo di volta in volta cosa fare.* We'll decide what to do as we go.
◆ **una cosa per volta** one thing at a time ◇ *Facciamo una cosa per volta.* Let's do one thing at a time.
◆ **C'era una volta...** Once upon a time there was...

voltare VERBO
to turn ◇ *Volta a sinistra e poi va' dritto.* Turn left and then go straight on. ◇ *Voltate pagina.* Turn the page.
◆ **voltarsi** to turn ◇ *Voltati dall'altra parte.* Turn the other way.
◆ **Si è allontanato senza voltarsi indietro.** He went off without looking back.

il voltastomaco NOME MASC
◆ **dare il voltastomaco a qualcuno** to make* somebody sick ◇ *Mi dà il voltastomaco.* It makes me sick.

il volume NOME MASC

volume ◇ *Potresti abbassare il volume?* Could you turn down the volume, please?

vomitare VERBO
to vomit

il vomito NOME MASC
vomit

la vongola NOME FEM
clam

vostro AGGETTIVO (FEM **vostra**)
vedi anche **vostro** PRONOME
your ◇ *i vostri libri* your books ◇ *È colpa vostra.* It's your fault.
◆ **un vostro amico** a friend of yours

vostro PRONOME (FEM **vostra**)
vedi anche **vostro** AGGETTIVO
yours ◇ *La nostra casa è più grande della vostra.* Our house is bigger than yours. ◇ *Di chi è questo? – È vostro.* Whose is this? – It's yours.

votare VERBO
to vote ◇ *Ho votato per loro.* I voted for them.

il voto NOME MASC
[1] mark (*a scuola*) ◇ *Ho preso un bel voto in matematica.* I got a good mark in maths.
[2] vote (*ad elezione*) ◇ *Hanno vinto per pochi voti.* They won by a few votes.

il vulcano NOME MASC
volcano

vuotare VERBO
to empty

vuoto AGGETTIVO (FEM **vuota**)
vedi anche **vuoto** NOME
empty ◇ *un appartamento vuoto* an empty flat
◆ **a mani vuote** empty-handed ◇ *È arrivato a mani vuote.* He arrived empty-handed.

il vuoto NOME MASC
vedi anche **vuoto** AGGETTIVO
[1] gap ◇ *La sua morte ha lasciato un vuoto tra di noi.* His death has left a real gap.
◆ **guardare nel vuoto** to gaze into space
◆ **avere paura del vuoto** to be* afraid of heights
◆ **assegno a vuoto** dud cheque
◆ **vuoto d'aria** air pocket
◆ **Ho fatto un viaggio a vuoto.** It was a wasted journey.
[2] empty (*bottiglia*) (PL empties)

W

il **wafer** NOME MASC (PL i **wafer**)
    wafer

il **water** NOME MASC (PL i **water**)
    toilet ◇ *L'ho gettato nel water.* I threw it in
    the toilet.

il **watt** NOME MASC (PL i **watt**)
    watt

il **W.C.** NOME MASC (PL i **W.C.**)
    W.C.

western AGGETTIVO, NOME MASC

- ◆ **un film western** a western
- ◆ **un western all'italiana** a spaghetti western

il **windsurf** NOME MASC (PL i **windsurf**)
     windsurfer (*tavola*)
     windsurfing (*attività*)
- ◆ **fare windsurf** to go* windsurfing

il **würstel** NOME MASC (PL i **würstel**)
    frankfurter ◇ *Vorrei un würstel con la*
    senape. I'd like a frankfurter with mustard.
- ◆ **un panino con il würstel** a hot dog

X

xenofobo AGGETTIVO (FEM **xenofoba**)
    xenophobic

lo **xilofono** NOME MASC
    xylophone

Y

lo **yacht** NOME MASC (PL gli **yacht**)
    yacht

lo **yoga** NOME MASC
    yoga

- ◆ **fare yoga** to do* yoga

lo **yogurt** NOME MASC (PL gli **yogurt**)
    yoghurt ◇ *uno yogurt alla fragola* a
    strawberry yoghurt

Z

lo **zafferano** NOME MASC
saffron

lo **zaino** NOME MASC
rucksack

la **zampa** NOME FEM
1 leg (*arto intero*)
2 paw (*parte che tocca terra*)
3 foot (PL feet) (*di elefante*)
+ **pantaloni a zampa d'elefante** flares
+ **a quattro zampe** on all fours
+ **zampe di gallina** (*rughe*) crow's feet

la **zanzara** NOME FEM
mosquito

la **zanzariera** NOME FEM
mosquito net

la **zattera** NOME FEM
raft

la **zebra** NOME FEM
zebra

la **zecca** NOME FEM (PL le **zecche**)
1 tick (*insetto*)
2 mint (*di monete*)

zeppo AGGETTIVO (FEM **zeppa**)
+ **zeppo di...** crammed with... ◊ *Era zeppo di gente.* It was crammed with people.

lo **zerbino** NOME MASC
doormat

lo **zero** NOME MASC
1 zero ◊ *tre, due, uno, zero* three, two, one, zero ◊ *trenta gradi sotto zero* thirty degrees below zero
2 O (*nei numeri di telefono*)
3 nil (*nel calcio*) ◊ *Hanno vinto tre a zero.* They won three-nil.
4 love (*nel tennis*) ◊ *trenta a zero* thirty love
+ **partire da zero** to start from scratch

la **zia** NOME FEM
aunt

lo **zigomo** NOME MASC
cheekbone

lo **zigzag** NOME MASC (PL gli **zigzag**)
+ **andare a zigzag** to zigzag

lo **zingaro**, la **zingara** NOME MASC, FEM
gypsy (PL gypsies)

lo **zio** NOME MASC
uncle
+ **i miei zii** (*zia e zio*) my aunt and uncle

zippare VERBO
to zip

la **zitella** NOME FEM
spinster

zitto AGGETTIVO (FEM **zitta**)
quiet ◊ *Sta' zitto!* Be quiet!

lo **zoccolo** NOME MASC
1 clog (*calzatura*)
2 hoof (PL hooves) (*di animale*)

zodiacale AGGETTIVO
+ **segno zodiacale** sign of the zodiac

lo **zodiaco** NOME MASC
zodiac

la **zolletta** NOME FEM
sugar lump

la **zona** NOME FEM
area ◊ *una zona malfamata* a rough area
+ **zona pedonale** pedestrian precinct

lo **zoo** NOME MASC (PL gli **zoo**)
zoo

zoppicare VERBO
to limp

zoppo AGGETTIVO (FEM **zoppa**)
lame

la **zucca** NOME FEM (PL le **zucche**)
pumpkin

zuccherare VERBO
to sugar

zuccherato AGGETTIVO (FEM **zuccherata**)
sweetened
+ **non zuccherato** unsweetened

la **zuccheriera** NOME FEM
sugar bowl

lo **zucchero** NOME MASC
sugar
+ **zucchero a velo** icing sugar
+ **zucchero di canna** cane sugar
+ **zucchero filato** candy floss, US: cotton candy

la **zucchina** NOME FEM
courgette
zucchini (PL zucchini) US

la **zuppa** NOME FEM
soup ◊ *una zuppa di verdura* a vegetable soup

zuppo AGGETTIVO (FEM **zuppa**)
soaked ◊ *Sono zuppo.* I'm soaked.

---

* I verbi seguiti da questo simbolo sono irregolari. Si veda anche alle pp.328–338.

ITALIAN IN ACTION

		ITALIANO ATTIVO
Games	304	Giochi
Correspondence	312	Corrispondenza
Telephone	316	Il telefono
Numbers	317	I numeri
Date	319	La data
Time	320	L'ora
False friends	321	Falsi amici

GAMES

GIOCHI

The wordgames on the following pages have been designed to give you practice in using your dictionary. Make sure you read the "Dictionary Skills" section at the front of this book before you start. Don't worry, there are answers at the end of the wordgames in case you get really stuck!

I giochi riportati alle pagine seguenti sono stati concepiti come esercizi per l'utilizzo del dizionario. Prima di cimentarsi con i giochi è meglio leggere la sezione "Come usare il dizionario" che si trova all'inizio del volume. Le soluzioni dei giochi si trovano alla fine di questa sezione.

WORDGAME 1

▶ OPPOSITES ◀

Complete the crossword by supplying opposites in Italian of the words below.
Use your dictionary to help.

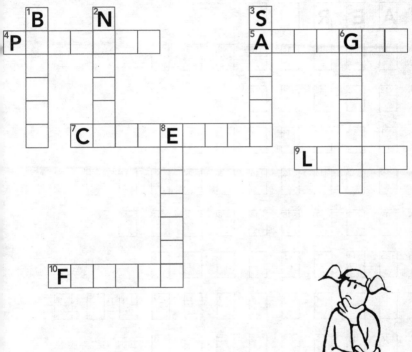

1. NERO
2. INTERESSANTE
3. SCENDERE
4. GRANDE
5. TRISTE
6. VECCHIO
7. INNOCENTE
8. USCIRE
9. CORTO
10. DIFFICILE

WORDGAME 2

▶ CODED WORDS ◀

Ten Italian words to do with transport have been spelled with numbers instead of letters. The same number always stands for the same letter. Try to crack the code and find the ten words. Use your dictionary to help.

1. | A¹ | E⁸ | R³ | .⁸ | ⁰ |

2. | 17 | 1 | 16 | 16 | 13 | 2 | 7 | 1 |

3. | 12 | 3 | 8 | 7 | 14 |

4. | 1 | 10 | 12 | 14 | 9 | 10 | 11 |

5. | 9 | 2 | 16 | 2 | 16 | 5 | 8 | 12 | 12 | 1 |

6. | 12 | 3 | 1 | 15 | 13 | 8 | 12 | 12 | 14 |

7. | 3 | 14 | 10 | 5 | 8 | 12 | 12 | 8 |

8. | 17 | 14 | 7 | 14 | 4 | 1 | 12 | 12 | 2 | 7 | 14 |

9. | 16 | 14 | 3 | 3 | 2 | 8 | 3 | 1 |

10. | 17 | 8 | 12 | 3 | 14 | 4 | 14 | 5 | 2 | 12 | 1 | 7 | |

306

WORDGAME 3

▶ KITCHEN SCRAMBLE ◀

Here is a list of Italian words to do with food and cooking. Rearrange the seven letters in the shaded boxes to find the missing Italian word.

1. orfon   Accendi il _____.

2. hcciuioca   un _____ di minestra

3. planote   L'acqua bolle nella _____.

4. gorif   Metti il burro in _____.

5. zazta   una _____ di caffè

6. tortinebu   Non hai chiuso il _____.

7. levolla   I piatti sporchi sono nel _____.

The word you are looking for is:

GIOCO 4

▶ TRADUZIONI DEL DIZIONARIO ◀

Completare il cruciverba inserendo le traduzioni in inglese delle parole italiane elencate nella parte inferiore della pagina. C'è tuttavia un piccolo inconveniente: tutte le parole hanno più di un significato in inglese, ma solo una delle traduzioni si adatta allo schema del cruciverba.

(Si ricordi che gli infiniti dei verbi in inglese vanno inseriti nel cruciverba senza il *to*. Nelle caselle non va quindi inserito "to go" ma solamente "go").

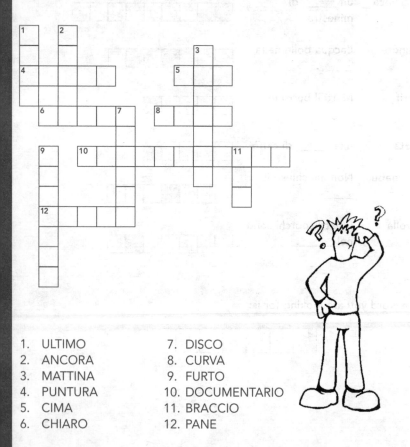

1. ULTIMO	7. DISCO
2. ANCORA	8. CURVA
3. MATTINA	9. FURTO
4. PUNTURA	10. DOCUMENTARIO
5. CIMA	11. BRACCIO
6. CHIARO	12. PANE

GIOCO 5

▶ PARTI DEL DISCORSO ◀

In ciascuna delle frasi riportate qui sotto è stata evidenziata una parola. Barrate la casella corrispondente alla funzione grammaticale della parola evidenziata.

FRASE	NOME	AGGETTIVO	AVVERBIO	VERBO
1. Are you going to wash your car?				
2. Hand me the hammer, please.				
3. Your dress is not very clean.				
4. Shall we go for a drive?				
5. We arrived just in time.				
6. The garage serviced my car last week.				
7. My feet are very cold.				
8. Are we having stew for dinner?				
9. They live in California.				
10. He switched off the light.				

GIOCO 6

▶ PAROLE IN CODICE ◀

Nelle caselle sottostanti le lettere che compongono le dieci parole inglesi sono state sostituite da numeri. Tenendo presente che a lettera uguale corrisponde numero uguale cercate di decifrare le dieci parole inglesi consultando il dizionario in caso di necessità.

Un piccolo aiuto: tutte e dieci le parole indicano mezzi di trasporto.

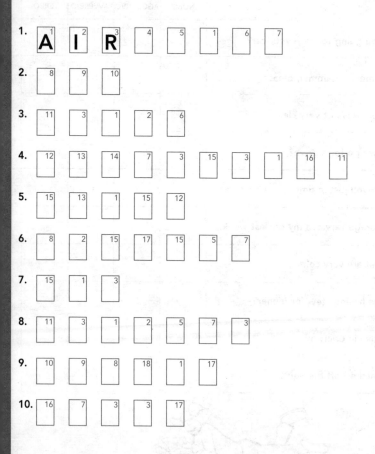

1. A¹ I² R³ ⁴ ⁵ 1 ⁶ ⁷

2. 8 9 10

3. 11 3 1 2 6

4. 12 13 14 7 3 15 3 1 16 11

5. 15 13 1 15 12

6. 8 2 15 17 15 5 7

7. 15 1 3

8. 11 3 1 2 5 7 3

9. 10 9 8 18 1 17

10. 16 7 3 3 17

WORDGAME 1

1. bianco
2. noioso
3. salire
4. piccolo
5. allegro
6. giovane
7. colpevole
8. entrare
9. corto
10. facile

WORDGAME 2

1. aereo
2. macchina
3. treno
4. autobus
5. bicicletta
6. traghetto
7. roulotte
8. monopattino
9. corriera
10. metropolitana

WORDGAME 3

1. forno
2. cucchiaio
3. pentola
4. frigo
5. tazza
6. rubinetto
7. lavello

Missing word –
CIOTOLA

GIOCO 4

1. last
2. still
3. morning
4. sting
5. top
6. clear
7. record
8. bend
9. robbery
10. documentary
11. arm
12. bread

GIOCO 5

1. Verbo
2. Verbo
3. Aggettivo
4. Nome
5. Avverbio
6. Verbo
7. Aggettivo
8. Nome
9. Verbo
10. Nome

GIOCO 6

1. airplane
2. bus
3. train
4. hovercraft
5. coach
6. bicycle
7. car
8. trailer
9. subway
10. ferry

CORRESPONDENCE

▶ LETTER

Date

Milano, 5 febbraio 2002

Cara Maria,
ti ringrazio moltissimo del biglietto che mi hai mandato per il mio compleanno, che è arrivato proprio il giorno della mia festa!

Mi dispiace che tu non sia potuta venire a Milano per il mio compleanno e spero che ti sia ripresa dopo l'influenza. Mi piacerebbe poterti incontrare presto perché ho molte novità da raccontarti. Forse tra due settimane verrò a Torino con degli amici. Pensi di essere libera il giorno 12? Ti telefono la prossima settimana, così ci mettiamo d'accordo.

Baci,

Anna

Or:
Un abbraccio
Con affetto

STARTING A PERSONAL LETTER

Ti ringrazio per la tua lettera.
Mi ha fatto piacere ricevere tue notizie.
Scusami se non ti ho scritto prima.

Thank you for your letter.
It was lovely to hear from you.
I'm sorry I didn't write sooner.

ENDING A PERSONAL LETTER

Scrivi presto!
Salutami tanto Lucia.
Tanti saluti anche da Paolo.

Write soon!
Give my love to Lucia.
Paolo sends his best wishes.

CORRISPONDENZA

▶ LA LETTERA

Indirizzo del mittente

18 Slateford Avenue
Leeds
L24 3PR

Data

14 September 2002

Dear Gran and Grandad,

Thank you both very much for the CDs which you sent me for my birthday. They are two of my favourite groups and I'll really enjoy listening to them.

There's not much news here. I seem to be spending most of my time studying for my exams which start in two weeks. I'm hoping to pass all of them but I'm not looking forward to the maths exam as that's my worst subject.

Mum says that you're off to Crete on holiday next week, so I hope that you have a great time and come back with a good tan.

With love from

Kerry

O:
With best wishes
Yours ever
Lots of love from

PER COMINCIARE LA LETTERA

Thank you for your letter.
It was lovely to hear from you.
I'm sorry I didn't write sooner.

Ti ringrazio per la tua lettera.
Mi ha fatto piacere ricevere tue notizie.
Scusami se non ti ho scritto prima.

PER TERMINARE LA LETTERA

Write soon!
Give my love to Vanessa.
Samuel sends his best wishes.

Scrivi presto!
Salutami tanto Vanessa.
Tanti saluti anche da Samuel.

CORRESPONDENCE

▶ EMAIL

To give your email address to someone in Italian, say:
"paolo punto rossi chiocciola posta punto i t"

	Nuovo messaggio
A:	paolo.rossi@posta.it
Da:	francesca@mail.it
Oggetto:	concerto
Cc:	elena@mail.it
Ccn:	

| Allegato | Invio |

Ciao, sei libera il prossimo fine settimana?

Ho un biglietto in pi per il concerto di sabato dato che una mia amica non pu venire. Fammi sapere se t interessa o se conosci qualcuno a cui possa interessare.

A presto.

Nuovo messaggio	New message
A	To
Da	From
Oggetto	Subject
Cc	cc
Ccn	bcc
Allegato	Attachment
Invio	Send

CORRISPONDENZA

▶ MESSAGGIO DI POSTA ELETTRONICA

> Per dare un indirizzo di posta
> elettronica in inglese si dice.
> **"gemma at n t net dot co dot ù k"**

	New Message
To:	gemma@ntnet.co.uk
From:	gordon@onemo.net
Subject:	concert next week
cc:	jeremy@blt.com
bcc:	

Attachment   Send

Hi guys

I ve just bought the new album by Rockstar, and it s brilliant!
I ve got two spare tickets to a concert they re giving in Edinburgh
next Wednesday evening, so I hope you can both make it.

See you soon!

New message	Nuovo messaggio
To	A
From	Da
Subject	Oggetto
cc	Cc
bcc	Ccn
Attachment	Allegato
Send	Invio

▶ WHEN YOUR NUMBER ANSWERS | ▶ QUANDO L'ABBONATO RISPONDE

- Hello! Could I speak to Sara, please?
- Potrei parlare con Sara, per favore?

- Could you ask him/her to call me back, please?
- Può chiedergli/chiederle di richiamarmi, per favore?

- I'll call back in half an hour.
- Richiamo fra una mezz'ora.

▶ ANSWERING THE TELEPHONE | ▶ PER RISPONDERE AL TELEFONO

- Hello! It's Paolo speaking.
- Pronto, sono Paolo.

- Speaking.
- Sono io.

- Who's speaking?
- Chi parla?

▶ WHEN THE SWITCHBOARD ANSWERS | ▶ RISPONDE IL CENTRALINO

- Who shall I say is calling?
- Chi devo dire?

- I'm putting you through.
- Le passo la comunicazione.

- Please hold.
- Attenda in linea.

- Would you like to leave a message?
- Vuole lasciare un messaggio?

▶ DIFFICULTIES | ▶ IN CASO DI DIFFICOLTÀ

- I can't get through.
- Non riesco a prendere la linea.

- I'm sorry, I've got the wrong number.
- Mi dispiace, ho sbagliato numero.

- This is a very bad line.
- La linea è molto disturbata.

- Their phone is out of order.
- Il loro telefono è guasto.

1	one	1	uno(a)
2	two	2	due
3	three	3	tre
4	four	4	quattro
5	five	5	cinque
6	six	6	sei
7	seven	7	sette
8	eight	8	otto
9	nine	9	nove
10	ten	10	diece
11	eleven	11	undici
12	twelve	12	dodici
13	thirteen	13	tredici
14	fourteen	14	quattordici
15	fifteen	15	quindici
16	sixteen	16	sedici
17	seventeen	17	diciassette
18	eighteen	18	diciotto
19	nineteen	19	diciannove
20	twenty	20	venti
21	twenty-one	21	ventuno
30	thirty	30	trenta
31	thirty-one	31	trentuno
40	forty	40	quaranta
41	forty-one	41	quarantuno
50	fifty	50	cinquanta
60	sixty	60	sessanta
70	seventy	70	settanta
80	eighty	80	ottanta
90	ninety	90	novanta
100	a hundred	100	cento
101	a hundred and one	101	centouno
200	two hundred	200	duecento
201	two hundred and one	201	duecentouno
1000	a thousand	1000	mille
1001	a thousand and one	1001	milleuno
1,000,000	a million	1,000,000	un milione

► EXAMPLES

on page nineteen
in chapter seven
on a scale of one to fifteen

► ESEMPI

a pagina diciannove
nel capitolo sette
su una scala da uno a quindici

1st	**first**		1°	**primo**
2nd	**second**		2°	**secondo**
3rd	**third**		3°	**terzo**
4th	**fourth**		4°	**quarto**
5th	**fifth**		5°	**quinto**
6th	**sixth**		6°	**sesto**
7th	**seventh**		7°	**settimo**
8th	**eighth**		8°	**ottavo**
9th	**ninth**		9°	**nono**
10th	**tenth**		10°	**decimo**
11th	**eleventh**		11°	**undicesimo**
12th	**twelfth**		12°	**dodicesimo**
13th	**thirteenth**		13°	**tredicesimo**
14th	**fourteenth**		14°	**quattordicesimo**
15th	**fifteenth**		15°	**quindicesimo**
16th	**sixteenth**		16°	**sedicesimo**
17th	**seventeenth**		17°	**diciassettesimo**
18th	**eighteenth**		18°	**diciottesimo**
19th	**nineteenth**		19°	**diciannovesimo**
20th	**twentieth**		20°	**ventesimo**
21st	**twenty-first**		21°	**ventunesimo**
30th	**thirtieth**		30°	**trentesimo**
100th	**hundredth**		100°	**centesimo**
101st	**hundred-and-first**		101°	**centunesimo**
1000th	**thousandth**		1000°	**millesimo**

▶FRACTIONS etc.

▶ LE FRAZIONI ecc

1/2	**a half**		1/2	**un mezzo**
1/3	**a third**		1/3	**un terzo**
1/4	**a quarter**		1/4	**un quarto**
1/5	**a fifth**		1/5	**un quinto**
0.5	**(nought) point five**		0,5	**zero virgola cinque**
3.4	**three point four**		3,4	**tre virgola quattro**
6.89	**six point eight nine**		6,89	**sei virgola ottantanove**
10%	**ten per cent**		10%	**dieci per cento**
100%	**a hundred per cent**		100%	**cento per cento**

▶ EXAMPLES

▶ ESEMPI

he lives on the fifth floor
he came in third
a quarter of the cake

abita al quinto piano
è arrivato terzo
un quarto della torta

DATE

▶ DAYS OF THE WEEK

Monday
Tuesday
Wednesday
Thursday
Friday
Saturday
Sunday

When?
on Monday
on Mondays
every Monday
last Tuesday
next Friday
a week on Saturday
two weeks on Saturday

▶ MONTHS OF THE YEAR

January
February
March
April
May
June
July
August
September
October
November
December

When?
in February
on December 1st *or* first 2002
in two thousand and two

What day is it?
It's ...
Monday, May 26th *o*
  Monday, May twenty-sixth

▶ GIORNI DELLA SETTIMANA

lunedì
martedì
mercoledì
giovedì
venerdì
sabato
domenica

Quando?
lunedì
di lunedì
tutti i lunedì
martedì scorso
venerdì prossimo
sabato della settimana prossima
sabato tra due settimane

▶ MESI DELL'ANNO

gennaio
febbraio
marzo
aprile
maggio
giugno
luglio
agosto
settembre
ottobre
novembre
dicembre

Quando?
in febbraio
il primo dicembre 2002
nel duemiladue

Che giorno è oggi?
È ...
lunedì, ventisei maggio

What time is it?	Che ora è?
What's the time?	Che ore sono?

It's one o'clock		È l'una.
It's ten past one		È l'una e dieci.
It's quarter past one		È l'una e un quarto.
It's half past one		È l'una e mezza.
It's twenty to two		Sono le due meno venti.
It's quarter to two		Sono le due meno un quarto.

What time?		A che ora?
at midnight		a mezzanotte
at midday		a mezzogiorno
at one o'clock (in the afternoon)		all'una (del pomeriggio)
at eleven o'clock (in the evening)		alle undici (di sera)

11:15 *o* eleven fifteen		le undici e quindici
8:45 *o* eight forty-five		le venti e quarantacinque

in twenty minutes	fra venti minuti
ten minutes ago	dieci minuti fa

Italiano ≠ English

attuale ≠ actual

Al momento **attuale**.	→	At the **present** moment.
What's the **actual** amount?	→	Qual è la cifra **effettiva**?

camera ≠ camera

Una **camera** grande.	→	A big **room**.
I have a **camera**.	→	Ho una **macchina fotografica**.

comprensivo ≠ comprehensive

È molto **comprensivo**.	→	He's very **understanding**.
A **comprehensive** guide to Greece.	→	Una guida **completa** della Grecia.

confetto ≠ confetti

Vuoi un **confetto**?	→	Do you want a **sugared amond**?
A bag of **confetti**.	→	Un sacchetto di **coriandoli**.

eventuale ≠ eventual

Siamo assicurati contro **eventuali** danni.	→	We're insured against **any** damage.
The **eventual** outcome.	→	Il risultato **finale**.

fabbrica ≠ fabric

Una **fabbrica** di mobili.	→	A furniture **factory**.
Red cotton **fabric**.	→	**Tessuto** rosso di cotone.

fastidioso ≠ fastidious

È un bambino **fastidioso**.	→	He's an **annoying** child.
He's very **fastidious**.	→	È molto **pignolo**.

fattoria ≠ factory

Vivono in una **fattoria**.	→	They live on a **farm**.
A car **factory**.	→	Una **fabbrica** di automobili.

firma ≠ firm

Una petizione con 500 **firme**.	→	A petition with 500 **signatures**.
Many **firms** were facing bankruptcy.	→	Molte **aziende** rischiavano il fallimento.

magazzino ≠ magazine

Lo tengono in un **magazzino**.	→	They keep it in a **warehouse**.
A monthly **magazine**.	→	Una **rivista** mensile.

occorrere ≠ occur

Mi **occorre** del denaro.	→	I **need** some money.
The accident **occurred** yesterday.	→	L'incidente è **successo** ieri.

parente ≠ parent

È un mio **parente**.	→	He's a **relative** of mine.
She changed when she became a **parent**.	→	È cambiata quando è diventata **madre**.

patente ≠ patent

Ho perso la **patente**.   →   I've lost my **driving licence**.

He applied for a **patent**.   →   Ha fatto **richiesta di brevetto**.

pretendere ≠ pretend

Pretende di essere pagato in anticipo.   →   He **expects** to be paid in advance.

To **pretend** to do something.   →   **Fare finta** di fare qualcosa.

puntura ≠ puncture

Gli ha fatto una **puntura** sul braccio.   →   She gave him an **injection** in his arm.

I had a **puncture** on the motorway.   →   Ho **forato** sull'autostrada.

rumore ≠ rumour

Cos'è questo **rumore**?   →   What's that **noise**?

There's a **rumour** that ...   →   Corre **voce** che ...

sensibile ≠ sensible

È un ragazzo **sensibile**.   →   He's a **sensitive** boy.

Be **sensible**!   →   Sii **ragionevole**!

sopportare ≠ support

Non lo **sopporto**.   →   I **can't stand** him.

My friends have always **supported** me.   →   I miei amici mi hanno sempre **appoggiato**.

vacanza ≠ vacancy

Ho fatto una lunga **vacanza**.   →   I had a long **holiday**.

There are no **vacancies** at the moment.   →   Non ci sono **posti disponibili** in questo momento.

LA CONIUGAZIONE DEI VERBI INGLESI

▶ INDICE

Introduzione   326

Tavole di coniugazione dei verbi

to WORK   331

to DO   332

to HAVE   333

to BE   334

CAN   335

Verbi irregolari inglesi   336

LA CONIUGAZIONE DEI VERBI INGLESI

Le tavole dei verbi inglesi e questa breve introduzione illustrano come va coniugato un verbo regolare modello (**to work**), i verbi irregolari e ausiliari **to do**, **to have** e **to be** e il verbo modale **can**.

Ciascuna tavola riporta le forme dell'infinito, del gerundio e del participio passato, oltre ad alcuni esempi sull'uso del verbo e alla coniugazione delle forme principali.

Alla fine di questa sezione si trova la tabella dei verbi irregolari inglesi, con le forme del PRESENTE, del PASSATO e del PARTICIPIO PASSATO.

▶ VERBI REGOLARI E IRREGOLARI – PRESENTE SEMPLICE

La forma AFFERMATIVA del PRESENTE SEMPLICE della maggior parte dei verbi inglesi è la stessa dell'infinito per tutte le persone, ad eccezione della terza persona singolare che normalmente si forma aggiungendo una **-s**:

> to say – I say, he says
> to speak – I speak, he speaks

Va ricordato che la terza persona singolare dei verbi che finiscono per **-ss**, **-sh**, **-ch** o **-x** si forma aggiungendo la desinenza **-es**:

> to pass – he passes
> to push – he pushes
> to reach – he reaches
> to mix – he mixes

Se un verbo termina con **-y** preceduta da vocale, la terza persona singolare presente si forma regolarmente aggiungendo una **-s**; se invece la **-y** è preceduta da consonante, la **y** cade e va aggiunta la desinenza **-ies**:

> to pay – he pays
> to try – he tries

Per la forma NEGATIVA si aggiunge **don't** o **do not** all'infinito senza il "to" del verbo da coniugare per tutte le persone ad eccezione della terza singolare, per la quale prima dell'infinito senza il "to" va posto **doesn't** o **does not**:

> to say – I **don't** say o **do not** say, he **doesn't** say o **does not** say, ecc.
> to try – I **don't** try o **do not** try, he **doesn't** try o **does not** try, ecc.

Per la forma INTERROGATIVA si aggiunge **do** all'INFINITO senza il "to" per tutte le persone ad eccezione della terza singolare, per la quale prima dell'infinito senza il "to" va posto **does**:

to speak – **do** you speak English?
      – **does** he speak English?, ecc.

▶ PASSATO SEMPLICE

In inglese il PASSATO SEMPLICE dei verbi regolari normalmente si forma per tutte le persone aggiungendo la terminazione **-ed** all'infinito:

to scream – I screamed, he screamed, ecc.

Se un verbo termina in **-e**, si aggiunge solamente **-d**:

to love – we loved, ecc.

Se un verbo termina con una sola vocale seguita da consonante e consta di una sola sillaba, la consonante raddoppia quando si aggiunge **-ed**:

to shop – they shopped, ecc.
to sob – she sobbed, ecc.

Lo stesso vale per i verbi con più sillabe dove l'accento cade sull'ultima sillaba.

to refer – they referred, ecc.

Negli altri casi il passato semplice si forma in genere senza raddoppiare la consonante finale.

to shout – they shouted ecc.
to seem – it seemed ecc.
to visit – they visited ecc.

La **-y** preceduta da consonante alla fine del verbo si trasforma in **-ied**:

to cry – she cried, ecc.
to worry – we worried, ecc.

Una nota a parte per i verbi che terminano con una sola vocale non accentata seguita da una **-l**: nell'inglese britannico la **-l** raddoppia per formare il passato, mentre nell'inglese americano non raddoppia:

to travel – (BRIT) he travelled – (US) he traveled

Nel caso dei verbi irregolari va consultato l'elenco alle pagine 336-338 che riporta le tre forme di ogni verbo. La seconda forma è quella del PASSATO che è uguale per tutte le persone:

to swim, swam, swum – he swam, they swam, ecc.

Le forme irregolari compaiono anche alla voce corrispondente al verbo sulla parte inglese-italiano del dizionario.

Per la forma NEGATIVA si usa, per tutte le persone, **didn't** o **did not** seguito dall'INFINITO del verbo senza il "to", sia con i verbi regolari che irregolari:

> to say – **did not** say o I **didn't** say, ecc.
> to go – **did not** go o I **didn't** go, ecc.

Per la forma INTERROGATIVA si utilizza **did** seguito dall'INFINITO senza il "to" per tutte le persone, sia con i verbi regolari che irregolari:

> to scream – **did** she scream?, ecc.
> to swim – **did** they swim?, ecc.

▶ ALTRI TEMPI VERBALI E L'USO DEI VERBI AUSILIARI

Gli altri tempi verbali si formano con i verbi ausiliari **have**, **will** e **be** che spesso si contraggono nell'inglese parlato.

Il PRESENT PERFECT si forma coniugando il verbo **have** (secondo il modello a pagina 333) e aggiungendo il PARTICIPIO PASSATO del verbo principale.

La forma NEGATIVA si forma collocando **not** o la forma contratta tra l'AUSILIARE e il VERBO PRINCIPALE. La forma INTERROGATIVA si forma invertendo l'ordine dell'AUSILIARE e del SOGGETTO.

to work

FORMA AFFERMATIVA:	I **have** o I'**ve** worked, he'**s** o he **has** worked, ecc.
FORMA NEGATIVA:	I **have not** o I **haven't** worked, he **hasn't** o he **has not** worked, ecc.
FORMA INTERROGATIVA:	**have** you worked, **has** he worked?, ecc.

to swim

FORMA AFFERMATIVA:	I'**ve** o I **have** swum, he'**s** o he **has** swum, ecc.
FORMA NEGATIVA:	I **haven't** o I **have not** swum, he **hasn't** o he **has not** swum, ecc.
FORMA INTERROGATIVA:	**have** you swum, **has** he swum?, ecc.

La forma del PARTICIPIO PASSATO dei verbi regolari termina in **-ed** come quella del PASSATO SEMPLICE. Per il PARTICIPIO PASSATO dei verbi irregolari si consulti la terza colonna dell'elenco alle pagine 336-338.

Per formare il FUTURO si deve usare il VERBO AUSILIARE **will** prima della forma dell'infinito senza il "to" del verbo che si vuole coniugare:

to work

FORMA AFFERMATIVA:	I'll o I **will** work, they'll o they **will** work, ecc.
FORMA NEGATIVA:	I **won't** o I **will not** work, he **won't** o he **will not** work, ecc.
FORMA INTERROGATIVA:	**will** you work, **will** he work?, ecc.

Per formare i TEMPI PROGRESSIVI (CONTINUOUS in inglese), si usa la forma coniugata del verbo **to be,** spesso contratta, seguita dal GERUNDIO:

to work

FORMA AFFERMATIVA – presente:	I'm o I **am** working, he's o he **is** working, ecc.
FORMA NEGATIVA – presente:	I'm **not** o I **am not** working, he's **not** o he **is not** working, ecc.
FORMA INTERROGATIVA – presente:	**are** you working, **is** he working?, ecc.
FORMA AFFERMATIVA – passato:	I **was** working, you **were** working, ecc.
FORMA NEGATIVA – passato:	I **wasn't** o I **was not** working, he **wasn't** o he **was not** working, ecc.
FORMA INTERROGATIVA – passato:	**were** you working, **was** he working?, ecc.

▶ FORMAZIONE DEL GERUNDIO

In inglese il GERUNDIO di tutti i verbi, sia regolari che irregolari, si forma normalmente aggiungendo la desinenza **-ing** all'INFINITO:

to scream – screaming

Se il verbo termina con una sola **-e**, questa scompare quando si aggiunge **-ing**:

to love – loving

Se il verbo termina con una sola vocale seguita da consonante ed è costituito da un'unica sillaba la consonante finale raddoppia quando si aggiunge **-ing**:

to shop – shopping
to sob – sobbing

Lo stesso vale per i verbi con più sillabe in cui l'accento cade sull'ultima sillaba:

to refer – referring

Negli altri casi il gerundio si forma in genere senza raddoppiare la consonante finale:

to shout – shouting
to seem – seeming
to visit – visiting

Una nota a parte per i verbi che terminano con una sola vocale non accentata seguita da una **-l**: nell'inglese britannico la **-l** raddoppia per formare il gerundio, mentre nell'inglese americano non raddoppia.

to travel – (BRIT) travelling – (US) traveling

▶ USO DELLE FORME SEMPLICI E PROGRESSIVE

In generale le FORME PROGRESSIVE (CONTINUOUS FORMS) si utilizzano per descrivere un'azione che si svolge o si svolgerà in un determinato momento:

Don't distract him, he **is preparing** for his exam.
This time tomorrow, she **will be travelling** down south.
When he came into the room I **was watching** TV.

Le forme progressive servono anche per indicare che l'azione non è finita o per descrivere una situazione transitoria:

The doorbell rang while I **was having** a shower.
I **am working** with Steve and Will at the moment.

Le forme semplici si utilizzano in riferimento ad azioni abituali oppure, nel caso del passato, ad azioni avvenute in un determinato momento:

I **visited** my grandmother regularly.
I **get up** at seven every morning.
He **cut** his knee when he fell.

Si confrontino le frasi riportate qui di seguito osservando l'uso delle forme verbali semplici e progressive:

I **was speaking** to my friend when the phone rang.
I **spoke** to my friend and then called my mother.

John **reads** the paper at the breakfast table every morning.
John **is** just **reading** the paper.

TAVOLE DI CONIUGAZIONE DEI VERBI

► to work

= lavorare

PAST PARTICIPLE

worked

GERUND

working

FUTURE

will work

PRESENT PERFECT

have/has worked

PRESENT PERFECT CONTINUOUS

have/has been working

ESEMPI

- *She **works** in a bookshop.*
  Lavora in una libreria.
- *Don't **work** so hard.*
  Non lavorare tanto.
- *He **worked** hard last month.*
  Ha lavorato molto il mese scorso.

SIMPLE PRESENT

I	work
you	work
he	works
we	work
you	work
they	work

SIMPLE PAST

I	worked
you	worked
he	worked
we	worked
you	worked
they	worked

PRESENT CONTINUOUS

I	am working
you	are working
he	is working
we	are working
you	are working
they	are working

PAST CONTINUOUS

I	was working
you	were working
he	was working
we	were working
you	were working
they	were working

TAVOLE DI CONIUGAZIONE DEI VERBI

▶ to do

= fare

PAST PARTICIPLE

done

GERUND

doing

FUTURE

will do

PRESENT PERFECT

have/has done

PRESENT PERFECT CONTINUOUS

have/has been doing

ESEMPI

- *What shall we **do** now?*
  Cosa facciamo adesso?
- *Where **did** you go on holiday?*
  Dove sei andato in vacanza?
- *He's **doing** his homework.*
  Sta facendo i compiti.

SIMPLE PRESENT

I	do
you	do
he	does
we	do
you	do
they	do

SIMPLE PAST

I	did
you	did
he	did
we	did
you	did
they	did

PRESENT CONTINUOUS

I	am doing
you	are doing
he	is doing
we	are doing
you	are doing
they	are doing

PAST CONTINUOUS

I	was doing
you	were doing
he	was doing
we	were doing
you	were doing
they	were doing

▸ to have

= avere

PAST PARTICIPLE	PRESENT PERFECT
had	have/has had

GERUND	PRESENT PERFECT CONTINUOUS
having	have/has been having

FUTURE	ESEMPI
will have	

ESEMPI

- *She **has** brown hair.*
  Ha i capelli castani.
- *I **had** two eggs for breakfast.*
  Ho mangiato due uova a colazione.
- *We're **having** a party tonight.*
  Stasera diamo una festa.

SIMPLE PRESENT

I	have
you	have
he	has
we	have
you	have
they	have

SIMPLE PAST

I	had
you	had
he	had
we	had
you	had
they	had

PRESENT CONTINUOUS

I	am having
you	are having
he	is having
we	are having
you	are having
they	are having

PAST CONTINUOUS

I	was having
you	were having
he	was having
we	were having
you	were having
they	were having

TAVOLE DI CONIUGAZIONE DEI VERBI

▶ to be

= essere

PAST PARTICIPLE

been

GERUND

being

FUTURE

will be

PRESENT PERFECT

have/has been

PRESENT PERFECT CONTINUOUS

have/has been being

ESEMPI

- *How **are** you?* Come stai?
- *She **is** thirteen years old.*
  Ha tredici anni.
- *It's cold today.* Oggi è freddo.
- *I'm hungry.* Ho fame.

SIMPLE PRESENT

I	am
you	are
he	is
we	are
you	are
they	are

SIMPLE PAST

I	was
you	were
he	was
we	were
you	were
they	were

PRESENT CONTINUOUS

I	am being
you	are being
he	is being
we	are being
you	are being
they	are being

PAST CONTINUOUS

I	was being
you	were being
he	was being
we	were being
you	were being
they	were being

► can

= potere, sapere

ESEMPI

- *She **can** swim well.* Sa nuotare bene.
- *I **can**'t speak French.* Non so parlare francese.
- *We **could**n't get the tickets.* Non siamo riusciti a prendere i biglietti.

PRESENT	
I	can
you	can
he	can
we	can
you	can
they	can

CONDITIONAL/SIMPLE PAST	
I	could
you	could
he	could
we	could
you	could
they	could

VERBI IRREGOLARI INGLESI

PRESENTE	PASSATO	PARTICIPIO PASSATO
awake	awoke	awoken
be (am, is, are; being)	was, were	been
bear	bore	born(e)
beat	beat	beaten
become	became	become
begin	began	begun
bend	bent	bent
bet	bet, betted	bet, betted
bite	bit	bitten
bleed	bled	bled
blow	blew	blown
break	broke	broken
breed	bred	bred
bring	brought	brought
build	built	built
burn	burnt, burned	burnt, burned
burst	burst	burst
buy	bought	bought
can	could	(been able)
catch	caught	caught
choose	chose	chosen
come	came	come
cost	cost	cost
creep	crept	crept
cut	cut	cut
deal	dealt	dealt
dig	dug	dug
do (does)	did	done
draw	drew	drawn
dream	dreamed, dreamt	dreamed, dreamt
drink	drank	drunk
drive	drove	driven
eat	ate	eaten
fall	fell	fallen
feed	fed	fed
feel	felt	felt
fight	fought	fought
find	found	found
fling	flung	flung
fly	flew	flown
forbid	forbad(e)	forbidden
forget	forgot	forgotten
forgive	forgave	forgiven
freeze	froze	frozen

PRESENTE	PASSATO	PARTICIPIO PASSATO
get	got	got, (US) gotten
give	gave	given
go (goes)	went	gone
grind	ground	ground
grow	grew	grown
hang	hung	hung
hang (execute)	hanged	hanged
have	had	had
hear	heard	heard
hide	hid	hidden
hit	hit	hit
hold	held	held
hurt	hurt	hurt
keep	kept	kept
kneel	knelt, kneeled	knelt, kneeled
know	knew	known
lay	laid	laid
lead	led	led
lean	leant, leaned	leant, leaned
leap	leapt, leaped	leapt, leaped
learn	learnt, learned	learnt, learned
leave	left	left
lend	lent	lent
let	let	let
lie (lying)	lay	lain
light	lit, lighted	lit, lighted
lose	lost	lost
make	made	made
may	might	—
mean	meant	meant
meet	met	met
mistake	mistook	mistaken
mow	mowed	mown, mowed
must	(had to)	(had to)
pay	paid	paid
put	put	put
quit	quit, quitted	quit, quitted
read	read	read
rid	rid	rid
ride	rode	ridden
ring	rang	rung
rise	rose	risen
run	ran	run
say	said	said
see	saw	seen
sell	sold	sold
send	sent	sent

PRESENTE	PASSATO	PARTICIPIO PASSATO
set	set	set
sew	sewed	sewn
shake	shook	shaken
shine	shone	shone
shoot	shot	shot
show	showed	shown
shrink	shrank	shrunk
shut	shut	shut
sing	sang	sung
sink	sank	sunk
sit	sat	sat
sleep	slept	slept
slide	slid	slid
smell	smelt, smelled	smelt, smelled
speak	spoke	spoken
speed	sped, speeded	sped, speeded
spell	spelt, spelled	spelt, spelled
spend	spent	spent
spill	spilt, spilled	spilt, spilled
spit	spat	spat
spoil	spoiled, spoilt	spoiled, spoilt
spread	spread	spread
stand	stood	stood
steal	stole	stolen
stick	stuck	stuck
sting	stung	stung
stink	stank	stunk
strike	struck	struck
swear	swore	sworn
sweep	swept	swept
swim	swam	swum
swing	swung	swung
take	took	taken
teach	taught	taught
tear	tore	torn
tell	told	told
think	thought	thought
throw	threw	thrown
tread	trod	trodden
wake	woke, waked	woken, waked
wear	wore	worn
weep	wept	wept
win	won	won
wind	wound	wound
write	wrote	written

ITALIAN VERBS

▶ CONTENTS

Introduction	340
Verb Tables:	
PARLARE	342
LAVARSI	343
CREDERE	344
DORMIRE	345
FINIRE	346
DIRE	347
DARE	348
ESSERE	349
AVERE	350
FARE	351
ANDARE	352
VOLERE	353
SAPERE	354
POTERE	355
DOVERE	356
STARE	357
Italian irregular verb forms	358
Other irregular verbs	364

ITALIAN VERB TABLES

This section contains 16 tables of very important Italian verbs (some regular and some irregular) that you need to learn. These are set out in full. These 16 verbs are followed by pages of other irregular verbs.

It is important to learn which Italian verbs are irregular. They are marked by an asterisk in the dictionary. When you see a verb on the Italian side of the dictionary which is marked with an asterisk you can look in the verb tables for the tense you need.

The tables are arranged in the following order:

▶ Regular verbs – parlare, lavarsi, credere, dormire and finire
▶ The most common irregular verbs

At the top of each full-page table you will find the infinitive, the imperative, the past participle and the gerund. The lower section of the table shows you how to form six tenses of the verb:

PRESENT
PAST HISTORIC
FUTURE
PRESENT SUBJUNCTIVE
IMPERFECT
PRESENT CONDITIONAL

▶ REGULAR VERBS

There are three groups of regular verbs:

"-ARE" verbs = verbs that end in -**are** like **parlare** on p342 or **lavarsi** on p343 (a reflexive verb, but otherwise a regular "-ARE" verb).
"-ERE" verbs = verbs that end in -**ere** like **credere** on p344
"-IRE" verbs = verbs that end in -**ire** like **dormire** on p345 or **finire** on p346

These are called regular verbs because they follow set patterns. When you have learned these patterns you will be able to form any regular verb.

The subject pronouns *io, tu, egli, noi, voi* and *essi* appear in brackets because they are not always necessary in Italian when **I, you, he** etc are used in English.

When subject pronouns are used in spoken Italian *lui* (he), *lei* (she) and *loro* (they) are more often used than the more formal *egli, essa, essi* and *esse*.

HOW TO FORM A REGULAR VERB

To form the present, imperfect, past historic, future, present conditional and present subjective, take the infinitive minus the last three letters. This is called the **stem** e.g. parlare → **parl-**, credere → **cred-**, dormire → **dorm-**, finire → **fin-**.

Next add the appropriate ending. You need to ask yourself three questions.

a) **What sort** of verb am I using (-ARE, -ERE, -IRE)?
b) **Who** is doing the verb? (io, tu, egli etc)?
c) **When** are they doing it (in the present, the past or the future)?

Look at the verb endings for **parlare**, **credere**, **dormire** and **finire**, ie at what is added on to the verb stem. These endings can be added onto the stem of any regular verb.

▶ THE MOST COMMON IRREGULAR VERBS

Many Italian verbs are irregular and this means you have to learn them individually. There are full-page tables for irregular verbs such as **potere**, **sapere** and **volere**. When you are translating from Italian and meet an unfamiliar verb form you may be able to guess from the context that it comes from one of these verbs, and you can then use the verb tables to check.

HOW TO USE THE VERB TABLES

You will find some useful examples at the top of each verb table, but if you don't find what you want to say in Italian there, use the table itself to help you. Imagine you want to find the Italian for "he wants". Here's how to do it:

● Look up **want** on the English-Italian side of the dictionary to find the Italian translation.
● The Italian translation is **volere**.
● Turn to the verb tables section of the dictionary and find **volere**.
● When does he want it? He wants it **now**, so look for the heading *PRESENT*.
● Who wants it? **He** does. The Italian for "he" is **egli** so look for egli under the *PRESENT* heading. The same form of the verb is also used if you are translating "she wants".
● The Italian for "he wants" is "**vuole**".

▶ OTHER IRREGULAR VERBS

On pages 358-363 there is an alphabetical list of further irregular verbs, with those tenses that are irregular set out in full. On page 364 are listed verbs that follow the same pattern as these verbs.

ITALIAN VERB TABLES

▶ parlare

= to speak

GERUND

parlando

IMPERATIVE

parla!

parli!
parliamo!
parlate!
parlino!

PAST PARTICIPLE

parlato

EXAMPLE PHRASES

- *Non **parlo** francese.* I don't speak French.
- *Ho **parlato** con tuo fratello ieri.* I spoke to your brother yesterday.
- ***Parlerò** con lei stasera.* I'll speak to her this evening.

PRESENT

(io)	parlo
(tu)	parli
(egli)	parla
(noi)	parliamo
(voi)	parlate
(essi)	parlano

PAST HISTORIC

(io)	parlai
(tu)	parlasti
(egli)	parlò
(noi)	parlammo
(voi)	parlaste
(essi)	parlarono

FUTURE

(io)	parlerò
(tu)	parlerai
(egli)	parlerà
(noi)	parleremo
(voi)	parlerete
(essi)	parleranno

PRESENT SUBJUNCTIVE

(io)	parli
(tu)	parli
(egli)	parli
(noi)	parliamo
(voi)	parliate
(essi)	parlino

IMPERFECT

(io)	parlavo
(tu)	parlavi
(egli)	parlava
(noi)	parlavamo
(voi)	parlavate
(essi)	parlavano

PRESENT CONDITIONAL

(io)	parlerei
(tu)	parleresti
(egli)	parlerebbe
(noi)	parleremmo
(voi)	parlereste
(essi)	parlerebbero

► lavarsi

* to wash oneself

GERUND	PAST PARTICIPLE
lavandosi	lavatosi

IMPERATIVE	EXAMPLE PHRASES
lavati!	• *Si sta **lavando***. He's washing.
si lavi!	• *Ti sei **lavato** le mani?*
laviamoci!	Did you wash your hands?
lavatevi!	• ***Lavati** i denti.* Brush your teeth.
si lavino!	

PRESENT

(io)	mi lavo
(tu)	ti lavi
(egli)	si lava
(noi)	ci laviamo
(voi)	vi lavate
(essi)	si lavano

PRESENT SUBJUNCTIVE

(io)	mi lavi
(tu)	ti lavi
(egli)	si lavi
(noi)	ci laviamo
(voi)	vi laviate
(essi)	si lavino

PAST HISTORIC

(io)	mi lavai
(tu)	ti lavasti
(egli)	si lavò
(noi)	ci lavammo
(voi)	vi lavaste
(essi)	si lavarono

IMPERFECT

(io)	mi lavavo
(tu)	ti lavavi
(egli)	si lavava
(noi)	ci lavavamo
(voi)	vi lavavate
(essi)	si lavavano

FUTURE

(io)	mi laverò
(tu)	ti laverai
(egli)	si laverà
(noi)	ci laveremo
(voi)	vi laverete
(essi)	si laveranno

PRESENT CONDITIONAL

(io)	mi laverei
(tu)	ti laveresti
(egli)	si laverebbe
(noi)	ci laveremmo
(voi)	vi lavereste
(essi)	si laverebbero

ITALIAN VERB TABLES

▶ credere

= to believe

GERUND

credendo

PAST PARTICIPLE

creduto

IMPERATIVE

credi!
creda!
crediamo!
credete!
credano!

EXAMPLE PHRASES

- **Credo** di sì. I think so.
- Gli ho **creduto**. I believed him.
- Non ci posso **credere**!
  I can't believe it!

PRESENT

(io)	credo
(tu)	credi
(egli)	crede
(noi)	crediamo
(voi)	credete
(essi)	credono

PRESENT SUBJUNCTIVE

(io)	creda
(tu)	creda
(egli)	creda
(noi)	crediamo
(voi)	crediate
(essi)	credano

PAST HISTORIC

(io)	credei or credetti
(tu)	credesti
(egli)	credè or credette
(noi)	credemmo
(voi)	credeste
(essi)	credettero

IMPERFECT

(io)	credevo
(tu)	credevi
(egli)	credeva
(noi)	credevamo
(voi)	credevate
(essi)	credevano

FUTURE

(io)	crederò
(tu)	crederai
(egli)	crederà
(noi)	crederemo
(voi)	crederete
(essi)	crederanno

PRESENT CONDITIONAL

(io)	crederei
(tu)	crederesti
(egli)	crederebbe
(noi)	crederemmo
(voi)	credereste
(essi)	crederebbero

► dormire

= to sleep

GERUND

dormendo

PAST PARTICIPLE

dormito

IMPERATIVE

dormi!
dorma!
dormiamo!
dormite!
dormano!

EXAMPLE PHRASES

- *I bambini **dormono**.*
  The children are sleeping.
- *Quando ha telefonato **dormivo**.*
  I was sleeping when he phoned.
- *Hai **dormito** bene?*
  Did you sleep well?

PRESENT

(io)	dormo
(tu)	dormi
(egli)	dorme
(noi)	dormiamo
(voi)	dormite
(essi)	dormono

PRESENT SUBJUNCTIVE

(io)	dorma
(tu)	dorma
(egli)	dorma
(noi)	dormiamo
(voi)	dormiate
(essi)	dormano

PAST HISTORIC

(io)	dormii
(tu)	dormisti
(egli)	dormì
(noi)	dormimmo
(voi)	dormiste
(essi)	dormirono

IMPERFECT

(io)	dormivo
(tu)	dormivi
(egli)	dormiva
(noi)	dormivamo
(voi)	dormivate
(essi)	dormivano

FUTURE

(io)	dormirò
(tu)	dormirai
(egli)	dormirà
(noi)	dormiremo
(voi)	dormirete
(essi)	dormiranno

PRESENT CONDITIONAL

(io)	dormirei
(tu)	dormiresti
(egli)	dormirebbe
(noi)	dormiremmo
(voi)	dormireste
(essi)	dormirebbero

ITALIAN VERB TABLES

▶ finire

= to finish

GERUND

finendo

IMPERATIVE

finisci!
finisca!
finiamo!
finite!
finiscano!

PAST PARTICIPLE

finito

EXAMPLE PHRASES

- *Le lezioni **finiscono** alle tre.*
  Classes finish at three.
- ***Finisci** i compiti!* Finish your
  homework!
- *Ho **finito**.* I've finished.

PRESENT

(io)	finisco
(tu)	finisci
(egli)	finisce
(noi)	finiamo
(voi)	finite
(essi)	finiscono

PAST HISTORIC

(io)	finii
(tu)	finisti
(egli)	finì
(noi)	finimmo
(voi)	finiste
(essi)	finirono

FUTURE

(io)	finirò
(tu)	finirai
(egli)	finirà
(noi)	finiremo
(voi)	finirete
(essi)	finiranno

PRESENT SUBJUNCTIVE

(io)	finisca
(tu)	finisca
(egli)	finisca
(noi)	finiamo
(voi)	finiate
(essi)	finiscano

IMPERFECT

(io)	finivo
(tu)	finivi
(egli)	finiva
(noi)	finivamo
(voi)	finivate
(essi)	finivano

PRESENT CONDITIONAL

(io)	finirei
(tu)	finiresti
(egli)	finirebbe
(noi)	finiremmo
(voi)	finireste
(essi)	finirebbero

dire

to say

GERUND

cendo

IMPERATIVE

i!
ica!
iciamo!
te!
icano!

PAST PARTICIPLE

detto

EXAMPLE PHRASES

- **Dice** sempre quello che pensa.
  She always says what she thinks.
- Mi ha **detto** una bugia.
  He told me a lie.
- **Diranno** che è colpa mia.
  They'll say it's my fault.

PRESENT

(io)	dico
(tu)	dici
(egli)	dice
(noi)	diciamo
(voi)	dite
(essi)	dicono

PAST HISTORIC

(io)	dissi
(tu)	dicesti
(egli)	disse
(noi)	dicemmo
(voi)	diceste
(essi)	dissero

FUTURE

(io)	dirò
(tu)	dirai
(egli)	dirà
(noi)	diremo
(voi)	direte
(essi)	diranno

PRESENT SUBJUNCTIVE

(io)	dica
(tu)	dica
(egli)	dica
(noi)	diciamo
(voi)	diciate
(essi)	dicano

IMPERFECT

(io)	dicevo
(tu)	dicevi
(egli)	diceva
(noi)	dicevamo
(voi)	dicevate
(essi)	dicevano

PRESENT CONDITIONAL

(io)	direi
(tu)	diresti
(egli)	direbbe
(noi)	diremmo
(voi)	direste
(essi)	direbbero

ITALIAN VERB TABLES

▶ dare

= to give

GERUND

dando

IMPERATIVE

da'! or dai!
dia!
diamo!
date!
diano!

PAST PARTICIPLE

dato

EXAMPLE PHRASES

- *Zia Maria ci dà le caramelle.*
  Aunt Maria gives us sweets.
- *Mi ha dato un libro.*
  He gave me a book.
- *Mi daranno una risposta domani.*
  They'll give me an answer
  tomorrow.

PRESENT

(io)	do
(tu)	dai
(egli)	dà
(noi)	diamo
(voi)	date
(essi)	danno

PAST HISTORIC

(io)	diedi or detti
(tu)	desti
(egli)	diede or dette
(noi)	demmo
(voi)	deste
(essi)	diedero or dettero

FUTURE

(io)	darò
(tu)	darai
(egli)	darà
(noi)	daremo
(voi)	darete
(essi)	daranno

PRESENT SUBJUNCTIVE

(io)	dia
(tu)	dia
(egli)	dia
(noi)	diamo
(voi)	diate
(essi)	diano

IMPERFECT

(io)	davo
(tu)	davi
(egli)	dava
(noi)	davamo
(voi)	davate
(essi)	davano

PRESENT CONDITIONAL

(io)	darei
(tu)	daresti
(egli)	darebbe
(noi)	daremmo
(voi)	dareste
(essi)	darebbero

essere

to be

GERUND

essendo

PAST PARTICIPLE

stato

IMPERATIVE

sii!
sia!
siamo!
siate!
siano!

EXAMPLE PHRASES

- **È inglese**. She's English.
- *Il film **era** molto bello.*
  The film was very good.
- **Saremo** in tanti alla festa.
  There'll be lots of us at the party.

PRESENT

(io)	sono
(tu)	sei
(egli)	è
(noi)	siamo
(voi)	siete
(essi)	sono

PAST HISTORIC

(io)	fui
(tu)	fosti
(egli)	fu
(noi)	fummo
(voi)	foste
(essi)	furono

FUTURE

(io)	sarò
(tu)	sarai
(egli)	sarà
(noi)	saremo
(voi)	sarete
(essi)	saranno

PRESENT SUBJUNCTIVE

(io)	sia
(tu)	sia
(egli)	sia
(noi)	siamo
(voi)	siate
(essi)	siano

IMPERFECT

(io)	ero
(tu)	eri
(egli)	era
(noi)	eravamo
(voi)	eravate
(essi)	erano

PRESENT CONDITIONAL

(io)	sarei
(tu)	saresti
(egli)	sarebbe
(noi)	saremmo
(voi)	sareste
(essi)	sarebbero

ITALIAN VERB TABLES

▶ avere

= to have

GERUND

avendo

PAST PARTICIPLE

avuto

IMPERATIVE

abbi!
abbia!
abbiamo!
abbiate!
abbiano!

EXAMPLE PHRASES

- **Ha** un fratello e una sorella.
  He has a brother and a sister.
- **Avevo** la febbre. I had a temperatu
- Domani **avranno** più tempo.
  They'll have more time tomorro

PRESENT		PRESENT SUBJUNCTIVE	
(io)	ho	(io)	abbia
(tu)	hai	(tu)	abbia
(egli)	ha	(egli)	abbia
(noi)	abbiamo	(noi)	abbiamo
(voi)	avete	(voi)	abbiate
(essi)	hanno	(essi)	abbiano

PAST HISTORIC		IMPERFECT	
(io)	ebbi	(io)	avevo
(tu)	avesti	(tu)	avevi
(egli)	ebbe	(egli)	aveva
(noi)	avemmo	(noi)	avevamo
(voi)	aveste	(voi)	avevate
(essi)	ebbero	(essi)	avevano

FUTURE		PRESENT CONDITIONAL	
(io)	avrò	(io)	avrei
(tu)	avrai	(tu)	avresti
(egli)	avrà	(egli)	avrebbe
(noi)	avremo	(noi)	avremmo
(voi)	avrete	(voi)	avreste
(essi)	avranno	(essi)	avrebbero

ITALIAN VERB TABLES

▶ fare

= to do, to make

GERUND

facendo

IMPERATIVE

fa'! or fai!
faccia!
facciamo!
fate!
facciano!

PAST PARTICIPLE

fatto

EXAMPLE PHRASES

- *Cosa stai **facendo**?*
  What are you doing?
- *Ho **fatto** i letti.* I've made the beds.
- *Ieri non abbiamo **fatto** niente.*
  We didn't do anything yesterday.

PRESENT

(io)	faccio
(tu)	fai
(egli)	fa
(noi)	facciamo
(voi)	fate
(essi)	fanno

PAST HISTORIC

(io)	feci
(tu)	facesti
(egli)	fece
(noi)	facemmo
(voi)	faceste
(essi)	fecero

FUTURE

(io)	farò
(tu)	farai
(egli)	farà
(noi)	faremo
(voi)	farete
(essi)	faranno

PRESENT SUBJUNCTIVE

(io)	faccia
(tu)	faccia
(egli)	faccia
(noi)	facciamo
(voi)	facciate
(essi)	facciano

IMPERFECT

(io)	facevo
(tu)	facevi
(egli)	faceva
(noi)	facevamo
(voi)	facevate
(essi)	facevano

PRESENT CONDITIONAL

(io)	farei
(tu)	faresti
(egli)	farebbe
(noi)	faremmo
(voi)	fareste
(essi)	farebbero

ITALIAN VERB TABLES

▶ andare

= to go

GERUND

andando

IMPERATIVE

va'! *or* vai!
vada!
andiamo!
andate!
vadano!

PAST PARTICIPLE

andato

EXAMPLE PHRASES

- *Ci* **vado** *spesso.* I go there often.
- **Andate** *via!* Go away!
- *Spero che* **vada** *bene.* I hope it goes well.

PRESENT

(io)	vado
(tu)	vai
(egli)	va
(noi)	andiamo
(voi)	andate
(essi)	vanno

PAST HISTORIC

(io)	andai
(tu)	andasti
(egli)	andò
(noi)	andammo
(voi)	andaste
(essi)	andarono

FUTURE

(io)	andrò
(tu)	andrai
(egli)	andrà
(noi)	andremo
(voi)	andrete
(essi)	andranno

PRESENT SUBJUNCTIVE

(io)	vada
(tu)	vada
(egli)	vada
(noi)	andiamo
(voi)	andiate
(essi)	vadano

IMPERFECT

(io)	andavo
(tu)	andavi
(egli)	andava
(noi)	andavamo
(voi)	andavate
(essi)	andavano

PRESENT CONDITIONAL

(io)	andrei
(tu)	andresti
(egli)	andrebbe
(noi)	andremmo
(voi)	andreste
(essi)	andrebbero

► volere

= to want

GERUND

volendo

IMPERATIVE

not used

PAST PARTICIPLE

voluto

EXAMPLE PHRASES

- *Cosa **vuoi**?* What do you want?
- ***Vorrei** andare in Australia.*
  I'd like to go to Australia.
- *Non ha **voluto** ammetterlo.*
  He didn't want to admit it.

PRESENT

(io)	voglio
(tu)	vuoi
(egli)	vuole
(noi)	vogliamo
(voi)	volete
(essi)	vogliono

PAST HISTORIC

(io)	volli
(tu)	volesti
(egli)	volle
(noi)	volemmo
(voi)	voleste
(essi)	vollero

FUTURE

(io)	vorrò
(tu)	vorrai
(egli)	vorrà
(noi)	vorremo
(voi)	vorrete
(essi)	vorranno

PRESENT SUBJUNCTIVE

(io)	voglia
(tu)	voglia
(egli)	voglia
(noi)	vogliamo
(voi)	vogliate
(essi)	vogliano

IMPERFECT

(io)	volevo
(tu)	volevi
(egli)	voleva
(noi)	volevamo
(voi)	volevate
(essi)	volevano

PRESENT CONDITIONAL

(io)	vorrei
(tu)	vorresti
(egli)	vorrebbe
(noi)	vorremmo
(voi)	vorreste
(essi)	vorrebbero

ITALIAN VERB TABLES

▶ sapere

= to know

GERUND

sapendo

IMPERATIVE

sappi!
sappia!
sappiamo!
sappiate!
sappiano!

PAST PARTICIPLE

saputo

EXAMPLE PHRASES

- *Non lo **so**.* I don't know.
- *Non ne **sapeva** niente.*
  He didn't know anything about it
- *Non ha **saputo** cosa fare.*
  He didn't know what to do.

PRESENT

(io)	so
(tu)	sai
(egli)	sa
(noi)	sappiamo
(voi)	sapete
(essi)	sanno

PAST HISTORIC

(io)	seppi
(tu)	sapesti
(egli)	seppe
(noi)	sapemmo
(voi)	sapeste
(essi)	seppero

FUTURE

(io)	saprò
(tu)	saprai
(egli)	saprà
(noi)	sapremo
(voi)	saprete
(essi)	sapranno

PRESENT SUBJUNCTIVE

(io)	sappia
(tu)	sappia
(egli)	sappia
(noi)	sappiamo
(voi)	sappiate
(essi)	sappiano

IMPERFECT

(io)	sapevo
(tu)	sapevi
(egli)	sapeva
(noi)	sapevamo
(voi)	sapevate
(essi)	sapevano

PRESENT CONDITIONAL

(io)	saprei
(tu)	sapresti
(egli)	saprebbe
(noi)	sapremmo
(voi)	sapreste
(essi)	saprebbero

► potere

= to be able

GERUND	PAST PARTICIPLE
potendo	potuto

IMPERATIVE	EXAMPLE PHRASES

not used	• **Puoi** venire con noi?
	  Can you come with us?
	• **Potrebbe** succedere.
	  It could happen.
	• Non ho **potuto** farlo ieri.
	  I couldn't do it yesterday.

PRESENT

(io)	posso
(tu)	puoi
(egli)	può
(noi)	possiamo
(voi)	potete
(essi)	possono

PRESENT SUBJUNCTIVE

(io)	possa
(tu)	possa
(egli)	possa
(noi)	possiamo
(voi)	possiate
(essi)	possano

PAST HISTORIC

(io)	potei
(tu)	potesti
(egli)	potè
(noi)	potemmo
(voi)	poteste
(essi)	poterono

IMPERFECT

(io)	potevo
(tu)	potevi
(egli)	poteva
(noi)	potevamo
(voi)	potevate
(essi)	potevano

FUTURE

(io)	potrò
(tu)	potrai
(egli)	potrà
(noi)	potremo
(voi)	potrete
(essi)	potranno

PRESENT CONDITIONAL

(io)	potrei
(tu)	potresti
(egli)	potrebbe
(noi)	potremmo
(voi)	potreste
(essi)	potrebbero

ITALIAN VERB TABLES

▶ dovere

= to have to

GERUND	PAST PARTICIPLE
dovendo	dovuto

IMPERATIVE	EXAMPLE PHRASES
not used	• *Ho **dovuto** dirglielo.* I had to tell him.
	• ***Dev**'essere tardi.* It must be late.
	• ***Dovresti** aiutarlo.* You should help him.

PRESENT		PRESENT SUBJUNCTIVE	
(io)	devo	(io)	deva
(tu)	devi	(tu)	deva
(egli)	deve	(egli)	deva
(noi)	dobbiamo	(noi)	dobbiamo
(voi)	dovete	(voi)	dobbiate
(essi)	devono	(essi)	devano

PAST HISTORIC		IMPERFECT	
(io)	dovetti	(io)	dovevo
(tu)	dovesti	(tu)	dovevi
(egli)	dovette	(egli)	doveva
(noi)	dovemmo	(noi)	dovevamo
(voi)	doveste	(voi)	dovevate
(essi)	dovettero	(essi)	dovevano

FUTURE		PRESENT CONDITIONAL	
(io)	dovrò	(io)	dovrei
(tu)	dovrai	(tu)	dovresti
(egli)	dovrà	(egli)	dovrebbe
(noi)	dovremo	(noi)	dovremmo
(voi)	dovrete	(voi)	dovreste
(essi)	dovranno	(essi)	dovrebbero

▸ stare

▪ to be

GERUND	PAST PARTICIPLE
tando	stato

IMPERATIVE	EXAMPLE PHRASES
ta'! or stai!	• *Come **stai**?* How are you?
tia!	• ***Sto** leggendo un libro.*
tiamo!	I'm reading a book.
tate!	• *Sei mai **stato** a Firenze?*
tiano!	Have you even been to Florence?

PRESENT

- (io) sto
- (tu) stai
- (egli) sta
- (noi) stiamo
- (voi) state
- (essi) stanno

PAST HISTORIC

- (io) stetti
- (tu) stesti
- (egli) stette
- (noi) stemmo
- (voi) steste
- (essi) stettero

FUTURE

- (io) starò
- (tu) starai
- (egli) starà
- (noi) staremo
- (voi) starete
- (essi) staranno

PRESENT SUBJUNCTIVE

- (io) stia
- (tu) stia
- (egli) stia
- (noi) stiamo
- (voi) stiate
- (essi) stiano

IMPERFECT

- (io) stavo
- (tu) stavi
- (egli) stava
- (noi) stavamo
- (voi) stavate
- (essi) stavano

PRESENT CONDITIONAL

- (io) starei
- (tu) staresti
- (egli) starebbe
- (noi) staremmo
- (voi) stareste
- (essi) starebbero

ITALIAN IRREGULAR VERB FORMS

Remember that when the auxiliary **essere** is used, the past participle agrees with the subject of the verb:

Paolo è uscito. Maria è uscita. I ragazzi sono usciti. Le ragazze sono uscite.

1 accendere

PAST PARTICIPLE	acceso
PAST HISTORIC	accesi, accendesti, accese, accendemmo, accendeste, accesero

2 accorgersi

PAST PARTICIPLE	accorso
PAST HISTORIC	mi accorsi, ti accorgesti, si accorse, ci accorgemmo, vi accorgeste, si accorsero

3 apparire - aux. *essere*

PAST PARTICIPLE	apparso
PRESENT	appaio, appari or apparisci, appare or apparisce, appariamo, apparite, appaiono or appariscono
PAST HISTORIC	apparvi, apparisti, apparve, apparimmo, appariste, apparvero
PRESENT SUBJUNCTIVE	appaia, appaia, appaia, appariamo, appariate, appaiano

4 appendere

PAST PARTICIPLE	appeso
PAST HISTORIC	appesi, appendesti, appese, appendemmo, appendeste, appesero

5 aprire

PAST PARTICIPLE	aperto
PAST HISTORIC	aprii, apristi, aprì, aprimmo, apriste, aprirono

6 assistere

PAST PARTICIPLE	assistito
PAST HISTORIC	assistei or assistetti, assistesti, assistette, assistemmo, assisteste, assisterono or assistettero

7 assumere

PAST PARTICIPLE	assunto
PAST HISTORIC	assunsi, assumesti, assunse, assumemmo, assumeste, assunsero

8 bere

PAST PARTICIPLE	bevuto
GERUND	bevendo
PRESENT	bevo, bevi, beve, beviamo, bevete, bevono
FUTURE	berrò, berrai, berrà, berremo, berrete, berranno
IMPERFECT	bevevo, bevevi, beveva, bevevamo, bevevate, bevevano
PRESENT SUBJUNCTIVE	beva, beva, beva, beviamo, beviate, bevano
PAST HISTORIC	bevvi or bevetti, bevesti, bevve or bevette, bevemmo, beveste, bevvero or bevettero
PRESENT CONDITIONAL	berrei, berresti, berrebbe, berremmo, berreste, berrebbero
IMPERATIVE	bevi!, beva!, beviamo!, bevete!, bevano!

9 cadere - aux. *essere*

FUTURE	cadrò, cadrai, cadrà, cadremo, cadrete, cadranno
PAST HISTORIC	caddi, cadesti, cadde, cademmo, cadeste, caddero
PRESENT CONDITIONAL	cadrei, cadresti, cadrebbe, cadremmo, cadreste, cadrebbero

10 chiedere

PAST PARTICIPLE	chiesto
PAST HISTORIC	chiesi, chiedesti, chiese, chiedemmo, chiedeste, chiesero

11 chiudere

PAST PARTICIPLE	chiuso
PAST HISTORIC	chiusi, chiudesti, chiuse, chiudemmo, chiudeste, chiusero

12 cogliere

PAST PARTICIPLE	colto
PRESENT	colgo, cogli, coglie, cogliamo, cogliete, colgono
PAST HISTORIC	colsi, cogliesti, colse, cogliemmo, coglieste, colsero
PRESENT SUBJUNCTIVE	colga, colga, colga, cogliamo, cogliate, colgan
IMPERATIVE	cogli!, colga!, cogliamo!, cogliete!, colgano!

13 confondere

PAST PARTICIPLE	confuso

14 conoscere

PAST PARTICIPLE	conosciuto
PAST HISTORIC	conobbi, conoscesti, conobbe, conoscemmo, conosceste, conobbero

15 correre - aux. avere/essere

PAST PARTICIPLE	corso
PAST HISTORIC	corsi, corresti, corse, corremmo, correste, corsero

16 crescere - aux. essere

PAST PARTICIPLE	cresciuto
PAST HISTORIC	crebbi, crescesti, crebbe, crescemmo, cresceste, crebbero

17 cuocere

PAST PARTICIPLE	cotto
PAST HISTORIC	cossi, cuocesti, cosse, cuocemmo, cuoceste, cossero

18 decidere

PAST PARTICIPLE	deciso
PAST HISTORIC	decisi, decidesti, decise, decidemmo, decideste, decisero

19 difendere

PAST PARTICIPLE	difeso
PAST HISTORIC	difesi, difendesti, difese, difendemmo, difendeste, difesero

20 dipingere

PAST PARTICIPLE	dipinto
PAST HISTORIC	dipinsi, dipingesti, dipinse, dipingemmo, dipingeste, dipinsero

21 dirigere

PAST PARTICIPLE	diretto
PAST HISTORIC	diressi, dirigesti, diresse, dirigemmo, dirigeste, diressero

22 discutere

PAST PARTICIPLE	discusso
PAST HISTORIC	discussi, discutesti, discusse, discutemmo, discuteste, discussero

23 distinguere

PAST PARTICIPLE	distinto

PAST HISTORIC	distinsi, distinguesti, distinse, distinguemmo, distingueste, distinsero

24 dividere

PAST PARTICIPLE	diviso
PAST HISTORIC	divisi, dividesti, divise, dividemmo, divideste, divisero

25 esigere

PAST PARTICIPLE	esatto (not common)
PAST HISTORIC	esigei or esigetti, esigesti, esigette, esigemmo, esigeste, esigettero

26 espellere

PAST PARTICIPLE	espulso
PAST HISTORIC	espulsi, espellesti, espulse, espellemmo, espelleste, espulsero

27 esplodere - aux. essere

PAST PARTICIPLE	esploso
PAST HISTORIC	esplosi, esplodesti, esplose, esplodemmo, esplodeste, esplosero

28 esprimere

PAST PARTICIPLE	espresso
PAST HISTORIC	espressi, esprimesti, espresse, esprimemmo, esprimeste, espressero

29 evadere - aux. essere

PAST PARTICIPLE	evaso
PAST HISTORIC	evasi, evadesti, evase, evademmo, evadeste, evasero

30 fingere

PAST PARTICIPLE	finto
PAST HISTORIC	finsi, fingesti, finse, fingemmo, fingeste, finsero

31 friggere

PAST PARTICIPLE	fritto
PAST HISTORIC	frissi, friggesti, frisse, friggemmo, friggeste, frissero

32 leggere

PAST PARTICIPLE	letto
PAST HISTORIC	lessi, leggesti, lesse, leggemmo, leggeste, lessero

33 mettere

PAST PARTICIPLE	messo
PAST HISTORIC	misi, mettesti, mise, mettemmo, metteste, misero

34 mordere

PAST PARTICIPLE	morso
PAST HISTORIC	morsi, mordesti, morse, mordemmo, mordeste, morsero

35 morire - aux. essere

PAST PARTICIPLE	morto
PRESENT	muoio, muori, muore, moriamo, morite, muoiono
PRESENT SUBJUNCTIVE	muoia, muoia, muoia, moriamo, moriate, muoiano

36 muovere

PAST PARTICIPLE	mosso
PAST HISTORIC	mossi, muovesti, mosse, muovemmo, muoveste, mossero

37 nascere - aux. essere

PAST PARTICIPLE	nato
PAST HISTORIC	nacqui, nascesti, nacque, nascemmo, nasceste, nacquero

38 nascondere

PAST PARTICIPLE	nascosto
PAST HISTORIC	nascosi, nascondesti, nascose, nascondemmo, nascondeste, nascosero

39 nuocere

PAST PARTICIPLE	nociuto or nuociuto
GERUND	nocendo or nuocendo
PRESENT	nuoccio, nuoci, nuoce, nuociamo, nuocete, nuocciono
PAST HISTORIC	nocqui, nuocesti, nocque, nuocemmo, nuoceste, nocquero

40 offrire

PAST PARTICIPLE	offerto
PAST HISTORIC	offrii, offristi, offrì, offrimmo, offriste, offrirono

41 parere - aux. essere

PAST PARTICIPLE	parso
PRESENT	pare, paiono
FUTURE	parrà, parranno
PAST HISTORIC	parve, parvero
PRESENT SUBJUNCTIVE	paia, paiano

42 perdere

PAST PARTICIPLE	perso or perduto
PAST HISTORIC	persi, perdesti, perse, perdemmo, perdeste, persero

43 piacere - aux. essere

PAST PARTICIPLE	piaciuto
PRESENT	piaccio, piaci, piace, piacciamo or piaciamo, piacete, piacciono
PAST HISTORIC	piacqui, piacesti, piacque, piacemmo, piaceste, piacquero
PRESENT SUBJUNCTIVE	piaccia, piaccia, piaccia, piacciamo, piacciate, piacciano

44 piangere

PAST PARTICIPLE	pianto
PAST HISTORIC	piansi, piangesti, pianse, piangemmo, piangeste, piansero

45 piovere

PAST PARTICIPLE	piovuto
PAST HISTORIC	piovve

46 porre

PAST PARTICIPLE	posto
PRESENT	pongo, poni, pone, poniamo, ponete, pongono
FUTURE	porrò, porrai, porrà, porremo, porrete, porranno
PAST HISTORIC	posi, ponesti, pose, ponemmo, poneste, posero
PRESENT SUBJUNCTIVE	ponga, ponga, ponga, poniamo, poniate, pongano

47 prefiggersi

PAST PARTICIPLE	prefisso
PAST HISTORIC	prefissi, prefiggesti, prefisse, prefiggemmo, prefiggeste, prefissero

48 prendere

PAST PARTICIPLE	preso
PAST HISTORIC	presi, prendesti, prese, prendemmo, prendeste, presero

49 proteggere

PAST PARTICIPLE	protetto
PAST HISTORIC	protessi, proteggesti, protesse, proteggemmo, proteggeste, protessero

50 pungere

PAST PARTICIPLE	punto
PAST HISTORIC	punsi, pungesti, punse, pungemmo, pungeste, punsero

51 radere

PAST PARTICIPLE	raso
PAST HISTORIC	rasi, radesti, rase, rademmo, radeste, rasero

52 reggere

PAST PARTICIPLE	retto
PAST HISTORIC	ressi, reggesti, resse, reggemmo, reggeste, ressero

53 rendere

PAST PARTICIPLE	reso
PAST HISTORIC	resi, rendesti, rese, rendemmo, rendeste, resero

54 ridere

PAST PARTICIPLE	riso
PAST HISTORIC	risi, ridesti, rise, ridemmo, rideste, risero

55 ridurre

PAST PARTICIPLE	ridotto
GERUND	riducendo
PRESENT	riduco, riduci, riduce, riduciamo, riducete, riducono
FUTURE	ridurrò, ridurrai, ridurrà, ridurremo, ridurrete, ridurranno
IMPERFECT	riducevo, riducevi, riduceva, riducevamo, riducevate, riducevano
PAST HISTORIC	ridussi, riducesti, ridusse, riducemmo, riduceste, ridussero
PRESENT SUBJUNCTIVE	riduca, riduca, riduca, riduciamo, riduciate, riducano

56 riempire

GERUND	riempiendo
PRESENT	riempio, riempi, riempie, riempiamo, riempite, riempiono

57 riflettere

PAST PARTICIPLE	riflettuto or riflesso

58 rimanere - aux. essere

PAST PARTICIPLE	rimasto
PRESENT	rimango, rimani, rimane, rimaniamo, rimanete, rimangono
FUTURE	rimarrò, rimarrai, rimarrà, rimarremo, rimarrete, rimarranno
PAST HISTORIC	rimasi, rimanesti, rimase, rimanemmo, rimaneste, rimasero
PRESENT	rimanga, rimanga, rimanga, rimaniamo, rimaniate, rimangano

59 risolvere

PAST PARTICIPLE	risolto
PAST HISTORIC	risolsi, risolvesti, risolse, risolvemmo, risolveste, risolsero

60 rispondere

PAST PARTICIPLE	risposto
PAST HISTORIC	risposi, rispondesti, rispose, rispondemmo, rispondeste, risposero

61 rivolgere

PAST PARTICIPLE	rivolto
PAST HISTORIC	rivolsi, rivolgesti, rivolse, rivolgemmo, rivolgeste, rivolsero

62 rompere

PAST PARTICIPLE	rotto
PAST HISTORIC	ruppi, rompesti, ruppe, rompemmo, rompeste, ruppero

63 salire - aux. avere/essere

PRESENT	salgo, sali, sale, saliamo, salite, salgono
PRESENT SUBJUNCTIVE	salga, salga, salga, saliamo, saliate, salgano
IMPERATIVE	sali!, salga!, saliamo!, salite!, salgano!

64 scegliere

PAST PARTICIPLE	scelto
PRESENT	scelgo, scegli, sceglie, scegliamo, scegliete, scelgono
PAST HISTORIC	scelsi, scegliesti, scelse, scegliemmo, sceglieste, scelsero
PRESENT SUBJUNCTIVE	scelga, scelga, scelga, scegliamo, scegliate, scelgano
IMPERATIVE	scegli!, scelga!, scegliamo!, scegliete!, scelgano!

65 scendere - aux. essere

PAST PARTICIPLE	sceso
PAST HISTORIC	scesi, scendesti, scese, scendemmo, scendeste, scesero

66 sciogliere

PAST PARTICIPLE	sciolto

PRESENT	sciolgo, sciogli, scioglie, sciogliamo, sciogliete, sciolgono
PAST HISTORIC	sciolsi, sciogliesti, sciolse, sciogliemmo, scioglieste, sciolsero
PRESENT SUBJUNCTIVE	sciolga, sciolga, sciolga, sciogliamo, sciogliate, sciolgano
IMPERATIVE	sciogli!, sciolga!, sciogliamo!, sciogliete!, sciolgano!

67 sconfiggere

PAST PARTICIPLE	sconfitto
PAST HISTORIC	sconfissi, sconfiggesti, sconfisse, sconfiggemmo, sconfiggeste, sconfissero

68 scorgere

PAST PARTICIPLE	scorto
PAST HISTORIC	scorsi, scorgesti, scorse, scorgemmo, scorgeste, scorsero

69 scrivere

PAST PARTICIPLE	scritto
PAST HISTORIC	scrissi, scrivesti, scrisse, scrivemmo, scriveste, scrissero

70 scuotere

PAST PARTICIPLE	scosso
PAST HISTORIC	scossi, scuotesti, scosse, scuotemmo, scuoteste, scossero

71 sedere

PRESENT	siedo, siedi, siede, sediamo, sedete, siedono
PRESENT SUBJUNCTIVE	sieda, sieda, sieda, sediamo, sediate, siedano

72 seppellire

PAST PARTICIPLE	sepolto or seppellito

73 soffrire

PAST PARTICIPLE	sofferto
PAST HISTORIC	soffrii, soffristi, soffrì, soffrimmo, soffriste, soffrirono

74 sorgere - aux. essere

PAST PARTICIPLE	sorto
PAST HISTORIC	sorse, sorsero

75 spargere

PAST PARTICIPLE	sparso
PAST HISTORIC	sparsi, spargesti, sparse, spargemmo, spargeste, sparsero

76 sparire - aux. essere

PAST HISTORIC	sparii, sparisti, sparì, sparimmo, spariste, sparirono

77 spegnere

PAST PARTICIPLE	spento
PRESENT	spengo, spegni, spegne, spegniamo, spegnete, spengono
PAST HISTORIC	spensi, spegnesti, spense, spegnemmo, spegneste, spensero
PRESENT SUBJUNCTIVE	spenga, spenga, spenga, spegniamo, spegnete, spengano

78 spendere

PAST PARTICIPLE	speso
PAST HISTORIC	spesi, spendesti, spese, spendemmo, spendeste, spesero

79 spingere

PAST PARTICIPLE	spinto
PAST HISTORIC	spinsi, spingesti, spinse, spingemmo, spingeste, spinsero

80 sporgersi

PAST PARTICIPLE	sporto
PAST HISTORIC	mi sporsi, ti sporgesti, si sporse, ci sporgemmo, vi sporgeste, si sporsero

81 stringere

PAST PARTICIPLE	stretto
PAST HISTORIC	strinsi, stringesti, strinse, stringemmo, stringeste, strinsero

82 succedere - aux. essere

PAST PARTICIPLE	successo
PAST HISTORIC	successi, succedesti, successe, succedemmo, succedeste, successero

83 tacere

PAST PARTICIPLE	taciuto
PRESENT	taccio, taci, tace, tacciamo, tacete, tacciono
PAST HISTORIC	tacqui, tacesti, tacque, tacemmo, taceste, tacquero
PRESENT SUBJUNCTIVE	taccia, taccia, taccia, tacciamo, tacciate, tacciano

84 tendere

PAST PARTICIPLE	teso
PAST HISTORIC	tesi, tendesti, tese, tendemmo, tendeste, tesero

85 tenere

PAST PARTICIPLE	tenuto
PRESENT	tengo, tieni, tiene, teniamo, tenete, tengono
FUTURE	terrò, terrai, terrà, terremo, terrete, terranno
PAST HISTORIC	tenni, tenesti, tenne, tenemmo, teneste, tennero
PRESENT SUBJUNCTIVE	tenga, tenga, tenga, teniamo, teniate, tengano
PRESENT CONDITIONAL	terrei, terresti, terrebbe, terremmo, terreste, terrebbero

86 togliere

PAST PARTICIPLE	tolto
PRESENT	tolgo, togli, toglie, togliamo, togliete, tolgono
PAST HISTORIC	tolsi, togliesti, tolse, togliemmo, toglieste, tolsero
PRESENT SUBJUNCTIVE	tolga, tolga, tolga, togliamo, togliate, tolgano
IMPERATIVE	togli!, tolga!, togliamo!, togliete!, tolgano!

87 trarre

PAST PARTICIPLE	tratto
GERUND	traendo
PRESENT	traggo, trai, trae, traiamo, traete, traggono
FUTURE	trarrò, trarrai, trarrà, trarremo, trarrete, trarranno
IMPERFECT	traevo, traevi, traeva, traevamo, traevate, traevano
PAST HISTORIC	trassi, traesti, trasse, traemmo, traeste, trassero
PRESENT SUBJUNCTIVE	tragga, tragga, tragga, traiamo, traiate, traggano

88 uccidere

PAST PARTICIPLE	ucciso
PAST HISTORIC	uccisi, uccidesti, uccise, uccidemmo, uccideste, uccisero

89 ungere

PAST PARTICIPLE	unto

PAST HISTORIC	unsi, ungesti, unse, ungemmo, ungeste, unsero

90 uscire - aux. essere

PRESENT	esco, esci, esce, usciamo, uscite, escono
PRESENT SUBJUNCTIVE	esca, esca, esca, usciamo, usciate, escano

91 valere - aux. essere

PAST PARTICIPLE	valso
PRESENT	valgo, vali, vale, valiamo, valete, valgono
FUTURE	varrò, varrai, varrà, varremo, varrete, varranno
PAST HISTORIC	valsi, valesti, valse, valemmo, valeste, valsero
PRESENT SUBJUNCTIVE	valga, valga, valga, valiamo, valiate, valgano

92 vedere

PAST PARTICIPLE	visto
FUTURE	vedrò, vedrai, vedrà, vedremo, vedrete, vedranno
PAST HISTORIC	vidi, vedesti, vide, vedemmo, vedeste, videro

93 venire - aux. essere

PAST PARTICIPLE	venuto
PRESENT	vengo, vieni, viene, veniamo, venite, vengono
FUTURE	verrò, verrai, verrà, verremo, verrete, verranno
PAST HISTORIC	venni, venisti, venne, venimmo, veniste, vennero
PRESENT SUBJUNCTIVE	venga, venga, venga, veniamo, veniate, vengano
IMPERATIVE	vieni!, venga!, veniamo!, venite!, vengano!

94 vincere

PAST PARTICIPLE	vinto
PAST HISTORIC	vinsi, vincesti, vinse, vincemmo, vinceste, vinsero

95 vivere - aux. essere

PAST PARTICIPLE	vissuto
PAST HISTORIC	vissi, vivesti, visse, vivemmo, viveste, vissero

96 volgere

PAST PARTICIPLE	volto
PAST HISTORIC	volsi, volgesti, volse, volgemmo, volgeste, volsero

OTHER IRREGULAR VERBS

The numbers on this list refer to model numbers shown on pages 376-379.

*accadere	9	pretendere	84
accogliere	12	prevedere	92
ammettere	33	produrre	55
appartenere	85	promuovere	36
avvenire	93	promettere	33
avvolgere	96	provenire	93
coinvolgere	96	raccogliere	12
commuoversi	36	respingere	79
contenere	85	restringere	81
contraddire	see DIRE	riconoscere	14
convenire	93	rifare	see FARE
convincere	94	rimettere	33
coprire	5	rimpiangere	44
correggere	52	rinchiudere	11
corrispondere	60	rincrescere	16
costringere	81	riuscire	90
deridere	54	rivedere	92
descrivere	69	scadere	9
dipendere	4	scommettere	33
distendere	84	scomparire	3
insistere	6	sconvolgere	96
intendere	84	scoprire	5
interrompere	62	scorrere	15
intervenire	93	smettere	33
intravedere	92	socchiudere	11
iscriversi	69	soccorrere	15
maledire	see DIRE	soddisfare	see FARE
mantenere	85	sorprendere	48
occorrere	15	sorridere	54
offendere	19	sospendere	4
ottenere	85	sostenere	85
percorrere	15	stendere	84
permettere	33	svenire	93
possedere	71	svolgere	96
predire	see DIRE	trasmettere	33
prescrivere	69	trattenere	85
presumere	7		

A

A [eɪ] NOUN

1. la A (*letter*)
2. ottimo (*school mark*) ◇ *I got an A for my essay.* Nel compito ho preso ottimo.
3. il la (PL i la) (*musical note*) ◇ *It's in A flat.* È in la bemolle.

a [eɪ, ə] ARTICLE

1. un MASC ◇ *a book* un libro ◇ *He's a friend.* È un amico.

*When the article comes before a masculine noun starting with impure s, gn, pn, ps, x, y or z use **uno**.*

◇ *an uncle* uno zio

2. una FEM ◇ *a letter* una lettera

*When the article comes before a feminine noun starting with a vowel use **un'**.*

◇ *She's a friend.* È un'amica. ◇ *a herring* un'aringa

a is sometimes translated by the Italian definite article.

◇ *He's a butcher.* Fa il macellaio. ◇ *I haven't got a car.* Non ho la macchina. ◇ *once a week* una volta alla settimana ◇ *seventy kilometres an hour* settanta chilometri all'ora

+ **a hundred pounds** cento sterline

AA [eɪ'eɪ] NOUN = **Automobile Association**
The Italian equivalent is the ACI.

aback [ə'bæk] ADVERB

+ **to be taken aback** rimanere* E sconcertato ◇ *I was taken aback by his reaction.* Sono rimasto sconcertato dalla sua reazione.

abandon [ə'bændən] VERB
abbandonare

abbey ['æbɪ] NOUN
l'abbazia

abbreviation [əbriːvɪ'eɪʃən] NOUN
l'abbreviazione FEM

ability [ə'bɪlɪtɪ] NOUN (PL **abilities**)
la capacità (PL le capacità) ◇ *Ian's got plenty of ability, but he doesn't work hard enough.* Ian ha le capacità ma non si applica abbastanza.

able ['eɪbl] ADJECTIVE

+ **to be able to do something** poter fare qualcosa

abolish [ə'bɒlɪʃ] VERB
abolire

abortion [ə'bɔːʃən] NOUN
l'aborto

+ **to have an abortion** abortire

about [ə'baʊt] PREPOSITION, ADVERB

1. a proposito di ◇ *I'm phoning you about tomorrow's meeting.* Ti chiamo a proposito della riunione di domani.
2. su ◇ *a book about London* un libro su Londra

+ **I don't know anything about it.** Non ne so niente.

+ **What's it about?** Di che si tratta?

3. circa ◇ *It takes about ten hours.* Ci vogliono circa dieci ore.

+ **at about eleven o'clock** verso le undici

+ **to be about to do something** stare* E per fare qualcosa ◇ *I was about to go out.* Stavo per uscire.

+ **What about me?** E io?

+ **How about?** E se? ◇ *How about going to the cinema?* E se andassimo al cinema?

above [ə'bʌv] PREPOSITION, ADVERB
sopra ◇ *He raised his hands above his head.* Ha sollevato le mani sopra la testa.

+ **the flat above** l'appartamento al piano di sopra

+ **above all** soprattutto

abroad [ə'brɔːd] ADVERB
all'estero ◇ *They decided to go abroad.* Hanno deciso di andare all'estero.

abrupt [ə'brʌpt] ADJECTIVE

1. brusco ◇ *He was a bit abrupt with me.* È stato un po' brusco con me.
2. improvviso ◇ *His abrupt departure aroused suspicion.* La sua improvvisa partenza ha sollevato dei sospetti.

abruptly [ə'brʌptlɪ] ADVERB
di scatto

absence ['æbsəns] NOUN

1. l'assenza ◇ *in my absence* in mia assenza
2. la mancanza

absent ['æbsənt] ADJECTIVE
assente

absent-minded ['æbsənt'maɪndɪd] ADJECTIVE
distratto

absolutely [æbsə'luːtlɪ] ADVERB
assolutamente ◇ *Jill's absolutely right.* Jill ha assolutamente ragione.

+ **Absolutely!** Altroché! ◇ *Do you think it's a good idea? – Absolutely!* Ti sembra una buona idea? – Altroché!

absorbed [əb'zɔːbd] ADJECTIVE

+ **to be absorbed in something** essere* E assorto in qualcosa

absorbent [əb'zɔːbənt] ADJECTIVE
assorbente

absorbent cotton [əb'zɔːbənt'kɒtn] NOUN
US
il cotone idrofilo

absurd [əb'sɜːd] ADJECTIVE
assurdo

abuse [ə'bjuːs] NOUN
see also **abuse** VERB

+ **child abuse** la violenza sui minori

+ **drug abuse** l'abuso di sostanze stupefacenti

to **abuse** [ə'bjuːz] VERB
see also **abuse** NOUN

+ **to abuse drugs** far uso di stupefacenti

+ **to be abused** subire* violenza ◇ *Children* ☞

who have been abused... I bambini che
hanno subito violenza...

abusive [ə'bjuːsɪv] ADJECTIVE
1. ingiurioso (*language*)
2. violento (*person, husband*)

academic [ækə'demɪk] ADJECTIVE
1. scolastico ◇ *his academic performance*
il suo rendimento scolastico
2. accademico ◇ *the academic year* l'anno
accademico
3. portato per gli studi ◇ *I'm not very
academic.* Non sono molto portato per gli
studi.

academy [ə'kædəmɪ] NOUN (PL **academies**)
l'accademia

to **accelerate** [æk'seləreɪt] VERB
accelerare

accelerator [æk'seləreɪtə'] NOUN
l'acceleratore MASC

accent ['æksent] NOUN
l'accento ◇ *He hasn't got an accent.* Non ha
deciso di accettare l'offerta.

to **accept** [ək'sept] VERB
accettare ◇ *I decided to accept the offer.* Ho
deciso di accettare l'offerta.
• **to accept responsibility for something**
assumersi E la responsabilità di qualcosa

acceptable [ək'septəbl] ADJECTIVE
accettabile

access ['ækses] NOUN
l'accesso ◇ *wheelchair access* accesso per
disabili
• **Her ex-husband has access to the children.**
Il suo ex marito ha diritto a vedere i bambini.
• **to gain access to something** (*files,
documents*) riuscire* E ad accedere a
qualcosa

accessible [æk'sesəbl] ADJECTIVE
accessibile

accessory [æk'sesərɪ] NOUN (PL **accessories**)
l'accessorio

accident ['æksɪdənt] NOUN
l'incidente MASC ◇ *The fog caused several
accidents.* La nebbia ha provocato diversi
incidenti.
• **by accident** per caso ◇ *They made the
discovery by accident.* La scoperta è
avvenuta per caso.
• **The burglar killed him by accident.** Il ladro lo
ha ucciso per errore.

accidental [æksɪ'dentl] ADJECTIVE
involontario

to **accommodate** [ə'kɔmədeɪt] VERB
alloggiare

accommodation [əkɔmə'deɪʃən] NOUN (US
accomodations)
l'alloggio

to **accompany** [ə'kʌmpənɪ] VERB
(**accompanied, accompanied**)
accompagnare

accord [ə'kɔːd] NOUN

• **of his own accord** spontaneamente

accordingly [ə'kɔːdɪŋlɪ] ADVERB
di conseguenza

according to [ə'kɔːdɪŋtuː] PREPOSITION
secondo ◇ *According to him, everyone had
left.* Secondo lui erano tutti andati via.

accordion [ə'kɔːdɪən] NOUN
la fisarmonica (PL le fisarmoniche)

account [ə'kaunt] NOUN
1. il conto ◇ *I've just opened an account.*
Ho appena aperto un conto.
• **a bank account** un conto in banca
• **the account number** il numero di conto
• **to do the accounts** tenere* la contabilità
2. il resoconto ◇ *He gave a detailed
account of what happened.* Ha fatto un
resoconto particolareggiato dell'accaduto.
• **to take something into account** prendere* in
considerazione qualcosa
• **by all accounts** a detta di tutti
• **on account of** a causa di ◇ *We couldn't go
out on account of the bad weather.* Non
siamo potuti uscire a causa del maltempo.

to **account for** [ə'kauntfɔː'] VERB
spiegare ◇ *If she was ill, that would account
for her poor results.* Se fosse malata si
spiegherebbero gli scarsi risultati.

accountable [ə'kauntəbl] ADJECTIVE
• **to be accountable to someone** dover
rendere* conto a qualcuno

accountancy [ə'kauntənsɪ] NOUN
la ragioneria

accountant [ə'kauntənt] NOUN
1. il/la commercialista (*graduate*)
2. il ragioniere
la ragioniera
(*bookkeeper*)

accuracy ['ækjurəsɪ] NOUN
l'accuratezza

accurate ['ækjurɪt] ADJECTIVE
accurato

accurately ['ækjurɪtlɪ] ADVERB
accuratamente

accusation [ækju'zeɪʃən] NOUN
l'accusa

to **accuse** [ə'kjuːz] VERB
• **to accuse somebody of something** accusare
qualcuno di qualcosa

ace [eɪs] NOUN
1. l'asso (*in cards*) ◇ *to play an ace* giocare
un asso
2. l'ace MASC (PL gli ace) (*in tennis*)

ache [eɪk] NOUN
see also **ache** VERB
il dolore ◇ *aches in your muscles* dolori ai
muscoli
• **to have stomach ache** avere* mal di
stomaco

to **ache** [eɪk] VERB
see also **ache** NOUN
far male ◇ *My leg's aching.* Mi fa male la

* Verbs followed by this symbol are irregular. See pp.339–364 for further details.

gamba.

achieve [ə'tʃiːv] VERB
ottenere* ◊ *You won't achieve anything.*
Non otterrai nulla.

achievement [ə'tʃiːvmənt] NOUN
il risultato ◊ *It was a fantastic achievement for our team.* È stato un risultato meraviglioso per la nostra squadra.

acid ['æsɪd] NOUN
l' acido ◊ *acid rain* pioggia acida

acne ['æknɪ] NOUN
l' acne FEM

acre ['eɪkə'] NOUN
l' acro
Un acro corrisponde a circa 4 ettari.

acrobat ['ækrəbæt] NOUN
l' acrobata MASC/FEM

across [ə'krɔs] PREPOSITION, ADVERB
dall'altra parte di ◊ *the shop across the road* il negozio dall'altra parte della strada
* **an expedition across the Sahara** una spedizione nel Sahara
* **to run across the road** attraversare di corsa la strada
* **across from** di fronte a ◊ *He sat down across from her.* Si è seduto di fronte a lei.

act [ækt] VERB
see also **act** NOUN
[1] agire ◊ *The police acted quickly.* La polizia ha agito prontamente.
* **to act as** fare* da ◊ *She acts as his interpreter.* Lei gli fa da interprete.
[2] recitare ◊ *She's acting the part of Juliet.* Recita il ruolo di Giulietta.

act [ækt] NOUN
see also **act** VERB
[1] l' atto ◊ *in the first act* nel primo atto
[2] la scena ◊ *It was all an act.* Era tutta una scena.

action ['ækʃən] NOUN
l' azione FEM ◊ *The film was full of action.* Nel film c'erano molte scene d'azione.
* **to take firm action against** prendere* misure energiche contro

action replay [ækʃən'riːpleɪ] NOUN
il replay (PL i replay)

active ['æktɪv] ADJECTIVE
attivo

activity [æk'tɪvɪtɪ] NOUN (PL **activities**)
l' attività (PL le attività) ◊ *outdoor activities* attività all'aria aperta

actor ['æktə'] NOUN
l' attore MASC

actress ['æktrɪs] NOUN (PL **actresses**)
l' attrice FEM

actual ['æktjuəl] ADJECTIVE
effettivo ◊ *What's the actual amount?* Qual è la cifra effettiva?
*Be careful not to translate **actual** by **attuale**.*

actually ['æktjuəlɪ] ADVERB
[1] effettivamente ◊ *You only pay for the electricity you actually use.* Si paga solo per l'elettricità effettivamente consumata.
actually is sometimes not translated.
◊ *I was so bored I actually fell asleep!* Ero così annoiato che mi sono addormentato!
◊ *I'm not a student, I'm a doctor, actually.* Non sono uno studente, sono un medico.
[2] veramente ◊ *Fiona's awful, isn't she? – Actually, I quite like her.* Fiona è odiosa, no? – Veramente a me è abbastanza simpatica.
*Be careful not to translate **actually** by **attualmente**.*

acupuncture ['ækjupʌŋktʃə'] NOUN
l' agopuntura

AD [eɪ'diː] ABBREVIAZIONE (= *Anno Domini*)
d.C. (= dopo Cristo) ◊ *in 800 AD* nell'anno 800 d.C.

ad [æd] NOUN
[1] l' annuncio ◊ *He put an ad in the paper.* Ha messo un annuncio sul giornale.
[2] la pubblicità (PL le pubblicità) ◊ *I saw an ad for the concert.* Ho visto la pubblicità del concerto.

to **adapt** [ə'dæpt] VERB
adattare
* **to adapt to something** adattarsi E a qualcosa

adaptor [ə'dæptə'] NOUN
[1] il riduttore (*for plug*)
[2] la presa multipla (*with several sockets*)

to **add** [æd] VERB
aggiungere* ◊ *Add a bit of sugar.* Aggiungi un po' di zucchero.

to **add up** [æd'ʌp] VERB
addizionare ◊ *If you add up the numbers...* Se addizioni i numeri...

addict ['ædɪkt] NOUN
il/la tossicomane

addicted [ə'dɪktɪd] ADJECTIVE
* **to be addicted to drugs** essere* E tossicodipendente
* **She's addicted to soaps.** È appassionata di telenovelas.

addition [ə'dɪʃən] NOUN
* **in addition** inoltre
* **in addition to** oltre a

address [ə'drɛs] NOUN (PL **addresses**)
l' indirizzo

adjective ['ædʒɛktɪv] NOUN
l' aggettivo

to **adjust** [ə'dʒʌst] VERB
regolare ◊ *You can adjust the height of the seat.* Si può regolare l'altezza della sedia.
* **to adjust to something** adattarsi E a qualcosa

adjustable [ə'dʒʌstəbl] ADJECTIVE
regolabile

administration [ədmɪnɪs'treɪʃən] NOUN
l' amministrazione FEM

admiral ['ædmərəl] NOUN
l' ammiraglio

to **admire** [əd'maɪə'] VERB
ammirare

admission [əd'mɪʃən] NOUN
l' ingresso ◇ *"admission free"* "ingresso gratuito"

to **admit** [əd'mɪt] VERB
1 ammettere* ◇ *I must admit that...* Devo ammettere che...
2 confessare ◇ *He admitted that he'd done it.* Ha confessato di averlo fatto.

admittance [əd'mɪtəns] NOUN
• **"no admittance"** "vietato l'ingresso"

adolescence [ædəu'lesns] NOUN
l' adolescenza

adolescent [ædəu'lesnt] NOUN
l' adolescente MASC / FEM

to **adopt** [ə'dɒpt] VERB
adottare

adopted [ə'dɒptɪd] ADJECTIVE
adottivo

adoption [ə'dɒpʃən] NOUN
l' adozione FEM

to **adore** [ə'dɔː'] VERB
adorare

Adriatic [eɪdrɪ'ætɪk] NOUN
• **the Adriatic** l'Adriatico

adult ['ædʌlt] NOUN
l' adulto
• **adult education** i corsi per adulti

to **advance** [əd'vɑːns] VERB
see also **advance** NOUN
1 avanzare ◇ *The troops are advancing.* Le truppe avanzano.
2 fare* progressi ◇ *Technology has advanced a great deal.* La tecnologia ha fatto grandi progressi.

advance [əd'vɑːns] NOUN
see also **advance** VERB
l' anticipo
• **in advance** in anticipo

advance booking [əd'vɑːns'bukɪŋ] NOUN
la prenotazione

advanced [əd'vɑːnst] ADJECTIVE
avanzato

advance warning [əd'vɑːns'wɔːnɪŋ] NOUN
il preavviso

advantage [əd'vɑːntɪdʒ] NOUN
il vantaggio ◇ *This is an advantage.* Questo è un vantaggio.
• **to take advantage of something** approfittare di qualcosa
• **to take advantage of somebody** approfittarsi[E] di qualcuno

adventure [əd'ventʃə'] NOUN
l' avventura

adverb ['ædvə:b] NOUN
l' avverbio

advert ['ædvə:t] NOUN
1 l' annuncio ◇ *He put an advert in the paper.* Ha messo un annuncio sul giornale.
2 la pubblicità ◇ *I saw an advert for the*

concert. Ho visto la pubblicità del concerto.

to **advertise** ['ædvətaɪz] VERB
fare* pubblicità ◇ *They're advertising the new model.* Stanno facendo pubblicità per il nuovo modello.
• **Jobs are advertised in the paper.** Il giornale pubblica annunci di lavoro.

advertisement [əd'və:tɪsmənt] NOUN
1 l' annuncio ◇ *He put an advertisement in the paper.* Ha messo un annuncio sul giornale.
2 la pubblicità ◇ *I saw an advertisement for the concert.* Ho visto la pubblicità del concerto.

advertising ['ædvətaɪzɪŋ] NOUN
la pubblicità

advice [əd'vaɪs] NOUN
il consiglio ◇ *Take my advice and stay away from him!* Segui il mio consiglio, tieniti alla larga da lui!
Unlike advice, consiglio is used with an article, and can be made plural.
• **some advice** dei consigli ◇ *He gave me some good advice.* Mi ha dato dei buoni consigli.

to **advise** [əd'vaɪz] VERB
consigliare ◇ *He advised me to wait.* Mi ha consigliato di aspettare.

aerial ['eərɪəl] NOUN
l' antenna

aerobics [eə'rəubɪks] NOUN PL
l' aerobica SING

aeroplane ['eərəpleɪn] NOUN
l' aeroplano

aerosol ['eərəsɔl] NOUN
l' aerosol MASC

affair [ə'feə'] NOUN
1 la faccenda ◇ *The government has mishandled the affair.* Il governo ha gestito male la faccenda.
2 la relazione ◇ *She's having an affair with a married man.* Ha una relazione con un uomo sposato.

to **affect** [ə'fekt] VERB
avere* un impatto su

affectionate [ə'fekʃənɪt] ADJECTIVE
affettuoso

to **afford** [ə'fɔːd] VERB
permettersi[E] ◇ *I can't afford a new pair of jeans.* Non mi posso permettere un altro paio di jeans.

afraid [ə'freɪd] ADJECTIVE
• **to be afraid of something** aver paura di qualcosa ◇ *I'm afraid of spiders.* Ho paura dei ragni.
• **I'm afraid I can't come.** Mi dispiace ma non posso venire.
• **I'm afraid so.** Temo di sì.
• **I'm afraid not.** Temo di no.

Africa ['æfrɪkə] NOUN
l' Africa

* Verbs followed by this symbol are irregular. See pp.339–364 for further details.

African ['æfrɪkən] ADJECTIVE
see also **African** NOUN
africano

African ['æfrɪkən] NOUN
see also **African** ADJECTIVE
l' africano
l' africana
◇ the Africans gli africani

after ['ɑːftə'] PREPOSITION, ADVERB, CONJUNCTION
1 dopo ◇ after dinner dopo cena ◇ after I'd had a rest dopo essermi riposato ◇ the day after il giorno dopo
2 dietro ◇ He ran after me. Mi è corso dietro. ◇ Shut the door after you. Chiudi la porta dietro di te.
♦ **after all** dopotutto

afternoon ['ɑːftə'nuːn] NOUN
il pomeriggio ◇ in the afternoon nel pomeriggio ◇ at four o'clock in the afternoon alle quattro del pomeriggio

afters ['ɑːftəz] NOUN
il dessert ◇ What's for afters? Cosa c'è per dessert?

aftershave ['ɑːftəʃeɪv] NOUN
il dopobarba (PL i dopobarba)

afterwards ['ɑːftəwədz] ADVERB
dopo

again [ə'gɛn] ADVERB
di nuovo ◇ They're friends again. Sono di nuovo amici.
♦ **not...again** non...più ◇ I won't go there again. Lì non ci torno più.
♦ **again and again** ripetutamente

against [ə'gɛnst] PREPOSITION
contro ◇ I'm against nuclear testing. Sono contro gli esperimenti nucleari.

age [eɪdʒ] NOUN
l' età (PL le età) ◇ at the age of sixteen all'età di sedici anni ◇ the age limit il limite d'età
♦ **the 40 to 50 age group** le persone fra i quaranta e i cinquant'anni
♦ **I haven't been to the cinema for ages.** Sono secoli che non vado al cinema.

aged [eɪdʒd] ADJECTIVE
♦ **aged ten** di dieci anni

agenda [ə'dʒɛndə] NOUN
l' ordine del giorno MASC

agent ['eɪdʒənt] NOUN
l' agente MASC/FEM ◇ an estate agent un agente immobiliare ◇ a travel agent un agente di viaggio

aggressive [ə'grɛsɪv] ADJECTIVE
aggressivo

agitated ['ædʒɪteɪtɪd] ADJECTIVE
turbato

ago [ə'gəu] ADVERB
fa ◇ two days ago due giorni fa ◇ not long ago poco tempo fa

agony ['ægənɪ] NOUN (PL **agonies**)
♦ **to be in agony** soffrire* moltissimo

♦ **It was agony!** È stata una tortura!

to **agree** [ə'griː] VERB
essere* E d'accordo ◇ I don't agree! Non sono d'accordo!
♦ **to agree to do something** accettare di fare qualcosa ◇ He agreed to go and pick her up. Ha accettato di andare a prenderla.
♦ **to agree that** ammettere* che ◇ I agree that it's difficult. Ammetto che è difficile.
♦ **Garlic doesn't agree with me.** L'aglio mi è indigesto.

agreed [ə'griːd] ADJECTIVE
stabilito ◇ at the agreed time all'ora stabilita

agreement [ə'griːmənt] NOUN
l' accordo
♦ **to be in agreement** essere* E d'accordo

agricultural [ægrɪ'kʌltʃərəl] ADJECTIVE
agricolo

agriculture ['ægrɪkʌltʃə'] NOUN
l' agricoltura

ahead [ə'hɛd] ADVERB
davanti ◇ She looked straight ahead. Guardava dritto davanti a sé.
♦ **ahead of time** in anticipo
♦ **to plan ahead** pianificare
♦ **to be ahead** (in sport) essere* E in vantaggio ◇ Italy is five points ahead. L'Italia è in vantaggio di cinque punti.
♦ **Go ahead!** Fai pure!

aid [eɪd] NOUN
gli aiuti ◇ humanitarian aid aiuti umanitari
♦ **in aid of charity** a scopo di beneficienza

AIDS [eɪdz] NOUN
l' A.I.D.S FEM

to **aim** [eɪm] VERB
see also **aim** NOUN
puntare ◇ He aimed the gun at me. Mi ha puntato contro la pistola.
♦ **to be aimed at** essere* E diretto a ◇ It's aimed at a young audience. È diretto ad un pubblico giovane.
♦ **to aim to do something** avere* intenzione di fare qualcosa

aim [eɪm] NOUN
see also **aim** VERB
l' obiettivo

air [ɛə'] NOUN
l' aria ◇ in the open air all'aria aperta
♦ **to travel by air** viaggiare in aereo

air-conditioned ['ɛəkən'dɪʃənd] ADJECTIVE
con l'aria condizionata

air conditioning ['ɛəkən'dɪʃənɪŋ] NOUN
l' aria condizionata

Air Force ['ɛəfɔːs] NOUN
l' aviazione militare FEM

air hostess ['ɛəhəustes] NOUN
la hostess (PL le hostess)

airline ['ɛəlaɪn] NOUN
la compagnia aerea

airmail ['ɛəmeɪl] NOUN ☞

♦ **by airmail** per via aerea

airplane ['ɛəpleɪn] NOUN US
l' aereoplano

airport ['ɛəpɔːt] NOUN
l' aeroporto

air traffic controller ['ɛətræfɪkkən'trəulə'] NOUN
il controllore di volo

aisle [aɪl] NOUN
1 il corridoio ◊ *an aisle seat* un posto sul corridoio
2 la navata ◊ *the central aisle of the church* la navata centrale della chiesa

alarm [ə'lɑːm] NOUN
l' allarme MASC ◊ *He raised the alarm.* Ha dato l'allarme.
♦ **a fire alarm** un allarme antincendio

alarm clock [ə'lɑːmklɔk] NOUN
la sveglia

album ['ælbəm] NOUN
l' album (PL gli album)

alcohol ['ælkəhɔl] NOUN
1 gli alcolici (*drinks*)
2 l'alcol MASC (*substance*)

alcoholic [ælkə'hɔlɪk] NOUN
see also **alcoholic** ADJECTIVE
l' alcolizzato
l' alcolizzata

alcoholic [ælkə'hɔlɪk] ADJECTIVE
see also **alcoholic** NOUN
alcolico ◊ *alcoholic drinks* bevande alcoliche FEM PL

alert [ə'lɜːt] ADJECTIVE
1 sveglio ◊ *He's a very alert baby.* È un bambino molto sveglio.
2 all'erta ◊ *We must stay alert.* Dobbiamo stare all'erta.

A level ['eɪlɛvl] NOUN
♦ **I did French at A level.** Il francese è una delle materie cho ho studiato per la matura.

ⓘ L'**A level** è il diploma di studi superiori che si ottiene a 17/18 anni superando l'esame omonimo, e che permette di accedere all'università. Le materie d'esame sono scelte dal candidato in relazione alla facoltà a cui si vuole iscrivere.

Algeria [æl'dʒɪərɪə] NOUN
l' Algeria

alike [ə'laɪk] ADVERB
♦ **to look alike** assomigliarsi E ◊ *The two sisters look alike.* Le due sorelle si assomigliano.

alive [ə'laɪv] ADJECTIVE
vivo

all [ɔːl] ADJECTIVE, PRONOUN, ADVERB
tutto ◊ *all alone* tutto solo ◊ *That's all I can remember.* È tutto ciò che ricordo.
♦ **after all** dopotutto
♦ **not at all** per niente ◊ *I'm not at all tired.*

Non sono per niente stanco.
♦ **all the time** tutto il tempo ◊ *We can't be together all the time.* Non possiamo stare assieme tutto il tempo.
♦ **She talks all the time.** Parla in continuazione.
♦ **The score is five all.** Il punteggio è di cinque a cinque.

allergic [ə'lɜːdʒɪk] ADJECTIVE
allergico

allergy ['ælədʒɪ] NOUN (PL **allergies**)
l' allergia (PL le allergie)

alley ['ælɪ] NOUN
il vicolo

to **allow** [ə'lau] VERB
permettere* ◊ *Smoking is not allowed.* Non è permesso fumare.
♦ **to allow somebody to do something** permettere* a qualcuno di fare qualcosa ◊ *His mum allowed him to go out.* Sua madre gli ha permesso di uscire.
♦ **to be allowed to do something** avere* il permesso di fare qualcosa ◊ *He's not allowed to go out at night.* Non ha il permesso di uscire la sera.

all right [ɔːl'raɪt] ADVERB, ADJECTIVE
bene ◊ *Everything turned out all right.* Tutto è andato bene.
♦ **All right!** Va bene!
♦ **to be all right (1)** (*person*) stare* E bene ◊ *I'm all right.* Sto bene.
♦ **to be all right (2)** (*thing*) andare* E bene ◊ *Is that all right with you?* Per te va bene?
♦ **The film was all right.** Il film non era male.

almond ['ɑːmənd] NOUN
la mandorla

almost ['ɔːlməust] ADVERB
quasi

alone [ə'ləun] ADJECTIVE, ADVERB
solo ◊ *The flight alone costs £500.* Solo il volo costa cinquecento sterline.
♦ **She lives alone.** Vive da sola.
♦ **Leave her alone!** Lasciala in pace!
♦ **Leave my things alone!** Lascia stare le mie cose!

along [ə'lɔŋ] PREPOSITION, ADVERB
lungo ◊ *Chris was walking along the beach.* Chris passeggiava lungo la spiaggia.
♦ **all along** fin dall'inizio ◊ *He was lying to me all along.* Mi ha mentito fin dall'inizio.

aloud [ə'laud] ADVERB
ad alta voce

alphabet ['ælfəbɛt] NOUN
l' alfabeto

Alps [ælps] NOUN PL
le Alpi

already [ɔːl'rɛdɪ] ADVERB
già ◊ *Liz had already gone.* Liz se n'era già andata.

also ['ɔːlsəu] ADVERB
anche

*Verbs followed by this symbol are irregular. See pp.339–364 for further details.

altar [ˈɔltə'] NOUN
l' altare MASC

to **alter** [ˈɔltə'] VERB
cambiare

alternate [ɔlˈtəːnɪt] ADJECTIVE
• **on alternate days** a giorni alterni

alternative [ɔlˈtəːnətɪv] NOUN
see also **alternative** ADJECTIVE
l' alternativa ◇ *You have no alternative.*
Non hai alternative.

alternative [ɔlˈtəːnətɪv] ADJECTIVE
see also **alternative** NOUN
alternativo ◇ *an alternative solution* una
soluzione alternativa ◇ *alternative
medicine* medicina alternativa
• **They made alternative plans.** Hanno fatto
altri piani.

alternatively [ɔlˈtəːnətɪvlɪ] ADVERB
altrimenti ◇ *Alternatively, we could just
stay at home.* Altrimenti potremmo
semplicemente stare a casa.

although [ɔːlˈðəu] CONJUNCTION
nonostante ◇ *Although she was tired, she
stayed up late.* Nonostante fosse stanca è
rimasta alzata fino a tardi.

altogether [ɔːltəˈgɛðə'] ADVERB
1 in tutto ◇ *You owe me twenty pounds
altogether.* In tutto mi devi venti sterline.
2 del tutto ◇ *I'm not altogether happy with
your work.* Non sono del tutto soddisfatto
del tuo lavoro.

aluminium [æljuˈmɪnɪəm] NOUN (US
aluminum)
l' alluminio

always [ˈɔːlweɪz] ADVERB
sempre ◇ *He's always moaning.* Si lamenta
sempre.

am [æm] VERB *see* **be**

a.m. [eɪˈɛm] ADVERB (= *ante meridiem*)
del mattino ◇ *at four a.m.* alle quattro del
mattino

amateur [ˈæmətə'] NOUN
il/la dilettante

amazed [əˈmeɪzd] ADJECTIVE
stupefatto ◇ *I was amazed that I managed
to do it.* Io stesso ero stupefatto di esserci
riuscito.

amazing [əˈmeɪzɪŋ] ADJECTIVE
1 incredibile ◇ *That's amazing news!* È
una notizia incredibile!
2 eccezionale ◇ *Vivian's an amazing cook.*
Vivian è una cuoca eccezionale.

ambassador [æmˈbæsədə'] NOUN
l' ambasciatore
l' ambasciatrice

amber [ˈæmbə'] ADJECTIVE
giallo ◇ *The light is amber!* È giallo!

ambition [æmˈbɪʃən] NOUN
l' ambizione FEM

ambitious [æmˈbɪʃəs] ADJECTIVE
ambizioso

ambulance [ˈæmbjuləns] NOUN
l' ambulanza

amenities [əˈmiːnɪtɪz] NOUN PL
• **The hotel has very good amenities.**
L'albergo è molto ben attrezzato dal punto di
vista ricreativo.
• **The town has many amenities.** La città gode
di strutture ricreative e commerciali.

America [əˈmɛrɪkə] NOUN
l' America

American [əˈmɛrɪkən] ADJECTIVE
see also **American** NOUN
americano

American [əˈmɛrɪkən] NOUN
see also **American** ADJECTIVE
l' americano
l' americana
◇ *the Americans* gli americani

among [əˈmʌŋ] PREPOSITION
tra ◇ *I was among friends.* Ero tra amici.

amount [əˈmaunt] NOUN
1 la quantità (PL le quantità) ◇ *a huge
amount of rice* una grossa quantità di riso
2 la somma ◇ *a large amount of money*
una grossa somma di denaro

amp [æmp] NOUN
1 l' ampere MASC (PL gli ampere) (*electricity*)
2 l' amplificatore MASC (*amplifier*)

amplifier [ˈæmplɪfaɪə'] NOUN
l' amplificatore MASC

to **amuse** [əˈmjuːz] VERB
divertire ◇ *He was most amused by the
story.* La storia lo divertì molto.

amusement [əˈmjuːzmənt] NOUN
il divertimento

amusement arcade [əˈmjuːzməntɑːˈkeɪd]
NOUN
la sala giochi

amusement park [əˈmjuːzməntˈpɑːk] NOUN
il luna park (PL i luna park)

an [æn,ən] ARTICLE *see* **a**

anaemic [əˈniːmɪk] ADJECTIVE
anemico

to **analyse** [ˈænəlaɪz] VERB (US **analyze**)
analizzare

analysis [əˈnæləsɪs] NOUN (PL **analyses**)
l' analisi (PL le analisi)

to **analyze** [ˈænəlaɪz] VERB US
analizzare

ancestor [ˈænsɪstə'] NOUN
l' antenato
l' antenata

anchor [ˈæŋkə'] NOUN
l' ancora

ancient [ˈeɪnʃənt] ADJECTIVE
antico ◇ *ancient Greece* la Grecia antica
• **an ancient monument** un monumento
storico

and [ænd] CONJUNCTION
e ◇ *you and me* tu ed io
• **Please try and come!** Cerca di venire! ☞

Verbs followed by the symbol "E" require the auxiliary "essere"

◆ **better and better** sempre meglio

anemic [əˈniːmɪk] ADJECTIVE US
anemico

angel [ˈeɪndʒəl] NOUN
l' angelo

anger [ˈæŋgə'] NOUN
la rabbia

angle [ˈæŋgl] NOUN
l' angolo ◇ *a right angle* un angolo retto

angler [ˈæŋglə'] NOUN
il pescatore

angling [ˈæŋglɪŋ] NOUN
la pesca con la lenza

angry [ˈæŋgrɪ] ADJECTIVE
arrabbiato ◇ *Your father looks very angry.*
Tuo padre ha l'aria molto arrabbiata.

◆ **You're making me angry.** Mi stai facendo arrabbiare.

◆ **to get angry** arrabbiarsi [E]

animal [ˈænɪməl] NOUN
l' animale MASC

ankle [ˈæŋkl] NOUN
la caviglia ◇ *I've twisted my ankle.* Mi sono slogato la caviglia.

anniversary [ænɪˈvɜːsərɪ] NOUN (PL **anniversaries**)
l' anniversario ◇ *It's their wedding anniversary.* È il loro anniversario di matrimonio.

to **announce** [əˈnauns] VERB
annunciare

announcement [əˈnaunsmənt] NOUN
l' annuncio ◇ *There's just been an announcement about our flight.* C'è stato un annuncio riguardo al nostro volo un attimo fa.

to **annoy** [əˈnɔɪ] VERB
dare* fastidio ◇ *He's really annoying me.*
Mi sta veramente dando fastidio.

◆ **to get annoyed** arrabbiarsi [E] ◇ *He got annoyed and put the phone down.* Si arrabbiò e mise giù il ricevitore.

◆ **Don't get so annoyed!** Non prendertela tanto!

annoying [əˈnɔɪɪŋ] ADJECTIVE
seccante

annual [ˈænjuəl] ADJECTIVE
annuale

anonymous [əˈnɒnɪməs] ADJECTIVE
anonimo

anorak [ˈænəræk] NOUN
la giacca a vento (PL le giacche a vento)

anorexic [ænəˈrɛksɪk] ADJECTIVE
anoressico

another [əˈnʌðə'] ADJECTIVE
un altro
un'altra
◇ *I've got another T-shirt in my bag.* Ho un'altra maglietta nella borsa.

to **answer** [ˈɑːnsə'] VERB
see also **answer** NOUN

rispondere* ◇ *Can you please answer the phone?* Puoi rispondere al telefono per favore?

◆ **to answer the door** andare* [E] ad aprire

answer [ˈɑːnsə'] NOUN
see also **answer** VERB
la risposta ◇ *We need an answer by Tuesday.* Dobbiamo avere una risposta entro martedì.

◆ **the answer to the problem** la soluzione del problema

answering machine [ˈɑːnsərɪŋ–] NOUN
la segreteria telefonica (PL le segreterie telefoniche)

ant [ænt] NOUN
la formica (PL le formiche)

Antarctic [æntˈɑːktɪk] NOUN
l' Antaride FEM

anthem [ˈænθəm] NOUN

◆ **the national anthem** l'inno nazionale

antibiotic [ˈæntɪbaɪˈɒtɪk] NOUN
l' antibiotico (PL gli antibiotici)

antidepressant [æntɪdrˈpresnt] NOUN
l' antidepressivo

antique [ænˈtiːk] NOUN
il pezzo d'antiquariato ◇ *I bought an antique.* Ho comprato un pezzo d'antiquariato.

antique dealer [ænˈtiːkdiːlə'] NOUN
l' antiquario
l' antiquaria

antique shop [anˈtiːkʃɒp] NOUN
il negozio d'antiquario

antiseptic [æntɪˈseptɪk] NOUN
il disinfettante

any [ˈɛnɪ] ADJECTIVE, PRONOUN
[1] qualche ◇ *Have you got any comment?*
Hai qualche commento?
[2] qualunque (*any at all*) ◇ *You can make the tart with any fruit you like.* Puoi fare la crostata con qualunque tipo di frutta.

◆ **any time you like** quando vuoi

*any is sometimes translated by **ne**.*
◇ *Sorry, I haven't got any.* Mi dispiace, non ne ho.

any is sometimes not translated.
◇ *I haven't got any money.* Non ho soldi.

◆ **any more** più ◇ *I don't love him any more.*
Non lo amo più.

anybody [ˈɛnɪbɒdɪ] PRONOUN
[1] qualcuno ◇ *Has anybody got a pen?*
Qualcuno ha una penna?
[2] nessuno
*Use **nessuno** in negative sentences.*
◇ *I can't see anybody.* Non vedo nessuno.
[3] chiunque (*anybody at all*) ◇ *Anybody can learn to swim.* Chiunque può imparare a nuotare.

anyhow [ˈɛnɪhau] ADVERB
comunque ◇ *He doesn't want to go out and anyhow he's not allowed.* Non vuole uscire

---

* Verbs followed by this symbol are irregular. See pp.339–364 for further details.

e comunque non ha il permesso di farlo.
+ **What business is it of yours, anyhow?** E tu di che t'impicci?

anyone ['ɛnɪwʌn] PRONOUN
[1] qualcuno ◇ *Has anyone got a pen?* Qualcuno ha una penna?
[2] nessuno
*Use **nessuno** in negative sentences.*
◇ *I can't see anyone.* Non vedo nessuno.
[3] chiunque (*anyone at all*) ◇ *Anyone can learn to swim.* Chiunque può imparare a nuotare.

anything ['ɛnɪθɪŋ] PRONOUN
[1] qualcosa ◇ *Do you need anything?* Ti serve qualcosa?
[2] niente
*Use **niente** in negative sentences.*
◇ *I can't hear anything.* Non sento niente.
[3] qualunque cosa (*anything at all*)
◇ *Anything could happen.* Potrebbe succedere qualunque cosa.

anyway ['ɛnɪweɪ] ADVERB
comunque ◇ *He doesn't want to go out and anyway he's not allowed.* Non vuole uscire e comunque non ha il permesso di farlo.
+ **What business is it of yours, anyway?** E tu di che t'impicci?

anywhere ['ɛnɪwɛə'] ADVERB
[1] da qualche parte ◇ *Have you seen my coat anywhere?* Hai visto il mio cappotto da qualche parte?
[2] da nessuna parte
*Use **da nessuna parte** in negative sentences.*
◇ *I can't find it anywhere.* Non riesco a trovarlo da nessuna parte.
[3] dovunque (*anywhere at all*) ◇ *You can buy stamps almost anywhere.* Puoi comprare i francobolli dovunque.

apart [ə'pɑːt] ADVERB
+ **The towns are ten kilometres apart.** Le città distano dieci chilometri.
+ **Nothing will keep them apart.** Niente li terrà lontani l'uno dall'altra.
+ **apart from** a parte ◇ *Apart from that, everything's fine.* A parte quello, va tutto bene.

apartment [ə'pɑːtmənt] NOUN
l' appartamento ◇ *a small apartment* un piccolo appartamento
+ **an apartment building** US uno stabile

to **apologize** [ə'pɒlədʒaɪz] VERB
chiedere* scusa ◇ *I apologize!* Chiedo scusa!

apology [ə'pɒlədʒɪ] NOUN (PL **apologies**)
le scuse ◇ *I owe you an apology.* Ti devo delle scuse.

apostrophe [ə'pɒstrəfɪ] NOUN
l' apostrofo

apparatus [æpə'reɪtəs] NOUN (PL **apparatus** or **apparatuses**)
[1] le apparecchiature ◇ *the apparatus in the chemistry lab* le apparecchiature del laboratorio chimico
[2] l' attrezzatura ◇ *the apparatus in the gym* l'attrezzatura della palestra

apparent [ə'pærənt] ADJECTIVE
apparente

apparently [ə'pærəntlɪ] ADVERB
+ **Apparently...** A quanto pare... ◇ *Apparently he was abroad when it happened.* A quanto pare era all'estero quando è successo il fatto.

to **appeal** [ə'piːl] VERB
see also **appeal** NOUN
chiedere* ◇ *They appealed for help from the international community.* Hanno chiesto aiuto alla comunità internazionale.
+ **Greece doesn't appeal to me.** La Grecia non mi attira.

appeal [ə'piːl] NOUN
see also **appeal** VERB
l' appello ◇ *They've launched an appeal.* Hanno lanciato un appello.

to **appear** [ə'pɪə'] VERB
[1] apparire* E ◇ *The bus appeared around the corner.* L'autobus è apparso all'angolo della strada.
[2] sembrare E ◇ *She appeared to be asleep.* Sembrava che dormisse.

appearance [ə'pɪərəns] NOUN
l' aspetto ◇ *She takes great care over her appearance.* Cura molto il suo aspetto.
+ **to make an appearance** fare* un'apparizione
+ **to put in an appearance** fare* atto di presenza

appendicitis [əpendɪ'saɪtɪs] NOUN
l' appendicite FEM

appetite ['æpɪtaɪt] NOUN
l' appetito ◇ *He has a big appetite.* Ha molto appetito.

to **applaud** [ə'plɔːd] VERB
applaudire

applause [ə'plɔːz] NOUN
gli applausi ◇ *laughter and applause* risa e applausi
+ **a round of applause** un applauso

apple ['æpl] NOUN
la mela

applicant ['æplɪkənt] NOUN
+ **There were a hundred applicants for that job.** Cento persone hanno fatto domanda per quel posto.
+ **They're interviewing four applicants this week.** Hanno colloqui con quattro candidati questa settimana.

application [æplɪ'keɪʃən] NOUN
la domanda ◇ *a job application* una domanda di lavoro

application form [æplɪ'keɪʃənfɔːm] NOUN
il modulo

to **apply** [ə'plaɪ] VERB (**applied, applied**)
+ **to apply for a job** fare* domanda per un ☞

posto di lavoro
+ **to apply to** riguardare* ◊ *This rule doesn't apply to us.* Questa norma non ci riguarda.

to **appoint** [ə'pɔɪnt] VERB
nominare

appointment [ə'pɔɪntmənt] NOUN
l' appuntamento ◊ *I've got a dental appointment.* Ho un appuntamento dal dentista.

to **appreciate** [ə'priːʃɪeɪt] VERB
+ **to appreciate something** essere* E riconoscente di qualcosa ◊ *I really appreciate your help.* Ti sono veramente riconoscente dell'aiuto.

apprentice [ə'prentɪs] NOUN
l' apprendista MASC/FEM

to **approach** [ə'prəʊtʃ] VERB
[1] avvicinarsi E a ◊ *He approached the house.* Si è avvicinato alla casa.
[2] affrontare ◊ *I'm not sure how to approach the problem.* Non so come affrontare il problema.

appropriate [ə'prəʊprɪɪt] ADJECTIVE
[1] adatto ◊ *an outfit appropriate to the job* un abbigliamento adatto al lavoro
[2] apposito ◊ *Tick the appropriate box.* Barrare l'apposita casella.
[3] corretto ◊ *appropriate behaviour* comportamento corretto

approval [ə'pruːvəl] NOUN
l' approvazione FEM

to **approve** [ə'pruːv] VERB
+ **to approve of** approvare ◊ *I don't approve of his choice.* Non approvo la sua scelta.

approximate [ə'prɒksɪmɪt] ADJECTIVE
approssimativo

apricot ['eɪprɪkɒt] NOUN
l' albicocca (PL le albicocche)

April ['eɪprəl] NOUN
aprile ◊ *in April* in aprile
+ **April Fool's Day** il primo aprile

apron ['eɪprən] NOUN
il grembiule da cucina

aquarium [ə'kweərɪəm] NOUN
l' acquario

Aquarius [ə'kweərɪəs] NOUN
l' Acquario ◊ *I'm Aquarius.* Sono dell'Acquario.

Arab ['ærəb] ADJECTIVE
see also **Arab** NOUN
arabo

Arab ['ærəb] NOUN
see also **Arab** ADJECTIVE
l' arabo
l' araba
◊ *the Arabs* gli arabi

Arabic ['ærəbɪk] NOUN
l' arabo (*language*)

arch [ɑːtʃ] NOUN (PL **arches**)
l' arcata

archaeologist [ɑːkɪ'ɒlədʒɪst] NOUN

l' archeologo
l' archeologa

archaeology [ɑːkɪ'ɒlədʒɪ] NOUN
l' archeologia

archbishop [ɑːtʃ'bɪʃəp] NOUN
l' arcivescovo

archeologist [ɑːkɪ'ɒlədʒɪst] NOUN US
l' archeologo
l' archeologa

archeology [ɑːkɪ'ɒlədʒɪ] NOUN US
l' archeologia

architect ['ɑːkɪtekt] NOUN
l' architetto

architecture ['ɑːkɪtektʃə'] NOUN
l' architettura

Arctic ['ɑːktɪk] NOUN
+ **the Arctic** l'Artico

are [ɑː'] VERB *see* be

area ['ɛərɪə] NOUN
[1] la zona ◊ *He lives in the Sheffield area.* Abita nella zona di Sheffield.
[2] il quartiere ◊ *My favourite area of London is Chelsea.* Il quartiere londinese che preferisco è Chelsea.
[3] la superficie ◊ *The field has an area of 2000 square metres.* Il campo ha una superficie di due mila metri quadrati.

area code ['ɛərɪəkəʊd] NOUN US
il prefisso (*for telephone*)

Argentina [ɑːdʒən'tiːnə] NOUN
l' Argentina

Argentinian [ɑːdʒən'tɪnɪən] NOUN
l' argentino
l' argentina

to **argue** ['ɑːgjuː] VERB
[1] litigare ◊ *They're always arguing.* Litigano sempre.
[2] sostenere* ◊ *She argued that her client had been misled.* Sosteneva che il suo cliente era stato tratto in inganno.

argument ['ɑːgjumənt] NOUN
[1] il motivo ◊ *There are strong arguments against lowering the price.* Ci sono motivi validi per non abbassare il prezzo.
[2] la discussione ◊ *a heated argument* un'accesa discussione
+ **to have an argument** litigare

Aries ['ɛəriːz] NOUN
l' Ariete MASC ◊ *I'm Aries.* Sono dell'Ariete.

arm [ɑːm] NOUN
il braccio (PL FEM le braccia) (*limb*)

armchair ['ɑːmtʃɛə'] NOUN
la poltrona

armour ['ɑːmə'] NOUN (US **armor**)
l' armatura

army ['ɑːmɪ] NOUN (PL **armies**)
l' esercito

around [ə'raʊnd] PREPOSITION, ADVERB
[1] intorno ◊ *She ignored the people around her.* Ha ignorato la gente che aveva intorno.

---

* Verbs followed by this symbol are irregular. See pp.339–364 for further details.

[2] circa ◇ *It costs around a hundred pounds.* Costa circa cento sterline.
[3] verso ◇ *Let's meet at around eight o'clock.* Troviamoci verso le otto.
♦ **around here** da queste parti ◇ *Is there a chemist's around here?* C'è una farmacia da queste parti?

○ **arrange** [ə'reɪndʒ] VERB
[1] organizzare ◇ *She arranged a trip to Scotland.* Ha organizzato un viaggio in Scozia.
♦ **to arrange to do something** mettersi[E] d'accordo per fare qualcosa ◇ *They arranged to go out together on Friday.* Si sono messi d'accordo per uscire venerdì.
[2] sistemare ◇ *The chairs were arranged in a circle.* Le sedie erano sistemate in cerchio.

arrangement [ə'reɪndʒmənt] NOUN
♦ **We have an arrangement.** Siamo d'accordo.
♦ **a flower arrangement** una composizione floreale
♦ **arrangements** preparativi ◇ *Pamela is in charge of the travel arrangements.* Pamela si occupa dei preparativi del viaggio.

○ **arrest** [ə'rɛst] VERB
see also **arrest** NOUN
arrestare

arrest [ə'rɛst] NOUN
see also **arrest** VERB
l' arresto ◇ *You're under arrest!* La dichiaro in arresto!

arrival [ə'raɪvl] NOUN
l' arrivo

○ **arrive** [ə'raɪv] VERB
arrivare[E] ◇ *We arrived at eight.* Siamo arrivati alle otto.

arrogant ['ærəgənt] ADJECTIVE
arrogante

arrow ['ærəʊ] NOUN
la freccia (PL le frecce)

art [ɑːt] NOUN
[1] l' arte FEM ◇ *Greek art.* L'arte greca.
[2] le materie artistiche ◇ *He's good at art.* È bravo nelle materie artistiche.

artery ['ɑːtəri] NOUN (PL **arteries**)
l' arteria

art gallery ['ɑːtgæləri] NOUN (PL **art galleries**)
la galleria d'arte

article ['ɑːtɪkl] NOUN
l' articolo

artificial [ɑːtɪ'fɪʃəl] ADJECTIVE
artificiale

artist ['ɑːtɪst] NOUN
l' artista MASC / FEM

artistic [ɑː'tɪstɪk] ADJECTIVE
artistico

art school ['ɑːtskuːl] NOUN
la scuola d'arte

as [æz,əz] CONJUNCTION, ADVERB
[1] quando ◇ *He came in as I was leaving.* È arrivato quando stavo uscendo.

[2] visto che ◇ *As it's Sunday, you can have a lie-in.* Visto che è domenica puoi restare a letto fino a tardi.
[3] come ◇ *He works as a waiter in the holidays.* Durante le vacanze lavora come cameriere.

There are various ways of translating **as...as** *when used in comparisons.*
◇ *Peter's as tall as Michael.* Peter è alto come Michael. ◇ *I haven't got as much money as you.* Non ho tanti soldi quanti ne hai tu. ◇ *Her coat cost twice as much as mine.* Il suo cappotto è costato il doppio del mio.
♦ **as soon as possible** prima possibile
♦ **as from tomorrow** a partire da domani
♦ **as if** come se
♦ **as though** come se ◇ *She acted as though she hadn't seen me.* Si comportava come se non mi avesse visto.

asap [eɪeseɪ'piː] ABBREVIAZIONE (= *as soon as possible*)
prima possibile

ash [æʃ] NOUN
la cenere (*from fire, cigarette*)

ashamed [ə'ʃeɪmd] ADJECTIVE
♦ **to be ashamed** vergognarsi[E] ◇ *You should be ashamed of yourself!* Dovresti vergognarti!

ashtray ['æʃtreɪ] NOUN
il portacenere (PL i portacenere)

Asia ['eɪʃə] NOUN
l' Asia

Asian ['eɪʃən] ADJECTIVE
see also **Asian** NOUN
asiatico

Asian ['eɪʃən] NOUN
see also **Asian** ADJECTIVE
l' asiatico
l' asiatica
◇ *the Asians* gli asiatici

to **ask** [ɑːsk] VERB
[1] chiedere* ◇ *"Have you finished?" she asked.* "Hai finito?" chiese.
♦ **to ask for something** chiedere* qualcosa ◇ *He asked for a cup of tea.* Ha chiesto una tazza di tè.
♦ **to ask about something** informarsi[E] su qualcosa ◇ *I asked about train times to Leeds.* Mi sono informato sugli orari dei treni per Leeds.
♦ **to ask somebody a question** fare* una domanda a qualcuno
[2] invitare ◇ *Have you asked Matthew to the party?* Hai invitato Matthew alla festa?
♦ **to ask somebody out** chiedere* a qualcuno di uscire ◇ *Peter asked her out.* Peter le ha chiesto di uscire con lui.

asleep [ə'sliːp] ADJECTIVE
♦ **to be asleep** dormire ◇ *He's asleep.* Dorme.
♦ **to fall asleep** addormentarsi[E] ◇ *I fell asleep in front of the TV.* Mi sono addormentato ☞

davanti alla TV.

asparagus [əs'pærəgəs] NOUN
gli asparagi

aspect ['æspekt] NOUN
l' aspetto

aspirin ['æsprɪn] NOUN
l' aspirina

asset ['æset] NOUN
il vantaggio ◇ Her experience will be an
asset to the firm. La sua esperienza sarà di
grande vantaggio per la ditta.

assignment [ə'saɪnmənt] NOUN
il compito ◇ We have to do three written
assignments. Dobbiamo fare tre compiti
scritti.

assistance [ə'sɪstəns] NOUN
l' aiuto

assistant [ə'sɪstənt] NOUN
1 il commesso
la commessa
(in shop)
2 l' assistente MASC / FEM (helper)

association [əsəʊsɪ'eɪʃən] NOUN
l' associazione FEM

assortment [ə'sɔːtmənt] NOUN
l' assortimento

to **assume** [ə'sjuːm] VERB
1 supporre ◇ I assume so. Suppongo di sì.
2 dare* per scontato ◇ I assumed he was
coming. Ho dato per scontato che venisse.

to **assure** [ə'ʃʊə'] VERB
assicurare ◇ He assured me he was coming.
Mi ha assicurato che sarebbe venuto.

asthma ['æsmə] NOUN
l' asma

to **astonish** [ə'stɒnɪʃ] VERB
stupire

astonishing [ə'stɒnɪʃɪŋ] ADJECTIVE
stupefacente

astrology [əs'trɒlədʒɪ] NOUN
l' astrologia

astronaut ['æstrənɔːt] NOUN
l' astronauta MASC / FEM

astronomy [əs'trɒnəmɪ] NOUN
l' astronomia

asylum seeker [ə'saɪləmsiːkə'] NOUN
• seven per cent of asylum seekers il sette per
cento di chi chiede asilo politico

at [æt] PREPOSITION
a ◇ at four o'clock alle quattro ◇ two at a
time due alla volta ◇ at school a scuola
• at the office in ufficio
• at night di notte

ate [eɪt] VERB see eat

Athens ['æθɪnz] NOUN
Atene FEM

athlete ['æθliːt] NOUN
l' atleta MASC / FEM

athletic [æθ'letɪk] ADJECTIVE
atletico

athletics [æθ'letɪks] NOUN SING

l' atletica

Atlantic [ət'læntɪk] NOUN
• the Atlantic l'Atlantico

atlas ['ætləs] NOUN (PL atlases)
l' atlante MASC

atmosphere ['ætməsfɪə'] NOUN
l' atmosfera

atom ['ætəm] NOUN
l' atomo

atomic [ə'tɒmɪk] ADJECTIVE
atomico

to **attach** [ə'tætʃ] VERB
attaccare ◇ They attached a rope to the car.
Hanno attaccato una corda alla macchina.

attached [ə'tætʃt] ADJECTIVE
• to be attached to somebody essere* E
affezionato a qualcuno
• Please find attached... Allego...

attachment [ə'tætʃmənt] NOUN
1 l' allegato (to email)
2 l' attaccamento ◇ His attachment to his
mother. Il suo attaccamento alla madre.

to **attack** [ə'tæk] VERB
see also **attack** NOUN
aggredire

attack [ə'tæk] NOUN
see also **attack** VERB
1 l' aggressione FEM ◇ a savage attack una
feroce aggressione
2 l' attacco (PL gli attacchi) ◇ a surprise
attack un attacco a sorpresa
• to be under attack essere* E attaccato

attempt [ə'tempt] NOUN
see also **attempt** VERB
il tentativo ◇ after several attempts dopo
diversi tentativi

to **attempt** [ə'tempt] VERB
see also **attempt** NOUN
• to attempt to do something tentare di fare
qualcosa ◇ I attempted to write a song. Ho
tentato di scrivere una canzone.

to **attend** [ə'tend] VERB
essere* E presente a ◇ He attended the
meeting. Era presente alla riunione.
Be careful not to translate **to attend** by
attendere.

attention [ə'tenʃən] NOUN
l' attenzione FEM
• to pay attention fare* attenzione

attic ['ætɪk] NOUN
la mansarda

attitude ['ætɪtjuːd] NOUN
l' atteggiamento

attorney [ə'tɜːnɪ] NOUN US
l' avvocato

to **attract** [ə'trækt] VERB
attirare ◇ The Lake District attracts lots of
tourists. La Regione dei Laghi attira molti
turisti.

attraction [ə'trækʃən] NOUN
l' attrazione FEM

* Verbs followed by this symbol are irregular. See pp.339–364 for further details.

attractive [ə'træktɪv] ADJECTIVE
attraente

aubergine ['əubəʒi:n] NOUN
la melanzana

auction ['ɔ:kʃən] NOUN
l' asta

audience ['ɔ:dɪəns] NOUN
il pubblico ◇ *a huge audience* un grandissimo pubblico
♦ **The concerts attracted huge audiences.** I concerti hanno attirato tantissima gente.

audition [ɔ:'dɪʃən] NOUN
l' audizione FEM

auditor ['ɔ:dɪtə'] NOUN
il revisore dei conti

August ['ɔ:gəst] NOUN
agosto ◇ *in August* in agosto

aunt [ɑ:nt] NOUN
la zia

aunty ['ɑ:ntɪ] NOUN (PL **aunties**)
la zia

au pair ['əu'peə'] NOUN
la ragazza alla pari

Australia [ɔs'treɪlɪə] NOUN
l' Australia

Australian [ɔs'treɪlɪən] ADJECTIVE
see also **Australian** NOUN
australiano

Australian [ɔs'treɪlɪən] NOUN
see also **Australian** ADJECTIVE
l' australiano
l' australiana
◇ *the Australians* gli australiani

Austria ['ɔstrɪə] NOUN
l' Austria

Austrian ['ɔstrɪən] ADJECTIVE
see also **Austrian** NOUN
austriaco

Austrian ['ɔstrɪən] NOUN
see also **Austrian** ADJECTIVE
l' austriaco
l' austriaca
◇ *the Austrians* gli austriaci

author ['ɔ:θə'] NOUN
l' autore
l' autrice

autobiography [ɔ:təbaɪ'ɔgrəfɪ] NOUN (PL
autobiographies)
l' autobiografia

autograph ['ɔ:təgrɑ:f] NOUN
l' autografo

automatic [ɔ:tə'mætɪk] ADJECTIVE
automatico

automatically [ɔ:tə'mætɪklɪ] ADVERB
automaticamente

autumn ['ɔ:təm] NOUN
l' autunno ◇ *in autumn* in autunno ◇ *last autumn* lo scorso autunno

availability [əveɪlə'bɪlɪtɪ] NOUN
la disponibilità

available [ə'veɪləbl] ADJECTIVE
[1] disponibile ◇ *the amount of money available* la cifra disponibile
[2] libero ◇ *Is Mr Cooke available today?* Mr Cooke è libero oggi?

avalanche ['ævəlɑ:nʃ] NOUN
la valanga (PL le valanghe)

avenue ['ævənju:] NOUN
il viale

average ['ævərɪdʒ] NOUN
see also **average** ADJECTIVE
la media ◇ *on average* in media

average ['ævərɪdʒ] ADJECTIVE
see also **average** NOUN
medio ◇ *the average price* il prezzo medio

avocado [ævə'kɑ:dəu] NOUN (PL **avocados**)
l' avocado (PL gli avocado)

to **avoid** [ə'vɔɪd] VERB
evitare ◇ *Avoid going out on your own at night.* Evita di uscire da sola di sera.

awake [ə'weɪk] ADJECTIVE
♦ **to be awake** essere* E sveglio

award [ə'wɔ:d] NOUN
il premio

aware [ə'weə'] ADJECTIVE
♦ **aware of** conscio di ◇ *They're aware of the danger.* Sono consci del pericolo.
♦ **to become aware of** accorgersi* E di

away [ə'weɪ] ADJECTIVE, ADVERB
[1] via ◇ *Jason was away on a business trip.* Jason era via per lavoro. ◇ *He's away for a week.* È andato via per una settimana.
♦ **Go away!** Vattene!
[2] di distanza ◇ *two kilometres away* a due chilometri di distanza ◇ *two hours away by car* a due ore di distanza in macchina
♦ **The holiday was two weeks away.** Mancavano due settimane alla vacanza.
♦ **away from his family and friends** lontano dalla famiglia e dagli amici
♦ **He was still working away in the library.** Stava ancora lavorando in biblioteca.

away match [ə'weɪmætʃ] NOUN (PL **away matches**)
la partita in trasferta

awful ['ɔ:fəl] ADJECTIVE
orribile ◇ *The weather's awful.* Il tempo è orribile.
♦ **I feel awful.** Mi sento malissimo.
♦ **an awful lot of...** un sacco di...

awfully ['ɔ:fəlɪ] ADVERB
terribilmente ◇ *I'm awfully sorry.* Sono terribilmente spiacente.

awkward ['ɔ:kwəd] ADJECTIVE
[1] imbarazzante ◇ *It's an awkward situation.* È una situazione imbarazzante.
[2] scomodo ◇ *It's a bit awkward for me to come and see you.* Mi è un po' scomodo passare da te.

axe [æks] NOUN (PL **axes**)
l' ascia (PL le asce)

B

BA [biːˈeɪ] NOUN (= *Bachelor of Arts*)
la <u>laurea</u> ◇ *She's got a BA in History.* Ha una laurea in storia.

baby [ˈbeɪbɪ] NOUN (PL **babies**)
il <u>bambino</u>
la <u>bambina</u>

baby carriage [ˈbeɪbɪkærɪdʒ] NOUN US
la <u>carrozzina</u>

to **babysit** [ˈbeɪbɪsɪt] VERB (**babysat, babysat**)
<u>fare* la babysitter</u>

babysitter [ˈbeɪbɪsɪtəʳ] NOUN
il/la <u>babysitter</u>

babysitting [ˈbeɪbɪsɪtɪŋ] NOUN
♦ **to go babysitting** fare* la babysitter

bachelor [ˈbætʃələʳ] NOUN
lo <u>scapolo</u>

back [bæk] NOUN
see also **back** ADJECTIVE, VERB
[1] la <u>schiena</u> ◇ *He's got a bad back.* Ha problemi alla schiena.
[2] la <u>groppa</u> ◇ *on the horse's back* sulla groppa del cavallo
[3] il <u>retro</u> ◇ *on the back of the cheque* sul retro dell'assegno ◇ *at the back of the house* sul retro della casa
[4] il <u>fondo</u> ◇ *at back of the class* in fondo alla classe
♦ **the back of a chair** lo schienale della sedia
♦ **in the back of the car** nel sedile posteriore dell'auto

back [bæk] ADJECTIVE, ADVERB
see also **back** NOUN, VERB
<u>posteriore</u> ◇ *the back seat* il sedile posteriore
♦ **the back door** la porta sul retro
♦ **to be back** tornare ᴱ ◇ *He's not back yet.* Non è ancora tornato.
♦ **We went there by bus and walked back.** Siamo andati in autobus e siamo ritornati a piedi.
♦ **to call somebody back** richiamare qualcuno

to **back** [bæk] VERB
see also **back** NOUN, ADJECTIVE
[1] <u>appoggiare</u> ◇ *The union is backing his claim for compensation.* Il sindacato appoggia la sua domanda di indennizzo.
♦ **to back a horse** puntare su un cavallo
[2] <u>fare* marcia indietro</u> ◇ *The road was blocked so I had to back.* La strada era bloccata e ho dovuto fare marcia indietro.
♦ **She backed into the parking space.** È entrata in parcheggio in retromarcia.

to **back out** [bækˈaʊt] VERB
<u>tirarsi ᴱ indietro</u> ◇ *They promised to help us and then backed out.* Avevano promesso di aiutarci, ma si sono tirati indietro.
♦ **He backed the car out of the garage.** È uscito in retromarcia dal garage.

to **back up** [bækˈʌp] VERB
<u>appoggiare</u> ◇ *She complained, and her colleagues backed her up.* Ha fatto reclamo e i suoi colleghi l'hanno appoggiata.
♦ **There's no evidence to back up his theory.** Non ci sono prove a sostegno della sua teoria.

backache [ˈbækeɪk] NOUN
il <u>mal di schiena</u> ◇ *I have backache.* Ho mal di schiena.

backbone [ˈbækbəʊn] NOUN
la <u>spina dorsale</u>

to **backfire** [bækˈfaɪəʳ] VERB
<u>avere* effetto contrario</u>

background [ˈbækgraʊnd] NOUN
lo <u>sfondo</u> ◇ *a house in the background* una casa sullo sfondo
♦ **background noise** rumori di fondo
♦ **his family background** il suo ambiente familiare

backhand [ˈbækhænd] NOUN
il <u>rovescio</u> (*tennis*)

backing [ˈbækɪŋ] NOUN
l' <u>appoggio</u> ◇ *They promised their backing.* Hanno garantito il loro appoggio.

backpack [ˈbækpæk] NOUN
lo <u>zaino</u>

backpacker [ˈbækpækəʳ] NOUN
una persona che viaggia con zaino e sacco a pelo

back pay [ˈbækpeɪ] NOUN
gli <u>arretrati</u> MASC PL

backside [ˈbæksaɪd] NOUN
il <u>sedere</u>

backstroke [ˈbækstrəʊk] NOUN
il <u>dorso</u>

backup [ˈbækʌp] NOUN
la <u>riserva</u> ◇ *They've got a generator as an emergency backup.* Hanno un generatore di riserva per le emergenze.
♦ **a backup file** un file di backup

backwards [ˈbækwədz] ADVERB
<u>indietro</u> ◇ *He took a step backwards.* Ha fatto un passo indietro.
♦ **to fall backwards** cadere* ᴱ all'indietro

back yard [bækˈjɑːd] NOUN
[1] il <u>cortile sul retro</u> (*paved*)
[2] il <u>giardino sul retro della casa</u> (*garden*) US

bacon [ˈbeɪkən] NOUN
la <u>pancetta</u> ◇ *bacon and eggs* uova con pancetta

bad [bæd] ADJECTIVE
[1] <u>cattivo</u> ◇ *He's in a bad mood.* È di cattivo umore. ◇ *You bad boy!* Cattivo!
[2] <u>brutto</u> ◇ *bad weather* brutto tempo
[3] <u>grave</u> ◇ *a bad accident* un grave incidente
♦ **to go bad** (*food*) andare* ᴱ a male
♦ **I feel bad about it.** Mi sento un po' in colpa.
♦ **not bad** niente male ◇ *That's not bad at all.*

---

* Verbs followed by this symbol are irregular. See pp.339–364 for further details.

Non è niente male.
+ **to be bad at something** non essere*[E] bravo in qualcosa ◊ *I'm really bad at maths.* Non sono bravo in matematica.
+ **bad language** parolacce FEM PL

badge [bædʒ] NOUN
il distintivo

badly ['bædlı] ADVERB
male ◊ *She behaved badly.* Si è comportata male. ◊ *badly paid* mal pagato
+ **badly wounded** gravemente ferito
+ **He badly needs a rest.** Ha assolutamente bisogno di riposare.

badminton ['bædmıntən] NOUN
il badminton

bad-tempered ['bæd'tempəd] ADJECTIVE
+ **to be bad-tempered (1)** (*always*) avere*[E] un brutto carattere
+ **to be bad-tempered (2)** (*at a particular time*) essere*[E] di malumore

baffle ['bæfl] VERB
lasciare perplesso

bag [bæg] NOUN
la borsa

baggage ['bægıdʒ] NOUN
i bagagli MASC PL
+ **baggage allowance** il peso consentito di bagaglio

baggage reclaim ['bægıdʒrıkleım] NOUN
il ritiro bagagli

baggy ['bægı] ADJECTIVE
sformato (*jumper, trousers*)

bagpipes ['bægpaıps] NOUN PL
la cornamusa SING

bake [beık] VERB
cuocere* al forno (*potatoes, fish*)
+ **to bake a cake** fare* un dolce

baked [beıkt] ADJECTIVE
cotto al forno ◊ *baked potatoes* patate cotte al forno con la buccia

baked beans [beıkt'bi:nz] NOUN PL
i fagioli in salsa rossa

baker ['beıkə'] NOUN
il fornaio

bakery ['beıkərı] NOUN (PL **bakeries**)
la panetteria

baking ['beıkıŋ] ADJECTIVE
+ **It's baking in here!** Qui dentro si muore di caldo!

balance ['bæləns] NOUN
l' equilibrio
+ **to lose one's balance** perdere* l'equilibrio

balanced ['bælənst] ADJECTIVE
equilibrato

balance sheet ['bælənsʃi:t] NOUN
il bilancio

balcony ['bælkənı] NOUN (PL **balconies**)
il terrazzo

bald [bɔ:ld] ADJECTIVE
calvo

ball [bɔ:l] NOUN

⊡ la palla ◊ *Pass the ball to me!* Passami la palla!
② la pallina ◊ *a tennis ball* una pallina da tennis
③ il pallone ◊ *a rugby ball* un pallone da rugby

ballet ['bæleı] NOUN
il balletto ◊ *We went to a ballet.* Siamo andati a vedere un balletto.
+ **ballet lessons** corso di danza classica

ballet dancer ['bæleıdɑ:nsə'] NOUN
il ballerino classico
la ballerina classica

ballet shoes ['bæleıʃu:z] NOUN PL
le scarpette da danza

balloon [bə'lu:n] NOUN
il palloncino ◊ *Lucy was holding a balloon.* Lucy teneva in mano un palloncino.
+ **a hot-air balloon** una mongolfiera

ballpoint pen ['bɔ:lpɔınt'pen] NOUN
la penna a sfera

ballroom dancing ['bɔ:lrum'dɑ:nsıŋ] NOUN
il ballo liscio

ban [bæn] NOUN
see also **ban** VERB
il divieto

to **ban** [bæn] VERB
see also **ban** NOUN
vietare

banana [bə'nɑ:nə] NOUN
la banana ◊ *a banana skin* una buccia di banana

band [bænd] NOUN
⊡ il gruppo ◊ *He plays the guitar in a band.* Suona la chitarra in un gruppo.
② la banda ◊ *The procession was led by a band.* La processione era preceduta da una banda.

bandage ['bændıdʒ] NOUN
see also **bandage** VERB
la fascia (PL le fasce)

to **bandage** ['bændıdʒ] VERB
see also **bandage** NOUN
fasciare

Band-Aid® ['bændeıd] NOUN [US]
il cerotto

bandit ['bændıt] NOUN
il bandito

bang [bæŋ] NOUN
see also **bang** VERB
⊡ lo scoppio ◊ *I heard a loud bang.* Ho sentito un forte scoppio.
② il colpo ◊ *a bang on the head* un colpo sulla testa
+ **bangs** [US] la frangetta SING

to **bang** [bæŋ] VERB
see also **bang** NOUN
sbattere* ◊ *I banged my head.* Ho sbattuto la testa.
+ **to bang on the door** picchiare alla porta

banger ['bæŋə'] NOUN ☞

la <u>salsiccia</u> (PL le salsicce) ◇ *bangers and mash* salsicce e purè di patate

bank [bæŋk] NOUN
  1 la <u>banca</u> (PL le banche) ◇ *The bank is closed.* La banca è chiusa.
  2 la <u>riva</u> ◇ *We walked along the bank.* Abbiamo camminato lungo la riva.

to **bank on** ['bæŋkɔn] VERB
  <u>contare su</u> ◇ *He was banking on a pay rise.* Contava su un aumento. ◇ *I wouldn't bank on it.* Non ci conterei.

bank account ['bæŋkəkaunt] NOUN
  il <u>conto in banca</u>

bank card ['bæŋkɑːd] NOUN
  la <u>carta assegni</u>

banker ['bæŋkə'] NOUN
  il <u>banchiere</u>

bank holiday ['bæŋk'hɔlɪdeɪ] NOUN
  la <u>festa</u> ◇ *Monday's a bank holiday.* Lunedì è festa.
  Le bank holidays sono giorni di festa per banche, aziende ecc. e cadono sempre di lunedì.

banknote ['bæŋknəut] NOUN
  la <u>banconota</u>

bankrupt ['bæŋkrʌpt] ADJECTIVE
  <u>fallito</u>
  ◆ **to go bankrupt** fallire

bar [bɑː'] NOUN
  1 il <u>bar</u> (PL i bar) *(pub)*
  2 il <u>banco</u> (PL i banchi) ◇ *Please order meals at the bar.* Si prega di ordinare le consumazioni al banco.
  ◆ **a bar of chocolate** una tavoletta di cioccolata
  ◆ **a bar of soap** una saponetta

barbaric [bɑː'bærɪk] ADJECTIVE
  <u>barbaro</u>

barbecue ['bɑːbɪkjuː] NOUN
  1 la <u>grigliata all'aperto</u> *(party)*
  2 la <u>griglia</u> *(equipment)*

barber ['bɑːbə'] NOUN
  il <u>barbiere</u>

bar code ['bɑːkəud] NOUN
  il <u>codice a barre</u>

bare [beə'] ADJECTIVE
  <u>nudo</u>

barefoot ['beəfut] ADJECTIVE, ADVERB
  <u>scalzo</u> ◇ *The children go around barefoot.* I bambini vanno in giro scalzi.

barely ['beəlɪ] ADVERB
  <u>a malapena</u> ◇ *I could barely hear what she was saying.* Sentivo a malapena quello che diceva.

bargain ['bɑːgɪn] NOUN
  l' <u>affare</u> MASC ◇ *It was a real bargain!* È stato un vero affare!

barge [bɑːdʒ] NOUN
  il <u>barcone</u>

to **bark** [bɑːk] VERB
  <u>abbaiare</u>

barmaid ['bɑːmeɪd] NOUN
  la <u>barista</u>

barman ['bɑːmən] NOUN (PL **barmen**)
  il <u>barista</u>

barn [bɑːn] NOUN
  il <u>fienile</u>

barrel ['bærəl] NOUN
  1 il <u>barile</u> ◇ *a barrel of beer* un barile di birra
  2 la <u>canna</u> *(of gun)*

barrier ['bærɪə'] NOUN
  la <u>barriera</u>

bartender ['bɑːtendə'] NOUN US
  il <u>barista</u>

base [beɪs] NOUN
  see also **base** VERB
  la <u>base</u>

to **base** [beɪs] VERB
  see also **base** NOUN
  ◆ **to base on** basare su ◇ *The film is based on a play by Shakespeare.* Il film è basato su una commedia di Shakespeare.
  ◆ **I'm based in London.** Vivo a Londra.

baseball ['beɪsbɔːl] NOUN
  il <u>baseball</u>
  ◆ **a baseball cap** un berretto da baseball

basement ['beɪsmənt] NOUN
  il <u>seminterrato</u> ◇ *a basement flat* un appartamento nel seminterrato

to **bash** [bæʃ] VERB
  see also **bash** NOUN
  <u>pestare</u>

bash [bæʃ] NOUN
  see also **bash** VERB
  ◆ **I'll have a bash.** Ci proverò.

basic ['beɪsɪk] ADJECTIVE
  1 <u>fondamentale</u> ◇ *It's one of the basic requirements.* È uno dei requisiti fondamentali.
  2 <u>base</u> MASC, FEM, PL ◇ *It's a basic model.* È un modello base.
  3 <u>modesto</u> ◇ *The accommodation is pretty basic.* L'alloggio è piuttosto modesto.

basically ['beɪsɪklɪ] ADVERB
  <u>fondamentalmente</u>

basics ['beɪsɪks] NOUN PL
  i <u>principi fondamentali</u>

basil ['bæzl] NOUN
  il <u>basilico</u>

basin ['beɪsn] NOUN
  1 la <u>terrina</u> ◇ *Put the sugar and flour in a basin.* Mettete lo zucchero e la farina in una terrina.
  2 il <u>lavandino</u> ◇ *He let the water out of the basin.* Ha fatto uscire l'acqua dal lavandino.

basis ['beɪsɪs] NOUN
  ◆ **on a daily basis** quotidianamente
  ◆ **on a regular basis** regolarmente

basket ['bɑːskɪt] NOUN
  il <u>cestino</u>

basketball ['bɑːskɪtbɔːl] NOUN
  la <u>pallacanestro</u>

---

* Verbs followed by this symbol are irregular. See pp.339–364 for further details.

bass [beɪs] NOUN (PL **basses**)
il basso
+ **double bass** contrabbasso

bass drum [beɪs'drʌm] NOUN
la grancassa

bassoon [bə'suːn] NOUN
il fagotto

bastard ['baːstəd] NOUN
il bastardo

bat [bæt] NOUN
[1] la mazza (for baseball, cricket)
[2] la racchetta (for ping pong)
[3] il pipistrello (animal)

bath [baːθ] NOUN
[1] il bagno ◊ I'll have a bath. Farò un bagno.
+ **a bath towel** un asciugamano da bagno
[2] la vasca da bagno (PL le vasche da bagno)
◊ There's a spider in the bath. C'è un ragno nella vasca da bagno.

bathe [beɪð] VERB
fare* il bagno ◊ It was too cold to bathe. Era troppo freddo per fare il bagno.

bathing suit ['beɪðɪŋsuːt] NOUN US
il costume da bagno

bathroom ['baːθrum] NOUN
il bagno

baths [baːðz] NOUN PL
+ **swimming baths** piscina SING

batter ['bætə'] NOUN
la pastella

battery ['bætərɪ] NOUN (PL **batteries**)
[1] la pila (for torch, toy)
[2] la batteria (in car)

battle ['bætl] NOUN
la battaglia

battleship ['bætlʃɪp] NOUN
la corazzata

bay [beɪ] NOUN
la baia ◊ San Francisco Bay la baia di San Francisco

bay leaf ['beɪliːf] NOUN
la foglia d'alloro

BC [biː'siː] ABBREVIAZIONE (= before Christ)
a.C. (= avanti Cristo)

be [biː] VERB (**is, was, been**)
[1] essere* E ◊ I'm tired. Sono stanco. ◊ I was very happy. Ero molto felice. ◊ You're late. Sei in ritardo. ◊ He is very tall. È molto alto. ◊ Aren't we lucky? Non siamo fortunati? ◊ They are very nice. Sono molto gentili. ◊ They're at home yesterday. Ieri erano in casa. ◊ It's one o'clock. È l'una.
Use **sono** for all times except one o'clock.
◊ It's four o'clock. Sono le quattro. ◊ It's a nice day, isn't it? È una bella giornata, no?
to be + the present participle is often translated by a simple tense in Italian.
◊ Are you coming? Vieni?
[2] fare* ◊ She's a doctor. Fa il medico. ◊ It was cold. Faceva freddo.

fare is used when talking about jobs and the weather.
[3] avere* ◊ I'm not cold. Non ho freddo.
Use **avere** when saying how old you are.
◊ I'm fourteen. Ho quattordici anni. ◊ How old are you? Quanti anni hai?
[4] stare* E ◊ I've never been to Paris. Non sono mai stato a Parigi.
Use **stare** to say what you're doing at the moment, and how you're feeling.
◊ What are you doing? Cosa stai facendo?
◊ How are you? Come stai? ◊ I'm fine. Sto bene.

beach [biːtʃ] NOUN (PL **beaches**)
la spiaggia (PL le spiagge)

bead [biːd] NOUN
la perlina

beak [biːk] NOUN
il becco (PL i becchi)

beam [biːm] NOUN
[1] il raggio ◊ a beam of light un raggio di luce
[2] la trave (of wood)

bean [biːn] NOUN
il fagiolo
+ **beans on toast** fagioli in salsa rossa sopra una fetta di pane tostato
+ **green beans** fagiolini

bean sprouts ['biːnsprauts] NOUN PL
i germogli di soia

bear [beə'] NOUN
see also **bear** VERB
l'orso

to **bear** [beə'] VERB (**bore, borne**)
see also **bear** NOUN
sopportare ◊ I can't bear it! Non lo sopporto! ◊ He bore his sufferings bravely. Ha sopportato con coraggio la sofferenza.
+ **If you would bear with me for a moment...** Se ha la cortesia di attendere un attimo...

beard [bɪəd] NOUN
la barba

bearded ['bɪədɪd] ADJECTIVE
barbuto

beat [biːt] NOUN
see also **beat** VERB
il ritmo

to **beat** [biːt] VERB (**beat, beaten**)
see also **beat** NOUN
battere ◊ We beat them three-nil. Li abbiamo battuti tre a zero. ◊ We were beaten. Siamo stati battuti.
+ **Beat it!** Fila!

to **beat up** [biːt'ʌp] VERB
picchiare

beautiful ['bjuːtɪful] ADJECTIVE
bello MASC (FEM bella, MASC PL belli, FEM PL belle)
◊ The weather was really beautiful. Il tempo è stato proprio bello. ◊ His sisters are beautiful. Le sue sorelle sono belle.
Use **bel** before a masculine noun starting ☞

Verbs followed by the symbol "E" require the auxiliary "essere"

with a consonant.
◇ *Thank you for the beautiful present.*
Grazie del bel regalo.
Use **bell'** before a masculine noun starting
with a vowel.
◇ *a beautiful old watch* un bell'orologio
antico
Use **bello** before a masculine noun starting
with impure s, gn, pn, ps, x, y or z.
◇ *a beautiful sapphire* un bello zaffiro
Use **bei** before a plural masculine noun
starting with a consonant.
◇ *Thanks for the beautiful flowers.* Grazie
dei bei fiori.
Use **begli** before a plural masculine noun
starting with a vowel, or with impure s, gn,
pn, ps, x, y or z.
◇ *He's got beautiful eyes.* Ha begli occhi.

beauty ['bjuːtɪ] NOUN (PL **beauties**)
la bellezza

beauty spot ['bjuːtɪspɒt] NOUN
la località pittoresca (PL le località
pittoresche)

became [bɪ'keɪm] VERB *see* **become**

because [bɪ'kɒz] CONJUNCTION
perché ◇ *I ate it because I was hungry.* L'ho
mangiato perché ero affamato.
+ **because of** a causa di

to **become** [bɪ'kʌm] VERB (**became, become**)
diventare[E] ◇ *He has become a professional
footballer.* È diventato un calciatore
professionista. ◇ *It became increasingly
difficult to cover costs.* È diventato sempre
più difficile far fronte ai costi.

bed [bɛd] NOUN
il letto ◇ *in bed* a letto
+ **to go to bed with somebody** andare*[E] a
letto con qualcuno

bed and breakfast ['bɛdən'brɛkfəst] NOUN
la pensione familiare (*place*)
+ **How much is it for bed and breakfast?**
Quanto costa la camera con prima
colazione?

bedclothes ['bɛdkləʊðz] NOUN PL
+ **the bedclothes** le coperte e le lenzuola

bedding ['bɛdɪŋ] NOUN
+ **the bedding** le coperte e le lenzuola

bedroom ['bɛdrum] NOUN
la camera da letto
+ **a three-bedroom house** una casa con tre
camere da letto

❶ In Italy the size of a house is indicated by
its floor area, as well as by the number of
rooms.

bedsit ['bɛdsɪt] NOUN
il monolocale

bedspread ['bɛdsprɛd] NOUN
il copriletto

bedtime ['bɛdtaɪm] NOUN

+ **Bedtime!** A nanna!
+ **Ten o'clock is my usual bedtime.**
Generalmente vado a letto alle dieci.

bee [biː] NOUN
l'ape FEM

beef [biːf] NOUN
il manzo
+ **roast beef** arrosto di manzo

beefburger ['biːfbɜːgəʳ] NOUN
l'hamburger (PL gli hamburger)

been [biːn] VERB *see* **be**

beer [bɪəʳ] NOUN
la birra

beetle ['biːtl] NOUN
lo scarabeo

beetroot ['biːtruːt] NOUN
la barbabietola

before [bɪ'fɔːʳ] PREPOSITION, CONJUNCTION,
ADVERB
[1] prima ◇ *before Tuesday* prima di
martedì ◇ *Before opening the packet, read
the instructions.* Prima di aprire il pacchetto
leggi le istruzioni.
[2] già ◇ *I've seen this film before.* Questo
film l'ho già visto.

beforehand [bɪ'fɔːhænd] ADVERB
prima

to **beg** [bɛg] VERB
[1] chiedere* l'elemosina ◇ *There were a
lot of people begging.* C'era molta gente che
chiedeva l'elemosina.
[2] pregare ◇ *He begged me to stop.* Mi ha
pregato di smettere.

began [bɪ'gæn] VERB *see* **begin**

beggar ['bɛgəʳ] NOUN
il/la mendicante

to **begin** [bɪ'gɪn] VERB (**began, begun**)
iniziare

Both **essere** and **avere** can be used as
auxiliaries.

◇ *It began to rain.* Ha iniziato a piovere.
◇ *The match began at 10 a.m.* La partita è
iniziata alle dieci del mattino. ◇ *The film has
just begun.* Il film è appena iniziato.

beginner [bɪ'gɪnəʳ] NOUN
il/la principiante

beginning [bɪ'gɪnɪŋ] NOUN
l'inizio
+ **in the beginning** all'inizio

begun [bɪ'gʌn] VERB *see* **begin**

behalf [bɪ'hɑːf] NOUN
+ **on behalf of...** per conto di...

to **behave** [bɪ'heɪv] VERB
comportarsi[E] ◇ *He behaved like an idiot.* Si
è comportato da stupido.
+ **to behave oneself** comportarsi[E] bene
◇ *Did the children behave themselves?* Si
sono comportati bene i bambini?
+ **Behave!** Comportati bene!

behaviour [bɪ'heɪvjəʳ] NOUN (US **behavior**)
il comportamento

* Verbs followed by this symbol are irregular. See pp.339–364 for further details.

B

behind [bɪ'haɪnd] PREPOSITION, ADVERB
see also **behind** NOUN
dietro ◊ *behind the television* dietro il
televisore
+ **to be behind** essere* E ◊ *I'm behind with
my revision.* Sono indietro con il ripasso.

behind [bɪ'haɪnd] NOUN
see also **behind** PREPOSITION, ADVERB
il didietro

beige [beɪʒ] ADJECTIVE
beige MASC, FEM, PL

Belgian ['bɛldʒən] ADJECTIVE
see also **Belgian** NOUN
belga MASC / FEM (MASC PL belgi, FEM PL belghe)

Belgian ['bɛldʒən] NOUN
see also **Belgian** ADJECTIVE
il/la belga
+ **the Belgians** i belgi

Belgium ['bɛldʒəm] NOUN
il Belgio

to **believe** [bɪ'liːv] VERB
credere ◊ *Do you believe in ghosts?* Credi
ai fantasmi?

bell [bɛl] NOUN
[1] il campanello ◊ *I rang the bell, but
nobody came.* Ho suonato il campanello,
ma non è arrivato nessuno.
[2] la campana ◊ *the church bell* la
campana della chiesa
[3] la campanella ◊ *The bell goes at half
past three.* La campanella suona alle tre e
mezza.
[4] il sonaglio ◊ *Our cat has a bell on its
collar.* Il nostro gatto ha un sonaglio al
collare.

belly ['bɛlɪ] NOUN (PL **bellies**)
la pancia (PL le pance)

to **belong** [bɪ'lɔŋ] VERB
[1] essere* E di ◊ *This ring belonged to my
grandmother.* Quest'anello era di mia
nonna. ◊ *Who does it belong to?* Di chi è?
◊ *That belongs to me.* È mio.
[2] far parte ◊ *Do you belong to any clubs?*
Fai parte di qualche club?
+ **Where does this belong?** Dove va questo?

belongings [bɪ'lɔŋɪŋz] NOUN PL
le cose ◊ *I collected my belongings and left.*
Ho raccolto le mie cose e me ne sono andato.
+ **your personal belongings** i suoi effetti
personali

below [bɪ'ləʊ] PREPOSITION, ADVERB
sotto ◊ *ten degrees below freezing* dieci
gradi sotto zero
+ **on the floor below** al piano di sotto

belt [bɛlt] NOUN
la cintura

beltway ['bɛltweɪ] NOUN US
[1] la circonvallazione
[2] l' autostrada (*motorway*)

bench [bɛntʃ] NOUN (PL **benches**)
la panchina

bend [bɛnd] NOUN
see also **bend** VERB
la curva

to **bend** [bɛnd] VERB (**bent, bent**)
see also **bend** NOUN
[1] piegare ◊ *I can't bend my arm.* Non
riesco a piegare il braccio.
[2] curvarsi E ◊ *It bends easily.* Si curva
facilmente.

to **bend down** [bɛnd'daʊn] VERB
chinarsi E ◊ *She bent down to pick a flower.*
Si è chinata a raccogliere un fiore.

to **bend over** [bɛnd'əʊvəʳ] VERB
chinarsi E

beneath [bɪ'niːθ] PREPOSITION
sotto

benefit ['bɛnɪfɪt] NOUN
see also **benefit** VERB
il beneficio ◊ *the benefits of this treatment* i
benefici di questa terapia
+ **unemployment benefit** l'indennità di
disoccupazione
+ **state benefits** sussidi statali
+ **to live on benefit** vivere* di sussidi

to **benefit** ['bɛnɪfɪt] VERB
see also **benefit** NOUN
+ **He'll benefit from the change.** Il
cambiamento gli farà bene.
+ **The scheme benefits children.** Il
programma si rivolge ai bambini.

bent [bɛnt] VERB *see* **bend**

bent [bɛnt] ADJECTIVE
curvo

beret ['bɛreɪ] NOUN
il berretto

berserk [bə'sɜːk] ADJECTIVE
+ **to go berserk** andare* E in bestia

berth [bɜːθ] NOUN
la cuccetta

beside [bɪ'saɪd] PREPOSITION
accanto ◊ *beside the television* accanto al
televisore
+ **to be beside oneself** essere* E fuori di sé
◊ *He was beside himself.* Era fuori di sé.
+ **That's beside the point.** Questo non c'entra
affatto.

besides [bɪ'saɪdz] ADVERB
inoltre ◊ *Besides, it's too expensive.* E
inoltre è troppo caro.
+ **...and much more besides.** ...e altro ancora.

best [bɛst] ADJECTIVE, ADVERB
[1] migliore ◊ *He's the best player in the
team.* È il migliore giocatore della squadra.
◊ *the best artist of his generation* il miglior
artista della sua generazione
[2] meglio ◊ *Emma sings best.* È Emma che
canta meglio.
+ **to do one's best** fare* del proprio meglio
◊ *It's not perfect, but I did my best.* Non è
perfetto, ma ho fatto del mio meglio.
+ **to make the best of it** accontentarsi E ☞

◇ *We'll have to make the best of it.* Dovremo accontentarci.

best man [best'mæn] NOUN (PL **best men**)
il testimone dello sposo

bet [bet] NOUN
see also **bet** VERB
la scommessa

to **bet** [bet] VERB (**bet, bet**)
see also **bet** NOUN
scommettere*
♦ **I bet you...** Scommetti...? ◇ *I bet you he won't come.* Scommetti che non viene?

to **betray** [bɪ'treɪ] VERB
tradire

better ['betə'] ADJECTIVE, ADVERB
1 migliore ◇ *This one's better than that one.* Questo è migliore di quello.
2 meglio ◇ *That's better!* Così va meglio! ◇ *Are you feeling better now?* Ti senti meglio ora?
♦ **better still** meglio ancora
♦ **to get better (1)** (*weather*) migliorare
♦ **to get better (2)** (*person*) rimettersi E
♦ **better off** più benestante ◇ *They're better off than us.* Sono più benestanti di noi.
had better is usually translated by the conditional of dovere.
◇ *You had better do it straight away.* Dovresti farlo subito. ◇ *I'd better go home.* Dovrei proprio tornare a casa.

betting shop ['betɪŋʃɒp] NOUN
la sala corse (PL le sale corse)

between [bɪ'twiːn] PREPOSITION
tra ◇ *between fifteen and twenty minutes* tra i quindici e i venti minuti

to **beware** [bɪ'wɛə'] VERB
♦ **Beware!** Attento!
♦ **to beware of...** stare* attento a...

to **bewilder** [bɪ'wɪldə'] VERB
sconcertare

beyond [bɪ'jɒnd] PREPOSITION, ADVERB
1 oltre ◇ *I heard footsteps beyond the door.* Ho sentito dei passi oltre la porta.
2 più in là ◇ *the wheat fields and the mountains beyond...* i campi di grano e le montagne più in là...
♦ **beyond belief** incredibile
♦ **beyond repair** irreparabile

biased ['baɪəst] ADJECTIVE
parziale

Bible ['baɪbl] NOUN
la Bibbia

bicycle ['baɪsɪkl] NOUN
la bicicletta

bifocals [baɪ'fəʊklz] NOUN PL
gli occhiali bifocali

big [bɪg] ADJECTIVE
1 grande ◇ *a big house* una casa grande
2 grosso ◇ *Taiwan's biggest companies* le più grosse aziende di Taiwan
♦ **my big brother** il mio fratello maggiore

♦ **Big deal!** Capirai!
♦ **It's no big deal.** Non è importante.

bigheaded ['bɪg'hedɪd] ADJECTIVE
♦ **to be bigheaded** darsi E un sacco di arie

bike [baɪk] NOUN
la bici (PL le bici)

bikini [bɪ'kiːnɪ] NOUN
il bikini (PL i bikini)

bilingual [baɪ'lɪŋgwəl] ADJECTIVE
bilingue

bill [bɪl] NOUN
1 il conto ◇ *Can we have the bill, please?* Il conto, per favore.
2 la bolletta ◇ *the gas bill* la bolletta del gas
3 la banconota US ◇ *a five-dollar bill* una banconota da cinque dollari

billiards ['bɪljədz] NOUN
il biliardo

billion ['bɪljən] NOUN
il miliardo

bin [bɪn] NOUN
il bidone

bingo ['bɪŋgəʊ] NOUN
la tombola

binoculars [bɪ'nɒkjʊləz] NOUN PL
il binocolo SING
♦ **a pair of binoculars** un binocolo

biochemistry [baɪə'kemɪstrɪ] NOUN
la biochimica

biography [baɪ'ɒgrəfɪ] NOUN (PL **biographies**)
la biografia

biology [baɪ'ɒlədʒɪ] NOUN
la biologia

bird [bɜːd] NOUN
l' uccello

bird-watching ['bɜːdwɒtʃɪŋ] NOUN
il bird-watching

Biro ® ['baɪərəʊ] NOUN
la biro ®

birth [bɜːθ] NOUN
la nascita ◇ *date of birth* data di nascita

birth certificate ['bɜːθsətɪfɪkɪt] NOUN
il certificato di nascita

birth control ['bɜːθkəntrəʊl] NOUN
il controllo delle nascite

birthday ['bɜːθdeɪ] NOUN
il compleanno ◇ *a birthday cake* una torta di compleanno ◇ *a birthday party* una festa di compleanno
♦ **a birthday card** un biglietto d'auguri

birth rate ['bɜːθreɪt] NOUN
l' indice di natalità MASC

biscuit ['bɪskɪt] NOUN
il biscotto

bishop ['bɪʃəp] NOUN
il vescovo

bit [bɪt] VERB *see* **bite**

bit [bɪt] NOUN
♦ **a bit (1)** un pezzo ◇ *a bit of cake* un pezzo di torta ◇ *Would you like another bit?* Ne vuoi

un altro pezzo?
* **a bit (2)** un po' ◊ *a bit of music* un po' di musica ◊ *He's a bit mad.* È un po' matto.
* **It's a bit of a nuisance.** È un po' una scocciatura.
* **Wait a bit!** Aspetta un attimo!
* **to fall to bits** cadere* E a pezzi
* **to take something to bits** smontare qualcosa
* **bit by bit** a poco a poco

bitch [bɪtʃ] NOUN (PL **bitches**)
⟦1⟧ la cagna ◊ *a bitch with three puppies* una cagna con tre cuccioli
⟦2⟧ la stronza (*rude*) ◊ *She's a bitch!* È una stronza!

to **bite** [baɪt] VERB (**bit, bitten**)
see also **bite** NOUN
⟦1⟧ mordere* ◊ *The dog bit him.* Il cane lo ha morso. ◊ *My dog's never bitten anyone.* Il mio cane non ha mai morso nessuno.
⟦2⟧ pungere* ◊ *I got bitten by mosquitoes.* Mi hanno punto le zanzare.
* **to bite one's nails** mangiarsi E le unghie

bite [baɪt] NOUN
see also **bite** VERB
⟦1⟧ la puntura ◊ *lots of mosquito bites* molte punture di zanzara
⟦2⟧ il morso ◊ *a dog bite* il morso di un cane
* **to have a bite to eat** mangiare un boccone

bitten ['bɪtn] VERB *see* **bite**

bitter ['bɪtə'] ADJECTIVE
see also **bitter** NOUN
amaro ◊ *It tastes bitter.* Ha un sapore amaro.
* **It's bitter today.** Oggi si gela.

bitter ['bɪtə'] NOUN
see also **bitter** ADJECTIVE
la birra rossa

black [blæk] ADJECTIVE
nero ◊ *She's black.* È nera. ◊ *black coffee* caffè nero

blackberry ['blækbərɪ] NOUN (PL **blackberries**)
la mora di rovo

blackbird ['blækbɜːd] NOUN
il merlo

blackboard ['blækbɔːd] NOUN
la lavagna

blackcurrant ['blæk'kʌrənt] NOUN
il ribes nero SING ◊ *blackcurrant jam* marmellata di ribes nero
* **blackcurrants** il ribes nero SING

blackmail ['blækmeɪl] NOUN
see also **blackmail** VERB
il ricatto

to **blackmail** ['blækmeɪl] VERB
see also **blackmail** NOUN
ricattare

black market [blæk'mɑːkɪt] NOUN
il mercato nero

blackout ['blækaut] NOUN

il black-out (PL i black-out)
* **to have a blackout** (*faint*) perdere* conoscenza

black pudding [blæk'pudɪŋ] NOUN
il sanguinaccio

blacksmith ['blæksmɪθ] NOUN
il fabbro

black spot ['blækspɒt] NOUN
luogo famigerato per gli incidenti (*on road*)

blade [bleɪd] NOUN
la lama

to **blame** [bleɪm] VERB
dare* la colpa a ◊ *Don't blame me!* Non dare la colpa a me!

blank [blæŋk] ADJECTIVE
see also **blank** NOUN
⟦1⟧ bianco ◊ *a blank sheet of paper* un foglio di carta bianca
⟦2⟧ vergine ◊ *a blank cassette* una cassetta vergine
* **My mind went blank.** Ho avuto un vuoto di memoria.

blank [blæŋk] NOUN
see also **blank** ADJECTIVE
lo spazio in bianco ◊ *Fill in the blanks.* Riempi gli spazi in bianco.

blank cheque [blæŋk'tʃɛk] NOUN
l' assegno in bianco

blanket ['blæŋkɪt] NOUN
la coperta

blast [blɑːst] NOUN
* **a bomb blast** un'esplosione

blatant ['bleɪtənt] ADJECTIVE
palese ◊ *a blatant lie* una bugia palese

blaze [bleɪz] NOUN
l' incendio

blazer ['bleɪzə'] NOUN
il blazer (PL i blazer)

bleach [bliːtʃ] NOUN (PL **bleaches**)
la candeggina

bleached [bliːtʃt] ADJECTIVE
* **bleached hair** capelli ossigenati MASC PL

bleak [bliːk] ADJECTIVE
⟦1⟧ poco promettente ◊ *The future looks bleak.* Il futuro sembra poco promettente.
⟦2⟧ desolato ◊ *a bleak area* un'area desolata

to **bleed** [bliːd] VERB (**bled, bled**)
sanguinare ◊ *My hand is bleeding.* Mi sanguina una mano.
* **to bleed to death** morire* E dissanguato

bleeper ['bliːpə'] NOUN
il cercapersone (PL i cercapersone)

blender ['blɛndə'] NOUN
il frullatore

to **bless** [blɛs] VERB
benedire ◊ *The priest blessed the children.* Il prete ha benedetto i bambini.
* **Bless you!** (*after sneezing*) Salute!

blew [bluː] VERB *see* **blow**

blind [blaɪnd] ADJECTIVE ☞

see also **blind** NOUN
cieco

blind [blaɪnd] NOUN
see also **blind** ADJECTIVE
l' avvolgibile

blindfold ['blaɪndfəuld] NOUN
see also **blindfold** VERB
la benda per occhi

to **blindfold** ['blaɪndfəuld] VERB
see also **blindfold** NOUN
bendare

to **blink** [blɪŋk] VERB
strizzare gli occhi

bliss [blɪs] NOUN
♦ **It was bliss!** È stato fantastico!

blister ['blɪstə'] NOUN
la vescica (PL le vesciche)

blizzard ['blɪzəd] NOUN
la bufera di neve

blob [blɒb] NOUN
la goccia (PL le gocce) ◇ *a blob of glue* una
goccia di colla

block [blɒk] NOUN
see also **block** VERB
[1] il palazzo ◇ *He lives in our block.* Abita
nel nostro palazzo.
[2] l' isolato ◇ *He walked around the block
three times.* Ha fatto tre volte il giro
dell'isolato.
♦ **a block of flats** un caseggiato

to **block** [blɒk] VERB
see also **block** NOUN
bloccare

blockage ['blɒkɪdʒ] NOUN
l' ingorgo (PL gli ingorghi)

block letters [blɒk'lɛtəz] NOUN PL
lo stampatello SING

bloke [bləuk] NOUN
il tipo ◇ *He's a really nice bloke.* È un tipo
veramente simpatico.

blonde [blɒnd] ADJECTIVE
biondo

blood [blʌd] NOUN
il sangue

blood pressure ['blʌdpreʃə'] NOUN
la pressione del sangue

blood sports ['blʌdspɔ:ts] NOUN PL
gli sport cruenti

blood test ['blʌdtest] NOUN
l' analisi del sangue (PL le analisi del sangue)

bloody ['blʌdɪ] ADJECTIVE
maledetto ◇ *that bloody television* quel
maledetto televisore
♦ **bloody difficult** maledettamente difficile
♦ **Bloody hell!** Porca miseria!

blouse [blauz] NOUN
la camicetta

blow [bləu] NOUN
see also **blow** VERB
il colpo

to **blow** [bləu] VERB (blew, blown)

see also **blow** NOUN
soffiare ◇ *A cold wind was blowing.*
Soffiava un vento freddo.
♦ **They were one-all when the whistle blew.**
Erano uno a uno quando l'arbitro ha
fischiato la fine.
♦ **to blow one's nose** soffiarsi E il naso ◇ *He
blew his nose loudly.* Si è soffiato il naso
rumorosamente.

to **blow out** [bləu'aut] VERB
spegnere* ◇ *Blow out the candles!* Spegni
le candeline! ◇ *He has blown out the
candles.* Ha spento le candeline.

to **blow up** [bləu'ʌp] VERB
[1] far saltare ◇ *They blew up a plane.*
Hanno fatto saltare un aereo.
[2] saltare E in aria ◇ *The house blew up.* La
casa è saltata in aria.
[3] gonfiare ◇ *We've blown up the
balloons.* Abbiamo gonfiato i palloncini.

blow-dry ['bləudraɪ] NOUN
la messa in piega con il fon

blown [bləun] VERB *see* **blow**

blue [blu:] ADJECTIVE
azzurro ◇ *a blue dress* un vestito azzurro
♦ **navy blue** blu MASC, FEM, PL
♦ **a blue film** un film porno
♦ **out of the blue** all'improvviso

blues [blu:z] NOUN PL
♦ **the blues** il blues

to **bluff** [blʌf] VERB
see also **bluff** NOUN
bluffare

bluff [blʌf] NOUN
see also **bluff** VERB
il bluff (PL i bluff)

blunder ['blʌndə'] NOUN
l' errore MASC

blunt [blʌnt] ADJECTIVE
[1] brusco ◇ *He was blunt with me.* È stato
brusco con me.
[2] spuntato ◇ *The knife was blunt.* Il
coltello era spuntato.

to **blush** [blʌʃ] VERB
arrossire E

board [bɔ:d] NOUN
[1] l' asse FEM (*plank*)
[2] la lavagna ◇ *Write it on the board.*
Scrivilo sulla lavagna.
[3] la bacheca (PL le bacheche) ◇ *There's a
notice on the board.* C'è un avviso in
bacheca.
[4] la scacchiera ◇ *There were six pawns on
the board.* C'erano sei pedoni sulla
scacchiera.
♦ **a chopping board** un tagliere
♦ **on board** a bordo
♦ **full board** pensione completa

boarder ['bɔ:də'] NOUN
il/la collegiale

board game ['bɔ:dgeɪm] NOUN

* Verbs followed by this symbol are irregular. See pp.339–364 for further details.

English ~ Italian

B

il gioco da tavolo (PL i giochi da tavolo)

boarding card ['bɔːdɪŋkɑːd] NOUN
la carta d'imbarco

boarding school ['bɔːdɪŋskuːl] NOUN
il collegio

boast [bəust] VERB
vantarsi[E]
♦ **to boast about something** vantarsi[E] di qualcosa

boat [bəut] NOUN
la barca (PL le barche)

body ['bɔdɪ] NOUN (PL **bodies**)
il corpo

bodybuilding ['bɔdɪ'bɪldɪŋ] NOUN
il culturismo

bodyguard ['bɔdɪgɑːd] NOUN
la guardia del corpo

bog [bɔg] NOUN
la palude

boil [bɔɪl] NOUN
see also **boil** VERB
il foruncolo

boil [bɔɪl] VERB
see also **boil** NOUN
1 far bollire ♦ Boil some water. Fai bollire dell'acqua.
2 bollire ♦ The water's boiling. L'acqua bolle.

boil over [bɔɪl'əuvə'] VERB
traboccare[E]

boiled [bɔɪld] ADJECTIVE
bollito ♦ boiled rice riso bollito
♦ **boiled potatoes** patate lesse
♦ **a boiled egg** un uovo alla coque

boiling ['bɔɪlɪŋ] ADJECTIVE
♦ **It's boiling in here!** Qui dentro si soffoca!
♦ **a boiling hot day** una giornata torrida

bolt [bəult] NOUN
1 il catenaccio ♦ There was a heavy bolt on the door. C'era un pesante catenaccio alla porta.
2 il bullone ♦ nuts and bolts dadi e bulloni

bomb [bɔm] NOUN
see also **bomb** VERB
la bomba

bomb [bɔm] VERB
see also **bomb** NOUN
bombardare

bomber ['bɔmə'] NOUN
1 il bombardiere (plane)
2 il dinamitardo
la dinamitarda
(person)

bombing ['bɔmɪŋ] NOUN
il bombardamento

bond [bɔnd] NOUN
il legame

bone [bəun] NOUN
1 l' osso (PL FEM le ossa)
The plural of **osso** is feminine when the bone is human.

♦ a broken bone un osso rotto
2 la lisca (PL le lische) (di pesce)

bone dry [bəun'draɪ] ADJECTIVE
asciuttissimo

bonfire ['bɔnfaɪə'] NOUN
il falò (PL i falò)

bonnet ['bɔnɪt] NOUN
il cofano (of car)

bonus ['bəunəs] NOUN (PL **bonuses**)
la gratifica (PL le gratifiche)

book [buk] NOUN
see also **book** VERB
il libro

to **book** [buk] VERB
see also **book** NOUN
prenotare

bookcase ['bukkeɪs] NOUN
la libreria

booklet ['buklɪt] NOUN
l' opuscolo

bookmark ['bukmɑːk] NOUN
il bookmark (PL i bookmark)

bookshelf ['bukʃelf] NOUN (PL **bookshelves**)
la mensola per libri

bookshop ['bukʃɔp] NOUN
la libreria

to **boost** [buːst] VERB
dare* una spinta a ♦ They're trying to boost the economy. Stanno cercando di dare una spinta all'economia.
♦ **to boost somebody's morale** sollevare il morale di qualcuno ♦ The win boosted the team's morale. La vittoria ha sollevato il morale della squadra.

boot [buːt] NOUN
1 il cofano (of car)
2 lo stivale (knee-high boot)
3 lo stivaletto (ankle boot)
4 lo scarpone (hiking boot)
♦ **football boots** scarpe da calcio

booze [buːz] NOUN
gli alcolici

border ['bɔːdə'] NOUN
il confine

bore [bɔː'] VERB see **bear**

bore [bɔː'] NOUN
la noia ♦ What a bore! Che noia!
♦ **John's a bore.** John è noioso.

bored [bɔːd] ADJECTIVE
annoiato
♦ **to get bored** annoiarsi[E]

boredom ['bɔːdəm] NOUN
la noia

boring ['bɔːrɪŋ] ADJECTIVE
noioso

born [bɔːn] ADJECTIVE
nato
♦ **to be born** nascere*[E] ♦ I was born in 1982. Sono nato nel 1982.

borne [bɔːn] VERB see **bear**

to **borrow** ['bɔrəu] VERB ☞

Verbs followed by the symbol "E" require the auxiliary "essere"

+ **Can I borrow your pen?** Mi presti la penna?
+ **to borrow something from somebody** farsi
  ^E prestare qualcosa da qualcuno

Bosnia ['bɔznɪə] NOUN
la Bosnia

Bosnian ['bɔznɪən] ADJECTIVE
bosniaco

boss [bɔs] NOUN (PL **bosses**)
il capo

to **boss around** [bɔsə'raund] VERB
+ **to boss somebody around** comandare* a
  bacchetta qualcuno

bossy ['bɔsɪ] ADJECTIVE
prepotente

both [bəuθ] ADJECTIVE, PRONOUN, ADVERB
tutt'e due ◇ *We both went.* Ci siamo andati
tutt'e due.
+ **Emma and Jane both went.** Sono andate sia
  Emma che Jane.

to **bother** ['bɔðə'] VERB
see also **bother** NOUN
⑴ preoccupare ◇ *What's bothering you?*
Cosa c'è che ti preoccupa?
⑵ disturbare ◇ *I'm sorry to bother you.*
Scusa se ti disturbo.
+ **Don't bother!** Lascia perdere!
+ **to bother to do something** darsi^E la pena di
  fare qualcosa ◇ *He didn't bother to tell me
  about it.* Non si è dato la pena di farmelo
  sapere.

bother ['bɔðə'] NOUN
see also **bother** VERB
la seccatura ◇ *It was too much bother to
report it to the police.* Sarebbe stata una
gran seccatura denunciare il fatto alla
polizia.
+ **Sliced bread is less bother.** Il pane già
  affettato è più comodo.
+ **No bother.** Non c'è problema.

bottle ['bɔtl] NOUN
la bottiglia

bottle bank ['bɔtlbæŋk] NOUN
il contenitore per la raccolta del vetro

bottle-opener ['bɔtləupnə'] NOUN
l'apribottiglie MASC (PL gli apribottiglie)

bottom ['bɔtəm] NOUN
see also **bottom** ADJECTIVE
⑴ il fondo ◇ *at the bottom of the page* in
fondo alla pagina
+ **to be bottom of** essere* ^E l'ultimo di ◇ *He
  was always bottom of the class.* Era sempre
  l'ultimo della classe.
⑵ il sedere ◇ *Do these trousers make my
bottom look big?* Questi pantaloni mi fanno
il sedere grosso?

bottom ['bɔtəm] ADJECTIVE
see also **bottom** NOUN
inferiore ◇ *the bottom shelf* il ripiano
inferiore

bought [bɔːt] VERB *see* **buy**

to **bounce** [bauns] VERB

rimbalzare ◇ *The ball bounced.* La palla è
rimbalzata.

bouncer ['baunsə'] NOUN
il buttafuori (PL i buttafuori)

bound [baund] ADJECTIVE
+ **He's bound to fail.** Fallirà sicuramente.
+ **There are bound to be price rises.** Ci sarà
  sicuramente un aumento dei prezzi.

boundary ['baundrɪ] NOUN (PL **boundaries**)
il confine

bow [bəu] NOUN
see also **bow** VERB
⑴ il fiocco (PL i fiocchi)
+ **to tie a bow** fare* un fiocco
⑵ l'arco (PL gli archi) ◇ *a bow and arrows*
arco e frecce

to **bow** [bau] VERB
see also **bow** NOUN
fare* un inchino

bowels ['bauəlz] NOUN PL
l'intestino SING

bowl [bəul] NOUN
see also **bowl** VERB
la scodella

to **bowl** [bəul] VERB
see also **bowl** NOUN
lanciare la palla (*in cricket*)

bowler ['bəulə'] NOUN
il lanciatore (*in cricket*)

bowling ['bəulɪŋ] NOUN
il bowling
+ **to go bowling** andare* ^E a giocare a bowling
+ **a bowling alley** una pista da bowling

bowls [bəulz] NOUN SING
le bocce ◇ *He play bowls.* Gioca a bocce.

bow tie [bəu'taɪ] NOUN
la cravatta a farfalla

box [bɔks] NOUN (PL **boxes**)
⑴ la scatola ◇ *a box of matches* una
scatola di fiammiferi
⑵ la casella ◇ *Tick the appropriate box.*
Barrare l'apposita casella.

boxer ['bɔksə'] NOUN
il pugile

boxer shorts ['bɔksəfɔːts] NOUN PL
i boxer

boxing ['bɔksɪŋ] NOUN
il pugilato

Boxing Day ['bɔksɪŋdeɪ] NOUN
+ **on Boxing Day** il ventisei dicembre

> **ⓘ //Boxing Day** è il primo giorno
> infrasettimanale dopo Natale; prende il
> nome dall'usanza di donare pacchi regalo
> natalizi a fornitori, dipendenti ecc.

box office ['bɔksɔfɪs] NOUN
la biglietteria

boy [bɔɪ] NOUN
⑴ il ragazzo ◇ *a boy of fifteen* un ragazzo di
quindici anni

---

* Verbs followed by this symbol are irregular. See pp.339–364 for further details.

B

[2] il bambino ◇ *a boy of seven* un bambino di sette anni

[3] il maschio ◇ *She has two boys and a girl.* Ha due maschi e una femmina.

● **a baby boy** un maschietto

boyfriend ['bɔɪfrend] NOUN
il ragazzo

bra [brɑ:] NOUN
il reggiseno

brace [breɪs] NOUN
l' apparecchio *(for teeth)* ◇ *Richard wears a brace.* Richard porta l'apparecchio.

bracelet ['breɪslɪt] NOUN
il braccialetto

brackets ['brækɪts] NOUN PL
le parentesi

● **in brackets** tra parentesi

brain [breɪn] NOUN
il cervello

brainy ['breɪnɪ] ADJECTIVE
intelligente

brake [breɪk] NOUN
see also **brake** VERB
il freno ◇ *The brakes failed.* I freni non hanno funzionato.

brake [breɪk] VERB
see also **brake** NOUN
frenare

brake light ['breɪklaɪt] NOUN
lo stop (PL gli stop)

branch [brɑ:ntʃ] NOUN (PL **branches**)
[1] il ramo *(of tree)*
[2] la filiale *(of bank)*

brand [brænd] NOUN
la marca (PL le marche) ◇ *a famous brand* una marca famosa

brand name ['brændneɪm] NOUN
la marca (PL le marche)

brand-new ['brænd'nju:] ADJECTIVE
nuovo di zecca

brandy ['brændɪ] NOUN (PL **brandies**)
il brandy (PL i brandy)

brass [brɑ:s] NOUN
l' ottone MASC

brass band [brɑ:s'bænd] NOUN
la banda

brat [bræt] NOUN
il moccioso ◇ *He's a spoiled brat.* È un moccioso viziato.

brave [breɪv] ADJECTIVE
coraggioso

Brazil [brə'zɪl] NOUN
il Brasile

bread [bred] NOUN
il pane ◇ *brown bread* pane integrale

break [breɪk] NOUN
see also **break** VERB
[1] la pausa ◇ *Let's take a break.* Facciamo una pausa.
[2] la ricreazione *(at school)*

● **the Christmas break** le vacanze di Natale

● **Give me a break!** Ma per carità!

to **break** [breɪk] VERB (**broke, broken**)
see also **break** NOUN
[1] rompere* ◇ *Careful, you'll break something!* Attento, o romperai qualcosa! ◇ *I've broken a glass.* Ho rotto un bicchiere.
[2] rompersi E ◇ *Careful, it'll break!* Stai attento che si rompe!

● **to break a promise** mancare a una promessa

● **to break a record** battere un record ◇ *He broke the world record.* Ha battuto il record mondiale.

to **break down** [breɪk'daʊn] VERB
rimanere* E in panne

to **break in** [breɪk'ɪn] VERB
entrare* E ◇ *The thief had broken in through a window.* Il ladro era entrato forzando una finestra.

to **break into** [breɪk'ɪntu] VERB
entrare* E in ◇ *Thieves broke into the house.* Dei ladri sono entrati in casa.

to **break off** [breɪk'ɔf] VERB
rompere*

to **break out** [breɪk'aʊt] VERB
scoppiare E *(war, fight)*

● **to break out in a rash** coprirsi E di brufoli

to **break up** [breɪk'ʌp] VERB
[1] disperdere* ◇ *Police broke up the demonstration.* La polizia ha disperso i dimostranti.
[2] finire E ◇ *More and more marriages break up.* Sono sempre più numerosi i matrimoni che finiscono.
[3] lasciarsi E ◇ *Richard and Marie have broken up.* Richard e Marie si sono lasciati.

● **to break up a fight** sedare una lite

● **We break up next Wednesday.** Mercoledì cominciano le vacanze.

breakdown ['breɪkdaʊn] NOUN
[1] la fine ◇ *the breakdown of their marriage* la fine del loro matrimonio
[2] l' esaurimento ◇ *He had a breakdown because of the stress.* Ha avuto un esaurimento dovuto allo stress.
[3] l' analisi FEM ◇ *a breakdown of the costs* un'analisi dei costi
[4] la panne

● **to have a breakdown** rimanere* E in panne ◇ *We had a breakdown near Leeds.* Siamo rimasti in panne vicino a Leeds.

● **a breakdown truck** un carro attrezzi

breakfast ['brekfəst] NOUN
la colazione

break-in ['breɪkɪn] NOUN
il furto con scasso

breast [brest] NOUN
il seno *(woman's)*

● **chicken breast** il petto di pollo

to **breast-feed** ['brestfi:d] VERB (**breast-fed, breast-fed**)
allattare

Verbs followed by the symbol "E" require the auxiliary "essere"

breaststroke ['brɛststrəuk] NOUN
la rana

breath [brɛθ] NOUN
1 l' alito ◊ *He's got bad breath.* Ha l'alito cattivo.
2 il fiato ◊ *I'm out of breath.* Sono senza fiato.

to **breathe** [bri:ð] VERB
respirare

to **breathe in** [bri:ð'ɪn] VERB
inspirare

to **breathe out** [bri:ð'aut] VERB
espirare

to **breed** [bri:d] VERB (**bred, bred**)
see also **breed** NOUN
riprodursi⁵ ◊ *They rarely breed in captivity.* In cattività si riproducono raramente.
♦ **to breed dogs** allevare cani

breed [bri:d] NOUN
see also **breed** VERB
la razza

breeze [bri:z] NOUN
la brezza

brewery ['bru:ərɪ] NOUN (PL **breweries**)
la fabbrica di birra (PL le fabbriche di birra)

bribe [braɪb] NOUN
see also **bribe** VERB
la bustarella

to **bribe** [braɪb] VERB
see also **bribe** NOUN
corrompere*

brick [brɪk] NOUN
il mattone

bricklayer ['brɪkleɪə'] NOUN
il muratore

bride [braɪd] NOUN
la sposa

bridegroom ['braɪdgru:m] NOUN
lo sposo

bridesmaid ['braɪdzmeɪd] NOUN
la damigella d'onore

bridge [brɪdʒ] NOUN
1 il ponte ◊ *a suspension bridge* un ponte sospeso
2 il bridge ◊ *He plays bridge.* Gioca a bridge.

brief [bri:f] ADJECTIVE
breve

briefcase ['bri:fkeɪs] NOUN
la valigetta ventiquattr'ore

briefly ['bri:flɪ] ADVERB
brevemente

briefs [bri:fs] NOUN PL
gli slip
♦ **a pair of briefs** un paio di slip

bright [braɪt] ADJECTIVE
1 vivace ◊ *a bright colour* un colore vivace
♦ **bright red** rosso vivo
2 sveglio ◊ *He's not very bright.* Non è molto sveglio.

brilliant ['brɪljənt] ADJECTIVE

1 fantastico ◊ *It's a brilliant idea!* È un'idea fantastica!
♦ **We had a brilliant time!** Ci siamo divertiti moltissimo!
2 geniale ◊ *a brilliant scientist* uno scienziato geniale

to **bring** [brɪŋ] VERB (**brought, brought**)
portare ◊ *Bring warm clothes.* Porta vestiti pesanti. ◊ *Can I bring a friend?* Posso portare un amico? ◊ *I've brought you a present.* Ti ho portato un regalo.

to **bring about** [brɪŋə'baut] VERB
causare

to **bring back** [brɪŋ'bæk] VERB
riportare ◊ *He's taken your drill. He'll bring it back tomorrow.* Ha preso il trapano. Lo riporterà domani.
♦ **That song brings back memories.** Quella canzone mi fa tornare in mente tanti ricordi.

to **bring forward** [brɪŋ'fɔ:wəd] VERB
anticipare ◊ *The meeting was brought forward.* La riunione è stata anticipata.

to **bring up** [brɪŋ'ʌp] VERB
allevare ◊ *She brought up five children on her own.* Ha allevato cinque figli da sola.

Britain ['brɪtən] NOUN
la Gran Bretagna

British ['brɪtɪʃ] ADJECTIVE
britannico
♦ **the British** i britannici

> ❶ *Italians often refer to the British as "gli inglesi".*

♦ **the British Isles** le Isole Britanniche

broad [brɔ:d] ADJECTIVE
largo ◊ *He's got broad shoulders.* Ha le spalle larghe.
♦ **in broad daylight** in pieno giorno

broad bean [brɔ:d'bi:n] NOUN
la fava

broadcast ['brɔ:dkɑ:st] NOUN
see also **broadcast** VERB
la trasmissione

to **broadcast** ['brɔ:dkɑ:st] VERB (**broadcast, broadcast**)
see also **broadcast** NOUN
trasmettere*
♦ **to broadcast live** trasmettere* in diretta

broad-minded ['brɔ:d'maɪndɪd] ADJECTIVE
di larghe vedute

broccoli ['brɒkəlɪ] NOUN SING
i broccoli MASC PL ◊ *The broccoli is delicious.* I broccoli sono buonissimi.

brochure ['brəuʃuə'] NOUN
il dépliant (PL i dépliant)

to **broil** [brɔɪl] VERB [US]
cuocere* a fuoco vivo

broke [brəuk] VERB *see* **break**

broke [brəuk] ADJECTIVE

---

* Verbs followed by this symbol are irregular. See pp.339–364 for further details.

B

▸ **to be broke** essere*^E al verde
broken ['brəukn] VERB *see* **break**
broken ['brəukn] ADJECTIVE
rotto ◇ *a broken glass* un vetro rotto
bronchitis [brɔŋ'kaɪtɪs] NOUN
la bronchite
bronze [brɔnz] NOUN
il bronzo ◇ *the bronze medal* la medaglia di
bronzo
brooch [brəutʃ] NOUN (PL **brooches**)
la spilla
broom [brum] NOUN
la scopa
brother ['brʌðə'] NOUN
il fratello
brother-in-law ['brʌðərɪnlɔ:] NOUN (PL
brothers-in-law)
il cognato
brought [brɔ:t] VERB *see* **bring**
brown [braun] ADJECTIVE
1 marrone (*shoes, clothes, eyes*)
2 castano (*hair*)
3 abbronzato (*tanned*)
▸ **brown bread** pane integrale
▸ **brown sugar** zucchero di canna
Brownie ['brauni] NOUN
la giovane esploratrice
browse [brauz] VERB
curiosare (*in bookshop*)
▸ **to browse on the Internet** fare* una ricerca
in Internet
browser ['brauzə'] NOUN
il browser (PL i browser)
bruise [bru:z] NOUN
il livido
brush [brʌʃ] NOUN (PL **brushes**)
see also **brush** VERB
1 la spazzola (*for hair*)
2 il pennello (*for painting*)
brush [brʌʃ] VERB
see also **brush** NOUN
spazzolare
▸ **to brush one's hair** spazzolarsi^E i capelli
▸ **to brush one's teeth** lavarsi^E i denti
▸ **to brush up one's English** rispolverare il
proprio inglese
Brussels ['brʌslz] NOUN
la Bruxelles
Brussels sprouts [brʌslz'sprauts] NOUN PL
i cavoletti di Bruxelles
brutal ['bru:tl] ADJECTIVE
brutale
BSc NOUN (= *Bachelor of Science*)
la laurea in scienze
BSE [bi:es'i:] NOUN (= *bovine spongiform
encephalopathy*)
l' encefalite bovina spongiforme
bubble ['bʌbl] NOUN
la bolla
bubble bath ['bʌblba:θ] NOUN
il bagnoschiuma (PL i bagnoschiuma)

bubble gum ['bʌblgʌm] NOUN
la gomma da masticare
bucket ['bʌkɪt] NOUN
il secchio
buckle ['bʌkl] NOUN
la fibbia
Buddhism ['budɪzəm] NOUN
il buddismo
Buddhist ['budɪst] ADJECTIVE
buddista
buddy ['bʌdɪ] NOUN (PL **buddies**) US
l' amico
budget ['bʌdʒɪt] NOUN
see also **budget** ADJECTIVE, VERB
il budget (PL i budget) ◇ *the defence budget*
il budget per la Difesa
▸ **the Budget** la legge finanziaria
▸ **to be on a tight budget** avere* un budget
limitato
budget ['bʌdʒɪt] ADJECTIVE
see also **budget** NOUN, VERB
▸ **budget prices** i prezzi ridotti
to **budget** ['bʌdʒɪt] VERB
see also **budget** NOUN, ADJECTIVE
gestire le proprie finanze ◇ *I'm learning
how to budget.* Sto imparando a gestire le
mie finanze.
budgie ['bʌdʒɪ] NOUN
il pappagallino
buffet ['bufeɪ] NOUN
il buffet (PL i buffet) ◇ *a cold buffet* un buffet
freddo
▸ **a buffet lunch** un buffet
buffet car ['bufeɪka:'] NOUN
il servizio ristoro
bug [bʌg] NOUN
1 l' insetto (*insect*)
2 il virus (PL i virus) ◇ *There's a bug going
round.* C'è in giro un virus.
▸ **a stomach bug** una gastroenterite
3 il baco (PL i bachi) (*in computer*)
bugged [bʌgd] ADJECTIVE
▸ **The room was bugged.** C'erano delle
microspie nella stanza.
to **build** [bɪld] VERB (**built, built**)
costruire ◇ *They're going to build houses
here.* Qui costruiranno delle case.
to **build up** [bɪld'ʌp] VERB
1 mettere* insieme ◇ *He has built up a
huge collection of stamps.* Ha messo
insieme una vasta collezione di francobolli.
2 accumularsi^E ◇ *Debts are building up.*
Si stanno accumulando i debiti.
builder ['bɪldə'] NOUN
1 l' imprenditore edile MASC (*boss*)
2 il muratore (*worker*)
building ['bɪldɪŋ] NOUN
l' edificio
building society ['bɪldɪŋsəsaɪətɪ] NOUN
la società immobiliare e finanziaria

> ❶ *Le* **building societies**, *oltre ad essere società immobiliari, forniscono diversi servizi bancari.*

built [bɪlt] VERB *see* **build**

bulb [bʌlb] NOUN
　[1] la lampadina ◊ *I'll change the bulb.* Cambierò la lampadina.
　[2] il bulbo (*of plant*)

bull [bul] NOUN
　il toro

bullet ['bulɪt] NOUN
　la pallottola

bulletin board ['bulɪtɪnbɔːd] NOUN
　la bacheca elettronica (PL le bacheche elettroniche)

bullfighting ['bulfaɪtɪŋ] NOUN
　la corrida

bullied ['bulɪd] VERB *see* **bully**

bullring ['bulrɪŋ] NOUN
　l' arena

bully ['bulɪ] NOUN (PL **bullies**)
　see also **bully** VERB
　il/la prepotente ◊ *He's a big bully.* È un grande prepotente.

to **bully** ['bulɪ] VERB (**bullied, bullied**)
　see also **bully** NOUN
　fare* il prepotente con

bum [bʌm] NOUN
　il sedere

bum bag ['bʌmbæg] NOUN
　il marsupio

bump [bʌmp] NOUN
　see also **bump** VERB
　[1] il bernoccolo ◊ *I've got a bump on my forehead.* Ho un bernoccolo sulla fronte.
　[2] la scossa ◊ *We felt a sudden bump.* Abbiamo sentito una scossa improvvisa.

to **bump** [bʌmp] VERB
　see also **bump** NOUN
　sbattere* ◊ *I bumped my head.* Ho sbattuto la testa.

to **bump into** [bʌmp'ɪntu] VERB
　incontrare per caso ◊ *I bumped into Paul yesterday.* Ho incontrato per caso Paul, ieri.

bumper ['bʌmpə'] NOUN
　il paraurti (PL i paraurti)

bumpy ['bʌmpɪ] ADJECTIVE
　accidentato

bun [bʌn] NOUN
　il panino dolce

bunch [bʌntʃ] NOUN (PL **bunches**)
　◆ **a bunch of flowers** un mazzo di fiori
　◆ **a bunch of grapes** un grappolo d'uva
　◆ **a bunch of bananas** un casco di banane

bunches ['bʌntʃəz] NOUN PL
　le codine

bungalow ['bʌŋgələu] NOUN
　la villetta ad un piano

bunk [bʌŋk] NOUN
　il letto a castello

burger ['bəːgə'] NOUN
　l' hamburger (PL gli hamburger)

burglar ['bəːglə'] NOUN
　lo scassinatore
　la scassinatrice

burglar alarm ['bəːglərəlɑːm] NOUN
　l' antifurto (PL gli antifurto)

to **burglarize** ['bəːgləraɪz] VERB US
　svaligiare

burglary ['bəːglərɪ] NOUN (PL **burglaries**)
　il furto con scasso

to **burgle** ['bəːgl] VERB
　svaligiare

buried ['berɪd] VERB *see* **bury**

burn [bəːn] NOUN
　see also **burn** VERB
　la bruciatura

to **burn** [bəːn] VERB (**burned** or **burnt, burned** or **burnt**)
　see also **burn** NOUN
　bruciare ◊ *I burned the cake.* Ho bruciato la torta.
　◆ **to burn oneself** bruciarsi [E]
　◆ **I've burned my hand.** Mi sono bruciato la mano.

to **burn down** [bəːn'daun] VERB
　◆ **The factory burned down.** La fabbrica è andata distrutta in un incendio.

to **burst** [bəːst] VERB (**burst, burst**)
　scoppiare [E] ◊ *The balloon burst.* Il palloncino è scoppiato.
　◆ **to burst out laughing** scoppiare [E] a ridere
　◆ **to burst into tears** scoppiare [E] in lacrime
　◆ **to burst into flames** prendere* fuoco

to **bury** ['berɪ] VERB (**buried, buried**)
　seppellire*

bus [bʌs] NOUN (PL **buses**)
　l' autobus (PL gli autobus) ◊ *the bus stop* la fermata dell'autobus
　◆ **the school bus** il pulmino della scuola

bush [buʃ] NOUN (PL **bushes**)
　il cespuglio

business ['bɪznɪs] NOUN (PL **businesses**)
　[1] l' impresa ◊ *He's got his own business.* Ha un'impresa in proprio.
　[2] gli affari MASC PL ◊ *He's away on business.* È via per affari. ◊ *It's none of my business.* Non sono affari miei.
　◆ **a business trip** un viaggio d'affari

businessman ['bɪznɪsmən] NOUN (PL **businessmen**)
　[1] l' uomo d'affari (gli uomini d'affari) (*in general*)
　[2] l' imprenditore MASC (*entrepreneur*)

businesswoman ['bɪznɪswumən] NOUN (PL **businesswomen**)
　[1] la donna d'affari (*in general*)
　[2] l' imprenditrice FEM (*entrepreneur*)

busker ['bʌskə'] NOUN
　il suonatore ambulante
　la suonatrice ambulante

---

* Verbs followed by this symbol are irregular. See pp.339–364 for further details.

bus pass ['bʌspɑːs] NOUN
la tessera ridotta dell'autobus

bus shelter ['bʌsʃeltə'] NOUN
la pensilina

bus station ['bʌssteɪʃən] NOUN
la stazione delle corriere

bust [bʌst] NOUN
il petto

busy ['bɪzɪ] ADJECTIVE
1 impegnato ◇ She's a very busy woman.
È una donna molto impegnata.
2 intenso ◇ I'd had a busy day and was
tired. Avevo avuto una giornata intensa ed
ero stanco.
3 animato ◇ The Strand is one of
London's busiest streets. Lo Strand è una
delle vie più animate di Londra.

busy signal ['bɪzɪsɪgnl] NOUN US
il segnale di occupato

but [bʌt] CONJUNCTION
ma ◇ strange but true strano ma vero
◆ all but tutti tranne ◇ They won all but two of
their matches. Hanno vinto tutte le partite
tranne due.
◆ the last but one il penultimo

butcher ['butʃə'] NOUN
il macellaio

butcher's ['butʃəz] NOUN
la macelleria

butter ['bʌtə'] NOUN
il burro

butterfly ['bʌtəflaɪ] NOUN (PL **butterflies**)
la farfalla

buttocks ['bʌtəks] NOUN PL
le natiche

button ['bʌtn] NOUN
1 il bottone
2 il distintivo US

to **buy** [baɪ] VERB (**bought, bought**)
see also **buy** NOUN
comprare ◇ I've bought my mother some
flowers. Ho comprato dei fiori per mia
madre.

buy [baɪ] NOUN
see also **buy** VERB
l' affare ◇ It was a good buy. È stato un buon
affare.

by [baɪ] PREPOSITION
1 da ◇ The thieves were caught by the
police. I ladri sono stati catturati dalla
polizia.
2 di ◇ a painting by Picasso un quadro di
Picasso
3 in ◇ by car in macchina
4 vicino a ◇ Where's the bank? – It's by the
post office. Dov'è la banca? – È vicino
all'ufficio postale.
5 entro ◇ We have to be there by 4 o'clock.
Dobbiamo essere lì entro le 4.
◆ by the time quando ◇ By the time I got
there it was too late. Quando sono arrivato
era troppo tardi. ◇ It'll be ready by the time
you get back. Sarà pronto per quando
ritorni.
◆ That's fine by me. Per me va benissimo.
◆ all by himself da solo ◇ I did it all by myself.
L'ho fatto da solo.
◆ by the way a proposito

bye ['baɪ] EXCLAMATION
ciao

bypass ['baɪpɑːs] NOUN (PL **bypasses**)
la circonvallazione

B

C

cab [kæb] NOUN
il taxi (PL i taxi)

cabbage ['kæbɪdʒ] NOUN
il cavolo

cabin ['kæbɪn] NOUN
la cabina (on ship)

cabin crew ['kæbɪnkru:] NOUN
l'equipaggio di bordo

cabinet ['kæbɪnɪt] NOUN
l'armadietto ◇ a bathroom cabinet un
armadietto del bagno
• **the Cabinet** il Consiglio dei Ministri

cable ['keɪbl] NOUN
il cavo

cable car ['keɪblkɑ:'] NOUN
la funivia

cable television ['keɪbl'telɪvɪʒən] NOUN
la televisione via cavo

cadet [kə'dɛt] NOUN
• **a police cadet** un allievo poliziotto
• **a cadet officer** un allievo ufficiale

café ['kæfeɪ] NOUN
il caffè (PL i caffè)

cafeteria [kæfɪ'tɪərɪə] NOUN
1 la mensa (in school, hospital)
2 il self-service (PL i self-service) (in store)

cage [keɪdʒ] NOUN
la gabbia

cagoule [kə'gu:l] NOUN
il K-Way ® (PL i K-Way)

cake [keɪk] NOUN
1 la torta (large) ◇ a chocolate cake una
torta al cioccolato
2 la pasta (small) ◇ a coffee and a cake un
caffè e una pasta
• **It's a piece of cake.** È un gioco da ragazzi.

to **calculate** ['kælkjuleɪt] VERB
calcolare ◇ They are calculating the likely
cost. Stanno calcolando quanto possa
costare.

calculation [kælkju'leɪʃən] NOUN
il calcolo

calculator ['kælkjuleɪtə'] NOUN
la calcolatrice

calendar ['kæləndə'] NOUN
il calendario

calf [kɑ:f] NOUN (PL **calves**)
1 il vitello ◇ a cow and her calf una mucca
e il suo vitello
2 il polpaccio (of leg)

call [kɔ:l] NOUN
see also **call** VERB
1 la chiamata ◇ Thanks for your call.
Grazie per la chiamata.
2 la visita ◇ He decided to pay a call on
Tom. Ha deciso di far visita a Tom.
• **a phone call** una telefonata
• **to be on call** (doctor) essere* E reperibile

to **call** [kɔ:l] VERB

see also **call** NOUN
1 chiamare ◇ We called the police.
Abbiamo chiamato la polizia.
• **to be called** chiamarsi E ◇ What's she
called? Come si chiama?
2 telefonare ◇ I'll tell him you called. Gli
dirò che hai telefonato.

to **call back** [kɔ:l'bæk] VERB
1 richiamare ◇ Can I call you back? Ti
posso richiamare?
2 ripassare E ◇ I'll call back later. Ripasso
più tardi.

to **call for** [kɔ:lfə:'] VERB
1 passare E a prendere ◇ Shall I call for
you at seven thirty? Passo a prenderti alle
sette e mezzo?
2 richiedere* ◇ This job calls for strong
nerves. Questo lavoro richiede nervi saldi.

to **call in** [kɔ:l'ɪn] VERB
passare E ◇ I'll call in at the office later.
Passerò più tardi in ufficio.

to **call off** [kɔ:l'ɔf] VERB
annullare ◇ The match was called off. La
partita è stata annullata.

to **call on** [kɔ:lɔn] VERB
invitare ◇ He was called on to give a speech.
Fu invitato a fare un discorso.

call box ['kɔ:lbɔks] NOUN (PL **call boxes**)
la cabina telefonica

call centre ['kɔ:lsentə'] NOUN
il call centre (PL i call centre)

calm [kɑ:m] ADJECTIVE
calmo

to **calm down** [kɑ:m'daun] VERB
1 calmarsi E ◇ Calm down! Calmati!
2 calmare ◇ He calmed her down. L'ha
calmata.

Calor gas ® ['kælərgæs] NOUN
il liquigas ®

calorie ['kælərɪ] NOUN
la caloria

calves [kɑ:vz] NOUN see **calf**

camcorder ['kæmkɔ:də'] NOUN
la videocamera

came [keɪm] VERB see **come**

camel ['kæməl] NOUN
1 il cammello (with two humps)
2 il dromedario (with one hump)

camera ['kæmərə] NOUN
1 la macchina fotografica (for photos)
2 la cinepresa (for filming, TV)

cameraman ['kæmərəmæn] NOUN (PL
cameramen)
il cameraman (PL i cameraman)

to **camp** [kæmp] VERB
see also **camp** NOUN
accamparsi E
• **to go camping** andare* E in campeggio
◇ We went camping in Cornwall. Siamo

andati in campeggio in Cornovaglia.

camp [kæmp] NOUN
see also **camp** VERB
[1] il campeggio ◇ *a summer camp* un campeggio estivo
♦ **a camp bed** una brandina
[2] il campo ◇ *a refugee camp* un campo profughi

campaign [kæm'peɪn] NOUN
see also **campaign** VERB
la campagna ◇ *an advertising campaign* una campagna pubblicitaria

campaign [kæm'peɪn] VERB
see also **campaign** NOUN
fare* una campagna ◇ *They are campaigning for a change in the law.* Stanno facendo una campagna per cambiare la legge.

camper ['kæmpə'] NOUN
il campeggiatore
la campeggiatrice

camper van ['kæmpəvæn] NOUN
il camper (PL i camper)

camping ['kæmpɪŋ] NOUN
il campeggio ◇ *I like camping.* Mi piace il campeggio.

camping gas ® ['kæmpɪŋgæs] NOUN
il butano

campsite ['kæmpsaɪt] NOUN
il campeggio ◇ *It's a nice campsite by the sea.* È un bel campeggio sul mare.

campus ['kæmpəs] NOUN (PL **campuses**)
il campus (PL i campus)

can [kæn] VERB (**could**)
see also **can** NOUN, **could** VERB
[1] potere (*be able, be allowed to*) ◇ *Can I use your phone?* Posso usare il telefono? ◇ *I'll do it as soon as I can.* Lo farò appena posso. ◇ *I can't do that.* Non posso farlo. ◇ *That can't be true!* Non può essere vero! ◇ *Our company cannot be held responsible for this.* La nostra ditta non può essere ritenuta responsabile di questo. ◇ *You can come to the party, can't you?* Puoi venire alla festa, vero?
can *is sometimes not translated.*
◇ *I can't hear you.* Non ti sento. ◇ *I can't remember.* Non ricordo. ◇ *Can you speak French?* Parli francese?
[2] sapere* (*know how to*) ◇ *I can swim.* So nuotare. ◇ *He can't drive.* Non sa guidare.

can [kæn] NOUN
see also **can** VERB
il barattolo (*tin*) ◇ *a can of peas* un barattolo di piselli
♦ **a can of beer** una lattina di birra

Canada ['kænədə] NOUN
il Canada

Canadian [kə'neɪdɪən] NOUN
see also **Canadian** ADJECTIVE
il/la canadese

Canadian [kə'neɪdɪən] ADJECTIVE
see also **Canadian** NOUN
canadese

canal [kə'næl] NOUN
il canale

Canaries [kə'neərɪz] NOUN PL
♦ **the Canaries** le Canarie

canary [kə'neərɪ] NOUN (PL **canaries**)
il canarino

to **cancel** ['kænsəl] VERB
[1] annullare ◇ *They cancelled their booking at the last moment.* Hanno annullato la prenotazione all'ultimo momento.
[2] disdire* ◇ *I had to cancel my appointment.* Ho dovuto disdire l'appuntamento.
[3] cancellare ◇ *Our flight was cancelled.* Il nostro volo è stato cancellato.
[4] sopprimere* ◇ *The train has been cancelled.* Il treno è stato soppresso.

cancellation [kænsə'leɪʃən] NOUN
[1] la disdetta (*of appointment*)
[2] l' annullamento (*of order, booking*)
[3] la cancellazione (*of flight*)
[4] la soppressione (*of train*)

Cancer ['kænsə'] NOUN
Cancro ◇ *I'm Cancer.* Sono del Cancro.

cancer ['kænsə'] NOUN
il cancro ◇ *He's got cancer.* Ha il cancro.

candidate ['kændɪdeɪt] NOUN
il candidato
la candidata

candle ['kændl] NOUN
[1] la candela ◇ *He lit a candle.* Ha acceso una candela.
[2] la candelina ◇ *a cake with fifteen candles* una torta con quindici candeline

candy ['kændɪ] NOUN US (PL **candies**)
[1] la caramella (*sweet*)
[2] i dolciumi (*confectionery*)

candyfloss ['kændɪflɒs] NOUN
lo zucchero filato

cannabis ['kænəbɪs] NOUN
la canapa indiana

canned [kænd] ADJECTIVE
in scatola (*food*)

cannot ['kænɒt] VERB = **can not**

to **canoe** [kə'nu:] VERB
see also **canoe** NOUN
andare*E in canoa ◇ *On holiday we canoed and swam.* In vacanza siamo andati in canoa e abbiamo nuotato.
♦ **We went canoeing.** Siamo andati in canoa.

canoe [kə'nu:] NOUN
see also **canoe** VERB
la canoa

canoeing [kə'nu:ɪŋ] NOUN
il canottaggio ◇ *I like canoeing.* Mi piace il canottaggio.

can opener ['kænəupnə'] NOUN ☞

C

l' apriscatole (PL gli apriscatole)

can't [kɑ:nt] VERB see **can**

canteen [kæn'ti:n] NOUN
la mensa ◇ I don't eat in the canteen. Non mangio in mensa.
*Be careful not to translate **canteen** by **cantina**.*

to **canter** ['kæntə'] VERB
andare* E a piccolo galoppo

canvas ['kænvəs] NOUN (PL **canvases**)
la tela

cap [kæp] NOUN
1 il tappo ◇ Please put the cap back on the toothpaste. Rimetti il tappo al dentifricio, per favore.
2 il berretto (with peak)
◆ This is his second cap for Scotland. È la seconda volta che veste la maglia della nazionale scozzese.

capable ['keɪpəbl] ADJECTIVE
capace ◇ They realized he was capable of murder. Capirono che era capace di uccidere.
◆ I think she's capable of achieving much more. Penso che sia in grado di ottenere molto di più.

capacity [kə'pæsɪtɪ] NOUN (PL **capacities**)
la capacità ◇ The tank has a 40-litre capacity. Il serbatoio ha una capacità di 40 litri.
◆ to have a capacity for hard work essere* E un gran lavoratore
◆ to work at full capacity lavorare a pieno ritmo
◆ to be filled to capacity essere* E pieno ◇ The auditorium was filled to capacity. La sala era piena.

cape [keɪp] NOUN
il capo ◇ Cape Horn capo Horn

capital ['kæpɪtl] NOUN
1 la capitale ◇ Cardiff is the capital of Wales. Cardiff è la capitale del Galles.
2 la maiuscola (letter) ◇ with a capital C con la C maiuscola
◆ in capitals in stampatello

capitalism ['kæpɪtəlɪzəm] NOUN
il capitalismo

capital punishment ['kæpɪtl'pʌnɪʃmənt] NOUN
la pena capitale

Capricorn ['kæprɪkɔ:n] NOUN
il Capricorno ◇ I'm Capricorn. Sono del Capricorno.

to **capsize** [kæp'saɪz] VERB
capovolgersi E ◇ The boat capsized. La barca si è capovolta.

captain ['kæptɪn] NOUN
il capitano

caption ['kæpʃən] NOUN
la didascalia

to **capture** ['kæptʃə'] VERB

catturare

car [kɑ:'] NOUN
1 la macchina ◇ We went by car. Siamo andati in macchina.
◆ a car bomb un'autobomba
◆ a car crash un incidente stradale
◆ a car ferry un traghetto
◆ car hire l'autonoleggio MASC
◆ a car park un parcheggio
◆ a car phone un telefonino per auto
◆ car rental l'autonoleggio MASC
◆ car radio autoradio
◆ a car wash un lavaggio auto
◆ a car boot sale un mercatino dell'usato

ⓘ / car boot sales sono mercatini dell'usato dove la merce viene esposta nei bagagliai aperti delle macchine.

2 la carrozza (carriage)
◆ the dining car la carrozza ristorante

caramel ['kærəməl] NOUN
la caramella gommosa

caravan ['kærəvæn] NOUN
la roulotte (PL le roulotte) ◇ a caravan site un campeggio per roulotte

card [kɑ:d] NOUN
1 il biglietto (greetings card) ◇ I'd like to send him a card for his birthday. Vorrei spedirgli un biglietto per il suo compleanno.
2 la cartolina ◇ I sent all my friends cards from New York. Ho mandato una cartolina da New York a tutti i miei amici.
3 la carta ◇ a card game un gioco di carte
◆ a credit card una carta di credito
◆ a membership card una tessera

cardboard ['kɑ:dbɔ:d] NOUN
il cartone ◇ a cardboard box una scatola di cartone

cardigan ['kɑ:dɪgən] NOUN
il cardigan (PL i cardigan)

cardphone ['kɑ:dfəun] NOUN
il telefono a scheda

care [keə'] NOUN
see also **care** VERB
la cura ◇ with care con cura
◆ children in care bambini sotto la custodia dello stato
◆ to take care of occuparsi E di ◇ I take care of the children on Saturdays. Io mi occupo dei bambini di sabato.
◆ Take care! (1) (be careful) Stai attento!
◆ Take care! (2) (look after yourself) Stammi bene!

to **care** [keə'] VERB
see also **care** NOUN
*care is often translated by **importare**, which is an impersonal verb. This means that in Italian you say, 'it matters to me' rather than 'I care about it.'*
◇ I don't care! Non mi importa! ◇ Of course

---

* Verbs followed by this symbol are irregular. See pp.339–364 for further details.

I care about him. Certo che m'importa di lui.
◇ *Who cares?* Chi se ne importa?
• **They don't care about their image.** Non si
curano della loro immagine.

care for [kɛəˈfɔːˈ] VERB
[1] voler bene a (*love*) ◇ *I still care a lot for
you.* Ti voglio ancora tanto bene.
[2] prendersi E cura di (*look after*) ◇ *They'll
employ a nurse to care for her.*
Assumeranno un'infermiera che si prenderà
cura di lei.

career [kəˈrɪəˈ] NOUN
la carriera ◇ *She had a successful career in
journalism.* Ha fatto una brillante carriera
come giornalista.

careers adviser [kəˈrɪəzədvaɪzəˈ] NOUN
il/la consulente d'orientamento
professionale

careful [ˈkɛəful] ADJECTIVE
attento ◇ *Be careful!* Sta' attento!

carefully [ˈkɛəfəlɪ] ADVERB
[1] accuratamente ◇ *She carefully avoided
talking about it.* Ha evitato accuratamente di
parlarne.
[2] attentamente ◇ *Think carefully!* Pensaci
attentamente!
[3] con prudenza ◇ *Drive carefully!* Guida
con prudenza.

careless [ˈkɛəlɪs] ADJECTIVE
[1] sbadato (*person*) ◇ *She's very careless.*
È molto sbadata.
[2] fatto con poco impegno (*work*)
• **a careless driver** un guidatore distratto
• **a careless mistake** un errore di distrazione

caretaker [ˈkɛəteɪkəˈ] NOUN
il custode (*of building*)
• **a school caretaker** un bidello

cargo [ˈkɑːgəʊ] NOUN (PL **cargoes**)
il carico (PL i carichi)

Caribbean [kærɪˈbiːən] ADJECTIVE
see also **Caribbean** NOUN
caraibico

Caribbean [kærɪˈbiːən] NOUN
see also **Caribbean** ADJECTIVE
• **the Caribbean** i Caraibi ◇ *We're going to the
Caribbean.* Andremo ai Caraibi.

caring [ˈkɛərɪŋ] ADJECTIVE
premuroso (*person*)
• **the caring professions**

❶ Per **caring professions** si intendono le
professioni in campo sociale o medico.

carnation [kɑːˈneɪʃən] NOUN
il garofano

carnival [ˈkɑːnɪvl] NOUN

❶ Il **carnival** è una festa con musica e balli e
non corrisponde al carnevale italiano. Il
"London Carnival" viene celebrato d'estate.

carol [ˈkærəl] NOUN
• **a Christmas carol** un canto natalizio

carpenter [ˈkɑːpɪntəˈ] NOUN
il carpentiere

carpentry [ˈkɑːpɪntrɪ] NOUN
la carpenteria

carpet [ˈkɑːpɪt] NOUN
[1] la moquette (PL le moquette) (*fitted*)
[2] il tappeto ◇ *a Persian carpet* un tappeto
persiano

carriage [ˈkærɪdʒ] NOUN
la carrozza

carrier bag [ˈkærɪəbæg] NOUN
la borsa di plastica

carrot [ˈkærət] NOUN
la carota

to carry [ˈkærɪ] VERB (**carried, carried**)
[1] portare ◇ *I'll carry your bag.* Porto io la
tua borsa.
[2] trasportare ◇ *A plane carrying 100
passengers crashed last week.* La scorsa
settimana è caduto un aereo che trasportava
100 passeggeri.

to carry on [kærɪˈɔn] VERB
continuare ◇ *She carried on talking.*
Continuò a parlare.
• **Carry on!** Va avanti! ◇ *Am I boring you? –
No, carry on!* Ti annoio? – No, va' avanti!

to carry out [kærɪˈaut] VERB
[1] eseguire ◇ *Make sure that he carries out
my orders.* Assicurati che esegua i miei
ordini.
[2] mettere* in pratica ◇ *I don't believe he'll
carry out his threat.* Non penso che metterà
in pratica la sua minaccia.

carrycot [ˈkærɪkɔt] NOUN
il porte-enfant (PL i porte-enfant)

cart [kɑːt] NOUN
see also **cart** VERB
[1] il carro ◇ *a horse and cart* un cavallo e
un carro
[2] il carrello US

to cart [kɑːt] VERB
see also **cart** NOUN
trascinare

carton [ˈkɑːtən] NOUN
il cartone (*of milk, fruit juice*)

cartoon [kɑːˈtuːn] NOUN
[1] il cartone animato (*film*)
[2] la vignetta (*in newspaper*)
• **a strip cartoon** un fumetto

cartridge [ˈkɑːtrɪdʒ] NOUN
la cartuccia (PL le cartucce)

to carve [kɑːv] VERB
tagliare ◇ *Dad carved the roast.* Il papà ha
tagliato l'arrosto.
• **a carved oak chair** una sedia di quercia
intagliata

case [keɪs] NOUN
[1] la valigia (PL le valigie *or* le valige) ◇ *I've
packed my case.* Ho fatto la valigia.

2 la cassa ◇ *a case of wine* una cassa di vini

3 il caso ◇ *in some cases* in alcuni casi ◇ *in any case* in ogni caso ◇ *in case of emergency* in caso di emergenza ◇ *The police are investigating the case.* La polizia sta indagando sul caso.

♦ **There's a case for banning smoking in public places.** Ci sono ottime ragioni per vietare il fumo nei luoghi pubblici.

♦ **just in case** per sicurezza ◇ *Take some money, just in case.* Prendi un po' di soldi per sicurezza.

♦ **in case it rains** caso mai dovesse piovere

♦ **a case in point** un tipico esempio

♦ **If this is the case...** Se è così...

cash [kæʃ] NOUN
i soldi ◇ *I'm a bit short of cash.* Sono un po' a corto di soldi.

♦ **in cash** in contanti ◇ *£200 in cash* 200 sterline in contanti

♦ **to pay cash** pagare in contanti

cash card [ˈkæʃkɑːd] NOUN
il tesserino per i prelievi automatici

cash desk [ˈkæʃdesk] NOUN
la cassa

cash dispenser [ˈkæʃdɪspensəˈ] NOUN
lo sportello automatico

cashew nut [kæˈʃuːnʌt] NOUN
l' anacardio

cash flow [ˈkæʃfləu] NOUN
la liquidità (PL le liquidità)

cashier [kæˈʃɪəˈ] NOUN
il cassiere
la cassiera

cashmere [ˈkæʃmɪəˈ] NOUN
il cashmere ◇ *a cashmere jumper* un maglione di cashmere

cash register [ˈkæʃredʒɪstəˈ] NOUN
il registratore di cassa

casino [kəˈsiːnəu] NOUN (PL **casinos**)
il casinò (PL i casinò)

casserole [ˈkæsərəul] NOUN
la casseruola ◇ *chicken casserole* pollo in casseruola

♦ **to make a casserole** fare* uno spezzatino

♦ **a casserole dish** una casseruola

cassette [kæˈset] NOUN
la cassetta

♦ **a cassette player** un riproduttore a cassette

♦ **a cassette recorder** un registratore a cassette

cast [kɑːst] NOUN
il cast (PL i cast) ◇ *After the play we met the cast.* Dopo la commedia abbiamo incontrato il cast.

castle [ˈkɑːsl] NOUN
il castello

casual [ˈkæʒjul] ADJECTIVE
1 sportivo ◇ *I prefer casual clothes.* Preferisco i vestiti sportivi.

2 noncurante ◇ *a casual attitude* un atteggiamento noncurante

3 poco importante ◇ *Before meeting him she'd had one or two casual affairs.* Prima di incontrarlo aveva avuto un paio di storie poco importanti.

4 saltuario ◇ *It's just a casual job.* È solo un lavoro saltuario.

♦ **a casual remark** un'osservazione buttata là

casually [ˈkæʒjulɪ] ADVERB

♦ **to dress casually** vestirsi ᴱ sportivo

casualty [ˈkæʒjultɪ] NOUN (PL **casualties**)
1 il pronto soccorso (*ward*)

2 il ferito (*injured person*) ◇ *There are no reports of casualties.* Non è stato segnalato nessun ferito.

3 la vittima ◇ *The casualties include a young boy killed by shellfire.* Tra le vittime c'è un ragazzo colpito in un bombardamento.

cat [kæt] NOUN
il gatto
la gatta

catalogue [ˈkætəlɔg] NOUN
il catalogo (PL i cataloghi)

catalytic converter [kætəˈlɪtɪkkənˈvɜːtəˈ] NOUN
la marmitta catalitica (PL le marmitte catalitiche)

catastrophe [kəˈtæstrəfɪ] NOUN
la catastrofe

to **catch** [kætʃ] VERB (**caught, caught**)
1 catturare ◇ *They caught the thief.* Hanno catturato il ladro.

2 prendere* ◇ *We caught the last train.* Abbiamo preso l'ultimo treno.

♦ **to catch a cold** prendere* il raffreddore

3 afferrare ◇ *I didn't catch his name.* Non ho afferrato il suo nome.

4 sorprendere* ◇ *He caught her stealing.* L'ha sorpresa a rubare.

to **catch up** [kætʃˈʌp] VERB
1 rimettersi* ᴱ in pari ◇ *I've got to catch up on my work.* Devo rimettermi in pari col lavoro.

2 raggiungere* ◇ *She caught me up.* Mi ha raggiunto.

catching [ˈkætʃɪŋ] ADJECTIVE
contagioso ◇ *Don't worry, it's not catching!* Non preoccuparti, non è contagioso!

catering [ˈkeɪtərɪŋ] NOUN
il servizio ristorazione

cathedral [kəˈθiːdrəl] NOUN
la cattedrale

Catholic [ˈkæθəlɪk] ADJECTIVE
see also **Catholic** NOUN
cattolico

Catholic [ˈkæθəlɪk] NOUN
see also **Catholic** ADJECTIVE
il cattolico (PL i cattolici)
la cattolica (PL le cattoliche)

* Verbs followed by this symbol are irregular. See pp.339–364 for further details.

◇ *I'm a Catholic.* Sono cattolico.

cattle ['kætl] NOUN PL
il bestiame

caught [kɔːt] VERB *see* **catch**

cauliflower ['kɔliflauə'] NOUN
il cavolfiore

cause [kɔːz] NOUN
see also **cause** VERB
la causa

cause [kɔːz] VERB
see also **cause** NOUN
causare

cautious ['kɔːʃəs] ADJECTIVE
cauto

cautiously ['kɔːʃəslɪ] ADVERB
con cautela

cave [keɪv] NOUN
la grotta

caviar ['kævɪɑː'] NOUN
il caviale

CCTV [siːsiːtiːˈviː] NOUN (= *closed circuit television*)
la televisione a circuito chiuso

CD [siːˈdiː] NOUN
il CD (PL i CD)

CD player [siːˈdiːpleɪə'] NOUN
il lettore CD

CD-ROM [siːdiːˈrɔm] NOUN
il CD-ROM (PL i CD-ROM)

ceasefire ['siːsfaɪə'] NOUN
il cessate il fuoco (PL i cessate il fuoco)

ceiling ['siːlɪŋ] NOUN
il soffitto

celebrate ['selɪbreɪt] VERB
festeggiare ◇ *I celebrated my birthday last week.* Ho festeggiato il mio compleanno la settimana scorsa.

celebrity [sɪˈlebrɪtɪ] NOUN (PL **celebrities**)
la celebrità (PL le celebrità)

celery ['selərɪ] NOUN
il sedano

cell [sel] NOUN
1️⃣ la cella ◇ *Prisoners spend many hours in their cells.* I prigionieri trascorrono molte ore in cella.
2️⃣ la cellula (*in biology*)

cellar ['selə'] NOUN
la cantina
♦ **in the cellar** in cantina
♦ **a wine cellar** una cantina

cello ['tʃeləu] NOUN (PL **cellos**)
il violoncello

cement [səˈment] NOUN
il cemento

cemetery ['semɪtrɪ] NOUN (PL **cemeteries**)
il cimitero

cent [sent] NOUN
il centesimo (*coin*)
♦ **per cent** per cento

centenary [senˈtiːnərɪ] NOUN (PL **centenaries**)
il centenario

center ['sentə'] NOUN [US]
il centro ◇ *a sports center* un centro sportivo ◇ *the city center* il centro della città

centigrade ['sentɪgreɪd] ADJECTIVE
centigrado ◇ *20 degrees centigrade* 20 gradi centigradi

centimetre ['sentɪmiːtə'] NOUN (US **centimeter**)
il centimetro

central ['sentrəl] ADJECTIVE
centrale

central heating ['sentrəl'hiːtɪŋ] NOUN
il riscaldamento autonomo

central reservation ['sentrəlrezə'veɪʃən] NOUN
la banchina spartitraffico (PL le banchine spartitraffico)

centre ['sentə'] NOUN
il centro ◇ *a sports centre* un centro sportivo ◇ *the city centre* il centro della città

century ['sentjurɪ] NOUN (PL **centuries**)
il secolo ◇ *the twenty first century* il ventunesimo secolo

cereal ['siːrɪəl] NOUN
i cereali ◇ *I have cereal for breakfast.* Mangio cereali per colazione.

ceremony ['serɪmənɪ] NOUN (PL **ceremonies**)
la cerimonia

certain ['sɜːtən] ADJECTIVE
certo ◇ *a certain person* una certa persona ◇ *I am certain he's not coming* Sono certo che non verrà.
♦ **for certain** per certo

certainly ['sɜːtənlɪ] ADVERB
sicuramente ◇ *I shall certainly be there.* Ci sarò sicuramente.
♦ **Certainly not!** No di certo!

certificate [səˈtɪfɪkɪt] NOUN
il certificato

CFCs [siːefsiːz] NOUN PL
i CFC

chain [tʃeɪn] NOUN
1️⃣ la catena ◇ *The gate was fastened with a chain.* Il cancello era chiuso con una catena.
2️⃣ la catenina ◇ *a gold chain* una catenina d'oro
♦ **a chain of events** una serie di avvenimenti

chair [tʃeə'] NOUN
1️⃣ la sedia ◇ *a table and four chairs* un tavolo e quattro sedie
2️⃣ la poltrona ◇ *a sofa and two chairs* un divano e due poltrone

chairlift ['tʃeəlɪft] NOUN
la seggiovia

chairman ['tʃeəmən] NOUN (PL **chairmen**)
il presidente

chalet ['ʃæleɪ] NOUN
1️⃣ il chalet (PL i chalet) (*in ski resort*)
2️⃣ il bungalow (PL i bungalow) (*in holiday camp*)

chalk [tʃɔːk] NOUN

il gesso

challenge [ˈtʃælɪndʒ] NOUN
  see also **challenge** VERB
  la sfida

to **challenge** [ˈtʃælɪndʒ] VERB
  see also **challenge** NOUN
  sfidare ◊ *She challenged me to a race.* Mi ha sfidato ad una gara.

challenging [ˈtʃælɪndʒɪŋ] ADJECTIVE
  impegnativo ◊ *a challenging job* un lavoro impegnativo

chambermaid [ˈtʃeɪmbəmeɪd] NOUN
  la cameriera

champagne [ʃæmˈpeɪn] NOUN
  lo champagne

champion [ˈtʃæmpɪən] NOUN
  il campione
  la campionessa

championship [ˈtʃæmpɪənʃɪp] NOUN
  il campionato

chance [tʃɑːns] NOUN
  see also **chance** ADJECTIVE
  1 la possibilità (PL le possibilità) ◊ *the team's chances of winning* le possibilità di vittoria della squadra ◊ *No chance!* Impossibile!
  2 l' opportunità (PL le opportunità) ◊ *I'll write when I get the chance.* Scriverò quando ne avrò l'opportunità.
  ◆ **by chance** per caso
  ◆ **to take a chance** rischiare ◊ *I'm taking no chances!* Non intendo rischiare!

chance [tʃɑːns] ADJECTIVE
  see also **chance** NOUN
  casuale ◊ *a chance meeting* un incontro casuale

Chancellor of the Exchequer
  [ˈtʃɑːnələrəvðɪksˈtʃekər] NOUN
  il Cancelliere dello Scacchiere

  ❶ //Chancellor of the Exchequer
  corrisponde al Ministro delle Finanze italiano.

chandelier [ʃændəˈlɪər] NOUN
  il lampadario

to **change** [tʃeɪndʒ] VERB
  see also **change** NOUN
  cambiare ◊ *The town has changed a lot.* La città è molto cambiata. ◊ *I'd like to change fifty pounds.* Vorrei cambiare 50 sterline. ◊ *He wants to change his job.* Vuole cambiare lavoro.
  ◆ **to change one's mind** cambiare idea ◊ *I've changed my mind.* Ho cambiato idea.
  ◆ **to change places** scambiarsi E di posto ◊ *We changed places.* Ci siamo scambiati di posto.

change [tʃeɪndʒ] NOUN
  see also **change** VERB
  1 il cambiamento ◊ *There's been a*

change of plan. C'è stato un cambiamento di programma.
  ◆ **a change of clothes** un cambio di vestiti
  ◆ **for a change** tanto per cambiare
  2 gli spiccioli ◊ *I haven't got any change.* Non ho spiccioli.
  ◆ **Can you give me change for a pound?** Mi può cambiare una sterlina?
  3 il resto ◊ *Here's your change.* Ecco il resto.

changeable [ˈtʃeɪndʒəbl] ADJECTIVE
  1 variabile ◊ *The weather's very changeable in autumn.* Il tempo è molto variabile in autunno.
  2 incostante (*person*)

change purse [ˈtʃeɪndʒpəːs] NOUN US
  il portamonete (PL i portamonete)

changing room [ˈtʃeɪndʒɪŋrum] NOUN
  1 il camerino ◊ *Three garments only allowed in the changing room.* Si possono portare solo tre articoli nel camerino.
  2 lo spogliatoio (*in gym*)

Channel [ˈtʃænl] NOUN
  ◆ **the Channel** il canale della Manica
  ◆ **the Channel Islands** le isole della Manica
  ◆ **the Channel Tunnel** il tunnel sotto la Manica

channel [ˈtʃænl] NOUN
  il canale (*on TV*)

chaos [ˈkeɪɔs] NOUN
  il caos

chap [tʃæp] NOUN
  il tipo ◊ *He's a nice chap.* È un tipo simpatico.

chapel [ˈtʃæpl] NOUN
  la cappella

chapter [ˈtʃæptər] NOUN
  il capitolo

character [ˈkærɪktər] NOUN
  1 il carattere ◊ *Can you give me some idea of his character?* Puoi descrivermi un po' il suo carattere?
  ◆ **She's quite a character.** È un tipo originale.
  2 il personaggio (*in film, book*)
  ◆ **a character reference** una referenza

characteristic [kærɪktəˈrɪstɪk] NOUN
  la caratteristica (PL le caratteristiche)

charcoal [ˈtʃɑːkəul] NOUN
  1 il carbone (*for barbecue*)
  2 il carboncino (*for sketching*)

charge [tʃɑːdʒ] NOUN
  see also **charge** VERB
  ◆ **Is there a charge for delivery?** C'è qualcosa da pagare per la spedizione?
  ◆ **an extra charge** un supplemento
  ◆ **free of charge** gratuito
  ◆ **I'd like to reverse the charges.** Vorrei fare una chiamata a carico del destinatario.
  ◆ **to be on a charge of** essere* E accusato di ◊ *He's on a charge of murder.* È stato accusato di omicidio.
  ◆ **to be in charge** essere* E responsabile

* Verbs followed by this symbol are irregular. See pp.339–364 for further details.

◇ *She was in charge of the group.* Era responsabile per il gruppo.

o **charge** [tʃɑːdʒ] VERB
see also **charge** NOUN
far* pagare a ◇ *How much did he charge you?* Quanto ti ha fatto pagare?

• **to charge somebody with...** accusare qualcuno di... ◇ *The police have charged him with murder.* La polizia lo ha accusato di omicidio.

charge card ['tʃɑːdʒkɑːd] NOUN
la carta acquisti

charity ['tʃærɪtɪ] NOUN (PL **charities**)
la beneficenza ◇ *He gave the money to charity.* Ha dato il denaro in beneficenza.

• **to collect for charity** raccogliere* denaro per beneficienza

• **a cancer charity** un'associazione per la raccolta di fondi contro il cancro

charity shop ['tʃærɪtɪʃɔp] NOUN

> **ⓘ** / **charity shops** sono negozi gestiti da volontari che vendono articoli di seconda mano e devolvono il ricavato in beneficenza.

charm [tʃɑːm] NOUN
il fascino ◇ *The charm of this region lies in its beautiful scenery.* Il fascino di questa regione sta nei suoi paesaggi stupendi.

charming ['tʃɑːmɪŋ] ADJECTIVE
delizioso ◇ *She's a charming girl.* È una ragazza deliziosa.

• **Prince Charming** il Principe azzurro

chart [tʃɑːt] NOUN
il grafico (PL i grafici) ◇ *The chart shows the rise of unemployment.* Il grafico mostra l'aumento della disoccupazione.

• **the charts** la Hit Parade ◇ *His record has been in the charts for ten weeks.* Il suo disco è rimasto nella classifica dei dischi più venduti per dieci settimane.

charter flight ['tʃɑːtəflaɪt] NOUN
il volo charter (PL i voli charter)

chase [tʃeɪs] NOUN
see also **chase** VERB
l'inseguimento ◇ *a car chase* un inseguimento in macchina

to **chase** [tʃeɪs] VERB
see also **chase** NOUN
1 inseguire ◇ *The policeman chased the thief.* Il poliziotto ha inseguito il ladro.
2 correre* E dietro a ◇ *He's always chasing the girls.* Corre sempre dietro alle ragazze.

to **chase away** [tʃeɪsə'weɪ] VERB
cacciare via

chat [tʃæt] NOUN
see also **chat** VERB
la chiacchierata

• **to have a chat** fare* una chiacchierata

to **chat** [tʃæt] VERB

see also **chat** NOUN
chiacchierare ◇ *I was chatting to my neighbour.* Stavo chiacchierando con il mio vicino.

to **chat up** [tʃæt'ʌp] VERB
abbordare ◇ *He's not very good at chatting up girls.* Non è molto bravo ad abbordare le ragazze.

chatroom ['tʃætrum] NOUN
la chatline (PL le chatline)

chat show ['tʃætʃəu] NOUN
il talk show (PL i talk show)

chauvinist ['ʃəuvɪnɪst] NOUN
• **a male chauvinist** un maschilista

cheap [tʃiːp] ADJECTIVE
1 economico ◇ *a cheap flight* un volo economico ◇ *The bus is cheaper.* L'autobus è più economico. ◇ *The cheapest seats are five pounds.* I posti più economici vengono cinque sterline.
2 scadente (poor quality) ◇ *She bought a dress made of a cheap material.* Ha comprato un vestito di stoffa scadente.
◇ *This stuff is cheap and nasty.* Questa roba è proprio scadente.

to **cheat** [tʃiːt] VERB
see also **cheat** NOUN
1 imbrogliare (at cards, in games) ◇ *You're cheating!* Stai imbrogliando!
2 copiare (in exam)

cheat [tʃiːt] NOUN
see also **cheat** VERB
l'imbroglione
l'imbrogliona

check [tʃɛk] NOUN
see also **check** VERB
1 il controllo ◇ *a thorough check* un controllo accurato
2 l'assegno (cheque) US

to **check** [tʃɛk] VERB
see also **check** NOUN
controllare ◇ *Could you check the oil, please?* Può controllare l'olio, per favore?

• **to check with somebody** chiedere* a qualcuno ◇ *I'll check with the driver what time the bus leaves.* Chiederò al conducente quando parte l'autobus.

to **check in** [tʃɛk'ɪn] VERB
1 fare* il check-in (at airport)
2 arrivare (in hotel)

to **check out** [tʃɛk'aut] VERB
lasciare la camera e saldare il conto (in hotel)

• **Check it out.** Vedi di che si tratta.

checked [tʃɛkt] ADJECTIVE
a quadretti

checkers ['tʃɛkəz] NOUN US
la dama

check-in ['tʃɛkɪn] NOUN (PL **check-ins**)
il banco del check-in

checking account ['tʃɛkɪŋəkaunt] NOUN
US

C

il conto corrente
checkout ['tʃɛkaut] NOUN
la cassa

check-up ['tʃɛkʌp] NOUN (PL check-ups)
il check-up (PL i check-up)

cheddar ['tʃɛdəʳ] NOUN
il cheddar

ⓘ *Il cheddar è un formaggio di latte di mucca molto diffuso in Gran Bretagna.*

cheek [tʃiːk] NOUN
la guancia (PL le guance) ◊ *a kiss on the cheek* un bacio sulla guancia
♦ **What a cheek!** Che faccia tosta!

cheeky ['tʃiːkɪ] ADJECTIVE
sfacciato ◊ *Don't be cheeky!* Non essere sfacciato!

cheer [tʃɪəʳ] NOUN
see also **cheer** VERB
l'urrà (PL gli urrà) ◊ *Three cheers for the winner!* Tre urrà per il vincitore!
♦ **Cheers! (1)** (*when drinking*) Cin cin!
♦ **Cheers! (2)** (*thank you*) Grazie!

to cheer [tʃɪəʳ] VERB
see also **cheer** NOUN
applaudire
♦ **to cheer somebody up** tirare qualcuno su di morale ◊ *I was trying to cheer him up.* Cercavo di tirarlo su di morale.
♦ **Cheer up!** Coraggio!

cheerful ['tʃɪəful] ADJECTIVE
allegro

cheerio [tʃɪərɪˈəu] EXCLAMATION
ciao

cheese [tʃiːz] NOUN
il formaggio

chef [ʃɛf] NOUN
lo chef (PL gli chef)

chemical ['kɛmɪkl] NOUN
il prodotto chimico (PL i prodotti chimici)

chemist ['kɛmɪst] NOUN
1 il/la farmacista (*person*)
2 la farmacia (PL le farmacie) (*shop*) ◊ *You get it from the chemist.* Si compra in farmacia.
3 il chimico (PL i chimici) (*scientist*)

chemistry ['kɛmɪstrɪ] NOUN
la chimica ◊ *the chemistry lab* il laboratorio di chimica

cheque [tʃɛk] NOUN
l'assegno ◊ *He wrote a cheque.* Ha fatto un assegno. ◊ *Can I pay by cheque?* Posso pagare con un assegno?

chequebook ['tʃɛkbuk] NOUN
il libretto degli assegni

cherry ['tʃɛrɪ] NOUN (PL cherries)
la ciliegia (PL le ciliegie *or* le ciliege)

chess [tʃɛs] NOUN
gli scacchi ◊ *He likes playing chess.* Gli piace giocare a scacchi.

chessboard ['tʃɛsbɔːd] NOUN
la scacchiera

chest [tʃɛst] NOUN
il petto ◊ *I've got a pain in my chest.* Ho un dolore al petto.
♦ **a chest of drawers** un cassettone

chestnut ['tʃɛsnʌt] NOUN
1 la castagna (*nut*)
2 il castagno (*tree*)

to chew [tʃuː] VERB
masticare

chewing gum ['tʃuːɪŋɡʌm] NOUN
la gomma da masticare

chick [tʃɪk] NOUN
il pulcino

chicken ['tʃɪkɪn] NOUN
il pollo ◊ *a chicken leg* una coscia di pollo

chickenpox ['tʃɪkɪnpɔks] NOUN
la varicella

chickpeas ['tʃɪkpiːz] NOUN PL
i ceci

chief [tʃiːf] NOUN
see also **chief** ADJECTIVE
il capo ◊ *the chief of security* il capo della sicurezza

chief [tʃiːf] ADJECTIVE
see also **chief** NOUN
principale ◊ *His chief reason for resigning was the low pay.* La ragione principale per cui si è licenziato è lo stipendio basso.

child [tʃaɪld] NOUN (PL children)
1 il bambino
la bambina
◊ *a child of six* un bambino di sei anni ◊ *I like children.* Mi piacciono i bambini.
2 il figlio
la figlia
◊ *Susan is our eldest child.* Susan è la nostra figlia maggiore. ◊ *They've got three children.* Hanno tre figli.

childish ['tʃaɪldɪʃ] ADJECTIVE
infantile

childminder ['tʃaɪldmaɪndəʳ] NOUN
la bambinaia

children ['tʃɪldrən] NOUN PL *see* child

Chile ['tʃɪlɪ] NOUN
il Cile

to chill [tʃɪl] VERB
see also **chill** NOUN
mettere* in fresco (*wine, food*)
♦ **serve chilled** servire fresco

chill [tʃɪl] NOUN
see also **chill** VERB
♦ **to catch a chill** prendere* un colpo di freddo

chilli ['tʃɪlɪ] NOUN
il peperoncino
♦ **chilli con carne** piatto di carne macinata e fagioli con il peperoncino

chilly ['tʃɪlɪ] ADJECTIVE
freddo

chimney ['tʃɪmnɪ] NOUN

* Verbs followed by this symbol are irregular. See pp.339–364 for further details.

il camino
chin [tʃɪn] NOUN
il mento
China ['tʃaɪnə] NOUN
la Cina
china ['tʃaɪnə] NOUN
la porcellana ◊ *a china plate* un piatto di porcellana
Chinese [tʃaɪ'ni:z] ADJECTIVE
see also **Chinese** NOUN
cinese
Chinese [tʃaɪ'ni:z] NOUN
see also **Chinese** ADJECTIVE
il cinese (*language*)
• **the Chinese** i cinesi
chip [tʃɪp] NOUN
[1] la patatina fritta (*to eat*)
[2] il chip (PL i chip) (*in computer*)
• **potato chips** [US] le patatine
chiropodist [kɪ'rɔpədɪst] NOUN
il/la callista
chives [tʃaɪvz] NOUN PL
l' erba cipollina
chocolate ['tʃɔklɪt] NOUN
[1] il cioccolato ◊ *a chocolate cake* una torta al cioccolato
[2] il cioccolatino ◊ *a box of chocolates* una scatola di cioccolatini
• **hot chocolate** la cioccolata calda
choice [tʃɔɪs] NOUN
la scelta ◊ *I had no choice.* Non avevo scelta.
choir ['kwaɪə'] NOUN
il coro
to **choke** [tʃəuk] VERB
soffocare ◊ *Help him, he's choking!* Aiutatelo, sta soffocando!
to **choose** [tʃu:z] VERB (**chose, chosen**)
scegliere ◊ *I don't know which to choose.* Non so quale scegliere. ◊ *She chose a pale pink skirt.* Ha scelto una gonna rosa pallido. ◊ *Have you already chosen?* Hai già scelto?
to **chop** [tʃɔp] VERB
see also **chop** NOUN
[1] tagliare a pezzetti (*meat, vegetables*)
[2] tritare (*onion*)
chop [tʃɔp] NOUN
see also **chop** VERB
la cotoletta ◊ *a pork chop* una cotoletta di maiale
chopsticks ['tʃɔpstɪks] NOUN PL
i bastoncini
chose, chosen [tʃəuz,'tʃəuzn] VERB *see* **choose**
Christ [kraɪst] NOUN
Cristo
christening ['krɪsnɪŋ] NOUN
il battesimo
Christian ['krɪstɪən] NOUN
see also **Christian** ADJECTIVE
il cristiano

la cristiana
Christian ['krɪstɪən] ADJECTIVE
see also **Christian** NOUN
cristiano
Christian name ['krɪstɪənneɪm] NOUN
il nome di battesimo
Christmas ['krɪsməs] NOUN
il Natale ◊ *Happy Christmas!* Buon Natale!
• **a Christmas card** un biglietto di auguri natalizi
• **Christmas Day** il giorno di Natale
• **Christmas Eve** la vigilia di Natale
• **Christmas pudding**

> ❶ //**Christmas pudding** è una specie di budino con frutta secca e spezie cotto a vapore.

chunk [tʃʌŋk] NOUN
il grosso pezzo ◊ *Cut the meat into chunks.* Taglia la carne a grossi pezzi.
church [tʃə:tʃ] NOUN (PL **churches**)
la chiesa
• **the Church of England** la chiesa anglicana
cider ['saɪdə'] NOUN
il sidro
cigar [sɪ'gɑ:'] NOUN
il sigaro
cigarette [sɪgə'ret] NOUN
la sigaretta ◊ *He's smoking a cigarette.* Sta fumando una sigaretta.
• **a cigarette end** un mozzicone
cigarette lighter [sɪgə'retlaɪtə'] NOUN
l' accendino
cinema ['sɪnəmə] NOUN
il cinema (PL i cinema)
cinnamon ['sɪnəmən] NOUN
la cannella
circle ['sə:kl] NOUN
il cerchio
circular ['sə:kjulə'] ADJECTIVE
circolare
circulation [sə:kju'leɪʃən] NOUN
[1] la circolazione ◊ *She has poor circulation.* Ha una cattiva circolazione.
[2] la tiratura ◊ *The newspaper has a circulation of around 8000.* Il giornale ha una tiratura di circa otto mila copie.
circumstances ['sə:kəmstənsɪz] NOUN PL
le circostanze ◊ *in the circumstances* date le circostanze
• **under no circumstances** in nessun caso
circus ['sə:kəs] NOUN (PL **circuses**)
il circo (PL i circhi)
citizen ['sɪtɪzn] NOUN
il cittadino
la cittadina
citizenship ['sɪtɪznʃɪp] NOUN
la cittadinanza
City ['sɪtɪ] NOUN
• **the City** la City di Londra

☞

❶ *La* **City** *di Londra è la parte della città dove si trovano le più importanti istituzioni finanziarie.*

city ['sɪtɪ] NOUN (PL **cities**)
la città (PL le città)
 • **the city centre** il centro
city technology college
['sɪtɪtekn'nɔlədʒɪ'kɔlɪdʒ] NOUN
l' istituto tecnico (PL gli istituti tecnici)

❶ *I* **city technology college** *sono scuole tecniche secondarie frequentate da ragazzi tra gli 11 e i 18 anni.*

civilization [sɪvɪlaɪ'zeɪʃən] NOUN
la civiltà
civil servant [sɪvɪl'sə:vənt] NOUN
il funzionario dello Stato
civil war [sɪvɪl'wɔ:'] NOUN
la guerra civile (PL le guerre civili)
to **claim** [kleɪm] VERB
see also **claim** NOUN
 [1] sostenere* ◇ *He claims he found the money.* Sostiene di aver trovato il denaro.
 [2] chiedere* ◇ *He's claiming compensation from the company.* Chiede un risarcimento da parte della società.
 [3] ricevere ◇ *She's claiming unemployment benefit.* Riceve il sussidio di disoccupazione.
claim [kleɪm] NOUN
see also **claim** VERB
 [1] l' affermazione FEM ◇ *The manufacturer's claims are obviously untrue.* Le affermazioni del fabbricante sono ovviamente false.
 [2] la richiesta di risarcimento ◇ *We sent in a claim to our insurance company.* Abbiamo mandato una richiesta di risarcimento alla nostra assicurazione.
 • **a claim form** un modulo di richiesta di risarcimento
 • **to put in a claim for a pay rise** chiedere* un aumento di stipendio
to **clap** [klæp] VERB
applaudire ◇ *Everybody clapped.* Tutti applaudirono.
 • **to clap one's hands** battere* le mani ◇ *Clap your hands.* Batti le mani.
clarinet [klærɪ'net] NOUN
il clarinetto
to **clash** [klæʃ] VERB
 [1] stonare ◇ *Red clashes with orange.* Il rosso stona con l'arancio.
 [2] coincidere ◇ *The date of the party clashes with the meeting.* La data della festa coincide con quella della riunione.
clasp [klɑ:sp] NOUN
il fermaglio (*of necklace, handbag*)
class [klɑ:s] NOUN (PL **classes**)

 [1] la classe ◇ *We're in the same class.* Siamo in classe insieme.
 [2] la lezione ◇ *I go to dancing classes.* Vado a lezione di ballo.
classic ['klæsɪk] ADJECTIVE
see also **classic** NOUN
classico ◇ *a classic example* un esempio classico
classic ['klæsɪk] NOUN
see also **classic** ADJECTIVE
il classico (PL i classici) ◇ *This song is a classic.* Questa canzone è un classico.
classical ['klæsɪkl] ADJECTIVE
classico ◇ *classical music* la musica classica
classmate ['klɑ:smeɪt] NOUN
il compagno di classe
la compagna di classe
classroom ['klɑ:srum] NOUN
la classe
clause [klɔ:z] NOUN
la proposizione
claw [klɔ:] NOUN
l' artiglio (*of dog, cat, bird*)
clean [kli:n] ADJECTIVE
see also **clean** VERB
pulito
to **clean** [kli:n] VERB
see also **clean** ADJECTIVE
pulire ◇ *He never cleans the bath.* Non pulisce mai la vasca da bagno.
 • **to clean one's teeth** lavarsi E i denti
cleaner ['kli:nə'] NOUN
 [1] l' addetto alle pulizie
l' addetta alle pulizie
(*person*)
 [2] il detersivo (*product*)
cleaner's ['kli:nəz] NOUN
la tintoria ◇ *He took his coat to the cleaner's.* Ha portato il cappotto in tintoria.
cleaning lady ['kli:nɪŋleɪdɪ] NOUN (PL **cleaning ladies**)
la donna delle pulizie
cleansing lotion ['klenzɪŋləuʃən] NOUN
il latte detergente
clear [klɪə'] ADJECTIVE
see also **clear** VERB
 [1] chiaro ◇ *a clear explanation* una spiegazione chiara ◇ *Have I made myself clear?* Sono stato chiaro?
 [2] libero ◇ *Wait till the road is clear.* Aspetta finché la strada sarà libera.
 [3] trasparente ◇ *a clear plastic bottle* una bottiglia di plastica trasparente
 • **a clear day** una giornata limpida
to **clear** [klɪə'] VERB
see also **clear** ADJECTIVE
 [1] liberare ◇ *They are clearing the road.* Stanno liberando la strada.
 [2] diradarsi E (*mist*)
 • **to be cleared of...** essere* E scagionato

* Verbs followed by this symbol are irregular. See pp.339–364 for further details.

dall'accusa di... ◇ *She was cleared of murder.* È stata scagionata dall'accusa di omicidio.

+ **to clear the table** sparecchiare la tavola

to **clear off** [klɪərˈɔf] VERB
andarsene [E] ◇ *Clear off and leave me alone!* Vattene e lasciami in pace!

to **clear up** [klɪərˈʌp] VERB
[1] mettere* in ordine ◇ *Who's going to clear all this up?* Chi metterà tutto in ordine?
[2] chiarire ◇ *I'm sure we can clear up this problem right away.* Sono sicuro che possiamo chiarire subito il problema.
[3] schiarire [E] (*weather*) ◇ *I think it's going to clear up.* Penso che schiarirà.

clearly ['klɪəlɪ] ADVERB
chiaramente ◇ *Clearly this project will cost money.* Chiaramente il progetto avrà un costo.

+ **to speak clearly** parlare chiaro

clementine ['klemantaɪn] NOUN
la clementina

to **clench** [klentʃ] VERB
stringere ◇ *She clenched her fists.* Strinse i pugni.

clerk [klɑːk] NOUN
l' impiegato
l' impiegata

clever ['klevə'] ADJECTIVE
[1] intelligente ◇ *She's very clever.* È molto intelligente.
[2] ingegnoso ◇ *a clever system* un sistema ingegnoso
[3] geniale ◇ *What a clever idea!* Che idea geniale!

click [klɪk] NOUN
see also **click** VERB
il click (PL i click)

to **click** [klɪk] VERB
see also **click** NOUN

+ **to click on** cliccare su

client ['klaɪənt] NOUN
il/la cliente

cliff [klɪf] NOUN
la scogliera

climate ['klaɪmɪt] NOUN
il clima

to **climb** [klaɪm] VERB
[1] scalare ◇ *Her ambition is to climb Mount Everest.* La sua ambizione è quella di scalare l'Everest.
[2] salire* [E] ◇ *We had to climb three flights of stairs to get there.* Abbiamo dovuto salire tre rampe di scale per arrivarci.
[3] salire* [E] su ◇ *They climbed a tree.* Sono saliti su un albero.

climber ['klaɪmə'] NOUN
il/la alpinista

climbing ['klaɪmɪŋ] NOUN
l' alpinismo

+ **to go climbing** andare* [E] a fare roccia

cling film ['klɪŋfɪlm] NOUN
la pellicola trasparente

clinic ['klɪnɪk] NOUN
la clinica (PL le cliniche)

clip [klɪp] NOUN
[1] il fermaglio (*for hair*)
[2] la sequenza ◇ *some clips from her latest film* alcune sequenze del suo ultimo film

clippers ['klɪpəz] NOUN

+ **nail clippers** il tagliaunghie

cloakroom ['kləʊkrʊm] NOUN
[1] il guardaroba (PL i guardaroba) (*for coats*)
[2] la toilette (PL le toilette) (*toilet*)

clock [klɔk] NOUN
l' orologio

+ **an alarm clock** una sveglia

+ **a clock-radio** una radiosveglia

+ **It's seven o'clock.** Sono le sette.

clockwork ['klɔkwɜːk] NOUN

+ **to go like clockwork** funzionare alla perfezione

clog [klɔg] NOUN
lo zoccolo

clone [kləʊn] NOUN
see also **clone** VERB
il clone

to **clone** [kləʊn] VERB
see also **clone** NOUN
clonare

close [kləʊs] ADJECTIVE, ADVERB
see also **close** VERB
[1] vicino ◇ *The shops are very close.* I negozi sono molto vicini. ◇ *Come closer.* Vieni più vicino.

+ **She was close to tears.** Stava per piangere.
[2] stretto ◇ *We're just inviting close relations.* Invitiamo solo i parenti più stretti.
[3] intimo ◇ *She's a close friend of mine.* È una mia amica intima.

+ **I'm very close to my sister.** Io e mia sorella siamo molto unite.
[4] combattuto ◇ *It was a very close contest.* È stata una gara molto combattuta.

+ **It's close this afternoon.** C'è afa questo pomeriggio.

to **close** [kləʊz] VERB
see also **close** ADJECTIVE
[1] chiudere ◇ *The shops close at five thirty.* I negozi chiudono alle cinque e mezza. ◇ *Please close the door.* Chiudi la porta, per favore.
[2] chiudersi [E] ◇ *The doors close automatically.* Le porte si chiudono automaticamente.

closed [kləʊzd] ADJECTIVE
chiuso

closely ['kləʊslɪ] ADVERB
da vicino (*look, examine*)

+ **a closely fought race** una gara molto combattuta

cloth [klɒθ] NOUN

la stoffa ◊ *five metres of cloth* cinque metri di stoffa
• **a cloth** uno straccio ◊ *Wipe it with a damp cloth.* Puliscilo con uno straccio umido.

clothes [kləʊðz] NOUN PL
i vestiti ◊ *smart clothes* vestiti eleganti
• **a clothes line** una corda per il bucato
• **a clothes horse** uno stendibiancheria
• **a clothes peg** una molletta

cloud [klaud] NOUN
la nuvola

cloudy ['klaudɪ] ADJECTIVE
nuvoloso

clove [kləuv] NOUN
• **a clove of garlic** uno spicchio d'aglio

clown [klaun] NOUN
il clown (PL i clown)

club [klʌb] NOUN
　① la mazza ◊ *a golf club* una mazza da golf
　② il circolo ◊ *the youth club* il circolo giovanile
　③ la discoteca (PL le discoteche) ◊ *We had dinner and went on to a club.* Abbiamo cenato e poi siamo andati in discoteca.
• **clubs** (*in cards*) i fiori

to **club together** [klʌbtə'geðə'] VERB
fare* colletta ◊ *We clubbed together to buy her a present.* Abbiamo fatto colletta per comprarle un regalo.

clubbing ['klʌbɪŋ] NOUN
• **to go clubbing** andare* E in discoteca

clue [klu:] NOUN
l' indizio ◊ *an important clue* un indizio importante
• **I haven't a clue.** Non ne ho la minima idea.

clumsy ['klʌmzɪ] ADJECTIVE
maldestro

cluster ['klʌstə'] NOUN
il gruppo

clutch [klʌtʃ] NOUN
see also **clutch** VERB
la frizione (*of car*)

to **clutch** [klʌtʃ] VERB
see also **clutch** NOUN
afferrare ◊ *She clutched my arm and begged me not to go.* Mi ha afferrato il braccio e mi ha pregato di non andarmene.

clutter ['klʌtə'] NOUN
il disordine ◊ *There's so much clutter in here.* C'è un gran disordine qua dentro.

coach [kəutʃ] NOUN (PL **coaches**)
　① la corriera ◊ *by coach* in corriera ◊ *the coach station* la stazione delle corriere
• **a coach trip** un viaggio in pullman
　② l' allenatore MASC (*of team*)

coal [kəul] NOUN
il carbone
• **a coal mine** una miniera di carbone
• **a coal miner** un minatore

coarse [kɔːs] ADJECTIVE
　① ruvido ◊ *The bag was made of coarse*

black cloth. La borsa era fatta di una stoffa nera ruvida.
　② grosso ◊ *The sand is very coarse on that beach.* La sabbia di quella spiaggia è molto grossa.

coast [kəust] NOUN
la costa

coastguard ['kəustgɑːd] NOUN
la guardia costiera

coat [kəut] NOUN
il cappotto ◊ *a nice warm coat* un bel cappotto caldo
• **a coat of paint** una mano di pittura

coat hanger ['kəuthæŋə'] NOUN
la gruccia (PL le grucce)

cobweb ['kɔbwɛb] NOUN
la ragnatela

cocaine [kə'keɪn] NOUN
la cocaina

cock [kɔk] NOUN
　① il gallo (*bird*)
　② il cazzo (*rude!*)

cockerel ['kɔkərl] NOUN
il gallo

cockney ['kɔknɪ] NOUN
• **He's got a cockney accent.** Ha un accento cockney.

> 🛈 *Il termine* **cockney** *indica sia gli abitanti che il dialetto parlato nell'East End, un quartiere popolare che si trova nella zona est di Londra.*

cocoa ['kəukəu] NOUN
il cacao

coconut ['kəukənʌt] NOUN
la noce di cocco

cod [kɔd] NOUN
il merluzzo

code [kəud] NOUN
　① il codice ◊ *It's written in code.* È scritto in codice.
　② il prefisso (*for telephone*) ◊ *What's the code for London?* Qual è il prefisso di Londra?

coffee ['kɔfɪ] NOUN
il caffè (PL i caffè) ◊ *a cup of coffee* una tazza di caffè

coffeepot ['kɔfɪpɔt] NOUN

> 🛈 *La* **coffeepot** *è una specie di teiera alta e stretta con il coperchio usata per servire il caffè.*

coffee table ['kɑfɪteɪbl] NOUN
il tavolino

coffin ['kɔfɪn] NOUN
la bara

coin [kɔɪn] NOUN
la moneta ◊ *a 50p coin* una moneta da 50 pence

---

* Verbs followed by this symbol are irregular. See pp.339–364 for further details.

English ~ Italian

coincidence [kəʊ'ɪnsɪdəns] NOUN
la coincidenza

coinphone ['kɔɪnfəʊn] NOUN
il telefono a monete

Coke ® [kəʊk] NOUN
la Coca ®

colander ['kɔləndə'] NOUN
il colapasta (PL i colapasta)

cold [kəʊld] ADJECTIVE
see also **cold** NOUN
freddo ◇ It's cold. Fa freddo.
* **to be cold** avere* freddo ◇ Are you cold?
Hai freddo?

cold [kəʊld] NOUN
see also **cold** ADJECTIVE
[1] il freddo ◇ I can't stand the cold. Non
sopporto il freddo.
[2] il raffreddore
* **to catch a cold** prendere* un raffreddore
* **to have a cold** avere* il raffreddore

cold sore ['kəʊldsɔː'] NOUN
la febbre

coleslaw ['kəʊlslɔː] NOUN
[l'] insalata di cavolo, carote e maionese

to **collapse** [kə'læps] VERB
[1] crollare^E ◇ The bridge collapsed during
the storm. Il ponte è crollato durante la
tempesta.
[2] avere* un collasso ◇ He collapsed while
playing tennis. Ha avuto un collasso mentre
giocava a tennis.

collar ['kɔlə'] NOUN
[1] il colletto (of coat, shirt)
[2] il collare (for animal)

collarbone ['kɔləbəʊn] NOUN
la clavicola

colleague ['kɔliːg] NOUN
il/la collega

to **collect** [kə'lekt] VERB
[1] raccogliere* ◇ The teacher collected the
exercise books. L'insegnante ha raccolto i
quaderni.
[2] fare* collezione di ◇ He collects stamps.
Fa collezione di francobolli.
[3] andare* a prendere^E ◇ Their mother
collects them from school. La mamma li va a
prendere a scuola.
[4] fare* una colletta ◇ I'm collecting for
UNICEF. Faccio una colletta per l'UNICEF.

collect call [kə'lektkɔːl] NOUN US
la telefonata con addebito al ricevente

collection [kə'lekʃən] NOUN
[1] la collezione ◇ my CD collection la mia
collezione di CD
[2] la colletta ◇ a collection for charity una
colletta per beneficienza

collector [kə'lektə'] NOUN
il/la collezionista

college ['kɔlɪdʒ] NOUN
[1] l' università (PL le università) ◇ I want to
go to college. Voglio andare^E all'università.

* **college students** gli studenti universitari
[2] il collegio (PL i collegi) (boarding school)
[3] la scuola (school)

to **collide** [kə'laɪd] VERB
scontrarsi^E

collie ['kɔli] NOUN
il collie (PL i collie)

colliery ['kɔlɪərɪ] NOUN (PL **collieries**)
la miniera di carbone

collision [kə'lɪʒən] NOUN
la collisione

colon ['kəʊlən] NOUN
i due punti (punctuation mark)

colonel ['kɜːnl] NOUN
il colonnello

colour ['kʌlə'] NOUN (US **color**)
il colore ◇ What colour is it? Di che colore è?
◇ It shouldn't matter what colour you are.
Non dovrebbe importare il colore della tua
pelle.
* **a colour TV** un televisore a colori

colourful ['kʌləful] ADJECTIVE (US **colorful**)
colorato

colouring ['kʌlərɪŋ] NOUN (US **coloring**)
il colorante (for food)

comb [kəʊm] NOUN
see also **comb** VERB
il pettine

to **comb** [kəʊm] VERB
see also **comb** NOUN
* **to comb one's hair** pettinarsi^E ◇ You
haven't combed your hair. Non ti sei
pettinato.

combination [kɔmbɪ'neɪʃən] NOUN
la combinazione

to **combine** [kəm'baɪn] VERB
[1] unire ◇ The film combines humour with
suspense. Il film unisce umorismo e
suspense.
[2] conciliare ◇ It's difficult to combine a
career with a family. È difficile conciliare la
carriera con la famiglia.

to **come** [kʌm] VERB (**came, come**)
[1] venire*^E ◇ Can I come too? Posso
venire anch'io? ◇ Come home. Vieni a casa.
◇ Come and see us soon. Vieni a trovarci
presto. ◇ Helen came with me. Helen è
venuta con me.
[2] arrivare^E ◇ They came late. Sono
arrivati tardi. ◇ The letter came this
morning. La lettera è arrivata stamattina.

to **come across** [kʌmə'krɔs] VERB
trovare per caso (by chance) ◇ I came
across a dress that I hadn't worn for years.
Ho trovato per caso un vestito che non
mettevo da anni.
* **to come across as** dare* l'impressione di
essere ◇ She comes across as a nice girl. Dà
l'impressione di essere una ragazza
simpatica.

to **come apart** [kʌmə'pɑːt] VERB 🖙

C

Verbs followed by the symbol "E" require the auxiliary "essere"

scucirsi ^E ◊ *My jacket is coming apart.* La mia giacca si sta scucendo.

to **come at** ['kʌmæt] VERB
avventarsi ^E su ◊ *He came at me with a knife.* Si è avventato su di me con un coltello.

to **come back** [kʌm'bæk] VERB
tornare ^E ◊ *He came back an hour later.* È tornato un'ora dopo.
• **Can I come back to you on that one?** Possiamo discuterne più tardi?

to **come down** [kʌm'daun] VERB
scendere* ^E

to **come for** ['kʌmfɔː'] VERB
passare ^E a prendere ◊ *I'll come for you at seven.* Passo a prenderti alle sette.

to **come forward** [kʌm'fɔːwəd] VERB
farsi ^E avanti

to **come in** [kʌm'ɪn] VERB
entrare* ^E ◊ *They came in together.* Entrarono insieme.
• **Come in!** Avanti!

to **come off** [kʌm'ɔf] VERB
[1] staccarsi ^E ◊ *A button came off my coat.* Mi si è staccato un bottone dal cappotto.
[2] andare* ^E via ◊ *I don't think this stain will come off.* Non penso che la macchia andrà via.

to **come on** [kʌm'ɔn] VERB
• **Come on! (1)** (*encouragement*) Avanti!
• **Come on! (2)** (*protest*) Ma dai!
• **I've got a cold coming on.** Mi sta venendo un raffreddore.

to **come out** [kʌm'aut] VERB
[1] uscire* ^E ◊ *We came out of the cinema at 10.* Siamo usciti dal cinema alle dieci. ◊ *Her book comes out in May.* Il suo libro esce in maggio.
[2] venire* ^E ◊ *None of my photos came out.* Non è venuta nessuna delle mie foto.

to **come round** [kʌm'raund] VERB
[1] passare ◊ *He is coming round to see us.* Passa a trovarci.
[2] riprendere* conoscenza ◊ *He came round after about ten minutes.* Ha ripreso conoscenza dopo circa dieci minuti.

to **come through** [kʌm'θruː] VERB
superare ◊ *They came through a difficult time in their marriage.* Hanno superato un periodo difficile nel loro matrimonio.

to **come to** [kʌm'tuː] VERB
riprendere* conoscenza ◊ *She came to in a hospital bed.* Ha ripreso conoscenza in un letto d'ospedale.

to **come up** [kʌm'ʌp] VERB
[1] saltare fuori ◊ *Something has come up so I'll be late home.* È saltato fuori un problema, per cui tornerò a casa tardi.
[2] avvicinarsi ^E ◊ *She came up to me and kissed me.* Mi si è avvicinata e mi ha baciato.

comedian [kə'miːdɪən] NOUN

il comico (PL i comici)

comedy ['kɔmɪdɪ] NOUN (PL **comedies**)
la commedia

comfortable ['kʌmfətəbl] ADJECTIVE
[1] comodo ◊ *comfortable shoes* scarpe comode ◊ *Are you comfortable sitting there?* Sei seduto comodo?
• **Make yourself comfortable.** Mettiti a tuo agio.
[2] confortevole ◊ *Their house is small but comfortable.* La loro casa è piccola ma confortevole.

comic ['kɔmɪk] NOUN
il giornalino (*magazine*)

comic strip ['kɔmɪkstrɪp] NOUN
la striscia (PL le strisce)

coming ['kʌmɪŋ] ADJECTIVE
prossimo ◊ *In the coming weeks, we will all have to work hard.* Dovremo lavorare sodo nelle prossime settimane.

comma ['kɔmə] NOUN
la virgola

command [kə'mɑːnd] NOUN
il comando

comment ['kɔment] NOUN
see also **comment** VERB
il commento ◊ *He made no comment.* Non fece commenti.

to **comment** ['kɔment] VERB
see also **comment** NOUN
fare* commenti ◊ *The police have not commented on these rumours.* La polizia non ha fatto commenti sulle voci.

commentary ['kɔməntərɪ] NOUN (PL **commentaries**)
[1] la telecronaca (PL le telecronache) (*on TV*)
[2] la radiocronaca (PL le radiocronache) (*on radio*)

commentator ['kɔmənteɪtə'] NOUN
[1] il/la telecronista (*on TV*)
[2] il/la radiocronista (*on radio*)

commercial [kə'məːʃəl] NOUN
see also **commercial** ADJECTIVE
lo spot pubblicitario (PL gli spot pubblicitari)

commercial [kə'məːʃəl] ADJECTIVE
see also **commercial** NOUN
commerciale

commission [kə'mɪʃən] NOUN
[1] la commissione ◊ *The bank charges 1% commission.* La banca fa pagare una commissione dell'uno per cento. ◊ *A commission has been set up to investigate the tragedy.* È stata nominata una commissione per indagare sulla tragedia.
[2] la provvigione (*on sales*) ◊ *He gets commission on top of his basic salary.* Oltre allo stipendio base prende una provvigione.
• **to work on commission** lavorare a provvigione

to **commit** [kə'mɪt] VERB

- **to commit a crime** commettere* un delitto
- **to commit suicide** suicidarsi [E]
- **to commit oneself** impegnarsi [E] ◇ *I don't want to commit myself.* Non voglio impegnarmi.

committee [kə'mɪtɪ] NOUN
la commissione

common ['kɔmən] ADJECTIVE
see also **common** NOUN
comune ◇ *It's a common name.* È un nome comune.

common ['kɔmən] NOUN
see also **common** ADJECTIVE
il parco comunale ◇ *a walk on the common* una passeggiata nel parco comunale
- **in common** in comune ◇ *We've got a lot in common.* Abbiamo molto in comune.

Commons ['kɔmənz] NOUN PL
- **the House of Commons** la Camera dei Comuni

common sense ['kɔmənsɛns] NOUN
il buonsenso

to **communicate** [kə'mju:nɪkeɪt] VERB
comunicare

communication [kəmju:nɪ'keɪʃən] NOUN
la comunicazione

communion [kə'mju:nɪən] NOUN
la comunione

communism ['kɔmjʊnɪzəm] NOUN
il comunismo

communist ['kɔmjʊnɪst] NOUN
see also **communist** ADJECTIVE
il/la comunista

communist ['kɔmjʊnɪst] ADJECTIVE
see also **communist** NOUN
comunista

community [kə'mju:nɪtɪ] NOUN (PL **communities**)
la comunità (PL le comunità) ◇ *the black community* la comunità nera ◇ *Mental patients now live in the community.* I malati di mente ora sono integrati all'interno della società.
- **community service**

ℹ️ *Il* **community service** *è un lavoro non pagato svolto come pena sostitutiva al carcere.*

to **commute** [kə'mju:t] VERB
fare* il pendolare ◇ *She commutes between Oxford and London.* Fa la pendolare tra Oxford e Londra.

compact disc [kəmpækt'dɪsk] NOUN
il compact disc (PL i compact disc)

compact disc player [kɔmpækt'dɪskpleɪə'] NOUN
il lettore di compact disc

companion [kəm'pænjən] NOUN
il compagno
la compagna

company ['kʌmpənɪ] NOUN (PL **companies**)
[1] la società (PL le società) ◇ *He works for a big company.* Lavora per una grossa società.
[2] la compagnia ◇ *an insurance company* una compagnia di assicurazione ◇ *a theatre company* una compagnia teatrale
- **to keep somebody company** fare* compagnia a qualcuno ◇ *I'll keep you company.* Ti farò compagnia.

comparatively [kəm'pærətɪvlɪ] ADVERB
relativamente ◇ *a comparatively easy exercise* un esercizio relativamente facile

to **compare** [kəm'peə'] VERB
[1] paragonare ◇ *They compared his work to that of Joyce.* Hanno paragonato la sua opera a quella di Joyce. ◇ *People always compare him with his brother.* Tutti lo paragonano sempre a suo fratello.
[2] mettere* a confronto ◇ *Compare the two illustrations.* Mettete a confronto le due illustrazioni.
- **compared with** rispetto a ◇ *Oxford is small compared with London.* Oxford è piccola rispetto a Londra.

comparison [kəm'pærɪsn] NOUN
il paragone

compartment [kəm'pɑ:tmənt] NOUN
[1] lo scompartimento ◇ *a first class compartment* uno scompartimento di prima classe
[2] lo scomparto (*in fridge, drawer*)

compass ['kʌmpəs] NOUN (PL **compasses**)
la bussola (*magnetic*)
- **compasses** compasso SING

compelling [kəm'pelɪŋ] ADJECTIVE
[1] avvincente ◇ *It's a violent yet compelling film.* È un film violento ma avvincente.
[2] convincente ◇ *He put forward a compelling argument against the death penalty.* Ha sollevato un argomento convincente contro la pena di morte.

compensation [kɔmpən'seɪʃən] NOUN
l' indennizzo (*money*)

compere ['kɔmpeə'] NOUN
il presentatore
la presentatrice

to **compete** [kəm'pi:t] VERB
- **to compete in** partecipare a ◇ *I'm competing in the marathon.* Partecipo alla maratona.
- **to compete for something** concorrere* per qualcosa ◇ *There are fifty students competing for six places.* Ci sono cinquanta studenti che concorrono per sei posti.

competent ['kɔmpɪtənt] ADJECTIVE
competente

competition [kɔmprɪ'tɪʃən] NOUN
[1] la gara ◇ *a singing competition* una gara di canto
[2] la concorrenza (*in business*)

☞

◇ *Competition in the computer sector is fierce.* C'è una grossa concorrenza nel settore informatico.

competitive [kəm'petɪtɪv] ADJECTIVE
competitivo ◇ *I'm a very competitive person.* Sono molto competitivo.

competitor [kəm'petɪtə'] NOUN
il/la concorrente

to **complain** [kəm'pleɪn] VERB
[1] presentare un reclamo ◇ *We're going to complain to the manager.* Presenteremo un reclamo al direttore.
[2] lamentarsi ᴱ ◇ *She's always complaining about her husband.* Si lamenta in continuazione di suo marito.

complaint [kəm'pleɪnt] NOUN
la lamentela

complete [kəm'pliːt] ADJECTIVE
completo

completely [kəm'pliːtlɪ] ADVERB
completamente

complexion [kəm'plekʃən] NOUN
la carnagione

complicated ['kɒmplɪkeɪtɪd] ADJECTIVE
complicato

compliment ['kɒmplɪmənt] NOUN
see also **compliment** VERB
il complimento ◇ *Thanks for the compliment.* Grazie del complimento.
♦ **to pay somebody a compliment** fare* un complimento a qualcuno ◇ *He's always paying her compliments.* Le fa sempre complimenti.
♦ **with our compliments** con i nostri omaggi
♦ **compliments of the season** auguri per le festività

to **compliment** ['kɒmplɪmɛnt] VERB
see also **compliment** NOUN
complimentarsi ᴱ ◇ *They complimented me on my Italian.* Si sono complimentati con me per il mio italiano.

complimentary [kɒmplɪ'mentərɪ] ADJECTIVE
♦ **a complimentary ticket** un biglietto omaggio

composer [kəm'pəuzə'] NOUN
il compositore
la compositrice

comprehension [kɒmprɪ'henʃən] NOUN
la comprensione

comprehensive [kɒmprɪ'hensɪv] ADJECTIVE
completo ◇ *a comprehensive guide to New Zealand* una guida completa della Nuova Zelanda
Be careful not to translate **comprehensive** by the Italian word **comprensivo**.

comprehensive school
[kɒmprɪ'hensɪvskuːl] NOUN
la scuola secondaria

🛈 La **comprehensive school** è una scuola statale britannica per i ragazzi dagli 11 ai 18

anni aperta a tutti.

compromise ['kɒmprəmaɪz] NOUN
see also **compromise** VERB
il compromesso

to **compromise** ['kɒmprəmaɪz] VERB
see also **compromise** NOUN
accettare un compromesso

compulsory [kəm'pʌlsərɪ] ADJECTIVE
obbligatorio

computer [kəm'pjuːtə'] NOUN
il computer (PL i computer)

computer game [kəm'pjuːtəgeɪm] NOUN
il gioco per il computer (PL i giochi per il computer)

computer programmer
[kəm'pjuːtə'prəugræmə'] NOUN
il programmatore
la programmatrice

computer science [kəm'pjuːtə'saɪəns] NOUN
l' informatica

computing [kəm'pjuːtɪŋ] NOUN
l' informatica

to **concentrate** ['kɒnsəntreɪt] VERB
concentrarsi ᴱ ◇ *I couldn't concentrate.* Non riuscivo a concentrarmi.

concentration [kɒnsən'treɪʃən] NOUN
la concentrazione

concept ['kɒnsept] NOUN
il concetto

concern [kən'sɜːn] NOUN
see also **concern** VERB
la preoccupazione ◇ *They expressed concern about the situation.* Hanno espresso la loro preoccupazione per la situazione.

to **concern** [kən'sɜːn] VERB
see also **concern** NOUN
[1] preoccupare ◇ *Their safety is what most concerns me.* Ciò che mi preoccupa maggiormente è la loro sicurezza. ◇ *They are more concerned to save money than to save lives.* Ciò che li preoccupa maggiormente è risparmiare denaro e non salvare vite umane.
[2] riguardare* ◇ *This matter does not concern you.* Questa faccenda non ti riguarda.
♦ **as far as I'm concerned** per quanto mi riguarda ◇ *As far as I'm concerned, you can come any time you like.* Per quanto mi riguarda, puoi venire quando vuoi.
♦ **As far as I'm concerned he's an idiot.** Secondo me è un idiota.
♦ **It was tragic for everyone concerned.** È stato tragico per tutti.

concerned [kən'sɜːnd] ADJECTIVE
preoccupato ◇ *His mother is concerned about him.* Sua madre è preoccupata per lui.

concerning [kən'sɜːnɪŋ] NOUN
il riguardo a ◇ *For further information*

* Verbs followed by this symbol are irregular. See pp.339–364 for further details.

concerning the job, contact Mr Ross. Per maggiori informazioni riguardo al lavoro, contatti il signor Ross.

concert ['kɔnsət] NOUN
il concerto

concrete ['kɔŋkri:t] NOUN
il calcestruzzo

condemn [kən'dɛm] VERB
condannare ◇ *The government has condemned the EU's decision.* Il governo ha condannato la decisione dell'Unione europea.

condition [kən'dɪʃən] NOUN
la condizione ◇ *I'll do it, on one condition...* Lo farò, ma ad una condizione... ◇ *in good condition* in buone condizioni

conditional [kən'dɪʃənl] NOUN
il condizionale

conditioner [kən'dɪʃənə'] NOUN
il balsamo *(for hair)*

condom ['kɔndəm] NOUN
il preservativo

conduct [kən'dʌkt] VERB
dirigere *(orchestra)*

conductor [kən'dʌktə'] NOUN
[1] il direttore d'orchestra *(musician)*
[2] il bigliettaio *(on bus)*

cone [kəun] NOUN
il cono ◇ *an ice-cream cone* un cono di gelato

conference ['kɔnfərəns] NOUN
la conferenza

confess [kən'fɛs] VERB
confessare ◇ *He confessed to the murder.* Ha confessato di aver commesso l'omicidio.

confession [kən'fɛʃən] NOUN
la confessione

confetti [kən'fɛti] NOUN SING
i coriandoli MASC PL

confidence ['kɔnfɪdns] NOUN
[1] la fiducia ◇ *I've got a lot of confidence in him.* Ho molta fiducia in lui.
[2] la fiducia in se stessi ◇ *She lacks confidence.* Non ha fiducia in se stessa.
♦ **in confidence** in via confidenziale ◇ *I'm telling you this in confidence.* Te lo dico in via confidenziale.

confident ['kɔnfɪdənt] ADJECTIVE
[1] sicuro ◇ *I'm confident everything will be okay.* Sono sicuro che tutto andrà bene.
[2] sicuro di sé ◇ *She seems very confident.* Sembra molto sicura di sé.

confidential [kɔnfɪ'dɛnʃəl] ADJECTIVE
confidenziale

confirm [kən'fə:m] VERB
confermare

confirmation [kɔnfə'meɪʃən] NOUN
la conferma

conflict ['kɔnflɪkt] NOUN
il conflitto

confuse [kən'fju:z] VERB
confondere

confused [kən'fju:zd] ADJECTIVE
confuso *(person, situation)*

confusing [kən'fju:zɪŋ] ADJECTIVE
confuso ◇ *It's all very confusing.* È tutto molto confuso.
♦ **All these messages are confusing for young people.** Tutti questi messaggi confondono i giovani.

confusion [kən'fju:ʒən] NOUN
la confusione

to **congratulate** [kən'grætjuleɪt] VERB
congratularsi con E ◇ *My friends congratulated me on passing my test.* I miei amici si sono congratulati con me per aver passato l'esame di guida.

congratulations [kəngrætju'leɪʃənz] NOUN PL
le congratulazioni ◇ *Congratulations on your new job!* Congratulazioni per il tuo nuovo lavoro!

conjunction [kən'dʒʌŋkʃən] NOUN
la congiunzione

conjurer ['kʌndʒərə'] NOUN
il prestigiatore

to **conjure up** [kʌndʒər'ʌp] VERB
rievocare *(memories)*

connection [kə'nɛkʃən] NOUN
[1] il rapporto ◇ *There's no connection between the two events.* Non c'è rapporto tra i due fatti.
[2] la coincidenza ◇ *We missed our connection.* Abbiamo perso la coincidenza.
♦ **connection to the Internet** collegamento ad Internet
♦ **a loose connection** un filo staccato

to **conquer** ['kɔŋkə'] VERB
[1] conquistare *(country)*
[2] vincere *(enemy)*

conscience ['kɔnʃəns] NOUN
la coscienza
♦ **to have a clear conscience** avere* la coscienza pulita
♦ **to have a guilty conscience** avere* la coscienza sporca

conscious ['kɔnʃəs] ADJECTIVE
[1] consapevole ◇ *She was conscious of it.* Ne era consapevole.
♦ **to make a conscious decision to** decidere* deliberatamente di ◇ *He made a conscious decision to tell nobody.* Ha deciso deliberatamente di non dirlo a nessuno.
[2] in sé ◇ *He was still conscious when the doctor arrived.* Era ancora in sé quando è arrivato il dottore.

consciousness ['kɔnʃəsnɪs] NOUN
la conoscenza ◇ *I lost consciousness.* Ho perso conoscenza.

consequence ['kɔnsɪkwəns] NOUN
la conseguenza

consequently ['kɔnsɪkwəntlɪ] ADVERB ☞

di conseguenza

conservation [kɒnsə'veɪʃən] NOUN
[1] la tutela ◇ *It's a report on the conservation of rain forests.* È una relazione sulla tutela delle foreste pluviali.
[2] la salvaguardia ambientale ◇ *a conservation project* un progetto di salvaguardia ambientale
- **People are aware of the need for conservation.** La gente sa che è necessario salvaguardare l'ambiente.
- **energy conservation** risparmio energetico

conservative [kən'sɜːvətɪv] ADJECTIVE
see also **conservative** NOUN
conservatore ◇ *the Conservative Party* il partito conservatore

conservative [kən'sɜːvətɪv] NOUN
see also **conservative** ADJECTIVE
il conservatore
la conservatrice
(*person*)
◇ *He votes Conservative.* Vota per i conservatori.

conservatory [kən'sɜːvətrɪ] NOUN (PL **conservatories**)
la veranda chiusa

to **consider** [kən'sɪdə'] VERB
[1] prendere* in considerazione ◇ *I'm considering the idea.* Sto prendendo in considerazione l'idea.
[2] ritenere* ◇ *He considers it a waste of time.* La ritiene una perdita di tempo.

considerate [kən'sɪdərɪt] ADJECTIVE
premuroso

considering [kən'sɪdərɪŋ] PREPOSITION
[1] dato che ◇ *Considering we were there for a month...* Dato che ci siamo rimasti per un mese...
[2] tutto sommato ◇ *I got a good mark, considering.* Tutto sommato ho preso un bel voto.

to **consist** [kən'sɪst] VERB
- **to consist of** consistere E di

consistent [kən'sɪstənt] ADJECTIVE
dal rendimento costante ◇ *consistent player* un giocatore dal rendimento costante
- **to be consistent with** essere* E coerente con ◇ *It is consistent with his views.* È coerente con il suo modo di pensare.

consonant ['kɒnsənənt] NOUN
la consonante

constant ['kɒnstənt] ADJECTIVE
costante ◇ *Meat must be kept at a constant temperature.* La carne deve essere tenuta a temperatura costante.

constantly ['kɒnstəntlɪ] ADVERB
in continuazione

constipated ['kɒnstɪpeɪtɪd] ADJECTIVE
stitico

to **construct** [kən'strʌkt] VERB
costruire

construction [kən'strʌkʃən] NOUN
la costruzione

consulate ['kɒnsjʊlɪt] NOUN
il consolato

to **consult** [kən'sʌlt] VERB
consultare

consumer [kən'sjuːmə'] NOUN
il consumatore
la consumatrice

contact ['kɒntækt] NOUN
see also **contact** VERB
il contatto ◇ *I'm in contact with her.* Sono in contatto con lei.

to **contact** ['kɒntækt] VERB
see also **contact** NOUN
contattare

contact lenses ['kɒntæktlɛnzɪz] NOUN PL
le lenti a contatto

to **contain** [kən'teɪn] VERB
contenere*

container [kən'teɪnə'] NOUN
il contenitore

contempt [kən'tempt] NOUN
il disprezzo

contents ['kɒntents] NOUN PL
il contenuto SING
- **the table of contents** l' indice MASC

contest ['kɒntest] NOUN
[1] la gara ◇ *a fishing contest* una gara di pesca
[2] la lotta ◇ *He won the leadership contest by a large margin.* Ha vinto la lotta per la leadership con un largo margine.
- **a beauty contest** un concorso di bellezza

contestant [kən'testənt] NOUN
il/la concorrente

context ['kɒntekst] NOUN
il contesto

continent ['kɒntɪnənt] NOUN
il continente
- **the Continent** l'Europa continentale

> **ⓘ** *I britannici, data la loro posizione insulare, chiamano il resto d'Europa "the Continent".*

continental breakfast ['kɒntɪnentl'brekfəst] NOUN
la colazione

> **ⓘ** *La* **continental breakfast** *è la colazione a base di pane, burro e marmellata servita negli alberghi in alternativa alla tradizionale colazione all'inglese con uova e pancetta.*

to **continue** [kən'tɪnjuː] VERB
[1] continuare ◇ *She continued talking to her friend.* Ha continuato a parlare alla sua amica.
[2] riprendere* (*after a break*) ◇ *We continued working after lunch.* Abbiamo ripreso a lavorare dopo pranzo.

* Verbs followed by this symbol are irregular. See pp.339–364 for further details.

continuous [kən'tɪnjuəs] ADJECTIVE
continuo

contraceptive [kɔntrə'septɪv] NOUN
il contraccettivo

contract ['kɔntrækt] NOUN
il contratto

to **contradict** [kɔntrə'dɪkt] VERB
contraddire

contrary ['kɔntrərɪ] NOUN
il contrario

♦ **on the contrary** al contrario

♦ **contrary to** contrariamente a ◊ *Contrary to what you may have heard, I am not resigning.* Contrariamente a quello che potete aver sentito, non mi dimetto.

contrast ['kɔntrɑːst] NOUN
il contrasto

to **contribute** [kən'trɪbjuːt] VERB
  1 contribuire ◊ *Everyone contributed to the success of the play.* Tutti hanno contribuito al successo della commedia.
  2 contribuire con ◊ *She contributed £10 to the collection.* Ha contribuito alla colletta con dieci sterline.
  3 partecipare ◊ *He didn't contribute to the discussion.* Non ha partecipato alla discussione.

contribution [kɔntrɪ'bjuːʃən] NOUN
il contributo

control [kən'trəul] NOUN
see also **control** VERB
il controllo ◊ *Everything is under control.* Tutto è sotto controllo.

♦ **He always seems to be in control.** Non perde mai il controllo della situazione.

♦ **to lose control** (*of car, oneself*) perdere* E il controllo

♦ **to keep control of** tenere* sotto controllo ◊ *She can't keep control of the class.* Non riesce a tenere la classe sotto controllo.

♦ **to be out of control** (*child*) essere* E scatenato

♦ **the controls** (*of car, plane*) i comandi

to **control** [kən'trəul] VERB
see also **control** NOUN
  1 dirigere (*country, organization*)
  2 tenere* sotto controllo ◊ *He can't control the class.* Non riesce a tenere la classe sotto controllo.
  3 controllare ◊ *Please control yourself, everyone's looking at us.* Per favore, controllati, tutti ci guardano.

control tower [kən'trəultauə'] NOUN
la torre di controllo

controversial [kɔntrə'vəːʃl] ADJECTIVE
controverso ◊ *Euthanasia is a controversial subject.* L'eutanasia è un argomento controverso.

convenient [kən'viːnɪənt] ADJECTIVE
  1 vicino (*place*) ◊ *The hotel's convenient for the airport.* L'albergo è vicino all'aeroporto.
  2 comodo ◊ *It is more convenient to eat in the kitchen.* È più comodo mangiare in cucina.

♦ **It's not a convenient time for me.** Non sono libero a quell'ora.

♦ **Would Monday be convenient for you?** Ti andrebbe bene lunedì?

*Be careful not to translate **convenient** by the Italian word **conveniente**.*

conventional [kən'venʃnl] ADJECTIVE
  1 tradizionalista ◊ *My parents are very conventional.* I miei genitori sono molto tradizionalisti.
  2 tradizionale ◊ *a conventional method* un metodo tradizionale

♦ **conventional weapons** le armi convenzionali

conversation [kɔnvə'seɪʃən] NOUN
la conversazione ◊ *We had a long conversation.* Abbiamo fatto una lunga conversazione.

to **convert** [kən'vəːt] VERB
trasformare ◊ *We've converted the loft into a bedroom.* Abbiamo trasformato la soffitta in una camera da letto.

to **convict** [kən'vɪkt] VERB
see also **convict** NOUN
dichiarare colpevole ◊ *He was convicted of the murder.* È stato dichiarato colpevole del delitto.

convict ['kɔnvɪkt] NOUN
see also **convict** VERB
il carcerato
la carcerata

conviction [kən'vɪkʃən] NOUN
  1 la convinzione ◊ *She spoke with great conviction.* Ha parlato con grande convinzione.
  2 la condanna ◊ *He has three previous convictions for robbery.* Ha tre precedenti condanne per furto.

to **convince** [kən'vɪns] VERB
convincere

to **cook** [kuk] VERB
see also **cook** NOUN
  1 cucinare ◊ *I can't cook.* Non so cucinare. ◊ *The chicken isn't cooked.* Il pollo non è cotto.
  2 preparare ◊ *She's cooking lunch.* Sta preparando il pranzo.

cook [kuk] NOUN
see also **cook** VERB
il cuoco (PL i cuochi)
la cuoca (PL le cuoche)

cookbook ['kukbuk] NOUN
il libro di cucina

cooker ['kukə'] NOUN
il fornello ◊ *a gas cooker* un fornello a gas

cookery ['kukərɪ] NOUN
la cucina

cookie ['kukɪ] NOUN US   ☞

C

il biscotto

cooking ['kukɪŋ] NOUN
la cucina ◇ French cooking la cucina
francese
 ♦ **I like cooking.** Mi piace cucinare.

cool [kuːl] ADJECTIVE
see also **cool** VERB
[1] fresco ◇ *a cool place* un luogo fresco
◇ *It's cool.* Fa fresco.
[2] leggero ◇ *a cool top* una maglietta
leggera
[3] figo ◇ *They think it's cool to do drugs.*
Pensano che sia figo drogarsi.
 ♦ **Keep your cool!** Calma!

to **cool** [kuːl] VERB
see also **cool** ADJECTIVE
raffreddare (*food*)
 ♦ **Just cool it!** Calmati!

cooperation [kəʊɔpəˈreɪʃən] NOUN
la cooperazione

cop [kɔp] NOUN
il poliziotto

to **cope** [kəʊp] VERB
farcela ◇ *It was hard, but we coped.* È stato
difficile ma ce l'abbiamo fatta.
 ♦ **to cope with** affrontare ◇ *She's got a lot of
problems to cope with.* Ha molti problemi
da affrontare.

copied ['kɔpɪd] VERB *see* **copy**

copper ['kɔpə'] NOUN
[1] il rame ◇ *a copper bracelet* un
braccialetto di rame
[2] il poliziotto ◇ *our friendly
neighbourhood copper* il cordiale poliziotto
del nostro quartiere

copy ['kɔpɪ] NOUN (PL **copies**)
see also **copy** VERB
la copia
 ♦ **rough copy** la brutta copia
 ♦ **fair copy** la bella copia

to **copy** ['kɔpɪ] VERB (**copied, copied**)
see also **copy** NOUN
copiare

core [kɔː'] NOUN
il torsolo (*of apple*)

cork [kɔːk] NOUN
[1] il tappo (*of bottle*)
[2] il sughero (*material*)

corkscrew ['kɔːkskruː] NOUN
il cavatappi (PL i cavatappi)

corn [kɔːn] NOUN
[1] il grano (*wheat*) ◇ *fields of corn* campi di
grano
[2] il granturco (*maize*)
 ♦ **corn on the cob** la pannocchia bollita

corner ['kɔːnə'] NOUN
l' angolo ◇ *the shop on the corner* il negozio
all'angolo ◇ *He lives just round the corner.*
Abita qua dietro l'angolo.
 ♦ **a corner kick** un calcio d'angolo

cornet ['kɔːnɪt] NOUN

[1] la cornetta (*instrument*)
[2] il cornetto (*ice cream*)

cornflakes ['kɔːnfleɪks] NOUN PL
i fiocchi di granturco

cornstarch ['kɔːnstɑːtʃ] NOUN US
la fecola di patate

Cornwall ['kɔːnwəl] NOUN
la Cornovaglia

corporal punishment ['kɔːpərl'pʌnɪʃmənt]
NOUN
la punizione corporale

corpse [kɔːps] NOUN
il cadavere

correct [kəˈrekt] ADJECTIVE
see also **correct** VERB
giusto ◇ *That's correct.* È giusto.
 ♦ **the correct answer** la risposta esatta
 ♦ **to be correct** avere* ragione ◇ *You're
absolutely correct.* Hai proprio ragione.

to **correct** [kəˈrekt] VERB
see also **correct** ADJECTIVE
correggere

correction [kəˈrekʃən] NOUN
la correzione
 ♦ **correction fluid** bianchetto

correctly [kəˈrektlɪ] ADVERB
correttamente

correspondent [kɔrɪsˈpɔndənt] NOUN
il/la corrispondente (*on paper*)

corridor ['kɔrɪdɔː'] NOUN
il corridoio

corruption [kəˈrʌpʃən] NOUN
la corruzione

Corsica ['kɔːsɪkə] NOUN
la Corsica

cosmetics [kɔzˈmetɪks] NOUN PL
i cosmetici

cosmetic surgery [kɔzmetɪk'səːdʒərɪ] NOUN
la chirurgia estetica

to **cost** [kɔst] VERB (**cost, cost**)
see also **cost** NOUN
costare^E ◇ *How much does it cost?* Quanto
costa?

cost [kɔst] NOUN
see also **cost** VERB
il costo ◇ *the cost of living* il costo della vita
 ♦ **at all costs** a tutti i costi
 ♦ **cost price** il prezzo all'ingrosso

costume ['kɔstjuːm] NOUN
il costume

cosy ['kəʊzɪ] ADJECTIVE
accogliente ◇ *a cosy room* una stanza
accogliente
 ♦ **to be cosy** (*person*) stare* bene ◇ *I'm very
cosy here.* Sto proprio bene qui.

cot [kɔt] NOUN
[1] il lettino (*for baby*)
[2] la brandina (*camp bed*) US

cottage ['kɔtɪdʒ] NOUN
la villetta

cottage cheese [kɔtɪdʒ'tʃiːz] NOUN

---
* Verbs followed by this symbol are irregular. See pp.339–364 for further details.

i fiocchi di latte

cotton [ˈkɔtn] NOUN
il cotone ◇ *a cotton shirt* una camicia di cotone

cotton candy [kɔtnˈkændɪ] NOUN
lo zucchero filato

cotton wool [kɔtnˈwul] NOUN
l' ovatta

couch [kautʃ] NOUN (PL **couches**)
il divano ◇ *He was sitting on the couch.* Era seduto sul divano.
♦ **couch potato** pigrone teledipendente

couchette [kuːˈʃet] NOUN
la cuccetta

to **cough** [kɔf] VERB
see also **cough** NOUN
tossire

cough [kɔf] NOUN
see also **cough** VERB
la tosse ◇ *I've got a cough.* Ho la tosse.
♦ **a cough mixture** uno sciroppo per la tosse

could [kud] VERB
see also **can** VERB

could *is often translated by conditional tenses of* **potere**.
◇ *Could you please close the window?* Potresti chiudere la finestra per favore?
◇ *You could be right.* Potresti avere ragione.
◇ *You could have killed me.* Avresti potuto uccidermi. ◇ *We couldn't wait.* Non abbiamo potuto aspettare.
When it means "couldn't manage to" **couldn't** *is often translated by the appropriate tense of* **riuscire**.
◇ *He couldn't concentrate because of the noise.* Non riusciva a concentrarsi a causa del rumore. ◇ *He said that he couldn't do it by next Friday.* Ha detto che non sarebbe riuscito a farlo per il venerdì seguente.
When it means "knew how to" **could** *is often translated by the appropriate tense of* **sapere**.
◇ *I thought you could drive.* Pensavo che sapessi guidare.
could *is sometimes not translated.*
◇ *I could see that something was wrong.* Capivo che c'era qualcosa che non andava.

council [ˈkaunsl] NOUN
il consiglio comunale (*in town*) ◇ *He's on the council.* Fa parte del consiglio comunale.
♦ **a council estate** un complesso di case popolari

ⓘ *Un* **council estate** *è un quartiere di edilizia popolare formato da palazzi o palazzine.*

♦ **a council house** una casa popolare
councillor [ˈkaunslə'] NOUN
♦ **a local councillor** un consigliere comunale
to **count** [kaunt] VERB
contare ◇ *You can count on me.* Puoi contare su di me.

counter [ˈkauntə'] NOUN
① il banco (PL i banchi) (*in shop*)
② lo sportello (*in post office, bank*)
③ il gettone (*for game*)

country [ˈkʌntrɪ] NOUN (PL **countries**)
① il paese ◇ *the border between the two countries* il confine tra i due paesi
② la campagna ◇ *I live in the country.* Vivo in campagna.
♦ **a country house** una villa in campagna
♦ **country dancing** danza popolare

countryside [ˈkʌntrɪsaɪd] NOUN
la campagna

county [ˈkauntɪ] NOUN (PL **counties**)
la contea

ⓘ *Una* **county** *è una regione avente un'amministrazione locale.*

♦ **the county council** il consiglio di contea
couple [ˈkʌpl] NOUN
① la coppia ◇ *the couple who live next door* la coppia che vive qui accanto
② il paio ◇ *a couple of hours* un paio d'ore

courage [ˈkʌrɪdʒ] NOUN
il coraggio

courgette [kuəˈʒet] NOUN
la zucchina

courier [ˈkurɪə'] NOUN
① l' accompagnatore turistico
l' accompagnatrice turistica
(*for tourists*)
② il corriere (*delivery service*) ◇ *They sent it by courier.* L'hanno spedito con il corriere.

course [kɔːs] NOUN
① il corso ◇ *a French course* un corso di francese
② la portata ◇ *the main course* la portata principale
♦ **the first course** il primo piatto
③ il campo ◇ *a golf course* un campo da golf
♦ **of course** certo ◇ *Do you love me? – Of course I do!* Mi ami? – Ma certo!

court [kɔːt] NOUN
la corte (*legal, royal*)
♦ **a tennis court** un campo da tennis

courtyard [ˈkɔːtjɑːd] NOUN
il cortile

cousin [ˈkʌzn] NOUN
il cugino
la cugina

cover [ˈkʌvə'] NOUN
see also **cover** VERB
① la copertina (*of book*)
② la coperta (*on bed*)

to **cover** [ˈkʌvə'] VERB
see also **cover** NOUN
coprire ◇ *He covered his face.* Si coprì il viso.

to **cover up** [kʌvər'ʌp] VERB
tenere* nascosto ◇ *The government tried to cover up the details of the accident.* Il governo ha cercato di tenere nascosti i particolari dell'incidente.

cover charge ['kʌvətʃɑːdʒ] NOUN
il coperto

cover-up ['kʌvərʌp] NOUN
l' occultamento di informazioni

cow [kau] NOUN
la mucca (PL le mucche)

coward ['kauəd] NOUN
il codardo
la codarda

cowardly ['kauədlɪ] ADJECTIVE
vigliacco

cowboy ['kaubɔɪ] NOUN
il cowboy (PL i cowboy)

crab [kræb] NOUN
il granchio

crack [kræk] NOUN
see also **crack** VERB
[1] la crepa (*in wall*)
[2] l' incrinatura (*in cup, plate*)
[3] il crack (*drug*)
◆ **to open the door a crack** aprire* la porta lasciandola accostata
◆ **I'll have a crack at it.** Ci proverò.

to **crack** [kræk] VERB
see also **crack** NOUN
[1] rompere (*egg, nut*)
[2] sbattere* ◇ *He cracked his head on the pavement.* Ha sbattuto la testa sul pavimento.
◆ **I think we've cracked it!** Penso che ci siamo!
◆ **to crack a joke** fare* una battuta

to **crack down on** [kræk'daunɔn] VERB
prendere* serie misure contro ◇ *The police are cracking down on motorists who drive too fast.* La polizia sta prendendo serie misure contro i motociclisti che vanno troppo veloci.

cracked [krækt] ADJECTIVE
incrinato (*cup, plate, window*)

cracker ['krækəʳ] NOUN
il cracker (PL i cracker) (*biscuit*)
◆ **a Christmas cracker** un mortaretto con sorpresa

❶ //**Christmas cracker** è una specie di grosso petardo di cartone che si tira alle estremità e che scoppia facendo uscire una piccola sorpresa.

cradle ['kreɪdl] NOUN
la culla

craft [krɑːft] NOUN
l' artigianato
◆ **a craft shop** un negozio che vende prodotti d'artigianato

craftsman ['krɑːftsmən] NOUN (PL **craftsmen**)

l' artigiano

to **cram** [kræm] VERB
[1] stipare ◇ *We crammed our stuff into the boot.* Abbiamo stipato la nostra roba nel bagagliaio.
[2] riempire ◇ *She crammed her bag with books.* Ha riempito la borsa di libri.
◆ **to cram for an exam** studiare come un pazzo per un esame

crammed [kræmd] ADJECTIVE
◆ **to be crammed with** essere* ᴱ pieno zeppo di ◇ *Her house was crammed with furniture.* La casa era piena zeppa di mobili.

crane [kreɪn] NOUN
la gru (PL le gru)

to **crash** [kræʃ] VERB
see also **crash** NOUN
[1] scontrarsi ᴱ ◇ *The two cars crashed.* Le due macchine si sono scontrate.
◆ **He's crashed his car.** Ha avuto un incidente con la macchina.
[2] precipitare ᴱ ◇ *The plane crashed.* L'aereo è precipitato.
[3] impiantarsi ᴱ ◇ *I'd nearly finished when my computer crashed.* Avevo quasi finito quando il computer si è impiantato.

crash [kræʃ] NOUN (PL **crashes**)
see also **crash** VERB
[1] l' incidente MASC (*car crash*)
[2] la caduta (*plane crash*)

crash course ['kræʃkɔːs] NOUN
il corso intensivo

crash helmet ['kræʃhelmɪt] NOUN
il casco di protezione (PL i caschi di protezione)

crash landing ['kræʃlændɪŋ] NOUN
l' atterraggio di fortuna

to **crawl** [krɔːl] VERB
see also **crawl** NOUN
andare* ᴱ gattoni (*baby*)

crawl [krɔːl] NOUN
see also **crawl** VERB
lo stile libero
◆ **to do the crawl** nuotare a stile libero

crazy ['kreɪzɪ] ADJECTIVE
pazzo ◇ *She's crazy about him.* È pazza di lui. ◇ *Paul is crazy about football.* Paul va pazzo per il calcio.

cream [kriːm] ADJECTIVE
see also **cream** NOUN
crema ◇ *a cream silk blouse* una camicetta di seta crema

cream [kriːm] NOUN
see also **cream** ADJECTIVE
[1] la panna ◇ *strawberries and cream* fragole con panna ◇ *a cream cake* una torta alla panna
◆ **cream cheese** formaggio cremoso
[2] la crema (*for skin*) ◇ *sun cream* crema solare

crease [kriːs] NOUN

---

* Verbs followed by this symbol are irregular. See pp.339–364 for further details.

la piega (PL le pieghe)

creased [kriːst] ADJECTIVE
spiegazzato

to **create** [kriːˈeɪt] VERB
creare

creation [kriːˈeɪʃən] NOUN
la creazione

creative [kriːˈeɪtɪv] ADJECTIVE
creativo

creature [ˈkriːtʃəʳ] NOUN
la creatura

crèche [krɛʃ] NOUN
l' asilo nido

credit [ˈkrɛdɪt] NOUN
il credito ◇ *on credit* a credito

credit card [ˈkrɛdɪtkɑːd] NOUN
la carta di credito

creep [kriːp] NOUN
+ **He's a creep.** È un tipo viscido.
+ **It gives me the creeps.** Mi fa venire la pelle d'oca.

to **creep up** [kriːpˈʌp] VERB (**crept, crept**)
+ **to creep up on somebody** avvicinarsi [E] quatto quatto a qualcuno

crept [krɛpt] VERB *see* **creep up**

cress [krɛs] NOUN
il crescione

crew [kruː] NOUN
l' equipaggio (*of ship, plane*)
+ **a film crew** una troupe cinematografica

crew cut [ˈkruːkʌt] NOUN
il taglio a spazzola

cricket [ˈkrɪkɪt] NOUN
[1] il cricket ◇ *I play cricket.* Gioco a cricket.
[2] il grillo (*insect*)

cried [kraɪd] VERB *see* **cry**

crime [kraɪm] NOUN
[1] il crimine ◇ *He committed a crime.* Ha commesso un crimine.
+ **the scene of the crime** la scena del delitto
[2] la criminalità ◇ *Crime is rising.* La criminalità è in aumento.

criminal [ˈkrɪmɪnl] NOUN
see also **criminal** ADJECTIVE
il/la criminale ◇ *a dangerous criminal* un pericoloso criminale

criminal [ˈkrɪmɪnl] ADJECTIVE
see also **criminal** NOUN
+ **a criminal offence** un reato
+ **to have a criminal record** avere* [E] precedenti penali

crippled [ˈkrɪpld] ADJECTIVE
+ **to be crippled in an accident** rimanere* [E] invalido in un incidente
+ **to be crippled with arthritis** soffrire* di una grave forma di artrite

crisis [ˈkraɪsɪs] NOUN (PL **crises**)
la crisi (PL le crisi)

crisp [krɪsp] ADJECTIVE
croccante (*food*)

crisps [krɪsps] NOUN PL

le patatine ◇ *a bag of crisps* un sacchetto di patatine

criterion [kraɪˈtɪəriən] NOUN (PL **criteria**)
[1] il criterio ◇ *I don't understand what their criteria were.* Non riesco a capire i criteri che hanno seguito.
+ **Price should not be the only criterion.** Il prezzo non dovrebbe essere l'unico criterio di scelta.
[2] il requisito ◇ *Only one candidate met all the criteria.* Un solo candidato soddisfava tutti i requisiti.

critic [ˈkrɪtɪk] NOUN
il critico (PL i critici)

critical [ˈkrɪtɪkl] ADJECTIVE
critico

criticism [ˈkrɪtɪsɪzəm] NOUN
la critica (PL le critiche)

to **criticize** [ˈkrɪtɪsaɪz] VERB
criticare

Croatia [krəʊˈeɪʃə] NOUN
la Croazia

to **crochet** [ˈkrəʊʃeɪ] VERB
lavorare all'uncinetto

crocodile [ˈkrɒkədaɪl] NOUN
il coccodrillo

crook [krʊk] NOUN
l' imbroglione ◇ *He's a crook.* È un imbroglione.
+ **a petty crook** un piccolo delinquente

crop [krɒp] NOUN
il raccolto

cross [krɒs] NOUN (PL **crosses**)
see also **cross** ADJECTIVE, VERB
la croce

cross [krɒs] ADJECTIVE
see also **cross** NOUN, VERB
arrabbiato ◇ *He was cross about something.* Era arrabbiato per qualcosa.

to **cross** [krɒs] VERB
see also **cross** ADJECTIVE, NOUN
attraversare (*street, bridge*)

to **cross out** [krɒsˈaʊt] VERB
cancellare

cross-country [krɒsˈkʌntri] NOUN
+ **a cross-country race** una corsa campestre
+ **cross-country skiing** sci da fondo MASC

crossing [ˈkrɒsɪŋ] NOUN
[1] la traversata ◇ *a ten-hour crossing* una traversata di dieci ore
[2] il passaggio pedonale ◇ *Always cross at the crossing.* Attraversa sempre sul passaggio pedonale.

crossroads [ˈkrɒsrəʊdz] NOUN SING
l' incrocio

crossword [ˈkrɒswɜːd] NOUN
le parole crociate

crow [krəʊ] NOUN
la cornacchia (PL le cornacchie)

crowd [kraʊd] NOUN
see also **crowd** VERB

Verbs followed by the symbol "E" require the auxiliary "essere"

la folla

to **crowd** [kraud] VERB
see also **crowd** NOUN
affollarsi^E ◇ *The children crowded round the model.* I bambini si sono affollati attorno al modellino.

crowded ['kraudɪd] ADJECTIVE
affollato

crown [kraun] NOUN
la corona
♦ **the crown jewels** i gioielli della Corona

crucifix ['kru:sɪfɪks] NOUN (PL **crucifixes**)
il crocefisso

crude [kru:d] ADJECTIVE
volgare ◇ *crude language* linguaggio volgare

cruel ['kruəl] ADJECTIVE
crudele

cruise [kru:z] NOUN
la crociera

crumb [krʌm] NOUN
la briciola

to **crush** [krʌʃ] VERB
see also **crush** NOUN
1 schiacciare (*can*)
2 tritare ◇ *Crush two cloves of garlic.* Tritate due spicchi d'aglio.

crush [krʌʃ] NOUN
see also **crush** VERB
♦ **to have a crush on somebody** avere* una cotta per qualcuno ◇ *She's had a crush on him for months.* Ha una cotta per lui da mesi.

crutch [krʌtʃ] NOUN (PL **crutches**)
la stampella

to **cry** [kraɪ] VERB (**cried, cried**)
see also **cry** NOUN
1 piangere ◇ *The baby's crying.* Il bambino sta piangendo.
2 gridare ◇ *"You're wrong," he cried.* "Hai torto," gridò.

cry [kraɪ] NOUN
see also **cry** VERB
1 il pianto ◇ *After he left she had a good cry.* Dopo che lui è partito lei si è fatta un bel pianto.
2 il grido (PL FEM le grida)
The plural of **grido** *is usually feminine.*
◇ *With a cry, she rushed forward.* Con un grido si lanciò in avanti.

crystal ['krɪstl] NOUN
il cristallo

CTC [si:ti:'si:] NOUN (= *city technology college*)
l' istituto tecnico (PL gli istituti tecnici)

cub [kʌb] NOUN
1 il cucciolo (*animal*)
2 il lupetto (*scout*)

cube [kju:b] NOUN
1 il cubetto ◇ *Cut the meat into cubes.* Tagliate la carne a cubetti.

2 la zolletta (*of sugar*)
3 il cubo (*in geometry*)

cubic ['kju:bɪk] ADJECTIVE
♦ **a cubic metre** un metro cubo

cucumber ['kju:kʌmbə'] NOUN
il cetriolo ◇ *tomatoes and cucumbers* pomodori e cetrioli
♦ **to be as cool as a cucumber** essere*^E imperturbabile

cuddle ['kʌdl] NOUN
see also **cuddle** VERB
la carezza ◇ *kisses and cuddles* baci e carezze
♦ **Come and give me a cuddle.** Vieni ad abbracciarmi.

to **cuddle** ['kʌdl] VERB
see also **cuddle** NOUN
abbracciare

cue [kju:] NOUN
la stecca (PL le stecche) (*for snooker, pool*)

culottes [kju'lɔts] NOUN PL
la gonna pantalone (PL le gonne pantalone)

culture ['kʌltʃə'] NOUN
la cultura

cunning ['kʌnɪŋ] ADJECTIVE
1 furbo (*person*)
2 ingegnoso ◇ *a cunning plan* un piano ingegnoso

cup [kʌp] NOUN
1 la tazza ◇ *a cup of coffee* una tazza di caffè
2 la coppa (*trophy*)

cupboard ['kʌbəd] NOUN
1 l' armadio (*anywhere*)
2 la credenza (*in kitchen*)

to **cure** [kjuə'] VERB
see also **cure** NOUN
guarire

cure [kjuə'] NOUN
see also **cure** VERB
la cura

curious ['kjuərɪəs] ADJECTIVE
curioso

curl [kɜ:l] NOUN
il ricciolo

curly ['kɜ:lɪ] ADJECTIVE
riccio ◇ *curly hair* capelli ricci

currant ['kʌrnt] NOUN
♦ **currants** uva passa SING
♦ **a currant bun** un panino con l'uva passa

currency ['kʌrnsɪ] NOUN (PL **currencies**)
la valuta ◇ *foreign currency* valuta estera

current ['kʌrnt] NOUN
see also **current** ADJECTIVE
la corrente

current ['kʌrnt] ADJECTIVE
see also **current** NOUN
1 attuale ◇ *The current situation is quite unacceptable.* La situazione attuale è del tutto inaccettabile.
2 corrente ◇ *the current financial year*

* Verbs followed by this symbol are irregular. See pp.339–364 for further details.

l'anno finanziario corrente

current account ['kʌrntɔkaunt] NOUN
il conto corrente

current affairs [kʌrntə'fɛəz] NOUN PL
l' attualità SING ◇ *She presents a current affairs programme on Monday evenings.* Presenta un programma d'attualità il lunedì sera.

curriculum [kə'rɪkjuləm] NOUN (PL **curriculums** or **curricula**)
il programma (PL i programmi)

curriculum vitae [kə'rɪkjuləm'vi:taɪ] (PL **curriculum vitaes**)
il curriculum vitae (PL i curriculum vitae)

curry ['kʌrɪ] NOUN (PL **curries**)
① il piatto al curry (*dish*)
♦ **to go out for a curry** andare* E al ristorante indiano
② il curry (*spice*) ◇ *a spoonful of curry* un cucchiaio di curry

> ❶ *Molto diffuso in Gran Bretagna, il* **curry** *è un piatto indiano a base di carne o verdure.*

curse [kə:s] NOUN
la maledizione

cursor ['kə:sə'] NOUN
il cursore

curtain ['kə:tn] NOUN
la tenda
♦ **to draw the curtains** tirare le tende

cushion ['kuʃən] NOUN
il cuscino

custard ['kʌstəd] NOUN
la crema pasticciera

custody ['kʌstədɪ] NOUN
l' affidamento (*of children*)
♦ **to be in custody** essere* E in arresto

custom ['kʌstəm] NOUN
l' usanza

customer ['kʌstəmə'] NOUN
il/la cliente

customs ['kʌstəmz] NOUN PL
la dogana
♦ **to go through customs** passare la dogana

customs officer ['kʌstəmzɔfisə'] NOUN
il doganiere

cut [kʌt] NOUN
> see also **cut** VERB
il taglio

to **cut** [kʌt] VERB (**cut, cut**)
> see also **cut** NOUN
tagliare
♦ **to cut oneself** tagliarsi E

to **cut down** [kʌt'daun] VERB
① abbattere (*tree*)
② ridurre ◇ *I'm cutting down on coffee and cigarettes.* Sto riducendo il caffè e le sigarette.

to **cut off** [kʌt'ɔf] VERB
tagliare ◇ *The electricity has been cut off.*

L'elettricità è stata tagliata.
♦ **We've been cut off.** (*while phoning*) È caduta la linea.

to **cut out** [kʌt'aut] VERB
① spegnersi E ◇ *The engine cut out at the traffic lights.* Il motore si è spento al semaforo.
② ritagliare ◇ *I'll cut the article out of the paper.* Ritaglierò l'articolo dal giornale.

to **cut up** [kʌt'ʌp] VERB
sminuzzare (*vegetables, meat*)

cutback ['kʌtbæk] NOUN
il taglio ◇ *Over the past year there have been many cutbacks in public services.* Nell'ultimo hanno ci sono stati molti tagli nei servizi pubblici.

cute [kju:t] ADJECTIVE
carino

cutlery ['kʌtlərɪ] NOUN
le posate FEM PL

cut-price ['kʌt'praɪs] ADJECTIVE
a prezzo ridotto MASC, FEM, PL

cutting ['kʌtɪŋ] NOUN
① il ritaglio (*from newspaper*)
② la talea (*from plant*)

CV [si:'vi:] NOUN
il curriculum vitae (PL i curriculum vitae)

cybercafé ['saɪbəkæfeɪ] NOUN
il cybercaffè (PL i cybercaffè)

cyberspace ['saɪbəspeɪs] NOUN
il ciberspazio

to **cycle** ['saɪkl] VERB
> see also **cycle** NOUN
andare* E in bicicletta ◇ *I cycle to school.* Vado a scuola in bicicletta.

cycle ['saɪkl] NOUN
> see also **cycle** VERB
la bicicletta ◇ *a cycle ride* un giro in bicicletta
♦ **cycle path** pista ciclabile

cycling ['saɪklɪŋ] NOUN
♦ **The roads round here are ideal for cycling.** Le strade qua attorno sono l'ideale per andare in bicicletta.

cyclist ['saɪklɪst] NOUN
il/la ciclista

cylinder ['sɪlɪndə'] NOUN
il cilindro

Cyprus ['saɪprəs] NOUN
Cipro FEM

Czech [tʃek] NOUN
> see also **Czech** ADJECTIVE
① il ceco
la ceca
(*person*)
♦ **the Czechs** i cechi
② il ceco (*language*)

Czech [tʃek] ADJECTIVE
> see also **Czech** NOUN
ceco
♦ **the Czech Republic** la Repubblica ceca

Verbs followed by the symbol "E" require the auxiliary "essere"

D

dad [dæd] NOUN
il papà (PL i papà) ◊ *I'll ask Dad.* Lo chiederò
al papà.

daddy ['dædɪ] NOUN (PL **daddies**)
il papà (PL i papà)

daffodil ['dæfədɪl] NOUN
il trombone

daft [dɑːft] ADJECTIVE
sciocco

daily ['deɪlɪ] ADJECTIVE
see also **daily** ADVERB
quotidiano ◊ *It's part of my daily routine.* Fa
parte del mio tran tran quotidiano.
+ **a daily paper** un quotidiano

daily ['deɪlɪ] ADVERB
see also **daily** ADJECTIVE
ogni giorno ◊ *The pool is open daily from
nine until six.* La piscina è aperta ogni
giorno dalle nove alle diciotto.

dairy ['deərɪ] NOUN (PL **dairies**)
la latteria

dairy products ['deərɪprɒdʌkts] NOUN PL
i latticini

daisy ['deɪzɪ] NOUN (PL **daisies**)
la margherita

dam [dæm] NOUN
la diga

damage ['dæmɪdʒ] NOUN
see also **damage** VERB
i danni MASC PL ◊ *The storm did a lot of
damage.* La tempesta ha causato molti
danni.

to **damage** ['dæmɪdʒ] VERB
see also **damage** NOUN
danneggiare

damn [dæm] NOUN
see also **damn** ADJECTIVE
+ **I don't give a damn!** Me ne frego!
+ **Damn!** Maledizione!

damn [dæm] ADJECTIVE
see also **damn** NOUN
+ **It's a damn nuisance!** Che gran seccatura!

damp [dæmp] ADJECTIVE
umido

dance [dɑːns] NOUN
see also **dance** VERB
1 il ballo ◊ *The last dance was a waltz.*
L'ultimo ballo era un valzer.
2 la danza ◊ *It's a Scottish dance.* È una
danza scozzese.

to **dance** [dɑːns] VERB
see also **dance** NOUN
ballare
+ **to go dancing** andare* E a ballare

dancer ['dɑːnsəʳ] NOUN
il ballerino
la ballerina

dandruff ['dændrəf] NOUN
la forfora

Dane [deɪn] NOUN
il/la danese
+ **the Danes** i danesi

danger ['deɪndʒəʳ] NOUN
il pericolo
+ **in danger** in pericolo
+ **to be in danger of** rischiare di ◊ *We were in
danger of missing the plane.* Rischiavamo
di perdere l'aereo.

dangerous ['deɪndʒrəs] ADJECTIVE
pericoloso

Danish ['deɪnɪʃ] ADJECTIVE
see also **Danish** NOUN
danese

Danish ['deɪnɪʃ] NOUN
see also **Danish** ADJECTIVE
il danese MASC (*language*)

Danish pastry [deɪnɪʃ'peɪstrɪ] NOUN
la focaccina

to **dare** [deəʳ] VERB
1 osare ◊ *I didn't dare tell my parents.*
Non osavo dirlo ai miei genitori.
2 sfidare ◊ *I dare you!* Ti sfido a farlo!
+ **I dare say...** Penso... ◊ *I dare say it'll be
okay.* Penso che andrà bene.

daring ['deərɪŋ] ADJECTIVE
audace

dark [dɑːk] ADJECTIVE
see also **dark** NOUN
1 buio ◊ *It's getting dark.* Si sta facendo
buio.
2 scuro ◊ *a dark green sweater* un
maglione verde scuro
3 bruno ◊ *He's tall, dark and handsome.* È
alto, bruno e bello.

dark [dɑːk] NOUN
see also **dark** ADJECTIVE
il buio
+ **after dark** quando fa buio

dark glasses [dɑːk'glɑːsɪz] NOUN PL
gli occhiali scuri

darkness ['dɑːknɪs] NOUN
l'oscurità

darling ['dɑːlɪŋ] NOUN
caro
cara

dart [dɑːt] NOUN
la freccetta
+ **to play darts** giocare a freccette

to **dash** [dæʃ] VERB
see also **dash** NOUN
1 precipitarsi E ◊ *Everyone dashed to the
window.* Tutti si sono precipitati alla
finestra.
2 scappare E ◊ *I've got to dash!* Devo
scappare!

dash [dæʃ] NOUN (PL **dashes**)
see also **dash** VERB
1 il goccio ◊ *a dash of vinegar* un goccio

---

* Verbs followed by this symbol are irregular. See pp.339–364 for further details.

d'aceto

[2] il trattino *(segno di interpunzione)*

dashboard ['dæʃbɔːd] NOUN
il cruscotto

data ['deɪtə] NOUN PL
i dati

database ['deɪtəbeɪs] NOUN
il database *(PL i database)*

data processing [deɪtə'prəusesɪŋ] NOUN
l' elaborazione elettronica dei dati FEM

date [deɪt] NOUN
[1] la data ◇ *my date of birth* la mia data di nascita
* **What's the date today?** Quanti ne abbiamo oggi?
* **out of date (1)** *(document, product)* scaduto
* **out of date (2)** *(technology, idea)* superato
* **up to date** *(dictionary, book)* aggiornato
[2] l' appuntamento ◇ *I have a date with Mark.* Ho un appuntamento con Mark.
[3] il dattero *(fruit)*

daughter ['dɔːtə'] NOUN
la figlia

daughter-in-law ['dɔːtərɪnlɔː] NOUN (PL **daughters-in-law**)
la nuora

dawn [dɔːn] NOUN
l' alba

day [deɪ] NOUN
[1] il giorno ◇ *every day* ogni giorno ◇ *during the day* di giorno
* **the day after tomorrow** dopodomani
* **the day before yesterday** l'altroieri
* **a day off** un giorno di ferie
* **a day return** un biglietto giornaliero di andata e ritorno
[2] la giornata ◇ *It's a nice day.* È una bella giornata.

dead [dɛd] ADJECTIVE
see also **dead** ADVERB
morto ◇ *He was dead.* Era morto.
* **to be shot dead** essere* E colpito a morte
* **to be a dead loss** non valere niente

dead [dɛd] ADVERB
see also **dead** ADJECTIVE
assolutamente ◇ *You're dead right!* Hai assolutamente ragione!
* **dead on time** in perfetto orario

dead end [dɛd'ɛnd] NOUN
il vicolo cieco

deadline ['dɛdlaɪn] NOUN
la scadenza ◇ *We'll never meet the deadline.* Ci sarà impossibile rispettare la scadenza.

deaf [dɛf] ADJECTIVE
sordo

deafening ['dɛfnɪŋ] ADJECTIVE
assordante

deal [diːl] NOUN
see also **deal** VERB
[1] l' affare MASC ◇ *It's a good deal.* È un

buon affare.
* **It's a deal!** Affare fatto!
[2] l' accordo ◇ *He made a deal with the kidnappers.* Ha fatto un accordo con i rapitori.
* **a great deal of** molto ◇ *a great deal of money* molto denaro

to **deal** [diːl] VERB (**dealt, dealt**)
see also **deal** NOUN
dare le carte ◇ *It's your turn to deal.* Tocca a te dare le carte.

to **deal with** ['diːlwɪð] VERB
occuparsi E di ◇ *He promised to deal with it immediately.* Ha promesso di occuparsene immediatamente.

dealer ['diːlə'] NOUN
* **a drug dealer** uno spacciatore
* **an antique dealer** un antiquario

dealt [dɛlt] VERB see **deal**

dear [dɪə'] ADJECTIVE
caro
* **Dear Paul** Caro Paul
* **Dear Mrs Smith** Gentile Signora Smith
* **Dear Sir/Madam** Egregio Signore/Signora
* **Oh dear!** Oh Dio!

> **ⓘ dear** viene spesso usato anche da commessi, bigliettai, controllori ecc. nel rivolgersi a clienti e passeggeri.

death [dɛθ] NOUN
la morte ◇ *I was bored to death.* Mi annoiavo a morte.

death penalty ['dɛθpɛnltɪ] NOUN
la pena di morte

debate [dɪ'beɪt] NOUN
see also **debate** VERB
il dibattito

to **debate** [dɪ'beɪt] VERB
see also **debate** NOUN
discutere*

debt [dɛt] NOUN
il debito ◇ *He's still paying off his debts.* Sta ancora pagando i debiti.
* **to be in debt** essere* E indebitato

decade ['dɛkeɪd] NOUN
il decennio

decaffeinated [dɪ'kæfɪneɪtɪd] ADJECTIVE
decaffeinato

decay [dɪ'keɪ] NOUN
see also **decay** VERB
* **tooth decay** la carie *(PL le carie)*

to **decay** [dɪ'keɪ] VERB
see also **decay** NOUN
cariarsi E *(teeth)* ◇ *a decaying mansion* una villa in rovina

to **deceive** [dɪ'siːv] VERB
ingannare

December [dɪ'sɛmbə'] NOUN
dicembre ◇ *in December* in dicembre

decent ['diːsənt] ADJECTIVE ☞

D

decente

to **decide** [dɪ'saɪd] VERB
　　① decidere ◇ *I decided to write to her.* Ho deciso di scriverle. ◇ *He decided not to go.* Ha deciso di non andare.
　　② decidersi E ◇ *I can't decide.* Non so decidermi.

to **decide on** [dɪ'saɪdɒn] VERB
　　scegliere

decimal ['desɪməl] ADJECTIVE
　　decimale ◇ *the decimal system* il sistema decimale
　• **decimal point** virgola

decision [dɪ'sɪʒən] NOUN
　　la decisione
　• **to make a decision** prendere* una decisione

decisive [dɪ'saɪsɪv] ADJECTIVE
　　risoluto (*person*)

deck [dek] NOUN
　　① il ponte di coperta (*of ship*)
　　② il piano (*of bus*)
　• **a deck of cards** il mazzo

deck chair ['dektʃeəʳ] NOUN
　　la sedia a sdraio

to **declare** [dɪ'kleəʳ] VERB
　　dichiarare

to **decline** [dɪ'klaɪn] VERB
　　① calare E ◇ *The birth rate is declining.* Il tasso di natalità sta calando.
　　② declinare ◇ *He declined the invitation.* Ha declinato l'invito.

to **decorate** ['dekəreɪt] VERB
　　① decorare (*cake*)
　　② pitturare (*paint*)
　　③ tappezzare (*wallpaper*)

decrease ['diːkriːs] NOUN
　　see also **decrease** VERB
　　la diminuzione ◇ *There has been a decrease in the number of people out of work.* C'è stata una diminuzione del numero dei disoccupati.

to **decrease** [diː'kriːs] VERB
　　see also **decrease** NOUN
　　diminuire ◇ *After three weeks I decreased the dose.* Dopo tre settimane ho diminuito la dose.
　　*When an auxiliary is needed to form past tenses use "essere" when **diminuire** does not have an object.*
　　◇ *The number has decreased* Il numero è diminuito

dedicated ['dedɪkeɪtɪd] ADJECTIVE
　• **a very dedicated teacher** un insegnante che ama molto il suo lavoro

to **deduct** [dɪ'dʌkt] VERB
　　detrarre

deep [diːp] ADJECTIVE
　　profondo ◇ *How deep is the lake?* Quanto è profondo il lago?
　• **to take a deep breath** fare* un respiro profondo

　• **to be deep in debt** essere* E nei debiti fino al collo

deeply ['diːplɪ] ADVERB
　　estremamente ◇ *deeply depressed* estremamente depresso

deer [dɪəʳ] NOUN (PL **deer**)
　　① il cervo (*red deer*)
　　② il daino (*fallow deer*)
　　③ il capriolo (*roe deer*)
　　*There is no general word in Italian for **deer**.*

defeat [dɪ'fiːt] NOUN
　　see also **defeat** VERB
　　la sconfitta

to **defeat** [dɪ'fiːt] VERB
　　see also **defeat** NOUN
　　sconfiggere

defect ['diːfekt] NOUN
　　il difetto

defence [dɪ'fens] NOUN
　　la difesa

to **defend** [dɪ'fend] VERB
　　difendere

defender [dɪ'fendəʳ] NOUN
　　il difensore

defense [dɪ'fens] NOUN US
　　la difesa

to **define** [dɪ'faɪn] VERB
　　definire

definite ['defɪnɪt] ADJECTIVE
　　① preciso ◇ *I haven't got any definite plans.* Non ho un programma preciso.
　　② definitivo ◇ *It's too soon to give a definite answer.* È troppo presto per dare una risposta definitiva.
　　③ sicuro ◇ *Maybe we'll go to Spain, but it's not definite.* Forse andremo in Spagna, ma non è sicuro.
　　④ categorico ◇ *He was definite about it.* È stato categorico a riguardo.
　　⑤ netto ◇ *It's a definite improvement.* È un netto miglioramento.

definitely ['defɪnɪtlɪ] ADVERB
　　decisamente ◇ *He's definitely the best player.* È decisamente il miglior giocatore.
　• **Yes, definitely!** Sicuramente!
　• **Definitely not!** No di certo!

definition [defɪ'nɪʃən] NOUN
　　la definizione

degree [dɪ'griː] NOUN
　　① il grado ◇ *a temperature of thirty degrees* una temperatura di trenta gradi
　　② la laurea ◇ *a degree in English* una laurea in inglese

　🛈 *Italian degrees on average take 4 to 5 years. Exams are both oral and written. In their final exam students are faced by examiners who ask questions about the thesis they have written on a chosen subject.*

to **delay** [dɪ'leɪ] VERB

D

see also **delay** NOUN
rimandare* ◇ *We decided to delay our departure.* Decidemmo di rimandare la partenza.
♦ **Don't delay!** Non perdere tempo!
♦ **to be delayed** subire* un ritardo ◇ *Our flight was delayed.* Il nostro volo ha subito un ritardo.

delay [dɪ'leɪ] NOUN
see also **delay** VERB
il ritardo ◇ *a delay of twenty minutes* un ritardo di venti minuti
♦ **without delay** immediatamente

to **delete** [dɪ'liːt] VERB
cancellare

deliberate [dɪ'lɪbərɪt] ADJECTIVE
intenzionale

deliberately [dɪ'lɪbərɪtlɪ] ADVERB
intenzionalmente

delicate ['delɪkɪt] ADJECTIVE
delicato

delicatessen [delɪkə'tesn] NOUN
la salumeria

> ⓘ *Per* **delicatessen**, *spesso abbreviato in "deli", si intende un negozio che vende salumi, formaggi e generi alimentari di qualità.*

delicious [dɪ'lɪfəs] ADJECTIVE
squisito

delight [dɪ'laɪt] NOUN
il piacere

delighted [dɪ'laɪtɪd] ADJECTIVE
contentissimo ◇ *He'll be delighted to see you.* Sarà contentissimo di vederti.

delightful [dɪ'laɪtful] ADJECTIVE
[1] delizioso ◇ *Lucy is a delightful child.* Lucy è una bambina deliziosa.
[2] incantevole ◇ *Thank you for a delightful evening.* Grazie per l'incantevole serata.

to **deliver** [dɪ'lɪvə'] VERB
consegnare ◇ *They delivered the parcel this morning.* Mi hanno consegnato il pacco stamattina.
♦ **to deliver a baby** far* nascere un bambino

delivery [dɪ'lɪvərɪ] NOUN (PL **deliveries**)
la consegna ◇ *Allow 28 days for delivery.* Calcola 28 giorni per la consegna.

to **demand** [dɪ'maːnd] VERB
see also **demand** NOUN
pretendere ◇ *I demand an explanation.* Pretendo una spiegazione.

demand [dɪ'maːnd] NOUN
see also **demand** VERB
la richiesta

demanding [dɪ'maːndɪŋ] ADJECTIVE
[1] impegnativo ◇ *It's a very demanding job.* È un lavoro molto impegnativo.
[2] esigente ◇ *a demanding child* un bambino esigente

demo ['deməu] NOUN (PL **demos**)
la manifestazione

democracy [dɪ'mɔkrəsɪ] NOUN (PL **democracies**)
la democrazia

democratic [demə'krætɪk] ADJECTIVE
democratico

to **demolish** [dɪ'mɔlɪʃ] VERB
demolire

to **demonstrate** ['demənstreɪt] VERB
[1] dimostrare ◇ *You have to demonstrate that you are reliable.* Devi dimostrare di essere affidabile.
[2] fare* una dimostrazione di ◇ *She demonstrated the technique.* Ha fatto una dimostrazione della tecnica.
[3] manifestare ◇ *They demonstrated outside the court.* Hanno manifestato fuori dal tribunale.

demonstration [demən'streɪʃən] NOUN
la dimostrazione

demonstrator ['demənstreɪtə'] NOUN
il/la dimostrante

denial [dɪ'naɪəl] NOUN
♦ **an official denial** una smentita ufficiale

denied [dɪ'naɪd] VERB *see* **deny**

denim ['denɪm] NOUN
♦ **a denim jacket** una giacca di jeans

denims ['denɪmz] NOUN PL
i blue jeans

Denmark ['denmɑːk] NOUN
la Danimarca

dense [dens] ADJECTIVE
[1] denso ◇ *Dense smoke prevented firemen from entering the building.* Un fumo denso impediva ai pompieri di entrare nell'edificio.
[2] ottuso ◇ *He's so dense!* È così ottuso!

dent [dent] NOUN
see also **dent** VERB
l' ammaccatura

to **dent** [dent] VERB
see also **dent** NOUN
ammaccare

dental ['dentl] ADJECTIVE
♦ **dental treatment** cure dentistiche FEM PL
♦ **a dental appointment** un appuntamento dal dentista

dental floss ['dentl'flɔs] NOUN
il filo interdentale

dentist ['dentɪst] NOUN
il/la dentista ◇ *Faith is a dentist.* Faith fa la dentista.

to **deny** [dɪ'naɪ] VERB (**denied, denied**)
negare

deodorant [diː'əudərənt] NOUN
il deodorante

to **depart** [dɪ'paːt] VERB
partire^E

department [dɪ'paːtmənt] NOUN
il reparto ◇ *the toy department* il reparto ☞

Verbs followed by the symbol "E" require the auxiliary "essere"

giocattoli
- **the English department (1)** (*in school*) i professori di inglese
- **the English department (2)** (*in university*) l'istituto di inglese

department store [dɪ'pɑːtmənstɔːʳ] NOUN
il grande magazzino

departure [dɪ'pɑːtʃəʳ] NOUN
la partenza ◇ *after his departure* dopo la sua partenza

departure lounge [dɪ'pɑːtʃəlaundʒ] NOUN
la sala d'attesa

to **depend** [dɪ'pend] VERB
dipendere*ᴱ ◇ *It depends...* Dipende...
- **to depend on** dipendere*ᴱ da ◇ *The price depends on the quality.* Il prezzo dipende dalla qualità.
- **depending on** a seconda di ◇ *depending on the weather* a seconda del tempo

to **deport** [dɪ'pɔːt] VERB
deportare

deposit [dɪ'pɒzɪt] NOUN
[1] l' acconto ◇ *You have to pay a deposit when you book.* Devi pagare un acconto alla prenotazione.
[2] la cauzione ◇ *You get the deposit back when you return the bike.* Quanto riporti la bici ti ridanno la cauzione.

deposit account [dɪ'pɒzɪtəkaunt] NOUN
il conto vincolato

depressed [dɪ'prest] ADJECTIVE
depresso

depressing [dɪ'presɪŋ] ADJECTIVE
deprimente

depth [depθ] NOUN
la profondità (PL le profondità)

to **descend** [dɪ'send] VERB
scendere*ᴱ ◇ *We descended to the cellar.* Scendemmo in cantina.
- **to descend on** invadere ◇ *Hordes of tourists descend on the village every summer.* Il paese è invaso ogni estate da orde di turisti.
- **to be descended from** discendere* da

to **describe** [dɪs'kraɪb] VERB
descrivere

description [dɪs'krɪpʃən] NOUN
la descrizione

desert ['dezət] NOUN
il deserto

desert island [dezət'aɪlənd] NOUN
l' isola deserta

to **deserve** [dɪ'zɜːv] VERB
meritare

design [dɪ'zaɪn] NOUN
see also **design** VERB
[1] il modello ◇ *a new design of lawnmower* un nuovo modello di tagliaerba
[2] il design (PL i design) ◇ *The design of the plane makes it safer.* Il design rende più sicuro l'aereo.

[3] la progettazione ◇ *a design fault* un difetto di progettazione ◇ *Garden design is a growth industry.* La progettazione di giardini è un'industria in espansione.
[4] il disegno ◇ *a geometric design* un disegno geometrico

to **design** [dɪ'zaɪn] VERB
see also **design** NOUN
[1] disegnare ◇ *She designed the dress herself.* Ha disegnato lei stessa il vestito.
[2] elaborare ◇ *We will design an exercise plan specially for you.* Elaboreremo un programma di esercizi apposta per te.

designer [dɪ'zaɪnəʳ] NOUN
lo/la stilista (*of clothes*)
- **a furniture designer** un designer di mobili una designer di mobili
- **designer clothes** abiti firmati

desire [dɪ'zaɪəʳ] NOUN
see also **desire** VERB
il desiderio

to **desire** [dɪ'zaɪəʳ] VERB
see also **desire** NOUN
desiderare

desk [desk] NOUN
[1] la scrivania (*in office*)
[2] il banco (PL i banchi) (*in school, hotel*)

despair [dɪs'peəʳ] NOUN
la disperazione
- **to be in despair** essere*ᴱ disperato

desperate ['despərɪt] ADJECTIVE
disperato ◇ *a desperate situation* una situazione disperata
- **to get desperate** essere*ᴱ sull'orlo della disperazione
- **to be desperate for** volere* disperatamente

desperately ['despərɪtlɪ] ADVERB
[1] estremamente ◇ *We're desperately worried.* Siamo estremamente preoccupati.
[2] disperatamente ◇ *He was desperately trying to persuade her.* Stava tentando disperatamente di convincerla.

to **despise** [dɪs'paɪz] VERB
disprezzare

despite [dɪs'paɪt] PREPOSITION
malgrado

dessert [dɪ'zɜːt] NOUN
il dessert (PL i dessert)

destination [destɪ'neɪʃən] NOUN
la destinazione

to **destroy** [dɪs'trɔɪ] VERB
distruggere

destruction [dɪs'trʌkʃən] NOUN
la distruzione

detail ['diːteɪl] NOUN
il dettaglio ◇ *I can't remember the details.* Non ricordo i dettagli.

detailed ['diːteɪld] ADJECTIVE
dettagliato

detective [dɪ'tektɪv] NOUN
l' investigatore

---

* Verbs followed by this symbol are irregular. See pp.339–364 for further details.

l' **investigatrice**
◇ *a private detective* un investigatore privato
+ **a detective story** un romanzo poliziesco

detention [dɪˈtɛnʃən] NOUN
+ **to get a detention** essere*[E] trattenuto a scuola

> ❶ *In Gran Bretagna i ragazzi possono venir trattenuti a scuola oltre l'orario come misura disciplinare.*

detergent [dɪˈtəːdʒənt] NOUN
il **detersivo**

determined [dɪˈtəːmɪnd] ADJECTIVE
determinato ◇ *She's a very determined woman.* È una donna molto determinata.
◇ *She's determined to succeed.* È determinata a riuscire.

detour [ˈdiːtuə'] NOUN
la **deviazione**

devaluation [dɪvæljuˈeɪʃən] NOUN
la **svalutazione**

devastated [ˈdevəsteɪtɪd] ADJECTIVE
sconvolto ◇ *I was devastated.* Ero sconvolto.

devastating [ˈdevəsteɪtɪŋ] ADJECTIVE
[1] **devastante** ◇ *Unemployment has a devastating effect on people.* La disoccupazione ha un effetto devastante sulle persone.
[2] **sconvolgente** (*news*) ◇ *She received some devastating news.* Ha ricevuto notizie sconvolgenti.

to **develop** [dɪˈvɛləp] VERB
sviluppare ◇ *I'll get the film developed.* Farò sviluppare la pellicola. ◇ *Girls develop faster than boys.* Le ragazze si sviluppano prima rispetto ai ragazzi.
+ **to develop into** trasformarsi[E] in ◇ *The argument developed into a fight.* La discussione si trasformò in una lite.

developing [dɪˈvɛləpɪŋ] ADJECTIVE
+ **a developing country** un paese in via di sviluppo

development [dɪˈvɛləpmənt] NOUN
lo **sviluppo** ◇ *the latest developments* gli ultimi sviluppi

device [dɪˈvaɪs] NOUN
il **congegno**

devil [ˈdɛvl] NOUN
il **diavolo**

to **devise** [dɪˈvaɪz] VERB
escogitare

to **devote** [dɪˈvəut] VERB
dedicare

devoted [dɪˈvəutɪd] ADJECTIVE
devoto (*husband, friend*)
+ **to be devoted to** essere*[E] molto attaccato a ◇ *He's completely devoted to her.* Le è estremamente attaccato.

diabetes [daɪəˈbiːtiːz] NOUN SING
il **diabete**

diabetic [daɪəˈbɛtɪk] ADJECTIVE
diabetico

diagonal [daɪˈægənl] ADJECTIVE
diagonale

diagram [ˈdaɪəgræm] NOUN
il **diagramma** (PL i diagrammi)

to **dial** [ˈdaɪəl] VERB
formare (*number*)

dialling tone [ˈdaɪəlɪŋˈtəun] NOUN (US **dialing tone**)
il **segnale di libero**

dialogue [ˈdaɪələg] NOUN
il **dialogo** (PL i dialoghi)

diamond [ˈdaɪəmənd] NOUN
il **diamante** ◇ *a diamond ring* un anello con diamante
+ **diamonds** (*in cards*) quadri

diaper [ˈdaɪəpə'] NOUN US
il **pannolino**

diarrhoea [daɪəˈriːə] NOUN (US **diarrhea**)
la **diarrea**

diary [ˈdaɪərɪ] NOUN (PL **diaries**)
[1] l' **agenda** ◇ *I've got her phone number in my diary.* Ho il suo numero di telefono nella mia agenda.
[2] il **diario** ◇ *Her diaries are being published.* I suoi diari saranno pubblicati.

dice [daɪs] NOUN (PL **dice**)
[1] il **dado** ◇ *Throw the dice.* Getta i dadi.
[2] il **cubetto** ◇ *Cut the vegetables into dice.* Tagliate le verdure a cubetti.

dictation [dɪkˈteɪʃən] NOUN
il **dettato**

dictionary [ˈdɪkʃənrɪ] NOUN (PL **dictionaries**)
il **dizionario**

did [dɪd] VERB see **do**

didn't [ˈdɪdnt] = **did not**

to **die** [daɪ] VERB
morire*[E] ◇ *He died last year.* È morto l'anno scorso. ◇ *I'm dying of boredom.* Muoio di noia.
+ **to be dying to do something** morire* dalla voglia di fare qualcosa

to **die down** [daɪˈdaun] VERB
calmarsi[E] ◇ *The wind died down.* Il vento si calmò.

diesel [ˈdiːzl] NOUN
[1] il **gasolio** ◇ *thirty litres of diesel* trenta litri di gasolio
[2] il **diesel** (PL i diesel) ◇ *Our car is a diesel.* La nostra macchina è un diesel.

diet [ˈdaɪət] NOUN
> see also **diet** VERB, ADJECTIVE

[1] l' **alimentazione** ◇ *a healthy diet* un'alimentazione sana
[2] la **dieta** (*slimming*) ◇ *I'm on a diet.* Sono in dieta.

diet [ˈdaɪət] ADJECTIVE
> see also **diet** NOUN, VERB

☞

D

Verbs followed by the symbol "E" require the auxiliary "essere"

dietetico ◇ *diet drinks* bibite dietetiche
♦ **diet yoghurt** yogurt magro

to **diet** ['daɪət] VERB

see also **diet** NOUN, ADJECTIVE

seguire una dieta ◇ *I've been dieting for two months.* Sto seguendo una dieta da due mesi.

difference ['dɪfrəns] NOUN
la differenza ◇ *There's not much difference in age between us.* Non c'è molta differenza d'età tra noi.
♦ **The new system has made a big difference.** Il nuovo sistema ha apportato un grosso miglioramento.
♦ **It makes no difference.** È uguale.

different ['dɪfrənt] ADJECTIVE
diverso ◇ *London is different from Rome.* Londra è diversa da Roma.

difficult ['dɪfɪkəlt] ADJECTIVE
difficile

difficulty ['dɪfɪkəltɪ] NOUN (PL **difficulties**)
la difficoltà (PL le difficoltà)

to **dig** [dɪg] VERB (**dug, dug**)
1 scavare ◇ *They're digging a hole in the road.* Stanno scavando un buco nella strada.
2 zappare ◇ *Dad's out digging the garden.* Il papà è fuori a zappare il giardino.

to **dig up** [dɪg'ʌp] VERB
1 sradicare ◇ *The cat's dug up my plants.* Il gatto ha sradicato le mie piante.
2 dissotterrare ◇ *The police have dug up a body.* La polizia ha dissotterrato un corpo.
3 tirar fuori ◇ *They're trying to dig up evidence against him.* Stanno cercando di tirar fuori delle prove contro di lui.

digestion [dɪ'dʒestʃən] NOUN
la digestione

digger ['dɪgə'] NOUN
l' escavatore

digital ['dɪdʒɪtl] ADJECTIVE
digitale
♦ **a digital camera** una macchina fotografica digitale
♦ **digital TV** TV digitale

dim [dɪm] ADJECTIVE
1 debole ◇ *a dim light* una luce debole
2 scarso ◇ *The prospects are dim.* Le prospettive sono scarse.
3 tonto (*person*)

dimension [daɪ'menʃən] NOUN
la dimensione

to **diminish** [dɪ'mɪnɪʃ] VERB
diminuire
*When an auxiliary is needed to form past tenses use "essere" when **diminuire** does not have an object.*
◇ *The threat of nuclear war has diminished.* La paura di una guerra nucleare è diminuita.

din [dɪn] NOUN
il chiasso

diner ['daɪnə'] NOUN US
la tavola calda

dinghy ['dɪŋgɪ] NOUN (PL **dinghies**)
♦ **a rubber dinghy** un gommone

dining car ['daɪnɪŋkɑː'] NOUN
il vagone ristorante (PL i vagoni ristorante)

dining room ['daɪnɪŋruːm] NOUN
la sala da pranzo

dinner ['dɪnə'] NOUN
la cena (*in the evening*) ◇ *Dinner is at seven o'clock.* La cena è alle sette.
♦ **to have dinner** cenare ◇ *Some schools provide breakfast as well as dinner.* In alcune scuole viene data sia la colazione che il pranzo. ◇ *It's half past twelve – nearly dinner time!* È mezzogiorno e mezza, è quasi ora di pranzo!
♦ **to have dinner** (*at midday*) pranzare ◇ *They have dinner at school.* Pranzano a scuola.
♦ **the dinner hour** l'intervallo del pranzo

🛈 *Nei ristoranti* **dinner** *indica sempre la cena.*

dinner jacket ['dɪnədʒækɪt] NOUN
lo smoking (PL gli smoking)

dinner party ['dɪnəpɑːtɪ] NOUN
1 la cena
2 il pranzo (*at midday*)

dinner time ['dɪnətaɪm] NOUN
l' ora di pranzo

dinosaur ['daɪnəsɔː'] NOUN
il dinosauro

dip [dɪp] NOUN

see also **dip** VERB

1 la salsa (*for vegetables, crisps*)
2 la nuotatina (*swim*)
♦ **to go for a dip** andare*[E] a fare una nuotatina

to **dip** [dɪp] VERB

see also **dip** NOUN

1 immergere ◇ *He dipped his hand in the water.* Ha immerso la mano nell'acqua.
♦ **He dipped a biscuit into his tea.** Ha inzuppato un biscotto nel tè.
2 scendere*[E] ◇ *The sun dipped below the horizon.* Il sole è sceso sotto l'orizzonte.

diploma [dɪ'pləʊmə] NOUN
il diploma (PL i diplomi)

diplomat ['dɪpləmæt] NOUN
il diplomatico (PL i diplomatici)

diplomatic [dɪplə'mætɪk] ADJECTIVE
diplomatico

direct [daɪ'rekt] ADJECTIVE, ADVERB

see also **direct** VERB

1 diretto ◇ *the most direct route* la strada più diretta
2 direttamente ◇ *You can go direct, without changing at Crewe.* Si può andarci direttamente senza cambiare a Crewe.

to **direct** [daɪ'rekt] VERB

see also **direct** ADJECTIVE

1 dirigere ◇ *Is that remark directed at me?*

---

* Verbs followed by this symbol are irregular. See pp.339–364 for further details.

È diretta a me questa osservazione?
[2] essere* ᴱ il regista di (film, programme)

direct debit [daɪrɛkt'debɪt] NOUN
l'addebito in conto corrente

direction [dɪ'rɛkʃən] NOUN
la direzione ◊ *We're going in the wrong direction.* Stiamo andando nella direzione sbagliata.
* **to ask somebody for directions** chiedere* a qualcuno la strada

direct object [daɪrɛkt'ɔbdʒɪkt] NOUN
il complemento oggetto

director [dɪ'rɛktə'] NOUN
[1] il/la dirigente (of company)
[2] il/la regista (of film, programme)

directory [dɪ'rɛktərɪ] NOUN (PL **directories**)
[1] l'elenco (PL gli elenchi) (phone book)
* **directory enquiries** informazioni elenco abbonati
[2] la directory (PL le directory) (in computing)

direct speech [daɪrɛkt'spiːtʃ] NOUN
il discorso diretto

dirt [dəːt] NOUN
la sporcizia

dirty ['dəːtɪ] ADJECTIVE
sporco ◊ *dirty socks* calzini sporchi
* **to get dirty** sporcarsi ᴱ
* **a dirty trick** un brutto scherzo

disabled [dɪs'eɪbld] ADJECTIVE
disabile
* **the disabled** i disabili

disadvantage [dɪsəd'vɑːntɪdʒ] NOUN
lo svantaggio

disagree [dɪsə'griː] VERB
non essere* ᴱ d'accordo ◊ *We always disagree.* Non siamo mai d'accordo. ◊ *He disagrees with me.* Non è d'accordo con me.

disagreement [dɪsə'griːmənt] NOUN
il disaccordo

disappear [dɪsə'pɪə'] VERB
scomparire* ᴱ

disappearance [dɪsə'pɪərəns] NOUN
la scomparsa ◊ *the disappearance of the money* la scomparsa del denaro

disappointed [dɪsə'pɔɪntɪd] ADJECTIVE
deluso

disappointing [dɪsə'pɔɪntɪŋ] ADJECTIVE
deludente

disappointment [dɪsə'pɔɪntmənt] NOUN
la delusione

disaster [dɪ'zɑːstə'] NOUN
il disastro

disastrous [dɪ'zɑːstrəs] ADJECTIVE
disastroso

disc [dɪsk] NOUN
il disco (PL i dischi)

discipline ['dɪsɪplɪn] NOUN
la disciplina

disc jockey ['dɪskdʒɔkɪ] NOUN
il/la disk jockey

disco ['dɪskəu] NOUN (PL **discos**)
la festa

> ⓘ *Per* **disco** *in inglese si intende una festa organizzata da scuole, circoli o ditte.*

to disconnect [dɪskə'nɛkt] VERB
staccare ◊ *If you don't pay the bill the phone will be disconnected.* Se non paghi la bolletta ti staccheranno il telefono.

discount ['dɪskaunt] NOUN
[1] la riduzione ◊ *a discount for students* una riduzione per studenti
[2] lo sconto ◊ *a twenty per cent discount* uno sconto del venti per cento

to discourage [dɪs'kʌrɪdʒ] VERB
scoraggiare
* **to get discouraged** scoraggiarsi ᴱ

to discover [dɪs'kʌvə'] VERB
scoprire

to discriminate [dɪs'krɪmɪneɪt] VERB
* **to discriminate against** fare* discriminazioni ai danni di

discrimination [dɪskrɪmɪ'neɪʃən] NOUN
la discriminazione

to discuss [dɪs'kʌs] VERB
* **to discuss something** discutere* di qualcosa ◊ *We discussed the topic at length.* Abbiamo discusso a lungo dell'argomento.

discussion [dɪs'kʌʃən] NOUN
la discussione

disease [dɪ'ziːz] NOUN
la malattia

disgraceful [dɪs'greɪsful] ADJECTIVE
scandaloso

disguise [dɪs'gaɪz] NOUN
il travestimento

disguised [dɪs'gaɪzd] ADJECTIVE
* **to be disguised as** essere* ᴱ travestito da

disgusted [dɪs'gʌstɪd] ADJECTIVE
disgustato

disgusting [dɪs'gʌstɪŋ] ADJECTIVE
disgustoso

dish [dɪʃ] NOUN (PL **dishes**)
il piatto ◊ *a vegetarian dish* un piatto vegetariano ◊ *Put the peas in a serving dish.* Metti i piselli in un piatto da portata.
* **to do the dishes** lavare i piatti
* **a satellite dish** un'antenna parabolica

dishonest [dɪs'ɔnɪst] ADJECTIVE
disonesto

dish soap ['dɪʃsəup] NOUN US
il detersivo liquido (per stoviglie)

dish towel ['dɪʃtauəl] NOUN US
lo strofinaccio dei piatti

dishwasher ['dɪʃwɔʃə'] NOUN
la lavastoviglie (PL le lavastoviglie)

disinfectant [dɪsɪn'fɛktənt] NOUN
il disinfettante

disk [dɪsk] NOUN ☞

D

il disco (PL i dischi) ◇ *the hard disk* il disco rigido
+ **the disk drive** il disk drive
diskette [dɪs'kɛt] NOUN
il dischetto
to dislike [dɪs'laɪk] VERB
see also **dislike** NOUN
+ **I dislike it.** Non mi piace.
dislike [dɪs'laɪk] NOUN
see also **dislike** VERB
+ **to take a dislike to somebody** prendere* in antipatia qualcuno
+ **my likes and dislikes** ciò che mi piace e ciò che non mi piace
dismal ['dɪzml] ADJECTIVE
misero ◇ *a dismal failure* un misero fallimento
to dismiss [dɪs'mɪs] VERB
[1] scartare ◇ *She dismissed the suggestion immediately.* Ha scartato subito il suggerimento.
[2] licenziare (*employee*)
disobedient [dɪsə'biːdɪənt] ADJECTIVE
disubbidiente
display [dɪs'pleɪ] NOUN
see also **display** VERB
la vetrina ◇ *The assistant took the watch out of the display.* Il commesso ha preso l'orologio dalla vetrina.
+ **to be on display** essere* E in mostra
+ **a firework display** uno spettacolo di fuochi d'artificio
to display [dɪs'pleɪ] VERB
see also **display** NOUN
[1] mostrare ◇ *She proudly displayed her medal.* Ha mostrato con orgoglio la sua medaglia.
[2] esporre ◇ *the watches displayed in the shop window* gli orologi esposti in vetrina
disposable [dɪs'pauzəbl] ADJECTIVE
usa e getta MASC, FEM, PL ◇ *a disposable razor* un rasoio usa e getta
+ **a disposable nappy** un pannolino
to disqualify [dɪs'kwɔlɪfaɪ] VERB (**disqualified, disqualified**)
squalificare
to disrupt [dɪs'rʌpt] VERB
interrompere ◇ *The meeting was disrupted by protesters.* La riunione è stata interrotta dai dimostranti.
+ **Train services are being disrupted by the strike.** Lo sciopero sta creando il caos nel trasporto ferroviario.
dissatisfied [dɪs'sætɪsfaɪd] ADJECTIVE
insoddisfatto ◇ *a dissatisfied customer* un cliente insoddisfatto
+ **to be dissatisfied with** non essere* E soddisfatti di ◇ *We were dissatisfied with the service.* Non eravamo soddisfatti del servizio.
to dissolve [dɪ'zɔlv] VERB

sciogliere
distance ['dɪstns] NOUN
la distanza ◇ *a distance of forty kilometres* una distanza di quaranta chilometri
+ **It's within walking distance.** Ci si arriva a piedi.
+ **in the distance** in lontananza
distant ['dɪstnt] ADJECTIVE
lontano
distillery [dɪs'tɪlərɪ] NOUN (PL **distilleries**)
la distilleria
distinction [dɪs'tɪŋkʃən] NOUN
la distinzione
+ **to make a distinction between** fare* una distinzione tra
+ **I got a distinction in my exam.** Ho ottenuto il massimo dei voti all'esame.
distinctive [dɪs'tɪŋktɪv] ADJECTIVE
tutto particolare
to distinguish [dɪs'tɪŋgwɪʃ] VERB
distinguere
to distract [dɪs'trækt] VERB
distrarre
to distribute [dɪs'trɪbjuːt] VERB
distribuire
district ['dɪstrɪkt] NOUN
[1] il quartiere (*of town*)
[2] il distretto (*of country*)
district attorney ['dɪstrɪktə'təːnɪ] NOUN
la pubblica accusa
to disturb [dɪs'təːb] VERB
disturbare ◇ *I'm sorry to disturb you.* Mi dispiace disturbarti.
ditch [dɪtʃ] NOUN (PL **ditches**)
see also **ditch** VERB
il fosso
to ditch [dɪtʃ] VERB
see also **ditch** NOUN
mollare ◇ *She's just ditched her boyfriend.* Ha appena mollato il suo ragazzo.
dive [daɪv] NOUN
see also **dive** VERB
il tuffo
to dive [daɪv] VERB (**dived** *or* **dove**)
see also **dive** NOUN
tuffarsi E
diver ['daɪvər] NOUN
il tuffatore
la tuffatrice
diversion [daɪ'vəːʃən] NOUN
la deviazione (*for traffic*)
to divide [dɪ'vaɪd] VERB
[1] dividere ◇ *Divide the pastry in half.* Dividete la pasta a metà.
[2] dividersi E ◇ *We divided into two groups.* Ci siamo divisi in due gruppi.
diving ['daɪvɪŋ] NOUN
i tuffi MASC PL (*sport*)
diving board ['daɪvɪŋbəːd] NOUN
il trampolino
division [dɪ'vɪʒən] NOUN

---

* Verbs followed by this symbol are irregular. See pp.339–364 for further details.

la divisione

divorce [dɪ'vɔːs] NOUN
il divorzio

divorced [dɪ'vɔːst] ADJECTIVE
divorziato

DIY [diːaɪ'waɪ] NOUN (= do-it-yourself)
il bricolage
+ **to do DIY** fare* bricolage
+ **a DIY shop** un negozio di bricolage

dizzy ['dɪzɪ] ADJECTIVE
+ **to feel dizzy** avere* il capogiro

DJ [diː'dʒeɪ] NOUN
il/la DJ (PL i/le DJ)

do [duː] VERB (**does, did, done**)
[1] fare* ◇ *He does chemistry.* Fa chimica.
◇ *What are you doing this evening?* Cosa fai
stasera? ◇ *She did it by herself.* L'ha fatto
da sola. ◇ *Have you done your homework?*
Hai fatto i compiti? ◇ *I want to do physics at
university.* Voglio fare fisica all'università.
+ **I could do with a holiday.** Avrei bisogno di
una vacanza.
[2] andare*E ◇ *She's doing well at school.*
Va bene a scuola.
+ **How are you doing?** Come va?
+ **How do you do?** Piacere.
[3] andare*E bene ◇ *It's not very good, but
it'll do.* Non è ottimo, ma andrà bene.
+ **That'll do, thanks.** Basta, grazie.
*When used as an auxiliary in questions, do is
not translated.*
◇ *Where does he live?* Dove vive? ◇ *What
does your father do?* Cosa fa tuo padre?
◇ *Where did you go for your holidays?* Dove
sei andato in vacanza?
*Use non in negative sentences for don't,
didn't etc.*
◇ *I don't understand.* Non capisco. ◇ *She
doesn't speak Italian.* Non parla italiano.
◇ *He didn't come.* Non è venuto. ◇ *Why
didn't you come?* Perché non sei venuto?
*When do is used with yes and no, it is not
translated.*
◇ *Do you speak English? – Yes, I do.* Parli
inglese? – Sì. ◇ *Do you like horses? – No, I
don't.* Ti piacciono i cavalli? – No. ◇ *Did you
tell him? – Yes, I did.* Gliel'hai detto? – Sì.
◇ *Did you like the film? – No, I didn't.* Ti è
piaciuto il film? – No.
+ **So do I.** Anch'io.
+ **Neither did I.** Neanch'io.
Use vero? to check information.
◇ *You go swimming on Fridays, don't you?*
Vai in piscina venerdì, vero? ◇ *You told him,
didn't you?* Gliel'hai detto, vero? ◇ *It
doesn't matter, does it?* Non importa, vero?

to **do up** [duː'ʌp] VERB
[1] allacciare (*shoes*)
[2] abbottonare (*shirt, cardigan*)
+ **Do up your zip!** Tirati su la lampo!
[3] rimettere* a nuovo (*house, room*)

to **do without** [duː'wɪð'aʊt] VERB

fare* a meno di ◇ *I couldn't do without my
computer.* Non potrei fare a meno del
computer.

dock [dɒk] NOUN
la darsena

doctor ['dɒktə'] NOUN
il dottore
la dottoressa
◇ *a good doctor* un bravo dottore

doctor's office ['dɒktəzɔfɪs] NOUN
lo studio medico

document ['dɒkjumənt] NOUN
il documento

documentary [dɒkju'mentərɪ] NOUN (PL
documentaries)
il documentario

to **dodge** [dɒdʒ] VERB
schivare (*attacker, blow*)

Dodgems ® ['dɒdʒəmz] NOUN PL
gli autoscontri

does [dʌz] VERB *see* **do**

doesn't ['dʌznt] = **does not**

dog [dɒg] NOUN
il cane

do-it-yourself ['duːɪtjɔː'self] NOUN
il fai da te

dole [dəul] NOUN
il sussidio di disoccupazione
+ **to be on the dole** ricevere il sussidio di
disoccupazione
+ **to go on the dole** fare* domanda per il
sussidio di disoccupazione

doll [dɒl] NOUN
la bambola

dollar ['dɒlə'] NOUN
il dollaro

dolphin ['dɒlfɪn] NOUN
il delfino

domestic [də'mestɪk] ADJECTIVE
[1] nazionale ◇ *a domestic flight* un volo
nazionale
[2] domestico ◇ *domestic chores* faccende
domestiche

dominoes ['dɒmɪnəuz] NOUN PL
il domino SING
+ **to have a game of dominoes** fare* una
partita a domino

to **donate** [də'neɪt] VERB
donare ◇ *He donated his collection to the
museum.* Ha donato la sua collezione al
museo.

done [dʌn] VERB *see* **do**

done [dʌn] ADJECTIVE
pronto ◇ *Is the pasta done?* È pronta la
pasta?

donkey ['dɒŋkɪ] NOUN
l' asino

donor ['dəunə'] NOUN
il donatore
la donatrice

don't [dəunt] = **do not**

D

to **doodle** ['duːdl] VERB
scarabocchiare

door [dɔːʳ] NOUN
[1] la porta ◇ the first door on the right la prima porta a destra
[2] la portiera (of car)
[3] lo sportello (of train)

doorbell ['dɔːbel] NOUN
il campanello

doorman ['dɔːmən] NOUN (PL **doormen**)
il portiere

doorstep ['dɔːstep] NOUN
la soglia

dormitory ['dɔːmɪtrɪ] NOUN (PL **dormitories**)
[1] il dormitorio ◇ the boys' dormitory il dormitorio dei ragazzi
[2] la casa dello studente US (at university)

dose [dəus] NOUN
la dose

dosh [dɔʃ] NOUN
la grana (money)

dot [dɔt] NOUN
[1] il puntino (on letter i)
[2] il punto (in email addresses)
♦ **on the dot** in punto

to **double** ['dʌbl] VERB
see also **double** ADJECTIVE, ADVERB
raddoppiare

double ['dʌbl] ADJECTIVE, ADVERB
see also **double** VERB
doppio ◇ a double helping una porzione doppia
♦ **to cost double** costare il doppio
♦ **a double bed** un letto matrimoniale
♦ **a double room** una camera matrimoniale

double bass [dʌbl'beɪs] NOUN
il contrabbasso

to **double-click** [dʌbl'klɪk] VERB
♦ **to double-click on** cliccare due volte su

double-decker bus ['dʌbldekə'bʌs] NOUN
l' autobus a due piani (PL gli autobus a due piani)

double glazing ['dʌbl'gleɪzɪŋ] NOUN
i doppi vetri MASC PL

doubles ['dʌblz] NOUN PL
il doppio (in tennis) ◇ to play mixed doubles fare un doppio misto

doubt [daut] NOUN
see also **doubt** VERB
il dubbio
♦ **if in doubt...** in caso di dubbio...
♦ **no doubt** sicuramente ◇ as you no doubt know... come saprai sicuramente...

to **doubt** [daut] VERB
see also **doubt** NOUN
dubitare di ◇ I don't doubt her honesty. Non dubito della sua onestà.
♦ **I doubt it.** Ne dubito.
♦ **to doubt that** dubitare che ◇ I doubt that he'll agree. Dubito che sarà d'accordo.

doubtful ['dautful] ADJECTIVE
poco convinto ◇ She sounds doubtful. Sembra poco convinta.
♦ **to be doubtful about doing something** essere* E incerto se fare qualcosa ◇ I'm doubtful about going by myself. Sono incerto se andare da solo.
♦ **It's doubtful.** Non è sicuro.

dough [dəu] NOUN
la pasta

doughnut ['dəunʌt] NOUN
il krapfen (PL i krapfen) ◇ a jam doughnut un krapfen con la marmellata

dove [dʌv] VERB see **dive**

down [daun] ADVERB, ADJECTIVE, PREPOSITION
[1] giù ◇ His office is down on the first floor. Il suo ufficio è giù al primo piano.
♦ **They live just down the road.** Abitano un po' più in giù.
♦ **down there** laggiù
[2] a terra ◇ He threw down his racket. Ha gettato a terra la racchetta.
♦ **to feel down** sentirsi E giù di morale
♦ **to be down** (computer) non funzionare

to **download** ['daunləud] VERB
scaricare

downpour ['daunpɔːʳ] NOUN
l' acquazzone

downstairs ['daun'steəz] ADVERB, ADJECTIVE
[1] al piano di sotto ◇ the people downstairs le persone che abitano al piano di sotto
[2] al piano terra ◇ the downstairs bathroom il bagno al piano terra

downtown ['daun'taun] ADVERB US
in città

to **doze** [dəuz] VERB
sonnecchiare

to **doze off** [dəuz'ɔf] VERB
appisolarsi E

dozen ['dʌzn] NOUN
la dozzina ◇ a dozen eggs una dozzina di uova ◇ two dozen due dozzine
♦ **dozens** (lots) centinaia ◇ I've told you that dozens of times. Te l'ho detto centinaia di volte.

drab [dræb] ADJECTIVE
triste (clothes)

draft [drɑːft] NOUN
[1] la bozza (of letter, speech)
[2] la corrente d'aria (draught) US

to **drag** [dræg] VERB
see also **drag** NOUN
trascinare (thing, person)
♦ **to drag and drop a file** spostare un file

drag [dræg] NOUN
see also **drag** VERB
♦ **It's a real drag!** È proprio una rompitura!
♦ **in drag** travestito da donna ◇ He was in drag. Era travestito da donna.

dragon ['drægn] NOUN
il drago (PL i draghi)

* Verbs followed by this symbol are irregular. See pp.339–364 for further details.

drain [dreɪn] NOUN
see also **drain** VERB
lo scarico (PL gli scarichi) ◊ *The drains are blocked.* Gli scarichi sono ostruiti.

drain [dreɪn] VERB
see also **drain** NOUN
scolare

draining board [ˈdreɪnɪŋbɔːd] NOUN
il piano del lavello

drainpipe [ˈdreɪnpaɪp] NOUN
il tubo di scarico

drama [ˈdrɑːmə] NOUN
1 il dramma (PL i drammi) ◊ *a TV drama* un dramma televisivo
2 la recitazione ◊ *Drama is my favourite subject.* La recitazione è la mia materia preferita.
♦ **drama school** scuola d'arte drammatica

dramatic [drəˈmætɪk] ADJECTIVE
1 straordinario ◊ *a dramatic improvement* un miglioramento straordinario
♦ **dramatic news** notizie sensazionali
2 drammatico ◊ *the dramatic arts* le arti drammatiche

drank [dræŋk] VERB *see* **drink**

drapes [dreɪps] NOUN PL US
le tende

drastic [ˈdræstɪk] ADJECTIVE
drastico
♦ **to take drastic action** agire in modo drastico

draught [drɑːft] NOUN
la corrente d'aria
♦ **draught beer** birra alla spina

draughts [drɑːfts] NOUN SING
la dama

draw [drɔː] NOUN
see also **draw** VERB
1 il pareggio ◊ *The game ended in a draw.* L'incontro è finito in pareggio.
2 l' estrazione FEM ◊ *The draw takes place on Saturday.* L'estrazione avviene sabato.

draw [drɔː] VERB (**drew, drawn**)
see also **draw** NOUN
1 disegnare ◊ *I can't draw.* Non so disegnare.
♦ **to draw a picture** fare* un disegno
♦ **to draw a picture of somebody** fare* il ritratto a qualcuno
♦ **to draw a line** tracciare una linea ◊ *He drew a line.* Ha tracciato una linea.
2 pareggiare (*in game*) ◊ *We drew two-all.* Abbiamo pareggiato due a due.
3 tirare ◊ *He drew her towards him.* La tirò verso di sé.
♦ **to draw the curtains** tirare le tende ◊ *She's drawn the curtains.* Ha tirato le tende.

draw on [ˈdrɔːɒn] VERB
fare* ricorso a ◊ *He drew on his own experience to write the book.* Ha fatto ricorso alla propria esperienza per scrivere il libro.

to **draw up** [drɔːˈʌp] VERB
compilare ◊ *She drew up a list of priorities.* Compilò un elenco di priorità.

drawback [ˈdrɔːbæk] NOUN
l' inconveniente MASC

drawer [drɔːˈ] NOUN
il cassetto

drawing [ˈdrɔːɪŋ] NOUN
il disegno

drawing pin [ˈdrɔːɪŋpɪn] NOUN
la puntina da disegno

drawing room [ˈdrɔːɪŋrum] NOUN
il salotto

drawn [drɔːn] VERB *see* **draw**

dreadful [ˈdredful] ADJECTIVE
1 terribile ◊ *a dreadful mistake* un terribile errore
2 orribile ◊ *The weather was dreadful.* Il tempo era orribile. ◊ *You look dreadful.* Hai un aspetto orribile.
♦ **I feel dreadful about it.** Me ne vergogno terribilmente.

to **dream** [driːm] VERB (**dreamed** *or* **dreamt, dreamed** *or* **dreamt**)
see also **dream** NOUN
sognare

dream [driːm] NOUN
see also **dream** VERB
il sogno

to **drench** [drentʃ] VERB
♦ **to get drenched** bagnarsi E fino all'osso

dress [dres] NOUN (PL **dresses**)
see also **dress** VERB
il vestito

to **dress** [dres] VERB
see also **dress** NOUN
1 vestirsi E ◊ *I got up, dressed, and went downstairs.* Mi alzai, mi vestii e scesi dabbasso.
♦ **to dress somebody** vestire qualcuno
♦ **to get dressed** vestirsi E
2 condire (*salad*)

to **dress up** [dresˈʌp] VERB
1 vestirsi E bene ◊ *There's no need to dress up.* Non c'è bisogno di vestirsi bene.
2 vestirsi E in maschera ◊ *Children like dressing up.* Ai bambini piace vestirsi in maschera.

dressed [drest] ADJECTIVE
vestito ◊ *I'm not dressed yet.* Non sono ancora vestito.
♦ **to be dressed in** indossare ◊ *She was dressed in a green jumper and jeans.* Indossava un maglione verde e un paio di jeans.

dresser [ˈdresə'] NOUN
la credenza (*piece of furniture*)

dressing [ˈdresɪŋ] NOUN
il condimento (*for salad*)

dressing gown [ˈdresɪŋgaun] NOUN ☞

la vestaglia

dressing table ['dresɪŋteɪbl] NOUN
la toilette (PL le toilette)

dress rehearsal ['dresrɪhɜːsəl] NOUN
la prova generale

drew [druː] VERB *see* **draw**

dried [draɪd] ADJECTIVE
secco ◇ *dried flowers* fiori secchi

drier ['draɪə'] NOUN
* **a tumble drier** un asciugabiancheria
* **a hair drier** un asciugacapelli

drift [drɪft] NOUN
see also **drift** VERB
* **a snow drift** un cumulo di neve

to **drift** [drɪft] VERB
see also **drift** NOUN
1 andare*E alla deriva (*boat*)
* **to drift into crime** scivolareE nell'illegalità
2 accumularsiE (*snow*)

drill [drɪl] NOUN
see also **drill** VERB
1 il trapano (*tool*)
2 l' esercizio orale ◇ *a grammar drill* un esercizio orale di grammatica

to **drill** [drɪl] VERB
see also **drill** NOUN
* **to drill a hole** fare* un buco con il trapano

to **drink** [drɪŋk] VERB (**drank, drunk**)
see also **drink** NOUN
bere* ◇ *What would you like to drink?* Cosa vuoi da bere? ◇ *She drank her tea.* Ha bevuto il suo tè. ◇ *He's drunk a lot.* Ha bevuto molto.
* **I don't drink.** Non bevo alcolici.

drink [drɪŋk] NOUN
see also **drink** VERB
la bibita ◇ *a cold drink* una bibita fresca
* **a hot drink** una bevanda calda
* **Would you like a drink?** Vuoi qualcosa da bere?
* **to go out for a drink** andare*E fuori a bere qualcosa
* **to have a drink** bere* qualcosa

drinking water ['drɪŋkɪŋwɔːtə'] NOUN
l' acqua potabile

drive [draɪv] NOUN
see also **drive** VERB
1 il giro
* **to go for a drive** andare*E a fare un giro
2 il vialetto ◇ *He parked his car in the drive.* Ha parcheggiato la macchina nel vialetto.

to **drive** [draɪv] VERB (**drove, driven**)
see also **drive** NOUN
1 guidare (*car*) ◇ *Can you drive?* Sai guidare? ◇ *He drove from London to Edinburgh.* Ha guidato da Londra ad Edimburgo.
2 andare*E in macchina (*travel by car*)
◇ *We never drive into the town centre.* Non andiamo mai in macchina in centro.

3 portare in macchina (*take by car*) ◇ *I'll drive you home.* Ti porto a casa in macchina.
* **to drive somebody mad** far diventare matto qualcuno ◇ *He drives her mad.* La fa diventare matta.

driver ['draɪvə'] NOUN
1 il guidatore
la guidatrice
◇ *He's a terrible driver.* È un pessimo guidatore.
2 l' autista MASC / FEM (*of bus, taxi*)

driver's license ['draɪvəzlaɪsəns] NOUN US
la patente

driving instructor ['draɪvɪŋɪn'strʌktə'] NOUN
l' istruttore di guida MASC
l' istruttrice di guida FEM

driving lesson ['draɪvɪŋlesn] NOUN
la lezione di guida

driving licence ['draɪvɪŋlaɪsns] NOUN
la patente

driving test ['draɪvɪŋtest] NOUN
l' esame di guida MASC
* **to take one's driving test** fare* l'esame di guida

drizzle ['drɪzl] NOUN
la pioggerellina

drop [drɔp] NOUN
see also **drop** VERB
1 la goccia (PL le gocce) ◇ *Would you like some milk? – Just a drop.* Vuoi del latte? – Solo una goccia.
2 il calo ◇ *a drop in temperature* un calo della temperatura

to **drop** [drɔp] VERB
see also **drop** NOUN
1 diminuireE ◇ *The temperature will drop tonight.* La temperatura diminuirà stanotte.
2 cadere*E ◇ *The book dropped onto the floor.* Il libro è caduto sul pavimento.
* **I dropped the glass.** Mi è caduto il bicchiere.
3 lasciare ◇ *Could you drop me at the station?* Puoi lasciarmi alla stazione?
4 non fare* più ◇ *I'm going to drop chemistry.* Ho intenzione di non fare più chimica.

drought [draut] NOUN
la siccità

drove [drəuv] VERB *see* **drive**

to **drown** [draun] VERB
annegareE

drug [drʌg] NOUN
1 la medicina (*medicine*)
2 la droga (*illegal*) ◇ *hard drugs* droghe pesanti ◇ *soft drugs* droghe leggere
* **to take drugs** drogarsiE
* **the drugs squad** la squadra narcotici

drug addict ['drʌgædɪkt] NOUN
il/la tossicodipendente

drug pusher ['drʌgpuʃə'] NOUN
lo spacciatore
la spacciatrice

---

* Verbs followed by this symbol are irregular. See pp.339–364 for further details.

English ~ Italian

drug smuggler ['drʌgsmʌglə'] NOUN
il contrabbandiere di droga

drugstore ['drʌgstɔː'] US NOUN

> ⓘ Negli Stati Uniti un **drugstore** è un negozio di generi vari e di articoli di farmacia con un bar.

drum [drʌm] NOUN
il tamburo (*instrument*)
* **a drum kit** una batteria
* **to play the drums** suonare la batteria

drum majorette ['drʌmmeɪdʒə'rɛt] NOUN
la majorette (PL le majorette)

drummer ['drʌmə'] NOUN
il/la batterista (*in rock group*)

drunk [drʌŋk] ADJECTIVE, NOUN
l' ubriaco
l' ubriaca
* **to get drunk** ubriacarsi ᴱ

drunk [drʌŋk] VERB see **drink**

dry [draɪ] ADJECTIVE
see also **dry** VERB
1 asciutto (*clothes, paint*)
2 secco ◇ *It's been exceptionally dry this spring.* Il clima è stato insolitamente secco in primavera.
* **a long dry period** un lungo periodo senza pioggia

dry [draɪ] VERB (**dried, dried**)
see also **dry** ADJECTIVE
1 asciugare ◇ *She was drying a customer's hair.* Stava asciugando i capelli ad una cliente.
2 far asciugare ◇ *There's nowhere to dry clothes here.* Qui non c'è posto per far asciugare i vestiti.
* **to dry one's hair** asciugarsi ᴱ i capelli

dry-cleaner's ['draɪ'kliːnəz] NOUN
il lavasecco (PL i lavasecco)

dryer ['draɪə'] NOUN
* **a tumble dryer** l' asciugabiancheria (PL gli asciugabiancheria)
* **a hair dryer** l' asciugacapelli (PL gli asciugacapelli)

DTP [diːtiːˈpiː] NOUN (= *desktop publishing*)
il desktop publishing

dubbed [dʌbd] ADJECTIVE
doppiato (*film*)

dubious ['djuːbɪəs] ADJECTIVE
dubbioso

duck [dʌk] NOUN
l' anatra

due [djuː] ADJECTIVE, ADVERB
* **He's due to arrive tomorrow.** Lo attendiamo per domani.
* **The plane's due in half an hour.** L'aereo è atteso tra mezz'ora.
* **When's the baby due?** Quando deve nascere il bambino?
* **due to** a causa di ◇ *The trip was cancelled due to bad weather.* Il viaggio è stato annullato a causa del maltempo.

dug [dʌg] VERB see **dig**

dull [dʌl] ADJECTIVE
1 noioso ◇ *He's nice, but a bit dull.* È simpatico, ma un po' noioso.
2 nuvoloso ◇ *a dull day* una giornata nuvolosa

dumb [dʌm] ADJECTIVE
1 muto
* **deaf and dumb** sordomuto
2 stupido ◇ *I was so dumb!* Che stupido sono stato!
* **a dumb thing** una stupidaggine ◇ *That was a really dumb thing I did!* Ho fatto proprio una stupidaggine!

dummy ['dʌmɪ] NOUN
il succhiotto (*for baby*)

dump [dʌmp] NOUN
see also **dump** VERB
1 la discarica (PL le discariche) ◇ *I'll take this stuff to the dump.* Porterò questa roba in discarica.
* **a rubbish dump** una discarica
2 il postaccio ◇ *It's a real dump!* È proprio un postaccio!

to dump [dʌmp] VERB
see also **dump** NOUN
1 mollare ◇ *We dumped our bags at the hotel and went to the beach.* Abbiamo mollato i bagagli all'albergo e siamo andati in spiaggia.
2 gettare (*rubbish*) ◇ *"no dumping"* "è vietato gettare rifiuti"

dungarees [dʌŋgə'riːz] NOUN PL
la salopette (PL le salopette)

dungeon ['dʌndʒən] NOUN
la prigione sotterranea

duration [djuə'reɪʃən] NOUN
la durata

during ['djuərɪŋ] PREPOSITION
durante

dusk [dʌsk] NOUN
il crepuscolo

dust [dʌst] NOUN
see also **dust** VERB
la polvere

to dust [dʌst] VERB
see also **dust** NOUN
spolverare

dustbin ['dʌstbɪn] NOUN
il bidone della spazzatura

dustman ['dʌstmən] NOUN (PL **dustmen**)
lo spazzino

dusty ['dʌstɪ] ADJECTIVE
polveroso

Dutch [dʌtʃ] ADJECTIVE
see also **Dutch** NOUN
olandese

Dutch [dʌtʃ] NOUN
see also **Dutch** ADJECTIVE

☞

Verbs followed by the symbol "E" require the auxiliary "essere"

l' olandese MASC (*language*)
* **the Dutch** gli olandesi
Dutchman ['dʌtʃmən] NOUN (PL **Dutchmen**)
* **a Dutchman** un olandese
Dutchwoman ['dʌtʃwumən] NOUN (PL **Dutchwomen**)
* **a Dutchwoman** un'olandese
duty ['djuːtɪ] NOUN (PL **duties**)
il dovere ◊ *It was his duty to tell the police.*
Era suo dovere dirlo alla polizia.
* **to be on duty (1)** (*policeman*) essere* ᴱ in servizio
* **to be on duty (2)** (*doctor, nurse*) essere* ᴱ di turno
duty-free ['djuːtɪ'friː] ADJECTIVE

esente da dazio
duvet ['duːveɪ] NOUN
il piumino
DVD [diːviː'diː] NOUN
il DVD (PL i DVD)
dwarf [dwɔːf] NOUN (PL **dwarves** or **dwarfs**)
il nano
la nana
dying ['daɪɪŋ] VERB *see* **die**
dynamic [daɪ'næmɪk] ADJECTIVE
dinamico
dyslexia [dɪs'leksɪə] NOUN
la dislessia

E

each [i:tʃ] ADJECTIVE, PRONOUN

1 ogni ◇ *each day* ogni giorno

2 ciascuno MASC
ciascuna FEM

◇ *They have ten points each.* Hanno dieci punti ciascuno. ◇ *The girls have two each.* Le ragazze ne hanno due ciascuna.

Use a reflexive verb to translate each other.

◇ *They hate each other.* Si odiano. ◇ *We write to each other.* Ci scriviamo.

eager [i:gə'] ADJECTIVE

impaziente ◇ *He was eager to tell us about his experiences.* Era impaziente di raccontarci le sue esperienze.

ear [ɪə'] NOUN

l' orecchio MASC (PL FEM le orecchie)

earache ['ɪəreɪk] NOUN

+ **to have earache** avere* mal d'orecchi

early ['ə:lɪ] ADVERB, ADJECTIVE

1 presto ◇ *I have to get up early.* Devo alzarmi presto.

+ **to have an early night** andare* [E] a letto presto

+ **to make an early start** iniziare presto

+ **earlier** prima ◇ *I get up earlier on weekdays.* Mi alzo prima durante la settimana. ◇ *I saw him earlier.* L'ho visto prima.

2 in anticipo ◇ *I arrived early to get a good seat.* Sono arrivato in anticipo per prendere un buon posto.

3 primo ◇ *his early films* i suoi primi film

earn [ə:n] VERB

guadagnare ◇ *She earns five pounds an hour.* Guadagna cinque sterline all'ora.

earnings ['ə:nɪŋz] NOUN PL

lo stipendio SING ◇ *Average earnings rose two percent last year.* L'anno scorso lo stipendio medio è aumentato del due per cento.

earring ['ɪərɪŋ] NOUN

l' orecchino

earth [ə:θ] NOUN

la terra

+ **the Earth** la terra

+ **What on earth...?** Cosa diavolo...?

earthquake ['ə:θkweɪk] NOUN

il terremoto

easily ['i:zɪlɪ] ADVERB

facilmente

east [i:st] ADVERB, ADJECTIVE

see also **east** NOUN

1 ad est *(to the east)*

+ **east of** a est di ◇ *It's east of London.* È a est di Londra.

2 verso est *(eastwards)* ◇ *We were travelling east.* Andavamo verso est.

3 orientale *(eastern)* ◇ *the east coast* la costa orientale

east [i:st] NOUN

see also **east** ADVERB, ADJECTIVE

l' est MASC ◇ *in the east* ad est

Easter ['i:stə'] NOUN

la Pasqua

+ **an Easter egg** un uovo di Pasqua

eastern ['i:stən] ADJECTIVE

orientale ◇ *France's eastern border* il confine orientale della Francia

+ **Eastern Europe** l'Europa dell'est

easy ['i:zɪ] ADJECTIVE

facile ◇ *It's easy to understand.* È facile da capire.

easy chair ['i:zɪtʃeə'] NOUN

la poltrona

easy-going ['i:zɪ'gəʊɪŋ] ADJECTIVE

+ **to be easy-going** avere* un buon carattere ◇ *She's very easy-going and gets on well with everybody.* Ha un buon carattere e va d'accordo con tutti.

to eat [i:t] VERB (**ate, eaten**)

mangiare ◇ *Would you like something to eat?* Vuoi mangiare qualcosa? ◇ *We slowly ate our sandwiches.* Abbiamo mangiato lentamente i nostri panini.

EC [i:'si:] NOUN (= *European Community*)

la CE (= Comunità Europea)

ECB [i:si:'bi:] NOUN (= *European Central Bank*)

la BCE (= Banca centrale europea)

eccentric [ɪk'sentrɪk] ADJECTIVE

eccentrico

echo ['ekəʊ] NOUN (PL **echoes**)

l' eco (PL gli echi)

eco-friendly ['i:kəʊ'frendlɪ] ADJECTIVE

ecologico

ecological [i:kə'lɒdʒɪkəl] ADJECTIVE

ecologico

ecology [ɪ'kɒlədʒɪ] NOUN

l' ecologia

e-commerce [i:kɒmə:s] NOUN

l' e-commerce MASC

economic [i:kə'nɒmɪk] ADJECTIVE

economico *(growth, development)*

economical [i:kə'nɒmɪkəl] ADJECTIVE

1 economico *(method, machine)*

2 economo *(person)*

economics [i:kə'nɒmɪks] NOUN

l' economia ◇ *He's doing economics at university.* Fa economia all'università.

to economize [ɪ'kɒnəmaɪz] VERB

fare* economia ◇ *We'll have to economize.* Dovremo fare economia.

+ **to economize on something** risparmiare su qualcosa

economy [ɪ'kɒnəmɪ] NOUN (PL **economies**)

l' economia

ecstasy ['ekstəsɪ] NOUN

l' ecstasy FEM *(drug)*

+ **to be in ecstasy** essere* [E] in estasi

ecu ['eɪkju:] NOUN (= *European Currency Unit*) ☞

Verbs followed by the symbol "E" require the auxiliary "essere"

l' ecu MASC (PL gli ecu)

eczema ['ɛksɪmə] NOUN
l' eczema MASC

edge [ɛdʒ] NOUN
il bordo ◇ *on the edge of the desk* sul bordo della scrivania
• **on the edge of the town** ai margini della città
• **to be on edge** essere* E nervoso
• **to be on the edge of extinction** stare* E per estinguersi
• **to have the edge over somebody** essere* E in vantaggio su qualcuno

edgy ['ɛdʒɪ] ADJECTIVE
nervoso

Edinburgh ['ɛdɪnbərə] NOUN
Edimburgo FEM

editor ['ɛdɪtəʳ] NOUN
1 il redattore
la redattrice
(*writer*)
◇ *the political editor* il redattore della pagina politica
2 il direttore
la direttrice
(*in charge of paper*)
Be careful not to translate **editor** by **editore**.

educated ['ɛdjukeɪtɪd] ADJECTIVE
istruito

education [ɛdju'keɪʃən] NOUN
l' istruzione FEM ◇ *She wants to complete her education.* Vuole completare la sua istruzione. ◇ *There should be more investment in education.* Si dovrebbero fare più investimenti nella scuola.

educational [ɛdju'keɪʃənl] ADJECTIVE
educativo (*experience, toy*)

effect [ɪ'fɛkt] NOUN
l' effetto ◇ *special effects* effetti speciali

effective [ɪ'fɛktɪv] ADJECTIVE
efficace

effectively [ɪ'fɛktɪvlɪ] ADVERB
1 efficacemente (*efficiently*)
2 in effetti (*in effect*)

efficient [ɪ'fɪʃənt] ADJECTIVE
1 efficiente ◇ *His secretary is very efficient.* La sua segretaria è molto efficiente.
2 efficace ◇ *It's a very efficient system.* È un sistema molto efficace.

effort ['ɛfət] NOUN
lo sforzo ◇ *He made no effort to hide his disappointment.* Non ha fatto alcuno sforzo per nascondere la sua delusione.
• **It wasn't worth the effort.** Non ne valeva la pena.

e.g. [iː'dʒiː] ABBREVIAZIONE (= *exempli gratia*)
es.

egg [ɛg] NOUN
l' uovo MASC (PL FEM le uova) ◇ *a hard-boiled egg* un uovo sodo ◇ *scrambled eggs* le uova strapazzate

egg cup ['ɛgkʌp] NOUN
il portauovo (PL i portauovo)

eggplant ['ɛgplɑːnt] NOUN US
la melanzana

Egypt ['iːdʒɪpt] NOUN
l' Egitto

eight [eɪt] NUMERAL
otto ◇ *She's eight.* Ha otto anni.

eighteen [eɪ'tiːn] NUMERAL
diciotto ◇ *She's eighteen.* Ha diciotto anni.

eighteenth [eɪ'tiːnθ] ADJECTIVE
diciottesimo ◇ *the eighteenth floor* il diciottesimo piano
• **the eighteenth of August** il diciotto agosto

eighth [eɪtθ] ADJECTIVE
ottavo ◇ *the eighth floor* l'ottavo piano
• **the eighth of August** l'otto agosto

eighty ['eɪtɪ] NUMERAL
ottanta ◇ *My grandad's eighty.* Mio nonno ha ottant'anni.

Eire ['ɛərə] NOUN
la Repubblica d'Irlanda

either ['aɪðəʳ] ADJECTIVE, CONJUNCTION, PRONOUN
neanche ◇ *I don't like milk, and I don't like eggs either.* Non mi piace il latte e neanche le uova. ◇ *I've never been to Spain. – I haven't either.* Non sono mai stato in Spagna. Neanch'io.
• **either...or...** o...o... ◇ *You can have either ice cream or yoghurt.* Puoi prendere o il gelato o lo yogurt.
• **I don't like either of them.** Non mi piace né l'uno né l'altro.
• **Take either of them.** Prendi quello che vuoi.
• **Do either of you smoke?** Uno di voi due fuma?

elastic [ɪ'læstɪk] NOUN
l' elastico

elastic band [ɪlæstɪk'bænd] NOUN
l' elastico

elbow ['ɛlbəu] NOUN
il gomito

elder ['ɛldəʳ] ADJECTIVE
maggiore ◇ *my elder sister* la mia sorella maggiore

elderly ['ɛldəlɪ] ADJECTIVE
anziano
• **the elderly** gli anziani

eldest ['ɛldɪst] ADJECTIVE
maggiore ◇ *my eldest sister* la maggiore delle mie sorelle

to **elect** [ɪ'lɛkt] VERB
eleggere

election [ɪ'lɛkʃən] NOUN
l' elezione FEM

electric [ɪ'lɛktrɪk] ADJECTIVE
elettrico ◇ *an electric fire* un stufa elettrica
• **electric chair** sedia elettrica

electrical [ɪ'lɛktrɪkl] ADJECTIVE
elettrico

---

* Verbs followed by this symbol are irregular. See pp.339–364 for further details.

English ~ Italian

◆ **an electrical engineer** un elettrotecnico

electrician [ɪlek'trɪʃən] NOUN
l' elettricista MASC/FEM

electricity [ɪlek'trɪsɪti] NOUN
l' elettricità

electronic [ɪlek'trɒnɪk] ADJECTIVE
elettronico

electronics [ɪlek'trɒnɪks] NOUN SING
l' elettronica

elegant ['elɪgənt] ADJECTIVE
elegante

elementary school [elɪ'mentərɪskuːl] NOUN
US
la scuola elementare

elephant ['elɪfənt] NOUN
l' elefante MASC

elevator ['elɪveɪtə'] NOUN US
l' ascensore MASC

eleven [ɪ'levn] NUMERAL
undici ◇ *She's eleven.* Ha undici anni.

eleventh [ɪ'levnθ] ADJECTIVE
undicesimo ◇ *the eleventh floor*
l'undicesimo piano

◆ **the eleventh of August** l'undici agosto

else [els] ADVERB
altro ◇ *somebody else* qualcun altro
◇ *nobody else* nessun altro ◇ *something
else* qualcos'altro ◇ *nothing else*
nient'altro

◆ **somewhere else** da qualche altra parte
◆ **or else** altrimenti ◇ *Give me the money, or
else I'll shoot.* Dammi i soldi, altrimenti
sparo.

e-mail ['iːmeɪl] NOUN
see also **e-mail** VERB
1 la posta elettronica ◇ *It's quicker by
e-mail.* È più veloce tramite posta
elettronica.
2 il messaggio di posta elettronica ◇ *I'll
send him an e-mail.* Gli manderò un
messaggio di posta elettronica.

e-mail ['iːmeɪl] VERB
see also **e-mail** NOUN
◆ **to e-mail somebody** mandare un
messaggio di posta elettronica a qualcuno
◇ *He e-mailed me.* Mi ha mandato un
messaggio di posta elettronica.

e-mail address ['iːmeɪlə'dres] NOUN (PL
e-mail addresses)
l' indirizzo di posta elettronica

embankment [ɪm'bæŋkmənt] NOUN
la massicciata (*of railway*)

embarrassed [ɪm'bærəst] ADJECTIVE
imbarazzato

embarrassing [ɪm'bærəsɪŋ] ADJECTIVE
imbarazzante

embassy ['embəsɪ] NOUN (PL **embassies**)
l' ambasciata

embroider [ɪm'brɔɪdə'] VERB
ricamare

embroidery [ɪm'brɔɪdərɪ] NOUN
il ricamo

emergency [ɪ'məːdʒənsɪ] NOUN (PL
emergencies)
l' emergenza ◇ *This is an emergency!*
Questa è un'emergenza!

◆ **in an emergency** in caso di emergenza
◆ **an emergency exit** un'uscita di sicurezza
◆ **an emergency landing** un atterraggio di
emergenza
◆ **the emergency services** i servizi di pronto
intervento

to emigrate ['emɪgreɪt] VERB
emigrare E

emotion [ɪ'məʊʃən] NOUN
l' emozione FEM

emotional [ɪ'məʊʃənl] ADJECTIVE
1 emotivo ◇ *She's very emotional.* È
molto emotiva.
◆ **to get emotional** commuoversi E ◇ *He got
very emotional at the farewell party.* Si è
molto commosso alla festa d'addio.
2 sentito ◇ *Euthanasia is a very emotional
issue.* L'eutanasia è una questione molto
sentita.

emperor ['empərə'] NOUN
l' imperatore MASC

to emphasize ['emfəsaɪz] VERB
sottolineare ◇ *He emphasized the
importance of the point.* Ha sottolineato
l'importanza della questione.

empire ['empaɪə'] NOUN
l' impero

to employ [ɪm'plɔɪ] VERB
dare* lavoro a ◇ *The factory employs six
hundred people.* La fabbrica dà lavoro a
seicento persone.

◆ **to be employed** lavorare ◇ *Thousands of
people are employed in tourism.* Migliaia di
persone lavorano nel settore turistico.

employee [ɪmplɔɪ'iː] NOUN
il/la dipendente

employer [ɪm'plɔɪə'] NOUN
il datore di lavoro
la datrice di lavoro

employment [ɪm'plɔɪmənt] NOUN
l' impiego ◇ *It's difficult to find
employment.* È difficile trovare un impiego.

◆ **their place of employment** il loro posto di
lavoro
◆ **employment agency** l' agenzia di
collocamento

empty ['emptɪ] ADJECTIVE
see also **empty** VERB
vuoto

to empty ['emptɪ] VERB (**emptied, emptied**)
see also **empty** ADJECTIVE
vuotare

to encourage [ɪn'kʌrɪdʒ] VERB
incoraggiare

encouragement [ɪn'kʌrɪdʒmənt] NOUN
l' incoraggiamento

Verbs followed by the symbol "E" require the auxiliary "essere"

encyclopedia [ɛnsaɪkləʊ'piːdɪə] NOUN
l' enciclopedia

end [ɛnd] NOUN
see also **end** VERB
1 la fine ◇ *the end of the film* la fine del film
♦ **in the end** alla fine
2 l' estremità (PL le estremità) ◇ *at the other end of the table* all'altra estremità del tavolo
♦ **at the end of the street** in fondo alla strada
♦ **for hours on end** per ore e ore
♦ **to come to an end** finire

to **end** [ɛnd] VERB
see also **end** NOUN
finire
*When an auxiliary is needed to form past tenses use "essere" when **finire** does not have an object.*
◇ *What time does the film end?* A che ora finisce il film?

to **end up** [ɛnd'ʌp] VERB
finire ◇ *She ended up in prison.* È finita in prigione.
♦ **He could have ended up a millionaire.** Avrebbe anche potuto diventare miliardario.

ending ['ɛndɪŋ] NOUN
il finale ◇ *I didn't like the ending.* Non mi è piaciuto il finale.
♦ **a happy ending** un lieto fine

endless ['ɛndlɪs] ADJECTIVE
interminabile

enemy ['ɛnəmɪ] NOUN (PL **enemies**)
il nemico (PL i nemici)
la nemica (PL le nemiche)

energetic [ɛnə'dʒɛtɪk] ADJECTIVE
attivo ◇ *She's very energetic.* È molto attiva.

energy ['ɛnədʒɪ] NOUN
l' energia

engaged [ɪn'geɪdʒd] ADJECTIVE
1 occupato (*telephone, toilet*)
2 fidanzato ◇ *She's engaged to Brian.* È fidanzata con Brian.
♦ **to get engaged** fidanzarsi E

engaged tone [ɪn'geɪdʒdtəʊn] NOUN
il segnale di occupato

engagement [ɪn'geɪdʒmənt] NOUN
il fidanzamento
♦ **an engagement ring** un'anello di fidanzamento

engine ['ɛndʒɪn] NOUN
1 il motore (*of car*)
2 la locomotiva (*pulling train*)

engineer [ɛndʒɪ'nɪəʳ] NOUN
l' ingegnere MASC
♦ **service engineer** il tecnico

engineering [ɛndʒɪ'nɪərɪŋ] NOUN
l' ingegneria

England ['ɪŋglənd] NOUN
l' Inghilterra

English ['ɪŋglɪʃ] ADJECTIVE
see also **English** NOUN
inglese ◇ *English students* gli studenti inglesi
♦ **English people** gli inglesi

English ['ɪŋglɪʃ] NOUN
see also **English** ADJECTIVE
l' inglese MASC (*language*) ◇ *Do you speak English?* Parli inglese? ◇ *the English teacher* l'insegnante di inglese

Englishman ['ɪŋglɪʃmən] NOUN (PL **Englishmen**)
♦ **an Englishman** un inglese

Englishwoman ['ɪŋglɪʃwumən] NOUN (PL **Englishwomen**)
♦ **an Englishwoman** un'inglese

to **enjoy** [ɪn'dʒɔɪ] VERB
♦ **Did you enjoy the film?** Ti è piaciuto il film?
♦ **to enjoy oneself** divertirsi E

enjoyable [ɪn'dʒɔɪəbl] ADJECTIVE
piacevole

enlargement [ɪn'lɑːdʒmənt] NOUN
l' ingrandimento (*of photo*)

enormous [ɪ'nɔːməs] ADJECTIVE
enorme

enough [ɪ'nʌf] ADJECTIVE
abbastanza ◇ *I didn't have enough money.* Non avevo abbastanza soldi. ◇ *I've had enough of his lies!* Ne ho abbastanza delle sue bugie!
♦ **That's enough.** Basta così.

to **enquire** [ɪn'kwaɪəʳ] VERB
♦ **to enquire about something** informarsi E su qualcosa

enquiry [ɪn'kwaɪərɪ] NOUN (PL **enquiries**)
l' inchiesta ◇ *There will be an enquiry into the accident.* Ci sarà un'inchiesta sull'incidente.
♦ **to make enquiries** chiedere* informazioni

to **enter** ['ɛntəʳ] VERB
1 entrare E in ◇ *There was a sudden silence when she entered the room.* Ci fu un improvviso silenzio quando entrò nella stanza.
2 immettere ◇ *They entered the name into the computer.* Hanno immesso il nome nel computer.
♦ **to enter a competition** partecipare ad una gara

to **entertain** [ɛntə'teɪn] VERB
1 divertire ◇ *He entertained us with his stories.* Ci ha divertito con le sue storie.
2 intrattenere (*guests*)

entertainer [ɛntə'teɪnəʳ] NOUN
l' intrattenitore
l' intrattenitrice

entertaining [ɛntə'teɪnɪŋ] ADJECTIVE
divertente

enthusiasm [ɪn'θuːzɪæzəm] NOUN
l' entusiasmo

enthusiast [ɪn'θuːzɪæst] NOUN

* Verbs followed by this symbol are irregular. See pp.339–364 for further details.

l' appassionato
l' appassionata
◇ *She's a DIY enthusiast.* È
un'appassionata di bricolage.

enthusiastic [ɪnθuːzɪ'æstɪk] ADJECTIVE
[1] entusiasta (*person*)
[2] entusiastico (*response*)

entire [ɪn'taɪə'] ADJECTIVE
intero ◇ *the entire world* il mondo intero

entirely [ɪn'taɪəlɪ] ADVERB
[1] completamente ◇ *an entirely new approach* un approccio completamente nuovo
[2] pienamente ◇ *I agree entirely.* Sono pienamente d'accordo.

entrance ['ɛntrəns] NOUN
l' ingresso
♦ **the entrance fee** il biglietto d'ingresso
♦ **an entrance exam** un esame di ammissione

entry ['ɛntrɪ] NOUN (PL **entries**)
l' ingresso
♦ **"no entry" (1)** (*on door*) "vietato l'ingresso"
♦ **"no entry" (2)** (*on road sign*) "divieto d'accesso"
♦ **an entry form** un modulo d'iscrizione

entry phone ['ɛntrɪfəʊn] NOUN
il citofono

envelope ['ɛnvələʊp] NOUN
la busta

envied ['ɛnvɪd] VERB *see* **envy**

envious ['ɛnvɪəs] ADJECTIVE
invidioso

environment [ɪn'vaɪərnmənt] NOUN
l' ambiente MASC

environmental [ɪnvaɪərn'mɛntl] ADJECTIVE
ambientale

environmentally-friendly
[ɪn'vaɪərnməntəlɪ'frendlɪ] ADJECTIVE
ecologico

envy ['ɛnvɪ] NOUN
see also **envy** VERB
l' invidia

to **envy** ['ɛnvɪ] VERB (**envied, envied**)
see also **envy** NOUN
invidiare

epileptic [ɛpɪ'lɛptɪk] NOUN
l' epilettico
l' epilettica

episode ['ɛpɪsəʊd] NOUN
l' episodio

equal ['iːkwl] ADJECTIVE
see also **equal** VERB
[1] uguale ◇ *equal numbers of men and women* un numero uguale di uomini e donne ◇ *Divide the mixture into three equal parts.* Dividi l'impasto in tre parti uguali.
[2] pari ◇ *Women demand equal rights at work.* Le donne chiedono di avere pari diritti sul lavoro.
♦ **to be on equal terms** essere* E su un piano di parità

to **equal** ['iːkwl] VERB
see also **equal** ADJECTIVE
[1] essere* E uguale a ◇ *Eight and twelve equals twenty.* Otto più dodici è uguale a venti.
[2] eguagliare ◇ *This score has never been equalled.* Questo punteggio non è stato mai eguagliato.

equality [iː'kwɔlɪtɪ] NOUN
l' uguaglianza

to **equalize** ['iːkwəlaɪz] VERB
pareggiare (*in sport*)

equator [ɪ'kweɪtə'] NOUN
l' equatore MASC

to **equip** [ɪ'kwɪp] VERB
preparare ◇ *Vocational courses equip you for a particular job.* I corsi di formazione professionale preparano per un lavoro specifico.
♦ **to equip somebody with something** fornire qualcosa a qualcuno

equipment [ɪ'kwɪpmənt] NOUN
l' attrezzatura ◇ *skiing equipment* attrezzatura da sci

equipped [ɪ'kwɪpt] ADJECTIVE
attrezzato ◇ *This caravan is equipped for four people.* Questa roulotte è attrezzata per quattro persone.
♦ **equipped with** dotato di ◇ *All rooms are equipped with phones, computers and faxes.* Tutte le stanze sono dotate di telefono, computer e fax.

equivalent [ɪ'kwɪvələnt] NOUN
see also **equivalent** ADJECTIVE
l' equivalente MASC

equivalent [ɪ'kwɪvələnt] ADJECTIVE
see also **equivalent** NOUN
equivalente

erratic [ɪ'rætɪk] ADJECTIVE
[1] discontinuo (*performance, service*)
[2] incostante (*behaviour*)

error ['ɛrə'] NOUN
l' errore MASC

escalator ['ɛskəleɪtə'] NOUN
la scala mobile

escape [ɪs'keɪp] NOUN
see also **escape** VERB
la fuga (PL le fughe) (*from prison*)
♦ **It was a narrow escape.** L'abbiamo scampata bella.

to **escape** [ɪs'keɪp] VERB
see also **escape** NOUN
scappare E ◇ *A lion has escaped.* È scappato un leone.
♦ **to escape unhurt** rimanere* E illeso ◇ *The passengers escaped unhurt.* I passeggeri sono rimasti illesi.
♦ **to escape from prison** evadere* E di prigione

escort ['ɛskɔːt] NOUN
la scorta ◇ *a police escort* una scorta di ☞

polizia

Eskimo ['eskɪməu] NOUN (PL **Eskimos**)
l'eschimese MASC/FEM

especially [ɪs'peʃlɪ] ADVERB
1 soprattutto ◇ *It's very hot there,
especially in the summer.* Fa molto caldo lì,
soprattutto d'estate.
2 particolarmente ◇ *The recession makes
finding work especially difficult.* La
recessione rende particolarmente difficile
trovare lavoro.

essay ['eseɪ] NOUN
il tema (PL i temi) ◇ *a history essay* un tema
di storia

essential [ɪ'senʃl] ADJECTIVE
essenziale

estate [ɪs'teɪt] NOUN
1 il complesso edilizio ◇ *I live on an new
estate.* Vivo in un nuovo complesso edilizio.
2 la tenuta ◇ *He's got a large estate in the
country.* Ha una grossa tenuta in campagna.

estate agent [ɪ'steɪteɪdʒənt] NOUN
l'agente immobiliare MASC/FEM

estate car [ɪ'steɪtkɑːʳ] NOUN
la station wagon (PL le station wagon)

to **estimate** ['estɪmeɪt] VERB
calcolare ◇ *They estimated it would take
three weeks.* Hanno calcolato che ci
sarebbero volute tre settimane.

etc [ɪt'setrə] ABBREVIAZIONE (= *et cetera*)
ecc.

Ethiopia [iːθɪ'əupɪə] NOUN
l'Etiopia

ethnic ['eθnɪk] ADJECTIVE
1 etnico ◇ *an ethnic minority* una
minoranza etnica
◆ **ethnic cleansing** pulizia etnica
2 tipico ◇ *Our local Greek restaurant
serves delicious ethnic food.* Nel nostro
ristorante greco locale fanno dei buonissimi
piatti tipici.

EU [iːˈjuː] NOUN (= *European Union*)
l'UE (= Unione europea)

euro ['juərəu] NOUN (PL **euros**)
l'euro (PL gli euro)

Eurocheque ['juərəutʃek] NOUN
l'eurocheque MASC (PL gli eurocheque)

Euroland ['juərəulænd] NOUN
Eurolandia

Europe ['juərəp] NOUN
l'Europa

European [juərə'piːən] ADJECTIVE
see also **European** NOUN
europeo

European [juərə'piːən] NOUN
see also **European** ADJECTIVE
l'europeo
l'europea

to **evacuate** [ɪ'vækjueɪt] VERB
evacuare

eve [iːv] NOUN

◆ **Christmas Eve** la vigilia di Natale
◆ **New Year's Eve** Santo Stefano

even ['iːvn] ADVERB
see also **even** ADJECTIVE
perfino ◇ *I like all animals, even snakes.* Mi
piacciono tutti gli animali, perfino i serpenti.
◆ **not even** neanche ◇ *He didn't even say
hello.* Non ha neanche salutato.
◆ **even if** anche se
◆ **even though** anche se
◆ **even more** ancora di più ◇ *You'll have even
more fun tomorrow.* Domani vi divertirete
ancora di più.

even ['iːvn] ADJECTIVE
see also **even** ADVERB
1 pari ◇ *an even number* un numero pari
◇ *The scores are even.* Sono a pari
punteggio.
2 costante ◇ *an even temperature* una
temperatura costante
◆ **an even surface** una superficie liscia

evening ['iːvnɪŋ] NOUN
la sera ◇ *in the evening* di sera ◇ *all
evening* tutta la sera
◆ **Good evening!** Buona sera!
◆ **evening class** il corso serale

event [ɪ'vent] NOUN
1 l'avvenimento ◇ *It was one of the most
important events in his life.* È stato uno degli
avvenimenti più importanti della sua vita.
2 la gara ◇ *She took part in two events at
the last Olympic Games.* Ha preso parte a
due gare alle ultime Olimpiadi.
◆ **a sporting event** una manifestazione
sportiva
◆ **social events for the students** iniziative per
gli studenti
◆ **in the event of** in caso di

eventful [ɪ'ventful] ADJECTIVE
movimentato

eventual [ɪ'ventʃuəl] ADJECTIVE
finale ◇ *the eventual outcome* il risultato
finale

Be careful not to translate **eventual** *by word*
eventuale*.*

eventually [ɪ'ventʃuəlɪ] ADVERB
alla fine

Be careful not to translate **eventually** *by
word* **eventualmente***.*

ever ['evəʳ] ADVERB
1 mai ◇ *Have you ever been to Germany?*
Sei mai stato in Germania? ◇ *the best I've
ever seen* il migliore che abbia mai visto
2 sempre ◇ *It will become ever more
complex.* Diventerà sempre più complicato.
◆ **for the first time ever** per la prima volta in
assoluto
◆ **ever since** da quando ◇ *ever since I met him*
da quando l'ho incontrato
◆ **ever since then** da allora

every ['evrɪ] ADJECTIVE
ogni ◇ *every pupil* ogni scolaro ◇ *every*

* Verbs followed by this symbol are irregular. See pp.339–364 for further details.

time ogni volta

+ **every one of** tutti ◇ *Every one of the components was faulty.* Tutti i componenti erano difettosi.

+ **every now and then** di tanto in tanto

everybody ['ɛvrɪbɒdɪ] PRONOUN
tutti ◇ *Everybody makes mistakes.* Tutti fanno errori.

everyone ['ɛvrɪwʌn] PRONOUN
tutti ◇ *Everyone makes mistakes.* Tutti fanno errori.

everything ['ɛvrɪθɪŋ] PRONOUN
tutto ◇ *You've thought of everything!* Hai pensato a tutto!

everywhere ['ɛvrɪwɛəʳ] ADVERB
[1] dappertutto ◇ *I looked everywhere, but I couldn't find it.* Ho cercato dappertutto, ma non l'ho trovato.
[2] ovunque ◇ *everywhere you go* ovunque tu vada

evil ['iːvl] ADJECTIVE
cattivo

ex [ɛks] NOUN (PL **exes**)
l' ex MASC/FEM (PL gli/le ex) ◇ *He's one of my exes.* È uno dei miei ex.

exact [ɪg'zækt] ADJECTIVE
esatto

exactly [ɪg'zæktlɪ] ADVERB
esattamente ◇ *exactly the same* esattamente uguale

+ **It's exactly ten o'clock.** Sono le dieci in punto.

to **exaggerate** [ɪg'zædʒəreɪt] VERB
esagerare

exaggeration [ɪgzædʒə'reɪʃən] NOUN
l' esagerazione FEM

exam [ɪg'zæm] NOUN
l' esame MASC ◇ *a French exam* un esame di francese ◇ *the exam results* i risultati degli esami

+ **to take an exam** fare* un esame

examination [ɪgzæmɪ'neɪʃən] NOUN
l' esame MASC

to **examine** [ɪg'zæmɪn] VERB
[1] controllare ◇ *He examined her passport.* Le ha controllato il passaporto.
[2] visitare ◇ *The doctor examined him.* Il dottore l'ha visitato.
[3] esaminare ◇ *Experts are examining the wreckage of the plane.* Gli esperti stanno esaminando il relitto dell'aereo.

examiner [ɪg'zæmɪnəʳ] NOUN
l' esaminatore
l' esaminatrice

example [ɪg'zɑːmpl] NOUN
l' esempio ◇ *for example* per esempio

excellent ['ɛksələnt] ADJECTIVE
eccellente ◇ *Her results were excellent.* I suoi risultati erano eccellenti.

+ **It was excellent fun.** È stato veramente divertente.

except [ɪk'sɛpt] PREPOSITION
tranne ◇ *everyone except me* tutti tranne me

+ **except for** ad eccezione di

+ **except that** salvo che

exception [ɪk'sɛpʃən] NOUN
l' eccezione FEM

exceptional [ɪk'sɛpʃənl] ADJECTIVE
eccezionale

to **exchange** [ɪks'tʃeɪndʒ] VERB
see also **exchange** NOUN
scambiare

exchange [ɪks'tʃeɪndʒ] NOUN
see also **exchange** VERB
lo scambio ◇ *I'd like to do an exchange with an Italian student.* Vorrei fare uno scambio con uno studente italiano.

+ **in exchange** in cambio ◇ *What will you give me in exchange?* Cosa mi darai in cambio?

+ **exchange rate** tasso di cambio

excited [ɪk'saɪtɪd] ADJECTIVE
eccitato

exciting [ɪk'saɪtɪŋ] ADJECTIVE
[1] entusiasmante ◇ *an exciting match* una partita entusiasmante
[2] appassionante ◇ *an exciting story* una storia appassionante
[3] eccitante ◇ *an exciting adventure* un'avventura eccitante

excuse [ɪks'kjuːs] NOUN
see also **excuse** VERB
la scusa

to **excuse** [ɪks'kjuːz] VERB
see also **excuse** NOUN

+ **Excuse me! (1)** (*to attract attention, apologize*) Scusi!

+ **Excuse me! (2)** (*when you want to get past*) Permesso!

+ **Excuse me?** Come, scusi?

to **execute** ['ɛksɪkjuːt] VERB
giustiziare (*prisoner*)

execution [ɛksɪ'kjuːʃən] NOUN
l' esecuzione FEM

executive [ɪg'zɛkjutɪv] NOUN
il/la dirigente

exercise ['ɛksəsaɪz] NOUN
[1] l' esercizio ◇ *page ten, exercise three* pagina dieci, esercizio numero tre

+ **an exercise book** un quaderno
[2] la ginnastica

+ **to take some exercise** fare* un po' di ginnastica

exercise bike ['ɛksəsaɪzbaɪk] NOUN
la cyclette (PL le cyclette)

exhaust [ɪg'zɔːst] NOUN
il tubo di scappamento

exhausted [ɪg'zɔːstɪd] ADJECTIVE
esausto

exhaust fumes [ɪg'zɔːstfjuːmz] NOUN PL
i gas di scarico

exhaust pipe [ɪg'zɔːst'paɪp] NOUN ☞

il tubo di scappamento

exhibition [eksɪ'bɪʃən] NOUN
la mostra

to **exist** [ɪg'zɪst] VERB
esistere [E]

exit ['eksɪt] NOUN
l' uscita

exotic [ɪg'zɔtɪk] ADJECTIVE
esotico

to **expect** [ɪks'pekt] VERB
[1] aspettare ◇ *I'm expecting him for dinner.* Lo aspetto per cena. ◇ *She's expecting a baby.* Sta aspettando un bambino.
[2] aspettarsi [E] ◇ *I didn't expect that from him.* Non me l'aspettavo da lui. ◇ *I didn't expect him to agree.* Non mi aspettavo che fosse d'accordo.
[3] pensare ◇ *I expect he'll be late.* Penso che arriverà tardi. ◇ *I expect so.* Penso di sì.

expedition [ekspə'dɪʃən] NOUN
la spedizione

to **expel** [ɪks'pel] VERB
 ♦ **to get expelled** essere* [E] espulso

expenses [ɪks'pensəz] NOUN PL
le spese ◇ *Can you claim this on expenses?* Puoi metterlo tra le spese?

expensive [ɪks'pensɪv] ADJECTIVE
costoso

experience [ɪks'pɪərɪəns] NOUN
see also **experience** VERB
l' esperienza

to **experience** [ɪks'pɪərɪəns] VERB
see also **experience** NOUN
[1] avere* ◇ *They're experiencing some problems.* Stanno avendo qualche problema.
[2] provare ◇ *He experienced fear and pain.* Ha provato paura e dolore.

experienced [ɪks'pɪərɪənst] ADJECTIVE
 ♦ **an experienced teacher** un insegnante che ha esperienza

experiment [ɪks'perɪmənt] NOUN
l' esperimento

expert ['ekspə:t] NOUN
see also **expert** ADJECTIVE
l' esperto
l' esperta

expert ADJECTIVE
see also **expert** NOUN
esperto

to **expire** [ɪks'paɪə'] VERB
scadere* [E] (*passport, ticket*)

to **explain** [ɪks'pleɪn] VERB
spiegare

explanation [eksplə'neɪʃən] NOUN
la spiegazione

to **explode** [ɪks'pləud] VERB
esplodere* [E]
When an auxiliary is needed to form past tenses use "essere" when **esplodere** *does not*

have an object.

to **exploit** [ɪks'plɔɪt] VERB
sfruttare

exploitation [eksplɔɪ'teɪʃən] NOUN
lo sfruttamento

to **explore** [ɪks'plɔ:'] VERB
esplorare (*place*)

explorer [ɪks'plɔ:rə'] NOUN
l' esploratore
l' esploratrice

explosion [ɪks'pləuʒən] NOUN
l' esplosione FEM

explosive [ɪks'pləusɪv] ADJECTIVE
see also **explosive** NOUN
esplosivo

explosive [ɪks'pləusɪv] NOUN
see also **explosive** ADJECTIVE
l' esplosivo

to **express** [ɪks'pres] VERB
esprimere
 ♦ **to express oneself** esprimersi [E]

expression [ɪks'preʃən] NOUN
l' espressione FEM

expressway [ɪks'presweɪ] NOUN [US]
l' autostrada che attraversa la città

extension [ɪks'tenʃən] NOUN
[1] l' annesso (*of building*)
[2] l' interno (*telephone*) ◇ *Extension three one three seven, please.* L'interno tre uno tre sette, per favore.
[3] la proroga ◇ *He's been given a six month extension.* Gli hanno dato una proroga di sei mesi.

extensive [ɪks'tensɪv] ADJECTIVE
[1] vasto ◇ *The hotel is set in extensive grounds.* L'albergo sorge su un vasto terreno.
[2] approfondito ◇ *extensive research* ricerche approfondite
 ♦ **to get extensive coverage** (*in press*) essere* [E] trattato ampiamente
 ♦ **extensive damage** danni ingenti MASC PL

extensively [ɪks'tensɪvlɪ] ADVERB
molto ◇ *He has travelled extensively.* Ha viaggiato molto.

extent [ɪks'tent] NOUN
l' entità FEM ◇ *The extent of the damage is not yet known.* Non è ancora nota l'entità dei danni.
 ♦ **to some extent** in una certa misura

exterior [eks'tɪərɪə'] ADJECTIVE
esterno

extinct [ɪks'tɪŋkt] ADJECTIVE
estinto ◇ *Dinosaurs are extinct.* I dinosauri sono estinti.
 ♦ **to become extinct** estinguersi [E]

extinguisher [ɪks'tɪŋgwɪʃə'] NOUN
l' estintore MASC

extortionate [ɪks'tɔ:ʃnɪt] ADJECTIVE
esorbitante

extra ['ekstrə] ADJECTIVE, ADVERB

* Verbs followed by this symbol are irregular. See pp.339–364 for further details.

in più ◇ *an extra blanket* una coperta in più
- **to pay extra** pagare extra
- **to be extra** essere* E a parte ◇ *Breakfast is extra.* La colazione è a parte.
- **Be extra careful!** Stai attentissimo!
- **extra time** tempi supplementari MASC PL ◇ *They won after extra time.* Hanno vinto dopo i tempi supplementari.

extraordinary [ɪksˈtrɔːdnrɪ] ADJECTIVE
straordinario

extravagant [ɪksˈtrævəgənt] ADJECTIVE
sprecone (*person*) ◇ *I'm not extravagant, but I do like nice clothes.* Non sono sprecone, ma mi piacciono i vestiti eleganti.
*Be careful not to translate **extravagant** by **stravagante**.*

extreme [ɪksˈtriːm] ADJECTIVE
estremo

extremely [ɪksˈtriːmlɪ] ADVERB
estremamente

extremist [ɪksˈtriːmɪst] NOUN
l' estremista MASC / FEM

eye [aɪ] NOUN
| *see also* **eye** VERB |
l' occhio ◇ *I've got green eyes.* Ho gli occhi verdi.
- **to keep an eye on something** tenere*

d'occhio qualcosa
- **to catch somebody's eye** attirare l'attenzione di qualcuno
- **to cry one's eyes out** piangere* a calde lacrime

to **eye** [aɪ] VERB
| *see also* **eye** NOUN |
scrutare ◇ *The children eyed the parcel with interest.* I bambini scrutavano il pacco con interesse.

eyebrow [ˈaɪbrau] NOUN
il sopracciglio

eyelash [ˈaɪlæʃ] NOUN (PL **eyelashes**)
il ciglio (PL FEM le ciglia)

eyelid [ˈaɪlɪd] NOUN
la palpebra

eyeliner [ˈaɪlaɪnəʳ] NOUN
l' eye-liner (PL gli eye-liner)

eye shadow [ˈaɪʃædəu] NOUN
l' ombretto

eyesight [ˈaɪsaɪt] NOUN
la vista

eyewitness [ˈaɪwɪtnɪs] NOUN (PL **eyewitnesses**)
il/la testimone oculare

E

F

fabric ['fæbrɪk] NOUN
la stoffa

fabulous ['fæbjuləs] ADJECTIVE
favoloso

face [feɪs] NOUN
see also **face** VERB
[1] la faccia (PL le facce) ◇ *He was red in the face.* Era rosso in faccia.
[2] la parete ◇ *the north face of the mountain* la parete nord della montagna
[3] il quadrante (*of watch*)
• **on the face of it** a prima vista
• **to take something at face value** giudicare qualcosa dalle apparenze
• **in the face of these difficulties** di fronte a queste difficoltà

to **face** [feɪs] VERB
see also **face** NOUN
[1] essere*ᴱ di fronte a ◇ *They faced each other.* Erano uno di fronte all'altro.
[2] trovarsiᴱ di fronte a ◇ *They will face serious problems.* Si troveranno di fronte a gravi problemi.
• **Let's face it...** Diciamocelo chiaramente...

to **face up to** [feɪsʌptu] VERB
accettare ◇ *He refuses to face up to his responsibilities.* Rifiuta di accettare le proprie responsabilità.

facecloth ['feɪsklɒθ] NOUN
il guanto di spugna

face lift ['feɪslɪft] NOUN
il lifting (PL i lifting)

facilities [fə'sɪlɪtiz] NOUN PL
le attrezzature ◇ *This school has excellent facilities.* Questa scuola ha ottime attrezzature.
• **The youth hostel has cooking facilities.** È possibile cucinare all'ostello.

fact [fækt] NOUN
il fatto ◇ *He finally accepted the fact that she didn't love him any more.* Alla fine ha accettato il fatto che lei non lo amasse più.
◇ *facts and figures* fatti e cifre
• **in fact** in effetti

factory ['fæktərɪ] NOUN (PL **factories**)
la fabbrica (PL le fabbriche) ◇ *a car factory* una fabbrica di automobili
• **factory farming** l'allevamento su scala industriale
Be careful not to translate **factory** by **fattoria**.

to **fade** [feɪd] VERB
[1] scolorirsiᴱ ◇ *My jeans have faded.* I miei jeans si sono scoloriti.
[2] svanireᴱ ◇ *Hopes of a peaceful solution are fading.* Sta svanendo ogni speranza di trovare una soluzione pacifica.

fag [fæg] NOUN
la cicca (PL le cicche)

to **fail** [feɪl] VERB
see also **fail** NOUN

[1] non superare (*exam*) ◇ *He failed his driving test.* Non ha superato l'esame di guida.
[2] essere*ᴱ bocciato (*fail to pass*) ◇ *A quarter of the students failed.* Un quarto degli studenti sono stati bocciati.
[3] non funzionare ◇ *The lorry's brakes failed.* I freni del camion non hanno funzionato.
[4] fallireᴱ ◇ *The plan failed.* Il piano è fallito.
• **to fail to do something** non riuscire*ᴱ a fare qualcosa ◇ *They failed to reach the quarter-finals.* Non sono riusciti a raggiungere i quarti di finale.

fail [feɪl] NOUN
see also **fail** VERB
• **D is a pass, E is a fail.** Con D si passa, con E si viene bocciati.
• **without fail** senz'altro

failure ['feɪljə'] NOUN
il fallimento ◇ *The attempt was a complete failure.* Il tentativo è stato un fallimento completo.
• **I feel a failure.** Mi sento un fallito.

faint [feɪnt] ADJECTIVE
see also **faint** VERB
debole ◇ *His voice was very faint.* La sua voce era molto debole.
• **I haven't the faintest idea.** Non ne ho la più pallida idea.
• **to feel faint** sentirsiᴱ svenire

to **faint** [feɪnt] VERB
see also **faint** ADJECTIVE
svenire*ᴱ

fair [feə'] ADJECTIVE
see also **fair** NOUN
[1] giusto ◇ *That's not fair!* Non è giusto!
[2] chiaro ◇ *people with fair skin* le persone con la pelle chiara
[3] discreto ◇ *I have a fair chance of winning.* Ho discrete probabilità di vincere.
• **That's a fair distance.** È una bella distanza.

fair [feə'] NOUN
see also **fair** ADJECTIVE
il parco dei divertimenti (PL i parchi dei divertimenti) ◇ *I won a furry dog at the fair.* Ho vinto un cane di peluche al parco dei divertimenti.
• **a trade fair** una fiera campionaria

fairground ['feəgraund] NOUN
il parco dei divertimenti (PL i parchi dei divertimenti)

fair-haired [feə'heəd] ADJECTIVE
biondo

fairly ['feəlɪ] ADVERB
[1] abbastanza ◇ *My car is fairly new.* La mia macchina è abbastanza nuova.
[2] equamente ◇ *The money was divided fairly.* Il denaro è stato diviso equamente.

* Verbs followed by this symbol are irregular. See pp.339–364 for further details.

F

fairness ['fɛənɪs] NOUN
+ **in all fairness** per una questione di giustizia
+ **In all fairness, I think we should check the facts.** Per una questione di giustizia, penso che dovremmo appurare i fatti.

fairy ['fɛərɪ] NOUN (PL **fairies**)
la fata

fairy tale ['fɛərɪteɪl] NOUN
la favola

faith [feɪθ] NOUN
1 la fiducia ◊ *People have lost faith in the government.* La gente ha perso fiducia nel governo.
+ **to put one's faith in** fidarsi ᴱ di
2 la fede (*religion*)

faithful ['feɪθful] ADJECTIVE
fedele

faithfully ['feɪθfəlɪ] ADVERB
+ **Yours faithfully...** Distinti saluti...

fake [feɪk] NOUN, ADJECTIVE
falso ◊ *The painting was a fake.* Il quadro era un falso. ◊ *a fake banknote* una banconota falsa
+ **a fake fur coat** una pelliccia sintetica

fall [fɔːl] NOUN
see also **fall** VERB
1 la caduta ◊ *She had a nasty fall.* Ha fatto una brutta caduta.
+ **a fall of snow** una nevicata
2 autunno US ◊ *in the fall* in autunno

to **fall** [fɔːl] VERB (**fell, fallen**)
see also **fall** NOUN
1 cadere* ᴱ ◊ *He tripped and fell.* È inciampato e caduto. ◊ *She's fallen.* È caduta.
+ **to fall in love** innamorarsi ᴱ
2 calare ᴱ ◊ *Prices are falling.* I prezzi stanno calando.

to **fall apart** [fɔːləˈpɑːt] VERB
cadere* ᴱ a pezzi

to **fall behind** [fɔːlbɪˈhaɪnd] VERB
rimanere* ᴱ indietro

to **fall for** [fɔːlˈfɔːʳ] VERB
1 cascarci ᴱ ◊ *They fell for it!* Ci sono cascati!
2 prendersi ᴱ una cotta per ◊ *Anne fell for him immediately.* Anne si è subito presa una cotta per lui.

to **fall off** [fɔːlˈɔf] VERB
1 cadere* ᴱ ◊ *The exhaust fell off.* È caduto il tubo di scarico.
2 diminuire ᴱ ◊ *Unemployment has fallen off.* La disoccupazione è diminuita.

to **fall out** [fɔːlˈaut] VERB
litigare ◊ *Sarah's fallen out with her boyfriend.* Sarah ha litigato col suo ragazzo.

to **fall through** [fɔːlˈθruː] VERB
fallire ᴱ

fallen ['fɔːlən] VERB *see* **fall**

false [fɔːls] ADJECTIVE
falso ◊ *a false alarm* un falso allarme

+ **under false pretences** con l'inganno
+ **false teeth** dentiera

fame [feɪm] NOUN
la fama

familiar [fəˈmɪlɪəʳ] ADJECTIVE
familiare ◊ *The name sounded familiar to me.* Il nome mi suonava familiare.
+ **to be familiar with something** conoscere* bene qualcosa ◊ *I'm familiar with his work.* Conosco bene i suoi lavori.

family ['fæmɪlɪ] NOUN (PL **families**)
la famiglia ◊ *the Cooke family* la famiglia Cooke
+ **a family doctor** un medico di famiglia

famine ['fæmɪn] NOUN
la carestia

famous ['feɪməs] ADJECTIVE
famoso

fan [fæn] NOUN
1 il tifoso
la tifosa
◊ *the England fans* i tifosi inglesi
2 l' ammiratore
l' ammiratrice
◊ *I'm one of his greatest fans.* Sono uno dei suoi più grandi ammiratori.
3 il patito
la patita
◊ *She's a jazz fan.* È una patita di jazz.
4 il ventaglio ◊ *a silk fan* un ventaglio di seta
+ **an electric fan** un ventilatore

fanatic [fəˈnætɪk] NOUN
il fanatico (PL i fanatici)
la fanatica (PL le fanatiche)

fan belt ['fænbelt] NOUN
la cinghia del ventilatore

to **fancy** ['fænsɪ] VERB (**fancied, fancied**)
+ **to fancy something** avere* voglia di qualcosa
+ **to fancy doing something** aver* voglia di fare qualcosa
+ **He fancies her.** Lei gli piace.

fancy dress ['fænsɪdres] NOUN
+ **a fancy dress ball** un ballo in maschera

fantastic [fænˈtæstɪk] ADJECTIVE
fantastico

far [fɑːʳ] ADJECTIVE, ADVERB
lontano ◊ *Is it far?* È lontano? ◊ *It's not far from London.* Non è lontano da Londra.
+ **It's far from easy.** Non è affatto facile.
+ **How far is it?** Quanto dista?
+ **How far have you got?** A che punto sei arrivato?
+ **at the far end of** all'altro lato di
+ **far better** molto meglio
+ **as far as I know** per quanto ne so
+ **so far** fino ad ora

fare [fɛəʳ] NOUN
la tariffa ◊ *Railway fares are very high in Britain.* La tariffe ferroviarie sono molto alte ☞

in Gran Bretagna.

◆ **He didn't have the bus fare, so he had to walk.** Non aveva i soldi per il biglietto dell'autobus, e così ha dovuto andare a piedi.

◆ **I spent a lot on taxi fares.** Ho speso molto per il taxi.

◆ **full fare** la tariffa intera

Far East [fɑːˈriːst] NOUN
l' Estremo Oriente MASC

farm [fɑːm] NOUN
la fattoria

farmer [ˈfɑːmə] NOUN
1 il coltivatore (*growing crops*)
2 l' allevatore (*raising animals*)

farmhouse [ˈfɑːmhaus] NOUN
la fattoria

farming [ˈfɑːmɪŋ] NOUN
l' agricoltura ◊ *organic farming* agricoltura biologica

◆ **sheep farming** l'allevamento di pecore

to **fascinate** [ˈfæsɪneɪt] VERB
affascinare

fascinating [ˈfæsɪneɪtɪŋ] ADJECTIVE
affascinante

fashion [ˈfæʃən] NOUN
la moda

◆ **in fashion** di moda

fashionable [ˈfæʃnəbl] ADJECTIVE
alla moda

fast [fɑːst] ADJECTIVE, ADVERB
veloce ◊ *a fast car* una macchina veloce

◆ **fast food** il fast food

◆ **to be fast** (*watch*) andare* [E] avanti

◆ **fast asleep** profondamente addormentato

fastidious [fæsˈtɪdɪəs] ADJECTIVE
pignolo

*Be careful not to translate **fastidious** by fastidioso.*

fat [fæt] ADJECTIVE
see also **fat** NOUN
grasso ◊ *She thinks she's too fat.* Pensa di essere troppo grassa.

fat [fæt] NOUN
see also **fat** ADJECTIVE
il grasso ◊ *It's very high in fat.* Contiene molti grassi.

fatal [ˈfeɪtl] ADJECTIVE
1 mortale ◊ *a fatal accident* un incidente mortale
2 fatale ◊ *a fatal mistake* un errore fatale

father [ˈfɑːðə] NOUN
il padre ◊ *my father* mio padre

◆ **Father Christmas** Babbo Natale

father-in-law [ˈfɑːðərənlɔː] NOUN (PL **fathers-in-law**)
il suocero

faucet [ˈfɔːsɪt] NOUN US
il rubinetto

fault [fɔːlt] NOUN
1 la colpa ◊ *It wasn't my fault.* Non è stata colpa mia.
2 il difetto ◊ *He has his faults, but I still like him.* Ha i suoi difetti, ma mi piace lo stesso.

◆ **a technical fault** un guasto tecnico

faulty [ˈfɔːltɪ] ADJECTIVE
difettoso

favour [ˈfeɪvə] NOUN (US **favor**)
il favore ◊ *Could you do me a favour?* Potresti farmi un favore?

◆ **to be in favour of something** essere* [E] a favore di qualcosa

favourite [ˈfeɪvrɪt] ADJECTIVE (US **favorite**)
see also **favourite** NOUN
preferito ◊ *It's my favourite.* È il mio preferito.

favourite [ˈfeɪvrɪt] NOUN (US **favorite**)
see also **favourite** ADJECTIVE
il favorito
la favorita
(*in sport*)

fawn [fɔːn] ADJECTIVE
marroncino

fax [fæks] NOUN (PL **faxes**)
see also **fax** VERB
il fax (PL i fax)

to **fax** [fæks] VERB
see also **fax** NOUN
spedire via fax (*letter, document*)

◆ **to fax somebody something** spedire via fax qualcosa a qualcuno ◊ *I'll fax you the document.* Ti spedirò via fax il documento.

fear [fɪə] NOUN
see also **fear** VERB
la paura

to **fear** [fɪə] VERB
see also **fear** NOUN
temere

feather [ˈfɛðə] NOUN
la piuma

feature [ˈfiːtʃə] NOUN
la caratteristica (PL le caratteristiche)

February [ˈfebruərɪ] NOUN
febbraio ◊ *in February* in febbraio

fed [fed] VERB *see* **feed**

fed up [fedˈʌp] ADJECTIVE

◆ **to be fed up with something** essere* [E] stufo di qualcosa

to **feed** [fiːd] VERB (**fed, fed**)
1 dar da mangiare a ◊ *Have you fed the cat?* Hai dato da mangiare al gatto?
2 mantenere ◊ *He worked hard to feed his family.* Lavorava sodo per mantenere la famiglia.

to **feel** [fiːl] VERB (**felt, felt**)
1 sentire ◊ *I didn't feel much pain.* Non sentivo molto dolore.
2 sentirsi [E] ◊ *I don't feel well.* Non mi sento bene. ◊ *I felt lonely.* Mi sento solo.

◆ **to feel hungry** avere* fame

◆ **to feel cold** avere* freddo

◆ **to feel like doing something** aver* voglia di

* Verbs followed by this symbol are irregular. See pp.339–364 for further details.

fare qualcosa ◊ *I don't feel like going out tonight.* Non ho voglia di uscire stasera.
* **Do you feel like an ice cream?** Hai voglia di un gelato?

feeling ['fiːlɪŋ] NOUN
[1] la sensazione ◊ *a burning feeling* una sensazione di bruciore
[2] il sentimento ◊ *He was afraid of hurting my feelings.* Aveva paura di urtare i miei sentimenti.
* **What are your feelings about it?** Cosa ne pensi?

feet [fiːt] NOUN PL *see* **foot**

fell [fɛl] VERB *see* **fall**

fellow ['fɛləu] ADJECTIVE
* **fellow students** compagni di studio
* **fellow workers** compagni di lavoro

felt [fɛlt] VERB *see* **feel**

felt-tip pen ['fɛlttɪp'pɛn] NOUN
il pennarello

female ['fiːmeɪl] ADJECTIVE
see also **female** NOUN
[1] femmina ◊ *Two of the puppies were female.* Due dei cuccioli erano femmine.
[2] femminile ◊ *the female sex* il sesso femminile
* **female MPs** le parlamentari
* **female students** le studentesse

female ['fiːmeɪl] NOUN
see also **female** ADJECTIVE
la femmina (*animal*)

feminine ['fɛmɪnɪn] ADJECTIVE
femminile

feminist ['fɛmɪnɪst] NOUN
la femminista

fence [fɛns] NOUN
lo steccato

fern [fəːn] NOUN
la felce

ferocious [fə'rəuʃəs] ADJECTIVE
feroce

ferry ['fɛrɪ] NOUN (PL **ferries**)
il traghetto

fertile ['fəːtaɪl] ADJECTIVE
fertile

fertilizer ['fəːtɪlaɪzəʳ] NOUN
il fertilizzante

festival ['fɛstɪvəl] NOUN
il festival (PL i festival) ◊ *a jazz festival* un festival di musica jazz

to **fetch** [fɛtʃ] VERB
[1] andare* E a prendere ◊ *Fetch the bucket.* Vai a prendere il secchio.
[2] essere* E venduto per ◊ *His painting fetched five thousand pounds.* Il suo quadro è stato venduto per cinquemila sterline.

fever ['fiːvəʳ] NOUN
la febbre ◊ *He's got a high fever.* Ha la febbre alta.
* **fever pitch** il colmo ◊ *Excitement has reached fever pitch.* L'eccitazione ha raggiunto il colmo.

few [fjuː] ADJECTIVE, PRONOUN
pochi (*not many*) ◊ *He has few friends.* Ha pochi amici.
* **a few** (*some*) alcuni ◊ *a few of them* alcuni di loro ◊ *I invited a few old friends.* Ho invitato alcuni vecchi amici.
* **quite a few people** un bel po' di gente

fewer ['fjuːəʳ] ADJECTIVE
meno ◊ *There were fewer people than yesterday.* C'era meno gente di ieri.

fiancé [fɪ'ɑːseɪ] NOUN
il fidanzato

fiancée [fɪ'ɑːseɪ] NOUN
la fidanzata

fiction ['fɪkʃən] NOUN
la narrativa

field [fiːld] NOUN
il campo ◊ *a field of wheat* un campo di grano
* **field sports** la caccia e la pesca

field events ['fiːldɪvɛnts] NOUN
le gare di salto e di lancio

fierce [fɪəs] ADJECTIVE
[1] feroce ◊ *a fierce Alsatian* un feroce cane lupo
[2] spietato ◊ *There's fierce competition between companies.* C'è una concorrenza spietata tra società.
[3] violento ◊ *a fierce attack* un violento attacco

fifteen [fɪf'tiːn] NUMERAL
quindici ◊ *I'm fifteen.* Ho quindici anni.

fifteenth [fɪf'tiːnθ] ADJECTIVE
quindicesimo
* **the fifteenth of August** il quindici agosto

fifth [fɪfθ] ADJECTIVE
quinto ◊ *the fifth floor* il quinto piano
* **the fifth of August** il cinque agosto

fifty ['fɪftɪ] NUMERAL
cinquanta ◊ *He's fifty.* Ha cinquant'anni.

fifty-fifty ['fɪftɪ'fɪftɪ] ADJECTIVE, ADVERB
a metà ◊ *They split the prize money fifty-fifty.* Hanno diviso a metà i soldi del premio.
* **a fifty-fifty chance** una probabilità su due

fight [faɪt] NOUN
see also **fight** VERB
[1] la rissa ◊ *There was a fight in the pub.* C'è stata una rissa al pub.
* **to have a fight with somebody** (*quarrel*) litigare con qualcuno ◊ *She had a fight with her best friend.* Ha litigato con la sua migliore amica.
[2] la lotta ◊ *the fight against cancer* la lotta contro il cancro
[3] incontro ◊ *Cassius Clay's last fight* l'ultimo incontro di Cassius Clay

to **fight** [faɪt] VERB (**fought, fought**)
see also **fight** NOUN
[1] azzuffarsi E ◊ *The fans started fighting.* I ☞

tifosi hanno cominciato ad azzuffarsi.

2 litigare (*quarrel*) ◇ *They fight sometimes, but they're good friends.* A volte litigano ma sono buoni amici.

3 lottare contro ◇ *She has fought racism all her life.* Ha lottato per tutta la vita contro il razzismo.

4 lottare ◇ *Let us fight for peace.* Lottiamo per la pace.

5 scontrarsi[E] ◇ *The demonstrators fought with the police.* I dimostranti si sono scontrati con la polizia.

to **fight back** [faɪtˈbæk] VERB
reagire ◇ *The attackers ran away when the man fought back.* Gli assalitori sono scappati quando l'uomo ha reagito.

fighting [ˈfaɪtɪŋ] NOUN
la rissa ◇ *Fighting broke out outside the pub.* È scoppiata una rissa fuori dal pub.

figure [ˈfɪgəʳ] NOUN
1 la cifra ◇ *Can you give me the exact figures?* Puoi darmi le cifre esatte?

2 figura ◇ *She's got a good figure.* Ha una bella figura.

3 linea ◇ *I have to watch my figure.* Devo stare attenta alla linea.

4 personaggio ◇ *She's an important political figure.* È un importante personaggio politico.

♦ **a figure of speech** una figura retorica

file [faɪl] NOUN
see also **file** VERB
1 la pratica (PL le pratiche) ◇ *There was stuff in that file that was private.* C'erano delle cose riservate in quella pratica.

♦ **The police have a file on him.** È schedato dalla polizia.

2 la cartella ◇ *She put the photocopy into her file.* Ha messo la fotocopia nella sua cartella.

3 la lima ◇ *a nail file* una lima per unghie
4 il file (PL i file) (*on computer*)

to **file** [faɪl] VERB
see also **file** NOUN
1 raccogliere* (*documents*)
2 limare ◇ *She was filing her nails.* Si stava limando le unghie.

to **fill** [fɪl] VERB
riempire* ◇ *She filled the glass with water.* Ha riempito il bicchiere d'acqua.

to **fill in** [fɪlˈɪn] VERB
1 riempire* ◇ *Can you fill this form in, please?* Può riempire questo modulo, per favore?

2 mettere* al corrente ◇ *I'll fill you in on what's been happening.* Ti metterò al corrente su quello che succede.

to **fill up** [fɪlˈʌp] VERB
♦ **Fill it up, please.** (*car*) Mi faccia il pieno, per favore.

film [fɪlm] NOUN
1 il film (PL i film) (*movie*)

2 il rullino ◇ *I need a 36 exposure film.* Vorrei un rullino da 36 foto.

film star [ˈfɪlmstɑːʳ] NOUN
il divo del cinema
la diva del cinema

filthy [ˈfɪlθɪ] ADJECTIVE
sudicio

final [ˈfaɪnl] ADJECTIVE
see also **final** NOUN
1 ultimo ◇ *a final attempt* un ultimo tentativo

2 definitiva ◇ *a final decision* una decisione definitiva

♦ **...and that's final!** ...e basta! ◇ *I'm not going and that's final!* Non ci vado e basta!

final [ˈfaɪnl] NOUN
see also **final** ADJECTIVE
la finale ◇ *Pete Sampras is in the final.* Pete Sampras è in finale.

finally [ˈfaɪnəlɪ] ADVERB
1 infine ◇ *Finally, I would like to say...* Vorrei dire, infine...

2 alla fine ◇ *They finally decided to leave on Saturday.* Alla fine hanno deciso di partire sabato.

to **find** [faɪnd] VERB (**found, found**)
trovare ◇ *I can't find the exit.* Non riesco a trovare l'uscita. ◇ *I've found it.* L'ho trovato.

to **find out** [faɪndˈaut] VERB
scoprire*
♦ **to find out about (1)** informarsi[E] su ◇ *Find out as much as possible about the town.* Informati il più possibile sulla città.

♦ **to find out about (2)** (*discover*) scoprire*

fine [faɪn] ADJECTIVE
see also **fine** NOUN
1 bene ◇ *How are you? – Fine, thanks!* Come stai? – Bene, grazie! ◇ *I feel fine.* Mi sento bene. ◇ *It'll be ready tomorrow. – That's fine, thanks.* Sarà pronto domani. – Va bene, grazie.

2 ottimo ◇ *He's a fine musician.* È un ottimo musicista.

3 bello ◇ *The weather is fine today.* Oggi il tempo è bello.

4 sottile ◇ *She's got very fine hair.* Ha i capelli molto sottili.

fine [faɪn] NOUN
see also **fine** ADJECTIVE
la multa

finger [ˈfɪŋgəʳ] NOUN
il dito (PL FEM le dita) ◇ *a ring on every finger* un anello su ogni dito

♦ **my little finger** il mignolo

fingernail [ˈfɪŋgəneɪl] NOUN
l' unghia

finish [ˈfɪnɪʃ] NOUN
see also **finish** VERB
la fine ◇ *from start to finish* dall'inizio alla fine

to **finish** [ˈfɪnɪʃ] VERB

---

* Verbs followed by this symbol are irregular. See pp.339–364 for further details.

English ~ Italian

finish with → fish fingers 449

see also finish NOUN
finire ◊ *I've finished!* Ho finito! ◊ *Have you finished eating?* Hai finito di mangiare?

o **finish with** ['fɪnɪʃwɪð] VERB
chiudere* con ◊ *She's finished with her boyfriend.* Ha chiuso con il suo ragazzo.

Finland ['fɪnlənd] NOUN
la Finlandia

Finn [fɪn] NOUN
il/la finlandese

Finnish ['fɪnɪʃ] ADJECTIVE
see also Finnish NOUN
finlandese

Finnish ['fɪnɪʃ] NOUN
see also Finnish ADJECTIVE
il finlandese (*language*)

fir [fəːʳ] NOUN
l' abete

fire ['faɪəʳ] NOUN
see also fire VERB
[1] il fuoco (PL i fuochi) ◊ *He made a fire to warm himself up.* Ha acceso un fuoco per scaldarsi.
 • **to be on fire** essere*E in fiamme
[2] l' incendio ◊ *The house was destroyed by a fire.* La casa è stata distrutta da un incendio.

to **fire** ['faɪəʳ] VERB
see also fire NOUN
[1] sparare ◊ *She fired at him.* Gli ha sparato.
 • **to fire a gun** fare fuoco
[2] licenziare ◊ *He was fired from his job.* È stato licenziato.

fire alarm ['faɪərəlɑːm] NOUN
l' allarme antincendio MASC (PL gli allarmi antincendio)

fire brigade ['faɪəbrɪgeɪd] NOUN
i vigili del fuoco MASC PL

fire department ['faɪədɪpɑːtmənt] NOUN
US
i vigili del fuoco MASC PL

fire engine ['faɪərendʒɪn] NOUN
l' autopompa

fire escape ['faɪərɪskeɪp] NOUN
la scala di sicurezza

fire extinguisher ['faɪərɪkstɪŋgwɪʃəʳ] NOUN
l' estintore MASC

fire fighter ['faɪəfaɪtəʳ] NOUN
il pompiere

fireman ['faɪəmən] NOUN (PL **firemen**)
il pompiere

fireplace ['faɪəpleɪs] NOUN
il caminetto

fire station ['faɪəsteɪʃən] NOUN
la caserma dei vigili del fuoco

fireworks ['faɪəwɜːks] NOUN PL
i fuochi d'artificio

firm [fəːm] ADJECTIVE
see also firm NOUN
[1] non troppo maturo (*fruit, vegetables*)

◊ *firm tomatoes* pomodori non troppo maturi
[2] rigido ◊ *a firm mattress* un materasso rigido
[3] saldo ◊ *a firm grip* una presa salda
[4] netto ◊ *a firm refusal* un netto rifiuto
[5] deciso
 • **to be firm with somebody** essere*E deciso con qualcuno

firm [fəːm] NOUN
see also firm ADJECTIVE
la ditta

first [fəːst] ADJECTIVE, NOUN, ADVERB
[1] primo ◊ *the first of September* il primo settembre ◊ *Rachel came first.* Rachel è arrivata prima.
 • **at first** all'inizio ◊ *It was difficult at first.* All'inizio è stato difficile.
[2] prima ◊ *I want to get a job, but first I have to pass my exams.* Voglio trovare un lavoro, ma prima devo passare gli esami.
 • **first of all** innanzitutto

first aid [fəːst'eɪd] NOUN
il pronto soccorso ◊ *a first aid kit* una cassetta del pronto soccorso

first-class [fəːst'klɑːs] ADJECTIVE
[1] di prima classe MASC, FEM, PL ◊ *a first-class ticket* un biglietto di prima classe
[2] eccellente ◊ *a first-class meal* un pranzo eccellente
 • **a first-class stamp** un francobollo per posta prioritaria

ⓘ *L'affrancatura* **first-class** *dovrebbe garantire la consegna entro un giorno dalla spedizione.*

first lady [fəːst'leɪdɪ] NOUN (PL **first ladies**)
la moglie del presidente

firstly ['fəːstlɪ] ADVERB
in primo luogo

first name [fəːst'neɪm] NOUN
il nome di battesimo

fish [fɪʃ] NOUN (PL **fish**)
see also fish VERB
il pesce ◊ *I caught three fish.* Ho pescato tre pesci. ◊ *I don't like fish.* Non mi piace il pesce.
 • **fish and chips** pesce impanato e patatine

ⓘ *Il* **fish and chips** *si compra nei "chip shops" o "fish and chip shops", ed è servito in contenitori di carta o di plastica.*

to **fish** [fɪʃ] VERB
see also fish NOUN
pescare

fisherman ['fɪʃəmən] NOUN (PL **fishermen**)
il pescatore

fish farm ['fɪʃfɑːm] NOUN
il vivaio

fish fingers [fɪʃ'fɪŋgəz] NOUN

Verbs followed by the symbol "E" require the auxiliary "essere"

i bastoncini di pesce

fishing ['fɪʃɪŋ] NOUN
la pesca
* **a fishing boat** un peschereccio
* **a fishing rod** la canna da pesca

fishing tackle ['fɪʃɪŋtækl] NOUN
l' attrezzatura da pesca

fishmonger's ['fɪʃmʌŋɡəz] NOUN
la pescheria

fish sticks ['fɪʃstɪks] NOUN PL US
i bastoncini di pesce

fist [fɪst] NOUN
il pugno

fit [fɪt] ADJECTIVE
see also **fit** VERB, NOUN
in forma ◊ *He felt relaxed and fit after his holiday.* Si sentiva rilassato e in forma dopo la vacanza.
* **to be fit to play** (*sport*) essere* ᴱ in condizione di giocare
* **They're not fit to govern.** Non sono in grado di governare.
* **Only two of the bikes were fit for the road.** Solo due bici erano utilizzabili.
* **The water wasn't fit to drink.** L'acqua non era potabile.

fit [fɪt] NOUN
see also **fit** ADJECTIVE, VERB
* **to have a fit (1)** (*epileptic*) avere* un attacco epilettico
* **to have a fit (2)** (*be angry*) andare* su tutte le furie

to **fit** [fɪt] VERB
see also **fit** ADJECTIVE, NOUN
1 andare* ᴱ bene (*clothes, shoes*) ◊ *Does it fit?* Ti va bene?
2 installare ◊ *It doesn't cost much to fit an alarm.* Non costa molto installare un allarme.

to **fit in** [fɪt'ɪn] VERB
1 inserire ◊ *She fitted the key in to the lock.* Ha inserito la chiave nella serratura.
* **The doctor can't fit you in today.** Il dottore non ha tempo di vederla oggi.
2 corrispondere ◊ *That story doesn't fit in with what he told us.* La storia non corrisponde a quanto ci ha detto.
3 ambientarsi ᴱ ◊ *She fitted in well at her new school.* Si è ambientata bene nella nuova scuola.

fitted carpet [fɪtɪd'kɑːpɪt] NOUN
la moquette (PL le moquette)

fitted kitchen ['fɪtɪd'kɪtʃɪn] NOUN
la cucina componibile

fitting room ['fɪtɪŋrum] NOUN
il camerino (*in shop*)

five [faɪv] NUMERAL
cinque ◊ *He's five.* Ha cinque anni.

to **fix** [fɪks] VERB
1 aggiustare ◊ *Can you fix my bike?* Puoi aggiustarmi la bici?

2 fissare ◊ *Let's fix a date for the party.* Fissiamo una data per la festa. ◊ *She fixed the picture to the wall.* Ha fissato il quadro al muro.
3 preparare ◊ *I'm fixing lunch.* Sto preparando da mangiare.

to **fix up** [fɪks'ʌp] VERB
1 fissare ◊ *I fixed up an appointment to see her.* Ho fissato un appuntamento per vederla.
2 sistemare ◊ *I've fixed up Paul's old room.* Ho sistemato la vecchia camera di Paul.

fixed [fɪkst] ADJECTIVE
fisso ◊ *fixed prices* prezzi fissi
* **at a fixed time** ad un'ora stabilita

fizzy ['fɪzɪ] ADJECTIVE
frizzante

flabby ['flæbɪ] ADJECTIVE
flaccido

flag [flæɡ] NOUN
la bandiera

flame [fleɪm] NOUN
la fiamma

flamingo [flə'mɪŋɡəʊ] NOUN (PL **flamingos** *or* **flamingoes**)
il fenicottero

flan [flæn] NOUN
1 la torta ◊ *a raspberry flan* una torta di lamponi
2 lo sformato ◊ *a cheese and onion flan* uno sformato di formaggio e cipolla

flannel ['flænl] NOUN
1 il guanto di spugna (*facecloth*)
2 la flanella (*material*)

to **flap** [flæp] VERB
battere (*wings*)

flash [flæʃ] NOUN (PL **flashes**)
see also **flash** VERB
il flash (PL i flash) (*of camera*)
* **a flash of lightning** un lampo
* **in a flash** in un baleno

to **flash** [flæʃ] VERB
see also **flash** NOUN
lampeggiare ◊ *A light was flashing.* Una luce stava lampeggiando. ◊ *A lorry driver flashed him.* Un camionista gli ha lampeggiato coi fari.
* **They flashed a torch in his face.** Gli hanno puntato una torcia in faccia.

flask [flɑːsk] NOUN
il thermos® (PL i thermos) (*vacuum flask*)

flat [flæt] ADJECTIVE
see also **flat** NOUN
piatto ◊ *a flat surface* una superficie piatta
* **flat shoes** scarpe basse
* **I've got a flat tyre.** Ho una gomma a terra.

flat [flæt] NOUN
see also **flat** ADJECTIVE
l' appartamento

to **flatter** ['flætə'] VERB

---

* Verbs followed by this symbol are irregular. See pp.339–364 for further details.

[1] adulare ◊ *She was just flattering me.* Mi stava solo adulando.
[2] donare a ◊ *clothes that flatter you* vestiti che ti donano

flattered ['flætəd] ADJECTIVE
lusingato

flavour ['fleɪvə'] NOUN (US **flavor**)
[1] il sapore ◊ *a very strong flavour* un sapore molto forte
[2] il gusto ◊ *Which flavour ice cream would you like?* Che gusto di gelato vuoi?

flavouring ['fleɪvərɪŋ] NOUN (US **flavoring**)
l' aroma MASC

flew [flu:] VERB *see* fly

flexible ['flɛksəbl] ADJECTIVE
flessibile

to **flick** [flɪk] VERB
dare* un colpetto a ◊ *He flicked the horse with his whip.* Ha dato un colpetto al cavallo con la frusta.
♦ **He flicked a mosquito off his leg.** Ha cacciato via la zanzara dalla gamba con un colpetto.
♦ **to flick through a book** sfogliare un libro

to **flicker** ['flɪkə'] VERB
tremolare (*light*)

flight [flaɪt] NOUN
il volo ◊ *What time is the flight to Paris?* A che ora è il volo per Parigi?
♦ **a flight of stairs** una rampa di scale

flight attendant ['flaɪtə'tendənt] NOUN
l' assistente di volo MASC / FEM

to **fling** [flɪŋ] VERB (**flung, flung**)
gettare ◊ *He flung the dictionary onto the floor.* Ha gettato il dizionario sul pavimento.

to **float** [fləut] VERB
galleggiare

flock [flɔk] NOUN
♦ **a flock of sheep** un gregge di pecore
♦ **a flock of birds** uno stormo di uccelli

flood [flʌd] NOUN
see also **flood** VERB
[1] l' inondazione FEM ◊ *The rain has caused serious floods.* La pioggia ha causato gravi inondazioni.
[2] la marea ◊ *He received a flood of letters.* Ha ricevuto una marea di lettere.

to **flood** [flʌd] VERB
see also **flood** NOUN
allagare ◊ *The river has flooded the village.* Il fiume ha allagato il paese.

flooding ['flʌdɪŋ] NOUN
l' inondazione FEM

floor [flɔ:'] NOUN
[1] il pavimento ◊ *a tiled floor* pavimento a piastrelle
♦ **on the floor** per terra
[2] il piano ◊ *the ground floor* il piano terra

flop [flɔp] NOUN
il fiasco (PL i fiaschi) ◊ *The film was a flop.* Il film è stato un fiasco.

floppy disk [flɔpɪ'dɪsk] NOUN
il floppy disk (PL i floppy disk)

Florence ['flɔrəns] NOUN
Firenze

florist ['flɔrɪst] NOUN
il fioraio
la fioraia

flour ['flauə'] NOUN
la farina

to **flow** [fləu] VERB
scorrere* E

flower ['flauə'] NOUN
see also **flower** VERB
il fiore ◊ *a bunch of flowers* un mazzo di fiori

to **flower** ['flauə'] VERB
see also **flower** NOUN
fiorire E

flowerbed ['flauəbɛd] NOUN
l' aiuola

flown [fləun] VERB *see* fly

flu [flu:] NOUN
l' influenza

fluent ['flu:ənt] ADJECTIVE
♦ **He speaks fluent French.** Parla il francese correntemente.

flung [flʌŋ] VERB *see* fling

flush [flʌʃ] NOUN
see also **flush** VERB
[1] il rossore ◊ *There was a slight flush on his cheeks.* C'era un leggero rossore sulle sue guance.
[2] lo sciacquone ◊ *He heard the flush of a toilet.* Ha sentito il rumore di uno sciacquone.

to **flush** [flʌʃ] VERB
see also **flush** NOUN
arrossire E ◊ *Irene flushed with embarrassment.* Irene è arrossita per l'imbarazzo.
♦ **to flush the toilet** tirare l'acqua

flute [flu:t] NOUN
il flauto

fly [flaɪ] NOUN (PL **flies**)
see also **fly** VERB
la mosca (PL le mosche)

to **fly** [flaɪ] VERB (**flew, flown**)
see also **fly** NOUN
[1] volare (*plane, bird*)
[2] andare* E in aereo ◊ *He flew from London to Glasgow.* È andato in aereo da Londra a Glasgow. ◊ *He's never flown.* Non è mai andato in aereo.

foal [fəul] NOUN
il puledro

focus ['fəukəs] NOUN (PL **focuses**)
see also **focus** VERB
il centro ◊ *He was the focus of attention.* Era al centro dell'attenzione.

to **focus** ['fəukəs] VERB
see also **focus** NOUN

F

mettere* a fuoco (*camera, binoculars*)
+ **to focus on something** concentrarsi ^E su qualcosa

focus group ['fəukəsgru:p] NOUN
il gruppo di discussione

fog [fɒg] NOUN
la nebbia

foggy ['fɒgɪ] ADJECTIVE
+ **It's foggy.** C'è nebbia.
+ **a foggy day** una giornata nebbiosa
+ **I haven't the foggiest idea.** Non ne ho la più pallida idea.

foil [fɔɪl] NOUN
la carta stagnola

fold [fəuld] NOUN
see also **fold** VERB
la piega (PL le pieghe)

to **fold** [fəuld] VERB
see also **fold** NOUN
piegare ◊ *He folded the newspaper in half.* Ha piegato a metà il giornale.
+ **to fold one's arms** incrociare le braccia

folder ['fəuldə'] NOUN
la cartella

folding ['fəuldɪŋ] ADJECTIVE
pieghevole

to **follow** ['fɒləu] VERB
seguire ◊ *You go first and I'll follow.* Vai tu per primo, io ti seguo.

to **follow up** [fɒləu'ʌp] VERB
seguire ◊ *The police are following up several leads.* La polizia sta seguendo diverse piste.

following ['fɒləuɪŋ] ADJECTIVE
seguente

fond [fɒnd] ADJECTIVE
+ **to be fond of somebody** voler bene a qualcuno

food [fu:d] NOUN
il cibo ◊ *I left some food for the cat.* Ho lasciato un po' di cibo per il gatto.
+ **We need to buy some food.** Dobbiamo comprare qualcosa da mangiare.
+ **Italian food is very popular.** La cucina italiana è molto popolare.

food poisoning ['fu:dpɔɪzənɪŋ] NOUN
l' intossicazione alimentare FEM

food processor ['fu:dprəusesə'] NOUN
il tritatutto elettrico (PL i tritatutto elettrici)

fool [fu:l] NOUN
lo sciocco
la sciocca

foot [fut] NOUN (PL **feet**)
1 il piede ◊ *She's got big feet.* Ha i piedi grandi.

🛈 *Un piede corrisponde a 30,4 centimetri.*

◊ *Dave is six foot tall.* Dave è alto circa un metro e ottanta.
+ **on foot** a piedi

2 la zampa (*of animal*)

football ['futbɔ:l] NOUN
1 il calcio ◊ *I like playing football.* Mi piace giocare a calcio.
2 il pallone ◊ *Paul threw the football over the fence.* Paul ha gettato il pallone oltre lo steccato.

footballer ['futbɔ:lə'] NOUN
il calciatore
la calciatrice

football player ['futbɔ:lpleɪə'] NOUN
il calciatore
la calciatrice

football pools ['futbɔ:lpu:lz] NOUN
il totocalcio

footpath ['futpɑ:θ] NOUN
il sentiero

footprint ['futprɪnt] NOUN
l' orma

footstep ['futstɛp] NOUN
il passo

for [fɔ:'] PREPOSITION
1 per ◊ *a present for me* un regalo per me ◊ *the train for London* il treno per Londra ◊ *He worked in France for two years.* Ha lavorato in Francia per due anni. ◊ *What for?* Per cosa?
+ **What did he do that for?** Perché lo ha fatto?
+ **What's it for?** A che cosa serve?
2 da

*When the perfect tense is used with **for** to describe actions or states that started in the past and are still going on, use **da** with the present tense of the Italian verb.*

◊ *He's been learning Italian for two years.* Studia italiano da due anni. ◊ *They've been here for ages.* Sono qui da moltissimo tempo.
+ **It's time for lunch.** È ora di mangiare.

to **forbid** [fə'bɪd] VERB (**forbade**, **forbidden**)
proibire
+ **to forbid somebody to do something** proibire a qualcuno di fare qualcosa

forbidden [fə'bɪdn] ADJECTIVE
vietato

force [fɔ:s] NOUN
see also **force** VERB
la forza ◊ *He's against the use of force.* È contrario all'uso della forza.
+ **UN forces** le forze dell'ONU
+ **in force** (*law*) in vigore

to **force** [fɔ:s] VERB
see also **force** NOUN
costringere (*person*)

forecast ['fɔ:kɑ:st] NOUN
+ **the weather forecast** le previsioni del tempo

foreground ['fɔ:graund] NOUN
il primo piano

forehead ['fɒrɪd] NOUN
la fronte

---

* Verbs followed by this symbol are irregular. See pp.339–364 for further details.

foreign ['fɒrɪn] ADJECTIVE
straniero ◊ *foreign countries* paesi
stranieri

foreigner ['fɒrɪnə'] NOUN
lo straniero
la straniera

foreign exchange [fɒrɪnɪks'tʃeɪndʒ] NOUN
la valuta estera

to **foresee** [fɔː'siː] VERB (**foresaw, foreseen**)
prevedere ◊ *He had foreseen the problem.*
Aveva previsto il problema.

forest ['fɒrɪst] NOUN
la foresta

forever [fə'revə'] ADVERB
[1] per sempre ◊ *yours forever* tuo per
sempre
◆ **Those days are gone forever.** Quei giorni
non torneranno più.
[2] sempre ◊ *She's forever complaining.* Si
lamenta sempre.

forgave [fə'geɪv] VERB *see* **forgive**

to **forge** [fɔːdʒ] VERB
falsificare ◊ *She forged his signature.* Ha
falsificato la sua firma.

forged [fɔːdʒd] ADJECTIVE
falso ◊ *forged documents* documenti falsi

to **forget** [fə'get] VERB (**forgot, forgotten**)
dimenticare ◊ *I've forgotten his name.* Ho
dimenticato il suo nome. ◊ *I'm sorry, I
completely forgot!* Scusa, me ne sono
completamente dimenticato!
◆ **If that's what you're hoping, you can forget
it!** Se questo è quello che speri puoi
scordartelo!

to **forgive** [fə'gɪv] VERB (**forgave, forgiven**)
perdonare ◊ *In the end he forgave me.* Alla
fine mi ha perdonato.
◆ **to forgive somebody for doing something**
perdonare qualcuno di aver fatto qualcosa

forgot, forgotten [fə'gɒt] VERB *see* **forget**

fork [fɔːk] NOUN
[1] la forchetta ◊ *Mix it with a fork.*
Mescolalo con una forchetta.
[2] il bivio ◊ *Take the left fork.* Al bivio volta
a sinistra.

form [fɔːm] NOUN
[1] il modulo
◆ **to fill in a form** riempire* un modulo
[2] la forma ◊ *I'm against all forms of
hunting.* Sono contrario a qualsiasi forma di
caccia.
◆ **in top form** in gran forma
[3] la classe ◊ *He's in my form.* È in classe
con me.

formal ['fɔːməl] ADJECTIVE
[1] ufficiale ◊ *a formal dinner* una cena
ufficiale
[2] formale ◊ *formal language* lingua
formale
◆ **formal clothes** abiti da cerimonia
◆ **His formal education ended when he was**

16. Ha smesso di andare a scuola a 16 anni.

former ['fɔːmə'] ADJECTIVE
ex MASC, FEM, PL ◊ *a former pupil* un ex alunno

formerly ['fɔːməlɪ] ADVERB
in passato

fort [fɔːt] NOUN
il forte

forth [fɔːθ] ADVERB
◆ **to go back and forth** andare*E avanti e
indietro
◆ **and so forth** e così via

forthcoming [fɔːθ'kʌmɪŋ] ADJECTIVE
prossimo ◊ *It will be discussed at the
forthcoming meeting.* Verrà discusso nella
prossima riunione.

fortnight ['fɔːtnaɪt] NOUN
quindici giorni MASC PL ◊ *for a fortnight* per
quindici giorni

fortunate ['fɔːtʃənɪt] ADJECTIVE
◆ **It's fortunate that I remembered the map.** È
una fortuna che mi sia ricordato della
cartina.

fortunately ['fɔːtʃənɪtlɪ] ADVERB
fortunatamente

fortune ['fɔːtʃən] NOUN
la fortuna ◊ *It cost a fortune.* È costato una
fortuna. ◊ *He made his fortune in Peru.* Ha
fatto fortuna in Perù.
◆ **to tell somebody's fortune** predire* il futuro
a qualcuno

forty ['fɔːtɪ] NUMERAL
quaranta ◊ *He's forty.* Ha quarant'anni.

to **forward** ['fɔːwəd] VERB
inoltrare (*letter*)

forward slash ['fɔːwədslæʃ] NOUN
la barra

to **foster** ['fɒstə'] VERB
avere* in affidamento ◊ *She has fostered
more than fifteen children.* Ha avuto in
affidamento più di quindici bambini.

foster child ['fɒstətʃaɪld] NOUN (PL **foster
children**)
il bambino in affidamento

fought [fɔːt] VERB *see* **fight**

foul [faul] ADJECTIVE
see also **foul** NOUN
[1] orribile ◊ *The weather was foul.* Il
tempo era orribile.
[2] disgustoso ◊ *It smells foul.* Ha un odore
disgustoso.
[3] pessimo ◊ *Brenda is in a foul mood.*
Brenda è di pessimo umore.

foul [faul] NOUN
see also **foul** ADJECTIVE
il fallo (*in sport*)

found [faund] VERB *see* **find**

to **found** [faund] VERB
fondare*

foundations [faun'deɪʃənz] NOUN PL
le fondamenta PL

fountain ['fauntɪn] NOUN ☞

la fontana ◇ *the fountains in Rome* le fontane di Roma

fountain pen ['fauntɪnpen] NOUN
la penna stilografica (PL le penne stilografiche)

four [fɔːʳ] NUMERAL
quattro ◇ *She's four.* Ha quattro anni.

fourteen ['fɔː'tiːn] NUMERAL
quattordici ◇ *I'm fourteen.* Ho quattordici anni.

fourteenth ['fɔː'tiːnθ] ADJECTIVE
quattordicesimo ◇ *the fourteenth floor* il quattordicesimo piano
• **the fourteenth of July** il quattordici luglio

fourth ['fɔːθ] ADJECTIVE
quarto ◇ *the fourth floor* il quarto piano
• **the fourth of July** il quattro luglio

fox [fɔks] NOUN (PL **foxes**)
la volpe

fragile ['frædʒaɪl] ADJECTIVE
fragile

frame [freɪm] NOUN
la cornice ◇ *a silver frame* una cornice d'argento
• **frames** la montatura SING ◇ *glasses with plastic frames* occhiali con la montatura di plastica

France [frɑːns] NOUN
la Francia

frantic ['fræntɪk] ADJECTIVE
frenetico ◇ *There was frantic activity backstage on the opening night.* C'era un'attività frenetica dietro le quinte la sera della prima.
• **to go frantic** perdere* la testa ◇ *I was going frantic.* Stavo perdendo la testa.
• **to be frantic with worry** essere* E fuori di sé dalla preoccupazione

fraud [frɔːd] NOUN
[1] la truffa ◇ *He was jailed for fraud.* È stato messo in prigione per truffa.
[2] l' impostore MASC ◇ *You're a fraud!* Sei un impostore!

freckles ['freklz] NOUN PL
le lentiggini

free [friː] ADJECTIVE
see also **free** VERB
[1] gratuito ◇ *a free brochure* un opuscolo gratuito
• **a free gift** un omaggio
[2] libero ◇ *Is this seat free?* È libero questo posto?

to **free** [friː] VERB
see also **free** ADJECTIVE
liberare

freedom ['friːdəm] NOUN
la libertà (PL le libertà)

free kick [friː'kɪk] NOUN
il calcio di punizione (PL i calci di punizione)

freeway ['friːweɪ] NOUN US
la superstrada

to **freeze** [friːz] VERB (**froze, frozen**)
[1] gelare E ◇ *The lake froze last winter.* Il lago è gelato lo scorso inverno.
[2] congelare (*food*)

freezer ['friːzəʳ] NOUN
il freezer (PL i freezer)

freezing ['friːzɪŋ] ADJECTIVE
• **It's freezing!** Si gela!
• **I'm freezing!** Sono congelato!
• **3 degrees below freezing** tre gradi sotto zero
• **freezing point** il punto di congelamento

freight [freɪt] NOUN
la merce
• **a freight train** US un treno merci

French [frentʃ] ADJECTIVE
see also **French** NOUN
francese

French [frentʃ] NOUN
see also **French** ADJECTIVE
il francese ◇ *I can speak French.* Parlo il francese. ◇ *the French teacher* l'insegnante di francese
• **the French** i francesi

French beans [frentʃ'biːnz] NOUN
i fagiolini MASC PL

French fries [frentʃ'fraɪz] NOUN
le patate fritte FEM PL

French horn [frentʃ'hɔːn] NOUN
il corno da caccia

French kiss [frentʃ'kɪs] NOUN
il bacio vero

French loaf [frentʃ'ləuf] NOUN (PL **French loaves**)
il filoncino

Frenchman ['frentʃmən] NOUN (PL **Frenchmen**)
• **a Frenchman** un francese

French windows [frentʃ'wɪndəuz] NOUN
la porta finestra SING

Frenchwoman ['frentʃwumən] NOUN (PL **Frenchwomen**)
• **a Frenchwoman** una francese

frequent ['friːkwənt] ADJECTIVE
frequente

fresh [freʃ] ADJECTIVE
fresco ◇ *Is the fish fresh?* Il pesce è fresco?
• **I need some fresh air.** Ho bisogno di un po' d'aria.
• **a teacher fresh from college** un insegnante appena uscito dall'università
• **fresh water** acqua dolce

to **freshen up** [freʃn'ʌp] VERB
rinfrescarsi E

freshwater ['freʃwɔːtəʳ] ADJECTIVE
d'acqua dolce ◇ *a freshwater fish* un pesce d'acqua dolce

to **fret** [fret] VERB
preoccuparsi E

Friday ['fraɪdɪ] NOUN
il venerdì (PL i venerdì)
• **on Friday** venerdì ◇ *I saw her on Friday.*

---

* Verbs followed by this symbol are irregular. See pp.339–364 for further details.

L'ho vista venerdì.
+ **on Fridays** di venerdì ◇ *I go swimming on Fridays.* Vado in piscina di venerdì.
fridge [frɪdʒ] NOUN
il frigo (PL i frighi)
fried [fraɪd] ADJECTIVE
fritto ◇ *fried chicken* pollo fritto
+ **a fried egg** un uovo al tegame
friend [frend] NOUN
l' amico (PL gli amici)
l' amica (PL le amiche)
◇ *He's a friend of mine.* È un mio amico.
friendly ['frendlɪ] ADJECTIVE
1 cordiale (*person*)
2 accogliente (*place*)
friendship ['frendʃɪp] NOUN
l' amicizia
fright [fraɪt] NOUN
lo spavento
+ **to get a fright** spaventarsi [E]
to **frighten** ['fraɪtn] VERB
fare* paura a ◇ *Horror films frighten him.* I film dell'orrore gli fanno paura.
frightened ['fraɪtnd] ADJECTIVE
+ **to be frightened** avere* paura
frightening ['fraɪtnɪŋ] ADJECTIVE
spaventoso
fringe [frɪndʒ] NOUN
la frangia (PL le frange) ◇ *I want my fringe cut.* Vorrei che mi tagliasse la frangia.
Frisbee® ['frɪzbɪ] NOUN
il Frisbee® (PL i Frisbee)
fro [frəu] ADVERB
+ **to go to and fro** andare* [E] avanti e indietro
frog [frɒg] NOUN
la rana
from [frɒm] PREPOSITION
da

The preposition comes at the beginning of the Italian question.

◇ *Where do you come from?* Da dove vieni?
◇ *The hotel is one kilometre from the beach.* L'albergo è ad un chilometro dalla spiaggia.
+ **Who's it from?** (*letter, card*) Chi lo manda?
+ **I'm from Wales.** Sono gallese.
front [frʌnt] NOUN
see also **front** ADJECTIVE
il davanti ◇ *the front of the house* il davanti della casa
+ **in front of** davanti a ◇ *Irene sits in front of me in class.* Irene è seduta davanti a me in classe.
+ **at the front of the train** in testa al treno
front [frʌnt] ADJECTIVE
see also **front** NOUN
1 primo ◇ *the front row* la prima fila
2 davanti ◇ *the front seats of the car* i sedili davanti della macchina
+ **the front door** la porta d'ingresso
+ **the front room** il salotto
frontier ['frʌntɪə'] NOUN

la frontiera
frost [frɒst] NOUN
il gelo
frosting ['frɒstɪŋ] NOUN US
la glassa
frosty ['frɒstɪ] ADJECTIVE
gelido ◇ *one frosty morning* una mattinata gelida ◇ *They gave him a frosty reception.* Gli hanno riservato un'accoglienza gelida.
to **frown** [fraun] VERB
aggrottare le sopracciglia
froze, frozen [frəuz] VERB *see* **freeze**
frozen ['frəuzn] ADJECTIVE
congelato
fruit [fruːt] NOUN
la frutta ◇ *Would you like some fruit?* Vuoi della frutta?
+ **fruit juice** succo di frutta
+ **fruit salad** macedonia
fruit machine ['fruːtməʃiːn] NOUN
la slot-machine (PL le slot-machine)
frustrated [frʌsˈtreɪtɪd] ADJECTIVE
frustrato
to **fry** [fraɪ] VERB (**fried, fried**)
friggere
frying pan ['fraɪŋpæn] NOUN
la padella
fuel ['fjuəl] NOUN
il carburante ◇ *The plane ran out of fuel.* L'aereo ha finito il carburante.
fuel tank ['fjuəltæŋk] NOUN
il serbatoio della benzina
to **fulfil** [fulˈfɪl] VERB
realizzare ◇ *He fulfilled his dream to visit China.* Ha realizzato il suo sogno di fare un viaggio in Cina.
+ **to fulfil a promise** mantenere una promessa
full [ful] ADJECTIVE
1 pieno ◇ *The tank's full.* Il serbatoio è pieno.
+ **full name** il nome completo e il cognome
+ **full board** pensione completa
2 sazio ◇ *I'm full.* Sono sazio.
+ **full information** tutte le informazioni
+ **at full speed** a tutta velocità
full stop [fulˈstɒp] NOUN
il punto (*punctuation mark*)
full-time ['fulˈtaɪm] ADJECTIVE, ADVERB
a tempo pieno
fully ['fulɪ] ADVERB
completamente
fumes [fjuːmz] NOUN PL
le esalazioni ◇ *poisonous fumes* esalazioni velenose
+ **exhaust fumes** gas di scarico
fun [fʌn] ADJECTIVE (*colloquiale*)
see also **fun** NOUN
1 simpatico (*person*)
2 bella (*evening, time*)
fun [fʌn] NOUN
see also **fun** ADJECTIVE

☞

+ **to have fun** divertirsi ^E
+ **It's fun!** È divertente!
+ **Have fun!** Divertiti!
+ **for fun** per divertimento
+ **to make fun of somebody** prendere in giro qualcuno

funds [fʌndz] NOUN PL
i fondi

+ **to raise funds** raccogliere* fondi

funeral ['fjuːnərəl] NOUN
il funerale

funfair ['fʌnfɛəʳ] NOUN
il luna park (PL i luna park)

funny ['fʌnɪ] ADJECTIVE
[1] divertente ◊ *It was so funny I couldn't stop laughing.* Era così divertente che non riuscivo a smettere di ridere.
[2] strano ◊ *There's something funny about him.* Ha qualcosa di strano.

fur [fɜːʳ] NOUN
[1] la pelliccia (PL le pellicce)
+ **a fur coat** una pelliccia
[2] il pelo ◊ *the cat's fur* il pelo del gatto

furious ['fjʊərɪəs] ADJECTIVE
furioso

furniture ['fɜːnɪtʃəʳ] NOUN
i mobili PL ◊ *The furniture is new.* I mobili sono nuovi.
+ **a piece of furniture** un mobile

further ['fɜːðəʳ] ADVERB, ADJECTIVE
[1] più lontano ◊ *London is further from here than Oxford.* Londra è più lontana da qui rispetto a Oxford.
+ **How much further is it?** Quanto manca ancora da qui?
+ **any further** più ◊ *I can't walk any further.* Non riesco a camminare più.
[2] ulteriore ◊ *Please write to us if you need any further information.* Ci scriva se ha bisogno di ulteriori informazioni.

further education ['fɜːðəredjuˈkeɪʃən] NOUN
i corsi di formazione ·

> ⓘ *Sono corsi dopo la scuola dell'obbligo per chi non si iscrive all'università.*

fuse [fjuːz] NOUN
il fusibile

fuss [fʌs] NOUN
le storie PL ◊ *What's all the fuss about?* Cosa sono tutte queste storie?

fussy ['fʌsɪ] ADJECTIVE
difficile ◊ *She is very fussy about her food.* Fa la difficile per il cibo.
+ **I'm not fussy.** Per me è lo stesso.

future ['fjuːtʃəʳ] NOUN
il futuro

G

gain [geɪn] VERB
guadagnare ◊ *What do you hope to gain by this?* Cosa speri di guadagnarci?
* **to gain experience** fare* esperienza ◊ *I gained valuable experience by working there.* Ho fatto molta esperienza lavorando lì.
* **to gain speed** acquistare velocità
* **to gain weight** aumentare di peso
* **to gain on somebody** avvicinarsi ^E a qualcuno

gallery ['gælərɪ] NOUN (PL **galleries**)
la galleria ◊ *an art gallery* una galleria d'arte

gamble ['gæmbl] VERB
see also **gamble** NOUN
[1] giocare ◊ *He gambled one hundred pounds at the casino.* Ha giocato cento sterline al casinò.
[2] puntare ◊ *Few firms want to gamble on new products.* Poche ditte vogliono puntare su prodotti nuovi.

gamble ['gæmbl] NOUN
see also **gamble** VERB
il rischio ◊ *It's a gamble.* È un rischio.

gambler ['gæmblə'] NOUN
il giocatore d'azzardo
la giocatrice d'azzardo

gambling ['gæmblɪŋ] NOUN
il gioco d'azzardo

game [geɪm] NOUN
[1] il gioco (PL i giochi) ◊ *The children were playing a game.* I bambini stavano facendo un gioco.
[2] la partita ◊ *a game of football* una partita di calcio ◊ *a game of cards* una partita a carte
[3] la selvaggina ◊ *There's game on the menu.* C'è selvaggina nel menù.

games console ['geɪmz'kɒnsəul] NOUN
la console dei videogame (PL le console dei videogame)

gang [gæŋ] NOUN
[1] la banda (*of thieves, troublemakers*)
[2] la comitiva (*of friends*)

gangster ['gæŋstə'] NOUN
il gangster (PL i gangster)

gang up [gæŋ'ʌp] VERB
* **to gang up on somebody** fare* comunella contro qualcuno

gap [gæp] NOUN
[1] il buco (PL i buchi) ◊ *There's a gap in the hedge.* C'è un buco nella siepe.
[2] l'intervallo ◊ *a gap of four years* un intervallo di quattro anni

gap year ['gæpjɪə'] NOUN
un anno di pausa preso prima di iniziare l'università, per lavorare o viaggiare

garage ['gærɑːʒ] NOUN

[1] il garage (PL i garage) (*of house*)
[2] l'officina (*for repairs*)
[3] la stazione di servizio (*petrol station*)

garbage ['gɑːbɪdʒ] NOUN US
[1] la spazzatura ◊ *garbage can* bidone della spazzatura ◊ *garbage collection* raccolta della spazzatura
[2] le fesserie FEM PL ◊ *That's garbage.* Sono fesserie.

garbage collector ['gɑːbɪdʒkə'lektə'] NOUN US
il netturbino

garden ['gɑːdn] NOUN
il giardino ◊ *a lovely garden* un bel giardino

garden centre ['gɑːdnsentə'] NOUN
il vivaio

gardener ['gɑːdnə'] NOUN
il giardiniere ◊ *He's a gardener.* Fa il giardiniere.

gardening ['gɑːdnɪŋ] NOUN
il giardinaggio

gardens ['gɑːdnz] NOUN PL
il giardino pubblico SING

garlic ['gɑːlɪk] NOUN
l'aglio

garment ['gɑːmənt] NOUN
l'indumento

gas [gæs] NOUN
[1] il gas (PL i gas) ◊ *a gas leak* una fuga di gas
* **a gas cooker** una cucina a gas
* **a gas cylinder** una bombola del gas
* **a gas fire** una stufa a gas
[2] la benzina (*petrol*) US ◊ *I'll stop soon and get gas.* Mi fermerò presto a fare* benzina.
* **a tank of gas** un pieno di benzina

gasoline ['gæsəliːn] NOUN US
la benzina

gas station ['gæsteɪʃən] NOUN US
la stazione di servizio

gate [geɪt] NOUN
[1] il cancello (*of garden, field*)
[2] l'uscita (*at airport*)

gateau ['gætəu] NOUN (PL **gateaux**)
la torta

to **gather** ['gæðə'] VERB
[1] riunirsi ^E (*meet*)
[2] raccogliere* (*information, material, things*)
* **to gather speed** acquistare velocità

gave [geɪv] VERB *see* **give**

gay [geɪ] ADJECTIVE
omosessuale

to **gaze** [geɪz] VERB
* **to gaze at** fissare ◊ *He was gazing at her.* La stava fissando.

GCSE [dʒiːsiːesˈiː] NOUN (= *General Certificate of Secondary Education*) ☞

il diploma di istruzione secondaria

❶ /GCSEs o *"GCSE examinations" sono gli esami che i ragazzi inglesi, gallesi e dell'Irlanda del Nord sostengono in varie materie, alcune obbligatorie ed altre facoltative, all'età di 15 o 16 anni.*

gear [gɪə'] NOUN
1 la marcia (PL le marce) ◇ *He left the car in gear.* Ha lasciato la macchina in marcia.
♦ **in first gear** in prima
2 l' attrezzatura ◇ *camping gear* attrezzatura da campeggio
♦ **sports gear** la roba da ginnastica

gear box ['gɪəbɔks] NOUN
la scatola del cambio

gear lever ['gɪəliːvə'] NOUN
la leva del cambio

gearshift ['gɪəʃɪft] NOUN US
la leva del cambio

geese [giːs] NOUN PL *see* **goose**

gel [dʒɛl] NOUN
il gel (PL i gel) ◇ *hair gel* gel per capelli

gem [dʒɛm] NOUN
la gemma

Gemini ['dʒɛmɪnaɪ] NOUN
i Gemelli ◇ *I'm Gemini.* Sono dei Gemelli.

gender ['dʒɛndə'] NOUN
il genere (*of noun*)

gene [dʒiːn] NOUN
il gene

general ['dʒɛnərl] NOUN
see also **general** ADJECTIVE
il generale

general ['dʒɛnərl] ADJECTIVE
see also **general** NOUN
generale ◇ *a general improvement* un miglioramento generale
♦ **in general** in generale
♦ **general election** elezioni politiche FEM PL

general knowledge ['dʒɛnərl'nɔlɪdʒ] NOUN
la cultura generale

generally ['dʒɛnrəlɪ] ADVERB •
in genere ◇ *It's generally true that...* In genere è vero che...
♦ **generally speaking...** parlando in generale...

general practitioner ['dʒɛnərlpræk'tɪʃənə'] NOUN
il medico di famiglia (PL i medici de famiglia)

generation [dʒɛnə'reɪʃən] NOUN
la generazione ◇ *the younger generation* la nuova generazione

generator ['dʒɛnəreɪtə'] NOUN
il generatore

generous ['dʒɛnərəs] ADJECTIVE
generoso ◇ *That's very generous of you.* È molto generoso da parte tua.

genetic [dʒɪ'nɛtɪk] ADJECTIVE
genetico

genetically-modified [dʒɪ'nɛtɪklɪ'mɔdɪfaɪd]
ADJECTIVE
geneticamente modificato

genetics [dʒɪ'nɛtɪks] NOUN
la genetica

Geneva [dʒɪ'niːvə] NOUN
Ginevra

genius ['dʒiːnɪəs] NOUN (PL **geniuses**)
il genio

Genoa ['dʒɛnəuə] NOUN
Genova

gentle ['dʒɛntl] ADJECTIVE
1 dolce (*person, voice*)
2 leggero (*wind, push*) ◇ *I gave him a gentle push.* Gli ho detto una leggera spinta.
Be careful not to translate **gentle** *by* **gentile**.

gentleman ['dʒɛntlmən] NOUN (PL **gentlemen**)
il signore

gently ['dʒɛntlɪ] ADVERB
1 dolcemente (*speak, smile*)
2 lievemente (*touch*)

gents [dʒɛnts] NOUN SING
la toilette degli uomini (PL le toilette degli uomini) ◇ *Can you tell me where the gents is, please?* Può dirmi dov'è la toilette degli uomini, per favore?
♦ **"gents"** (*on sign*) "uomini"

genuine ['dʒɛnjuɪn] ADJECTIVE
1 vero ◇ *These are genuine diamonds.* Questi sono diamanti veri.
2 sincero ◇ *She's a very genuine person.* È una persona molto sincera.

geography [dʒɪ'ɔgrəfɪ] NOUN
la geografia

germ [dʒɜːm] NOUN
il germe

German ['dʒɜːmən] ADJECTIVE
see also **German** NOUN
tedesco

German ['dʒɜːmən] NOUN
see also **German** ADJECTIVE
1 il tedesco
la tedesca
(*person*)
♦ **the Germans** i tedeschi
2 il tedesco (*language*) ◇ *our German teacher* il nostro insegnante di tedesco

German measles ['dʒɜːmən'miːzlz] NOUN
la rosolia

German shepherd [dʒɜːmən'ʃɛpəd] NOUN
il cane lupo

Germany ['dʒɜːmənɪ] NOUN
la Germania

gesture ['dʒɛstjə'] NOUN
il gesto ◇ *She made a threatening gesture.* Ha fatto un gesto minaccioso.
♦ **a mere gesture** un gesto simbolico

to **get** [gɛt] VERB (**got**, **got** *or* **gotten**) *
There are several ways of translating **get**. *Scan the examples for one similar to what you want to say.*

---

* Verbs followed by this symbol are irregular. See pp.339–364 for further details.

1 ~~ricevere~~ ◇ *I got lots of presents.* Ho ricevuto molti regali. ◇ *He got first prize.* Ha ricevuto il primo premio. ◇ *The book's gotten good reviews.* Il libro ha ricevuto buone critiche.
2 ~~ottenere~~* ◇ *Jackie got good exam results.* Jackie ha ottenuto un buon risultato all'esame.
3 ~~prendere~~* ◇ *They've got the thief.* Hanno preso il ladro. ◇ *I'm getting the bus into town.* Prendo l'autobus per andare* in città.
4 ~~capire~~ ◇ *I don't get the joke.* Non capisco lo scherzo.
5 ~~arrivare~~^E ◇ *He should get here soon.* Dovrebbe arrivare presto. ◇ *How do you get to the cinema?* Come si arriva al cinema?
6 ~~andare~~*^E a cercare ◇ *Quick, get help!* Svelto, vai a cercare aiuto!
7 ~~procurare~~
♦ **to get something for somebody** procurare qualcosa a qualcuno ◇ *The bookshop got the book for me.* Il libraio mi ha procurato il libro.
♦ **I'll get it! (1)** (*phone*) Rispondo io!
♦ **I'll get it! (2)** (*door*) Vado io!
♦ **to have got** (*own*) avere* ◇ *How many have you got?* Quanti ne hai?

*When **got** is used colloquially without "have", it is translated by the present tense in Italian.*

◇ *You got any identification?* Ha un documento di identificazione?
♦ **to get something done** farsi^E fare* qualcosa ◇ *I got my hair cut.* Mi sono fatto tagliare i capelli.
*to **have got to** is translated by **dovere**.*
◇ *I've got to tell him.* Devo dirglielo.
*to **get** + an adjective is often translated by a specific verb in Italian.*
◇ *to get old* invecchiare ◇ *to get angry* arrabbiarsi ◇ *to get tired* stancarsi
♦ **It's getting late.** Si sta facendo tardi.

get ahead [getə'hed] VERB
♦ **to get ahead of somebody** superare qualcuno

get around [getə'raund] VERB
~~superare~~ (*problema*)

get away [getə'weɪ] VERB
1 ~~andare~~*^E via ◇ *What time can you get away?* A che ora puoi andare* via?
2 ~~scappare~~^E ◇ *One of the burglars got away.* Uno dei ladri è scappato.

get away with [getə'weɪwɪð] VERB
♦ **to get away with it** passarla liscia ◇ *You'll never get away with it.* Non riuscirai a passarla liscia.

get back [get'bæk] VERB
1 ~~tornare~~^E ◇ *What time did you get back?* A che ora sei tornato?
2 ~~riavere indietro~~ ◇ *He got his money back.* Ha riavuto indietro i suoi soldi.

to **get down** [get'daun] VERB
1 ~~scendere~~*^E ◇ *Get down from there!* Scendi da lì!
2 ~~buttare giù~~ ◇ *His constant grumbling really gets me down.* Il suo continuo brontolare mi butta proprio giù.
3 ~~annotare~~ ◇ *He spoke so fast I couldn't get it all down.* Parlava così veloce che non sono riuscito ad annotare tutto.

to **get in** [get'ɪn] VERB
1 ~~rientrare~~^E ◇ *What time did you get in last night?* A che ora sei rientrato ieri sera?
2 ~~arrivare~~^E ◇ *The train gets in at half past three.* Il treno arriva alle tre e mezza.

to **get into** [get'ɪntu] VERB
~~salire~~*^E in ◇ *Sharon got into the car.* Sharon è salita in macchina.

to **get off** [get'ɔf] VERB
1 ~~scendere~~*^E da ◇ *Isobel got off the train.* Isobel è scesa dal treno.
2 ~~andare~~*^E via da ◇ *He managed to get off early from work yesterday.* Ieri è riuscito ad andar via presto dal lavoro.

to **get on** [get'ɔn] VERB
1 ~~montare~~^E su ◇ *Phyllis got on the bus.* Phyllis è montata sull'autobus.
2 ~~andare~~*^E d'accordo ◇ *We got on really well.* Andavamo molto d'accordo.
♦ **How are you getting on?** Come va?

to **get out** [get'aut] VERB
1 ~~scendere~~*^E ◇ *She got out of the car.* È scesa dalla macchina.
2 ~~tirare fuori~~ ◇ *She got the map out.* Ha tirato fuori la cartina.

to **get over** [get'əuvə'] VERB
1 ~~rimettersi~~^E da ◇ *It took her a long time to get over the illness.* Ci è voluto molto tempo perché si rimettesse dalla malattia.
2 ~~superare~~ ◇ *He managed to get over the problem.* È riuscito a superare il problema.

to **get round to** [get'raundtu] VERB
~~trovare il tempo per~~ ◇ *I'll get round to it eventually.* Prima o poi troverò il tempo per farlo.

to **get together** [gettə'geðə'] VERB
~~trovarsi~~^E ◇ *Could we get together this evening?* Possiamo trovarci questa sera?

to **get up** [get'ʌp] VERB
~~alzarsi~~^E ◇ *What time do you get up?* A che ora ti alzi?

ghetto ['getəu] NOUN
il ~~ghetto~~ ◇ *the black ghettos* i ghetti della gente di colore

ghetto blaster ['getəu'blɑːstə'] NOUN
il ~~maxistereo portatile~~ (PL i maxistereo portatili)

ghost [gəust] NOUN
il ~~fantasma~~ (PL i fantasmi) ◇ *ghost story* storia di fantasmi

giant ['dʒaɪənt] ADJECTIVE
see also **giant** NOUN

G

gigante

giant ['dʒaɪənt] NOUN
see also **giant** ADJECTIVE
il gigante

gift [gɪft] NOUN
il regalo ◇ *a lovely gift* un bel regalo
* **to have a gift for something** essere* E
portato per qualcosa ◇ *Dave's got a gift for
painting.* Dave è portato per la pittura.

gifted ['gɪftɪd] ADJECTIVE
di talento ◇ *Janice is a gifted dancer.* Janice
è una ballerina di talento.
* **one of the most gifted artists** uno degli
artisti più dotati

gift shop ['gɪftʃɒp] NOUN
il negozio di articoli da regalo

gift token ['gɪfttəukən] NOUN
il buono omaggio (PL i buoni omaggio)

gift-wrapped ['gɪftræpt] ADJECTIVE
impacchettato

gigantic [dʒaɪˈgæntɪk] ADJECTIVE
gigantesco

to **giggle** ['gɪgl] VERB
ridacchiare

gin [dʒɪn] NOUN
il gin (PL i gin)

ginger ['dʒɪndʒəʳ] NOUN
see also **ginger** ADJECTIVE
lo zenzero

ginger ['dʒɪndʒəʳ] ADJECTIVE
see also **ginger** NOUN
rossiccio ◇ *She's got ginger hair.* Ha i
capelli rossicci.

ginger ale [dʒɪndʒərˈeɪl] NOUN
la bibita gassata allo zenzero

giraffe [dʒɪˈrɑːf] NOUN
la giraffa

girl [gəːl] NOUN
[1] la bambina ◇ *a five-year-old girl* una
bambina di cinque anni
[2] la ragazza ◇ *an English girl* una ragazza
inglese
[3] la femmina ◇ *They've got a girl and two
boys.* Hanno una femmina e due maschi.

girlfriend ['gəːlfrend] NOUN
[1] la ragazza ◇ *Paul's girlfriend is called
Lee.* La ragazza di Paul si chiama Lee.
[2] l' amica (PL le amiche) ◇ *She often went
out with her girlfriends.* Usciva spesso con
le sue amiche.

to **give** [gɪv] VERB (**gave, given**)
dare* *

dare is used with the preposition a.

* **to give somebody something** dare*
qualcosa a qualcuno ◇ *I gave my sister
some money.* Ho dato dei soldi a mia
sorella.
*When give is followed by a pronoun, use an
indirect pronoun in Italian.*
◇ *He gave me ten pounds.* Mi ha dato dieci
sterline. ◇ *I gave him some money.* Gli ho

dato dei soldi.
* **to give somebody a present** fare* un regalo
a qualcuno ◇ *They gave their teacher a
present.* Hanno fatto un regalo alla maestra.
* **to give way** (*in car*) dare* la precedenza

to **give away** [gɪvəˈweɪ] VERB
[1] dar via ◇ *We have six copies to give
away.* Abbiamo sei copie da dare* via.
[2] tradire ◇ *Her accent gave her away.* Il
suo accento l'ha tradita.

to **give back** [gɪvˈbæk] VERB
tornare ◇ *I gave the book back to him.* Gli
ho tornato il libro.

to **give in** [gɪvˈɪn] VERB
[1] cedere ◇ *His Mum gave in and let him go
out.* Sua madre ha ceduto e lo ha lasciato
uscire*.
[2] arrendersi* E ◇ *I give in.* Mi arrendo.

to **give out** [gɪvˈaut] VERB
distribuire ◇ *He gave out leaflets in the
street.* Distribuiva manifestini per strada.

to **give up** [gɪvˈʌp] VERB
lasciar perdere* ◇ *I couldn't do it, so I gave
up.* Non sono riuscito a farlo, così ho
lasciato perdere*.
* **to give oneself up** arrendersi* E ◇ *He gave
himself up.* Si è arreso.
* **to give up doing something** smettere* di
fare* qualcosa ◇ *He gave up smoking.* Ha
smesso di fumare.

given ['gɪvn] VERB see **give**

glad [glæd] ADJECTIVE
contento

glamorous ['glæmərəs] ADJECTIVE
affascinante (*person*)

to **glance** [glɑːns] VERB
see also **glance** NOUN
* **to glance at** dare* un'occhiata a ◇ *Peter
glanced at his watch.* Peter ha dato
un'occhiata all'orologio.

glance [glɑːns] NOUN
see also **glance** VERB
l' occhiata ◇ *We exchanged glances.* Ci
siamo scambiati un'occhiata.
* **at first glance** a prima vista
* **at a glance** a colpo d'occhio

to **glare** [gleəʳ] VERB
* **to glare at somebody** fulminare qualcuno
con lo sguardo

glaring ['gleərɪŋ] ADJECTIVE
* **a glaring mistake** un errore palese

glass [glɑːs] NOUN (PL **glasses**)
[1] il bicchiere ◇ *a glass of milk* un bicchiere
di latte
[2] il vetro ◇ *a glass door* una porta di vetro

glasses ['glɑːsəs] NOUN PL
gli occhiali ◇ *He wears glasses.* Porta gli
occhiali.

to **gleam** [gliːm] VERB
brillare ◇ *Her eyes gleamed with
excitement.* Le brillavano gli occhi

---

* Verbs followed by this symbol are irregular. See pp.339–364 for further details.

dall'eccitazione.

glider ['glaɪdə'] NOUN
l' aliante MASC

gliding ['glaɪdɪŋ] NOUN
il volo con l'aliante ◇ My hobby is gliding. Il mio hobby è il volo con l'aliante.

glimpse [glɪmps] NOUN
+ **to catch a glimpse of somebody** intravedere* qualcuno

glitter ['glɪtə'] VERB
luccicare

global ['gləʊbl] ADJECTIVE
mondiale ◇ on a global scale su scala mondiale
+ **a global view** una visione globale

global warming ['gləʊbl'wɔːmɪŋ] NOUN
il riscaldamento dell'atmosfera terrestre

globe [gləʊb] NOUN
il globo

gloomy ['gluːmɪ] ADJECTIVE
[1] tetro ◇ a huge gloomy church un'enorme chiesa tetra
[2] depresso ◇ She's been feeling very gloomy recently. Ultimamente è stata molto depressa.

glorious ['glɔːrɪəs] ADJECTIVE
splendido

glove [glʌv] NOUN
il guanto ◇ a pair of gloves un paio di guanti

glove compartment ['glʌvkəmpɑːtmənt] NOUN
il vano portaoggetti

glow [gləʊ] VERB
fare* luce (cigarette, fire)
+ **to glow with health** sprizzare salute da tutti i pori

glue [gluː] NOUN
see also **glue** VERB
la colla

glue [gluː] VERB
see also **glue** NOUN
incollare

GM [dʒiːˈɛm] ADJECTIVE
(= genetically-modified)
+ **GM foods** alimenti geneticamente modificati

GMO [dʒiːɛmˈəʊ] ABBREVIAZIONE
(= genetically-modified organism)
l' organismo geneticamente modificato

go [gəʊ] NOUN
see also **go** VERB
+ **to have a go at doing something** provare a fare* qualcosa
+ **Whose go is it?** A chi tocca?

go [gəʊ] VERB (went, gone)
see also **go** NOUN
[1] andare* E ◇ I'm going to the cinema tonight. Vado al cinema stasera. ◇ My car won't go. La mia macchina non va. ◇ How did it go? Com'è andata? ◇ We went home. Siamo andati a casa.

+ **to go for a walk** andare* a fare* una passeggiata ◇ He went for a walk. È andato a fare* una passeggiata.
+ **to go past something** passare accanto a qualcosa
[2] andare* via ◇ Where's Judy? – She's gone. Dov'è Judy? – È andata via. ◇ I'm going now. Adesso vado via.
+ **to be going to**
Use the future tense in Italian to say what you're going to do, or what's going to happen.
◇ I'm going to do it tomorrow. Lo farò domani. ◇ It's going to be difficult. Sarà difficile.

to **go ahead** [gəʊəˈhɛd] VERB
proseguire ◇ The show went ahead as planned. Lo spettacolo proseguì come previsto.
+ **to go ahead with** mettere* in atto ◇ We'll go ahead with your suggestion. Metteremo in atto il tuo suggerimento.

to **go after** [gəʊˈɑːftə'] VERB
rincorrere* E ◇ Quick, go after them! Veloce, rincorrili!

to **go around** [gəʊəˈraʊnd] VERB
circolare ◇ There's a rumour going around that... Circola voce che...

to **go away** [gəʊəˈweɪ] VERB
andarsene E ◇ Go away! Vattene!

to **go back** [gəʊˈbæk] VERB
ritornare E ◇ We went back to the same place. Siamo ritornati allo stesso posto.

to **go by** [gəʊˈbaɪ] VERB
passare E ◇ Two policemen went by. Sono passati due poliziotti.

to **go down** [gəʊˈdaʊn] VERB
scendere* E ◇ He went down the stairs. Ha sceso le scale. ◇ The price of computers has gone down. Il prezzo dei computer è sceso.
+ **to go down with** (illness) beccarsi E ◇ My brother's gone down with flu. Mio fratello si è beccato l'influenza.

to **go for** ['gəʊfɔː'] VERB
[1] scegliere* ◇ I think I'll go for a more casual look. Penso che sceglierò un look più casual.
[2] attaccare ◇ Suddenly the dog went for me. Improvvisamente il cane mi ha attaccato.
+ **Go for it!** Forza!

to **go in** [gəʊˈɪn] VERB
entrare E ◇ They all went in. Sono entrati tutti.

to **go off** [gəʊˈɔf] VERB
[1] andarsene ◇ They went off after lunch. Se ne sono andati dopo pranzo.
+ **to go off with something** portare via qualcosa
+ **I've gone off the idea.** L'idea non mi piace più.
[2] scoppiare E ◇ The bomb went off at ten ☞

G

Verbs followed by the symbol "E" require the auxiliary "essere"

o'clock. La bomba è scoppiata alle 10.

• **The gun went off by accident.** È partito un colpo accidentalmente.

   ③ suonare ◇ *My alarm goes off at seven.* La sveglia suona alle sette.

   ④ spegnersi ◇ *All the lights went off.* Si sono spente tutte le luci.

   ⑤ andare*ᴱ a male ◇ *This milk has gone off.* Il latte è andato a male.

to **go on** [gəʊ'ɒn] VERB

   ① succedere*ᴱ ◇ *What's going on?* Cosa succede?

   ② durareᴱ ◇ *The concert went on until eleven o'clock.* Il concerto è durato fino alle undici.

   ③ continuare ◇ *He went on reading.* Ha continuato a leggere*.

• **to go on about something** non finirla più con qualcosa

• **Go on!** Forza! ◇ *Go on, tell me what the problem is!* Forza, dimmi qual è il problema!

to **go out** [gəʊ'aʊt] VERB

   ① uscire*ᴱ ◇ *I went out with Steven last night.* Ieri sera sono uscita con Steven.

• **to be going out with somebody** stare*ᴱ insieme a qualcuno ◇ *I've been going out with him for two months.* Sono due mesi che stiamo insieme.

• **to go out for a meal** andare*ᴱ a mangiare fuori

   ② spegnersiᴱ ◇ *Suddenly, the lights went out.* Improvvisamente si sono spente le luci.

to **go past** [gəʊ'pɑːst] VERB

passareᴱ vicino a ◇ *The bus goes past the school.* L'autobus passa vicino alla scuola.

to **go round** [gəʊ'raʊnd] VERB

   ① visitare ◇ *We want to go round the museum today.* Oggi vogliamo visitare il museo.

• **to go round to somebody's house** andare*ᴱ da qualcuno ◇ *We're all going round to Paul's house tonight.* Andiamo tutti da Paul stasera.

   ② essere*ᴱ in circolazione ◇ *There's a bug going round.* C'è un virus in circolazione.

• **Is there enough food to go round?** C'è abbastanza da mangiare per tutti?

to **go through** [gəʊ'θruː] VERB

   ① passareᴱ ◇ *I know what you're going through.* So cosa stai passando.

   ② leggere* da cima a fondo ◇ *I went through his essay with him.* Ho letto il suo tema da cima a fondo assieme a lui.

   ③ riesaminare da cima a fondo ◇ *They went through the plan again.* Hanno riesaminato il piano da cima a fondo.

   ④ frugare tra ◇ *Someone had gone through her things.* Qualcuno aveva frugato tra le sue cose.

to **go up** [gəʊ'ʌp] VERB

salire*ᴱ ◇ *She went up the stairs.* Ha salito

le scale. ◇ *The price has gone up.* Il prezzo è salito.

• **to go up in flames** andare*ᴱ in fiamme

to **go with** [gəʊ'wɪð] VERB

andare*ᴱ con ◇ *Does this blouse go with that skirt?* Questa camicia va con quella gonna?

goal [gəʊl] NOUN

   ① il gol (PL i gol) ◇ *He scored the first goal.* Ha segnato il primo gol.

   ② l' obiettivo ◇ *His goal is to become the world champion.* Il suo obiettivo è quello di diventare campione del mondo.

goalkeeper [ˈgəʊlkiːpə'] NOUN

il portiere

goat [gəʊt] NOUN

la capra ◇ *goat's cheese* formaggio di capra

god [gɒd] NOUN

il dio (PL gli dei) ◇ *I believe in God.* Credo in Dio.

goddaughter [ˈgɒdɔːtə'] NOUN

la figlioccia (PL le figliocce)

godfather [ˈgɒdfɑːðə'] NOUN

il padrino

godmother [ˈgɒdmʌðə'] NOUN

la madrina

godson [ˈgɒdsʌn] NOUN

il figlioccio

goggles [ˈgɒglz] NOUN PL

la maschera SING

gold [gəʊld] NOUN

l' oro ◇ *a gold necklace* una collana d'oro

goldfish [ˈgəʊldfɪʃ] NOUN (PL **goldfish**)

il pesce rosso

gold-plated [ˈgəʊldˈpleɪtɪd] ADJECTIVE

placcato oro

golf [gɒlf] NOUN

il golf

• **a golf club** una mazza da golf

• **a golf course** un campo da golf

gone [gɒn] VERB *see* **go**

good [gʊd] ADJECTIVE

   ① bello ◇ *It's a very good film.* È un film molto bello.

Use **bel** *before a masculine noun starting with a consonant.*

◇ *a good film* un bel film

Use **bell'** *before a masculine noun starting with a vowel.*

◇ *a good pay rise* un bell'aumento

Use **bello** *before a masculine noun starting with impure s, gn, pn, ps, x, y or z.*

◇ *a good salary* un bello stipendio

Use **bei** *before a plural masculine noun starting with a consonant.*

◇ *good books* bei libri

Use **begli** *before a plural masculine noun starting with a vowel, or with impure s, gn, pn, ps, x, y or z.*

◇ *good salaries* begli stipendi

   ② gentile ◇ *They were very good to me.*

* Verbs followed by this symbol are irregular. See pp.339–364 for further details.

Sono stati molto gentili con me. ◊ *That's very good of you.* È molto gentile da parte tua.

[3] <u>bravo</u> ◊ *He's the best in the class.* È il più bravo della classe.

◆ **to be good at something** essere* [E] bravo in qualcosa ◊ *Jane's very good at maths.* Jane è molto brava in matematica.

[4] <u>buono</u> ◊ *Be good!* Sii buono! ◊ *They make very good soup here.* Qui fanno una minestra molto buona.

Use **buon** *before a masculine noun starting with a consonant or a vowel.*

◊ *a good number* un buon numero ◊ *a good friend* un buon amico

Use **buono** *before a masculine noun starting with impure s, gn, pn, ps, x, y or z.*

◊ *a good rucksack* un buono zaino

Use **buon'** *before a feminine noun starting with a vowel.*

◊ *Good idea!* Buon'idea!

◆ **Good morning!** Buongiorno!
◆ **Good afternoon!** Buon pomeriggio!
◆ **Good evening!** Buona sera!
◆ **Good night!** Buona notte!
◆ **Have a good journey!** Buon viaggio!
◆ **Good!** Bene!
◆ **to feel good** sentirsi [E] bene ◊ *I'm feeling really good today.* Oggi mi sento proprio bene.
◆ **to be good for somebody** far bene a qualcuno ◊ *Vegetables are good for you.* La verdura ti fa bene.
◆ **It's no good complaining.** Non vale la pena lamentarsi.
◆ **for good** per sempre ◊ *The theatre has closed for good.* Il teatro ha chiuso per sempre.
◆ **as good as** praticamente ◊ *as good as new* praticamente nuovo

goodbye! [gud'baɪ] EXCLAMATION
<u>arrivederci</u>!

Good Friday [gud'fraɪdɪ] NOUN
il <u>venerdì santo</u>

good-looking ['gud'lukɪŋ] ADJECTIVE
<u>bello</u>

good-natured ['gud'neɪtʃəd] ADJECTIVE
di <u>buon carattere</u>

goods ['gudz] NOUN PL
la <u>merce</u> ◊ *faulty goods* merce difettosa
◆ **a goods train** un treno merci

goose [guːs] NOUN (PL **geese**)
l' <u>oca</u> (PL le oche) ◊ *a flock of geese* un branco di oche

gooseberry ['guzbrɪ] NOUN (PL **gooseberries**)
l' <u>uva spina</u>

gorgeous ['gɔːdʒəs] ADJECTIVE
<u>stupendo</u>

gorilla [gə'rɪlə] NOUN
il <u>gorilla</u> (PL i gorilla)

gospel ['gɔspl] NOUN

il <u>vangelo</u>

gossip ['gɔsɪp] NOUN
see also **gossip** VERB
[1] i <u>pettegolezzi</u> PL ◊ *It's just gossip.* Sono solo pettegolezzi.
◆ **Tell me the gossip!** Dimmi le ultime!
[2] il <u>pettegolo</u>
la <u>pettegola</u>

to **gossip** ['gɔsɪp] VERB
see also **gossip** NOUN
<u>chiacchierare</u> ◊ *They were always gossiping.* Chiacchieravano in continuazione.

got [gɔt] VERB *see* **get**

gotta ['gɔtə] VERB = **have got to**

gotten ['gɔtn] VERB US *see* **get**

government ['gʌvnmənt] NOUN
il <u>governo</u>

GP [dʒiː'piː] NOUN (= General Practitioner)
il <u>medico di famiglia</u> (PL i medici di famiglia)

to **grab** [græb] VERB
<u>afferrare</u> ◊ *He grabbed my arm.* Mi ha afferrato il braccio.
◆ **to grab something from somebody** strappare qualcosa di mano a qualcuno

graceful ['greɪsful] ADJECTIVE
<u>aggraziato</u> (*person, movements*)

grade [greɪd] NOUN
[1] il <u>livello</u> ◊ *the grade II exam* un esame di secondo livello
[2] il <u>voto</u> (*mark*)

grade crossing ['greɪdkrɔsɪŋ] NOUN US
il <u>passaggio a livello</u> (PL i passaggi a livello)

grade school ['greɪdskuːl] NOUN US
la <u>scuola elementare</u>

gradual ['grædjuəl] ADJECTIVE
<u>graduale</u>

gradually ['grædjuəlɪ] ADVERB
<u>gradualmente</u>

graduate ['grædjuit] NOUN
see also **graduate** VERB
il <u>laureato</u>
la <u>laureata</u>

to **graduate** ['grædjueɪt] VERB
see also **graduate** NOUN
<u>laurearsi</u> [E] ◊ *He graduated from London University last year.* Si è laureato alla London University l'anno scorso.
◆ **to graduate from high school** diplomarsi [E]

graffiti [grə'fiːtɪ] NOUN PL
i <u>graffiti</u>

grain [greɪn] NOUN
[1] il <u>chicco</u> (PL i chicchi) ◊ *a grain of rice* un chicco di riso
◆ **a grain of truth** un briciolo di verità
[2] i <u>cereali</u> ◊ *grain producers* produttori di cereali

gram [græm] NOUN
il <u>grammo</u>

grammar ['græmə'] NOUN
la <u>grammatica</u> ◊ *a grammar book* un libro ☞

G

di grammatica

grammar school ['græməsku:l] NOUN
il liceo

> **ⓘ** In Gran Bretagna la **grammar school** è una scuola secondaria selettiva, oggi sempre meno diffusa. Negli Stati Uniti, invece, per **grammar school** si intende la scuola elementare.

grammatical [grə'mætɪkl] ADJECTIVE
grammaticale

gramme [græm] NOUN
il grammo

grand [grænd] ADJECTIVE
sontuoso ◇ Her house is very grand. La sua casa è molto sontuosa.
◆ **We had a grand time.** Ce la siamo proprio spassata.
◆ **a grand total of two thousand pounds** una somma complessiva di duemila sterline

grandchild ['græntʃaɪld] NOUN (PL **grandchildren**)
il/la nipote (di nonni)

grandchildren ['græntʃɪldrən] NOUN PL see **grandchild**

granddad ['grændæd] NOUN
il nonno

granddaughter ['grændɔːtər] NOUN
la nipote (di nonni)

grandfather ['grændfɑːðər] NOUN
il nonno

grandma ['grænmɑː] NOUN
la nonna

grandmother ['grænmʌðər] NOUN
la nonna

grandpa ['grænpɑː] NOUN
il nonno

grandparents ['grændpeərənts] NOUN PL
i nonni

grand piano [grændpɪ'ænəu] NOUN
il pianoforte a coda

grandson ['grænsʌn] NOUN
il nipote (di nonni)

granny ['grænɪ] NOUN (PL **grannies**)
la nonna

grant [grɑːnt] NOUN
see also **grant** VERB
1 la sovvenzione ◇ a grant to restore the church una sovvenzione per il restauro della chiesa
2 la borsa di studio ◇ Some students get grants. Alcuni studenti ottengono delle borse di studio.

to **grant** [grɑːnt] VERB
see also **grant** NOUN
concedere* ◇ He grants few interviews. Concede poche interviste.
◆ **to take somebody for granted** non rendersi conto di quanto qualcuno sia importante
◆ **to take something for granted** dare*

qualcosa per scontato

grapefruit ['greɪpfruːt] NOUN
il pompelmo

grapes [greɪps] NOUN PL
l' uva SING ◇ a bunch of grapes un grappolo d'uva

graph [grɑːf] NOUN
il grafico (PL i grafici)

graphics ['græfɪks] NOUN
la grafica

to **grasp** [grɑːsp] VERB
afferrare

grass [grɑːs] NOUN
l' erba ◇ Keep off the grass. Vietato calpestare l'erba.

grasshopper ['grɑːshɒpər] NOUN
la cavalletta

to **grate** [greɪt] VERB
grattugiare

grateful ['greɪtful] ADJECTIVE
grato

grave [greɪv] NOUN
la tomba

gravel ['grævl] NOUN
la ghiaia

graveyard ['greɪvjɑːd] NOUN
il cimitero

gravy ['greɪvɪ] NOUN
il sugo della carne

gray [greɪ] ADJECTIVE US
grigio ◇ a gray suit un vestito grigio
◆ **to go gray** ingrigirsi E

grease [griːs] NOUN
il grasso

greasy ['griːsɪ] ADJECTIVE
grasso ◇ He has greasy hair. Ha i capelli grassi.

great [greɪt] ADJECTIVE
1 grande ◇ a great oak tree una grande quercia
◆ **He took great care to explain clearly.** Ha cercato in ogni modo di dare* una spiegazione chiara.
◆ **a great many** moltissimi
2 fantastico ◇ That's great! È fantastico!

Great Britain [greɪt'brɪtən] NOUN
la Gran Bretagna

> **ⓘ** La **Gran Bretagna** è formata da Inghilterra, Galles e Scozia; assieme all'Irlanda del Nord costituisce il Regno Unito.

great-grandfather [greɪt'grænfɑːðər] NOUN
il bisnonno

great-grandmother [greɪt'grænmʌðər] NOUN
la bisnonna

Greece [griːs] NOUN
la Grecia

greedy ['griːdɪ] ADJECTIVE
1 ingordo ◇ Don't be greedy. Leave some

* Verbs followed by this symbol are irregular. See pp.339–364 for further details.

cake for Helen. Non essere* ingordo. Lascia un po' di torta per Helen.
2 avido ◇ *greedy for power* avido di potere*

Greek [gri:k] ADJECTIVE
see also **Greek** NOUN
greco

Greek [gri:k] NOUN
see also **Greek** ADJECTIVE
1 il greco
la greca
(*person*)
◆ **the Greeks** i greci
2 il greco (*language*)

green [gri:n] ADJECTIVE
see also **green** NOUN
verde ◇ *a green car* una macchina verde
◆ **the Green Party** i Verdi

green [gri:n] NOUN
see also **green** ADJECTIVE
il verde ◇ *dark green* verde scuro
◆ **greens** la verdura SING
◆ **the Green Party** i Verdi

green belt ['gri:nbelt] NOUN
la cintura di verde

green card ['gri:nkɑ:d] NOUN
la carta verde

greengrocer ['gri:nɡrəʊsəʳ] NOUN
il fruttivendolo
◆ **to go to the greengrocer's** andare* dal fruttivendolo

greenhouse ['gri:nhaʊs] NOUN
la serra ◇ *the greenhouse effect* l'effetto serra
◆ **greenhouse gas** il gas responsabile dell'effetto serra (PL i gas responsabili dell'effetto serra)

Greenland ['gri:nlənd] NOUN
la Groenlandia

greet [gri:t] VERB
salutare ◇ *He greeted me with a kiss.* Mi ha salutata con un bacio.
◆ **to greet something with** accogliere* qualcosa con

greetings ['gri:tɪŋz] NOUN PL
i saluti ◇ *Greetings from London!* Saluti da Londra!
◆ **"Season's greetings"** (*on card*) "Buone Feste"

greetings card ['gri:tɪŋzkɑ:d] NOUN
il biglietto d'auguri

grew [gru:] VERB *see* **grow**

grey [greɪ] ADJECTIVE
grigio ◇ *a grey suit* un completo grigio
◆ **to go grey** ingrigirsi E

grey-haired [greɪˈheəd] ADJECTIVE
dai capelli grigi

grid [ɡrɪd] NOUN
1 la rete ◇ *a grid of streets* una rete di strade
2 la grata (*made of metal*)

grief [gri:f] NOUN
il dolore

to **grieve** [gri:v] VERB
◆ **to grieve over** piangere* ◇ *She was grieving over the death of her husband.* Stava piangendo la morte di suo marito.
◆ **The family is still grieving.** La famiglia è ancora in lutto.
◆ **I need time to grieve.** Ho bisogno di tempo per piangere* la sua morte.

grill [ɡrɪl] NOUN
see also **grill** VERB
la griglia (*of cooker*)
◆ **a mixed grill** una grigliata mista

to **grill** [ɡrɪl] VERB
see also **grill** NOUN
cucinare alla griglia

grim [ɡrɪm] ADJECTIVE
deprimente ◇ *The outskirts of the city are very grim.* La periferia della città è un luogo molto deprimente.

to **grin** [ɡrɪn] VERB
see also **grin** NOUN
fare* un gran sorriso ◇ *Dave grinned at me.* Dave mi fece un gran sorriso.

grin [ɡrɪn] NOUN
see also **grin** VERB
il sorriso smagliante

to **grind** [ɡraɪnd] VERB (**ground, ground**)
1 macinare (*coffee, pepper*) ◇ *Have you ground the coffee?* Hai macinato il caffè?
2 tritare (*meat*) US

to **grip** [ɡrɪp] VERB
afferrare

gripping ['ɡrɪpɪŋ] ADJECTIVE
avvincente

grit [ɡrɪt] NOUN
la ghiaia

to **groan** [ɡrəʊn] VERB
see also **groan** NOUN
gemere ◇ *He groaned with pain.* Gemette dal dolore.

groan [ɡrəʊn] NOUN
see also **groan** VERB
il gemito

grocer ['ɡrəʊsəʳ] NOUN
il/la negoziante di generi alimentari

groceries ['ɡrəʊsərɪz] NOUN PL
i generi alimentari ◇ *a shop selling groceries* un negozio che vende generi alimentari
◆ **a bag of groceries** una borsa di roba da mangiare
◆ **to get some groceries** fare* un po' di spesa

grocer's ['ɡrəʊsəz] NOUN
il negozio di alimentari

grocery store ['ɡrəʊsərɪstɔ:ʳ] NOUN
il negozio di alimentari (PL i negozi di alimentari)

groom [gru:m] NOUN
lo sposo ◇ *the groom and his best man* lo ☞

G

sposo e il suo testimone

to **grope** [grəʊp] VERB
- **to grope for something** cercare qualcosa a tentoni ◇ *He groped for the light switch.* Cercò a tentoni l'interruttore della luce.

gross [grəʊs] ADJECTIVE
1. lordo ◇ *gross interest* interesse lordo
2. disgustoso ◇ *It was really gross!* È stato veramente disgustoso!
3. obeso (*fat*)

grossly ['grəʊslɪ] ADVERB
decisamente ◇ *We're grossly underpaid.* Siamo decisamente sottopagati.

ground [graʊnd] VERB *see* grind

ground [graʊnd] NOUN
see also **ground** ADJECTIVE
1. la terra ◇ *The ground's wet.* La terra è bagnata.
- **on the ground** per terra
- **to get off the ground (1)** (*scheme*) prendere* il via
- **to get off the ground (2)** (*plane*) decollare
2. il campo ◇ *a football ground* un campo di calcio
- **grounds** motivo SING ◇ *We've got grounds for complaint.* Abbiamo motivo di lamentarci.

ground [graʊnd] ADJECTIVE
see also **ground** NOUN, VERB
- **ground coffee** caffè macinato
- **ground meat** carne macinata

ground floor [graʊnd'flɔːʳ] NOUN
il pianterreno
- **on the ground floor** al pianterreno

group [gruːp] NOUN
il gruppo

to **grow** [grəʊ] VERB (**grew, grown**)
1. crescere* E ◇ *Haven't you grown!* Come sei cresciuto!
- **to grow a beard** farsi E crescere* la barba ◇ *I'm growing a beard.* Mi sto facendo crescere* la barba. ◇ *He grew a moustache.* Si è fatto crescere* i baffi.
2. aumentare E (*number*)
3. coltivare ◇ *He grew vegetables in his garden.* Coltivava ortaggi in giardino. ◇ *Lettuce was grown by the Ancient Romans.* Gli antichi romani coltivavano l'insalata.

to **grow out of** [grəʊ'aʊtəv] VERB
1. non entrare più in (*clothes*) ◇ *He's grown out of his jacket.* Non entra più nella giacca.
2. perdere* (*habit*)

to **grow up** [grəʊ'ʌp] VERB
crescere* E ◇ *I grew up in Rome.* Sono cresciuto a Roma.
- **Oh, grow up!** Non fare* il bambino!

to **growl** [graʊl] VERB
ringhiare

grown [grəʊn] VERB *see* grow

growth [grəʊθ] NOUN
la crescita ◇ *economic growth* crescita economica

grub [grʌb] NOUN
1. il bruco (PL i bruchi) (*insect*)
2. qualcosa da mangiare ◇ *Get yourself some grub.* Prenditi qualcosa da mangiare.

grudge [grʌdʒ] NOUN
il rancore
- **to have a grudge against somebody** serbare rancore a qualcuno

gruesome ['gruːsəm] ADJECTIVE
orrendo

guarantee [gærən'tiː] NOUN
see also **guarantee** VERB
la garanzia ◇ *a five-year guarantee* una garanzia di cinque anni ◇ *It's still under guarantee.* È ancora in garanzia.

to **guarantee** [gærən'tiː] VERB
see also **guarantee** NOUN
garantire ◇ *I can't guarantee he'll come.* Non posso garantire che venga.

to **guard** [gɑːd] VERB
see also **guard** NOUN
fare* la guardia a ◇ *They guarded the palace.* Facevano la guardia al palazzo.

guard [gɑːd] NOUN
see also **guard** VERB
1. la guardia ◇ *security guard* guardia giurata
- **to catch somebody off guard** prendere* qualcuno alla sprovvista
2. il capotreno (*on train*)

guard dog ['gɑːddɔg] NOUN
il cane da guardia

to **guess** [ges] VERB
see also **guess** NOUN
1. indovinare ◇ *Can you guess what it is?* Indovina cos'è!
- **Guess what!** Sai l'ultima?
2. supporre* ◇ *I guess so.* Suppongo di sì.

guess [ges] NOUN (PL **guesses**)
see also **guess** VERB
la supposizione ◇ *It's just a guess.* È solo una supposizione.
- **Have a guess!** Prova a indovinare!

guest [gest] NOUN
l' ospite MASC/FEM ◇ *We have guests staying with us.* Abbiamo degli ospiti da noi.

guest house ['gesthaʊs] NOUN
la pensione

guide [gaɪd] NOUN
la guida (*book, person*)
- **the Guides** le Giovani esploratrici

guidebook ['gaɪdbʊk] NOUN
la guida

guide dog ['gaɪddɔg] NOUN
il cane per ciechi

guilty ['gɪltɪ] ADJECTIVE
colpevole ◇ *She was found guilty.* È stata riconosciuta colpevole.

---

* Verbs followed by this symbol are irregular. See pp.339–364 for further details.

English ~ Italian

+ **to feel guilty** sentirsi^E in colpa ◇ *He felt guilty about lying to her.* Si sentiva in colpa per averle mentito.
+ **to have a guilty conscience** avere* la coscienza sporca

guinea pig ['gɪnɪpɪg] NOUN
la cavia

guitar [gɪ'tɑːʳ] NOUN
la chitarra

gum [gʌm] NOUN
la gomma ◇ *I'm chewing gum.* Sto masticando una gomma.
+ **gums** le gengive ◇ *My gums are bleeding.* Le gengive mi sanguinano.

gun [gʌn] NOUN
1. la pistola (*handgun*)
2. il fucile (*rifle*)

gunpoint ['gʌnpɔɪnt] NOUN
+ **at gunpoint** sotto la minaccia delle armi

gust [gʌst] NOUN
+ **gust of wind** raffica di vento

guy [gaɪ] NOUN
il tipo ◇ *Who's that guy?* Chi è quel tipo?

gym [dʒɪm] NOUN
la palestra ◇ *I go to the gym every day.* Vado in palestra ogni giorno.
+ **gym classes** un corso di ginnastica

gymnast ['dʒɪmnæst] NOUN
il/la ginnasta

gymnastics [dʒɪm'næstɪks] NOUN
la ginnastica

gym shoes ['dʒɪmʃuːz] NOUN
le scarpe da ginnastica

gypsy ['dʒɪpsɪ] NOUN (PL **gypsies**)
lo zingaro
la zingara

G

H

habit ['hæbɪt] NOUN
l'abitudine FEM

to **hack** [hæk] VERB
- **to hack into a system** inserirsi[E] illegalmente in un sistema

hacker ['hækə'] NOUN
il pirata informatico (PL i pirati informatici)

had [hæd] VERB *see* **have**

haddock ['hædək] NOUN (PL **haddock**)
l'eglefino

hadn't ['hædnt] = **had not**

hail [heɪl] NOUN
see also **hail** VERB
la grandine

to **hail** [heɪl] VERB
see also **hail** NOUN
1. acclamare ◇ *He was hailed in the press as a hero.* La stampa lo acclamava come un eroe.
2. grandinare[E] ◇ *It's hailing.* Grandina.

hair [heə'] NOUN
1. i capelli PL ◇ *Her hair is lovely.* Ha dei bei capelli.
- **to have one's hair cut** farsi[E] tagliare i capelli
- **He's got hairs on his chest.** Ha il petto peloso.
2. il pelo (*of animal*)

hairbrush ['heəbrʌʃ] NOUN (PL **hairbrushes**)
la spazzola

haircut ['heəkʌt] NOUN
il taglio ◇ *a nice haircut* un bel taglio
- **to have a haircut** farsi[E] tagliare i capelli

hairdresser ['heədresə'] NOUN
il parrucchiere
la parrucchiera
◇ *at the hairdresser's* dal parrucchiere

hair dryer ['heədraɪə'] NOUN
l'asciugacapelli MASC (PL gli asciugacapelli)

hair gel ['heədʒel] NOUN
il gel (PL i gel)

hairgrip ['heəgrɪp] NOUN
la molletta

hair spray ['heəspreɪ] NOUN
la lacca (PL le lacche)

hairstyle ['heəstaɪl] NOUN
la pettinatura

hairy ['heərɪ] ADJECTIVE
peloso

half [hɑːf] NOUN (PL **halves**)
see also **half** ADJECTIVE, ADVERB
la metà (PL le metà) ◇ *half of the cake* metà torta ◇ *I can do the job in half the time.* Posso fare* il lavoro in metà del tempo.
- **Half the time I don't know what he's talking about.** Spesso non so di che cosa stia parlando.
- **two and a half** due e mezzo
- **half an hour** mezz'ora
- **half past ten** dieci e mezza

- **half a kilo** mezzo chilo
- **to cut something in half** tagliare qualcosa a metà
- **One and two halves, please.** Un biglietto intero e due ridotti, per favore.

half [hɑːf] ADJECTIVE, ADVERB
see also **half** NOUN
mezzo ◇ *a half chicken* mezzo pollo ◇ *He was half asleep.* Era mezzo addormentato.
- **She half expected him to refuse.** Era quasi convinta che avrebbe rifiutato.

half-hour [hɑːf'auə'] NOUN
la mezz'ora

half-price ['hɑːf'praɪs] ADJECTIVE, ADVERB
a metà prezzo ◇ *I bought it half-price.* L'ho comprato a metà prezzo.

half-term [hɑːf'tɜːm] NOUN
la vacanza di metà quadrimestre

> **ⓘ** In Gran Bretagna a metà di ogni trimestre scolastico i ragazzi hanno una vacanza di alcuni giorni.

half-time [hɑːf'taɪm] NOUN
l'intervallo

halfway [hɑːf'weɪ] ADVERB
1. a metà strada ◇ *Reading is halfway between Oxford and London.* Reading è a metà strada tra Oxford e Londra.
2. a metà ◇ *halfway through the film* a metà del film

hall [hɔːl] NOUN
1. l'ingresso ◇ *He hung his coat in the hall.* Ha appeso il cappotto nell'ingresso.
2. il corridoio US ◇ *Her room is down the hall.* La sua camera è in fondo al corridoio.
3. la sala ◇ *a concert hall* una sala concerti
- **a sports hall** una palestra
- **village hall** sala comunale a disposizione del pubblico

hall of residence [hɔːləv'rezɪdəns] NOUN
la casa dello studente

Hallowe'en ['hæləʊ'iːn] NOUN
la vigilia di Ognissanti

> **ⓘ** Secondo la tradizione **Hallowe'en**, la notte del 31 ottobre, è la notte delle streghe. I bambini, mascherati e con in mano lanterne ricavate da zucche, vanno di casa in casa per raccogliere dolci e piccoli doni.

hallway ['hɔːlweɪ] NOUN
l'ingresso

halt [hɔːlt] NOUN
see also **halt** VERB
- **to come to a halt** fermarsi[E]

to **halt** [hɔːlt] VERB
see also **halt** NOUN
arrestare ◇ *The government failed to halt economic decline.* Il governo non è riuscito

---

* Verbs followed by this symbol are irregular. See pp.339–364 for further details.

ad arrestare il declino economico.

halves [hɑːvz] NOUN PL *see* **half**

ham [hæm] NOUN
il prosciutto ◊ *a ham sandwich* un panino al prosciutto

hamburger ['hæmbə:gə'] NOUN
l' hamburger (PL gli hamburger)

hammer ['hæmə'] NOUN
il martello

hamster ['hæmstə'] NOUN
il criceto

hand [hænd] NOUN
see also **hand** VERB
[1] la mano ◊ *Wash your hands!* Lavati le mani!
[2] la lancetta (*of clock*)
✦ **on the one hand..., on the other hand...** da un lato..., dall'altro...

hand [hænd] VERB
see also **hand** NOUN
passare ◊ *He handed me the book.* Mi ha passato il libro.

hand in [hænd'ɪn] VERB
consegnare ◊ *Martin handed his exam paper in.* Martin ha consegnato il compito scritto.

hand out [hænd'aut] VERB
distribuire ◊ *The teacher handed out the books.* L'insegnante ha distribuito i libri.

hand over [hænd'əuvə'] VERB
consegnare ◊ *She handed the keys over to me.* Mi ha consegnato le chiavi.

handbag ['hændbæg] NOUN
la borsetta

handball ['hændbɔːl] NOUN
[1] la pallamano ◊ *We played handball.* Giocavamo a pallamano.
[2] il fallo di mano (*in football*)

handbook ['hændbuk] NOUN
il manuale

handcuffs ['hændkʌfs] NOUN PL
le manette

handkerchief ['hæŋkətʃɪf] NOUN
il fazzoletto

handle ['hændl] NOUN
see also **handle** VERB
[1] la maniglia ◊ *He was too small to reach the door handle.* Era troppo piccolo per arrivare alla maniglia della porta.
[2] il manico (PL i manici) ◊ *a knife with a plastic handle* un coltello con il manico di plastica

handle ['hændl] VERB
see also **handle** NOUN
[1] occuparsi [E] di ◊ *Kath handled the travel arrangements.* Kath si è occupata dell'organizzazione del viaggio.
[2] gestire ◊ *It was a difficult situation, but he handled it well.* Era una situazione difficile, ma l'ha gestita bene.
[3] trattare ◊ *She's good at handling*

children. Sa come trattare i bambini.
✦ **"handle with care"** "fragile"

handlebars ['hændlbɑːz] NOUN PL
il manubrio SING

handmade ['hænd'meɪd] ADJECTIVE
fatto a mano

handsome ['hænsəm] ADJECTIVE
bello ◊ *My father's very handsome.* Mio padre è proprio un bell'uomo.

handwriting ['hændraɪtɪŋ] NOUN
la scrittura

handy ['hændɪ] ADJECTIVE
[1] pratico ◊ *This knife's very handy.* Questo coltello è molto pratico.
[2] a portata di mano ◊ *Have you got a pen handy?* Hai una penna a portata di mano?
✦ **to come in handy** tornare [E] utile ◊ *The money came in very handy.* Il denaro è tornato molto utile.

to **hang** [hæŋ] VERB (hung, hung)
[1] appendere* ◊ *Mike hung the painting on the wall.* Mike ha appeso il quadro al muro.
[2] pendere* ◊ *There was a red bulb hanging from the ceiling.* C'era una lampadina rossa che pendeva dal soffitto.
[3] impiccare ◊ *In the past criminals were hanged.* In passato i criminali venivano impiccati.

to **hang around** [hæŋə'raund] VERB
[1] gironzolare (*loiter*)
[2] restare ad aspettare (*wait*)

to **hang on** [hæŋ'ɒn] VERB
aspettare ◊ *Hang on a minute please.* Aspetta un momento per favore.

to **hang up** [hæŋ'ʌp] VERB
[1] appendere* (*clothes*)
[2] riattaccare (*phone*)
✦ **to hang up on somebody** mettere* giù il ricevitore a qualcuno

hanger ['hæŋə'] NOUN
la gruccia (PL le grucce) (*for clothes*)

hang-gliding ['hæŋglaɪdɪŋ] NOUN
il deltaplano

hangover ['hæŋəuvə'] NOUN
i postumi della sbornia ◊ *I woke up with a hangover.* Mi sono svegliato coi postumi della sbornia.

to **happen** ['hæpən] VERB
succedere* [E] ◊ *What happened?* Cos'è successo?
✦ **as it happens** per combinazione
✦ **Do you happen to know if...** Sai per caso se...

happily ['hæpɪlɪ] ADVERB
[1] felicemente ◊ *He's happily married.* È felicemente sposato.
✦ **...and they lived happily ever after.** ...e vissero felici e contenti.
[2] fortunatamente ◊ *Happily, everything went well.* Fortunatamente tutto è andato ☞

H

bene.

happiness ['hæpɪnɪs] NOUN
la felicità

happy ['hæpɪ] ADJECTIVE
1 felice ◇ *Janet looks happy.* Janet sembra felice.
2 soddisfatto ◇ *I'm very happy with your work.* Sono molto soddisfatto del tuo lavoro.
+ **Happy birthday!** Buon compleanno!
+ **a happy ending** un lieto fine

happy hour ['hæpɪaʊəʳ] NOUN
[l'] orario in cui i pub hanno prezzi ridotti

harassment ['hærəsmənt] NOUN SING
+ **sexual harassment** molestie sessuali FEM PL

harbour ['hɑːbəʳ] NOUN (US **harbor**)
il porto

hard [hɑːd] ADJECTIVE, ADVERB
1 duro ◇ *This cheese is very hard.* Questo formaggio è proprio duro.
2 difficile ◇ *This exercise is too hard for me.* Quest'esercizio è troppo difficile per me.
+ **to work hard** lavorare sodo
+ **hard cash** il denaro in contanti
+ **to be hard up** essere* ᴱ a corto di soldi

hard disk [hɑːd'dɪsk] NOUN
il disco rigido (PL i dischi rigidi)

hardly ['hɑːdlɪ] ADVERB
appena ◇ *I hardly know you.* Ti conosco appena.
+ **I've got hardly any money.** Ho pochissimo denaro.
+ **hardly ever** quasi mai
+ **hardly anything** quasi niente

hard shoulder [hɑːd'ʃəʊldəʳ] NOUN
la corsia d'emergenza

hare [hɛəʳ] NOUN
la lepre

to **harm** [hɑːm] VERB
see also **harm** NOUN
+ **to harm somebody** far male a qualcuno
+ **to harm something** danneggiare qualcosa

harm [hɑːm] NOUN
see also **harm** VERB ◇ *It might do more harm than good.* Potrebbe fare* più male che bene.
+ **There's no harm trying.** Tentar non nuoce.

harmful ['hɑːmful] ADJECTIVE
dannoso

harmless ['hɑːmlɪs] ADJECTIVE
innocuo

harsh [hɑːʃ] ADJECTIVE
1 severo ◇ *harsh punishment* una punizione severa
2 sgradevole ◇ *She's got a very harsh voice.* Ha una voce molto sgradevole.

has [hæz] VERB *see* **have**

hasn't ['hæznt] = **has not**

hat [hæt] NOUN
il cappello

to **hate** [heɪt] VERB
odiare

hatred ['heɪtrɪd] NOUN
l' odio

haunted ['hɔːntɪd] ADJECTIVE
+ **a haunted castle** un castello infestato dagli spiriti

to **have** [hæv] VERB (**had, had**)
1 avere* ◇ *Do you have any brothers or sisters?* Hai fratelli o sorelle? ◇ *He has one brother and two sisters.* Ha un fratello e due sorelle. ◇ *I had no idea you were here.* Non avevo idea che fossi qui.
*When translating perfect tenses remember that some Italian verbs take **avere** and others take **essere**. When a verb has an object the auxiliary is always **avere**.*
◇ *I've already seen that film.* Ho già visto quel film. ◇ *If you had phoned me I would have come round.* Se mi avessi telefonato sarei venuto.
*When the Italian verb takes **essere**, the past participle agrees with the subject of the sentence.*
◇ *They've arrived.* Sono arrivati. ◇ *Has he ever been to Paris?* È mai stato a Parigi? ◇ *Has she gone?* È andata via?
*Reflexive verbs always take **essere**.*
◇ *Lucy has hurt herself.* Lucy si è fatta male.
*The reply to a question containing **to have** either has no verb in Italian, or the verb in full.*
◇ *Have you read that book? – Yes, I have.* Hai letto quel libro? – Sì, l'ho letto. ◇ *Has he told you? – No, he hasn't.* Te l'ha detto? – No.
+ **You've done it, haven't you?** Lo hai fatto, vero?
+ **to have got** avere* ◇ *He's got blue eyes.* Ha gli occhi azzurri. ◇ *Have you got any brothers or sisters?* Hai fratelli o sorelle?
2 fare* ◇ *He's already had breakfast.* Ha già fatto colazione. ◇ *We're going to have a party.* Faremo una festa.
3 prendere* ◇ *I'll have a coffee.* Prendo un caffè.
+ **to have to do something** dover fare* qualcosa ◇ *She had to do it.* Ha dovuto farlo.
+ **She has got to do it.** Deve farlo.
+ **to have one's hair cut** farsi ᴱ tagliare i capelli
+ **to have a look** dare* un'occhiata

haven't ['hævnt] = **have not**

hay [heɪ] NOUN
il fieno

hay fever ['heɪfiːvəʳ] NOUN
la febbre da fieno

hazelnut ['heɪzlnʌt] NOUN
la nocciola

he [hiː] PRONOUN
lui ◇ *He loves dogs.* Lui ama i cani.
***he** is often not translated.*
◇ *"Come here," he said.* "Vieni qui," disse.
***lui** is the pronoun used in spoken and informal written Italian. The more formal word for **he** is "egli".*

* Verbs followed by this symbol are irregular. See pp.339–364 for further details.

head [hɛd] NOUN
see also **head** VERB

[1] la testa ◇ *Mind your head!* Attento alla testa! ◇ *He lost his head and started screaming.* Ha perso la testa e ha cominciato a gridare.
+ **I've got no head for figures.** Sono negato per la matematica.
+ **Heads or tails? – Heads.** Testa o croce? – Testa.
+ **to keep one's head** mantenere* la calma ◇ *She always manages to keep her head in difficult situations.* Riesce sempre a mantenere* la calma nelle situazioni difficili.
[2] il/la preside (*of school*)
+ **a head of state** un capo di stato

head [hɛd] VERB
see also **head** NOUN

essere*[E] in cima a ◇ *She headed the list.* Era in cima all'elenco.
+ **to head the ball** colpire la palla di testa
+ **to head for...** dirigersi[E] verso... ◇ *They headed for the church.* Si sono diretti verso la chiesa.

headache ['hɛdeɪk] NOUN
il mal di testa ◇ *I've got a headache.* Ho mal di testa.

headlight ['hɛdlaɪt] NOUN
il faro

headline ['hɛdlaɪn] NOUN
il titolo

headmaster [hɛd'mɑːstəʳ] NOUN
il preside

headmistress [hɛd'mɪstrɪs] NOUN
la preside

head office [hɛd'ɔfɪs] NOUN
la sede centrale

headphones ['hɛdfəunz] NOUN PL
la cuffia

headquarters ['hɛdkwɔːtəz] NOUN PL
la sede centrale SING (*of organization*)

head teacher [hɛd'tiːtʃəʳ] NOUN
il/la preside

head waiter [hɛd'weɪtəʳ] NOUN
il capocameriere

heal [hiːl] VERB
guarire[E]

When an auxiliary is needed to form past tenses use "essere" when **guarire** does not have an object.

◇ *The wound healed.* La ferte è guarita.

health [hɛlθ] NOUN
la salute ◇ *She's in good health.* È in buona salute.
+ **the Department of Health** il Ministero della Sanità

healthy ['hɛlθɪ] ADJECTIVE
sano

heap [hiːp] NOUN
il mucchio ◇ *a heap of stones* un mucchio di sassi
+ **There's heaps of time.** C'è un sacco di tempo.

to hear [hɪəʳ] VERB (**heard, heard**)
sentire ◇ *I didn't hear anything.* Non ho sentito niente. ◇ *She can't hear very well.* Non sente molto bene. ◇ *Can you hear me?* Mi senti?
+ **to hear about something** sentir parlare* di qualcosa
+ **to hear from somebody** ricevere notizie da qualcuno

heart [hɑːt] NOUN
il cuore ◇ *heart trouble* disturbi di cuore
+ **the ace of hearts** l'asso di cuori
+ **to learn something by heart** imparare qualcosa a memoria

heart attack ['hɑːtətæk] NOUN
l'infarto
+ **to have a heart attack** avere* un infarto

heartbroken ['hɑːtbrəukən] ADJECTIVE
+ **to be heartbroken** avere* il cuore infranto

heart failure ['hɑːtfeɪljəʳ] NOUN
l'arresto cardiaco

heat [hiːt] NOUN
see also **heat** VERB

il calore ◇ *the heat of the sun* il calore del sole
+ **Take the pan off the heat.** Togli la pentola dal fuoco.

to heat [hiːt] VERB
see also **heat** NOUN

scaldare ◇ *Heat gently for five minutes.* Scaldare a fuoco lento per cinque minuti.

to heat up [hiːt'ʌp] VERB
riscaldare

heater ['hiːtəʳ] NOUN
[1] la stufa ◇ *I had the heater on and the window open.* Avevo la stufa accesa e la finestra aperta.
+ **an electric heater** una stufa elettrica
+ **a water heater** uno scaldaacqua
[2] il riscaldamento (*in car*) ◇ *Could you put on the heater?* Puoi accendere* il riscaldamento?

heather ['hɛðəʳ] NOUN
l'erica

heating ['hiːtɪŋ] NOUN
il riscaldamento

heaven ['hɛvn] NOUN
il paradiso

heavily ['hɛvɪlɪ] ADVERB
[1] molto ◇ *It rained heavily in the night.* Ha piovuto molto durante la notte. ◇ *He drinks heavily.* Beve molto.
[2] pesantemente ◇ *She sat down heavily on the sofa.* Si è seduta pesantemente sul divano.
+ **He's a heavily built man.** È un uomo di corporatura robusta.

heavy ['hɛvɪ] ADJECTIVE
[1] pesante ◇ *This bag's very heavy.* 🖙

H

Questa borsa è molto pesante.

[2] **forte** ◇ *heavy rain* forte pioggia

◆ **to be a heavy drinker** essere* [E] un forte bevitore

he'd [hiːd] = **he would, he had**

hedge [hedʒ] NOUN
la siepe

hedgehog ['hedʒhɒg] NOUN
il riccio

heel [hiːl] NOUN

[1] il tacco (PL i tacchi) ◇ *high heels* tacchi alti

[2] il tallone (*part of foot*)

height [haɪt] NOUN
l' altezza

heir [ɛəʳ] NOUN
l' erede MASC

heiress ['ɛərɛs] NOUN
l' erede FEM

held [held] VERB *see* **hold**

helicopter ['helɪkɒptəʳ] NOUN
l' elicottero

hell [hel] NOUN
l' inferno ◇ *He'll go to hell.* Andrà all'inferno.

◆ **Hell!** Porca miseria!

◆ **It's a hell of a mess!** È un casino!

he'll [hiːl] = **he will, he shall**

hello [hə'ləʊ] EXCLAMATION

[1] ciao (*to somebody you address as "tu"*)

[2] salve (*also to somebody you address as "lei"*)

***hello** non si usa mai per congedarsi.*

[3] pronto (*on the phone*)

helmet ['helmɪt] NOUN
il casco (PL i caschi)

to **help** [help] VERB
see also **help** NOUN
aiutare ◇ *Can you help me?* Mi puoi aiutare? ◇ *I'll help you carry it.* Ti aiuto a portarlo.

◆ **Help yourself!** Serviti pure!

◆ **I couldn't help laughing.** Non ho potuto fare* a meno di ridere*.

help [help] NOUN
see also **help** VERB
l' aiuto

helpful ['helpful] ADJECTIVE

[1] disponibile ◇ *The staff are always friendly and helpful.* Il personale è sempre amichevole e disponibile.

[2] utile ◇ *He gave me some helpful advice.* Mi ha dato dei consigli utili.

hen [hen] NOUN
la gallina

her [həʳ] ADJECTIVE
see also **her** PRONOUN

[1] il suo MASC (PL i suoi) ◇ *her address* il suo indirizzo ◇ *her parents* i suoi genitori

[2] la sua FEM (PL le sue) ◇ *her house* la sua casa ◇ *Ann and her two best friends* Ann e

le sue due migliori amiche

[3] suo MASC (PL suoi) ◇ *Sarah and her father* Sarah e suo padre

[4] sua FEM (PL sue) ◇ *her aunt* sua zia

her *is often not translated.*

◇ *She's lost her wallet.* Ha perduto il portafoglio. ◇ *with her hands in her pockets* con le mani in tasca ◇ *She took off her coat.* Si è tolta il cappotto. ◇ *She washed her hair this morning.* Si è lavata i capelli stamattina.

her [həʳ] PRONOUN
see also **her** ADJECTIVE

[1] la ◇ *I saw her.* L'ho vista. ◇ *Look at her!* Guardala!

[2] le (*to her*) ◇ *I gave her a book.* Le ho dato un libro.

[3] lei

lei *is used after a preposition.*

◇ *I'm going with her.* Vado con lei. ◇ *I'm older than her.* Sono più vecchio di lei.

herb [hɜːb] NOUN
l' erba aromatica (PL le erbe aromatiche) (*for cooking*)

here [hɪəʳ] ADVERB
qui ◇ *I live here.* Vivo qui.

◆ **here is** ecco ◇ *Here he is!* Eccolo qui!

◆ **here are** ecco ◇ *Here are the books.* Ecco i libri.

heritage ['herɪtɪdʒ] NOUN

◆ **cultural heritage** il patrimonio culturale

hero ['hɪərəʊ] NOUN (PL **heroes**)
l' eroe MASC

heroin ['herəʊɪn] NOUN
l' eroina (*drug*)

◆ **heroin addict** l' eroinomane MASC / FEM

heroine ['herəʊɪn] NOUN
l' eroina (*of novel*)

hers [hɜːz] PRONOUN

The Italian pronoun agrees with the noun it is replacing.

[1] il suo MASC (PL i suoi) ◇ *my dog and hers* il mio cane e il suo ◇ *my parents and hers* i miei genitori e i suoi

[2] la sua FEM (PL le sue) ◇ *My car is older than hers.* La mia macchina è più vecchia della sua. ◇ *my friends and hers* le mie amiche e le sue

[3] suo MASC (PL suoi) (*her property*) ◇ *Whose is this? – It's hers.* Di chi è questo? – È suo.

[4] sua FEM (PL sue) (*her property*) ◇ *Is that car hers?* È sua quella macchina?

◆ **a friend of hers** una sua amica

herself [hə'self] PRONOUN

[1] si

*A verb + **herself** is often translated by a reflexive verb in Italian.*

◇ *She's hurt herself.* Si è fatta male. ◇ *She looked at herself in the mirror.* Si è guardata allo specchio.

[2] lei (*emphatic use*) ◇ *She did it herself.* L'ha fatto lei.

---

* Verbs followed by this symbol are irregular. See pp.339–364 for further details.

[3] sé (following preposition) ◊ She talked mainly about herself. Parlava principalmente di sé.
+ **by herself** da sola ◊ She doesn't like travelling by herself. Non le piace viaggiare da sola.

he's [hi:z] = **he is, he has**

to **hesitate** ['hezɪteɪt] VERB
esitare

heterosexual ['hetərəu'seksjuəl] ADJECTIVE
eterosessuale

hi [haɪ] EXCLAMATION
[1] ciao (to somebody you address as "tu")
[2] salve (also to somebody you address as "lei")

hi non si usa mai per congedarsi.

hiccup ['hɪkʌp] NOUN
il problemino ◊ The project is on course, despite one or two hiccups. Il programma è in atto nonostante uno o due problemini.
+ **to have hiccups** avere* il singhiozzo

to **hide** [haɪd] VERB (**hid, hidden**)
[1] nascondere* ◊ Paula hid the present. Paula ha nascosto il regalo.
[2] nascondersi E ◊ He hid behind a bush. Si è nascosto dietro ad un cespuglio.

hide-and-seek ['haɪdən'si:k] NOUN
+ **to play hide-and-seek** giocare a nascondino

hideous ['hɪdɪəs] ADJECTIVE
orribile

hi-fi ['haɪfaɪ] NOUN
l' hi-fi MASC (PL gli hi-fi)

high [haɪ] ADJECTIVE, ADVERB
[1] alto ◊ The wall's two metres high. Il muro è alto due metri. ◊ Prices are higher in Germany. I prezzi sono più alti in Germania. ◊ The plane flew high over the mountains. L'aereo volava alto sulle montagne.
+ **to be high in something** avere* un alto contenuto di qualcosa ◊ It's very high in fat. Ha un altissimo contenuto di grassi.
[2] forte ◊ There's high unemployment in Europe. C'è una forte disoccupazione in Europa.
[3] acuto ◊ She's got a very high voice. Ha una voce molto acuta.
+ **to be high** (on drugs) essere* E fatto
+ **the high season** l'alta stagione
+ **the high street** la via principale

high-heeled [haɪ'hi:ld] ADJECTIVE
con i tacchi alti

high jump ['haɪdʒʌmp] NOUN
il salto in alto

highlight ['haɪlaɪt] NOUN
see also **highlight** VERB
[1] il clou (PL i clou) ◊ the highlight of the evening il clou della serata
[2] il momento più bello ◊ the highlight of the holiday il momento più bello della vacanza

to **highlight** ['haɪlaɪt] VERB

see also **highlight** NOUN
mettere* in evidenza

highlighter ['haɪlaɪtə'] NOUN
l' evidenziatore MASC

high-rise ['haɪraɪz] ADJECTIVE
+ **a high-rise building** un palazzone

high school ['haɪsku:l] NOUN
la scuola secondaria

> ❶ In Gran Bretagna i ragazzi frequentano la **high school** tra gli 11 e i 18 anni, negli Stati Uniti tra i 14 e i 18 anni. È obbligatoria fino ai 16 anni.

to **hijack** ['haɪdʒæk] VERB
dirottare

hijacker ['haɪdʒækə'] NOUN
il dirottatore
la dirottatrice

hike [haɪk] NOUN
l' escursione a piedi FEM

hiking ['haɪkɪŋ] NOUN
+ **to go hiking** fare* escursioni a piedi

hilarious [hɪ'leərɪəs] ADJECTIVE
spassosissimo

hill [hɪl] NOUN
la collina

hill-walking ['hɪlwɔ:kɪŋ] NOUN
+ **to go hill-walking** fare* passeggiate in collina

him [hɪm] PRONOUN
[1] lo ◊ I saw him. L'ho visto. ◊ Look at him! Guardalo!
[2] gli (to him) ◊ I gave him a book. Gli ho dato un libro.
[3] lui

lui is used after a preposition.
◊ I'm going with him. Vado con lui. ◊ I'm older than him. Sono più vecchio di lui.

himself [hɪm'self] PRONOUN
[1] si

A verb + himself is often translated by a reflexive verb in Italian.
◊ He's hurt himself. Si è fatto male. ◊ He was looking at himself in the mirror. Si guardava allo specchio.
[2] lui (emphatic use) ◊ He did it himself. L'ha fatto lui.
[3] sé (following preposition) ◊ He talked mainly about himself. Parlava principalmente di sé.
+ **by himself** da solo ◊ He doesn't like travelling by himself. Non gli piace viaggiare da solo.

Hindu ['hɪndu:] ADJECTIVE
indù MASC, FEM, PL

hint [hɪnt] NOUN
see also **hint** VERB
+ **to give a hint** dare* almeno un'indicazione ◊ Give me a hint. Dammi almeno un'indicazione.

H

- **to drop a hint** lasciar capire ◇ *He dropped a hint that he'd like to see her more often.* Le ha lasciato capire che voleva vederla più spesso.
- **to take a hint** capire l'antifona ◇ *I told him I was a bit tired, but he didn't take the hint.* Gli ho detto che ero un po' stanca, ma non ha capito l'antifona.
- **a hint of garlic** una puntina d'aglio

to **hint** [hɪnt] VERB

> see also **hint** NOUN

lasciar capire ◇ *He hinted that I had a good chance of getting the job.* Ha lasciato capire che avevo buone probabilità di ottenere* il lavoro.

hip [hɪp] NOUN

il fianco (PL i fianchi) ◇ *She put her hands on her hips.* Si è messa le mani sui fianchi.

hippie ['hɪpɪ] NOUN

1 l' hippy MASC (PL gli hippy)
2 la hippy (PL le hippy)

hippo ['hɪpəu] NOUN

l' ippopotamo

to **hire** ['haɪə'] VERB

> see also **hire** NOUN

1 noleggiare ◇ *We hired a car.* Abbiamo noleggiato una macchina.
2 assumere* ◇ *They hired a lawyer.* Hanno assunto un avvocato.

hire ['haɪə'] NOUN

> see also **hire** VERB

il noleggio

- **car hire** noleggio dell'auto
- **for hire** a noleggio
- **a hire car** un'auto a noleggio

his [hɪz] ADJECTIVE

> see also **his** PRONOUN

1 il suo MASC (PL i suoi) ◇ *his address* il suo indirizzo ◇ *his parents* i suoi genitori
2 la sua FEM (PL le sue) ◇ *his house* la sua casa ◇ *his opinions* le sue opinioni
3 suo MASC (PL suoi) ◇ *Joe and his father* Joe e suo padre
4 sua FEM (PL sue) ◇ *his aunt* sua zia
his is often not translated.
◇ *He took off his coat.* Si è tolto il cappotto.
◇ *He's washing his hair.* Si sta lavando i capelli.

his [hɪz] PRONOUN

> see also **his** ADJECTIVE

The Italian pronoun agrees with the noun it is replacing.

1 il suo MASC (PL i suoi) ◇ *my dog and his* il mio cane e il suo ◇ *my parents and his* i miei genitori e i suoi
2 la sua FEM (PL le sue) ◇ *My car is older than his.* La mia macchina è più vecchia della sua. ◇ *my shoes and his* le mie scarpe e le sue
3 suo MASC (PL suoi) (*his property*)
◇ *Whose is this? – It's his.* Di chi è questo? – È suo.

4 sua FEM (PL sue) (*his property*) ◇ *Is that car his?* È sua quella macchina?

- **a friend of his** un suo amico

history ['hɪstərɪ] NOUN

la storia

to **hit** [hɪt] VERB (**hit, hit**)

> see also **hit** NOUN

1 colpire ◇ *He hit the ball.* Ha colpito la palla.

- **to hit the target** colpire il bersaglio
2 picchiare ◇ *Andrew hit him.* Andrew l'ha picchiato.
3 urtare ◇ *He was hit by a car.* È stato urtato da una macchina.

- **to hit it off with somebody** andare* E d'accordo con qualcuno

hit [hɪt] NOUN

> see also **hit** VERB

il successo ◇ *the band's latest hit* l'ultimo successo del complesso

hitch [hɪtʃ] NOUN

l' intoppo ◇ *There's been a slight hitch.* C'è stato un piccolo intoppo.

to **hitchhike** ['hɪtʃhaɪk] VERB

fare* autostop

hitchhiker ['hɪtʃhaɪkə'] NOUN

l' autostoppista MASC / FEM

hitchhiking ['hɪtʃhaɪkɪŋ] NOUN

l' autostop MASC

hit man ['hɪtmæn] NOUN (PL **hit men**)

il sicario

HIV-negative [eɪtʃaɪviːˈnɛɡətɪv] ADJECTIVE

sieronegativo

HIV-positive [eɪtʃaɪviːˈpɒzɪtɪv] ADJECTIVE

sieropositivo

hobby ['hɒbɪ] NOUN (PL **hobbies**)

l' hobby (PL gli hobby)

hockey ['hɒkɪ] NOUN

l' hockey MASC

to **hold** [həuld] VERB (**held, held**)

1 tenere* ◇ *He was holding her in his arms.* La teneva tra le braccia.
2 tenere* in braccio ◇ *She was holding the baby.* Teneva in braccio il bambino.
◇ *He held the pistol in his right hand.* Teneva la pistola con la mano destra.
3 contenere* ◇ *It holds ten litres.* Contiene dieci litri.

- **Hold the line!** (*on the phone*) Resti in linea!
- **Hold it!** Fermati!
- **to get hold of something** procurarsi E qualcosa

to **hold on** [həuldˈɒn] VERB

aspettare ◇ *Hold on, I'm coming!* Aspettami, arrivo!

- **Hold on!** (*on the phone*) Resti in linea!

to **hold on to** [həuldˈɒntu] VERB

1 tenersi E stretto a ◇ *Hold on to the rail.* Tieniti stretto alla ringhiera.
2 conservare ◇ *He managed to hold on to his job.* È riuscito a conservare il posto di

* Verbs followed by this symbol are irregular. See pp.339–364 for further details.

lavoro.

to **hold up** [həuld'ʌp] VERB
  1 alzare ◇ *Peter held up his hand.* Peter ha alzato la mano.
  2 trattenere* ◇ *I was held up at the office.* Sono stato trattenuto in ufficio.
  3 rapinare (*bank*)

hold-up ['həuldʌp] NOUN
  1 la rapina ◇ *A bank clerk was injured in the hold-up.* Un impiegato di banca è rimasto ferito nella rapina.
  2 l'intoppo ◇ *No one explained the reason for the hold-up.* Nessuno ha spiegato i motivi dell'intoppo.
  3 l'ingorgo (PL gli ingorghi) ◇ *a hold-up on the motorway* un ingorgo sull'autostrada

hole [həul] NOUN
  il buco (PL i buchi)

holiday ['hɒlɪdeɪ] NOUN
  1 la vacanza ◇ *the school holidays* le vacanze scolastiche
  • **on holiday** in vacanza
  2 la festa ◇ *Next Monday is a holiday.* Lunedì prossimo è festa.
  3 le ferie (*time off work*) ◇ *He took a day's holiday.* Ha preso un giorno di ferie.

holiday rep ['hɒlɪdeɪrep] NOUN
  il/la rappresentante dell'agenzia di viaggio

Holland ['hɒlənd] NOUN
  l'Olanda

hollow ['hɒləu] ADJECTIVE
  cavo

holly ['hɒlɪ] NOUN
  l'agrifoglio

holy ['həulɪ] ADJECTIVE
  santo

home [həum] NOUN, ADVERB
  la casa ◇ *at home* a casa ◇ *I'll be home at five o'clock.* Sarò a casa alle cinque.
  • **Make yourself at home.** Fai come se fossi a casa tua.
  • **to get home** arrivare a casa
  • **a children's home** un istituto per l'infanzia

home address [həumə'drɛs] NOUN
  l'indirizzo di casa

homeland ['həumlænd] NOUN
  la patria

homeless ['həumlɪs] ADJECTIVE, NOUN
  il senzatetto
  • **the homeless** i senzatetto

home match ['həummætʃ] NOUN
  la partita in casa

Home Office ['həumɒfɪs] NOUN
  il ministero degli Interni

homeopathy [həumɪ'ɒpəθɪ] NOUN
  l'omeopatia

home page ['həumpeɪdʒ] NOUN
  l'home page (PL le home page)

Home Secretary [həum'sɛkrətərɪ] NOUN
  il ministro degli Interni

homesick ['həumsɪk] ADJECTIVE

  • **to be homesick** avere* nostalgia di casa

homework ['həumwɜːk] NOUN
  i compiti MASC PL ◇ *Have you done your homework?* Hai fatto i compiti?

homosexual [hɒməu'sɛksjuəl] ADJECTIVE
  omosessuale

honest ['ɒnɪst] ADJECTIVE
  onesto ◇ *an honest man* un uomo onesto
  • **To be honest...** Onestamente...
  • **Tell me your honest opinion.** Dimmi cosa ne pensi sinceramente.

honestly ['ɒnɪstlɪ] ADVERB
  onestamente ◇ *Did you honestly think we wouldn't notice?* Pensavi onestamente che non l'avremmo notato?

honesty ['ɒnɪstɪ] NOUN
  l'onestà

honey ['hʌnɪ] NOUN
  il miele ◇ *a pot of honey* un vaso di miele
  • **Hi honey, I'm here!** Ciao cara, sono qui!

honeymoon ['hʌnɪmuːn] NOUN
  il viaggio di nozze

honour ['ɒnəʳ] NOUN (US **honor**)
  l'onore MASC ◇ *I would consider it an honour.* Sarebbe un onore per me.

honours degree ['ɒnəzdɪgriː] NOUN
  la laurea
  • **to get an honours degree** laurearsi E

> ❶ *All'università è possibile scegliere tra due corsi di laurea, l'***honours degree***, più impegnativo, e l'"ordinary degree".*

hood [hud] NOUN
  1 il cappuccio ◇ *a coat with a hood* un cappotto con il cappuccio
  2 il cofano (*of car*) US

hook [huk] NOUN
  1 il gancio ◇ *He hung the painting on the hook.* Ha appeso il quadro al gancio.
  2 l'amo ◇ *He felt a fish pull at his hook.* Ha sentito che un pesce abboccava all'amo.
  • **to take the phone off the hook** staccare il ricevitore

hooligan ['huːlɪgən] NOUN
  il teppista

hooray [huː'reɪ] EXCLAMATION
  urrà!

Hoover® ['huːvəʳ] NOUN
  l'aspirapolvere (PL gli aspirapolvere)

to **hoover** ['huːvəʳ] VERB
  passare l'aspirapolvere

to **hop** [hɒp] VERB
  1 saltellare (*animal*)
  2 saltellare su un piede (*person*)

to **hope** [həup] VERB
  see also **hope** NOUN
  sperare ◇ *I hope he comes.* Spero che venga. ◇ *I hope so.* Spero di sì. ◇ *I hope not.* Spero di no.

hope [həup] NOUN

see also **hope** VERB
la speranza

♦ **to give up hope** abbandonare le speranze

hopeful ['həupful] ADJECTIVE

1. ottimista ◇ *I'm hopeful.* Sono ottimista.

♦ **He's hopeful of winning.** Conta di vincere*.

2. incoraggiante ◇ *The prospects look hopeful.* Le prospettive sembrano incoraggianti.

hopefully ['həupfulı] ADVERB

♦ **Hopefully he'll make it in time.** Si spera che arrivi in tempo.

hopeless ['həuplıs] ADJECTIVE

1. impossibile ◇ *It is a hopeless task.* È un compito impossibile.

2. inutile ◇ *It's hopeless to try and change her mind.* È inutile cercare di farle cambiare idea.

♦ **Many young people feel hopeless about job prospects.** Molti giovani sentono di non avere* prospettive di lavoro.

♦ **to be hopeless at something** essere* E completamente negato per qualcosa

♦ **a hopeless case** un caso disperato

horizon [hə'raızn] NOUN
l' orizzonte MASC

horizontal [hɒrı'zɒntl] ADJECTIVE
orizzontale

horn [hɔːn] NOUN

1. il clacson (PL i clacson) ◇ *He sounded the horn.* Ha suonato il clacson.

2. il corno (*of animal*)

horoscope ['hɒrəskəup] NOUN
l' oroscopo

horrible ['hɒrıbl] ADJECTIVE
orribile

to **horrify** ['hɒrıfaı] VERB
lasciare inorridito ◇ *I was horrified by the news.* La notizia mi ha lasciato inorridito.

horrifying ['hɒrıfaııŋ] ADJECTIVE
spaventoso

horror ['hɒrə'] NOUN

1. l' orrore MASC ◇ *To my horror I discovered I was locked out.* Ho scoperto con orrore di essere* rimasto chiuso fuori.

2. il terrore ◇ *She has a horror of spiders.* Ha il terrore dei ragni.

♦ **a horror film** un film dell'orrore

horse [hɔːs] NOUN
il cavallo

horse-racing ['hɔːsreısıŋ] NOUN
l' ippica

horseshoe ['hɔːsʃuː] NOUN
il ferro di cavallo

hose [həuz] NOUN
il tubo di gomma

hosepipe ['həuzpaıp] NOUN
il tubo di gomma

hospital ['hɒspıtl] NOUN
l' ospedale MASC

hospitality [hɒspı'tælıtı] NOUN

l' ospitalità

host [həust] NOUN

1. l' ospite MASC ◇ *We thanked our hosts.* Abbiamo ringraziato i nostri ospiti.

2. il mucchio ◇ *a host of problems* un mucchio di problemi

hostage ['hɒstıdʒ] NOUN
l' ostaggio

♦ **to take somebody hostage** prendere* qualcuno in ostaggio

hostel ['hɒstl] NOUN
l' ostello ◇ *youth hostel* ostello della gioventù

hostess ['həustıs] NOUN

1. l' ospite FEM ◇ *We thanked our hostess.* Abbiamo ringraziato la nostra ospite.

2. l' hostess (PL le hostess) (*on plane*)

hostile ['hɒstaıl] ADJECTIVE
ostile

hot [hɒt] ADJECTIVE

1. caldo ◇ *a hot bath* un bagno caldo ◇ *I'm hot.* Ho caldo. ◇ *It's hot today.* Fa caldo oggi.

2. piccante ◇ *Indian food's too hot for me.* Il cibo indiano è troppo piccante per me.

hot dog ['hɒtdɒg] NOUN
l' hot-dog (PL gli hot-dog)

hotel [həu'tel] NOUN
l' albergo (PL gli alberghi)

hour ['auə'] NOUN
l' ora ◇ *a quarter of an hour* un quarto d'ora ◇ *two and a half hours* due ore e mezza ◇ *half an hour* mezz'ora

♦ **They work long hours.** Hanno una giornata lavorativa molto lunga.

hourly ['auəlı] ADJECTIVE, ADVERB

♦ **There are hourly buses.** Ci sono autobus ogni ora.

♦ **to be paid hourly** essere* E pagato all'ora

house [haus] NOUN
la casa ◇ *at his house* a casa sua

House of Commons [hausəv'kɒmənz] NOUN
la Camera dei Comuni

House of Lords [hausəv'lɔːdz] NOUN
la Camera dei Lord

ⓘ *In Gran Bretagna il Parlamento è composto da due camere, la "House of Commons", i cui membri sono eletti dal popolo, e la* **House of Lords**, *cui si accede tramite nomina o carica ereditaria.*

---

housewife ['hauswaıf] NOUN (PL **housewives**)
la casalinga (PL le casalinghe)

housework ['hauswɜːk] NOUN
i lavori di casa MASC PL

hovercraft ['hɒvəkrɑːft] NOUN
l' hovercraft (PL gli hovercraft)

how [hau] ADVERB

come ◇ *How are you?* Come stai? ◇ *How do you say "apple" in Italian?* Come si traduce "apple" in italiano?

+ **How many?** Quanti?
+ **How much?** Quanto?
+ **How old are you?** Quanti anni hai?
+ **How far is it to Edinburgh?** Quanto dista Edimburgo?
+ **How long have you been here?** Da quanto tempo sei qui?
+ **How long does it take?** Quanto tempo ci vuole?

however [hau'ɛvə'] CONJUNCTION
tuttavia

to **howl** [haul] VERB
1 ululare ◇ *The dog howled all night.* Il cane ha ululato tutta la notte.
2 urlare ◇ *He howled with pain.* Urlava dal dolore.

HTML [eitʃti:ɛm'el] NOUN
l' HTML

to **Hug** [hʌg] VERB
see also **hug** NOUN
abbracciare

hug [hʌg] NOUN
see also **hug** VERB
+ **to give somebody a hug** abbracciare qualcuno

huge [hju:dʒ] ADJECTIVE
enorme

to **hum** [hʌm] VERB
canticchiare

human ['hju:mən] ADJECTIVE
umano
+ **a human being** un essere* umano

humble ['hʌmbl] ADJECTIVE
umile

humour ['hju:mə'] NOUN (US **humor**)
l' umorismo
+ **to have a sense of humour** avere* il senso dell'umorismo

hundred ['hʌndrəd] NUMERAL
+ **a hundred** cento
*When **hundred** follows any number except one, "-cento" is added to the number.*
◇ *three hundred boys and five hundred girls* trecento ragazzi e cinquecento ragazze
+ **hundreds of people** centinaia di persone

hung [hʌŋ] VERB *see* **hang**

Hungary ['hʌŋgəri] NOUN
l'Ungheria

hunger ['hʌŋgə'] NOUN
la fame

hungry ['hʌŋgri] ADJECTIVE
+ **to be hungry** avere* fame ◇ *I'm not hungry.* Non ho fame.

to **hunt** [hʌnt] VERB
1 dare* la caccia a ◇ *They hunt foxes.* Danno la caccia alle volpi.
+ **to go hunting** andare* E a caccia
2 cercare ◇ *The police are hunting the killer.* La polizia sta cercando il killer.
+ **to hunt for something** cercare qualcosa ◇ *I hunted everywhere for that book.* Ho cercato quel libro dappertutto.

hunting ['hʌntɪŋ] NOUN
la caccia ◇ *fox hunting* caccia alla volpe

hurdle ['hə:dl] NOUN
l' ostacolo
+ **the 100 metres hurdles** i 100 metri ad ostacoli

hurricane ['hʌrɪkən] NOUN
l' uragano

to **hurry** ['hʌrɪ] VERB
see also **hurry** NOUN
affrettarsi E ◇ *Sharon hurried back home.* Sharon si affrettò a tornare a casa.
+ **Hurry up!** Sbrigati!

hurry ['hʌrɪ] NOUN
see also **hurry** VERB
la fretta ◇ *There's no hurry.* Non c'è fretta.
+ **to be in a hurry** avere* fretta
+ **to do something in a hurry** fare* qualcosa in fretta

to **hurt** [hə:t] VERB (**hurt, hurt**)
see also **hurt** ADJECTIVE
1 fare* male ◇ *That hurts.* Fa male.
+ **to hurt somebody** fare* male a qualcuno ◇ *You're hurting me!* Mi fai male! ◇ *Have you hurt yourself?* Ti sei fatto male? ◇ *My leg hurts.* Mi fa male la gamba.
2 ferire ◇ *His criticisms really hurt me.* Le sue critiche mi hanno proprio ferito.

hurt [hə:t] ADJECTIVE
see also **hurt** VERB
ferito ◇ *Is he badly hurt?* È ferito gravemente?
+ **to get hurt** farsi E male ◇ *Luckily, nobody got hurt.* Fortunatamente nessuno si è fatto male.

husband ['hʌzbənd] NOUN
il marito

hut [hʌt] NOUN
la capanna

hymn [hɪm] NOUN
l' inno

hypermarket ['haɪpəmɑ:kɪt] NOUN
l' ipermercato

hypertext ['haɪpətekst] NOUN
l' ipertesto

hyphen ['haɪfn] NOUN
il trattino

H

I

I [aɪ] PRONOUN
io ◇ *Ann and I* Ann ed io
I is often not translated.
◇ *I love cats.* Amo i gatti.

ice [aɪs] NOUN
il ghiaccio ◇ *a sheet of ice* una lastra di ghiaccio

iceberg ['aɪsbə:g] NOUN
l' iceberg MASC (PL gli iceberg)

icebox ['aɪsbɔks] NOUN (PL **iceboxes**) US
il frigorifero

ice cream [aɪs'kri:m] NOUN
il gelato ◇ *a vanilla ice cream* un gelato alla vaniglia

ice cube ['aɪskju:b] NOUN
il cubetto di ghiaccio

ice hockey ['aɪshɔki] NOUN
l' hockey su ghiaccio MASC

Iceland ['aɪslənd] NOUN
l' Islanda

ice lolly [aɪs'lɔli] NOUN (PL **ice lollies**)
il ghiacciolo

ice rink ['aɪsrɪŋk] NOUN
la pista di pattinaggio su ghiaccio

ice-skating ['aɪsskeɪtɪŋ] NOUN
il pattinaggio su ghiaccio
+ **to go ice-skating** andare* E a pattinare sul ghiaccio

icing ['aɪsɪŋ] NOUN
la glassa (*on cake*)
+ **icing sugar** zucchero a velo

icon ['aɪkɔn] NOUN
l' icona

icy ['aɪsɪ] ADJECTIVE
1 gelido ◇ *an icy wind* un vento gelido
2 ghiacciato ◇ *The roads are icy.* Le strade sono ghiacciate.

I'd [aɪd] = **I had, I would**

idea [aɪ'dɪə] NOUN
l' idea

ideal [aɪ'dɪəl] ADJECTIVE
ideale

identical [aɪ'dentɪkl] ADJECTIVE
identico

identification [aɪdentɪfɪ'keɪʃən] NOUN
1 il documento d'identità ◇ *Have you got any identification?* Ha un documento d'identità?
2 l' individuazione FEM ◇ *the identification of genes* l'individuazione dei geni
3 l' identificazione FEM ◇ *the identification of bodies* l'identificazione dei corpi

to **identify** [aɪ'dentɪfaɪ] VERB (**identified, identified**)
1 individuare ◇ *We managed to identify the problem.* Siamo riusciti ad individuare il problema.
2 identificare ◇ *The police have identified the body.* La polizia ha identificato il corpo.

identity [aɪ'dentɪtɪ] NOUN
l' identità

identity card [aɪ'dentɪtɪkɑːd] NOUN
la carta d'identità

ⓘ *All Italians have an identity card.*

idiom ['ɪdɪəm] NOUN
l' espressione idiomatica FEM

idiot ['ɪdɪət] NOUN
l' idiota MASC / FEM

idiotic [ɪdɪ'ɔtɪk] ADJECTIVE
idiota

idle ['aɪdl] ADJECTIVE
+ **It's just idle gossip.** Sono solo chiacchiere futili.
+ **I asked out of idle curiosity.** L'ho chiesto per pura curiosità.
+ **to be idle** (*person*) non avere* niente da fare*

i.e. [aɪ'iː] ABBREVIAZIONE (= *id est*)
cioè

if [ɪf] CONJUNCTION
se ◇ *You can have it if you like.* Puoi prenderlo se vuoi. ◇ *If I were you...* Se fossi in te...
+ **if only** se solo ◇ *If only I had more money!* Se solo avessi più denaro!
+ **if not** altrimenti ◇ *Are you coming? If not, I'll go with Mark.* Vieni? Altrimenti vado con Mark.
+ **if so** allora ◇ *Are you coming? If so, I'll wait.* Vieni? Allora ti aspetto.

ignorant ['ɪgnərənt] ADJECTIVE
ignorante

to **ignore** [ɪg'nɔː'] VERB
ignorare

I'll [aɪl] = **I will**

ill [ɪl] ADJECTIVE
ammalato ◇ *He's seriously ill.* È gravemente ammalato.
+ **to be taken ill** ammalarsi E ◇ *She was taken ill.* Si è ammalata.
+ **ill at ease** a disagio

illegal [ɪ'liːgl] ADJECTIVE
illegale

illegible [ɪ'ledʒɪbl] ADJECTIVE
illeggibile

ill feeling [ɪl'fiːlɪŋ] NOUN
il rancore

illness ['ɪlnɪs] NOUN (PL **illnesses**)
la malattia

illusion [ɪ'luːʒən] NOUN
l' illusione FEM

illustration [ɪlə'streɪʃən] NOUN
l' illustrazione FEM

I'm [aɪm] = **I am**

image ['ɪmɪdʒ] NOUN
l' immagine FEM ◇ *The company has*

---

* Verbs followed by this symbol are irregular. See pp.339–364 for further details.

changed its image. La società ha cambiato immagine.

imagination [ˌɪmædʒɪ'neɪʃən] NOUN
l'immaginazione FEM ◇ *She has no imagination.* Non ha immaginazione.

imagine [ɪ'mædʒɪn] VERB
immaginare

imitate ['ɪmɪteɪt] VERB
imitare

imitation [ˌɪmɪ'teɪʃən] NOUN
l'imitazione FEM
◆ **imitation leather** finta pelle

immediate [ɪ'miːdɪət] ADJECTIVE
immediato

immediately [ɪ'miːdɪətlɪ] ADVERB
immediatamente

immigrant ['ɪmɪɡrənt] NOUN
l'immigrato
l'immigrata

immigration [ˌɪmɪ'ɡreɪʃən] NOUN
l'immigrazione FEM

immoral [ɪ'mɒrl] ADJECTIVE
immorale

impartial [ɪm'pɑːʃl] ADJECTIVE
imparziale

impatience [ɪm'peɪʃəns] NOUN
l'impazienza

impatient [ɪm'peɪʃənt] ADJECTIVE
impaziente ◇ *She was impatient to get back home.* Era impaziente di tornare a casa.
◆ **to get impatient** spazientirsi[E] ◇ *People are getting impatient.* La gente si sta spazientendo.

impatiently [ɪm'peɪʃəntlɪ] ADVERB
con impazienza

impersonal [ɪm'pɜːsənl] ADJECTIVE
impersonale

implement ['ɪmplɪment] VERB
attuare ◇ *It'll take a few months to implement the plan.* Ci vorranno alcuni mesi per attuare il piano.

imply [ɪm'plaɪ] VERB
insinuare ◇ *Are you implying I did it on purpose?* Stai insinuando che l'ho fatto apposta?

importance [ɪm'pɔːtns] NOUN
l'importanza

important [ɪm'pɔːtənt] ADJECTIVE
importante

impose [ɪm'pəuz] VERB
imporre*

impossible [ɪm'pɒsɪbl] ADJECTIVE
impossibile

impress [ɪm'pres] VERB
[1] colpire ◇ *What impressed him most was...* Quello che l'ha colpito di più è stato...
◇ *He really impressed me!* Mi ha veramente colpito!
[2] fare* buona impressione su ◇ *a group of students trying to impress their teacher* un gruppo di studenti che cercavano di fare* buona impressione sull'insegnante

impressed [ɪm'prest] ADJECTIVE
colpito ◇ *I'm impressed!* Sono colpito!
*Be careful not to translate **impressed** by* *impressionato.*

impression [ɪm'preʃən] NOUN
l'impressione FEM ◇ *I was under the impression that...* Avevo l'impressione che...

impressive [ɪm'presɪv] ADJECTIVE
[1] notevole ◇ *an impressive achievement* un risultato notevole
[2] imponente (*building*)

to improve [ɪm'pruːv] VERB
migliorare ◇ *He's improved his technique.* Ha migliorato la tecnica.
*When an auxiliary is needed to form past tenses use "essere" when **migliorare** does not have an object.*
◇ *My Italian improved a lot.* Il mio italiano è migliorato molto.

improvement [ɪm'pruːvmənt] NOUN
il miglioramento

in [ɪn] PREPOSITION, ADVERB
[1] in ◇ *in the house* in casa ◇ *in the country* in campagna ◇ *in town* in città ◇ *in two thousand and two* nel duemila due ◇ *I did it in 3 hours.* L'ho fatto in tre ore. ◇ *in English* in inglese
◆ **in time** in tempo
[2] a ◇ *in school* a scuola ◇ *in hospital* all'ospedale ◇ *in London* a Londra ◇ *It was written in pencil.* Era scritto a matita.
[3] di ◇ *the best pupil in the class* il migliore studente della classe ◇ *at six in the morning* alle sei del mattino ◇ *an increase in road accidents* un aumento degli incidenti stradali
◆ **to be in** (*at home, work*) esserci[E] ◇ *He wasn't in.* Non c'era.
◆ **to ask somebody in** invitare qualcuno ad entrare ◇ *Why don't you ask John in?* Perché non inviti John ad entrare?
◆ **the boy in the blue shirt** il ragazzo con la camicia azzurra
◆ **I'll see you in three weeks.** Ci vediamo tra tre settimane.
◆ **You look good in that dress.** Quel vestito ti sta bene.
◆ **in here** qui dentro
◆ **in the rain** sotto la pioggia
◆ **one person in ten** una persona su dieci
◆ **in writing** per iscritto
◆ **the in thing** la cosa che va di moda

inaccurate [ɪn'ækjurət] ADJECTIVE
inesatto

inadequate [ɪn'ædɪkwət] ADJECTIVE
inadeguato

incentive [ɪn'sentɪv] NOUN
l'incentivo ◇ *There's no incentive to work.* Non c'è alcun incentivo a lavorare.

inch [ɪntʃ] NOUN (PL **inches**) 🖙

Verbs followed by the symbol "E" require the auxiliary "essere"

il pollice

ⓘ *Un* **inch** *corrisponde a circa 2,54 centimetri.*

incident ['ɪnsɪdnt] NOUN
l'incidente MASC ◇ *a minor incident* un piccolo incidente

inclined [ɪn'klaɪnd] ADJECTIVE
• **I'm inclined to agree with you.** Credo di essere* d'accordo con te.
• **Nobody seemed inclined to argue with Steve.** Nessuno sembrava propenso a litigare con Steve.
• **He was inclined to self-pity.** Tendeva ad autocommiserarsi.

to **include** [ɪn'kluːd] VERB
comprendere* ◇ *Service is not included.* Il servizio non è compreso.

including [ɪn'kluːdɪŋ] PREPOSITION
compreso ◇ *It will be two hundred pounds, including tax.* Sono duecento sterline tasse comprese.

inclusive [ɪn'kluːsɪv] ADJECTIVE
tutto compreso ◇ *The inclusive price is two hundred pounds.* Il prezzo tutto compreso è di duecento sterline.
• **inclusive of VAT** IVA compresa

income ['ɪnkʌm] NOUN
il reddito ◇ *low income families* famiglie a basso reddito

income tax ['ɪnkʌmtæks] NOUN
l'imposta sul reddito

incompetent [ɪn'kɔmpɪtnt] ADJECTIVE
incompetente

incomplete [ɪnkəm'pliːt] ADJECTIVE
incompleto

inconsistent [ɪnkən'sɪstnt] ADJECTIVE
incostante ◇ *Your work this year has been very inconsistent.* Il tuo rendimento quest'anno è stato incostante.
• **to be inconsistent with** essere* E in contraddizione con

inconvenience [ɪnkən'viːnjəns] NOUN
il disturbo ◇ *I don't want to cause any inconvenience.* Non vorrei dare* disturbo.

inconvenient [ɪnkən'viːnjənt] ADJECTIVE
• **Is it an inconvenient time for you?** Ti è scomodo a quest'ora?

incorrect [ɪnkə'rɛkt] ADJECTIVE
1 inesatto ◇ *The information he gave me was incorrect.* Le informazioni che mi ha dato erano inesatte.
2 scorretto ◇ *His backache is caused by incorrect posture.* Il suo mal di schiena è causato dalla postura scorretta.

increase ['ɪnkriːs] NOUN
see also **increase** VERB
l'aumento ◇ *an increase in road accidents* un aumento degli incidenti stradali ◇ *a salary increase* un aumento di stipendio

to **increase** [ɪn'kriːs] VERB
see also **increase** NOUN
aumentare ◇ *They've increased the price.* Hanno aumentato il prezzo.
When an auxiliary is needed to form past tenses use "essere" when **aumentare** *does not have an object.*
◇ *The number increased.* Il numero è aumentato.

incredible [ɪn'krɛdɪbl] ADJECTIVE
incredibile

indecisive [ɪndɪ'saɪsɪv] ADJECTIVE
indeciso (*person*)

indeed [ɪn'diːd] ADVERB
1 veramente ◇ *It's very hard indeed.* È veramente molto difficile.
2 certamente ◇ *Know what I mean?* – *Indeed I do.* Sai cosa intendo? – Certamente.
• **Thank you very much indeed!** Grazie infinite!

independence [ɪndɪ'pɛndns] NOUN
l'indipendenza

independent [ɪndɪ'pɛndnt] ADJECTIVE
indipendente ◇ *Two independent studies have been carried out.* Sono stati condotti due studi indipendenti.
• **an independent school** una scuola privata

index ['ɪndɛks] NOUN (PL **indexes**)
l'indice MASC ◇ *Look in the index.* Guarda nell'indice.

index finger ['ɪndɛksfɪŋgə'] NOUN
l'indice MASC

India ['ɪndɪə] NOUN
l'India

Indian ['ɪndɪən] ADJECTIVE
see also **Indian** NOUN
indiano

Indian ['ɪndɪən] NOUN
see also **Indian** ADJECTIVE
l'indiano
l'indiana
• **American Indians** gli indiani d'America

to **indicate** ['ɪndɪkeɪt] VERB
1 indicare ◇ *This indicates a change in US policy.* Questo indica un cambiamento della politica statunitense.
2 mettere* la freccia (*when driving*)

indigestion [ɪndɪ'dʒɛstʃən] NOUN
• **I've got indigestion.** Ho qualcosa sullo stomaco.

individual [ɪndɪ'vɪdjuəl] ADJECTIVE
see also **individual** NOUN
individuale

individual [ɪndɪ'vɪdjuəl] NOUN
see also **individual** ADJECTIVE
l'individuo

indoor ['ɪndɔː'] ADJECTIVE
coperto ◇ *an indoor swimming pool* una piscina coperta

indoors [ɪn'dɔːz] ADVERB
dentro ◇ *They're indoors.* Sono dentro.

* Verbs followed by this symbol are irregular. See pp.339–364 for further details.

English ~ Italian

industrial [ɪn'dʌstrɪəl] ADJECTIVE
industriale

industrial estate [ɪn'dʌstrɪəl'steɪt] NOUN
la zona industriale

industry ['ɪndəstrɪ] NOUN (PL **industries**)
l'industria ◇ *the oil industry* l'industria petrolifera
- **the tourist industry** il turismo

inefficient [ɪnɪ'fɪʃənt] ADJECTIVE
inefficiente

inevitable [ɪn'evɪtəbl] ADJECTIVE
inevitabile

inexpensive [ɪnɪk'spensɪv] ADJECTIVE
poco costoso

inexperienced [ɪnɪk'spɪərɪənst] ADJECTIVE
inesperto

infant school ['ɪnfəntsku:l] NOUN
la scuola elementare

> **ⓘ** *In Gran Bretagna la* **infant school** *è frequentata da bambini dai 5 ai 7 anni di età.*

infection [ɪn'fekʃən] NOUN
l'infezione FEM ◇ *an ear infection* un'infezione all'orecchio
- **a throat infection** un'angina

infectious [ɪn'fekʃəs] ADJECTIVE
infettivo

infinitive [ɪn'fɪnɪtɪv] NOUN
l'infinito

infirmary [ɪn'fɜ:mərɪ] NOUN (PL **infirmaries**)
l'ospedale MASC

inflatable [ɪn'fleɪtəbl] ADJECTIVE
gonfiabile

inflation [ɪn'fleɪʃən] NOUN
l'inflazione FEM

influence ['ɪnfluəns] NOUN
see also **influence** VERB
l'influenza ◇ *He's a bad influence on her.* Ha una cattiva influenza su di lei.

o **influence** ['ɪnfluəns] VERB
see also **influence** NOUN
influenzare

influenza [ɪnflu'enzə] NOUN
l'influenza

o **inform** [ɪn'fɔ:m] VERB
informare ◇ *Nobody informed me of the change of plan.* Nessuno mi ha informato del cambiamento di piani.

informal [ɪn'fɔ:ml] ADJECTIVE
- **informal language** linguaggio colloquiale
- **an informal visit** una visita non ufficiale
- **an informal party** una festa tra amici
- **"informal dress"** "non è richiesto l'abito da sera"

information [ɪnfə'meɪʃən] NOUN
l'informazione FEM ◇ *Where did you get this information?* Dove hai avuto questa informazione? ◇ *Could you give me some information about...* Potrebbe darmi qualche informazione su...

> *informazione* is often used in the plural.
> ◇ *For further information contact the number below.* Per ulteriori informazioni contattate il numero sottostante.
- **a piece of information** un'informazione

information office [ɪnfə'meɪʃənɔfɪs] NOUN
l'ufficio informazioni (PL gli uffici informazioni)

infuriating [ɪn'fjʊərɪeɪtɪŋ] ADJECTIVE
estremamente irritante

ingenious [ɪn'dʒi:njəs] ADJECTIVE
ingegnoso

ingredient [ɪn'gri:dɪənt] NOUN
l'ingrediente MASC

inhabitant [ɪn'hæbɪtnt] NOUN
l'abitante MASC/FEM

to **inherit** [ɪn'herɪt] VERB
ereditare

initials [ɪ'nɪʃlz] NOUN PL
le iniziali

initiative [ɪ'nɪʃətɪv] NOUN
l'iniziativa

to **inject** [ɪn'dʒekt] VERB
iniettare
- **to inject with** fare* un'iniezione di ◇ *They injected me with antibiotics.* Mi hanno fatto un'iniezione di antibiotici.
- **to inject oneself** farsi E un'iniezione ◇ *He needs to inject himself twice a day.* Deve farsi un'iniezione due volte al giorno.

injection [ɪn'dʒekʃən] NOUN
l'iniezione FEM ◇ *The doctor gave me an injection.* Il dottore mi ha fatto un'iniezione.

to **injure** ['ɪndʒə'] VERB
ferire

injured ['ɪndʒəd] ADJECTIVE
ferito

injury ['ɪndʒərɪ] NOUN (PL **injuries**)
la ferita ◇ *a serious injury* una ferita grave

injury time ['ɪndʒərɪtaɪm] NOUN
i minuti di recupero MASC PL

injustice [ɪn'dʒʌstɪs] NOUN
l'ingiustizia

ink [ɪŋk] NOUN
l'inchiostro

in-laws ['ɪnlɔ:z] NOUN PL
[1] la famiglia del marito (*husband's family*)
[2] la famiglia della moglie (*wife's family*)

inn [ɪn] NOUN
la locanda

inner ['ɪnə'] ADJECTIVE
[1] interno ◇ *an inner office* un ufficio interno
[2] profondo ◇ *her inner sense of security* il suo profondo senso di sicurezza
- **the inner city** i quartieri in degrado del centro

inner tube ['ɪnətju:b] NOUN
la camera d'aria

innocent ['ɪnəsnt] ADJECTIVE
innocente

Verbs followed by the symbol "E" require the auxiliary "essere"

inquest ['ɪnkwɛst] NOUN
l' inchiesta ufficiale

to **inquire** [ɪn'kwaɪəʳ] VERB
domandare ◇ *"Is something wrong?" he inquired.* "C'è qualcosa che non va?", domandò.
◆ **to inquire about something** informarsi ᴱ su qualcosa

inquiries office [ɪn'kwaɪərɪz'ɔfɪs] NOUN
l' ufficio informazioni (PL gli uffici informazioni)

inquiry [ɪn'kwaɪərɪ] NOUN (PL **inquiries**)
l' inchiesta ◇ *There will be an inquiry into the accident.* Ci sarà un'inchiesta sull'incidente.
◆ **to make inquiries** chiedere* informazioni

inquisitive [ɪn'kwɪzɪtɪv] ADJECTIVE
curioso

insane [ɪn'seɪn] ADJECTIVE
pazzo

inscription [ɪn'skrɪpʃən] NOUN
l' iscrizione FEM (*on stone, plaque*)

insect ['ɪnsɛkt] NOUN
l' insetto

insect repellent ['ɪnsɛktrɪpɛlənt] NOUN
l' insettifugo (PL gli insettifughi)

insensitive [ɪn'sɛnsɪtɪv] ADJECTIVE
insensibile

to **insert** [ɪn'sɜːt] VERB
inserire

inside ['ɪn'saɪd] NOUN
see also **inside** ADVERB
l' interno

inside ['ɪn'saɪd] ADVERB, PREPOSITION
see also **inside** NOUN
dentro ◇ *Come inside!* Vieni dentro!
◆ **inside the house** in casa
◆ **inside out** alla rovescia ◇ *He put his jumper on inside out.* Si è messo il maglione alla rovescia.

inside lane [ɪnsaɪd'leɪn] NOUN
la corsia di marcia

insincere [ɪnsɪn'sɪəʳ] ADJECTIVE
falso

to **insist** [ɪn'sɪst] VERB
1 insistere* ◇ *I didn't want to, but he insisted.* Non volevo, ma ha insistito.
◆ **to insist on doing something** insistere* per fare* qualcosa ◇ *She insisted on paying.* Ha insistito per pagare.
2 sostenere* ◇ *He insisted that he was innocent.* Sosteneva di essere* innocente.

inspector [ɪn'spɛktəʳ] NOUN
l' ispettore
l' ispettrice
◆ **the ticket inspector** il controllore

to **install** [ɪn'stɔːl] VERB
installare

instalment [ɪn'stɔːlmənt] NOUN (US **installment**)
la puntata (*of serial*)

◆ **to pay in instalments** pagare a rate

instance ['ɪnstəns] NOUN
il caso ◇ *in many instances* in molti casi
◆ **for instance** per esempio

instant ['ɪnstənt] ADJECTIVE
see also **instant** NOUN
immediato ◇ *It was an instant success.* È stato un successo immediato.
◆ **instant coffee** caffè solubile

instant ['ɪnstənt] NOUN
see also **instant** ADJECTIVE
l' istante MASC

instantly ['ɪnstəntlɪ] ADVERB
immediatamente

instead [ɪn'stɛd] PREPOSITION, ADVERB
◆ **instead of** invece di ◇ *We played tennis instead of going swimming.* Abbiamo giocato a tennis invece di andare* a nuotare.
◆ **He went instead of Peter.** È andato al posto di Peter.
◆ **The pool was closed, so we played tennis instead.** La piscina era chiusa e così abbiamo giocato a tennis.

instinct ['ɪnstɪŋkt] NOUN
l' istinto

institute ['ɪnstɪtjuːt] NOUN
l' istituto

institution [ɪnstɪ'tjuːʃən] NOUN
l' istituzione FEM

to **instruct** [ɪn'strʌkt] VERB
◆ **to instruct somebody to do something** ordinare a qualcuno di fare* qualcosa ◇ *She instructed us to wait outside.* Ci ha ordinato di aspettare fuori.

instructions [ɪn'strʌkʃənz] NOUN PL
le istruzioni

instructor [ɪn'strʌktəʳ] NOUN
l' istruttore
l' istruttrice
◇ *my driving instructor* il mio istruttore di guida
◆ **a skiing instructor** un maestro di sci

instrument ['ɪnstrumənt] NOUN
lo strumento ◇ *Do you play an instrument?* Suoni qualche strumento?

insufficient [ɪnsə'fɪʃənt] ADJECTIVE
insufficiente

insulin ['ɪnsjulɪn] NOUN
l' insulina

insult ['ɪnsʌlt] NOUN
see also **insult** VERB
l' insulto

to **insult** [ɪn'sʌlt] VERB
see also **insult** NOUN
insultare

insurance [ɪn'ʃuərəns] NOUN
l' assicurazione FEM ◇ *his car insurance* la sua assicurazione della macchina
◆ **an insurance policy** una polizza di assicurazione

intelligent [ɪn'tɛlɪdʒənt] ADJECTIVE

* Verbs followed by this symbol are irregular. See pp.339–364 for further details.

intelligente

intend [ɪn'tɛnd] VERB
- **to intend to do something** avere* intenzione di fare* qualcosa ◇ *I intend to do languages at university.* Ho intenzione di fare* lingue all'università.

intense [ɪn'tɛns] ADJECTIVE
  1. intenso ◇ *intense heat* calore intenso
  2. vivo ◇ *intense interest* vivo interesse

intensive [ɪn'tɛnsɪv] ADJECTIVE
intensivo

intention [ɪn'tɛnʃən] NOUN
l' intenzione FEM

intercom ['ɪntəkɔm] NOUN
l' interfono

interest ['ɪntrɪst] NOUN
see also **interest** VERB
l' interesse MASC ◇ *She has a wide range of interests.* Ha moltissimi interessi. ◇ *5% interest* un interesse del 5%
- **to lose interest** perdere* l'interesse
- **to have no interest in** non interessarsi^E di

interest ['ɪntrɪst] VERB
see also **interest** NOUN
interessare
- **to be interested in something** interessarsi^E di qualcosa ◇ *I'm not interested in politics.* Non mi interesso di politica.

interest-free ['ɪntrɪst'friː] ADJECTIVE
senza interessi

interesting ['ɪntrɪstɪŋ] ADJECTIVE
interessante

interest rate ['ɪntrɪstreɪt] NOUN
il tasso di interesse

interior [ɪn'tɪərɪə] NOUN
l' interno

interior designer [ɪn'tɪərɪədɪ'zaɪnə] NOUN
l' arredatore
l' arredatrice

intermediate [ɪntə'miːdɪət] ADJECTIVE
intermedio

internal [ɪn'təːnl] ADJECTIVE
interno

international [ɪntə'næʃənl] ADJECTIVE
internazionale

Internet ['ɪntənɛt] NOUN
Internet MASC ◇ *on the Internet* su Internet

Internet café ['ɪntənɛt'kæfeɪ] NOUN
il cybercaffè (PL i cybercaffè)

Internet user ['ɪntənɛt'juːzə] NOUN
l' utente Internet MASC / FEM

interpret [ɪn'təːprɪt] VERB
  1. tradurre* (for speaker)
  2. interpretare (law, theory)

interpreter [ɪn'təːprɪtə] NOUN
l' interprete MASC / FEM

interrupt [ɪntə'rʌpt] VERB
interrompere*

interruption [ɪntə'rʌpʃən] NOUN
l' interruzione FEM

interval ['ɪntəvl] NOUN
l' intervallo

interview ['ɪntəvjuː] NOUN
see also **interview** VERB
  1. l' intervista (on TV, radio)
  2. il colloquio (for job)

interview ['ɪntəvjuː] VERB
see also **interview** NOUN
intervistare ◇ *I seized the chance to interview one of the actors.* Ho colto l'opportunità per intervistare uno degli attori.
- **to be interviewed for a job** avere* un colloquio di lavoro

interviewer ['ɪntəvjuə] NOUN
l' intervistatore
l' intervistatrice

intimate ['ɪntɪmət] ADJECTIVE
intimo

into ['ɪntu] PREPOSITION
in ◇ *I'm going into town.* Vado in città.
◇ *Translate it into Italian.* Traducilo in italiano. ◇ *He got into the car.* È salito in macchina.
- **He walked into a lampost.** Ha battuto contro un lampione.

intranet ['ɪntrənɛt] NOUN
- **the intranet** Intranet MASC

introduce [ɪntrə'djuːs] VERB
  1. presentare ◇ *He introduced me to his parents.* Mi ha presentato ai suoi genitori.
  2. introdurre* ◇ *A new system is to be introduced.* Verrà introdotto un nuovo sistema.

introduction [ɪntrə'dʌkʃən] NOUN
  1. l' introduzione FEM ◇ *the introduction of the new system* l'introduzione del nuovo sistema
  2. la presentazione ◇ *a letter of introduction* una lettera di presentazione

intruder [ɪn'truːdə] NOUN
l' intruso
l' intrusa

intuition [ɪntjuː'ɪʃn] NOUN
l' intuito

invade [ɪn'veɪd] VERB
invadere*

invalid ['ɪnvəlɪd] NOUN
see also **invalid** ADJECTIVE
l' invalido
l' invalida

invalid [ɪn'vælɪd] ADJECTIVE
see also **invalid** NOUN
non valido

invent [ɪn'vɛnt] VERB
inventare

invention [ɪn'vɛnʃən] NOUN
l' invenzione FEM

inventor [ɪn'vɛntə] NOUN
l' inventore
l' inventrice

investigation [ɪnvɛstɪ'ɡeɪʃən] NOUN ☞

Verbs followed by the symbol "E" require the auxiliary "essere"

l' indagine FEM

investment [ɪn'vɛstmənt] NOUN
l' investimento

invigilator [ɪn'vɪdʒɪleɪtə'] NOUN
l' adetto alla sorveglianza in sede d'esame

❶ Si chiamano **invigilators** gli addetti alla sorveglianza dei candidati durante gli esami.

invisible [ɪn'vɪzɪbl] ADJECTIVE
invisibile

invitation [ɪnvɪ'teɪʃən] NOUN
l' invito

to **invite** [ɪn'vaɪt] VERB
invitare ◊ You're invited to a party at Claire's house. Sei invitato ad una festa a casa di Claire.

to **involve** [ɪn'vɒlv] VERB
1 comportare ◊ It involves a lot of work. Comporta un sacco di lavoro.
2 coinvolgere* ◊ We won't involve him. Non lo coinvolgeremo.
◆ **to be involved in something** essere* E coinvolto in qualcosa ◊ I don't want to be involved in the argument. Non voglio essere* coinvolto nella discussione.
◆ **She was involved in politics.** Si occupava di politica.
◆ **to be involved with somebody** avere* una relazione con qualcuno ◊ She was involved with a married man. Aveva una relazione con un uomo sposato.

IQ [aɪ'kju:] NOUN (= intelligence quotient)
il QI (= quoziente d'intelligenza)

Iran [ɪ'rɑ:n] NOUN
l' Iran MASC

Iraq [ɪ'rɑ:k] NOUN
l' Iraq MASC

Iraqi [ɪ'rɑ:kɪ] ADJECTIVE
see also **Iraqi** NOUN
iracheno

Iraqi [ɪ'rɑ:kɪ] NOUN
see also **Iraqi** ADJECTIVE
l' iracheno
l' irachena

Ireland [ˈaɪələnd] NOUN
l' Irlanda

Irish [ˈaɪrɪʃ] ADJECTIVE
see also **Irish** NOUN
irlandese

Irish [ˈaɪrɪʃ] NOUN
see also **Irish** ADJECTIVE
l' irlandese MASC (language)
◆ **the Irish** gli irlandesi

Irishman [ˈaɪrɪʃmən] NOUN (PL **Irishmen**)
◆ **an Irishman** un irlandese

Irishwoman [ˈaɪrɪʃwʊmən] NOUN (PL **Irishwomen**)
◆ **an Irishwoman** un'irlandese

iron [ˈaɪən] NOUN
see also **iron** VERB

1 il ferro ◊ an iron gate un cancello di ferro
2 il ferro da stiro (for clothes)

to **iron** [ˈaɪən] VERB
see also **iron** NOUN
stirare

ironic [aɪ'rɒnɪk] ADJECTIVE
ironico ◊ an ironic remark un commento ironico

ironing [ˈaɪənɪŋ] NOUN
◆ **to do the ironing** stirare
◆ **I hate ironing.** Odio stirare.
◆ **ironing board** tavola da stiro

ironing board [ˈaɪənɪŋbɔːd] NOUN
la tavola da stiro

ironmonger's [ˈaɪənmʌŋgəz] NOUN
la ferramenta

irrelevant [ɪ'rɛləvənt] ADJECTIVE
1 non pertinente ◊ He either ignored the questions or gave irrelevant answers. O ignorava le domande o dava risposte non pertinenti.
◆ **That's irrelevant.** Non c'entra.
2 non importante ◊ If he has the qualifications, his age is irrelevant. Se ha le qualifiche la sua età non è importante.

irresponsible [ɪrɪ'spɒnsɪbl] ADJECTIVE
irresponsabile

irritating [ˈɪrɪteɪtɪŋ] ADJECTIVE
irritante

is [ɪz] VERB see **be**

Islam [ˈɪzlɑ:m] NOUN
l' Islam MASC

Islamic [ɪz'læmɪk] ADJECTIVE
islamico ◊ Islamic countries paesi islamici

island [ˈaɪlənd] NOUN
l' isola

isle [aɪl] NOUN
◆ **the Isle of Man** l'isola di Man
◆ **the Isle of Wight** l'isola di Wight

isn't [ˈɪznt] = **is not**

isolated [ˈaɪsəleɪtɪd] ADJECTIVE
isolato

ISP [aɪɛs'pi:] NOUN (= Internet Service Provider)
il provider (PL i provider)

Israel [ˈɪzreɪl] NOUN
l' Israele MASC

Israeli [ɪz'reɪlɪ] ADJECTIVE
see also **Israeli** NOUN
israeliano

Israeli [ɪz'reɪlɪ] NOUN
see also **Israeli** ADJECTIVE
l' israeliano
l' israeliana

issue [ˈɪʃjuː] NOUN
see also **issue** VERB
1 la questione ◊ a controversial issue una questione controversa
◆ **to make an issue of something** fare* un problema di qualcosa
2 il numero (of magazine) ◊ the March

---

* Verbs followed by this symbol are irregular. See pp.339–364 for further details.

issue il numero di marzo

to **issue** ['ɪʃjuː] VERB
> see also **issue** NOUN

rilasciare ◇ *The minister issued a statement yesterday.* Ieri il ministro ha rilasciato una dichiarazione.

♦ **Staff will be issued with new uniforms.** Al personale verranno consegnate nuove uniformi.

it [ɪt] PRONOUN
When the subject of the sentence, it is not translated.
◇ *Where's my book? – It's on the table.* Dov'è il mio libro? – È sul tavolo. ◇ *It's raining.* Piove. ◇ *It's Friday tomorrow.* Domani è venerdì. ◇ *Who is it? – It's me.* Chi è? – Sono io.
Use a plural verb when telling the time.
◇ *It's six o'clock.* Sono le sei.
When the object of the sentence, it is translated by lo or la, depending on whether the noun referred to is masculine or feminine.
◇ *It's a good film. Did you see it?* È un bel film. Lo hai visto? ◇ *There's a croissant left. Do you want it?* C'è ancora una brioche. La vuoi?
ne is the translation for of it and is used when the Italian verb takes di.
◇ *I'm sure of it.* Ne sono sicuro. ◇ *They don't know anything about it.* Non ne sanno nulla. ◇ *Have you told him about the party? – Yes I told him about it yesterday.* Gli hai detto della festa? – Sì, gliel'ho detto ieri. ◇ *I doubt it.* Ne dubito.

Italian [ɪ'tæljən] ADJECTIVE
> see also **Italian** NOUN

italiano

Italian [ɪ'tæljən] NOUN
> see also **Italian** ADJECTIVE

1 l' italiano
l' italiana
(*person*)

♦ **the Italians** gli italiani

2 l' italiano (*language*) ◇ *Can you speak*

Italian? Parli italiano? ◇ *our Italian teacher* il nostro insegnante di italiano

italics [ɪ'tælɪks] NOUN PL
il corsivo SING ◇ *in italics* in corsivo

Italy ['ɪtəlɪ] NOUN
l' Italia ◇ *Do you like Italy?* Ti piace l'Italia?

to **itch** [ɪtʃ] VERB
prudere

itchy ['ɪtʃɪ] ADJECTIVE
♦ **My arm is itchy.** Ho prurito al braccio.

it'd ['ɪtd] = **it had, it would**

item ['aɪtəm] NOUN
1 l' articolo ◇ *a collector's item* un articolo da collezione
2 l' oggetto ◇ *The first item he bought was an alarm clock.* Il primo oggetto che ha comprato è stato una sveglia.
3 la voce ◇ *He checked the items on his bill.* Ha controllato le voci del conto.
4 il punto ◇ *The next item on the agenda is...* Il prossimo punto all'ordine del giorno è...

♦ **an item of news** una notizia

itinerary [aɪ'tɪnərərɪ] NOUN (PL **itineraries**)
l' itinerario

it'll ['ɪtl] = **it will**

its [ɪts] ADJECTIVE
il suo ◇ *The party has concluded its annual conference.* Il partito ha concluso la sua conferenza annuale.
its is often not translated.
◇ *The dog is losing its hair.* Il cane sta perdendo il pelo.

it's [ɪts] = **it is, it has**

itself [ɪt'sɛlf] PRONOUN
1 si ◇ *The dog has hurt itself.* Il cane si è fatto male. ◇ *The heating switches itself off.* Il riscaldamento si spegne da solo.
2 stesso ◇ *life itself* la vita stessa

♦ **by itself** da solo
♦ **in itself** di per sé ◇ *It's not a problem in itself.* Non è un problema di per sé.

I've [aɪv] = **I have**

I

J

jab [dʒæb] NOUN
see also **jab** VERB
la puntura

to **jab** [dʒæb] VERB
see also **jab** NOUN
conficcare ◊ *She jabbed the needle into my arm.* Mi ha conficcato l'ago nel braccio.

jack [dʒæk] NOUN
1 il cric (PL i cric) ◊ *The jack's in the boot.* Il cric è nel cofano.
2 il fante (*in cards*)

jacket ['dʒækɪt] NOUN
la giacca (PL le giacche) ◊ *a wool jacket* una giacca di lana
♦ **jacket potatoes** patate cotte in forno

> ❶ Le **jacket potatoes** sono patate cotte al forno, intere e con la buccia.

jackpot ['dʒækpɒt] NOUN
il primo premio ◊ *He won the jackpot.* Ha vinto il primo premio.
♦ **to hit the jackpot** fare* centro

jail [dʒeɪl] NOUN
see also **jail** VERB
la prigione
♦ **to go to jail** andare*E in prigione

to **jail** [dʒeɪl] VERB
see also **jail** NOUN
mandare in prigione

jam [dʒæm] NOUN
see also **jam** VERB
la marmellata ◊ *strawberry jam* marmellata di fragole
♦ **a traffic jam** un ingorgo

to **jam** [dʒæm] VERB
see also **jam** NOUN
bloccare ◊ *Demonstrators jammed the city centre.* I manifestanti hanno bloccato il centro.
♦ **Twenty people jammed into the tiny office.** Venti persone erano ammassate nel piccolo ufficio.

jam jar ['dʒæmdʒɑːʳ] NOUN
il vasetto da marmellata

jammed [dʒæmd] ADJECTIVE
bloccato ◊ *The window's jammed.* La finestra è bloccata.

jam-packed [dʒæm'pækt] ADJECTIVE
pieno zeppo ◊ *The hall was jam-packed.* La sala era piena zeppa.

janitor ['dʒænɪtəʳ] NOUN
il custode

January ['dʒænjuərɪ] NOUN
gennaio ◊ *in January* in gennaio

Japan [dʒə'pæn] NOUN
il Giappone

Japanese [dʒæpə'niːz] ADJECTIVE (PL **Japanese**)
see also **Japanese** NOUN
giapponese

Japanese [dʒæpə'niːz] NOUN
see also **Japanese** ADJECTIVE
il giapponese (*language*)
♦ **the Japanese** i giapponesi

jar [dʒɑːʳ] NOUN
il vasetto ◊ *a jar of honey* un vasetto di miele

jaundice ['dʒɔːndɪs] NOUN
l' itterizia

javelin ['dʒævlɪn] NOUN
il giavellotto

jaw [dʒɔː] NOUN
la mascella

jazz [dʒæz] NOUN
il jazz

jealous ['dʒeləs] ADJECTIVE
geloso

jeans [dʒiːnz] NOUN PL
i jeans

to **jeer** [dʒɪəʳ] VERB
fischiare

Jehovah's Witness [dʒɪ'həuvəz'wɪtnɪs] NOUN (PL **Jehovah's Witnesses**)
il/la testimone di Geova

Jell-o ® ['dʒeləu] NOUN US
la gelatina

jelly ['dʒelɪ] NOUN (PL **jellies**)
1 la gelatina ◊ *fruit jelly* gelatina di frutta
2 la marmellata (*jam*) US

jellyfish ['dʒelɪfɪʃ] NOUN (PL **jellyfish**)
la medusa

jersey ['dʒɜːzɪ] NOUN
la maglia (*jumper*)

Jesus ['dʒiːzəs] NOUN
Gesù

jet [dʒet] NOUN
il jet (PL i jet)

jet lag ['dʒetlæg] NOUN
♦ **to be suffering from jet lag** essere*E scombussolato per il cambiamento di fuso orario

jetty ['dʒetɪ] NOUN (PL **jetties**)
l' imbarcadero

Jew [dʒuː] NOUN
l' ebreo
l' ebrea
♦ **the Jews** gli ebrei

jewel ['dʒuːəl] NOUN
il gioiello

jeweller ['dʒuːələʳ] NOUN (US **jeweler**)
il gioielliere

jeweller's shop ['dʒuːələzʃɒp] NOUN (US **jeweler's shop**)
la gioielleria

jewellery ['dʒuːəlrɪ] NOUN (US **jewelry**)
i gioielli MASC PL

Jewish ['dʒuːɪʃ] ADJECTIVE

---

* Verbs followed by this symbol are irregular. See pp.339–364 for further details.

1 ebreo ◊ *He's Jewish.* È ebreo.

2 ebraico ◊ *a Jewish festival* una festività ebraica

jigsaw ['dʒɪgsɔ:] NOUN
il puzzle (PL i puzzle)

job [dʒɔb] NOUN
1 il lavoro ◊ *a part-time job* un lavoro part-time ◊ *You've done a good job!* Hai fatto un ottimo lavoro!
2 il compito ◊ *It's not my job to make the tea.* Fare il tè non è compito mio.

job centre ['dʒɔbsɛntə'] NOUN
l' ufficio di collocamento

jobless ['dʒɔblɪs] ADJECTIVE
disoccupato

jockey ['dʒɔkɪ] NOUN
il fantino

to **jog** [dʒɔg] VERB
fare* jogging

jogging ['dʒɔgɪŋ] NOUN
il jogging
♦ **to go jogging** andare* E a fare* jogging

john [dʒɔn] NOUN US
il gabinetto

to **join** [dʒɔɪn] VERB
1 iscriversi* E a ◊ *I'm going to join the ski club.* Ho intenzione di iscrivermi ad uno sci club.
2 raggiungere* ◊ *I'll join you later.* Ti raggiungo più tardi.
♦ **Hi Tony, come and join us!** Ciao Tony, siediti qui con noi!
♦ **Do you mind if I join you?** Posso venire* con voi?
♦ **Will you join me for a coffee?** Vieni a bere* un caffè?
3 collegare ◊ *The car parks are joined by a footpath.* I parcheggi sono collegati da un sentiero.

to **join in** [dʒɔɪn'ɪn] VERB
partecipare

joiner ['dʒɔɪnə'] NOUN
il falegname

joint [dʒɔɪnt] NOUN
1 l' articolazione FEM ◊ *I've got pains in my joints.* Mi fanno male le articolazioni.
♦ **a joint of pork** un pezzo di maiale da arrosto
2 lo spinello (*drugs*)

joke [dʒəuk] NOUN
see also **joke** VERB
1 lo scherzo ◊ *Don't get upset, it was only a joke.* Non prendertela, era solo uno scherzo.
2 la barzelletta
♦ **to tell a joke** raccontare una barzelletta

to **joke** [dʒəuk] VERB
see also **joke** NOUN
scherzare ◊ *You must be joking!* Stai scherzando!

jolly ['dʒɔlɪ] ADJECTIVE, ADVERB
1 allegro (*person*)

♦ **a jolly party** una bella festa
2 molto ◊ *You were jolly unlucky.* Sei stato molto sfortunato.

Jordan ['dʒɔ:dən] NOUN
la Giordania

to **jot down** [dʒɔt'daun] VERB
annotare (*address, phone number*)

jotter ['dʒɔtə'] NOUN
il blocchetto per appunti

journalism ['dʒə:nəlɪzəm] NOUN
il giornalismo

journalist ['dʒə:nəlɪst] NOUN
il/la giornalista MASC / FEM

journey ['dʒə:nɪ] NOUN
il viaggio ◊ *a five-hour journey* un viaggio di cinque ore
♦ **My journey to school takes about half an hour.** Ci vuole una mezz'ora per andare* a scuola.
♦ **to go on a journey** fare* un viaggio

joy [dʒɔɪ] NOUN
la gioia

joystick ['dʒɔɪstɪk] NOUN
il joystick (PL i joystick)

judge [dʒʌdʒ] NOUN
see also **judge** VERB
il giudice MASC

to **judge** [dʒʌdʒ] VERB
see also **judge** NOUN
giudicare

judo ['dʒu:dəu] NOUN
il judo

jug [dʒʌg] NOUN
la brocca (PL le brocche)

juggler ['dʒʌglə'] NOUN
il giocoliere

juice [dʒu:s] NOUN
il succo (PL i succhi) ◊ *orange juice* succo d'arancia

July [dʒu:'laɪ] NOUN
luglio ◊ *in July* in luglio

jumble ['dʒʌmbl] NOUN
il miscuglio ◊ *a meaningless jumble of words* un miscuglio di parole senza senso

jumble sale ['dʒʌmblseɪl] NOUN
la vendita di beneficenza di roba usata

to **jump** [dʒʌmp] VERB
saltare ◊ *They jumped over the wall.* Hanno saltato oltre il muro.
♦ **You made me jump!** Mi hai spaventato!

jumper ['dʒʌmpə'] NOUN
il maglione

junction ['dʒʌŋkʃən] NOUN
l' incrocio (*of roads*)

June [dʒu:n] NOUN
giugno ◊ *in June* in giugno

jungle ['dʒʌŋgl] NOUN
la giungla

junior ['dʒu:nɪə'] ADJECTIVE, NOUN
♦ **a junior minister** un sottosegretario
♦ **He's three years my junior.** Ha tre anni ☞

J

meno di me.

junior school ['dʒuːnɪəskuːl] NOUN
la <u>scuola elementare</u>

junk [dʒʌŋk] NOUN
la <u>robaccia</u> ◇ *The attic's full of junk.* La soffitta è piena di robaccia.
+ **to eat junk food** mangiare porcherie
+ **a junk shop** un rigattiere

junk mail ['dʒʌŋkmeɪl] NOUN
la <u>posta spazzatura</u>

jury ['dʒuərɪ] NOUN (PL **juries**)
la <u>giuria</u>

just [dʒʌst] ADVERB
1 <u>proprio</u> ◇ *I did it just now.* L'ho fatto proprio adesso.
+ **just now** in questo momento ◇ *I'm rather busy just now.* In questo momento sono molto occupato.
2 <u>appena</u> ◇ *just in time* appena in tempo ◇ *He's just arrived.* È appena arrivato. ◇ *We had just enough money.* Il denaro ci è bastato appena.
3 <u>solo</u> ◇ *I just thought that...* Pensavo solo che...
+ **Just a minute!** Aspetta un attimo!
+ **just about** quasi
+ **just after Christmas** poco dopo Natale
+ **I'm just coming!** Arrivo subito!

justice ['dʒʌstɪs] NOUN
la <u>giustizia</u>

to **justify** ['dʒʌstɪfaɪ] VERB (**justified, justified**)
<u>giustificare</u>

K

kangaroo [kæŋgə'ru:] NOUN
il canguro

karaoke [kærə'əʊkɪ] NOUN
il karaoke

karate [kə'rɑːtɪ] NOUN
il karate

kebab [kə'bæb] NOUN
lo spiedino ◇ *a lamb kebab* uno spiedino di agnello

keen [ki:n] ADJECTIVE
1 entusiasta ◇ *He doesn't seem very keen.* Non sembra molto entusiasta.
2 attento e interessato ◇ *She's a keen student.* È una studentessa attenta e interessata.
• **I'm not very keen on maths.** Non mi piace molto la matematica.
• **He's keen on her.** Lei gli piace molto.
• **to be keen on doing something** avere* una gran voglia di fare* qualcosa

to **keep** [ki:p] VERB (**kept, kept**)
1 tenere* ◇ *You can keep it.* Lo puoi tenere*. ◇ *The noise kept him awake.* Il rumore lo teneva sveglio.
2 stare*[E] ◇ *Keep still!* Stai fermo! ◇ *Keep quiet!* Stai zitto!
3 continuare ◇ *Keep straight on.* Continua dritto.
• **I keep forgetting my keys.** Continuo a dimenticare le chiavi.
• **Keep trying!** Prova ancora!
• **"keep out"** "vietato l'ingresso"
• **"keep off the grass"** "non calpestare l'erba"

to **keep back** [ki:p'bæk] VERB
1 tenere* da parte ◇ *Keep back some of the strawberries to decorate the cake.* Tieni da parte qualche fragola per guarnire la torta.
2 nascondere* ◇ *I'm sure she's keeping something back.* Sono sicuro che sta nascondendo qualcosa.

to **keep on** [ki:p'ɔn] VERB
continuare ◇ *The car keeps on breaking down.* La macchina continua a rompersi.

to **keep up** [ki:p'ʌp] VERB
star[E] dietro a ◇ *Matthew walks so fast I can't keep up.* Matthew cammina così veloce che non riesco a stargli dietro.

keep-fit [ki:p'fit] NOUN
la ginnastica ◇ *I go to keep-fit classes.* Vado ad un corso di ginnastica.

kennel ['kɛnl] NOUN
il canile

kept [kɛpt] VERB *see* **keep**

kerosene ['kɛrəsiːn] NOUN [US]
il cherosene

ketchup ['kɛtʃəp] NOUN
il ketchup

kettle ['kɛtl] NOUN
il bollitore

key [ki:] NOUN
see also **key** ADJECTIVE
1 la chiave ◇ *a bunch of keys* un mazzo di chiavi
2 il tasto *(of computer)*

key [ki:] ADJECTIVE
see also **key** NOUN
chiave MASC, FEM, PL ◇ *Yes, this is a key point.* Sì, è un punto chiave.

keyboard ['ki:bɔːd] NOUN
la tastiera

key ring ['ki:rɪŋ] NOUN
il portachiavi (PL i portachiavi)

kick [kɪk] NOUN
see also **kick** VERB
il calcio

to **kick** [kɪk] VERB
see also **kick** NOUN
• **to kick somebody** dare* un calcio a qualcuno ◇ *He kicked me.* Mi ha dato un calcio. ◇ *He kicked the ball hard.* Ha dato un forte calcio alla palla.
• **to kick off** dare* il calcio d'inizio *(in football)*

kick-off ['kɪkɔf] NOUN
• **The kick-off is at 10 o'clock.** La partita inizia alle dieci.

kid [kɪd] NOUN
see also **kid** VERB
1 il bambino
la bambina
◇ *One of the kids was crying.* Uno dei bambini stava piangendo.
2 il figlio
la figlia
◇ *They've got three kids.* Hanno tre figli.
• **a gang of kids on motorbikes** una banda di ragazzi in motorino

to **kid** [kɪd] VERB
see also **kid** NOUN
scherzare

to **kidnap** ['kɪdnæp] VERB
rapire

kidney ['kɪdnɪ] NOUN
1 il rene ◇ *He's got kidney trouble.* Ha disturbi ai reni.
2 il rognone ◇ *I don't like kidneys.* Non mi piace il rognone.

to **kill** [kɪl] VERB
uccidere* ◇ *She killed her husband.* Ha ucciso suo marito. ◇ *Sixteen people were killed in the accident.* Nell'incidente sono rimaste uccise sedici persone.
• **He was killed in a car accident.** È morto in un incidente stradale.
• **Luckily, nobody was killed.** Fortunatamente non ci sono state vittime.
• **to kill oneself** uccidersi[E] ◇ *He killed himself.* Si è ucciso.

Verbs followed by the symbol "E" require the auxiliary "essere"

killer ['kɪlə'] NOUN
1 l' assassino
l' assassina
◇ *The police are searching for the killer.* La polizia sta cercando l'assassino.
♦ **Meningitis can be a killer.** Si può morire* di meningite.
2 il/la killer (PL i/le killer) (*hitman*)

kilo ['ki:ləu] NOUN (PL **kilos**)
il chilo ◇ *£5 a kilo* cinque sterline al chilo

kilometre ['kɪləmi:tə'] NOUN (US **kilometer**)
il chilometro

kilt [kɪlt] NOUN
il kilt (PL i kilt)

kind [kaɪnd] ADJECTIVE
see also **kind** NOUN
gentile
♦ **to be kind to somebody** essere* E gentile con qualcuno
♦ **Thank you for being so kind.** Grazie mille.

kind [kaɪnd] NOUN
see also **kind** ADJECTIVE
la specie ◇ *It's a kind of sausage.* È una specie di salsiccia.

kindergarten ['kɪndəgɑːtn] NOUN
l' asilo

kindly ['kaɪndlɪ] ADVERB
gentilmente ◇ *They kindly offered to lend me some money.* Si sono offerti gentilmente di prestarmi il denaro.
♦ **"Don't worry," she said kindly.** "Non preoccuparti," disse con dolcezza.
♦ **Kindly refrain from smoking.** Si prega di non fumare.

kindness ['kaɪndnɪs] NOUN
la gentilezza

king [kɪŋ] NOUN
il re (PL i re)

kingdom ['kɪŋdəm] NOUN
il regno

kiosk ['ki:ɒsk] NOUN
il chiosco (PL i chioschi) (*small shop*)
♦ **a telephone kiosk** una cabina telefonica

kipper ['kɪpə'] NOUN
l' aringa affumicata (PL le aringhe affumicate)

kiss [kɪs] NOUN (PL **kisses**)
see also **kiss** VERB
il bacio

to **kiss** [kɪs] VERB
see also **kiss** NOUN
1 baciare ◇ *He kissed her passionately.* L'ha baciata appassionatamente.
2 baciarsi E ◇ *They kissed.* Si sono baciati.

kit [kɪt] NOUN
1 la roba ◇ *I've forgotten my gym kit.* Ho dimenticato la roba da ginnastica.
2 il kit (PL i kit) ◇ *a tool kit* un kit di attrezzi ◇ *a sewing kit* un kit da cucito
♦ **a first aid kit** una cassetta del pronto soccorso

♦ **a puncture repair kit** l'attrezzatura per riparare la gomma
♦ **a drum kit** una batteria

kitchen ['kɪtʃɪn] NOUN
la cucina ◇ *a fitted kitchen* una cucina componibile ◇ *the kitchen units* gli elementi della cucina ◇ *a kitchen knife* un coltello da cucina

kite [kaɪt] NOUN
l' aquilone MASC

kitten ['kɪtn] NOUN
il gattino

knee [ni:] NOUN
il ginocchio (PL le ginocchia) ◇ *I've hurt my knee.* Mi sono fatto male al ginocchio.
♦ **to be on one's knees** essere* E in ginocchio

to **kneel** [ni:l] VERB (**knelt** or **kneeled, knelt** or **kneeled**)
inginocchiarsi E

knew [nju:] VERB *see* **know**

knickers ['nɪkəz] NOUN PL
gli slip
♦ **a pair of knickers** un paio di slip

knife [naɪf] NOUN (PL **knives**)
il coltello ◇ *a sharp knife* un coltello affilato

to **knit** [nɪt] VERB
lavorare a maglia

knitting ['nɪtɪŋ] NOUN
♦ **I like knitting.** Mi piace lavorare a maglia.

knives [naɪvz] NOUN PL *see* **knife**

knock [nɒk] NOUN
see also **knock** VERB
il colpo

to **knock** [nɒk] VERB
see also **knock** NOUN
bussare ◇ *Someone's knocking at the door.* Qualcuno sta bussando alla porta.

to **knock down** [nɒk'daun] VERB
investire ◇ *She was knocked down by a car.* È stata investita da una macchina.

to **knock out** [nɒk'aut] VERB
1 eliminare ◇ *They were knocked out early in the tournament.* Sono stati eliminati all'inizio del torneo.
2 stordire ◇ *They knocked out the watchman.* Hanno stordito il guardiano.

knot [nɒt] NOUN
il nodo
♦ **to tie a knot in something** fare* un nodo a qualcosa

to **know** [nəu] VERB (**knew, known**)
Use **sapere** *for knowing facts,* **conoscere** *for knowing people and places.*
1 sapere* ◇ *Yes, I know.* Sì, lo so. ◇ *I don't know.* Non so. ◇ *I don't know any German.* Non so una parola di tedesco. ◇ *He knows a lot about cars.* Sa molte cose sulle macchine. ◇ *How should I know?* Come vuoi che lo sappia? ◇ *You never know!* Non si sa mai! ◇ *I knew it.* Lo sapevo.
♦ **to know that** sapere* che

---

* Verbs followed by this symbol are irregular. See pp.339–364 for further details.

2 conoscere* ◇ *I know her.* La conosco.
◇ *I know London well.* Conosco bene
Londra.
♦ **to get to know somebody** conoscere*
qualcuno
know-all ['nəʊɔːl] NOUN
il sapientone
la sapientona
◇ *He's such a know-all!* È un gran
sapientone!
know-how ['nəʊhaʊ] NOUN
il know-how
knowledge ['nɔlɪdʒ] NOUN

la conoscenza

knowledgeable ['nɔlɪdʒəbl] ADJECTIVE
♦ **to be knowledgeable about something**
essere* E ben informato su qualcosa

known [nəʊn] VERB *see* **know**

Koran [kɔˈrɑːn] NOUN
il Corano

Korea [kəˈrɪə] NOUN
la Corea

kosher ['kəʊʃəʳ] ADJECTIVE
kasher MASC, FEM, PL

K

L

lab [læb] NOUN
il laboratorio ◇ *a lab technician* un tecnico di laboratorio

label ['leɪbl] NOUN
see also **label** VERB
l'etichetta

to **label** ['leɪbl] VERB
see also **label** NOUN
◆ **to be labelled** essere* ᴱ etichettato

labor ['leɪbəʳ] NOUN US
◆ **the labor market** il mercato del lavoro
◆ **to be in labor** avere* le doglie

laboratory [ləˈbɒrətərɪ] NOUN (PL **laboratories**)
il laboratorio

Labour ['leɪbəʳ] NOUN (US **Labor**)
il/la laburista ◇ *the Labour Party* il partito laburista ◇ *My parents vote Labour.* I miei genitori votano per i laburisti.

labour ['leɪbəʳ] NOUN
◆ **the labour market** il mercato del lavoro
◆ **to be in labour** avere* le doglie

labourer ['leɪbərəʳ] NOUN (US **laborer**)
il manovale (*construction worker*)
◆ **a farm labourer** un bracciante agricolo

lace [leɪs] NOUN
1 il laccio ◇ *a pair of laces* un paio di lacci
2 il pizzo ◇ *a lace collar* un colletto di pizzo

lack [læk] NOUN
la mancanza ◇ *He got the job, despite his lack of experience.* Ha ottenuto il lavoro nonostante la mancanza d'esperienza.

lacquer ['lækəʳ] NOUN
la lacca (PL le lacche)

lad [læd] NOUN
il ragazzo

ladder ['lædəʳ] NOUN
la scala a pioli

lady ['leɪdɪ] NOUN (PL **ladies**)
la signora ◇ *Ladies and gentlemen...* Signore e signori...
◆ **What can I do for you, young lady?** Cosa posso fare* per te, cara?
◆ **the ladies** la toilette delle signore

ladybird ['leɪdɪbɜːd] NOUN
la coccinella

ladybug ['leɪdɪbʌg] NOUN US
la coccinella

to **lag behind** [lægbɪˈhaɪnd] VERB
restare indietro

lager ['lɑːgəʳ] NOUN
la birra chiara
◆ **a can of lager** una lattina di birra
◆ **a lager lout** un giovinastro ubriaco

laid [leɪd] VERB *see* **lay**

laid-back [leɪdˈbæk] ADJECTIVE
tranquillo e rilassato ◇ *his laid-back attitude* il suo atteggiamento tranquillo e rilassato

lain [leɪn] VERB *see* **lie**

lake [leɪk] NOUN
il lago (PL i laghi)

lamb [læm] NOUN
l'agnello ◇ *a lamb chop* una cotoletta d'agnello

lame [leɪm] ADJECTIVE
1 zoppo ◇ *She was lame in one leg.* Era zoppa da un piede.
2 zoppicante ◇ *a lame excuse* una scusa zoppicante

lamp [læmp] NOUN
la lampada

lamppost ['læmppəʊst] NOUN
il lampione

land [lænd] NOUN
see also **land** VERB
la terra ◇ *Fewer people work on the land now.* Oggi c'è meno gente che lavora la terra.

to **land** [lænd] VERB
see also **land** NOUN
atterrare ᴱ ◇ *The plane landed at 5 o'clock.* L'aereo è atterrato alle cinque.

landing ['lændɪŋ] NOUN
1 l'atterraggio (*of plane*)
2 il pianerottolo (*of staircase*)
◆ **a landing strip** una pista d'atterraggio

landlady ['lændleɪdɪ] NOUN (PL **landladies**)
la padrona di casa

landlord ['lændlɔːd] NOUN
1 il padrone di casa (*of rented property*)
2 il proprietario (*of pub*)

landmark ['lændmɑːk] NOUN
il punto di riferimento ◇ *Big Ben is a London landmark.* La torre del Big Ben è un punto di riferimento a Londra.

landscape ['lændskeɪp] NOUN
il paesaggio

lane [leɪn] NOUN
1 la stradina ◇ *a country lane* una stradina di campagna
2 la corsia ◇ *the outside lane* la corsia esterna

language ['læŋgwɪdʒ] NOUN
la lingua ◇ *a foreign language* una lingua straniera
◆ **to use bad language** dire* parolacce

language laboratory ['læŋgwɪdʒləˈbɒrətərɪ] NOUN (PL **language laboratories**)
il laboratorio linguistico (PL i laboratori linguistici)

lap [læp] NOUN
il giro ◇ *I ran ten laps.* Ho fatto dieci giri di corsa.
◆ **Andrew was sitting on his mother's lap.** Andrew era seduto in braccio a sua madre.

laptop ['læptɒp] NOUN
il computer portatile (PL i computer portatili)

larder ['lɑːdəʳ] NOUN

---

* Verbs followed by this symbol are irregular. See pp.339–364 for further details.

English ~ Italian

la dispensa

large [lɑːdʒ] ADJECTIVE
- [1] grande ◇ *a large house* una casa grande
- [2] grosso ◇ *a large amount* una grossa cifra
- **a large, cheerful woman** un donnone allegro
- **a large number of people** molte persone

largely [ˈlɑːdʒlɪ] ADVERB
in gran parte

laser [ˈleɪzə] NOUN
il laser (PL i laser)

laser printer [ˈleɪzəprɪntə] NOUN
la stampante laser (PL le stampanti laser)

lass [læs] NOUN (PL **lasses**)
la ragazza

> **ⓘ lass** *è usato specialmente nell'Inghilterra settentrionale e in Scozia.*

last [lɑːst] ADJECTIVE, ADVERB
see also **last** VERB
- [1] scorso ◇ *last Friday* venerdì scorso
- [2] ultimo ◇ *the last time* l'ultima volta
  ◇ *He arrived last.* È arrivato ultimo.
- [3] per l'ultima volta ◇ *I've lost my bag. – When did you see it last?* Ho perso la borsa. – Dove l'hai vista per l'ultima volta?
- **last night (1)** ieri notte ◇ *I couldn't sleep last night.* Ieri notte non sono riuscito a dormire*.
- **last night (2)** ieri sera ◇ *I got home at midnight last night.* Ieri sera sono arrivata a casa a mezzanotte.
- **at last** finalmente

to **last** [lɑːst] VERB
see also **last** ADJECTIVE
durare[E] ◇ *The concert lasts two hours.* Il concerto dura due ore.

lastly [ˈlɑːstlɪ] ADVERB
infine ◇ *Lastly I'd like to mention...* Infine vorrei accennare a...

late [leɪt] ADJECTIVE, ADVERB
- [1] tardi ◇ *Hurry up or you'll be late!* Sbrigati o farai tardi! ◇ *I went to bed late.* Sono andato a letto tardi.
- [2] in ritardo ◇ *I'm often late for school.* Arrivo spesso in ritardo a scuola.
- **to arrive late** arrivare[E] in ritardo
- **in the late afternoon** nel tardo pomeriggio
- **in late May** verso la fine di maggio

lately [ˈleɪtlɪ] ADVERB
ultimamente ◇ *I haven't seen him lately.* Ultimamente non l'ho visto.

later [ˈleɪtə] ADVERB
più tardi ◇ *I'll do it later.* Lo farò più tardi.
- **See you later!** Ci vediamo dopo!

latest [ˈleɪtɪst] ADJECTIVE
ultimo ◇ *their latest album* il loro ultimo album
- **at the latest** al più tardi ◇ *by ten o'clock at the latest* alle dieci al più tardi

Latin [ˈlætɪn] NOUN
il latino ◇ *I do Latin.* Studio latino.

Latin America [ˈlætɪnəˈmɛrɪkə] NOUN
l'America Latina

Latin American [ˈlætɪnəˈmɛrɪkən] ADJECTIVE
sudamericano

latter [ˈlætə] ADJECTIVE, NOUN
l'ultimo
l'ultima
◇ *the latter part of the match* l'ultima parte della partita
- **the former..., the latter...** il primo..., il secondo...

laugh [lɑːf] NOUN
see also **laugh** VERB
la risata ◇ *with a laugh* con una risata
- **It was a good laugh.** È stato molto divertente.

to **laugh** [lɑːf] VERB
see also **laugh** NOUN
ridere*
- **to laugh at somebody** ridere* di qualcuno

to **launch** [lɔːntʃ] VERB
lanciare ◇ *They're about to launch the new model.* Stanno per lanciare il nuovo modello.

launderette® [lɔːnˈdrɛt] NOUN
la lavanderia a gettone

Laundromat® [ˈlɔːndrəmæt] NOUN [US]
la lavanderia a gettone

laundry [ˈlɔːndrɪ] NOUN
il bucato ◇ *She does my laundry.* Mi fa lei il bucato.

lavatory [ˈlævətərɪ] NOUN (PL **lavatories**)
il gabinetto

lavender [ˈlævəndə] NOUN
la lavanda

law [lɔː] NOUN
la legge ◇ *It's against the law.* È contro la legge.
- **law and order** l'ordine pubblico

law court [ˈlɔːkɔːt] NOUN
il tribunale

lawn [lɔːn] NOUN
il prato all'inglese

lawnmower [ˈlɔːnməuə] NOUN
il tagliaerba (PL i tagliaerba)

law school [ˈlɔːskuːl] NOUN [US]
la facoltà di legge (PL le facoltà di legge)

lawyer [ˈlɔːjə] NOUN
l'avvocato

to **lay** [leɪ] VERB (**laid, laid**)
> **lay** *is also the past of* **to lie.**
- [1] mettere* ◇ *She laid the baby in her cot.* Ha messo la bambina nel suo lettino.
- [2] posare ◇ *He laid a sheet of newspaper on the floor.* Ha posato un foglio di giornale sul pavimento.
- **to lay the table** apparecchiare la tavola ◇ *I haven't laid the table yet.* Non ho ancora apparecchiato la tavola.

to **lay off** [leɪˈɒf] VERB
　licenziare ◇ *My father's been laid off.* Mio
　padre è stato licenziato.
　• **Lay off me!** Piantala!

to **lay on** [leɪˈɒn] VERB
　[1] fornire ◇ *They laid on extra buses.*
　Hanno fornito autobus supplementari.
　[2] organizzare ◇ *They laid on a special
　meal.* Hanno organizzato un pranzo
　speciale.

lay-by [ˈleɪbaɪ] NOUN (PL **lay-bys**)
　la piazzola di sosta

layer [ˈleɪəʳ] NOUN
　lo strato

layout [ˈleɪaʊt] NOUN
　la disposizione (*of house*)

lazy [ˈleɪzɪ] ADJECTIVE
　pigro

lb. ABBREVIAZIONE (= *pound*)
　libbra

　🛈 *Una libbra equivale a 0,454 Kg.*

lead (1) [liːd] NOUN
　see also **lead** VERB
　[1] il filo (*cable*)
　[2] il guinzaglio ◇ *Dogs must be kept on a
　lead.* I cani devono essere* tenuti al
　guinzaglio.
　[3] il vantaggio
　• **to be in the lead** essere* E in vantaggio

lead (2) [lɛd] NOUN
　il piombo ◇ *a lead pipe* un tubo di piombo

to **lead** [liːd] VERB (**led, led**)
　see also **lead (1)** NOUN
　[1] portare ◇ *the street that leads to the
　station* la strada che porta alla stazione
　◇ *The incident led to serious trouble.*
　L'incidente ha portato a problemi seri.
　[2] guidare ◇ *He led the party for five years.*
　Ha guidato il partito per cinque anni.
　• **to lead the way** fare* strada

to **lead away** [liːdəˈweɪ] VERB
　condurre* via

leaded petrol [lɛdɪdˈpɛtrəl] NOUN
　la benzina con piombo

leader [ˈliːdəʳ] NOUN
　il capo

lead-free [ˈlɛdfriː] ADJECTIVE
　• **lead-free petrol** benzina verde

lead singer [liːdˈsɪŋəʳ] NOUN
　il/la cantante solista

leaf [liːf] NOUN (PL **leaves**)
　la foglia

leaflet [ˈliːflɪt] NOUN
　il dépliant (PL i dépliant)

league [liːg] NOUN
　il campionato ◇ *They are at the top of the
　league.* Sono in testa al campionato.
　• **the Premier League** la prima divisione

leak [liːk] NOUN

see also **leak** VERB
　[1] la fuga (PL le fughe) ◇ *a gas leak* una fuga
　di gas
　[2] la perdita ◇ *a leak in the radiator* una
　perdita del radiatore

to **leak** [liːk] VERB
　see also **leak** NOUN
　perdere* ◇ *The pipe is leaking.* Il tubo
　perde.

to **lean** [liːn] VERB (**leant** or **leaned, leant** or
　leaned)
　appoggiare ◇ *He leaned the ladder against
　the wall.* Ha appoggiato la scala al muro.
　• **to be leaning against something** essere* E
　appoggiato a qualcosa ◇ *The ladder was
　leaning against the wall.* La scala era
　appoggiata al muro.

to **lean forward** [liːnˈfɔːwəd] VERB
　piegarsi E in avanti

to **lean on** [ˈliːnɒn] VERB
　[1] appoggiarsi E ◇ *She leant on his arm.* Si
　appoggiò al suo braccio.
　[2] spingere* ◇ *She leant on him to
　contribute to the fund.* Lo ha spinto a
　contribuire alla raccolta di fondi.

to **lean out** [liːnˈaʊt] VERB
　sporgersi E ◇ *She leant out of the window.*
　Si è sporta dal finestrino.

to **lean over** [liːnˈəʊvəʳ] VERB
　chinarsi E ◇ *Don't lean over too far.* Non
　chinarti troppo.

to **leap** [liːp] VERB (**leapt** or **leaped, leapt** or
　leaped)
　see also **leap** NOUN
　saltare E ◇ *He leapt out of his chair when his
　team scored.* È saltato in piedi quando la sua
　squadra ha segnato.

leap [liːp] NOUN
　see also **leap** VERB
　il salto ◇ *a leap in the dark* un salto nel buio

leap year [ˈliːpjɪəʳ] NOUN
　l'anno bisestile

to **learn** [ləːn] VERB (**learned** or **learnt, learned** or
　learnt)
　imparare ◇ *I'm learning to ski.* Sto
　imparando a sciare.

learner [ˈləːnəʳ] NOUN
　• **She's a quick learner.** Impara in fretta.

learner driver [ləːnəˈdraɪvəʳ] NOUN
　il/la principiante

least [liːst] ADJECTIVE, PRONOUN, ADVERB
　[1] minimo ◇ *I haven't the least idea.* Non
　ne ho la minima idea. ◇ *It's the least I can
　do.* È il minimo che possa fare*.
　[2] meno ◇ *Go for the ones with least fat.*
　Scegli quelli con meno grassi. ◇ *the least
　expensive hotel* l'albergo meno costoso
　◇ *It takes the least time.* È quello per cui ci
　vuole meno tempo. ◇ *History is the subject I
　like the least.* La storia è la materia che mi
　piace di meno.

* Verbs followed by this symbol are irregular. See pp.339–364 for further details.

3 ultimo ◇ *That's the least of my worries.*
È l'ultima delle mie preoccupazioni.
+ **at least** almeno ◇ *...but at least nobody was hurt.* ...ma almeno nessuno si è fatto male.

leather ['lɛðə'] NOUN
la pelle ◇ *a black leather jacket* una giacca di pelle nera

leave [li:v] NOUN
　see also **leave** VERB
1 il permesso (*from work*)
2 la licenza (*from army*) ◇ *My brother is on leave for a week.* Mio fratello è in licenza per una settimana.

leave [li:v] VERB (**left, left**)
　see also **leave** NOUN
1 lasciare ◇ *Don't leave your wallet in the car.* Non lasciare il portafoglio in macchina.
2 partire^E ◇ *The bus leaves at eight.* L'autobus parte alle otto. ◇ *They left yesterday.* Sono partiti ieri.
3 partire^E da ◇ *We leave London at six o'clock.* Partiamo da Londra alle sei.
4 andare*^E via ◇ *She's just left.* È appena andata via.
+ **to leave home** andarsene^E di casa ◇ *She left home when she was sixteen.* Se n'è andata di casa quando aveva sedici anni.
+ **to leave somebody alone** lasciare in pace qualcuno ◇ *Leave me alone!* Lasciami in pace!

leave behind [li:vbɪ'haɪnd] VERB
dimenticare ◇ *I left my umbrella behind in the shop.* Ho dimenticato l'ombrello nel negozio.

leave out [li:v'aut] VERB
escludere* ◇ *Not knowing the language, I felt really left out.* Mi sentivo proprio escluso dato che non sapevo la lingua.

leaves [li:vz] NOUN PL *see* **leaf**

Lebanon ['lɛbənən] NOUN
il Libano

lecture ['lɛktʃə'] NOUN
　see also **lecture** VERB
1 la conferenza ◇ *a public lecture* una conferenza pubblica
2 la lezione (*at university*)

lecture ['lɛktʃə'] VERB
　see also **lecture** NOUN
1 insegnare ◇ *She lectures at the technical college.* Insegna all'istituto tecnico.
2 rimproverare ◇ *He's always lecturing us.* Ci rimprovera sempre.

lecturer ['lɛktʃərə'] NOUN
il/la docente

led [lɛd] VERB *see* **lead**

leek [li:k] NOUN
il porro

left [lɛft] VERB *see* **leave**

left [lɛft] ADJECTIVE, ADVERB
　see also **left** NOUN
1 sinistro ◇ *my left hand* la mia mano

sinistra
2 a sinistra ◇ *Turn left at the traffic lights.* Volta a sinistra al semaforo.
+ **I haven't got any money left.** Non ho più denaro.
+ **Is there any ice cream left?** C'è ancora del gelato?

left [lɛft] NOUN
　see also **left** ADJECTIVE
la sinistra
+ **on the left** a sinistra

left-hand ['lɛfthænd] ADJECTIVE
+ **the left-hand side** il lato sinistro

left-handed [lɛft'hændɪd] ADJECTIVE
mancino

left-luggage office [lɛft'lʌgɪdʒ'ɔfɪs] NOUN
il deposito bagagli

leg [lɛg] NOUN
la gamba ◇ *She's broken her leg.* Si è rotta la gamba.
+ **a leg of lamb** una coscia d'agnello

legal ['li:gl] ADJECTIVE
legale

leggings ['lɛgɪŋz] NOUN PL
i fuseaux

leisure ['lɛʒə'] NOUN
+ **leisure time** tempo libero
+ **leisure activities** attività ricreative

leisure centre ['lɛʒəsentə'] NOUN
il centro ricreativo pubblico (PL i centri ricreativi pubblici)

lemon ['lɛmən] NOUN
il limone

lemonade [lɛmə'neɪd] NOUN
la limonata

to **lend** [lɛnd] VERB (**lent, lent**)
prestare ◇ *I can lend you some money.* Posso prestarti del denaro. ◇ *He lent me £10.* Mi ha prestato dieci sterline.

length [lɛŋθ] NOUN
la lunghezza
+ **It's about a metre in length.** È lungo circa un metro.

lens [lɛnz] NOUN (PL **lenses**)
1 la lente (*of microscope*)
2 l' obiettivo (*of camera*) ◇ *contact lenses* lenti a contatto

Lent [lɛnt] NOUN
la Quaresima

lent [lɛnt] VERB *see* **lend**

lentil ['lɛntɪl] NOUN
la lenticchia

Leo ['li:əu] NOUN
il Leone ◇ *I'm Leo.* Sono del Leone.

leotard ['li:ətɑ:d] NOUN
il body (PL i body)

lesbian ['lɛzbɪən] NOUN
la lesbica (PL le lesbiche)

less [lɛs] ADJECTIVE, PRONOUN, ADVERB
meno ◇ *A bit less, please.* Un po' meno, per favore. ◇ *It's less than a kilometre from* ☞

L

Verbs followed by the symbol "E" require the auxiliary "essere"

here. È a meno di un chilometro da qui.
◇ *less than half* meno della metà
♦ **less and less** sempre meno

lesson ['lɛsn] NOUN
la lezione ◇ *an English lesson* una lezione d'inglese

to **let** [lɛt] VERB (**let, let**)
☐1 lasciare
♦ **to let somebody do something** lasciar fare* qualcosa a qualcuno ◇ *Let me go!* Lasciami andare*!
♦ **to let somebody know something** far sapere* qualcosa a qualcuno ◇ *I'll let you know as soon as possible.* Ti farò sapere* qualcosa prima possibile.
♦ **to let in** far entrare ◇ *They wouldn't let me in because I'm under 18.* Non mi hanno fatto entrare perché sono minorenne.
☐2 affittare ◇ *"to let"* "affittasi"
When making suggestions, use the "-iamo" form of the Italian verb.
◇ *Let's go to the cinema!* Andiamo al cinema! ◇ *Let's have a break! – Yes, let's.* Facciamo una pausa! – Va bene.

to **let down** [lɛt'daʊn] VERB
deludere* ◇ *I won't let you down.* Non ti deluderò.

letter ['lɛtə'] NOUN
la lettera

letter bomb ['lɛtəbɒm] NOUN
la lettera esplosiva

letterbox ['lɛtəbɒks] NOUN (PL **letterboxes**)
☐1 la buca delle lettere sulla porta (PL le buche delle lettere sulla porta)

ℹ️ *In genere per* **letterbox** *si intende la fessura sulla porta di casa dove il postino infila la posta.*

◇ *She pushed the key through the letterbox.* Infilò la chiave nella buca delle lettere sulla porta.
☐2 la cassetta per la posta (*in entrance hall*)

lettuce ['lɛtɪs] NOUN
la lattuga (PL le lattughe)

leukaemia [luːˈkiːmɪə] NOUN (US **leukemia**)
la leucemia

level ['lɛvl] ADJECTIVE
see also **level** NOUN
piano ◇ *a level surface* una superficie piana

level ['lɛvl] NOUN
see also **level** ADJECTIVE
il livello ◇ *The level of the river is rising.* Il livello del fiume sta salendo.

level crossing [lɛvlˈkrɒsɪŋ] NOUN
il passaggio a livello (PL i passaggi a livello)

lever ['liːvə'] NOUN
la leva

liable ['laɪəbl] ADJECTIVE
♦ **He's liable to panic.** È facile che si lasci prendere* dal panico.

liar ['laɪə'] NOUN
il bugiardo
la bugiarda

liberal ['lɪbərl] ADJECTIVE
liberale ◇ *liberal views* vedute liberali
♦ **the Liberal Democrats** i liberaldemocratici

liberation [lɪbəˈreɪʃən] NOUN
la liberazione

Libra ['liːbrə] NOUN
la Bilancia ◇ *I'm Libra.* Sono della Bilancia.

librarian [laɪˈbrɛərɪən] NOUN
il bibliotecario
la bibliotecaria

library ['laɪbrərɪ] NOUN (PL **libraries**)
la biblioteca (PL le biblioteche)

Libya ['lɪbɪə] NOUN
la Libia

licence ['laɪsns] NOUN (US **license**)
la patente ◇ *He lost his licence for a year.* Gli hanno ritirato la patente per un anno.
♦ **a television licence** un abbonamento alla TV

license plate ['laɪsnspleɪt] NOUN [US]
la targa (PL le targhe)

to **lick** [lɪk] VERB
leccare

lid [lɪd] NOUN
il coperchio (*of box, pan*)

lie [laɪ] NOUN
see also **lie** VERB
la bugia
♦ **to tell a lie** dire* una bugia

to **lie** [laɪ] VERB (**lied, lied**)
see also **lie** NOUN
☐1 mentire (*tell untruths*) ◇ *I know she's lying.* So che sta mentendo. ◇ *You lied to me!* Mi hai mentito!
☐2 essere* E disteso (*be lying down*)
Quando **to lie** *ha questo significato è un verbo irregolare: il passato è* **lay** *e il participio è* **lain**.
◇ *He was lying on the sofa.* Era disteso sul divano. ◇ *He had lain there for hours.* È rimasto disteso lì per ore.

to **lie down** [laɪˈdaʊn] VERB
distendersi E ◇ *Why not go and lie down for a bit?* Perché non vai a distenderti per un po'?
♦ **to be lying down** essere* E disteso

lie-in ['laɪɪn] NOUN
♦ **to have a lie-in** rimanere* E a letto

lieutenant [lɛfˈtɛnənt] NOUN
il tenente

life [laɪf] NOUN (PL **lives**)
la vita ◇ *all my life* tutta la vita
♦ **life insurance** assicurazione sulla vita FEM
♦ **life jacket** giubbotto di salvataggio
♦ **life sentence** ergastolo

lifebelt ['laɪfbɛlt] NOUN
il salvagente

lifeboat ['laɪfbəʊt] NOUN
la scialuppa di salvataggio

* Verbs followed by this symbol are irregular. See pp.339–364 for further details.

lifeguard [ˈlaɪfɡɑːd] NOUN
il bagnino

life-saving [ˈlaɪfseɪvɪŋ] NOUN
il salvataggio ◇ *I've done a course in life-saving.* Ho fatto un corso di salvataggio.

lifestyle [ˈlaɪfstaɪl] NOUN
lo stile di vita

lift [lɪft] VERB
see also **lift** NOUN
sollevare ◇ *It's too heavy, I can't lift it.* È troppo pesante, non riesco a sollevarlo.

lift [lɪft] NOUN
see also **lift** VERB
[1] l' ascensore MASC ◇ *The lift isn't working.* L'ascensore non funziona.
[2] il passaggio ◇ *He gave me a lift to the cinema.* Mi ha dato un passaggio al cinema.

light [laɪt] ADJECTIVE
see also **light** NOUN, VERB
[1] leggero ◇ *a light jacket* una giacca leggera ◇ *a light meal* un pasto leggero
[2] chiaro ◇ *a light blue sweater* una maglia azzurro chiaro

light [laɪt] NOUN
see also **light** ADJECTIVE, VERB
la luce ◇ *He switched on the light.* Ha acceso la luce. ◇ *He switched off the light.* Ha spento la luce.
♦ **Have you got a light?** Ha da accendere*?
♦ **the traffic lights** il semaforo SING

light [laɪt] VERB (**lit, lit**)
see also **light** ADJECTIVE, NOUN
accendere* ◇ *She lit the candles on the cake.* Ha acceso le candeline sulla torta.

light bulb [ˈlaɪtbʌlb] NOUN
la lampadina

lighter [ˈlaɪtəʳ] NOUN
l' accendino

lighthouse [ˈlaɪthaus] NOUN
il faro

lightning [ˈlaɪtnɪŋ] NOUN SING
i fulmini MASC PL ◇ *thunder and lightning* tuoni e fulmini
♦ **a flash of lightning** un fulmine

like [laɪk] VERB
see also **like** PREPOSITION
*When saying what you like, remember that the Italian verb **piacere** is impersonal. This means that instead of saying what you like, you say what is pleasing to you. If this is singular the verb is singular, if it is plural the verb is plural.*
◇ *I like Tom.* Tom mi piace. ◇ *I don't like dogs.* Non mi piacciono i cani. ◇ *I like riding.* Mi piace cavalcare. ◇ *How did you like the trip?* Ti è piaciuto il viaggio?
*When **would like** means "want" it is translated by the conditional of **volere**.*
◇ *I'd like an orange juice, please.* Vorrei un'aranciata, per favore. ◇ *I'd like to wash my hands.* Vorrei lavarmi le mani. ◇ *He'd like to leave early.* Vorrebbe andarsene

presto.
♦ **Would you like...?** Vuoi...? ◇ *Would you like to come?* Vuoi venire*?
♦ **What would you like?** Cosa vuoi?

like [laɪk] PREPOSITION
see also **like** VERB
come ◇ *a city like Paris* una città come Parigi ◇ *What was Turkey like?* Com'era la Turchia?
♦ **What's the weather like?** Che tempo fa?
♦ **It's a bit like salmon.** Assomiglia un po' al salmone.
♦ **It's fine like that.** Così va bene.
♦ **Do it like this.** Fallo così.
♦ **something like that** qualcosa del genere
♦ **to look like somebody** assomigliare a qualcuno ◇ *You look like my brother.* Assomigli a mio fratello.
♦ **What does she look like?** Che aspetto ha?

likely [ˈlaɪklɪ] ADJECTIVE
probabile ◇ *That's not very likely.* Non è molto probabile.
♦ **She's not likely to come.** È difficile che venga.

Lilo ® [ˈlaɪləu] (PL **Lilos**) NOUN
il materassino gonfiabile

lily of the valley [lɪlɪəvðəˈvælɪ] NOUN
il mughetto

lime [laɪm] NOUN
la limetta (*fruit*)
♦ **lime green** giallo-verdino

limit [ˈlɪmɪt] NOUN
il limite ◇ *The speed limit is 70 mph.* Il limite di velocità è di settanta miglia all'ora.

limousine [ˈlɪməziːn] NOUN
la limousine (PL le limousine)

to **limp** [lɪmp] VERB
see also **limp** NOUN
zoppicare

limp [lɪmp] NOUN
see also **limp** VERB
♦ **to have a limp** zoppicare

line [laɪn] NOUN
see also **line** VERB
[1] la linea ◇ *a straight line* una linea retta ◇ *our best-selling line* la linea che vendiamo di più
♦ **to draw a line under something** dimenticare qualcosa ◇ *I want to draw a line under the experience.* Voglio dimenticare quell'esperienza.
[2] la fila ◇ *a line of people* una fila di persone
♦ **to stand in line** US stare* E in fila
[3] la riga (PL le righe) ◇ *He wrote a few lines.* Ha scritto qualche riga.
♦ **a railway line** una linea ferroviaria
♦ **a phone line** una linea telefonica
♦ **Hold the line, please.** Attenda in linea, per favore.
♦ **It's a very bad line.** La comunicazione è disturbata.

L

Verbs followed by the symbol "E" require the auxiliary "essere"

to **line** [laɪn] VERB

see also **line** NOUN

rivestire ◇ *Line the tin with greaseproof paper.* Rivesti la tortiera con carta oleata.

◆ **Crowds lined the street.** C'erano molte persone ai bordi della strada.

◆ **The street was lined with trees.** La strada era alberata.

to **line up** [laɪn'ʌp] VERB

mettersi [E] in fila ◇ *Line up in twos.* Mettetevi in fila per due.

linen [ˈlɪnɪn] NOUN

il lino ◇ *a linen jacket* una giacca di lino

liner [ˈlaɪnə'] NOUN

la nave di linea

linguist [ˈlɪŋgwɪst] NOUN

◆ **to be a good linguist** essere* [E] portato per le lingue

lining [ˈlaɪnɪŋ] NOUN

la fodera (*of coat, jacket*)

link [lɪŋk] NOUN

see also **link** VERB

il collegamento ◇ *the link between smoking and cancer* il collegamento tra fumo e cancro ◇ *There's a link to another site.* C'è un collegamento ad un altro sito.

◆ **cultural links** rapporti culturali

to **link** [lɪŋk] VERB

see also **link** NOUN

collegare

lino [ˈlaɪnəu] NOUN

il linoleum

lion [ˈlaɪən] NOUN

il leone

lioness [ˈlaɪənɪs] NOUN (PL **lionesses**)

la leonessa

lip [lɪp] NOUN

il labbro (PL FEM le labbra)

◆ **red lips** labbra rosse

to **lip-read** [ˈlɪpriːd] VERB (**lip-read, lip-read**)

leggere* le labbra

lip salve [ˈlɪpsælv] NOUN

il burro di cacao

lipstick [ˈlɪpstɪk] NOUN

il rossetto

liqueur [lɪˈkjuə'] NOUN

il liquore

liquid [ˈlɪkwɪd] NOUN, ADJECTIVE

liquido

liquidizer [ˈlɪkwɪdaɪzə'] NOUN

il frullatore

list [lɪst] NOUN

see also **list** VERB

la lista

to **list** [lɪst] VERB

see also **list** NOUN

elencare

to **listen** [ˈlɪsn] VERB

ascoltare ◇ *Listen to this!* Ascolta!

listener [ˈlɪsnə'] NOUN

l'ascoltatore

l'ascoltatrice

lit [lɪt] VERB *see* **light**

liter [ˈliːtə'] NOUN ⟨US⟩

il litro

literally [ˈlɪtrəlɪ] ADVERB

letteralmente ◇ *It was literally impossible to find a seat.* Era letteralmente impossibile trovare un posto.

literature [ˈlɪtrɪtʃə'] NOUN

la letteratura

litre [ˈliːtə'] NOUN (US **liter**)

il litro

litter [ˈlɪtə'] NOUN SING

i rifiuti MASC PL

◆ **a litter bin** un cestino dei rifiuti

little [ˈlɪtl] ADJECTIVE

see also **little** NOUN

1 piccolo ◇ *a little girl* una bambina piccola

2 poco ◇ *It makes little difference.* Fa poca differenza. ◇ *We've got very little time.* Abbiamo molto poco tempo.

little [ˈlɪtl] NOUN

see also **little** ADJECTIVE

poco ◇ *Little is known about his childhood.* Si sa poco della sua infanzia. ◇ *It's changed very little.* È cambiato molto poco.

◆ **a little** un po' ◇ *How much would you like? – Just a little.* Quanto ne vuoi? – Solo un po'. ◇ *It's okay, we've still got a little time.* Va bene, abbiamo ancora un po' di tempo.

◆ **little by little** a poco a poco

live [laɪv] ADJECTIVE

see also **live** VERB

vivo ◇ *I'm against tests on live animals.* Sono contrario agli esperimenti su animali vivi.

◆ **a live broadcast** una trasmissione in diretta

◆ **a live concert** un concerto dal vivo

to **live** [lɪv] VERB

see also **live** ADJECTIVE

1 vivere* [E] ◇ *I live with my grandmother.* Vivo con mia nonna. ◇ *How can people live like that?* Come si può vivere* così?

2 abitare ◇ *Where do you live?* Dove abiti? ◇ *I live in Edinburgh.* Abito ad Edimburgo.

to **live together** [lɪvtəgeðə'] VERB

convivere [E]

lively [ˈlaɪvlɪ] ADJECTIVE

vivace ◇ *She's got a lively personality.* È una persona vivace.

liver [ˈlɪvə'] NOUN

il fegato

lives [laɪvz] NOUN *see* **life**

living [ˈlɪvɪŋ] NOUN

◆ **to make a living** guadagnarsi [E] da vivere*

◆ **What does she do for a living?** Come si guadagna da vivere*?

◆ **living standards** il tenore di vita SING

living room [ˈlɪvɪŋruːm] NOUN

---

* Verbs followed by this symbol are irregular. See pp.339–364 for further details.

English ~ Italian

il salotto

lizard ['lɪzəd] NOUN
la lucertola

load [ləud] NOUN
see also **load** VERB
il carico (PL i carichi) ◊ _a heavy load_ un pesante carico
* **loads of** un sacco di ◊ _They've got loads of money._ Hanno un sacco di soldi.
* **a load of rubbish** un mucchio di sciocchezze ◊ _You're talking a load of rubbish!_ Stai dicendo un mucchio di sciocchezze!

load [ləud] VERB
see also **load** NOUN
caricare ◊ _I can't load the program._ Non riesco a caricare il programma.

loaf [ləuf] NOUN (PL **loaves**)
la pagnotta

loan [ləun] NOUN
see also **loan** VERB
il prestito

loan [ləun] VERB
see also **loan** NOUN
dare* in prestito

loathe [ləuð] VERB
detestare ◊ _I loathe her._ La detesto.

loaves [ləuvz] NOUN _see_ **loaf**

lobster ['lɒbstə'] NOUN
l' aragosta

local ['ləukl] ADJECTIVE
locale ◊ _the local paper_ il giornale locale
* **local anaesthetic** l'anestesia locale
* **a local call** una chiamata urbana

local authority [ləuklɔː'θɒrɪtɪ] NOUN
l' autorità locale

loch [lɒx] NOUN

> **ⓘ** /loch sono laghi o profonde insenature che si trovano in Scozia.

lock [lɒk] NOUN
see also **lock** VERB
la serratura (_of door_)

lock [lɒk] VERB
see also **lock** NOUN
chiudere* a chiave ◊ _Make sure you lock your door._ Non dimenticare di chiudere* la porta a chiave.

lock out [lɒk'aut] VERB
chiudere* fuori ◊ _The door slammed and I was locked out._ La porta si è chiusa di colpo e sono rimasto chiuso fuori.

locker ['lɒkə'] NOUN
l' armadietto ◊ _left-luggage lockers_ armadietti per deposito bagagli

locker room ['lɒkərum] NOUN
lo spogliatoio

locket ['lɒkɪt] NOUN
il medaglione portaritratti

lodger ['lɒdʒə'] NOUN
il/la pensionante

loft [lɒft] NOUN
la soffitta

log [lɒg] NOUN
il ciocco (PL i ciocchi) (_piece of wood_)

logical ['lɒdʒɪkl] ADJECTIVE
logico

to **log in** [lɒg'ɪn] VERB
registrarsi E

to **log off** [lɒg'ɒf] VERB
scollegarsi E

to **log on** [lɒg'ɒn] VERB
registrarsi E (_to computer_)
* **to log on to the Net** collegarsi E in rete

lollipop ['lɒlɪpɒp] NOUN
il lecca lecca (PL i lecca lecca)

lolly ['lɒlɪ] NOUN (PL **lollies**)
* **an ice lolly** un ghiacciolo

London ['lʌndən] NOUN
Londra ◊ _I'm from London._ Sono di Londra.

Londoner ['lʌndənə'] NOUN
il/la londinese

loneliness ['ləunlɪnɪs] NOUN
la solitudine

lonely ['ləunlɪ] ADJECTIVE
[1] solo (_person_) ◊ _I sometimes feel lonely._ Qualche volta mi sento solo.
[2] isolato (_place_) ◊ _a lonely cottage_ una villetta isolata

lonesome ['ləunsəm] ADJECTIVE
* **to feel lonesome** sentirsi E solo

long [lɒŋ] ADJECTIVE, ADVERB
see also **long** VERB
lungo ◊ _She's got long hair._ Ha i capelli lunghi. ◊ _The room is six metres long._ La stanza è lunga sei metri.
* **a long time** molto tempo ◊ _It takes a long time._ Ci vuole molto tempo. ◊ _I've been waiting a long time._ Aspetto da molto tempo.
* **as long as** sempre che ◊ _I'll come as long as it's not too expensive._ Verrò, sempre che non costi troppo.
* **How long did you stay there?** Per quanto tempo sei rimasto lì?
* **How long is the flight?** Quanto dura il volo?
* **How long will it take?** Quanto ci vorrà?
Sentences with **how long** and the perfect tense are translated by an Italian verb in the present tense.
◊ _How long have you been here?_ Da quanto sei qui? ◊ _How long has he been learning Italian?_ Da quanto studia l'italiano?

to **long** [lɒŋ] VERB
see also **long** ADJECTIVE
* **to long to do something** morire* dalla voglia di fare* qualcosa

long-distance [lɒŋ'dɪstəns] ADJECTIVE
* **a long-distance call** una chiamata interurbana

longer ['lɒŋgə'] ADVERB
see also **long** ADJECTIVE

L

☞

♦ **no longer** non...più ◇ *They're no longer going out together.* Non escono più insieme. ◇ *I can't stand it any longer.* Non lo sopporto più.

long jump ['lɒŋdʒʌmp] NOUN
il salto in lungo

loo [luː] NOUN
il gabinetto

look [luk] NOUN
see also **look** VERB
l' occhiata ◇ *Have a look at this!* Dai un'occhiata a questo!

♦ **I don't like the look of it.** Non mi piace per niente.

to **look** [luk] VERB
see also **look** NOUN
[1] guardare

♦ **to look at something** guardare qualcosa ◇ *Look at the picture on page three.* Guardate la figura a pagina tre.
[2] sembrare ^E ◇ *She looks surprised.* Sembra sorpresa. ◇ *That cake looks nice.* La torta sembra buona.

♦ **Look out!** Attento!

♦ **to look like somebody** assomigliare a qualcuno ◇ *He looks like his brother.* Assomiglia a suo fratello.

♦ **What does she look like?** Che aspetto ha?

to **look after** [luk'ɑːftəʳ] VERB
occuparsi ^E di ◇ *I look after my little sister.* Mi occupo della mia sorellina.

to **look for** ['lukfɔːʳ] VERB
cercare ◇ *I'm looking for my passport.* Sto cercando il mio passaporto.

to **look forward to** [luk'fɔːwədtuː] VERB
non veder l'ora di ◇ *I'm looking forward to meeting you.* Non vedo l'ora di incontrarti.

♦ **I'm looking forward to the holidays.** Non vedo l'ora che arrivino le vacanze.

♦ **Looking forward to hearing from you...** Aspettando tue notizie...

to **look round** [luk'raund] VERB
[1] voltarsi ^E ◇ *I shouted and he looked round.* Ho gridato e lui si è voltato.
[2] dare* un'occhiata ◇ *I'm just looking round.* Sto solo dando un'occhiata.

♦ **to look round an exhibition** visitare una mostra

to **look up** [luk'ʌp] VERB
cercare ◇ *If you don't know a word, look it up in the dictionary.* Se non conosci qualche parola cercala sul dizionario.

loose [luːs] ADJECTIVE
largo ◇ *a loose shirt* una camicia larga

♦ **a loose screw** una vite allentata

♦ **loose change** spiccioli MASC PL

lord [lɔːd] NOUN
il signore (*feudal*)

♦ **the House of Lords** la Camera dei Lord

Lord [lɔːd] NOUN

♦ **the Lord** il Signore

♦ **Good Lord!** Mio Dio!

lorry ['lɒrɪ] NOUN (PL **lorries**)
il camion (PL i camion)

♦ **a lorry driver** un/una camionista ◇ *He's a lorry driver.* Fa il camionista.

to **lose** [luːz] VERB (**lost, lost**)
perdere* ◇ *I've lost my purse.* Ho perso il portamonete. ◇ *They lost the match.* Hanno perso la partita.

♦ **to get lost** perdersi ^E ◇ *I was afraid I'd get lost.* Avevo paura di perdermi.

♦ **to lose weight** dimagrire ^E

loser ['luːzəʳ] NOUN
il/la perdente

♦ **to be a bad loser** non saper perdere*

loss [lɒs] NOUN (PL **losses**)
la perdita

lost [lɒst] VERB see **lose**

lost [lɒst] ADJECTIVE
perso ◇ *I realized I was lost.* Ho capito che mi ero perso.

lost-and-found [lɒstən'faund] NOUN US
l' ufficio oggetti smarriti

lost property office [lɒst'prɒpətɪ'ɒfɪs] NOUN
l' ufficio oggetti smarriti

lot [lɒt] NOUN

♦ **a lot** molto ◇ *She talks a lot.* Parla molto. ◇ *Do you like football? – Not a lot.* Ti piace il calcio? – Non molto.

♦ **a lot of** molto ◇ *I drink a lot of coffee.* Bevo molto caffè. ◇ *We saw a lot of interesting things.* Abbiamo visto molte cose interessanti.

♦ **lots of** molto ◇ *He's got lots of friends.* Ha molti amici. ◇ *She's got lots of self-confidence.* Ha molta fiducia in se stessa.

♦ **That's the lot.** È tutto.

lottery ['lɒtərɪ] NOUN (PL **lotteries**)
la lotteria

♦ **to win the lottery** vincere* alla lotteria

loud [laud] ADJECTIVE
forte

loudly ['laudlɪ] ADVERB
forte

loudspeaker [laud'spiːkəʳ] NOUN
l' altoparlante MASC

lousy ['lauzɪ] ADJECTIVE
pessimo ◇ *The food's lousy.* Il cibo è pessimo.

♦ **I feel lousy.** Sto da cani.

love [lʌv] NOUN
see also **love** VERB
l' amore MASC ◇ *true love* vero amore

♦ **to be in love** essere* ^E innamorato ◇ *She's in love with Paul.* È innamorata di Paul.

♦ **to fall in love** innamorarsi ^E

♦ **to make love** fare* l'amore

♦ **Give Gloria my love.** Salutami Gloria.

♦ **Love, Rosemary.** (*in letter*) Con affetto, Rosemary.

to **love** [lʌv] VERB

see also **love** NOUN

1 amare ◇ *I love you.* Ti amo.

2 voler bene a ◇ *Everybody loves her.* Tutti le vogliono bene.

◆ **I love chocolate.** Mi piace molto la cioccolata.

◆ **I'd love to...** Mi piacerebbe molto... ◇ *I'd love to come.* Mi piacerebbe molto venire.

◆ **Would you like to come? – I'd love to.** Vuoi venire*? – Mi piacerebbe molto.

love affair ['lʌvəfeə'] NOUN
la relazione

lovely ['lʌvlɪ] ADJECTIVE

1 bello ◇ *What a lovely surprise!* Che bella sorpresa! ◇ *They've got a lovely house.* Hanno una bella casa.

2 buonissimo ◇ *Is your meal okay? – Yes, it's lovely.* Ti piace il pranzo? – Sì, è buonissimo.

3 delizioso ◇ *She's a lovely person.* È una persona deliziosa.

◆ **Have a lovely time!** Divertiti!

lover ['lʌvə'] NOUN
l' amante MASC / FEM

low [ləʊ] ADJECTIVE, ADVERB
basso ◇ *That plane is flying very low.* Quell'aereo vola molto basso. ◇ *in the low season* in bassa stagione

lower ['ləʊə'] VERB
abbassare ◇ *They have lowered interest rates.* Hanno abbassato i tassi d'interesse.

lower ['ləʊə'] ADJECTIVE
inferiore ◇ *a lower standard* un livello inferiore

◆ **the lower sixth** il biennio conclusivo della scuola secondaria

> ❶ *Il* **lower sixth** *è il primo anno del "sixth form", cioè del biennio che i ragazzi frequentano dai 16 ai 18 anni per prepararsi per gli esami chiamati A levels.*

low-fat ['ləʊ'fæt] ADJECTIVE
magro

loyalty ['lɔɪəltɪ] NOUN
la lealtà

loyalty card ['lɔɪəltɪkɑːd] NOUN
la carta fedeltà (PL le carte fedeltà) (*of shop*)

lozenge ['lɒzɪndʒ] NOUN
la pastiglia (*for throat*)

L-plates ['elpleɪts] NOUN PL

> ❶ *Le* **L-plates** *sono tabelle bianche con una L rossa che i guidatori principianti, i "learners", devono applicare alla propria autovettura finché non hanno ottenuto la patente.*

luck [lʌk] NOUN
la fortuna

◆ **Good luck!** Buona fortuna!

◆ **Bad luck!** Che sfortuna!

◆ **Just my luck!** La mia solita sfortuna!

luckily ['lʌkɪlɪ] ADVERB
fortunatamente

lucky ['lʌkɪ] ADJECTIVE
fortunato ◇ *He's lucky, he's got a job.* È fortunato. Ha un lavoro.

◆ **Black cats are lucky in Britain.** I gatti neri portano fortuna in Gran Bretagna.

◆ **That was lucky!** Per fortuna!

◆ **a lucky horseshoe** un ferro di cavallo portafortuna

luggage ['lʌgɪdʒ] NOUN (PL **luggage**)
i bagagli MASC PL ◇ *My luggage was left behind.* Hanno dimenticato i miei bagagli.

lukewarm ['luːkwɔːm] ADJECTIVE
tiepido

lump [lʌmp] NOUN

1 il pezzo ◇ *a lump of butter* un pezzo di burro

2 il bernoccolo ◇ *He's got a lump on his forehead.* Ha un bernoccolo sulla fronte.

lump sum [lʌmp'sʌm] NOUN
la somma forfettaria

lunatic ['luːnətɪk] NOUN
il pazzo
la pazza
◇ *He's an absolute lunatic.* È completamente pazzo.

lunch [lʌntʃ] NOUN (PL **lunches**)
il pranzo ◇ *a delicious lunch* un pranzo squisito

◆ **to have lunch** pranzare ◇ *We have lunch at 12 30.* Pranziamo a mezzogiorno e mezza.

luncheon voucher ['lʌntʃənvautʃə'] NOUN
il buono pasto (PL i buoni pasto)

lung [lʌŋ] NOUN
il polmone ◇ *lung cancer* il cancro ai polmoni

luscious ['lʌʃəs] ADJECTIVE
succoso (*fruit*)

lush [lʌʃ] ADJECTIVE
lussureggiante

lust [lʌst] NOUN
il desiderio

Luxembourg ['lʌksəmbəːg] NOUN
il Lussemburgo

luxurious [lʌg'zjuəriəs] ADJECTIVE
lussuoso
Be careful not to translate **luxurious** *by lussurioso.*

luxury ['lʌkʃərɪ] NOUN (PL **luxuries**)
il lusso ◇ *It was luxury!* È stato un vero lusso! ◇ *a luxury hotel* un albergo di lusso
Be careful not to translate **luxury** *by lussuria.*

lying ['laɪɪŋ] VERB *see* **lie**

lyrics ['lɪrɪks] NOUN PL
le parole

L

M

mac [mæk] NOUN
l' impermeabile MASC

macaroni [mækəˈrəʊnɪ] NOUN SING
i maccheroni MASC PL

machine [məˈʃiːn] NOUN
1 la macchina ◇ It's a complicated machine. È una macchina complicata.
2 la lavatrice ◇ I put clothes in the machine. Ho messo i vestiti in lavatrice.

machine gun [məˈʃiːngʌn] NOUN
la mitragliatrice

machinery [məˈʃiːnərɪ] NOUN SING
i macchinari MASC PL ◇ The machinery in the factory was outdated. I macchinari della fabbrica erano superati.

mackerel [ˈmækrl] NOUN (PL **mackerel**)
lo sgombro

mad [mæd] ADJECTIVE
1 pazzo ◇ You're mad! Tu sei pazzo!
♦ **to go mad** impazzire E ◇ Have you gone mad? Sei impazzito?
♦ **to be mad about** andare* E matto per ◇ He's mad about football. Va matto per il calcio.
♦ **mad cow disease** morbo della mucca pazza
2 furioso ◇ She'll be mad when she finds out. Sarà furiosa quando lo scoprirà.

madam [ˈmædəm] NOUN
la signora ◇ How may I help you Madam? La signora desidera?

> ❶ **madam** è una formula di cortesia che viene usata principalmente nei negozi e nei ristoranti per rivolgersi alle clienti.

made [meɪd] VERB see **make**

madly [ˈmædlɪ] ADVERB
♦ **They're madly in love.** Sono follemente innamorati.

madman [ˈmædmən] NOUN (PL **madmen**)
il pazzo

madness [ˈmædnɪs] NOUN
la pazzia ◇ It's absolute madness. È pura pazzia.

magazine [mægəˈziːn] NOUN
la rivista

> Be careful not to translate **magazine** by **magazzino**.

maggot [ˈmægət] NOUN
il baco (PL i bachi)

magic [ˈmædʒɪk] NOUN
see also **magic** ADJECTIVE
la magia

magic [ˈmædʒɪk] ADJECTIVE
see also **magic** NOUN
1 magico ◇ a magic potion una pozione magica
2 miracoloso ◇ There's no magic solution. Non ci sono soluzioni miracolose.

3 fantastico ◇ It was magic! È stato fantastico!

magician [məˈdʒɪʃən] NOUN
1 l' illusionista MASC / FEM (entertainer)
2 il mago (PL i maghi) (in stories)

magnet [ˈmægnɪt] NOUN
la calamita

magnificent [mægˈnɪfɪsnt] ADJECTIVE
1 magnifico ◇ a magnificent view una vista magnifica
2 grosso ◇ It is a magnificent achievement. È un grosso risultato.

magnifying glass [ˈmægnɪfaɪɪŋˈglɑːs] NOUN
la lente d'ingrandimento

maid [meɪd] NOUN
1 la cameriera (in hotel)
2 la domestica (PL le domestiche) (in house)
♦ **an old maid** una vecchia zitella

maiden name [ˈmeɪdnneɪm] NOUN
il nome da ragazza

mail [meɪl] NOUN
see also **mail** VERB
la posta ◇ by mail per posta

to **mail** [meɪl] VERB
see also **mail** NOUN
1 spedire per posta ◇ He mailed me the contract. Mi ha spedito il contratto per posta.
2 imbucare ◇ I forgot to mail the letter. Ho dimenticato di imbucare la lettera.

mailbox [ˈmeɪlbɒks] NOUN (PL **mailboxes**) US
la cassetta delle lettere

mailing list [ˈmeɪlɪŋlɪst] NOUN
la mailing list (PL le mailing list)

mailman [ˈmeɪlmæn] NOUN (PL **mailmen**) US
il postino

main [meɪn] ADJECTIVE
principale ◇ the main points i punti principali

mainly [ˈmeɪnlɪ] ADVERB
principalmente

main road [meɪnˈrəʊd] NOUN
la strada principale

to **maintain** [meɪnˈteɪn] VERB
1 mantenere* ◇ Teachers try hard to maintain standards. Gli insegnanti ce la mettono tutta per mantenere* un certo livello scolastico.
2 sostenere* ◇ She had always maintained her innocence. Aveva sempre sostenuto la propria innocenza.

maintenance [ˈmeɪntənəns] NOUN
1 la manutenzione ◇ car maintenance la manutenzione della macchina
2 gli alimenti MASC PL ◇ His father has to pay maintenance. Suo padre deve pagare gli alimenti.

maize [meɪz] NOUN

---

* Verbs followed by this symbol are irregular. See pp.339–364 for further details.

il granturco

majesty ['mædʒɪstɪ] NOUN (PL **majesties**)
la maestà

major ['meɪdʒəʳ] ADJECTIVE
[1] grosso ◇ *Drugs are a major problem.* La droga è un grosso problema.
[2] importante ◇ *a major new film* un importante nuovo film

Majorca [məˈjɔːkə] NOUN
Maiorca

majority [məˈdʒɒrɪtɪ] NOUN (PL **majorities**)
la maggioranza ◇ *the vast majority of our products* la grande maggioranza dei nostri prodotti

make [meɪk] NOUN
see also **make** VERB
la marca (PL le marche)

to **make** [meɪk] VERB (**made, made**)
see also **make** NOUN
[1] fare* ◇ *I'd like to make a phone call.* Vorrei fare* una telefonata. ◇ *I make my bed every morning.* Mi faccio il letto ogni mattina. ◇ *What time do you make it?* Che ora fai? ◇ *It's well made.* È ben fatto.
[2] fabbricare ◇ *It was made in Italy.* È stato fabbricato in Italia.
[3] guadagnare ◇ *He makes a lot of money.* Guadagna un sacco di soldi.
[4] arrivare E a ◇ *We made Exeter by seven o'clock.* Siamo arrivati ad Exeter alle sette.
♦ **to make somebody do something** obbligare qualcuno a fare* qualcosa ◇ *My mother makes me do my homework.* Mia madre mi obbliga a fare* i compiti.
♦ **to make do with** accontentarsi E di ◇ *You'll have to make do with a cheaper alternative.* Dovrai accontentarti di qualcosa che costi meno.
♦ **Sorry, I can't make it to the party.** Mi dispiace, ma non riesco a venire* alla festa.
♦ **I make the total cost £1200.** Penso che il costo complessivo sia di milleduecento sterline.

to **make off** [meɪkˈɒf] VERB
svignarsela E

to **make out** [meɪkˈaut] VERB
[1] decifrare ◇ *I can't make out the address on the label.* Non riesco a decifrare l'indirizzo sull'etichetta.
[2] capire ◇ *I can't make her out at all.* Non riesco proprio a capirla.
[3] voler far credere ◇ *They're making out it was my fault.* Vogliono far credere che sia colpa mia.
♦ **to make a cheque out to somebody** intestare un assegno a qualcuno

to **make up** [meɪkˈʌp] VERB
♦ **Women make up thirteen per cent of the police force.** Il tredici percento del corpo di polizia è formato da donne.
[1] inventare ◇ *He made up the whole story.* Ha inventato tutta la storia.

[2] fare* la pace ◇ *They had a quarrel, but soon made up.* Hanno litigato, ma hanno subito fatto la pace.
[3] truccarsi E ◇ *She spends hours making herself up.* Passa delle ore a truccarsi.

to **make up for** [meɪkˈʌpfɔːʳ] VERB
compensare ◇ *Money can't make up for the stress I've suffered.* Il denaro non può compensare lo stress che ho subito.

to **make up to** [meɪkˈʌptu] VERB
♦ **I'll make it up to you somehow, I promise.** La ricompenserò in qualche modo.

maker ['meɪkəʳ] NOUN
il produttore ◇ *Italy's biggest car maker* il più grosso produttore di automobili in Italia

make-up ['meɪkʌp] NOUN
il trucco
♦ **to put on one's make-up** truccarsi E ◇ *She put on her make-up.* Si è truccata.

male [meɪl] ADJECTIVE
maschio ◇ *Most football players are male.* Quasi tutti i giocatori di calcio sono maschi.
♦ **Sex: Male** Sesso: Maschile
♦ **a male nurse** un infermiere
♦ **a male chauvinist** un maschilista

mall [mɔːl] NOUN
il centro commerciale

Malta ['mɔːltə] NOUN
Malta

mammoth ['mæməθ] ADJECTIVE
see also **mammoth** NOUN
mostruoso ◇ *a mammoth task* un lavoro mostruoso

mammoth ['mæməθ] NOUN
see also **mammoth** ADJECTIVE
il mammut (PL i mammut)

man [mæn] NOUN (PL **men**)
l' uomo (PL gli uomini)

to **manage** ['mænɪdʒ] VERB
[1] riuscire* E ◇ *Luckily I managed to pass the exam.* Fortunatamente sono riuscito a passare l'esame.
[2] farcela ◇ *Can you manage?* Ce la fai?
♦ **Can you manage a bit more?** Posso mettertene ancora un po'?
[3] arrangiarsi E ◇ *We haven't got much money, but we manage.* Non abbiamo molto denaro, ma ci arrangiamo.
[4] dirigere* ◇ *She manages a big store.* Dirige un grande negozio.

manageable ['mænɪdʒəbl] ADJECTIVE
accettabile ◇ *It was a manageable task.* Era un compito accettabile.

management ['mænɪdʒmənt] NOUN
la gestione ◇ *The restaurant is under new management.* Il ristorante ha una nuova gestione.
♦ **management and workers** dirigenti e lavoratori

manager ['mænɪdʒəʳ] NOUN
[1] il direttore

M

la direttrice
◊ *I complained to the manager.* Mi sono lamentato con il direttore.
[2] il commissario tecnico (PL i commissari tecnici) ◊ *the England manager* il commissario tecnico dell'Inghilterra

manageress [mænɪdʒəˈrɛs] NOUN (PL **manageresses**)
la direttrice

mandarin [ˈmændərɪn] NOUN
il mandarino

mango [ˈmæŋgəʊ] NOUN (PL **mangos** or **mangoes**)
il mango (PL i manghi)

maniac [ˈmeɪnɪæk] NOUN
[1] il maniaco (PL i maniaci)
la maniaca (PL le maniache)
◊ *a dangerous maniac* un pericoloso maniaco
[2] il pazzo
la pazza
◊ *He drives like a maniac.* Guida come un pazzo.

to **manipulate** [məˈnɪpjuleɪt] VERB
manipolare ◊ *She used her position to manipulate people.* Usava la sua posizione per manipolare le persone.
• **He tried to manipulate the situation.** Ha cercato di pilotare la situazione a proprio vantaggio.

man-made [ˈmænˈmeɪd] ADJECTIVE
artificiale

manner [ˈmænə'] NOUN
il modo ◊ *She was behaving in an odd manner.* Si comportava in modo strano.
• **a confident manner** un modo di fare* molto sicuro
• **good manners** buona educazione SING
• **Her manners are appalling.** Non conosce le buone maniere.
• **It's bad manners to speak with your mouth full.** È da maleducati parlare* con la bocca piena.

manpower [ˈmænpaʊə'] NOUN
la manodopera

mansion [ˈmænʃən] NOUN
la casa signorile

mantelpiece [ˈmæntlpiːs] NOUN
il caminetto

manual [ˈmænjuəl] NOUN
il manuale

to **manufacture** [mænjuˈfæktʃə'] VERB
fabbricare

manufacturer [mænjuˈfæktʃərə'] NOUN
il produttore

manure [məˈnjuə'] NOUN
il concime

manuscript [ˈmænjuskrɪpt] NOUN
il manoscritto

many [ˈmɛnɪ] ADJECTIVE, PRONOUN
molti ◊ *He hasn't got many friends.* Non ha

molti amici.
• **many people** molta gente
• **How many?** Quanti? ◊ *How many do you want?* Quanti ne vuoi?
• **too many** troppi ◊ *Sixteen people? That's too many.* Sedici persone? Sono troppe.
• **so many** tanti ◊ *He told so many lies.* Ha detto tante bugie.
• **as many as** quanti ◊ *Take as many as you like.* Prendine quanti ne vuoi.

map [mæp] NOUN
[1] la carta geografica (PL le carte geografiche) ◊ *a map of Egypt* una carta geografica dell'Egitto
[2] la cartina ◊ *maps and guide books* cartine e guide
• **a map of the city** una pianta della città

marathon [ˈmærəθən] NOUN
la maratona

marble [ˈmɑːbl] NOUN
il marmo ◊ *a marble statue* una statua di marmo

March [mɑːtʃ] NOUN
marzo ◊ *in March* in marzo

to **march** [mɑːtʃ] VERB
see also **march** NOUN
[1] sfilare ◊ *The demonstrators were marching along the main street.* I dimostranti stavano sfilando sulla via principale.
[2] marciare ◊ *The soldiers marched 50 miles.* I soldati hanno marciato per cinquanta miglia.

march [mɑːtʃ] NOUN (PL **marches**)
see also **march** VERB
la marcia (PL le marce)

mare [mɛə'] NOUN
la cavalla

margarine [mɑːdʒəˈriːn] NOUN
la margarina

margin [ˈmɑːdʒɪn] NOUN
il margine

marijuana [mærɪˈwɑːnə] NOUN
la marijuana

marina [məˈriːnə] NOUN
la marina (*for leisure craft*)

marital status [mærɪtlˈsteɪtəs] NOUN
lo stato civile

mark [mɑːk] NOUN
see also **mark** VERB
[1] il voto ◊ *I get good marks for French.* Prendo bei voti in francese.
[2] il segno ◊ *There were red marks all over his back.* Aveva segni rossi su tutta la schiena.
[3] la macchia ◊ *You've got a mark on your shirt.* Hai una macchia sulla camicia.
[4] il marco (PL i marchi) ◊ *three million marks* tre milioni di marchi

to **mark** [mɑːk] VERB
see also **mark** NOUN

---

* Verbs followed by this symbol are irregular. See pp.339–364 for further details.

[1] correggere* ◇ *The teacher hasn't marked my homework yet.* Il professore non mi ha ancora corretto il compito.
[2] segnare ◇ *Mark its position on the map.* Segna il posto in cui si trova sulla cartina.

to **mark down** [mɑːk'daun] VERB
ribassare ◇ *The shirts were marked down at the beginning of the week.* Le camicie sono state ribassate all'inizio della settimana.

market ['mɑːkɪt] NOUN
il mercato
+ **market research** indagini di mercato FEM PL

marketing ['mɑːkɪtɪŋ] NOUN
il marketing

marketplace ['mɑːkɪtpleɪs] NOUN
la piazza del mercato

marmalade ['mɑːm�əleɪd] NOUN
la marmellata d'arance

maroon [mə'ruːn] ADJECTIVE
bordeaux MASC, FEM, PL

marriage ['mærɪdʒ] NOUN
il matrimonio
+ **marriage certificate** il certificato di matrimonio

married ['mærɪd] ADJECTIVE
sposato

marrow ['mærəʊ] NOUN
la zucca (PL le zucche) (*vegetable*)
+ **bone marrow** il midollo osseo

to **marry** ['mærɪ] VERB (**married, married**)
sposare ◇ *He wants to marry her.* Vuole sposarla.
+ **to get married** sposarsi E ◇ *My sister's getting married in June.* Mia sorella si sposa in giugno.

marvellous ['mɑːvləs] ADJECTIVE (US **marvelous**)
stupendo ◇ *The weather was marvellous.* Il tempo era stupendo.

marzipan ['mɑːzɪpæn] NOUN
il marzapane

mascara [mæs'kɑːrə] NOUN
il mascara (PL i mascara)

masculine ['mæskjʊlɪn] ADJECTIVE
maschile

to **mash** [mæʃ] VERB
schiacciare (*vegetables, fruit*)

mashed potatoes [mæʃtpə'teɪtəʊz] NOUN
il purè di patate SING

mask [mɑːsk] NOUN
la maschera

masked [mɑːskt] ADJECTIVE
mascherato

mass [mæs] NOUN (PL **masses**)
[1] la massa ◇ *a mass of books and papers* una massa di libri e carte
[2] la messa ◇ *Sunday mass* messa della domenica

massage ['mæsɑːʒ] NOUN
il massaggio

massive ['mæsɪv] ADJECTIVE
enorme

to **master** ['mɑːstər] VERB
impadronirsi E di ◇ *She soon mastered the technique.* Si è impadronita rapidamente della tecnica.

masterpiece ['mɑːstəpiːs] NOUN
il capolavoro

mat [mæt] NOUN
il tappetino (*doormat*)
+ **a table mat** una tovaglietta all'americana

match [mætʃ] NOUN (PL **matches**)
see also **match** VERB
[1] la partita ◇ *Are you going to the match?* Vai alla partita?
[2] il fiammifero ◇ *a box of matches* una scatola di fiammiferi

to **match** [mætʃ] VERB
see also **match** NOUN
[1] intonarsi E con ◇ *The jacket matches the trousers.* La giacca si intona con i pantaloni.
[2] far corrispondere* ◇ *Match the pictures to the titles.* Fai corrispondere* le immagini ai titoli.

matching ['mætʃɪŋ] ADJECTIVE
intonato

mate [meɪt] NOUN
l'amico (PL gli amici) ◇ *He always goes on holiday with his mates.* Va sempre in vacanza con i suoi amici.

material [mə'tɪərɪəl] NOUN
[1] la stoffa ◇ *The curtains are made of thin material.* Le tende sono fatte di una stoffa sottile.
[2] il materiale ◇ *I'm collecting material for my project.* Sto raccogliendo materiale per la mia ricerca.
+ **raw materials** materie prime

maths [mæθs] NOUN (US **math**)
la matematica

matron ['meɪtrən] NOUN
l'infermiera capo FEM (PL le infermiere capo)

matter ['mætər] NOUN
see also **matter** VERB
la questione ◇ *It's a matter of life and death.* È una questione di vita o di morte.
+ **What's the matter?** Cosa c'è che non va?
+ **as a matter of fact** per dire* la verità

to **matter** ['mætər] VERB
see also **matter** NOUN
importare E ◇ *I can't give you the money today. – It doesn't matter.* Non ti posso dare* i soldi oggi. – Non importa.
+ **Shall I phone today or tomorrow? – Whenever, it doesn't matter.** Devo telefonare oggi o domani? – Quando vuoi, è uguale.
+ **It matters a lot to me.** È molto importante per me.

mattress ['mætrɪs] NOUN (PL **mattresses**)
il materasso

mature [mə'tjʊər] ADJECTIVE ☞

M

maturo

maximum ['mæksɪməm] NOUN, ADJECTIVE
il massimo

May [meɪ] NOUN
maggio ◇ *in May* in maggio
• **May Day** il primo maggio

ℹ️ **May Day** *è il primo maggio, giorno in cui si festeggia l'arrivo della primavera.*

may [meɪ] VERB
*may is usually translated by **potere.***
◇ *May I smoke?* Posso fumare? ◇ *It may rain.* Potrebbe piovere*.
• **Are you going to the party? – I don't know, I may...** Vai alla festa? – Non so, forse...
• **He may come.** Può darsi che venga.
• **They may have thought you were joking.** Forse hanno pensato che scherzassi.

maybe ['meɪbi:] ADVERB
forse

mayonnaise [meɪə'neɪz] NOUN
la maionese

mayor [mɛəʳ] NOUN
il sindaco (PL i sindaci)

maze [meɪz] NOUN
il labirinto

me [mi:] PRONOUN
1 mi ◇ *Excuse me!* Mi scusi! ◇ *Could you lend me your pen?* Puoi prestarmi la penna? ◇ *Look at me!* Guardami!
2 me ◇ *Come with me!* Vieni con me!
• **without me** senza di me
• **It's me.** Sono io.

meal [mi:l] NOUN
il pasto ◇ *before meals* prima dei pasti
• **Enjoy your meal!** Buon appetito!

mealtime ['mi:ltaɪm] NOUN
• **at mealtimes** all'ora dei pasti

to **mean** [mi:n] VERB (**meant, meant**)
see also **mean** ADJECTIVE
1 significare ◇ *What does "trap" mean?* Cosa significa "trap"? ◇ *You mean a lot to me.* Significhi molto per me.
2 intendere* ◇ *That's not what I meant.* Non era quello che intendevo. ◇ *Do you mean me?* Intendi me?
3 volere* ◇ *I didn't mean to hurt you.* Non volevo farti del male.
• **Do you really mean it?** Parli sul serio?
• **He means what he says.** Parla sul serio.

mean [mi:n] ADJECTIVE
see also **mean** VERB
1 avaro ◇ *He's too mean to buy presents.* È troppo avaro per comprare regali.
2 meschino ◇ *That's a really mean thing to say!* Che cosa meschina da dire*!
3 cattivo ◇ *You're being mean to me.* Sei cattivo con me.

meaning ['mi:nɪŋ] NOUN
il significato

means [mi:nz] NOUN SING
il mezzo ◇ *He'll do it by any possible means.* Lo farò con ogni mezzo possibile.
• **a means of transport** un mezzo di trasporto
• **by means of** per mezzo di
• **Can I come? – By all means!** Posso venire*? – Ma certamente!

meant [ment] VERB *see* **mean**

meanwhile ['mi:nwaɪl] ADVERB
nel frattempo

measles ['mi:zlz] NOUN SING
il morbillo

to **measure** ['mɛʒəʳ] VERB
misurare ◇ *They regularly measure pollution levels.* Misurano regolarmente il grado di inquinamento.

measurements ['mɛʒəmənts] NOUN PL
le misure ◇ *Are you sure the measurements are correct?* Sei sicuro che le misure siano giuste?

meat [mi:t] NOUN
la carne ◇ *I don't eat meat.* Non mangio carne.

Mecca ['mɛkə] NOUN
la Mecca

mechanic [mɪ'kænɪk] NOUN
il meccanico (PL i meccanici)

medal ['medl] NOUN
la medaglia

medallion [mɪ'dælɪən] NOUN
il medaglione

media ['mi:dɪə] NOUN PL
• **the media** i mass media

median strip [mi:dɪən'strɪp] NOUN PL US
la banchina spartitraffico (PL le banchine spartitraffico)

medical ['medɪkl] ADJECTIVE
see also **medical** NOUN
medico ◇ *medical treatment* cure mediche
FEM PL

medical ['medɪkl] NOUN
see also **medical** ADJECTIVE
la visita medica (PL le visite mediche) ◇ *He had his medical last week.* Ha fatto una visita medica la settimana scorsa.

medicine ['medsɪn] NOUN
la medicina

Mediterranean [medɪtə'reɪnɪən] ADJECTIVE
mediterraneo

medium ['mi:dɪəm] ADJECTIVE
medio ◇ *Small, medium or large?* Piccola, media o grande?
• **a medium size town** una città di dimensioni medie

to **meet** [mi:t] VERB (**met, met**)
1 incontrare ◇ *I met Paul in town.* Ho incontrato Paul in città.
2 incontrarsi[E] ◇ *We met by chance.* Ci siamo incontrati per caso.
3 trovarsi[E] ◇ *I'm going to meet my friends at the swimming pool.* Mi trovo con i miei

---

* Verbs followed by this symbol are irregular. See pp.339–364 for further details.

amici in piscina.

[4] andare* [E] a prendere* ◊ *I'll meet you at the station.* Vengo a prenderti in stazione.

[5] conoscere* ◊ *Come and meet my dad.* Vieni a conoscere* mio padre.

• **Pleased to meet you.** Piacere di conoscerla.

to **meet up** [miːtʌp] VERB
incontrarsi [E] ◊ *They arranged to meet up with the others at eight o'clock.* Hanno stabilito di incontrarsi con gli altri alle otto.

meeting ['miːtɪŋ] NOUN
[1] l' incontro ◊ *their first meeting* il loro primo incontro
[2] la riunione ◊ *a business meeting* una riunione di lavoro

mega ['mɛgə] ADJECTIVE
• **He's mega rich.** È straricco.

melody ['mɛlədɪ] NOUN (PL **melodies**)
la melodia

melon ['mɛlən] NOUN
il melone

to **melt** [mɛlt] VERB
[1] sciogliere* ◊ *Melt two ounces of butter in a saucepan.* Sciogliete sessanta grammi di burro in una casseruola.
[2] sciogliersi [E] ◊ *The snow is melting.* La neve si sta sciogliendo.

member ['mɛmbə'] NOUN
[1] il membro ◊ *a member of NATO* un membro della NATO
• **a member of the public** un privato cittadino una privata cittadina
[2] il socio (*of club*) ◊ *"members only"* "riservato ai soci"
• **a Member of Parliament** un deputato una deputata

membership ['mɛmbəʃɪp] NOUN
l' iscrizione FEM ◊ *I'm going to apply for membership.* Farò domanda d'iscrizione.

membership card ['mɛmbəʃɪpkɑːd] NOUN
la tessera

memento [mə'mɛntəu] NOUN (PL **mementos** or **mementoes**)
il ricordo

memorial [mɪ'mɔːrɪəl] ADJECTIVE
see also **memorial** NOUN
• **a memorial service** una funzione commemorativa

memorial [mɪ'mɔːrɪəl] NOUN
see also **memorial** ADJECTIVE
• **a war memorial** un monumento ai caduti

to **memorize** ['mɛməraɪz] VERB
imparare a memoria

memory ['mɛmərɪ] NOUN (PL **memories**)
[1] la memoria ◊ *I've got a terrible memory.* Ho una pessima memoria.
[2] il ricordo ◊ *happy memories* bei ricordi

men [mɛn] NOUN PL see **man**

to **mend** [mɛnd] VERB
aggiustare

meningitis [mɛnɪn'dʒaɪtɪs] NOUN
la meningite

mental ['mɛntl] ADJECTIVE
mentale ◊ *a mental illness* una malattia mentale
• **a mental hospital** un ospedale psichiatrico

mentality [mɛn'tælɪtɪ] NOUN
la mentalità (PL le mentalità)

to **mention** ['mɛnʃən] VERB
[1] parlare* di ◊ *He didn't mention it to me.* Non me ne ha parlato.
[2] accennare a ◊ *She didn't mention her unpleasant experience.* Non ha accennato alla sua spiacevole esperienza.
[3] dire* ◊ *I mentioned she might come later.* Ho detto che poteva passare più tardi.
• **Thank you! – Don't mention it!** Grazie! – Di niente!

menu ['mɛnjuː] NOUN
il menù (PL i menù) ◊ *a set menu* un menù a prezzo fisso

merchant ['mɜːtʃənt] NOUN
il/la commerciante ◊ *a wine merchant* un commerciante di vini

merchant navy ['mɜːtʃənt'neɪvɪ] NOUN
la marina mercantile

mercy ['mɜːsɪ] NOUN
la pietà

mere [mɪə'] ADJECTIVE
semplice ◊ *It's a mere formality.* È una semplice formalità.
• **a mere five percent** solo il cinque per cento
• **the merest** il minimo ◊ *the merest hint of criticism* il minimo accenno di critica

meringue [mə'ræŋ] NOUN
la meringa (PL le meringhe)

merry ['mɛrɪ] ADJECTIVE
• **Merry Christmas!** Buon Natale!

merry-go-round ['mɛrɪgəuraund] NOUN
la giostra

mess [mɛs] NOUN
[1] il disordine
• **to be a mess** essere* [E] in disordine ◊ *My hair's a mess, it needs cutting.* Ho i capelli in disordine: devo tagliarli.
[2] il guaio ◊ *I'll be in a mess if I fail the exam.* Sarò in un bel guaio se non passerò l'esame.

to **mess about** [mɛsə'baut] VERB
trafficare ◊ *Stop messing about with my computer!* Smettetela di trafficare con il mio computer!
• **I didn't do much at the weekend, just messed about with friends.** Non ho fatto granché per il fine settimana, sono stato con degli amici.

message ['mɛsɪdʒ] NOUN
il messaggio

to **mess up** [mɛsʌp] VERB
incasinare ◊ *You've messed up my cassettes!* Hai incasinato i miei cassetti.
• **I messed up my chemistry exam.** Mi è ☞

M

andato male l'esame di chimica.

messenger ['mesɪndʒə'] NOUN
il messaggero
la messaggera

messy ['mesɪ] ADJECTIVE
pasticcione ◇ *She's such a messy person!* È
una persona talmente pasticciona!
+ **Painting can be a messy activity.** Dipingere
è un'attività con cui ci si può sporcare molto.
+ **Her writing is very messy.** Ha una
scritturaccia.

met [met] VERB *see* **meet**

metal ['metl] NOUN
il metallo

meter ['miːtə'] NOUN
1 il parchimetro (*parking meter*)
2 il contatore (*for gas, electricity*)
3 il metro (*metre*) US

method ['meθəd] NOUN
il metodo

Methodist ['meθədɪst] NOUN
il/la metodista MASC/FEM

metre ['miːtə'] NOUN
il metro

metric ['metrɪk] ADJECTIVE
metrico

Mexico ['meksɪkəu] NOUN
il Messico

to **miaow** [miːˈau] VERB
miagolare

mice [maɪs] NOUN *see* **mouse**

microchip ['maɪkrəutʃɪp] NOUN
il microcircuito integrato

microphone ['maɪkrəfəun] NOUN
il microfono

microscope ['maɪkrəskəup] NOUN
il microscopio

microwave ['maɪkrəuweɪv] NOUN
il forno a microonde

mid [mɪd] ADJECTIVE
+ **in mid May** a metà maggio
+ **He's in his mid twenties.** Avrà circa
venticinque anni.

midday [mɪdˈdeɪ] NOUN
il mezzogiorno

middle ['mɪdl] NOUN
see also **middle** ADJECTIVE
+ **in the middle** in mezzo ◇ *In the middle let's
put...* E in mezzo mettiamo...
+ **in the middle of** in mezzo a ◇ *The car was in
the middle of the road.* La macchina era in
mezzo alla strada.
+ **The potatoes were still raw in the middle.**
Le patate erano ancora crude dentro.
+ **She was in the middle of her exams.** Era
sotto esame.
+ **in the middle of the night** nel cuore della
notte

middle ['mɪdl] ADJECTIVE
see also **middle** NOUN
di mezzo ◇ *the middle seat* il sedile di mezzo

+ **the middle finger** il medio
+ **middle name** secondo nome

middle-aged [mɪdl'eɪdʒd] ADJECTIVE
di mezza età

Middle Ages [mɪdl'eɪdʒəz] NOUN PL
+ **the Middle Ages** il Medioevo

middle-class [mɪdl'klɑːs] ADJECTIVE
borghese

Middle East [mɪdl'iːst] NOUN
il Medio Oriente

middle name ['mɪdlneɪm] NOUN
il secondo nome

midge [mɪdʒ] NOUN
il moscerino

midnight ['mɪdnaɪt] NOUN
la mezzanotte

midwife ['mɪdwaɪf] NOUN (PL **midwives**)
l' ostetrica (PL le ostetriche)

might [maɪt] VERB

*might is often translated by the conditional
of potere.*

◇ *We might go to Spain next year.*
Potremmo andare* in Spagna il prossimo
anno. ◇ *She might not have understood.*
Potrebbe non aver capito. ◇ *He might come
later.* Forse potrebbe arrivare più tardi.
+ **I suppose you might as well come with us.**
Tanto vale che tu venga con noi, suppongo.

migraine ['miːɡreɪn] NOUN
l' emicrania

mike [maɪk] NOUN
il microfono

Milan [mɪˈlæn] NOUN
Milano FEM

mild [maɪld] ADJECTIVE
1 mite ◇ *The winters are quite mild.* Gli
inverni sono abbastanza miti.
+ **It's very mild today.** Oggi non fa affatto
freddo.
2 delicato ◇ *a mild flavour* un sapore
delicato
+ **mild soap** sapone neutro

mile [maɪl] NOUN
il miglio (PL FEM le miglia)

❶ *In Gran Bretagna le distanze sono
espresse in miglia invece che in chilometri.
Un miglio corrisponde a 1,609 metri.*

+ **We walked for miles!** Abbiamo fatto
chilometri a piedi!

military ['mɪlɪtərɪ] ADJECTIVE
militare

milk [mɪlk] NOUN
see also **milk** VERB
il latte ◇ *tea with milk* tè con il latte

to **milk** [mɪlk] VERB
see also **milk** NOUN
mungere*

milk chocolate [mɪlk'tʃɒklɪt] NOUN

* Verbs followed by this symbol are irregular. See pp.339–364 for further details.

il cioccolato al latte

milkman ['mɪlkmən] NOUN (PL **milkmen**)
il lattaio

milk shake ['mɪlkʃeɪk] NOUN
il frappé (PL i frappé)

mill [mɪl] NOUN
il mulino ◇ *an old mill* un vecchio mulino
* **a woollen mill** un lanificio
* **a pepper mill** un macinapepe

millennium [mɪˈlenɪəm] NOUN PL
il millennio

millimetre ['mɪlɪmiːtə'] NOUN (US **millimeter**)
il millimetro

million ['mɪljən] NOUN
il milione ◇ *two million lire* due milioni di lire

millionaire [mɪljəˈneə'] NOUN
il miliardario
la miliardaria

to **mimic** ['mɪmɪk] VERB (**mimicked, mimicked**)
imitare

mince [mɪns] NOUN
la carne macinata ◇ *lean mince* carne macinata magra

mince pie [mɪnsˈpaɪ] NOUN
il tortino natalizio

> **❶** *Un* **mince pie** *è un tortino natalizio ripieno di frutta secca.*

to **mind** [maɪnd] VERB
see also **mind** NOUN
[1] fare* attenzione a ◇ *Mind you don't fall.* Fa' attenzione a non cadere*.
* **Mind the step!** Attenzione al gradino!
[2] occuparsi^E di ◇ *Could you mind the baby this afternoon?* Puoi occuparti del bambino questo pomeriggio?
[3] guardare ◇ *Could you mind my bags for a few minutes?* Può guardarmi le borse per qualche minuto?
* **Do you mind if I open the window? – No, I don't mind.** Le dispiace se apro la finestra? – Faccia pure.
* **I don't mind getting up early.** Non mi dispiace alzarmi presto.
* **I don't mind the noise.** Il rumore non mi dà fastidio.
* **Never mind!** Non fa niente!

mind [maɪnd] NOUN
see also **mind** VERB
la mente ◇ *What have you got in mind?* Che cos'hai in mente? ◇ *It never crossed my mind.* Non mi ha mai sfiorato la mente.
* **to make up one's mind** decidere* ◇ *I haven't made up my mind yet.* Non ho ancora deciso.
* **to change one's mind** cambiare idea ◇ *He's changed his mind.* Ha cambiato idea.
* **to bear something in mind** tener presente ◇ *I'll bear that in mind.* Lo terrò presente.
* **Are you out of your mind?** Sei impazzito?

* **It'll keep your mind off the exam.** Ti distrarrà dall'esame.
* **She's got a mind of her own.** Pensa con la sua testa.

mine [maɪn] PRONOUN
see also **mine** NOUN
The Italian pronoun agrees with the noun it is replacing.
[1] il mio MASC (PL i miei) ◇ *Is this your coat? – No, mine's black.* È tuo questo cappotto? – No, il mio è nero. ◇ *Your marks are better than mine.* I tuoi voti sono migliori dei miei.
[2] la mia FEM (PL le mie) ◇ *Is this your scarf? – No, mine's red.* È tua questa sciarpa? No, la mia è rossa. ◇ *Her shoes are nicer than mine.* Le sue scarpe sono più belle delle mie.
[3] mio MASC (PL miei) (*my property*) ◇ *That book's mine.* Quel libro è mio.
* **He's a friend of mine.** È un mio amico.
[4] mia FEM (PL mie) (*my property*) ◇ *These pencils are mine.* Queste matite sono mie.
* **She's friend of mine.** È una mia amica.

mine [maɪn] NOUN
see also **mine** PRONOUN
[1] la miniera ◇ *a coal mine* una miniera di carbone
[2] la mina ◇ *There are still many unexploded mines in Kosovo.* Ci sono ancora molte mine inesplose in Kosovo.

miner ['maɪnə'] NOUN
il minatore

mineral ['mɪnərəl] ADJECTIVE
minerale

mineral water ['mɪnərəlwɔːtə'] NOUN
l'acqua minerale

miniature ['mɪnətʃə'] ADJECTIVE
in miniatura

minibus ['mɪnɪbʌs] NOUN (PL **minibuses**)
il pulmino

minicab ['mɪnɪkæb] NOUN
il taxi (PL i taxi)

> **❶** *I* **minicabs** *sono radiotaxi privati in genere meno costosi dei tradizionali taxi neri, maggiormente regolamentati.*

Minidisc ® ['mɪnɪdɪsk] NOUN
il minidisco (PL i minidischi)

minimum ['mɪnɪməm] ADJECTIVE, NOUN
il minimo

miniskirt ['mɪnɪskəːt] NOUN
la minigonna

minister ['mɪnɪstə'] NOUN
[1] il ministro ◇ *the Education Minister* il ministro della Pubblica Istruzione
[2] il pastore (*of church*)

ministry ['mɪnɪstrɪ] NOUN (PL **ministries**)
il ministero

mink [mɪŋk] NOUN
il visone ◇ *a mink coat* una pelliccia di ☞

M

visone

minor ['maɪnə'] ADJECTIVE
1 secondario ◇ *a minor problem* un problema secondario
2 piccolo ◇ *a minor operation* una piccola operazione

minority [maɪ'nɔrɪtɪ] NOUN (PL **minorities**)
la minoranza

mint [mɪnt] NOUN
1 la mentina ◇ *Would you like a mint?* Vuoi una mentina?
2 la menta (*herb*)
• **mint sauce** la salsa alla menta

❶ *La* **mint sauce** *è una salsa alla menta servita con l'agnello.*

minus ['maɪnəs] PREPOSITION
1 meno ◇ *sixteen minus three* sedici meno tre ◇ *I got a B minus for my French.* Ho ricevuto B meno in francese.

❶ *Nei paesi anglosassoni i voti sono espressi con le lettere A, B, C e D.*

• **minus two degrees** due gradi sotto zero
2 ma senza ◇ *I found my wallet, minus the money.* Ho ritrovato il mio portafoglio, ma senza il denaro.

minute ['mɪnɪt] NOUN
see also **minute** ADJECTIVE
il minuto ◇ *ten minutes* dieci minuti

minute [maɪ'njuːt] ADJECTIVE
see also **minute** NOUN
minuscolo ◇ *Her flat is minute.* Il suo appartamento è minuscolo.
• **a minute amount** una quantità minima

miracle ['mɪrəkl] NOUN
il miracolo

mirror ['mɪrə'] NOUN
1 lo specchio ◇ *She looked at herself in the mirror.* Si è guardata allo specchio.
2 lo specchietto ◇ *She got in the car and adjusted the mirror.* È entrata in macchina e ha regolato lo specchietto.

to **misbehave** [mɪsbɪ'heɪv] VERB
comportarsi [E] male

miscellaneous [mɪsɪ'leɪnɪəs] ADJECTIVE
vario ◇ *miscellaneous items* articoli vari

mischief ['mɪstʃɪf] NOUN
• **She's always up to mischief.** Ne combina sempre una.
• **full of mischief** birichino

mischievous ['mɪstʃɪvəs] ADJECTIVE
birichino

miser ['maɪzə'] NOUN
l'avaro
l'avara

miserable ['mɪzərəbl] ADJECTIVE
infelice ◇ *a miserable life* una vita infelice

• **to feel miserable** essere* [E] giù di morale
• **miserable weather** brutto tempo
• **a miserable failure** un fiasco

misery ['mɪzərɪ] NOUN
1 la tristezza ◇ *All that money brought nothing but misery.* Tutto quel denaro non ha portato che tristezza.
2 la lagna ◇ *She's a real misery.* È proprio una lagna.

misfortune [mɪs'fɔːtʃən] NOUN
la sfortuna

mishap ['mɪshæp] NOUN
la disavventura ◇ *a minor mishap* una piccola disavventura
• **without mishap** senza incidenti

to **misjudge** [mɪs'dʒʌdʒ] VERB
1 giudicare male ◇ *I may have misjudged him.* Posso averlo giudicato male.
2 valutare male ◇ *The driver misjudged the bend.* Il guidatore ha valutato male la curva.

to **mislay** [mɪs'leɪ] VERB (**mislaid, mislaid**)
smarrire

to **mislead** [mɪs'liːd] VERB (**misled, misled**)
trarre* in inganno

misleading [mɪs'liːdɪŋ] ADJECTIVE
fuorviante

misprint ['mɪsprɪnt] NOUN
l'errore di stampa MASC

Miss [mɪs] NOUN
la signorina ◇ *Miss Peters wants to see you.* La signorina Peters vuole vederla.

❶ *When* **miss** *is used to address a secondary school teacher it is translated by "professoressa". "Maestra" would be used for a primary school teacher.*

miss [mɪs] NOUN
see also **miss** VERB
• **He decided to give the film a miss.** Ha deciso di non andare* a vedere* quel film.
• **We had a near miss.** Per poco non ci è successo un incidente.

to **miss** [mɪs] VERB
see also **miss** NOUN
1 perdere* ◇ *Hurry or you'll miss the bus.* Affrettati o perderai l'autobus. ◇ *It's too good an opportunity to miss.* È un'opportunità da non perdere* assolutamente.
2 mancare ◇ *He missed the target.* Ha mancato il bersaglio.
3 saltare ◇ *You've missed a page.* Hai saltato una pagina.
4 sentire la mancanza di ◇ *I miss my family.* Sento la mancanza della mia famiglia.

to **miss out** [mɪs'aut] VERB
saltare ◇ *What about Sally? You've missed her out.* E Sally? L'hai saltata.

---

* Verbs followed by this symbol are irregular. See pp.339–364 for further details.

missing ['mɪsɪŋ] ADJECTIVE
mancante ◊ *the missing link* l'anello mancante

◆ **to be missing (1)** (*thing*) mancare [E]
◆ **to be missing (2)** (*person*) mancare [E] all'appello
◆ **a missing person** un disperso

missionary ['mɪʃənrɪ] NOUN (PL **missionaries**)
il missionario
la missionaria

mist [mɪst] NOUN
la foschia

mistake [mɪs'teɪk] NOUN
see also **mistake** VERB
l'errore MASC ◊ *a spelling mistake* un errore di ortografia ◊ *There must be some mistake.* Dev'esserci un errore. ◊ *He makes a lot of mistakes when he speaks English.* Fa molti errori quando parla in inglese.

◆ **by mistake** per sbaglio

to **mistake** [mɪs'teɪk] VERB (**mistook, mistaken**)
see also **mistake** NOUN
scambiare ◊ *He mistook me for my sister.* Mi ha scambiato per mia sorella.

mistaken [mɪs'teɪkən] ADJECTIVE
◆ **to be mistaken** sbagliarsi [E] ◊ *If you think I'm going to pay, you're mistaken.* Se pensi che ho intenzione di pagare ti sbagli.

mistakenly [mɪs'teɪkənlɪ] ADVERB
erroneamente

mistletoe ['mɪsltəʊ] NOUN
il vischio

> ❶ *In Gran Bretagna e negli Stati Uniti per Natale c'è l'usanza di baciarsi sotto il vischio.*

mistook [mɪs'tʊk] VERB *see* **mistake**

mistress ['mɪstrɪs] NOUN (PL **mistresses**)
[1] l'amante FEM ◊ *He's got a mistress.* Ha un'amante.
[2] la professoressa ◊ *our English mistress* la nostra professoressa di inglese

mistrust [mɪs'trʌst] NOUN
la diffidenza ◊ *a deep mistrust of politicians* una profonda diffidenza nei confronti dei politici

misty ['mɪstɪ] ADJECTIVE
nebbioso

to **misunderstand** [mɪsʌndə'stænd] VERB (**misunderstood, misunderstood**)
fraintendere ◊ *Maybe I misunderstood you.* Forse ho frainteso.

misunderstanding ['mɪsʌndə'stændɪŋ] NOUN
il fraintendimento ◊ *I think there's been some misunderstanding.* Penso che ci sia stato un fraintendimento.

misunderstood [mɪsʌndə'stʊd] VERB *see* **misunderstand**

mix [mɪks] NOUN (PL **mixes**)
see also **mix** VERB
il misto ◊ *The film is a mix of science fiction and comedy.* Il film è un misto di fantascienza e commedia.

◆ **a cake mix** un preparato per torte

to **mix** [mɪks] VERB
see also **mix** NOUN
[1] mescolare ◊ *Mix the flour with the sugar.* Mescolate la farina con lo zucchero.
[2] unire ◊ *He's mixing business with pleasure.* Unisce l'utile al dilettevole.
[3] legare ◊ *He doesn't mix much.* Non lega molto con gli altri.

◆ **to mix with** frequentare ◊ *I like mixing with all sorts of people.* Mi piace frequentare persone di tutti i tipi.

to **mix up** [mɪks'ʌp] VERB
confondere* ◊ *The travel agent mixed up the bookings.* L'agente di viaggio ha confuso le prenotazioni.

mixed [mɪkst] ADJECTIVE
[1] misto ◊ *a mixed grill* una grigliata mista
[2] contrastante ◊ *I've got mixed feelings about it.* Ho dei sentimenti contrastanti a riguardo.
[3] variabile ◊ *The weather was mixed.* C'era tempo variabile.

mixed up [mɪkst'ʌp] ADJECTIVE
[1] disorientato ◊ *I'm getting mixed up.* Sono disorientato.
[2] confuso ◊ *a mixed up teenager* un adolescente confuso

◆ **to be mixed up with** avere* a che fare* con ◊ *He's mixed up with drug dealers.* Ha a che fare* con degli spacciatori.
◆ **to get something mixed up** scambiare qualcosa ◊ *He got their names mixed up.* Ha scambiato i loro nomi.

mixer ['mɪksə'] NOUN
il frullatore

mixture ['mɪkstʃə'] NOUN
il miscuglio ◊ *a mixture of spices* un miscuglio di spezie

mix-up ['mɪksʌp] NOUN
la confusione

to **moan** [məʊn] VERB
lamentarsi [E] ◊ *She's always moaning about something.* Ha sempre qualcosa di cui lamentarsi.

mobile ['məʊbaɪl] ADJECTIVE
see also **mobile** NOUN
◆ **She's ninety, but still mobile.** Ha novant'anni ma riesce ancora a camminare.

mobile ['məʊbaɪl] NOUN
see also **mobile** ADJECTIVE
il cellulare ◊ *You can get me on my mobile.* Mi puoi trovare sul cellulare.

mobile home [məʊbaɪl'həʊm] NOUN
la grande roulotte

mobile phone [məʊbaɪl'fəʊn] NOUN
il telefono cellulare

M

to **mock** [mɔk] VERB
> see also **mock** ADJECTIVE
canzonare

mock [mɔk] ADJECTIVE
> see also **mock** VERB
* **a mock exam** una simulazione d'esame

> ❶ / mock exams *servono a saggiare la preparazione degli studenti in vista degli esami ufficiali.*

mod cons [mɔd'kɔnz] NOUN PL
* **with all mod cons** con tutti i comfort

model ['mɔdl] NOUN, ADJECTIVE
> see also **model** VERB
1 il modello ◇ *It's the basic model.* È il modello base.
2 il modellino ◇ *a model of the castle* un modellino del castello
* **a model railway** un trenino in miniatura
3 la modella ◇ *She's a famous model.* È una modella famosa.

to **model** ['mɔdl] VERB
> see also **model** NOUN
indossare

modem ['məudem] NOUN
il modem (PL i modem)

moderate ['mɔdərət] ADJECTIVE
moderato ◇ *His views are quite moderate.* Ha opinioni abbastanza moderate.
* **a moderate amount of** un po' di ◇ *I do a moderate amount of exercise.* Faccio un po' di ginnastica.

modern ['mɔdən] ADJECTIVE
moderno

to **modernize** ['mɔdənaɪz] VERB
modernizzare

modest ['mɔdɪst] ADJECTIVE
modesto

to **modify** ['mɔdɪfaɪ] VERB (**modified, modified**)
modificare

moist [mɔɪst] ADJECTIVE
1 umido ◇ *Sow the seeds in moist soil.* Piantate i semi nel terreno umido.
2 soffice ◇ *This cake is very moist.* Questa torta è molto soffice.

moisture ['mɔɪstʃə'] NOUN
l'umidità

moisturizer ['mɔɪstʃəraɪzə'] NOUN
la crema idratante

moldy ['məuldɪ] ADJECTIVE US
ammuffito

mole [məul] NOUN
1 il neo ◇ *I've got a mole on my back.* Ho un neo sulla schiena.
2 la talpa (*animal, spy*)

moment ['məumənt] NOUN
il momento ◇ *any moment now* da un momento all'altro

momentous [məu'mentəs] ADJECTIVE
di grande importanza

monarch ['mɔnək] NOUN
il monarca (PL i monarchi)

monarchy ['mɔnəkɪ] NOUN (PL **monarchies**)
la monarchia

monastery ['mɔnəstərɪ] NOUN (PL **monasteries**)
il monastero

Monday ['mʌndɪ] NOUN
il lunedì (PL i lunedì)
* **on Monday** lunedì ◇ *I saw her on Monday.* L'ho vista lunedì.
* **on Mondays** di lunedì ◇ *I go swimming on Mondays.* Vado in piscina di lunedì.

money ['mʌnɪ] NOUN
i soldi MASC PL ◇ *I need to change some money.* Devo cambiare dei soldi.

mongrel ['mʌŋgrəl] NOUN
il bastardo ◇ *My dog's a mongrel.* Il mio cane è un bastardo.

monk [mʌŋk] NOUN
il monaco (PL i monaci)

monkey ['mʌŋkɪ] NOUN
la scimmia

monkey nut ['mʌŋkɪnʌt] NOUN
la nocciolina americana

monopoly ® [mə'nɔpəlɪ] NOUN
il monopolio ◇ *a state monopoly* un monopolio di stato
* **to play Monopoly** ® giocare a Monopoli ®

monster ['mɔnstə'] NOUN
il mostro

month [mʌnθ] NOUN
il mese ◇ *last month* il mese scorso

monthly ['mʌnθlɪ] ADJECTIVE
mensile

mood [mu:d] NOUN
l'umore MASC ◇ *He was in a bad mood.* Era di cattivo umore.

moody ['mu:dɪ] ADJECTIVE
1 lunatico ◇ *He's moody and unpredictable.* È lunatico e imprevedibile.
2 malinconico ◇ *moody lyrics* parole malinconiche

moon [mu:n] NOUN
la luna ◇ *There's a full moon tonight.* Stanotte c'è la luna piena.
* **She's over the moon about it.** È al settimo cielo.

moor [muə'] NOUN
> see also **moor** VERB
la brughiera

to **moor** [muə'] VERB
> see also **moor** NOUN
ormeggiare

mop [mɔp] NOUN
il mocio ®

moped ['məuped] NOUN
il motorino

moral ['mɔrl] NOUN
la morale ◇ *The moral of the story is...* La morale della storia è...

---

* Verbs followed by this symbol are irregular. See pp.339–364 for further details.

◆ **morals** moralità SING

morale [mɔˈrɑːl] NOUN
il morale ◇ *Morale was low.* Il morale era basso.

more [mɔːʳ] ADJECTIVE, PRONOUN, ADVERB
1 più ◇ *There isn't any more.* Non ce n'è più.
2 di più ◇ *It costs a lot more.* Costa molto di più.
3 ancora ◇ *A bit more?* Ancora un po'? ◇ *Is there any more?* Ce n'è ancora? ◇ *It'll take a few more days.* Ci vorrà ancora qualche giorno.

◆ **more than** più di ◇ *I spent more than ten pounds.* Ho speso più di dieci sterline. ◇ *He's more intelligent than me.* È più intelligente di me.
◆ **more or less** più o meno
◆ **more than ever** più che mai
◆ **more and more** sempre più ◇ *I got more and more depressed.* Ero sempre più depresso. ◇ *more and more often* sempre più spesso

moreover [mɔːˈrəʊvəʳ] ADVERB
inoltre

Mormon [ˈmɔːmən] NOUN
il/la mormone

morning [ˈmɔːnɪŋ] NOUN
la mattina ◇ *at seven o'clock in the morning* alle sette di mattina
◆ **I'll do it first thing in the morning.** Lo farò domani mattina appena mi sveglio.
◆ **this morning** stamattina
◆ **the morning papers** i giornali del mattino

Moscow [ˈmɒskəʊ] NOUN
Mosca ◇ *He's in Moscow.* È a Mosca.

Moslem [ˈmɒzləm] NOUN, ADJECTIVE
il mussulmano
la mussulmana

mosque [mɒsk] NOUN
la moschea

mosquito [mɒsˈkiːtəʊ] NOUN (PL **mosquitoes**)
la zanzara ◇ *a mosquito bite* una puntura di zanzara

mosquito repellent [mɒsˈkiːtəʊriˈpelənt] NOUN
l' insettifugo (PL gli insettifughi)

most [məʊst] ADJECTIVE, PRONOUN, ADVERB
di più ◇ *the thing she most feared* la cosa che temeva di più ◇ *He's the one who talks most.* Lui è quello che parla di più.
◆ **the most** il più ◇ *the most expensive restaurant* il ristorante più caro
◆ **He won the most votes.** Ha avuto più voti degli altri.
◆ **most of** gran parte di ◇ *I know most of them.* Conosco gran parte di loro. ◇ *most of the time* gran parte del tempo ◇ *I did most of the work.* Ho fatto gran parte del lavoro.
◆ **most people** quasi tutti ◇ *Most people go out on Friday night.* Quasi tutti escono venerdì sera.

◆ **at the most** al massimo ◇ *two hours at the most* due ore al massimo
◆ **to make the most of** sfruttare al massimo ◇ *He made the most of his holiday.* Ha sfruttato al massimo la vacanza.

mostly [ˈməʊstlɪ] ADVERB
in genere ◇ *The teachers are mostly quite nice.* In genere gli insegnanti sono abbastanza gentili.

MOT [ɛməʊˈtiː] NOUN
la revisione

> ❶ *L'* **MOT** *è una revisione annuale obbligatoria per autoveicoli che hanno più di tre anni.*

◇ *My car has failed its MOT.* La mia macchina non ha passato la revisione.

moth [mɒθ] NOUN
1 la falena (*butterfly*)
2 la tarma (*clothes moth*)

mother [ˈmʌðəʳ] NOUN
la madre ◇ *my mother* mia madre
◆ **mother tongue** madrelingua

mother-in-law [ˈmʌðərɪnlɔː] NOUN (PL **mothers-in-law**)
la suocera

Mother's Day [ˈmʌðəzdeɪ] NOUN
la festa della mamma

M

> ❶ **Mother's Day** *in Italy is the second Sunday in May, while in Britain it is the fourth Sunday of Lent.*

motionless [ˈməʊʃənlɪs] ADJECTIVE
immobile

motivated [ˈməʊtɪveɪtɪd] ADJECTIVE
motivato ◇ *He's highly motivated.* È fortemente motivato.

motivation [məʊtɪˈveɪʃən] NOUN
la motivazione

motive [ˈməʊtɪv] NOUN
1 il movente ◇ *the motive for the killing* il movente dell'omicidio
2 l' intenzione FEM ◇ *for the best of motives* con la migliore delle intenzioni
◆ **an ulterior motive** un secondo fine

motor [ˈməʊtəʳ] NOUN
il motore ◇ *a boat with a motor* una barca a motore

motorbike [ˈməʊtəbaɪk] NOUN
la motocicletta

motorboat [ˈməʊtəbəʊt] NOUN
il motoscafo

motorcycle [ˈməʊtəsaɪkl] NOUN
la motocicletta

motorcyclist [ˈməʊtəsaɪklɪst] NOUN
il/la motociclista

motorist [ˈməʊtərɪst] NOUN
l' automobilista

motor mechanic [ˈməʊtəmɪˈkænɪk] NOUN ☞

il meccanico (PL i meccanici)

motor racing ['məʊtəreɪsɪŋ] NOUN
le corse automobilistiche FEM PL

motorway ['məʊtəweɪ] NOUN
l'autostrada ◇ on the motorway in
autostrada

ⓘ *In Italy you have to pay a toll on
motorways.*

mouldy ['məʊldɪ] ADJECTIVE (US **moldy**)
ammuffito

to **mount** [maʊnt] VERB
[1] organizzare ◇ They're mounting a
publicity campaign. Stanno organizzando
una campagna pubblicitaria.
[2] aumentare^E ◇ Tension is mounting. La
tensione sta aumentando.

to **mount up** [maʊnt'ʌp] VERB
[1] accumularsi^E ◇ Letters and bills
mounted up while we were on holiday.
Lettere e fatture si sono accumulate mentre
eravamo in vacanza.
[2] aumentare^E ◇ My savings are
mounting up gradually. I miei risparmi
aumentano a poco a poco.

mountain ['maʊntɪn] NOUN
la montagna
• **in the mountains** in montagna
• **mountain rescue** soccorso alpino

mountain bike ['maʊntɪnbaɪk] NOUN
la mountain bike (PL le mountain bike)

mountaineer [maʊntɪ'nɪə'] NOUN
l'alpinista

mountaineering [maʊntɪ'nɪərɪŋ] NOUN
l'alpinismo
• **to go mountaineering** fare* alpinismo

mountainous ['maʊntɪnəs] ADJECTIVE
montagnoso

mouse [maʊs] NOUN (PL **mice**)
[1] il topo (animal)
[2] il mouse (PL i mouse) (of computer)

mouse mat ['maʊsmæt] NOUN
il tappetino del mouse

mouse pad ['maʊspæd] NOUN
il tappetino del mouse

mousse [muːs] NOUN
[1] la mousse (PL le mousse) ◇ chocolate
mousse mousse di cioccolata
[2] la schiuma (for hair)

moustache [məs'tɑːʃ] NOUN
i baffi MASC PL

mouth [maʊθ] NOUN
la bocca (PL le bocche)

mouthful ['maʊθful] NOUN
[1] il boccone (of food)
[2] la sorsata (of liquid)

mouth organ ['maʊθɔːgən] NOUN
l'armonica a bocca (PL le armoniche a bocca)

mouthwash ['maʊθwɒʃ] NOUN
il colluttorio

move [muːv] NOUN
see also **move** VERB
[1] la mossa ◇ That was a good move! Bella
mossa!
• **It's your move.** Tocca a te giocare.
[2] il trasloco (PL i traslochi) ◇ our move
from Oxford to Luton il nostro trasloco da
Oxford a Luton
• **Get a move on!** Sbrigati!

to **move** [muːv] VERB
see also **move** NOUN
[1] muoversi^E ◇ Don't move! Non
muovetevi!
[2] spostare ◇ Could you move your stuff
please? Può spostare le sue cose per
favore?
[3] traslocare ◇ We're moving in July.
Traslochiamo in luglio.
[4] avanzare^E ◇ The car was moving very
slowly. La macchina avanzava molto
lentamente.
[5] commuovere* ◇ The book moved me
deeply. Il libro mi ha commossa
profondamente.

to **move away** [muːvə'weɪ] VERB
andarsene^E ◇ Our neighbours are moving
away. I nostri vicini se ne vanno.

to **move back** [muːv'bæk] VERB
ritornare^E ◇ They had no intention of
moving back to Britain. Non avevano
intenzione di ritornare in Gran Bretagna.

to **move in** [muːv'ɪn] VERB
arrivare^E ◇ When are the new neighbours
moving in? Quando arrivano i nuovi vicini?

to **move on** [muːv'ɒn] VERB
cambiare ◇ I felt it was time to move on.
Sentii che era arrivato il momento di
cambiare.
• **Let's move on to the next question.**
Passiamo alla prossima domanda.
• **The policeman told them to move on.** Il
poliziotto ha ordinato loro di andare* via.

to **move over** [muːv'əʊvə'] VERB
spostarsi^E ◇ Could you move over a bit?
Puoi spostarti un po'?

movement ['muːvmənt] NOUN
[1] il movimento ◇ a sudden movement un
movimento brusco
[2] lo spostamento ◇ He was asked to
account for his movements. Gli è stato
chiesto di rendere* conto dei suoi
spostamenti.

movie ['muːvɪ] NOUN
il film (PL i film)
• **the movies** il cinema

moving ['muːvɪŋ] ADJECTIVE
[1] in movimento ◇ a moving bus un
autobus in movimento
[2] commovente ◇ a moving story una
storia commovente

to **mow** [məʊ] VERB (**mowed, mowed** or **mown**)
tagliare ◇ I sometimes mow the lawn. A

---

* Verbs followed by this symbol are irregular. See pp.339–364 for further details.

volte taglio l'erba del prato.

mower ['məuə'] NOUN
il tagliaerba (PL i tagliaerba)

mown [məun] VERB see **mow**

MP [ɛm'piː] NOUN
il deputato
la deputata

mph [ɛmpiː'eɪtʃ] ABBREVIAZIONE (= miles per hour)

> **ⓘ** Speeds in Italy are measured in kilometres per hour. 50 mph is about 80 km/h.

Mr ['mɪstə'] NOUN
il signor

Mrs ['mɪsɪz] NOUN
la signora

MS [ɛm'ɛs] NOUN (= multiple sclerosis)
la sclerosi multipla ◊ She's got MS. Ha la sclerosi multipla.

Ms [mɪz] NOUN
la signora

> **ⓘ** Ms si usa quasi esclusivamente nella lingua scritta per evitare di distinguere tra signora (Mrs) e signorina (Miss).

MSc [ɛmɛs'siː] NOUN
il Master in scienze naturali ◊ She's got a MSc. Ha un Master in scienze naturali.

much [mʌtʃ] ADJECTIVE, PRONOUN, ADVERB
molto ◊ I feel much better now. Ora mi sento molto meglio. ◊ I haven't got much money. Non ho molto denaro. ◊ Have you got a lot of luggage? – No, not much. Ha molto bagaglio? – No, non molto.
+ **very much** moltissimo ◊ I enjoyed myself very much. Mi sono divertito moltissimo.
+ **Thank you very much.** Mille grazie.
+ **how much** quanto ◊ How much is it? Quanto costa?
+ **too much** troppo ◊ They give us too much homework. Ci danno troppi compiti.
+ **so much** così tanto ◊ I like it so much. Mi piace così tanto.

mud [mʌd] NOUN
il fango

muddle ['mʌdl] NOUN
il disordine
+ **in a muddle** in disordine ◊ The photos are in a muddle. Le foto sono in disordine.

to **muddle up** [mʌdl'ʌp] VERB
confondere* ◊ He muddles me up with my sister. Mi confonde con mia sorella.
+ **to get muddled up** essere*E confuso ◊ I'm getting muddled up. Sono confuso.

muddy ['mʌdɪ] ADJECTIVE
fangoso

muffler ['mʌflə'] NOUN [US]
la marmitta

mug [mʌg] NOUN

see also **mug** VERB
la tazza ◊ a mug of coffee una tazza di caffè
+ **a beer mug** un boccale

to **mug** [mʌg] VERB
see also **mug** NOUN
aggredire ◊ He was mugged in the city centre. È stato aggredito in centro.

mugger ['mʌgə'] NOUN
lo scippatore

mugging ['mʌgɪŋ] NOUN
l'aggressione

muggy ['mʌgɪ] ADJECTIVE
+ **It's muggy today.** Oggi c'è afa.

multiple ['mʌltɪpl] ADJECTIVE
multiplo ◊ multiple injuries ferite multiple

multiple choice test [mʌltɪpl'tʃɔɪstest] NOUN
gli esercizi a scelta multipla MASC PL

multiple sclerosis ['mʌltɪplsklɪ'rəusɪs] NOUN
la sclerosi multipla

to **multiply** ['mʌltɪplaɪ] VERB (multiplied, multiplied)
moltiplicare

multi-storey car park [mʌltɪstɔːrɪ'kɑːpɑːk] NOUN
il parcheggio a più piani

mum [mʌm] NOUN
la mamma ◊ I'll ask mum. Chiederò alla mamma. ◊ my mum la mia mamma

mummy ['mʌmɪ] NOUN (PL **mummies**)
1 la mamma ◊ I want my mummy. Voglio la mia mamma.
2 la mummia (Egyptian)

mumps [mʌmps] NOUN SING
gli orecchioni

Munich ['mjuːnɪk] NOUN
Monaco di Baviera

murder ['mɜːdə'] NOUN
see also **murder** VERB
l'omicidio ◊ a terrible murder un terribile omicidio
+ **the murder weapon** l'arma del delitto
+ **She gets away with murder.** Se la cava sempre.

to **murder** ['mɜːdə'] VERB
see also **murder** NOUN
assassinare

murderer ['mɜːdərə'] NOUN
l'assassino
l'assassina

muscle ['mʌsl] NOUN
il muscolo

muscular ['mʌskjulə'] ADJECTIVE
muscoloso ◊ He's got muscular legs. Ha gambe muscolose.

museum [mjuː'zɪəm] NOUN
il museo

mushroom ['mʌʃrum] NOUN
il fungo (PL i funghi)

music ['mjuːzɪk] NOUN
la musica

M

musical ['mju:zɪkl] ADJECTIVE
see also **musical** NOUN
1 musicale ◇ *a musical instrument* uno strumento musicale
2 portato per la musica ◇ *I'm not musical.* Non sono portato per la musica.

musical ['mju:zɪkl] NOUN
see also **musical** ADJECTIVE
la commedia musicale

music centre ['mju:zɪksentə'] NOUN
lo stereo compatto (PL gli stereo compatti)

musician [mju:'zɪʃən] NOUN
il/la musicista

Muslim ['mʌzlɪm] NOUN, ADJECTIVE
il mussulmano
la mussulmana

mussel ['mʌsl] NOUN
la cozza

must [mʌst] VERB
see also **must** NOUN
must is often translated by dovere.
dovere* ◇ *I must do it.* Devo farlo. ◇ *You mustn't forget to send her a card.* Non devi dimenticare di mandarle una cartolina.
◇ *There must be some problem.* Dev'esserci qualche problema. ◇ *You must come again next year.* Devi assolutamente tornare il prossimo anno.
♦ **You must be joking!** Stai scherzando!

must [mʌst] NOUN
see also **must** VERB
♦ **to be a must** essere* E d'obbligo ◇ *For a celebration champagne is a must.* Per celebrare qualcosa lo champagne è d'obbligo.

mustard ['mʌstəd] NOUN
la senape

mustn't ['mʌsnt] = **must not**

to **mutter** ['mʌtə'] VERB
borbottare

mutton ['mʌtn] NOUN
la carne di montone

mutual ['mju:tʃuəl] ADJECTIVE
reciproco ◇ *The feeling was mutual.* Il sentimento era reciproco.
♦ **a mutual friend** un amico comune

my [maɪ] ADJECTIVE
1 il mio MASC (PL i miei) ◇ *my friend* il mio amico ◇ *my parents* i miei genitori
2 la mia FEM (PL le mie) ◇ *my car* la mia macchina ◇ *my opinions* le mie opinioni
3 mio MASC (PL miei) ◇ *my father* mio padre
4 mia FEM (PL mie) ◇ *my aunt* mia zia
my is not always translated.
◇ *I've lost my wallet.* Ho perduto il portafoglio. ◇ *with my hands in my pockets* con le mani in tasca
♦ **I want to wash my hair.** Voglio lavarmi i capelli.
♦ **I've hurt my foot.** Mi sono fatto male ad un piede.

myself [maɪ'self] PRONOUN
1 mi
A verb + myself is often translated by a reflexive verb in Italian.
◇ *I've hurt myself.* Mi sono fatto male. ◇ *I looked at myself in the mirror.* Mi sono guardato allo specchio.
2 me ◇ *a beginner like myself* un principiante come me
3 io ◇ *I made it myself.* L'ho fatto io.
♦ **by myself** da solo ◇ *I don't like travelling by myself.* Non mi piace viaggiare da solo.

mysterious [mɪs'tɪərɪəs] ADJECTIVE
misterioso

mystery ['mɪstərɪ] NOUN (PL **mysteries**)
il mistero ◇ *It's a mystery!* È un mistero!
♦ **a murder mystery** un romanzo giallo

myth [mɪθ] NOUN
il mito ◇ *a Greek myth* un mito greco
♦ **That's a myth.** È una credenza falsa.

mythology [mɪ'θɒlədʒɪ] NOUN
la mitologia

N

naff [næf] ADJECTIVE
kitsch MASC, FEM, PL

nag [næg] VERB
tormentare ◇ *She's always nagging me.* Mi tormenta in continuazione.

nail [neɪl] NOUN
[1] il chiodo ◇ *He hammered a nail into the wall.* Ha messo un chiodo nel muro.
[2] l' unghia ◇ *She bites her nails.* Si mangia le unghie.

nail brush ['neɪlbrʌʃ] NOUN
lo spazzolino per unghie

nail file ['neɪlfaɪl] NOUN
la limetta per le unghie

nail polish ['neɪlpɒlɪʃ] NOUN
lo smalto per unghie

nail scissors ['neɪlsɪzəz] NOUN PL
le forbicine per unghie

nail varnish ['neɪlvɑːnɪʃ] NOUN
lo smalto per unghie

nail varnish remover ['neɪlvɑːnɪʃrɪ'muːvə'] NOUN
l' acetone MASC

naked ['neɪkɪd] ADJECTIVE
nudo

name [neɪm] NOUN
il nome ◇ *his real name* il suo vero nome
♦ **What's your name?** Come ti chiami?

nanny ['nænɪ] NOUN (PL **nannies**)
la bambinaia

nap [næp] NOUN
il pisolino ◇ *She likes to have a nap in the afternoon.* Le piace fare* un pisolino di pomeriggio.

napkin ['næpkɪn] NOUN
il tovagliolo

Naples ['neɪplz] NOUN
Napoli FEM

nappy ['næpɪ] NOUN (PL **nappies**)
il pannolino

narrow ['nærəu] ADJECTIVE
stretto

narrow-minded [nærəu'maɪndɪd] ADJECTIVE
♦ **to be narrow-minded** essere* E di idee ristrette

nasty ['nɑːstɪ] ADJECTIVE
[1] brutto ◇ *a nasty cold* un brutto raffreddore
[2] cattivo ◇ *a nasty smell* un cattivo odore
♦ **a nasty look** un'occhiataccia ◇ *He gave me a nasty look.* Mi ha dato un'occhiataccia.

nation ['neɪʃən] NOUN
la nazione

national ['næʃənl] ADJECTIVE
nazionale

national anthem ['næʃənl'ænθəm] NOUN
l' inno nazionale

National Health Service ['næʃənl'hɛlθsəːvɪs] NOUN

il servizio sanitario nazionale

nationalism ['næʃnəlɪzəm] NOUN
il nazionalismo

nationalist ['næʃnəlɪst] NOUN, ADJECTIVE
il/la nazionalista

nationality [næʃə'nælɪtɪ] NOUN (PL **nationalities**)
la nazionalità (PL le nazionalità)

National Lottery ['næʃənl'lɒtərɪ] NOUN
la lotteria nazionale

national park ['næʃənl'pɑːk] NOUN
il parco nazionale (PL i parchi nazionali)

native ['neɪtɪv] ADJECTIVE
natale ◇ *my native country* il mio paese natale
♦ **native language** lingua madre ◇ *English isn't their native language.* L'inglese non è la loro lingua madre.
♦ **a Native American** un discendente di tribù dell'America settentrionale

naturalist ['nætʃrəlɪst] NOUN
lo studioso di scienze naturali
la studiosa di scienze naturali

naturally ['nætʃrəlɪ] ADVERB
naturalmente ◇ *Naturally, we were very disappointed.* Naturalmente siamo rimasti molto delusi.
♦ **Her hair's naturally curly.** È riccia naturale.

nature ['neɪtʃə'] NOUN
la natura ◇ *the ambitious nature of the project* la natura ambiziosa del progetto
♦ **nature study** l'osservazione della natura FEM

naughty ['nɔːtɪ] ADJECTIVE
cattivo ◇ *Naughty girl!* Cattiva!

navy ['neɪvɪ] NOUN (PL **navies**)
la marina ◇ *He's in the navy.* È in marina.

navy-blue [neɪvɪ'bluː] ADJECTIVE
blu scuro MASC, FEM, PL ◇ *a navy-blue skirt* una gonna blu scuro

near [nɪə'] ADJECTIVE, PREPOSITION, ADVERB
[1] vicino ◇ *It's quite near.* È abbastanza vicino. ◇ *It's very near to the school.* È molto vicino alla scuola. ◇ *Where's the nearest service station?* Dov'è la stazione di servizio più vicina? ◇ *The nearest shops were three kilometres away.* I negozi più vicini erano a tre chilometri di distanza. ◇ *Is there a bank near here?* C'è una banca qui vicino?
♦ **That was a near miss.** C'è mancato poco.
[2] vicino a ◇ *I live near Liverpool.* Abito vicino a Liverpool.

nearby [nɪə'baɪ] ADJECTIVE, ADVERB
[1] vicino ◇ *a nearby village* un paese vicino
[2] qui vicino ◇ *There's a supermarket nearby.* C'è un supermercato qui vicino.

nearly ['nɪəlɪ] ADVERB
quasi ◇ *Dinner's nearly ready.* La cena è ☞

N

quasi pronta. ◇ *I'm nearly fifteen.* Ho quasi quindici anni.
* **I nearly missed the train.** Per poco non ho perso il treno.

neat [niːt] ADJECTIVE
  1 ordinato ◇ *Everything was neat and tidy.* Era tutto pulito e ordinato.
  2 stupendo (*great*) US

neatly ['niːtlɪ] ADVERB
con cura ◇ *neatly folded* piegato con cura

necessarily ['nɛsɪsrɪlɪ] ADVERB
* **not necessarily** non necessariamente

necessary ['nɛsɪsrɪ] ADJECTIVE
necessario

necessity [nɪ'sɛsɪtɪ] NOUN (PL **necessities**)
la necessità (PL le necessità)

neck [nɛk] NOUN
il collo ◇ *a V-neck sweater* un maglione con il collo a V
* **a stiff neck** un torcicollo

necklace ['nɛklɪs] NOUN
la collana

to **need** [niːd] VERB
see also **need** NOUN
aver bisogno di ◇ *I need you.* Ho bisogno di te.
* **You don't need to go.** Non c'è bisogno che tu vada.
* **You needn't worry.** Non devi preoccuparti.

need [niːd] NOUN
see also **need** VERB
il bisogno ◇ *There's no need to book.* Non c'è bisogno di prenotare.
* **to be in need of** avere* bisogno di ◇ *It's in need of a wash.* Ha bisogno di una lavata.

needle ['niːdl] NOUN
l' ago ◇ *used needles* aghi già usati

negative ['nɛgətɪv] NOUN
see also **negative** ADJECTIVE
la negativa (*of photo*)

negative ['nɛgətɪv] ADJECTIVE
see also **negative** NOUN
negativo ◇ *He's got a very negative attitude.* Ha un atteggiamento molto negativo.

neglected [nɪ'glɛktɪd] ADJECTIVE
trascurato ◇ *The garden is neglected.* Il giardino è trascurato.

to **negotiate** [nɪ'gəʊʃɪeɪt] VERB
negoziare

negotiations [nɪgəʊʃɪ'eɪʃənz] NOUN PL
le trattative

neighbour ['neɪbə'] NOUN (US **neighbor**)
il vicino
la vicina

neighbourhood ['neɪbəhud] NOUN (US **neighborhood**)
il quartiere

neither ['naɪðə'] ADJECTIVE, CONJUNCTION, PRONOUN
  1 nessuno dei due ◇ *Carrots or peas? –*

Neither, thanks. Vuoi carote o piselli? – Nessuno dei due, grazie. ◇ *Neither of them is coming.* Non viene nessuno dei due.
  2 neanche ◇ *I don't like him. – Neither do I!* Non mi è simpatico. – Neanche a me! ◇ *I've never been to Spain. – Neither have I.* Non sono mai stato in Spagna. – Neanch'io.
* **neither...nor...** né...né... ◇ *Neither Sarah nor Tamsin is coming to the party.* Alla festa non vengono né Sarah né Tamsin.

neon ['niːɔn] NOUN
il neon ◇ *a neon light* una luce al neon

nephew ['nɛvjuː] NOUN
il nipote (*di zii*)

nerve [nɜːv] NOUN
  1 il nervo ◇ *She sometimes gets on my nerves.* Certe volte mi dà ai nervi.
  2 la faccia tosta ◇ *He's got a nerve!* Ha una bella faccia tosta!

nerve-racking ['nɜːvrækɪŋ] ADJECTIVE
snervante

nervous ['nɜːvəs] ADJECTIVE
teso ◇ *I bite my nails when I'm nervous.* Quando sono teso mi mangio le unghie. ◇ *I'm a bit nervous about the exams.* Sono un po' tesa per gli esami.
* **a nervous breakdown** un esaurimento nervoso

nest [nɛst] NOUN
il nido

Net [nɛt] NOUN
la Rete ◇ *on the Net* in Rete
* **to surf the Net** navigare in Internet

net [nɛt] NOUN
see also **net** ADJECTIVE
la rete ◇ *a fishing net* una rete da pesca

net [nɛt] ADJECTIVE
see also **net** NOUN
netto

netball ['nɛtbɔːl] NOUN
la pallacanestro

Netherlands ['nɛðələndz] NOUN PL
i Paesi Bassi

network ['nɛtwɜːk] NOUN
la rete

neurotic [njuə'rɔtɪk] ADJECTIVE
nevrotico

never ['nɛvə'] ADVERB
mai ◇ *Have you ever been to Germany? – No, never.* Sei mai stato in Germania? – No, mai. ◇ *Never leave valuables in your car.* Non lasciare mai oggetti di valore in macchina.
* **Never again!** Mai più!
* **Never mind.** Non fa niente.

new [njuː] ADJECTIVE
nuovo ◇ *her new boyfriend* il suo nuovo ragazzo
* **new moon** luna nuova

newcomer ['njuːkʌmə'] NOUN
il nuovo arrivato

---

* Verbs followed by this symbol are irregular. See pp.339–364 for further details.

la nuova arrivata

news [njuːz] NOUN SING

[1] le notizie PL ◇ *good news* buone notizie ◇ *It was nice to have your news.* Mi ha fatto piacere* avere* tue notizie.

[2] la notizia ◇ *That's wonderful news!* Che bella notizia!

[3] il telegiornale ◇ *I watch the news every evening.* Guardo il telegiornale ogni sera.

[4] il giornale radio ◇ *I listen to the news every morning.* Ascolto il giornale radio ogni mattina.

newsagent ['njuːzeɪdʒənt] NOUN
il giornalaio

news dealer ['njuːzdiːlə'] NOUN US
il giornalaio

newspaper ['njuːzpeɪpə'] NOUN
il giornale

newsreader ['njuːzriːdə'] NOUN
il/la giornalista

New Year [njuːˈjɪə'] NOUN
l' anno nuovo ◇ *to celebrate New Year* festeggiare l'anno nuovo

◆ **Happy New Year!** Buon anno!

◆ **New Year's Day** Capodanno

◆ **New Year's Eve** la vigilia di Capodanno

◆ **a New Year's Eve party** un veglione di Capodanno

New Zealand [njuːˈziːlənd] NOUN
la Nuova Zelanda

New Zealander [njuːˈziːləndə'] NOUN
il/la neozelandese

next [nɛkst] ADJECTIVE, ADVERB, PREPOSITION

[1] prossimo ◇ *next Saturday* sabato prossimo ◇ *the next time* la prossima volta

◆ **Next please!** Avanti il prossimo!

[2] dopo ◇ *What did you do next?* Cos'hai fatto dopo? ◇ *What happened next?* Cos'è successo dopo? ◇ *The next day we visited Verona.* Il giorno dopo abbiamo visitato Verona.

[3] accanto MASC, FEM, PL ◇ *the next room* la stanza accanto

◆ **next to** accanto a ◇ *next to the bank* accanto alla banca

◆ **next door** della porta accanto ◇ *the girl next door* la ragazza della porta accanto

◆ **They live next door.** Abitano nella casa accanto.

NHS [enetʃ'es] NOUN (= *National Health Service*)
il servizio sanitario nazionale

nice [naɪs] ADJECTIVE

[1] simpatico ◇ *Your parents are very nice.* I tuoi genitori sono molto simpatici.

[2] gentile ◇ *She was always very nice to me.* È sempre stata gentile con me.

[3] carino ◇ *That's a nice dress!* Che vestito carino! ◇ *It was nice of you to remember my birthday.* Sei stata carina a ricordarti del mio compleanno.

[4] buono ◇ *This pasta is very nice.* Questa pasta è molto buona.

[5] bello ◇ *Pisa is a nice town.* Pisa è una bella città. ◇ *nice weather* bel tempo ◇ *It's a nice day.* È una bella giornata. ◇ *a nice cup of coffee* una bella tazza di caffè

◆ **Have a nice time!** Divertiti!

nickname ['nɪkneɪm] NOUN
il soprannome

niece [niːs] NOUN
la nipote (*di zii*)

Nigeria [naɪˈdʒɪərɪə] NOUN
la Nigeria

night [naɪt] NOUN

[1] la notte ◇ *I want a single room for two nights.* Vorrei una camera singola per due notti.

◆ **at night** di notte

[2] la sera ◇ *We went to a party last night.* Ieri sera siamo andati ad una festa.

nightdress ['naɪtdrɛs] NOUN
la camicia da notte (PL le camicie da notte)

nightie ['naɪtɪ] NOUN
la camicia da notte (PL le camicie da notte)

nightlife ['naɪtlaɪf] NOUN
la vita notturna

nightmare ['naɪtmɛə'] NOUN
l' incubo ◇ *The whole trip was a nightmare.* Il viaggio è stato un vero incubo.

night shift ['naɪtʃɪft] NOUN
il turno di notte

nightshirt ['naɪtʃəːt] NOUN
la camicia da notte (PL le camicie da notte)

nil [nɪl] NOUN
lo zero ◇ *We won one-nil.* Abbiamo vinto uno a zero.

nine [naɪn] NUMERAL
nove ◇ *She's nine.* Ha nove anni.

nineteen ['naɪnˈtiːn] NUMERAL
diciannove ◇ *She's nineteen.* Ha diciannove anni.

nineteenth [naɪnˈtiːnθ] NUMERAL
diciannovesimo ◇ *the nineteenth floor* il diciannovesimo piano

◆ **the nineteenth of July** il diciannove luglio

ninety ['naɪntɪ] NUMERAL
novanta

ninth [naɪnθ] ADJECTIVE
nono ◇ *the ninth floor* il nono piano

◆ **the ninth of August** il nove agosto

no [nəʊ] ADVERB, ADJECTIVE

[1] no ◇ *Are you coming? – No.* Vieni? – No. ◇ *Would you like some more? – No thank you.* Ne vuoi ancora? – No grazie.

[2] non ◇ *There's no hot water.* Non c'è acqua calda. ◇ *There are no trains on Sundays.* La domenica non ci sono treni.

◆ **I've got no idea.** Non ne ho la minima idea.

◆ **no one** nessuno ◇ *Who's going with you? – No one.* Chi ti accompagna? – Nessuno. ◇ *There was no one in the office.* In ufficio non c'era nessuno. ☞

N

+ **No way!** Neanche per sogno!
+ **"no smoking"** "vietato fumare"

nobody ['nəʊbədɪ] PRONOUN
nessuno ◊ *Who's going with you?* –
Nobody. Chi ti accompagna? – Nessuno.
◊ *There was nobody in the office.* In ufficio
non c'era nessuno. ◊ *Nobody likes him.*
Non è simpatico a nessuno.

to **nod** [nɒd] VERB
fare* un cenno col capo

noise [nɔɪz] NOUN
il rumore ◊ *Please make less noise.* Per
favore fate meno rumore.

noisy ['nɔɪzɪ] ADJECTIVE
rumoroso ◊ *the noisiest city in the world* la
città più rumorosa del mondo

to **nominate** ['nɒmɪneɪt] VERB
candidare

none [nʌn] PRONOUN
nessuno ◊ *How many sisters have you got?*
– None. Quante sorelle hai? – Nessuna.
◊ *None of my friends wanted to come.*
Nessuno dei miei amici è voluto venire*.
+ **There's none left.** Non ce n'è più.
+ **There are none left.** Non ce ne sono più.

nonsense ['nɒnsəns] NOUN
le sciocchezze FEM PL ◊ *She talks a lot of*
nonsense. Dice un sacco di sciocchezze.
◊ *Nonsense!* Che sciocchezze!

non-smoker ['nɒn'sməʊkə'] NOUN
il non fumatore
la non fumatrice
+ **to be a non-smoker** non fumare

non-smoking ['nɒn'sməʊkɪŋ] ADJECTIVE
+ **non-smoking area** settore riservato ai non
fumatori
+ **Smoking or non-smoking?** Fumatori o non
fumatori?

non-stop ['nɒn'stɒp] ADJECTIVE, ADVERB
[1] diretto ◊ *a non-stop flight* un volo
diretto ◊ *We flew non-stop.* Abbiamo preso
un volo diretto.
[2] ininterrottamente ◊ *He talks non-stop.*
Parla ininterrottamente.

noodles ['nuːdlz] NOUN PL
[1] i tagliolini (*Italian*)
[2] gli spaghetti cinesi (*Chinese*)

noon [nuːn] NOUN
il mezzogiorno

nor [nɔː'] CONJUNCTION
neanche ◊ *I haven't seen him. – Nor have I.*
Non l'ho visto. – Neanch'io. ◊ *I didn't like*
the film. – Nor did I. Il film non mi è piaciuto.
– Neanche a me.
+ **neither...nor** né...né ◊ *neither the cinema*
nor the swimming pool né il cinema né la
piscina

normal ['nɔːməl] ADJECTIVE
normale

normally ['nɔːməlɪ] ADVERB
normalmente

north [nɔːθ] NOUN, ADVERB, ADJECTIVE
[1] il nord ◊ *in the north* al nord
[2] verso nord ◊ *We were travelling north.*
Viaggiavamo verso nord.
+ **north of** a nord di ◊ *It's north of London.* È a
nord di Londra.
[3] settentrionale ◊ *the north coast* la costa
settentrionale

North America [nɔː'θə'mɛrɪkə] NOUN
l' America del Nord

northbound ['nɔːθbaʊnd] ADJECTIVE
diretto a nord

northeast [nɔːθ'iːst] NOUN
il nord-est

northern ['nɔːðən] ADJECTIVE
settentrionale ◊ *Northern Europe* l'Europa
settentrionale

Northern Ireland [nɔːðən'aɪələnd] NOUN
l' Irlanda del nord

North Pole [nɔː'θ'pəʊl] NOUN
il Polo nord

North Sea [nɔːθ'siː] NOUN
il mare del Nord

northwest [nɔːθ'wɛst] NOUN
il nord-ovest

Norway ['nɔːweɪ] NOUN
la Norvegia

Norwegian [nɔː'wiːdʒən] ADJECTIVE
see also **Norwegian** NOUN
norvegese

Norwegian [nɔː'wiːdʒən] NOUN
see also **Norwegian** ADJECTIVE
[1] il/la norvegese (*person*)
[2] il norvegese (*language*)

nose [nəʊz] NOUN
il naso

nosebleed ['nəʊzbliːd] NOUN
l' emorragia nasale (PL le emorragie nasali)

nosy ['nəʊzɪ] ADJECTIVE
+ **She's very nosy.** È una vera ficcanaso.

not [nɒt] ADVERB
[1] no ◊ *Are you coming or not?* Vieni o no?
◊ *I hope not.* Spero di no.
[2] non ◊ *I'm not sure.* Non sono sicuro.
◊ *He isn't coming.* Non viene. ◊ *Have you*
finished? – Not yet. Hai finito? – Non ancora.
+ **not at all** non...affatto ◊ *I'm not at all sure*
it's a good idea. Non sono affatto sicuro che
sia una buona idea.
+ **Thank you very much. – Not at all.** Grazie
infinite. – Di niente.

note [nəʊt] NOUN
[1] l' appunto ◊ *Remember to take notes.*
Ricordati di prendere* appunti.
[2] la nota ◊ *I'll drop her a note.* Le lascerò
una nota.
[3] il biglietto ◊ *a five pound note* un
biglietto da cinque sterline

to **note down** [nəʊt'daʊn] VERB
prendere* nota di ◊ *I noted down the main*
points. Ho preso nota dei punti principali.

---

* Verbs followed by this symbol are irregular. See pp.339–364 for further details.

notebook ['nəutbuk] NOUN
il blocchetto per appunti

note pad ['nəutpæd] NOUN
il bloc notes (PL i bloc notes)

notepaper ['nəutpeɪpə'] NOUN
la carta da lettere

nothing ['nʌθɪŋ] PRONOUN
niente ◇ *nothing special* niente di speciale
◇ *He does nothing.* Non fa niente. ◇ *He ate nothing for breakfast.* Non ha mangiato niente a colazione.

notice ['nəutɪs] VERB
see also **notice** NOUN
accorgersi*ᴱ

notice ['nəutɪs] NOUN
see also **notice** VERB
[1] l' avviso ◇ *There's a notice on the board about the trip.* In bacheca c'è un avviso a proposito del viaggio. ◇ *"until further notice"* "fino a nuovo avviso"
[2] il preavviso ◇ *He was transferred without notice.* È stato trasferito senza preavviso.
✦ **to hand in one's notice** dare* le dimissioni ◇ *She handed in her notice yesterday.* Ha dato le dimissioni ieri.
✦ **a warning notice** un avvertimento
✦ **Don't take any notice of him!** Non far caso a lui!

notice board ['nəutɪsbɔːd] NOUN
la bacheca (PL le bacheche)

nought [nɔːt] NOUN
lo zero

noun [naun] NOUN
il nome

novel ['nɒvl] NOUN
il romanzo

novelist ['nɒvəlɪst] NOUN
il romanziere
la romanziera

November [nəu'vembə'] NOUN
novembre ◇ *in November* in novembre

now [nau] ADVERB, CONJUNCTION
ora ◇ *What are you doing now?* Cosa fai ora?
✦ **just now** in questo momento ◇ *I'm very busy just now.* In questo momento sono molto occupato.
✦ **I did it just now.** L'ho appena fatto.
✦ **by now** ormai ◇ *It should be ready by now.* Ormai dovrebbe essere* pronto.
✦ **from now on** d'ora in poi
✦ **now and then** ogni tanto

nowhere ['nəuweə'] ADVERB
da nessuna parte ◇ *nowhere else* da nessun'altra parte

nuclear ['njuːklɪə'] ADJECTIVE
nucleare ◇ *nuclear power* energia nucleare

nude [njuːd] ADJECTIVE, NOUN
nudo

nudist ['njuːdɪst] NOUN
il/la nudista

nuisance ['njuːsns] NOUN
[1] la seccatura ◇ *It's a real nuisance.* È una vera seccatura.
[2] lo scocciatore
la scocciatrice
◇ *You're a nuisance!* Sei uno scocciatore!

numb [nʌm] ADJECTIVE
✦ **numb with cold** intirizzito dal freddo

number ['nʌmbə'] NOUN
il numero ◇ *They live at number five.* Abitano al numero cinque. ◇ *What's your phone number?* Qual è il tuo numero di telefono? ◇ *You've got the wrong number.* Ha sbagliato numero.
✦ **a large number of people** moltissima gente

number plate ['nʌmbəpleɪt] NOUN
la targa (PL le targhe) (*on car*)

nun [nʌn] NOUN
la suora

nurse [nəːs] NOUN
l' infermiere
l' infermiera

nursery ['nəːsərɪ] NOUN (PL **nurseries**)
[1] il vivaio (*for plants*)
[2] l' asilo (*for children*)

nursery rhyme ['nəːsərɪraɪm] NOUN
la filastrocca (PL le filastrocche)

nursery school ['nəːsərɪskuːl] NOUN
la scuola materna

nursery slope ['nəːsərɪsləup] NOUN
la pista da sci per principianti

nut [nʌt] NOUN
[1] la noce (*walnut*)
[2] la nocciola (*hazlenut*)
[3] la nocciolina (*peanut*)
In Italian there is no general word for **nut.**
✦ **nuts** frutta secca SING
[4] il dado (*made of metal*)
✦ **He's nuts.** È pazzo.

nutmeg ['nʌtmeg] NOUN
la noce moscata

nutritious [njuː'trɪʃəs] ADJECTIVE
nutriente

nutter ['nʌtə'] NOUN
✦ **He's a nutter.** È completamente matto.

O

oak [əuk] NOUN
la quercia (PL le querce)

oar [ɔːʳ] NOUN
il remo

oats [əuts] NOUN PL
l' avena

obedient [əˈbiːdɪənt] ADJECTIVE
ubbidiente

to **obey** [əˈbeɪ] VERB
ubbidire
- **to obey the rules** rispettare il regolamento

object [ˈɒbdʒɪkt] NOUN
see also **object** VERB
l' oggetto

to **object** [əbˈdʒɛkt] VERB
see also **object** NOUN
obiettare ◊ *A lot of people objected to the proposal.* Molti hanno obiettato alla proposta.

objection [əbˈdʒɛkʃən] NOUN
l' obiezione FEM

objective [əbˈdʒɛktɪv] ADJECTIVE, NOUN
l' obiettivo

oblong [ˈɒblɒŋ] ADJECTIVE
rettangolare

oboe [ˈəubəu] NOUN
l' oboe (PL gli oboe)

obscene [əbˈsiːn] ADJECTIVE
osceno

observant [əbˈzɜːvənt] ADJECTIVE
- **You're very observant!** Hai molto spirito di osservazione!
*Be careful not to translate **observant** by osservante.*

to **observe** [əbˈzɜːv] VERB
osservare

obsessed [əbˈsɛst] ADJECTIVE
- **He's obsessed with western movies.** Ha una fissazione per i film western.

obsession [əbˈsɛʃən] NOUN
la fissazione ◊ *It's getting to be an obsession with you.* Sta diventando una fissazione per te.
- **Football's an obsession of mine.** Sono un maniaco del calcio.

obsolete [ˈɒbsəliːt] ADJECTIVE
sorpassato

obstacle [ˈɒbstəkl] NOUN
l' ostacolo

obstinate [ˈɒbstɪnɪt] ADJECTIVE
ostinato

to **obstruct** [əbˈstrʌkt] VERB
bloccare ◊ *A lorry was obstructing the traffic.* Un camion bloccava il traffico.

to **obtain** [əbˈteɪn] VERB
ottenere*

obvious [ˈɒbvɪəs] ADJECTIVE
ovvio

obviously [ˈɒbvɪəslɪ] ADVERB

ovviamente ◊ *Obviously I'd be sorry if we didn't go.* Ovviamente mi dispiacerebbe non andarci.
- **She was obviously exhausted.** Si vedeva che era stanca.
- **Obviously not!** Certo che no!

occasion [əˈkeɪʒən] NOUN
l' occasione FEM
- **on several occasions** in varie occasioni

occasionally [əˈkeɪʒənəlɪ] ADVERB
ogni tanto

occupation [ɒkjuˈpeɪʃən] NOUN
la professione

to **occupy** [ˈɒkjupaɪ] VERB (**occupied, occupied**)
occupare ◊ *The toilet was occupied.* Il bagno era occupato.

to **occur** [əˈkɜːʳ] VERB
succedere* E ◊ *The accident occurred yesterday.* L'incidente è successo ieri.
- **to occur to somebody** venire* E in mente a qualcuno ◊ *It suddenly occurred to me that...* Improvvisamente mi è venuto in mente che...
*Be careful not to translate **to occur** by occorrere.*

ocean [ˈəuʃən] NOUN
l' oceano

o'clock [əˈklɒk] ADVERB
- **It's one o'clock.** È l'una.
Except for one o'clock, use the plural article and a plural verb when telling the time.
- **at four o'clock** alle quattro
- **It's five o'clock.** Sono le cinque.

October [ɒkˈtəubəʳ] NOUN
ottobre MASC ◊ *in October* in ottobre

odd [ɒd] ADJECTIVE
1 strano ◊ *That's odd!* Che strano!
2 dispari ◊ *an odd number* un numero dispari
- **odd jobs** lavori occasionali

of [ɒv,əv] PREPOSITION
di ◊ *a boy of ten* un bambino di dieci anni ◊ *a kilo of oranges* un chilo di arance ◊ *It's made of wood.* È di legno.
- **There were three of us.** Eravamo in tre.
- **a friend of mine** un mio amico
- **the 14th of September** il quattordici settembre
- **That's very kind of you.** È molto gentile da parte tua.

off [ɒf] ADJECTIVE, ADVERB, PREPOSITION
1 spento (*heating, light, TV*) ◊ *All the lights are off.* Tutte le luci sono spente.
2 chiuso (*tap, gas*) ◊ *Are you sure the tap is off?* Sei sicuro che il rubinetto sia chiuso?
- **to be off sick** essere* E assente per malattia
- **a day off** un giorno di ferie ◊ *She took a day off work to go to the wedding.* Ha preso un giorno di ferie per andare* al matrimonio.
- **I've got tomorrow off.** Domani ho un giorno

---

* Verbs followed by this symbol are irregular. See pp.339–364 for further details.

libero.
+ **She's off school today.** Oggi non è a scuola.
+ **I must be off now.** Ora devo andare*.
+ **I'm off.** Io me ne vado.
+ **10% off** sconto del 10%
+ **It's just off Baker Street.** È una trasversale di Baker Street.
+ **Sorry, the lasagne is off.** Mi dispiace, le lasagne sono terminate.
+ **The match is off.** La partita non si gioca più.

offence [əˈfens] NOUN (US **offense**)
il reato

offensive [əˈfensɪv] ADJECTIVE
offensivo

offer [ˈɔfəʳ] NOUN
see also **offer** VERB
l' offerta ◇ *"on special offer"* "in offerta speciale"

o **offer** [ˈɔfəʳ] VERB
see also **offer** NOUN
[1] offrire* ◇ *Can I offer you a drink?* Posso offrirti qualcosa da bere*?
[2] offrirsi ᴱ ◇ *He offered to help me.* Si è offerto di aiutarmi.

office [ˈɔfɪs] NOUN
l' ufficio
+ **office hours** orario d'ufficio

officer [ˈɔfɪsəʳ] NOUN
l' ufficiale MASC (*in the army*)
+ **a police officer** un agente di polizia

official [əˈfɪʃl] ADJECTIVE
ufficiale

off-licence [ˈɔflaɪsns] NOUN
la rivendita di alcolici

off-peak [ˈɔfpiːk] ADVERB
[1] in bassa stagione ◇ *It's cheaper to go on holiday off-peak.* Costa meno andare* in vacanza in bassa stagione.
[2] al di fuori dell'ora di punta ◇ *Train tickets are cheaper off-peak.* I biglietti ferroviari sono più economici al di fuori dell'ora di punta.

offside [ˈɔfsaɪd] ADJECTIVE
fuorigioco

often [ˈɔfn] ADVERB
spesso ◇ *It often rains.* Spesso piove.
+ **How often?** Ogni quanto? ◇ *How often do you go to the gym?* Ogni quanto vai in palestra?

o **oil** [ɔɪl] VERB
see also **oil** NOUN
lubrificare

oil [ɔɪl] NOUN
see also **oil** VERB
[1] l' olio (*for salad*)
[2] il petrolio (*crude oil*)

oil rig [ˈɔɪlrɪg] NOUN
la piattaforma petrolifera

oil slick [ˈɔɪlslɪk] NOUN
la chiazza di petrolio

oil well [ˈɔɪlwel] NOUN
il pozzo petrolifero

ointment [ˈɔɪntmənt] NOUN
la pomata

okay [əuˈkeɪ] EXCLAMATION, ADJECTIVE
va bene ◇ *Is that okay?* Va bene? ◇ *I'll do it tomorrow, if that's okay with you.* Lo faccio domani, se per te va bene.
+ **Are you okay?** Tutto ok?
+ **The film was okay.** Il film non era male.

old [əuld] ADJECTIVE
vecchio ◇ *My grandfather is very old.* Mio nonno è molto vecchio. ◇ *He's older than me.* È più vecchio di me.
+ **an old man** un vecchio
+ **old people** gli anziani
+ **How old are you?** Quanti anni hai?
+ **He's ten years old.** Ha dieci anni.
+ **my older brother** il mio fratello maggiore
+ **She's two years older than me.** Ha due anni più di me.

old age pensioner [əuldeɪdʒˈpenʃənəʳ] NOUN
il pensionato
la pensionata

old-fashioned [ˈəuldfæʃnd] ADJECTIVE
[1] fuori moda (*clothes*)
[2] all'antica ◇ *My parents are rather old-fashioned.* I miei sono un po' all'antica.

olive [ˈɔlɪv] NOUN
l' oliva

olive oil [ˈɔlɪvɔɪl] NOUN
l' olio d'oliva

olive tree [ˈɔlɪvtriː] NOUN
l' olivo

Olympic [əuˈlɪmpɪk] ADJECTIVE
olimpico
+ **the Olympics** le Olimpiadi

on [ɔn] PREPOSITION, ADVERB
see also **on** ADJECTIVE
[1] su ◇ *on the table* sul tavolo ◇ *on an island* su un'isola ◇ *It's on Channel four.* È su Canale quattro.
[2] a ◇ *on the left* a sinistra ◇ *on TV* alla TV
+ **on foot** a piedi ◇ *It's about ten minutes on foot.* A piedi ci vogliono circa dieci minuti.
[3] in ◇ *I go to school on my bike.* Vado a scuola in bicicletta. ◇ *on holiday* in vacanza
When used with dates and days on is generally not translated.
◇ *on June twentieth* il venti giugno ◇ *on my birthday* il giorno del mio compleanno ◇ *on Christmas Day* il giorno di Natale ◇ *on Friday* venerdì
+ **on Fridays** di venerdì
+ **He's on drugs.** È un tossicodipendente.
+ **She was on antibiotics for a week.** Ha preso antibiotici per una settimana.
+ **Is the party still on?** Si fa sempre la festa?
+ **I've got a lot on this weekend.** Questo fine settimana sono molto impegnata.
+ **The coffee is on the house.** Il caffè lo offre la casa.

☞

O

♦ **What is he on about?** Cosa va dicendo?

on [ɔn] ADJECTIVE

see also **on** PREPOSITION, ADVERB

[1] acceso (*light, TV, heating*) ◊ *I think I left the light on.* Mi pare di aver lasciato la luce accesa.

[2] aperto (*tap, gas*) ◊ *Leave the tap on.* Lascia il rubinetto aperto.

[3] in funzione ◊ *Is the dishwasher on?* È in funzione la lavastoviglie?

♦ **What's on at the cinema?** Cosa danno al cinema?

once [wʌns] ADVERB

una volta ◊ *once more* ancora una volta ◊ *I've been to Italy once before.* Sono già stato in Italia una volta. ◊ *once a week* una volta alla settimana

♦ **Once upon a time...** C'era una volta...

♦ **once in a while** una volta ogni tanto

♦ **once and for all** una volta per tutte

♦ **at once** immediatamente

one [wʌn] NUMERAL, PRONOUN

[1] uno (FEM una) ◊ *I've got one brother and one sister.* Ho un fratello e una sorella. ◊ *I need a smaller one.* Me ne serve uno più piccolo.

♦ **The big ones cost more.** Quelli grandi costano di più.

[2] si (*impersonal*) ◊ *One never knows.* Non si sa mai.

♦ **this one** questo ◊ *Which foot is hurting? – This one.* Qual è il piede che ti fa male? – Questo.

♦ **that one** quello ◊ *Which bag is yours? – That one.* Qual è la tua borsa? – Quella.

oneself [wʌnˈsɛlf] PRONOUN

[1] si

A verb + **oneself** *is often translated by a reflexive verb in Italian.*

◊ *One asks oneself how it could happen.* Ci si chiede come sia potuto succedere*.

[2] da solo MASC (FEM da sola) ◊ *It's quicker to do it oneself.* Si fa più in fretta a farlo da solo.

one-way [wʌnweɪ] ADJECTIVE

[1] a senso unico ◊ *a one-way street* una strada a senso unico

[2] di sola andata ◊ *a one-way ticket* un biglietto di sola andata

onion [ˈʌnjən] NOUN

la cipolla

online ADJECTIVE, ADVERB

on line ◊ *an online catalogue* un catalogo on line

♦ **to be online** essere* E in Internet

only [ˈəʊnlɪ] ADVERB, ADJECTIVE, CONJUNCTION

solo ◊ *How much was it? – Only ten pounds.* Quanto è costato? – Solo dieci sterline. ◊ *We only want to stay for one night.* Vorremmo stare* solo una notte.

♦ **only child** figlio unico ◊ *She's an only child.* È figlia unica.

onwards [ˈɔnwədz] ADVERB

in poi ◊ *from July onwards* da luglio in poi

open [ˈəʊpn] ADJECTIVE

see also **open** VERB

aperto ◊ *The shop's open on Sunday morning.* Il negozio è aperto la domenica mattina.

♦ **in the open air** all'aperto

to **open** [ˈəʊpn] VERB

see also **open** ADJECTIVE

[1] aprire* ◊ *What time do the shops open?* A che ora aprono i negozi?

[2] aprirsi E ◊ *The door opens automatically.* La porta si apre automaticamente.

opening hours [ˈəʊpnɪŋauəz] NOUN PL

l'orario di apertura

opera [ˈɒpərə] NOUN

l'opera (*music*)

to **operate** [ˈɒpəreɪt] VERB

[1] funzionare ◊ *I don't know how the electoral system operates in Italy.* Non so come funziona il sistema elettorale italiano.

[2] far funzionare ◊ *Can you operate the video?* Sai far funzionare il videoregistratore?

[3] operare (*perform surgery*)

♦ **to operate on someone** operare qualcuno

operation [ɒpəˈreɪʃən] NOUN

l'operazione FEM ◊ *a minor operation* una piccola operazione

♦ **to have an operation** essere* E operato ◊ *I've never had an operation.* Non sono mai stato operato.

operator [ˈɒpəreɪtə'] NOUN

il/la centralinista

opinion [əˈpɪnjən] NOUN

l'opinione FEM

♦ **in my opinion** secondo me

♦ **What's your opinion?** Cosa ne pensi?

opinion poll [əˈpɪnjənpəʊl] NOUN

il sondaggio d'opinione

opponent [əˈpəʊnənt] NOUN

l'avversario
l'avversaria

opportunity [ɒpəˈtjuːnɪtɪ] NOUN (PL **opportunities**)

l'opportunità (PL le opportunità) ◊ *I've never had the opportunity to go to Spain.* Non ho mai avuto l'opportunità di andare* in Spagna.

opposing [əˈpəʊzɪŋ] ADJECTIVE

avversario ◊ *the opposing team* la squadra avversaria

opposite [ˈɒpəzɪt] ADJECTIVE, ADVERB, PREPOSITION

[1] opposto ◊ *It's in the opposite direction.* È nella direzione opposta.

[2] di fronte ◊ *They live opposite.* Abitano di fronte.

[3] di fronte a ◊ *the girl sitting opposite me* la ragazza seduta di fronte a me

---

* Verbs followed by this symbol are irregular. See pp.339–364 for further details.

♦ **the opposite sex** l'altro sesso

opposition [ɔpə'zɪʃən] NOUN
  1 l'opposizione FEM ◇ *The plan met considerable opposition.* Il progetto ha incontrato una notevole opposizione.
  2 la squadra avversaria ◇ *What are the opposition like?* Com'è la squadra avversaria?

optician [ɔp'tɪʃən] NOUN
  l'ottico (PL gli ottici)

optimist ['ɔptɪmɪst] NOUN
  il/la ottimista ◇ *I'm an optimist.* Sono ottimista.

optimistic [ɔptɪ'mɪstɪk] ADJECTIVE
  ottimista
♦ **Let's be optimistic.** Cerchiamo di essere* ottimisti.

option ['ɔpʃən] NOUN
  1 la scelta ◇ *I've got no option.* Non ho scelta.
  2 la materia facoltativa ◇ *I'm doing geology as my option.* Come materia facoltativa studio geologia.

optional ['ɔpʃənl] ADJECTIVE
  facoltativo

or [ɔː'] CONJUNCTION
  1 o ◇ *Would you like tea or coffee?* Vuoi del tè o del caffè?
  2 altrimenti ◇ *Hurry up or you'll miss the bus.* Sbrigati, altrimenti perdi l'autobus.
♦ **not...or...** né...né... ◇ *I don't eat meat or fish.* Non mangio né carne né pesce. ◇ *She can't dance or sing.* Non sa né ballare né cantare.

oral ['ɔːrəl] ADJECTIVE
  see also **oral** NOUN
  orale ◇ *an oral exam* un esame orale

oral ['ɔːrəl] NOUN
  see also **oral** ADJECTIVE
  l'orale MASC ◇ *I've got my Italian oral soon.* Tra poco avrò l'orale d'italiano.

orange ['ɔrɪndʒ] NOUN
  see also **orange** ADJECTIVE
  l'arancia (PL le arance)
♦ **an orange juice** un succo d'arancia

orange ['ɔrɪndʒ] ADJECTIVE
  see also **orange** NOUN
  arancione ◇ *an orange jumper* un maglione arancione

orchard ['ɔːtʃəd] NOUN
  il frutteto

orchestra ['ɔːkɪstrə] NOUN
  l'orchestra

order ['ɔːdə'] NOUN
  see also **order** VERB
  1 l'ordine MASC ◇ *in alphabetical order* in ordine alfabetico
  2 l'ordinazione FEM ◇ *The waiter took our order.* Il cameriere ha preso la nostra ordinazione.
♦ **an order form** un modulo d'ordine
♦ **in order to** per ◇ *He does it in order to earn*

money. Lo fa per guadagnare qualcosa.
♦ **"out of order"** "guasto"

to **order** ['ɔːdə'] VERB
  see also **order** NOUN
  ordinare ◇ *We ordered steak and chips.* Abbiamo ordinato bistecca e patatine.
  ◇ *Are you ready to order?* Volete ordinare?

to **order about** VERB ['ɔːdə'ə'baut] VERB
  dare* ordini ◇ *He tries to order me about.* Cerca di darmi ordini.

ordinary ['ɔːdnrɪ] ADJECTIVE
  1 come tanti ◇ *an ordinary day* una giornata come tante ◇ *He's just an ordinary guy.* È uno come tanti.
  2 normale ◇ *It has 25 calories less than ordinary ice cream.* Ha 25 calorie in meno rispetto ad un gelato normale.

organ ['ɔːgən] NOUN
  l'organo

organic [ɔː'gænɪk] ADJECTIVE
  biologico (*fruit, vegetables*)

organization [ɔːgənaɪ'zeɪʃən] NOUN
  l'organizzazione FEM

to **organize** ['ɔːgənaɪz] VERB
  organizzare

origin ['ɔrɪdʒɪn] NOUN
  l'origine FEM

original [ə'rɪdʒɪnl] ADJECTIVE
  originale

originally [ə'rɪdʒɪnəlɪ] ADVERB
  in origine

Orkneys ['ɔːkniz] NOUN PL
  le Orcadi

ornament ['ɔːnəmənt] NOUN
  il soprammobile (*on shelf, mantelpiece*)

orphan ['ɔːfn] NOUN
  l'orfano
  l'orfana

ostrich ['ɔstrɪtʃ] NOUN (PL **ostriches**)
  lo struzzo

other ['ʌðə'] ADJECTIVE, PRONOUN
  1 altro MASC (PL altri)
  2 altra FEM (PL altre) ◇ *Have you got these jeans in other colours?* Avete questi jeans in altri colori?
♦ **the other one** l'altro (FEM l'altra) ◇ *This one? – No, the other one.* Questo? – No, l'altro.
♦ **the others** gli altri (FEM le altre) ◇ *The others are going but I'm not.* Gli altri ci vanno ma io no.

otherwise ['ʌðəwaɪz] ADVERB, CONJUNCTION
  1 altrimenti ◇ *Note down the number, otherwise you'll forget it.* Scrivi il numero, altrimenti te lo dimentichi.
  2 a parte ciò ◇ *I'm tired, but otherwise I'm fine.* Sono stanco, ma a parte ciò sto bene.

ought [ɔːt] VERB
  ought is usually translated by the conditional of dovere.
  ◇ *I ought to phone my parents.* Dovrei telefonare ai miei. ◇ *You ought not to do* ☞

O

that. Non dovresti farlo. ◊ *He ought to win.* Dovrebbe vincere* lui.

ounce [auns] NOUN
l' oncia (PL le once)

ℹ️ Un'oncia *corrisponde a 28,349 grammi.*

our ['auə'] ADJECTIVE
[1] il nostro MASC (PL i nostri) ◊ *our dog* il nostro cane ◊ *our neighbours* i nostri vicini
[2] la nostra FEM (PL le nostre) ◊ *our school* la nostra scuola ◊ *our opinions* le nostre opinioni
[3] nostro MASC (PL nostri) ◊ *our father* nostro padre
[4] nostra FEM (PL nostre) ◊ *our aunt* nostra zia
our is not always translated.
◊ *We took off our coats.* Ci siamo tolti i cappotti. ◊ *We washed our hair.* Ci siamo lavati i capelli.

ours [auəz] PRONOUN
The Italian pronoun agrees with the noun it is replacing.
[1] il nostro MASC (PL i nostri) ◊ *Your garden is much bigger than ours.* Il vostro giardino è molto più grande del nostro. ◊ *Our teachers are strict. – Ours are too.* I nostri professori sono severi. – Anche i nostri.
[2] la nostra FEM (PL le nostre) ◊ *Your house is big, ours is much smaller.* Casa tua è grande, la nostra è molto più piccola.
[3] nostro MASC (PL nostri) (*our property*)
◊ *Whose is this? – It's ours.* Di chi è questo? – È nostro. ◊ *Those tickets are ours.* Quei biglietti sono nostri.
[4] nostra FEM (PL nostre) (*our property*)
◊ *That car is ours.* Quella macchina è nostra.
◆ **He is a friend of ours.** È un nostro amico.
◆ **She is a friend of ours.** È una nostra amica.

ourselves [auə'sɛlvz] PRONOUN
[1] ci
*A verb + **ourselves** is often translated by a reflexive verb in Italian.*
◊ *We really enjoyed ourselves.* Ci siamo divertiti moltissimo.
[2] noi (*emphatic use*) ◊ *We built our garage ourselves.* Il garage l'abbiamo costruito noi.
◆ **by ourselves** da soli (FEM da sole) ◊ *We don't like travelling by ourselves.* Non ci piace viaggiare da soli.

out [aut] ADVERB
see also **out** ADJECTIVE
fuori ◊ *It's cold out.* Fuori fa freddo. ◊ *a night out with my friends* una serata fuori con gli amici ◊ *That's out of the question.* Questo è fuori discussione.
◆ **out of town** fuori città ◊ *He's out of town this week.* Questa settimana è fuori città.
◆ **She's out.** È uscita.
◆ **She's out for the afternoon.** Starà via tutto il pomeriggio.

◆ **to drink out of a bottle** bere* dalla bottiglia
◆ **out of curiosity** per curiosità
◆ **to be out of something** aver finito qualcosa
◊ *We're out of milk.* Abbiamo finito il latte.
◆ **in nine cases out of ten** in nove casi su dieci
◆ **three kilometres out of town** a tre chilometri dalla città
◆ **out of work** senza lavoro
◆ **"way out"** "uscita"
◆ **"now out on video"** "ora su videocassetta"

out [aut] ADJECTIVE
see also **out** ADVERB
[1] spento ◊ *All the lights are out.* Le luci sono tutte spente.
[2] eliminato ◊ *Liverpool are out.* Il Liverpool è stato eliminato.

outbreak ['autbreɪk] NOUN
[1] l' epidemia ◊ *an outbreak of cholera* un'epidemia di colera
[2] lo scoppio ◊ *the outbreak of war* lo scoppio della guerra

outcome ['autkʌm] NOUN
il risultato

outdoor [aut'dɔː'] ADJECTIVE
◆ **an outdoor swimming pool** una piscina scoperta
◆ **outdoor activities** attività all'aperto FEM PL

outdoors [aut'dɔːz] ADVERB
all'aria aperta

outgoing ['autgəʊɪŋ] ADJECTIVE
estroverso ◊ *She's very outgoing.* È molto estroversa.

outing ['autɪŋ] NOUN
la gita
◆ **to go on an outing** andare* E in gita

outline ['autlaɪn] NOUN
[1] l' abbozzo ◊ *This is an outline of the plan.* Questo è un abbozzo del progetto.
[2] il contorno ◊ *the outline of the building* il contorno dell'edificio

outlook ['autluk] NOUN
la visione ◊ *It changed my outlook on life.* Ha cambiato la mia visione della vita.

outrageous [aut'reɪdʒəs] ADJECTIVE
[1] scandaloso ◊ *Her behaviour was outrageous.* Il suo comportamento è stato scandaloso.
[2] esorbitante ◊ *The prices they charge are outrageous.* Hanno prezzi esorbitanti.

outset ['autset] NOUN
l' inizio ◊ *at the outset* all'inizio

outside [aut'saɪd] ADJECTIVE, NOUN
see also **outside** ADVERB, PREPOSITION
esterno ◊ *the outside walls* le mura esterne ◊ *the outside of the house* l'esterno della casa

outside [aut'saɪd] ADVERB, PREPOSITION
see also **outside** ADJECTIVE, NOUN
[1] fuori ◊ *It's very cold outside.* Fa molto freddo fuori.
[2] fuori di ◊ *outside the school* fuori della

* Verbs followed by this symbol are irregular. See pp.339–364 for further details.

scuola
- **outside school hours** al di fuori dell'orario scolastico

outsize ['autsaɪz] ADJECTIVE
- **outsize clothes** abiti per taglie forti

outskirts ['autskɜːts] NOUN PL
la periferia
- **on the outskirts of town** in periferia

outstanding [aut'stændɪŋ] ADJECTIVE
eccellente

oval ['əʊvl] ADJECTIVE
ovale

oven ['ʌvn] NOUN
il forno

over ['əʊvə'] ADJECTIVE
see also **over** PREPOSITION, ADVERB
finito ◇ *I'll be happy when the exams are over.* Sarò contento quando gli esami saranno finiti.

over ['əʊvə'] PREPOSITION, ADVERB
see also **over** ADJECTIVE
[1] sopra ◇ *There's a mirror over the washbasin.* Sopra il lavandino c'è uno specchio.
[2] oltre ◇ *The ball went over the wall.* La palla è andata oltre il muro. ◇ *It's over twenty kilos.* Pesa oltre venti chili.
[3] durante ◇ *over the summer* durante l'estate ◇ *over Christmas* durante il periodo natalizio
[4] dall'altra parte di ◇ *The shop is over the road.* Il negozio è dall'altra parte della strada.
[5] su ◇ *I spilled coffee over my shirt.* Mi sono versato del caffè sulla camicia.
- **over here** qua
- **over there** là
- **all over Scotland** in tutta la Scozia

overall [əʊvər'ɔːl] ADJECTIVE, ADVERB
nel complesso ◇ *What was your overall impression?* Nel complesso che impressione ti ha fatto? ◇ *Overall I was disappointed.* Nel complesso sono rimasto deluso.

overalls ['əʊvərɔːlz] NOUN PL
la tuta da lavoro

overcast ['əʊvəkɑːst] ADJECTIVE
coperto (*sky*)

to **overcharge** [əʊvə'tʃɑːdʒ] VERB
fare* pagare troppo ◇ *They overcharged us for the meal.* Ci hanno fatto pagare troppo per il pranzo.

overdone [əʊvə'dʌn] ADJECTIVE
troppo cotto

overdose ['əʊvədəʊs] NOUN
l' overdose (PL le overdose)

to **overestimate** [əʊvər'estɪmeɪt] VERB
sopravvalutare

overhead projector ['əʊvəhedprə'dʒektə'] NOUN
la lavagna luminosa

to **overlook** [əʊvə'lʊk] VERB
[1] dare* su ◇ *The hotel overlooked the beach.* L'albergo dava sulla spiaggia.
[2] trascurare ◇ *He had overlooked one important problem.* Aveva trascurato un problema importante.

overseas [əʊvə'siːz] ADVERB
all'estero

oversight ['əʊvəsaɪt] NOUN
la svista

to **oversleep** [əʊvə'sliːp] VERB (**overslept, overslept**)
non svegliarsi[E] in tempo ◇ *I overslept this morning.* Non mi sono svegliato in tempo stamattina.

to **overtake** [əʊvə'teɪk] VERB (**overtook, overtaken**)
sorpassare

overtime ['əʊvətaɪm] NOUN
lo straordinario
- **to work overtime** fare* lo straordinario

overweight [əʊvə'weɪt] ADJECTIVE
sovrappeso

to **owe** [əʊ] VERB
dovere* ◇ *How much do I owe you?* Quanto le devo?

owing to ['əʊɪŋtu] PREPOSITION
a causa di ◇ *owing to bad weather* a causa del maltempo

owl [aʊl] NOUN
il gufo

to **own** [əʊn] VERB
see also **own** ADJECTIVE
possedere* ◇ *everything I own* tutto ciò che possiedo
- **The golf course is owned by a Japanese company.** Il campo da golf appartiene ad una società giapponese.

to **own up** VERB [əʊn'ʌp] VERB
confessare

own [əʊn] ADJECTIVE
see also **own** VERB
- **This is my own recipe.** È una mia ricetta.
- **He can't trust his own judgement.** Non si può fidare del proprio giudizio.
- **of my own** tutto per me ◇ *I wish I had a room of my own.* Mi piacerebbe avere* una camera tutta per me.
- **on his own** da solo
- **on their own** da soli

owner ['əʊnə'] NOUN
il proprietario
la proprietaria

oxygen ['ɒksɪdʒən] NOUN
l' ossigeno

oyster ['ɔɪstə'] NOUN
l' ostrica (PL le ostriche)

ozone ['əʊzəʊn] NOUN
l' ozono
- **the ozone layer** lo strato d'ozono

O

P

PA [pi:'eɪ] NOUN (= *personal assistant*)
la segretaria di direzione
+ **the PA system** l'impianto di amplificazione

pace [peɪs] NOUN
il passo ◇ *He was walking at a brisk pace.*
Camminava a passo spedito.

Pacific [pə'sɪfɪk] NOUN
+ **the Pacific** il Pacifico

pacifier ['pæsɪfaɪəʳ] NOUN US
il succhiotto

to **pack** [pæk] VERB
see also **pack** NOUN
fare* i bagagli ◇ *I'll help you pack.* Ti aiuto a
fare i bagagli.
+ **to pack one's case** fare* la valigia ◇ *I've
already packed my case.* Ho già fatto la
valigia.
+ **Pack it in!** Piantala!

pack [pæk] NOUN
see also **pack** VERB
1 il pacco (PL i pacchi) ◇ *He was carrying a
heavy pack on his back.* Portava un grosso
pacco sulle spalle.
2 la confezione ◇ *a six-pack* una
confezione da sei
+ **an information pack** una serie di opuscoli
informativi
+ **a pack of cigarettes** una stecca di sigarette
+ **a pack of cards** un mazzo di carte

package ['pækɪdʒ] NOUN
il pacco (PL i pacchi) ◇ *a small package* un
piccolo pacco
+ **a package holiday** un viaggio organizzato

packed [pækt] ADJECTIVE
affollato ◇ *The cinema was packed.* Il
cinema era affollato.

packed lunch [pækt'lʌntʃ] NOUN
il pranzo al sacco

packet ['pækɪt] NOUN
1 il pacchetto ◇ *a packet of cigarettes* un
pacchetto di sigarette
2 il sacchetto ◇ *a packet of crisps* un
sacchetto di patatine

pad [pæd] NOUN
il bloc-notes (PL i bloc-notes)

to **paddle** ['pædl] VERB
see also **paddle** NOUN
1 sguazzare (*in water*)
2 pagaiare (*in a boat*)

paddle ['pædl] NOUN
see also **paddle** VERB
la pagaia (*oar*)
+ **to go for a paddle** sguazzare nell'acqua

padlock ['pædlɒk] NOUN
il lucchetto

Padua ['pædʒuə] NOUN
Padova FEM

page [peɪdʒ] NOUN
see also **page** VERB

la pagina ◇ *on page three* a pagina tre

to **page** [peɪdʒ] VERB
see also **page** NOUN
chiamare col cercapersone

pager ['peɪdʒəʳ] NOUN
il cercapersone (PL i cercapersone)

paid [peɪd] VERB *see* pay

paid [peɪd] ADJECTIVE
pagato ◇ *three weeks' paid holiday* tre
settimane di ferie pagate

pail [peɪl] NOUN
il secchio

pain [peɪn] NOUN
1 il dolore ◇ *a terrible pain* un dolore
insopportabile
+ **I've got a pain in my stomach.** Mi fa male lo
stomaco.
+ **to be in pain** soffrire* ◇ *She's in a lot of
pain.* Soffre molto.
2 il/la rompiscatole ◇ *He's a real pain.* È un
gran rompiscatole.

painful ['peɪnful] ADJECTIVE
doloroso

painkiller ['peɪnkɪləʳ] NOUN
l'analgesico (PL gli analgesici)

paint [peɪnt] NOUN
see also **paint** VERB
la vernice

to **paint** [peɪnt] VERB
see also **paint** NOUN
1 verniciare ◇ *He decided to paint it green.*
Ha deciso di verniciarlo di verde.
2 dipingere* ◇ *When did he paint the
picture?* Quando ha dipinto il quadro?
+ **He painted her portrait.** Le ha fatto il ritratto.

paintbrush ['peɪntbrʌʃ] NOUN (PL
paintbrushes)
il pennello

painter ['peɪntəʳ] NOUN
1 l'imbianchino ◇ *The painter is coming
tomorrow to redecorate the house.* Domani
viene l'imbianchino per ridipingere la casa.
2 il pittore
la pittrice
◇ *a famous 13th century painter* un famoso
pittore del tredicesimo secolo

painting ['peɪntɪŋ] NOUN
1 il quadro ◇ *a painting by Picasso* un
quadro di Picasso
2 la pittura ◇ *My hobby is painting.* Il mio
hobby è la pittura.

pair [peəʳ] NOUN
il paio (PL FEM le paia) ◇ *a pair of shoes* un
paio di scarpe ◇ *a pair of scissors* un paio di
forbici
+ **in pairs** a coppie ◇ *We work in pairs.*
Lavoriamo a coppie.

pajamas [pə'dʒɑːməz] NOUN PL US
il pigiama ◇ *my pajamas* il mio pigiama

---

* Verbs followed by this symbol are irregular. See pp.339–364 for further details.

Pakistan [pɑːkɪˈstɑːn] NOUN
il Pakistan

Pakistani [pɑːkɪˈstɑːnɪ] ADJECTIVE
see also **Pakistani** NOUN
pachistano

Pakistani [pɑːkɪˈstɑːnɪ] NOUN
see also **Pakistani** ADJECTIVE
il pachistano
la pachistana

pal [pæl] NOUN
l' amico (PL gli amici)
l' amica (PL le amiche)

palace [ˈpæləs] NOUN
il palazzo

pale [peɪl] ADJECTIVE
pallido ◇ *She still looks very pale.* È ancora molto pallida.
• **pale pink** rosa pallido
• **pale blue** celeste
• **pale green** verdolino

Palestine [ˈpælɪstaɪn] NOUN
la Palestina

Palestinian [pælɪsˈtɪnɪən] ADJECTIVE
see also **Palestinian** NOUN
palestinese

Palestinian [pælɪsˈtɪnɪən] NOUN
see also **Palestinian** ADJECTIVE
il/la palestinese

palm [pɑːm] NOUN
il palmo (*of hand*)
• **a palm tree** una palma
• **Palm Sunday** la domenica delle Palme

pamphlet [ˈpæmflət] NOUN
il dépliant (PL i dépliant)

pan [pæn] NOUN
la pentola

pancake [ˈpænkeɪk] NOUN
la crêpe (PL le crêpe)

panic [ˈpænɪk] NOUN
see also **panic** VERB
il panico (PL i panici)

to **panic** [ˈpænɪk] VERB (**panicked, panicked**)
see also **panic** NOUN
farsi* ᴱ prendere dal panico ◇ *He panicked when he saw the blood.* Quando ha visto il sangue si è fatto prendere dal panico.
• **Don't panic!** Non agitarti!

panther [ˈpænθəʳ] NOUN
la pantera

panties [ˈpæntɪz] NOUN PL
le mutandine

pantomime [ˈpæntəmaɪm] NOUN
la recita natalizia per bambini

❶ *Si tratta di una libera interpretazione delle favole più conosciute messa in scena a teatro durante il periodo natalizio.*

pants [pænts] NOUN PL
1 le mutande ◇ *bra and pants* reggiseno e mutande

2 i pantaloni (*trousers*) US

pantyhose [ˈpæntɪhəʊz] NOUN US
il collant (PL i collant)

paper [ˈpeɪpəʳ] NOUN
1 la carta ◇ *a paper towel* una salvietta di carta ◇ *a paper hankie* un fazzoletto di carta
• **paper clip** graffetta
2 il giornale ◇ *I saw an advert in the paper.* Ho visto un annuncio sul giornale.
• **to do a paper round** recapitare i giornali a domicilio
• **an exam paper** una prova scritta

paperback [ˈpeɪpəbæk] NOUN
il tascabile (*book*)

paper boy [ˈpeɪpəbɔɪ] NOUN
il ragazzo che recapita i giornali a domicilio

paper girl [ˈpeɪpəgəːl] NOUN
la ragazza

paper round [ˈpeɪpəraʊnd] NOUN
il giro di distribuzione dei giornali

paperweight [ˈpeɪpəweɪt] NOUN
il fermacarte (PL i fermacarte)

paperwork [ˈpeɪpəwəːk] NOUN
le pratiche ◇ *I've got a lot of paperwork to do.* Ho un sacco di pratiche da sbrigare.

parachute [ˈpærəʃuːt] NOUN
il paracadute

parade [pəˈreɪd] NOUN
la sfilata

paradise [ˈpærədaɪs] NOUN
il paradiso

paraffin [ˈpærəfɪn] NOUN
la paraffina
• **paraffin wax** la paraffina solida
• **a paraffin lamp** una lampada a petrolio

paragraph [ˈpærəgrɑːf] NOUN
il paragrafo

parallel [ˈpærəlɛl] ADJECTIVE
parallelo

paralysed [ˈpærəlaɪzd] ADJECTIVE
paralizzato

paramedic [pærəˈmɛdɪk] NOUN
il paramedico (PL i paramedici)

parcel [ˈpɑːsl] NOUN
il pacco (PL i pacchi)

pardon [ˈpɑːdn] NOUN
see also **pardon** VERB
• **Pardon?** Prego?

to **pardon** [ˈpɑːdn] VERB
see also **pardon** NOUN
scusare

parent [ˈpɛərənt] NOUN
1 il padre (*father*)
2 la madre ◇ *She changed when she became a parent.* È cambiata quando è diventata madre.
• **my parents** i miei genitori
Be careful not to translate **parent** *by* **parente**.

Paris [ˈpærɪs] NOUN
Parigi FEM

Parisian [pəˈrɪzɪən] NOUN ☞

P

il parigino
la parigina

park [pɑːk] NOUN
see also **park** VERB
il parco (PL i parchi) ◇ *Why don't we go for a walk in the park?* Andiamo a fare una passeggiata al parco?
- **a national park** un parco nazionale
- **a theme park** un parco a tema
- **a car park** un parcheggio

to **park** [pɑːk] VERB
see also **park** NOUN
parcheggiare ◇ *Where can I park my car?* Dove posso parcheggiare l'auto?

parking [ˈpɑːkɪŋ] NOUN
- **Parking is difficult in the city centre.** È difficile trovare un posto per la macchina in centro.
- **"no parking"** "divieto di sosta"

parking lot [ˈpɑːkɪŋlɒt] NOUN US
il parcheggio

parking meter [ˈpɑːkɪŋmiːtəʳ] NOUN
il parchimetro

parking place [ˈpɑːkɪŋpleɪs] NOUN
il posto per la macchina

parking ticket [ˈpɑːkɪŋtɪkɪt] NOUN
la multa per sosta vietata

parliament [ˈpɑːləmənt] NOUN
il parlamento

parole [pəˈrəʊl] NOUN
- **on parole** in libertà vigilata

parrot [ˈpærət] NOUN
il pappagallo

parsley [ˈpɑːslɪ] NOUN
il prezzemolo

part [pɑːt] NOUN
see also **part** VERB
[1] la parte ◇ *The first part of the play was boring.* La prima parte della commedia era noiosa. ◇ *She got a part in the film.* Ha ottenuto una parte nel film.
- **to take part in something** partecipare a qualcosa ◇ *A lot of people took part in the demonstration.* Alla manifestazione ha partecipato molta gente.
- **in part exchange** in pagamento parziale
[2] il pezzo ◇ *spare parts* pezzi di ricambio
[3] la riga *(parting)* US

to **part** [pɑːt] VERB
see also **part** NOUN
separarsi E ◇ *They are parting after six years.* Si stanno separando dopo sei anni.
- **to part with something** separarsi E da qualcosa ◇ *I hate to part with this lamp.* Mi dispiace separarmi da questa lampada.

particular [pəˈtɪkjʊləʳ] ADJECTIVE
particolare
- **to place particular emphasis on something** dare* particolare importanza a qualcosa
- **nothing in particular** nulla di particolare

particularly [pəˈtɪkjʊləlɪ] ADVERB

particolarmente

parting [ˈpɑːtɪŋ] NOUN
la riga (PL le righe) *(in hair)*

partly [ˈpɑːtlɪ] ADVERB
in parte

partner [ˈpɑːtnəʳ] NOUN
il/la partner (PL i/le partner)

part-time [ˈpɑːtˈtaɪm] ADJECTIVE, ADVERB
part time MASC, FEM, PL ◇ *a part-time job* un lavoro part time ◇ *She works part-time.* Lavora part time.

party [ˈpɑːtɪ] NOUN (PL **parties**)
[1] la festa ◇ *a birthday party* una festa di compleanno
[2] il partito ◇ *the Conservative Party* il partito conservatore
[3] la comitiva ◇ *a party of tourists* una comitiva di turisti

pass [pɑːs] NOUN (PL **passes**)
see also **pass** VERB
[1] il passaggio *(in football)* ◇ *a brilliant pass* un bel passaggio
[2] il valico (PL i valichi) ◇ *The pass was blocked with snow.* Il valico era bloccato dalla neve.
- **to get a pass** *(in exam)* avere* la sufficienza ◇ *I got six passes.* Ho avuto la sufficienza in sei materie.
- **a bus pass** un tesserino dell'autobus

to **pass** [pɑːs] VERB
see also **pass** NOUN
[1] passare E ◇ *Could you pass me the salt, please?* Mi passi il sale, per favore?
*Use **essere** to form past tenses when **passare** does not have an object.*
◇ *The time has passed quickly.* Il tempo è passato molto in fretta. ◇ *I hope I'll pass the exam.* Spero di passare l'esame.
[2] passare E davanti a ◇ *I pass his house on my way to school.* Andando a scuola passo davanti a casa sua.

to **pass out** [pɑːsˈaʊt] VERB
svenire* E

passage [ˈpæsɪdʒ] NOUN
[1] il brano ◇ *Read the passage carefully.* Leggi attentamente il brano.
[2] il passaggio *(corridor)*

passenger [ˈpæsɪndʒəʳ] NOUN
il passeggero
la passeggera

passion [ˈpæʃən] NOUN
la passione

passive [ˈpæsɪv] ADJECTIVE
passivo ◇ *passive smoking* fumo passivo

Passover [ˈpɑːsəʊvəʳ] NOUN
la Pasqua ebraica

passport [ˈpɑːspɔːt] NOUN
il passaporto ◇ *passport control* il controllo passaporti

password [ˈpɑːswɜːd] NOUN
la parola d'ordine

* Verbs followed by this symbol are irregular. See pp.339–364 for further details.

past [pɑːst] ADVERB, PREPOSITION
see also **past** NOUN
oltre ◊ *It's on the right, just past the station.*
È sulla destra, appena oltre la stazione.
• **to go past** passare ᴱ ◊ *The bus went past
without stopping.* L'autobus è passato
senza fermarsi.
• **The bus goes past our house.** L'autobus
passa davanti a casa nostra.
• **It's half past ten.** Sono le dieci e mezzo.
• **It's quarter past nine.** Sono le nove e un
quarto.
• **It's ten past eight.** Sono le otto e dieci.
• **It's past midnight.** È mezzanotte passata.

past [pɑːst] NOUN
see also **past** ADVERB
il passato ◊ *She lives in the past.* Vive nel
passato.

pasta ['pæstə] NOUN
la pasta

paste [peɪst] NOUN
la colla (*glue*)

pasteurized ['pæstʃəraɪzd] ADJECTIVE
pastorizzato

pastime ['pɑːstaɪm] NOUN
il passatempo

pastry ['peɪstrɪ] NOUN (PL **pastries**)
la pasta

patch [pætʃ] NOUN (PL **patches**)
la toppa ◊ *jackets with patches on the
elbows* giacche con le toppe sui gomiti
• **a patch of land** un appezzamento
• **a patch of grass** un pezzetto di prato
• **a bald patch** una calvizie incipiente
• **a bad patch** un periodaccio ◊ *They're going
through a bad patch.* Stanno attraversando
un periodaccio.

patched [pætʃt] ADJECTIVE
rattoppato ◊ *a pair of patched jeans* un paio
di jeans rattoppati

pâté ['pæteɪ] NOUN
il pâté (PL i pâté)

path [pɑːθ] NOUN
il sentiero

pathetic [pə'θetɪk] ADJECTIVE
[1] penoso ◊ *his pathetic excuses* le sue
scuse penose
[2] patetico ◊ *a pathetic sight* un spettacolo
patetico

patience ['peɪʃns] NOUN
[1] la pazienza ◊ *He hasn't got much
patience.* Non ha molta pazienza.
[2] il solitario ◊ *She was playing patience.*
Stava facendo un solitario.

patient ['peɪʃnt] NOUN, ADJECTIVE
il/la paziente

patio ['pætɪəʊ] NOUN (PL **patios**)
l'area pavimentata (*in garden*)

patriotic [pætrɪ'ɒtɪk] ADJECTIVE
patriottico

patrol [pə'trəʊl] NOUN
la pattuglia
• **on patrol** di pattuglia

patrol car [pə'trəʊlkɑː'] NOUN
l'autopattuglia

pattern ['pætən] NOUN
[1] lo schema (PL gli schemi) ◊ *The three
attacks follow the same pattern.* Le tre
aggressioni seguono lo stesso schema.
[2] il motivo ◊ *a geometric pattern* un
motivo geometrico
• **a sewing pattern** un cartamodello

pause [pɔːz] NOUN
la pausa

pavement ['peɪvmənt] NOUN
il marciapiede
Be careful not to translate **pavement** *by*
pavimento.

paw [pɔː] NOUN
la zampa

pay [peɪ] NOUN
see also **pay** VERB
la paga
• **a pay slip** un foglio paga
• **pay phone** cabina telefonica

to **pay** [peɪ] VERB (**paid, paid**)
see also **pay** NOUN
pagare ◊ *They pay me more on Sundays.*
La domenica mi pagano di più. ◊ *I'll pay you
back tomorrow.* Ti restituisco i soldi
domani. ◊ *Can I pay by cheque?* Posso
pagare con un assegno? ◊ *I paid by credit
card.* Ho pagato con la carta di credito.
• **to pay for something** pagare qualcosa ◊ *I
paid fifty pounds for it.* L'ho pagato
cinquanta sterline.
• **to pay attention** fare* attenzione ◊ *I wasn't
paying attention to what the teacher was
saying.* Non ho fatto attenzione a quello che
diceva l'insegnante.
• **Don't pay any attention to him!** Non dargli
retta!
• **to pay somebody a visit** andare* ᴱ a trovare
qualcuno ◊ *Paul paid us a visit last night.*
Paul è venuto a trovarci ieri sera.

payable ['peɪəbl] ADJECTIVE
• **Who shall I make the cheque payable to?** A
chi devo intestare l'assegno?

payment ['peɪmənt] NOUN
il pagamento

payphone ['peɪfəʊn] NOUN
la cabina telefonica

PC [piː'siː] NOUN
il personal computer (PL i personal
computer)

PE [piː'iː] NOUN (= *physical education*)
l'educazione fisica FEM

pea [piː] NOUN
il pisello

peace [piːs] NOUN
la pace
• **peace talks** i negoziati di pace ☞

P

• **a peace treaty** un trattato di pace

peaceful ['piːsful] ADJECTIVE
1. tranquillo ◇ *a peaceful afternoon* un pomeriggio tranquillo
2. pacifico ◇ *a peaceful demonstration* una manifestazione pacifica

peach [piːtʃ] NOUN (PL **peaches**)
la pesca (PL le pesche)

peacock ['piːkɔk] NOUN
il pavone

peak [piːk] NOUN
1. la cima (*of mountain*)
2. l' apice MASC ◇ *His career was at its peak.* La sua carriera era all'apice.

• **peak season** l'alta stagione

peak rate ['piːkreɪt] NOUN
la tariffa ore di punta (*for phone*)

peanut ['piːnʌt] NOUN
la nocciolina americana ◇ *a packet of peanuts* un pacchetto di noccioline americane

peanut butter ['piːnʌtbʌtəʳ] NOUN
il burro di arachidi

pear [pɛəʳ] NOUN
la pera

pearl [pəːl] NOUN
la perla

pebble ['pɛbl] NOUN
il ciottolo

peckish ['pɛkɪʃ] ADJECTIVE
• **to feel peckish** avere* un languorino

peculiar [pɪ'kjuːlɪəʳ] ADJECTIVE
strano ◇ *He's a peculiar person.* È un tipo strano. ◇ *It tastes peculiar.* Ha un sapore strano.

pedal ['pɛdl] NOUN
il pedale

pedestrian [pɪ'dɛstrɪən] NOUN
il pedone ◇ *cyclists and pedestrians* ciclisti e pedoni

pedestrian crossing [pɪ'dɛstrɪən'krɔsɪŋ] NOUN
l' attraversamento pedonale

pedestrianized [pɪ'dɛstrɪənaɪzd] ADJECTIVE
• **a pedestrianized street** una via pedonalizzata

pedestrian precinct [pɪ'dɛstrɪən'priːsɪŋkt] NOUN
la zona pedonale

pedigree ['pɛdɪgriː] ADJECTIVE
di razza ◇ *a pedigree dog* un cane di razza

pee [piː] NOUN
• **to have a pee** fare* la pipì

peek [piːk] NOUN
• **to have a peek at** dare* una sbirciatina a ◇ *I had a peek at his diary.* Ho dato una sbirciatina al suo diario.

peel [piːl] NOUN
see also **peel** VERB
1. la buccia (PL le bucce) ◇ *apple peel* buccia di mela

2. la scorza ◇ *orange peel* scorza d'arancio

to **peel** [piːl] VERB
see also **peel** NOUN
1. sbucciare ◇ *Shall I peel the potatoes?* Sbuccio le patate?
2. spellarsi[E] ◇ *My nose is peeling.* Mi si sta spellando il naso.

peg [pɛg] NOUN
1. l' attaccapanni (PL gli attaccapanni) (*for clothes*)
2. la molletta (*for washing*)

• **a tent peg** un picchetto

Pekinese [piːkɪ'niːz] NOUN (PL **Pekinese**)
il pechinese (*dog*)

pellet ['pɛlɪt] NOUN
il pallino (*for gun*)

pelvis ['pɛlvɪs] NOUN (PL **pelvises**)
il bacino

pen [pɛn] NOUN
la penna ◇ *I haven't got a pen.* Non ho una penna.

• **a pen name** uno pseudonimo

penalty ['pɛnltɪ] NOUN (PL **penalties**)
1. la pena ◇ *The penalty for this offence is life imprisonment.* La pena per questo reato è l'ergastolo.

• **the death penalty** la pena di morte
2. il calcio di rigore (*in football*)

• **a penalty shoot-out** i rigori

pence [pɛns] NOUN PL
i penny ◇ *24 pence* ventiquattro penny

pencil ['pɛnsl] NOUN
la matita ◇ *in pencil* a matita

pencil case ['pɛnslkeɪs] NOUN
il portamatite (PL i portamatite)

pencil sharpener ['pɛnslʃɑːpnəʳ] NOUN
il temperamatite (PL i temperamatite)

pendant ['pɛndnt] NOUN
il pendaglio

pen-friend ['pɛnfrɛnd] NOUN
l' amico di penna (PL gli amici di penna)
l' amica di penna (PL le amiche di penna)

penguin ['pɛŋgwɪn] NOUN
il pinguino

penicillin [pɛnɪ'sɪlɪn] NOUN
la penicillina

penis ['piːnɪs] NOUN (PL **penises**)
il pene

penitentiary [pɛnɪ'tɛnʃərɪ] NOUN (PL **penitentiaries**) [US]
il penitenziario

penknife ['pɛnnaɪf] NOUN (PL **penknives**)
il temperino

penny ['pɛnɪ] NOUN (PL **pence**)
il penny (PL i penny)

pension ['pɛnʃən] NOUN
la pensione

pensioner ['pɛnʃənəʳ] NOUN
il pensionato
la pensionata

pentathlon [pɛn'tæθlən] NOUN

* Verbs followed by this symbol are irregular. See pp.339–364 for further details.

il pentathlon

people ['pi:pl] NOUN PL

[1] la gente SING ◇ *a lot of people* un sacco di gente

*Use a singular verb with **gente**.*

◇ *The people were nice.* La gente era simpatica.

[2] le persone ◇ *six people* sei persone
◇ *several people* diverse persone

* **How many people are there in your family?** Quanti siete in famiglia?
* **Italian people** gli italiani
* **People say that...** Si dice che...

pepper ['pepə'] NOUN

[1] il pepe ◇ *Pass the pepper, please.* Mi passi il pepe, per favore?

[2] il peperone ◇ *a green pepper* un peperone verde

peppermill ['pepəmɪl] NOUN

il macinapepe (PL i macinapepe)

peppermint ['pepəmɪnt] NOUN

la caramella alla menta ◇ *Would you like a peppermint?* Vuoi una caramella alla menta?

* **peppermint tea** il tè alla menta

per [pə:'] PREPOSITION

a ◇ *per day* al giorno ◇ *per week* alla settimana ◇ *30 miles per hour* trenta miglia all'ora

* **per annum** all'anno
* **per cent** per cento ◇ *fifty per cent* cinquanta per cento

percolator ['pə:kəleɪtə'] NOUN

la caffettiera a filtro

percussion [pə'kʌʃən] NOUN

le percussioni FEM PL ◇ *I play percussion.* Suono le percussioni.

perfect ['pə:fɪkt] ADJECTIVE

see also **perfect** NOUN

perfetto ◇ *That's perfect!* Perfetto!

perfect ['pə:fɪkt] NOUN

see also **perfect** ADJECTIVE

* **the perfect** il passato composto

perfectly ['pə:fɪktlɪ] ADVERB

perfettamente

perform [pə'fɔ:m] VERB

[1] compiere ◇ *He performed many acts of bravery.* Ha compiuto molti atti di coraggio.

[2] rappresentare ◇ *This play was first performed in 1890.* Questa commedia è stata rappresentata per la prima volta nel 1890.

* **to perform a task** svolgere* un compito
* **to perform brilliantly** (*team*) fornire un'ottima prestazione

performance [pə'fɔ:məns] NOUN

[1] lo spettacolo ◇ *The performance lasts two hours.* Lo spettacolo dura due ore.

[2] l'interpretazione FEM ◇ *his performance as Hamlet* la sua interpretazione di Amleto

[3] la prestazione ◇ *the team's disappointing performance* la deludente prestazione della squadra

perfume [pə:fju:m] NOUN

il profumo

perhaps [pə'hæps] ADVERB

forse ◇ *Perhaps he's ill.* Forse è malato.

period ['pɪərɪəd] NOUN

[1] il periodo ◇ *for a limited period* per un periodo limitato

[2] l'epoca ◇ *the Victorian period* l'epoca vittoriana

[3] le mestruazioni FEM PL ◇ *I'm having my period.* Ho le mestruazioni.

[4] la lezione ◇ *Each period lasts forty minutes.* Ogni lezione dura quaranta minuti.

[5] il punto (*full stop*) US ◇ *Comma or period?* Virgola o punto?

perm [pə:m] NOUN

la permanente ◇ *She's got a perm.* Ha la permanente.

permanent ['pə:mənənt] ADJECTIVE

permanente ◇ *a permanent ban* un divieto permanente

* **a permanent job** un lavoro fisso

permission [pə'mɪʃən] NOUN

il permesso ◇ *You'll have to ask permission.* Dovrai chiedere il permesso.

permit ['pə:mɪt] NOUN

il permesso ◇ *a work permit* un permesso di lavoro

* **a fishing permit** una licenza di pesca

Persian ['pə:ʃən] ADJECTIVE

persiano ◇ *a Persian cat* un gatto persiano

persistent [pə'sɪstənt] ADJECTIVE

tenace

person ['pə:sn] NOUN

la persona

personal ['pə:snl] ADJECTIVE

personale ◇ *a personal opinion* un'opinione personale

personal assistant ['pə:snlə'sɪstənt] NOUN

la segretaria di direzione

personal column ['pə:snl'kɔləm] NOUN

la colonna dei piccoli annunci

personality [pə:sə'nælɪtɪ] NOUN (PL **personalities**)

la personalità (PL le personalità)

personally ['pə:snəlɪ] ADVERB

personalmente ◇ *Personally I don't agree.* Personalmente non sono d'accordo.

personal stereo ['pə:snl'stɪərɪəu] NOUN

il walkman ® (PL i walkman)

personnel [pə:sə'nɛl] NOUN

il personale

perspiration [pə:spɪ'reɪʃən] NOUN

la traspirazione

to **persuade** [pə'sweɪd] VERB

convincere* ◇ *She persuaded me to go with her.* Mi ha convinto ad andare con lei.

pessimist ['pesɪmɪst] NOUN

il/la pessimista

pessimistic [pesɪ'mɪstɪk] ADJECTIVE ☞

P

pessimista

pest [pɛst] NOUN
- ☐1 l' insetto nocivo ◇ *garden pests* gli insetti nocivi del giardino
- ☐2 il/la rompiscatole ◇ *He's a real pest!* È un gran rompiscatole!

to **pester** ['pɛstə'] VERB
tormentare ◇ *He's always pestering me.* Mi tormenta in continuazione.

pet [pɛt] NOUN
l' animale domestico (PL gli animali domestici) ◇ *Have you got any pets?* Hai qualche animale domestico?
- ◆ **the teacher's pet** il cocco dell'insegnante

petition [pə'tɪʃən] NOUN
la petizione

petrified ['pɛtrɪfaɪd] ADJECTIVE
terrorizzato ◇ *I was petrified.* Ero terrorizzato.

petrol ['pɛtrəl] NOUN
la benzina ◇ *They spend a lot on petrol.* Spendono molto per la benzina.
- ◆ **unleaded petrol** la benzina verde
- ◆ **a petrol pump** una pompa di benzina
Be careful not to translate petrol by petrolio.

petrol station ['pɛtrəlsteɪʃən] NOUN
la stazione di servizio

petrol tank ['pɛtrəltæŋk] NOUN
il serbatoio della benzina

phantom ['fæntəm] NOUN
il fantasma (PL i fantasmi)

pharmacy ['fɑ:məsɪ] NOUN (PL **pharmacies**)
la farmacia

pheasant ['fɛznt] NOUN
il fagiano

philosophy [fɪ'lɒsəfɪ] NOUN (PL **philosophies**)
la filosofia

phobia ['fəubjə] NOUN
la fobia

to **phone** [fəun] VERB
see also **phone** NOUN
telefonare ◇ *I'll phone the station.* Telefono alla stazione.
- ◆ **to phone back** richiamare

phone [fəun] NOUN
see also **phone** VERB
il telefono
- ◆ **by phone** per telefono
- ◆ **to be on the phone** essere* E al telefono ◇ *She's on the phone at the moment.* In questo momento è al telefono.

phone bill ['fəunbɪl] NOUN
la bolletta del telefono

phone book ['fəunbuk] NOUN
l' elenco telefonico (PL gli elenchi telefonici)

phone box ['fəunbɔks] NOUN
la cabina telefonica (PL le cabine telefoniche)

phone call ['fəunkɔ:l] NOUN
la telefonata ◇ *to make a phone call* fare una telefonata

phonecard ['fəunkɑ:d] NOUN

la scheda telefonica (PL le schede telefoniche)

phone number ['fəunnʌmbə'] NOUN
il numero di telefono

photo ['fəutəu] NOUN (PL **photos**)
la foto (PL le foto)
- ◆ **to take a photo** fare* una foto ◇ *I took a photo of the bride and groom.* Ho fatto una foto agli sposi.

photocopy ['fəutəukɔpɪ] NOUN (PL **photocopies**)
see also **photocopy** VERB
la fotocopia

to **photocopy** ['fəutəukɔpɪ] VERB (**photocopied, photocopied**)
see also **photocopy** NOUN
fotocopiare

photograph ['fəutəgræf] NOUN
see also **photograph** VERB
la fotografia

to **photograph** ['fəutəgræf] VERB
see also **photograph** NOUN
fotografare

photographer [fə'tɒgrəfə'] NOUN
il fotografo
la fotografa
◇ *She's a photographer.* Fa la fotografa.

photography [fə'tɒgrəfɪ] NOUN
la fotografia ◇ *My hobby is photography.* Il mio hobby è la fotografia.

phrase [freɪz] NOUN
la frase

phrase book ['freɪzbuk] NOUN
il manuale di conversazione

physical ['fɪzɪkl] ADJECTIVE
see also **physical** NOUN
fisico

physical ['fɪzɪkl] NOUN US
see also **physical** ADJECTIVE
la visita medica

physicist ['fɪzɪsɪst] NOUN
il fisico ◇ *a nuclear physicist* un fisico nucleare

physics ['fɪzɪks] NOUN
la fisica ◇ *She teaches physics.* Insegna fisica.

physiotherapist [fɪzɪəu'θɛrəpɪst] NOUN
il/la fisioterapista

physiotherapy [fɪzɪəu'θɛrəpɪ] NOUN
la fisioterapia

pianist ['pi:ənɪst] NOUN
il/la pianista

piano [pɪ'ænəu] NOUN (PL **pianos**)
il pianoforte

pick [pɪk] NOUN
see also **pick** VERB
il piccone ◇ *pick and shovel* pala e piccone
- ◆ **Take your pick!** Scegli quello che vuoi!
Use "quella" if what you may pick is feminine, and "quelli" or "quelle" if it is plural.

to **pick** [pɪk] VERB

see also **pick** NOUN

[1] scegliere* ◇ *I picked the biggest piece.* Ho scelto il pezzo più grosso.

[2] cogliere* ◇ *I picked some strawberries.* Ho colto un po' di fragole.

• **to pick on somebody** prendersela* E con qualcuno ◇ *She's always picking on me.* Se la prende sempre con me.

pick out [pɪk'aut] VERB

scegliere* ◇ *I like them all – it's difficult to pick one out.* Mi piacciono tutti, è difficile sceglierne uno.

pick up [pɪk'ʌp] VERB

[1] prendere* ◇ *We'll come to the airport to pick you up.* Veniamo a prenderti all'aeroporto.

[2] raccogliere* ◇ *Could you help me pick up the toys?* Mi aiuti a raccogliere i giocattoli?

[3] imparare ◇ *I picked up some Spanish during my holiday.* Ho imparato un po' di spagnolo in vacanza.

[4] prendersi* E ◇ *They picked up a nasty infection.* Si sono presi una brutta infezione.

pickpocket ['pɪkpɔkɪt] NOUN
il borseggiatore
la borseggiatrice

picnic ['pɪknɪk] NOUN
il picnic (PL i picnic)

• **to have a picnic** fare* un picnic

picture ['pɪktʃə'] NOUN
see also **picture** VERB

[1] l' illustrazione FEM ◇ *Children's books have lots of pictures.* Ci sono molte illustrazioni nei libri per bambini.

[2] la foto (PL le foto) ◇ *My picture was in the paper.* C'era la mia foto sul giornale.

[3] il quadro ◇ *There were pictures on the walls.* C'erano dei quadri alle pareti.

• **to paint a picture of something** dipingere* qualcosa

[4] il disegno ◇ *a nice picture* un bel disegno

• **to draw a picture of something** disegnare qualcosa

• **the pictures** il cinema SING ◇ *Shall we go to the pictures?* Andiamo al cinema?

picture ['pɪktʃə'] VERB
see also **picture** NOUN

immaginare ◇ *I can just picture it!* Me lo immagino!

picturesque [pɪktʃə'rɛsk] ADJECTIVE
pittoresco

pie [paɪ] NOUN

[1] la torta ◇ *an apple pie* una torta di mele
[2] il pasticcio in crosta (*savoury*)

piece [piːs] NOUN
il pezzo ◇ *A small piece, please.* Un pezzo piccolo, per favore.

• **a piece of furniture** un mobile
• **a piece of advice** un consiglio
• **a 10p piece** una moneta da dieci penny

pie chart ['paɪtʃɑːt] NOUN
il grafico a torta (PL i grafici a torta)

Piedmont ['piːdmɔnt] NOUN
il Piemonte

pier [pɪə'] NOUN
il pontile

to pierce [pɪəs] VERB
perforare ◇ *A bullet pierced his chest.* Un proiettile gli ha perforato il petto.

• **to have one's ears pierced** farsi* E fare i buchi alle orecchie

pierced [pɪəst] ADJECTIVE

• **to have pierced ears** avere* i buchi per gli orecchini ◇ *I've got pierced ears.* Ho i buchi per gli orecchini.

piercing ['pɪəsɪŋ] NOUN
il piercing (PL i piercing) ◇ *She has several piercings.* Ha diversi piercing.

pig [pɪg] NOUN
il maiale

pigeon ['pɪdʒən] NOUN
il piccione

piggyback ['pɪgɪbæk] NOUN

• **to give a piggyback** portare a cavalluccio ◇ *I can't give you a piggyback, you're too heavy.* Non posso portarti a cavalluccio, sei troppo pesante.

piggy bank ['pɪgɪbæŋk] NOUN
il salvadanaio

pigtail ['pɪgteɪl] NOUN
la treccia (PL le trecce)

pile [paɪl] NOUN
la pila ◇ *There were piles of dirty dishes in the kitchen.* C'erano pile di piatti sporchi in cucina.

piles [paɪlz] NOUN PL
le emorroidi

pile-up ['paɪlʌp] NOUN
il tamponamento a catena

pill [pɪl] NOUN
la pillola

• **to be on the pill** prendere* la pillola

pillar ['pɪlə'] NOUN
il pilastro ◇ *marble pillars* pilastri di marmo

pillar box ['pɪləbɔks] NOUN
la buca delle lettere (PL le buche delle lettere)

pillow ['pɪləu] NOUN
il guanciale

pilot ['paɪlət] NOUN
il/la pilota ◇ *He's a pilot.* Fa il pilota.

pilot light ['paɪlətlaɪt] NOUN
la fiamma pilota

pimple ['pɪmpl] NOUN
il brufolo

PIN [pɪn] NOUN (= *personal identification number*)
il numero di codice segreto

pin [pɪn] NOUN
see also **pin** VERB
lo spillo ◇ *fastened with a pin* fissato con uno spillo ☞

P

• **pins and needles** il formicolio ◇ *I've got pins and needles.* Ho un formicolio.

to **pin** [pɪn] VERB
see also **pin** NOUN
appuntare ◇ *They pinned a notice on the board.* Hanno appuntato un avviso in bacheca.

pinafore ['pɪnəfɔːʳ] NOUN
il grembiule

pinball ['pɪnbɔːl] NOUN
il flipper ◇ *They're playing pinball.* Giocano a flipper.

pinball machine ['pɪnbɔːlməʃiːn] NOUN
il flipper (PL i flipper)

to **pinch** [pɪntʃ] VERB
[1] pizzicare ◇ *He pinched me!* Mi ha pizzicato!
[2] fregare ◇ *Who's pinched my pen?* Chi mi ha fregato la penna?

pine [paɪn] NOUN
il pino

pineapple ['paɪnæpl] NOUN
l' ananas (PL gli ananas)

pink [pɪŋk] ADJECTIVE
rosa MASC, FEM, PL

pint [paɪnt] NOUN
la pinta

ⓘ *Una* pinta *equivale a 0,568 litri.*

• **a pint of beer** una birra grande
• **half a pint of beer** una birra piccola
• **to have a pint** bere* una birra
• **to go out for a pint** uscire*[E] a bere una birra

pipe [paɪp] NOUN
[1] il tubo ◇ *a plastic pipe* un tubo di plastica
[2] la pipa ◇ *He smokes a pipe.* Fuma la pipa.
• **the pipes** la cornamusa SING ◇ *He plays the pipes.* Suona la cornamusa.

pirate ['paɪərət] NOUN
il pirata (PL i pirati)

pirated ['paɪərətɪd] ADJECTIVE
pirata MASC, FEM, PL ◇ *a pirated video* una videocassetta pirata

Pisces ['paɪsiːz] NOUN
i Pesci ◇ *I'm Pisces.* Sono dei Pesci.

pissed [pɪst] ADJECTIVE
bevuto

pitch [pɪtʃ] NOUN (PL **pitches**)
see also **pitch** VERB
il campo ◇ *a football pitch* un campo di calcio

to **pitch** [pɪtʃ] VERB
see also **pitch** NOUN
[1] lanciare ◇ *He pitched the bottle into the lake.* Ha lanciato la bottiglia nel lago.
[2] piantare ◇ *We pitched our tent near the beach.* Abbiamo piantato la tenda vicino alla spiaggia.

pity ['pɪtɪ] NOUN
see also **pity** VERB
la compassione
• **to feel pity for somebody** provare compassione per qualcuno
• **What a pity!** Che peccato!

to **pity** ['pɪtɪ] VERB (**pitied, pitied**)
see also **pity** NOUN
compatire ◇ *I don't hate him, I pity him.* Non lo odio, lo compatisco.

pizza ['piːtsə] NOUN
la pizza

place [pleɪs] NOUN
see also **place** VERB
il posto ◇ *It's a quiet place.* È un posto tranquillo. ◇ *There are a lot of interesting places to visit.* Ci sono tanti posti interessanti da vedere. ◇ *a university place* un posto all'università
• **to change places** scambiarsi[E] di posto
• **to take place** avere* luogo ◇ *Elections will take place on November 25th.* Le elezioni avranno luogo il 25 novembre.
• **at your place** a casa tua ◇ *Shall we meet at your place?* Ci incontriamo a casa tua?

to **place** [pleɪs] VERB
see also **place** NOUN
posare ◇ *He placed his hand on hers.* Ha posato la mano sulla sua.

placement ['pleɪsmənt] NOUN
lo stage (PL gli stage)
• **to do a work placement** fare* uno stage

plain [pleɪn] ADJECTIVE
[1] in tinta unita ◇ *a plain tie* una cravatta in tinta unita
[2] semplice ◇ *a plain white blouse* una camicetta bianca, semplice
• **in plain clothes** in borghese

plain chocolate ['pleɪn'tʃɔklɪt] NOUN
il cioccolato fondente

plait [plæt] NOUN
la treccia (PL le trecce)

plan [plæn] NOUN
see also **plan** VERB
[1] il programma (PL i programmi) ◇ *What are your plans for the holidays?* Che programmi hai per le vacanze?
• **to make plans** fare* progetti
• **according to plan** come previsto
◇ *Everything went according to plan.* È andato tutto come previsto.
[2] la piantina ◇ *a plan of the campsite* una piantina del campeggio

to **plan** [plæn] VERB
see also **plan** NOUN
[1] progettare ◇ *We're planning a trip to France.* Stiamo progettando un viaggio in Francia.
[2] organizzare ◇ *Plan your revision carefully.* Organizza bene il ripasso.
• **to plan to do something** avere* intenzione

di fare qualcosa ◇ *I'm planning to get a job in the holidays.* Ho intenzione di trovare un lavoro per le vacanze.

plane [pleɪn] NOUN
l' aereo ◇ *by plane* in aereo

planet ['plænɪt] NOUN
il pianeta (PL i pianeti)

planning ['plænɪŋ] NOUN
* **The trip needs careful planning.** Bisogna organizzare bene il viaggio.
* **planning permission** permesso di costruzione
* **family planning** pianificazione familiare

plant [plɑːnt] VERB
see also **plant** NOUN
piantare

plant [plɑːnt] NOUN
see also **plant** VERB
[1] la pianta ◇ *I water my plants every week.* Annaffio le piante ogni settimana.
[2] la fabbrica (PL le fabbriche) ◇ *a chemical plant* una fabbrica chimica

plant pot ['plɑːntpɒt] NOUN
il vaso per piante

plaque [plæk] NOUN
[1] la targa (PL le targhe) (*commemorative*)
[2] la placca (*on teeth*)

plaster ['plɑːstə'] NOUN
[1] il cerotto ◇ *Have you got a plaster, by any chance?* Hai un cerotto, per caso?
[2] il gesso ◇ *Her leg's in plaster.* Ha una gamba in gesso.

plastic ['plæstɪk] NOUN
see also **plastic** ADJECTIVE
la plastica ◇ *It's made of plastic.* È di plastica.

plastic ['plæstɪk] ADJECTIVE
see also **plastic** NOUN
di plastica ◇ *a plastic bag* un sacchetto di plastica

plate [pleɪt] NOUN
il piatto

platform ['plætfɔːm] NOUN
[1] il binario ◇ *at platform four* al binario quattro
[2] la banchina ◇ *They were waiting on the platform.* Aspettavano sulla banchina.
[3] il palco (PL i palchi) ◇ *The soloist had just left the platform.* Il solista aveva appena lasciato il palco.

play [pleɪ] NOUN
see also **play** VERB
[1] la commedia ◇ *a play by Shakespeare* una commedia di Shakespeare
* **to put on a play** mettere* in scena una commedia
[2] il gioco ◇ *work and play* lavoro e gioco

play [pleɪ] VERB
see also **play** NOUN
[1] giocare ◇ *He's playing with his friends.* Sta giocando con gli amici.

[2] giocare contro ◇ *Italy will play Scotland next month.* Il mese prossimo l'Italia giocherà contro la Scozia.
[3] giocare a ◇ *I play hockey.* Gioco a hockey. ◇ *Can you play pool?* Sai giocare a biliardo?
[4] suonare ◇ *I play the guitar.* Suono la chitarra.
[5] ascoltare ◇ *She's always playing that record.* Ascolta sempre quel disco.
[6] recitare il ruolo di ◇ *I would like to play Cleopatra.* Mi piacerebbe recitare il ruolo di Cleopatra.

to **play down** [pleɪ'daun] VERB
minimizzare ◇ *He tried to play down his illness.* Ha cercato di minimizzare la sua malattia.

to **play up** [pleɪ'ʌp] VERB
[1] fare* i capricci ◇ *The car's playing up.* La macchina fa i capricci.
[2] far* male ◇ *My leg's playing up.* La gamba mi fa male.

player ['pleɪə'] NOUN
il giocatore
la giocatrice
* **a football player** un calciatore
* **a piano player** un pianista
* **a saxophone player** un sassofonista

playful ['pleɪful] ADJECTIVE
giocherellone

playground ['pleɪgraund] NOUN
[1] il cortile per la ricreazione (*at school*)
[2] il campo giochi (*in park*)

playgroup ['pleɪgruːp] NOUN
l' asilo

playing card ['pleɪŋkɑːd] NOUN
la carta da gioco

playing field ['pleɪŋfiːld] NOUN
il campo sportivo

playtime ['pleɪtaɪm] NOUN
la ricreazione

playwright ['pleɪraɪt] NOUN
il commediografo
la commediografa

pleasant ['plezənt] ADJECTIVE
piacevole

please [pliːz] EXCLAMAZIONE
per favore ◇ *Two coffees, please.* Due caffè, per favore.
* **Yes please.** Sì, grazie.

pleased [pliːzd] ADJECTIVE
contento ◇ *My mother's not going to be very pleased.* Mia madre non sarà molto contenta. ◇ *It's beautiful: she'll be pleased with it.* È bellissimo, ne sarà contenta.
* **Pleased to meet you!** Piacere!

pleasure ['pleʒə'] NOUN
il piacere

plenty ['plentɪ] PRONOUN
abbastanza ◇ *I've got plenty.* Ne ho abbastanza.

P

- **I've got plenty to do.** Ho un sacco di cose da fare.
- **plenty of** un sacco di ◇ *We've got plenty of time.* Abbiamo un sacco di tempo.
- **I've got plenty of money.** Ho soldi a sufficienza.

pliers ['plaɪəz] NOUN PL
le pinze

plot [plɒt] NOUN
see also **plot** VERB
[1] la trama ◇ *a complicated plot* una trama complicata
[2] il complotto ◇ *a plot against the president* un complotto contro il presidente
- **a vegetable plot** un orticello

to **plot** [plɒt] VERB
see also **plot** NOUN
complottare

plug [plʌg] NOUN
[1] la spina ◇ *The plug is faulty.* La spina è difettosa.
[2] il tappo (*for sink, bath*)

to **plug in** [plʌgˈɪn] VERB
attaccare ◇ *Is the iron plugged in?* È attaccato il ferro da stiro?

plum [plʌm] NOUN
la prugna

plumber ['plʌmər] NOUN
l'idraulico (PL gli idraulici) ◇ *He's a plumber.* Fa l'idraulico.

plump [plʌmp] ADJECTIVE
grassoccio

to **plunge** [plʌndʒ] VERB
tuffarsi E ◇ *She plunged into the pool.* Si è tuffata nella piscina.

plural ['pluərl] NOUN
il plurale

plus [plʌs] CONJUNCTION, ADJECTIVE
[1] più ◇ *4 plus 3 equals 7.* Quattro più tre fa sette.
[2] e ◇ *three children plus a dog* tre bambini e un cane
- **I got B plus for my essay.** Ho ricevuto B più nel tema.

> ⓘ *Nei paesi anglosassoni i voti sono espressi con le lettere A, B, C e D.*

plus point ['plʌspɔɪnt] NOUN
il vantaggio

p.m. [piːˈɛm] ADVERB (= *post meridiem*)
- **at eight p.m.** alle otto di sera
- **at two p.m.** alle quattordici

pneumonia [njuːˈməʊnɪə] NOUN
la polmonite

poached [pəʊtʃt] ADJECTIVE
- **a poached egg** un uovo affogato

pocket ['pɒkɪt] NOUN
la tasca (PL le tasche) ◇ *He had his hands in his pockets.* Aveva le mani in tasca.

pocket calculator ['pɒkɪtˈkælkjəleɪtəʳ] NOUN
la calcolatrice tascabile

pocket money ['pɒkɪtmʌnɪ] NOUN
la paghetta ◇ *£8 a week pocket money* una paghetta settimanale di otto sterline

poem ['pəʊɪm] NOUN
la poesia

poet ['pəʊɪt] NOUN
la poeta
la poetessa

poetry ['pəʊɪtrɪ] NOUN
la poesia

point [pɔɪnt] NOUN
see also **point** VERB
[1] il punto ◇ *a point on the horizon* un punto all'orizzonte ◇ *They scored five points.* Hanno segnato cinque punti. ◇ *At that point, we decided to leave.* A quel punto abbiamo deciso di andarcene.
- **a point of view** un punto di vista
- **to get to the point** arrivare E al punto
[2] l'osservazione FEM ◇ *He made some interesting points.* Ha fatto delle osservazioni interessanti.
[3] la punta ◇ *a pencil with a sharp point* una matita con la punta
[4] la virgola (*in decimals*) ◇ *two point five (2.5)* due virgola cinque (2,5)
- **to get somebody's point** capire ciò che qualcuno vuole dire ◇ *Yes, I get your point.* Sì, capisco ciò che vuoi dire.
- **That's a good point!** Giusto!
- **There's no point.** È inutile. ◇ *There's no point waiting.* È inutile aspettare.
- **What's the point?** Perché? ◇ *What's the point of leaving so early?* Perché partire così presto?

to **point** [pɔɪnt] VERB
see also **point** NOUN
indicare col dito ◇ *Don't point!* Non indicare col dito!
- **to point at somebody** indicare qualcuno col dito ◇ *She pointed at Anne.* Ha indicato Anna col dito.
- **to point a gun at somebody** puntare una pistola contro qualcuno

to **point out** [pɔɪntˈaʊt] VERB
[1] indicare ◇ *The guide pointed out Big Ben to us.* La guida ci ha indicato il Big Ben.
[2] far* presente ◇ *She pointed out our mistakes.* Ci ha fatto presente i nostri errori.
- **I'd like to point out that...** Vorrei far notare che...

pointless ['pɔɪntlɪs] ADJECTIVE
inutile ◇ *It's pointless to argue.* È inutile discutere.

poison ['pɔɪzn] NOUN
see also **poison** VERB
il veleno

to **poison** ['pɔɪzn] VERB
see also **poison** NOUN
avvelenare

poisonous ['pɔɪznəs] ADJECTIVE

---

* Verbs followed by this symbol are irregular. See pp.339–364 for further details.

[1] <u>velenoso</u> ◇ *poisonous snakes* serpenti velenosi

[2] <u>tossico</u> ◇ *poisonous fumes* vapori tossici

to **poke** [pəuk] VERB
* **He poked me in the eye.** Mi ha ficcato un dito nell'occhio.

poker ['pəukə'] NOUN
il <u>poker</u> ◇ *I play poker.* Gioco a poker.

Poland ['pəuland] NOUN
la <u>Polonia</u>

polar bear ['pəuləbɛə'] NOUN
l' <u>orso bianco</u> (PL gli orsi bianchi)

Pole [pəul] NOUN
il <u>polacco</u>
la <u>polacca</u>

pole [pəul] NOUN
[1] il <u>palo</u> ◇ *a telegraph pole* un palo del telegrafo
* **a tent pole** un paletto per la tenda
* **a ski pole** una racchetta da sci
[2] il <u>polo</u> ◇ *the earth's poles* i poli terrestri
* **the North Pole** il polo nord
* **the South Pole** il polo sud

pole vault ['pəulvɔ:lt] NOUN
il <u>salto con l'asta</u>

police [pə'li:s] NOUN
la <u>polizia</u> SING ◇ *We called the police.* Abbiamo chiamato la polizia.

police car [pə'li:skɑ:'] NOUN
l' <u>auto della polizia</u> (PL le auto della polizia)

policeman [pə'li:smən] NOUN (PL **policemen**)
il <u>poliziotto</u>

police station [pə'li:sstɛiʃən] NOUN
il <u>comando di polizia</u>

policewoman [pə'li:swumən] NOUN (PL **policewomen**)
la <u>donna poliziotto</u> (PL le donne poliziotto)

polio ['pəuliəu] NOUN
il <u>polio</u>

Polish ['pəuliʃ] ADJECTIVE
<u>polacco</u>

polish ['pɔliʃ] NOUN (PL **polishes**)
see also **polish** VERB
[1] il <u>lucido</u> ◇ *shoe polish* lucido per scarpe
[2] la <u>cera</u> (*for furniture*)

to **polish** ['pɔliʃ] VERB
see also **polish** NOUN
<u>lucidare</u> (*shoes, furniture*)

polite [pə'laɪt] ADJECTIVE
<u>educato</u>

politely [pə'laɪtlɪ] ADVERB
<u>educatamente</u>

politeness [pə'laɪtnɪs] NOUN
l' <u>educazione</u> FEM ◇ *out of politeness* per educazione

political [pə'lɪtɪkl] ADJECTIVE
<u>politico</u>

politician [pɔlɪ'tɪʃən] NOUN
il <u>politico</u> (PL i politici)

politics ['pɔlɪtɪks] NOUN PL

la <u>politica</u> ◇ *I'm not interested in politics.* Non m'interesso di politica.

poll [pəul] NOUN
il <u>sondaggio</u> ◇ *A recent poll revealed that...* Un recente sondaggio ha rivelato che...

pollen ['pɔlən] NOUN
il <u>polline</u>

to **pollute** [pə'lu:t] VERB
<u>inquinare</u>

polluted [pə'lu:tɪd] ADJECTIVE
<u>inquinato</u>

pollution [pə'lu:ʃən] NOUN
l' <u>inquinamento</u>

polo ['pəuləu] NOUN
il <u>polo</u> (*sport*)

polo neck ['pəuləunɛk] NOUN
il <u>maglione dolcevita</u>

polo-necked ['pəuləunɛkt] ADJECTIVE
* **a polo-necked sweater** un maglione dolcevita

polo shirt ['pəuləuʃə:t] NOUN
la <u>polo</u> (PL le polo)

polythene bag ['pɔlɪθi:n'bæg] NOUN
il <u>sacchetto di plastica</u>

pond [pɔnd] NOUN
[1] lo <u>stagno</u> (*natural*)
[2] il <u>laghetto</u> (*artificial*)

pony ['pəunɪ] NOUN (PL **ponies**)
il <u>pony</u> (PL i pony)
* **to go pony trekking** fare* un'escursione a cavallo

ponytail ['pəunɪtɛɪl] NOUN
[1] la <u>coda di cavallo</u> ◇ *She's got a ponytail.* Ha la coda di cavallo.
[2] il <u>codino</u> (*man's*)

poodle ['pu:dl] NOUN
il <u>barboncino</u>

pool [pu:l] NOUN
see also **pool** VERB
[1] la <u>pozza</u> ◇ *a pool of blood* una pozza di sangue
[2] lo <u>stagno</u> (*pond*)
[3] la <u>piscina</u> (*swimming bath*)
[4] il <u>biliardo</u> ◇ *Let's play pool.* Giochiamo a biliardo.
* **the pools** il totocalcio
* **to do the pools** giocare la schedina

to **pool** [pu:l] VERB
see also **pool** NOUN
<u>mettere</u>* insieme

poor [puə'] ADJECTIVE
[1] <u>povero</u> ◇ *a poor family* una famiglia povera ◇ *Poor David, he's very unlucky!* Povero David, è proprio sfortunato!
* **the poor** i poveri
[2] <u>mediocre</u> ◇ *a poor mark* un voto mediocre

poorly ['puəlɪ] ADJECTIVE
* **to be poorly** sentirsi E poco bene

pop [pɔp] ADJECTIVE
see also **pop** VERB

P

☞

pop MASC, FEM, PL ◇ *a pop group* un gruppo pop

to **pop** [pɒp] VERB

> *see also* **pop** ADJECTIVE

① scoppiare^E ◇ *The balloon popped.* Il pallone è scoppiato.

② mettere* ◇ *He popped a sweet into his mouth.* Si è messo una caramella in bocca.

③ fare* ◇ *I'll just pop to the toilet.* Farò un salto alla toilette. ◇ *I'm just popping round to John's.* Faccio un salto da John.

to **pop up** [pɒp'ʌp] VERB
apparire*^E

popcorn ['pɒpkɔ:n] NOUN
il popcorn

Pope [pəup] NOUN
♦ **the Pope** il Papa

poppy ['pɒpɪ] NOUN (PL **poppies**)
il papavero

Popsicle ® ['pɒpsɪkl] NOUN US
il ghiacciolo

popular ['pɒpjulə'] ADJECTIVE

① in voga ◇ *This is a very popular style.* Questo stile è molto in voga.

② popolare ◇ *the popular press* la stampa popolare ◇ *He's the most popular politician in France.* È il personaggio politico più popolare in Francia.

♦ **Madame Tussaud's is very popular with tourists.** Madame Tussaud piace molto ai turisti.

③ simpatica ◇ *She's a very popular girl.* È molto simpatica a tutti.

population [pɒpju'leɪʃən] NOUN
la popolazione

porch [pɔ:tʃ] NOUN (PL **porches**)
la veranda

pork [pɔ:k] NOUN
la carne di maiale ◇ *I don't eat pork.* Non mangio carne di maiale.

♦ **a pork chop** una braciola di maiale

porn [pɔ:n] NOUN

> *see also* **porn** ADJECTIVE

la pornografia

porn [pɔ:n] ADJECTIVE

> *see also* **porn** NOUN

porno MASC, FEM, PL

pornographic [pɔ:nə'græfɪk] ADJECTIVE
pornografico

pornography [pɔ:'nɒgrəfɪ] NOUN
la pornografia

porridge ['pɒrɪdʒ] NOUN
il porridge

port [pɔ:t] NOUN
il porto

portable ['pɔ:təbl] ADJECTIVE
portatile ◇ *a portable TV* una TV portatile

porter ['pɔ:tə'] NOUN

① il portiere (*in hotel*)

② il facchino (*at station*)

portion ['pɔ:ʃən] NOUN
la porzione

portrait ['pɔ:treɪt] NOUN
il ritratto

Portugal ['pɔ:tjugl] NOUN
il Portogallo

Portuguese [pɔ:tju'gi:z] ADJECTIVE

> *see also* **Portuguese** NOUN

portoghese

Portuguese [pɔ:tju'gi:z] NOUN

> *see also* **Portuguese** ADJECTIVE

il portoghese (*language*)

♦ **the Portuguese** i portoghesi

posh [pɒʃ] ADJECTIVE

① di lusso ◇ *a posh hotel* un albergo di lusso

② snob MASC, FEM, PL ◇ *posh people* gente snob

position [pə'zɪʃən] NOUN
la posizione ◇ *an uncomfortable position* una posizione scomoda

positive ['pɒzɪtɪv] ADJECTIVE

① positivo ◇ *a positive attitude* un atteggiamento positivo

② sicuro ◇ *I'm positive.* Ne sono sicuro.

possession [pə'zɛʃən] NOUN
il possesso ◇ *in possession of* in possesso di

♦ **one's possessions** le sue cose ◇ *Have you got all your possessions?* Hai tutte le tue cose?

possibility [pɒsɪ'bɪlɪtɪ] NOUN (PL **possibilities**)
la possibilità (PL le possibilità) ◇ *the possibility of a strike* la possibilità di uno sciopero

♦ **It's a possibility.** È possibile.

possible ['pɒsɪbl] ADJECTIVE
possibile ◇ *as soon as possible* al più presto possibile

possibly ['pɒsɪblɪ] ADVERB
forse ◇ *Are you coming to the party? – Possibly.* Vieni alla festa? – Forse.

♦ **...if you possibly can.** ...se ti è possibile.

♦ **I can't possibly come.** Non posso proprio venire.

to **post** [pəust] VERB

> *see also* **post** NOUN

imbucare ◇ *I've got some cards to post.* Devo imbucare delle cartoline.

post [pəust] NOUN

> *see also* **post** VERB

① la posta ◇ *by post* per posta ◇ *Is there any post for me?* C'è posta per me?

② il palo ◇ *The ball hit the post.* Il pallone ha colpito il palo.

postage ['pəustɪdʒ] NOUN
l' affrancatura

postbox ['pəustbɒks] NOUN (PL **postboxes**)
la buca delle lettere (PL le buche delle lettere)

postcard ['pəustkɑ:d] NOUN
la cartolina

postcode ['pəustkəud] NOUN

---

* Verbs followed by this symbol are irregular. See pp.339–364 for further details.

il codice postale

poster ['pəustə'] NOUN
[1] il poster (PL i poster) ◇ *I've got posters on my bedrooms walls.* Ho dei poster sulle pareti di camera mia.
[2] il manifesto ◇ *There are posters all over town.* Ci sono manifesti in tutta la città.

postman ['pəustmən] NOUN (PL **postmen**)
il postino ◇ *He's a postman.* Fa il postino.

postmark ['pəustmɑːk] NOUN
il timbro postale

post office ['pəustɒfɪs] NOUN
l' ufficio postale

to **postpone** [pəus'pəun] VERB
rinviare ◇ *The match has been postponed.* La partita è stata rinviata.

postwoman ['pəustwumən] NOUN (PL **postwomen**)
la postina ◇ *She's a postwoman.* Fa la postina.

pot [pɒt] NOUN
[1] la pentola ◇ *a pot of soup* una pentola di zuppa
♦ **pots and pans** le pentole
[2] il vasetto ◇ *a pot of jam* un vasetto di marmellata
♦ **a pot plant** una pianta in vaso
[3] l' erba (*marijuana*) ◇ *to smoke pot* fumare erba

potato [pə'teɪtəu] NOUN (PL **potatoes**)
la patata
♦ **mashed potatoes** il purè di patate SING
♦ **a baked potato** una patata cotta al forno con la buccia
♦ **potato chips** (*crisps*) US le patatine

potential [pə'tenʃl] NOUN
see also **potential** ADJECTIVE
♦ **He has great potential.** È promettente.

potential [pə'tenʃl] ADJECTIVE
see also **potential** NOUN
potenziale ◇ *a potential problem* un potenziale problema

pothole ['pɒthəul] NOUN
la buca (PL le buche)

pottery ['pɒtərɪ] NOUN (PL **potteries**)
la ceramica
♦ **pottery classes** un corso di ceramica

pound [paund] NOUN
see also **pound** VERB
[1] la libbra

❶ *Una libbra corrisponde a 0,454 chilogrammi.*

♦ **a pound of carrots** mezzo chilo di carote
[2] la sterlina ◇ *twenty pounds* venti sterline ◇ *a pound coin* una moneta da una sterlina

to **pound** [paund] VERB
see also **pound** NOUN
battere forte ◇ *My heart was pounding.* Mi batteva forte il cuore.

to **pour** [pɔː'] VERB
[1] versare ◇ *She poured some water into the pan.* Ha versato dell'acqua nella pentola. ◇ *She poured him a drink.* Gli ha versato da bere. ◇ *Shall I pour you a cup of tea?* Ti verso del tè?
[2] diluviare ◇ *It's pouring.* Sta diluviando.
♦ **in the pouring rain** sotto una pioggia torrenziale

poverty ['pɒvətɪ] NOUN
la povertà

powder ['paudə'] NOUN
la polvere ◇ *white powder* polvere bianca
♦ **face powder** cipria
♦ **powder room** toilette delle signore

power ['pauə'] NOUN
[1] il potere ◇ *The Tories were in power for 18 years.* I conservatori sono stati al potere per diciotto anni.
[2] la corrente ◇ *The power's off.* La corrente è staccata.
[3] l' energia ◇ *nuclear power* energia nucleare ◇ *solar power* energia solare

power cut ['pauəkʌt] NOUN
l' interruzione di corrente FEM

powerful ['pauəful] ADJECTIVE
potente

power point ['pauəpɔɪnt] NOUN
la presa di corrente

power station ['pauəsteɪʃən] NOUN
la centrale elettrica (PL le centrali elettriche)

practical ['præktɪkl] ADJECTIVE
pratico ◇ *a practical suggestion* un consiglio pratico ◇ *She's very practical.* È una tipa molto pratica.

practically ['præktɪklɪ] ADVERB
praticamente ◇ *It's practically impossible.* È praticamente impossibile.

practice ['præktɪs] NOUN
l' allenamento ◇ *football practice* allenamento di calcio ◇ *I'm out of practice.* Sono fuori allenamento.
♦ **piano practice** esercizi al piano MASC PL
♦ **in practice** in pratica ◇ *In practice it's more difficult.* In pratica è più difficile.
♦ **a medical practice** uno studio medico

to **practise** ['præktɪs] VERB (US **practice**)
[1] esercitarsi E ◇ *I ought to practise more.* Dovrei esercitarmi di più.
[2] esercitarsi E a ◇ *I practise the flute every evening.* Mi esercito al flauto ogni sera.
[3] fare* pratica di ◇ *I practised my Italian when I was on holiday.* Ho fatto pratica d'italiano quand'ero in vacanza.
[4] allenarsi E ◇ *The team practises on Thursdays.* La squadra si allena di giovedì.

practising ['præktɪsɪŋ] ADJECTIVE (US **practicing**)
praticante ◇ *She's a practising Catholic.* È ☞

P

cattolica praticante.

pram [præm] NOUN
la carrozzina

prawn [prɔːn] NOUN
il gamberetto

prawn cocktail [prɔːn'kɔkteɪl] NOUN
il cocktail di gamberetti (PL i cocktail di gamberetti)

to **pray** [preɪ] VERB
pregare

prayer [preə'] NOUN
la preghiera

precaution [prɪ'kɔːʃən] NOUN
la precauzione

preceding [prɪ'siːdɪŋ] ADJECTIVE
precedente

precinct ['priːsɪŋkt] NOUN
• **a shopping precinct** un centro commerciale
• **a pedestrian precinct** una zona pedonale

precious ['preʃəs] ADJECTIVE
prezioso

precise [prɪ'saɪs] ADJECTIVE
preciso ◇ *at that precise moment* in quel preciso istante

precisely [prɪ'saɪslɪ] ADVERB
precisamente ◇ *Precisely!* Precisamente!
• **at 10 a.m. precisely** alle dieci precise

to **predict** [prɪ'dɪkt] VERB
predire

predictable [prɪ'dɪktəbl] ADJECTIVE
prevedibile

prefect ['priːfekt] NOUN

ⓘ *Il* **prefect** *è un allievo delle classi superiori che è incaricato della disciplina e gode di alcuni privilegi.*

to **prefer** [prɪ'fɜː'] VERB
preferire ◇ *Which would you prefer?* Quale preferisci? ◇ *I prefer chemistry to maths.*
Preferisco la chimica alla matematica.

preference ['prefrəns] NOUN
la preferenza

pregnant ['pregnənt] ADJECTIVE
incinta ◇ *She's six months pregnant.* È incinta di sei mesi.

prehistoric ['priːhɪs'tɔrɪk] ADJECTIVE
preistorico

prejudice ['predʒudɪs] NOUN
il pregiudizio ◇ *There's a lot of racial prejudice.* Ci sono molti pregiudizi razziali.

prejudiced ['predʒudɪst] ADJECTIVE
• **to be prejudiced against somebody** essere* E prevenuto contro qualcuno

premature ['premətʃuə'] ADJECTIVE
prematuro ◇ *a premature baby* un neonato prematuro

premier ['premɪə'] NOUN
il primo ministro ◇ *the Australian premier* il primo ministro australiano
• **the Premier League** la prima divisione

premises ['premɪsɪz] NOUN PL
i locali ◇ *They're moving to new premises.*
Si trasferiscono in nuovi locali.

premonition [premə'nɪʃən] NOUN
il presentimento

preoccupied [priː'ɔkjupaɪd] ADJECTIVE
tutto preso ◇ *They're preoccupied with the forthcoming wedding.* Sono tutti presi dall'imminente matrimonio.

prep [prep] NOUN
i compiti MASC PL ◇ *history prep* compiti di storia

preparation [prepə'reɪʃən] NOUN
la preparazione ◇ *months of preparation* mesi di preparazione
• **in preparation for** in vista di
• **preparations** i preparativi ◇ *Preparations are being made for the visit of the Queen.*
Sono in atto i preparativi per la visita della regina.

to **prepare** [prɪ'peə'] VERB
preparare ◇ *Teachers have to prepare lessons in the evening.* La sera gli insegnanti devono preparare le lezioni.
• **to prepare for something** fare* i preparativi per qualcosa ◇ *We're preparing for our skiing holiday.* Stiamo facendo i preparativi per le vacanze in montagna.

prepared [prɪ'peəd] ADJECTIVE
• **to be prepared to do something** essere* E pronto a fare qualcosa ◇ *I'm prepared to help you.* Sono pronto ad aiutarti.

prep school ['prepskuːl] NOUN
la scuola privata

Presbyterian [prezbɪ'tɪərɪən] NOUN
il presbiteriano
la presbiteriana

to **prescribe** [prɪ'skraɪb] VERB
prescrivere*

prescription [prɪ'skrɪpʃən] NOUN
la ricetta medica (PL le ricette mediche)

presence ['prezns] NOUN
la presenza ◇ *presence of mind* presenza di spirito

present ['prezənt] ADJECTIVE
see also **present** NOUN, VERB
1 attuale ◇ *the present situation* la situazione attuale
2 presente ◇ *He wasn't present at the meeting.* Non era presente alla riunione.
• **the present tense** il presente
• **the present perfect** il passato composto

present ['prezənt] NOUN
see also **present** ADJECTIVE, VERB
1 il regalo
• **to give somebody a present** fare* un regalo a qualcuno ◇ *He gave me a lovely present.*
Mi ha fatto un bel regalo.
2 il presente ◇ *the past and the present* il passato e il presente
• **for the present** per il momento

* Verbs followed by this symbol are irregular. See pp.339–364 for further details.

* **at present** al momento

to **present** [prɪˈzɛnt] VERB

see also **present** ADJECTIVE, NOUN

* **to present somebody with something** consegnare qualcosa a qualcuno ◊ _The Mayor presented the winner with a medal._ Il sindaco ha consegnato una medaglia al vincitore.
* **if the opportunity presents itself** se si presenterà l'opportunità

presenter [prɪˈzɛntə'] NOUN

il presentatore

la presentatrice

presently [ˈprɛzntlɪ] ADVERB

1 tra poco ◊ _You'll feel better presently._ Tra poco ti sentirai meglio.

2 al momento ◊ _They're presently on tour._ Al momento sono in tournée.

president [ˈprɛzɪdənt] NOUN

il presidente

press [prɛs] NOUN

see also **press** VERB

* **the press** la stampa

to **press** [prɛs] VERB

see also **press** NOUN

1 premere* ◊ _Don't press so hard!_ Non premere così forte!

2 stirare ◊ _She was pressing her blouse._ Si stava stirando la camicetta.

* **They pressed me to stay.** Hanno insistito perché restassi.

press conference [ˈprɛskɔnfərəns] NOUN

la conferenza stampa

pressed [prɛst] ADJECTIVE

* **to be pressed for time** avere* poco tempo

press-up [ˈprɛsʌp] NOUN

* **to do press-ups** fare* flessioni sulle braccia

pressure [ˈprɛʃə'] NOUN

see also **pressure** VERB

la pressione

* **to be under pressure** essere*[E] sotto pressione ◊ _He's been under a lot of pressure recently._ Ultimamente è stato molto sotto pressione.
* **a pressure group** un gruppo di pressione

to **pressure** [ˈprɛʃə'] VERB

see also **pressure** NOUN

fare* pressioni su ◊ _My parents are pressuring me to stay on at school._ I miei fanno pressioni su di me perché continui gli studi.

to **pressurize** [ˈprɛʃəraɪz] VERB

* **to pressurize somebody to do something** fare* pressione su qualcuno perché faccia qualcosa

prestige [prɛsˈtiːʒ] NOUN

il prestigio

prestigious [prɛsˈtɪdʒəs] ADJECTIVE

prestigioso

presumably [prɪˈzjuːməblɪ] ADVERB

presumibilmente

to **presume** [prɪˈzjuːm] VERB

presumere* ◊ _I presume so._ Presumo di sì. ◊ _I presume he'll come._ Presumo che venga.

to **pretend** [prɪˈtɛnd] VERB

* **to pretend to do something** fare* finta di fare qualcosa ◊ _He pretended to be asleep._ Ha fatto finta di dormire.

pretty [ˈprɪtɪ] ADVERB

see also **pretty** ADJECTIVE

piuttosto ◊ _The weather was pretty awful._ Il tempo era piuttosto brutto.

* **pretty much** praticamente ◊ _It's pretty much the same._ È praticamente la stessa cosa.

pretty [ˈprɪtɪ] ADJECTIVE

see also **pretty** ADVERB

carino ◊ _She's very pretty._ È molto carina.

* **pretty weather** US bel tempo

to **prevent** [prɪˈvɛnt] VERB

impedire

* **to prevent somebody from doing something** impedire a qualcuno di fare qualcosa ◊ _The police prevented the protesters from entering the building._ La polizia ha impedito ai dimostranti di entrare nell'edificio.
* **to prevent something happening again** fare* in modo che qualcosa non si ripeta

previous [ˈpriːvɪəs] ADJECTIVE

precedente

previously [ˈpriːvɪəslɪ] ADVERB

precedentemente

prey [preɪ] NOUN

la preda ◊ _Tourists are easy prey._ I turisti sono una facile preda.

* **a bird of prey** un uccello rapace

price [praɪs] NOUN

il prezzo ◊ _I'll ask the price._ Chiederò il prezzo.

* **to go up in price** aumentare[E] ◊ _Petrol went up in price last week._ La benzina è aumentata la settimana scorsa.
* **to come down in price** calare[E] di prezzo

price list [ˈpraɪslɪst] NOUN

il listino prezzi

to **prick** [prɪk] VERB

pungere ◊ _I've pricked my finger._ Mi sono punto un dito.

pride [praɪd] NOUN

1 l' orgoglio ◊ _wounded pride_ orgoglio ferito

2 la superbia ◊ _His pride may be his downfall._ La superbia potrebbe essere la sua rovina.

priest [priːst] NOUN

il prete

primary [ˈpraɪmərɪ] ADJECTIVE

principale ◊ _The primary reason for my choice was..._ La principale ragione della mia scelta è stata...

P

primary school ['praɪmərɪskuːl] NOUN
la scuola elementare

prime [praɪm] ADJECTIVE
principale ◇ *my prime concern* la mia
preoccupazione principale

prime minister [praɪm'mɪnɪstə'] NOUN
il primo ministro

primitive ['prɪmɪtɪv] ADJECTIVE
primitivo

prince [prɪns] NOUN
il principe ◇ *the Prince of Wales* il principe
di Galles

princess [prɪn'ses] NOUN (PL **princesses**)
la principessa

principal ['prɪnsɪpl] ADJECTIVE
see also **principal** NOUN
principale

principal ['prɪnsɪpl] NOUN
see also **principal** ADJECTIVE
il/la preside

principle ['prɪnsɪpl] NOUN
il principio ◇ *on principle* per principio

print [prɪnt] NOUN
see also **print** VERB
[1] la foto (PL le foto) ◇ *colour prints* foto a
colori
[2] l'impronta digitale ◇ *The policeman
took his prints.* Il poliziotto gli ha preso le
impronte digitali.
[3] la stampa ◇ *a framed print* una stampa
incorniciata
♦ **in small print** a caratteri piccoli

to **print** [prɪnt] VERB
see also **print** NOUN
[1] stampare ◇ *It was printed in Hong Kong.*
È stato stampato ad Hong Kong.
[2] scrivere* in stampatello ◇ *Please print
your name and address.* Per favore, scrivi il
tuo nome ed indirizzo in stampatello.

printer ['prɪntə'] NOUN
la stampante

priority [praɪ'ɒrɪtɪ] NOUN (PL **priorities**)
[1] la priorità (PL le priorità) ◇ *The
government's priority is to build more
power plants.* La priorità del governo è
quella di costruire più centrali elettriche.
♦ **my first priority** la mia priorità
[2] la precedenza
♦ **to take priority over something** avere* la
precedenza su qualcosa ◇ *My family takes
priority over my work.* La mia famiglia ha la
precedenza sul lavoro.

prison ['prɪzn] NOUN
il carcere
♦ **to send somebody to prison for five years**
condannare qualcuno a cinque anni di
carcere
♦ **a prison officer** un agente di custodia

prisoner ['prɪznə'] NOUN
[1] il detenuto
la detenuta

◇ *Prisoners have to share cells.* I detenuti
devono dividere le celle.
[2] il prigioniero
la prigioniera
(*prisoner of war*)

privacy ['prɪvəsɪ] NOUN
la privacy

private ['praɪvɪt] ADJECTIVE
privato ◇ *a private school* una scuola
privata
♦ **private property** la proprietà privata
♦ **"private"** (*on envelope*) "riservato"

private eye [praɪvɪt'aɪ] NOUN
l'investigatore privato MASC

to **privatize** ['praɪvɪtaɪz] VERB
privatizzare

privilege ['prɪvɪlɪdʒ] NOUN
il privilegio

prize [praɪz] NOUN
il premio ◇ *She won first prize.* Ha vinto il
primo premio.

prize-giving ['praɪzgɪvɪŋ] NOUN
la premiazione

prizewinner ['praɪzwɪnə'] NOUN
il vincitore
la vincitrice

pro [prəʊ] NOUN (PL **pros**)
♦ **the pros and cons** i pro e i contro ◇ *We
weighed up the pros and cons.* Abbiamo
valutato i pro e i contro.

probability [prɒbə'bɪlɪtɪ] NOUN
la probabilità (PL le probabilità)

probable ['prɒbəbl] ADJECTIVE
probabile

probably ['prɒbəblɪ] ADVERB
probabilmente

problem ['prɒbləm] NOUN
il problema (PL i problemi) ◇ *No problem!*
Non c'è problema!
♦ **What's the problem?** Che cosa c'è?

to **proceed** [prə'siːd] VERB
[1] procedere ◇ *Work was proceeding
normally.* Il lavoro procedeva
normalmente.
[2] recarsi^E ◇ *Please proceed to gate
thirty-two.* Vi preghiamo di recarvi all'uscita
trentadue.
♦ **to proceed to do something** cominciare a
fare qualcosa ◇ *He then proceeded to tell
me the whole story.* Quindi cominciò a
raccontarmi tutta la storia.

proceeds ['prəʊsiːdz] NOUN PL
il ricavato SING ◇ *The proceeds from the
concert will go to charity.* Il ricavato del
concerto sarà devoluto in beneficenza.

process ['prəʊses] NOUN (PL **processes**)
il processo ◇ *the peace process* il processo
di pace
♦ **We're in the process of painting the kitchen.**
Stiamo ridipingendo la cucina.

procession [prə'seʃən] NOUN

---

* Verbs followed by this symbol are irregular. See pp.339–364 for further details.

la processione

to **produce** [prə'dju:s] VERB
produrre

producer [prə'dju:sə'] NOUN
il produttore
la produttrice

product ['prɔdʌkt] NOUN
il prodotto

production [prə'dʌkʃən] NOUN
1 la produzione ◊ *They're increasing production of luxury models.* Stanno aumentando la produzione di modelli di lusso.
• **the production line** la catena di lavorazione
2 la rappresentazione ◊ *a production of "Hamlet"* una rappresentazione di "Amleto"

profession [prə'feʃən] NOUN
la professione

professional [prə'feʃənl] NOUN
see also **professional** ADJECTIVE
il/la professionista

professional [prə'feʃənl] ADJECTIVE
see also **professional** NOUN
professionista ◊ *a professional musician* un musicista professionista
• **a very professional piece of work** un lavoro da professionista

professionally [prə'feʃnəlɪ] ADVERB
• **She sings professionally.** È una cantante professionista.

professor [prə'fesə'] NOUN
il/la docente

profit ['prɔfɪt] NOUN
il guadagno ◊ *a profit of ten thousand pounds* un guadagno di diecimila sterline

profitable ['prɔfɪtəbl] ADJECTIVE
redditizio

program ['prəugræm] NOUN
see also **program** VERB
• **a computer program** un programma per computer

to **program** ['prəugræm] VERB
see also **program** NOUN
programmare

programme ['prəugræm] NOUN (US **program**)
il programma (PL i programmi)

programmer ['prəugræmə'] NOUN
il programmatore
la programmatrice
◊ *She's a programmer.* Fa la programmatrice.

progress ['prəugres] NOUN
il progresso ◊ *That's progress!* Questo è il progresso!
• **to make progress** fare* progressi ◊ *You're making progress!* Stai facendo progressi!

to **prohibit** [prə'hɪbɪt] VERB
vietare ◊ *Smoking is prohibited.* È vietato fumare.

project ['prɔdʒekt] NOUN

see also **project** VERB
1 il piano ◊ *a development project* un piano di sviluppo
2 la ricerca (PL le ricerche) ◊ *I'm doing a project on the greenhouse effect.* Sto facendo una ricerca sull'effetto serra.

to **project** [prə'dʒekt] VERB
see also **project** NOUN
1 prevedere ◊ *A population rise of five per cent is projected.* È previsto un aumento della popolazione del cinque per cento.
2 proiettare (*film*)

projector [prə'dʒektə'] NOUN
il proiettore

promenade [prɔmə'nɑ:d] NOUN
il lungomare (PL i lungomare)

promise ['prɔmɪs] NOUN
see also **promise** VERB
la promessa ◊ *He made me a promise.* Mi ha fatto una promessa.
• **It's a promise!** Promesso!

to **promise** ['prɔmɪs] VERB
see also **promise** NOUN
promettere* ◊ *She promised to write.* Ha promesso di scrivere.

promising ['prɔmɪsɪŋ] ADJECTIVE
promettente ◊ *a promising player* un giocatore promettente

to **promote** [prə'məut] VERB
• **to be promoted** avere* una promozione ◊ *She was promoted after six months.* Ha avuto una promozione dopo sei mesi.

promotion [prə'məuʃən] NOUN
la promozione

prompt [prɔmpt] ADJECTIVE, ADVERB
see also **prompt** VERB
1 sollecito ◊ *a prompt reply* una risposta sollecita
2 puntuale ◊ *He's always very prompt.* È sempre puntualissimo.
3 in punto ◊ *at eight o'clock prompt* alle otto in punto

to **prompt** [prɔmpt] VERB
see also **prompt** ADJECTIVE, ADVERB
• **to prompt somebody to do something** spingere* qualcuno a fare qualcosa

promptly ['prɔmptlɪ] ADVERB
puntualmente ◊ *We left promptly at seven.* Siamo partiti puntualmente alle sette.

pronoun ['prəunaun] NOUN
il pronome

to **pronounce** [prə'nauns] VERB
pronunciare ◊ *How do you pronounce that word?* Come si pronuncia quella parola?

pronunciation [prənʌnsɪ'eɪʃən] NOUN
la pronuncia

proof [pru:f] NOUN
la prova

proper ['prɔpə'] ADJECTIVE
1 vero ◊ *We didn't have a proper lunch, just sandwiches.* Non abbiamo mangiato un ☞

Verbs followed by the symbol "E" require the auxiliary "essere"

vero pranzo, solo dei panini.

[2] adatto ◇ *You have to have the proper equipment.* Bisogna avere l'attrezzatura adatta.

[3] corretto ◇ *This is the proper way to do it.* Questo è il modo corretto per farlo.

♦ **at the proper time** all'ora giusta ◇ *If you had come at the proper time...* Se fossi venuto all'ora giusta...

properly ['prɔpəlɪ] ADVERB
[1] come si deve ◇ *You're not doing it properly.* Non lo stai facendo come si deve.
[2] in modo adeguato ◇ *Dress properly for your interview.* Vestiti in modo adeguato per il colloquio.

property ['prɔpətɪ] NOUN (PL **properties**)
[1] la proprietà (PL le proprietà)
♦ **"private property"** "proprietà privata"
[2] la casa ◇ *a new property* una nuova casa
♦ **The value of property in the area is rising.** Il valore degli immobili della zona sta salendo.

proportional [prə'pɔːʃənl] ADJECTIVE
proporzionale ◇ *proportional representation* rappresentanza proporzionale

proposal [prə'pəuzl] NOUN
la proposta

to **propose** [prə'pəuz] VERB
proporre* ◇ *What do you propose to do?* Cosa proponi di fare?
♦ **to propose to somebody** fare* una proposta di matrimonio a qualcuno

to **prosecute** ['prɔsɪkjuːt] VERB
perseguire a norma di legge ◇ *"Shoplifters will be prosecuted"* "I taccheggiatori saranno perseguiti a norma di legge"

prospect ['prɔspɛkt] NOUN
la prospettiva ◇ *His future prospects are good.* Ha delle buone prospettive.

prospectus [prə'spɛktəs] NOUN (PL **prospectuses**)
il prospetto

prostitute ['prɔstɪtjuːt] NOUN
la prostituta (*female*)
♦ **a male prostitute** un prostituto

to **protect** [prə'tɛkt] VERB
proteggere

protection [prə'tɛkʃən] NOUN
la protezione

protein ['prəutiːn] NOUN
la proteina

protest ['prəutest] NOUN
see also **protest** VERB
la protesta ◇ *He ignored their protests.* Ha ignorato le loro proteste. ◇ *a protest march* una manifestazione di protesta

to **protest** [prə'test] VERB
see also **protest** NOUN
protestare

Protestant ['prɔtɪstənt] NOUN
see also **Protestant** ADJECTIVE
il/la protestante

Protestant ['prɔtɪstənt] ADJECTIVE
see also **Protestant** NOUN
protestante

protester [prə'tɛstə'] NOUN
il/la dimostrante MASC / FEM

proud [praud] ADJECTIVE
fiero ◇ *Her parents are proud of her.* I suoi sono fieri di lei.

to **prove** [pruːv] VERB
dimostrare ◇ *The police couldn't prove it.* La polizia non è riuscita a dimostrarlo.

proverb ['prɔvəːb] NOUN
il proverbio

to **provide** [prə'vaɪd] VERB
fornire
♦ **to provide somebody with something** fornire qualcosa a qualcuno ◇ *They provided us with maps.* Ci hanno fornito delle cartine.

to **provide for** [prə'vaɪdfɔː'] VERB
mantenere* ◇ *He can't provide for his family any more.* Non è più in grado di mantenere la famiglia.

provided [prə'vaɪdɪd] CONJUNCTION
sempre che ◇ *He'll play in the next match provided he's fit.* Giocherà nella prossima partita sempre che sia in forma.

prowler ['praulə'] NOUN
♦ **There was a prowler in the garden.** C'era un tipo sospetto che si aggirava in giardino.

prune [pruːn] NOUN
la prugna secca (PL le prugne secche)

to **pry** [praɪ] VERB
impicciarsi[E] ◇ *He's always prying into other people's affairs.* S'impiccia sempre degli affari altrui.

pseudonym ['sjuːdənɪm] NOUN
lo pseudonimo

psychiatrist [saɪ'kaɪətrɪst] NOUN
lo/la psichiatra MASC / FEM

psychoanalyst [saɪkəu'ænəlɪst] NOUN
lo/la psicanalista MASC / FEM

psychological [saɪkə'lɔdʒɪkl] ADJECTIVE
psicologico

psychologist [saɪ'kɔlədʒɪst] NOUN
lo psicologo (PL gli psicologi)
la psicologa (PL le psicologhe)

psychology [saɪ'kɔlədʒɪ] NOUN
la psicologia

PTO [piːtiː'əu] ABBREVIAZIONE (= *please turn over*)
vedi retro

pub [pʌb] NOUN
il pub (PL i pub)

public ['pʌblɪk] NOUN
see also **public** ADJECTIVE
♦ **the public** il pubblico ◇ *open to the public* aperto al pubblico
♦ **in public** in pubblico

public ['pʌblɪk] ADJECTIVE

* Verbs followed by this symbol are irregular. See pp.339–364 for further details.

see also **public** NOUN

pubblico ◇ *a public place* un luogo pubblico

♦ **to be in the public eye** essere* ^{E} un personaggio in vista

public address system
[pʌblɪkə'dressɪstəm] NOUN
l' impianto di amplificazione

publican ['pʌblɪkən] NOUN
il gestore di un pub

public holiday [pʌblɪk'hɔlɪdeɪ] NOUN
la festa nazionale

publicity [pʌb'lɪsɪtɪ] NOUN
la pubblicità

public opinion [pʌblɪkə'pɪnjən] NOUN
l' opinione pubblica FEM

public school [pʌblɪk'sku:l] NOUN
la scuola superiore privata

public transport [pʌblɪk'trænspɔ:t] NOUN
i mezzi pubblici MASC PL

to **publish** ['pʌblɪʃ] VERB
pubblicare

publisher ['pʌblɪʃə'] NOUN
la casa editrice (*company*)

pudding ['pudɪŋ] NOUN
il dessert (PL i dessert) ◇ *What's for pudding?* Cosa c'è per dessert?

♦ **a rice pudding** un budino di riso

♦ **black pudding** il sanguinaccio

puddle ['pʌdl] NOUN
la pozzanghera

puff pastry ['pʌf'peɪstrɪ] NOUN
la pasta sfoglia

to **pull** [pul] VERB
tirare ◇ *She pulled my hair.* Mi ha tirato i capelli. ◇ *Pull!* Tira!

♦ **to pull the trigger** premere* il grilletto

♦ **to pull a muscle** farsi* ^{E} uno strappo muscolare

♦ **You're pulling my leg!** Mi stai prendendo in giro!

♦ **Pull yourself together!** Datti una mossa!

to **pull down** [pul'daun] VERB
demolire ◇ *The old school was pulled down last year.* L'anno scorso hanno demolito la vecchia scuola.

to **pull in** [pul'ɪn] VERB
fermarsi ^{E} ◇ *She pulled in at the side of the road.* Si fermò a lato della strada.

to **pull out** [pul'aut] VERB
1 spostarsi ^{E} sulla destra (*in Great Britain*) ◇ *The car pulled out to overtake.* L'auto si è spostata sulla destra per sorpassare.
2 ritirarsi ^{E} ◇ *She pulled out of the tournament.* Si è ritirata dal torneo.

to **pull through** [pul'θru:] VERB
cavarsela ^{E} ◇ *They think he'll pull through.* Pensano che se la caverà.

to **pull up** [pul'ʌp] VERB
fermarsi ^{E} ◇ *A black car pulled up beside me.* Una macchina nera si è fermata accanto a me.

pullover ['puləuvə'] NOUN
il pullover (PL i pullover)

pulse [pʌls] NOUN
il polso ◇ *The nurse took his pulse.* L'infermiera gli ha tastato il polso.

pulses ['pʌlsəz] NOUN PL
i legumi secchi

pump [pʌmp] NOUN
see also **pump** VERB
1 la pompa ◇ *a bicycle pump* una pompa di bicicletta

♦ **a petrol pump** un distributore di benzina

2 la scarpa da ginnastica ◇ *She was wearing a leotard and black pumps.* Indossava un body e scarpe da ginnastica nere.

to **pump** [pʌmp] VERB
see also **pump** NOUN
pompare (*water, blood*)

♦ **to pump up** gonfiare

pumpkin ['pʌmpkɪn] NOUN
la zucca (PL le zucche)

punch [pʌntʃ] NOUN (PL **punches**)
see also **punch** VERB
il pugno

to **punch** [pʌntʃ] VERB
see also **punch** NOUN
1 dare* un pugno a ◇ *He punched me!* Mi ha dato un pugno!
2 forare ◇ *He forgot to punch my ticket.* Si è dimenticato di forarmi il biglietto.

punctual ['pʌŋktjuəl] ADJECTIVE
puntuale

punctuation [pʌŋktju'eɪʃən] NOUN
la punteggiatura

puncture ['pʌŋktʃə'] NOUN

♦ **to have a puncture** forare ◇ *I had a puncture on the motorway.* Ho forato sull'autostrada.

Be careful not to translate **puncture** *by* **puntura**.

to **punish** ['pʌnɪʃ] VERB
punire

punishment ['pʌnɪʃmənt] NOUN
la punizione

punk [pʌŋk] NOUN, ADJECTIVE
il/la punk (PL i/le punk)

pupil ['pju:pl] NOUN
l' allievo
l' allieva

puppet ['pʌpɪt] NOUN
il burattino

puppy ['pʌpɪ] NOUN (PL **puppies**)
il cucciolo

to **purchase** ['pə:tʃɪs] VERB
acquistare

pure [pjuə'] ADJECTIVE
puro ◇ *pure orange juice* puro succo d'arancia ◇ *He's doing pure maths.* Fa matematica pura.

purple ['pə:pl] ADJECTIVE

P

viola MASC, FEM, PL

purpose ['pɜːpəs] NOUN
lo scopo ◇ *What is the purpose of these changes?* Qual è lo scopo di questi cambiamenti? ◇ *his purpose in life* lo scopo della sua vita
* **on purpose** apposta ◇ *He did it on purpose.* L'ha fatto apposta.

to **purr** [pəːʳ] VERB
fare* le fusa

purse [pɜːs] NOUN
[1] il portamonete (PL i portamonete) ◇ *I've got ten pounds in my purse.* Ho dieci sterline nel portamonete.
[2] la borsa (*handbag*) [US]

to **pursue** [pə'sjuː] VERB
[1] proseguire (*career*)
[2] inseguire (*person, vehicle*)

pursuit [pə'sjuːt] NOUN
[1] la ricerca ◇ *the pursuit of success* la ricerca del successo
[2] l'attività (PL le attività) ◇ *outdoor pursuits* attività all'aperto

push [puʃ] NOUN (PL **pushes**)
see also **push** VERB
la spinta
* **to give somebody a push** dare* una spinta a qualcuno ◇ *He gave me a push.* Mi ha dato una spinta.

to **push** [puʃ] VERB
see also **push** NOUN
spingere*
* **to push somebody to do something** spingere* qualcuno a fare qualcosa ◇ *My parents are pushing me to go to university.* I miei mi spingono ad andare all'università.
* **to push drugs** spacciare droga
* **Push off!** Sparisci!
* **Don't push your luck!** Non tirare troppo la corda!
* **to push one's way through** farsi*ᴱ largo ◇ *I pushed my way through till I reached the front.* Mi sono fatto largo fino ad arrivare davanti.

to **push around** [puʃə'raund] VERB
dare* ordini ◇ *He likes pushing people around.* Gli piace dare ordini a tutti.

to **push on** [puʃ'ɒn] VERB
andare*ᴱ avanti ◇ *I've got a lot to do, so I must push on now.* Ho molto da fare, quindi devo andare avanti.

pushchair ['puʃtʃeəʳ] NOUN
il passeggino

pushed [puʃt] ADJECTIVE
* **to be pushed for** essere*ᴱ a corto di ◇ *I'm a bit pushed for money.* Sono un po' a corto di denaro.
* **I'm pushed for time today.** Oggi non ho un minuto di tempo.

pusher ['puʃəʳ] NOUN
lo spacciatore
la spacciatrice

push-up ['puʃʌp] NOUN
la flessione sulle braccia
* **to do push-ups** fare* flessioni sulle braccia

to **put** [put] VERB (**put, put**)
mettere* ◇ *Where shall I put my things?* Dove metto le mie cose? ◇ *She's putting the baby to bed.* Sta mettendo a letto il bambino.

to **put across** [putə'krɒs] VERB
riuscire*ᴱ a comunicare ◇ *He finds it hard to put his ideas across.* Trova difficile riuscire a comunicare le proprie idee.

to **put aside** [putə'said] VERB
tenere* da parte ◇ *Can you put this aside for me till tomorrow?* Me lo può tenere da parte fino a domani?

to **put away** [putə'wei] VERB
[1] riporre* ◇ *Can you put away the dishes, please?* Ti dispiace riporre i piatti?
[2] mettere* dentro (*in prison*) ◇ *I hope they put him away for a long time.* Spero che lo mettano dentro per un bel pezzo.

to **put back** [put'bæk] VERB
[1] rimettere* a posto ◇ *Put it back when you've finished with it.* Rimettilo a posto quando hai finito.
[2] rinviare ◇ *The meeting's been put back till two o'clock.* La riunione è stata rinviata alle due.
[3] mettere* indietro ◇ *Remember to put your watch back.* Ricorda di mettere indietro l'orologio.

to **put down** [put'daun] VERB
[1] posare ◇ *I'll put these bags down for a minute.* Poso un attimo queste borse.
[2] buttare giù ◇ *I've put down a few ideas.* Ho buttato giù alcune idee.
[3] far abbattere ◇ *We had to have our dog put down.* Abbiamo dovuto far abbattere il cane.

to **put in** [put'in] VERB
presentare ◇ *He's put in a request for an assistant.* Ha presentato richiesta per avere un assistente.
* **to put in a lot of work** lavorare sodo

to **put off** [put'ɒf] VERB
[1] spegnere ◇ *Shall I put the light off?* Spengo la luce?
[2] rimandare ◇ *I keep putting it off.* Continuo a rimandarlo.
[3] distrarre* ◇ *Stop putting me off!* Smettila di distrarmi!
[4] scoraggiare ◇ *He's not easily put off.* Non si lascia scoraggiare facilmente.

to **put on** [put'ɒn] VERB
[1] mettersi*ᴱ ◇ *I'll put my coat on.* Mi metto il cappotto.
[2] accendere* ◇ *Shall I put the heating on?* Accendo il riscaldamento?
[3] mettere* in scena ◇ *We're putting on "Bugsy Malone".* Stiamo mettendo in scena "Bugsy Malone".

---

* Verbs followed by this symbol are irregular. See pp.339–364 for further details.

◆ **She's not ill: she's just putting it on.** Non è
malata, sta solo facendo finta.
[4] mettere* a cuocere ◇ *I'll put the
potatoes on.* Metto a cuocere le patate.
[5] ingrassare[E] di ◇ *I put on four pounds.*
Sono ingrassata di due chili.
◆ **to put on weight** ingrassare[E] ◇ *He's put on
a lot of weight.* È ingrassato parecchio.

to **put out** [put'aut] VERB
[1] spegnere ◇ *It took them five hours to put
out the fire.* Ci sono volute cinque ore per
spegnere l'incendio.
[2] tendere ◇ *He smiled and put out his
hand.* Ha sorriso tendendo la mano.
◆ **to be put out** essere*[E] seccato ◇ *He's a bit
put out that nobody came.* È un po' seccato
che non sia venuto nessuno.

to **put through** [put'θru:] VERB
passare ◇ *Can you put me through to the
manager?* Mi passa il direttore, per favore?
◆ **I'm putting you through.** Le dò la
comunicazione.

to **put up** [put'ʌp] VERB
[1] appendere ◇ *The poster's great. I'll put it
up on my wall.* Il poster è fantastico, lo
appendo alla parete.
[2] montare ◇ *We put up our tent in a field.*
Abbiamo montato la tenda in un prato.
[3] aumentare ◇ *They've put up the price.*
Hanno aumentato il prezzo.

[4] ospitare ◇ *A friend will put me up for the
night.* Un amico mi ospita per la notte.
[5] alzare ◇ *If you have any questions, put
up your hand.* Se avete domande alzate la
mano.
◆ **to put up with something** sopportare
qualcosa ◇ *I'm not going to put up with it
any longer.* Non ho intenzione di
sopportarlo oltre.
◆ **to put up for sale** mettere* in vendita
◇ *They're going to put their house up for
sale.* Metteranno in vendita la casa.

puzzle ['pʌzl] NOUN
il puzzle (PL i puzzle)

puzzled ['pʌzld] ADJECTIVE
perplesso ◇ *You look puzzled!* Hai un'aria
perplessa!

puzzling ['pʌzlɪŋ] ADJECTIVE
sconcertante

pyjamas [pə'dʒɑːməz] NOUN PL
il pigiama SING ◇ *my pyjamas* il mio pigiama
◇ *They were already in their pyjamas.*
Erano già in pigiama.
◆ **a pair of pyjamas** un pigiama

pyramid ['pɪrəmɪd] NOUN
la piramide

Pyrenees [pɪrə'niːz] NOUN PL
i Pirenei

P

Q

quaint [kweɪnt] ADJECTIVE
pittoresco (*house*)

qualification [kwɔlɪfɪˈkeɪʃən] NOUN
1 la qualifica (PL le qualifiche) ◇ *What qualifications do they require?* Che qualifiche richiedono?
+ **vocational qualifications** qualifiche professionali
2 il titolo di studio ◇ *He left school without any qualifications.* Ha lasciato la scuola senza alcun titolo di studio.

qualified [ˈkwɔlɪfaɪd] ADJECTIVE
1 abilitato ◇ *a qualified teacher* un insegnante abilitato
2 diplomato ◇ *a qualified nurse* un'infermiera diplomata
+ **to be well qualified** (*for job*) avere* tutti i requisiti necessari

to **qualify** [ˈkwɔlɪfaɪ] VERB (**qualified, qualified**)
1 ottenere* l'abilitazione ◇ *She qualified as a teacher last year.* Ha ottenuto l'abilitazione all'insegnamento l'anno scorso.
2 qualificarsi^E ◇ *Our team didn't qualify for the finals.* La nostra squadra non si è qualificata per le finali.

quality [ˈkwɔlɪtɪ] NOUN (PL **qualities**)
la qualità
+ **good-quality paper** carta di buona qualità

quantity [ˈkwɔntɪtɪ] NOUN (PL **quantities**)
la quantità (PL le quantità)

quarantine [ˈkwɔrəntiːn] NOUN
la quarantena ◇ *in quarantine* in quarantena

quarrel [ˈkwɔrl] NOUN
see also **quarrel** VERB
la lite ◇ *after their last quarrel* dopo la loro ultima lite
+ **to have a quarrel** litigare ◇ *We had a quarrel.* Abbiamo litigato.

to **quarrel** [ˈkwɔrl] VERB
see also **quarrel** NOUN
litigare

quarry [ˈkwɔrɪ] NOUN (PL **quarries**)
la cava

quart [kwɔːt] NOUN
+ **a quart** due pinte FEM PL

> **ⓘ** *Un* **quart** *corrisponde a 0,946 litri.*

quarter [ˈkwɔːtə^r] NOUN
1 il quarto ◇ *three quarters* tre quarti ◇ *a quarter of an hour* un quarto d'ora ◇ *a quarter past ten* le dieci e un quarto
+ **a quarter to eleven** le dieci e tre quarti
+ **a quarter of ten** US le nove e tre quarti
2 la moneta da venticinque centesimi (*coin*) US

quarter-finals [kwɔːtəˈfaɪnls] NOUN PL
i quarti di finale

quartet [kwɔːˈtɛt] NOUN
il quartetto ◇ *a string quartet* un quartetto di archi

quay [kiː] NOUN
la banchina

queasy [ˈkwiːzɪ] ADJECTIVE
+ **to feel queasy** avere* la nausea

queen [kwiːn] NOUN
la regina ◇ *Queen Elizabeth* la regina Elisabetta ◇ *the queen of hearts* la regina di cuori
+ **the Queen Mother** la regina madre

query [ˈkwɪərɪ] NOUN (PL **queries**)
see also **query** VERB
la domanda

to **query** [ˈkwɪərɪ] VERB
see also **query** NOUN
mettere* in dubbio ◇ *No one queried my decision.* Nessuno ha messo in dubbio la mia decisione.
+ **They queried the bill.** Hanno chiesto spiegazioni sul conto.

to **question** [ˈkwɛstʃən] VERB
see also **question** NOUN
interrogare ◇ *He was questioned by the police.* È stato interrogato dalla polizia.

question [ˈkwɛstʃən] NOUN
see also **question** VERB
1 la domanda ◇ *Can I ask a question?* Posso fare* una domanda?
2 la questione ◇ *That's a difficult question.* È una questione difficile.
+ **It's out of the question.** È fuori discussione.

question mark [ˈkwɛstʃənmɑːk] NOUN
il punto di domanda

questionnaire [kwɛstʃəˈnɛə^r] NOUN
il questionario

queue [kjuː] NOUN
see also **queue** VERB
la fila ◇ *People were standing in a queue outside the cinema.* La gente era in fila fuori dal cinema.

to **queue** [kjuː] VERB
see also NOUN
fare* la fila ◇ *We had to queue for tickets.* Abbiamo dovuto fare* la fila per i biglietti.

quick [kwɪk] ADJECTIVE, ADVERB
veloce ◇ *a quick lunch* un pranzo veloce ◇ *It's quicker by train.* È più veloce in treno.
+ **Be quick!** Fa' presto!
+ **She's a quick learner.** Impara presto.

quickly [ˈkwɪklɪ] ADVERB
velocemente

quiet [ˈkwaɪət] ADJECTIVE
1 silenzioso ◇ *You're very quiet today.* Sei molto silenzioso oggi. ◇ *The engine's very quiet.* Il motore è molto silenzioso.
2 tranquillo ◇ *a quiet little town* una cittadina tranquilla ◇ *a quiet weekend* un

---

* Verbs followed by this symbol are irregular. See pp.339–364 for further details.

tranquillo fine settimana
+ **Be quiet!** Fate silenzio!
+ **Quiet!** Silenzio!

quietly ['kwaɪətlɪ] ADVERB
[1] piano ◇ *"She's dead," he said quietly.* "È morta," disse piano.
[2] senza far rumore ◇ *He quietly opened the door.* Ha aperto la porta senza far rumore.

quilt [kwɪlt] NOUN
il piumino

to **quit** [kwɪt] VERB (**quit, quit**)
[1] lasciare ◇ *I quit my job last week.* Ho lasciato il lavoro la settimana scorsa.
+ **I've been given notice to quit.** Mi hanno dato lo sfratto.
[2] smettere* ◇ *I've quit smoking.* Ho smesso di fumare.

quite [kwaɪt] ADVERB
[1] piuttosto ◇ *It's quite warm today.* Fa piuttosto caldo oggi. ◇ *It's quite a long way.* È piuttosto lontano.
+ **quite a lot** un bel po' ◇ *It costs quite a lot to go abroad.* Costa un bel po' andare* all'estero. ◇ *quite a lot of money* un bel po' di denaro
+ **I've been there quite a lot.** Ci sono stato un bel po' di volte.
+ **There were quite a few people there.** C'era un bel po' di gente.
[2] abbastanza ◇ *I quite liked the film, but...* Il film mi è piaciuto abbastanza, ma...

+ **How was the film? – Quite good.** Com'era il film? – Non era male.
[3] del tutto ◇ *I'm not quite sure.* Non sono del tutto sicuro.
[4] proprio ◇ *It was quite a shock.* È stato proprio uno shock. ◇ *It's not quite the same.* Non è proprio lo stesso.

quiz [kwɪz] NOUN (PL **quizzes**)
il quiz (PL i quiz)

quota ['kwəʊtə] NOUN
la quota

quotation [kwəʊ'teɪʃən] NOUN
[1] la citazione ◇ *a quotation from Shakespeare* una citazione da Shakespeare
[2] il preventivo ◇ *I asked the firm to give me a quotation.* Ho chiesto alla ditta di farmi un preventivo.

quotation marks [kwəʊ'teɪʃənmɑːks] NOUN PL
le virgolette

quote [kwəʊt] NOUN
see also **quote** VERB
[1] la citazione ◇ *a Shakespeare quote* una citazione da Shakespeare
[2] il preventivo ◇ *Can you give me a quote?* Può farmi un preventivo?
+ **quotes** virgolette FEM PL ◇ *in quotes* tra virgolette

to **quote** [kwəʊt] VERB
see also **quote** NOUN
citare

Q

R

rabbi ['ræbaɪ] NOUN (PL **rabbis**)
il rabbino

rabbit ['ræbɪt] NOUN
il coniglio
  ◆ **a rabbit hutch** una conigliera

rabies ['reɪbiːz] NOUN SING
la rabbia ◇ *a dog with rabies* un cane con la rabbia

race [reɪs] NOUN
  see also **race** VERB
  [1] la gara ◇ *a cycle race* una gara ciclistica
  [2] la corsa ◇ *a race against time* una corsa contro il tempo
  [3] la razza ◇ *students of all races* studenti di tutte le razze
  ◆ **race relations** rapporti interrazziali
  ◆ **the human race** il genere umano

to **race** [reɪs] VERB
  see also **race** NOUN
  correre* ◇ *We raced to catch the bus.* Abbiamo corso per prendere* l'autobus.
  ◆ **I'll race you!** Facciamo a gara!

racecourse ['reɪskɔːs] NOUN
  l' ippodromo

racehorse ['reɪshɔːs] NOUN
  il cavallo da corsa

racer ['reɪsə'] NOUN
  [1] la bicicletta da corsa ◇ *a red racer* una bicicletta da corsa rossa
  [2] il corridore (*person*)

racetrack ['reɪstræk] NOUN
  la pista

racial ['reɪʃl] ADJECTIVE
  razziale ◇ *racial discrimination* discriminazione razziale

racing car ['reɪsɪŋkɑː'] NOUN
  la macchina da corsa

racing driver ['reɪsɪŋdraɪvə'] NOUN
  il corridore automobilistico (PL i corridori automobilistici)

racism ['reɪsɪzəm] NOUN
  il razzismo

racist ['reɪsɪst] ADJECTIVE, NOUN
  razzista

rack [ræk] NOUN
  [1] il portabagagli (PL i portabagagli) (*in train*)
  [2] il portapacchi (PL i portapacchi) (*on car*)
  [3] l' appendiabiti (PL gli appendiabiti) (*for clothes*)
  [4] la rastrelliera (*for bikes*)

racket ['rækɪt] NOUN
  [1] il baccano ◇ *They were making a terrible racket.* Stavano facendo un terribile baccano.
  [2] la racchetta (*tennis racket*)

racquet ['rækɪt] NOUN
  la racchetta

radar ['reɪdɑː'] NOUN
  il radar (PL i radar)

radiation [reɪdɪ'eɪʃən] NOUN
  la radiazione

radiator ['reɪdɪeɪtə'] NOUN
  il radiatore

radio ['reɪdɪəu] NOUN (PL **radios**)
  la radio (PL le radio)
  ◆ **on the radio** alla radio
  ◆ **a radio station** una stazione radio

radioactive ['reɪdɪəu'æktɪv] ADJECTIVE
  radioattivo

radio cassette ['reɪdɪəukə'set] NOUN
  il radioregistratore

radio-controlled ['reɪdɪəukən'trəuld] ADJECTIVE
  radiocomandato

radish ['rædɪʃ] NOUN (PL **radishes**)
  il ravanello

RAF [ɑːreɪ'ef] NOUN (= *Royal Air Force*)
  [l'] areonautica militare britannica

raffle ['ræfl] NOUN
  la lotteria di beneficenza

raft [rɑːft] NOUN
  la zattera

rag [ræg] NOUN
  lo straccio ◇ *dressed in rags* vestito di stracci

rage [reɪdʒ] NOUN
  la rabbia ◇ *He was trembling with rage.* Tremava dalla rabbia.
  ◆ **mad with rage** arrabbiatissimo
  ◆ **to be in a rage** essere* E furioso
  ◆ **It's all the rage.** Fa furore.

raid [reɪd] NOUN
  see also **raid** VERB
  [1] la rapina ◇ *a bank raid* una rapina in banca
  [2] il raid (PL i raid) ◇ *a police raid* un raid della polizia

to **raid** [reɪd] VERB
  see also **raid** NOUN
  [1] rapinare (*bank*)
  [2] fare* un raid in ◇ *The police raided a club in Soho.* La polizia ha fatto un raid in una discoteca di Soho.

rail [reɪl] NOUN
  [1] il corrimano ◇ *He climbed the stairs, holding the rail.* Salì le scale tenendosi al corrimano.
  [2] il parapetto ◇ *He leaned over the rail.* Si è sporto dal parapetto.
  [3] la rotaia (*for train*) ◇ *between the rails* tra le rotaie
  ◆ **by rail** in treno
  ◆ **a rail strike** uno sciopero dei treni
  [4] l' appendiabiti (PL gli appendiabiti) (*for clothes*)

railcard ['reɪlkɑːd] NOUN
  la tessera di riduzione ferroviaria

---

* Verbs followed by this symbol are irregular. See pp.339–364 for further details.

railroad ['reɪlrəud] NOUN US
la ferrovia

railway ['reɪlweɪ] NOUN
la ferrovia
* **a railway line** una linea ferroviaria
* **the railway station** la stazione ferroviaria

rain [reɪn] NOUN
see also **rain** VERB
la pioggia (PL le piogge) ◊ *in the rain* sotto la pioggia ◊ *It looks like rain.* C'è aria di pioggia.

to **rain** [reɪn] VERB
see also **rain** NOUN
piovere*

rainbow ['reɪnbəu] NOUN
l' arcobaleno

raincoat ['reɪnkəut] NOUN
l' impermeabile MASC

rainfall ['reɪnfɔːl] NOUN
la piovosità

rainforest ['reɪnfɔrɪst] NOUN
la foresta pluviale

rainy ['reɪnɪ] ADJECTIVE
piovoso

to **raise** [reɪz] VERB
[1] sollevare ◊ *He raised his hand.* Ha sollevato la mano.
[2] migliorare ◊ *They want to raise standards in schools.* Vogliono migliorare il livello qualitativo delle scuole.
[3] far sorgere* *(doubts, suspicions)*
* **to raise money** raccogliere* fondi

raisins ['reɪznz] NOUN PL
l' uvetta SING

rake [reɪk] NOUN
il rastrello

rally ['rælɪ] NOUN (PL **rallies**)
[1] il raduno ◊ *a pre-election rally* un raduno pre-elettorale
[2] il rally (PL i rally) ◊ *a rally driver* un pilota di rally
[3] lo scambio *(in tennis)*

ram [ræm] NOUN
see also **ram**
il montone

to **ram** [ræm] VERB
see also **ram** NOUN
cozzare contro

ramble ['ræmbl] NOUN
* **to go for a ramble** fare* un'escursione

rambler ['ræmblə'] NOUN
l' escursionista MASC / FEM

ramp [ræmp] NOUN
la rampa d'accesso

ran [ræn] VERB *see* **run**

ranch [rænʃ] (PL **ranches**)   NOUN
il ranch (PL i ranch)

random ['rændəm] ADJECTIVE
* **a random selection** una selezione effettuata a caso
* **at random** a caso

* **random access** l'accesso casuale

rang [ræŋ] VERB *see* **ring**

range [reɪndʒ] NOUN
see also **range** VERB
la gamma ◊ *There's a wide range of colours.* C'è una vasta gamma di colori.
* **a range of subjects** diverse materie
* **It's out of my price range.** Non è alla mia portata.
* **a range of mountains** una catena di montagne

to **range** [reɪndʒ] VERB
see also **range** NOUN
* **to range from...to** andare* E da...a ◊ *Tickets range from four pounds to twenty pounds.* I prezzi vanno dalle quattro alle venti sterline.

rank [ræŋk] NOUN
see also **rank** VERB
il grado ◊ *the rank of captain* il grado di capitano
* **a taxi rank** un posteggio di taxi

to **rank** [ræŋk] VERB
see also **rank** NOUN
classificare

ransom ['rænsəm] NOUN
il riscatto

rap [ræp] NOUN
il rap *(music)*
* **There was a rap on the door.** Hanno bussato alla porta.

rape [reɪp] NOUN
see also **rape** VERB
lo stupro

to **rape** [reɪp] VERB
see also **rape** NOUN
stuprare

rapids ['ræpɪdz] [ræpɪds] NOUN PL
le rapide

rapist ['reɪpɪst] NOUN
lo stupratore

rare [reə'] ADJECTIVE
[1] raro ◊ *a rare disease* una malattia rara
[2] al sangue *(meat)*

rash [ræʃ] NOUN (PL **rashes**)
see also **rash** ADJECTIVE
l' eritema MASC (PL gli eritemi) ◊ *I've got a rash on my chest.* Ho uno eritema sul petto.

rash [ræʃ] ADJECTIVE
see also **rash** NOUN
avventato

rasher ['ræʃə'] NOUN
* **a rasher of bacon** una fettina di pancetta

raspberry ['rɑːzbərɪ] NOUN (PL **raspberries**)
il lampone

rat [ræt] NOUN
il ratto ◊ *a huge rat* un ratto enorme
* **rat race** la corsa al successo

rate [reɪt] NOUN
see also **rate** VERB
[1] la tariffa ◊ *There are reduced rates for students.* Ci sono tariffe ridotte per gli

R

☞

studenti.

[2] il tasso ◊ *a high rate of interest* un alto tasso d'interesse

[3] la velocità (PL le velocità) ◊ *at a slow rate* a bassa velocità

to **rate** [reɪt] VERB

see also **rate** NOUN

considerare ◊ *He was rated the best.* Era considerato il migliore.

rather ['rɑːðəʳ] ADVERB

piuttosto ◊ *I was rather disappointed.* Ero piuttosto deluso.

+ **rather a lot** molto ◊ *I've got rather a lot of homework to do.* Ho molti compiti da fare*.

+ **I'd rather** preferirei ◊ *I'd rather stay in tonight.* Preferirei stare* a casa, stasera.

rattle ['rætl] NOUN

il sonaglio (*baby's*)

rattlesnake ['rætlsneɪk] NOUN

il serpente a sonagli

to **rave** [reɪv] VERB

see also **rave** NOUN

farneticare ◊ *She cried and raved for weeks.* Ha urlato e farneticato per settimane.

+ **to rave about** essere* E assolutamente entusiasta di ◊ *They raved about the film.* Erano assolutamente entusiasti del film.

rave [reɪv] NOUN

see also **rave** VERB

il rave (PL i rave)

raven ['reɪvən] NOUN

il corvo

ravenous ['rævənəs] ADJECTIVE

+ **to be ravenous** avere* una fame da lupi

raving ['reɪvɪŋ] ADJECTIVE

+ **raving mad** matto da legare

raw [rɔː] ADJECTIVE

crudo ◊ *raw carrots* carote crude

+ **to get a raw deal** essere* E bidonato

+ **raw materials** materie prime

razor ['reɪzəʳ] NOUN

il rasoio ◊ *disposable razors* rasoi usa e getta

+ **a razor blade** una lametta da barba

RE [ɑːrˈiː] NOUN (= *religious education*)

la religione

reach [riːtʃ] NOUN

see also **reach** VERB

+ **out of reach** fuori portata

+ **Keep medicine out of reach of children.** Non lasciare medicinali alla portata dei bambini.

+ **within easy reach of** in prossimità di ◊ *The hotel is within easy reach of the town centre.* L'albergo è in prossimità del centro.

to **reach** [riːtʃ] VERB

see also **reach** NOUN

[1] arrivare E a ◊ *We reached the hotel at seven o'clock.* Siamo arrivati all'albergo alle sette. ◊ *Eventually they reached a decision.* Alla fine hanno preso una decisione.

[2] contattare ◊ *We need to be able to reach*

him in an emergency. Dobbiamo essere* in grado di contattarlo in caso di emergenza.

+ **He reached for his gun.** Ha fatto per prendere* la pistola.

to **react** [riːˈækt] VERB

reagire

reaction [riːˈækʃən] NOUN

la reazione

reactor [riːˈæktəʳ] NOUN

il reattore

to **read** [riːd] VERB (**read, read**)

leggere* ◊ *I read a lot.* Leggo molto.

to **read out** [riːdˈaut] VERB

leggere* a voce alta

reader ['riːdəʳ] NOUN

il lettore

la lettrice

readily ['rɛdɪlɪ] ADVERB

prontamente

reading ['riːdɪŋ] NOUN

la lettura ◊ *reading and writing* lettura e scrittura

+ **I like reading.** Mi piace leggere*.

ready ['rɛdɪ] ADJECTIVE

pronto ◊ *She was always ready to help.* Era sempre pronta ad aiutare.

+ **to get ready** prepararsi E

+ **to get something ready** preparare qualcosa

real [rɪəl] ADJECTIVE

vero ◊ *He wasn't a real policeman.* Non era un vero poliziotto.

+ **in real life** in realtà

+ **in real time** in tempo reale

real estate ['riːlɪsteɪt] NOUN US

i beni immobili MASC PL

realistic [rɪəˈlɪstɪk] ADJECTIVE

realistico

reality [riːˈælɪtɪ] NOUN

la realtà (PL le realtà)

to **realize** ['rɪəlaɪz] VERB

rendersi E conto ◊ *I suddenly realized he was lying.* Improvvisamente mi sono reso conto che stava mentendo.

+ **to realize something** rendersi E conto di qualcosa ◊ *Once they realized their mistake...* Dopo che si erano resi conto del loro errore...

really ['rɪəlɪ] ADVERB

[1] davvero ◊ *I'm learning German. – Really?* Sto studiando tedesco. – Davvero?

[2] proprio ◊ *She's really nice.* È proprio simpatica. ◊ *I really don't like Tom.* Tom non mi piace proprio.

+ **Did he hurt you? – Not really.** Ti ha fatto male? – Non è niente di grave.

Realtor® ['rɪəltɔːʳ] NOUN US

l' agente immobiliare MASC / FEM

rear [rɪəʳ] ADJECTIVE

see also **rear** NOUN

posteriore ◊ *the rear wheel* la ruota posteriore

---

* Verbs followed by this symbol are irregular. See pp.339–364 for further details.

rear [rɪə'] NOUN

see also **rear** ADJECTIVE

il retro ◇ *the rear of the building* il retro dell'edificio

♦ **at the rear of the train** in coda al treno

reason ['riːzn] NOUN

la ragione ◇ *for security reasons* per ragioni di sicurezza

reasonable ['riːznəbl] ADJECTIVE

[1] ragionevole ◇ *Be reasonable!* Sii ragionevole!

[2] discreto ◇ *He wrote a reasonable essay.* Ha fatto un tema discreto.

reasonably ['riːznəblɪ] ADVERB

♦ **reasonably well** discretamente ◇ *The team played reasonably well.* La squadra ha giocato discretamente.

♦ **reasonably priced accommodation** alloggi a prezzi ragionevoli

to **reassure** [riːə'ʃuə'] VERB

rassicurare

reassuring [riːə'ʃuərɪŋ] ADJECTIVE

rassicurante

rebel ['rɛbəl] NOUN

see also **rebel** VERB

il/la ribelle

to **rebel** [rɪ'bɛl] VERB

see also **rebel** NOUN

ribellarsi^E

rebellious [rɪ'bɛljəs] ADJECTIVE

ribelle

receipt [rɪ'siːt] NOUN

la ricevuta

to **receive** [rɪ'siːv] VERB

ricevere

receiver [rɪ'siːvə'] NOUN

la cornetta ◇ *She picked up the receiver.* Ha sollevato la cornetta.

recent ['riːsnt] ADJECTIVE

recente ◇ *recent events* avvenimenti recenti

♦ **in recent weeks** nelle ultime settimane

recently ['riːsntlɪ] ADVERB

di recente ◇ *I haven't seen him recently.* Non l'ho visto di recente.

reception [rɪ'sɛpʃən] NOUN

[1] la reception (PL le reception) ◇ *Please leave your key at reception.* Si prega di lasciare le chiavi alla reception.

[2] il ricevimento ◇ *The reception will be at a big hotel.* Il ricevimento si terrà in un grande albergo.

[3] l'accoglienza ◇ *His speech got a cool reception.* Il suo discorso ha ricevuto una fredda accoglienza.

receptionist [rɪ'sɛpʃənɪst] NOUN

il/la receptionist (PL i/le receptionist)

recession [rɪ'sɛʃən] NOUN

la recessione

recipe ['rɛsɪpɪ] NOUN

la ricetta

to **reckon** ['rɛkən] VERB

pensare ◇ *What do you reckon?* Cosa ne pensi?

reclining [rɪ'klaɪnɪŋ] ADJECTIVE

♦ **reclining seat** sedile reclinabile MASC

recognizable ['rɛkəgnaɪzəbl] ADJECTIVE

riconoscibile

to **recognize** ['rɛkəgnaɪz] VERB

riconoscere*

to **recommend** [rɛkə'mɛnd] VERB

consigliare ◇ *What do you recommend?* Che cosa ci consiglia?

to **reconsider** [riːkən'sɪdə'] VERB

riconsiderare

record ['rɛkəd] NOUN

see also **record** VERB

[1] il record (PL i record) ◇ *the world record* il record mondiale ◇ *in record time* a tempo di record

♦ **a record holder** un primatista

[2] il disco (PL i dischi) ◇ *one of my favourite records* uno dei miei dischi preferiti

[3] la traccia (PL le tracce) ◇ *There is no record of your booking.* Non c'è traccia della vostra prenotazione.

♦ **to keep a record of something** tenere* nota di qualcosa

♦ **to have a criminal record** avere* precedenti penali

♦ **records** archivio ◇ *I'll check in the records.* Controllo in archivio.

to **record** [rɪ'kɔːd] VERB

see also **record** NOUN

registrare

recorded delivery [rɪ'kɔːdɪd'lɪvərɪ] NOUN

♦ **to send something recorded delivery** spedire qualcosa per raccomandata

recorder [rɪ'kɔːdə'] NOUN

il flauto dolce

♦ **to play the recorder** suonare il flauto dolce

recording [rɪ'kɔːdɪŋ] NOUN

la registrazione

record player ['rɛkədpleɪə'] NOUN

il giradischi (PL i giradischi)

to **recover** [rɪ'kʌvə'] VERB

riprendersi^E ◇ *It took her half an hour to recover.* Le ci è voluta mezz'ora per riprendersi.

Be careful not to translate **recover** *by* **ricoverare**.

recovery [rɪ'kʌvərɪ] NOUN

la ripresa

rectangle ['rɛktæŋgl] NOUN

il rettangolo

rectangular [rɛk'tæŋgjulə'] ADJECTIVE

rettangolare

to **recycle** [riː'saɪkl] VERB

riciclare

recycling [riː'saɪklɪŋ] NOUN

il riciclaggio

red [rɛd] ADJECTIVE ☞

R

rosso ◊ *a red light* un semaforo rosso
* **to go through a red light** passare [E] col rosso
Red Cross [ˌredˈkrɔs] NOUN
la Croce Rossa

redcurrant [ˈredkʌrənt] NOUN
il ribes rosso ◊ *redcurrant jelly* marmellata di ribes rosso
* **redcurrants** ribes rosso SING

to **redecorate** [riːˈdekəreɪt] VERB
1 tinteggiare di nuovo (*repaint*)
2 tappezzare di nuovo (*repaper*)

red-haired [ˌredˈhɛəd] ADJECTIVE
dai capelli rossi

red-handed [ˌredˈhændɪd] ADJECTIVE
* **to catch somebody red-handed** prendere* qualcuno con le mani nel sacco

redhead [ˈredhɛd] NOUN
il rosso

to **redo** [riːˈduː] VERB (**redid, redone**)
rifare*

red tape [ˌredˈteɪp] NOUN
la burocrazia

to **reduce** [rɪˈdjuːs] VERB
ridurre* ◊ *at a reduced price* a prezzo ridotto
* **"reduce speed now"** "rallentare"

reduction [rɪˈdʌkʃən] NOUN
la riduzione ◊ *reductions in staff* riduzioni di personale
* **"huge reductions!"** "ribassi!"

redundancy [rɪˈdʌndənsɪ] NOUN (PL **redundancies**)
il licenziamento
* **a redundancy payment** un'indennità di licenziamento

redundant [rɪˈdʌndnt] ADJECTIVE
* **to be made redundant** essere* [E] licenziato

reed [riːd] NOUN
la canna di palude

reel [riːl] NOUN
il rocchetto

to **refer** [rɪˈfɜː] VERB
* **to refer to** fare* accenno a ◊ *He referred to a recent trip to Canada.* Ha fatto accenno ad un recente viaggio in Canada.

referee [ˌrefəˈriː] NOUN
l'arbitro

reference [ˈrefrəns] NOUN
il riferimento ◊ *With reference to...* In riferimento a...
* **a reference number** un numero di riferimento
* **references** (*for job*) referenze ◊ *They require references.* Chiedono delle referenze.
* **a reference book** un testo di consultazione

to **refill** [riːˈfɪl] VERB
riempire* di nuovo

refinery [rɪˈfaɪnərɪ] NOUN (PL **refineries**)
la raffineria

to **reflect** [rɪˈflekt] VERB

riflettere*

reflection [rɪˈflekʃən] NOUN
il riflesso

reflex [ˈriːfleks] NOUN (PL **reflexes**)
il riflesso

reflexive [rɪˈfleksɪv] ADJECTIVE
riflessivo ◊ *a reflexive verb* un verbo riflessivo

refresher course [rɪˈfreʃəkɔːs] NOUN
il corso di aggiornamento

refreshing [rɪˈfreʃɪŋ] ADJECTIVE
1 rinfrescante (*drink*)
2 piacevole ◊ *It was a refreshing change.* È stato un piacevole cambiamento.

refreshments [rɪˈfreʃmənts] NOUN PL
i rinfreschi

refrigerator [rɪˈfrɪdʒəreɪtə] NOUN
il frigorifero

to **refuel** [riːˈfjuəl] VERB
rifornirsi [E] di carburante

refuge [ˈrefjuːdʒ] NOUN
il rifugio

refugee [ˌrefjuˈdʒiː] NOUN
il profugo (PL i profughi)
la profuga (PL le profughe)

refund [ˈriːfʌnd] NOUN
see also **refund** VERB
il rimborso

to **refund** [rɪˈfʌnd] VERB
see also **refund** NOUN
rimborsare

refusal [rɪˈfjuːzəl] NOUN
il rifiuto

to **refuse** [rɪˈfjuːz] VERB
see also **refuse** NOUN
rifiutare

refuse [ˈrefjuːs] NOUN
see also **refuse** VERB
i rifiuti MASC PL
* **refuse collection** la raccolta dei rifiuti

to **regain** [rɪˈgeɪn] VERB
* **to regain control** riacquistare il controllo
* **to regain consciousness** riprendere conoscenza

regard [rɪˈgɑːd] NOUN
see also **regard** VERB
* **with regard to** riguardo a
* **regards** saluti ◊ *Give my regards to Alice.* Saluti a Alice.
* **with kind regards** cordiali saluti

to **regard** [rɪˈgɑːd] VERB
see also **regard** NOUN
* **to regard something as** considerare qualcosa come
* **as regards** per quel che riguarda

regarding [rɪˈgɑːdɪŋ] PREPOSITION
riguardante ◊ *the laws regarding the export of animals* le leggi riguardanti l'esportazione di animali

regardless [rɪˈgɑːdlɪs] ADVERB
* **to carry on regardless** continuare come se

* Verbs followed by this symbol are irregular. See pp.339–364 for further details.

niente fosse

regiment ['redʒɪmənt] NOUN
il reggimento

region ['ri:dʒən] NOUN
la regione

regional ['ri:dʒənl] ADJECTIVE
regionale

register ['redʒɪstə'] NOUN
see also **register** VERB
il registro ◊ the hotel register il registro dell'albergo
• **to call the register** fare* l'appello

register ['redʒɪstə'] VERB
see also **register** NOUN
iscriversi* ᴱ (enrol) ◊ We have to register tomorrow. Dobbiamo iscriverci domani.
• **He registered the birth of his son.** Ha denunciato all'anagrafe la nascita del figlio.

registered ['redʒɪstəd] ADJECTIVE
• **a registered letter** un'assicurata

registration [redʒɪs'treɪʃən] NOUN
[1] l' iscrizione FEM ◊ registration of voters iscrizione alle liste elettorali dei votanti
[2] l' appello (at school) ◊ English is the first lesson after registration. La prima lezione dopo l'appello è quella d'inglese.

registration number [redʒɪs'treɪʃənnʌmbə']
NOUN
il numero di targa

regret [rɪ'gret] NOUN
see also **regret** VERB
il rimpianto

regret [rɪ'gret] VERB
see also **regret** NOUN
pentirsi ᴱ ◊ Try it, you won't regret it! Provalo, non te ne pentirai!
• **to regret doing something** rimpiangere* di aver fatto qualcosa

regular ['regjulə'] ADJECTIVE
[1] regolare ◊ at regular intervals a intervalli regolari
• **to take regular exercise** fare* moto regolarmente
[2] abituale ◊ He's a regular customer. È un cliente abituale.
[3] medio ◊ a regular portion of fries una porzione media di patatine fritte

regularly ['regjuləlɪ] ADVERB
regolarmente

regulation [regju'leɪʃən] NOUN
la norma ◊ safety regulations norme di sicurezza

rehearsal [rɪ'hə:səl] NOUN
la prova
• **the dress rehearsal** la prova generale

rehearse [rɪ'hə:s] VERB
provare

reindeer ['reɪndɪə'] NOUN (PL **reindeer**)
la renna

reins [reɪnz] NOUN PL
le redini

to reject [rɪ'dʒekt] VERB
scartare (idea, suggestion)

relapse [rɪ'læps] NOUN
la ricaduta

related [rɪ'leɪtɪd] ADJECTIVE
imparentato ◊ We're related. Siamo imparentati.
• **The two events were not related.** Non c'è alcun rapporto tra i due avvenimenti.

relation [rɪ'leɪʃən] NOUN
[1] il/la parente ◊ He's a distant relation. È un lontano parente.
[2] il rapporto ◊ It has no relation to reality. Non ha nessun rapporto con la realtà.
• **in relation to** con riferimento a

relationship [rɪ'leɪʃənʃɪp] NOUN
[1] il rapporto ◊ We have a good relationship. Abbiamo un bel rapporto.
[2] la relazione (with partner) ◊ I'm not in a relationship at the moment. Al momento non ho una relazione.

relative ['relətɪv] NOUN
il/la parente

relatively ['relətɪvlɪ] ADVERB
relativamente

to relax [rɪ'læks] VERB
rilassarsi ᴱ

relaxation [ri:læk'seɪʃən] NOUN
il relax

relaxed [rɪ'lækst] ADJECTIVE
rilassato

relaxing [rɪ'læksɪŋ] ADJECTIVE
rilassante

relay ['ri:leɪ] NOUN (PL **relays**)
see also **relay** VERB
• **a relay race** una corsa a staffetta

to relay [rɪ'leɪ] VERB
see also **relay** NOUN
trasmettere*

to release [rɪ'li:s] VERB
see also **release** NOUN
[1] rimettere* in libertà (prisoner)
[2] rendere* noto (news, report)
[3] far uscire* (record, video)

release [rɪ'li:s] NOUN
see also **release** VERB
la liberazione ◊ the release of Nelson Mandela la liberazione di Nelson Mandela
• **the band's latest release** l'ultimo disco del gruppo

relegated ['reləgeɪtɪd] ADJECTIVE
• **to be relegated** essere* ᴱ retrocesso

relevant ['reləvənt] ADJECTIVE
[1] pertinente ◊ Make sure that what you say is relevant. Cerca di dire* qualcosa di pertinente.
• **Education should be relevant to real life.** L'istruzione dovrebbe avere* un riscontro nella vita reale.
[2] del caso ◊ They passed all relevant information to the police Hanno passato ☞

R

tutte le informazioni del caso alla polizia.
+ **That's not relevant.** Questo non c'entra.
Be careful not to translate relevant by
rilevante.

reliable [rɪ'laɪəbl] ADJECTIVE
affidabile

relief [rɪ'li:f] NOUN
il sollievo ◊ *That's a relief!* Che sollievo!

to **relieve** [rɪ'li:v] VERB
alleviare

relieved [rɪ'li:vd] ADJECTIVE
sollevato

religion [rɪ'lɪdʒən] NOUN
la religione

religious [rɪ'lɪdʒəs] ADJECTIVE
religioso

reluctant [rɪ'lʌktənt] ADJECTIVE
+ **to be reluctant to do something** essere* E
restio a fare* qualcosa

reluctantly [rɪ'lʌktəntlɪ] ADVERB
a malincuore

to **rely on** [rɪ'laɪɒn] VERB (**relied, relied**)
contare su ◊ *I'm relying on you.* Conto su di
te.

to **remain** [rɪ'meɪn] VERB
restare E
+ **to remain silent** restare E in silenzio

remaining [rɪ'meɪnɪŋ] ADJECTIVE
+ **the remaining ingredients** il resto degli
ingredienti

remains [rɪ'meɪnz] NOUN PL
i resti ◊ *the remains of the picnic* i resti del
picnic ◊ *human remains* resti umani
+ **Roman remains** le rovine romane

remake ['ri:meɪk] NOUN
il remake (PL i remake)

remark [rɪ'mɑ:k] NOUN
see also **remark** VERB
il commento

to **remark** [rɪ'mɑ:k] VERB
see also **remark** NOUN
osservare

remarkable [rɪ'mɑ:kəbl] ADJECTIVE
straordinario

remarkably [rɪ'mɑ:kəblɪ] ADVERB
straordinariamente

to **remarry** [ri:'mærɪ] VERB (**remarried,**
remarried)
risposarsi E

remedy ['rɛmədɪ] NOUN (PL **remedies**)
il rimedio

to **remember** [rɪ'mɛmbəʳ] VERB
ricordarsi E ◊ *I can't remember his name.*
Non mi ricordo come si chiama.
◊ *Remember to post that letter.* Ricordati di
imbucare la lettera. ◊ *I don't remember*
saying that. Non mi ricordo di aver detto
una cosa del genere.

Remembrance Day [rɪ'mɛmbrənsdeɪ]
NOUN
giorno della commemorazione dei caduti in

guerra

❶ *Si celebra la domenica più vicina all'undici*
novembre, ricorrenza dell'Armistizio. È
consuetudine portare all'occhiello un finto
papavero, i proventi della cui vendita vanno
a favore delle associazioni dei reduci.

to **remind** [rɪ'maɪnd] VERB
ricordare ◊ *The scenery here reminds me of*
Scotland. Il paesaggio mi ricorda la Scozia.
◊ *Remind me to speak to Daniel.* Ricordami
di parlare* a Daniel.

remnant ['rɛmnənt] NOUN
+ **the remnants of the defeated army** ciò che
restava dell'esercito sconfitto

remorse [rɪ'mɔ:s] NOUN
il rimorso

remote [rɪ'məut] ADJECTIVE
isolato ◊ *a remote village* un paesino
isolato

remote control [rɪməutkən'trəul] NOUN
il telecomando

remotely [rɪ'məutlɪ] ADVERB
vagamente ◊ *There was nobody remotely*
resembling this description. Non c'era
nessuno che corrispondesse neanche
vagamente alla descrizione.
+ **I suppose it is remotely possible that...**
Suppongo che ci sia una remota possibilità
che...

removable [rɪ'mu:vəbl] ADJECTIVE
staccabile

removal [rɪ'mu:vəl] NOUN
⬚1 l'asportazione FEM ◊ *the removal of a*
small lump in her breast l'asportazione di un
piccolo nodulo al seno
⬚2 il trasloco (PL i traslochi)
+ **a removal van** un furgone per traslochi

to **remove** [rɪ'mu:v] VERB
togliere* ◊ *Please remove your bag from*
my seat. Le dispiace togliere* la borsa dal
mio sedile?

rendezvous ['rɒndɪvu:] NOUN (PL
rendezvous)
l'appuntamento

to **renew** [rɪ'nju:] VERB
rinnovare (*passport, licence*)

renewable [rɪ'nju:əbl] ADJECTIVE
rinnovabile

to **renovate** ['rɛnəveɪt] VERB
restaurare

renowned [rɪ'naund] ADJECTIVE
rinomato

rent [rɛnt] NOUN
see also **rent** VERB
l'affitto

to **rent** [rɛnt] VERB
see also **rent** NOUN
⬚1 affittare (*house*)
⬚2 noleggiare (*car, bike*)

* Verbs followed by this symbol are irregular. See pp.339–364 for further details.

rental ['rɛntl] NOUN
il noleggio

rental car ['rɛntlkɑːʳ] NOUN
la macchina a nolo

to **reorganize** [riːˈɔːɡənaɪz] VERB
riorganizzare

rep [rɛp] NOUN
il/la rappresentante

repaid [riˈpeɪd] VERB see **repay**

to **repair** [rɪˈpɛəʳ] VERB
see also **repair** NOUN
aggiustare
♦ **to get something repaired** far aggiustare qualcosa ◊ *I got the washing machine repaired.* Ho fatto aggiustare la lavatrice.

repair [rɪˈpɛəʳ] NOUN
see also **repair** VERB
la riparazione

to **repay** [riˈpeɪ] VERB (**repaid, repaid**)
rimborsare
♦ **I don't know how I can ever repay you.** Come potrò mai ricompensarti?

repayment [riˈpeɪmənt] NOUN
♦ **debt repayment** il rimborso del debito pubblico
♦ **mortgage repayments** le rate del mutuo

to **repeat** [rɪˈpiːt] VERB
see also **repeat** NOUN
ripetere

repeat [rɪˈpiːt] NOUN
see also **repeat** VERB
la replica (PL le repliche) ◊ *There are too many repeats on TV.* Ci sono troppe repliche in TV.

repeatedly [rɪˈpiːtɪdlɪ] ADVERB
ripetutamente

repellent [rɪˈpɛlənt] NOUN
♦ **insect repellent** l'insettifugo

repetitive [rɪˈpɛtɪtɪv] ADJECTIVE
ripetitivo

to **replace** [rɪˈpleɪs] VERB
[1] rimpiazzare ◊ *Computers have replaced typewriters.* I computer hanno rimpiazzato le macchine da scrivere*.
[2] riattaccare (*receiver*)

replay ['riːpleɪ] NOUN
see also **replay** VERB
la partita di spareggio

to **replay** [riːˈpleɪ] VERB
see also **replay** NOUN
[1] rigiocare (*match*)
[2] riascoltare (*record, tape*)

replica ['rɛplɪkə] NOUN
la replica (PL le repliche)

reply [rɪˈplaɪ] NOUN (PL **replies**)
see also **reply** VERB
la risposta

to **reply** [rɪˈplaɪ] VERB (**replied, replied**)
see also **reply** NOUN
rispondere*

report [rɪˈpɔːt] NOUN
see also **report** VERB
[1] la relazione ◊ *The committee will today publish its report.* La commissione pubblicherà oggi la sua relazione.
[2] l' articolo ◊ *There's a report in today's paper.* C'è un articolo sul giornale di oggi.
[3] la pagella (*at school*) ◊ *He got a terrible report.* Ha ricevuto una bruttissima pagella.
♦ **a report card** una pagella

to **report** [rɪˈpɔːt] VERB
see also **report** NOUN
[1] denunciare ◊ *I reported the theft to the police.* Ho denunciato il furto alla polizia.
[2] presentarsi E ◊ *Report to reception when you arrive.* Si presenti alla reception al suo arrivo.

to **report back** [rɪpɔːtˈbæk] VERB
riferire ◊ *I'll report back as soon as I hear anything.* Appena ho notizie te lo faccio sapere*.

reporter [rɪˈpɔːtəʳ] NOUN
il/la reporter (PL i/le reporter)

to **represent** [rɛprɪˈzɛnt] VERB
rappresentare

representative [rɛprɪˈzɛntətɪv] ADJECTIVE
rappresentativo

reproduction [riːprəˈdʌkʃən] NOUN
la riproduzione

reptile ['rɛptaɪl] NOUN
il rettile

republic [rɪˈpʌblɪk] NOUN
la repubblica (PL le repubbliche)

repulsive [rɪˈpʌlsɪv] ADJECTIVE
ripugnante

reputable ['rɛpjutəbl] ADJECTIVE
degno di fiducia

reputation [rɛpjuˈteɪʃən] NOUN
la reputazione

request [rɪˈkwɛst] NOUN
see also **request** VERB
la richiesta

to **request** [rɪˈkwɛst] VERB
see also **request** NOUN
richiedere*

to **require** [rɪˈkwaɪəʳ] VERB
richiedere* ◊ *What qualifications are required?* Che qualifiche si richiedono?

requirement [rɪˈkwaɪəmənt] NOUN
il requisito ◊ *What are the requirements for the job?* Quali sono i requisiti necessari per il lavoro?
♦ **entry requirements** i criteri d'ammissione

to **rescue** ['rɛskjuː] VERB
see also **rescue** NOUN
salvare

rescue ['rɛskjuː] NOUN
see also **rescue** VERB
[1] il salvataggio ◊ *a rescue operation* un'operazione di salvataggio
[2] il soccorso ◊ *a mountain rescue team* una squadra di soccorso alpino

R

☞

Verbs followed by the symbol "E" require the auxiliary "essere"

♦ **to come to somebody's rescue** venire* E in aiuto di qualcuno

research [rɪˈsɜːtʃ] NOUN
  [1] la ricerca ◇ *He's doing research.* Fa ricerca.
  [2] le ricerche PL ◇ *She's doing some research in the library.* Sta facendo delle ricerche in biblioteca.

resemblance [rɪˈzɛmbləns] NOUN
  la somiglianza

to **resent** [rɪˈzɛnt] VERB
  ♦ **to resent somebody** provare risentimento nei confronti di qualcuno
  ♦ **I resent being dependent on her.** Non sopporto di dipendere* da lei.

resentful [rɪˈzɛntfəl] ADJECTIVE
  pieno di risentimento
  ♦ **to feel resentful towards somebody** essere* pieno di risentimento nei confronti di qualcuno

reservation [rɛzəˈveɪʃən] NOUN
  [1] la prenotazione ◇ *I've got a reservation for two nights.* Ho una prenotazione per due notti.
  [2] la riserva ◇ *I've got reservations about it.* Ho delle riserve a riguardo.

reserve [rɪˈzɜːv] NOUN
  see also **reserve** VERB
  la riserva

to **reserve** [rɪˈzɜːv] VERB
  see also **reserve** NOUN
  riservare ◇ *I'd like to reserve a table for tomorrow evening.* Vorrei riservare un tavolo per domani sera.

reserved [rɪˈzɜːvd] ADJECTIVE
  riservato

reservoir [ˈrɛzəvwɑːˈ] NOUN
  il bacino idrico (PL i bacini idrici)

resident [ˈrɛzɪdənt] NOUN
  l' abitante MASC/FEM ◇ *local residents* gli abitanti della zona

residential [rɛzɪˈdɛnʃəl] ADJECTIVE
  residenziale ◇ *a residential area* una zona residenziale

to **resign** [rɪˈzaɪn] VERB
  dare* le dimissioni

resistance [rɪˈzɪstəns] NOUN
  la resistenza

to **resit** [riːˈsɪt] VERB (**resat, resat**)
  ripresentarsi E a ◇ *I'm resitting the exam in December.* Mi ripresento all'esame in dicembre.

resolution [rɛzəˈluːʃən] NOUN
  [1] il buon proposito ◇ *Have you made any New Year resolutions?* Hai fatto dei buoni propositi per l'anno nuovo?
  [2] la risoluzione ◇ *a UN resolution* una risoluzione dell'ONU

resort [rɪˈzɔːt] NOUN
  la località turistica (PL le località turistiche)
  ♦ **a seaside resort** una stazione balneare

♦ **a ski resort** una stazione sciistica
♦ **as a last resort** come ultima risorsa

resource [rɪˈzɔːs] NOUN
  la risorsa

respect [rɪsˈpɛkt] NOUN
  see also **respect** VERB
  il rispetto ◇ *I have tremendous respect for Dean.* Ho un grandissimo rispetto per Dean.
  ♦ **in some respects** sotto certi aspetti

to **respect** [rɪsˈpɛkt] VERB
  see also **respect** NOUN
  rispettare

respectable [rɪsˈpɛktəbl] ADJECTIVE
  [1] rispettabile ◇ *a respectable family* una famiglia rispettabile
  [2] discreto ◇ *My marks were respectable.* I miei voti erano discreti.

respectively [rɪsˈpɛktɪvlɪ] ADVERB
  rispettivamente

responsibility [rɪspɒnsɪˈbɪlɪtɪ] NOUN (PL **responsibilities**)
  la responsabilità (PL le responsabilità)

responsible [rɪsˈpɒnsɪbl] ADJECTIVE
  responsabile
  ♦ **to be responsible for something** essere* E responsabile di qualcosa
  ♦ **a responsible job** un posto di responsabilità

rest [rɛst] NOUN
  see also **rest** VERB
  [1] il riposo ◇ *five minutes' rest* cinque minuti di riposo
  ♦ **a rest home** una casa di riposo
  ♦ **to have a rest** riposarsi E
  [2] il resto ◇ *I'll do the rest.* Faccio io il resto.
  ◇ *the rest of the money* il resto dei soldi
  ♦ **the rest of them** gli altri ◇ *The rest of them went swimming.* Gli altri sono andati a nuotare.

to **rest** [rɛst] VERB
  see also **rest** NOUN
  [1] riposare ◇ *She's resting in her room.* È in camera sua a riposare.
  [2] non affaticare ◇ *He has to rest his knee.* Non deve affaticare il ginocchio.
  [3] appoggiare ◇ *I rested my bike against the window.* Ho appoggiato la bici alla finestra.

restaurant [ˈrɛstərɒn] NOUN
  il ristorante
  ♦ **the restaurant car** il vagone ristorante

restful [ˈrɛstful] ADJECTIVE
  riposante

restless [ˈrɛstlɪs] ADJECTIVE
  irrequieto

restoration [rɛstəˈreɪʃən] NOUN
  il restauro

to **restore** [rɪˈstɔːˈ] VERB
  [1] ripristinare ◇ *They restored order.* Hanno ripristinato l'ordine.
  ♦ **to restore somebody's confidence** far riacquistare fiducia a qualcuno

2 restaurare ◇ *The picture has been restored.* Il quadro è stato restaurato.

to **restrict** [rɪs'trɪkt] VERB
limitare

restroom ['restruːm] NOUN [US]
la toilette (PL le toilette)

result [rɪ'zʌlt] NOUN
see also **result** VERB
il risultato ◇ *an excellent result* un risultato eccellente.

♦ **as a result** di conseguenza ◇ *...and as a result, morale is low.* ...e di conseguenza il morale è basso.

to **result** [rɪ'zʌlt] VERB
see also **result** NOUN

♦ **to result in** causare ◇ *Many accidents result in head injuries.* Molti incidenti causano delle lesioni craniche.

♦ **The enquiry resulted in her being sacked.** L'inchiesta ha portato al suo licenziamento.

to **resume** [rɪ'zjuːm] VERB
riprendere ◇ *They've resumed work.* Hanno ripreso il lavoro.

résumé ['reɪzjumeɪ] NOUN [US]
il curriculum vitae (PL i curriculum vitae)

to **retire** [rɪ'taɪəʳ] VERB
andare* ᴱ in pensione

retired [rɪ'taɪəd] ADJECTIVE
in pensione ◇ *a retired teacher* un insegnante in pensione

retirement [rɪ'taɪəmənt] NOUN

♦ **since his retirement** da quando è andato in pensione

to **retrace** [riː'treɪs] VERB

♦ **to retrace one's steps** ritornare ᴱ sui propri passi

return [rɪ'tɜːn] NOUN
see also **return** VERB
1 il ritorno ◇ *on our return* al nostro ritorno

♦ **the return journey** il viaggio di ritorno

♦ **a return match** una partita di ritorno
2 il biglietto di andata e ritorno ◇ *A return to Bangor, please.* Vorrei un biglietto di andata e ritorno per Bangor.

♦ **in return** in cambio ◇ *...and I help her in return.* ...e io in cambio aiuto lei.

♦ **in return for** in cambio di

♦ **Many happy returns!** Cento di questi giorni!
3 invio (*key*) ◇ *Hit return.* Premere invio.

to **return** [rɪ'tɜːn] VERB
see also **return** NOUN
1 tornare ᴱ ◇ *I've just returned from holiday.* Sono appena tornato dalle vacanze.
2 restituire ◇ *She borrows my things and doesn't return them.* Prende le mie cose e poi non le restituisce.

reunion [riːˈjuːnɪən] NOUN
la riunione

to **reuse** [riːˈjuːz] VERB
riutilizzare

to **reveal** [rɪ'viːl] VERB
rivelare

revenge [rɪ'vendʒ] NOUN
la vendetta ◇ *This is my revenge.* Questa è la mia vendetta.

♦ **to take revenge** vendicarsi ᴱ

to **reverse** [rɪ'vɜːs] VERB
see also **reverse** ADJECTIVE
1 fare* retromarcia ◇ *He reversed without looking.* Ha fatto retromarcia senza guardare.
2 invertire ◇ *They are trying to reverse this trend.* Stanno cercando di invertire la tendenza.

♦ **to reverse one's decision** tornare ᴱ sulla propria decisione

♦ **to reverse the charges** fare* una telefonata a carico del destinatario

reverse [rɪ'vɜːs] ADJECTIVE
see also **reverse** VERB
inverso ◇ *in reverse order* in ordine inverso

♦ **in reverse gear** in retromarcia

♦ **a reverse charge call** una telefonata a carico del destinatario

review [rɪ'vjuː] NOUN
see also **review** VERB
la recensione ◇ *The book got good reviews.* Il libro ha avuto recensioni favorevoli.

♦ **to be under review** essere* ᴱ preso in esame

to **review** [rɪ'vjuː] VERB
see also **review** NOUN
fare* la recensione di

to **revise** [rɪ'vaɪz] VERB
ripassare ◇ *I haven't started revising yet.* Non ho ancora cominciato a ripassare.

♦ **to revise one's opinion** cambiare idea

revision [rɪ'vɪʒən] NOUN
il ripasso

to **revive** [rɪ'vaɪv] VERB
rianimare ◇ *The nurses tried to revive him.* Gli infermieri cercarono di rianimarlo.

revolting [rɪ'vəʊltɪŋ] ADJECTIVE
disgustoso

revolution [revə'luːʃən] NOUN
la rivoluzione

revolutionary [revə'luːʃənrɪ] ADJECTIVE
rivoluzionario

revolver [rɪ'vɒlvəʳ] NOUN
il revolver (PL i revolver)

reward [rɪ'wɔːd] NOUN
la ricompensa

rewarding [rɪ'wɔːdɪŋ] ADJECTIVE
gratificante ◇ *a rewarding job* un lavoro gratificante

to **rewind** [riː'waɪnd] VERB (**rewound, rewound**)
riavvolgere

rheumatism ['ruːmətɪzəm] NOUN
il reumatismo

Rhine [raɪn] NOUN

♦ **the Rhine** il Reno

R

Verbs followed by the symbol "E" require the auxiliary "essere"

rhinoceros [raɪˈnɒsərəs] NOUN
il rinoceronte

Rhone [rəun] NOUN
* **the Rhone** il Rodano

rhubarb [ˈruːbɑːb] NOUN
il rabarbaro

rhythm [ˈrɪðm] NOUN
il ritmo

rib [rɪb] NOUN
la costola

ribbon [ˈrɪbən] NOUN
il nastro

rice [raɪs] NOUN
il riso
* **rice pudding** il budino di riso

rich [rɪtʃ] ADJECTIVE
ricco
* **the rich** i ricchi

to **rid** [rɪd] VERB (**rid, rid**)
liberare ◇ *an attempt to rid the house of mice* un tentativo di liberare la casa dai topi
* **to get rid of** sbarazzarsi [E] di

to **ride** [raɪd] VERB (**rode, ridden**)
see also **ride** NOUN
cavalcare ◇ *I'm learning to ride.* Sto imparando a cavalcare.
* **to ride a horse** cavalcare
* **to ride a bike** andare* [E] in bicicletta ◇ *Can you ride a bike?* Sai andare* in bicicletta? ◇ *He rode to school on his new bike.* È andato a scuola con la bici nuova.
* **to ride the bus** US prendere* l'autobus

ride [raɪd] NOUN
see also **ride** VERB
* **to go for a ride (1)** (*on horse*) andare* [E] a fare* una cavalcata
* **to go for a ride (2)** (*on bike*) andare* [E] a fare* un giro in bicicletta
* **It's a short bus ride to the town centre.** In autobus il centro non è lontano.

rider [ˈraɪdər] NOUN
[1] il cavallerizzo
la cavallerizza
◇ *She's a good rider.* È una buona cavallerizza.
[2] il/la ciclista (*cyclist*)

ridiculous [rɪˈdɪkjuləs] ADJECTIVE
ridicolo

riding [ˈraɪdɪŋ] NOUN
l'equitazione FEM
* **to go riding** fare* equitazione
* **a riding school** una scuola d'equitazione

rifle [ˈraɪfl] NOUN
il fucile

rig [rɪg] NOUN
* **an oil rig** una piattaforma petrolifera

right [raɪt] ADJECTIVE, ADVERB
see also **right** NOUN
[1] giusto ◇ *It isn't the right size.* Non è la taglia giusta.
[2] esatto ◇ *Do you have the right time?* Hai

l'ora esatta? ◇ *the right answer* la risposta esatta ◇ *That's right!* Esatto!
* **to be right** (*person*) avere* ragione ◇ *You were right!* Avevi ragione!
[3] bene ◇ *Did I pronounce it right?* L'ho pronunciato bene? ◇ *Right! Let's get started.* Bene, cominciamo! ◇ *It's not right to behave like that.* Non sta bene fare* così.
* **to do the right thing** fare* bene ◇ *I think you did the right thing.* Secondo me hai fatto bene.
[4] destro ◇ *my right hand* la mano destra
[5] a destra ◇ *Turn right at the traffic lights.* Al semaforo gira a destra.
* **right away** subito ◇ *I'll do it right away.* Lo faccio subito.

right [raɪt] NOUN
see also **right** ADJECTIVE
[1] il diritto ◇ *You've got no right to do that.* Non hai diritto di farlo.
* **to have right of way** (*person*) avere* la precedenza
[2] la destra
* **on the right** a destra

right angle [ˈraɪtæŋgl] NOUN
l'angolo retto

right-hand [ˈraɪthænd] ADJECTIVE
destra ◇ *the right-hand side* il lato destro
* **to be on the right-hand side** essere* [E] sulla destra

right-handed [raɪtˈhændɪd] ADJECTIVE
* **I'm right-handed.** Scrivo con la destra.

rightly [ˈraɪtlɪ] ADVERB
[1] giustamente ◇ *She rightly decided that he was lying.* Concluse, giustamente, che lui mentiva.
[2] bene ◇ *If I remember rightly.* Se mi ricordo bene.

rim [rɪm] NOUN
l'orlo ◇ *the rim of a cup* l'orlo della tazza
* **rims** montatura SING ◇ *glasses with wire rims* occhiali con montatura metallica

ring [rɪŋ] NOUN
see also **ring** VERB
[1] l'anello ◇ *He gave her a silver ring.* Le ha regalato un anello d'argento.
* **a wedding ring** una fede
[2] il cerchio ◇ *They were sitting in a ring.* Erano seduti in cerchio.
[3] lo squillo (*of phone, bell*) ◇ *He answered at the first ring.* Ha risposto al primo squillo.
* **to give somebody a ring** telefonare a qualcuno

to **ring** [rɪŋ] VERB (**rang, rung**)
see also **ring** NOUN
[1] telefonare ◇ *Your mother rang this morning.* Stamattina ha telefonato tua madre. ◇ *Several friends have rung to congratulate me.* Mi hanno telefonato diversi amici per congratularsi.
* **to ring somebody** telefonare a qualcuno
[2] squillare ◇ *The phone's ringing.* Sta

squillando il telefono.
* **to ring the bell** suonare il campanello
* **to ring back** richiamare ◇ *I'll ring back later.* Richiamerò più tardi.
* **to ring up** telefonare

ring binder ['rɪŋbaɪndə'] NOUN
il classificatore ad anelli

ring road ['rɪŋrəud] NOUN
la circonvallazione

rink [rɪŋk] NOUN
la pista di pattinaggio

to **rinse** [rɪns] VERB
sciacquare

riot ['raɪət] NOUN
see also **riot** VERB
la sommmossa
* **police in riot gear** polizia in tenuta antisommossa

to **riot** ['raɪət] VERB
see also **riot** NOUN
fare* una sommossa

to **rip** [rɪp] VERB
strappare ◇ *I accidentally ripped the envelope.* Senza volere* ho strappato la busta.
* **I've ripped my jeans.** Mi si sono strappati i jeans.

to **rip off** [rɪp'ɔf] VERB
pelare ◇ *The hotel ripped us off.* All'albergo ci hanno pelato.

to **rip up** [rɪp'ʌp] VERB
strappare ◇ *He read the note and then ripped it up.* Ha letto il biglietto e poi l'ha strappato.

ripe [raɪp] ADJECTIVE
maturo

rip-off ['rɪpɔf] NOUN
* **It's a rip-off!** È un furto!

rise [raɪz] NOUN
see also **rise** VERB
l' aumento

to **rise** [raɪz] VERB (rose, risen)
see also **rise** NOUN
[1] aumentare E ◇ *Prices rose sharply last month.* I prezzi sono aumentati notevolmente il mese scorso.
[2] sorgere* E (*sun*)
* **to rise to one's feet** alzarsi E in piedi ◇ *He rose to his feet.* Si alzò in piedi.

riser ['raɪzə'] NOUN
* **to be an early riser** essere* E mattutino

risk [rɪsk] NOUN
see also **risk** VERB
il rischio
* **to take risks** correre* dei rischi
* **It's at your own risk.** È a tuo rischio e pericolo.

to **risk** [rɪsk] VERB
see also **risk** NOUN
rischiare

risky ['rɪskɪ] ADJECTIVE

rischioso

rival ['raɪvl] NOUN
see also **rival** ADJECTIVE, VERB
il/la rivale

rival ['raɪvl] ADJECTIVE
see also **rival** NOUN, VERB
[1] rivale ◇ *a rival gang* una banda rivale
[2] concorrente ◇ *a rival company* una ditta concorrente

to **rival** ['raɪvl] VERB
see also **rival** ADJECTIVE, NOUN
competere con ◇ *Cassette recorders cannot rival the sound quality of CD players.* I registratori a cassette non possono competere con la qualità del suono dei riproduttori CD.

rivalry ['raɪvlrɪ] NOUN (PL **rivalries**)
la rivalità (PL le rivalità)

river ['rɪvə'] NOUN
il fiume ◇ *across the river* dall'altra parte del fiume
* **the river bank** l'argine MASC

Riviera [rɪvɪ'ɛərə] NOUN
* **the French Riviera** la Costa Azzurra
* **the Italian Riviera** la riviera ligure

road [rəud] NOUN
la strada

road accident ['rəudæksɪdənt] NOUN
l' incidente stradale MASC

road map ['rəudmæp] NOUN
la carta stradale

road rage ['rəudreɪdʒ] NOUN
l' aggressività al volante

road sign ['rəudsaɪn] NOUN
il cartello stradale

roadworks ['rəudwɜːks] NOUN PL
i lavori stradali

roast [rəust] ADJECTIVE
arrosto ◇ *roast chicken* pollo arrosto
* **roast pork** arrosto di maiale
* **roast beef** arrosto di manzo

to **rob** [rɔb] VERB
derubare ◇ *I've been robbed.* Sono stato derubato.
* **to rob somebody of something** rubare qualcosa a qualcuno ◇ *He was robbed of his wallet.* Gli hanno rubato il portafoglio.
* **to rob a bank** svaligiare una banca

robber ['rɔbə'] NOUN
il rapinatore
la rapinatrice
◇ *armed robbers* rapinatori armati

robbery ['rɔbərɪ] NOUN (PL **robberies**)
[1] la rapina (*in bank, shop*)
* **a bank robbery** una rapina in banca
* **an armed robbery** una rapina a mano armata
[2] il furto ◇ *He was arrested for robberies on trains.* È stato arrestato per aver commesso vari furti sui treni.

robin ['rɔbɪn] NOUN ☞

R

il pettirosso

robot ['rəubɒt] NOUN
il robot (PL i robot)

rock [rɒk] NOUN
see also **rock** VERB
[1] la roccia (PL le rocce) ◊ *I sat on a rock.* Mi sono seduto su una roccia.
• **Morale was at rock bottom.** Il morale era a terra.
• **Prices have hit rock bottom.** I prezzi sono scesi tantissimo.
[2] la pietra ◊ *The crowd started to throw rocks.* La folla cominciò a lanciare sassi.
[3] il rock ◊ *a rock concert* un concerto rock
• **rock and roll** il rock and roll
• **a stick of rock** un bastoncino di zucchero d'orzo

to **rock** [rɒk] VERB
see also **rock** NOUN
[1] far oscillare ◊ *The tremor rocked the building.* Il terremoto ha fatto oscillare l'edificio.
[2] cullare (*baby*)

rockery ['rɒkəri] NOUN
il giardino roccioso

rocket ['rɒkɪt] NOUN
il razzo

rocking chair ['rɒkɪŋtʃeə'] NOUN
la sedia a dondolo

rocking horse ['rɒkɪŋhɔːs] NOUN
il cavallo a dondolo

rod [rɒd] NOUN
la canna da pesca

rode [rəud] VERB *see* **ride**

role [rəul] NOUN
il ruolo

role play ['rəulpleɪ] NOUN
il gioco di ruolo (PL i giochi di ruolo) ◊ *to do a role play* fare* un gioco di ruolo

roll [rəul] NOUN
see also **roll** VERB
[1] il rotolo ◊ *a toilet roll* un rotolo di carta igienica
• **a roll of film** un rullino fotografico
[2] il panino ◊ *a cheese roll* un panino al formaggio
• **roll call** (*at school*) l'appello

to **roll** [rəul] VERB
see also **roll** NOUN
rotolare ◊ *The ball rolled into the net.* La palla rotolò in rete.

to **roll out** [rəul'aut] VERB
spianare (*pastry*)

to **roll up** [rəul'ʌp] VERB
rimboccare (*sleeves*)

roller ['rəulə'] NOUN
il bigodino (*for hair*)

Rollerblades® ['rəuləbleɪdz] NOUN PL
i pattini in linea

to **roller-blade** ['rəuləbleɪd] VERB
pattinare

rollercoaster ['rəuləkəustə'] NOUN
le montagne russe FEM PL

roller skates ['rəuləskeɪts] NOUN PL
i pattini a rotelle

roller-skating ['rəuləskeɪtɪŋ] NOUN
il pattinaggio a rotelle

rolling pin ['rəulɪŋpɪn] NOUN
il mattarello

Roman ['rəumən] ADJECTIVE, NOUN
il romano
la romana
◊ *the Roman empire* l'impero romano
• **the Romans** i romani

Roman Catholic ['rəumən'kæθəlɪk] NOUN
il cattolico
la cattolica

romance [rə'mæns] NOUN
[1] l' amore MASC ◊ *a holiday romance* un amore estivo
[2] il fascino ◊ *the romance of Paris* il fascino di Parigi
[3] il romanzo rosa (PL i romanzi rosa) ◊ *She writes romances.* Scrive romanzi rosa.

Romania [rəu'meɪnɪə] NOUN
la Romania

Romanian [rəu'meɪnɪən] ADJECTIVE
rumeno

romantic [rə'mæntɪk] ADJECTIVE
romantico

Rome [rəum] NOUN
Roma FEM

roof [ruːf] NOUN
il tetto ◊ *a sloping roof* un tetto spiovente

roof rack ['ruːfræk] NOUN
il portapacchi (PL i portapacchi)

room [ruːm] NOUN
[1] la stanza ◊ *the biggest room in the house* la stanza più grande della casa
[2] la camera ◊ *She's in her room.* È in camera sua.
• **a single room** una camera singola
• **a double room** una camera matrimoniale
[3] la sala ◊ *the music room* la sala musica
[4] il posto ◊ *There's no room for that box.* Non c'è posto per quella scatola.

roommate ['ruːmmeɪt] NOUN
il compagno di stanza
la compagna di stanza

room service ['ruːmsɜːvɪs] NOUN
il servizio in camera

root [ruːt] NOUN
see also **root** VERB
la radice

to **root** [ruːt] VERB
see also **root** NOUN
mettere* radici

to **root around** [ruːtə'raund] VERB
rovistare

to **root out** [ruːt'aut] VERB
eliminare ◊ *They are determined to root out corruption.* Sono decisi ad eliminare la

---

* Verbs followed by this symbol are irregular. See pp.339–364 for further details.

corruzione.

rope [rəup] NOUN
la corda

to **rope** [rəup] VERB
legare ◇ *The climbers were roped together.*
I rocciatori erano legati assieme.

to **rope in** [rəup'ɪn] VERB
tirar dentro ◇ *I was roped in to help with the
refreshments.* Mi hanno tirato dentro a
dare* una mano con i rinfreschi.

rose [rəuz] VERB *see* rise

rose [rəuz] NOUN
la rosa

to **rot** [rɒt] VERB
[1] marcire[E] ◇ *The wood had rotted.* Il
legno era marcito.
[2] cariare ◇ *Sugar rots your teeth.* Lo
zucchero caria i denti.

rotten ['rɒtn] ADJECTIVE
marcio ◇ *a rotten apple* una mela marcia
• **rotten weather** tempo da cani
• **That's a rotten thing to do.** Che carognata!
• **to feel rotten** sentirsi[E] da cani

rough [rʌf] ADJECTIVE, ADVERB
[1] ruvido ◇ *My hands are rough.* Ho le
mani ruvide.
[2] violento ◇ *Rugby's a rough sport.* Il
rugby è uno sport violento.
[3] poco raccomandabile ◇ *It's a rough
area.* È una zona poco raccomandabile.
[4] mosso ◇ *The sea was rough.* Il mare era
mosso.
[5] approssimativo ◇ *I've got a rough idea.*
Ne ho un'idea approssimativa.
• **to feel rough** sentirsi[E] poco bene
• **to sleep rough** dormire* per strada ◇ *A lot
of people sleep rough in London.* A Londra
tanta gente dorme per strada.

roughly ['rʌflɪ] ADVERB
pressapoco ◇ *It weighs roughly twenty
kilos.* Pesa pressapoco venti chili.
• **Roughly chop the tomatoes and peppers.**
Tagliare i pomodori e i peperoni a pezzi
grossi.

round [raund] ADJECTIVE, ADVERB, PREPOSITION
see also **round** NOUN
[1] rotondo ◇ *a round table* un tavolo
rotondo
[2] intorno a ◇ *We were sitting round the
table.* Eravamo seduti intorno al tavolo.
• **a round number** una cifra tonda
• **round the corner** dietro l'angolo
• **to go round to somebody's house** andare*[E]
a casa di qualcuno
• **to have a look round** dare* un'occhiata in
giro
• **to go round a museum** visitare un museo
• **round here** da queste parti ◇ *Is there a
chemist's round here?* C'è una farmacia da
queste parti?
• **all round** tutt'intorno ◇ *There were
vineyards all round.* Tutt'intorno c'erano

delle vigne.
• **all year round** tutto l'anno
• **round about** circa ◇ *It costs round about a
hundred pounds.* Costa circa cento sterline.
• **round about eight o'clock** verso le otto

round [raund] NOUN
see also **round** ADJECTIVE, ADVERB, PREPOSITION
[1] il round (PL i round) (*in boxing*) ◇ *He was
knocked out in the tenth round.* È andato al
tappeto al decimo round.
[2] il giro ◇ *another round of talks* un altro
giro di consultazioni
[3] la fettina ◇ *a few rounds of cucumber*
alcune fettine di cetriolo
• **to buy a round of drinks** (*in pub*) offrire* un
giro
• **I think it's my round.** Tocca a me offrire* da
bere*.
• **a round of golf** una partita di golf
• **a round of sandwiches** un tramezzino

to **round off** [raund'ɔf] VERB
terminare ◇ *They rounded off the meal with
liqueurs.* Hanno terminato il pranzo con dei
liquori.

to **round up** [raund'ʌp] VERB
[1] fare* una retata (*suspects*)
[2] arrotondare (*sum, number*)

roundabout ['raundəbaut] NOUN
[1] la rotatoria (*at junction*)
[2] la giostra (*in fairground*)

rounders ['raundəz] NOUN

> ℹ️ **ll rounders** è un gioco per bambini simile
> al baseball.

round trip ['raundtrɪp] NOUN US
l' andata e ritorno

route [ruːt] NOUN
l' itinerario ◇ *a different route* un itinerario
diverso
• **a bus route** un percorso dell'autobus

routine [ruː'tiːn] NOUN
see also **routine** ADJECTIVE
• **my daily routine** le mie occupazioni
quotidiane

routine [ruː'tiːn] ADJECTIVE
see also **routine** NOUN
di routine ◇ *a routine check* un controllo di
routine

row (1) [rəu] NOUN
see also **row** VERB
la fila ◇ *a row of houses* una fila di case ◇ *in
the front row* in prima fila ◇ *five times in a
row* cinque volte di fila

row (2) [rau] NOUN
[1] il baccano ◇ *What's that terrible row?*
Cos'è quel baccano?
[2] il litigio ◇ *their latest row* il loro ultimo
litigio
• **to have a row** litigare ◇ *They've had a row.*
Hanno litigato.

to **row** [rəu] VERB ☞

R

see also **row (1)** NOUN
remare (*in boat*)

rowboat ['rəubaut] NOUN US
la barca a remi (PL le barche a remi)

rowing ['rəuɪŋ] NOUN
il canottaggio ◇ *I like rowing.* Mi piace il canottaggio.

♦ **a rowing boat** una barca a remi

royal ['rɔɪəl] ADJECTIVE, NOUN
reale

♦ **the royals** i reali

to **rub** [rʌb] VERB
sfregare ◇ *She gently rubbed the stain.* Ha sfregato leggermente la macchia. ◇ *She rubbed her eyes.* Si sfregò gli occhi.

to **rub out** [rʌb'aut] VERB
cancellare

rubber ['rʌbə'] NOUN
[1] la gomma ◇ *rubber soles* suole di gomma
[2] la gomma da cancellare (*eraser*) ◇ *You'll need a pencil and a rubber.* Occorre una matita e una gomma da cancellare.

♦ **a rubber band** un elastico

rubber plant ['rʌbəplɑːnt] NOUN
il ficus (PL i ficus)

rubbish ['rʌbɪʃ] NOUN
see also **rubbish** ADJECTIVE
[1] le immondizie FEM PL ◇ *The rubbish is collected on Mondays.* Le immondizie vengono portate via di lunedì. ◇ *He threw the bottle in the rubbish.* Ha buttato la bottiglia nelle immondizie.

♦ **the rubbish bin** la pattumiera
[2] le porcherie FEM PL ◇ *Children eat a lot of rubbish.* I bambini mangiano molte porcherie.
[3] le sciocchezze FEM PL ◇ *Don't talk rubbish!* Non dire* sciocchezze! ◇ *That's a load of rubbish!* Tutte sciocchezze!

rubbish ['rʌbɪʃ] ADJECTIVE
see also **rubbish** NOUN

♦ **They're a rubbish team!** È una squadra che non vale niente!

rubbish dump ['rʌbɪʃdʌmp] NOUN
la discarica (PL le discariche)

RUC [ɑːjuːˈsiː] ABBREVIAZIONE (= *Royal Ulster Constabulary*)
[le] forze di polizia dell'Irlanda del Nord

rucksack ['rʌksæk] NOUN
lo zaino

rude [ruːd] ADJECTIVE
[1] maleducato ◇ *It's rude to interrupt.* È maleducato interrompere*. ◇ *He was very rude to me.* È stato molto maleducato nei miei confronti.
[2] volgare ◇ *a rude joke* una barzelletta sporca

♦ **a rude word** una parolaccia

rug [rʌg] NOUN
[1] il tappeto (*carpet*)

[2] la coperta (*blanket*)

rugby ['rʌgbɪ] NOUN
il rugby

ruin ['ruːɪn] NOUN
see also **ruin** VERB
la rovina ◇ *the ruins of the castle* le rovine del castello

to **ruin** ['ruːɪn] VERB
see also **ruin** NOUN
rovinare

rule [ruːl] NOUN
see also **rule** VERB
la regola

♦ **as a rule** di regola
♦ **It's against the rules.** È contro il regolamento.

to **rule** [ruːl] VERB
see also **rule** NOUN
governare ◇ *He has ruled the country since 1996.* Governa il paese dal 1996.

to **rule out** [ruːl'aut] VERB
escludere*

ruler ['ruːlə'] NOUN
il righello

rum [rʌm] NOUN
il rum

rumour ['ruːmə'] NOUN (US **rumor**)

♦ **There's a rumour that...** Corre voce che...
Be careful not to translate **rumour** by **rumore**.

rump steak ['rʌmpsteɪk] NOUN
la bistecca di girello

run [rʌn] NOUN
see also **run** VERB
[1] la corsa

♦ **to go for a run** andare* a correre* ◇ *I go for a run every morning.* Vado a correre* ogni mattina.
♦ **to be on the run** essere* latitante ◇ *The criminals are still on the run.* I criminali sono ancora latitanti.
[2] il punto (*in cricket*)
[3] la pista (*ski run*)
♦ **in the long run** alla lunga

to **run** [rʌn] VERB (**ran, run**)
see also **run** NOUN
[1] correre* ◇ *He was running towards her.* Correva verso di lei. ◇ *I ran five kilometres.* Ho corso cinque chilometri.

♦ **to run a marathon** partecipare ad una maratona
[2] dirigere* ◇ *He runs a large company.* Dirige una grossa società.
[3] organizzare ◇ *They run music courses in the holidays.* Organizzano corsi di musica durante le vacanze.
[4] portare (*in car*) ◇ *I can run you to the station.* Ti porto alla stazione.
♦ **to leave the tap running** lasciare il rubinetto aperto
♦ **to run a bath** preparare il bagno

to **run away** [rʌnəˈweɪ] VERB

---

* Verbs followed by this symbol are irregular. See pp.339–364 for further details.

scappare[E] ◇ *They ran away before the police came.* Sono scappati prima che arrivasse la polizia.

to **run out** [rʌn'aut] VERB
finire*[E] ◇ *The supplies have run out.* Le provviste sono finite.
◆ **to run out of** rimanere*[E] senza ◇ *We ran out of money.* Siamo rimasti senza soldi.

to **run over** [rʌn'əuvə'] VERB
investire
◆ **to get run over** essere*[E] investito

rung [rʌŋ] VERB *see* **ring**

runner ['rʌnə'] NOUN
il corridore

runner beans ['rʌnəbi:nz] NOUN PL
i fagiolini

runner-up [rʌnər'ʌp] NOUN (PL **runners-up**)
il secondo arrivato
la seconda arrivata

running ['rʌnɪŋ] NOUN
1 la corsa (*sport*) ◇ *running shoes* scarpe da corsa
2 la gestione (*management*) ◇ *the running of the business* la gestione dell'attività
◆ **running costs** costi d'esercizio MASC PL
3 l' organizzazione FEM ◇ *They have a part in the running of the competition.* Partecipano all'organizzazione della gara.
◆ **to be out of the running** non essere*[E] più in lizza

run-up [rʌnʌp] NOUN
◆ **in the run-up to Christmas** nel periodo che precede Natale

runway ['rʌnweɪ] NOUN
la pista

rural ['ruərl] ADJECTIVE
rurale

to **rush** [rʌʃ] VERB
  see also **rush** NOUN
1 affrettarsi[E] ◇ *There's no need to rush.* Non c'è bisogno di affrettarsi.
2 precipitarsi[E] ◇ *Everyone rushed outside.* Tutti si precipitarono fuori.

rush [rʌʃ] NOUN
  see also **rush** VERB
la fretta ◇ *There's no rush.* Non c'è fretta.
◆ **in a rush** in fretta
◆ **to be in a rush** avere* fretta

rush hour ['rʌʃauə'] NOUN
l' ora di punta

rusk [rʌsk] NOUN
la fetta biscottata

Russia ['rʌʃə] NOUN
la Russia

Russian ['rʌʃən] NOUN
  see also **Russian** ADJECTIVE
1 il russo
la russa
(*person*)
◆ **the Russians** i russi
2 il russo (*language*)

Russian ['rʌʃən] ADJECTIVE
  see also **Russian** NOUN
russo

rust [rʌst] NOUN
la ruggine

rusty ['rʌstɪ] ADJECTIVE
arrugginito

ruthless ['ru:θlɪs] ADJECTIVE
spietato

rye [raɪ] NOUN
la segale
◆ **rye bread** il pane di segale

R

S

Sabbath ['sæbəθ] NOUN
  [1] il sabato (*Jewish*)
  [2] la domenica (*Christian*)

sack [sæk] NOUN
  see also **sack** VERB
  il sacco (PL i sacchi) ◇ *a sack of potatoes* un sacco di patate
  ♦ **to get the sack** essere* E licenziato

to **sack** [sæk] VERB
  see also **sack** NOUN
  licenziare

sacred ['seɪkrɪd] ADJECTIVE
  sacro

sacrifice ['sækrɪfaɪs] NOUN
  il sacrificio

sad [sæd] ADJECTIVE
  triste

saddle [sædl] NOUN
  la sella

saddlebag ['sædlbæg] NOUN
  la bisaccia (PL le bisacce)

sadly ['sædlɪ] ADVERB
  [1] tristemente ◇ *"She's gone," he said sadly.* "Se n'è andata" disse tristemente.
  [2] sfortunatamente ◇ *Sadly, it was too late.* Sfortunatamente era troppo tardi.

safe [seɪf] NOUN
  see also **safe** ADJECTIVE
  la cassaforte (PL le casseforti)

safe [seɪf] ADJECTIVE
  see also **safe** NOUN
  [1] sicuro ◇ *This car isn't safe.* Questa macchina non è sicura.
  ♦ **Don't worry, it's perfectly safe.** Non preoccuparti, non c'è alcun pericolo.
  ♦ **safe to drink** potabile ◇ *Is the water safe to drink?* È potabile l'acqua?
  [2] al sicuro ◇ *You're safe now.* Ora sei al sicuro.
  ♦ **to feel safe** sentirsi* E al sicuro

safety ['seɪftɪ] NOUN
  la sicurezza ◇ *safety belt* cintura di sicurezza
  ♦ **a safety pin** una spilla da balia

Sagittarius [sædʒɪ'tɛərɪəs] NOUN
  il Sagittario ◇ *I'm Sagittarius.* Sono del Sagittario.

Sahara [sə'hɑːrə] NOUN
  ♦ **the Sahara desert** il Deserto del Sahara

said [sed] VERB *see* say

sail [seɪl] NOUN
  see also **sail** VERB
  la vela

to **sail** [seɪl] VERB
  see also **sail** NOUN
  salpare E ◇ *The boat sails at eight o'clock.* Il battello salpa alle otto.
  ♦ **to sail round the world** fare il giro del mondo a vela

sailing ['seɪlɪŋ] NOUN

  la vela (*sport*)
  ♦ **to go sailing** fare vela
  ♦ **a sailing ship** un veliero

sailor ['seɪlə'] NOUN
  il marinaio

saint [seɪnt] NOUN
  il santo

sake [seɪk] NOUN
  ♦ **for the sake of the children** per il bene dei bambini
  ♦ **for the sake of argument** a titolo d'esempio
  ♦ **For goodness sake!** Per amor del cielo!

salad ['sæləd] NOUN
  l' insalata ◇ *green salad* insalata verde
  ♦ **salad dressing** il condimento

salami [sə'lɑːmɪ] NOUN SING
  il salame

salary ['sælərɪ] NOUN (PL **salaries**)
  lo stipendio

sale [seɪl] NOUN
  [1] la vendita ◇ *the sale of the company* la vendita della ditta ◇ *on sale* in vendita
  ♦ **for sale** in vendita ◇ *The house is for sale.* La casa è in vendita.
  ♦ **"for sale"** "vendesi"
  [2] i saldi MASC PL ◇ *There's a sale on at Harrods.* Da Harrods ci sono i saldi.

sales assistant ['seɪlzəsɪstənt] NOUN
  il commesso
  la commessa

sales clerk ['seɪlzklɑːk] NOUN US
  il commesso
  la commessa

salesman ['seɪlzmən] NOUN (PL **salesmen**)
  [1] il rappresentante di commercio (*sales rep*)
  [2] il commesso (*assistant*)
  ♦ **a car salesman** un rivenditore di auto

sales rep ['seɪlzrep] NOUN
  il/la rappresentante di commercio

saleswoman ['seɪlzwumən] NOUN (PL **saleswomen**)
  [1] la rappresentante di commercio (*sales rep*)
  [2] la commessa (*assistant*)

salmon ['sæmən] NOUN
  il salmone

salon ['sælɔn] NOUN
  il salone ◇ *hair salon* il salone da parrucchiere
  ♦ **beauty salon** istituto di bellezza

saloon car [sə'luːnkɑː'] NOUN
  la berlina

salt [sɔːlt] NOUN
  il sale

salty ['sɔːltɪ] ADJECTIVE
  salato

to **salute** [sə'luːt] VERB
  fare* il saluto militare (*soldier*)

---

* Verbs followed by this symbol are irregular. See pp.339–364 for further details.

same [seɪm] ADJECTIVE

[1] stesso ◇ the same model lo stesso modello ◇ It's not the same. Non è lo stesso. ◇ It's all the same to me. Per me fa lo stesso.

[2] uguale ◇ They're exactly the same. Sono esattamente uguali.

sample ['sɑːmpl] NOUN

il campione ◇ a free sample of perfume un campione gratuito di profumo

sand [sænd] NOUN

la sabbia ◇ sand dune duna di sabbia

sandal ['sændl] NOUN

il sandalo

sandwich ['sændwɪtʃ] NOUN (PL sandwiches)

il sandwich (PL i sandwich)

sang [sæŋ] VERB see sing

sanitary napkin ['sænɪtrɪ'næpkɪn] NOUN US

l' assorbente igienico MASC (PL gli assorbenti igienici)

sanitary towel ['sænɪtrɪ'tauəl] NOUN

l' assorbente igienico MASC (PL gli assorbenti igienici)

sank [sæŋk] VERB see sink

Santa Claus [sæntə'klɔːz] NOUN

Babbo Natale

sarcastic [sɑː'kæstɪk] ADJECTIVE

sarcastico

Sardinia [sɑː'dɪnɪə] NOUN

la Sardegna

sat [sæt] VERB see sit

satchel ['sætʃl] NOUN

la cartella

satellite ['sætəlaɪt] NOUN

il satellite ◇ satellite television televisione via satellite

♦ a satellite dish un'antenna parabolica

satisfactory [sætɪs'fæktərɪ] ADJECTIVE

soddisfacente

satisfied ['sætɪsfaɪd] ADJECTIVE

soddisfatto

Saturday ['sætədɪ] NOUN

il sabato

♦ on Saturday sabato ◇ I saw her on Saturday. L'ho vista sabato.

♦ on Saturdays di sabato ◇ I go swimming on Saturdays. Vado in piscina di sabato.

♦ Saturday job

> **❶** In Gran Bretagna non si va a scuola di sabato e molti ragazzi trovano un lavoretto, comunemente chiamato **Saturday job**, per guadagnare qualcosa.

sauce [sɔːs] NOUN

la salsa

saucepan ['sɔːspən] NOUN

la pentola

saucer ['sɔːsə'] NOUN

il piattino

Saudi Arabia [saudɪə'reɪbɪə] NOUN

l' Arabia Saudita

sauna ['sɔːnə] NOUN

la sauna

sausage ['sɔsɪdʒ] NOUN

la salsiccia (PL le salsicce)

♦ a sausage roll un involtino di pasta sfoglia con salsiccia

to **save** [seɪv] VERB

[1] mettere* da parte ◇ I've saved fifty pounds already. Ho già messo da parte cinquanta sterline.

[2] risparmiare ◇ I saved money by staying in youth hostels. Ho risparmiato alloggiando negli ostelli della gioventù. ◇ It saved us time. Ci ha fatto risparmiare tempo.

[3] salvare ◇ She saved his life. Gli ha salvato la vita.

[4] memorizzare ◇ I saved the file onto a diskette. Ho memorizzato il file su un dischetto.

to **save up** [seɪv'ʌp] VERB

risparmiare ◇ I'm saving up for a new bike. Sto risparmiando per comprare una bici nuova.

savings ['seɪvɪŋz] NOUN PL

i risparmi ◇ She spent all her savings on a computer. Ha speso tutti i risparmi per comprare un computer.

savoury ['seɪvərɪ] ADJECTIVE (US savory)

salato ◇ Is it sweet or savoury? È dolce o salato?

saw [sɔː] VERB see see

saw [sɔː] NOUN

la sega (PL le seghe)

sax [sæks] NOUN (PL saxes)

il sax (PL i sax)

saxophone ['sæksəfəun] NOUN

il sassofono

to **say** [seɪ] VERB (said, said)

dire* ◇ What did he say? Cos'ha detto? ◇ David said he'd come. David ha detto che sarebbe venuto.

♦ to say again ripetere ◇ Could you say that again? Potresti ripetere?

♦ It goes without saying that... Va da sé che...

saying ['seɪɪŋ] NOUN

il detto

scale [skeɪl] NOUN

[1] la scala ◇ a large-scale map una carta geografica su larga scala

[2] la portata ◇ He underestimated the scale of the problem. Ha sottovalutato la portata del problema.

scales [skeɪlz] NOUN PL

la bilancia SING

♦ bathroom scales la bilancia pesapersone SING

scampi ['skæmpɪ] NOUN PL

gli scampi

scandal ['skændl] NOUN ☞

S

lo scandalo ◇ *It caused a scandal.* Ha fatto scandalo.

Scandinavia [skændɪ'neɪvɪə] NOUN
la Scandinavia

Scandinavian [skændɪ'neɪvɪən] ADJECTIVE
scandinavo

scar [skɑ:] NOUN
la cicatrice

scarce [skeəs] ADJECTIVE
scarso

scarcely ['skeəslɪ] ADVERB
appena ◇ *I scarcely knew him.* Lo conoscevo appena.

scare [skeəʳ] NOUN
see also **scare** VERB
lo spavento ◇ *We had a bit of a scare.* Abbiamo preso uno spavento.
♦ **a bomb scare** un allarme per sospetta presenza di una bomba

to **scare** [skeəʳ] VERB
see also **scare** NOUN
spaventare ◇ *You scared me!* Mi hai spaventato!

scarecrow ['skeəkrəʊ] NOUN
lo spaventapasseri (PL gli spaventapasseri)

scared ['skeəd] ADJECTIVE
♦ **to be scared** aver paura ◇ *Are you scared of him?* Hai paura di lui?
♦ **to be scared stiff** essere* E mezzo morto di paura

scarf [skɑ:f] NOUN (PL **scarfs** or **scarves**)
[1] la sciarpa (*woollen*)
[2] il foulard (PL i foulard) (*silk*)

scary ['skeərɪ] ADJECTIVE
♦ **to be scary** fare paura ◇ *It was really scary.* Faceva veramente paura.
♦ **a scary film** un film del brivido

scene [si:n] NOUN
la scena ◇ *It was an amazing scene.* È stata una scena incredibile.
♦ **the scene of the crime** il luogo del delitto
♦ **to make a scene** fare una scenata

scenery ['si:nərɪ] NOUN
il paesaggio

scent [sent] NOUN
il profumo

schedule ['ʃedju:l] NOUN
see also **schedule** VERB
il programma (PL i programmi) ◇ *a busy schedule* un programma fitto d'impegni
♦ **on schedule** in orario
♦ **to be behind schedule** essere E in ritardo sulla tabella di marcia

to **schedule** ['ʃedju:l] VERB
see also **schedule** NOUN
fissare ◇ *The meeting is scheduled for Monday.* La riunione è fissata per lunedì.

scheduled flight ['ʃedju:ld'flaɪt] NOUN
il volo di linea

scheme [ski:m] NOUN
il progetto ◇ *a road-widening scheme* un

progetto di ampliamento della strada

scholarship ['skɒləʃɪp] NOUN
la borsa di studio

school [sku:l] NOUN
la scuola

schoolbook ['sku:lbʊk] NOUN
il libro scolastico (PL i libri scolastici)

schoolboy ['sku:lbɔɪ] NOUN
lo scolaro

schoolchildren ['sku:ltʃɪldrən] NOUN
gli scolari

schoolgirl ['sku:lgə:l] NOUN
la scolara

science ['saɪəns] NOUN
la scienza

science fiction ['saɪəns'fɪkʃən] NOUN
la fantascienza

scientific [saɪən'tɪfɪk] ADJECTIVE
scientifico

scientist ['saɪəntɪst] NOUN
lo scienziato
la scienziata

scissors ['sɪzəz] NOUN PL
le forbici

to **scoff** [skɒf] VERB
ridere* ◇ *My friends scoffed at the idea.* I miei amici hanno riso dell'idea.

scone [skɒn] NOUN

ⓘ *Un dolcetto che si spalma di burro, marmellata e panna.*

scooter ['sku:təʳ] NOUN
[1] lo scooter (PL gli scooter) ◇ *He was riding a scooter.* Era in sella ad uno scooter.
[2] il monopattino (*for children*)

score [skɔ:ʳ] NOUN
see also **score** VERB
il punteggio ◇ *The score was three nil.* Il punteggio era tre a zero.
♦ **scores of** molti ◇ *scores of times* molte volte

to **score** [skɔ:ʳ] VERB
see also **score** NOUN
[1] segnare ◇ *He scored a goal.* Ha segnato una rete.
[2] tenere* il punteggio ◇ *Who's going to score?* Chi tiene il punteggio?
♦ **to score six out of ten** totalizzare un punteggio di sei su dieci

Scorpio ['skɔ:pɪəʊ] NOUN
lo Scorpione ◇ *I'm Scorpio.* Sono dello Scorpione.

Scot [skɒt] NOUN
lo/la scozzese

Scotch tape® ['skɒtʃteɪp] NOUN US
lo scotch ®

Scotland ['skɒtlənd] NOUN
la Scozia

Scots [skɒts] ADJECTIVE
scozzese ◇ *a Scots accent* un accento

---

* Verbs followed by this symbol are irregular. See pp.339–364 for further details.

scozzese

Scotsman ['skɔtsmən] NOUN (PL **Scotsmen**)
lo scozzese

Scotswoman ['skɔtswumən] NOUN (PL
Scotswomen)
la scozzese

Scottish ['skɔtɪʃ] ADJECTIVE
scozzese

♦ **the Scottish Parliament** il Parlamento
scozzese

> **ℹ** **Il Parlamento scozzese** è stato fondato nel
> 1999 e ha sede ad Edimburgo.

scout [skaut] NOUN
il boy-scout (PL i boy-scout)

scrambled eggs ['skræmbld'egz] NOUN PL
le uova strapazzate

scrap [skræp] NOUN
see also **scrap** VERB
il pezzo ◊ *a scrap of paper* un pezzo di carta

♦ **There wasn't a scrap of evidence.** Non c'era
la benché minima prova.

♦ **to sell for scrap** vendere come ferrovecchio

♦ **scrap iron** ferraglia

♦ **to get into a scrap** azzuffarsi ᴱ ◊ *He got into
a scrap with a bigger boy.* Si è azzuffato con
un ragazzo più grande.

to **scrap** [skræp] VERB
see also **scrap** NOUN
scartare ◊ *In the end the plan was scrapped.*
Alla fine il progetto venne scartato.

scrapbook ['skræpbuk] NOUN
l' album (PL gli album)

to **scratch** [skrætʃ] VERB
see also **scratch** NOUN
[1] grattarsi ᴱ ◊ *He scratched his head.* Si è
grattato la testa.
[2] graffiare ◊ *The cat scratched me.* Il gatto
mi ha graffiato.

scratch [skrætʃ] NOUN (PL **scratches**)
see also **scratch** VERB
il graffio (*on skin*)

♦ **to start from scratch** cominciare da zero

♦ **a scratch card** un gratta e vinci ®

scream [skriːm] NOUN
see also **scream** VERB
il grido (PL FEM le grida)

to **scream** [skriːm] VERB
see also **scream** NOUN
gridare

screen [skriːn] NOUN
lo schermo

screen saver ['skriːnseɪvə'] NOUN
lo screensaver (PL gli screensaver)

screw [skruː] NOUN
la vite

screwdriver ['skruːdraɪvə'] NOUN
il cacciavite

to **scribble** ['skrɪbl] VERB
scribacchiare

to **scrub** [skrʌb] VERB
sfregare

sculpture ['skʌlptʃə'] NOUN
la scultura

sea [siː] NOUN
il mare

seafood ['siːfuːd] NOUN
i frutti di mare MASC PL

seagull ['siːgʌl] NOUN
il gabbiano

seal [siːl] NOUN
see also **seal** VERB
[1] la foca (PL le foche) (*animal*)
[2] il sigillo (*on envelope*)

to **seal** [siːl] VERB
see also **seal** NOUN
sigillare

seaman ['siːmən] NOUN (PL **seamen**)
il marinaio

to **search** [sɜːtʃ] VERB
see also **search** NOUN

♦ **to search for** cercare ◊ *They're searching
for the missing climbers.* Stanno cercando
gli alpinisti dispersi.
[1] perquisire ◊ *The police searched him for
drugs.* La polizia l'ha perquisito alla ricerca
di droga.
[2] perlustrare ◊ *They searched the woods
for the little girl.* Hanno perlustrato i boschi
alla ricerca della bambina.

search [sɜːtʃ] NOUN (PL **searches**)
see also **search** VERB
la ricerca (PL le ricerche) ◊ *The search was
abandoned.* La ricerca fu abbandonata.

♦ **She went in search of Paul.** È andata a
cercare Paul.

search engine ['sɜːtʃendʒɪn] NOUN
il motore di ricerca

search party ['sɜːtʃpɑːtɪ] NOUN (PL **search
parties**)
la squadra di ricerca

seashore ['siːʃɔː'] NOUN
la riva del mare

seasick ['siːsɪk] ADJECTIVE

♦ **to be seasick** avere il mal di mare

seaside ['siːsaɪd] NOUN
il mare ◊ *at the seaside* al mare

♦ **seaside resort** la località balneare (PL le
località balneari)

season ['siːzn] NOUN
see also **season** VERB
la stagione ◊ *out of season* fuori stagione

♦ **during the holiday season** nel periodo delle
vacanze

♦ **a season ticket** una tessera d'abbonamento

to **season** ['siːzn] VERB
see also **season** NOUN
condire ◊ *Season with salt and pepper.*
Condite con sale e pepe.

seat [siːt] NOUN
[1] il sedile ◊ *on the back seat of the car* sul 🖙

S

Verbs followed by the symbol "E" require the auxiliary "essere"

sedile posteriore della macchina
+ **Please take a seat.** Si accomodi.
  [2] il posto ◇ *Are there any seats left?* Ci
  sono ancora posti?
  [3] il seggio ◇ *The party hopes to win more
  seats in the next election.* Il partito spera di
  ottenere più seggi alle prossime elezioni.

seat belt ['si:tbɛlt] NOUN
  la cintura di sicurezza

seaweed ['si:wi:d] NOUN
  le alghe FEM PL

second ['sɛkənd] ADJECTIVE, NOUN
  il secondo
+ **to come second** arrivare [E] secondo
+ **to travel second class** viaggiare in seconda
  classe
+ **the second of March** il due marzo
+ **to have second thoughts** ripensarci

secondary school ['sɛkəndrɪsku:l] NOUN
  la scuola secondaria

second-class ['sɛkənd'klɑ:s] ADJECTIVE,
ADVERB
+ **second-class citizen** cittadino di serie B
+ **to send a letter second-class** mandare una
  lettera per posta ordinaria

> **❶** *In Gran Bretagna, l'affrancatura*
> **second-class** *è più economica della "first
> class" e consente il recapito della posta dopo
> due o tre giorni.*

secondhand ['sɛkənd'hænd] ADJECTIVE
  di seconda mano

secondly ['sɛkəndlɪ] ADVERB
+ **firstly..., secondly...** in primo luogo..., in
  secondo luogo...

secret ['si:krɪt] ADJECTIVE, NOUN
  il segreto ◇ *a secret mission* una missione
  segreta ◇ *Can you keep a secret?* Sai tenere
  un segreto?
+ **in secret** in segreto

secretary ['sɛkrətərɪ] NOUN (PL **secretaries**)
  la segretaria

secretly ['si:krɪtlɪ] ADVERB
  segretamente

section ['sɛkʃən] NOUN
  la sezione

security [sɪ'kjuərɪtɪ] NOUN
  la sicurezza ◇ *They are trying to improve
  airport security.* Cercano di migliorare la
  sicurezza dell'aeroporto.
+ **to have no job security** non avere la
  garanzia del posto di lavoro
+ **a security guard** una guardia giurata

sedan [sɪ'dæn] NOUN US
  la berlina

to **see** [si:] VERB (**saw, seen**)
  vedere* ◇ *I can't see anything.* Non vedo
  niente. ◇ *I saw him yesterday.* L'ho visto
  ieri. ◇ *Have you seen that film?* Hai visto
  quel film?

+ **See you!** Ci vediamo!
+ **See you soon!** A presto!

to **see to** ['si:tu:] VERB
  occuparsi [E] di ◇ *The shower isn't working.
  Can you see to it please?* La doccia non
  funziona. Se ne può occupare, per favore?

seed [si:d] NOUN
  il seme ◇ *sunflower seeds* semi di girasole

to **seek** [si:k] VERB (**sought, sought**)
  cercare ◇ *people seeking work* le persone
  che cercano lavoro ◇ *They are seeking a
  solution to the problem.* Cercano di trovare
  una soluzione al problema. ◇ *He sought to
  calm them down.* Ha cercato di
  tranquillizzarli.
+ **to seek help** chiedere aiuto

to **seem** [si:m] VERB
  sembrare [E] ◇ *That seems like a good idea.*
  Mi sembra una buona idea.
+ **It seems that...** Pare che... ◇ *It seems she's
  getting married.* Pare che si sposi.

seen [si:n] VERB *see* **see**

seesaw ['si:sɔ:] NOUN
  l' altalena a bilico

see-through ['si:θru:] ADJECTIVE
  trasparente

seldom ['sɛldəm] ADVERB
  raramente

to **select** [sɪ'lɛkt] VERB
  selezionare

selection [sɪ'lɛkʃən] NOUN
  la selezione

self-assured [sɛlfə'ʃuəd] ADJECTIVE
  sicuro di sé

self-catering [sɛlf'keɪtərɪŋ] ADJECTIVE
+ **self-catering apartment** appartamento con
  cucina

self-centred [sɛlf'sɛntəd] ADJECTIVE (US
  self-centered)
  egocentrico

self-confidence [sɛlf'kɒnfɪdns] NOUN
  la fiducia in se stesso

self-conscious [sɛlf'kɒnʃəs] ADJECTIVE
  [1] impacciato ◇ *She was very
  self-conscious at first.* All'inizio era molto
  impacciata.
  [2] complessato ◇ *She was self-conscious
  about her height.* Era complessata per la
  statura.

self-contained [sɛlfkən'teɪnd] ADJECTIVE
  indipendente

self-control [sɛlfkən'trəul] NOUN
  l' autocontrollo

self-defence [sɛlfdɪ'fɛns] NOUN (US
  self-defense)
  la difesa personale ◇ *self-defence classes*
  corso di difesa personale
+ **She killed him in self-defence.** L'ha ucciso
  per legittima difesa.

self-discipline [sɛlf'dɪsɪplɪn] NOUN
  l' autodisciplina

---

* Verbs followed by this symbol are irregular. See pp.339–364 for further details.

self-employed [sɛlfɪm'plɔɪd] ADJECTIVE
- **to be self-employed** lavorare in proprio
- **the self-employed** i lavoratori autonomi

selfish ['sɛlfɪʃ] ADJECTIVE
egoista

self-respect [sɛlfrɪ'spɛkt] NOUN
la dignità

self-service [sɛlf'sɜːvɪs] ADJECTIVE
self-service MASC, FEM, PL

to **sell** [sɛl] VERB (**sold, sold**)
vendere* ◇ *They're selling the house.*
Stanno vendendo la casa. ◇ *He sold his car to his sister.* Ha venduto la macchina alla sorella.
- **Do you sell stamps?** Avete francobolli?

to **sell off** [sɛl'ɔf] VERB
svendere*

to **sell out** [sɛl'aut] VERB
andare*ᴱ esaurito ◇ *The tickets sold out in three hours.* I biglietti sono andati esauriti in tre ore.

sell-by date ['sɛlbaɪdeɪt] NOUN
la data di scadenza

Sellotape ® ['sɛləuteɪp] NOUN
lo scotch ®

semi ['sɛmɪ] NOUN
la villa bifamiliare

> **ⓘ semi** è l'abbreviazione di "semi-detached house", la tipica casa britannica costituita da due abitazioni con un muro divisorio in comune e con giardino davanti e sul retro.

semicircle ['sɛmɪsɜːkl] NOUN
il semicerchio

semicolon [sɛmɪ'kəulən] NOUN
il punto e virgola

semi-final [sɛmɪ'faɪnl] NOUN
la semifinale

semi-skimmed milk ['sɛmɪskɪmd'mɪlk] NOUN
il latte parzialmente scremato

to **send** [sɛnd] VERB (**sent, sent**)
[1] spedire ◇ *Have you sent the letter?* Hai spedito la lettera?
[2] mandare ◇ *She sent me a birthday card.* Mi ha mandato un biglietto d'auguri.

to **send back** [sɛnd'bæk] VERB
rispedire

to **send off** [sɛnd'ɔf] VERB
[1] spedire ◇ *We sent off your order yesterday.* Ieri abbiamo spedito il suo ordinativo.
[2] espellere (*player*) ◇ *He was sent off.* L'hanno espulso.

to **send off for** [sɛnd'ɔfɔːʳ] VERB
ordinare per posta
- **I'll send off for a brochure.** Mi farò spedire un depliant.

to **send out** [sɛnd'aut] VERB
inviare ◇ *She sent out a hundred invitations.* Ha inviato cento inviti.
- **to send out for** farsiᴱ portare ◇ *Let's send out for a pizza.* Facciamoci portare una pizza.

sender ['sɛndəʳ] NOUN
il/la mittente

senior ['siːnɪəʳ] ADJECTIVE, NOUN
di grado superiore ◇ *senior management* i dirigenti di grado superiore
- **She's five years my senior.** Ha cinque anni più di me.
- **senior pupils** gli studenti delle classi superiori

senior citizen ['siːnɪə'sɪtɪzən] NOUN
il pensionato
la pensionata

senior school ['siːnɪəskuːl] NOUN
il liceo

sensational [sɛn'seɪʃənl] ADJECTIVE
sensazionale

sense [sɛns] NOUN
[1] il senso ◇ *It makes sense.* Ha senso. ◇ *It doesn't make sense.* Non ha senso. ◇ *the five senses* i cinque sensi ◇ *sense of humour* senso dell'umorismo
- **a keen sense of smell** un olfatto finissimo
[2] il buonsenso ◇ *Have a bit of sense!* Un po' di buonsenso, via!

senseless ['sɛnslɪs] ADJECTIVE
[1] insensato ◇ *acts of senseless violence* atti di violenza insensata
[2] privo di sensi ◇ *She fell senseless to the ground.* Cadde a terra priva di sensi.

sensible ['sɛnsɪbl] ADJECTIVE
ragionevole ◇ *Be sensible!* Sii ragionevole! ◇ *It would be sensible to check first.* Sarebbe meglio controllare prima.
Be careful not to translate **sensible** *by* **sensibile**.

sensitive ['sɛnsɪtɪv] ADJECTIVE
sensibile

sensuous ['sɛnsjuəs] ADJECTIVE
sensuale

sent [sɛnt] VERB *see* **send**

sentence ['sɛntns] NOUN
see also **sentence** VERB
[1] la frase ◇ *He wrote a sentence.* Ha scritto una frase.
[2] la condanna ◇ *the death sentence* la condanna a morte ◇ *He served a long sentence.* Ha scontato una lunga condanna.
- **He got a life sentence.** Ha avuto l'ergastolo.

to **sentence** ['sɛntns] VERB
see also **sentence** NOUN
- **to sentence somebody to life imprisonment** condannare qualcuno all'ergastolo
- **to sentence somebody to death** condannare a morte qualcuno

sentimental [sɛntɪ'mɛntl] ADJECTIVE
sentimentale

separate ['sɛpərət] ADJECTIVE ☞

S

see also **separate** VERB

[1] separato ◇ *They have separate rooms.* Hanno camere separate.

[2] diverso ◇ *on separate occasions* in diverse occasioni

[3] altro ◇ *I wrote it on a separate sheet.* L'ho scritto su un altro foglio di carta.

to **separate** ['sepəreɪt] VERB

see also **separate** ADJECTIVE

[1] separare ◇ *The police tried to separate the two groups.* La polizia ha cercato di separare i due gruppi.

[2] separarsi [E] ◇ *They separated seven years ago.* Si sono separati sette anni fa.

separately ['seprɪtlɪ] ADVERB
separatamente

separation [sepə'reɪʃən] NOUN
la separazione

September [sep'tembə'] NOUN
settembre ◇ *in September* in settembre

sequel ['si:kwl] NOUN
il seguito

sequence ['si:kwəns] NOUN

[1] la serie ◇ *the sequence of events that led to the murder* la serie di avvenimenti che ha portato all'omicidio

[2] l'ordine MASC ◇ *in sequence* in ordine

[3] la sequenza (*in film*)

sergeant ['sɑ:dʒənt] NOUN
il sergente

serial ['sɪərɪəl] NOUN
il serial (PL i serial)

series ['sɪərɪz] NOUN (PL **series**)
la serie (PL le serie)

serious ['sɪərɪəs] ADJECTIVE

[1] serio ◇ *You're looking very serious.* Hai un'aria molto seria.

◆ **Are you serious?** Parli sul serio?

[2] grave ◇ *a serious illness* una grave malattia

seriously ['sɪərɪəslɪ] ADVERB
seriamente ◇ *We'll have to think about it seriously.* Dovremo pensarci seriamente.

◆ **No, but seriously...** No, scherzi a parte...

◆ **to take somebody seriously** prendere sul serio qualcuno

◆ **seriously injured** gravemente ferito

sermon ['sɜ:mən] NOUN
il sermone

servant ['sɜ:vənt] NOUN
il domestico (PL i domestici)
la domestica (PL le domestiche)

to **serve** [sɜ:v] VERB

see also **serve** NOUN

[1] servire ◇ *Dinner is served.* La cena è servita.

◆ **It's Agassi's turn to serve.** È Agassi al servizio.

[2] scontare (*sentence*)

◆ **to serve time** essere* [E] in prigione

◆ **It serves you right.** Ben ti sta.

serve [sɜ:v] NOUN

see also **serve** VERB
il servizio (*in tennis*)

server ['sɜ:və'] NOUN
il server (PL i server)

to **service** ['sɜ:vɪs] VERB

see also **service** NOUN
revisionare (*car*)

service ['sɜ:vɪs] NOUN

see also **service** VERB

[1] il servizio ◇ *Service is included.* Il servizio è compreso. ◇ *the postal service* il servizio postale

[2] la revisione (*of car*)

[3] la funzione (*religious*)

◆ **the armed services** le forze armate

service area ['sɜ:vɪsɛərɪə] NOUN
l'area di servizio

service charge ['sɜ:vɪstʃɑ:dʒ] NOUN
il servizio ◇ *There's no service charge.* Il servizio è compreso.

serviceman ['sɜ:vɪsmən] NOUN (PL **servicemen**)
il militare

service station ['sɜ:vɪsteɪʃən] NOUN
la stazione di servizio

serviette [sɜ:vɪ'et] NOUN
il tovagliolo

session ['seʃən] NOUN
la sessione

set [set] NOUN

see also **set** VERB

[1] la serie (PL le serie) ◇ *a set of calculations* una serie di calcoli

◆ **a set of keys** una serie completa di chiavi

◆ **The sofa and chairs are sold only as a set.** Il divano e le poltrone non si possono vendere separatamente.

◆ **a chess set** un gioco di scacchi

◆ **a train set** un trenino elettrico

[2] il set (PL i set) ◇ *She was leading five-one in the first set.* Conduceva il primo set cinque a uno.

to **set** [set] VERB (**set, set**)

see also **set** NOUN

[1] mettere* ◇ *I set the alarm for seven o'clock.* Ho messo la sveglia alle sette.

[2] stabilire ◇ *The world record was set last year.* Il record mondiale è stato stabilito l'anno scorso.

[3] tramontare ◇ *The sun was setting.* Il sole stava tramontando.

◆ **to be set** (*novel, film*) essere* [E] ambientato ◇ *The film is set in Morocco.* Il film è ambientato in Marocco.

◆ **to set sail** salpare

◆ **to set the table** apparecchiare la tavola

to **set off** [set'ɔf] VERB
partire [E] ◇ *We set off after breakfast.* Siamo partiti dopo colazione.

to **set out** [set'aut] VERB

partire[E] ◇ *We set out for London at nine o'clock.* Siamo partiti per Londra alle nove.

settee [sɛ'ti:] NOUN
il divano

settings ['sɛtɪŋz] NOUN PL
le impostazioni

to **settle** ['sɛtl] VERB
[1] risolvere* ◇ *That should settle the problem.* Questo dovrebbe risolvere il problema.
[2] saldare ◇ *I'll settle the bill tomorrow.* Salderò il conto domani.

to **settle down** [sɛtl'daun] VERB
sistemarsi[E] ◇ *I want to settle down and start a family.* Voglio sistemarmi e metter su famiglia. ◇ *Things will settle down eventually.* Le cose si sistemeranno alla fine.

to **settle in** [sɛtl'ɪn] VERB
ambientarsi[E]

to **settle on** ['sɛtlɔn] VERB
decidere* per

seven ['sɛvn] NUMERAL
sette ◇ *She's seven.* Ha sette anni.

seventeen [sɛvn'ti:n] NUMERAL
diciassette ◇ *He's seventeen.* Ha diciassette anni.

seventeenth [sɛvn'ti:nθ] ADJECTIVE
diciassettesimo ◇ *the seventeenth floor* il diciassettesimo piano
♦ **the seventeenth of August** il diciassette agosto

seventh ['sɛvnθ] ADJECTIVE
settimo ◇ *the seventh floor* il settimo piano
♦ **the seventh of August** il sette agosto

seventy ['sɛvntɪ] NUMERAL
settanta

several ['sɛvərl] ADJECTIVE, PRONOUN
diversi MASC
diverse FEM
◇ *several times* diverse volte

to **sew** [səu] VERB (**sewed, sewn**)
cucire ◇ *She was sewing.* Cuciva. ◇ *It was sewn by hand.* Era cucito a mano.

to **sew up** [səu'ʌp] VERB
rammendare

sewing ['səuɪŋ] NOUN
♦ **I like sewing.** Mi piace cucire.
♦ **a sewing machine** una macchina da cucire

sewn [səun] VERB *see* **sew**

sex [sɛks] NOUN (PL **sexes**)
il sesso ◇ *the opposite sex* il sesso opposto
♦ **to have sex with somebody** avere rapporti sessuali con qualcuno
♦ **sex education** educazione sessuale

sexism ['sɛksɪzəm] NOUN
il sessismo

sexist ['sɛksɪst] ADJECTIVE
sessista

sexual ['sɛksjuəl] ADJECTIVE
sessuale ◇ *sexual discrimination* la discriminazione sessuale ◇ *sexual harassment* molestie sessuali

sexuality [sɛksju'ælɪtɪ] NOUN
la sessualità

sexy ['sɛksɪ] ADJECTIVE
sexy MASC, FEM, PL

shabby ['ʃæbɪ] ADJECTIVE
trasandato

shade [ʃeɪd] NOUN
[1] l' ombra ◇ *It was thirty five degrees in the shade.* C'erano trentacinque gradi all'ombra.
[2] la tonalità (PL le tonalità) ◇ *a beautiful shade of blue* una bella tonalità d'azzurro

shadow ['ʃædəu] NOUN
l' ombra
♦ **the shadow cabinet** il governo ombra

to **shake** [ʃeɪk] VERB (**shook, shaken**)
[1] scuotere ◇ *Donald shook his head.* Donald scosse il capo.
[2] tremare ◇ *He was shaking with cold.* Tremava di freddo.
♦ **to shake hands with somebody** stringere* la mano a qualcuno ◇ *They shook hands.* Si strinsero la mano.

shaken ['ʃeɪkn] ADJECTIVE
scosso ◇ *I was feeling a bit shaken.* Ero un po' scosso.

shaky ['ʃeɪkɪ] ADJECTIVE
[1] incerto ◇ *The team got off to a shaky start.* La partita ha avuto un avvio incerto per la squadra.
[2] tremante ◇ *He answered in a shaky voice.* Ha risposto con voce tremante.
♦ **to feel shaky** sentirsi[E] debole

shall [ʃæl] VERB
shall I and shall we are translated by the present tense.
◇ *Shall I shut the window?* Chiudo la finestra? ◇ *Shall we ask him to come with us?* Gli chiediamo di venire con noi?
When shall means "will", it is translated by the future tense.
◇ *I shall know more next week, I hope.* Ne saprò qualcosa di più la prossima settimana, spero.

shallow ['ʃæləu] ADJECTIVE
poco profondo

shambles ['ʃæmblz] NOUN SING
il disastro ◇ *It's a complete shambles.* È un disastro totale.

shame [ʃeɪm] NOUN
la vergogna ◇ *I'd die of shame!* Morirei di vergogna!
♦ **What a shame!** Che peccato!
♦ **It's a shame that...** È un peccato che...

shampoo [ʃæm'pu:] NOUN (PL **shampoos**)
lo shampoo (PL gli shampoo)

shandy ['ʃændɪ] NOUN (PL **shandies**)
la birra con gazzosa

shan't [ʃɑːnt] = **shall not**

S

Verbs followed by the symbol "E" require the auxiliary "essere"

shape [ʃeɪp] NOUN
la forma ◊ *a strange shape* una strana forma

+ **to be in good shape** (*person*) essere^E in forma

share [ʃeəʳ] NOUN
see also **share** VERB

1 la parte ◊ *I want a fair share.* Ne voglio una parte equa.

2 l' azione FEM ◊ *They've got shares in British Gas.* Hanno delle azioni della British Gas.

3 la quota ◊ *He refused to pay his share of the bill.* Ha rifiutato di pagare la sua quota del conto.

to **share** [ʃeəʳ] VERB
see also **share** NOUN
dividere* ◊ *I share the room with Helen.* Divido la stanza con Helen.

to **share out** [ʃeəʳˈaʊt] VERB
distribuire ◊ *They shared the sweets out among the children.* Hanno distribuito i dolci ai bambini.

shark [ʃɑːk] NOUN
lo squalo

sharp [ʃɑːp] ADJECTIVE

1 affilato ◊ *Be careful, that knife's sharp!* Stai attento, quel coltello è affilato!

2 brusco e notevole ◊ *a sharp rise in prices* un brusco e notevole aumento dei prezzi

3 sveglio ◊ *She's very sharp.* È molto sveglia.

+ **at two o'clock sharp** alle due in punto

+ **a sharp bend** una curva a gomito

to **shave** [ʃeɪv] VERB
see also **shave** NOUN
farsi*^E la barba ◊ *He's shaving.* Si fa la barba.

+ **to shave one's legs** depilarsi^E le gambe

shave [ʃeɪv] NOUN
see also **shave** VERB

+ **I need a shave.** Devo farmi la barba.

+ **That was a close shave!** Ce la siamo cavata per un pelo!

shaver [ˈʃeɪvəʳ] NOUN

+ **electric shaver** rasoio elettrico

shaving cream [ˈʃeɪvɪŋkriːm] NOUN
la crema da barba

shaving foam [ˈʃeɪvɪŋfəʊm] NOUN
la schiuma da barba

she [ʃiː] PRONOUN
lei ◊ *She was fifteen then.* Allora lei aveva quindici anni.
she is often not translated.
◊ *She's very tall.* È molto alta.
lei is the pronoun used in spoken and informal written Italian. The more formal word for **she** *is "ella".*

shed [ʃed] NOUN
la rimessa

she'd [ʃiːd] = **she had, she would**

sheep [ʃiːp] NOUN (PL **sheep**)
la pecora

sheepdog [ˈʃiːpdɔg] NOUN
il cane da pastore

sheer [ʃɪəʳ] ADJECTIVE
puro ◊ *It's sheer greed.* È pura avidità.

sheet [ʃiːt] NOUN
il lenzuolo (PL FEM le lenzuola) ◊ *cotton sheets* lenzuola di cotone

+ **a sheet of paper** un foglio di carta

shelf [ʃelf] NOUN (PL **shelves**)

1 la mensola (*on wall*)

2 il ripiano (*in cupboard*)

shell [ʃel] NOUN

1 la conchiglia (*on beach, snail*)

2 il guscio ◊ *an egg shell* un guscio d'uovo

3 la granata ◊ *an unexploded shell* una granata inesplosa

she'll [ʃiːl] = **she will**

shellfish [ˈʃelfɪʃ] NOUN
i frutti di mare MASC PL

shell suit [ˈʃelsuːt] NOUN
la tuta di acetato

shelter [ˈʃeltəʳ] NOUN
il riparo

+ **to take shelter** mettersi^E al riparo

+ **a bus shelter** una pensilina d'autobus

shelves [ʃelvz] NOUN PL *see* **shelf**

shepherd [ˈʃepəd] NOUN
il pastore ◊ *a shepherd with his dog* un pastore con il suo cane

shepherd's pie [ʃepədzˈpaɪ] NOUN
timballo di patate e carne macinata, per lo più d'agnello

sheriff [ˈʃerɪf] NOUN
lo sceriffo

sherry [ˈʃerɪ] NOUN (PL **sherries**)
lo sherry (PL gli sherry)

she's [ʃiːz] = **she is, she has**

Shetland Islands [ˈʃetlənd'aɪləndz] NOUN PL
le isole Shetland

shield [ʃiːld] NOUN
lo scudo

shift [ʃɪft] NOUN
see also **shift** VERB
il turno ◊ *the night shift* il turno di notte

+ **to do shift work** fare i turni

to **shift** [ʃɪft] VERB
see also **shift** NOUN
spostare ◊ *I couldn't shift the wardrobe on my own.* Non riuscivo a spostare l'armadio da solo. ◊ *Shift yourself!* Spostati!

shifty [ˈʃɪftɪ] ADJECTIVE

1 losco ◊ *He looked shifty.* Aveva un'aria losca.

2 sfuggente (*eyes*)

shin [ʃɪn] NOUN
lo stinco (PL gli stinchi)

to **shine** [ʃaɪn] VERB (**shone, shone**)

* Verbs followed by this symbol are irregular. See pp.339–364 for further details.

splendere ◇ *The sun was shining.*
Splendeva il sole.
shiny ['ʃaɪnɪ] ADJECTIVE
lucido
ship [ʃɪp] NOUN
la nave
shipbuilding ['ʃɪpbɪldɪŋ] NOUN
la costruzione navale
shipwreck ['ʃɪprɛk] NOUN
il naufragio
shipwrecked ['ʃɪprɛkt] ADJECTIVE
✦ **to be shipwrecked** fare naufragio
shipyard ['ʃɪpjɑːd] NOUN
il cantiere navale
shirt [ʃɜːt] NOUN
la camicia (PL le camicie)
shit [ʃɪt] EXCLAMATION
merda (*rude*)
to **shiver** ['ʃɪvə'] VERB
rabbrividire ᴱ
shock [ʃɒk] NOUN
see also **shock** VERB
[1] lo shock (PL gli shock) ◇ *The news came as a shock.* La notizia è stata uno shock.
[2] la scossa ◇ *I got a shock when I touched the switch.* Quando ho toccato l'interruttore ho preso la scossa.
✦ **an electric shock** una scossa elettrica
to **shock** [ʃɒk] VERB
see also **shock** NOUN
[1] scioccare ◇ *They were shocked by what happened.* Erano scioccati per ciò che era successo.
[2] scandalizzare ◇ *After twenty years in the police nothing shocks him.* Dopo vent'anni di lavoro in polizia non lo scandalizza più niente.
shocked [ʃɒkt] ADJECTIVE
scioccato
shocking ['ʃɒkɪŋ] ADJECTIVE
[1] scandaloso ◇ *It's shocking!* È scandaloso!
[2] vergognoso ◇ *a shocking waste* uno spreco vergognoso
[3] orribile ◇ *The weather was shocking.* Il tempo era orribile.
shoe [ʃuː] NOUN
la scarpa ◇ *shoe polish* lucido per scarpe ◇ *shoe shop* negozio di scarpe
shoelace ['ʃuːleɪs] NOUN
il laccio di scarpa
shone [ʃɒn] VERB *see* **shine**
shook [ʃʊk] VERB *see* **shake**
to **shoot** [ʃuːt] VERB (**shot, shot**)
[1] colpire ◇ *He was shot by a sniper.* È stato colpito da un cecchino.
✦ **to shoot somebody dead** colpire a morte qualcuno
[2] fucilare ◇ *He was shot at dawn.* È stato fucilato all'alba.
[3] sparare ◇ *Don't shoot!* Non sparare!

◇ *He shot himself with a revolver.* Si è sparato con un revolver.
✦ **to shoot at somebody** sparare a qualcuno
[4] girare ◇ *The film was shot in Prague.* Il film è stato girato a Praga.
[5] tirare
✦ **to shoot wide** tirare a vuoto
[6] sfrecciare ◇ *A car shot past me.* Una macchina mi è sfrecciata accanto.
✦ **to shoot an arrow** scoccare una freccia
shooting ['ʃuːtɪŋ] NOUN
[1] gli spari MASC PL ◇ *They heard shooting.* Hanno sentito degli spari.
✦ **a shooting** una sparatoria
[2] la caccia ◇ *shooting and fishing* la caccia e la pesca
shop [ʃɒp] NOUN
see also **shop** VERB
il negozio ◇ *a sports shop* un negozio di articoli sportivi
✦ **the workers on the shop floor** gli operai
to **shop** [ʃɒp] VERB
see also **shop** NOUN
andare* ᴱ a fare compere ◇ *They shop in expensive stores.* Vanno a fare compere in negozi costosi.
shop assistant ['ʃɒpəsɪstənt] NOUN
il commesso
la commessa
shopkeeper ['ʃɒpkiːpə'] NOUN
il/la negoziante
shoplifting ['ʃɒplɪftɪŋ] NOUN
il taccheggio
shopping ['ʃɒpɪŋ] NOUN
la spesa ◇ *Can you get the shopping from the car?* Puoi prendere la spesa dalla macchina?
✦ **I love shopping.** Adoro fare shopping.
✦ **a shopping bag** una borsa per la spesa
✦ **a shopping centre** un centro commerciale
shop window [ʃɒp'wɪndəu] NOUN
la vetrina
shore [ʃɔː'] NOUN
la riva ◇ *boats on the shore* barche sulla riva
✦ **on shore** a terra

S

short [ʃɔːt] ADJECTIVE
[1] corto ◇ *a short skirt* una gonna corta ◇ *short hair* capelli corti
✦ **to be short of something** essere ᴱ a corto di qualcosa
[2] breve ◇ *a short break* una breve pausa ◇ *It was a great holiday, but too short.* È stata una bella vacanza, ma troppo breve.
[3] basso ◇ *She's quite short.* È piuttosto bassa.
✦ **at short notice** con poco preavviso
✦ **in short** per farla breve ◇ *In short, the answer is no.* Per farla breve, la risposta è no.
shortage ['ʃɔːtɪdʒ] NOUN
la scarsità (PL le scarsità)
short cut ['ʃɔːtkʌt] NOUN   ☞

la scorciatoia

shorthand [ˈʃɔːθænd] NOUN
la stenografia

short list [ˈʃɔːtlɪst] NOUN
la rosa dei candidati

shortly [ˈʃɔːtlɪ] ADVERB
tra poco

shorts [ʃɔːts] NOUN PL
gli shorts

short-sighted [ʃɔːtˈsaɪtɪd] ADJECTIVE
miope

short story [ˈʃɔːtˈstɔːrɪ] NOUN (PL **short stories**)
il racconto

shot [ʃɒt] VERB see **shoot**

shot [ʃɒt] NOUN
[1] lo sparo ◇ *A witness said he heard a shot.* Un testimone ha detto di aver sentito uno sparo.
[2] la foto (PL le foto) ◇ *a shot of Edinburgh castle* una foto del castello di Edimburgo
[3] l' iniezione FEM ◇ *They gave him shots.* Gli hanno fatto delle iniezioni.
♦ **to have a shot at doing something** provare a fare qualcosa
♦ **He had only one shot at goal.** Ha avuto solo una possibilità di segnare.

shotgun [ˈʃɒtgʌn] NOUN
il fucile da caccia

should [ʃʊd] VERB

> ***should** is usually translated by the conditional of **dovere**.*
>
> ◇ *You should take more exercise.* Dovresti fare più moto. ◇ *He should be there by now.* A quest'ora dovrebbe essere arrivato.
> ◇ *That shouldn't be too hard.* Non dovrebbe essere troppo difficile. ◇ *I should have told you before.* Avrei dovuto dirtelo prima.

♦ **I should go if I were you.** Se fossi in te ci andrei.
♦ **I should be so lucky!** Sarebbe bello!

shoulder [ˈʃəʊldəʳ] NOUN
la spalla ◇ *broad shoulders* spalle larghe
♦ **a shoulder bag** una borsa a tracolla

shoulder blade [ˈʃəʊldəbleɪd] NOUN
la scapola

shouldn't [ˈʃʊdnt] = **should not**

to **shout** [ʃaʊt] VERB
see also **shout** NOUN
urlare ◇ *Don't shout!* Non urlare! ◇ *"Go away!" he shouted.* "Vattene!" urlò.

shout [ʃaʊt] NOUN
see also **shout** VERB
l' urlo (PL FEM le urla)

shovel [ˈʃʌvl] NOUN
la pala

show [ʃəʊ] NOUN
see also **show** VERB
[1] lo spettacolo ◇ *We're seeing a show this evening.* Stasera andiamo a vedere uno spettacolo.

♦ **a fashion show** una sfilata di moda
♦ **the motor show** il salone dell'automobile
[2] il programma (PL i programmi) (*on TV*)
◇ *He's now got his own show.* Ora ha un suo programma.
[3] la dimostrazione ◇ *a show of strength* una dimostrazione di forza

to **show** [ʃəʊ] VERB (**showed, shown**)
see also **show** NOUN
[1] mostrare
♦ **to show somebody something** mostrare qualcosa a qualcuno ◇ *He showed me the flat he shares with Emma.* Mi ha mostrato l'appartamento che divide con Emma.
◇ *Have you shown the article to your boss?* Hai mostrato l'articolo al tuo capo?
[2] dimostrare ◇ *She showed great courage.* Ha dimostrato un gran coraggio.
♦ **It shows.** Si vede. ◇ *I've never been riding before. – It shows.* Non sono mai andato a cavallo prima d'ora. – Si vede.

to **show off** [ʃəʊˈɒf] VERB
mettersi*ᴱ in mostra

to **show up** [ʃəʊˈʌp] VERB
presentarsiᴱ ◇ *He showed up late as usual.* Si è presentato in ritardo, come al solito.

show business [ˈʃəʊbɪznɪs] NOUN
il mondo dello spettacolo

shower [ˈʃaʊəʳ] NOUN
[1] la doccia (PL le docce) (*in bathroom*)
♦ **to have a shower** fare la doccia
[2] il rovescio (*of rain*)

showerproof [ˈʃaʊəpruːf] ADJECTIVE
impermeabile

showing [ˈʃəʊɪŋ] NOUN
la proiezione (*of film*)

shown [ʃəʊn] VERB see **show**

show-off [ˈʃəʊɒf] NOUN (PL **show-offs**)
l' esibizionista MASC / FEM

shrank [ʃræŋk] VERB see **shrink**

to **shriek** [ʃriːk] VERB
strillare

shrimps [ʃrɪmps] NOUN PL
i gamberetti

to **shrink** [ʃrɪŋk] VERB (**shrank, shrunk**)
restringersi*ᴱ ◇ *My sweater shrank in the wash.* Il mio maglione si è ristretto durante il lavaggio. ◇ *All my jumpers have shrunk.* Mi si sono ristretti tutti i maglioni.

Shrove Tuesday [ʃrəʊvˈtjuːzdɪ] NOUN
il martedì grasso

> ❶ *In occasione dello* **Shrove Tuesday** *in Gran Bretagna è tradizione mangiare "pancakes", le crêpe.*

to **shrug** [ʃrʌg] VERB
♦ **to shrug one's shoulders** fare* spallucce

shrunk [ʃrʌŋk] VERB see **shrink**

to **shudder** [ˈʃʌdəʳ] VERB
rabbrividireᴱ

to **shuffle** ['ʃʌfl] VERB
strascicare i piedi ◇ *She shuffled along the corridor.* Strascicava i piedi lungo il corridoio.
- **to shuffle the cards** mescolare le carte

to **shut** [ʃʌt] VERB (**shut, shut**)
chiudere* ◇ *What time do the shops shut?* A che ora chiudono i negozi?

to **shut down** [ʃʌt'daun] VERB
chiudere* i battenti ◇ *The cinema shut down last year.* Il cinema ha chiuso i battenti l'anno scorso.

to **shut off** [ʃʌt'ɔf] VERB
spegnere*

to **shut up** [ʃʌt'ʌp] VERB
stare* zitto ◇ *Shut up!* Stai zitto!

shutters ['ʃʌtəz] NOUN PL
le imposte

shuttle ['ʃʌtl] NOUN
la navetta

shuttlecock ['ʃʌtlkɔk] NOUN
il volano

shy [ʃaɪ] ADJECTIVE
timido

Sicily ['sɪsɪlɪ] NOUN
la Sicilia

sick [sɪk] ADJECTIVE
[1] malato ◇ *She looks after her sick mother.* Si occupa della madre malata.
[2] di cattivo gusto ◇ *That's really sick!* È veramente di cattivo gusto!
- **to be sick** vomitare ◇ *I was sick twice last night.* Ho vomitato due volte, ieri notte.
- **I feel sick.** Ho la nausea.
- **to be sick of something** averne abbastanza di qualcosa ◇ *I'm sick of your lies.* Ne ho abbastanza delle tue bugie.

sickening ['sɪknɪŋ] ADJECTIVE
nauseante

sick leave ['sɪkliːv] NOUN
il congedo per malattia

sickness ['sɪknɪs] NOUN (PL **sicknesses**)
la malattia

sick note ['sɪknəut] NOUN
[1] la giustificazione per assenza (*for pupil*)
[2] il certificato di malattia (*for employee*)

sick pay ['sɪkpeɪ] NOUN
indennità di malattia e infortuni

side [saɪd] NOUN
[1] il lato ◇ *He was driving on the wrong side of the road.* Guidava sul lato sbagliato della strada.
- **a side entrance** un ingresso laterale
[2] il bordo ◇ *at the side of the road* sul bordo della strada
- **by the side of the lake** sulla riva del lago
[3] il fianco (PL i fianchi) ◇ *She was lying on her side.* Era sdraiata su un fianco. ◇ *side by side* fianco a fianco
[4] la parte ◇ *I'm on your side* Sto dalla tua parte.

- **to take sides with somebody** schierarsi E con qualcuno
[5] la squadra ◇ *Manchester was the stronger side.* Il Manchester era la squadra più forte.

sideboard ['saɪdbɔːd] NOUN
la credenza

side-effect ['saɪdɪfɛkt] NOUN
l'effetto collaterale

side street ['saɪdstriːt] NOUN
la traversa

sidewalk ['saɪdwɔːk] NOUN US
il marciapiede

sideways ['saɪdweɪz] ADVERB
di lato ◇ *I took a step sideways.* Ho fatto un passo di lato.
- **sideways on** di profilo

sieve [sɪv] NOUN
il setaccio

sigh [saɪ] NOUN
see also **sigh** VERB
il sospiro

to **sigh** [saɪ] VERB
see also **sigh** NOUN
sospirare

sight [saɪt] NOUN
[1] la vista ◇ *My sight is failing.* La vista mi sta calando.
- **to know somebody by sight** conoscere di vista qualcuno
- **in sight** visibile
- **Keep out of sight!** Non farti vedere!
[2] lo spettacolo ◇ *It was an amazing sight.* Era uno spettacolo incredibile.
- **the sights** le attrazioni turistiche
- **to see the sights of London** visitare Londra

sightseeing ['saɪtsiːɪŋ] NOUN
- **to go sightseeing** fare un giro turistico

sign [saɪn] NOUN
see also **sign** VERB
[1] il cartello ◇ *There was a big sign saying "private".* C'era un grande cartello con la scritta "privato".
- **a road sign** un segnale stradale
[2] il segno ◇ *There's no sign of improvement.* Non c'è alcun segno di miglioramento. ◇ *What sign are you?* Di che segno sei?

to **sign** [saɪn] VERB
see also **sign** NOUN
firmare ◇ *Sign here, please.* Firmi qui, per favore.

to **sign up** [saɪn'ʌp] VERB
iscriversi* E
- **to sign up for** iscriversi* E a

signal ['sɪgnl] NOUN
see also **signal** VERB
il segnale

to **signal** ['sɪgnl] VERB
see also **signal** NOUN
- **to signal to somebody** fare* segno a ☞

S

qualcuno

signature ['sɪgnətʃə'] NOUN
la firma ◊ *a petition containing one thousand signatures* una petizione con mille firme

signature tune ['sɪgnətʃətjuːn] NOUN
la sigla musicale

significance [sɪg'nɪfɪkəns] NOUN
l' importanza

significant [sɪg'nɪfɪkənt] ADJECTIVE
[1] importante ◊ *a significant development* uno sviluppo importante
[2] notevole ◊ *a significant improvement* un miglioramento notevole

sign language ['saɪnlæŋgwɪdʒ] NOUN
il linguaggio dei segni

signpost ['saɪnpəʊst] NOUN
l' indicatore stradale MASC

silence ['saɪləns] NOUN
il silenzio

silent ['saɪlənt] ADJECTIVE
silenzioso

silicon ['sɪlɪkən] NOUN
il silicio
*Be careful not to translate **silicon** by **silicone**.*

silicon chip ['sɪlɪkən'tʃɪp] NOUN
il chip (PL i chip)

silicone ['sɪlɪkəʊn] NOUN
il silicone

silk [sɪlk] NOUN
la seta ◊ *a silk scarf* un foulard di seta

silky ['sɪlkɪ] ADJECTIVE
di seta

silly ['sɪlɪ] ADJECTIVE
sciocco

silver ['sɪlvə'] NOUN
l' argento ◊ *a silver medal* una medaglia d'argento

similar ['sɪmɪlə'] ADJECTIVE
simile

simple ['sɪmpl] ADJECTIVE
[1] semplice ◊ *The answer is simple.* La risposta è semplice.
◆ **the simple past** il passato semplice
[2] sprovveduto ◊ *He's a bit simple.* È un po' sprovveduto.

simply ['sɪmplɪ] ADVERB
semplicemente

simultaneous [sɪməl'teɪnɪəs] ADJECTIVE
simultaneo

sin [sɪn] NOUN
see also **sin** VERB
il peccato

to **sin** [sɪn] VERB .
see also **sin** NOUN
peccare

since [sɪns] PREPOSITION, ADVERB, CONJUNCTION
[1] da ◊ *since Christmas* da Natale ◊ *since then* da allora
When describing a state or action that started in the past and is still continuing, translate

since *by* **da** *and use the present tense of the Italian verb.*
◊ *I've been here since the beginning of June.* Sono qua dall'inizio di giugno.
◊ *We've been waiting for him since three o'clock.* Siamo qui ad aspettarlo dalle tre.
[2] da allora ◊ *I haven't seen him since.* Non lo vedo da allora.
◆ **ever since** da allora
[3] da quando ◊ *I haven't seen her since she left.* Non l'ho più vista da quando è partita.
[4] dato che ◊ *Since you're tired, let's stay at home.* Dato che sei stanco restiamo a casa.

sincere [sɪn'sɪə'] ADJECTIVE
sincero

sincerely [sɪn'sɪəlɪ] ADVERB
◆ **Yours sincerely...** Distinti saluti...

to **sing** [sɪŋ] VERB (**sang, sung**)
cantare ◊ *She sang in the school choir.* Cantava nel coro della scuola. ◊ *He has sung in the choir for two years.* Canta nel coro da due anni.

singer ['sɪŋə'] NOUN
il/la cantante

singing ['sɪŋɪŋ] NOUN
il canto

single ['sɪŋgl] ADJECTIVE
see also **single** NOUN
[1] singolo ◊ *a single room* una stanza singola
[2] solo ◊ *She hadn't said a single word.* Non aveva detto una sola parola.
◆ **a single bed** un letto a una piazza
◆ **in single file** in fila indiana
[3] single MASC, FEM, PL ◊ *a single mother* una madre single
◆ **a single parent** un genitore che alleva i figli da solo
◆ **a single parent family** una famiglia monoparentale

single ['sɪŋgl] NOUN
see also **single** ADJECTIVE
[1] il biglietto di sola andata ◊ *A single to Oxford, please.* Un biglietto di sola andata per Oxford, per favore.
[2] il singolo ◊ *a CD single* un CD singolo

singles ['sɪŋglz] NOUN PL
il singolare SING ◊ *the women's singles* il singolare femminile

singular ['sɪŋgjulə'] NOUN
il singolare ◊ *in the singular* al singolare

sinister ['sɪnɪstə'] ADJECTIVE
sinistro

sink [sɪŋk] NOUN
see also **sink** VERB
[1] il lavello (*in kitchen*)
[2] il lavandino (*in bathroom*)

to **sink** [sɪŋk] VERB (**sank, sunk**)
see also **sink** NOUN
affondare ◊ *The ship sank.* La nave è affondata. ◊ *The ship was sunk in the war.*

* Verbs followed by this symbol are irregular. See pp.339–364 for further details.

La nave venne affondata durante la guerra.

sir [sɜ'] NOUN
il signore

siren ['saɪərn] NOUN
la sirena

sister ['sɪstə'] NOUN
[1] la sorella ◊ *This is my sister.* Questa è mia sorella.
[2] l' infermiera caposala (PL le infermiere caposala) ◊ *She's a sister at the infirmary.* È infermiera caposala all'ospedale.

sister-in-law ['sɪstərɪnlɔ:] NOUN (PL **sisters-in-law**)
la cognata

to **sit** [sɪt] VERB (**sat, sat**)
essere* E seduto ◊ *He was sitting in front of the TV.* Era seduto davanti alla TV. ◊ *We sat in the front row.* Eravamo seduti in prima fila.
◆ **to sit an exam** sostenere* un esame

to **sit down** [sɪt'daʊn] VERB
sedersi* E ◊ *He sat down at his desk.* Si sedette alla scrivania.

sitcom ['sɪtkɔm] NOUN
la situation comedy (PL le situation comedy)

site [saɪt] NOUN
[1] il luogo (PL i luoghi) ◊ *the site of the disaster* il luogo del disastro
[2] il campeggio (*for tents*)
[3] il sito (*website*)
◆ **to visit a site** visitare un sito
◆ **an archaeological site** una zona archeologica

sitting room ['sɪtɪŋru:m] NOUN
il soggiorno

situated ['sɪtjueɪtɪd] ADJECTIVE
◆ **to be situated** essere E situato

situation [sɪtju'eɪʃən] NOUN
la situazione

six [sɪks] NUMERAL
sei ◊ *He's six.* Ha sei anni.

sixteen [sɪks'ti:n] NUMERAL
sedici ◊ *He's sixteen.* Ha sedici anni.

sixteenth [sɪks'ti:nθ] ADJECTIVE
sedicesimo ◊ *the sixteenth floor* il sedicesimo piano
◆ **the sixteenth of August** il sedici agosto

sixth [sɪksθ] ADJECTIVE
sesto ◊ *the sixth floor* il sesto piano
◆ **the sixth of August** il sei agosto
◆ **sixth form**
gli ultimi due anni della scuola superiore

❶ *Dopo la scuola dell'obbligo, e quindi dopo i 16 anni, si può continuare gli studi per due anni frequentando la "lower sixth form" e la "upper sixth form" e preparando gli esami "A levels" da sostenere a 18 anni.*

sixty ['sɪkstɪ] NUMERAL
sessanta

size [saɪz] NOUN
[1] la grandezza ◊ *plates of various sizes* piatti di varia grandezza
◆ **to be the size of** essere E grande come ◊ *Leeds is about the size of Florence.* Leeds è grande più o meno come Firenze.
[2] la taglia ◊ *What size do you take?* Che taglia porti?
[3] il numero (*of shoes*)

to **skate** [skeɪt] VERB
pattinare
◆ **to go skating** fare* pattinaggio
◆ **figure skating** pattinaggio artistico
◆ **skating rink** pista di pattinaggio

skateboard ['skeɪtbɔ:d] NOUN
lo skateboard (PL gli skateboard)

skateboarding ['skeɪtbɔ:dɪŋ] NOUN
◆ **I like skateboarding.** Mi piace andare sullo skateboard.

skates [skeɪts] NOUN PL
i pattini

skating ['skeɪtɪŋ] NOUN
il pattinaggio

skeleton ['skelɪtn] NOUN
lo scheletro

sketch [sketʃ] NOUN (PL **sketches**)
[see also **sketch** VERB]
l' abbozzo
◆ **sketch pad** blocco per schizzi

to **sketch** [sketʃ] VERB
[see also **sketch** NOUN]
abbozzare (*picture*)

to **ski** [ski:] VERB
[see also **ski** NOUN]
sciare
◆ **to go skiing** andare* E a sciare

ski [ski:] NOUN
[see also **ski** VERB]
lo sci (PL gli sci)
◆ **ski boots** scarponi da sci
◆ **ski lift** impianto di risalita
◆ **ski pants** pantaloni da sci
◆ **ski pass** ski pass
◆ **ski pole** bastoncino da sci
◆ **ski slope** pista da sci
◆ **ski suit** tuta da sci

to **skid** [skɪd] VERB
scivolare E

skier ['skɪə'] NOUN
lo sciatore
la sciatrice

skiing ['ski:ɪŋ] NOUN
lo sci (*sport*)
◆ **to go on a skiing holiday** fare una vacanza sulla neve

skilful ['skɪlful] ADJECTIVE (**skillful**) US
abile

skill [skɪl] NOUN
la capacità (PL le capacità) ◊ *It requires a lot of skill.* Richiede molta abilità.

skilled [skɪld] ADJECTIVE

S

* **a skilled worker** un operaio specializzato

skimmed milk [skɪmd'mɪlk] NOUN
il latte scremato

skimpy ['skɪmpɪ] ADJECTIVE
1 succinto (clothes)
2 frugale (meal)

skin [skɪn] NOUN
la pelle ◇ skin cancer cancro della pelle

skinhead ['skɪnhɛd] NOUN
il/la skinhead (PL gli/le skinhead)

skinny ['skɪnɪ] ADJECTIVE
magro

skin-tight ['skɪntaɪt] ADJECTIVE
aderente

skip [skɪp] NOUN
see also **skip** VERB
la benna

to **skip** [skɪp] VERB
see also **skip** NOUN
saltare ◇ You should never skip breakfast.
Non si dovrebbe mai saltare la colazione.

* **to skip school** marinare la scuola

skirt [skəːt] NOUN
la gonna

skittles ['skɪtlz] NOUN PL
i birilli

to **skive** [skaɪv] VERB
fare* il lavativo ◇ It's Monday morning, and
she's skiving as usual. È lunedì mattina e
come al solito fa la lavativa.

* **to skive off school** marinare la scuola

skull [skʌl] NOUN
1 il cranio (of someone alive)
2 il teschio (of skeleton)

sky [skaɪ] NOUN (PL **skies**)
il cielo

skyscraper ['skaɪskreɪpə'] NOUN
il grattacielo

slack [slæk] ADJECTIVE
1 allentato (rope)
2 negligente (person)

to **slag off** [slæg'ɔf] VERB
sputtanare

to **slam** [slæm] VERB
sbattere ◇ She slammed the door. Ha
sbattuto la porta.

slang [slæŋ] NOUN
il gergo

slap [slæp] NOUN
see also **slap** VERB
lo schiaffo

to **slap** [slæp] VERB
see also **slap** NOUN
dare* uno schiaffo a

slate [sleɪt] NOUN
1 l'ardesia ◇ a slate roof un tetto
d'ardesia
2 la tegola d'ardesia ◇ a missing slate una
tegola d'ardesia mancante

sledge [slɛdʒ] NOUN
la slitta

sledging ['slɛdʒɪŋ] NOUN
* **to go sledging** andare[E] in slitta

sleep [sliːp] NOUN
see also **sleep** VERB
il sonno ◇ a couple of hours' sleep un paio
di ore di sonno

* **to walk in one's sleep** camminare nel sonno
* **to go to sleep** addormentarsi[E]

to **sleep** [sliːp] VERB (**slept, slept**)
see also **sleep** NOUN
dormire* ◇ I couldn't sleep last night. Ieri
notte non riuscivo a dormire. ◇ The baby
slept during the journey. Il bambino ha
dormito lungo il tragitto.

to **sleep around** [sliːpə'raʊnd] VERB
andare*[E] a letto con tutti

to **sleep in** [sliːp'ɪn] VERB
dormire* fino a tardi

to **sleep together** ['sliːptəgɛðə'] VERB
avere* rapporti sessuali

to **sleep with** ['sliːpwɪð] VERB
andare*[E] a letto con

sleeping bag ['sliːpɪŋbæg] NOUN
il sacco a pelo (PL i sacchi a pelo)

sleeping car ['sliːpɪŋkɑː'] NOUN
il vagone letto (PL i vagoni letto)

sleeping pill ['sliːpɪŋpɪl] NOUN
il sonnifero

sleepy ['sliːpɪ] ADJECTIVE
* **to feel sleepy** essere[E] assonnato
* **a sleepy little village** un paesino tranquillo

sleet [sliːt] NOUN
il nevischio

sleeve [sliːv] NOUN
1 la manica (PL le maniche) (of shirt, coat)
2 la copertina (of record)

sleigh [sleɪ] NOUN
lo slittino

slept [slɛpt] VERB see **sleep**

slice [slaɪs] NOUN
see also **slice** VERB
la fetta

to **slice** [slaɪs] VERB
see also **slice** NOUN
affettare

slick [slɪk] NOUN
see also **slick** ADJECTIVE
* **an oil slick** una chiazza di petrolio

slick [slɪk] ADJECTIVE
see also **slick** NOUN
impeccabile ◇ a slick performance una
performance impeccabile

to **slide** [slaɪd] VERB (**slid, slid**)
see also **slide** NOUN
scivolare[E]

slide [slaɪd] NOUN
see also **slide** VERB
1 lo scivolo ◇ some swings and a slide
alcune altalene ed uno scivolo
2 la diapositiva ◇ He showed us his slides.
Ci ha mostrato le sue diapositive.

---

* Verbs followed by this symbol are irregular. See pp.339–364 for further details.

English ~ Italian

[3] il fermacapelli (PL i fermacapelli) (for hair)

slight [slaɪt] ADJECTIVE
+ **a slight problem** un piccolo problema
+ **a slight improvement** un leggero miglioramento

slightly ['slaɪtlɪ] ADVERB
leggermente ◇ They are slightly more expensive. Sono leggermente più costosi.

slim [slɪm] ADJECTIVE
see also **slim** VERB
magro

to **slim** [slɪm] VERB
see also **slim** ADJECTIVE
dimagrire ◇ She's trying to slim. Sta cercando di dimagrire.
+ **I'm slimming.** Sono a dieta.

sling [slɪŋ] NOUN
see also **sling** VERB
la fascia a tracolla

to **sling** [slɪŋ] VERB (**slung, slung**)
see also **sling** NOUN
buttare ◇ He slung his bag onto the back seat. Ha buttato la borsa sul sedile posteriore.

slip [slɪp] NOUN
see also **slip** VERB
[1] lo sbaglio ◇ There must be no slips. Non ci devono essere sbagli.
[2] la sottoveste ◇ a white slip una sottoveste bianca
+ **a slip of paper** un pezzo di carta
+ **a slip of the tongue** un lapsus
+ **slip road** rampa di accesso

to **slip** [slɪp] VERB
see also **slip** NOUN
scivolare[E] ◇ He slipped on the ice. È scivolato sul ghiaccio.

to **slip up** [slɪpʌp] VERB
fare* un errore

slipper ['slɪpə'] NOUN
le pantofola

slippery ['slɪpərɪ] ADJECTIVE
scivoloso

slip-up ['slɪpʌp] NOUN
lo sbaglio

slope [sləʊp] NOUN
il pendio ◇ a steep slope un pendio ripido

sloppy ['slɒpɪ] ADJECTIVE
trascurato

slot [slɒt] NOUN
[1] la fessura ◇ Put the money in the slot. Inserite il denaro nella fessura.
[2] lo spazio (in programme)

slot machine ['slɒtməʃiːn] NOUN
la slot-machine (PL le slot-machine)

slow [sləʊ] ADJECTIVE, ADVERB
lento ◇ a slow lorry un camion lento
+ **in slow motion** al rallentatore
+ **to go slow** andare[E] piano ◇ Go slower! Vai più piano!
+ **The clock's slow.** L'orologio è indietro.

to **slow down** [sləʊ'daʊn] VERB
rallentare
Use "essere" to form past tenses when rallentare does not have an object.

slowly ['sləʊlɪ] ADVERB
lentamente

slug [slʌg] NOUN
la lumaca (PL le lumache)

slum [slʌm] NOUN
il quartiere povero

slush [slʌʃ] NOUN
la fanghiglia

sly [slaɪ] ADJECTIVE
scaltro ◇ She's sly! È scaltra!
+ **a sly smile** un sorriso sornione

smack [smæk] NOUN
see also **smack** VERB
il ceffone

to **smack** [smæk] VERB
see also **smack** NOUN
dare* un ceffone a

small [smɔːl] ADJECTIVE
piccolo ◇ a small car una macchina piccola
+ **small change** spiccioli MASC PL
+ **small talk** chiacchiere FEM PL

smart [smɑːt] ADJECTIVE
[1] elegante ◇ a smart navy blue suit un elegante vestito blu
[2] intelligente ◇ He thinks he's smarter than Sarah. Pensa di essere più intelligente di Sarah.

smart card ['smɑːtkɑːd] NOUN
la smart card (PL le smart card)

smash [smæʃ] NOUN (PL **smashes**)
see also **smash** VERB
lo scontro

to **smash** [smæʃ] VERB
see also **smash** NOUN
[1] rompere* ◇ They smashed the windows. Hanno rotto le finestre.
[2] rompersi*[E] ◇ The glass smashed. Il bicchiere si è rotto.
+ **to smash into tiny pieces** andare*[E] in frantumi

smashing ['smæʃɪn] ADJECTIVE
formidabile ◇ I think he's smashing. Io lo trovo formidabile.

smell [smɛl] NOUN
see also **smell** VERB
l' odore MASC ◇ a nice smell un buon odore
+ **the sense of smell** l'odorato

to **smell** [smɛl] VERB (**smelled** or **smelt, smelled** or **smelt**)
see also **smell** NOUN
[1] puzzare ◇ That dog smells! Quel cane puzza!
+ **to smell of something** avere odore di qualcosa ◇ It smells of petrol. Ha odore di benzina.
[2] sentire odore di ◇ I can smell gas. Sento odore di gas.

S

smelly ['smɛlɪ] ADJECTIVE
puzzolente

smile [smaɪl] NOUN
see also **smile** VERB
il sorriso

to **smile** [smaɪl] VERB
see also **smile** NOUN
sorridere*

smiley ['smaɪlɪ] NOUN
la faccina

smoke [sməʊk] NOUN
see also **smoke** VERB
il fumo

to **smoke** [sməʊk] VERB
see also **smoke** NOUN
fumare
   ♦ **to stop smoking** smettere* di fumare

smoker ['sməʊkə'] NOUN
il fumatore
la fumatrice

smoking ['sməʊkɪŋ] NOUN
   ♦ **Smoking is bad for you.** Il fumo fa male.
   ♦ **"no smoking"** "vietato fumare"

smooth [smu:ð] ADJECTIVE
   [1] liscio ◊ *It keeps your skin soft and smooth.* Mantiene la pelle morbida e liscia.
   [2] mellifluo ◊ *He's too smooth for my liking.* È troppo mellifluo per i miei gusti.

smudge [smʌdʒ] NOUN
la sbavatura

smug [smʌg] ADJECTIVE
compiaciuto

to **smuggle** ['smʌgl] VERB
contrabbandare ◊ *They smuggle arms and drugs.* Contrabbandano armi e droga.
   ♦ **to smuggle in** far* entrare di contrabbando
   ♦ **to smuggle out** far* uscire clandestinamente

smuggler ['smʌglə'] NOUN
il contrabbandiere
la contrabbandiera

smuggling ['smʌglɪŋ] NOUN
il contrabbando

smutty ['smʌtɪ] ADJECTIVE
sconcio ◊ *a smutty magazine* un giornale sconcio
   ♦ **smutty jokes** barzellette sporche FEM PL

snack [snæk] NOUN
lo spuntino
   ♦ **to have a snack** fare uno spuntino

snack bar ['snækbɑ:'] NOUN
lo snack bar (PL gli snack bar)

snail [sneɪl] NOUN
la lumaca (PL le lumache)

snake [sneɪk] NOUN
il serpente

to **snap** [snæp] VERB
spezzare^E di netto ◊ *The branch snapped.* Il ramo si è spezzato di netto.
   ♦ **to snap one's fingers** schioccare le dita

snapshot ['snæpʃɔt] NOUN

la foto (PL le foto)

to **snarl** [snɑ:l] VERB
ringhiare

to **snatch** [snætʃ] VERB
   ♦ **to snatch something from somebody** strappare a qualcosa a qualcuno ◊ *He snatched the keys from my hand.* Mi ha strappato di mano le chiavi.
   ♦ **My bag was snatched.** Mi hanno scippato.

to **sneak** [sni:k] VERB
   ♦ **to sneak a look at something** dare* una sbirciatina a qualcosa
   ♦ **to sneak in** entrare*^E di nascosto
   ♦ **to sneak out** uscire*^E di nascosto
   ♦ **to sneak up on** avvicinarsi^E senza far rumore

sneaker ['sni:kə'] NOUN [US]
la scarpa da ginnastica

to **sneeze** [sni:z] VERB
starnutire

to **sniff** [snɪf] VERB
   [1] tirare su col naso ◊ *Stop sniffing!* Smettila di tirare su col naso!
   [2] annusare ◊ *The dog sniffed my hand.* Il cane mi ha annusato la mano.
   ♦ **to sniff glue** sniffare colla

snob [snɔb] NOUN
lo/la snob (PL gli/le snob)

snooker ['snu:kə'] NOUN
il biliardo

snooze [snu:z] NOUN
il pisolino
   ♦ **to have a snooze** fare un pisolino

to **snore** [snɔ:'] VERB
russare

snow [snəʊ] NOUN
see also **snow** VERB
la neve

to **snow** [snəʊ] VERB
see also **snow** NOUN
nevicare ◊ *It's snowing.* Nevica.

snowball ['snəʊbɔ:l] NOUN
la palla di neve

snowflake ['snəʊfleɪk] NOUN
il fiocco di neve (PL i fiocchi di neve)

snowman ['snəʊmæn] NOUN (PL **snowmen**)
il pupazzo di neve

so [səʊ] CONJUNCTION, ADVERB
   [1] così ◊ *It was raining, so I got wet.* Pioveva, e così mi sono bagnato. ◊ *It was so heavy!* Era così pesante! ◊ *He was talking so fast I couldn't understand.* Parlava così in fretta che non capivo. ◊ *That's not so.* Non è così.
   [2] allora ◊ *So, have you always lived in London?* Allora, hai sempre vissuto a Londra?
   ♦ **So what?** E con questo?
   ♦ **How's your father? – Not so good.** Come sta tuo padre? – Non tanto bene.
   ♦ **so much** tanto ◊ *I love you so much.* Ti

---

* Verbs followed by this symbol are irregular. See pp.339–364 for further details.

voglio tanto bene. ◇ *I've got so much work.* Ho tanto lavoro.

• **so many** tanti ◇ *I've got so many things to do today.* Ho così tante cose da fare oggi.

• **so do I** anch'io ◇ *I love horses. – So do I.* Adoro i cavalli. – Anch'io.

• **so have we** anche noi ◇ *I've been waiting for an hour. – So have we.* È un'ora che aspetto. – Anche noi.

• **I think so.** Penso di sì.

• **I hope so.** Lo spero.

• **so far** finora ◇ *It's been easy so far.* Finora è stato facile.

• **so far so good** fin qui tutto bene

• **ten or so people** circa una decina di persone

• **at five o'clock or so** verso le cinque

to **soak** [səuk] VERB
mettere* in ammollo ◇ *Soak it in cold water.* Mettilo in ammollo nell'acqua fredda.

• **to soak up the sun** rosolarsi ^E al sole

soaked [səukt] ADJECTIVE
bagnato fradicio

soaking ['səukɪŋ] ADJECTIVE
zuppo ◇ *Your shoes are soaking.* Hai le scarpe zuppe.

soap [səup] NOUN
  1. il sapone (*to wash with*)
  2. la soap opera (PL le soap opera) (*on TV*)

soap powder ['səuppaudə'] NOUN
il detersivo in polvere

to **sob** [sɔb] VERB
singhiozzare

sober ['səubə'] ADJECTIVE
sobrio

to **sober up** [səubər'ʌp] VERB
smaltire la sbornia

soccer ['sɔkə'] NOUN
il calcio ◇ *a game of soccer* una partita di calcio

• **a soccer player** un calciatore

social ['səuʃl] ADJECTIVE
sociale ◇ *social problems* problemi sociali

socialism ['səuʃəlɪzəm] NOUN
il socialismo

socialist ['səuʃəlɪst] NOUN
see also **socialist** ADJECTIVE
il/la socialista

socialist ['səuʃəlɪst] ADJECTIVE
see also **socialist** NOUN
socialista

social security ['səuʃəlsɪ'kuərɪti] NOUN
la previdenza sociale

• **to be on social security** ricevere sussidi dalla previdenza sociale

social worker ['səuʃəlwə:kə'] NOUN
l'assistente sociale MASC/FEM

society [sə'saɪəti] NOUN (PL **societies**)
  1. la società (PL le società) ◇ *We live in a multi-cultural society.* Viviamo in una società multiculturale.
  2. l'associazione FEM ◇ *a literary society* un'associazione letteraria

sociology [səusi'ɔlədʒi] NOUN
la sociologia

sock [sɔk] NOUN
il calzino

socket ['sɔkɪt] NOUN
la presa di corrente

soda ['səudə] NOUN
il selz (PL i selz)

soda pop ['səudəpɔp] NOUN [US]
la gassosa

sofa ['səufə] NOUN
il divano

soft [sɔft] ADJECTIVE
  1. morbido ◇ *a nice soft towel* un asciugamano bello morbido
  2. soffice ◇ *The mattress is too soft.* Il materasso è troppo soffice.

• **to be soft on somebody** essere ^E indulgente con qualcuno

• **soft cheeses** formaggi a pasta molle

• **a soft drink** una bibita analcolica

• **soft drugs** droghe leggere

• **a soft option** la scelta più facile

software ['sɔftwɛə'] NOUN
il software

soggy ['sɔgi] ADJECTIVE
molliccio

soil [sɔil] NOUN
la terra

solar ['səulə'] ADJECTIVE
solare ◇ *solar panel* pannello solare ◇ *solar power* energia solare

sold [səuld] VERB *see* **sell**

soldier ['səuldʒə'] NOUN
il soldato

sold out [səuld'aut] ADJECTIVE
esaurito ◇ *The tickets are all sold out.* I biglietti sono tutti esauriti.

solicitor [sə'lɪsɪtə'] NOUN
  1. l'avvocato (*for lawsuits*)
  2. il notaio (*for wills, property*)

solid ['sɔlɪd] ADJECTIVE
solido ◇ *a solid wall* un muro solido

• **solid gold** oro massiccio

• **for three solid hours** per tre ore filate

solo ['səuləu] NOUN (PL **solos**)
l'assolo ◇ *a guitar solo* un assolo di chitarra

solution [sə'lu:ʃən] NOUN
la soluzione

to **solve** [sɔlv] VERB
risolvere*

some [sʌm] ADJECTIVE, PRONOUN
  1. del MASC
  della FEM
  ◇ *some bread* del pane ◇ *some beer* della birra

  Use dello before a masculine noun if it starts with gn, pn, ps, x, y, z or s + another consonant.

  ◇ *some yoghurt* dello yogurt

S

☞

*Use **dell'** before nouns starting with vowels.*
◇ *some salad* dell'insalata
* **some of it** un po' ◇ *I only took some of it.* Ne ho preso solo un po'.
* **Would you like some coffee? – No thanks, I've got some.** Vuoi del caffè? – No grazie, ne ho.
2 alcuni MASC PL
alcune FEM PL
◇ *You have to be careful with mushrooms: some are poisonous.* Bisogna stare attenti con i funghi, alcuni sono velenosi.
* **some of them** alcuni ◇ *I only sold some of them.* Ne ho venduto solo alcuni.
* **some people** alcuni
* **some day** un giorno ◇ *Some day you'll understand.* Un giorno capirai.

somebody ['sʌmbədɪ] PRONOUN
qualcuno

somehow ['sʌmhau] ADVERB
in un modo o nell'altro ◇ *I'll do it somehow.* Lo farò, in un modo o nell'altro.
* **Somehow I don't think he believed me.** Qualcosa mi dice che non mi ha creduto.

someone ['sʌmwʌn] PRONOUN
qualcuno

someplace ['sʌmpleɪs] ADVERB US
da qualche parte ◇ *I've left my keys someplace.* Ho lasciato le chiavi da qualche parte.

something ['sʌmθɪŋ] PRONOUN
qualcosa ◇ *something special* qualcosa di speciale ◇ *Wear something warm.* Mettiti qualcosa di pesante.
* **His name is Peter or something.** Si chiama Peter o qualcosa del genere.
* **...or something like that** ...o giù di lì ◇ *It cost a hundred pounds, or something like that.* È costato cento sterline o giù di lì.
* **It would be really something!** Non sarebbe mica male!

sometime ['sʌmtaɪm] ADVERB
1 un giorno o l'altro ◇ *I want to go to Spain sometime.* Voglio andare in Spagna un giorno o l'altro.
2 uno di questi giorni ◇ *You must come and see us sometime.* Vieni a trovarci uno di questi giorni.
* **sometime last month** il mese scorso

sometimes ['sʌmtaɪmz] ADVERB
a volte ◇ *Sometimes I think Carol hates me.* A volte ho l'impressione che Carol mi detesti.

somewhere ['sʌmwɛəʳ] ADVERB
da qualche parte ◇ *I've left my keys somewhere.* Ho lasciato le chiavi da qualche parte.
* **I'd like to go on holiday, somewhere exotic.** Vorrei andare in vacanza, in qualche località esotica.

son [sʌn] NOUN
il figlio

song [sɒŋ] NOUN
la canzone

son-in-law ['sʌnɪnlɔː] NOUN (PL **sons-in-law**)
il genero

soon [suːn] ADVERB
presto ◇ *very soon* prestissimo
* **soon afterwards** poco dopo
* **as soon as possible** il più presto possibile

sooner ['suːnəʳ] ADVERB
prima ◇ *Can't you come a bit sooner?* Non puoi venire un po' prima?
* **sooner or later** prima o poi
* **the sooner the better** prima è meglio è

soot [sut] NOUN
la fuliggine

soppy ['sɒpɪ] ADJECTIVE
sentimentale

soprano [sə'prɑːnəu] NOUN (PL **sopranos**)
il/la soprano

sorcerer ['sɔːsərəʳ] NOUN
lo stregone

sore [sɔːʳ] ADJECTIVE
see also **sore** NOUN
* **It's sore.** Mi fa male.
* **a sore point** un punto delicato

sore [sɔːʳ] NOUN
see also **sore** ADJECTIVE
la piaga (PL le piaghe)

sorry ['sɒrɪ] ADJECTIVE
* **Sorry!** Scusi!
* **Sorry?** Come, scusa?
* **I'm very sorry.** Mi dispiace tanto.
* **I'm sorry I'm late.** Scusa il ritardo.
* **You'll be sorry!** Te ne pentirai!
* **to feel sorry for somebody** dispiacersi ᴱ per qualcuno

sort [sɔːt] NOUN
see also **sort** VERB
il tipo ◇ *What sort of bike have you got?* Che tipo di bici hai?

to **sort** [sɔːt] VERB
see also **sort** NOUN
suddividere ᴱ ◇ *The students are sorted into three groups.* Gli studenti sono suddivisi in tre gruppi.

to **sort out** [sɔːt'aut] VERB
1 riordinare (*things*)
2 risolvere* (*problem*)

so-so ['səusəu] ADVERB
così così ◇ *How are you feeling? – So-so.* Come ti senti? – Così così.

sought [sɔːt] VERB *see* **seek**

soul [səul] NOUN
l'anima

sound [saund] NOUN
see also **sound** VERB, ADJECTIVE
1 il rumore ◇ *Don't make a sound!* Non fare rumore! ◇ *the sound of footsteps* il rumore di passi
2 il suono ◇ *the speed of sound* la velocità del suono

* *Verbs followed by this symbol are irregular. See pp.339–364 for further details.*

• **sound effects** effetti sonori

3 l' audio ◊ *Can I turn the sound down?* Posso abbassare l'audio?

to **sound** [saʊnd] VERB

see also **sound** NOUN, ADJECTIVE

sembrare E ◊ *That sounds interesting.* Mi sembra interessante. ◊ *It sounds as if she's doing well at school.* Sembra che stia andando bene a scuola. ◊ *That sounds like a good idea.* Sembra una buona idea.

sound [saʊnd] ADJECTIVE, ADVERB

see also **sound** NOUN, VERB

buono ◊ *Julian gave me some sound advice.* Julian mi ha dato un buon consiglio.

• **sound asleep** profondamente addormentato

soundtrack ['saʊndtræk] NOUN la colonna sonora

soup [suːp] NOUN la minestra

sour ['saʊər] ADJECTIVE acido

south [saʊθ] NOUN, ADJECTIVE, ADVERB

1 il sud ◊ *the South of France* il sud della Francia ◊ *South Wales* il Galles del sud

• **in the south** a sud

• **south of** a sud di ◊ *It's south of London.* È a sud di Londra.

2 verso sud ◊ *We were travelling south.* Viaggiavamo verso sud.

3 meridionale ◊ *the south coast* la costa meridionale

South Africa [saʊθ'æfrɪkə] NOUN il Sudafrica

South America [saʊθə'mɛrɪkə] NOUN il Sudamerica

South American [saʊθə'mɛrɪkən] NOUN

see also **South American** ADJECTIVE

sudamericano
sudamericana

South American [saʊθə'mɛrɪkən] ADJECTIVE

see also **South American** NOUN

sudamericano

southbound ['saʊθbaʊnd] ADJECTIVE diretto a sud

south-east [saʊθ'iːst] NOUN il sud-est

southern ['sʌðən] ADJECTIVE meridionale ◊ *the southern part of the island* la zona meridionale dell'isola ◊ *Southern England* l'Inghilterra meridionale

South Pole [saʊθ'pəʊl] NOUN il Polo sud

south-west [saʊθ'wɛst] NOUN il sud-ovest

souvenir [suːvə'nɪər] NOUN il souvenir (PL i souvenir) ◊ *a souvenir shop* un negozio di souvenir

Soviet ['səʊvɪət] ADJECTIVE sovietico

soya ['sɔɪə] NOUN la soia

soy sauce ['sɔɪsɔːs] NOUN la salsa di soia

space [speɪs] NOUN lo spazio ◊ *There isn't enough space.* Non c'è abbastanza spazio. ◊ *in the space of a few minutes* nello spazio di pochi minuti

• **a parking space** un parcheggio

spacecraft ['speɪskrɑːft] NOUN (PL **spacecraft**) il veicolo spaziale

spade [speɪd] NOUN la pala ◊ *spade and fork* pala e forcone

• **spades** picche ◊ *the ace of spades* l'asso di picche

Spain [speɪn] NOUN la Spagna

Spaniard ['spænjəd] NOUN lo spagnolo
la spagnola

spaniel ['spænjəl] NOUN lo spaniel (PL gli spaniel)

Spanish ['spænɪʃ] ADJECTIVE

see also **Spanish** NOUN

spagnolo

Spanish ['spænɪʃ] NOUN

see also **Spanish** ADJECTIVE

lo spagnolo (*language*)

• **the Spanish** gli spagnoli

to **spank** [spæŋk] VERB sculacciare

spanner ['spænər] NOUN la chiave fissa

spare [spɛər] ADJECTIVE

see also **spare** VERB, NOUN

di scorta ◊ *spare batteries* pile di scorta

• **Any spare change, please?** Ha qualche spicciolo, per favore?

• **a spare part** un pezzo di ricambio

• **a spare room** una stanza degli ospiti

• **spare time** il tempo libero

• **the spare wheel** la ruota di scorta

to **spare** [spɛər] VERB

see also **spare** ADJECTIVE, NOUN

• **Can you spare a moment?** Hai un attimo di tempo?

• **I can't spare the time.** Non ho tempo.

• **They've got no money to spare.** Non hanno poi tanti soldi.

• **We arrived with time to spare.** Siamo arrivati un po' in anticipo.

spare [spɛər] NOUN

see also **spare** ADJECTIVE, VERB

l' altro MASC
l' altra FEM

◊ *I've lost my key. – Have you got a spare?* Ho perso la chiave. – Ne hai un'altra?

sparkling ['spɑːklɪŋ] ADJECTIVE frizzante ◊ *sparkling wine* vino frizzante

sparrow ['spærəʊ] NOUN il passero

S

spat [spæt] VERB *see* spit

to **speak** [spi:k] VERB (**spoke, spoken**)
parlare* ◇ *Do you speak English?* Parli
inglese? ◇ *Have you spoken to him?* Gli hai
parlato? ◇ *I've spoken to her about it.*
Gliene ho parlato. ◇ *I spoke to her
yesterday.* Le ho parlato ieri. ◇ *She spoke to
him about it.* Gliene ho parlato.
- **Speaking!** (*on phone*) Sono io! ◇ *Could I
speak to Alison? – Speaking!* Posso parlare
con Alison? – Sono io!

to **speak out** [spi:k'aut] VERB
parlare* ◇ *He finally decided to speak out.*
Alla fine si è deciso a parlare.

speaker ['spi:kə'] NOUN
1 l' altoparlante MASC (*loudspeaker*)
2 l' oratore MASC
l' oratrice FEM (*person*)

special ['spɛʃl] ADJECTIVE
speciale

specialist ['spɛʃəlɪst] NOUN
lo/la specialista

speciality [spɛʃi'ælɪtɪ] NOUN (PL **specialities**)
la specialità (PL le specialità)

to **specialize** ['spɛʃəlaɪz] VERB
specializzarsi^E

specially ['spɛʃlɪ] ADVERB
1 specialmente ◇ *It can be very cold here,
specially in January.* Qui può fare molto
freddo, specialmente in gennaio.
- **not specially** non particolarmente ◇ *Do you
like opera? – Not specially.* Ti piace l'opera?
– Non particolarmente.
2 apposta ◇ *It's specially designed for
teenagers.* È concepito apposta per i
giovani.

species ['spi:ʃi:z] NOUN
la specie (PL le specie)

specific [spə'sɪfɪk] ADJECTIVE
1 specifico ◇ *certain specific issues* certi
problemi specifici
2 preciso ◇ *Could you be more specific?*
Puoi essere più preciso?

specifically [spə'sɪfɪklɪ] ADVERB
1 appositamente ◇ *It's specifically
designed for teenagers.* È appositamente
concepito per i giovani.
2 specificamente ◇ *In Britain, or more
specifically in England...* In Gran Bretagna, o
più specificamente in Inghilterra...
3 chiaramente ◇ *I specifically said that...*
Avevo chiaramente detto che...

specs [spɛks] NOUN PL
gli occhiali

spectacles ['spɛktəklz] NOUN PL
gli occhiali

spectacular [spɛk'tækjulə'] ADJECTIVE
fantastico

spectator [spɛk'teɪtə'] NOUN
lo spettatore
la spettatrice

speech [spi:tʃ] NOUN (PL **speeches**)
il discorso ◇ *He made a speech at the
conference.* Ha fatto un discorso alla
conferenza.

speechless ['spi:tʃlɪs] ADJECTIVE
- **to be speechless** rimanere^E senza parole

speed [spi:d] NOUN
la velocità (PL le velocità) ◇ *at top speed* ad
alta velocità
- **a ten-speed bike** una bicicletta a dieci marce

speedboat ['spi:dbəut] NOUN
il motoscafo

speeding ['spi:dɪŋ] NOUN
l' eccesso di velocità ◇ *He was fined for
speeding.* Ha preso la multa per eccesso di
velocità.

speed limit ['spi:dlɪmɪt] NOUN
il limite di velocità
- **to break the speed limit** superare il limite di
velocità

speedometer [spɪ'dɔmɪtə'] NOUN
il tachimetro

to **speed up** [spi:d'ʌp] VERB
accelerare

to **spell** [spɛl] VERB (**spelled** *or* **spelt, spelled** *or*
spelt)
see also **spell** NOUN
- **How do you spell your name?** Come si
scrive il tuo nome?
- **Can you spell that please?** Come si scrive?
- **I can't spell.** Faccio errori di ortografia.

spell [spɛl] NOUN
see also **spell** VERB
l' incantesimo
- **to cast a spell on somebody** fare un
incantesimo a qualcuno
- **to be under somebody's spell** essere^E
stregato da qualcuno

spelling ['spɛlɪŋ] NOUN
l' ortografia ◇ *a spelling mistake* un errore
di ortografia
- **My spelling is terrible.** Faccio molto errori di
ortografia.

to **spend** [spɛnd] VERB (**spent, spent**)
1 spendere* ◇ *They spend an enormous
amount of money on advertising.*
Spendono grosse cifre per la pubblicità.
2 trascorrere* ◇ *He spent a month in
France.* Ha trascorso un mese in Francia.
- **to spend time on** dedicare del tempo a ◇ *He
spends a lot of time on his hobbies.* Dedica
un sacco di tempo ai suoi hobby.

spice [spaɪs] NOUN
la spezia

spicy ['spaɪsɪ] ADJECTIVE
piccante

spider ['spaɪdə'] NOUN
il ragno

to **spill** [spɪl] VERB (**spilled** *or* **spilt, spilled** *or*
spilt)
1 rovesciare^E ◇ *He spilled coffee on his*

---

* Verbs followed by this symbol are irregular. See pp.339–364 for further details.

trousers. S'è rovesciato il caffè sui pantaloni.

[2] fuoriuscire*[E] ◊ *Oil is spilling from the tanker.* Il petrolio sta fuoriuscendo dalla petroliera.

to **spin** [spɪn] VERB (**spun, spun**)
[1] girare ◊ *He spun the wheel sharply.* Ha girato il volante bruscamente.
[2] tessere ◊ *She spins the wool from her own sheep.* Fila la lana delle sue pecore.
[3] centrifugare (*washing*)

spinach ['spɪnɪtʃ] NOUN
gli spinaci MASC PL ◊ *The spinach is delicious.* Gli spinaci sono ottimi.

spin drier [spɪn'draɪəʳ] NOUN
la centrifuga (PL le centrifughe)

spin doctor ['spɪndɔktəʳ] NOUN
il curatore d'immagine
la curatrice d'immagine

spine [spaɪn] NOUN
la colonna vertebrale

spinster ['spɪnstəʳ] NOUN
la zitella

spire ['spaɪəʳ] NOUN
la guglia

spirit ['spɪrɪt] NOUN
[1] lo spirito ◊ *the human spirit* lo spirito umano
[2] il coraggio ◊ *Everyone who knew her admired her spirit.* Tutti quelli che la conoscevano ammiravano il suo coraggio.

spirit level ['spɪrɪtlɛvl] NOUN
la livella a bolla

spirits ['spɪrɪts] NOUN
i superalcolici ◊ *I don't drink spirits.* Non bevo superalcolici.
• **to be in good spirits** essere[E] su di morale

spiritual ['spɪrɪtjuəl] ADJECTIVE
spirituale

spit [spɪt] NOUN
see also **spit** VERB
lo sputo

to **spit** [spɪt] VERB (**spat, spat**)
see also **spit** NOUN
sputare ◊ *They spat at me.* Mi hanno sputato adosso.

to **spit out** [spɪt'aut] VERB
sputare ◊ *It tasted horrible and I spat it out.* Aveva un saporaccio e l'ho sputato.

spite [spaɪt] NOUN
see also **spite** VERB
• **in spite of** magrado
• **out of spite** per dispetto

to **spite** [spaɪt] VERB
see also **spite** NOUN
fare* dispetto a ◊ *He just did it to spite me.* L'ha fatto solo per farmi dispetto.

spiteful ['spaɪtful] ADJECTIVE
dispettoso

to **splash** [splæʃ] VERB
see also **splash** NOUN

[1] schizzare ◊ *Don't splash me!* Non schizzarmi!
[2] spruzzare ◊ *He splashed water on his face.* Si spruzzò acqua sul viso.

splash [splæʃ] NOUN (PL **splashes**)
see also **splash** VERB
il tonfo ◊ *I heard a splash.* Ho sentito un tonfo.
• **a splash of colour** un tocco di colore

splendid ['splɛndɪd] ADJECTIVE
splendido

splint [splɪnt] NOUN
la stecca (PL le stecche)

splinter ['splɪntəʳ] NOUN
la scheggia (PL le schegge)

to **split** [splɪt] VERB (**split, split**)
[1] spaccare ◊ *He split the wood with an axe.* Spaccava la legna con l'ascia.
[2] spaccarsi[E] ◊ *The ship hit a rock and split in two.* La nave ha urtato contro una roccia e s'è spaccata in due.
[3] dividere* ◊ *They decided to split the profits.* Hanno deciso di dividere i guadagni.

to **split up** [splɪt'ʌp] VERB
separarsi[E]

to **spoil** [spɔɪl] VERB (**spoiled** or **spoilt, spoiled** or **spoilt**)
[1] rovinare ◊ *Don't let it spoil your holiday!* Non lasciare che ti rovini la vacanza!
[2] viziare ◊ *Grandparents like to spoil their grandchildren.* Ai nonni piace viziare i nipotini.

spoilsport ['spɔɪlspɔːt] NOUN
il/la guastafeste

spoke [spəuk] VERB *see* **speak**

spoke [spəuk] NOUN
il raggio

spoken ['spəukn] VERB *see* **speak**

spokesman ['spəuksmən] NOUN (PL **spokesmen**)
il portavoce (PL i portavoce)

spokeswoman ['spəukswumən] NOUN (PL **spokeswomen**)
la portavoce (PL le portavoce)

sponge [spʌndʒ] NOUN
la spugna ◊ *a wet sponge* una spugna bagnata
• **sponge bag** nécessaire MASC
• **sponge cake** pan di Spagna

sponsor ['spɔnsəʳ] NOUN
see also **sponsor** VERB
lo sponsor (PL gli sponsor)

to **sponsor** ['spɔnsəʳ] VERB
see also **sponsor** NOUN
sponsorizzare ◊ *The tournament was sponsored by local firms.* Il torneo è stato sponsorizzato da imprese locali.
• **She got all her friends to sponsor her.** Ha chiesto a tutti gli amici di contribuire alla colletta.

S

ℹ *Spesso in Gran Bretagna vengono organizzate manifestazioni sportive i cui partecipanti chiedono agli amici di raccogliere denaro da dare in beneficienza.*

spontaneous [spɒn'teɪnɪəs] ADJECTIVE
spontaneo

spooky ['spu:kɪ] ADJECTIVE
sinistro ◊ *The house has a spooky atmosphere.* La casa ha un'atmosfera sinistra.

spoon [spu:n] NOUN
il cucchiaio

sport [spɔ:t] NOUN
lo sport (PL gli sport) ◊ *I'm not interested in sport.* Lo sport non mi interessa.
* **sports bag** la sacca sportiva
* **sports car** l'auto sportiva
* **sports jacket** la giacca sportiva
* **Go on, be a sport!** Dai, sii buono!

sportsman ['spɔ:tsmən] NOUN (PL **sportsmen**)
lo sportivo

sportswear ['spɔ:tsweə'] NOUN
l' abbigliamento sportivo

sportswoman ['spɔ:tswumən] NOUN (PL **sportswomen**)
la sportiva

sporty ['spɔ:tɪ] ADJECTIVE
sportivo

spot [spɒt] NOUN
see also **spot** VERB
1 la macchia ◊ *There's a spot on your shirt.* Hai una macchia sulla camicia.
2 il pallino ◊ *a red dress with white spots* un vestito rosso a pallini bianchi
3 il brufolo ◊ *He's covered in spots.* È pieno di brufoli.
4 il posto ◊ *It's a lovely spot for a picnic.* È un posto ideale per un picnic.
* **on the spot (1)** immediatamente ◊ *They offered her the job on the spot.* Le hanno offerto immediatamente il lavoro.
* **on the spot (2)** sul posto ◊ *Troops are on the spot.* Le truppe sono sul posto.
* **a spot check** un controllo senza preavviso

to **spot** [spɒt] VERB
see also **spot** NOUN
notare ◊ *I spotted a mistake.* Ho notato un errore.

spotless ['spɒtlɪs] ADJECTIVE
immacolato

spotlight ['spɒtlaɪt] NOUN
il riflettore

spotty ['spɒtɪ] ADJECTIVE
brufoloso

spouse [spaʊs] NOUN
il/la coniuge

to **sprain** [spreɪn] VERB
see also **sprain** NOUN
slogarsi[E] ◊ *She's sprained her ankle.* S'è slogata una caviglia.

sprain [spreɪn] NOUN
see also **sprain** VERB
la slogatura

spray [spreɪ] NOUN
see also **spray** VERB
lo spray (PL gli spray)

to **spray** [spreɪ] VERB
see also **spray** NOUN
spruzzare ◊ *She sprayed perfume on my hand.* Mi ha spruzzato del profumo sulla mano.
* **Graffiti were sprayed on the wall.** C'erano dei graffiti sul muro.

spread [spred] NOUN
see also **spread** VERB
* **cheese spread** formaggio da spalmare
* **chocolate spread** cioccolata da spalmare

to **spread** [spred] VERB (**spread, spread**)
see also **spread** NOUN
1 spalmare ◊ *Spread the whipped cream on the top of the cake.* Spalma la panna montata sopra la torta.
2 diffondersi[E] ◊ *The news spread rapidly.* La notizia si diffuse rapidamente.

to **spread out** [spred'aʊt] VERB
1 sparpagliarsi[E] ◊ *The soldiers spread out across the field.* I soldati si sparpagliarono nel campo.
2 spiegare ◊ *He spread the map out on the table.* Ha spiegato la cartina sul tavolo.

spreadsheet ['spredʃi:t] NOUN
il foglio elettronico (PL i fogli elettronici)

spring [sprɪŋ] NOUN
see also **spring** ADJECTIVE, VERB
1 la primavera ◊ *in spring* in primavera ◊ *last spring* la scorsa primavera
2 la molla ◊ *a broken spring* una molla rotta
3 la sorgente ◊ *water from a spring* acqua di sorgente

spring [sprɪŋ] ADJECTIVE
see also **spring** NOUN, VERB
primaverile ◊ *spring weather* tempo primaverile

spring-cleaning [sprɪŋ'kli:nɪŋ] NOUN
le pulizie di primavera FEM PL

spring onion [sprɪŋ'ʌnjən] NOUN
la cipollina

springtime ['sprɪŋtaɪm] NOUN
la primavera

sprinkler ['sprɪŋklə'] NOUN
l' irrigatore MASC

sprint [sprɪnt] NOUN
see also **sprint** VERB
lo sprint (PL gli sprint) ◊ *in a sprint finish* con uno sprint finale
* **the women's 100 metres sprint** i cento metri piani femminili

to **sprint** [sprɪnt] VERB
see also **sprint** NOUN

* *Verbs followed by this symbol are irregular. See pp.339–364 for further details.*

fare* una corsa ◇ *She sprinted for the bus.*
Ha fatto una corsa per prendere l'autobus.

sprinter ['sprɪntə'] NOUN
il/la velocista

sprouts [sprauts] NOUN PL
◆ **Brussels sprouts** cavoletti di Bruxelles

spun [spʌn] VERB *see* **spin**

spy [spaɪ] NOUN (PL **spies**)
la spia

spying ['spaɪɪŋ] NOUN
lo spionaggio

to **spy on** ['spaɪɒn] VERB (**spied, spied**)
spiare

to **squabble** ['skwɒbl] VERB
bisticciare ◇ *Stop squabbling!* Smettetela
di bisticciare!

square [skwɛə'] NOUN
see also **square** ADJECTIVE
[1] il quadrato ◇ *a square and a triangle* un
quadrato e un triangolo
[2] la piazza ◇ *the main square* la piazza
principale

square [skwɛə'] ADJECTIVE
see also **square** NOUN
quadrato ◇ *a square table* un tavolo
quadrato ◇ *two square metres* due metri
quadrati
◆ **It's two metres square.** Misura due metri
per due.

squash [skwɒʃ] NOUN
see also **squash** VERB
[1] lo squash (*sport*)
◆ **a squash court** un campo da squash
◆ **a squash racket** una racchetta da squash
[2] la zucca (*vegetable*)
◆ **orange squash** sciroppo di arancia

to **squash** [skwɒʃ] VERB
see also **squash** NOUN
schiacciare ◇ *You're squashing me.* Mi stai
schiacciando.

to **squeak** [skwiːk] VERB
[1] scricchiolare ◇ *The door squeaked as it
opened.* La porta scricchiolò aprendosi.
[2] lanciare un gridolino ◇ *She squeaked
with delight.* Ha lanciato un gridolino di
gioia.

to **squeeze** [skwiːz] VERB
[1] spremere ◇ *Squeeze two large lemons.*
Spremete due limoni grossi.
[2] stringere* ◇ *She squeezed my hand
reassuringly.* Mi ha stretto la mano con fare
rassicurante.
◆ **The thieves squeezed through a tiny
window.** I ladri si sono introdotti attraverso
una finestrella.
◆ **I can squeeze you in at two o'clock.** Le
posso dare un appuntamento alle due.

to **squint** [skwɪnt] VERB
see also **squint** NOUN
strizzare gli occhi

squint [skwɪnt] NOUN

see also **squint** VERB
lo strabismo
◆ **to have a squint** essere ᴱ strabico

squirrel ['skwɪrəl] NOUN
lo scoiattolo

to **stab** [stæb] VERB
accoltellare

stable ['steɪbl] NOUN
see also **stable** ADJECTIVE
la stalla

stable ['steɪbl] ADJECTIVE
see also **stable** NOUN
[1] stabile ◇ *a stable relationship* una
relazione stabile
[2] stazionario ◇ *The injured man is in a
stable condition.* Le condizioni del ferito
sono stazionarie.

stack [stæk] NOUN
la pila ◇ *There was a stack of books on the
table.* Sul tavolo c'era una pila di libri.
◆ **stacks of** un sacco di ◇ *They've got stacks
of money.* Hanno un sacco di soldi.

stadium ['steɪdɪəm] NOUN
lo stadio

staff [stɑːf] NOUN
il personale

staffroom ['stɑːfrum] NOUN
la sala professori

stage [steɪdʒ] NOUN
see also **stage** VERB
[1] la fase ◇ *at this stage in the negotiations*
in questa fase dei negoziati
[2] la tappa ◇ *the final stage of their world
tour* la tappa conclusiva della loro tournée
mondiale
[3] il palco (PL i palchi) ◇ *She went on stage
and did her act.* È salita sul palco e ha fatto il
suo show.
◆ **to go on the stage** fare del teatro

to **stage** [steɪdʒ] VERB
see also **stage** NOUN
[1] organizzare (*event*)
[2] mettere* in scena (*play, show*)

to **stagger** ['stægə'] VERB
barcollare

stain [steɪn] NOUN
see also **stain** VERB
la macchia ◇ *a large stain* una grande
macchia

to **stain** [steɪn] VERB
see also **stain** NOUN
macchiare

stainless steel ['steɪnlɪs'stiːl] NOUN
l' acciaio inossidabile

stain remover ['steɪnrɪ'muːvə'] NOUN
lo smacchiatore

stair [stɛə'] NOUN
il gradino ◇ *He left the bag on the bottom
stair.* Ha lasciato la borsa sull'ultimo
gradino.

staircase ['stɛəkeɪs] NOUN

S

☞

la scala

stairs [steəz] NOUN PL
le scale ◇ *a flight of stairs* una rampa di scale

stale [steɪl] ADJECTIVE
* **stale bread** pane raffermo

stalemate ['steɪlmeɪt] NOUN
il punto morto ◇ *The negotiations have reached a stalemate.* I negoziati sono arrivati ad un punto morto.

stall [stɔːl] NOUN
la bancarella (*in market*)
* **the stalls** (*in theatre*) la platea

stamina ['stæmɪnə] NOUN
la resistenza fisica

stammer ['stæmə'] NOUN
* **He's got a stammer.** È balbuziente.

stamp [stæmp] NOUN
see also **stamp** VERB
[1] il francobollo ◇ *I collect stamps.* Faccio collezione di francobolli.
* **a stamp album** un album per francobolli
[2] il timbro ◇ *an official stamp* un timbro ufficiale
Be careful not to translate **stamp** *by* **stampa.**

to **stamp** [stæmp] VERB
see also **stamp** NOUN
timbrare ◇ *He looked at her ticket, and stamped it.* Le ha guardato il biglietto e l'ha timbrato.
* **to stamp one's feet** battere i piedi ◇ *The audience stamped their feet.* Il pubblico batteva i piedi.

stamped [stæmpt] ADJECTIVE
* **stamped addressed envelope** busta già affrancata per la risposta

stand [stænd] NOUN
see also **stand** VERB
lo stand (PL gli stand) ◇ *our stand in the trade fair* il nostro stand alla fiera

to **stand** [stænd] VERB (**stood, stood**)
see also **stand** NOUN
[1] stare*[E] in piedi ◇ *He was standing by the door.* Stava in piedi vicino alla porta.
[2] essere*[E] situato ◇ *The house stands on top of a hill.* La casa è situata in cima ad una collina.
[3] sopportare ◇ *I can't stand this noise.* Non sopporto questo chiasso.

to **stand down** [stænd'daun] VERB
farsi*[E] da parte

to **stand for** ['stændfɔː'] VERB
[1] essere*[E] l'abbreviazione di ◇ *"BT" stands for "British Telecom".* "BT" è l'abbreviazione di "British Telecom".
[2] tollerare ◇ *I won't stand for it any more!* Non ho intenzione di tollerarlo oltre!

to **stand in for** [stænd'ɪnfɔː'] VERB
sostituire

to **stand out** [stænd'aut] VERB
spiccare

to **stand up** [stænd'ʌp] VERB
alzarsi*[E] in piedi

to **stand up for** [stænd'ʌpfɔː'] VERB
difendere* ◇ *Stand up for your rights!* Difendi i tuoi diritti!

standard ['stændəd] ADJECTIVE
see also **standard** NOUN
[1] lo standard (PL gli standard) ◇ *standard English* inglese standard
[2] di serie (*accessories*)

standard ['stændəd] NOUN
see also **standard** ADJECTIVE
il livello qualitativo ◇ *The standard is very high.* Il livello qualitativo è molto alto.
* **She's got high standards.** È molto esigente.
* **standard of living** tenore di vita

standard lamp ['stændəd'læmp] NOUN
la lampada a stelo

stand-by ticket ['stænbaɪ'tɪkɪt] NOUN
il biglietto stand-by

standpoint ['stændpɔɪnt] NOUN
il punto di vista

stands [stændz] NOUN PL
la tribuna SING

stank [stæŋk] VERB *see* **stink**

staple ['steɪpl] NOUN
see also **staple** ADJECTIVE, VERB
il punto metallico (PL i punti metallici)

to **staple** ['steɪpl] VERB
see also **staple** ADJECTIVE, NOUN
cucire con punti metallici

staple ['steɪpl] ADJECTIVE
see also **staple** NOUN, VERB
principale ◇ *Rice is their staple food.* Il loro alimento principale è il riso.

stapler ['steɪplə'] NOUN
la cucitrice

star [stɑː'] NOUN
see also **star** VERB
la stella ◇ *the moon and stars* la luna e le stelle
* **a TV star** una star della TV
* **the stars** l'oroscopo

to **star** [stɑː'] VERB
see also **star** NOUN
avere* come protagonista ◇ *The film stars Sharon Stone.* Il film ha come protagonista Sharon Stone.
* **...starring Johnny Depp** ...con Johnny Depp
* **to star in a film** essere*[E] protagonista di un film

to **stare** [steə'] VERB
guardare fisso

stark [stɑːk] ADVERB
* **stark naked** completamente nudo

start [stɑːt] NOUN
see also **start** VERB
l'inizio ◇ *It's not much, but it's a start.* Non è molto ma è pur sempre un inizio.
* **to make a start** cominciare ◇ *Shall we make a start on the washing-up?*

---

* Verbs followed by this symbol are irregular. See pp.339–364 for further details.

Cominciamo a lavare i piatti?

♦ **for a start** per cominciare ◊ *For a start you need to check all the names.* Per cominciare devi controllare tutti i nomi.

to **start** [stɑːt] VERB

see also **start** NOUN

[1] iniziare ◊ *What time does it start?* A che ora inizia?

♦ **to start doing something** iniziare a fare qualcosa

[2] avviare ◊ *He wants to start his own business.* Vuole avviare un'attività in proprio.

[3] lanciare ◊ *She started a campaign against drugs.* Ha lanciato una campagna contro la droga.

[4] far* partire ◊ *He couldn't start the car.* Non riusciva a far partire la macchina.

[5] partire[E] ◊ *The car wouldn't start.* La macchina non partiva.

to **start off** [stɑːtˈɔf] VERB

mettersi* [E] in viaggio ◊ *We started off first thing in the morning.* Ci siamo messi in viaggio di buon mattino.

starter [ˈstɑːtə] NOUN

l' antipasto

to **starve** [stɑːv] VERB

morire* [E] di fame ◊ *People are starving.* La gente muore di fame.

♦ **I'm starving!** Ho una fame da lupo!

state [steɪt] NOUN

see also **state** VERB

[1] lo stato ◊ *It's an independent state.* È uno stato indipendente.

[2] le condizioni FEM PL ◊ *He was in no state to drive.* Non era in condizioni di guidare.

♦ **to be in a state of shock** essere* [E] sotto shock

♦ **to be in a real state** (*person*) essere* [E] tutto agitato

♦ **the States** gli Stati Uniti

to **state** [steɪt] VERB

see also **state** NOUN

dichiarare ◊ *He stated his intention to resign.* Ha dichiarato di essere intenzionato a dimettersi.

♦ **Please state your name and address.** Fornisca nome e indirizzo.

stately home [steɪtlɪˈhəʊm] NOUN

la dimora signorile

ⓘ La **stately home** è una dimora signorile di interesse storico e artistico, aperta al pubblico.

statement [ˈsteɪtmənt] NOUN

[1] la dichiarazione ◊ *He made a statement to the police.* Ha fatto una dichiarazione alla polizia.

[2] l' affermazione ◊ *I found this statement vague and unclear.* Ho trovato vaga e poco chiara l'affermazione.

[3] l' estratto conto (*bank statement*)

♦ **a bank statement** un estratto conto bancario

station [ˈsteɪʃən] NOUN

la stazione

♦ **the bus station** la stazione degli autobus

♦ **the police station** il commissariato di polizia

♦ **a radio station** una stazione radiofonica

stationer's [ˈsteɪʃənəz] NOUN

la cartoleria

station wagon [ˈsteɪʃənwægən] NOUN [US]

la station wagon

statue [ˈstætjuː] NOUN

la statua

stay [steɪ] NOUN

see also **stay** VERB

il soggiorno ◊ *my stay in Italy* il mio soggiorno in Italia

to **stay** [steɪ] VERB

see also **stay** NOUN

[1] restare [E] ◊ *Stay here!* Resta qui!

[2] stare* [E] ◊ *She's staying with friends.* Sta presso amici.

[3] alloggiare ◊ *Where are you staying?* Dove alloggi?

♦ **to stay the night** passare [E] la notte

to **stay in** VERB

restare [E] a casa

to **stay up** VERB

rimanere* [E] alzato ◊ *We stayed up till midnight.* Siamo rimasti alzati fino a mezzanotte.

steady [ˈstɛdɪ] ADJECTIVE

[1] regolare ◊ *a steady income* un reddito regolare

[2] fermo ◊ *You need a steady hand for this job.* Ci vuole mano ferma per fare questo lavoro.

[3] fisso ◊ *a steady job* un lavoro fisso

♦ **steady progress** progresso costante

♦ **Steady on!** Calma!

steak [steɪk] NOUN

la bistecca (PL le bistecche)

to **steal** [stiːl] VERB (**stole, stolen**)

rubare ◊ *Thieves broke in and stole the video.* Sono entrati i ladri e hanno rubato il videoregistratore. ◊ *My car was stolen last week.* Mi hanno rubato la macchina la settimana scorsa.

steam [stiːm] NOUN

see also **steam** VERB

il vapore ◊ *a steam engine* una locomotiva a vapore

to **steam** [stiːm] VERB

see also **steam** NOUN

cuocere a vapore (*vegetables*)

to **steam up** [stiːmˈʌp] VERB

appannarsi [E] (*windows*)

steel [stiːl] NOUN

l' acciaio

steep [stiːp] ADJECTIVE ☞

S

Verbs followed by the symbol "E" require the auxiliary "essere"

ripido

steeple ['sti:pl] NOUN
il campanile

to **steer** [stɪə'] VERB
guidare ◇ *My father let me steer the car.*
Mio padre mi ha lasciato guidare la
macchina. ◇ *He steered us into the nearest
seats.* Ci ha guidati fino ai posti più vicini.

steering wheel ['stɪərɪŋwi:l] NOUN
il volante

step [stɛp] NOUN
see also **step** VERB
[1] il passo ◇ *He took a step forward.* Fece
un passo in avanti.
[2] il gradino ◇ *She tripped over the step.*
Ha inciampato sul gradino.

to **step** [stɛp] VERB
see also **step** NOUN
fare* un passo ◇ *I tried to step forward.* Ho
cercato di fare un passo in avanti.
♦ **Step this way, please.** Da questa parte, per
favore.

to **step aside** [stɛpə'saɪd] VERB
farsi* E da parte

to **step back** [stɛp'bæk] VERB
indietreggiare

to **step up** [stɛp'ʌp] VERB
intensificare

stepbrother ['stɛpbrʌðə'] NOUN
il fratellastro

stepdaughter ['stɛpdɔ:tə'] NOUN
la figliastra

stepfather ['stɛpfɑ:ðə'] NOUN
il patrigno

stepladder ['stɛplædə'] NOUN
la scala a libretto

stepmother ['stɛpmʌðə'] NOUN
la matrigna

stepsister ['stɛpsɪstə'] NOUN
la sorellastra

stepson ['stɛpsʌn] NOUN
il figliastro

stereo ['stɛrɪəu] NOUN (PL **stereos**)
lo stereo (PL gli stereo)

sterling ['stɜ:lɪŋ] ADJECTIVE
♦ **pound sterling** lira sterlina

stew [stju:] NOUN
lo spezzatino

steward ['stju:əd] NOUN
lo steward (PL gli steward)

stewardess ['stu:ədɪs] NOUN
la hostess (PL le hostess)

stick [stɪk] NOUN
see also **stick** VERB
il bastone ◇ *walking stick* bastone da
passeggio

to **stick** [stɪk] VERB (**stuck, stuck**)
see also **stick** NOUN
[1] attaccare ◇ *Stick the stamps on the
envelope.* Attacca i francobolli sulla busta.
[2] attaccarsi E ◇ *The rice stuck to the pan.* Il

riso s'è attaccato.
[3] ficcare ◇ *He picked up the papers and
stuck them in his briefcase.* Ha raccolto i
documenti e li ha ficcati nella valigetta.
♦ **I can't stick it any longer.** Non ne posso più.

to **stick by** [stɪk'baɪ] VERB
rimanere* E al fianco di ◇ *She stuck by him
through it all.* È sempre rimasta al suo
fianco.

to **stick out** [stɪk'aut] VERB
[1] tirare fuori ◇ *The little girl stuck out her
tongue.* La bambina tirò fuori la lingua.
[2] spiccare ◇ *It sticks out because of the
colour.* Spicca a causa del colore.

to **stick up for** [stɪk'ʌpfɔ:'] VERB
battersi E per

sticker ['stɪkə'] NOUN
l' autoadesivo

sticky ['stɪkɪ] ADJECTIVE
[1] appiccicoso ◇ *My hands are sticky.* Ho
le mani appiccicose.
[2] adesivo ◇ *a sticky label* un'etichetta
adesiva

stiff [stɪf] ADJECTIVE, ADVERB
rigido ◇ *stiff material* stoffa rigida
♦ **to have a stiff neck** avere il torcicollo
♦ **to feel stiff** sentirsi E indolenzito
♦ **to be bored stiff** essere E annoiato a morte
♦ **to be frozen stiff** essere E congelato
♦ **to be scared stiff** essere E morto di paura

still [stɪl] ADVERB
see also **still** ADJECTIVE
[1] ancora ◇ *I still haven't finished!* Non ho
ancora finito! ◇ *Are you still in bed?* Sei
ancora a letto? ◇ *better still* meglio ancora
[2] ciò nonostante ◇ *She knows I don't like
it, but she still does it.* Sa che non mi piace,
ma ciò nonostante lo fa lo stesso.
[3] in fondo ◇ *Still, it's the thought that
counts.* In fondo è il pensiero che conta.

still [stɪl] ADJECTIVE
see also **still** ADVERB
fermo ◇ *Keep still!* Stai fermo!
♦ **still mineral water** acqua minerale naturale
♦ **a still life** una natura morta

sting [stɪŋ] NOUN
see also **sting** VERB
la puntura ◇ *a bee sting* una puntura d'ape

to **sting** [stɪŋ] VERB (**stung, stung**)
see also **sting** NOUN
pungere* ◇ *I got stung by a wasp.* Mi ha
punto una vespa.

stingy ['stɪndʒɪ] ADJECTIVE
avaro

to **stink** [stɪŋk] VERB (**stank, stunk**)
see also **stink** NOUN
puzzare ◇ *The room stank of cigarettes.* La
stanza puzzava di fumo.

stink [stɪŋk] NOUN
see also **stink** VERB
la puzza

* Verbs followed by this symbol are irregular. See pp.339–364 for further details.

English ~ Italian

to **stir** [stəːʳ] VERB
   mescolare ◊ *Stir the mixture well.*
   Mescolare bene l'impasto.

to **stir up** [stəːrˈʌp] VERB
   1 fomentare (*ill feeling*)
   2 provocare (*trouble*)

to **stitch** [stɪtʃ] VERB
   see also **stitch** NOUN
   cucire

stitch [stɪtʃ] NOUN (PL **stitches**)
   see also **stitch** VERB
   il punto ◊ *I had five stitches.* Mi hanno
   messo cinque punti.

stock [stɔk] NOUN
   see also **stock** VERB
   1 la scorta ◊ *a small stock of medicines*
   una piccola scorta di medicine
   ◆ **in stock** disponibile ◊ *Yes, we've got your*
   size in stock. Sì, abbiamo la sua taglia.
   ◆ **out of stock** esaurito ◊ *I'm sorry, they're*
   both out of stock. Mi dispiace, sono esauriti
   tutt'e due.
   2 il brodo ◊ *chicken stock* brodo di pollo

to **stock** [stɔk] VERB
   see also **stock** NOUN
   vendere* ◊ *Do you stock camping stoves?*
   Vendete fornellini da campeggio?

to **stock up** [stɔkˈʌp] VERB
   fare* provvista ◊ *I must stock up on*
   candles. Devo fare provvista di candele.

stock cube [ˈstɔkkjuːb] NOUN
   il dado da brodo

stock exchange [ˈstɔkɪkstʃeɪndʒ] NOUN
   la Borsa

stockings [ˈstɔkɪŋz] NOUN PL
   le calze ◊ *a pair of nylon stockings* un paio
   di calze di nailon

stock market [ˈstɔkmɑːkɪt] NOUN
   il mercato azionario

stole, stolen [stəul, ˈstəuln] VERB *see* **steal**

stomach [ˈstʌmək] NOUN
   lo stomaco (PL gli stomachi)
   ◆ **to have stomach ache** avere mal di stomaco

stone [stəun] NOUN
   1 la pietra ◊ *a stone wall* un muro di pietra
   2 il nocciolo ◊ *a peach stone* un nocciolo
   di pesca

   ❶ *Uno* **stone** *equivale a 6,35 chilogrammi.*

stood [stud] VERB *see* **stand**

stool [stuːl] NOUN
   lo sgabello

to **stop** [stɔp] VERB
   see also **stop** NOUN
   fermarsi^E ◊ *The bus doesn't stop there.*
   L'autobus non si ferma lì.
   ◆ **Stop that!** Smettila!
   ◆ **to stop doing something** smettere* di fare
   qualcosa ◊ *I must stop smoking.* Devo
   smettere di fumare.

   ◆ **to stop somebody doing something**
   impedire a qualcuno di fare qualcosa
   ◆ **to stop to do something** fermarsi^E per fare
   qualcosa ◊ *He stopped to look at the view.*
   Si è fermato per guardare il panorama.

stop [stɔp] NOUN
   see also **stop** VERB
   la fermata ◊ *a bus stop* una fermata
   d'autobus

stopwatch [ˈstɔpwɔtʃ] NOUN (PL
   stopwatches)
   il cronometro

store [stɔːʳ] NOUN
   see also **store** VERB
   1 il negozio ◊ *a furniture store* un negozio
   di mobili
   2 la scorta ◊ *my secret store of biscuits* la
   mia scorta segreta di biscotti
   ◆ **to lie in store for somebody** aspettare
   qualcuno ◊ *We had no idea what lay in store*
   for us. Non avevamo idea di cosa ci
   aspettasse.

to **store** [stɔːʳ] VERB
   see also **store** NOUN
   conservare

storey [ˈstɔːrɪ] NOUN (US **story**)
   il piano ◊ *a three-storey building* un
   palazzo a tre piani

storm [stɔːm] NOUN
   1 la tempesta ◊ *Their boat sank in a storm.*
   La barca è affondata durante una tempesta.
   2 il temporale ◊ *There was a power cut*
   because of the storm. C'è stato un blackout
   a causa del temporale.

stormy [ˈstɔːmɪ] ADJECTIVE
   tempestoso

story [ˈstɔːrɪ] NOUN (PL **stories**)
   la storia

stove [stəuv] NOUN
   1 la cucina ◊ *an electric stove* una cucina
   elettrica
   2 il fornello ◊ *a camping stove* un fornello
   da campeggio

straight [streɪt] ADJECTIVE, ADVERB
   1 dritto ◊ *a straight road* una strada dritta
   ◆ **a straight line** una linea retta
   2 liscio ◊ *straight hair* capelli lisci
   3 eterosessuale ◊ *I'm sure he's straight.*
   Sono sicura che sia eterosessuale.
   4 subito ◊ *I'll come straight back.* Torno
   subito.
   ◆ **straight away** subito
   ◆ **straight on** sempre dritto

straightforward [streɪtˈfɔːwəd] ADJECTIVE
   1 semplice ◊ *The question seemed*
   straightforward enough. La questione
   sembrava abbastanza semplice.
   2 onesto ◊ *She's a very straightforward*
   girl. È una ragazza molto onesta.

strain [streɪn] NOUN
   see also **strain** VERB
   la pressione ◊ *She is under considerable*   ☞

S

strain. È molto sotto pressione.
+ **It was a strain.** È stata dura.

to **strain** [streɪn] VERB
> see also **strain** NOUN
  1. sforzare *(eyes)*
  2. mettere sotto pressione ◊ *The volume of flights is straining the air traffic control system.* Il gran numero di voli sta mettendo sotto pressione il sistema di controllo del traffico aereo.
+ **to strain one's back** farsi [E] male alla schiena
+ **to strain a muscle** farsi [E] uno strappo muscolare

strained [streɪnd] ADJECTIVE
+ **a strained muscle** uno strappo muscolare

stranded ['strændɪd] ADJECTIVE
+ **to be stranded** rimanere [E] bloccato

strange [streɪndʒ] ADJECTIVE
strano

stranger ['streɪndʒəʳ] NOUN
lo sconosciuto
la sconosciuta
◊ *Don't speak to strangers.* Non parlare con gli sconosciuti.
+ **I'm a stranger here.** Non sono del posto.

to **strangle** ['stræŋgl] VERB
strangolare

strap [stræp] NOUN
  1. la tracolla ◊ *the strap of her bag* la tracolla della borsa
  2. il cinturino ◊ *I need a new strap for my watch.* Ho bisogno di un cinturino nuovo per l'orologio.
  3. la spallina ◊ *a top with thin straps* un top con le spalline strette

straw [strɔː] NOUN
  1. la paglia ◊ *a straw hat* un cappello di paglia
  2. la cannuccia (PL le cannucce) ◊ *He sucked the juice through a straw.* Ha bevuto il succo di frutta con la cannuccia.
+ **That's the last straw!** Questa è la goccia che fa traboccare il vaso!

strawberry ['strɔːbərɪ] NOUN (PL **strawberries**)
la fragola

stray [streɪ] ADJECTIVE
randagio ◊ *a stray cat* un gatto randagio

stream [striːm] NOUN
il ruscello

street [striːt] NOUN
la strada ◊ *a narrow street* una strada stretta
+ **a street plan** una cartina della città

street car ['striːtkɑːʳ] NOUN [US]
il tram (PL i tram)

streetlamp ['striːtlæmp] NOUN
il lampione

streetwise ['striːtwaɪz] ADJECTIVE
+ **to be streetwise** sapersela [E] cavare
+ **a streetwise kid** un ragazzo smaliziato

strength [streŋθ] NOUN
la forza

to **stress** [stres] VERB
> see also **stress** NOUN
sottolineare ◊ *I would like to stress that...* Vorrei sottolineare che...

stress [stres] NOUN
> see also **stress** VERB
  1. lo stress ◊ *a stress-related illness* una malattia legata allo stress
+ **I'm under stress.** Sono sotto pressione.
  2. l' accento ◊ *The stress is on the first syllable.* L'accento cade sulla prima sillaba.

stretch [stretʃ] NOUN
> see also **stretch** VERB
  1. il pezzo ◊ *a stretch of road* un pezzo di strada
  2. l' esercizio di stretching ◊ *We'll begin with a few stretches.* Cominceremo con qualche esercizio di stretching.

to **stretch** [stretʃ] VERB
> see also **stretch** NOUN
  1. stiracchiarsi [E] ◊ *The dog woke up and stretched.* Il cane s'è svegliato e s'è stiracchiato.
  2. allargarsi [E] ◊ *My sweater stretched when I washed it.* Il maglione s'è allargato durante il lavaggio.
  3. tendere* ◊ *They stretched a rope between two trees.* Hanno teso una corda tra due alberi.

to **stretch out** [stretʃaʊt] VERB
  1. distendersi* [E] ◊ *There wasn't enough room to stretch out.* Non c'era abbastanza spazio per distendersi.
  2. allungare ◊ *She stretched out an arm and grabbed me.* Ha allungato un braccio per afferrarmi.

stretcher ['stretʃəʳ] NOUN
la barella

stretchy ['stretʃɪ] ADJECTIVE
elastico

strict [strɪkt] ADJECTIVE
severo

strike [straɪk] NOUN
> see also **strike** VERB
lo sciopero
+ **to be on strike** essere [E] in sciopero
+ **to go on strike** scioperare

to **strike** [straɪk] VERB (**struck, struck**)
> see also **strike** NOUN
  1. fare* sciopero ◊ *They decided to strike.* Hanno deciso di fare sciopero.
  2. colpire ◊ *He struck the ball hard.* Ha colpito forte la palla. ◊ *They fear the killer may strike again.* Temono che il killer possa colpire di nuovo.
  3. suonare ◊ *The clock struck three.* L'orologio ha suonato le tre.
+ **to strike a match** accendere* un fiammifero

striker ['straɪkəʳ] NOUN
  1. lo/la scioperante ◊ *The strikers wanted*

more money. Gli scioperanti volevano più soldi.

[2] l' **attaccante** MASC/FEM ◇ *the Manchester striker* l'attaccante del Manchester

striking ['straɪkɪŋ] ADJECTIVE
notevole ◇ *a striking resemblance* una notevole somiglianza

string [strɪŋ] NOUN

[1] lo spago ◇ *a piece of string* un pezzo di spago

[2] la corda (*of violin, guitar*)

[3] la serie (PL le serie) ◇ *a string of victories* una serie di vittorie

string bean [strɪŋ'biːn] NOUN
il fagiolino

to **strip** [strɪp] VERB
see also **strip** NOUN
spogliarsi[E]

strip [strɪp] NOUN
see also **strip** VERB

[1] la striscia (PL le strisce) ◇ *a strip of material* una striscia di stoffa

[2] la divisa ◇ *the Manchester strip* la divisa del Manchester

strip cartoon [strɪpkɑː'tuːn] NOUN
il fumetto

stripe [straɪp] NOUN
la striscia (PL le strisce)

striped [straɪpt] ADJECTIVE
a righe ◇ *a striped skirt* una gonna a righe

stripper ['strɪpə'] NOUN
lo/la spogliarellista

stripy ['straɪpɪ] ADJECTIVE
a righe

to **stroke** [strəʊk] VERB
see also **stroke** NOUN
accarezzare

stroke [strəʊk] NOUN
see also **stroke** VERB
l' ictus (PL gli ictus) ◇ *He had a stroke.* Ha avuto un ictus.

♦ **a stroke of luck** un colpo di fortuna

stroll [strəʊl] NOUN

♦ **to go for a stroll** andare[E] a fare due passi

stroller ['strəʊlə'] NOUN US
il passeggino

strong [strɒŋ] ADJECTIVE
forte ◇ *She's stronger than me.* Lei è più forte di me.

♦ **Punctuality isn't my strong point.** La puntualità non è il mio forte.

strongly ['strɒŋlɪ] ADVERB

♦ **We recommend strongly that...** Raccomandiamo vivamente di...

♦ **to smell strongly of something** avere un forte odore di qualcosa

♦ **strongly built** robusto

♦ **I don't feel strongly about it.** Per me fa lo stesso.

struck [strʌk] VERB see **strike**

to **struggle** ['strʌgl] VERB

see also **struggle** NOUN

[1] divincolarsi[E] ◇ *He struggled, but he couldn't escape.* Si divincolò ma non riuscì a liberarsi.

[2] lottare ◇ *He struggled to get custody of his daughter.* Ha lottato per ottenere la custodia della figlia.

♦ **They struggle to pay their bills.** Riescono a stento a pagare le bollette.

struggle ['strʌgl] NOUN
see also **struggle** VERB
la lotta ◇ *a violent struggle* una lotta violenta

♦ **It was a struggle.** È stata dura.

stub [stʌb] NOUN
il mozzicone

stubborn ['stʌbən] ADJECTIVE
testardo

to **stub out** [stʌb'aʊt] VERB
spegnere*

stuck [stʌk] VERB see **stick**

stuck [stʌk] ADJECTIVE
bloccato

♦ **to get stuck** rimanere[E] bloccato ◇ *We got stuck in a traffic jam.* Siamo rimasti bloccati nel traffico.

stuck-up [stʌk'ʌp] ADJECTIVE
presuntuoso

stud [stʌd] NOUN

[1] l' orecchino ◇ *gold studs* orecchini d'oro

[2] il tacchetto (*in football boots*)

student ['stjuːdənt] NOUN
lo studente
la studentessa

studio ['stjuːdɪəʊ] NOUN (PL **studios**)
lo studio ◇ *a TV studio* uno studio televisivo

♦ **a studio flat** un monolocale

to **study** ['stʌdɪ] VERB (**studied, studied**)
studiare

stuff [stʌf] NOUN
la roba ◇ *Have you got all your stuff?* Hai tutta la tua roba?

♦ **I need some stuff for hay fever.** Mi serve qualcosa per il raffreddore da fieno.

stuffy ['stʌfɪ] ADJECTIVE

♦ **It's stuffy in here.** Si soffoca qui dentro.

to **stumble** ['stʌmbl] VERB
inciampare

stung [stʌŋ] VERB see **sting**

stunk [stʌŋk] VERB see **stink**

stunned [stʌnd] ADJECTIVE
sbalordito

stunning ['stʌnɪŋ] ADJECTIVE
fantastico

stunt [stʌnt] NOUN

[1] la trovata ◇ *a publicity stunt* una trovata pubblicitaria

[2] la scena pericolosa ◇ *He performed his own stunts.* Ha girato personalmente le scene pericolose.

S

stuntman ['stʌntmæn] NOUN (PL **stuntmen**)
lo stuntman (PL gli stuntman)

stupid ['stjuːpɪd] ADJECTIVE
stupido

to **stutter** ['stʌtə'] VERB
see also **stutter** NOUN
balbettare

stutter ['stʌtə'] NOUN
see also **stutter** VERB

♦ **He's got a stutter.** È balbuziente.

style [staɪl] NOUN
lo stile ◊ *That's not his style.* Non è nel suo stile.

subject ['sʌbdʒɪkt] NOUN
1 l' argomento ◊ *The subject of my project is the Internet.* L'argomento della mia ricerca è Internet.
2 la materia ◊ *What's your favourite subject?* Quale materia preferisci?
3 il soggetto (*of sentence*)

subjunctive [səb'dʒʌŋktɪv] NOUN
il congiuntivo

submarine [sʌbmə'riːn] NOUN
il sottomarino

subscription [səb'skrɪpʃən] NOUN
l' abbonamento (*to magazine*)

♦ **to take out a subscription** abbonarsi E

subsequently ['sʌbsɪkwəntlɪ] ADVERB
in seguito

to **subsidize** ['sʌbsɪdaɪz] VERB
sovvenzionare

subsidy ['sʌbsɪdɪ] NOUN (PL **subsidies**)
la sovvenzione

substance ['sʌbstəns] NOUN
la sostanza

substitute ['sʌbstɪtjuːt] NOUN
see also **substitute** VERB
1 il sostituto ◊ *He's looking for a substitute.* Sta cercando un sostituto.

♦ **There's no substitute for personal contact.** Non c'è niente di meglio dei contatti personali.
2 la riserva (*in sport*) ◊ *A substitute came on in the 71st minute.* È entrata una riserva al 71° minuto.

to **substitute** ['sʌbstɪtjuːt] VERB
see also **substitute** NOUN
sostituire ◊ *They want to substitute gas for coal.* Vogliono sostituire il carbone con il gas.

subtitled ['sʌbtaɪtld] ADJECTIVE
sottotitolato

subtitles ['sʌbtaɪtlz] NOUN PL
i sottotitoli

subtle ['sʌtl] ADJECTIVE
sottile

to **subtract** [səb'trækt] VERB
sottrarre

suburb ['sʌbəːb] NOUN
il sobborgo (PL i sobborghi) ◊ *a London suburb* un sobborgo di Londra

♦ **in the suburbs** in periferia ◊ *They live in the suburbs.* Abitano in periferia.

suburban [sə'bəːbən] ADJECTIVE
periferico ◊ *a suburban street* una via periferica

♦ **a suburban shopping centre** un centro commerciale fuori città

subway ['sʌbweɪ] NOUN
1 il sottopassaggio (*for pedestrians*)
2 la metropolitana (*train*)

to **succeed** [sək'siːd] VERB
riuscire* E

♦ **to succeed in doing something** riuscire* E a fare qualcosa ◊ *They succeeded in persuading her.* Sono riusciti a persuaderla.
♦ **The plan did not succeed.** Il piano è fallito.

success [sək'ses] NOUN (PL **successes**)
il successo

successful [sək'sesful] ADJECTIVE
riuscito ◊ *a successful attempt* un tentativo riuscito

♦ **to be successful in doing something** riuscire a fare qualcosa
♦ **a successful lawyer** un avvocato affermato

successfully [sək'sesfəlɪ] ADVERB
con successo

successive [sək'sesɪv] ADJECTIVE
consecutivo ◊ *He was the winner for a second successive year.* Ha vinto per il secondo anno consecutivo.

such [sʌtʃ] ADJECTIVE, ADVERB
così ◊ *such nice people* gente così simpatica ◊ *such a lot* così tanto ◊ *such a lot of work* così tanto lavoro

♦ **It was such a waste of time.** Era una tale perdita di tempo.
♦ **such a thing** una cosa del genere ◊ *I wouldn't dream of doing such a thing.* Non mi sognerei di fare una cosa del genere.
♦ **such as** come ◊ *hot countries such as India* paesi caldi, come l'India
♦ **There's no such thing.** Non esiste.
♦ **He's not an expert as such, but...** Non è un vero e proprio esperto, però...

such-and-such ['sʌtʃənsʌtʃ] ADJECTIVE
tale ◊ *such-and-such a place* il tale posto

to **suck** [sʌk] VERB
succhiare ◊ *She sucks her thumb.* Si succhia il pollice.

sudden ['sʌdn] ADJECTIVE
improvviso ◊ *a sudden change* un cambiamento improvviso

♦ **all of a sudden** all'improvviso

suddenly ['sʌdnlɪ] ADVERB
improvvisamente

suede [sweɪd] NOUN
la pelle scamosciata ◊ *a suede jacket* una giacca di pelle scamosciata

to **suffer** ['sʌfə'] VERB
soffrire*

♦ **to suffer from something** soffrire di

---

* Verbs followed by this symbol are irregular. See pp.339–364 for further details.

qualcosa ◊ *I suffer from hay fever.* Soffro di raffreddore da fieno.

to **suffocate** ['sʌfəkeɪt] VERB
soffocare

sugar ['ʃugəʳ] NOUN
lo zucchero

to **suggest** [sə'dʒɛst] VERB
1 proporre* ◊ *She suggested going out for a pizza.* Ha proposto di andare a mangiare la pizza.
2 consigliare ◊ *I suggested they set off early.* Ho consigliato loro di partire presto.
3 insinuare ◊ *What are you trying to suggest?* Cosa vuoi insinuare?

suggestion [sə'dʒɛstʃən] NOUN
la proposta

suicide ['suːɪsaɪd] NOUN
il suicidio ◊ *a case of attempted suicide* un caso di tentato suicidio
♦ **to commit suicide** suicidarsi[E]

suit [suːt] NOUN
see also **suit** VERB
1 l'abito (*man's*)
2 il tailleur (PL i tailleur) (*woman's*)

to **suit** [suːt] VERB
see also **suit** NOUN
1 andare*[E] bene ◊ *What time would suit you?* A che ora ti andrebbe bene? ◊ *That suits me fine.* Per me va benissimo.
2 stare*[E] bene a ◊ *That dress really suits you.* Quel vestito ti sta benissimo.
♦ **Suit yourself!** Fa' come ti pare!

suitable ['suːtəbl] ADJECTIVE
1 conveniente ◊ *a suitable time* un'ora conveniente
2 adatto ◊ *suitable clothing* vestiti adatti

suitcase ['suːtkeɪs] NOUN
la valigia (PL le valigie)

suite [swiːt] NOUN
la suite (PL le suite) ◊ *a suite at the Paris Hilton* una suite all'Hilton di Parigi
♦ **a bedroom suite** (*furniture*) una camera da letto
♦ **a three-piece suite** un divano e due poltrone

to **sulk** [sʌlk] VERB
fare* il broncio

sulky ['sʌlkɪ] ADJECTIVE
imbronciato

sultana [sʌl'tɑːnə] NOUN
♦ **sultanas** l'uva sultanina SING

sum [sʌm] NOUN
1 la somma ◊ *a sum of money* una somma di denaro
2 l'addizione FEM ◊ *We do sums.* Facciamo le addizioni.

to **summarize** ['sʌməraɪz] VERB
riassumere

summary ['sʌmərɪ] NOUN (PL **summaries**)
il riassunto

summer ['sʌməʳ] NOUN
see also **summer** ADJECTIVE

l'estate FEM ◊ *in the summer* d'estate ◊ *last summer* l'estate scorsa

summer ['sʌməʳ] ADJECTIVE
see also **summer** NOUN
estivo ◊ *summer clothes* abiti estivi ◊ *the summer holidays* le vacanze estive

summertime ['sʌmətaɪm] NOUN
l'estate FEM

summit ['sʌmɪt] NOUN
1 il vertice ◊ *the NATO summit in Rome* il vertice della NATO a Roma
2 la cima ◊ *After six hours we reached the summit.* Dopo sei ore abbiamo raggiunto la cima.

to **sum up** [sʌm'ʌp] VERB
riassumere* ◊ *To sum up...* Per riassumere...

sun [sʌn] NOUN
il sole ◊ *in the sun* al sole

to **sunbathe** ['sʌnbeɪð] VERB
prendere* il sole

sun block ['sʌnblɔk] NOUN
la protezione solare totale

sunburn ['sʌnbəːn] NOUN
la scottatura

sunburnt ['sʌnbəːnt] ADJECTIVE
scottato dal sole ◊ *sunburnt shoulders* spalle scottate dal sole
♦ **to get sunburnt** scottarsi[E]

Sunday ['sʌndɪ] NOUN
la domenica
♦ **on Sunday** domenica ◊ *I saw her on Sunday.* L'ho vista domenica.
♦ **on Sundays** di domenica ◊ *I go swimming on Sundays.* Vado in piscina di domenica.

Sunday school ['sʌndɪskuːl] NOUN
la scuola di catechismo

sunflower ['sʌnflauəʳ] NOUN
il girasole

sung [sʌŋ] VERB see **sing**

sunglasses ['sʌnglɑːsɪz] NOUN PL
gli occhiali da sole

sunk [sʌŋk] VERB see **sink**

sunlight ['sʌnlaɪt] NOUN
la luce solare

sunny ['sʌnɪ] ADJECTIVE
♦ **It's sunny.** C'è il sole.
♦ **a sunny day** una bella giornata

sunrise ['sʌnraɪz] NOUN
l'alba ◊ *before sunrise* prima dell'alba

sunroof ['sʌnruːf] NOUN
il tettuccio apribile

sunscreen ['sʌnskriːn] NOUN
la crema solare protettiva

sunset ['sʌnset] NOUN
il tramonto

sunshine ['sʌnʃaɪn] NOUN
il sole ◊ *six hours of sunshine* sei ore di sole ◊ *in the sunshine* al sole

sunstroke ['sʌnstrəuk] NOUN
l'insolazione FEM

S

+ **to get sunstroke** prendere un'insolazione

suntan ['sʌntæn] NOUN
l' abbronzatura ◊ *her usual suntan* la sua solita abbronzatura
+ **a suntan lotion** una lozione abbronzante
+ **suntan oil** olio abbronzante

super ['su:pə'] ADJECTIVE
fantastico

superb [su:'pə:b] ADJECTIVE
magnifico

supermarket ['su:pəmɑ:kɪt] NOUN
il supermercato

supernatural [su:pə'nætʃərəl] ADJECTIVE
soprannaturale

superstitious [su:pə'stɪʃəs] ADJECTIVE
superstizioso

to **supervise** ['su:pəvaɪz] VERB
vigilare

supervisor ['su:pəvaɪzə'] NOUN
[1] il/la sorvegliante ◊ *a supervisor in the factory* un sorvegliante della fabbrica
[2] il capocommesso
la capocommessa
(*in shop*)
◊ *He's a supervisor in a big store.* È capocommesso in un grande magazzino.

supper ['sʌpə'] NOUN
la cena

supplement ['sʌplɪmənt] NOUN
il supplemento

to **supply** [sə'plaɪ] VERB (**supplied, supplied**)
see also **supply** NOUN
fornire
+ **to supply somebody with something** fornire qualcosa a qualcuno ◊ *The centre supplied us with all the equipment.* Il centro ci ha fornito tutta l'attrezzatura.

supply [sə'plaɪ] NOUN (PL **supplies**)
see also **supply** VERB
[1] la provvista ◊ *a supply of paper* una provvista di carta
[2] la fornitura ◊ *the water supply* la fornitura dell'acqua
+ **supplies** rifornimenti
+ **medical supplies** medicinali

supply teacher [sə'plaɪti:tʃə'] NOUN
il/la supplente

to **support** [sə'pɔ:t] VERB
see also **support** NOUN
[1] appoggiare ◊ *My friends have always supported me.* I miei amici mi hanno sempre appoggiato.
[2] tifare per ◊ *What team do you support?* Per quale squadra tifi?
[3] mantenere* ◊ *She had to support five children on her own.* Ha dovuto mantenere cinque figli da sola.
Be careful not to translate **to support** *by* **sopportare.**

support [sə'pɔ:t] NOUN
see also **support** VERB
l' appoggio

supporter [sə'pɔ:tə'] NOUN
[1] il tifoso
la tifosa
◊ *a Liverpool supporter* un tifoso del Liverpool
[2] il/la simpatizzante ◊ *a supporter of the Labour Party* un simpatizzante del partito Laburista
[3] il sostenitore
la sostenitrice
◊ *a major supporter of the tax reform plan* un importante sostenitore del piano di riforma fiscale

to **suppose** [sə'pəuz] VERB
supporre* ◊ *I suppose he's late.* Suppongo che sia in ritardo.
+ **I suppose so.** Credo di sì.
+ **He's supposed to...** Dovrebbe... ◊ *He's supposed to leave on Sunday.* Dovrebbe partire domenica.
+ **You're not supposed to smoke in the toilet.** Non è consentito fumare nel bagno.
+ **It's supposed to be...** Sembra che... ◊ *It's supposed to be the best hotel in the city.* Sembra che sia il miglior albergo della città.

supposing [sə'pəuzɪŋ] CONJUNCTION
+ **supposing that** mettiamo che ◊ *Supposing you won the lottery...* Mettiamo che tu vinca alla lotteria...

to **suppress** [sə'pres] VERB
reprimere

surcharge ['sə:tʃɑ:dʒ] NOUN
il sovrapprezzo

sure [ʃuə'] ADJECTIVE
sicuro ◊ *Are you sure?* Sei sicuro?
+ **Sure!** Certo!
+ **to make sure that** assicurarsi^E che ◊ *I'm going to make sure the door's locked.* Voglio assicurarmi che la porta sia chiusa a chiave.

surely ['ʃuəlɪ] ADVERB
+ **Surely you don't believe that?** Non ci crederai davvero?

to **surf** [sə:f] VERB
see also **surf** NOUN
fare* surf
+ **to go surfing** fare* surf
+ **to surf the net** navigare in Internet

surf [sə:f] NOUN
see also **surf** VERB
la spuma

surface ['sə:fɪs] NOUN
la superficie

surfboard ['sə:fbɔ:d] NOUN
la tavola da surf

surfing ['sə:fɪŋ] NOUN
il surf (*sport*)

surgeon ['sə:dʒən] NOUN
il chirurgo (PL i chirurghi)

surgery ['sə:dʒərɪ] NOUN (PL **surgeries**)
l' ambulatorio ◊ *surgery hours* orario di

---

* Verbs followed by this symbol are irregular. See pp.339–364 for further details.

ambulatorio

surname [ˈsɜːneɪm] NOUN
il cognome

surprise [səˈpraɪz] NOUN
la sorpresa

surprised [səˈpraɪzd] ADJECTIVE
sorpreso ◊ *I was surprised to see him.* Ero
sorpreso di vederlo.

surprising [səˈpraɪzɪŋ] ADJECTIVE
sorprendente

to **surrender** [səˈrendəʳ] VERB
see also **surrender** NOUN
arrendersi ᴱ

surrender [səˈrendəʳ] NOUN
see also **surrender** VERB
la resa

to **surround** [səˈraund] VERB
circondare

surroundings [səˈraundɪŋz] NOUN PL
◆ **in beautiful surroundings** in una bellissima
posizione

survey [ˈsɜːveɪ] NOUN
see also **survey** VERB
l' indagine FEM ◊ *They did a survey of a
thousand students.* È stata fatta un'indagine
su un campione di mille studenti.

to **survey** [səˈveɪ] VERB
see also **survey** NOUN
[1] condurre* un'indagine su ◊ *They have
surveyed a number of companies.* Hanno
condotto un'indagine su diverse società.
[2] esaminare ◊ *He surveyed the room.* Ha
esaminato la stanza.
[3] fare un rilevamento di ◊ *They have
surveyed the area.* Hanno fatto un
rilevamento della zona.

surveyor [səˈveɪəʳ] NOUN
[1] il perito geometra (*of buildings*)
[2] l' agrimensore MASC (*of land*)

survivor [səˈvaɪvəʳ] NOUN
il/la superstite ◊ *There were no survivors.*
Non ci sono stati superstiti.

to **suspect** [səsˈpekt] VERB
see also **suspect** NOUN
sospettare

suspect [ˈsʌspekt] NOUN
see also **suspect** VERB
il sospetto
la sospetta

to **suspend** [səsˈpend] VERB
sospendere*

suspenders [səsˈpendəz] NOUN US
le bretelle (*braces*)

suspense [səsˈpens] NOUN
[1] l' attesa ◊ *The suspense was terrible.*
L'attesa era terribile.
[2] la suspense ◊ *a film with lots of
suspense* un film ricco di suspense

suspension [səsˈpenʃən] NOUN
la sospensione

suspicious [səsˈpɪʃəs] ADJECTIVE

[1] sospettoso ◊ *He was suspicious at first.*
All'inizio era sospettoso.
[2] sospetto ◊ *suspicious behaviour* un
comportamento sospetto

to **swallow** [ˈswɒləu] VERB
inghiottire

swam [swæm] VERB *see* **swim**

swan [swɒn] NOUN
il cigno

to **swap** [swɒp] VERB
[1] scambiare* ◊ *He swapped the vouchers
for tickets.* Ha scambiato i voucher con i
biglietti.
[2] fare* scambio ◊ *Do you want to swap?*
Vuoi fare scambio?

to **swat** [swɒt] VERB
schiacciare

to **sway** [sweɪ] VERB
oscillare

to **swear** [sweəʳ] VERB (**swore, sworn**)
[1] giurare ◊ *I swear I didn't know.* Giuro
che non lo sapevo. ◊ *He swore he wouldn't
do it again.* Ha giurato che non l'avrebbe
rifatto.
[2] imprecare ◊ *He swore under his breath.*
Ha imprecato sottovoce.

swearword [ˈsweəwɜːd] NOUN
la parolaccia (PL le parolacce)

sweat [swet] NOUN
see also **sweat** VERB
il sudore

to **sweat** [swet] VERB
see also **sweat** NOUN
sudare

sweater [ˈswetəʳ] NOUN
il maglione

sweatshirt [ˈswetʃɜːt] NOUN
la felpa

sweaty [ˈswetɪ] ADJECTIVE
sudato

Swede [swiːd] NOUN
lo/la svedese

swede [swiːd] NOUN
la rapa svedese (*vegetable*)

Sweden [ˈswiːdn] NOUN
la Svezia

Swedish [ˈswiːdɪʃ] ADJECTIVE
see also **Swedish** NOUN
svedese

Swedish [ˈswiːdɪʃ] NOUN
see also **Swedish** ADJECTIVE
lo svedese

to **sweep** [swiːp] VERB (**swept, swept**)
spazzare ◊ *She swept the floor.* Ha spazzato
il pavimento.

sweet [swiːt] NOUN
see also **sweet** ADJECTIVE
[1] la caramella ◊ *a bag of sweets* un
sacchetto di caramelle
[2] il dolce ◊ *Are you going to have a sweet?*
Prendi il dolce?

S

sweet [swiːt] ADJECTIVE
see also **sweet** NOUN
1 dolce ◊ *a sweet wine* un vino dolce
2 carino ◊ *That was really sweet of you.* È stato molto carino da parte tua.
• **sweet and sour pork** maiale in agrodolce

sweetcorn ['swiːtkɔːn] NOUN
il mais

sweltering ['sweltərɪŋ] ADJECTIVE
• **It was sweltering.** Faceva un caldo soffocante.

swept [swept] VERB *see* **sweep**

to **swerve** [swɜːv] VERB
sterzare ◊ *I swerved to avoid the cyclist.* Ho sterzato per evitare il ciclista.

swim [swɪm] NOUN
see also **swim** VERB
la nuotata ◊ *Let's go for a swim.* Andiamo a fare una nuotata.

to **swim** [swɪm] VERB (**swam, swum**)
see also **swim** NOUN
nuotare ◊ *Can you swim?* Sai nuotare? ◊ *I swam for an hour.* Ho nuotato per un'ora. ◊ *I've never swum in the sea.* Non ho mai nuotato nel mare.
• **to go swimming** andare* E a nuotare
• **to swim across...** attraversare...a nuoto ◊ *She swam across the river.* Ha attraversato il fiume a nuoto.

swimmer ['swɪmə'] NOUN
il nuotatore
la nuotatrice

swimming ['swɪmɪŋ] NOUN
il nuoto ◊ *swimming and cycling* il nuoto ed il ciclismo
• **Do you like swimming?** Ti piace nuotare?
• **a swimming cap** una cuffia da bagno
• **a swimming costume** un costume da bagno
• **swimming trunks** calzoncini da bagno

swimming pool ['swɪmɪŋpuːl] NOUN
la piscina

swimsuit ['swɪmsuːt] NOUN
il costume da bagno

swing [swɪŋ]
see also **swing** VERB NOUN
l' altalena ◊ *a slide and some swings* uno scivolo e alcune altalene
• **a mood swing** un cambiamento d'umore

to **swing** [swɪŋ] VERB (**swung, swung**)
see also **swing** NOUN
dondolare ◊ *A large key swung from his belt.* Dalla cintura gli dondolava una grossa chiave.
• **to swing round** rigirarsi E ◊ *The canoe suddenly swung round.* La canoa si rigirò all'improvviso.
• **He swung the bag over his shoulder.** Si mise la borsa sulla spalla.
• **The gate swung shut.** Il cancello si è chiuso.

Swiss [swɪs] ADJECTIVE
see also **Swiss** NOUN

svizzero

Swiss [swɪs] NOUN
see also **Swiss** ADJECTIVE
lo svizzero
• **the Swiss** gli svizzeri

switch [swɪtʃ] NOUN (PL **switches**)
see also **switch** VERB
l' interruttore MASC

to **switch** [swɪtʃ] VERB
see also **switch** NOUN
cambiare ◊ *We switched partners.* Abbiamo cambiato partner.

to **switch off** [swɪtʃ'ɔf] VERB
spegnere* (*TV, engine, machine*)

to **switch on** [swɪtʃ'ɔn] VERB
accendere* (*TV, engine, machine*)

Switzerland ['swɪtsələnd] NOUN
la Svizzera

swollen ['swəulən] ADJECTIVE
gonfio ◊ *My ankle is swollen.* Ho una caviglia gonfia.

to **swop** [swɔp] VERB
1 scambiare* ◊ *He swopped the vouchers for tickets.* Ha scambiato i voucher con i biglietti.
2 fare* scambio ◊ *Do you want to swop?* Vuoi fare scambio?

sword [sɔːd] NOUN
la spada

swore, sworn [swɔː',swɔːn] VERB *see* **swear**

to **swot** [swɔt] VERB
see also **swot** NOUN
sgobbare
• **to swot for an exam** sgobbare per un esame

swot [swɔt] NOUN
see also **swot** VERB
lo sgobbone
la sgobbona

swum [swʌm] VERB *see* **swim**

swung [swʌŋ] VERB *see* **swing**

syllabus ['sɪləbəs] NOUN (PL **syllabuses**)
il programma (PL i programmi)

symbol ['sɪmbl] NOUN
il simbolo

sympathetic [sɪmpə'θetɪk] ADJECTIVE
comprensivo ◊ *I told my teacher and she was sympathetic.* L'ho detto all'insegnante e lei è stata comprensiva.
Be careful not to translate **sympathetic** *by* **simpatico.**

to **sympathize** ['sɪmpəθaɪz] VERB
• **to sympathize with somebody** capire qualcuno

sympathy ['sɪmpəθɪ] NOUN
la compassione

symptom ['sɪmptəm] NOUN
il sintomo

syringe [sɪ'rɪndʒ] NOUN
la siringa (PL le siringhe)

system ['sɪstəm] NOUN
il sistema (PL i sistemi)

* Verbs followed by this symbol are irregular. See pp.339–364 for further details.

T

table ['teɪbl] NOUN
il tavolo ◊ *It's on the table.* È sul tavolo.
• **to lay the table** apparecchiare la tavola

tablecloth ['teɪblklɔθ] NOUN
la tovaglia

tablespoon ['teɪblspuːn] NOUN
il cucchiaio ◊ *a tablespoonful of sugar* un cucchiaio di zucchero

tablet ['tæblɪt] NOUN
la pastiglia

table tennis ['teɪbltenɪs] NOUN
il ping-pong

tabloid ['tæblɔɪd] NOUN
il tabloid (PL i tabloid)

ℹ️ *I* **tabloid** *sono quotidiani a larga diffusione di tipo scandalistico e sensazionalistico.*

---

tackle ['tækl] NOUN
see also **tackle** VERB
[1] il contrasto (*in football*)
[2] il placcaggio (*in rugby*)
• **fishing tackle** l'attrezzatura da pesca

to **tackle** ['tækl] VERB
see also **tackle** NOUN
[1] contrastare (*in football*)
[2] placcare (*in rugby*)
• **to tackle a problem** affrontare un problema

tact [tækt] NOUN
il tatto

tactful ['tæktful] ADJECTIVE
pieno di tatto

tactics ['tæktɪks] NOUN PL
la tattica SING

tactless ['tæktlɪs] ADJECTIVE
privo di tatto (*person*)
• **a tactless remark** un'osservazione indelicata

tadpole ['tædpəul] NOUN
il girino

tag [tæg] NOUN
l'etichetta

tail [teɪl] NOUN
la coda (*of animal*)
• **Heads or tails?** Testa o croce?
• **the tail end** la fine

tail coat ['teɪlkəut] NOUN
la marsina

tailor ['teɪlə'] NOUN
il sarto

to **take** [teɪk] VERB (**took, taken**)
[1] prendere* ◊ *He took a plate out of the cupboard.* Ha preso un piatto dall'armadietto.
[2] portare ◊ *Don't forget to take your camera.* Non scordarti di portare la macchina fotografica. ◊ *He goes to London every week, but he never takes me.* Va a Londra tutte le settimane ma non mi porta

mai con sé.
[3] volerci ^E ◊ *It takes about an hour.* Ci vuole circa un'ora. ◊ *It won't take long.* Non ci vorrà molto. ◊ *It takes a lot of money to do that.* Ci vogliono un sacco di soldi per farlo.
[4] sopportare ◊ *He can't take being criticized.* Non sopporta di essere* criticato.
[5] fare* ◊ *Have you taken your driving test yet?* Hai già fatto l'esame di guida? ◊ *He took a photograph.* Ha fatto una fotografia.

to **take after** [teɪk'ɑːftə'] VERB
assomigliare a ◊ *She takes after her mother.* Assomiglia a sua madre.

to **take apart** [teɪkə'pɑːt] VERB
• **to take something apart** smontare qualcosa

to **take away** [teɪkə'weɪ] VERB
[1] portare via ◊ *They took away all his belongings.* Gli hanno portato via tutte le sue cose.
• **hot meals to take away** piatti pronti da asporto
[2] togliere* ◊ *She was afraid her children would be taken away from her.* Temeva che le togliessero i bambini.
[3] sottrarre* ◊ *You need to take this amount away from the total.* Devi sottrarre* questa cifra dal totale.
• **sixteen take away three** sedici meno tre

to **take back** [teɪk'bæk] VERB
[1] riportare ◊ *I took it back to the shop.* L'ho riportato al negozio.
[2] ritirare ◊ *I take it all back!* Ritiro tutto quello che ho detto!

to **take down** [teɪk'daun] VERB
prendere* nota di ◊ *The policeman took down the details.* Il poliziotto ha preso nota dei particolari.

to **take in** [teɪk'ɪn] VERB
[1] capire ◊ *I didn't really take it in.* Non avevo capito bene.
[2] abbindolare ◊ *They were taken in by his story.* Si sono lasciati abbindolare dalla sua storia.

to **take off** [teɪk'ɔf] VERB
[1] decollare ◊ *The plane took off twenty minutes late.* L'aereo ha decollato con venti minuti di ritardo.
[2] levarsi ^E ◊ *Take your coat off.* Levati il cappotto.

to **take out** [teɪk'aut] VERB
tirare fuori ◊ *He opened his wallet and took out some money.* Ha aperto il portafoglio e ha tirato fuori dei soldi.
• **to take somebody out to...** portare qualcuno a... ◊ *He took her out to the theatre.* L'ha portata a teatro.

to **take over** [teɪk'əuvə'] VERB
assumere* il controllo di ◊ *They took over the company last year.* Hanno assunto il controllo della società l'anno scorso.

☞

- **I'll take over now.** Ti dò il cambio.
- **to take over from somebody** subentrare[E] a qualcuno

takeaway ['teɪkəweɪ] NOUN
  ① il piatto pronto (da asporto) (*food*)
  ② la tavola calda con piatti pronti (da asporto) (*restaurant*)

taken ['teɪkən] VERB *see* **take**

takeoff ['teɪkɔf] NOUN
  il decollo

talcum powder ['tælkəm'paudə'] NOUN
  il talco

tale [teɪl] NOUN
  il racconto

talent ['tælnt] NOUN
  il talento ◇ *He's got a lot of talent.* Ha molto talento.
- **to have a talent for** essere*[E] portato per ◇ *He's got a real talent for languages.* È molto portato per le lingue.

talented ['tæləntɪd] ADJECTIVE
  di talento ◇ *She's a talented pianist.* È una pianista di talento.

talk [tɔːk] NOUN
  see also **talk** VERB
  ① la conversazione
- **to have a talk about** parlare* di ◇ *I had a talk with my Mum about it.* Ne ho parlato con mia mamma.
- **to give a talk on** fare* un intervento su ◇ *She gave a talk on ancient Egypt.* Ha fatto un intervento sull'antico Egitto.
  ② le chiacchiere ◇ *It's just talk.* Sono solo chiacchiere.
- **a talk show** un talk show

to **talk** [tɔːk] VERB
  see also **talk** NOUN
  parlare* ◇ *What did you talk about?* Di che cosa avete parlato?
- **to talk something over with somebody** discutere* qualcosa con qualcuno ◇ *I'll talk it over with my wife.* Ne discuterò con mia moglie.

talkative ['tɔːkətɪv] ADJECTIVE
  loquace

tall [tɔːl] ADJECTIVE
  alto
- **to be two metres tall** essere*[E] alto due metri

tame [teɪm] ADJECTIVE
  addomesticato (*animal*)

tampon ['tæmpɔn] NOUN
  il tampone

tan [tæn] NOUN
  l' abbronzatura

tangerine [tændʒə'riːn] NOUN
  il mandarino

tangle ['tæŋgl] NOUN
  il groviglio ◇ *a tangle of wires* un groviglio di fili

tank [tæŋk] NOUN
  ① il serbatoio (*for fuel*)
- **a fish tank** un acquario
  ② il carro armato ◇ *The army sent in its tanks.* L'esercito ha inviato i carri armati.

tanker ['tæŋkə'] NOUN
  l' autocisterna (*lorry*)
- **an oil tanker** una petroliera

to **tantalize** ['tæntəlaɪz] VERB
  tormentare

tap [tæp] NOUN
  see also **tap** VERB
  ① il rubinetto ◇ *the hot tap* il rubinetto dell'acqua calda
  ② il colpetto ◇ *a tap on the door* un colpetto alla porta

to **tap** [tæp] VERB
  see also **tap** NOUN
  dare* un colpetto a ◇ *I tapped him on the shoulder.* Gli ho dato un colpetto sulla spalla.

tap-dancing ['tæpdɑːnsɪŋ] NOUN
  il tip tap

to **tape** [teɪp] VERB
  see also **tape** NOUN
  registrare ◇ *Did you tape the film last night?* Hai registrato il film di ieri sera?

tape [teɪp] NOUN
  see also **tape** VERB
  ① il nastro ◇ *adhesive tape* nastro adesivo
  ② la cassetta ◇ *a tape of Oasis* una cassetta degli Oasis

tape deck ['teɪpdek] NOUN
  la piastra di registrazione

tape measure ['teɪpmeʒə'] NOUN
  il metro a nastro

tape recorder ['teɪprɪkɔːdə'] NOUN
  il registratore a cassette

target ['tɑːgɪt] NOUN
  see also **target** VERB
  ① il bersaglio ◇ *The bullet hit the target.* Il proiettile ha colpito il bersaglio.
  ② l' obiettivo ◇ *He achieved his target.* Ha raggiunto il suo obiettivo.

to **target** ['tɑːgɪt] VERB
  see also **target** NOUN
  puntare su ◇ *The company targets well-off childless couples.* L'azienda punta sulle coppie benestanti senza figli.

Tarmac® ['tɑːmæk] NOUN
  l' asfalto

tart [tɑːt] NOUN
  la crostata

tartan ['tɑːtn] ADJECTIVE
  scozzese ◇ *a tartan scarf* una sciarpa scozzese

task [tɑːsk] NOUN
  il compito ◇ *a difficult task* un compito difficile

taste [teɪst] NOUN
  see also **taste** VERB
  ① il sapore ◇ *It's got a really strange taste.*

---
* Verbs followed by this symbol are irregular. See pp.339–364 for further details.

Ha un sapore veramente strano.
+ **Would you like a taste?** Vuoi assaggiare?
  2 il gusto ◇ *a joke in bad taste* uno scherzo di cattivo gusto
to **taste** [teɪst] VERB
  see also **taste** NOUN
  1 assaggiare ◇ *Would you like to taste it?* Vuoi assaggiare?
+ **You can taste the garlic in it.** Si sente il sapore dell'aglio.
  2 sapere* ◇ *It tastes of fish.* Sa di pesce.
tasteful ['teɪstful] ADJECTIVE
  di buon gusto
tasteless ['teɪstlɪs] ADJECTIVE
  1 insipido ◇ *The soup was tasteless.* La minestra era insipida.
  2 di cattivo gusto ◇ *a tasteless remark* un'osservazione di cattivo gusto
tasty ['teɪstɪ] ADJECTIVE
  saporito
tattoo [tə'tu:] NOUN
  il tatuaggio
taught [tɔ:t] VERB *see* **teach**
Taurus ['tɔ:rəs] NOUN
  il Toro ◇ *I'm Taurus.* Sono del Toro.
tax [tæks] NOUN (PL **taxes**)
  1 la tassa ◇ *the tax on cigarettes* la tassa sulle sigarette
  2 le tasse ◇ *Nobody wants to pay more tax.* Nessuno vuole pagare più tasse.
+ **tax disc** il bollo
taxi ['tæksɪ] NOUN
  il taxi (PL i taxi)
taxi driver ['tæksɪdraɪvə'] NOUN
  il/la tassista
taxi rank ['tæksɪræŋk] NOUN
  il posteggio di taxi (PL i posteggi di taxi)
TB [ti:'bi:] NOUN (= *tuberculosis*)
  la tubercolosi
tea [ti:] NOUN
  1 il tè (PL i tè) ◇ *Would you like some tea?* Vuoi del tè? ◇ *a cup of tea* una tazza di tè
+ **tea leaves** le foglie di tè
  2 la cena (*evening meal*) ◇ *We're having sausages and beans for tea.* Per cena abbiamo salsicce e fagioli.
tea bag ['ti:bæg] NOUN
  la bustina di tè
tea break ['ti:breɪk] NOUN
  la pausa per il tè
to **teach** [ti:tʃ] VERB (**taught, taught**)
  insegnare ◇ *She teaches physics.* Insegna fisica. ◇ *My sister taught me to swim.* Mia sorella mi ha insegnato a nuotare.
+ **That'll teach you!** Così impari!
teacher ['ti:tʃə'] NOUN
  l' insegnante MASC/FEM
+ **He's the teacher's pet.** È il cocco della maestra.
tea cloth ['ti:klɔθ] NOUN
  lo strofinaccio (PL gli strofinacci)

team [ti:m] NOUN
  la squadra
teapot ['ti:pɔt] NOUN
  la teiera
tear (1) [tɪə'] NOUN
  la lacrima ◇ *a few tears* qualche lacrima
+ **to burst into tears** scoppiare E a piangere*
tear (2) [tɛə'] NOUN
  see also **tear** VERB
  lo strappo ◇ *There was a small tear in the sleeve.* C'era un piccolo strappo sulla manica.
to **tear** [tɛə'] VERB (**tore, torn**)
  see also **tear (2)** NOUN
  1 strappare ◇ *Be careful or you'll tear the page.* Stai attento o strapperai la pagina. ◇ *He tore his jacket.* Gli si è strappata la giacca. ◇ *I've torn my jeans.* Mi si sono strappati i jeans.
  2 strapparsi E ◇ *It won't tear, it's very strong.* Non si strappa, è molto resistente.
to **tear up** [tɛə'ʌp] VERB
  strappare ◇ *He tore the letter up.* Ha strappato la lettera.
tear gas ['tɪəgæs] NOUN
  il gas lacrimogeno
to **tease** [ti:z] VERB
  1 tormentare ◇ *Stop teasing that poor animal!* Smettila di tormentare quella povera bestia!
  2 prendere* in giro ◇ *He's teasing you.* Ti sta prendendo in giro. ◇ *I was only teasing.* Ti stavo solo prendendo in giro.
teaspoon ['ti:spu:n] NOUN
  il cucchiaino ◇ *a teaspoonful of sugar* un cucchiaino di zucchero
teatime ['ti:taɪm] NOUN
+ **at teatime** all'ora del tè

  ❶ Per **teatime** in genere si intendono le cinque o le sei di sera.

+ **Teatime!** A tavola!
tea towel ['ti:tauəl] NOUN
  lo strofinaccio (PL gli strofinacci)
technical ['tɛknɪkl] ADJECTIVE
  tecnico
technical college ['tɛknɪkəl'kɔlɪdʒ] NOUN
  l' istituto tecnico (PL gli istituti tecnici)
technician [tɛk'nɪʃən] NOUN
  il tecnico (PL i tecnici)
technique [tɛk'ni:k] NOUN
  la tecnica (PL le tecniche)
techno ['tɛknəu] NOUN
  la musica techno
technological [tɛknə'lɔdʒɪkl] ADJECTIVE
  tecnologico
technology [tɛk'nɔlədʒɪ] NOUN (PL **technologies**)
  la tecnologia

T

teddy bear ['tɛdɪbeə'] NOUN
l'orsacchiotto

teenage ['tiːneɪdʒ] ADJECTIVE
1 per ragazzi ◇ *a teenage magazine* una
rivista per ragazzi
2 adolescente ◇ *She has two teenage
daughters.* Ha due figlie adolescenti.

teenager ['tiːneɪdʒə'] NOUN
l'adolescente MASC / FEM

teens [tiːnz] NOUN PL
• **She's in her teens.** È un'adolescente.

tee-shirt ['tiːʃəːt] NOUN
la maglietta

teeth [tiːθ] NOUN PL *see* tooth

to **teethe** [tiːð] VERB
mettere* i denti

teetotal ['tiːˈtəutl] ADJECTIVE
astemio

telecommunications
['telɪkəmjuːnɪˈkeɪʃənz] NOUN PL
le telecomunicazioni

teleconference ['telɪkɒnfərəns] NOUN
la teleconferenza

telephone ['telɪfəun] NOUN
il telefono
• **a telephone call** una telefonata
• **the telephone directory** l'elenco telefonico
• **a telephone number** un numero di telefono

telesales ['telɪseɪlz] NOUN PL
la vendita per telefono

telescope ['telɪskəup] NOUN
il telescopio

television ['telɪvɪʒən] NOUN
la televisione ◇ *on television* alla
televisione
• **television licence** l'abbonamento alla
televisione

television set ['telɪvɪʒənset] NOUN
il televisore

teleworking ['telɪwəːkɪŋ] NOUN
il telelavoro

to **tell** [tel] VERB (**told, told**)
dire*
• **to tell lies** dire* bugie
• **to tell somebody something** dire* qualcosa
a qualcuno ◇ *Did you tell your mother?*
L'hai detto a tua madre? ◇ *I told him I was
going on holiday.* Gli ho detto che andavo in
vacanza. ◇ *Who told you?* Chi te l'ha detto?
• **to tell somebody to do something** dire* a
qualcuno di fare* qualcosa ◇ *He told me to
wait a moment.* Mi ha detto di aspettare un
attimo.
• **to tell a story** raccontare una storia
• **I can't tell the difference between them.**
Non riesco a distinguerli uno dall'altro.
• **You can tell he's not serious.** Si vede che sta
scherzando.

to **tell off** [telˈɒf] VERB
sgridare

telly ['telɪ] NOUN (PL **tellies**)

la tivù (PL le tivù)

temper ['tempə'] NOUN
il carattere ◇ *He's got a terrible temper.* Ha
un pessimo carattere.
• **to be in a bad temper** essere* [E] in collera
• **to lose one's temper** arrabbiarsi [E] ◇ *I lost
my temper.* Mi sono arrabbiato.

temperature ['temprətʃə'] NOUN
la temperatura
• **to have a temperature** avere* la febbre

temple ['templ] NOUN
il tempio

temporary ['tempərərɪ] ADJECTIVE
temporaneo

to **tempt** [tempt] VERB
tentare ◇ *I'm very tempted!* Sono proprio
tentato!
• **to tempt somebody to do something**
cercare di indurre* qualcuno a fare*
qualcosa

temptation [tempˈteɪʃən] NOUN
la tentazione

tempting ['temptɪŋ] ADJECTIVE
allettante

ten [ten] NUMERAL
dieci ◇ *She's ten.* Ha dieci anni.

tenant ['tenənt] NOUN
l'inquilino
l'inquilina

to **tend** [tend] VERB
• **to tend to do something** avere* la tendenza
a fare* qualcosa

tender ['tendə'] ADJECTIVE
tenero

tennis ['tenɪs] NOUN
il tennis
• **a tennis ball** una pallina da tennis
• **a tennis court** un campo da tennis
• **a tennis racket** una racchetta da tennis
• **tennis shoes** scarpe da tennis

tennis player ['tenɪspleɪə'] NOUN
il/la tennista

tenor ['tenə'] NOUN
il tenore

tenpin bowling ['tenpɪnˈbəulɪŋ] NOUN
il bowling

tense [tens] ADJECTIVE
see also **tense** NOUN
teso

tense [tens] NOUN
see also **tense** ADJECTIVE
il tempo
• **the present tense** il presente

tension ['tenʃən] NOUN
la tensione

tent [tent] NOUN
la tenda
• **a tent peg** un picchetto da tenda
• **a tent pole** un montante da tenda

tenth [tenθ] ADJECTIVE
decimo ◇ *the tenth floor* il decimo piano

* Verbs followed by this symbol are irregular. See pp.339–364 for further details.

+ **the tenth of August** il dieci agosto

term [tə:m] NOUN

[1] il quadrimestre ◇ *It's nearly the end of term.* È quasi la fine del quadrimestre.

🛈 *Nelle scuole britanniche l'anno accademico si divide in 3* **terms**.

[2] il termine ◇ *a short-term solution* una soluzione a breve termine

+ **to be on good terms with** essere* ᴱ in buoni rapporti con
+ **to come to terms with** accettare ◇ *He hasn't yet come to terms with his disability.* Non ha ancora accettato la propria invalidità.

terminal ['tə:mɪnl] ADJECTIVE

see also **terminal** NOUN

terminale

terminal ['tə:mɪnl] NOUN

see also **terminal** ADJECTIVE

+ **a computer terminal** un terminale
+ **an air terminal** un terminal

terminally ['tə:mɪnlɪ] ADVERB

+ **the terminally ill** i malati terminali

terrace ['tɛrəs] NOUN

la terrazza ◇ *We were sitting on the terrace.* Eravamo seduti in terrazza.

+ **Our house is in a terrace.** Abitiamo in una casa a schiera.
+ **the terraces** (*in stadium*) le gradinate

terraced ['tɛrəst] ADJECTIVE

+ **a terraced house** una casa a schiera

terrible ['tɛrɪbl] ADJECTIVE

terribile ◇ *a terrible nightmare* un incubo terribile

+ **to feel terrible** sentirsi ᴱ malissimo

terribly ['tɛrɪblɪ] ADVERB

[1] terribilmente ◇ *I'm terribly sorry.* Mi spiace terribilmente.

[2] moltissimo ◇ *He suffered terribly.* Ha sofferto moltissimo.

terrific [tə'rɪfɪk] ADJECTIVE

fantastico ◇ *That's terrific!* Fantastico!

+ **You look terrific!** Stai benissimo!

terrified ['tɛrɪfaɪd] ADJECTIVE

terrorizzato ◇ *I was terrified.* Ero terrorizzata.

terrorism ['tɛrərɪzəm] NOUN

il terrorismo

terrorist ['tɛrərɪst] NOUN

il/la terrorista ◇ *a group of terrorists* un gruppo di terroristi

+ **a terrorist attack** un attentato terroristico

to **test** [tɛst] VERB

see also **test** NOUN

[1] provare ◇ *Test the water with your wrist.* Prova l'acqua con il polso.

[2] sperimentare ◇ *The drug was tested on rats.* La medicina è stata sperimentata sui ratti.

+ **to test something out** testare qualcosa
  [3] interrogare ◇ *He tested us on the new vocabulary.* Ci ha interrogato sui nuovi vocaboli.
+ **to be tested for drugs** essere* ᴱ sottoposto all'antidoping
+ **to test positive for** risultare ᴱ positivo al test di

test [tɛst] NOUN

see also **test** VERB

[1] l'esperimento ◇ *nuclear tests* esperimenti nucleari ◇ *tests on animals* esperimenti sugli animali

[2] l'analisi (PL le analisi) ◇ *They're going to do some more tests.* Devono fare* altre analisi.

+ **to have a blood test** fare* le analisi del sangue
  [3] il compito in classe ◇ *We've got an English test tomorrow.* Abbiamo un compito in classe di inglese domani.
+ **a driving test** un esame di guida

test match ['tɛstmætʃ] NOUN

la partita internazionale

test tube ['tɛsttju:b] NOUN

la provetta

tetanus ['tɛtənəs] NOUN

il tetano

+ **tetanus injection** antitetanica

textbook ['tɛkstbuk] NOUN

il libro di testo

textiles ['tɛkstaɪlz] NOUN PL

i tessuti (*fabrics*)

Thames [tɛmz] NOUN

il Tamigi

than [ðæn,ðən] CONJUNCTION

[1] di ◇ *She's taller than me.* È più alta di me. ◇ *more than once* più d'una volta

[2] che ◇ *I've got more CDs than tapes.* Ho più CD che cassette.

to **thank** [θæŋk] VERB

ringraziare ◇ *Don't forget to write and thank them.* Mi raccomando, scrivi per ringraziarli.

+ **thank you** grazie
+ **thank you very much** grazie mille

thanks [θæŋks] EXCLAMATION

grazie

that [ðæt] ADJECTIVE

see also **that** PRONOUN, CONJUNCTION, ADVERB

quel MASC (FEM quella) ◇ *that day* quel giorno ◇ *that time* quella volta

Use **quell'** when the word following starts with a vowel

◇ *that man* quell'uomo ◇ *that university* quell'università

Use **quello** when word following starts with gn, pn, ps, x, y, z or s + another consonant.

◇ *that rucksack* quello zaino

+ **that one** quello là (FEM quella là) ◇ *Do you like this photo? – No, I prefer that one.* Ti piace questa foto? – No, preferisco quella là.

T

that [ðæt] PRONOUN

see also **that** ADJECTIVE, CONJUNCTION, ADVERB

[1] quello MASC (FEM quella) (*demonstrative*)
◇ *What's that?* Cos'è quello? ◇ *Who's that?* Chi è quello?
* **Is that you?** Sei tu?

[2] che (*in relative clause*) ◇ *the man that we saw* l'uomo che abbiamo visto
* **the man that we spoke to** l'uomo con cui abbiamo parlato

that [ðæt] CONJUNCTION

see also **that** ADJECTIVE, PRONOUN, ADVERB

che ◇ *He thought that Henry was ill.* Credeva che Henry fosse malato. ◇ *I know that she likes chocolate.* So che le piace la cioccolata.

that [ðæt] ADVERB

see also **that** ADJECTIVE, PRONOUN, CONJUNCTION

così ◇ *It was that big.* Era grande così. ◇ *It's not that difficult.* Non è poi così difficile.

thatched [θætʃt] ADJECTIVE
* **a thatched cottage** un cottage con il tetto di paglia

the [ði:,ðə] ARTICLE

Use il before a masculine noun, la before a feminine noun and l' before nouns starting with vowels. If a masculine noun starts with gn, pn, ps, x, y, z or s + another consonant, use lo.

◇ *the boy* il bambino ◇ *the girl* la ragazza ◇ *the murderer* l'assassino ◇ *the rucksack* lo zaino

For plural nouns use i for masculine and le for feminine. If a masculine plural noun starts with a vowel or gn, pn, ps, x, y, z or s + another consonant use gli.

◇ *the knives* i coltelli ◇ *the forks* le forchette ◇ *the friends* gli amici ◇ *the spaghetti* gli spaghetti
the is sometimes not translated.
◇ *on the Internet* su Internet ◇ *paid by the hour* pagato a ore

theatre ['θɪətə'] (US **theater**) NOUN
il teatro

theft [θɛft] NOUN
il furto

their [ðeə'] ADJECTIVE

[1] il loro MASC (PL i loro) ◇ *their money* il loro denaro ◇ *their parents* i loro genitori

[2] la loro FEM (PL le loro) ◇ *their house* la loro casa ◇ *their girlfriends* le loro ragazze
their is sometimes not translated.
◇ *They took off their coats.* Si sono tolti il cappotto. ◇ *They washed their hair.* Si sono lavati i capelli. ◇ *Someone has left their bag here.* Qualcuno ha lasciato qui la borsa.

theirs [ðeəz] PRONOUN

The Italian pronoun agrees with the noun it is replacing.

[1] il loro MASC (PL i loro) (*their one*) ◇ *Our garden is smaller than theirs.* Il nostro giardino è più piccolo del loro.

[2] la loro FEM (PL le loro) (*their one*) ◇ *It's not our car, it's theirs.* Non è la nostra auto, è la loro.

[3] loro (*their property*) ◇ *Is this car theirs?* È loro questa macchina?
* **a friend of theirs** un loro amico

them [ðəm] PRONOUN

[1] li MASC (FEM le)
Use li or le when them is the direct object of the verb in the sentence.
◇ *I didn't see them.* Non li ho visti. ◇ *I'm looking for the tickets, have you seen them?* Sto cercando i biglietti, li hai visti? ◇ *Where are the sweets, have you eaten them?* Dove sono le caramelle? Le hai mangiate?

[2] loro
Use loro when them means to them.
◇ *I gave them some brochures.* Ho dato loro alcuni depliant.
loro is also used after prepositions.
◇ *Sally came with them.* Sally è venuta con loro. ◇ *It's for them.* È per loro.

theme [θi:m] NOUN
il tema (PL i temi)

theme park ['θi:mpɑ:k] NOUN
il parco dei divertimenti a tema (PL i parchi dei divertimenti a tema)

themselves [ðəm'sɛlvz] PRONOUN

[1] si
A verb + themselves is often translated by a reflexive verb in Italian.
◇ *Did they hurt themselves?* Si sono fatti male?

[2] loro (*following an English preposition*)
◇ *beginners like themselves* dei principianti come loro
* **They built it themselves.** L'hanno costruito da soli.
* **by themselves** da soli ◇ *They never travel by themselves.* Non viaggiano mai da soli.

then [ðen] ADVERB, CONJUNCTION

[1] poi ◇ *I get dressed, then I have breakfast.* Mi vesto e poi faccio colazione.

[2] allora ◇ *My pen's run out. – Use a pencil then!* È finita la penna. – Allora usa una matita! ◇ *There was no electricity then.* Allora non c'era l'elettricità.
* **now and then** ogni tanto

therapy ['θerəpɪ] NOUN (PL **therapies**)
la terapia

there [ðeə'] ADVERB

[1] lì ◇ *Put it there, on the table.* Mettilo lì sul tavolo.
* **over there** là
* **in there** là dentro
* **on there** là sopra
* **up there** lassù
* **down there** laggiù
* **There he is!** Eccolo!

[2] ci ◇ *He went there on Friday.* Ci è andato venerdì.
* **there is** c'è ◇ *There's a factory near my*

---

house. Vicino a casa mia c'è una fabbrica.
* **there are** ci sono ◇ *There are two apples each.* Ci sono due mele per ciascuno.
* **There's been a lot of rain.** È piovuto molto.

therefore ['ðɛəfɔːʳ] ADVERB
perciò

there's ['ðɛəz] = **there is, there has**

thermometer [θə'mɒmɪtəʳ] NOUN
il termometro

Thermos ® ['θɜːməs] NOUN
il thermos ® (PL i thermos)

these [ðiːz] ADJECTIVE, PRONOUN
questi MASC (FEM queste) ◇ *these shoes* queste scarpe ◇ *I want these!* Voglio questi!
* **these ones** questi qui MASC (FEM queste qui) ◇ *These ones are very interesting.* Questi qui sono molto interessanti.

they [ðeɪ] PRONOUN
loro ◇ *Who are they?* Chi sono loro?
they is often not translated.
◇ *They were watching TV.* Stavano guardando la TV. ◇ *They're horrible.* Sono bruttissimi.
* **They say that...** Si dice che...
loro is the pronoun used in spoken and informal written Italian. The more formal words for they are "essi" and "esse".

they'd [ðeɪd] = **they had, they would**

they'll [ðeɪl] = **they will**

they're [ðɛəʳ] = **they are**

they've [ðeɪv] = **they have**

thick [θɪk] ADJECTIVE
[1] spesso ◇ *It's very thick.* È molto spesso.
* **The walls are one metre thick.** I muri hanno uno spessore di un metro.
[2] tonto ◇ *He's a bit thick.* È un po' tonto.

thief [θiːf] NOUN (PL **thieves**)
[1] il ladro
[2] la ladra

thigh [θaɪ] NOUN
la coscia (PL le cosce)

thin [θɪn] ADJECTIVE
[1] sottile ◇ *a thin slice* una fettina sottile
[2] magro ◇ *She's very thin.* È molto magra.

thing [θɪŋ] NOUN
[1] la cosa ◇ *Where shall I put my things?* Dove metto le mie cose?
[2] il coso ◇ *What's that thing called?* Come si chiama quel coso?
* **You poor thing!** Poverino!

to **think** [θɪŋk] VERB (**thought, thought**)
pensare ◇ *What do you think of it?* Cosa ne pensi? ◇ *Think carefully before you reply.* Pensaci bene prima di rispondere*. ◇ *What are you thinking about?* A cosa stai pensando? ◇ *Have you thought about it?* Ci hai pensato? ◇ *I think so.* Penso di sì.
* **I don't think so.** Non credo.
* **think tank** gruppo di esperti
* **I'll think it over.** Ci penserò su.

third [θɜːd] ADJECTIVE, NOUN
il terzo ◇ *the third time* la terza volta ◇ *I came third.* Sono arrivato terzo. ◇ *a third of the population* un terzo della popolazione
* **the third of March** il tre marzo

thirdly ['θɜːdlɪ] ADVERB
in terzo luogo

Third World ['θɜːd'wɜːld] NOUN
il terzo mondo

thirst [θɜːst] NOUN
la sete

thirsty ['θɜːstɪ] ADJECTIVE
* **to be thirsty** avere* sete

thirteen [θɜː'tiːn] NUMERAL
tredici ◇ *I'm thirteen.* Ho tredici anni.

thirteenth [θɜː'tiːnθ] ADJECTIVE
tredicesimo ◇ *the thirteenth floor* il tredicesimo piano
* **the thirteenth of March** il tredici marzo

thirty ['θɜːtɪ] NUMERAL
trenta

this [ðɪs] ADJECTIVE, PRONOUN
questo MASC (FEM questa) ◇ *this man* quest'uomo ◇ *this apple* questa mela ◇ *What's this?* Cos'è questo?
* **this one** questo qui MASC (FEM questa qui) ◇ *Pass me that pen. – This one?* Passami quella penna. – Questa qui?
* **This is Gavin speaking.** Sono Gavin. (*on the phone*)

thistle ['θɪsl] NOUN
il cardo

thorough ['θʌrə] ADJECTIVE
[1] minuzioso ◇ *a thorough check* un controllo minuzioso
[2] meticoloso ◇ *She's very thorough.* È molto meticolosa.

thoroughly ['θʌrəlɪ] ADVERB
[1] meticolosamente ◇ *I checked the car thoroughly.* Ho controllato la macchina meticolosamente.
[2] bene ◇ *Mix the ingredients thoroughly.* Mescolare bene gli ingredienti.
[3] moltissimo ◇ *I thoroughly enjoyed myself.* Mi sono divertito moltissimo.

those [ðəʊz] ADJECTIVE
see also **those** PRONOUN
[1] quei MASC (FEM quelle) ◇ *those days* quei giorni ◇ *those pages* quelle pagine
[2] quegli MASC
Use quegli when word following starts with a vowel, gn, pn, ps, x, y, z or s + another consonant.
◇ *those students* quegli studenti
* **those ones** quelli lì MASC (FEM quelle lì) ◇ *Pass me those books. – Those ones?* Passami quei libri. – Quelli lì?

those [ðəʊz] PRONOUN
see also **those** ADJECTIVE
quelli MASC (FEM quelle) ◇ *I want those!* Voglio quelli!

T

though [ðəʊ] CONJUNCTION
anche se ◇ *Though it's raining...* Anche se
piove... ◇ *He's a nice person, though he's
not very clever.* È simpatico, anche se non è
molto sveglio.

thought [θɔːt] VERB *see* **think**

thought [θɔːt] NOUN
[1] il pensiero ◇ *It was a nice thought, thank
you.* È stato un pensiero carino, grazie.
[2] l'idea ◇ *I've just had a thought.* Ho
un'idea.

thoughtful ['θɔːtful] ADJECTIVE
[1] pensieroso ◇ *She had a thoughtful
expression on her face.* Aveva
un'espressione pensierosa.
[2] premuroso ◇ *a thoughtful and caring
man* un uomo premuroso ed attento

thoughtless ['θɔːtlɪs] ADJECTIVE
poco delicato ◇ *It was thoughtless of her to
mention it.* È stato poco delicato da parte
sua parlarne.

thousand ['θaʊzənd] NUMERAL
♦ **a thousand** mille ◇ *a thousand pounds*
mille sterline
When **thousand** *follows any number except
one, "-mila" is added to the number.*
◇ *three thousand boys and five thousand
girls* tremila ragazzi e cinquemila ragazze
♦ **thousands of people** migliaia di persone

thousandth ['θaʊzəntθ] ADJECTIVE, NOUN
il millesimo

thread [θred] NOUN
il filo

threat [θret] NOUN
la minaccia (PL le minacce)

to **threaten** ['θretn] VERB
minacciare
♦ **to threaten to do something** minacciare di
fare* qualcosa

three [θriː] NUMERAL
tre ◇ *She's three.* Ha tre anni.

three-dimensional [θriːdɪ'menʃənl]
ADJECTIVE
tridimensionale

three-piece suite ['θriːpiːs'swiːt] NOUN
un divano e due poltrone

threw [θruː] VERB *see* **throw**

thrifty ['θrɪftɪ] ADJECTIVE
parsimonioso

thrill [θrɪl] NOUN
l'emozione FEM ◇ *It was a great thrill to see
my team win.* Che emozione vedere*
vincere* la mia squadra!

thrilled [θrɪld] ADJECTIVE
♦ **I was thrilled.** Ero felicissimo.

thriller ['θrɪlə'] NOUN
il thriller (PL i thriller)

thrilling ['θrɪlɪŋ] ADJECTIVE
entusiasmante ◇ *a thrilling match* una
partita entusiasmante

throat [θrəʊt] NOUN
la gola
♦ **to have a sore throat** avere* il mal di gola

to **throb** [θrɒb] VERB
♦ **My arm's throbbing.** Ho delle fitte al braccio.
♦ **a throbbing pain** un dolore pulsante

throne [θrəʊn] NOUN
il trono

through [θruː] PREPOSITION, ADJECTIVE
[1] attraverso ◇ *through the crowd*
attraverso la folla
♦ **to go through Birmingham** passare[E] per
Birmingham
♦ **to look through a telescope** guardare con
un telescopio
♦ **to walk through the woods** attraversare i
boschi
♦ **a through train** un treno diretto
♦ **"no through road"** "strada senza uscita"
[2] tramite ◇ *I know her through my sister.*
La conosco tramite mia sorella.

throughout [θruː'aʊt] PREPOSITION
♦ **throughout Britain** in tutta la Gran Bretagna
♦ **throughout the year** per tutto l'anno

to **throw** [θrəʊ] VERB **(threw, thrown)**
[1] lanciare ◇ *He threw the ball to me.* Mi ha
lanciato la palla.
[2] sconcertare ◇ *That really threw him.*
L'ha veramente sconcertato.
♦ **to throw a party** dare* una festa

to **throw away** [θrəʊə'weɪ] VERB
buttare via ◇ *He threw it away.* Lo ha
buttato via.

to **throw out** [θrəʊ'aʊt] VERB
buttare fuori

to **throw up** [θrəʊ'ʌp] VERB
vomitare

thug [θʌg] NOUN
il teppista

thumb [θʌm] NOUN
il pollice

thumbtack ['θʌmtæk] NOUN US
la puntina da disegno

to **thump** [θʌmp] VERB
picchiare

thunder ['θʌndə'] NOUN
il tuono

thunderstorm ['θʌndəstɔːm] NOUN
il temporale

thundery ['θʌndərɪ] ADJECTIVE
temporalesco

Thursday ['θɜːzdɪ] NOUN
il giovedì (PL i giovedì)
♦ **on Thursday** giovedì ◇ *I saw her on
Thursday.* L'ho vista giovedì.
♦ **on Thursdays** di giovedì ◇ *I go swimming
on Thursdays.* Vado in piscina di giovedì.

thyme [taɪm] NOUN
il timo

Tiber ['taɪbə'] NOUN
il Tevere

tick [tɪk] NOUN

---

* Verbs followed by this symbol are irregular. See pp.339–364 for further details.

see also **tick** VERB
1. il visto ◇ _Put a tick in the appropriate box._ Metti un visto nell'apposita casella.
2. il ticchettio ◇ _the loud tick of the alarm clock_ il forte ticchettio della sveglia
+ **in a tick** in un attimo

to **tick** [tɪk] VERB
see also **tick** NOUN
fare* un segno accanto a ◇ _Tick the right answer._ Fai un segno accanto alla risposta esatta.

to **tick off** [tɪk'ɔf] VERB
1. spuntare ◇ _He ticked the names off the list._ Ha spuntato i nomi dalla lista.
2. sgridare ◇ _She ticked me off for being late._ Mi ha sgridato per il ritardo.

ticket ['tɪkɪt] NOUN
1. il biglietto ◇ _the man inspecting the tickets_ l'uomo che controlla i biglietti
2. la multa per sosta vietata (_for parking_)

ticket inspector ['tɪkɪtɪnspɛktə'] NOUN
il controllore

ticket office ['tɪkɪtɔfɪs] NOUN
la biglietteria

to **tickle** ['tɪkl] VERB
fare* il solletico

ticklish ['tɪklɪʃ] ADJECTIVE
+ **to be ticklish** soffrire* il solletico

tide [taɪd] NOUN
la marea ◇ _high tide_ alta marea ◇ _low tide_ bassa marea

tidy ['taɪdɪ] ADJECTIVE
see also **tidy** VERB
ordinato

to **tidy** ['taɪdɪ] VERB (**tidied, tidied**)
see also **tidy** ADJECTIVE
mettere* in ordine ◇ _Go and tidy your room._ Vai a mettere* in ordine la tua camera.

to **tidy up** [taɪdɪ'ʌp] VERB
riordinare

tie [taɪ] NOUN
see also **tie** VERB
1. la cravatta ◇ _a red tie_ una cravatta rossa
2. il pareggio ◇ _The match ended in a tie._ La partita è finita in pareggio.

to **tie** [taɪ] VERB
see also **tie** NOUN
1. legare ◇ _He tied the handles of the bag together._ Ha legato assieme i manici della borsa.
+ **to tie a knot** fare* un nodo
2. pareggiare ◇ _They tied three-all._ Hanno pareggiato tre a tre.

to **tie up** [taɪ'ʌp] VERB
legare

tiger ['taɪgə'] NOUN
la tigre

tight [taɪt] ADJECTIVE
1. stretto ◇ _This dress is a bit tight._ Questo vestito è un po' stretto.

2. attillato ◇ _tight jeans_ jeans attillati

to **tighten** ['taɪtn] VERB
tendere* ◇ _He tightened the rope._ Ha teso la corda.
+ **to tighten one's grip** stringere* la presa
+ **to tighten security** aumentare la sicurezza

tightly ['taɪtlɪ] ADVERB
stretto
+ **to hold something tightly** tenere* stretto qualcosa ◇ _She held his hand tightly._ Gli tenne stretta la mano.
+ **tightly closed** saldamente chiuso

tights [taɪts] NOUN PL
i collant

tile [taɪl] NOUN
1. la tegola ◇ _roofs with red tiles_ tetti con le tegole rosse
2. la piastrella ◇ _black and white tiles_ piastrelle bianche e nere

tiled [taɪld] ADJECTIVE
1. di tegole ◇ _a tiled roof_ un tetto di tegole
2. piastrellato ◇ _tiled walls_ pareti piastrellate

till [tɪl] NOUN
see also **till** PREPOSITION
la cassa ◇ _Pay at the till._ Pagare alla cassa.

till [tɪl] PREPOSITION
see also **till** NOUN
fino a ◇ _I waited till ten o'clock._ Ho aspettato fino alle dieci.
+ **not...till** non...prima di ◇ _It won't be ready till next week._ Non sarà pronto prima della settimana prossima.
+ **till now** finora
+ **till then** fino ad allora

time [taɪm] NOUN
1. l'ora ◇ _What time is it?_ Che ora è?
◇ _What time do you get up?_ A che ora ti alzi?
◇ _It was two o'clock, Italian time._ Erano le due, ora italiana.
2. il tempo ◇ _I'm sorry, I haven't got time._ Scusa, non ho tempo. ◇ _a long time_ molto tempo
+ **Have you lived here for a long time?** È da tanto che abiti qui?
+ **in time** in tempo ◇ _just in time_ appena in tempo ◇ _We arrived in time for lunch._ Siamo arrivati in tempo per il pranzo.
3. la volta ◇ _this time_ questa volta ◇ _two at a time_ due alla volta ◇ _How many times?_ Quante volte?
+ **at times** certe volte
+ **two times two is four** due per due fa quattro
+ **to be on time** essere* [E] puntuale
+ **He never arrives on time.** Non è mai puntuale.
+ **in no time** prestissimo ◇ _It will ready in no time._ Sarà pronto prestissimo.
+ **from time to time** di tanto in tanto
+ **for the time being** per il momento
+ **in a week's time** tra una settimana
+ **any time now** da un momento all'altro

T

☞

♦ **Come and see us any time.** Vieni a trovarci quando vuoi.

♦ **to have a good time** divertirsi ^E ◇ *Did you have a good time?* Vi siete divertiti?

♦ **to take time out** assentarsi ^E

♦ **a time limit** un limite di tempo

time off [taɪm'ɔf] NOUN
il tempo libero

timer ['taɪmə'] NOUN
il contaminuti (PL i contaminuti)

time scale ['taɪmskeɪl] NOUN
i tempi d'esecuzione PL

time-share ['taɪmʃɛə'] NOUN
la casa in multiproprietà

timetable ['taɪmteɪbl] NOUN
1 l' orario ◇ *the train timetable* l'orario del treno
2 il programma (PL i programmi) ◇ *History is one of the most important subjects on the timetable.* Storia è una delle materie più importanti in programma.

time zone ['taɪmzəʊn] NOUN
il fuso orario

tin [tɪn] NOUN
1 il barattolo ◇ *a tin of beans* un barattolo di fagioli

♦ **a biscuit tin** una scatola per biscotti
2 lo stagno (*metal*)

tin foil ['tɪnfɔɪl] NOUN
la carta stagnola

tinned [tɪnd] ADJECTIVE
in scatola ◇ *tinned peaches* pesche in scatola

tin opener ['tɪnəʊpnə'] NOUN
l' apriscatole (PL gli apriscatole)

tinsel ['tɪnsl] NOUN
i fili argentati MASC PL

tinted ['tɪntɪd] ADJECTIVE
colorato (*glasses, window*)

tiny ['taɪnɪ] ADJECTIVE
minuscolo

tip [tɪp] NOUN
see also **tip** VERB
1 la mancia (PL le mance) ◇ *He didn't leave a tip.* Non ha lasciato la mancia.
2 il consiglio ◇ *a useful tip* un buon consiglio
3 la punta ◇ *It's on the tip of my tongue.* Ce l'ho sulla punta della lingua.
4 la discarica (PL le discariche) ◇ *I took the old sofa to the tip.* Ho portato il vecchio divano in discarica.

♦ **This place is a complete tip!** Che porcile!

to **tip** [tɪp] VERB
see also **tip** NOUN
1 vuotare ◇ *She tipped the leftovers in the bin.* Ha vuotato gli avanzi nella pattumiera.
2 dare* la mancia a ◇ *He tipped the waiter.* Ha dato la mancia al cameriere.

♦ **to tip back** inclinare all'indietro ◇ *She tipped back her head.* Ha inclinato la testa all'indietro.

tipsy ['tɪpsɪ] ADJECTIVE
brillo

tiptoe ['tɪptəu] NOUN
♦ **on tiptoe** in punta di piedi

tired ['taɪəd] ADJECTIVE
stanco ◇ *I'm tired.* Sono stanco.

♦ **to be tired of** essere* ^E stufo di ◇ *I'm tired of waiting.* Sono stufa di aspettare.

tiring ['taɪərɪŋ] ADJECTIVE
stancante

tissue ['tɪʃuː] NOUN
1 il tessuto ◇ *muscle tissue* tessuto muscolare
2 il fazzolettino di carta ◇ *She blew her nose on a tissue.* Si è soffiata il naso con un fazzolettino di carta.

tissue paper ['tɪʃuːpeɪpə'] NOUN
la carta velina

title ['taɪtl] NOUN
il titolo ◇ *author and title* autore e titolo

title role ['taɪtlrəul] NOUN
il ruolo principale

to [tuː,tə] PREPOSITION
1 a ◇ *I go to school.* Vado a scuola.
◇ *ready to go* pronto a partire

♦ **from...to...** da...a... ◇ *from nine o'clock to half past three* dalle nove alle tre e mezza
2 da ◇ *He's been to the doctor.* È stato dal medico. ◇ *Let's go to Anne's house.* Andiamo da Anne. ◇ *something to drink* qualcosa da bere* ◇ *I've got things to do.* Ho da fare*. ◇ *It's easy to remember.* È facile da ricordare.
3 in ◇ *We're going to go to Portugal.* Abbiamo intenzione di andare* in Portogallo.
4 fino a ◇ *Count to ten!* Conta fino a dieci!
5 per ◇ *the train to London* il treno per Londra ◇ *I did it to help you.* L'ho fatto per aiutarti. ◇ *She's too young to go to school.* È troppo piccola per andare* a scuola.

♦ **to be kind to** essere* ^E gentile con

♦ **the key to the front door** la chiave della porta d'ingresso

♦ **It's difficult to say.** È difficile dirlo.

toad [təud] NOUN
il rospo

toadstool ['təudstuːl] NOUN
il fungo velenoso (PL i funghi velenosi)

toast [təust] NOUN
1 il pane tostato ◇ *a piece of toast* una fetta di pane tostato
2 il brindisi (PL i brindisi)

♦ **to drink a toast to somebody** brindare a qualcuno

toaster ['təustə'] NOUN
il tostapane (PL i tostapane)

toastie ['təustɪ] NOUN
il toast (PL i toast)

tobacco [tə'bækəu] NOUN (PL **tobaccos**)

---

* Verbs followed by this symbol are irregular. See pp.339–364 for further details.

il tabacco

tobacconist's [təˈbækənɪsts] NOUN
la tabaccheria

toboggan [təˈbɔgən] NOUN
lo slittino

tobogganing [təˈbɔgənɪŋ] NOUN
♦ **to go tobogganing** andare* [E] in slittino

today [təˈdeɪ] ADVERB
oggi

toddler [ˈtɔdlə'] NOUN
il bambino che impara a camminare

toe [təu] NOUN
il dito del piede (PL FEM le dita del piede)

toffee [ˈtɔfɪ] NOUN
la caramella mou (PL le caramelle mou)

together [təˈgɛðə'] ADVERB
insieme ◇ Are they still together? Stanno
ancora insieme?

toilet [ˈtɔɪlət] NOUN
la toilette (PL le toilette) ◇ Where's the toilet?
Dov'è la toilette?

toilet bag [ˈtɔɪlɪtbæg] NOUN
il nécessaire da toilette

toilet paper [ˈtɔɪlɪtpeɪpə'] NOUN
la carta igienica

toiletries [ˈtɔɪlətrɪz] NOUN PL
gli articoli da toilette

toilet roll [ˈtɔɪlɪtrəul] NOUN
il rotolo di carta igienica

token [ˈtəukən] NOUN
♦ **as a token of our respect** come segno di
rispetto
♦ **a token gesture** un gesto simbolico
♦ **a gift token** un buono omaggio

told [təuld] VERB see **tell**

tolerant [ˈtɔlərnt] ADJECTIVE
tollerante

toll [təul] NOUN
il pedaggio

tomato [təˈmɑːtəu] NOUN (PL **tomatoes**)
il pomodoro

tomboy [ˈtɔmbɔɪ] NOUN
il maschiaccio ◇ She's a tomboy. È un
maschiaccio.

tomorrow [təˈmɔrəu] ADVERB
domani
♦ **the day after tomorrow** dopodomani

ton [tʌn] NOUN
la tonnellata

tongue [tʌŋ] NOUN
la lingua
♦ **to say something tongue in cheek** dire*
qualcosa ironicamente

tonic [ˈtɔnɪk] NOUN
l'acqua tonica ◇ a bottle of tonic una
bottiglia di acqua tonica
♦ **a gin and tonic** un gin tonic

tonight [təˈnaɪt] ADVERB
1 stasera ◇ Are you going out tonight?
Esci stasera?
2 stanotte ◇ I'll sleep well tonight.

Stanotte dormirò bene.

tonsillitis [tɔnsɪˈlaɪtɪs] NOUN
la tonsillite

tonsils [ˈtɔnslz] NOUN PL
le tonsille

too [tuː] ADVERB, ADJECTIVE
1 anche ◇ My sister came too. È venuta
anche mia sorella.
2 troppo ◇ The water's too hot. L'acqua è
troppo calda. ◇ We arrived too late. Siamo
arrivati troppo tardi.
♦ **too much** troppo
♦ **too many** troppi
♦ **Too bad!** Tanto peggio!

took [tuk] VERB see **take**

tool [tuːl] NOUN
l'attrezzo ◇ a tool box una cassetta degli
attrezzi

tooth [tuːθ] NOUN (PL **teeth**)
il dente

toothache [ˈtuːθeɪk] NOUN
il mal di denti

toothbrush [ˈtuːθbrʌʃ] NOUN (PL
toothbrushes)
lo spazzolino da denti

toothpaste [ˈtuːθpeɪst] NOUN
il dentifricio

top [tɔp] NOUN
see also **top** ADJECTIVE
1 la cima ◇ at the top of the page in cima
alla pagina ◇ from top to bottom da cima a
fondo
2 il coperchio (of jar)
3 il tappo (of bottle)
4 la maglia ◇ a cotton top una maglia di
cotone
♦ **a bikini top** il pezzo di sopra di un bikini
♦ **the top of the table** la superficie del tavolo
♦ **on top of** sopra ◇ on top of the cupboard
sopra l'armadio
♦ **There's a surcharge on top of that.** In più c'è
un sovrapprezzo.

top [tɔp] ADJECTIVE
see also **top** NOUN
grande ◇ a top surgeon un grande chirurgo
♦ **a top model** una top model
♦ **top marks** ottimi voti MASC PL ◇ He always
gets top marks in Italian. Ha sempre degli
ottimi voti in italiano.
♦ **the top floor** l'ultimo piano

top hat [tɔpˈhæt] NOUN
il cilindro

topic [ˈtɔpɪk] NOUN
l'argomento ◇ The essay can be on any
topic. Per il tema si può scegliere* un
argomento qualunque.

topical [ˈtɔpɪkl] ADJECTIVE
d'attualità ◇ a topical issue un problema
d'attualità

topless [ˈtɔplɪs] ADJECTIVE
♦ **to go topless** mettersi [E] in topless

T

top-secret ['tɒp'siːkrɪt] ADJECTIVE
top secret

torch [tɔːtʃ] NOUN (PL **torches**)
la torcia elettrica (PL le torce elettriche)

tore, torn [tɔːʳ,tɔːn] VERB see **tear**

tortoise ['tɔːtəs] NOUN
la tartaruga (PL le tartarughe)

torture ['tɔːtʃəʳ] NOUN
see also **torture** VERB
la tortura

to **torture** ['tɔːtʃəʳ] VERB
see also **torture** NOUN
torturare

Tory ['tɔːrɪ] NOUN (PL **Tories**)
il conservatore
la conservatrice
◇ the Tories i conservatori

to **toss** [tɒs] VERB
1 lanciare ◇ She tossed me a can of beer.
Mi ha lanciato una lattina di birra.
2 mescolare ◇ Toss the salad in the
dressing. Mescola l'insalata con il
condimento.
◆ to toss pancakes far saltare le crêpes
◆ Shall we toss for it? Facciamo a testa o
croce?

total ['təʊtl] ADJECTIVE
see also **total** NOUN
totale

total ['təʊtl] NOUN
see also **total** ADJECTIVE
il totale

totally ['təʊtəlɪ] ADVERB
completamente

touch [tʌtʃ] NOUN
see also **touch** VERB
◆ at the touch of a button premendo un
bottone
◆ to get in touch with somebody mettersi E in
contatto con qualcuno
◆ to keep in touch with somebody tenersi E in
contatto con qualcuno ◇ I'll keep in touch
with Ann. Mi terrò in contatto con Ann.
◆ I haven't kept in touch with Hilary. Non
sono rimasta in contatto con Hilary.
◆ Keep in touch! Fatti vivo!
◆ to lose touch perdersi E di vista
◆ to lose touch with somebody perdere* di
vista qualcuno

to **touch** [tʌtʃ] VERB
see also **touch** NOUN
1 toccare ◇ Don't touch that! Non
toccare!
2 commuovere* ◇ The story touched me
deeply. La storia mi ha commosso
profondamente.

touchdown ['tʌtʃdaʊn] NOUN
l' atterraggio

touched [tʌtʃt] ADJECTIVE
commosso ◇ I was really touched. Ero
veramente commosso.

touching ['tʌtʃɪŋ] ADJECTIVE
commovente

touchline ['tʌtʃlaɪn] NOUN
la linea laterale (on football pitch)

touchpad ['tʌtʃpæd] NOUN
il touchpad (PL i touchpad)

touchy ['tʌtʃɪ] ADJECTIVE
suscettibile

tough [tʌf] ADJECTIVE
1 duro ◇ It was tough, but I managed
okay. È stata dura ma ce l'ho fatta. ◇ The
meat is tough. La carne è dura. ◇ He thinks
he's a tough guy. Crede di essere* un duro.
2 resistente ◇ tough leather gloves guanti
di pelle resistenti
◆ Tough luck! Tanto peggio!

to **tour** ['tʊəʳ] VERB
see also **tour** NOUN
visitare ◇ The Prime Minister is touring the
country. Il primo ministro sta visitando il
paese.
◆ The band is touring Europe. Il complesso è
in tournée in Europa.

tour ['tʊəʳ] NOUN
see also **tour** VERB
1 il giro ◇ a tour of the city un giro della
città
◆ a package tour un viaggio organizzato
2 la tournée (PL le tournée) ◇ on tour in
tournée
◆ to go on tour fare* una tournée

tour guide ['tʊəgaɪd] NOUN
la guida turistica (PL le guide turistiche)

tourism ['tʊərɪzm] NOUN
il turismo

tourist ['tʊərɪst] NOUN
il/la turista ◇ There were lots of tourists.
C'erano molti turisti.
◆ tourist information office l'ufficio
informazioni turistiche

tournament ['tʊənəmənt] NOUN
il torneo

tour operator ['tʊərɒpəreɪtəʳ] NOUN
l' operatore turistico MASC (PL gli operatori
turistici)

towards [tə'wɔːdz] PREPOSITION (US **toward**)
1 verso ◇ He came towards me. È venuto
verso di me.
2 nei confronti di ◇ my feelings towards
him i miei sentimenti nei suoi confronti

towel ['taʊəl] NOUN
l' asciugamano

tower ['taʊəʳ] NOUN
la torre ◇ the towers of the castle le torri del
castello

tower block ['taʊəblɒk] NOUN
il palazzone

town [taʊn] NOUN
la città (PL le città) ◇ a town plan una
piantina della città
◆ the town centre il centro cittadino

---

* Verbs followed by this symbol are irregular. See pp.339–364 for further details.

town hall ['taun'hɔ:l] NOUN
il municipio (PL i municipi)

town planning [taun'plænɪŋ] NOUN
l'urbanistica

tow truck ['təutrʌk] NOUN
il carro attrezzi (PL i carri attrezzi)

toy [tɔɪ] NOUN
il giocattolo ◊ *a toy shop* un negozio di
giocattoli
♦ **a toy car** un'automobilina

trace [treɪs] NOUN
see also **trace** VERB
la traccia (PL le tracce) ◊ *There was no trace
of the robbers.* Non c'era traccia dei ladri.

to **trace** [treɪs] VERB
see also **trace** NOUN
[1] rintracciare ◊ *The police are trying to
trace witnesses.* La polizia sta cercando di
rintracciare i testimoni.
[2] ricalcare (*map, picture*)

tracing paper ['treɪsɪŋpeɪpə'] NOUN
la carta da ricalco

track [træk] NOUN
[1] il sentiero ◊ *a mountain track* un
sentiero di montagna
[2] il binario ◊ *A woman fell onto the tracks.*
Una donna è caduta sui binari.
[3] la pista ◊ *two laps of the track* due giri di
pista
[4] il pezzo (*song*) ◊ *This is my favourite
track.* Questo è il mio pezzo preferito.
[5] la traccia (PL le tracce) ◊ *They followed
the tracks for miles.* Hanno seguito le tracce
per miglia.

to **track down** [træk'daun] VERB
trovare ◊ *The police never tracked down
the killer.* La polizia non ha mai trovato
l'assassino.

tracksuit ['træksu:t] NOUN
la tuta da ginnastica

tractor ['træktə'] NOUN
il trattore

trade [treɪd] NOUN
see also **trade** VERB
[1] il commercio ◊ *the arms trade* il
commercio di armi
♦ **free trade** il libero scambio
♦ **a trade agreement** un accordo commerciale
[2] il mestiere ◊ *to learn a trade* imparare
un mestiere

to **trade** [treɪd] VERB
see also **trade** NOUN
[1] commerciare ◊ *They have traded with
France for centuries.* Commerciano con la
Francia da secoli.
[2] scambiare ◊ *I'd like to trade some cards.*
Vorrei scambiare alcune figurine.
♦ **They traded insults.** Si sono insultati a
vicenda.

trade fair ['treɪdfeə'] NOUN
la fiera campionaria

trade union [treɪd'ju:njən] NOUN
il sindacato

trade unionist [treɪd'ju:njənɪst] NOUN
il/la sindacalista

tradition [trə'dɪʃən] NOUN
la tradizione

traditional [trə'dɪʃənl] ADJECTIVE
tradizionale

traffic ['træfɪk] NOUN
il traffico ◊ *heavy traffic* traffico pesante

traffic circle ['træfɪksə:kl] NOUN US
la rotonda

traffic jam ['træfɪkdʒæm] NOUN
l'ingorgo stradale (PL gli ingorghi stradali)

traffic lights ['træfɪklaɪts] NOUN PL
il semaforo SING

traffic warden ['træfɪkwɔ:dən] NOUN
il vigile urbano

tragedy ['trædʒədɪ] NOUN (PL **tragedies**)
la tragedia

tragic ['trædʒɪk] ADJECTIVE
tragico

trailer ['treɪlə'] NOUN
[1] il rimorchio ◊ *a car and trailer* un'auto
con rimorchio
[2] il trailer (PL i trailer) (*of film*)
[3] la roulotte (PL le roulotte) (*caravan*) US
◊ *They live in a trailer.* Vivono in una
roulotte.
♦ **a trailer park** US un accampamento

train [treɪn] NOUN
see also **train** VERB
il treno

to **train** [treɪn] VERB
see also **train** NOUN
[1] allenarsi [E]
♦ **to train for a race** allenarsi[E] per una gara
♦ **to train as a teacher** fare* tirocinio come
insegnante
[2] addestrare (*animal*)

trained [treɪnd] ADJECTIVE
qualificato ◊ *highly trained workers* operai
altamente qualificati
♦ **She's a trained nurse.** È infermiera
diplomata.

trainee [treɪ'ni:] NOUN
l'apprendista MASC/FEM ◊ *a trainee plumber*
un apprendista idraulico
♦ **She's a trainee.** Sta facendo il tirocinio.

trainer ['treɪnə'] NOUN
[1] l'allenatore MASC
l'allenatrice FEM (*of team*)
[2] l'addestratore MASC
l'addestratrice FEM (*of animals*)
♦ **a language trainer** un/un'insegnante di
lingua

trainers ['treɪnəz] NOUN PL
le scarpe da ginnastica

training ['treɪnɪŋ] NOUN
[1] la formazione ◊ *a training course* un
corso di formazione ☞

T

2 l' allenamento ◇ *He strained a muscle in training.* Si è fatto uno strappo durante l'allenamento.

tram [træm] NOUN
il tram (PL i tram)

tramp [træmp] NOUN
il vagabondo
la vagabonda

trampoline ['træmpəli:n] NOUN
il trampolino

tranquillizer ['træŋkwɪlaɪzə'] NOUN
il tranquillante ◇ *She's on tranquillizers.* Prende tranquillanti.

transfer ['trænsfə'] NOUN
see also **transfer** VERB
1 il trasferimento ◇ *a bank transfer* un trasferimento bancario
♦ **the transfer of power** il passaggio di potere*
2 la decalcomania (*with design*)

to **transfer** [træns'fə:'] VERB
see also **transfer** NOUN
trasferire*

transfusion [træns'fju:ʒən] NOUN
la trasfusione

transistor [træn'zɪstə'] NOUN
il transistor (PL i transistor)

transit ['trænzɪt] NOUN
il transito ◇ *in transit* in transito

transit lounge ['trænzɪtlaʊndʒ] NOUN
la sala di transito

to **translate** [trænz'leɪt] VERB
tradurre*

translation [trænz'leɪʃən] NOUN
la traduzione

translator [trænz'leɪtə'] NOUN
il traduttore
la traduttrice

transparent [træns'pærnt] ADJECTIVE
trasparente

transplant ['trænsplɑ:nt] NOUN
il trapianto ◇ *a heart transplant* un trapianto cardiaco

transport ['trænspɔ:t] NOUN
see also **transport** VERB
1 il trasporto ◇ *rail transport* il trasporto ferroviario
2 il mezzo di trasporto ◇ *Have you got your own transport?* Hai un tuo mezzo di trasporto?
♦ **public transport** i trasporti pubblici

to **transport** [træns'pɔ:t] VERB
see also **transport** NOUN
trasportare

trap [træp] NOUN
see also **trap** VERB
la trappola

to **trap** [træp] VERB
see also **trap** NOUN
catturare ◇ *They trapped rabbits.* Catturavano conigli usando delle trappole.

♦ **to be trapped** rimanere* E intrappolato ◇ *Six people were trapped in the burning building.* Sei persone sono rimaste intrappolate nell'edificio in fiamme.

trash [træʃ] NOUN US
la spazzatura ◇ *I'll take out the trash.* Porto fuori la spazzatura.
♦ **the trash can** il secchio della spazzatura

trashy ['træʃɪ] ADJECTIVE
scadente ◇ *a trashy film* un film scadente

traumatic [trɔ:'mætɪk] ADJECTIVE
traumatico

to **travel** ['trævl] VERB
see also **travel** NOUN
viaggiare ◇ *I prefer to travel by train.* Preferisco viaggiare in treno.
♦ **We travelled over 800 kilometres.** Abbiamo fatto più di ottocento chilometri.
♦ **to travel round the world** girare il mondo
♦ **News travels fast!** Le notizie volano!

travel ['trævl] NOUN
see also **travel** VERB
♦ **Air travel is cheap these days.** Viaggiare in aereo non costa molto di questi tempi.
♦ **travel insurance** assicurazione di viaggio

travel agency ['trævleɪdʒənsɪ] NOUN
l' agenzia di viaggi

travel agent ['trævleɪdʒənt] NOUN
l' agente di viaggio MASC/FEM

traveller ['trævlə'] NOUN (US **traveler**)
il viaggiatore
la viaggiatrice

traveller's cheque ['trævləztʃɛk] NOUN
il traveller's cheque (PL i traveller's cheque)

travelling ['trævlɪŋ] NOUN (US **traveling**)
♦ **I love travelling.** Adoro viaggiare.

travel sickness ['trævlsɪknɪs] NOUN
1 il mal d'auto (*in car*)
2 il mal d'aria (*in plane*)

tray [treɪ] NOUN
il vassoio (PL i vassoi)

to **tread** [trɛd] VERB (**trod, trodden**)
calpestare
♦ **to tread on something** calpestare qualcosa ◇ *He trod on a piece of glass.* Ha calpestato un pezzo di vetro.
♦ **He trod on her foot.** Le ha pestato un piede.

treasure ['trɛʒə'] NOUN
il tesoro

treat [tri:t] NOUN
see also **treat** VERB
1 il regalo ◇ *as a birthday treat* come regalo di compleanno
2 la sorpresa ◇ *They're taking me out to dinner as a treat.* Per farmi una sorpresa mi portano fuori a cena.
♦ **to give somebody a treat** fare* una sorpresa a qualcuno
3 la leccornia (*to eat*)

to **treat** [tri:t] VERB
see also **treat** NOUN

---

* Verbs followed by this symbol are irregular. See pp.339–364 for further details.

☐1 trattare ◇ *The hostages were well treated.* Gli ostaggi sono stati trattati bene.
☐2 curare ◇ *She was treated for a minor head wound.* Le hanno curato una ferita superficiale al capo.
◆ **to treat somebody to something** offrire* qualcosa a qualcuno
◆ **I'll treat you!** Offro io!

treatment ['tri:tmənt] NOUN
☐1 la cura ◇ *an effective treatment for eczema* una cura efficace per l'eczema
☐2 il trattamento ◇ *We don't want any special treatment.* Non vogliamo un trattamento di favore.

to **treble** ['trɛbl] VERB
see also **treble** ADVERB
triplicare

treble ['trɛbl] ADVERB
see also **treble** VERB
il triplo ◇ *He now earns treble what he did.* Guadagna il triplo rispetto a prima.

tree [tri:] NOUN
l' albero

to **tremble** ['trɛmbl] VERB
tremare

tremendous [trɪ'mɛndəs] ADJECTIVE
☐1 fantastico ◇ *He was a tremendous person.* Era una persona fantastica.
☐2 strepitoso ◇ *a tremendous success* un successo strepitoso
Be careful not to translate **tremendous** *by* tremendo.

trend [trɛnd] NOUN
la moda ◇ *the latest trend* l'ultima moda
◆ **There's a trend towards part-time employment.** Il lavoro part-time è sempre più diffuso.

trendy ['trɛndɪ] ADJECTIVE
trendy MASC, FEM, PL

trial ['traɪəl] NOUN
☐1 il processo ◇ *the witnesses at the trial* i testimoni del processo
☐2 la prova ◇ *a trial period* un periodo di prova

triangle ['traɪæŋgl] NOUN
il triangolo

tribe [traɪb] NOUN
la tribù (PL le tribù)

trick [trɪk] NOUN
see also **trick** VERB
il trucco (PL i trucchi) ◇ *It's not easy, there's a trick to it.* Non è facile, c'è un trucco per farlo.
◆ **to play a trick on somebody** giocare un tiro a qualcuno

to **trick** [trɪk] VERB
see also **trick** NOUN
imbrogliare

tricky ['trɪkɪ] ADJECTIVE
difficile

tricycle ['traɪsɪkl] NOUN
il triciclo

trifle ['traɪfl] NOUN
la zuppa inglese ◇ *Trifle or ice cream?* Zuppa inglese o gelato?
◆ **a trifle...** un po'... ◇ *That seems a trifle ambitious.* Sembra un po' ambizioso.

to **trim** [trɪm] VERB
see also **trim** NOUN, ADJECTIVE
☐1 spuntare (*hair*)
☐2 tagliare (*grass*)

trim [trɪm] VERB
see also **trim** VERB, ADJECTIVE
◆ **to have a trim** farsi ^{E} spuntare i capelli

trim [trɪm] ADJECTIVE
see also **trim** VERB, NOUN
snello ◇ *a trim figure* una figura snella

trip [trɪp] NOUN
see also **trip** VERB
il viaggio
◆ **to go on a trip** fare* un viaggio ◇ *Have a good trip!* Buon viaggio!
◆ **a day trip** una gita di un giorno

to **trip** [trɪp] VERB
see also **trip** NOUN
inciampare

triple ['trɪpl] ADJECTIVE
triplo

triplets ['trɪplɪts] NOUN PL
◆ **to have triplets** avere* tre gemelli

trivial ['trɪvɪəl] ADJECTIVE
insignificante
Be careful not to translate **trivial** *by* triviale.

trod, trodden [trɔd, 'trɔdn] VERB *see* **tread**

trolley ['trɔlɪ] NOUN
il carrello

trombone [trɔm'bəʊn] NOUN
il trombone

troops [tru:ps] NOUN PL
le truppe

trophy ['trəʊfɪ] NOUN (PL **trophies**)
il trofeo

tropical ['trɔpɪkl] ADJECTIVE
tropicale

to **trot** [trɔt] VERB
trottare

trouble ['trʌbl] NOUN
il problema (PL i problemi) ◇ *The trouble is, it's too expensive.* Il problema è che costa troppo.
◆ **to be in trouble** essere* ^{E} nei guai
◆ **What's the trouble?** Cosa c'è che non va?
◆ **stomach trouble** disturbi gastrici MASC PL
◆ **to take a lot of trouble over something** mettere* molto impegno in qualcosa

troublemaker ['trʌblmeɪkə'] NOUN
l' elemento perturbatore

trousers ['traʊzəz] NOUN PL
i pantaloni

trout [traʊt] NOUN
la trota

truant ['truːənt] NOUN
◆ **to play truant** marinare la scuola

T

truck [trʌk] NOUN
il camion (PL i camion)

truck driver ['trʌkdraɪvə'] NOUN
il/la camionista

trucker ['trʌkə'] NOUN US
il/la camionista

true [truː] ADJECTIVE
vero ◇ *That can't be true!* Non può essere*
vero!
♦ **to come true** avverarsi ᴱ ◇ *I hope my dream
will come true.* Spero che il mio sogno si
avveri.

truly ['truːlɪ] ADVERB
veramente ◇ *It was a truly remarkable
victory.* È stata veramente una vittoria
straordinaria.
♦ **Yours truly...** Distinti saluti...

trumpet ['trʌmpɪt] NOUN
la tromba

trunk [trʌŋk] NOUN
[1] il tronco (PL i tronchi) ◇ *a tree trunk* un
tronco d'albero
[2] la proboscide (*of elephant*)
[3] il baule (*luggage*)
[4] il portabagagli (PL i portabagagli) (*boot*)
US ◇ *Put it in the trunk.* Mettilo nel
portabagagli.
♦ **swimming trunks** calzoncini da bagno

trust [trʌst] NOUN
see also **trust** VERB
la fiducia

to **trust** [trʌst] VERB
see also **trust** NOUN
fidarsi ᴱ di ◇ *Don't you trust me?* Non ti fidi
di me? ◇ *Trust me!* Fidati di me!

trusting ['trʌstɪŋ] ADJECTIVE
fiducioso

truth [truːθ] NOUN
la verità

truthful ['truːθful] ADJECTIVE
sincero

try [traɪ] NOUN (PL **tries**)
see also **try** VERB
il tentativo ◇ *his third try* il suo terzo
tentativo
♦ **to have a try** provare
♦ **to give something a try** provare qualcosa
♦ **It's worth a try.** Vale la pena di tentare.

to **try** [traɪ] VERB (**tried, tried**)
see also **try** NOUN
[1] tentare ◇ *I tried, but failed.* Ho tentato,
ma non ci sono riuscito. ◇ *You must try
harder.* Devi tentare ancora.
♦ **to try to do something** provare a fare*
qualcosa
♦ **to try again** ritentare
[2] assaggiare ◇ *Would you like to try
some?* Vuoi assaggiare?

to **try on** [traɪˈɒn] VERB
provare (*clothes*)

to **try out** [traɪˈaut] VERB
provare (*machine, system*)

T-shirt ['tiːʃəːt] NOUN
la maglietta

tube [tjuːb] NOUN
[1] il tubetto ◇ *a tube of toothpaste* un
tubetto di dentifricio
[2] il tubo ◇ *a cardboard tube* un tubo di
cartone
♦ **the Tube** la metropolitana di Londra

tuberculosis [tjubəːkjuˈləusɪs] NOUN
la tubercolosi

Tuesday ['tjuːzdɪ] NOUN
il martedì (PL i martedì)
♦ **on Tuesday** martedì ◇ *I saw her on
Tuesday.* L'ho vista martedì.
♦ **on Tuesdays** di martedì ◇ *I go swimming on
Tuesdays.* Vado in piscina di martedì.
♦ **Shrove Tuesday** martedì grasso

tug-of-war [tʌgəvˈwɔː'] NOUN
il tiro alla fune

tuition [tjuːˈɪʃən] NOUN
le lezioni PL
♦ **private tuition** lezioni private

tulip ['tjuːlɪp] NOUN
il tulipano

to **tumble** ['tʌmbl] VERB
fare* un capitombolo ◇ *He tumbled down
the steps.* Ha fatto un capitombolo giù dalle
scale.

tumble dryer ['tʌmbldraɪə'] NOUN
l' asciugatrice FEM

tummy ['tʌmɪ] NOUN (PL **tummies**)
la pancia (PL le pance)
♦ **tummy ache** mal di pancia

tuna ['tjuːnə] NOUN
il tonno

tune [tjuːn] NOUN
la melodia ◇ *a familiar tune* una melodia
familiare
♦ **to play in tune** essere* ᴱ accordato
♦ **to sing out of tune** stonare

Tunisia [tjuːˈnɪzɪə] NOUN
la Tunisia

tunnel ['tʌnl] NOUN
il tunnel (PL i tunnel)

Turin ['tjuəˈrɪn] NOUN
Torino

Turk [təːk] NOUN
il turco
la turca
♦ **the Turks** i turchi

Turkey ['təːkɪ] NOUN
la Turchia

turkey ['təːkɪ] NOUN
il tacchino

Turkish ['təːkɪʃ] ADJECTIVE
see also **Turkish** NOUN
turco

Turkish ['təːkɪʃ] NOUN
see also **Turkish** ADJECTIVE
il turco (*language*)

* Verbs followed by this symbol are irregular. See pp.339–364 for further details.

turn [təːn] NOUN
see also **turn** VERB
[1] la svolta ◇ *Take the next turn left.* Prendi la prossima svolta a sinistra.
♦ **"no left turn"** "divieto di svolta a sinistra"
[2] il turno
♦ **to take turns** fare* a turno
♦ **It's my turn!** Tocca a me!

to **turn** [təːn] VERB
see also **turn** NOUN
[1] girare ◇ *Turn right at the lights.* Al semaforo gira a destra.
[2] diventare[E] ◇ *When he's drunk he turns nasty.* Quando è ubriaco diventa cattivo.
♦ **The weather turned cold.** La temperatura è scesa.
♦ **to turn into** trasformarsi[E] in ◇ *The holiday turned into a nightmare.* La vacanza si è trasformata in un incubo.

to **turn back** [təːn'bæk] VERB
tornare[E] indietro ◇ *We turned back.* Siamo tornati indietro.

to **turn down** [təːn'daun] VERB
[1] rifiutare ◇ *He turned down the offer.* Ha rifiutato l'offerta.
[2] abbassare ◇ *Shall I turn the heating down?* Abbasso il riscaldamento?

to **turn off** [təːn'ɔf] VERB
[1] spegnere* ◇ *I'll turn off the radio.* Spegnerò la radio.
[2] chiudere* ◇ *You haven't turned off the tap.* Non hai chiuso il rubinetto.

to **turn on** [təːn'ɔn] VERB
[1] accendere* ◇ *Shall I turn on the light?* Accendo la luce?
[2] aprire* ◇ *She turned on the tap.* Ha aperto il rubinetto.

to **turn out** [təːn'aut] VERB
risultare[E] ◇ *It turned out to be a mistake.* È risultato essere* un errore. ◇ *It turned out that she was right.* È risultato che aveva ragione lei.

to **turn round** [təːn'raund] VERB
[1] girare (*car*)
[2] voltarsi[E] (*person*)

to **turn up** [təːn'ʌp] VERB
[1] arrivare[E] ◇ *She never turned up.* Non è mai arrivata.
[2] saltare[E] fuori ◇ *The painting turned up in an old house in Devon.* Il dipinto è saltato fuori in una vecchia casa nel Devon.
[3] alzare ◇ *Can you turn up the volume?* Puoi alzare il volume?

turning ['təːnɪŋ] NOUN
la svolta ◇ *We took the wrong turning.* Non abbiamo preso la svolta giusta.
♦ **a turning point** una svolta decisiva

turnip ['təːnɪp] NOUN
la rapa

turquoise ['təːkwɔɪz] ADJECTIVE
turchese

turtle ['təːtl] NOUN
la testuggine

Tuscany ['tʌskənɪ] NOUN
la Toscana

tutor ['tjuːtə'] NOUN
l'insegnante privato
l'insegnante privata

tuxedo [tʌk'siːdəu] NOUN [US]
lo smoking (PL gli smoking)

TV [tiː'viː] NOUN
la TV (PL le TV)

tweezers ['twiːzəz] NOUN PL
la pinzetta

twelfth [twɛlfθ] ADJECTIVE
dodicesimo ◇ *the twelfth floor* il dodicesimo piano
♦ **the twelfth of August** il dodici agosto

twelve [twɛlv] NUMERAL
dodici ◇ *She's twelve.* Ha dodici anni.

twentieth ['twɛntɪθ] ADJECTIVE
ventesimo ◇ *the twentieth floor* il ventesimo piano
♦ **the twentieth of May** il venti maggio

twenty ['twɛntɪ] NUMERAL
venti ◇ *He's twenty.* Ha vent'anni.

twice [twaɪs] ADVERB
due volte ◇ *I tried twice.* Ho provato due volte.
♦ **twice as much** il doppio

twin [twɪn] NOUN
il gemello ◇ *my twin brother* mio fratello gemello
♦ **twin beds** letti gemelli
♦ **a twin room** una camera con due letti

twinned [twɪnd] ADJECTIVE
gemellato ◇ *Nottingham is twinned with Minsk.* Nottingham è gemellata con Minsk.

to **twist** [twɪst] VERB
[1] attorcigliare (*hair*)
♦ **to twist one's ankle** slogarsi[E] la caviglia
[2] travisare ◇ *You're twisting my words.* Stai travisando le mie parole.

twit [twɪt] NOUN
il cretino
la cretina

two [tuː] NUMERAL
due ◇ *She's two.* Ha due anni.

type [taɪp] NOUN
see also **type** VERB
il tipo ◇ *What type of camera have you got?* Che tipo di macchina fotografica hai?

to **type** [taɪp] VERB
see also **type** NOUN
battere a macchina

typewriter ['taɪpraɪtə'] NOUN
la macchina da scrivere*

typical ['tɪpɪkl] ADJECTIVE
tipico ◇ *That's just typical!* Tipico!

tyre ['taɪə'] NOUN (US **tire**)
lo pneumatico
♦ **tyre pressure** pressione dei pneumatici

T

Verbs followed by the symbol "E" require the auxiliary "essere"

U

UFO [juːfˈəʊ] NOUN (PL **UFOs**) (= *Unidentified Flying Object*)
l' <u>ufo</u> (PL gli ufo)

ugh [əːh] EXCLAMATION
<u>puah!</u>

ugly [ˈʌglɪ] ADJECTIVE
<u>brutto</u>

UK [juːˈkeɪ] NOUN (= *United Kingdom*)
il <u>Regno Unito</u>

ulcer [ˈʌlsəˈ] NOUN
l' <u>ulcera</u> ◊ *a stomach ulcer* un'ulcera allo stomaco

♦ **a mouth ulcer** un'afta

Ulster NOUN
l' <u>Ulster</u> MASC

ultimate [ˈʌltɪmət] ADJECTIVE
<u>supremo</u> ◊ *the ultimate challenge* la sfida suprema

♦ **the ultimate in luxury** il massimo del lusso

ultimately [ˈʌltɪmətlɪ] ADVERB
<u>in fin dei conti</u> ◊ *Ultimately, it's your decision.* In fin dei conti, la decisione è tua.

umbrella [ʌmˈbrɛlə] NOUN
l' <u>ombrello</u>

umpire [ˈʌmpaɪəˈ] NOUN
[1] l' <u>arbitro</u> (*in cricket*)
[2] il <u>giudice di gara</u> (*in tennis*)

UN [juːˈɛn] NOUN (= *United Nations*)
l' <u>ONU</u> FEM

unable [ʌnˈeɪbl] ADJECTIVE
♦ **to be unable to do something** non poter fare* qualcosa ◊ *Unfortunately, he was unable to come.* Purtroppo non è potuto venire*.

unacceptable [ʌnəkˈsɛptəbl] ADJECTIVE
<u>inaccettabile</u>

unanimous [juːˈnænɪməs] ADJECTIVE
<u>unanime</u>

unattended [ʌnəˈtɛndɪd] ADJECTIVE
<u>incustodito</u> ◊ *Please do not leave your luggage unattended.* Non lasciare il bagaglio incustodito.

unavoidable [ʌnəˈvɔɪdəbl] ADJECTIVE
<u>inevitabile</u>

unaware [ʌnəˈwɛəˈ] ADJECTIVE
♦ **to be unaware of** non essere*ᴱ a conoscenza di ◊ *She was unaware of the regulations.* Non era a conoscenza del regolamento.

♦ **She was unaware that she was being filmed.** Non si era resa conto di essere* filmata.

unbearable [ʌnˈbɛərəbl] ADJECTIVE
<u>insopportabile</u>

unbeatable [ʌnˈbiːtəbl] ADJECTIVE
<u>imbattibile</u>

unbelievable [ʌnbɪˈliːvəbl] ADJECTIVE
<u>incredibile</u>

unborn [ʌnˈbɔːn] ADJECTIVE

♦ **the unborn child** il feto

unbreakable [ʌnˈbreɪkəbl] ADJECTIVE
<u>infrangibile</u>

uncanny [ʌnˈkænɪ] ADJECTIVE
<u>strano</u> ◊ *That's uncanny!* È strano!

♦ **an uncanny resemblance** una rassomiglianza stupefacente

uncertain [ʌnˈsəːtn] ADJECTIVE
<u>incerto</u> ◊ *The future is uncertain.* L'avvenire* è incerto.

uncivilized [ʌnˈsɪvɪlaɪzd] ADJECTIVE
<u>incivile</u>

uncle [ˈʌŋkl] NOUN
lo <u>zio</u> (PL gli zii)

uncomfortable [ʌnˈkʌmfətəbl] ADJECTIVE
[1] <u>scomodo</u> ◊ *an uncomfortable position* una posizione scomoda
[2] <u>a disagio</u> ◊ *The way he talks makes me feel uncomfortable.* Il modo in cui parla mi mette a disagio.

unconscious [ʌnˈkɔnʃəs] ADJECTIVE
<u>svenuto</u>

uncontrollable [ʌnkənˈtrəʊləbl] ADJECTIVE
<u>irrefrenabile</u>

unconventional [ʌnkənˈvɛnʃənl] ADJECTIVE
[1] <u>anticonformista</u> (*person*)
[2] <u>poco convenzionale</u> (*technique*)

under [ˈʌndəˈ] PREPOSITION
<u>sotto</u> ◊ *The cat's under the table.* Il gatto è sotto il tavolo. ◊ *The tunnel goes under the Channel.* Il tunnel passa sotto il Canale della Manica.

♦ **under there** lì sotto ◊ *What's under there?* Cosa c'è lì sotto?

♦ **children under ten** bambini al di sotto dei dieci anni

♦ **under twenty people** meno di venti persone

under-age [ʌndərˈeɪdʒ] ADJECTIVE
♦ **He's under-age.** È minorenne.

undercover [ʌndəˈkʌvəˈ] ADJECTIVE, ADVERB
[1] <u>segreto</u> ◊ *an undercover agent* un agente segreto
[2] <u>in incognito</u> ◊ *She was working undercover.* Agiva in incognito.

underdog [ˈʌndədɔg] NOUN
♦ **Inter were the underdogs on this occasion.** In questa occasione l'Inter era la squadra sfavorita.

to **underestimate** [ˈʌndərˈɛstɪmeɪt] VERB
<u>sottovalutare</u>

to **undergo** [ʌndəˈgəʊ] VERB (**underwent, undergone**)
<u>sottoporsi</u>ᴱ a

underground [ˈʌndəgraʊnd] ADJECTIVE, ADVERB
see also **underground** NOUN
[1] <u>sotterraneo</u> ◊ *an underground car park* un parcheggio sotterraneo
[2] <u>sottoterra</u> ◊ *Moles live underground.* Le

* Verbs followed by this symbol are irregular. See pp.339–364 for further details.

talpe vivono sottoterra.

♦ **to go underground** (*political group, terrorist*)
entrare in clandestinità

underground ['ʌndəgraund] NOUN
see also **underground** ADJECTIVE, ADVERB
la metropolitana

to **underline** [ʌndə'laɪn] VERB
sottolineare

underneath [ʌndə'niːθ] PREPOSITION, ADVERB
sotto ◇ *underneath the carpet* sotto la
moquette ◇ *I got out of the car and looked
underneath.* Sono sceso dalla macchina e
ho guardato sotto.

underpaid [ʌndə'peɪd] ADJECTIVE
sottopagato

underpants ['ʌndəpænts] NOUN PL
le mutande da uomo

underpass ['ʌndəpɑːs] NOUN (PL
underpasses)
il sottopassaggio

undershirt ['ʌndəʃɜːt] NOUN US
1 la canottiera (*sleeveless*)
2 la maglietta (*with short sleeves*)

underskirt ['ʌndəskɜːt] NOUN
la sottogonna

to **understand** [ʌndə'stænd] VERB
(**understood, understood**)
capire ◇ *Do you understand?* Capisci? ◇ *I
don't understand the question.* Non ho
capito la domanda.

♦ **Is that understood?** È chiaro?

understanding [ʌndə'stændɪŋ] ADJECTIVE
comprensivo

understood [ʌndə'stud] VERB see
understand

undertaker ['ʌndəteɪkə'] NOUN
l'impresario di pompe funebri

underwater ['ʌndə'wɔːtə'] ADJECTIVE, ADVERB
1 subacqueo ◇ *underwater photography*
fotografia subacquea
2 sott'acqua ◇ *This sequence was filmed
underwater.* Questa scena è stata girata
sott'acqua.

underwear ['ʌndəweə'] NOUN
la biancheria intima

underwent [ʌndə'went] VERB see **undergo**

to **undo** [ʌn'duː] VERB (**undid, undone**)
1 sbottonare ◇ *She undid her coat.* Si è
sbottonata il cappotto.
2 sciogliere* ◇ *I can't undo the knot.* Non
riesco a sciogliere* il nodo.

♦ **Your laces are undone.** Hai le scarpe
slacciate.

to **undress** [ʌn'dres] VERB
spogliarsi E

uneconomic [ʌniːkə'nɒmɪk] ADJECTIVE
poco redditizio

unemployed [ʌnɪm'plɔɪd] ADJECTIVE
disoccupato

♦ **the unemployed** i disoccupati

unemployment [ʌnɪm'plɔɪmənt] NOUN
la disoccupazione

unexpected [ʌnɪks'pektɪd] ADJECTIVE
inatteso

unexpectedly [ʌnɪks'pektɪdlɪ] ADVERB
inaspettatamente

unfair [ʌn'feə'] ADJECTIVE
ingiusto

unfamiliar [ʌnfə'mɪlɪə'] ADJECTIVE
sconosciuto ◇ *I heard an unfamiliar voice.*
Ho sentito una voce sconosciuta.

unfashionable [ʌn'fæʃnəbl] ADJECTIVE
fuori moda

unfit [ʌn'fɪt] ADJECTIVE
fuori forma ◇ *I'm really unfit at the moment.*
Al momento sono proprio fuori forma.

♦ **to be unfit for work** essere* E inabile al
lavoro

to **unfold** [ʌn'fəuld] VERB
spiegare ◇ *She unfolded the map.* Ha
spiegato la cartina.

unforgettable [ʌnfə'getəbl] ADJECTIVE
indimenticabile

unfortunately [ʌn'fɔːtʃənətlɪ] ADVERB
sfortunatamente

unfriendly [ʌn'frendlɪ] ADJECTIVE
antipatico ◇ *The waiters are a bit
unfriendly.* I camerieri sono un po'
antipatici.

ungrateful [ʌn'greɪtful] ADJECTIVE
ingrato

unhappy [ʌn'hæpɪ] ADJECTIVE
infelice ◇ *He was very unhappy as a child.*
Da bambino era molto infelice.

♦ **to look unhappy** avere* l'aria triste

unhealthy [ʌn'helθɪ] ADJECTIVE
malaticcio ◇ *an unhealthy girl* una ragazza
malaticcia

♦ **He's unhealthy and depressed.** Non sta
bene ed è depresso.

♦ **an unhealthy diet** una dieta poco equilibrata

uni ['juːnɪ] NOUN
l'università (PL le università) ◇ *He's at uni.* È
all'università.

uniform ['juːnɪfɔːm] NOUN
see also **uniform** ADJECTIVE
l'uniforme FEM

♦ **school uniform** la divisa scolastica

uniform ['juːnɪfɔːm] ADJECTIVE
see also **uniform** NOUN
uniforme

uninhabited [ʌnɪn'hæbɪtɪd] ADJECTIVE
disabitato

union ['juːnjən] NOUN
il sindacato ◇ *Do you belong to a union?*
Appartieni ad un sindacato?

Union Jack ['juːnjən'dʒæk] NOUN
la bandiera del Regno Unito

unique [juː'niːk] ADJECTIVE
unico

unit ['juːnɪt] NOUN
l'unità (PL le unità) ◇ *a unit of measurement* ☞

U

Verbs followed by the symbol "E" require the auxiliary "essere"

un'unità di misura

* **a kitchen unit** un elemento componibile della cucina

United Kingdom [juːˈnaɪtɪdˈkɪŋdəm] NOUN
il Regno Unito

United Nations [juːˈnaɪtɪdˈneɪʃənz] NOUN
le Nazioni Unite

United States [juːˈnaɪtɪdˈsteɪts] NOUN PL
gli Stati Uniti

universe [ˈjuːnɪvɜːs] NOUN
l' universo

university [juːnɪˈvɜːsɪtɪ] NOUN (PL
universities)
l' università (PL le università)

unleaded petrol [ʌnlɛdɪdˈpɛtrəl] NOUN
la benzina verde

unless [ʌnˈlɛs] CONJUNCTION
se non ◇ *We won't get there in time unless we leave earlier.* Se non partiamo prima non arriveremo in tempo. ◇ *unless I am mistaken...* se non mi sbaglio...

unlike [ʌnˈlaɪk] PREPOSITION
a differenza di ◇ *Unlike Tom, I really enjoy flying.* Io, a differenza di Tom, adoro viaggiare in aereo.

unlikely [ʌnˈlaɪklɪ] ADJECTIVE
poco probabile ◇ *He's unlikely to come.* È poco probabile che venga.

unlisted [ʌnˈlɪstɪd] ADJECTIVE US
* **an unlisted number**
un numero che non è sull'elenco del telefono

to **unload** [ʌnˈləʊd] VERB
scaricare

to **unlock** [ʌnˈlɒk] VERB
aprire* ◇ *He unlocked the door of the car.* Ha aperto la portiera dell'auto.

unlucky [ʌnˈlʌkɪ] ADJECTIVE
* **to be unlucky (1)** (*person*) non avere* fortuna
* **to be unlucky (2)** (*number, thing*) portare sfortuna

unmarried [ʌnˈmærɪd] ADJECTIVE
non sposato ◇ *an unmarried couple* una coppia non sposata
* **an unmarried mother** una ragazza madre

unnatural [ʌnˈnætʃrəl] ADJECTIVE
poco naturale

unnecessary [ʌnˈnɛsəsərɪ] ADJECTIVE
non necessario

unofficial [ʌnəˈfɪʃl] ADJECTIVE
ufficioso ◇ *unofficial figures* cifre ufficiose
* **an unofficial strike** uno sciopero non autorizzato

to **unpack** [ʌnˈpæk] VERB
1 disfare* ◇ *I unpacked my suitcase.* Ho disfatto la valigia.
* **I haven't unpacked my clothes yet.** Non ho ancora tolto i vestiti dalla valigia.
2 disfare* le valigie ◇ *I went to my room to unpack.* Sono andato in camera mia a

disfare* le valigie.

unpleasant [ʌnˈplɛznt] ADJECTIVE
1 spiacevole ◇ *an unpleasant situation* una situazione spiacevole
2 sgradevole ◇ *an unpleasant smell* un odore sgradevole
3 antipatico (*person*)

to **unplug** [ʌnˈplʌg] VERB
staccare la presa di ◇ *She unplugs the TV before going to bed.* Stacca la presa della TV prima di andare* a letto.

unpopular [ʌnˈpɒpjʊləʳ] ADJECTIVE
impopolare

unpredictable [ʌnprɪˈdɪktəbl] ADJECTIVE
imprevedibile

unreal [ʌnˈrɪəl] ADJECTIVE
1 irreale ◇ *an unreal situation* una situazione irreale
2 falso ◇ *unreal expectations* false aspettative
3 incredibile ◇ *It was unreal!* Era incredibile!

unrealistic [ˈʌnrɪəˈlɪstɪk] ADJECTIVE
non realistico

unreasonable [ʌnˈriːznəbl] ADJECTIVE
irragionevole ◇ *Her attitude was completely unreasonable.* Il suo atteggiamento era del tutto irragionevole.

unreliable [ʌnrɪˈlaɪəbl] ADJECTIVE
inaffidabile ◇ *It's a nice car, but a bit unreliable.* È una bella macchina ma un po' inaffidabile.

to **unroll** [ʌnˈrəʊl] VERB
srotolare

unsatisfactory [ˈʌnsætɪsˈfæktərɪ] ADJECTIVE
poco soddisfacente

to **unscrew** [ʌnˈskruː] VERB
svitare

unshaven [ʌnˈʃeɪvn] ADJECTIVE
non rasato

unskilled [ʌnˈskɪld] ADJECTIVE
* **an unskilled worker** un operaio non specializzato

unstable [ʌnˈsteɪbl] ADJECTIVE
instabile

unsteady [ʌnˈstɛdɪ] ADJECTIVE
malsicuro

unsuccessful [ʌnsəkˈsɛsfʊl] ADJECTIVE
fallito ◇ *an unsuccessful artist* un artista fallito
* **The attempt was unsuccessful.** Il tentativo fallì.

unsuitable [ʌnˈsuːtəbl] ADJECTIVE
non adatto

untidy [ʌnˈtaɪdɪ] ADJECTIVE
1 in disordine (*place*)
2 disordinato (*person*)

to **untie** [ʌnˈtaɪ] VERB
1 sciogliere* ◇ *He couldn't untie the knots.* Non riusciva a sciogliere* i nodi.
2 slegare (*animal, person*)

* Verbs followed by this symbol are irregular. See pp.339–364 for further details.

until [ən'tɪl] PREPOSITION, CONJUNCTION
fino a ◊ *I waited until ten o'clock.* Ho
aspettato fino alle dieci.
+ **It won't be ready until next week.** Non sarà
pronto prima della settimana prossima.
+ **until now** finora ◊ *It's never been a
problem until now.* Non è mai stato un
problema, finora.
+ **until then** fino ad allora ◊ *Until then I'd
never been to Italy.* Fino ad allora non ero
mai stato in Italia.

unusual [ʌn'juːʒuəl] ADJECTIVE
[1] insolito ◊ *an unusual shape* una forma
insolita
[2] raro ◊ *It's unusual to get snow at this
time of year.* È raro che nevichi in questa
stagione.

unwilling [ʌn'wɪlɪŋ] ADJECTIVE
+ **He was unwilling to help me.** Non era
disposto ad aiutarmi.

to **unwind** [ʌn'waɪnd] VERB (**unwound,
unwound**)
[1] rilassarsi [E] ◊ *I need time to unwind.* Ho
bisogno di tempo per rilassarmi.
[2] srotolare ◊ *He unwound the rope.* Ha
srotolato la fune.

unwise [ʌn'waɪz] ADJECTIVE
imprudente

to **unwrap** [ʌn'ræp] VERB
aprire* ◊ *After lunch we unwrapped the
presents.* Dopo pranzo abbiamo aperto i
regali.

up [ʌp] PREPOSITION, ADVERB
su ◊ *up on the hill* su in collina
+ **up here** quassù
+ **up there** lassù
+ **up north** su al nord
+ **to be up** essersi [E] alzato ◊ *We were up at
six.* Ci siamo alzati alle sei. ◊ *He's not up
yet.* Non si è ancora alzato.
+ **What's up?** Che c'è?
+ **What's up with her?** Che cos'ha?
+ **to go up** salire* ◊ *The bus went up the hill.*
L'autobus salì su per la collina.
+ **to go up to somebody** avvicinarsi [E] a
qualcuno ◊ *She came up to me.* Mi si
avvicinò.
+ **up to** fino a ◊ *to count up to fifty* contare
fino a cinquanta ◊ *up to three hours* fino a
tre ore
+ **up to now** finora
+ **It's up to you.** Sta a te decidere*.
+ **up to date (1)** moderno ◊ *the most up to
date electric power stations* le centrali
elettriche più moderne
+ **up to date (2)** aggiornato ◊ *an up-to-date
timetable* un orario aggiornato
+ **to bring somebody up-to-date on
something** aggiornare qualcuno su
qualcosa

upbringing ['ʌpbrɪŋɪŋ] NOUN
l' educazione FEM

uphill ['ʌp'hɪl] ADJECTIVE
+ **It was an uphill struggle.** È stata dura.

upper ['ʌpə'] ADJECTIVE
superiore ◊ *on the upper floor* al piano
superiore

upper sixth [ʌpə'sɪksθ] NOUN
l' ultimo anno della scuola superiore

upright ['ʌpraɪt] ADJECTIVE
+ **to stand upright** stare* [E] dritto

upset ['ʌpset] NOUN
see also **upset** ADJECTIVE, VERB
+ **to have a stomach upset** avere* lo stomaco
scombussolato

upset [ʌp'set] ADJECTIVE
see also **upset** NOUN, VERB
turbato ◊ *She's still a bit upset.* È ancora un
po' turbata.
+ **to have an upset stomach** avere* lo
stomaco scombussolato
+ **to get upset** prendersela [E] ◊ *Don't get
upset.* Non te la prendere*.

to **upset** [ʌp'set] VERB (**upset, upset**)
see also **upset** NOUN, ADJECTIVE
+ **to upset somebody** turbare qualcuno
◊ *You'll only upset her if you mention it.*
Riuscirai solo a turbarla menzionandolo.
+ **Don't upset yourself.** Non te la prendere*.

upside down [ʌpsaɪd'daun] ADVERB
alla rovescia ◊ *The painting was hung
upside down.* Il quadro era appeso alla
rovescia.

upstairs [ʌp'stɛəz] ADVERB
di sopra ◊ *Where's your coat? – It's upstairs.*
Dov'è il tuo cappotto? – È di sopra. ◊ *He
went upstairs to bed.* È andato di sopra a
coricarsi.

uptight [ʌp'taɪt] ADJECTIVE
nervoso

upwards ['ʌpwədz] ADVERB
verso l'alto

urgent ['əːdʒənt] ADJECTIVE
urgente

urine ['juərɪn] NOUN
l' urina

US [juːˈes] NOUN (= *United States*)
gli Stati Uniti

us [ʌs] PRONOUN
[1] ci ◊ *They helped us.* Ci hanno aiutato.
[2] noi
*Use **noi** after a preposition.*
◊ *Why don't you come with us?* Perché non
vieni con noi?

USA [juːes'eɪ] NOUN (= *United States of
America*)
gli USA

use [juːs] NOUN
see also **use** VERB
l' uso ◊ *"directions for use"* "istruzioni per
l'uso"
+ **It's no use...** È inutile... ◊ *It's no use
shouting, she's deaf.* È inutile gridare, è

U

sorda.

to **use** [juːz] VERB

> see also **use** NOUN

usare ◊ *a used car* una macchina usata

used to *+ verb is usually translated by the Italian imperfect.*

◊ *I used to live in London.* Una volta abitavo a Londra. ◊ *I didn't use to like maths when I was at school.* La matematica non mi piaceva quando andavo a scuola.

- ◆ **to be used to something** essere* E abituato a qualcosa
- ◆ **to be used to doing something** essere* E abituato a fare* qualcosa ◊ *He wasn't used to driving on the right.* Non era abituato a guidare sulla destra. ◊ *Don't worry, I'm used to it.* Non preoccuparti, ci sono abituato.

to **use up** [juːzˈʌp] VERB

finire* ◊ *We've used up all the paint.* Abbiamo finito tutta la vernice.

useful [ˈjuːsful] ADJECTIVE
utile

useless [ˈjuːslɪs] ADJECTIVE
  1 inutile ◊ *It's useless!* È inutile!
  2 impedito ◊ *I'm useless at tennis!* A tennis sono un impedito!

user [ˈjuːzəʳ] NOUN
l' utente MASC / FEM

user-friendly [ˈjuːzəˈfrɛndlɪ] ADJECTIVE
di facile uso

usual [ˈjuːʒuəl] ADJECTIVE
solito
- ◆ **as usual** come al solito

usually [ˈjuːʒuəlɪ] ADVERB
di solito

utility room [juːˈtɪlɪtɪrum] NOUN
la stanza adibita a lavanderia

U-turn [ˈjuːtəːn] NOUN
l' inversione a U FEM (*by driver*)

V

vacancy ['veɪkənsɪ] NOUN (PL **vacancies**)
1 il posto vacante (*job*) ◊ *There were no vacancies.* Non c'erano posti vacanti.
- **They have vacancies for programmers.** Cercano programmatori.
2 la camera disponibile (*in hotel*)
- **"no vacancies"** "completo"
*Be careful not to translate **vacancy** by vacanza.*

vacant ['veɪkənt] ADJECTIVE
libero

vacation [veɪ'keɪʃən] NOUN US
la vacanza

to **vaccinate** ['væksɪneɪt] VERB
vaccinare

to **vacuum** ['vækjum] VERB
*see also **vacuum** NOUN*
passare l'aspirapolvere in ◊ *to vacuum the lounge* passare l'aspirapolvere nel salotto

vacuum ['vækjum] NOUN
*see also **vacuum** VERB*
il vuoto ◊ *Their departure has left a vacuum.* La loro partenza ha lasciato un vuoto.

vacuum cleaner ['vækjumkliːnə'] NOUN
l'aspirapolvere MASC

vagina NOUN
la vagina

vague [veɪg] ADJECTIVE
vago

vain [veɪn] ADJECTIVE
1 vano ◊ *a vain hope* una speranza vana
2 vanitoso ◊ *He's terribly vain.* È terribilmente vanitoso.
- **in vain** invano

Valentine card ['væləntaɪnkɑːd] NOUN
il biglietto di auguri per San Valentino

Valentine's Day ['væləntaɪnzdeɪ] NOUN
il San Valentino

valid ['vælɪd] ADJECTIVE
valido

valley ['vælɪ] NOUN (PL **valleys**)
la valle

valuable ['væljuəbl] ADJECTIVE
1 di valore ◊ *a valuable painting* un quadro di valore
2 prezioso ◊ *valuable help* un aiuto prezioso

valuables ['væljuəblz] NOUN PL
gli oggetti di valore

value ['væljuː] NOUN
il valore
- **value added tax** l'imposta sul valore aggiunto

van [væn] NOUN
il furgone

vandal NOUN
il vandalo

vandalism NOUN
il vandalismo

to **vandalize** ['vændəlaɪz] VERB
rovinare

vanilla [və'nɪlə] NOUN
la vaniglia

to **vanish** ['vænɪʃ] VERB
sparire* E

variable ['veərɪəbl] ADJECTIVE
variabile

varied ['veərɪd] ADJECTIVE
vario

variety [və'raɪətɪ] NOUN (PL **varieties**)
la varietà (PL le varietà)

various ['veərɪəs] ADJECTIVE
vario ◊ *We visited various villages in the area.* Abbiamo visitato vari paesini della zona.

to **vary** ['veərɪ] VERB (**varied, varied**)
variare

vase [vɑːz] NOUN
il vaso

VAT [væt] NOUN
l'IVA

VCR [viːsiːɑːr] NOUN (= *video cassette recorder*)
il videoregistratore

VDU [viːdiːjuː] NOUN (= *visual display unit*)
il videoterminale

veal [viːl] NOUN
la carne di vitello

vegan ['viːgən] NOUN
il vegetaliano
la vegetaliana

vegetable ['vɛdʒtəbl] NOUN
la verdura ◊ *vegetable soup* minestra di verdura

vegetarian [vɛdʒɪ'teərɪən] ADJECTIVE
*see also **vegetarian** NOUN*
vegetariano

vegetarian [vɛdʒɪ'teərɪən] NOUN
*see also **vegetarian** ADJECTIVE*
il vegetariano
la vegetariana

vehicle ['viːɪkl] NOUN
il veicolo

vein [veɪn] NOUN
la vena

velvet ['vɛlvɪt] NOUN
il velluto

vending machine ['vɛndɪŋməʃiːn] NOUN
il distributore automatico

Venetian blind [vɪniːʃən'blaɪnd] NOUN
la veneziana

Venice ['vɛnɪs] NOUN
Venezia FEM

verb [vəːb] NOUN
il verbo

verdict ['vəːdɪkt] NOUN
la sentenza

V

Verbs followed by the symbol "E" require the auxiliary "essere"

vertical ['vɜːtɪkl] ADJECTIVE
verticale

vertigo ['vɜːtɪgəʊ] NOUN
le vertigini ◇ I get vertigo. Mi vengono le vertigini.

very ['vɛrɪ] ADVERB
molto ◇ very tall molto alto ◇ not very interesting non molto interessante
♦ **very much** moltissimo

vest [vɛst] NOUN
1 la canottiera ◇ a thermal vest una canottiera termica
2 il gilè (PL i gilè) (waistcoat) US

vet [vɛt] NOUN
il veterinario

via ['vaɪə] PREPOSITION
passando per ◇ We went to Rome via London. Siamo andati a Roma passando per Londra.

vicar ['vɪkə'] NOUN
il pastore

vice [vaɪs] NOUN
1 il vizio ◇ vices and virtues vizi e virtù
2 la morsa ◇ held in a vice stretto in una morsa

vice versa ['vaɪsɪ'vɜːsə] ADVERB
viceversa

vicious ['vɪʃəs] ADJECTIVE
1 brutale ◇ a vicious attack un attacco brutale
2 cattivo (dog, person)
♦ **a vicious circle** un circolo vizioso

victim ['vɪktɪm] NOUN
la vittima ◇ He was the victim of a mugging. È stato vittima di un'aggressione.

victory ['vɪktərɪ] NOUN (PL **victories**)
la vittoria

to **video** ['vɪdɪəʊ] VERB
see also **video** NOUN
1 registrare (from TV) ◇ I'll video the programme. Registrerò il programma.
2 filmare (with camera)

video ['vɪdɪəʊ] NOUN (PL **videos**)
see also **video** VERB
1 la videocassetta ◇ It's out on video. È uscito su videocassetta. ◇ She lent me a video. Mi ha prestato una videocassetta.
2 il videoregistratore ◇ Have you got a video? Hai il videoregistratore?
♦ **a video camera** una videocamera
♦ **a video cassette** una videocassetta
♦ **a video recorder** un videoregistratore
♦ **a video shop** un videonoleggio

video game ['vɪdɪəʊgeɪm] NOUN
il videogioco (PL i videogiochi)

Vietnam [vjet'næm] NOUN
il Vietnam

Vietnamese [vjetnə'miːz] ADJECTIVE
vietnamita INV

view [vjuː] NOUN
see also **view** VERB

1 la vista ◇ There's an amazing view. C'è una vista fantastica.
2 l' avviso ◇ in my view a mio avviso

to **view** [vjuː] VERB
see also **view** NOUN
considerare ◇ How do you view this development? Come consideri questo sviluppo?

viewer ['vjuːə'] NOUN
il telespettatore
la telespettatrice

viewpoint ['vjuːpɔɪnt] NOUN
il punto di vista

vile [vaɪl] ADJECTIVE
disgustoso

villa NOUN
la villa

village ['vɪlɪdʒ] NOUN
il paese

villain ['vɪlən] NOUN
il/la malvivente
♦ **the villain** (of film, story) il cattivo

vine [vaɪn] NOUN
la vite

vinegar ['vɪnɪgə'] NOUN
l' aceto

vineyard ['vɪnjɑːd] NOUN
il vigneto

viola [vɪ'əʊlə] NOUN
la viola

violence ['vaɪələns] NOUN
la violenza

violent ['vaɪələnt] ADJECTIVE
violento

violin [vaɪə'lɪn] NOUN
il violino

violinist [vaɪə'lɪnɪst] NOUN
il/la violinista

virgin ['vɜːdʒɪn] NOUN
la vergine

Virgo ['vɜːgəʊ] NOUN
la Vergine ◇ I'm Virgo. Sono della Vergine.

virtual ['vɜːtjuəl] ADJECTIVE
♦ **It's a virtual certainty.** È praticamente una certezza.

virtual reality ['vɜːtjuəlrɪ'ælɪtɪ] NOUN
la realtà virtuale

virus ['vaɪərəs] NOUN (PL **viruses**)
il virus (PL i virus)

visa ['viːzə] NOUN
il visto (in passport)

vise [vaɪs] NOUN US
la morsa

visible ['vɪzəbl] ADJECTIVE
visibile

visit ['vɪzɪt] NOUN
see also **visit** VERB
la visita

to **visit** ['vɪzɪt] VERB
see also **visit** NOUN
1 andare*ᴱ a trovare ◇ I visited my

grandmother last week. Sono andato a
trovare mia nonna la settimana scorsa.
[2] visitare ◇ *We'd like to visit the castle.* Ci
piacerebbe visitare il castello.
visitor ['vɪzɪtə'] NOUN
il visitatore
la visitatrice
◇ *important visitors* visitatori importanti
✦ **to have a visitor** avere* una visita
visual ['vɪzjuəl] ADJECTIVE
visivo
to **visualize** ['vɪzjuəlaɪz] VERB
immaginare
vital ['vaɪtl] ADJECTIVE
d'importanza vitale ◇ *vital information*
informazioni d'importanza vitale
✦ **It's vital to sterilize the equipment.** È
essenziale sterilizzare l'attrezzatura.
vitamin ['vɪtəmɪn] NOUN
la vitamina
vivid ['vɪvɪd] ADJECTIVE
vivo (*colour*)
✦ **to have a vivid imagination** avere* una
fervida immaginazione
vocabulary [vəu'kæbjulərɪ] NOUN (PL
vocabularies)
il vocabolario
vocational [vəu'keɪʃənl] ADJECTIVE
professionale ◇ *vocational training*
formazione professionale
vodka NOUN
la vodka
voice [vɔɪs] NOUN
la voce ◇ *I heard voices.* Sentivo delle voci.
voice mail ['vɔɪsmeɪl] NOUN
il servizio di messaggeria vocale
volcano [vɔl'keɪnəu] NOUN (PL **volcanoes**)
il vulcano

volleyball ['vɔlɪbɔːl] NOUN
la pallavolo
volt NOUN
il volt (PL **i volt**)
voltage ['vəultɪdʒ] NOUN
il voltaggio
voluntary ['vɔləntərɪ] ADJECTIVE
[1] volontario ◇ *voluntary contributions*
contributi volontari
[2] facoltativo ◇ *Attendance is voluntary.*
La frequenza è facoltativa.
✦ **to do voluntary work** fare* volontariato
volunteer [vɔlən'tɪə'] NOUN
see also **volunteer** VERB
il volontario
la volontaria
to **volunteer** [vɔlən'tɪə'] VERB
see also **volunteer** NOUN
✦ **to volunteer to do something** offrirsi ᴱ
volontario per fare* qualcosa
to **vomit** ['vɔmɪt] VERB
vomitare
to **vote** [vəut] VERB
see also **vote** NOUN
votare
vote [vəut] NOUN
see also **vote** VERB
[1] il voto ◇ *They won by two votes.* Hanno
vinto per due voti.
[2] la votazione ◇ *Now let's take a vote.*
Passiamo ora alla votazione.
voucher ['vautʃə'] NOUN
il buono ◇ *a gift voucher* un buono acquisto
vowel ['vauəl] NOUN
la vocale
vulgar ['vʌlgə'] ADJECTIVE
volgare

V

W

wafer ['weɪfə'] NOUN
la cialda

wage [weɪdʒ] NOUN
la paga ◇ *a low wage* una paga bassa
* **the minimum wage** il salario minimo garantito
* **wages** la paga SING ◇ *He collected his wages.* Ha ritirato la paga.

wage packet ['weɪdʒpækɪt] NOUN
la busta paga (PL le buste paga)

waist [weɪst] NOUN
la vita ◇ *He put his arm round her waist.* Le ha messo un braccio attorno alla vita.

waistcoat ['weɪskəut] NOUN
il gilè (PL i gilè)

to **wait** [weɪt] VERB
aspettare ◇ *How long have you been waiting?* Da quanto tempo stai aspettando?
* **to wait for something** aspettare qualcosa
* **to wait for somebody** aspettare qualcuno ◇ *I'll wait for you.* Ti aspetto. ◇ *Wait for me!* Aspettami!
* **to keep somebody waiting** fare* aspettare qualcuno ◇ *They kept us waiting for hours.* Ci hanno fatto aspettare per delle ore.
* **I can't wait for the holidays.** Non vedo l'ora che arrivino le vacanze.
* **I can't wait to see him again.** Non vedo l'ora di rivederlo.
* **to wait on somebody** (*waiter*) servire qualcuno

to **wait up** [weɪt'ʌp] VERB
* **to wait up for somebody** rimanere*ᴱ alzato ad aspettare qualcuno ◇ *Don't wait up for me.* Non rimanere* alzato ad aspettarmi.

waiter ['weɪtə'] NOUN
il cameriere

waiting list ['weɪtɪŋlɪst] NOUN
la lista d'attesa

waiting room ['weɪtɪŋruːm] NOUN
la sala d'attesa

waitress ['weɪtrɪs] NOUN (PL **waitresses**)
la cameriera

to **wake** [weɪk] VERB (**woke, woken**)
1 svegliarsiᴱ ◇ *I woke at six o'clock.* Mi sono svegliato alle sei.
2 svegliare ◇ *Please would you wake me at seven o'clock?* Mi può svegliare alle sette, per favore? ◇ *I was woken at seven.* Mi hanno svegliato alle sette.

to **wake up** [weɪk'ʌp] VERB (**woke up, woken up**)
1 svegliarsiᴱ ◇ *He's just woken up.* Si è appena svegliato.
2 svegliare ◇ *Don't wake him up!* Non svegliarlo!

Wales [weɪlz] NOUN
il Galles ◇ *the Prince of Wales* il Principe di Galles

to **walk** [wɔːk] VERB
see also **walk** NOUN
1 camminare ◇ *They walked in silence for a while.* Hanno camminato in silenzio per un po'. ◇ *We walked 10 kilometres.* Abbiamo camminato per dieci chilometri.
2 andare*ᴱ a piedi ◇ *Are you walking or going by bus?* Ci vai a piedi o in autobus?
* **to walk the dog** portare fuori il cane
* **to walk out on somebody** abbandonare qualcuno ◇ *He walked out on his wife and family.* Ha abbandonato la moglie e la famiglia.
* **He walked out of the meeting in protest.** Ha abbandonato la riunione in segno di protesta.

walk [wɔːk] NOUN
see also **walk** VERB
la passeggiata ◇ *We went for a walk.* Abbiamo fatto una passeggiata.
* **It's 10 minutes' walk from here.** Ci vogliono dieci minuti a piedi da qui.

walkie-talkie ['wɔːkɪ'tɔːkɪ] NOUN (PL **walkie-talkies**)
il walkie-talkie (PL i walkie-talkie)

walking ['wɔːkɪŋ] NOUN
l'escursionismo ◇ *I did some walking in the Alps last summer.* Ho fatto escursionismo sulle Alpi, l'estate scorsa.

walking shoes ['wɔːkɪŋʃuːz] NOUN
le scarpe per camminare

walking stick ['wɔːkɪŋstɪk] NOUN
il bastone da passeggio

Walkman ® ['wɔːkmən] (PL **Walkmans**) NOUN
il Walkman ® (PL i Walkman)

wall [wɔːl] NOUN
il muro

wallet ['wɒlɪt] NOUN
il portafoglio

wallpaper ['wɔːlpeɪpə'] NOUN
la carta da parati

walnut ['wɔːlnʌt] NOUN
la noce

to **wander** ['wɒndə'] VERB
* **to wander around** gironzolare ◇ *I just wandered around for a while.* Ho gironzolato per un po'.

to **want** [wɒnt] VERB
volere* ◇ *Do you want some cake?* Vuoi un po' di torta?
* **to want to do something** volere* fare* qualcosa ◇ *What do you want to do tomorrow?* Che cosa vuoi fare* domani?
* **He is wanted by the police.** È ricercato dalla polizia.

war [wɔː'] NOUN
la guerra

ward [wɔːd] NOUN
il reparto (*in hospital*)

* Verbs followed by this symbol are irregular. See pp.339–364 for further details.

warden ['wɔːdn] NOUN
il guardiano

wardrobe ['wɔːdrəub] NOUN
l' armadio

warehouse ['weəhaus] NOUN
il magazzino

warm [wɔːm] ADJECTIVE
see also **warm** VERB
1 caldo ◇ *warm water* acqua calda ◇ *It's warm in here.* Fa caldo qui. ◇ *I'm too warm.* Ho troppo caldo.
2 caloroso ◇ *a warm welcome* una calorosa accoglienza

to **warm** [wɔːm] VERB
see also **warm** ADJECTIVE
scaldare ◇ *She warmed her hands by the fire.* Si è scaldata le mani vicino al fuoco.

to **warm up** [wɔːm'ʌp] VERB
1 riscaldare ◇ *I'll warm up some lasagne for you.* Ti riscaldo delle lasagne.
2 fare* riscaldamento (*in gym*) ◇ *Spend the first five minutes warming up.* Innanzitutto, fai cinque minuti di riscaldamento.

to **warn** [wɔːn] VERB
avvertire ◇ *Well, I warned you!* Beh, ti avevo avvertito!
◆ **to warn somebody not to do something** consigliare a qualcuno di non fare* qualcosa

warning ['wɔːnɪŋ] NOUN
l' avvertimento

warning light ['wɔːnɪŋlaɪt] NOUN
la spia luminosa

warning triangle [wɔːnɪŋ'traɪæŋgl] NOUN
il triangolo

Warsaw ['wɔːsɔː] NOUN
Varsavia

wart [wɔːt] NOUN
la verruca (PL le verruche)

was [wɒz] VERB *see* be

wash [wɒʃ] NOUN
see also **wash** VERB
◆ **to have a wash** lavarsi[E]
◆ **to give something a wash** lavare qualcosa

to **wash** [wɒʃ] VERB
see also **wash** NOUN
1 lavare ◇ *I'll wash the dishes.* Lavo io i piatti.
2 lavarsi[E] ◇ *He washed his hands.* Si è lavato le mani. ◇ *Have you washed your hair?* Ti sei lavata i capelli?

to **wash away** [wɒʃə'weɪ] VERB
spazzare via

to **wash up** [wɒʃ'ʌp] VERB
lavare i piatti

washbasin ['wɒʃbeɪsn] NOUN
il lavandino

washcloth ['wɒʃklɔθ] NOUN
il guanto di spugna

washing ['wɒʃɪŋ] NOUN
il bucato

◆ **to do the washing** fare* il bucato
◆ **dirty washing** roba da lavare

washing machine ['wɒʃɪŋməʃiːn] NOUN
la lavatrice

washing powder ['wɒʃɪŋpaudə'] NOUN
il detersivo in polvere per bucato

washing-up [wɒʃɪŋ'ʌp] NOUN
◆ **to do the washing-up** fare* i piatti

washing-up liquid [wɒʃɪŋ'ʌplɪkwɪd] NOUN
il detersivo liquido per stoviglie

wasn't ['wɒznt] = was not

wasp [wɒsp] NOUN
la vespa

waste [weɪst] NOUN
see also **waste** VERB
1 lo spreco (PL gli sprechi) ◇ *It's such a waste!* È un tale spreco!
◆ **It's a waste of time.** È tempo sprecato.
2 scorie ◇ *nuclear waste* scorie nucleari
◆ **the waste pipe** il tubo di scarico

to **waste** [weɪst] VERB
see also **waste** NOUN
sprecare ◇ *I don't like wasting money.* Non mi piace sprecare i soldi.
◆ **to waste time** perdere* tempo ◇ *There's no time to waste.* Non c'è tempo da perdere*.

wastepaper basket ['weɪstpeɪpəbɑːskɪt] NOUN
il cestino per la cartaccia

watch [wɒtʃ] NOUN (PL **watches**)
see also **watch** VERB
l' orologio ◇ *He was wearing an expensive watch.* Portava un orologio costoso.

to **watch** [wɒtʃ] VERB
see also **watch** NOUN
1 guardare ◇ *I was watching TV.* Stavo guardando la TV.
2 sorvegliare ◇ *The police were watching the house.* La polizia sorvegliava la casa.
◆ **Watch out!** Attento!

water ['wɔːtə'] NOUN
see also **water** VERB
l' acqua ◇ *a glass of water* un bicchiere d'acqua

to **water** ['wɔːtə'] VERB
see also **water** NOUN
annaffiare ◇ *She's watering the geraniums.* Sta annaffiando i gerani.

to **water down** [wɔːtə'daun] VERB
1 annacquare (*wine*)
2 indebolire (*suggestions, rules*)

waterfall ['wɔːtəfɔːl] NOUN
la cascata

water heater ['wɔːtəhiːtə'] NOUN
lo scaldabagno

watering can ['wɔːtərɪŋkæn] NOUN
l' annaffiatoio

watermelon ['wɔːtəmɛlən] NOUN
il cocomero

waterproof ['wɔːtəpruːf] ADJECTIVE
impermeabile

W

water-skiing ['wɔ:təski:ɪŋ] NOUN
lo sci d'acqua

water tank ['wɔ:tətæŋk] NOUN
il serbatoio d'acqua (PL i serbatoi d'acqua)

wave [weɪv] NOUN
> see also **wave** VERB

1 l' onda ◇ *He was knocked over by a big wave.* È stato gettato a terra da una grossa onda.

2 il cenno (*of the hand*) ◇ *a friendly wave* un cenno amichevole

+ **to give somebody a wave** salutare qualcuno con la mano

to **wave** [weɪv] VERB
> see also **wave** NOUN

fare* un cenno con la mano ◇ *He waved at me.* Mi ha fatto un cenno con la mano.

+ **to wave goodbye** salutare con la mano

wavy ['weɪvɪ] ADJECTIVE
ondulato ◇ *a wavy line* una linea ondulata

+ **wavy hair** i capelli mossi

wax [wæks] NOUN (PL **waxes**)
la cera

way [weɪ] NOUN

1 il modo ◇ *She looked at me in a strange way.* Mi ha guardato in modo strano.

2 la strada ◇ *I don't know the way.* Non so la strada.

+ **Do you know the way to the hotel?** Sai come arrivare all'albergo?

+ **on the way** per strada

+ **He lost it on the way to school.** Lo ha perso andando a scuola.

3 la parte ◇ *Which way is it?* Da che parte è? ◇ *The supermarket is this way.* Il supermercato è da questa parte.

+ **in a way** in un certo senso

+ **a way of life** uno stile di vita

+ **It's a long way.** È lontano.

+ **He's on his way.** Sta arrivando.

+ **"way in"** "entrata"

+ **"way out"** "uscita"

+ **by the way...** a proposito...

we [wi:] PRONOUN
noi ◇ *We aren't so lucky.* Noi non siamo così fortunati.

we is often not translated.
◇ *We'll arrive tomorrow.* Arriveremo domani.

weak [wi:k] ADJECTIVE
debole

wealthy ['welθɪ] ADJECTIVE
ricco

weapon ['wepən] NOUN
l' arma

to **wear** [wɛə'] VERB (**wore, worn**)
portare ◇ *She was wearing a black coat.* Portava un cappotto nero.

+ **She was wearing black.** Era vestita di nero.
◇ *He wore black trousers and a T-shirt.* Portava pantaloni neri ed una maglietta.

+ **This is the first time I've worn these shoes.** È la prima volta che metto queste scarpe.

to **wear off** [wɛər'ɔf] VERB
svanire E ◇ *The feeling soon wore off.* Presto la sensazione svanì.

to **wear out** [wɛər'aut] VERB

1 consumare ◇ *He wore out his shoes wandering round the city.* Ha consumato le scarpe gironzolando per la città.

2 stancarsi E tanto ◇ *Don't wear yourself out!* Non stancarti tanto!

weather ['weðə'] NOUN
il tempo ◇ *What's the weather like?* Che tempo fa?

weather forecast ['weðəfɔ:kɑ:st] NOUN
le previsioni del tempo

weather man ['weðəmæn] NOUN (PL **weather men**)
il meteorologo (PL i meteorologhi)

web [web] NOUN

+ **the web** il Web

web browser ['webbrauzə'] NOUN
il browser (PL i browser)

webmaster ['webmɑ:stə'] NOUN
il webmaster (PL i webmaster)

web page ['webpeɪdʒ] NOUN
la pagina Web

website ['websaɪt] NOUN
il sito Internet

webzine ['webzi:n] NOUN
la rivista web

we'd [wi:d] = **we had, we would**

wedding ['wedɪŋ] NOUN
il matrimonio

+ **a wedding anniversary** un anniversario di matrimonio

+ **a wedding dress** un abito da sposa

wedding ring ['wedɪŋrɪŋ] NOUN
la fede

Wednesday ['wednzdɪ] NOUN
il mercoledì (PL i mercoledì)

+ **on Wednesday** mercoledì ◇ *I saw her on Wednesday.* L'ho vista mercoledì.

+ **on Wednesdays** di mercoledì ◇ *I go swimming on Wednesdays.* Vado in piscina di mercoledì.

weed [wi:d] NOUN
> see also **weed** VERB

l' erbaccia (PL le erbacce) ◇ *The garden's full of weeds.* Il giardino è pieno di erbacce.

to **weed** [wi:d] VERB
> see also **weed** NOUN

diserbare

week [wi:k] NOUN
la settimana ◇ *in a week's time* tra una settimana

+ **a week on Friday** venerdì a otto

weekday ['wi:kdeɪ] NOUN
il giorno feriale

+ **on weekdays** durante la settimana

weekend [wi:k'end] NOUN
il fine settimana (PL i fine settimana) ◇ *last*

---

* Verbs followed by this symbol are irregular. See pp.339–364 for further details.

_ *weekend* l'altro fine settimana

to **weep** [wi:p] VERB (**wept, wept**)
piangere* ◇ *She wept for hours.* Pianse per ore.

to **weigh** [weɪ] VERB
pesare ◇ *How much do you weigh?* Quanto pesi?
- **to weigh oneself** pesarsi [E]

to **weigh down** [weɪ'daun] VERB
appesantire

to **weigh up** [weɪ'ʌp] VERB
valutare

weight [weɪt] NOUN
il peso ◇ *the weight of the load* il peso del carico
- **to lose weight** dimagrire [E]
- **to put on weight** ingrassare [E]
- **to do weight training** fare* pesi

weightlifter ['weɪtlɪftə'] NOUN
il sollevatore di pesi

weightlifting ['weɪtlɪftɪŋ] NOUN
il sollevamento pesi

weird [wɪəd] ADJECTIVE
strano

welcome ['welkəm] NOUN
see also **welcome** VERB
l'accoglienza
- **a warm welcome** un'accoglienza calorosa
- **Welcome!** Benvenuto!

to **welcome** ['welkəm] VERB
see also **welcome** NOUN
1 accogliere* ◇ *Everyone was there to welcome me.* Erano tutti lì ad accogliermi.
2 apprezzare ◇ *They did not welcome the suggestion.* Non hanno apprezzato il suggerimento.
- **Thank you! – You're welcome!** Grazie! – Di niente!

well [wel] ADJECTIVE, ADVERB
see also **well** NOUN
1 bene ◇ *You did that really well.* L'hai fatto proprio bene.
- **to do well** andare* [E] bene ◇ *She's doing really well at school.* Va molto bene a scuola.
- **to be well** stare* [E] bene ◇ *I'm not very well at the moment.* Non sto molto bene in questo periodo.
- **Get well soon!** Guarisci presto!
- **Well done!** Bravo!
2 beh ◇ *It's enormous! Well, quite big anyway.* È gigantesco! Beh, diciamo molto grande.
- **as well** anche ◇ *We worked hard, but we had some fun as well.* Abbiamo lavorato sodo ma ci siamo anche divertiti. ◇ *We went to Verona as well as Venice.* Siamo stati a Venezia e anche a Verona.

well [wel] NOUN
see also **well** ADJECTIVE, ADVERB
il pozzo

we'll [wi:l] = **we will**

well-behaved ['welbɪ'heɪvd] ADJECTIVE
beneducato

well-dressed ['wel'drest] ADJECTIVE
elegante

wellingtons ['welɪŋtənz] NOUN PL
gli stivali di gomma

well-known ['wel'nəun] ADJECTIVE
famoso ◇ *a well-known film star* un famoso divo del cinema

well-off ['wel'ɔf] ADJECTIVE
benestante

Welsh [welʃ] ADJECTIVE
see also **Welsh** NOUN
gallese
- **the Welsh Assembly** il parlamento gallese

> ❶ *Il parlamento gallese ha responsabilità limitate e non può imporre tasse.*

Welsh [welʃ] NOUN
see also **Welsh** ADJECTIVE
il gallese (*language*)
- **the Welsh** i gallesi

Welshman ['welʃmən] NOUN (PL **Welshmen**)
il gallese

Welshwoman ['welʃwumən] NOUN (PL **Welshwomen**)
la gallese

went [went] VERB *see* **go**

wept [wept] VERB *see* **weep**

were [wəː'] VERB *see* **be**

we're [wɪə'] = **we are**

weren't [wəːnt] = **were not**

west [west] NOUN, ADVERB, ADJECTIVE
1 l' ovest MASC ◇ *in the west* ad ovest
- **west of** a ovest di ◇ *Stroud is west of Oxford.* Stroud è a ovest di Oxford.
2 verso ovest ◇ *We were travelling west.* Andavamo verso ovest.
3 occidentale ◇ *the west coast* la costa occidentale
- **the West Country** il sud-ovest dell'Inghilterra

westbound ['westbaund] ADJECTIVE
diretto ad ovest

western ['westən] NOUN
see also **western** ADJECTIVE
il western (PL i western)

western ['westən] ADJECTIVE
see also **western** NOUN
occidentale ◇ *the western coast of Scotland* la costa occidentale della Scozia

West Indian [west'ɪndɪən] ADJECTIVE
see also **West Indian** NOUN
caraibico ◇ *the West Indian team* la squadra caraibica ◇ *the West Indian community* la comunità caraibica

West Indian [west'ɪndɪən] NOUN
see also **West Indian** ADJECTIVE
il caraibico
la caraibica

W

West Indies [west'ɪndɪz] NOUN
i Caraibi

wet [wɛt] ADJECTIVE
bagnato ◇ *wet clothes* abiti bagnati
* **to get wet** bagnarsi[E]
* **dripping wet** gocciolante
* **wet weather** tempo piovoso
* **It was wet all week.** È piovuto tutta la settimana.

wet blanket [wɛt'blæŋkɪt] NOUN
il/la guastafeste (PL i/le guastafeste)

wet suit ['wɛtsuːt] NOUN
la muta subacquea

we've [wiːv] = **we have**

whale [weɪl] NOUN
la balena

what [wɔt] ADJECTIVE, PRONOUN
[1] che ◇ *What subjects are you studying?* Che materie studi? ◇ *What colour is it?* Di che colore è? ◇ *What a mess!* Che disordine!
[2] quale ◇ *What's the capital of Finland?* Qual è la capitale della Finlandia? ◇ *What's her telephone number?* Qual è il suo numero di telefono?
[3] che cosa ◇ *Tell me what you did.* Dimmi che cosa hai fatto. ◇ *What are you doing?* Che cosa fai? ◇ *What did you say?* Che cos'hai detto? ◇ *What is it?* Che cos'è? ◇ *What's the matter?* Che cosa c'è? ◇ *What happened?* Che cos'è successo?
[4] quello che ◇ *I saw what happened.* Ho visto quello che è successo. ◇ *I heard what he said.* Ho sentito quello che ha detto.
* **What? (1)** Come? (*what did you say?*)
* **What? (2)** Cosa? (*what do you want?*)
* **What? (3)** Cosa? (*surprised*)

wheat [wiːt] NOUN
il grano

wheel [wiːl] NOUN
la ruota ◇ *the front wheel* la ruota davanti
* **a wheel clamp** un morsetto bloccaruota
* **the steering wheel** il volante

wheelchair ['wiːltʃɛəʳ] NOUN
la sedia a rotelle

when [wɛn] ADVERB, CONJUNCTION
quando ◇ *When did he go?* Quando è partito? ◇ *She was reading when I came in.* Quando sono entrato stava leggendo.

where [wɛəʳ] ADVERB, CONJUNCTION
dove ◇ *Where do you live?* Dove abiti? ◇ *Where are you going?* Dove stai andando?

whether ['wɛðəʳ] CONJUNCTION
se ◇ *I don't know whether to go or not.* Non so se andare* o no.

which [wɪtʃ] PRONOUN, ADJECTIVE
[1] quale ◇ *Which would you like?* Quale vuoi? ◇ *Which of these are yours?* Quali di questi sono tuoi?
* **Which one?** Quale? ◇ *I know his sister. –*

Which one? Conosco sua sorella. – Quale?
[2] che ◇ *Which flavour do you want?* Che gusto vuoi? ◇ *the CD which is playing now* il CD che stiamo ascoltando

while [waɪl] CONJUNCTION
see also **while** NOUN
mentre ◇ *You hold the torch while I look inside.* Tieni la pila mentre io guardo dentro. ◇ *Isobel is very dynamic, while Kay is more laid-back.* Isobel è molto attiva mentre Kay è più tranquilla.

while [waɪl] NOUN
see also **while** CONJUNCTION
* **a while** un po' di tempo
* **after a while** dopo un po'
* **a while ago** poco fa ◇ *He was here a while ago.* Era qui poco fa.
* **for a while** per un po' ◇ *I lived in London for a while.* Ho abitato a Londra per un po'.
* **quite a while** tanto tempo ◇ *I haven't seen him for quite a while.* È da tanto tempo che non lo vedo.

whip [wɪp] NOUN
see also **whip** VERB
la frusta

to **whip** [wɪp] VERB
see also **whip** NOUN
[1] frustare (*horse*)
[2] montare ◇ *Whip the cream.* Montate la panna.
[3] sbattere* ◇ *Whip the egg whites.* Sbattete gli albumi.

whipped cream [wɪpt'kriːm] NOUN
la panna montata

whisk [wɪsk] NOUN
see also **whisk** VERB
il frullino

to **whisk** [wɪsk] VERB
see also **whisk** NOUN
[1] trascinare ◇ *He was whisked away in a police car.* È stato trascinato via in una macchina della polizia.
[2] sbattere* ◇ *Whisk the yolks with the sugar.* Sbattete i tuorli e lo zucchero.

whiskers ['wɪskəz] NOUN PL
i baffi

whisky ['wɪskɪ] NOUN (US **whiskey**)
il whisky (PL i whisky)

to **whisper** ['wɪspəʳ] VERB
sussurrare

whistle ['wɪsl] NOUN
see also **whistle** VERB
[1] il fischietto (*thing*)
[2] il fischio (*noise*)
* **The referee blew his whistle.** L'arbitro ha fischiato.

to **whistle** ['wɪsl] VERB
see also **whistle** NOUN
fischiare

white [waɪt] ADJECTIVE
bianco ◇ *He's got white hair.* Ha i capelli

---

* Verbs followed by this symbol are irregular. See pp.339–364 for further details.

bianchi.
* **white wine** vino bianco
* **white bread** pane bianco
* **white coffee** caffè macchiato
* **a white man** un bianco
* **white people** i bianchi

Whitsun ['wɪtsn] NOUN
la Pentecoste

who [hu:] PRONOUN
[1] chi ◊ *Who said that?* Chi l'ha detto?
◊ *Who is it?* Chi è?
[2] che ◊ *the man who saw us* l'uomo che ci
ha visto ◊ *the man who spoke to him*
l'uomo che gli ha parlato

whole [həʊl] ADJECTIVE
| *see also* **whole** NOUN |
intero ◊ *the whole class* la classe intera ◊ *a
whole box of chocolates* un'intera scatola di
cioccolatini
* **the whole afternoon** tutto il pomeriggio
* **the whole world** tutto il mondo

whole [həʊl] NOUN
| *see also* **whole** ADJECTIVE |
* **the whole of** tutto ◊ *the whole of August*
tutto agosto ◊ *The whole of Wales was
affected.* Tutto il Galles è stato colpito.
* **on the whole** nel complesso

wholemeal ['həʊlmi:l] ADJECTIVE
integrale ◊ *wholemeal bread* pane
integrale

wholewheat ['həʊlwi:t] ADJECTIVE [US]
integrale ◊ *wholewheat bread* pane
integrale

whom [hu:m] PRONOUN
[1] chi ◊ *Whom did you see?* Chi hai visto?
[2] cui ◊ *the man to whom I spoke* l'uomo
con cui ho parlato

whose [hu:z] PRONOUN
[1] di chi ◊ *Whose is this?* Di chi è questo?
◊ *I know whose it is.* Io lo so di chi è.
◊ *Whose book is this?* Di chi è questo libro?
[2] il cui
la cui
◊ *the girl whose picture was in the paper* la
ragazza la cui foto era sul giornale

why [waɪ] ADVERB
perché ◊ *Why did you do it?* Perchè l'hai
fatto? ◊ *That's why he did it.* Ecco perché
l'ha fatto.

wicked ['wɪkɪd] ADJECTIVE
[1] cattivo ◊ *a wicked deed* un gesto cattivo
[2] un po' malizioso ◊ *She has a wicked
sense of humour.* Ha un senso
dell'umorismo un po' malizioso.

wicket ['wɪkɪt] NOUN
la porta (*in cricket*)

wide [waɪd] ADJECTIVE, ADVERB
[1] largo ◊ *a wide road* una strada larga
[2] ampio ◊ *a wide choice of hotels*
un'ampia scelta di alberghi
* **wide open** spalancato ◊ *The door was wide
open.* La porta era spalancata.

* **wide awake** completamente sveglio

widow ['wɪdəʊ] NOUN
la vedova

widower ['wɪdəʊə'] NOUN
il vedovo

width [wɪdθ] NOUN
la larghezza

wife [waɪf] NOUN (PL **wives**)
la moglie

wig [wɪg] NOUN
la parrucca (PL le parrucche)

wild [waɪld] ADJECTIVE
[1] selvatico ◊ *a wild animal* un animale
selvatico
[2] pazzo ◊ *She's a bit wild.* È un po' pazza.

wild card ['waɪldkɑːd] NOUN
il carattere jolly

wildlife ['waɪldlaɪf] NOUN
la natura

will [wɪl] NOUN
| *see also* **will** VERB |
[1] il testamento ◊ *He made a will.* Ha fatto
testamento.
[2] la volontà ◊ *a strong will* una forte
volontà

will [wɪl] VERB
| *see also* **will** NOUN |
*When will + verb refers to the future, it can be
translated both by the future tense of the
Italian verb, and by the present.*
◊ *I will finish it tomorrow.* Lo finirò domani.
◊ *It won't take long.* Non ci vorrà molto.
◊ *She'll love that card.* Quel biglietto le
piacerà moltissimo. ◊ *Will you do it? – No, I
won't.* Lo farai? – No. ◊ *Will you help me?*
Mi aiuti? ◊ *I won't go there again.* Lì non ci
ritorno.
*When will + verb refers to the present, it is
translated by the present tense of the Italian
verb.*
◊ *I'll show you your room.* Ti mostro la tua
stanza. ◊ *I'll give you a hand.* Ti dò una
mano. ◊ *Will you be quiet!* Fai silenzio!
◊ *That will be the postman.* Dev'essere* il
postino.
*When **won't** means "refuses to" it is
translated by the present tense of **volere**.*
◊ *She won't listen to me.* Non mi vuol dar
retta.

willing ['wɪlɪŋ] ADJECTIVE
* **to be willing to do something** essere* [E]
disposto a fare* qualcosa

to **win** [wɪn] VERB (**won, won**)
| *see also* **win** NOUN |
vincere* ◊ *Did you win?* Hai vinto? ◊ *He
won a gold medal.* Ha vinto una medaglia
d'oro.
* **to win the lottery** vincere* alla lotteria

win [wɪn] NOUN
| *see also* **win** VERB |
la vittoria

W

wind [wɪnd] NOUN
see also **wind** VERB
il vento ◇ *a strong wind* un vento forte
• **a wind instrument** uno strumento a fiato
• **wind power** l'energia eolica

to **wind** [waɪnd] VERB (**wound, wound**)
see also **wind** NOUN
[1] avvolgere* ◇ *He wound the rope round a tree.* Ha avvolto la fune attorno ad un albero.
[2] snodarsi [E] (*road, river*)

to **wind up** [waɪnd'ʌp] VERB
[1] chiudere* ◇ *The company will be wound up.* La società verrà chiusa.
[2] finire* [E] ◇ *He'll wind up in jail.* Finirà in prigione.

windmill ['wɪndmɪl] NOUN
il mulino a vento

window ['wɪndəu] NOUN
[1] la finestra ◇ *the kitchen window* la finestra della cucina
[2] il finestrino ◇ *He wound down the window.* Ha abbassato il finestrino.
[3] il vetro ◇ *a broken window* un vetro rotto
• **a window pane** un vetro
• **a shop window** una vetrina

window box ['wɪndəubɒks] NOUN
la cassetta per i fiori

window cleaner ['wɪndəukliːnə'] NOUN
il/la lavavetri (PL i/le lavavetri)

windscreen ['wɪndskriːn] NOUN
il parabrezza (PL i parabrezza)

windscreen wiper ['wɪndskriːnwaɪpə'] NOUN
il tergicristalli (PL i tergicristalli)

windshield ['wɪndʃiːld] NOUN [US]
il parabrezza (PL i parabrezza)

windshield wiper ['wɪndʃiːldwaɪpə'] NOUN [US]
il tergicristalli (PL i tergicristalli)

windsurfing ['wɪndsə:fɪŋ] NOUN
il windsurf

windy ['wɪndɪ] ADJECTIVE
ventoso ◇ *a windy day* una giornata ventosa
• **It's windy.** C'è vento.

wine [waɪn] NOUN
il vino ◇ *white wine* vino bianco ◇ *red wine* vino rosso ◇ *a glass of wine* un bicchiere di vino ◇ *a wine glass* un bicchiere da vino
• **a wine bar**

❶ *Un* **wine bar** *è un bar con ampia scelta di vini e cocktail.*

• **the wine list** la carta dei vini
• **a wine tasting** una degustazione dei vini

wing [wɪŋ] NOUN
l'ala (PL le ali)

to **wink** [wɪŋk] VERB
• **to wink at somebody** fare* l'occhiolino a qualcuno

winner ['wɪnə'] NOUN
il vincitore
la vincitrice

winning ['wɪnɪŋ] ADJECTIVE
vincitore ◇ *the winning team* la squadra vincitrice
• **the winning goal** il gol della vittoria
• **the winning post** il traguardo

winter ['wɪntə'] NOUN
see also **winter** ADJECTIVE
l'inverno ◇ *in winter* d'inverno ◇ *last winter* lo scorso inverno

winter ['wɪntə'] ADJECTIVE
see also **winter** NOUN
invernale ◇ *winter clothes* vestiti invernali ◇ *winter sports* sport invernali

to **wipe** [waɪp] VERB
pulire
• **to wipe one's feet** pulirsi [E] i piedi

to **wipe out** [waɪp'aut] VERB
spazzare via

to **wipe up** [waɪp'ʌp] VERB
asciugare

wire ['waɪə'] NOUN
il filo ◇ *copper wire* filo di rame ◇ *electrical wire* filo elettrico ◇ *the telephone wire* il filo del telefono

wise [waɪz] ADJECTIVE
saggio

wisdom tooth ['wɪzdəmtu:θ] NOUN (PL **wisdom teeth**)
il dente del giudizio

to **wish** [wɪʃ] VERB
see also **wish** NOUN
volere* ◇ *I wish to make a complaint.* Voglio fare* reclamo. ◇ *I wish you were here!* Come vorrei che tu fossi qui!
• **I wish you'd told me!** Se solo me l'avessi detto!
• **to wish for something** desiderare qualcosa
• **to wish somebody happy birthday** augurare buon compleanno a qualcuno

wish [wɪʃ] NOUN (PL **wishes**)
see also **wish** VERB
[1] la voglia ◇ *She had no wish for conversation.* Non aveva alcuna voglia di conversare.
[2] il desiderio ◇ *Make a wish.* Esprimi un desiderio.
• **"best wishes"** "tanti auguri"
• **"with best wishes, Kathy"** "cari saluti, Kathy"

wit [wɪt] NOUN
lo spirito ◇ *He was known for his intelligence and wit.* Era conosciuto per la sua intelligenza e il suo spirito.
• **to be at one's wits' end** non sapere* più cos'altro fare* ◇ *I'm at my wits' end!* Non

so più cos'altro fare*!

with [wɪð,wɪθ] PREPOSITION

1 con ◇ *Come with me.* Vieni con me. ◇ *a woman with blue eyes* una donna con gli occhi azzurri

2 a casa di ◇ *We stayed with friends.* Siamo stati a casa di amici.

3 di ◇ *green with envy* verde d'invidia ◇ *He was shaking with fear.* Tremava di paura. ◇ *Fill the jug with water.* Riempi la brocca d'acqua.

within [wɪð'ɪn] PREPOSITION

1 all'interno di ◇ *communication within the organization* la comunicazione all'interno dell'organizzazione

2 entro ◇ *within the week* entro questa settimana

♦ **within easy reach** vicino ◇ *The shops are within easy reach.* I negozi sono vicini.

without [wɪð'aut] PREPOSITION

senza ◇ *without a coat* senza il cappotto ◇ *without speaking* senza parlare*

witness ['wɪtnɪs] NOUN (PL **witnesses**)

il/la testimone ◇ *There were no witnesses.* Non c'erano testimoni.

♦ **the witness box** il banco dei testimoni

♦ **the witness stand** US il banco dei testimoni

witty ['wɪtɪ] ADJECTIVE

spiritoso

wives [waɪvz] NOUN *see* **wife**

woke, woken [wəuk, 'wəukn] VERB *see* **wake**

wolf [wulf] NOUN (PL **wolves**)

il lupo

woman ['wumən] NOUN (PL **women**)

la donna ◇ *a man and two women* un uomo e due donne

♦ **a woman doctor** una dottoressa

won [wʌn] VERB *see* **win**

to **wonder** ['wʌndə'] VERB

chiedersi E ◇ *I wonder why she said that.* Mi chiedo perché l'abbia detto.

♦ **I wonder what that means.** Chissà cosa vuol dire*.

wonderful ['wʌndəful] ADJECTIVE

meraviglioso

won't [wəunt] = **will not**

wood [wud] NOUN

1 il legno ◇ *It's made of wood.* È di legno.

2 il bosco (PL i boschi) ◇ *We went for a walk in the wood.* Siamo andati a passeggiare nel bosco.

wooden ['wudn] ADJECTIVE

di legno ◇ *a wooden chair* una sedia di legno

woodwork ['wudwə:k] NOUN

la falegnameria (*school subject*)

wool [wul] NOUN

la lana

word [wə:d] NOUN

la parola ◇ *The word "ginseng" is Chinese.* La parola "ginseng" è cinese.

♦ **in other words** in altri termini

♦ **to have a word with somebody** parlare* con qualcuno ◇ *Can I have a word with you?* Posso parlarti?

word processing ['wə:dprəusesɪŋ] NOUN

l' elaborazione testi FEM

word processor ['wə:d'prəusesə'] NOUN

il word processor (PL i word processor)

wore [wɔ:'] VERB *see* **wear**

work [wə:k] NOUN

see also **work** VERB

il lavoro ◇ *She's looking for work.* Sta cercando lavoro.

♦ **It's hard work.** È faticoso.

♦ **to be off work** essere* E in congedo

♦ **to be out of work** essere* E disoccupato

to **work** [wə:k] VERB

see also **work** NOUN

1 lavorare ◇ *She works in a shop.* Lavora in un negozio. ◇ *They are working hard.* Lavorano sodo.

2 funzionare ◇ *The heating isn't working.* Il riscaldamento non funziona. ◇ *My plan worked perfectly.* Il mio piano ha funzionato a meraviglia.

to **work out** [wə:k'aut] VERB

1 fare* ginnastica ◇ *I work out twice a week.* Faccio ginnastica due volte alla settimana.

2 andare* E bene ◇ *I hope it will all work out.* Spero che tutto vada bene.

3 capire ◇ *I just couldn't work it out.* Non riuscivo proprio a capire.

♦ **It works out at £10 each.** Fanno dieci sterline a testa.

worker ['wə:kə'] NOUN

il lavoratore

la lavoratrice

◇ *a good worker* un bravo lavoratore

♦ **a factory worker** un operaio

un'operaia

work experience ['wə:kɪkspɪərɪəns] NOUN

1 l' esperienza lavorativa ◇ *They have little work experience.* Hanno poca esperienza lavorativa.

2 il tirocinio ◇ *I'm going to do work experience in a factory.* Farò tirocinio in una fabbrica.

working class ['wə:kɪŋ'klɑ:s] ADJECTIVE

operaio ◇ *a working class family* una famiglia operaia

♦ **I'm working class.** Vengo da una famiglia operaia.

workman ['wə:kmən] NOUN (PL **workmen**)

l' operaio

works [wə:ks] NOUN SING

la fabbrica

worksheet ['wə:kʃi:t] NOUN

la scheda (*at school*)

Verbs followed by the symbol "E" require the auxiliary "essere"

workshop [ˈwəːkʃɔp] NOUN
il laboratorio ◇ *a drama workshop* un laboratorio teatrale

workstation [ˈwəːksteɪʃən] NOUN
la stazione di lavoro

world [wəːld] NOUN
il mondo ◇ *the world champion* il campione del mondo
• **the World Wide Web** il Web

worm [wəːm] NOUN
il verme

worn [wɔːn] VERB *see* **wear**

worn [wɔːn] ADJECTIVE
logoro ◇ *The carpet is a bit worn.* La moquette è un po' logora.
• **worn out (1)** logoro ◇ *worn out shoes* scarpe logore
• **worn out (2)** sfinito ◇ *I'm worn out!* Sono sfinito!

worried [ˈwʌrɪd] ADJECTIVE
preoccupato ◇ *I was worried about my job.* Ero preoccupato per il mio lavoro.
• **to look worried** avere* l'aria preoccupata

to **worry** [ˈwʌrɪ] VERB (**worried, worried**)
preoccuparsi^E ◇ *Don't worry!* Non preoccuparti!

worse [wəːs] ADJECTIVE, ADVERB
1 peggiore ◇ *It was even worse than mine.* Era anche peggiore del mio.
2 peggio ◇ *I'm feeling worse.* Mi sento peggio.
• **to get worse** peggiorare^E ◇ *In March the weather will get worse.* In marzo il tempo peggiorerà.
• **He is now worse off than before.** Ora è in condizioni peggiori di prima.

to **worship** [ˈwəːʃɪp] VERB
adorare

worst [wəːst] ADJECTIVE
see also **worst** NOUN
• **the worst** il peggiore ◇ *the worst student in the class* il peggior studente della classe
• **my worst enemy** il mio peggior nemico

worst [wəːst] NOUN
see also **worst** ADJECTIVE
il peggio ◇ *The worst of it is that...* Il peggio è che...
• **at worst** alla peggio
• **if the worst comes to the worst** nel peggiore dei casi

worth [wəːθ] ADJECTIVE
• **to be worth** valere*^E ◇ *It's worth a lot of money.* Vale un sacco di soldi. ◇ *How much is it worth?* Quanto vale?
• **It's worth it.** Ne vale la pena. ◇ *Is it worth it?* Ne vale la pena? ◇ *It's not worth it.* Non ne vale la pena.

would [wʊd] VERB
would you like is translated by volere, or by the conditional of piacere.
◇ *Would you like a biscuit?* Vuoi un

biscotto? ◇ *Would you like to go and see a film?* Ti piacerebbe andare* al cinema?
When would you + verb is used to ask somebody to do something it can be translated by the imperative.
◇ *Would you close the door please?* Chiudi la porta per favore.
When would + verb indicates the conditional it is translated by the conditional of the Italian verb.
◇ *It wouldn't cost much.* Non costerebbe tanto. ◇ *He'd probably do it.* Probabilmente lo farebbe. ◇ *If you asked him he'd do it.* Se glielo chiedessi lo farebbe. ◇ *If you had asked him he would have done it.* Se glielo avessi chiesto lo avrebbe fatto.
In indirect speech the perfect conditional of the Italian verb is used.
◇ *I said I would do it.* Ho detto che l'avrei fatto.
• **I'd like...** Mi piacerebbe... ◇ *I'd like to go to America.* Mi piacerebbe andare* in America.
When wouldn't means "refused to" it is translated by the past tense of volere.
◇ *He wouldn't lend me the money.* Non mi ha voluto prestare i soldi.

wouldn't [ˈwʊdnt] = **would not**

wound [wuːnd] NOUN
see also **wound** VERB
la ferita

to **wound** [wuːnd] VERB
see also **wound** NOUN
ferire

wound [waʊnd] VERB *see* **wind**

to **wrap** [ræp] VERB
incartare ◇ *She's wrapping her Christmas presents.* Sta incartando i regali di Natale.
• **Can you wrap it for me please?** Mi può fare* una confezione regalo, per favore?

to **wrap up** [ræpˈʌp] VERB
avvolgere*

wrapping paper [ˈræpɪŋpeɪpəˈ] NOUN
la carta da regalo

wreck [rek] NOUN
see also **wreck** VERB
1 il rottame ◇ *That car is a wreck!* Quella macchina è un rottame!
2 l'incidente MASC ◇ *He was killed in a car wreck.* È rimasto ucciso in un incidente automobilistico.
• **to be a complete wreck** essere*^E distrutto ◇ *After the exams I was a complete wreck.* Dopo gli esami ero distrutto.

to **wreck** [rek] VERB
see also **wreck** NOUN
1 distruggere* ◇ *The explosion wrecked the whole house.* L'esplosione ha completamente distrutto la casa.
2 rovinare ◇ *The trip was wrecked by bad weather.* Il brutto tempo ha rovinato la gita.

wreckage [ˈrekɪdʒ] NOUN

---

* Verbs followed by this symbol are irregular. See pp.339–364 for further details.

[1] i rottami MASC PL ◇ *the wreckage of the coach* i rottami della corriera
[2] le macerie FEM PL ◇ *the wreckage of the building* le macerie dell'edificio

wrestler ['rɛslə'] NOUN
il lottatore

wrestling ['rɛslɪŋ] NOUN
la lotta libera

wrinkled ['rɪŋkld] ADJECTIVE
[1] pieno di rughe ◇ *I'm old and wrinkled.* Sono vecchio e pieno di rughe.
[2] stropicciato ◇ *His suit was wrinkled.* Il suo vestito era stropicciato.

wrist [rɪst] NOUN
il polso

to **write** [raɪt] VERB (**wrote, written**)
scrivere* ◇ *I was writing a letter.* Stavo scrivendo una lettera. ◇ *Have you written the letter?* Hai scritto la lettera? ◇ *He wrote me a letter last week.* Mi ha scritto una lettera la settimana scorsa.
◆ **to write to somebody** scrivere* a qualcuno

to **write down** [raɪt'daun] VERB
[1] annotare ◇ *I wrote down the address.* Ho annotato l'indirizzo.
[2] scrivere* ◇ *Can you write it down for me, please?* Me lo può scrivere*, per favore?

writer ['raɪtə'] NOUN
lo scrittore
la scrittrice

writing ['raɪtɪŋ] NOUN
la scrittura ◇ *I can't read your writing.* Non riesco a leggere* la tua scrittura.
◆ **in writing** per iscritto

written ['rɪtn] VERB *see* **write**

wrong [rɔŋ] ADJECTIVE, ADVERB
sbagliato ◇ *The information they gave us was wrong.* Ci hanno dato le informazioni sbagliate. ◇ *the wrong answer* la risposta sbagliata
◆ **You've got the wrong number.** Ha sbagliato numero.
◆ **to be wrong** sbagliarsi [E] ◇ *You're wrong about that.* Ti sbagli.
◆ **to do something wrong** sbagliare ◇ *You've done it wrong.* Hai sbagliato.
◆ **to go wrong** andare* [E] male ◇ *The robbery went wrong and they got caught.* La rapina è andata male e li hanno presi.
◆ **Lying is wrong.** Non si dicono le bugie.
◆ **What's wrong?** Cosa c'è che non va?
◆ **Something must be wrong.** Dev'esserci qualcosa che non va.
◆ **What's wrong with her?** Cos'ha?

wrote [rəut] VERB *see* **write**

WWW [dʌbljudʌbljuˈdʌblju] NOUN (= *World Wide Web*)
il Web

W

X

Xerox ® ['zɪərɔks] NOUN
see also **xerox** VERB
la fotocopiatrice

to **xerox** ['zɪərɔks] VERB
see also **Xerox** NOUN
fotocopiare

Xmas ['ɛksməs] NOUN
il Natale

to **X-ray** ['ɛksreɪ] VERB
see also **X-ray** NOUN
fare* una radiografia a ◊ *They X-rayed my arm.* Mi hanno fatto una radiografia al braccio.

X-ray ['ɛksreɪ] NOUN
see also **X-ray** VERB
la radiografia
+ **to have an X-ray** farsi ᴱ fare* una radiografia
+ **X-rays** raggi X

xylophone ['zaɪləfəun] NOUN
lo xilofono

Y

Y2K [waɪtuːˈkeɪ] NOUN
l' anno 2000

yacht NOUN
lo yacht (PL gli yacht)

yard [jɑːd] NOUN
[1] la iarda (*measurement*)

> ❶ *Una* **iarda** *corrisponde a 91,44 centimetri.*

[2] il cortile ◊ *There's a small yard behind the house.* C'è un piccolo cortile dietro alla casa.
[3] il giardino (*garden*) US

to **yawn** [jɔːn] VERB
see also **yawn** NOUN
sbadigliare

yawn [jɔːn] NOUN
see also **yawn** VERB
lo sbadiglio

year [jɪəʳ] NOUN
l' anno ◊ *last year* l'anno scorso
+ **to be 15 years old** avere* quindici anni
+ **an eight-year-old child** un bambino di otto anni
+ **She's in the fifth year.** È in quinta.

to **yell** [jɛl] VERB
see also **yell** NOUN
urlare

yell [jɛl] NOUN
see also **yell** VERB
l' urlo
The plural of **urlo** *is usually* "le urla".

yellow ['jɛləu] ADJECTIVE
giallo

yes [jɛs] ADVERB
sì ◊ *Do you like it? – Yes.* Ti piace? – Sì.

yesterday ['jɛstədɪ] ADVERB
ieri

yet [jɛt] ADVERB
[1] ancora (*still*) ◊ *A settlement might yet be possible.* È ancora possibile trovare un accordo.
+ **not yet** non ancora ◊ *It's not finished yet.*

Non è ancora finito.
+ **as yet** per ora ◊ *There's no news as yet.* Per ora non ci sono notizie.
[2] già (*already*) ◊ *Have you told your parents yet?* Lo hai già detto ai tuoi genitori?

to **yield** [jiːld] VERB US
dare* la precedenza

yob [jɔb] NOUN
il teppista

yoghurt ['jəugət] NOUN
lo yogurt (PL gli yogurt)

yolk [jəuk] NOUN
il tuorlo

you [juː] PRONOUN
[1] tu (*informal: 1 person*) ◊ *It's you!* Sei tu!
[2] te (*following preposition*) ◊ *I'll come with you.* Vengo con te.
[3] ti (*object*) ◊ *I told you what I thought.* Ti ho detto quello che pensavo.
[4] voi (*plural*) ◊ *I'd like to come with you.* Vorrei venire* con voi. ◊ *all of you* tutti voi
[5] vi (*plural, object*) ◊ *I'll take you to the station.* Vi porto in stazione.
[6] lei (*polite singular*) ◊ *You're a good teacher.* Lei è una brava insegnante. ◊ *This is for you.* Questo è per lei.
[7] la (*polite singular, direct object*) ◊ *I'll call you later.* La chiamo più tardi.
[8] le (*polite singular, indirect object*) ◊ *As I was telling you...* Come le stavo dicendo...
[9] si (*one*) ◊ *I doubt it, but you never know.* Ne dubito, ma non si sa mai.
you is sometimes not translated.
◊ *Where are you going?* Dove state andando?

young [jʌŋ] ADJECTIVE
giovane ◊ *You're too young.* Sei troppo giovane.
+ **young people** i giovani
+ **young children** bambini piccoli
+ **younger** più giovane ◊ *He's younger than me.* È più giovane di me.
+ **my younger brother** il mio fratello minore
+ **my youngest brother** il mio fratello minore
+ **the youngest (1)** (*masculine*) il più giovane

---

* Verbs followed by this symbol are irregular. See pp.339–364 for further details.

◇ *He's the youngest.* È il più giovane.

◆ **the youngest (2)** *(feminine)* la più giovane
◇ *She's the youngest in the class.* È la più giovane della classe.

◆ **She is the youngest competitor.** È la concorrente più giovane.

your [jɔːʳ] ADJECTIVE

1. il tuo MASC (PL i tuoi)
la tua FEM (PL le tue) *(informal singular form)*
◇ *your address* il tuo indirizzo ◇ *your parents* i tuoi genitori ◇ *your pen* la tua penna

2. tuo (PL tuoi)
tua (PL tue)
◇ *your father* tuo padre ◇ *your mother* tua madre

3. il vostro MASC (PL i vostri)
la vostra FEM (PL le vostre)
◇ *Children, give these letters to your parents.* Ragazzi, date queste lettere ai vostri genitori. ◇ *Children, give these letters to your mothers.* Ragazzi, date queste lettere alle vostre madri.

4. vostro (PL vostri)
vostra FEM (PL vostre)
◇ *your father* vostro padre ◇ *your mother* vostra madre

5. il suo MASC (PL i suoi)
la sua FEM (PL le sue) *(polite singular form)*
◇ *Your ticket, madam.* Il suo biglietto, signora. ◇ *Your car, madam.* La sua macchina, signora.

6. suo MASC (PL suoi)
sua FEM (PL sue)
◇ *your father* suo padre ◇ *your mother* sua madre

your *is not always translated.*
◇ *Wash your hands.* Lavati le mani.
◇ *Remember to take your umbrella, sir.* Non dimentichi di prendere* l'ombrello.

yours [jɔːz] PRONOUN

The Italian pronoun agrees with the noun it is replacing.

1. il tuo MASC (PL i tuoi)
la tua FEM (PL le tue) *(familiar form)*
◇ *My garden is smaller than yours.* Il mio giardino è più piccolo del tuo. ◇ *That bag's not mine, it's yours.* Questa borsa non è la mia, è la tua.

2. tuo MASC (PL tuoi)
tua FEM (PL tue) *(your property)*
◇ *Is this yours?* È tuo questo?

◆ **a friend of yours** un tuo amico ◇ *Is this bag yours?* È tua questa borsa?

3. il vostro MASC (PL i vostri)
la vostra FEM (PL le vostre)
◇ *our parents and yours* i nostri genitori ed i vostri ◇ *My car is older than yours.* La mia

macchina è più vecchia della vostra.

4. vostro MASC (PL vostri)
vostra FEM (PL vostre) *(your property)*
◇ *Is that dog yours?* È vostro quel cane?
◇ *Is that car yours?* È vostra quella macchina?

5. il suo MASC (PL i suoi)
la sua FEM (PL le sue) *(polite form)*
◇ *my luggage and yours* il mio bagaglio ed il suo ◇ *My house is smaller than yours.* La mia casa è più piccola della sua.

6. suo MASC (PL suoi)
sua FEM (PL sue) *(your property)*
◇ *Excuse me, madam. Is this yours?* Mi scusi signora. È suo questo? ◇ *Is that car yours, sir?* È sua quella macchina, signore?

yourself [jɔːˈsɛlf] PRONOUN

1. ti *(familiar form)*
A verb + yourself is often translated by a reflexive verb in Italian.
◇ *Have you looked at yourself in the mirror?* Ti sei guardato allo specchio?

2. te *(familiar form, following an English preposition)* ◇ *a beginner like yourself* un principiante come te

3. si *(polite form)*
A verb + yourself is often translated by a reflexive verb in Italian.
◇ *Did you enjoy yourself, sir?* Si è divertito, signore?

4. lei *(polite form, following an English preposition)* ◇ *an important person like yourself* una persona importante come lei

◆ **by yourself** da solo (FEM da sola) ◇ *Do you like travelling by yourself?* Ti piace viaggiare da solo?

yourselves [jɔːˈsɛlvz] PRONOUN

1. vi
A verb + yourselves is often translated by a reflexive verb in Italian.
◇ *Have you looked at yourselves in the mirror?* Vi siete guardati allo specchio?

2. voi *(following an English preposition)*
◇ *important people like yourselves* persone importanti come voi

◆ **by yourselves** da soli (FEM da sole) ◇ *Do you like travelling by yourselves?* Vi piace viaggiare da soli?

youth [juːθ] NOUN

◆ **in my youth** quand'ero giovane

youth club [ˈjuːθklʌb] NOUN
il circolo giovanile

youth hostel [ˈjuːθhɒstl] NOUN
l' ostello della gioventù

Yugoslavia [ˈjuːgəuˈslɑːvɪə] NOUN
l' lugoslavia

◆ **in the former Yugoslavia** nell'ex lugoslavia

Y

Z

zany ['zeɪnɪ] ADJECTIVE
un po' pazzo

zebra NOUN
la zebra

zebra crossing [zi:brə'krɔsɪŋ] NOUN
il passaggio pedonale (PL i passaggi pedonali)

zero ['zɪərəu] NOUN (PL **zeros** or **zeroes**)
lo zero

Zimbabwe [zɪm'bɑ:bwɪ] NOUN
lo Zimbabwe

Zimmer frame® ['zɪməfreɪm] NOUN
il deambulatore

zip [zɪp] NOUN
see also **zip** VERB
la cerniera lampo (PL le cerniere lampo)
◇ The zip's stuck. La cerniera lampo è inceppata.

to **zip** [zɪp] VERB
see also **zip** NOUN
1 sfrecciare E ◇ A sports car zipped past me. Una macchina sportiva mi è sfrecciata accanto.

2 zippare (file)

zip code ['zɪpkəud] NOUN US
il codice di avviamento postale

zipper ['zɪpə'] NOUN US
la cerniera lampo

zit [zɪt] NOUN US
il brufolo

zodiac ['zəudɪæk] NOUN
lo zodiaco

zone [zəun] NOUN
la zona

zoo NOUN
lo zoo (PL gli zoo)

to **zoom** [zu:m] VERB
sfrecciare E ◇ The police car zoomed by very close to him. La macchina della polizia gli è sfrecciata accanto vicinissima.

zoom lens ['zu:mlɛnz] NOUN
lo zoom (PL gli zoom)

zucchini [zu:'ki:nɪ] NOUN SING US
la zucchina ◇ potatoes and zucchini patate e zucchine

---

* Verbs followed by this symbol are irregular. See pp.339–364 for further details.